The Law of Social Security

The Law of
Social Security

Third edition

A I Ogus BCL MA
Professor of Law, University of Manchester

E M Barendt BCL, MA
of Gray's Inn, Barrister;
Fellow of St Catherine's College, Oxford
Chairman, Social Security Appeal Tribunals

T G Buck LLB (Hons)
Senior Lecturer in Law, Lancashire Polytechnic

T Lynes

Butterworths
London
1988

United Kingdom	Butterworth & Co (Publishers) Ltd, 88 Kingsway, LONDON WC2B 6AB and 4 Hill Street, EDINBURGH
Australia	Butterworths Pty Ltd, SYDNEY, MELBOURNE, BRISBANE, ADELAIDE, PERTH, CANBERRA and HOBART
Canada	Butterworths Canada Ltd, TORONTO and VANCOUVER
Ireland	Butterworth (Ireland) Ltd, DUBLIN
Malaysia	Malayan Law Journal Sdn Bhd, KUALA LUMPUR
New Zealand	Butterworths of New Zealand Ltd, WELLINGTON and AUCKLAND
Singapore	Butterworth & Co (Asia) Pte Ltd, SINGAPORE
USA	Butterworths Legal Publishers, ST PAUL, Minnesota, SEATTLE, Washington, BOSTON, Massachusetts, AUSTIN, Texas and D & S Publishers, CLEARWATER, Florida

A CIP Catalogue record for this book is available from the British Library.

First edition 1978
Second edition 1982

ISBN Hardcover 0 406 63372 X
      Softcover 0 406 63370 3

Typeset by Colset Private Limited, Singapore
Printed and bound in Great Britain by
Billing and Sons Limited, Worcester

Preface to third edition

When the second edition of this book was published in 1982, the Conservative government had begun, but had far from completed, its major reappraisal of social security law and policy. The process reached its climax in the publication of the Fowler Reviews in 1985, the main proposals of which were enacted in the following year and brought into force in April 1988. As a conseqence of these and other reforms a substantial proportion of the book had to be rewritten. We now subsume in one chapter the much altered law on maternity and death benefits. The principles governing unemployment benefit, disability benefits, retirement pensions and industrial injuries benefits have all been subject to major changes, as have the arrangements for administration and adjudication, and much new material is to be found in the relevant chapters. War pensions alone remain substantially unaffected by the reform process — they constitute perhaps the 'sacred cow' of the social security system.

The restructuring of the means-tested (now to be known as 'income-related') benefits is undoubtedly the most important and most widely discussed of the reforms. This has resulted in four chapters on, respectively, income support, family credit, housing benefit and the social fund, replacing the two chapters in the previous edition on supplementary benefit and family income supplement. We felt it imperative to include in this edition treatment of housing benefit even though it falls outside the pragmatic definition of 'social security' which we have adopted hitherto, namely administration by the DHSS (now the DSS), because on almost any other criterion it is clearly now to be regarded as a social security benefit. The facts that the legislative framework is laid down in the Social Security Act 1986 and that the rules of entitlement have been integrated with those applied to the other income-related benefits support this proposition.

Reference ought also to be made to two relatively minor changes in our exposition of the law. First, following a suggestion by a reviewer, we have tabulated in an Appendix the current rates of benefit and contributions. Secondly, when a consolidated statute or statutory instrument has been amended we have not, mainly for reasons of economy of space, attempted to incorporate in footnotes references to the amending measure; rather, we have confined the citation to the original statute (or instrument) as amended. A new consolidation of the Social Security Act 1975 and its very many amendments is badly overdue and rumour has it that such a measure is being prepared. Fortunately for us (if not for our readers) it did not surface before the manuscript went to press. One change that we have *not* made relates to our

v

treatment of genders. Like the legislature, but unlike many other authors, we have, with few exceptions, stuck resolutely to the masculine form where a statement might apply to persons of either sex. Paraphrasing the often convoluted language of statutes and regulations has proved to be difficult enough, without assuming the additional burden of rendering it in alternative forms.

Our original plans for the authorship of this edition could not be adhered to. We are enormously grateful to Trevor Buck and Tony Lynes who joined the team at a relatively late stage and who responded with considerable energy and enthusiasm to our request for assistance. Responsibility for the product is divided in the following way: Anthony Ogus prepared chapters 1–4 and 6–9, Eric Barendt chapters 10 and 15–17, Tony Lynes chapter 5, and Trevor Buck and Anthony Ogus (jointly) chapters 11–14. We have attempted to state the law as we understand it to be in June 1988, though we have been able to accommodate some later changes.

Finally, we wish to acknowledge the assistance of Martin Davey, Tina McKevitt and Ashley Wilton for their contributions to, and criticisms of, several chapters. As ever, the editorial staff of Butterworths have been tolerant of our shortcomings and efficient in the processing of the manuscript.

A.I.O.
E.M.B.

August 1988

Foreword to the first edition

by the Rt. Hon. Lord Scarman, OBE, Lord of Appeal in Ordinary

Social security is now the subject of rights and duties. Inevitably, therefore, it is a legal subject. Anthony Ogus and Eric Barendt by this work have committed themselves, without compromise or condition, to this basic proposition: and I commend their work to all who understand the need of a legal approach to a legal subject. But they do not — nor I for that matter — underrate the value of the contributions other disciplines make to the development of a coherent and well-grounded national system of social security; and, of course, no lawyer can understand, or help forward, the law unless he is capable of an inter-disciplinary approach.

I expect this book to become one of the indispensable textbooks of the law. Certainly an authoritative, and independent, work is needed. At present, tribunals and practitioners have to rely heavily on the material produced, but not invariably published, by the Department of Health and Social Security. The department does a fine job: but it is not, and never has been, the office of a government department to declare or interpret the law. If law is to be administered justly, the independence, as well as the skills, of the lawyer must be mobilised. *Ogus and Barendt* will become, I hope, a name as familiar to the lawyer as Chitty, Salmond, Buckley, and Simon.

Finally, this work gives us an opportunity of measuring the extent to which our social security law satisfies the obligations accepted by the United Kingdom as a signatory of the European Social Charter 1961 and the International Covenant on Economic, Social, and Cultural Rights 1966. If any doubt should continue to be entertained that social security has to be part and parcel of English law, our international obligations are the answer.

I commend this book to lawyers primarily — but also to members of the other disciplines concerned with the behaviour of man in society; to politicians; and to all who are concerned to ensure that humanity and compassion are secured by law as well as by generosity.

Scarman

Extract from preface to the first edition

The growth of interest in social security law, both of teachers and practitioners, has been rapid in the last few years. The process has not been free from controversy: opinions differ both as to the academic merit of the subject and to the preferred method of presentation. Some contend that the social security system has not sufficient intellectual weight for the serious student of law; others view the educational objective more in terms of fostering the arithmetic ability to calculate the entitlement of a given individual to benefit rather than of providing any analysis of the principles of the system as a whole. A third approach stresses the desirability of covering, within one university course, broad and diverse areas of the welfare system including not only social security but also housing, education and legal services. We do not adopt these perspectives. The book has been written from a conviction that social security should take its place alongside other, more traditional, legal subjects as fully worthy of critical study, and its unity and technical character make it, in our view, more suitable for this purpose than the necessarily vague outlines of 'welfare' or 'poverty' law.

Legal education has tended in the past to concentrate on law as a method of determining relationships between individuals. While public law — the relationship between the state and the individual — has not been neglected, attention has been focussed for the most part on the formal or constitutional nature of the relationship rather than on its substance. The emphasis has been on the individual's ability to invoke judicial controls over unlawful executive activity rather than on the content of the rights conferred on the individual by the state within the proper exercise of its powers. While social security law raises problems of the constitutional limits of executive powers, it also lays down in considerable detail rules which materially affect the lives of all members of the community. As a body of law, it consists of a complex network of primary and subordinate legislation and case-law (notably Commissioners' decisions, though in some areas judicial rulings are not unimportant), the scrutiny of which provides an excellent training in the handling of a variety of legal instruments. As a reflection of competing social and economic policies, it reveals the way in which a very important branch of state activity has evolved, and how general objectives and strategies are translated into particular principles and rules of law.

In contrast to their counterparts in most other countries, the British universities have accepted 'social administration' as an intellectual discipline in its own right, though necessarily it has relied on other disciplines such as economics, history and sociology for its tools of analysis. Social security, in the context of general social policy, has featured prominently in its publications. This work does not attempt to compete with such studies. Quite apart from the limits to our own competence, we have not the space here both to expound a complex area of law and to subject the policies on which it is based to rigorous interdisciplinary analysis. At the same time, we have sought to explain the law in terms of its policy background and the insights offered by other disciplines, as we believe that the functioning of a social security system cannot be understood without reference to the objectives and values which it incorporates.

This goal has, with other factors, created the problem of preserving a satisfactory balance between historical and policy background, general principle and technical rules. In writing this book we have had in mind not only law students but also practitioners and other professional groups with an interest in this area. To accomplish these various objectives, we have adopted a compromise solution. We have inset not only, as is customary in legal texts, quotations and case summaries, but also technical rules which do not raise issues of legal principle.

A.I.O.
E.M.B.

Oxford
April 1978

Contents

Chronological table of statutes

References in this Table to *Statutes* are to Halsbury's Statutes of England (Fourth Edition) showing the volume and page at which the annotated text of an Act will be found.

Chronological table of statutory instruments

List of British cases

Table of EC cases

Note on citation of Social Security Commissioner Decisions

Reported decisions of the Social Security (formerly National Insurance) Commissioners provide a most important source of social security law. There has been a standard method for citing these decisions since 1951. It starts with the prefix 'R', indicating that the case is reported. There then follows in parenthesis the series initial, denoting the particular social security benefit involved in the case. There are now eleven series:

(A)   Attendance allowance
(F)   Child benefit, and formerly family allowances
(FC)   Family credit
(G)   General — miscellaneous benefits (maternity allowance and statutory maternity pay, guardian's allowance, widow's benefit and invalid care allowance, and formerly child's special allowance and the maternity and death grants)
(I)   Industrial injuries benefits
(IS)   Income support
(M)   Mobility allowance
(P)   Retirement pensions
(S)   Sickness and invalidity benefits, and severe disablement allowance
(SSP) Statutory sick pay
(U)   Unemployment benefit

Although supplementary benefits and family income supplement have been abolished and their series discontinued, some decisions on these benefits are referred to in this book as providing guidance on interpretation of the new benefit rules: their series initials were (SB) and (FIS) respectively.

After the series initial, the number and (after an oblique stroke) the year of the case follow. For example, *R(P) 9/55* refers to the ninth reported retirement pensions case in 1955, and *R(I) 12/75* refers to the twelfth reported decision on industrial injuries benefits in 1975. The heading of reported decisions indicates if they are decisions of a Tribunal of three Commissioners (see p. 580); in this book such decisions are indicated by the initial 'T' in parenthesis after the number and year of the case: for example, *R(U) 4/88 (T)*. The decisions are published individually by HMSO, and then bound every four years. (Until 1976 industrial injuries cases were bound in separate volumes.)

Unreported decisions may be read at the Commissioners' offices. A few of these decisions are discussed in this book. They are identified by reference to two letters ('C' standing for Commissioner, and the relevant series letter), followed by the appropriate number and year. Thus, *CG 17/69* refers to the seventeenth numbered case in 1969 concerning one of the miscellaneous benefits, e.g. guardian's allowance or widow's benefit.

Before 1951 a reported case was referred to simply by its number and series initial, with the addition of the suffix 'K' or 'KL'. For both unpublished decisions, and reported decisions until the end of 1950, the letter 'S' or 'W' was added after the 'C' to denote a Scottish or Welsh case. Thus *CSU 14/48 (KL)* refers to the fourteenth Scottish case on unemployment benefit in 1948 — and a reported case. Now a reported decision merely indicates in its heading whether it is a Scottish or Welsh case.

Some reference is made in this book to decisions of the Northern Ireland Commissioners. Their decisions are cited in much the same way as British cases, though the number and year precede the series initial. These initials also differ from those used in Britain. They are:

(AA)   Attendance allowance
(FA)   Child benefit, and formerly family allowances
(ICA) Invalid care allowance
(II)   Industrial injuries benefits
(IVB) Invalidity benefits
(MB)   Maternity benefits
(P)   Retirement pensions, widow's benefit and guardian's allowance
(SB)   Sickness benefit
(UB)   Unemployment benefit

Thus, *R 10/60 (UB)* refers to the tenth reported Northern Ireland decision during 1960 on unemployment benefit. Before 1960 the letter 'R' was omitted.

Table of decisions

Decisions of the Social Security Commissioner

Decisions of the Northern Ireland Commissioner

Abbreviations

Statutes

CBA	Child Benefit Act
FAA	Family Allowances Act
FANIA	Family Allowances and National Insurance Act
FISA	Family Income Supplements Act
IIDA	Industrial Injuries and Diseases (Old Cases) Act
NAA	National Assistance Act
NHIA	National Health Insurance Act
NIA	National Insurance Act
NI(II)A	National Insurance (Industrial Injuries) Act
SBA	Supplementary Benefits Act
SSA	Social Security Act
SSBA	Social Security Benefits Act
SSCA	Social Security (Contributions) Act
SSHBA	Social Security and Housing Benefits Act
SS(MP)A	Social Security (Miscellaneous Provisions) Act
SSPA	Social Security Pensions Act
UIA	Unemployment Insurance Act
WCA	Workmen's Compensation Act

Books

Calvert	*Social Security Law* (2nd edn)
Cane	*Atiyah's Accidents, Compensation and the Law* (4th edn)
George	*Social Security: Beveridge and After* (1968)
Harris	*William Beveridge* (1977)
Housing Benefit Guidance Manual	DHSS *The Housing Benefit Guidance Manual* (1977)
Kaim-Caudle	*Comparative Social Policy and Social Security* (1973)
Lewis	*Compensation for Industrial Injury* (1987)
Ogus	(ed) Köhler and Zacher *A Century of Social Insurance* (1982) pp. 150–264
Social Fund Manual	DHSS *Social Fund Manual* (1987)
Townsend	*Poverty in the United Kingdom* (1979)
Walley	*Social Security: Another British Failure?* (1972)
Williams	*Social Security Taxation* (1982)

Reports and Papers

Beveridge	Social Insurance and Allied Services (1942, Cmd 6404)
Finer	Report of the Committee on One-Parent Families (1974, Cmnd 5629)
Fisher	Report of the Committee on Abuse of Social Security Benefits (1973, Cmnd 5228)
Green Paper 1985	Green Paper: Reform of Social Security (1985) Vol 1 (Cmnd 9517), Vol 2 Programme for Change (Cmnd 9518), Vol 3 Background Papers (Cmnd 9519)
Housing Benefit Review	Housing Benefit Review, Report of the Review Team (1985, Cmnd 9520)
Industrial Injuries Compensation	DHSS Discussion Document, *Industrial Injuries Compensation* (1980)
McCarthy	Report of the Royal Commission of Inquiry: Social Security in New Zealand (1972)
Pearson	Report of the Royal Commission on Civil Liability and Compensation for Personal Injury (1978, Cmnd 7054–1), vol 1
Reform of the Industrial Injuries Scheme	White Paper: Social Security Act 1975 — Reform of the Industrial Injuries Scheme (1981, Cmnd 8402)
Social Assistance	DHSS Review of the Supplementary Benefits Scheme (1978)
Social Insurance Part I	White Paper: Social Insurance, Part I (1944, Cmd 6550)
Social Insurance Part II	White Paper: Social Insurance, Part II, Workmen's Compensation (1944, Cmd 6551)
White Paper 1985	White Paper: Reform of Social Security — Programme for Action (1985, Cmnd 9691)

Chapter 1
Social security and social policy

Part 1   Introduction

Social security is a massive public enterprise. In 1985–86 the budget was about £40 billion, a third of all public expenditure and just over 11 per cent of the gross domestic product.[1] There are very few individuals who do not, at some stage of their lives, exercise their legal right to benefit of some kind, and the vast majority also pay social security contributions. At any one time, approximately three-quarters of the households in Great Britain derive some of their income from the system.[2] As will be seen, it is governed by a mass of complex statutory principles and regulations, the application of which generates a considerable number of disputes. In 1985, nearly 300,000 appeals by claimants were registered at the social security appeal tribunals.[3]

To gain a proper understanding of the system as a whole, it is necessary first to address the many theoretical issues to which social security gives rise. After a brief account of its evolution in Britain (Part 2), we then explore possible objectives for the system in the light of social, political and economic values (Part 3). In the remainder of the chapter, we consider the different strategies available to meet these objectives.

Part 2   Evolution of social security in Britain[4]
A The family and the Poor Law

In the period of emergent industrialism and capitalism, welfare was to be achieved through personal effort complemented by family interdependence. There was thought to be work available for anyone who wanted it, and destitution was therefore seen as resulting not from social or economic forces but rather from personal failings, a view bolstered by the Puritan ethic of work.[5] Moreover, poverty constituted not only a deviation from moral discipline, but also a threat to civil order, as it was typically associated with crime and

1 *Green Paper 1985* para 3.1
2 Bradshaw in Bean, Ferris and Whynes (eds) *In Defence of Welfare* (1985) p.228.
3 Social Security Statistics 1986, Table 49.01B.
4 See, generally, Gilbert *The Evolution of National Insurance in Great Britain* (1966); Gilbert *British Social Policy 1914–1939* (1970); Bruce *The Rise of the Welfare State* (1973); Fraser *The Evolution of the British Welfare State* (1973); *Ogus*; Wood *The British Welfare State 1900–1950* (1982).
5 Tawney *Religion and the Rise of Capitalism* (1921) pp. 218–249.

political unrest.[6] In this context relief of the poor was necessarily repressive and punitive: a generous system of welfare would have encouraged more idleness and therefore more social chaos. The poor law perfectly reflected this ideology: relief was granted to able-bodied persons only if they were willing to subject themselves to the rigours of the workhouse, where life was intentionally made harsh and repellant.[7] The guiding principle was the so-called doctrine of 'less eligibility'.[8] In the words of the Poor Law Commissioners,

> the first and most essential of all conditions is that the situation of the individual relieved shall not be made really or apparently so eligible as the situation of the independent labourer of the lowest class.[9]

Some mitigation of the doctrine was granted only where it was patent that the individual's plight arose from accident rather than from personal inaptitude, thus for the blind, the crippled and the aged.[10]

B   Voluntary devices for dealing with poverty

Victorian society reaffirmed faith in self-help and personal thrift: protection against the hazards of illness, old age and death was to be achieved through voluntary saving for which purpose friendly societies, trade unions and insurance companies provided the institutional arrangements.[11] At the same time, humanitarian ideals gave rise to a huge philanthropic movement.[12] But the poor law remained as the only state interventionist measure concerned with poverty as such; legislative responses to hardships created by industrialisation concentrated on improvements to health and environmental conditions.

C   National insurance and means-tested assistance

The 1911 legislation which established national insurance in Britain was the culmination of complex social and political developments.[13] The condition of the poor had been investigated by the new social sciences[14] which had challenged the traditional assumption that poverty resulted from moral failings. In particular, most forms of unemployment were seen to have economic causes,[15] a finding of the utmost importance to the movement for unemployment insurance which the market could not provide on a general basis. Protection against the consequences of sickness was more widespread but, outside the poor law, medical care was 'organised' on a haphazard basis, particularly in poorer neighbourhoods where much depended on charitable efforts, and only one half of the working population were insured (usually with friendly societies) against earnings loss.[16] The most important measure

---

6 Fraser n.4, above, pp. 28–31.
7 The classic study is Webb and Webb *History of English Local Government* (1972) vol 7. See also Marshall *The Old Poor Law 1795–1834* (1968), and Rose *The English Poor Law 1780–1930* (1971).
8 Webb and Webb, n.7, above, at pp. 215–264.
9 Report of Royal Commission on Poor Law (1834), para 228.
10 The so-called system of 'out-relief': see Bruce n.4, above, pp. 117–128.
11 Gosden *Self-Help: Voluntary Associations in 19th Century Britain* (1973).
12 Harrison 9 Victorian Studies 360.
13 Hay *The Origins of the Liberal Welfare Reforms 1906–1914* (1975); Ogus pp. 156–187.
14 Booth *Life and Labour of the People in London* (1902); Rowntree *Poverty: A Study of Town Life* (1901)
15 Beveridge *Unemployment, A Problem of Industry* (1909).
16 Bruce, n.4, above, p.214.

directly concerned with income was the introduction in 1908 of a means-tested pension for those aged over 70. While the conditions of entitlement were somewhat narrowly drawn and included a test of character – 'it was a pension for the very old, the very poor and the very respectable'[17] – nevertheless it constituted the first system of financial aid for a social hazard funded from general resources, administered centrally and independent of the poor law.

Means-tested welfare was not, however, to be the general solution. Lloyd George, who visited Germany to study its system of social insurance, became convinced that this was the best method of making 'provisions against the accidents of life which bring so much undeserved poverty to hundreds of thousands of homes, accidents which are quite inevitable such as the death of a breadwinner or his premature breakdown in health'.[18] Insurance was an attractive solution since it would engender the traditional virtue of individual responsibility and investment of personal resources, and would not be far removed from the typical market economy device of the 'exchange' transaction.[19] The notion that such risks were something which the community as a whole should bear received partial recognition by the sharing of insurance costs between the employer (who would pass it on in the form of prices) and the employee; but in order that individual initiative should not be stifled and to discourage idleness, benefit would be paid at only a survival level. This was the scheme adopted for unemployment and sickness under the National Insurance Act 1911. It was also applied by analogy in 1925 to those risks against which individuals might be expected to provide – old age or premature death – but which, in the case of low-earners, typically went unprotected.

There was left a hard core of poverty cases outside these two categories, either because the individual's contribution record was inadequate, or because the duration of the interruption of employment was excessive. The cases might be undeserving and in 1909 the Majority of the Royal Commission on the Poor Law could still argue that it was necessary to treat them as a distinct group of society whose predicament was, in some way, attributable to defects in moral character.[20] But humanitarian sentiments were allowed to prevail. As we have seen, a means-tested financial benefit had already in 1908 been introduced to protect the aged from the poor law, and a similar device, in the form of unemployment assistance, was adopted for the vast numbers of unemployed who during the inter-war period had exhausted their right to insurance benefit.

D Beveridge and comprehensive social security

The pattern established by the end of the 1930s – social insurance covering the major causes of income loss and conferring benefit at a flat-rate survival level, combined with a scheme of residual means-tested assistance for those remaining – was in its essence left unaltered by the programme instituted in 1946–47 and inspired by the Beveridge Report. His primary aims were to make the insurance scheme universal and more comprehensive, to substitute 'subsistence' for 'survival' as the minimum level and to unify its administration. The significance of the Report for the history of British social security lay not so much in these specific aims but rather in the comprehensive review

17 Thane *The Origins of British Social Policy* (1978) pp. 103–104.
18 Quoted in Fraser, n.4, above, p.150.
19 Pinker *Social Theory and Social Policy* (1971) pp. 135–144.
20 (1909, Cd 4499) p.643.

which he undertook of social risks and the methods of meeting them. The primacy of social insurance was reaffirmed: 'benefit in return for contributions, rather than free allowances from the State, is what the people of Britain desire',[1] but it was not to undermine individual responsibility and freedom:

> Social security must be achieved by cooperation between the State and the individual.. . . . The State in organising security should not stifle incentive, opportunity, responsibility; in establishing a national minimum, it should leave room and encouragement for voluntary action by each individual to provide more than that minimum for himself and his family.[2]

Hence the British approach, flat-rate benefits for flat-rate contributions, was to remain distinct from the traditional continental model of earnings-related social insurance.[3]

Equally important, though sometimes overlooked, is the fact that Beveridge was confident that the comprehensive system of national insurance and means-tested assistance would ensure 'freedom from want' only if it was combined with three policies external to the system: full employment, family endowment and a national health service.[4] The government adopted the policies: a commitment to 'the maintenance of a high and stable level of employment';[5] the introduction of family allowances; and the replacement of medical benefits under national health insurance by the national health service.

E Modifications to the Beveridge model

Government complacency engendered by the popularity of the post-war welfare measures was not to last. Empirical studies undertaken by the newly developed discipline of 'social administration', under the inspired leadership of Richard Titmuss,[6] claimed to have 'rediscovered poverty',[7] especially among the aged.[8] National insurance benefits did not provide the level of minimum subsistence which had been promised. The principle of flat-rate contributions meant that the latter had to be set at a level which the lowest paid could afford and the government felt that more subsidy from the Exchequer would undermine the insurance basis of the scheme. Beveridge's assumption that individuals would boost national insurance benefits with private and occupational schemes proved to be well-founded only for the more affluent workers. Provision under superannuation schemes meant that they could look forward to a relatively small drop in living standards when no longer in active employment, whereas the typical manual worker, without such protection, had to fall back on a combination of the flat-rate but inadequate national insurance pension and means-tested national assistance.

In the 1960s and early 1970s attention was focused on two other disadvantaged groups. Family poverty resulted, in part, from a failure of successive governments to maintain the value of family allowance and, in part, from the rapid growth in the number of single-parent families,[9] a

---

1 Para 21.
2 Para 9.
3 Ogus in Zacher (ed) *Bedingungen für die Entstehung und Entwicklung von Sozialversicherung* (1979) pp. 337–348.
4 Para 301.
5 White Paper *Employment Policy* (1944, Cmd 6527) para 3.
6 Reisman *Richard Titmuss: Welfare and Society* (1977).
7 Abel-Smith and Townsend *The Poor and the Poorest* (1965).
8 Townsend *The Family Life of Old People* (1957).
9 *Finer* (1974).

phenomenon which had not been anticipated. National insurance provided less than adequate coverage for the severely disabled both because their needs were often greater than those of other beneficiaries and because many had not been able to participate in the labour market sufficiently to establish a title to benefit.[10]

There was a sustained effort in the mid-1970s to deal with these problems. More resources were allocated to child benefit, which replaced the family allowance. A number of non-contributory, but also non-means tested, allowances were introduced for the disabled. Perhaps most significantly, a new earnings-related pension scheme was introduced and contributions to the national insurance fund, even for the flat-rate benefits, also became earnings-related – British social security thus began to resemble the European systems.[11]

F Wither the Welfare State?[12]

By an unhappy coincidence, the reforms described in the last paragraph occurred at the time of the international economic crisis.[13] The period thereafter has been marked by reversals in social security policy, both in Britain and abroad.[14] The rapid growth of unemployment placed a double strain on the financing of the systems: not only from the costs of income maintenance of the unemployed, but also from the fact that the latter were not contributing to the national insurance fund. Moreover, there was concern that future generations of earners would be unable to meet the obligations of pension schemes to the ever increasing aged population. The economic and political philosophy of the New Right began to exert a profound influence: monetarist policy demanded reductions in public expenditure; social security programmes should guard against the creation of work disincentives and barriers to labour mobility; resources should be targetted on those whose need is greatest; individual responsibility for, and choice of, welfare provision should be maintained.[15]

The impact of these policies was evident in the reforms carried out by the first Thatcher administration – reductions were made to the value of many benefits and responsibility for income maintenance during short periods of sickness was transferred from the state to the employer – but was more explicit in the Green and White Papers of 1985 which followed what was, perhaps, the most important and comprehensive review of the social security system to be undertaken since Beveridge.[16] Legislation in 1986 implemented most of the proposals:[17] reduction to future entitlement under the state earnings-related pension scheme; the encouragement of personal and occupational pensions as alternatives to the state scheme; transfer to the employer of responsibility for maternity payments; and restructuring of the means-tested benefits (henceforth to be known as 'income-related benefits')

10 OPCS Survey of Handicapped and Impaired Persons in Great Britain (1971–72).
11 Ogus, n.3, above.
12 Cf Seldon IEA Occasional Paper 60 (1981).
13 Cf OECD *The Welfare State in Crisis* (1981); EISS Yearbook 1980–81, Part II, *Social Security and the Economic Crisis* (1982).
14 Oyen *Comparing Welfare States and their Futures* (1986).
15 Seldon, n.12, above, and for critical commentary, see Plant in Bean, Ferris and Whynes (eds) *In Defence of Welfare* (1985) ch 1 and Harris *Justifying State Welfare* (1987) ch 1.
16 *Green Paper 1985* vol 1, esp chs 1–6 and 13; *White Paper 1985*, esp ch 1.
17 SSA 1986.

including, most controversially, replacement of rights to single and urgent needs payments by a social fund, administered on a discretionary basis and subject to cash limits.

Part 3   Objectives

A   Private and public systems of welfare

Society has always, been, and for the indefinite future will remain, afflicted by the problem of scarce resources. To deal with the problem of scarcity, and to avoid anarchy, systems of resource allocation must be developed. Clearly, social security is one such system: the state, by means of legislation, allocates some of the scarce resources to those who satisfy certain conditions, typically assumed, or demonstrated, need. But equally clearly, in capitalist and mixed economies, it competes with, and is complementary to, a system which preceded it historically: the market. To understand the existence and content of the social security system, it is, therefore, necessary to analyze the market method of dealing with resources and the shortcomings to which it gives rise.

i The market model of welfare

The basic features of the market model are easily grasped.[18] Individuals, motivated by profit, supply goods and services for which other individuals are prepared to pay. Price plays a key role in the process: it enables potential buyers to communicate the intensity of their demand for a particular good or service; and it allows potential suppliers to compare what they would earn from putting their resources to that use, as opposed to other uses – in the language of economics, supply is determined by opportunity cost. Provided that there is competition, the process is said to generate 'efficiency': competition between buyers ensures that resources move to their most highly valued uses; and competition between suppliers ensures that the goods or services are produced at the lowest cost. Enshrined in the process are the values of liberty – individuals are treated as autonomous and responsible for securing the welfare of themselves and their families – and decentralisation – the state does not determine the production or distribution of resources; its role is limited to preserving law and order and upholding property and contract rights.

The notion of welfare incorporated in this model means not only that individuals are expected to choose how best to exploit resources (typically labour) at their disposal and thus to maximise their income but also that they should make rational decisions on how to cope with contingencies affecting their earning potential, notably, sickness, invalidity, unemployment, old age and death. This will involve some sacrifice of current consumption to 'save for the rainy day'. And the market will respond to the demand to maximise the value of such savings by means of pension and insurance schemes.

ii Limitations of the market model

What we have described above is, of course, an idealised model and, while it can be used to explain the early history of social policy, particularly in the

18 See, generally: McKenzie and Tullock *Modern Political Economy* (1978) chs 1–4 and Creedy and Disney *Social Insurance in Transition* (1985) ch 1.

nineteenth century, it is difficult to reconcile with social reality, at least as it is perceived in modern times.[19] First, it assumes that individuals have the infor-mation available and the capacity to make rational, wise decisions con-cerning current and future welfare; unhappily, that is not always a realistic assumption. The growth of social security may, then, be attributed either to the greater knowledge possessed by bureaucracies on the risks to an indivi-dual's livelihood or to a paternalist policy pursued by governments on the basis that they know better than the individual what is good for him.[20]

Secondly, the insistence on individual decisionmaking fails to take account of the fact that such decisions may affect other people, beneficially or detri-mentally. The problem lies not so much in relation to the obvious and imme-diate effects on the individual's family, because the model assumes that their welfare is identified with his own. The concern is rather with more wide-spread and longer-term effects: society needs a healthy and well-educated workforce to produce goods; poverty is linked to crime and infectious dis-eases; and the existence of deprivation may adversely affect the welfare of others, because a sight of it is 'distasteful' to them, or because they genuinely care about the plight of the less fortunate.[1] Of course, there is nothing to stop those affected in this way from themselves taking steps to alleviate depri-vation in a manner not inconsistent with the market model. Charitable gifts and the like may be rationalised on this basis, but quite apart from the fact that the recipients may find this form of transfer stigmatising this solution, in its turn, gives rise to what is generally referred to as the 'free rider' problem.[2] Potential donors should appreciate that they will derive benefit from the alle-viation of poverty when others make the necessary gifts and they provide nothing. They may, then, make a contribution only if it is matched by con-tributions from others. In the absence of legislative compulsion, this is diffi-cult to organise; hence the case for forced transfers, financed by taxes or social security contributions.

Thirdly, there may be technical problems in the market meeting the demand for protection against risks to income. Private, voluntary insurance has to cope with the problem of 'adverse selection'.[3] An insurance company may begin by assessing a given risk, for example, sickness across a group of individuals defined by (say) age, sex and occupation, and calculating the pre-miums payable for each within the group on the basis of the average risk for the group as a whole. Those for whom the risk is of higher probability than the average will have an incentive to be insured at this level of premium, while individuals with lower than average risks may find the premium excessive for their needs.[4] A spiralling effect may well ensue: as more low-risk indivi-duals forego insurance, the density of high-risk individuals in the group increases, necessitating a higher premium which may now prove unattractive to those with risks nearer the average. To counter the problem, the insurance company has to engage in some degree of individual risk-rating, so that individuals pay premiums proportionate to their own risk. In itself, this is a costly exercise which will be reflected in the premiums; it also means that

19 Cf Bean et al, n.15, above, chs 5–6.
20 Sugden *Who Cares?* IEA Occasional Paper 67 (1983).
 1 Culyer *The Political Economy of Social Policy* (1980).
 2 Friedman *Capitalism and Freedom* (1962) pp. 190–191.
 3 Bean et al, n.15, above, pp. 130–131.
 4 It should be noted, however, that the demand for protection will vary according to the indivi-dual's degree of 'risk aversion', which is independent of the objectively determined risk itself: *Bowles Law and the Economy* (1982) pp. 45–46.

high-risk individuals will be charged premiums that they may not be able to afford. Social insurance, because it is compulsory, can obtain an appropriate balance between high-risk and low-risk individuals. Private insurance companies are, moreover, loth to offer any coverage for some important risks to livelihood, notably unemployment.[5] It is, actuarially, extremely difficult to assess the risk of unemployment because it is primarily a consequence of general economic circumstances which do not follow consistent patterns or trends; and it is also difficult to verify the validity of claims, that individuals are not gainfully employed. The fact that social insurance schemes can be financed on a 'pay as you go' basis enables them to solve the actuarial problem and the existence of broad investigatory powers, to deal with the verification problem, is less controversial if associated with state machinery. Finally, insurance private, or public,[6] because it deals with future, uncertain risks cannot deal with adverse conditions which have already arisen. Some individuals may have been prevented by, for example, congenital disablement, from ever having been able to enter the labour market. Non-contributory benefits must be made available if they are to be protected.

This last example is, in fact, indicative of the fourth and most fundamental problem, concerned with distributional justice: are the processes and the outcomes which they generate *fair*? The welfare obtained by individuals by means of the market depends crucially on their ex ante situation, the property and other resources, including natural endowments like skill and intelligence, at their disposal before the process of exchange begins. If, according to some criterion, the initial distribution of resources is regarded as unjust then the process of exchange will tend to reinforce and even aggravate the injustice. Affluence enables individuals legitimately to purchase the means – for example, education or expertise – to add to their affluence, and illegitimate means, such as barriers to entry and other restrictive practices, may be used to entrench advantages secured in the labour market.[7]

iii Theories of distributional justice
It is one thing to recognise the importance of the distribution justice problem and that social security programmes may be used to pursue distributional goals; it is quite another to reach agreements on what is a just distribution. A variety of theories have been advanced, each with important implications for the design of welfare systems.[8] The extreme position on the Right taken by libertarians is that distributions are just so long as the process by which the resources were acquired were just and this includes, notably, inheritance and purchase.[9] Interventions by the state to reorganise distributions constitutes an infringement of personal liberty; in particular, income tax is equivalent to forced labour and a tax on capital to an unwarranted seizure of goods.[10]

5 Malinvaud 10 Geneva Papers on Risk and Insurance 6.
6 Though public insurance schemes can adapt to the problem by, for example, crediting contributions.
7 On the segmentation of the labour market and the cycle of deprivation, see Reich et al in Atkinson *Wealth, Income and Inequality* (2nd edn) pp. 381–389.
8 George and Wilding *Ideology and Social Welfare* (rev edn); Barr *The Economics of the Welfare State* (1987) ch 3; Harris *Justifying State Welfare* (1987).
9 Nozick *Anarchy, State and Utopia* (1974). The original acquisition of a resource through an application of an individual's labour is justified by the property right residing in the individual's person: cf Locke *Second Treatise of Civil Government* (Everyman ed) s.43.
10 Nozick, n.9, above, pp. 169–172. Some libertarians are, however, prepared to admit that a minimum degree of material support for disadvantaged persons may be necessary if they are to be able to exercise their political rights, which are highly valued: Buchanan in Dworkin, Bermont and Brown *Markets and Morals* (1977) ch 6.

Exponents of liberal theories are prepared to temper acceptance of the market order and respect for individual liberty with some concern for distributional consequences. Typical is the well-known proposition advanced by Rawls that individuals, if prevented by a veil of ignorance from knowing their station in society, would agree that social and economic inequalities are justified only if they improve the position of everyone, especially the least advantaged.[11] The state should redress unjustified inequalities by interventionist measures[12] but the vagueness of the criterion makes it difficult to spell out what degree of redistribution is called for.

More explicit, in this respect, are theories based on notions of citizenship; the goal is to

> ensure that everyone is able to enjoy a standard of living much like that of the rest of the community, and thus is able to feel a sense of participation in and belonging to the community.[13]

This leads to a notion of citizenship rights conferred as an act of social policy on those whose resources are inadequate for full participation in the community and existing alongside the more traditional rights, such as property, associated with the market model.[14] As will be seen, approaches of this kind raise difficult questions of how to measure need.

Egalitarian theories involve a more direct attack on the market method of allocating resources.[15] They go beyond advocating equality of opportunity but, typically, fall short of advocating equality of income,[16] primarily because they recognise that effort and responsibility should be rewarded. Social policy should be directed towards *reducing* inequalities and opinions obviously differ on how far this process should be taken.

Marxists argue that the very existence of market relationships is incompatible with notions of just distribution and needs to be replaced by another system of economic organisation which will enable resources to move 'from each according to his ability to each according to his need'.[17]

iv Economic constraints

Policymakers, convinced of the unfairness of the market model and intent on devising social security measures to redistribute resources in the light of one or more of the theories described in the last section, may nevertheless be concerned with the general economic consequences of such measures. On the face of it, social security benefits are simply 'transfer payments'[18] from one group to another and the aggregate wealth of society is not affected. Indeed, it can be argued that, in terms of utility, redistribution from the rich to the poor makes society 'better off' since £1 in the hands of a poor transferee is worth more to him than it was in the hands of the richer transferor.[19]

---

11 *A Theory of Justice* (1972), esp chs 11–14. It should be noted, however, that the principle ranks second in priority below that of equal liberty.
12 Ibid, ch 43.
13 *McCarthy* p.65.
14 Marshall *Sociology at the Crossroads and Other Essays* (1963) ch 4; Parker *Social Policy and Citizenship* (1975) ch 9.
15 George and Wilding, n.8, above, ch 4; Harris, n.8, above, ch 5.
16 George and Wilding, n.8, above, p.65.
17 Marx *Criticism of the Gotha Programme* in Feuer (ed) *Marx and Engels: Basic Writings on Politics and Philosophy* (1969) p.160 and, generally, ch 5.
18 Cf McClements *The Economics of Social Security* (1978) ch 7.
19 Cf Culyer *The Political Economy of Social Policy* (1980) ch 4. However, interpersonal comparisons of this kind are subject to many theoretical difficulties: ibid, p.23.

However, welfare transfers may involve sacrifices to general economic welfare in three different ways:[20] first, high levels of benefit may create work disincentives and thus productivity losses; secondly, the marginal tax rates necessary to finance progressive redistribution may have the same effect and may also reduce the amount available for investment, thus depleting the capital stocks of society; thirdly, the administration of the transfers is itself costly, employing resources which could be put to more productive use.

B Political factors

The attribution of stages in the evolution of the social security system to the theories of distribution outlined above would appear to be plausible: nineteenth century approaches match libertarian ideologies; the combination of national insurance and means-tested assistance endorses the liberal approach (which is made explicit in the Beveridge Report); the notion of citizenship can be located in, for example, the non-contributory benefits for the disabled; and egalitarian ideals may lie behind family allowances and child benefit. To explain policy developments by reference to goals is, however, necessarily simplistic because it ignores the political dimension – how policy is implemented.

Political scientists and others have developed several competing theories to explain changes in welfare legislation.[1] On a broad 'macro' level, there are theories which regard such changes as inseparably linked to wider socio-economic factors, such as the degree of industrialization.[2] Analogously, Marxists argue that social welfare measures are typically a response by capitalists to the threat to stability and order posed by the class struggle.[3]

Less ambitious theories offer, perhaps, more promising hypotheses. One focuses on intellectual activity and perceives policy change to proceed from the way new information is collected and new ideas formulated by professionals and academics and then communicated to the policymaker.[4] The difficulty with this view it is that it takes no account of political structures and institutions and explanations of change in terms of the latter command the widest support among theorists. Some purport to find the key in the party structure: the envisaged reform must be consistent with the traditional set of values held by the party with dominant power at the time.[5] Others take more seriously the democratic basis of the legislative process: policy is seen as a product of competition to win electoral support.[6] A third view stresses the role of bureaucrats: the real power, it is alleged, is held by those within the departments of government who can force their opinion on politicians, often because of greater expertise and superior information.[7] Finally, on the fourth approach, policy is viewed as the outcome of conflict between different interest groups: it balances the power between these groups, with bureaucrats providing the technical expertise to fashion the appropriate compromise.[8]

As will be seen from a comparison of the two most recent periods of social

20 McClements, n.18, above, ch 4.
 1 See, esp, Banting *Poverty, Politics and Policy* (1979).
 2 Wilensky *The Welfare State and Equality* (1975).
 3 Kincaid *Poverty and Equality in Britain* (1973).
 4 Lindblom *The Intelligence of Democracy* (1965).
 5 Beer *Modern British Politics* (1965).
 6 Downs *An Economic Theory of Democracy* (1957).
 7 Rose *The Problem of Party Government* (1974).
 8 Wootten *Pressure Politics in Contemporary Britain* (1978).

security reform, it is not easy to reach general conclusions on these rival theories. The modifications to the Beveridge model enacted in the period 1965 to 1975 would seem to reflect the cumulative importance of different influences on social policy.[9] The reforms had their origin in intellectual activity – the rediscovery of poverty by the academics – but required the efforts of pressure groups to give the campaign momentum. Thereafter, bureaucrats played the decisive role in the way they formulated alternative strategies for their political masters.[10] Party politics and electoral considerations became involved only at a relatively late stage and, arguably, had little influence on the eventual outcome.[11]

· The story of the Thatcher reforms is very different.[12] As regards intellectual inspiration, Conservative politicians have been somewhat contemptuous of traditional sociological research and have preferred to commission studies of the social security system from within government.[13] The primary role of bureaucrats in formulating policy options has been maintained but the emphasis has changed: the parameters within which reform is perceived as possible have been determined by politicians rather than administrators. The impact of most of the interest groups appears to have been substantially reduced. While the proposals have been published for public consultation at an interim stage, seemingly the government has only been prepared to make compromise when pressure has been exerted from within its own supporters.[14]

C Other values

i Demographic aims

In some countries the level of family endowment is thought to have a significant impact on the birth rate and in this sense social security has been regarded as an instrument of demographic policy.[15] Undeniably it played an important role in the introduction of family allowances in Britain.[16] In the recent discussions of family endowment, however, demographic issues have been relatively neglected.

A second demographic goal, that of labour mobility, features more prominently in social policy, particularly under the Thatcher government.[17] On the one hand, the social security system provides positive incentives notably through maintaining an individual's contribution record and preserving the right to benefit during periods of retraining or rehabilitation,[18] and by insisting on the portability of occupational pension rights.[19] Much of the international law in this field, particularly that of the European Communities, is

9 Ogus 1034 Acta Universitatis Wratislaviensis 49.
10 Hall et al *Change, Choice and Conflict in Social Policy* (1975) pp. 69–72.
11 Banting, n.1, above, pp. 87–100.
12 Taylor-Gooby in Klein and O'Higgins (eds) *The Future of Welfare* (1985) ch 5; Ogus, n.9, above, pp. 61–64.
13 Notably, the Fowler reviews, summarised in *Green Paper 1985* vols 2–4.
14 Eg abandoning the proposal to abolish the earnings-related pension scheme between the publications of the Green and White Papers 1985.
15 *Kaim-Caudle*, pp. 18–21, Mirinoff [1980] Soc Services Rev 301.
16 Hall, Land, Parker and Webb *Change, Choice and Conflict in Social Policy* (1975) pp. 170–174.
17 See *White Paper 1985*, para 1, 12 and, more generally, Sinfield *What Unemployment Means* (1981) pp. 106–118.
18 Pp. 58–59, below.
19 Pp. 214–216, below.

designed to encourage the mobility of labour between countries.[20] On the other hand, there are negative sanctions involving the withdrawal of benefit where individuals fail to avail themselves of work opportunities.[1]

ii The family

On a superficial analysis it may appear as if the social security system serves to undermine the integrity of the family unit. In an historical sense, it is true that originally support by other family members was the first and sometimes the only refuge from destitution,[2] and that this function has to a considerable extent been superseded by state financial provision. But while dependence on remoter family relationships may, to some extent, have diminished in importance, the legal interdependence of the inner family unit has in fact increased and is in no way overridden by the social security system which intervenes to replace maintenance obligations only when they remain unfulfilled.[3] Moreover, social security can have a positive effect on family relationships by materially enabling individuals to care for their weaker relatives.

Another argument turns on the extent of support for natural, as opposed to legal, family relationships. It has been said that recognition of *de facto* relationships acts as an incentive to marital breakdown.[4] It must be conceded that for some, but by no means all, purposes, social security has regard to the consequences of such a relationship rather than the legal family as the basic unit. But there is little evidence to suggest that such state support as exists for *de facto* families acts as an incentive to marriage breakdown.[5] Even if it does, the consequent evil has to be weighed against the competing desire to protect the welfare of children by not forcing couples to continue to cohabit when a marriage has already disintegrated, and by recognising new obligations that may arise from alternative relationships.[6] Whether for the purposes of social security the 'family' is that recognised by the law generally or a broader concept, it is indisputable that its economic welfare constitutes one of the primary objectives of the system. This is evident not only from the attempts to make child benefit and family credit underwrite intra-family maintenance, but also from the way in which, in sharp contrast to that of some other countries, British law has traditionally concentrated its income maintenance programme on family needs rather than earnings replacement.

iii Sex equality

There have always been significant differences in social security systems between the treatment of men and women.[7] Although this area of law was deliberately excluded from the sex discrimination legislation, nevertheless as a result of membership of the European Economic Community[8] recent

20 Ch 17, below.
 1 Pp. 104–109 and 452–458, below.
 2 Eekelaar *Family Law and Social Policy* (2nd edn) pp. 17–21.
 3 See generally *Finer* Part 4, and pp. 458–464, below.
 4 The argument is stated and repudiated in Friedmann *Law in a Changing Society* (2nd edn) pp. 287–289. See also *Finer* para 2.7.
 5 Cf. *Finer* pp. 6–18.
 6 The issue has been very fully discussed in the context of divorce legislation: see Eekelaar, n.2, above, ch 2.
 7 See generally Land in Barker and Allen (eds) *Sexual Divisions and Society* (1976) pp. 108–132; Townsend *Sociology and Social Policy* (1975) ch 17; Wilson *Women and the Welfare State* (1977); ISSA Studies and Research no 5, *Women and Social Security* (1973).
 8 Esp the Directive on Equal Treatment in Social Security Benefits: Dir 79/7, OJ 1979 L 6/24, on which see Atkins [1978–79] JSWL 244.

governments have made steady progress towards greater sex equality. As regards single women, the pre-war discrimination based on the assumption that they were 'poor risks' was abolished in 1945[9] and the only difference remaining is that the pensionable age for women is five years earlier than that for men.[10]

The different treatment of married women stemmed in part from the practice of regarding the family as a single financial unit. The model which traditionally dominated social policy thinking was that of the wife doing the housework and rearing the children while the husband was the breadwinner. The structure of national insurance was based on the assumption that a married woman's earnings were subsidiary and, in the words of Beveridge, her earnings were 'a means not of subsistence but of a standard of living above subsistence', and thus in the case of unemployment or sickness she could fall back on her husband's support.[11] A complex set of rules was formulated to reflect this lower status, including notably the ability to opt out of the insurance scheme. With changing social attitudes, and the increasing participation of married women in the labour market,[12] this option was abolished for those marrying after April 1977. There followed a series of further reforms to other social security provisions. Since 1983, either member of a couple may claim a means-tested benefit and not, as was typically the case before, only the husband or male partner.[13] Married women were previously excluded from the invalid care allowance and had to satisfy special conditions for the non-contributory invalidity pension but the provisions have now been altered, though in the case of the former benefit only as a result of a decision of the European Court of Justice, that the legislation infringed the EEC Directive on Equal Treatment.[14] The principles governing the entitlement of husbands and wives to increases to a contributory benefit for a dependent spouse have now been harmonised.[15]

However the logic of these reforms has not been pursued in the case of survivor benefits. A widow receives substantial benefit and thus is not expected to maintain herself by earnings if she has dependent children, or is aged over 55.[16] But outside the war pension scheme, and unless he is an invalid, a husband receives no benefit on the death of his wife: the assumption must be that husbands are not financially dependent on wives and that, as regards housework and care, it is easier for them to find a replacement spouse.[17] Nor at present does there appear to be any inclination to follow the Swedish example of establishing a paternity allowance payable to fathers who temporarily cease work to care for a new-born child.[18] The more radical proposals, made by feminists and others, for state benefits for child-carers or housewives[19] have

---

9 Cf *Beveridge* para 123.
10 Proposals for a common pensionable age have been rejected by the government on the grounds of cost: p.187, below.
11 Para 108.
12 Beveridge relied on the fact that before the Second World War only about 12½ per cent of married women of working age were gainfully employed (para 108). In 1978 the figure was 62 per cent: General Household Survey 1978, Table 5.1.
13 P.424, below.
14 Pp. 145 and 169, below.
15 P.341, below.
16 Pp. 240–242, below.
17 Clarke and Ogus, 5 Br J Law and Son 7. Statistics, however, show that the remarriage rate of widowers is higher than that of widows.
18 See Baude in Lipman-Blumen and Berhard, *Sex Roles and Social Policy* (1979) ch 4.
19 Bennett in Segal (ed) *What Is To Be Done About The Family?* (1983) ch 8; Esam, Good and Middleton *Who's to Benefit?* (1985) ch 4.

proved to be even less acceptable. They emanate from a concern that the principle of aggregating a couple's resources for the purposes of means-tested benefits and the consequent need to formulate and enforce rules on cohabitation[20] in practice discriminate against women and reinforce notions of dependency.

Part 4   Strategies

A   Introduction

In Part 2 we considered the range of objectives that a social security system might adopt. In this part we discuss the different strategies available to meet these objectives. In section B, we consider how recipients of cash benefits may be selected and classified according to their needs. Section C is concerned with the principles for assessing benefits, and section D with the methods of financing them. Finally, in section E we contrast the cash benefit system with two other types of social welfare: benefits in kind, and fiscal relief.

B   Selection and classification of need

i   General

The primary question arising under a system of cash benefits relates to the circumstances in which and the persons to whom benefits are paid. To postulate that a social security system must be 'selective' is merely to state the obvious. The same benefits cannot be enjoyed to the same degree by all members of society. Even the most 'universal' of schemes, such as the social dividend proposal (described later in this chapter[1]) which purports to grant benefit to all, nevertheless effectively takes it back from many through the medium of taxation. The debate on 'universality versus selectivity'[2] is thus concerned not with a choice between two extreme alternatives but rather on the nature and extent of the selectivity process. At a very broad level, two fundamentally different approaches should be distinguished. In the first, generally referred to as the means test method, the target is poverty as such, and the primary condition of entitlement is a level of resources below a stipulated amount. The second attempts to focus on presumed needs (often but not exclusively involving income deprivation) arising from certain circumstances, e.g. unemployment, disability, old age, the maintenance of children. The one approach is not necessarily coterminous with the other – it is possible that entitlement to a particular benefit may depend on conditions both of non-financial circumstances and of income – but the relative weight to be given to each strategy raises an important issue of social policy.

ii   Means-tested benefits

The primary assumption behind the means test approach is that deprivation of income and other resources constitutes the greatest need on which the

20 Pp. 354–357, below.
 1 P.29, below.
 2 See esp. *McCarthy* ch 14; Titmuss *Commitment to Welfare* (2nd edn) ch 10; Davies *Universality, Selectivity and Effectiveness in Social Policy* (1978) ch 7 Garfinkel (ed) *Income-Tested Transfer Programs: The Case For and Against* (1982); Wilson and Wilson *The Political Economy of the Welfare State* (1982) ch 4; Deacon and Bradshaw *Reserved for the Poor* (1983) ch 4.

social security system should concentrate. It is typically combined with concern that welfare expenditure (which involves a substantial degree of redistribution) should be limited to cases of *demonstrated* need and that the conditions for receipt should be kept within carefully observed limits.[3] The process has, however, been attacked by a battery of arguments.[4] Means tests are regarded as socially divisive not the least because those who are subject to them are conscious of the continuity of a tradition dating back to the poor law. They imply strong control functions by governments and bureaucrats whose attitudes may be coloured by their own moral judgments of poverty. This leads to a conclusion that 'there is a general discouragement to use means-tested services which is built into their operating rules and administration by a society which sets great store by self-help and thrift'.[5] Perhaps the most frequently voiced objection is that means-tests are stigmatising[6] and for that, and other reasons result in a lower than desirable take-up rate.[7] Finally, means-testing, as a means of selecting beneficiaries, is expensive to administer,[8] and the additional costs borne by claimants (waiting, frustration, travelling) must also be taken into account.[9]

General considerations of the merits of means tests leave open the question as to the form such tests might take. The McCarthy Royal Commission in New Zealand was quick to assert what appeared to it to be a fundamental distinction between 'means tests' and 'income tests': the former but not the latter take into account the claimant's capital resources.[10] The income test was less stigmatising as the claimant's total circumstances need not be opened to public scrutiny; it also avoided any incentive to dissipate capital resources to gain entitlement. In Britain, while the level of capital resources disregarded under the present income-related schemes is reasonably generous,[11] the tradition has always been to take them into account not only because someone with substantial capital is assumed not to be in need but also because to disregard them creates inequities between claimants. This same problem is inherent in the difficult choice between simplicity and comprehensiveness[12]: to do justice to each recipient involves a rigorous scrutiny of all his circumstances which is both expensive and disagreeable. If the objective is to be achieved by rules conferring rights, there is a danger of creating a complex and unwieldy body of law which those directly concerned would be unlikely fully to understand. If the more flexible alternative of a wide discretion is preferred, this creates the risk of bureaucratic power and apparent arbitrariness.

There has been no consistent development in British social policy in relation to means-tested benefits.[13] The early forms of welfare were, of course,

3 Harris and Seldon *Over-ruled on Welfare* (1979); Dilnot, Kay and Morris *The Reform of Social Security* (1984) pp. 113–118; *Green Paper 1985* para 6.3.
4 *McCarthy* ch 14; National Consumer Council *Means-Tested Benefits* (1976) and the references cited in n.2, above.
5 *Townsend* p.880.
6 The evidence and arguments are reviewed in Spicker *Stigma and Social Welfare* (1984).
7 Deacon and Bradshaw, n.2, above, ch 7, which contains inter alia recent statistics on take-up rates.
8 Eg in 1981–82 the administration of supplementary benefit cost 10.5 per cent of benefit expenditure, compared with 1.5 per cent for retirement pensions and 8.3 per cent for unemployment benefit: Dilnot et al, n.3, above, Table 2.1, p.45.
9 Collard in Bull (ed) *Family Poverty* (2nd edn) p.42.
10 *McCarthy* p.139.
11 See pp. 447–449, below.
12 *Social Assistance* ch 3; Wilding in Adler and Bradley (eds) *Justice, Discretion and Poverty* (1976) ch 4; Titmuss 42 Political Q 113.
13 Deacon and Bradshaw, n.2, above.

almost wholly dependent on this method. As we have seen, between the wars unemployment assistance became a necessary complement to national insurance; and, though Beveridge's aim was to reduce reliance on means-tested welfare to a minimum, the very opposite occurred. Today, it is accepted as an inevitable and major feature of the social security system – over 7 million individuals now depend on means-tested benefits to a greater or lesser extent[14] – and indeed is consistent with the Conservative government's explicit policy to target resources more effectively.[15] But policies have varied on the form and structure of the schemes.[16] In the early 1980s, the emphasis was on detailed rights and regulation. The latest reforms reversed the trend, as the government sought to restrain the costs and the complexities by subjecting important areas of need to discretionary decisionmaking. At the same time, an effort was made to coordinate the different schemes.

iii Criterion of assumed needs

The alternative strategy of selecting circumstances or individuals whose present or future needs are assumed rather than demonstrated is more widely favoured. Inevitably it raises the fundamental question of what is comprehended by 'needs' and of whether their satisfaction is properly the subject of state intervention as opposed to individual initiative.[17] A fundamental goal of all social security systems is to make provision for economic insecurity and thus it is a question of identifying the typical causes of such insecurity.[18] The variety of circumstances causing financial hardship is infinite. While some are regarded uncontroversially as properly the subject of individual initiative, for example, property loss through fire, theft or vandalism,[19] and others are endemic in a society of mixed cultures and values, for example, lack of ambition, idleness, personal extravagance,[20] there is a broad category of hazards which in most industrially developed societies are regarded as appropriate for state intervention. They may be divided into three groups.

a *Earnings loss*

Social security systems have always centred on providing some compensation for the interruption or deprivation of earnings resulting from one or more of the standard risks: unemployment, sickness, invalidity, maternity and old age. Income maintenance in these circumstances is provided primarily by the contributory (formerly national insurance) benefits.

b *Loss of maintenance*

Impairment of the breadwinner's income can also have adverse consequences on dependants and additions are available to some of the contributory benefits for this purpose but the death of the breadwinner is the only cause of loss of maintenance which, under the British system, gives rise to substantial protection, in the form of widow's benefits and the guardian's allowance. The breakdown of marriage, while a major source of deprivation, has never been

14 Bradshaw in Bean et al *In Defence of Welfare* (1985) p.230.
15 *White Paper* 1985 para 1.5.
16 Pp. 414–417, 473–476 and 487–491, below.
17 Harris *Justifying State Welfare* (1987) ch 7.
18 Cf *Beveridge* paras 311–312; Turnbull, Williams and Cheit *Economic and Social Security* (4th edn) pp. 3–4.
19 *Beveridge,* para 312.
20 Rejda *Social Insurance and Economic Security* (1976) pp. 8–9.

treated as equivalent to death and special relief is limited to an increased rate of child benefit for single parents.[1]

c *Special expenses*
Priority has been conferred on the partial indemnification of two categories of expenditure: the costs of rearing children and those incurred by seriously disabled persons. Maternity and funeral expenses used to be the subject of universal grants but assistance with these expenses is now means-tested, as is help with housing costs.

C Levels of cash benefit

i Flat-rate or earnings-related
Having determined the circumstances in which a cash benefit will be payable, the social security system must then decide on what principle that benefit will be calculated. Where it is intended as some replacement for the interruption or loss of earnings, the fundamental issue arises whether the benefit should be flat-rate or earnings-related. The main theoretical argument in favour of the latter approach is that based on free-enterprise incentives, a predictably popular creed in the United States of America:

> A free-enterprise society which stresses the rewards of individual initiative should also embody incentive principles: that the higher income secured by the higher-paid worker should be reflected in high social security benefits when he cannot work.[2]

Allied to this is the notion, popular with some trade-unions, that benefit is merely a 'deferred wage' and therefore should reflect the collective bargaining process which determined the amount of that wage.[3] The argument is a compelling one in a wholly state-controlled economy where the state is both the employer and the provider of benefits, on the assumption that the initial wage level accords with the distributional dictates of its conception of social justice.[4] For this very reason it is opposed by those who argue that an earnings-related scheme reinforces differentials, on the whole dictated by market forces, and which may therefore be inequitable.[5] This viewpoint is linked to the principle that the social welfare system should operate as a mechanism for redistribution rather than merely as a compensation for losses incurred through social risks.

The debate may involve fundamental issues of social philosophy but typically the matter is decided by more pragmatic considerations. Increasing affluence, as manifest in post-war industrial societies, reinforces concern for the preservation of differentials.[6] Hence there is a substantial demand at least from middle and higher socio-economic groups for benefits, particularly pensions, to reflect those differentials. If the state system does not meet this demand, the market will.[7] The issue of earnings-related benefits depends then

1 The recommendation of the Finer Committee that a guaranteed maintenance allowance be introduced for this group has not been implemented.
2 Burns *Social Security and Public Policy* (1956) p.40 See also Richardson *Economic and Financial Aspects of Social Security* (1960) p.42, and *Walley* p.145.
3 *Burns*, n.2, above, at p.41; *George* p.36.
4 *McCarthy* p.173.
5 Kincaid *Poverty and Equality in Britain* (1973) pp. 236–237; Esam, Good and Middleton *Who's to Benefit?* (1985) pp. 37–38.
6 *George* p.36, and see the Swedish Report *Social Policy and How It Works* (1969).
7 Cf Silburn (ed) *The Future of Social Security* (1985) pp. 68–69.

on the relationship between public and private provision, on which there have been dramatic changes in the period since the Second World War.

Beveridge regarded protection of resources above the subsistence level as a matter for individual initiative but the principle of flat-rate benefits led to a glaring disparity between those who were able and willing to augment state provision by occupational schemes and those who were not. The Conservative government's solution, a modest graduated pension scheme, proved to be inadequate and the Labour party drew up plans for a national superannuation programme of earnings-related provision which nevertheless was slow to be implemented. Earnings-related supplements to the short-term benefits for sickness and unemployment were introduced in 1966 but the state earnings-related pension scheme (SERPS) was enacted only in 1975. The concern of the Thatcher administration to encourage expansion of private provision and to broaden choice naturally led to a reversal of the trend. The earnings-related supplements to the short-term benefits were abolished in 1982 and though the original intention of abolishing SERPS was abandoned the 1986 legislation reduced entitlements under the scheme.

ii Determination of benefits according to need
A large number of benefits payable under the current system are not related to earnings. These include not only the flat-rate components in the standard income-replacement benefits for sickness, unemployment and retirement, but also those designed to accommodate special expenses or needs and those which are means-tested. For all within this category, decisions must be taken on the appropriate level of financial support. There has been a considerable amount of literature devoted to this question, much of it concerned with theoretical problems of assessing need and defining poverty. Less well treated are the political and other pressures which in practice operate on governmental decision-makers in this area.

a *Assessing needs*
The Beveridge objective, it will be recalled, was that of a minimum level of 'subsistence' on the basis of 'normal needs'. How were such needs to be assessed? Already earlier in the century some scientific measurement had been attempted, notably by Rowntree. He drew up a list of 'consumption necessities', e.g. food, clothing and housing expenditure.[8] The method was adopted by Beveridge as a guide;[9] he applied a variable of age and also added a margin for inefficiency in spending. In another respect, however, his criteria were more stringent than those proposed by Rowntree who had allowed a small amount for 'personal sundries', e.g. trade union subscriptions, newspapers, radio, beer, tobacco.[10] Of course, as determinants for individual needs, these models were deficient, in that they had to be based on perceived averages.[11] Any shortfall was therefore to be remedied by supplementary schemes based on detailed means tests. This handicap was only one of a number of aspects which were vigorously criticised by commentators in the 1950s and 1960s. The most comprehensive and widely publicised was

8 *Poverty – A Study of Town Life* (1901); *Human Needs of Labour* (1937).
9 Paras 217–232; cf *Harris* pp. 396–399.
10 *Human Needs of Labour* (1973) p.61.
11 Cf *Social Assistance* para 5.5. The problem of variations in rent Beveridge felt to be particularly acute but after some hesitation decided that to make a separate award for household needs would be impracticable: paras 193–216.

that of Townsend.[12] He rejected any absolute objective notion of poverty based on subsistence requirements: he regarded it instead as a relative concept to be measured only by reference to the living standards of a particular society at a particular time. Others have stressed that poverty is a psychological state dependent on an individual's own expectations:[13] this may be conditioned by his own or his neighbour's previous level of earnings or standard of living. Finally there is the perspective which has regard to the effect of deprivation on the lives of individuals within the community – a state of 'virtual non-participation'.[14] In the latest large scale survey of poverty, Townsend sought to incorporate these broader dimensions by focusing not only on objective standards as reflected in data on the distribution of resources but also on individuals' perceptions of what constitutes poverty, the effect of environmental factors, and the relevance to deprivation of categorisation into one of the social minorities (e.g. single parents, non-whites, unemployed).[15]

b *Fixing scales of benefit*
Undoubtedly the data available on the needs of particular disadvantaged groups influence to a certain extent governmental decisions on the level of benefits, but it is important to appreciate that there are other factors which may play an equal if not primary role. Regard has typically been had not only to the level of prices but also to the general level of earnings: a system in which benefits are significantly above the incomes of the lower paid is likely to be politically unacceptable, if for no other reason than it is thought to have an effect on work incentives.[16] Further, fixing the amount of some flat-rate benefits, such as retirement pensions, may be influenced by the fact that many beneficiaries receive also an earnings-related component. Conversely, account may be taken of equity considerations when determining the relationship between different categories of social security benefit, for example, between contributory and non-contributory benefits.[17] The level of social security payments is also necessarily dependent on the general economic policy pursued by government. The restraints imposed on public expenditure by the current Conservative administration which have resulted in reductions in the real value of benefits are considered to be crucial to the control of inflation and the revitalisation of the economy.[18] However controversial this policy may be, it is at least consistent with general strategy and in this sense is 'rational'.[19] As such it is to be contrasted with the way in which decisions as to social welfare spending have been reached on purely political grounds: for example, the raising of benefits to a generous level in the year before a general election is by no means unknown. A remarkable feature of the past two

12 (1954) Br Jo of Sociology 330 and (1962), ibid, 210. See also the collection of essays, Townsend (ed) *The Concept of Poverty* (1970).
13 E.g. Runciman *Relative Deprivation and Social Justice* (1966).
14 See Economic Council of Canada *The Challenge of Growth and Change* (1968). The definition won the approval of the NZ Royal Commission: *McCarthy* pp. 104–105. See also Goldthorpe in Wedderburn (ed) *Poverty, Inequality and Class Struture* (1974) ch 11.
15 *Townsend*.
16 *McCarthy* ch 19; *Fisher* paras 35–36; Burns *Social Security and Public Policy* (1956) ch 4. The argument has been attacked by e.g. Kincaid *Poverty and Equality in Britain* (1973) ch 12 and Jordan *Poor Parents* (1974) ch 4.
17 P.145, below.
18 White Paper, The Government's Expenditure Plans 1980–81 (1979, Cmnd 7746).
19 Though see the criticisms of the Commons' Social Services Committee, 3rd Report 1979–80, HC 702.

decades or so has been the growth of pressure groups identified with particular categories of beneficiaries or disadvantaged people.[20] They have had a significant influence on decision-making, especially in the area of family[1] and disability[2] benefits.

c *The problem of inflation*

Of course, the level of a particular benefit depends not only on the policy (or politics) prevailing at the time the benefit was introduced but also on whether governments are prepared to maintain its value relative to changes in prices and earnings.[3] Indeed, inflation can be used to alter policy on particular benefits without direct legislative reform. For example, successive governments allowed the real value of the death and maternity grants to erode so substantially over the period since the Second World War that in recent years they no longer served their original purpose. Politically, it then became easier to argue for their abolition as universal benefits, since the cost of administering payment was very high relative to their value.[4] Nevertheless, as regards the major income maintenance programmes, social *security* would be a misnomer if beneficiaries could not rely on some degree of protection against inflation, particularly, as in the 1970s, when the rate was high.[5] There has·been a widespread consensus that legislative duties to up-rate benefits, in some form, should be imposed on governments but, as will be revealed in a later chapter,[6] the provisions have been modified several times since their original enactment in 1973. Perhaps most significant was the repeal of the obligation to link pensions to rises in earnings, a decision which generated very substantial savings in social security expenditure.[7] Such constraints on public expenditure were considered by the Thatcher administration to be the most effective means of controlling inflation. However, the argument that social security beneficiaries should share the burden of the struggle with fellow citizens[8] carries less weight if their incomes are already very low.[9]

iii Determination of earnings-related benefits

Some of the problems inherent in relating benefits to a claimant's previous earnings are of a practical nature; for example, the type of earnings of which account may be taken and the nature of proof required.[10] Others raise delicate questions of social policy. To achieve equity as between those, typically manual workers, whose optimal earnings are reached at an early age and those, typically white-collar workers, who reach their earnings peak later in life, it may be necessary to have regard to widely divergent periods as the basis for the calculation.[11] In systems where short-term benefits are earnings-related, regard is generally had to the claimant's wages in the period imme-

---

20 Donnison *The Politics of Poverty* (1982) pp. 126–134.
 1 Banting *Poverty, Politics and Policy* (1979).
 2 Walker in Jones (ed) *Yearbook of Social Policy 1975* pp. 204–207.
 3 See, generally, Wilson (ed) *Pensions, Inflation and Growth* (1974) and Hirsch and Goldthorpe (eds) *The Political Economy of Inflation* (1978) ch 4.
 4 Some of the industrial injury benefits have been subject to the same process: p.310, below.
 5 Trinder in Willmott (ed) *Sharing Inflation* (1976) chs 2–4.
 6 Pp. 379–381, below.
 7 Lynes *Maintaining the Value of Benefits* (1985) pp. 18–19.
 8 See the government's reply to the 3rd report of the Commons' Social Services Committee (1980, Cmnd 8086) para 34.
 9 See the First Report of the Social Security Advisory Committee (1982) para 3.22.
10 Pp. 373–379, below.
11 Cf White Paper, Better Pensions (1974, Cmnd 5713), p.iii.

diately before that of entitlement;[12] but for long-term benefits, it is thought fairer to take account of that period when the earnings were highest in real terms.[13] Neither of these approaches copes adequately with the case where an individual is rendered unemployable. It is rare indeed for a social security system (in contrast to the common law method of awarding damages for future lost earnings) to base the earnings award on future hypothetical income, though the New Zealand Accident Compensation scheme has, to a certain extent, incorporated the principle.[14]

Between what limits of earnings should the base for the calculation be set? Of course, all schemes must set an upper limit: to allow a millionaire to claim as sickness benefit a proportion of all his lost earnings would offend notions of social justice. Typically, where contributions are earnings-related a ceiling is imposed to limit the liability of high salary-earners and at least on analogy with the principles of insurance (though not in accordance with redistributive objectives), there should be a correlation between liability and entitlement. Imposing a lower earnings limit is not an invariable practice, but in terms of administrative costs it makes little sense to have regard to earnings below the subsistence level where the earnings-related benefit constitutes a supplement to a flat-rate benefit designed to provide maintenance at that level.

The question of what proportion of lost earnings should be recoverable is not susceptible to a precise answer as it depends on several factors. First, there is the ubiquitous issue of work incentives: most systems regard 100 per cent indemnities as inadvisable on this ground. Secondly, regard must be had to the circumstances of the typical beneficiary: most people expect to tolerate some drop in living standards when no longer earning. On the other hand, the needs of some, particularly those disabled, may well increase. Thirdly, account has to be taken of tax considerations.[15] Finally, and most problematically, account has clearly to be taken of the fact that in the British system, unlike many others,[16] the earnings-related component is combined with a flat-rate component, originally designed to cover subsistence needs.

D Financing of benefits

There are two main methods of financing social security benefits: by a fund the contributions to which are earmarked exclusively for the purpose, and by general taxation. The first approach is often, though as will emerge largely misleadingly, referred to as the 'insurance' method. It may itself involve either flat-rate or earnings-related contributions.

i The insurance concept
At the heart of the British system are the benefits financed by contributions and known, until 1973, as 'national insurance'. Although the latter term has

---

12 E.g. France: Saint-Jours *Le Droit de la Sécurité Sociale* (1980) p.212. The rules for calculating the British earnings-related supplement which was abolished in 1982 meant that there was often a substantial gap between the period of reference and the period of benefit: see the first edition of this book, p.426.
13 Until recent reforms the British pensions scheme had regard to the claimant's best 20 years of working life; earnings-related components are now based on the working-life average: p.209 below.
14 Accident Compensation Act 1972, ss. 117–118.
15 Cf pp. 28–29, below.
16 *Kaim-Caudle* pp. 306–308.

disappeared from the statute book, the concept of insurance is deeply rooted in the history of social security.[17] Private insurance to cover what are today regarded as social risks, e.g. retirement and premature death, was widespread in the nineteenth century[18] and greatly influenced the German and British developments in social welfare. Under the National Insurance Act 1911 benefit was seen to rest on past economic performance rather than need per se, and bad risks, those employed in certain industries, women and children, were excluded. The scheme was popular with the middle classes for it seemed to encourage thrift and also with the working classes because it created, for the first time, a framework of legal rights to welfare.[19] As was pointed out by Beveridge,[20] and has since been stated by many others,[1] the analogy between the contributory schemes and private insurance is an inappropriate one. In a private insurance scheme premiums are based on the risk attendant on the particular circumstances of the insured person (age, sex, health, occupation, family commitments). Provided that the risk-rating is sufficiently precise, there can properly be no redistribution between insured individuals except in the very limited sense that those for whom the risk does not materialise will support those who become subject to it. The trend in social security legislation has been almost wholly against relating contributions to the degree of risk. Thus at an early stage unemployment insurance and workmen's compensation were extended to industries particularly sensitive to the hazards in question, without varying the rates of contributions. The separate categorisation of married women was abolished in 1975 so that, apart from minor exceptions,[2] all that remains is the very broad division between the employed, the self-employed and the non-employed. There is, it should be noted, an argument that, at least as regards certain hazards which might be avoided by more careful management, employers' contributions should be 'experience-rated'.[3] But in Britain, in sharp contrast to some other systems,[4] the incentive or prevention objectives of social welfare have been kept distinct from the financing provisions.

The second important respect in which contributory schemes differ from private insurance relates to the actuarial basis of their administration. The latter must be actuarially sound in the sense that the funds available from contributions and investment yields must be sufficient to finance predicted future benefits. A social security fund, on the other hand, may adopt the 'pay as you go' approach so that benefits payable at a particular time are related not to previous accumulations of contributions but to the finances made available from current contributions.[5] As a result there may be redistribution as between generations of insured persons.

ii Types of contribution
The first question arising under a contributory scheme is whether both

---

17 *Ogus* pp. 232–236; Burns *Social Security and Public Policy* (1956) ch 2; Titmuss *Social Policy* (1974) ch 7.
18 Gosden *Self-Help: Voluntary Associations in the 19th Century* (1973).
19 Pinker *Social Theory and Social Policy* (1971) p.90.
20 Paras 24–25.
  1 E.g. *McCarthy* pp. 145–146; McClements *Economics of Social Security* (1978) pp. 32–33; Barr *The Economics of the Welfare State* (1987).
  2 Pp. 52–53, below.
  3 Barr, n.1. above, p.197. and pp. 254–255, below.
  4 *Kaim-Caudle* pp. 100–101, 231–232, 294–295.
  5 See generally Wilson *Pensions, Inflation and Growth* (1974) pp. 35–42; Barr, n.1, above, ch 9.

employers and employees should participate. Some would argue that the problem is an unreal one, for whichever group pays, the net effect is, in the long run, the same: an employer paying the contributions will pay less in the form of wages.[6] Most economists, however, regard the problem as a complex one:[7] the proportions in which the cost will be distributed between consumer (through higher prices), investor (through lower profits) and employee (through lower wages) will vary according to such factors as the elasticity of demand for the goods or services in question, the bargaining power of the wage-earners and the level of unemployment. To the extent that the burden falls on consumers, the distributional effect is likely to be regressive since lower-income groups spend proportionately more on consumption. Conversely, Beveridge contended that social security provision was one of the costs of production which should be reflected in the price of the product if competition was not to be distorted.[8] The other arguments he deployed for employers' contributions were of a more amorphous character: it is in the interest of the employer that his employees' health and welfare should be protected; he should feel 'concerned for the lives of those who work under (his) control, should think of them not as instruments in production but as human beings';[9] finally it was desirable that employers should have a basis for participation in the administration and strategies of the scheme. Whatever weight be given to these various factors, there is, it is submitted, one overriding consideration: a tax on employers is an easy source of revenue and one that tends to be politically popular.[10]

Should contributions be flat-rate or related to the ability to pay? The principle of the flat-rate contributions was as central to Beveridge's philosophy as that of flat-rate benefit: taxation according to capacity

> involves a departure from existing practice, for which there is neither need nor justification and which conflicts with the wishes and feelings of the British democracy. . . . Contribution means that in their capacity as possible recipients of benefits the poorer man and the richer man are treated alike.[11]

The rhetoric in this passage should not be allowed to cloud the real issue: the extent of redistribution to be admitted as a central objective of the system. Beveridge's commitment to the 'insurance' principle led him to forswear a substantial degree of redistribution which would have resulted from financing by progressive taxation methods, but the alleged dichotomy between on the one hand an 'insurance fund' and on the other hand earnings-related contributions is a false one. There is no reason, in principle, why the 'fund' or 'earmarked taxes' approach, even if used to finance flat-rate benefits, should not be combined with earnings-related contributions.[12] Beveridge's dogmatic preference for flat-rate contributions was indeed one of the reasons why his plan eventually failed. The burden on the lower paid of contributions sufficient to support an adequate level of benefits was too great.

The shift to earnings-related contributions, accomplished in 1975, was an inevitable corollary to the introduction of a broadly-based earnings-related pension scheme – continuance of a flat-rate method would, of course, have resulted in regressive redistribution. Similarity to the predominantly

6 Kincaid *Poverty and Equality in Britain* (1973) pp. 89–90.
7 Cf Creedy and Disney *Social Insurance in Transition* (1985) ch 11.
8 Para 276.
9 Ibid.
10 *George* p.48.
11 Para 273.
12 Cf Lister *Social Security: The Case for Reform* (1975), Poverty Pamphlet No 22, pp. 39–41.

progressive income tax method of raising funds was increased as a result of two other developments: the extension of contributions liability to individuals deriving profits from business activities; and, most recently in 1985, the scaling of contribution rates according to the level of earnings and the abolition of an upper limit to the contributions paid by employers. The primary aim of the latter reforms was to encourage employers to engage low-earners but it also has progressive redistributional consequences.[13] Some remaining differences from income tax should, however, be noted: first, contributions are payable on total earnings, not merely those above the threshold; secondly, liability is non-cumulative, in the sense that it is calculated on the basis of each week's earnings, whatever the amounts earned or not earned in other weeks; thirdly, an *employee* is not liable on earnings above an upper limit; and finally, contributions are not payable on unearned income.

In determining the principles and level of contributions there is clearly a need to maintain equity as between different sections of the community. Within the broad category of employed persons, and in sharp contrast to private insurance methods, it is not regarded as appropriate to differentiate according to susceptibility to risk – healthy individuals in secure employment pay the same rates as those with a record of illness or with an unstable participation in the labour market.[14] Differentials may be applied when a class of contributors can have no recourse to a benefit or group of benefits.[15] Those opting out of the state earnings-related pension scheme, for example, pay a lower rate of contributions and the liability of the self-employed, without entitlement to unemployment, industrial injury and earnings-related benefits, is calculated on a different basis.[16]

iii General taxation
Under Beveridge's plan and consistently thereafter, a place in the contributory scheme was alloted to general taxation but it was a small one (between 10 per cent and 20 per cent).[17] It was thought desirable not on redistributional principles but because it was clear that contributions recovered by the flat-rate method would otherwise be insufficient. With the introduction in 1975 of earnings-related contributions, this rationale lapsed and the policy of the Conservative administration has been substantially to reduce the Exchequer contribution to the National Insurance Fund: from 18 per cent in 1981 to 5 per cent in 1988. Non-contributory benefits are, of course, funded by general taxation and the massive growth of these programmes (most obviously the means-tested benefits, but also those payable to the disabled) has meant that about 40 per cent of current social security expenditure is derived from this source.[18]

There has been much discussion, particularly by economists,[19] on the respective merits of contributory schemes and general taxation as methods for

13 Barr, n.1, above, p.182.
14 Members of HM forces constitute an exception: pp. 52–53, below.
15 On this basis, married women have in the past been treated as a special category: cf *Beveridge* paras 107–117.
16 Though, they frequently argue that it is unfairly high for the benefits offered: e.g. National Federation of Self Employed *Policy, Strategy and Tactics Committee Research Paper No 3* (1977). See also DHSS Discussion Document *The Self-Employed and National Insurance* (1980).
17 *Beveridge* para 282.
18 Barr, n.1, above, p.175.
19 Culyer *The Economics of Social Policy* (1975) pp. 202–204; Rejda *Social Insurance and Economic Security* (1976) pp. 162–172; Creedy and Disney, n.7, above, ch 10.

funding social security benefits. The arguments are difficult to unravel because not only do the contributory schemes themselves contain several different strategies (employer or employee, flat-rate or earnings-related), but also because the effect of the methods on industrial growth and level of earnings is still highly controversial. The general consensus of opinion is, however, as one might expect, that the taxation approach is more redistributional, and therefore preferable on grounds of social justice, while the contribution approach tends to greater economic efficiency and therefore increased overall welfare. As important as these theoretical studies are, they do not feature much in the discussions within the political arena. Instead, we tend to be confronted with broad vague sentiments based on what the public allegedly wants. Thus Beveridge felt able to report that

> benefit in return for contributions, rather than free allowances from the State, is what the people of Britain desire,[20]

and the mood was echoed in the government White Paper which followed it.[1] The Crossman Paper on National Superannuation discredited arguments for a move to general taxation methods:

> people do not want to be *given* rights to pensions and benefits; they want to *earn* them by their contributions.[2]

The vacuity of these statements may be self-evident, but their very existence provides the key to understanding why in the British and other systems the contributory approach remains the primary strategy for social security provision: the popularity of the method rests on its psychological appeal.[3] People are prepared to subscribe more by way of contributions, which they see as offering returns in the form of personal and family security, than they would be willing to pay by taxation, which might be diverted to a wide variety of uses.[4] They are led to believe that because of their contributions to the scheme they are participating in its administration and may thus exercise closer political control on its development.[5] As has been observed, however, the same degree of public scrutiny should operate through the parliamentary supervision of public spending generally, if our political system is functioning properly.[6] Indeed, the Royal Commission in New Zealand regarded as an important reason for preferring the taxation approach the flexibility inherent in a system which does not tie funds down to a particular form of social welfare but rather allows different political administrations to take different views on social priorities.[7] One undeniably genuine and important factor is that of stigma. Sociologists have shown that we have been conditioned to bestow greater esteem on systems built on exchanges (benefits in *return* for contributions) than those incorporating unilateral transfers.[8] Nevertheless, one may question whether this is an attitude which our social system should foster, and whether it is appropriate to perpetuate beliefs in

20 Para 21.
  1 *Social Insurance* Part I, para 6.
  2 White Paper, National Superannuation and Social Insurance (1969, Cmnd 3883), para 25. See also *Green Paper 1985*, para 6.8
  3 *McCarthy* p.158; Wilson *Pensions, Inflation and Growth* (1974) p.28.
  4 National Superannuation, n.2, above, at para 25.
  5 *Beveridge* para 274.
  6 *Culyer*, n.19, above, at p.203.
  7 *McCarthy* p.158.
  8 Pinker *Social Theory and Social Policy* (1971) ch 4; Pruger 2 Jo Soc Pol 289.

what are, in most respects, unreal differences between general and earmarked taxation. In the words of one commentator, the main effect of our 'contributory system' is 'to create confusion among the contributors/tax payers and fiscal illusion'.[9]

E Other forms of welfare provision

The policy-maker concerned to confer welfare on different groups within society has three broad strategies available to him. He may arrange for cash payments to be made (what we refer to as 'social security'), he may provide for benefits in kind (typically known as 'social services'), or he may exploit possibilities created by the fiscal systems, through e.g. tax reliefs. In this section we explore the relationship between social security and the other forms of welfare, and discuss some of the issues involved in the choice between the various strategies.

i Benefits in cash or in kind

Social welfare, as broadly construed, embraces a wide range of benefits in kind, among many others those for health, education and housing. On a simple view, these services may be regarded as complementary to, and independent from, the cash benefits which form the subject-matter of this book: cash benefits, it might be said, are designed for income maintenance, whereas the services are designed to fulfil other objectives of social policy. But since income is necessary, above all, to purchase essential items for living and those items could be provided directly for those in need, the policymaker is clearly faced with a choice between these strategies. Two opposing theories may be considered.[10]

According to the more traditional liberal, individualist view, welfare measures are necessary to redress inequalities of resources. Since the beneficiary knows best how to maximise his utility from the spending of money, cash transfers must generate at least as much utility as benefits in kind and often more. Moreover, they are cheaper to administer, involve a less intrusive role for the state and avoid the distortion of prices which results from large-scale public purchases. Legal enforcement is also easier: an individual deprived of a cash benefit may without undue difficulty appeal against the decision, whereas his counterpart with a grievance against the social services may find either that the agency concerned was under no duty to provide it, or, if it was, that a court will not be prepared to enforce it.[11] Not surprisingly economists tend to prefer this form of welfare and indeed argue that some services traditionally provided in kind, such as education, could instead be the subject of choice and purchase through cash vouchers.[12]

These views are challenged by those who adopt a less individualist approach to welfare. It is argued, first that certain types of good, for example, health or education, are not proper subjects for the operation of

9 *Culyer*, n.19, above at p.204. See also Dilnot, Kay and Morris *The Reform of Social Security* (1984) p.29.
10 Tobin 12 J Law Econ 263; ISSA Studies and Research No 6, *The Role of Social Services in Social Security* (1974); Thurow in Dworkin, Bermont and Brown (eds) *Market and Morals* (1977) ch 6.
11 Lebel in ISSA Studies and Research No 6, n.10, above, p.125.
12 Jenks *Education Vouchers* (1970); Culyer *The Political Economy of Social Policy* (1980) pp. 246–248.

market forces either because the social costs of mistaken decisions are too great or because, adopting a paternalist stance, it is not to be assumed that in such areas individuals always act as rational maximisers of their own welfare.[13] Secondly, the model ignores the causes of poverty; by the careful use of services to prevent as well as to react to social hazards, the problem of inadequate income, may, in some cases, be avoided.[14] Thirdly, the income redistribution technique is less sensitive to specific needs and less personal in its administration – the individual guidance implicit in the social service model may both respond in a humane way to individual circumstances and at the same time encourage greater social activity and participation.[15]

ii Social security and taxation

The relationship between the social security and taxation systems constitutes an important feature of the policy issues arising under social legislation.[16] There are three independent but related matters which call for discussion: first, the manner in which the tax system may, through its granting of reliefs, itself operate as a direct instrument of income maintenance; secondly, the extent to which social security benefits are taxable, and the implications which this has on the degree of redistribution; thirdly, the desirability or otherwise of integrating taxation with social security.

a *Tax as an instrument for income support*

Since the introduction of progressive taxation in 1907 there has been what Titmuss has described as 'a remarkable development of social policy operating through the medium of the fiscal system'.[17] Most significantly this has taken the form of family support, through the granting of children's and other dependants' allowances[18] – the amount of income permitted to be accumulated before tax is imposed. Such a system may be regarded as equitable as between those taxpayers who have, and those who do not have, family commitments but within a broader social perspective the position is different. It can benefit only those with resources sufficient to attract tax and, if it is applied consistently throughout the tax structure, the system of reliefs has a regressive effect, for the value of the relief increases as the rate of tax increases. For political reasons, it has nevertheless proved to be difficult to modify arrangements in the light of these considerations. The introduction of family allowances in 1945 did not affect the tax relief on children then available.[19] In 1968, a compromise solution was reached: by means of the so-called 'clawback', the amount by which family allowances were increased was in effect deducted from the individual's tax relief.[20] The replacement of family allowances by child benefit in 1975 signalled the

---

13 Titmuss *Commitment to Welfare* (1968) pp. 147–150; *Culyer*, n.19, above, ch 7.
14 Crosland *The Future of Socialism* (1961) pp. 145–146; Lebel in ISSA Studies and Research No 6, n.10, above, at pp. 126–127.
15 *Lebel*, n.10, above, at p.125; *Crosland*, n.14, above, at p. 148; *Titmuss*, n.13, above, at p.150.
16 See in general Atkinson 1 Jo Soc Pol 135–148, Kay and King *The British Tax System* (3rd edn) ch 8.
17 *Essays on the Welfare State* (2nd edn) p.45.
18 There are also minor forms of tax relief for the blind and disabled; see Simon *Taxes* (3rd edn) para E 2.8.
19 See White Paper on Family Allowances: Memorandum by the Chancellor of the Exchequer (1942, Cmd 6134), p.5 and *Beveridge* para 422.
20 See, generally, Lynes in Bull (ed) *Family Poverty* (2nd edn) ch 10.

government's intention also to abolish tax allowances for children and this was finally achieved in 1979.[1] Since then the question has been raised whether tax relief for dependent spouses should also be replaced by cash benefits.[2] While this proposal would be to the significant advantage of couples below the tax threshold and thus can be justified on distributional grounds,[3] it has been rejected by the government, primarily on grounds of cost.[4]

b *Tax liability of beneficiaries*
In the last paragraph we saw how the value of tax reliefs increases in proportion to the taxable income of an individual. If a social security benefit is not taxable, there is a similar problem, for its value will also vary according to the tax liabilities of the recipient. The consequent possibility of inequity as between different beneficiaries might be thought to be academic since most social security benefits are payable only when the claimant has no earnings. But income tax liability is cumulative over the tax year and so a beneficiary who has sufficient income during the rest of the tax year to take him above the tax threshold will gain from the fact if the benefit does not form part of his taxable income. Quite apart from this problem of equity, such a situation may also give rise to significant work disincentives. First, with tax thresholds set at their currently low level, a beneficiary with a large number of dependants may be better off out of work than when employed. The anomaly is increased if, as is often the case with white-collar workers who would otherwise be liable for a substantial amount of tax, support is forthcoming also from occupational schemes.[5] Secondly, the existence of the progressive system of taxation collected by the PAYE method means that during spells of unemployment or sickness an employee may be entitled to weekly refunds of tax paid on his anticipated annual earnings, thus creating a kind of 'parallel system of . . . benefits . . . calculated on the mythical basis that the worker, during his unemployment or sickness, had no social security income at all'.[6]

The policy of the post-war government was that all income-maintenance benefits[7] should be taxed. On grounds of impracticability the policy had to be reversed in 1949 with regard to the short-term benefits: beneficiaries could not be incorporated into the PAYE scheme and taxes had thus to to be collected retrospectively; the recovery of millions of small debts by the Inland Revenue was uneconomic.[8] Given the circumstances then prevailing, the decision was not unreasonable. Since 1949, however, the situation has changed dramatically. On the one hand, the real value of benefits has increased so that the amounts involved are no longer negligible. On the other hand, the administration of tax and social security is more clearly integrated than it was – indeed, the records of taxpayers are now kept under their national insurance numbers. In 1980 the Conservative government announced its intention of extending taxation to most income-maintenance benefit.[9] Widow's benefits,[10] retirement and invalidity pensions were already

1 Pp. 390 and 392, below.
2 Green Paper on Taxation of Husband and Wife (1983, Cmnd 8093).
3 Cf First Report of Social Security Advisory Committee (1983), paras 2.21–2.27.
4 Green Paper on the Reform of Personal Taxation (1986, Cmnd 9756), Part III.
5 Houghton *Paying for the Social Services* (1968), IEA Occasional Paper 16, p.29.
6 *Walley* p.207.
7 Though anomalously not industrial injury benefit.
8 *Houghton* n.5, above, at p.28, and see Report of the Committee on the Taxation of Pensions for Retirement (1954, Cmd 9063), paras 271–294.
9 Sir G Howe, Chancellor of the Exchequer, 980 HC Official Report (5th series), col 1460.
10 But not those payable under the war pensions scheme.

taxable.[11] The contributory and means-tested benefits payable to the unemployed were added to the list in 1981,[12] and the same applied to statutory sick pay and statutory maternity pay which in 1983 and 1988 respectively replaced for most beneficiaries' sickness benefit and maternity allowance.[13]

c *Integration of tax and social security*
The perceived need both to rationalise the existing relationship between taxation and social security and remove anomalies created by untaxed benefits was joined by a third force which saw in an integrated tax-welfare scheme the way to abolish poverty altogether. The movement which attracted considerable attention in the 1970s developed from various sources. The first was located in the United States of America and was based on a concern to target assistance to the poor as efficiently as possible. This could best be done by extending the tax system downwards so that those below a poverty threshold would receive instead of pay the negative income tax.[14] A moderate version was promoted by the Nixon administration but it failed to pass through Congress.[15] The idea won support this side of the Atlantic, as a means not only of rationalising the cumbersome coexistence of various benefit schemes but also of dealing with the problems of stigma and take-up associated with traditional means-tests.[16] A slightly less ambitious, but arguably more practical, plan to cover employed persons and national insurance beneficiaries was advanced by the Conservative government in 1972.[17] The Tax Credit scheme, as it was called, though in general endorsed by a Parliamentary Select Committee[18] never reached the stage of draft legislation.

A third stream of influence extends back to 1943 when, as an alternative to the Beveridge plan, Lady Rhys Williams urged the adoption of a 'social dividend', the payment to all members of society of weekly amounts necessary for the ordinary needs of living.[19] As developed by others,[20] such a scheme would involve, by means of taxation, a 'clawback' of resources from those with adequate income from other sources. As such, in essence, if not in administrative arrangements, it is similar to the negative income tax proposals.

It is not difficult to understand why these proposals failed to reach the statute book: either the marginal rate of taxation for those above or around the poverty threshold[1] was unacceptably high or the level of that threshold was so low as to defeat the goals of the scheme.[2] The more recent proposals have concentrated on ways of meeting these problems, typically with more

---

11 See Simon *Taxes* (3rd edn) para C4. 122.
12 Finance Act 1981, s.29.
13 See now Taxes Act 1970, s.219(1)(b)–(c), as amended.
14 Friedman *Capitalism and Freedom* (1962); Green *Negative Taxes and the Poverty Problem* (1967).
15 Moynihan *The Politics of a Guaranteed Income* (1973).
16 Lees, Lloyds Bank Rev, October 1967, 1–15; Institute of Economic Affairs *Policy for Poverty* (1970). The idea of using tax returns for national assistance claims was published in the Labour Party Election Manifesto 1964.
17 Green Paper, Proposals for a Tax-Credit System (Cmnd 5116).
18 1972–73 HC 341.
19 Rhys Williams *Something to Look Forward To* (1943)
20 Notably Brown and Dawson *Personal Taxation, Incentives and Tax Reform* (1969).
 1 This includes indirect taxation resulting from the withdrawal of benefits, as income rises.
 2 Barr *The Economics of the Welfare State* (1987) pp. 256–268.

modest aims, but also with more sophisticated principles of taxation.[3] The enormous complexity of the issues involved which must respond, in particular, to the variables of family size, employment status and the impact of existing benefit systems has given rise to an intimidating critical literature,[4] a detailed account of which is beyond the scope of this book. Nevertheless, some general considerations do call for further comment.

The strongest argument for universal schemes of the type proposed is that they generate information on the existence of poverty and, at the same time, enable claims to be made without the problems of stigma and low take-up. More controversial is the fact that most proposals define eligibility for financial assistance by reference solely to economic criteria (primarily levels of income), thus abandoning the conditions of entitlement traditionally associated with contributory schemes (unemployment, sickness, retirement etc). No doubt, this enables the system to become at once more comprehensive and simpler; it would also focus on those in greatest need. Such objectives are obviously appealing but it may be objected that elimination of the categories is neither possible nor desirable. To avoid abuse, it would presumably be necessary for the unemployed to register as available for work or be relieved from this obligation for a specific reason, e.g. sickness, retirement or family responsibilities, and thus for administrative purposes some categorisation is inevitable. Further, it may be appropriate to differentiate between various categories of claimants on the grounds that their needs are not identical: it is not obvious, for example, that a man retired at 55 should be paid the same as someone considerably older, or that a disabled person should receive no more than if he had been made redundant. Finally, no system of computerised assessment would be able to deal adequately with special circumstances which occur suddenly and which require immediate assistance so that some form of discretionary aid would have to complement the general scheme.

It is, perhaps, safe to conclude that there is no prospect of a major integration of the tax and social security systems within the foreseeable future. A Green Paper on the Reform of Personal Taxation, published in 1986,[5] revealed the government's disinclination to proceed with proposals which conflict with the principle of contributory benefits or which would involve high marginal rates of taxation for earners. Ideas for streamlining the relationship between tax and social security, for example, by amalgamating income tax liability with Class 1 contributions are, however, being actively considered.

---

3 Notably Dilnot, Kay and Morris *The Reform of Social Security* (1984). For a useful summary of this and other proposals see Aktinson 84 New Society 426.
4 Creedy and Disney *Social Insurance in Transition* (1985) chs 9–12; Barr, n.2, above, ch 11, and the references there cited.
5 Cmnd 9756.

Chapter 2
Contributions

Part 1 Introduction

In chapter 1 the various methods of financing social security benefits were considered, and it was seen how British policy has continued to favour the contributory approach. In this chapter we describe the liability to pay contributions and the general principles governing the fulfilment of contribution conditions.[1] The basic concepts are derived from the insurance schemes existing before the Second World War but their character has since changed in several fundamental respects.

A Risk-related insurance

As has already been explained,[2] private insurance influenced the development of national insurance, and this is particularly evident in the early efforts of the state schemes to relate liability to the risks attached to particular categories of individuals or employments. The first unemployment insurance of 1911 covered only those trades in which the employment pattern was thought to be reasonably stable. Moreover, employers of men who by the age of 60 had paid more by way of contribution than they had received by way of benefit were entitled to a refund.[3] This right lasted only until 1920, at which time also insurance coverage was extended to all manual workers engaged under a contract of service, and non-manual workers of a similar description whose income was below a certain level.[4] However, the principle of differentiation was not totally abandoned, for industries with particularly low unemployment might adopt their own special scheme and, with the approval of the Minister, opt out of national insurance,[5] an arrangement permitted for the finance and banking industries until 1946.[6] Unemployment insurance was extended to agriculture only in 1936 and then at special rates of benefit and contribution.[7] Other forms of insurance did not call for the same degree of differentiation but the health scheme was administered by Approved Societies, who could offer by way of benefit in return for the nationally determined

1 See generally, *Williams*.
2 P.2, above.
3 NIA 1911, s.94.
4 UIA 1920.
5 Ibid, s.18.
6 See SR & O 1938/589 and 656.
7 UI (Agriculture) Act 1936.

31

rate of contributions whatever they wished above the national minimum.[8] Finally, mention should be made of the low rates of contribution paid, and the even lower benefits received, by women on the ground that they were 'poor risks'.[9]

B Comprehensive insurance

One of the primary objectives of the Beveridge plan, and the legislation which implemented it, was to abolish such vestiges of the risk-related approach which remained, and to establish a fully comprehensive system in which all would share in supporting the burden of those subjected to the prescribed social risks:

> The term 'social insurance' . . . implies both that it is compulsory and that men stand together with their fellows.[10]

The policy gave rise to four important modifications of the pre-war schemes. First, compulsory insurance was extended to those previously above the income limits. Secondly, it included those substantially free from one or more of the social risks (e.g. civil servants in relation to unemployment) or with sufficient protection under their terms of employment (e.g. the police in relation to sickness and old age – though members of HM Forces in a somewhat analogous position were allowed to pay a lower rate of contributions[11]). Thirdly, the Approved Societies were no longer to administer health insurance, and the special arrangements for agriculture, banking and finance were also abolished. Finally, the self-employed were covered for all purposes except unemployment and industrial injury. The special status of women as such was also eradicated; instead, the legislation singled out for special treatment those who were married. They could opt out of insurance in their own right, and, if they elected to stay in, would pay lower contributions and receive lower benefits.[12] The comprehensive coverage was completed by the compulsory insurance of all remaining persons over 16 who were not gainfully employed: in return for their weekly contributions, they qualified for all benefits except those for unemployment, sickness and industrial injury.[13] Contributions could not, of course, be extracted from those on very low incomes and the problem was met by, on the one hand, exempting from liability (and also therefore from entitlement to all benefits) those whose income did not exceed £2 a week,[14] and, on the other hand, excusing from the payment of contributions, but nevertheless crediting for certain purposes, those unemployed or incapable of work or undergoing education or training.[15] While Beveridge's assumption was that many would participate in occupational schemes to lift their income above the standard subsistence rate of benefit, there was no question of using this as an argument to justify exemption from the national scheme. Different considerations were, however, to prevail when earnings-related pensions were introduced, first with the limited

---

8 P.129, below.
9 Land in Barker and Allen (eds) *Sexual Divisions and Society* (1976) p.109.
10 *Beveridge* para 26.
11 P.52, below.
12 P.51, below.
13 NIA 1946, s.4(2)(c).
14 Ibid, s.5(1)(a)(iii).
15 Ibid, s.5(1)(a)(i)–(ii).

graduated scheme of 1959,[16] and subsequently with the more comprehensive approach of 1975.[17] In both cases, contributions to the state earnings-related element was voluntary in the sense that those with sufficient coverage elsewhere might opt out.

C Liability according to capacity

The policy issues raised by the nature of the contributions payable have already been discussed in chapter 1.[18] Here it is necessary merely to relate how the insurance system gradually evolved towards a principle of liability according to capacity to pay. Under the early schemes, flat-rate contributions of the worker were matched by those of his employer, generally on an equal basis,[19] and the fund was augmented by a grant from the Exchequer. Certain concessions were, however, made for low-wage earners; they paid a reduced contribution.[20] The principles were maintained under the 1946 reconstruction, except that the liability of the employer was somewhat lower than that of the employee.[1] The flat-rate approach, of which Beveridge was such an enthusiastic advocate, proved insufficient to finance benefits at the desired level and a shift to an earnings-related method became inevitable. Under the graduated pensions scheme, those contributing paid 4½ per cent of their earnings between £9 and £15, the employer being liable for a similar amount.[2] The hybrid system for those in employment of flat-rate and graduated contributions was replaced in 1973–75 by a single system of contributions paid on earnings between a much wider band, but with a reduction for those contracting out of the new earnings-related pensions scheme.[3] The assimilation to an income tax method of financing was taken even further by imposing on the self-employed, in addition to a flat-rate liability, a charge on profits and gains,[4] notwithstanding that the earnings-related supplements for sickness, maternity and widow's benefits continued to be unavailable to this group. Two further structural changes in 1985, while consistent with the capacity to pay principle, were designed also to encourage more low-paid employments:[5] the rate of contributions payable by both employers and employees on low earnings was reduced; and the upper limit on employers' contributions was abolished.[6]

D Unity of administration

Before the co-ordinating legislation of 1946 there were in effect three independent insurance schemes: those for unemployment and for health, both dating from 1911, and that for widows', orphans' and old age pensions

---

16 Pp. 205–206, below.
17 Pp. 211–212, below.
18 Pp. 22–24, above.
19 Though not under the original national health scheme to which the employer paid 3d a week and the male employee 4d: NIA 1911, Sch 2.
20 See e.g. NHIA 1924, Sch 2.
 1 The ratio was approximately 55–45: NIA 1946, Sch 1.
 2 NIA 1959, s.1(1).
 3 P.43, below.
 4 P.49, below.
 5 *Green Paper 1985* vol 1, ch 11.
 6 SSA 1985, s.7, p.45, below.

established in 1925. But the financing of the health and pensions schemes was amalgamated so that in practice each insured person had to maintain two insurance records, in the form of cards to which stamps representing weekly contributions were affixed. In 1946 the three schemes were replaced by a single national insurance system, with the weekly contribution stamp serving for all the contributory benefits. The independent industrial injuries scheme superseded the workmen's compensation legislation, which had imposed liability for compensation on the individual employer, but the contributions to this insurance fund were added automatically to those payable for employed persons under the main scheme. In 1973 the separate industrial injuries fund was abolished and henceforth benefits were financed by the ordinary National Insurance Fund. The introduction of earnings-related contributions necessarily made their calculation and collection more complicated and under the legislation of 1973–75 administration was simplified by combining the process with that of income tax assessment, notably for employed persons through the PAYE system. The tax system is currently being computerised and it will be rendered compatible with the social security computer system.[7] The affixing of stamps to an insurance card remains only for the flat-rate contributions by the self-employed, and even they can be paid by direct debit from the contributor's bank or by National Giro.[8]

E   Outline of system

The monies collected from social security contributions are neither used exclusively for the financing of social security benefits nor do they provide the funds necessary for all such benefits.

i *Social security benefits financed by contributions*   All contributory benefits (formerly insurance benefits), viz those for unemployment, sickness, invalidity, widowhood, retirement (Categories A and B), maternity allowance, and benefits for industrial injuries (including old workmen's compensation cases) are so derived.

ii *Social security benefits financed by general taxation*   All remaining social security benefits are financed from the Exchequer.

iii *Other purposes financed by contributions*   Social security contributions finance indirectly statutory sick pay and statutory maternity pay, in that the employer's payments under these schemes are offset against his contributions liability.[9] Allocations are also made to the National Health Service and to the Redundancy Fund for employment protection purposes.[10]

The funds collected under the Social Security Act 1975 are derived from three sources: insured persons, employers and the Exchequer. The Exchequer contributes currently 5 per cent per year of the amount of all other contributions used for contributory benefits (i.e. excluding the sums payable for the National Health Service and the Redundancy Fund).[11] Contributions from insured persons and employers are divided into four categories:

7 *Green Paper 1985* vol 2, para 6.25.
8 SI 1979/591, reg 54(3).
9 SSHBA 1982, s.9; SSA 1986, Sch 4, para 5.
10 SSA 1975, ss.1(1) and 134, as amended. The national insurance surcharge which enabled governments to raise funds for general purposes by imposing an additional burden on employer contributions was abolished by the Finance Act 1984, s.117.
11 SSA 1975, s.1(5), as amended.

Class 1 Primary contributions from 'employed earners' and secondary contributions from 'employers and other persons paying earnings', both being earnings-related.

Class 2 Flat-rate contributions from self-employed earners;

Class 3 Voluntary flat-rate contributions from earners and others;

Class 4 Contributions payable on the basis of profits or gains arising from a trade, profession or vocation.

Part 2 describes the principles of categorisation, the methods of assessing liability and also the grounds on which persons may be exempt from contributions. In Part 3 we consider the position of married women, widows and other special categories of contributions. Finally, Part 4 is concerned with the contribution conditions which must be satisfied for entitlement to benefit and the rules to assist those otherwise unable to qualify.

Part 2 Classification of contributions

A General

This Part is devoted to the principles governing liability to pay contributions of Classes 1, 2 and 4 and entitlement to pay those in Classes 2 and 3. Under the pre-1973 legislation insured *persons* were categorised accordingly.[12] Under the new scheme, the classification is of *contributions*. The important reason for this change of terminology is that an insured person may now be liable to pay contributions both as an employed (Class 1), and as a self-employed, person (Classes 2 and 4). The law defining the various categories remains, however, substantially unchanged. In particular, regard must be had to the complex case-law distinguishing between employed and self-employed persons. In this connection, it is worth observing that adjudication of disputes as to classification and the fulfilment of contribution conditions is within the jurisdiction not of the normal adjudicating authorities, viz adjudication officer, social security appeal tribunals and Commissioner, but of the Secretary of State.[13] A question of law arising from any such decision may be referred for final determination to the High Court (or in Scotland the Court of Session) either by the Secretary of State if he thinks fit or by a person aggrieved by the decision.[14] Many of the High Court decisions are of course published in the ordinary law reports, and for the period 1950–60, HMSO published selected decisions of the Minister on classification questions.[15]

B Primary Class 1 contributions

Class 1 contributions may confer title to any contributory benefit. The primary contributions of this class are payable by 'employed earners'.[16] An 'employed earner' is defined as

> a person who is gainfully employed in Great Britain either under a contract of service, *or* in an office (including elective office) with emoluments chargeable to income tax under Schedule E.[17]

12 NIA 1965, s.1(2).
13 SSA 1975, s.93: cf p.567, below.
14 SSA 1975, s.94.
15 The 'M' Decisions. It is not clear why publication ceased in 1960.
16 SSA 1975, s.1(2).
17 Ibid, s.2(1)(a).

The second alternative was added in 1973,[18] the intention being to correlate Class 1 contributors with Schedule E tax payers and thus to facilitate the collection of contributions through the PAYE system.

i Gainfully employed

For both alternative formulations, the contributor must be 'gainfully employed'. This replaces the phrase 'gainfully occupied' used in the earlier legislation.[19] The significance of the modification is unclear. A body of case-law had been built around the interpretation of 'gainfully occupied' for the purposes not only of the classification of contributors but also in relation to retirement pensions[20] and increases for dependants.[1] One possible view is that, in the light of different policy considerations, it was thought desirable to keep distinct the interpretation of the phrase in its various contexts. If so, this would justify the authorities approaching the changed statutory formula *de novo*. A more likely explanation is that the notion of 'occupation' was thought to be too restrictive when applied to the new category of 'office with emoluments'.[2] If this is correct, it should follow that the interpretation of the concept has remained substantially unchanged. The basic idea is that the contributor

> receives from his master under the contract of employment something by way of remuneration for the services which he is contractually bound to render to the master under the contract of service.[3]

Under the former legislation, it was important to determine what was to be regarded as 'remuneration'. Under the current system the problem no longer arises because contributions are earnings-related and there is a body of rules, described below,[4] governing the nature and calculation of 'earnings' for this purpose.

ii Contract of service

The classification of individuals into employed and self-employed persons, as characterised by the distinction between a 'contract of service' and a 'contract for services', has been a regular legal conundrum and not only in social security law.[5] The Social Security Act 1975 makes only a marginal effort to alleviate the problems by prescribing that 'contract of service' means

> any contract of service or apprenticeship, whether written or oral and whether expressed or implied.[6]

Resort must therefore be had to the case-law.[7] As implied above, decisions on the matter are not limited to social security law: many other legal consequences flow from the existence of a contract of service, for example, the

---

18 SSA 1973, s.1(7).
19 NIA 1965, s.1(2).
20 Ibid, s.30(2), cf pp. 192–193, below.
 1 NIA 1965, s.43(1)(b).
 2 Cf *R(P) 2/76*, para 22, R J A Temple, Chief Comr.
 3 Per Slade J, *Vandyk v Minister of Pensions and National Insurance* [1955] 1 QB 29 at 38.
 4 Pp. 43–44, below.
 5 For a particularly valuable discussion, see Davies and Freedland *Labour Law* (2nd edn) pp. 80–111 and for an empirical study of the issue, Leighton *Contractual Arrangements in Selected Industries* (1983).
 6 Sch 20.
 7 There is a useful analysis in *Williams* ch 3, as well as the standard labour law texts.

right to a redundancy payment and the imposition of vicarious liability on the employer. The question arises whether courts and tribunals, interpreting the relevant legislative provisions, should reach uniform answers. The view most popular with judges[8] and writers[9] is that since different legal consequences give rise to different policy considerations, it is dangerous to cross legal boundaries. It can be argued that a classification which only affects the reciprocal rights and duties of two persons, the employer and employee, does not involve the public interest, which is clearly relevant in determining liability to pay social security contributions. There are also policy considerations which apply only in the social security context; for example, whether the nature of the occupation is such that insurance against unemployment and industrial injuries, exclusive to Class 1 contributors, is regarded as appropriate. On the other hand, confusion and administrative inconvenience ensue if an individual is an 'employee' for some purposes and not for others and there is, therefore, a pragmatic argument for uniform solutions.[10] As a matter of statutory interpretation, Parliament when using the term 'contract of service' might be assumed to have in mind traditional judicial interpretations of the phrase.

The principles governing the distinction between a contract of service and one for services are not easy to state for two reasons: first, because there are differing views on the extent to which the issue is one of law rather than of fact (and thus within the jurisdiction of the High Court or Court of Session);[11] secondly, because judicial views on the nature of the distinction have changed substantially over the years and there is currently no uniformly accepted criterion which can be applied to all cases.

The classical nineteenth-century test was one of supervision and control: 'a servant is a person subject to the command of his master as to the manner in which he shall do his work'.[12] The first High Court decisions under the National Insurance Act 1946 placed great reliance on this criterion,[13] but its limitations in the modern technological and commercial world soon provoked a more critical attitude. It was obvious in the first place that there could be little or no direct control over the work of a professional or skilled employee, such as a doctor working in a hospital,[14] a theatrical or circus artist[15] or a political columnist,[16] nor where the employer was a corporate entity and the employee was of a high status, e.g. a company director.[17] Secondly, it is imprecise. The 'employer' of an independent contractor, for example, may reserve to himself the right to direct not only what is to be done, but in broad outlines how it is to be done.[18]

8 E.g. *Tyne & Clyde Warehouses Ltd v Hamerton* [1978] ICR 661; *President of the Methodist Conference v Parfitt* [1984] QB 368, [1983] 3 All ER 747.
9 *Calvert*, p.18; *Williams* para 3–05.
10 Cf *O'Kelly v Trusthouse Forte plc* [1984] QB 90 at 115, [1983] 3 All ER 456 at 472, per Ackner LJ.
11 See generally p.569, below.
12 Per Bramwell B, *Yewens v Noakes* (1880) 6 QBD 530 at 532–533.
13 *Gould v Minister of National Insurance* [1951] 1 KB 731, [1951] 1 All ER 368; *Stagecraft v Minister of National Insurance* 1952 SC 288.
14 *Cassidy v Minister of Health* [1951] 2 KB 243, [1951] 1 All ER 574.
15 *Whittaker v Minister of Pensions and National Insurance* [1967] 1 QB 156, [1966] 3 All ER 531.
16 *Beloff v Pressdram* [1973] 1 All ER 241.
17 *Lee v Lee's Air Farming* [1961] AC 12, [1960] 3 All ER 420. NB by virtue of his 'office', such a person is now a Class 1 contributor; p.41, below.
18 E.g. *Construction Industry Training Board v Labour Forces* [1970] 3 All ER 220 (contract construction labourer); *Addison v London Philharmonic Orchestra Ltd* [1981] ICR 261 (orchestral musician); M25 (tailoring outworker); M48 (BBC interviewer).

Dissatisfaction with the control test prompted Denning LJ (as he then was) to formulate a new criterion, whether the alleged employee was 'part and parcel of the organisation',[19] whether he was 'employed as part of the business, and his work is done as an integral part of the business'.[20] This approach, and an analogous test of 'economic reality' emanating from the United States Supreme Court,[1] have attracted some support.[2] They have the advantage of directing attention to the admittedly important issue of whose assets are involved in the undertaking and who stands to profit or lose on its outcome, but it can be objected that, though these are factors to be taken into account, they are no more decisive than was (or is) the control element. It has indeed become obvious, and is readily acknowledged in almost all recent cases on the subject,[3] that it is a question of having regard to a number of factors, any number or combination of which might be relevant in a given case. The mere reference to such factors does not, of course, indicate how they are to be deployed, or what weight is to be given to each. For the most part, judges have refused to be drawn on this issue, contenting themselves with the general proposition that the relative importance of the different factors will vary from case to case.[4]

Some of the more important factors, to which the Secretary of State should attribute such weight as in his discretion seems appropriate, may be described as follows.

a *Supervision of work*   Though the control test has rightly been repudiated as the sole or decisive criterion, close and regular supervision of the work process clearly remains an important factor, especially for less skilled occupations.[5]

b *Powers of appointment and dismissal*   This factor is often mentioned,[6] but if it refers to the appointment and dismissal of the person whose classification is in question it is generally helpful only in indicating to which of two 'employers' he is contractually engaged.[7] More important for the pre-

19 *Bank voor Handel en Scheepvaart v Slatford* [1953] 1 QB 248 at 295.
20 *Stevenson, Jordan and Harrison v Macdonald and Evans* [1952] 1 TLR 101 at 111.
 1 *United States v Silk* 331 US 704 (1946). See also a dictum of Lord Wright in *Montreal Locomotive Works v Montreal and A–G* [1947] 1 DLR 161 at 164.
 2 Notably in *Market Investigations v Minister of Social Security* [1969] 2 QB 173, [1968] 3 All ER 732; *Young and Woods v West* [1980] IRLR 201; *Midland Sinfonia Concert Society Ltd v Secretary of State for Social Services* [1981] ICR 454; *Warner Holidays Ltd v Secretary of State for Social Services* [1983] ICR 440.
 3 Especially, *Ready Mixed Concrete South East Ltd v Minister of Pensions and National Insurance* [1968] 2 QB 497, [1968] 1 All ER 433; *Willy Scheidegger Swiss Typewriting School (London) Ltd v Minister of Social Security* (1968) 5 KIR 65; *Argent v Minister of Social Security* [1968] 3 All ER 208, [1968] 1 WLR 7749; *Rennison & Son v Minister of Social Security* (1970) 10 KIR 65; *Ferguson v John Dawson & Partners (Contractors)* [1976] 3 All ER 817, [1976] 1 WLR 346.
 4 E.g. Cooke J in *Construction Training Board* case, n.18, above, at 224; Bridge J in *Rennison's* case, n.3, above, at 68. This is a question of fact not law *O'Kelly v Trusthouse Fork* (Ackner LJ diss), above n.10.
 5 *Amalgamated Engineering Union v Minister of Pensions and National Insurance* [1963] 1 All ER 864, [1963] 1 WLR 441; *Construction Training Board* case, n.18, above; *Thames Television Ltd v Wallis* [1979] IRLR 136; *Hitchcock v Post Office* [1980] ICR 100; *Narich Pty v Commissioner of Pay-Roll Tax* [1984] ICR 286.
 6 E.g. by Lord Thankerton in one of the first judicial attempts to enumerate the relevant factors: *Short v Henderson* (1946) 62 TLR 427 at 429.
 7 E.g. *Mersey Docks and Harbour Board v Coggins and Griffith (Liverpool) Ltd* [1947] AC 1, [1946] 2 All ER 345; M5; M14; M35; and see p.45, below.

sent purpose is whether the 'employee' has the power to employ a substitute to assist him or to whom his duties may be delegated.[8]

c *Form of remuneration* The typical contract of service provides for regular remuneration in the form of a salary or wages, while the typical contract for services prescribes a fixed sum for the job. The distinction accords well with the 'economic reality' theory. In the words of Lord Widgery CJ, 'if a man agrees to perform an operation for a fixed sum and thus stands to lose if the work is delayed, and to profit if it is done quickly, that is the man who on the face of it appears to be an independent contractor working under a contract for services'.[9] While the method of payment may thus provide some guideline,[10] it is not a very reliable criterion. There have been cases where an individual paid on the basis of time has been held to be self-employed.[11] Conversely, the courts have not shown great reluctance to find a contract of service where the employee is paid a fixed rate for the job[12] or where both parties have sought artificially to transform the nature of the contract by converting wages into a different form of payment, e.g. the so-called 'lump'.[13]

d *Duration of contract* Again, there is a tendency for the duration of contracts for services to be determined according to a specific undertaking, or a specific (and often short) time period, whereas a contract of service will often be of an indefinite period or at least contain some element of continuity.[14] The factor has been adverted to in some cases,[15] but it can at best play a subordinate role. There are many occupations where the pattern is reversed.[16]

e *Equipment* The question whether the 'employee' is bound to use his own plant or equipment is perhaps of greater assistance. It too is related to the 'economic reality' idea. A worker who uses his own equipment is investing his own resources in the undertaking and thus there is a strong argument for not categorising him as an employee.[17] But the criterion carries force only where such an investment is on a large scale.[18] In many occupations it is customary for an employee under a contract of service to provide his own tools.

f *Place of work* If the work is undertaken at the individual's own premises he is more likely to be regarded as self-employed. If, on the other hand, the

---

8 *Ready Mixed Concrete* case, n.3, above; M23; M25; M34; M48.
9 *Global Plant v Secretary of State for Health and Social Security* [1971] 3 All ER 385 at 391.
10 E.g. *Gould's* case, n.13, above; *Construction Training Board* case, n.18, above; *Challinor v Taylor*, n.3, above.
11 E.g. *Ready Mixed Concrete* case, n.3, above.
12 E.g. *Market Investigations* case, n.2, above.
13 *Ferguson v John Dawson*, n.3, above; and see further p.42, below.
14 *Wickens v Champion Employment* [1984] ICR 365.
15 E.g. *Argent v Minister of Social Security* [1968] 3 All ER 208, [1968] 1 WLR 1749; M48.
16 E.g. *Stagecraft v Minister of National Insurance* 1952 SC 288; *Construction Industry Training Board v Labour Forces* [1970] 3 All ER 220; *Ready Mixed Concrete* case, n.3, above; *Willy Scheidegger* case, n.3, above.
17 *BSM (1257) Ltd v Secretary of State for Social Services* [1978] ICR 894; *Midland Sinfonia Concert Society* case, n.2, above.
18 E.g. *Inglefield v Macey* (1967) 2 KIR 146; *Ready Mixed Concrete* case, n.3, above.

occupation is peripatetic (e.g. a sales representative) the question is usually resolved by the degree of supervision exercised by the 'employer'.[19]

g *Obligation to work*   Under some contracts, it is left to the person 'employed' to decide how much, if at all, he is to work. If so, it is very persuasive evidence that he is self-employed.[20] The case must be contrasted with that in which the individual is given an option whether or not to work for a specific period (e.g. a day) and in which, if he so agrees, he is under an obligation to perform specific tasks during that period. Such a contract will often be one of service.[1]

h *Discretion on hours of work*   A related idea is that the more discretion an individual has as to when he performs his duties, the more likely he is to be classified as self-employed.[2] But the criterion is in no way decisive, and there are instances of contracts of service being held to confer such a broad discretion.[3]

The question remains as to the weight, if any, to be given to any attempts by the parties themselves conclusively to determine the issue by a declaration in the contract. It is a question which has assumed, in recent years, increased importance, in the light of efforts, particularly in the construction industry, to avoid the financial burdens of the employment relationship arising from both fiscal and social security legislation.[4] The approach taken by the judiciary has, with one notable exception,[5] been uniform. While regard must be had to the obligations arising from the explicit terms of the contract to see whether they are more consistent with a contract of service or a contract for services, the exact terminology in fact used may be of no legal significance.[6] Two alternative justifications have been advanced for this approach. Some judges purport to search for the true 'intentions' of the parties which, they argue, are to be found in the obligations arising under the contract rather than from the exact terminology employed. The problem with this argument is that in many cases the terminology will indeed represent the intentions of the parties.[7] To overcome this objection other judges have relied overtly on public policy considertions. 'I think that it would be contrary to the public

---

19 E.g. *Ready Mixed Concrete* case, n.3, above; *Willy Scheidegger* case, n.3, above; *Market Investigations* case, n.2, above; *Global Plant* case, n.9, above; M22; M33.
20 E.g. *Willy Scheidegger* case, n.3, above; *Addison v London Philharmonic Orchestra Ltd*, n.2, above; M9; M11; M17; M47; M51; M65; *WHPT Housing Association Ltd v Secretary of State for Social Services* [1981] ICR 737.
 1 E.g. *Market Investigations* case, n.2, above.
 2 Especially in cases of casual workers: *O'Kelly v Trusthouse Fork plc* [1984] QB 90 [1983] 3 All ER 456. See also *Willy Scheidegger* case, n.3, above; M9; M11; M13; M17; M25; M44.
 3 E.g. *Market Investigations v Minister of Social Security* [1969] 2 QB 173, [1968] 3 All ER 732; *Global Plant* case, n.9, above; M40; M60.
 4 See the Report of The Committee of Inquiry under Professor Phelps Brown into Certain Matters Concerning Labour (1968, Cmnd 3714); Davies and Freedland *Labour Law* (2nd edn) pp. 94–98; and de Clark 30 MLR 6.
 5 Lawton LJ in *Ferguson v John Dawson* [1976] 3 All ER 817 at 827–829.
 6 *Inglefield v Macey*, n.18, above; *Ready Mixed Concrete v Minister of Pensions and National Insurance* [1968] 2 QB 497, [1968] 1 All ER 433; *Construction Industry Training Board v Labour Forces* [1970] 3 All ER 220; *Rennison v Minister of Social Security* (1970) 10 KIR 65; *Ferguson v John Dawson* (majority judgments), n.5, above; *BSM (1257) Ltd* case, n.17, above; *Narich Pty v Commissioner of Pay-Roll Tax* [1984] ICR 286; *Young and Woods v West* [1980] IRLR 201.
 7 See Lawton LJ in *Ferguson v John Dawson*, n.5, above, at 828.

interest if . . . the parties, by their own whim, by the use of a verbal formula, unrelated to the reality of the relationship, could influence the decision . . . .'[8] If there is such a principle of public policy, it is one which is both obscure in its origins[9] and vague in its scope. The efforts of the judiciary to distinguish between genuine and bogus self-employment have been matched by a variety of responses from the legislature. On the one hand, the increased burden of contributions under Classes 2 and 4 resulting from the 1973–75 legislation has made the status of self-employment less attractive.[10] On the other hand, the Secretary of State has been given power to make regulations for securing that the liability to pay Class 1 contributions is not avoided by 'abnormal practice' in relation to the payment of earnings.[11]

iii Office with emoluments

The second category of primary Class 1 contributions was introduced to ensure that Class 1 was co-extensive with tax liability under Schedule E. The term 'office' has never been rigourously defined but it has been employed in tax legislation for well over a century and has acquired there a special meaning, to distinguish it from 'employment', 'profession' or 'vocation'.[12] In the leading case of *Edwards (Inspector of Taxes) v Clinch*,[13] a majority of the House of Lords reaffirmed that it involves 'a degree of continuance (not necessarily continuity) and of independent existence: it must connote a post to which a person can be appointed, which he can vacate and to which a successor can be appointed'.[14] So, someone appointed to conduct a public inquiry on a temporary, ad hoc and personal basis was not an 'office-holder'. There are, of course, many honorary office-holders, but if emoluments – statutorily defined as including 'salaries, fees, wages, perquisites and profit'[15] – are payable, they are chargeable to income tax under Schedule E and thus give rise to liability for Class 1 contributions. Examples of those who have been so classified are: company directors (where there is no contract of service),[16] trustees and executors,[17] consultants under the National Health Service,[18] accountants acting as company auditors,[19] solicitors acting as company registrars.[20]

iv Classification by the Secretary of State

As has already been indicated, decisions on the classification of individual cases are in the first instance made by the Secretary of State. Quite independently of this jurisdiction, he has reserved to him two further powers, the exercise of which affects the classification of an individual or an occupation.

8 Per Megaw LJ in *Ferguson v John Dawson*, n.5, above, at 825.
9 Some authority may be found in the landlord/tenant case of *Addiscombe Garden Estates v Crabbe* [1958] 1 QB 513, [1957] 3 All ER 563.
10 See pp. 49–51, below.
11 SSA 1975, Sch 1, para 4(c)–(d).
12 See e.g. Simon *Taxes* (3rd edn) para E4.201.
13 [1981] 3 All ER 543 (Lords Edmund-Davies and Bridge dissenting).
14 Per Lord Wilberforce, ibid, at 546.
15 Income and Corporation Taxes Act 1970, s.183(1), on which see *Hamblett v Godfrey* [1987] 1 All ER 916, [1987] 1 WLR 357.
16 *McMillan v Guest* [1942] AC 561, [1942] 1 All ER 606 and see SI 1979/591, reg 19B.
17 *Dale v IRC* [1954] AC 11, [1953] 2 All ER 671.
18 *Mitchell and Edon v Ross* [1962] AC 814, [1961] 3 All ER 49.
19 *Ellis v Lucas* [1967] Ch 856, [1966] 2 All ER 935.
20 *IRC v Brander and Cruickshank* [1971] 1 All ER 36, [1971] 1 WLR 212.

Under the first, intended to counter the practice of 'lump' payments by means of which employers and employees collaborate in an attempt to avoid Class 1 contributions, he may

> where he is satisfied as to the existence of any practice in respect of the payment of earnings whereby the incidence of earnings-related contributions is avoided or reduced by means of irregular or unequal payments, give directions for securing that such contributions are payable as if that practice were not followed.[1]

A rather unhappy feature of this provision is that it appears to confer an absolute discretion, there being no right of appeal to the High Court or other authorities. The second, of a more traditional nature, confers on him the power to shift earners in prescribed occupations from one class to another.[2] In some cases, the power will be exercised where there is genuine doubt as to the appropriate classification of a given occupation. In others, it will be a conscious act of policy to extend or reduce insurance cover where this is deemed appropriate in the light of the social needs and circumstances of the occupation in question.[3] Perhaps the most important issue is whether an occupation, otherwise to be categorised as Class 1, should be excluded from unemployment benefit, and, conversely, an occupation, otherwise characterised as Class 2, should be so included. The prevailing Categorisation of Earners Regulations fall into two groups.

a *Employments treated as Class 1*[4]   These are: (a) office cleaners, (b) certain part-time lecturers, teachers and instructors,[5] (c) ministers of religion receiving a stipend or salary, (d) employment by a spouse for the purposes of that spouse's employment, and (e) workers supplied by agencies, rendering personal services and subject to supervision or control,[6] where the agency is paid by the 'employer' (though excluding entertainers, models, and homeworkers).

b *Employments disregarded*[7]   The second group comprises employments which are excluded from both Classes 1 and 2, viz employment by a member of the family in a private home occupied by both the employer and employee which is not employment for the purposes of the trade or business of that employer; self-employment, where this is not the individual's ordinary employment; employment as a returning or counting officer in an election or referendum; and employment in this country in connection with the Visiting Forces Act 1952 or the International Headquarters and Defence Organisation Act 1964.

There is another set of Regulations which extend and restrict the concept of employed earner's employment for the purposes of the industrial injury scheme.[8] This is considered below in chapter 8.[9]

---

1 SI 1979/591, reg 22.
2 SSA 1975, s.2(2).
3 The principle was made explicit by the National Insurance Advisory Committee in its various pronoucements on classification issues: see e.g. its Report of Share Fishermen 1947–48 HC 137, and on Actors, Artistes and Entertainers (1952, Cmd 8549).
4 SI 1978/1689, Sch 1, Part 1.
5 For details, see ibid, para 4, as amended.
6 This implies that the 'employer' has the right not only to tell the worker what to do but how to do it: *Staples v Secretary of State for Social Services* (15 March 1985, unreported).
7 SI 1978/1689, Sch 1, Part III, as amended.
8 SI 1975/467.
9 Pp. 256–257, below.

v Residence or presence

The Act refers to gainful employment in Great Britain.[10] The more detailed conditions as to residence and presence are contained in the Contributions Regulations.[11]

(1) The major condition is that at the time of employment the earner is resident or present in GB – temporary absences being disregarded – or is then ordinarily resident in GB.

(2) If, however, he is not normally resident or employed in the UK, but, in pursuance of employment which is mainly abroad for an employer whose place of business is also outside the UK, he works for a time in GB, contributions are payable only when he has been continuously resident in GB for 52 contribution weeks. The same proviso applies also to other non-residents who, on vacation from full-time studies abroad, are in GB on temporary employment in some way connected with their studies and to those working in GB as apprentices for foreign masters.

(3) Even if an employee is working abroad, he may still be liable to contribute if he is ordinarily resident in GB, was resident there before the commencement of the employment and (most important of all) his employer has a place of business in GB. The liability exists only for the first 52 contribution weeks of the foreign employment.

vi Age

To be liable, the earner must be over 16 and under pensionable age (65 for men, 60 for women).[12]

vii Calculation of contributions

Those with very low earnings are exempt from liability to contribute. The threshold is supplied by the statutory lower earnings limit, a figure fixed annually by the Secretary of State and roughly equal to the basic state pension. Persons with earnings above the threshold pay contributions on *all* earnings up to an upper earnings limit, which is about seven times the lower limit. As a result of a major reform in 1985, the contribution rates are no longer uniform; they are now graduated (5, 7 and 9 per cent respectively) for those with weekly earnings between three different brackets.[13] Those opting out of the state earnings-related pension scheme pay 2 per cent less on earnings between the lower and upper earnings limits[14] (they pay the normal rate on earnings below the lower limit).

The earnings on which the calculation is based are the individual's gross remuneration from his employment or employments.[15] This is deemed by legislation to include sick pay,[16] maternity pay and certain other payments made by employers under the Employment Protection (Consolidation) Act

10 SSA 1975, s.2(1).
11 SI 1979/591, regs 119–120. For 'resident' and 'ordinarily resident', see pp. 362–364, below.
12 SSA 1975, s.4(2)(a) and SSPA 1975, s.4(1). Liability attaches to earnings received after the relevant 60th or 65th birthday but which would normally fall to be paid before that date: SI 1985/397, reg 3.
13 SSA 1975, s.4(6)–(6B), as amended.
14 SSPA 1975, s.27(2).
15 SSA 1975, s.3(1), and Sch 1, para 1; SI 1979/591, reg. 18. For the rules governing the determination of earnings periods, see SI 1979/591, regs 2–6A, as amended. To calculate contributions where the individual is engaged in both contracted-out and non-contracted-out employment, see SSA 1975, Sch 1, paras 1A–1D.
16 SSHBA 1982, ss. 23 and 37, and see SI 1983/395, reg 2.

1978.[17] Without specific authority, it is regarded by the DHSS as also including payments to cover travel between home and work.[18] However, the following items are disregarded.[19]

(1) payments on account of a person's earnings, comprising sums on which contributions have already been made;
(2) holiday payments where a number of employers contribute to a central holiday fund (as in the construction industry);
(3) gratuities not paid directly or indirectly by the employer;[20]
(4) payments in kind (if not of a beneficial interest in a security);
(5) certain payments from trustees (before 6 April 1990);
(6) pension payments;
(7) VAT payable on earnings;
(8) fees received by ministers of religion not forming part of the stipend or salary;
(9) travelling expenses paid to disabled persons;
(10) payments under profit-sharing schemes;
(11) redundancy payments;
(12) reimbursement of expenses incurred in the employment;
(13) parts of sick pay or maternity pay attributable to an employee's own contributions.

If husband and wife are jointly engaged in employment and the earnings therefrom are paid jointly, the amounts of earnings upon which the calculation of contributions is based are the same as those assessed by the Inland Revenue for the purposes of income tax.[1]

C Secondary Class 1 contributions

i Designation of contributors

Secondary Class 1 contributions are payable by 'employers and other persons paying earnings'.[2] The statutory definition of the contributor depends on the status of the earner: if he works under a contract of service, the secondary contributor is his employer,[3] if he is engaged in an office with emoluments, it is either 'such person as may be prescribed in relation to that office', or if no such person is prescribed 'the government department, public authority or body of persons responsible for paying the emoluments of the office'.[4] There is little to add to the provisions concerning an office-holder. As regards employment under a contract of service, the principles elaborated under that head should assist in determining not only the existence of such a contract, but also the parties to it. Where it is clear that an earner is employed under a contract of service, but unclear with which of two parties the contract was made, the issue should be resolved by answering such questions as: who supervised the work? who paid the employee? who had the right to appoint

---

17 SS(MP)A 1977, s.13, as amended.
18 See Leaflet NP 15, para 13.
19 SI 1979/591, reg 19, as amended.
20 See for discussion NIAC Report on Draft Contribution Amendment Regulations (1980, Cmnd 8117).
1 SI 1975/591, reg 16 and see Pinson *Revenue Law* (17th edn) paras 8.23–8.30.
2 SSA 1975, s.1(2).
3 Ibid, s.4(4)(a).
4 Ibid, s.4(4)(b).

and dismiss him?[5] Cases of doubt, and cases where the party legally cate-gorised as an employer under a contract of service is regarded as an inappro-priate secondary contributor, may be regulated by the Secretary of State's power to transfer liability to another prescribed person.[6] Under current regulations:[7]

(1) An office cleaner is employed by the person for whom the work is done, unless he/she is supplied and paid by an agency, in which case the agency is the employer.
(2) In other cases, where an employee renders personal services under an agreement with an agency, the agency is treated as the employer.
(3) Where the earner is employed in a company which has gone into volun-tary liquidation but which carries on business under a liquidator, the per-son holding the office of liquidator at the time of the employment is treated as the employer.
(4) A barrister's clerk is treated as being employed by the head of his chambers.
(5) In respect of Anglican ministers of religion, the secondary contributions are payable by the Church Commissioners; for other ministers, by the administrators of the fund from which the minister's remuneration is paid.

Where an earner is employed under two or more independent contracts of service, and is paid by each employer an amount equal to or exceeding the lower earnings limit, both will be liable to contribute. However, if the earn-ings in one or more of the employments are lower than that limit, and the rele-vant employer carries on business in association with another employer, the earnings may be aggregated to achieve the necessary liability and the con-tributions are then payable by each of those employers on a proportionate basis.[8]

ii Residence
Liability for secondary contributions arises only where the party otherwise liable is resident or present in Great Britain or has a place of business there.[9] The same regulation optimistically adds that even if these conditions are not met an employer may pay the contributions 'if he so wishes'.

iii Amount
The employer's liability for secondary contributions is wider than that of the employee in three respects:[10] first, it extends to earnings after the latter has reached pensionable age; secondly, there is no upper earnings limit and so contributions are payable on all earnings; and thirdly, there are four earnings brackets in respect of which the employer pays, respectively, 5, 7, 9 and 10.45 per cent. There is a reduction of 3.8 per cent on earnings between the lower and upper limits for contracted-out employments.[11]

5 Atiyah *Vicarious Liability* (1966) pp. 160–161; and see Lord Porter in *Mersey Docks and Harbour Board v Coggins and Griffith (Liverpool) Ltd* [1974] AC 1 at 17. Two reported deci-sions of the Minister, M14 and M35, by implication, apply these criteria.
6 SSA 1975, s.4(5)(b).
7 SI 1978/1689, Sch 3.
8 SI 1979/591, reg 13.
9 Ibid, reg 119(1)(b).
10 See SSA 1985, s.7, amending SSA 1975, s.4.
11 SSPA 1975, s.27(2), as amended.

D Class 2 contributions

Contributions under Class 2 may confer title to any contributory benefit except unemployment benefit, and the earnings-related additional components in pensions.[12] They are payable by self-employed earners[13] and differ from Class 1 contributions in three important respects: since *ex hypothesi* there is no contract of service, there is for each employment only one contributor; the contribution is payable on a flat-rate basis; a self-employed person who is not liable to contribute because, for example, his earnings are too small or he does not satisfy the residence conditions may pay voluntarily.

i Persons liable

A self-employed person is defined as

> a person who is gainfully employed in Great Britain otherwise than in employed earner's employment (whether or not he is also employed in such employment).[14]

a *Combinations of employments*

The negative and rather confusing formulation means that if a person is in a gainful employment for which Class contributions are not payable[15] he is necessarily self-employed[16] even though he may concurrently and independently be employed in a Class 1 employment. The liability to pay under both classes (and as we shall see also under Class 4) was a major innovation of the Social Security Act 1973. The justification for the new approach is not immediately apparent but may readily be inferred from general policy considerations. The acceptance of an earnings-related principle for contributions naturally led to the conclusion that a proportionate part of a self-employed person's profits should be payable whether or not he was also employed under a contract of service: hence Class 4. But as will be seen, it was thought too expensive administratively to impose such a charge on profits below a certain figure.[17] The flat-rate contribution under Class 2 is therefore fixed so that it roughly represents the same percentage of that figure as the Class 4 contribution does of liable income above it.[18]

b *Gainful employment*

The shift in terminology from 'gainfully occupied in employment' to 'gainfully employed' has already been the subject of comment in relation to Class 1 contributions.[19] As was suggested there, the authorities on the interpretation of the earlier formulation should be used as guidelines for the term currently employed. In the present context, the matter is of more than academic interest, for while there is no liability to pay where earnings are below a certain level, the self-employed earner if 'gainfully employed' may in such circumstances voluntarily contribute. Thus an individual undertaking a new

12 SSA 1975, s.13(1), (3).
13 Ibid, s.1(2).
14 Ibid, s.2(1)(b).
15 This includes the single case where the Secretary of State has prescribed that someone employed under a contract of service shall nevertheless be treated as a self-employed earner: SI 1978/1689, Sch 1, Part II.
16 Unless disregarded, p.42, above.
17 DHSS Discussion Document, *The Self-Employed and National Insurance* (1980), paras 8, 39.
18 Ibid, para 18.
19 P.36, above.

enterprise will be *entitled* to pay Class 2 contributions as soon as he is 'gainfully employed', notwithstanding that his current failure to make substantial profits exempts him from *liability* to pay. 'Gainfully occupied' under the former legislation was held not necessarily to imply the making of a net profit on an enterprise.[20] Thus in relation to self-employment, it was said that

> the question is not to be posed at any particular time, has he in fact received some net profit from his activities . . . but does he hold himself out as being anxious to become employed for purpose of gain?[1]

The answer to this latter question is a matter of fact for the determining authority. But assistance may be derived from decisions on analogous issues within other areas of social security law, notably in relation to retirement pensions.[2]

c *Continuing employment*
The boundaries of self-employment are not always easy to determine. To a certain extent, the answer will be supplied by the 'gainfully employed' criterion discussed in the last paragraph. To reinforce the notion that regard should be had to an individual's endeavours over a substantial period rather than to short-term and spasmodic profit/loss accounting, the Regulations prescribe that where a person is a self-employed earner (or is treated as such) 'the employment shall . . . be treated as continuing unless and until he is no longer ordinarily employed in that employment.'[3]

d *Residence*
A self-employed earner is liable to pay contributions only if he is either ordinarily resident in Great Britain or was resident there for a period of at least 26 of the immediately preceding 52 contribution weeks.[4] Where he is not liable under these rules an earner may nevertheless voluntarily contribute.[5]

e *Age*
The contributor must be over 16 years and under pensionable age (men 65, women 60).[6]

ii **Exceptions**
There are two grounds on which a self-employed person may be excepted from liability to pay contributions: inability to earn, and low earnings. As regards the first, he must show that throughout the week for which the exception is claimed (excluding Sunday or an equivalent rest day), he received sickness or invalidity benefit, invalid care or maternity allowance, or was in prison or detained in legal custody.[7] An exception for low earnings has existed ever since self-employed persons were compulsorily insured in 1946,[8] the

20 *Vandyk v Minister of Pensions and National Insurance* [1955] 1 QB 29.
1 Per Slade J, ibid at 38.
2 Pp. 192–195, below.
3 SI 1978/1689, Sch 2.
4 SI 1979/591, reg 119(1)(d). For 'resident' and 'ordinarily resident' see pp. 362–364, below.
5 But only if he is either present in GB, in the week in question, or if abroad, had been resident there and had paid Class 1 or 2 contributions for three years immediately preceding his departure: SI 1979/591, regs 119(1)(c) and 121.
6 SSA 1975, s.7(1), as amended, and SSPA 1975, s.4(2).
7 SI 1979/591, reg 23.
8 See in general, NIAC Report on Liability for Contributions of Pensions with Small Incomes (1955, Cmd 9432).

justifications being to exclude occasional profit makers and to reduce administrative expenditure. Earnings, for this purpose, means 'net earnings' from the employment,[9] and is effectively such income as is chargeable to income tax under Schedule D:[10] thus from gross earnings may be deducted expenses necessarily incurred in connection with the employment.[11] In furtherance of this policy of integrating contributions and tax liability, the regulations adopt the Inland Revenue rule of allowing assessments to be based on earnings from a preceding tax year.[12] Earnings for a particular year are treated as less than the threshold if, in the preceding year, the individual's earnings were less than that amount and there had since been no material change of circumstances, or if in the year for which exception is claimed the earnings are expected to be less than that amount.[13] The onus is on the self-employed earner to claim exception, and if he is successful he will be granted a certificate of exception. When an exception is granted on either of the two grounds specified in this paragraph, the self-employed person may voluntarily pay contributions (either of Class 2 or of Class 3).[14]

iii Amount

Whether contributions are mandatory or voluntary, a weekly flat-rate contribution is payable. A higher rate is paid by share fishermen who, exceptionally, may be entitled to unemployment benefit on the basis of Class 2 contributions.[15]

E Class 3 contributions

Beveridge's conception of social insurance was a comprehensive one – all of working age were to be included. Under his scheme, as implemented in the 1946 legislation, there was to be a third class of *compulsory* contributions, for those who would need provision for medical treatment, retirement and funeral expenses, and who were not in a gainful occupation but were of working age.[16] Typically included were students, unmarried women engaged in unremunerated domestic work, those retiring early under an occupational pension scheme, and persons in receipt of private income. Of course they must have had resources to pay contributions, and so there were exemptions for those below a minimum income level. This class of contributions, so defined, was abolished by the 1973 Act. The new Class 3 allows only for *voluntary* contributions, and these may be paid either by non-employed persons or those contributing in Class 1 or 2, but with deficiencies in their contribution record. They may enable a person to qualify only for widow's benefit and retirement pensions (Categories A and B).[17] A weekly flat-rate is payable, just marginally below the amount paid by Class 2 contributors.

---

9 SI 1979/591, reg 25(2).
10 See Pinson *Revenue Law* (17th edn) chs 2, 4, 5.
11 Ibid, paras 2.51–2.78.
12 Ibid, paras 2.79–2.84.
13 SI 1979/591, reg 25(1)(b).
14 Ibid, regs 23(3) and 26(b).
15 Ibid, reg 98, as amended.
16 Paras 310 and 317.
17 SSA 1975, s.13(1).

i Persons entitled to contribute

The contributor must be over 16[18] and under pensionable age (65 for men, 60 for women),[19] and with some exceptions resident in Great Britain during the year for which he makes his contribution.[20]

ii Making up a reckonable year

The 1975 Act prescribes that:

> payment of Class 3 contributions shall be allowed only with a view to enabling the contributor to satisfy contribution conditions of entitlement to benefit.[1]

As will be seen, for those benefits for which Class 3 payments may count, a year of contributions will only qualify towards entitlement if a minimum number of contributions has been made. At the end of each contribution year a Class 1 contributor is sent a statement of his account indicating any shortage, and how many Class 3 contributions will be necessary to make up a reckonable year. Class 2 contributors with an incomplete record may, as already indicated, voluntarily pay additional contributions of that class, but if they wish to secure entitlement only to the more limited benefits available to Class 3 contributors, they may in the alternative make up the number with additional payments of the latter class. There are rules to prevent an individual making unnecessary contributions, e.g. where his record is complete for a given year, or where he will be credited with contributions for that year.[2] If such payments have nevertheless been made, the contributor is entitled to a refund,[3] though he may, if he prefers, have the extra contributions appropriated to satisfy conditions for another tax year.[4]

F Class 4 contributions

It was evident that if the self-employed were to make earnings-related contributions to the National Insurance Fund, this in practice could be achieved only by integrating assessment and administration with the fiscal system.[5] A fourth category of contributions was therefore created which would effectively coincide with tax liability under Schedule D of the Income Tax Acts. Entitlement to benefit, however, is established by reference only to contributions of Classes 1, 2 or 3; Class 4 is simply the most convenient means of securing earnings-related contributions from those paying Class 2 contributions. The principle of coincidence with tax liability is stated in the Social Security Act thus:

> Class 4 contributions shall be payable in respect of all annual profits or gains immediately derived from the carrying on or exercise of one or more trades, professions or vocations, being profits or gains chargeable to income tax under Case I or Case II of Schedule D . . . and the contributions shall be payable (a) in the same

18 Ibid, s.8(1).
19 SI 1979/591, reg 28(1)(e).
20 Ibid, reg 119(1)(e). Those abroad can contribute on the same conditions as are prescribed in relation to Class 2 voluntary contributions: n.14, above.
1 SSA 1975, s.8(2).
2 SSPA 1975, s.5(1) and SI 1979/591, reg 28.
3 Ibid, regs 32–33.
4 SSA 1975, s.8(2)(a) and SI 1979/591, reg 30.
5 For the policy considerations relevant to the liability of the self-employed, see pp. 23–24, above.

manner as any income tax . . . and (b) by the person on whom the income tax is (or would be) charged, in accordance with assessments made from time to time under the Income Tax Acts.[6]

For the nature and extent of this liability, then, reference should be made to the standard texts on taxation.[7] What follows is an account of those aspects of the assessment which are peculiar to Class 4 contributions.

i Persons liable

The condition of residence in the United Kingdom is that applied under the Income Tax Acts,[8] but in contrast to that legislation, liability for contributions does not extend to earners who are under 16 or over pensionable age.[9] As with income tax, a husband and wife may either aggregate their income or be assessed separately. In the case of the latter, the wife's separate assessment will be treated as the base for her contributions.[10] If income is, however, aggregated, as under tax law, the husband will be liable to pay contributions on his wife's profits and gains, though they will nevertheless be regarded as her contributions.[11] In the case of partnerships, as under tax law, each partner is liable according to his share of the profits,[12] but contributions are not payable by those liable to tax as trustees, administrators, executors and other nominal holders of property.[13]

A person charged for income tax under both Schedule E and Schedule D, because he is both employed under a contract of service and derives profits from a trade or business, for that reason will also be liable to pay contributions of both Classes 1 and 4, provided that in either case his earnings or profits exceed the relevant lower limit. Some difficulty is caused where tax and social security liability do not correspond in this way. Thus, while actors, musicians and those working for agencies pay Class 1 contributions, their earnings or profits are nevertheless chargeable to tax under Schedule D. The solution provided by the regulations is to deduct from the profits and gains chargeable to Schedule D, the amount of earnings on the basis of which the Class 1 contributions were assessed, so that liability for Class 4 will be attracted only if the remainder exceeds the threshold.[14] Conversely, a person paying Class 2 contributions but whose earnings are chargeable to tax under Schedule E, will be liable for Class 4 at the same rate as other self-employed persons, though in this case liability is deferred until the end of the relevant tax year and any payments will thereafter be recovered by the DHSS and not the Inland Revenue.[15]

ii Amount of liability

Class 4 contributions involve the payment of a prescribed proportion (currently 6.3 per cent) of profits and gains between a lower and upper level.

---

6 SSA 1975, s.9(1). For an interesting, if hopeless, challenge to the constitutional validity of this provision, see *Martin v O'Sullivan* [1984] STC 258, 57 TC 709.
7 E.g. Pinson *Revenue Law* (17th edn) chs 2, 4, 5.
8 Ibid, paras 7.17–7.24.
9 SSA 1975, s.9(8), as amended.
10 Ibid, Sch 2, para 4(1).
11 Ibid, para 4(3).
12 Ibid, para 5.
13 Ibid, para 6.
14 SI 1979/591, reg 61.
15 SSA 1975, s.10 and SI 1979/591, regs 71 and 78.

The profits and gains in question are those which are chargeable to income tax under Schedule D. Account must therefore be taken of such deductions and reliefs as are there provided,[16] but the following tax reliefs do not apply for the purposes of Class 4 contributions:[17] personal allowances;[18] payments under annuity contracts and trust schemes;[19] the carrying forward of losses;[20] the payment of interest.[1] Someone liable for both Class 1 and Class 4 contributions will not have to pay, in aggregate, more than the maximum which would have been payable on contributions of a single class.[2]

Part 3   Special categories

A Married women

Under the Beveridge plan of national insurance, married women required special treatment.[3] This was derived from his view of the family as a single economic unit, the wife doing the housework for the husband, who in return maintained her. According to the figures then available,[4] over 80 per cent of married women of working age regarded marriage as their sole occupation. Even if a wife was an earner, she was different from a single woman in that employment was liable to interruption for childbirth, and, more significantly, her earnings were 'a means, not of subsistence but of a standard of living above subsistence'.[5] It followed that in sickness or unemployment she did not need compensation on the same scale as the primary breadwinner; she could fall back on her husband's income, or his benefit if his earnings were interrupted. It was therefore proposed that a married woman who was an earner could choose either to opt out of the scheme, and thus become wholly dependent on her husband's contributions for retirement pension and maternity grant, or else to contribute in her own right.[6] These proposals were implemented in full by the 1946 legislation, and with some modifications, remained in force until 1975.

By the 1970s, the social and economic climate had changed considerably. Over 60 per cent of married women of working age were now in paid employment.[7] The movement against sex discrimination had intensified, and the social security position of married women was a prime target.[8] The Labour government, in consequence, decided to abolish the married woman's option as part of its programme for pension reform. The ability, for the purpose of pension entitlement, to take into consideration years during which a woman

---

16 See *Pinson*, n.7, above.
17 SSA 1975, Sch 2, para 3(2).
18 Under Income and Corporation Taxes Act 1970, Part 1, ch II.
19 Ibid, ss. 226–227.
20 Ibid, s.173.
1 Ibid, s.175 and Finance Act 1972, s.75.
2 SI 1979/591, reg 71.
3 Para 108.
4 Beveridge relied on the 1931 census. He regarded the much higher figures for wartime work (see Thomas *Women at Work: Wartime Social Survey* (1944)) as a temporary phenomenon.
5 *Beveridge* para 108.
6 As a non-earner, she might similarly opt between contributions under Class IV and relying on her husband's contributions.
7 General Household Survey 1978, Table 5.7.
8 See e.g. Report of Labour Party Study Group *Towards Equality: Women and Social Security* (1969).

was 'precluded from regular employment by responsibilities at home'[9] was regarded as the key provision which would ensure a fair return for her contributions. However, in order that existing family arrangements should not be unduly prejudiced by the decision to abolish the option, those already married or widowed when the new provisions came into force were allowed to choose between 'full' and 'reduced' liability.

To benefit from the reduced liability provisions, married women must either have opted out of liability under the previous contributory system or have elected for reduced liability under the transitional provisions.[10] The period of reduced liability then runs until pensionable age (60) is reached, but it terminates earlier:

(1) on the date of a dissolution of marriage by divorce or annulment; or
(2) at the end of the tax year in which she ceases to be qualified to the relevant widow's benefit; or
(3) at the end of the tax year in which she revokes her election for reduced liability; or
(4) at the end of any two consecutive tax years subsequent to 5 April 1978 during which she is neither a self-employed earner nor is engaged in employment which attracts Class 1 contributions liability.[11]

Reduced liability confers on a married woman who has so elected exemption from paying Class 2 contributions[12] and disentitles her from paying Class 3 contributions.[13] But the obligation to pay those of Class 4 remains unaffected and, as regards Class 1, the liability is reduced to 3.85 per cent rather than excluded altogether.[14] These payments are more akin to taxes than to contributions for they cannot assist in gaining title to any benefits or to the crediting of contributions during periods of sickness, unemployment or domestic responsibilities.[15]

B Other special cases

Certain categories of occupation are selected for special treatment either because provision is not necessary for some hazards (e.g. unemployment) or because there are difficulties in fulfilling the normal conditions for contributions.

i HM forces

One of the consequences of the Beveridge principle of universality was to extend insurance to Crown employees, who had previously been excluded from the national schemes. The principle, affirmed in the Social Security Act 1975, is that the provisions apply 'to persons employed by or under the

---

9 See p.200, below.
10 SI 1979/591, Part VIII, Case D, and *Williams* ch 10.
11 SI 1979/591, reg 101(1).
12 Ibid, reg 100(1)(b).
13 Ibid, reg 105.
14 Ibid, reg 104, as amended. The liability of the employer for secondary Class 1 contributions remains unaffected.
15 SSPA 1975, s.3(4), does enable regulations to be made so that reduced liability contributions may be used to satisfy the relevant contribution conditions but the power has not been exercised in relation to married women and widows.

Crown in like manner as if they were employed by a private person'.[16] However, members of HM forces are in a special position:

- During the currency of their service, they do not lose earnings for reasons of sickness, invalidity or unemployment and benefit is not payable for these contingencies. In their case, the aim is merely to ensure that they will be sufficiently covered, in terms of contributions, for needs arising after they have returned to civilian life. Class 1 contributions are therefore payable, but the rate is reduced by 0.9 per cent (primary) and 0.95 per cent (secondary).[17] For the purposes of satisfying the residence conditions for contributions, a serving member of the forces[18] is treated as 'present in Great Britain'.[18]

ii Employment on the Continental Shelf
The problem here is simply that of satisfying the residence requirements. Regulations therefore prescribe that

- an employment in an area designated under the Continental Shelf Act 1964 in connection with the exploitation of resources, or the exploration, of the sea bed and subsoil, is deemed to be employment within GB.[19]

iii Airmen
Similar considerations apply to airmen:

- Provided that the employer has a place of business in GB, if the aircraft is British, or the principal place of business is in GB, in the case of other aircraft, the airman is treated as present in GB,[20] though if he is neither domiciled nor has a place of residence there, no contributions are payable.[1]

iv Mariners and registered dock workers
- For a person employed as a mariner,[2] the normal residence requirements for contributions are replaced by the simple condition that he is domiciled or resident in GB.[3] If the mariner's employment is wholly or partly on a 'foreign-going ship', the secondary liability is reduced by 0.5 per cent.[4] There are also special methods of calculating earnings for the purpose of earnings-related contributions.[5]

v Volunteer Development Workers
The object is to enable those working abroad in volunteer development but

16 SSA 1975, s.127(1).
17 SI 1979/591, reg 115(1), as amended.
18 Ibid, reg 114.
19 Ibid, reg 85.
20 Ibid, reg 82(1). For the definition of 'airmen' and 'British aircraft' see ibid, reg 81.
 1 Ibid, reg 82(2).
 2 For definition, see ibid, reg 86.
 3 Ibid, reg 87.
 4 Ibid, reg 89(1)(b).
 5 Ibid, regs 90-97, as amended.

ordinarily resident in Great Britain to make contributions. If such work does not render such individuals liable to pay Class 1 contributions, they are exempt from, but may opt to pay, Class 2 contributions at a specially high rate.[6]

Part 4   Contribution conditions

Under the system in force before 1975, contributions were predominantly flat-rate. It was therefore convenient to express the conditions of contributions for the various benefits in terms of the number of weekly contributions paid (or credited) during a specified period (often a 'contribution year'). With the adoption of the earnings-related system and the interdependence with tax liability, such concepts were no longer feasible, and so they were replaced by 'earnings factors' (representing the amount of earnings on which liability to contribute is based) and the 'tax year' (6 April–5 April) as the usual contributory period.

A   Earnings factors

Contributions to Class 1 are earnings-related, those of Class 2 and Class 3 are flat-rate. In any one tax year, an individual might combine contributions of one class with those of either or both of the other classes. It was therefore necessary to create some common denominator whereby equivalent conditions could be exacted from those paying different types of contributions, hence the 'earnings factor'. For Class 1 contributions, this is simply the earnings on which such contributions are paid or treated as paid.[7] For Class 2 or 3 contributions (which are flat-rate) it is the lower earnings limit for Class 1 contributions multiplied by the number of contributions made in the relevant tax year.[8] Similar principles govern the calculation of the earnings factors derived from credited and contracted-out contributions,[9] though these are calculated separately from factors derived from contributions actually paid in non-contracted-out employment.

One important function of the earnings factors is to determine the amount of the earnings-related component in the pensions scheme.[10] Because of what is often a substantial gap in time between the payment of the contributions and the receipt of the benefit, it is necessary to 'revalue' the earnings factors to keep pace with inflation. Under the Pensions Act, therefore, the Secretary of State is directed to review in each tax year the general level of earnings obtaining in Great Britain, and if he concludes that the earnings factors for any previous tax year have not maintained their value in relation to the general level of earnings, he must make an order directing that the earnings

6 SI 1986/485.
7 SSA 1975, s.13(2), as amended. For the technically precise mode of calculation, see SI 1979/676, Sch 1, Part I, as amended. No earnings factors are derived from secondary Class 1 contributions or from reduced liability contributions (married women and widows): SSA 1975, s.13(3).
8 Ibid, s.13(5)(b), as amended, and SI 1975/468, Sch 1, Part II.
9 Ibid, Part I, paras 4–7.
10 Pp. 206–208, below.

factors shall be increased by such percentages as he thinks necessary to restore their values.[11]

B Conditions for benefit

In the section of the book devoted to the individual contributory benefits, the contribution conditions of each will be specified. At this stage, it will be convenient to review the general pattern of rules. The aim of these rules has been to preserve a fair balance between the average contributor and the average beneficiary.[12] This objective of equity has given rise to two fundamental principles. The first is that the claimant's record of contributions should be sufficient in terms both of initial establishment in the scheme and of consistency over a period of time. The second is that there should be a difference according to whether he is claiming a short-term or a long-term benefit. In the case of the latter, where he will draw heavily on the fund's resources, it is appropriate that the tests should be more stringent. The conditions for the short-term benefits have traditionally been relatively easy to satisfy. The Conservative government in recent years has been concerned that unemployment benefit, in particular, was payable to many claimants whose employment record was only marginal[13] and in 1988 imposed more onerous conditions.[14] The state maternity allowance forms a category of its own: the conditions are easily satisfied because the benefit is now intended for a residual group of women not covered by the new statutory maternity pay scheme.[15] The contribution rules are expressed in terms of earnings factors, but it should be noted that claimants to long-term benefits may satisfy an alternative set of conditions formulated in terms of pre-1975 contributions.[16]

i Initial condition

The first test, based on the idea of initial establishment in the scheme, can be satisfied only by contributions actually paid, i.e. credits do not qualify. In the case of unemployment benefit, the claimant must have paid in either of the two last tax years before the year of the claim contributions, the earnings factor from which is at least 25 times the lower earnings limit for that year.[17] As regards sickness benefit and widow's payment, the test can be satisfied for any tax year.[18] For those contributors at the lower end of the income scale (or making flat-rate Class 2 contributions) this will mean approximately six months' contributions. For the long-term benefits (retirement pensions, Categories A and B, and the remaining widow's benefits – but not invalidity benefit, entitlement to which depends on fulfilling the conditions for sickness benefit) the qualifying earnings factor is 52 times the lower earnings limit (equivalent to one year's contributions at the lowest end of the scale).[19]

11 SSPA 1975, s.21(2),(3), as amended.
12 See NIAC Report on the Question of Contribution Conditions and Credits Provisions (1956, Cmd 9854) para 36.
13 Mr J Moore, Secretary of State, 121 HC Official Report (6th series), col 659.
14 SSA 1988, s.6.
15 Pp. 228–229, below.
16 See SI 1979/643.
17 SSA 1975, Sch 3, para 1(2), as amended.
18 Ibid, paras 1(2) and 4(1).
19 Ibid, para 5.

ii Continuing condition

For the second qualifying condition, credits are equivalent to paid contributions, but the difference between the short-term and long-term benefits becomes considerable. For the former, the earnings factor derived from contributions paid or credited during each of the two tax year immediately preceding the year during which the entitlement to benefit falls must have been at least 50 times the lower earnings limit.[20] For the latter, the position is more complicated as the contributions determine entitlement not merely to the basic component in the benefit, but also to the earnings-related additional component. To qualify for the basic component, for each of not less than 90 per cent of the tax years of his working life (viz between 16 and pensionable age) the claimant must have paid, or been credited with, contributions the earnings factor of which was 52 times the lower earnings limit.[1] Alternatively, that earnings factor must be achieved for one half of 90 per cent of the working life (or 20 years, if that is less) and during each of the remaining years of working life the contributor was 'precluded from regular employment by responsibilities at home'.[2] The additional component is based on the surplus of earnings factors above the minimum qualifying factor for each tax year.[3] It should be observed, however, that entitlement to the additional component is not conditional on satisfying the contribution requirements for the basic component; thus someone without title to the basic component because, for example, his contribution record was not sufficient over the relevant proportion of the working life will still receive the additional component based on those years when he did achieve a surplus of earnings factors.

C Credits

The system of crediting contributions is designed to assist those who are already established in the scheme but, for reasons beyond their control, have been unable to continue to make the requisite payments, sufficient to satisfy the second condition.[4] To the extent that crediting is permitted, the beneficiaries are being subsidised by other contributors and for this reason it has been said both that there must be 'real and substantial justification' for the granting of the facility,[5] and that the beneficiary must show a significant degree of participation in the scheme during non-credited periods.[6] It is for the latter reason that married women who have elected for reduced liability[7] generally cannot be credited with Class 1 contributions.[8] With this exception, there are six main categories of contributors entitled to credits: those unemployed or otherwise incapable of work; those caring full-time for invalids; those approaching retirement; new entrants; those engaged in full-time education or training; and women whose marriage has been terminated.

---

20 Ibid, para 1(3). For widow's payment, the test needs to be satisfied only in relation to the last tax year before the benefit year: ibid, para 4(3).
 1 Ibid, para 5.
 2 Ibid, para 5(6). See, further, SI 1978/508 and p.200, below.
 3 SSPA 1975, s.6(4) and see generally below, pp. 207–209.
 4 SI 1975/556, reg 3. A credited Class 1 contribution is equivalent to a payment at the lower earnings limit then current.
 5 NIAC Report in Credits for Approved Training Courses (1953, Cmd 8860), paras 17–18. See also Report on Contribution Conditions and Credits, n.12, above.
 6 Mr S Orme, Minister for Social Security, 928 HC Official Report (5th series), cols 1475–1476.
 7 See pp. 51–52, above.
 8 SI 1978/409, reg 2(2).

i Unemployed or incapable of work

A Class 1 credit is available in respect of each week of unemployment or incapacity,[9] effectively for periods which would have counted for the purposes of entitlement to unemployment benefit,[10] sickness benefit,[11] or maternity allowance[12] if an appropriate claim had been made.[13] However, someone claiming unemployment benefit, sickness benefit or maternity allowance can only avail himself of these credit facilities if he satisfies one of the following conditions:[14]

(1) at some time during the tax year of the credits in question he actually paid contributions amounting to an earnings factor of at least 13 times the lower earnings limit;
(2) at some time during that year he made a claim, and satisfied the contribution conditions, for unemployment benefit, sickness benefit or maternity allowance;
(3) at some time during that year he was in receipt of invalidity pension, invalid care allowance, or a training allowance;
(4) the credits in question related to a period when his entitlement to unemployment or sickness benefit had expired or he would have received sickness benefit, if not entitled to statutory sick pay.

ii Full-time care of invalid

As will be seen,[15] the invalid care allowance is intended for those who care for an invalid but who otherwise would be in full-time employment. Their position is therefore similar to that of the unemployed or incapable and they are granted Class 1 credits for each week for which they are paid the allowance.[16]

iii Persons approaching retirement

Class 1 contributions may be credited for the tax year in which an individual reaches 60 and for the four subsequent tax years, sufficient to make the year in question a 'reckonable year' for the purposes of entitlement, without the condition of being either incapable of work or having registered for employment.[17] The aim is to encourage early retirement without adding to the number of registered unemployed. There is, however, a condition that the individual be present in Great Britain for six months of the tax year in question.[18]

iv Starting credits

Individuals begin contributing to the scheme at different ages, according to their circumstances. Many will commence employment on reaching the

9 SI 1975/556, reg 9(1); also for periods of jury service: ibid, reg 9B.
10 Pp. 71–77, below.
11 P.140, below.
12 P.232, below.
13 SI 1975/556, reg 9(2)–(5), as amended. The unemployed will normally have to register, and those incapable provide medical evidence. Very short periods of work during the week are disregarded. Periods of statutory sick pay only give rise to credits when the amount of such pay is less than the lower earnings limit and hence there is no contributions liability: SI 1983/197.
14 SI 1975/556, reg 9(9), as amended.
15 Pp. 168–171, below.
16 SI 1975/556, reg 7A. Widows who would have been paid the allowance but for the Overlapping Regulations are also entitled to the credit.
17 Ibid, reg 9A.
18 Ibid, reg 9A(4).

school-leaving age of 16; others will remain in full-time education for several more years. At whatever time the entry is made, it will rarely coincide with the tax year (the base period of contribution conditions) and unless concessions are made a substantial number of payments will have no insurance significance. The system of credits has traditionally attempted to maintain equity between these various categories of entrants. However, the facility for the purpose of claims to the short-term benefits was withdrawn in 1988[19] and all that remains is a small concession for someone claiming a retirement pension or a widow's benefit: such a person is entitled to the number of Class 3 credits necessary to bring the relevant earnings factor up to a reckonable year for the first three years of possible employment, viz the tax year during which he reached the age of 16 and the two following tax years.[20]

v Education and training

The next set of rules makes concessions for those who start contributing late, or interrupt their contribution record, because they are engaged in education or training. It is not, however, thought appropriate that all persons engaged in education or training courses at whatever age and for whatever purpose should be subsidised by the fund.[1]

a *Course begun before age 21*

In this case, the policy is an ungenerous one: it is simply to grant credits for the year in which full-time education, apprenticeship or a training course approved by the Secretary of State ended, so that the year may be constituted a reckonable year for the purposes of entitlement to unemployment benefit or sickness benefit.[2]

b *Interruptions for approved training courses*

Clearly it is felt desirable to encourage individuals to improve their capacity for a job or equip themselves with the necessary skills for a new one. This form of vocational training, it may be argued, is in the national interest, and therefore justifies some form of subsidisation by the National Insurance Fund.[3] Thus the Regulations prescribe that[4] a contributor shall be granted credits for each week during any part of which he was engaged in a course of full-time training approved by the Secretary of State, provided that all of the following conditions are satisfied:

(1) the course was not in pursuance of his employment;
(2) he had reached 18 before the beginning of the tax year during which the week in question began;
(3) the course was not intended to last more than one year,[5] and

19 Ibid, reg 5, revoked by SI 1988/1230.
20 Ibid, reg 4(1).
 1 See NIAC Report on Credits for Approved Training Courses, n.5, above.
 2 SI 1975/556, reg 8, as amended.
 3 NIAC Report, n.5, above, at paras 20–21.
 4 SI 1975/556, reg 7.
 5 Though if it was training of a disabled person under the Employment and Training Act 1973, it may be permitted for 'such longer period as is reasonable in the circumstances': SI 1975/556, reg 7(2)(b).

(4) for at least one of the last three tax years before the course began, he had paid or had been credited with contributions amounting to at least 50 times the lower earnings limit for that year.[6]

vi Termination of marriage

A woman may obtain employment for the first time where a marriage has been terminated by death or dissolution or when children cease to require full-time attention. The position of such a woman is analogous to that of new entrants and similar credit facilities are available.

(1) For the purpose of satisfying the 'continuing' condition of unemployment benefit, sickness benefit, and maternity allowance, a woman whose marriage has been terminated may be credited with the necessary number of Class 1 contributions for any year during the whole or any part of which the marriage was subsisting. During one year which was either the last year before the marriage terminated or any subsequent year, she must, however, have paid Class 1 or Class 2 contributions, the earnings factor derived from which was at least 25 times the lower earnings limit for that year.[7]

(2) For the same purpose, a widow who ceases to be entitled to widowed mother's allowance (because she has no longer dependent children of the relevant age to care for) will be credited with the requisite number of Class 1 contributions for every year up to and including that in which she ceased to be entitled to the allowance.[8]

(3) For the purposes of entitlement to retirement pension, a widow is credited with such Class 3 contributions as are necessary to enable her to acquire the requisite earnings factor for periods before 5 April 1978 during which she was entitled to a widow's benefit (other than the age-related widow's pension, or, if she was widowed before 6 April 1975, the widow's basic pension).[9]

D Other assistance in satisfying contribution conditions

i Aggregate of contributions by new entrants

The credit facilities available to new entrants serve to assist them only in satisfying the second of the two contribution conditions. The fortuitous timing of their entry in relation to the relevant tax years may constitute an obstacle to the fulfilment of the first condition. The legislation makes a further concession for entitlement to widow's payment (the equivalent facility for claimants to other short-term benefits was abrogated in 1988).

– Where the last complete tax year, before the beginning of the year in which occurred the event for which benefit is claimed, was either the year in which the claimant's former husband first became liable for contributions of Classes 1 or 2, or the year preceding that year, she may for the purposes of satisfying the first contribution condition for widow's payment

6 This condition may be waived if 'in the circumstances of the case there is reasonable ground': ibid, reg 7(2)(a).
7 SI 1974/2010, reg 2.
8 Ibid, reg 3(1)(b).
9 Ibid, reg 6, as amended.

aggregate the contributions which he has actually paid, and that aggregate is then treated as having been paid in the last complete year.[10]

ii Widows deemed to satisfy first condition

Widows joining, or rejoining, the scheme once their entitlement to widowed mother's allowance has expired are faced with a similar problem, and for the purposes of entitlement to unemployment and sickness benefit or maternity allowance, they are deemed to have satisfied the first contribution condition.[11]

iii Invalidity pensioners

The first condition for a widowed mother's allowance, a widow's pension, or a retirement pension (Categories A and B) is deemed to be satisfied if the relevant contributor was entitled to an invalidity pension at any time during the year in which he reached pensionable age or died, or the year preceding that year.[12]

iv Employment abroad

For the purpose of claims for unemployment and sickness benefit and maternity allowance, a person who is employed abroad but who is ordinarily resident in Great Britain is, subject to certain conditions, treated as if he paid Class 1 contributions at the lower earnings limit for the period of absence.[13]

v Spouse's contributions and retirement pensions

As will be revealed in chapter 5, a woman who is, or has been, married or a widower may rely on the spouse's contributions for the purposes of a Category B retirement pension;[14] where a marriage has been terminated by death or divorce, a similar facility is available for the purposes of a Category A pension.[15]

vi Industrial accidents and diseases

When the short-term benefit for those rendered incapable of work by an industrial accident or disease was abolished in 1983, it was necessary to provide financial support if the individual was not entitled to statutory sick pay or could not satisfy the contribution conditions for sickness benefit.[16] In such a case, the latter conditions are deemed to be satisfied.[17] Following the abolition of industrial death benefit in 1988, a similar facility is granted to the

---

10 SSA 1975, Sch 3, para 8, as amended. She is deemed to satisfy this condition if she has been able successfully to apply the aggregation principle to a previous claim for another short-term benefit and the contributions in question were of the appropriate class.
11 SI 1974/2010, reg 3(1)(a), as amended.
12 SSA 1975, Sch 3, para 5(5).
13 SI 1975/564, reg 18, and SI 1975/553, reg 11, both as amended. Of course, this facility only applies to periods during which he is not liable to pay contributions under the rules stated above, p.43.
14 P. 201, below.
15 Pp. 202–204, below. For assistance granted to widows and widowers in relation to the invalidity benefit, see pp. 143 and 244, below.
16 P.283, below.
17 SSA 1975, s.50A.

widow of someone who died as the result of an industrial accident or disease.[18]

E Partial satisfaction of contribution conditions

Too rigid an application of the contribution conditions, particularly the second, would lead to an 'all or nothing' result. In consequence, for long-term benefit (retirement pensions Categories A and B, widowed mother's allowance and widow's pension), the legislation provides for a reduced benefit where the second contribution condition has been only partially satisfied: the basic component is calculated according to the proportion of reckonable years (i.e. years in which the qualifying earnings factor has been achieved) to the number of years prescribed for the benefit in question.[19] Increases for adult dependants are subject to the same reduction but increases for child dependants are payable in full. However, if the percentage is less than 25 per cent, neither the basic component nor the increase for the dependant (adult or child) is payable.

Analogous provisions used to be available for the purposes of entitlement to short-term benefits but these were abolished in 1986.[20] The argument was that the administrative costs were disproportionately high relative to the small sums that were paid out to beneficiaries.[1]

18 SSA 1986, Sch 3, para 10.
19 SSA 1975, s.33(1) and SI 1979/642, reg 6. Entitlement to any additional, earnings-related, component is unaffected.
20 SSA 1986, s.42.
 1 See Mr T Newton, Standing Committee B Debates on the 1986 Bill, col 1498.

Chapter 3

Unemployment benefit

Part 1 Introduction

A General

Unemployment, as a major cause of earnings loss and financial hardship, has from the beginning been an object for protection under social security legislation. Yet it differs from other social hazards similarly so protected in one important respect: unlike the natural phenomena of sickness, old age, birth and death, it results in a large degree from the interplay of economic forces. As such, the level of unemployment to be tolerated, the means of combating it and the extent of financial support granted to victims, can be influenced by a government as part of its overall economic policy.[1] By its control of investment, rates of interest, taxation, pay and prices, it may stimulate demand for goods and services which will induce a high level of employment.[2] According to neo-classical economic theory, 'full employment' can typically be achieved by such interventionist measures only at the cost of inflation and reduced productivity and hence has been largely forsworn by the current Conservative administration. Nevertheless, a bewildering variety of specific schemes have been introduced, most of which are administered by the Manpower Services Commission, to reduce numbers on the employment register.[3] Some are directed against the supply side of the labour market: for example, the Job Release Scheme, under which an elderly employee who vocates a post, thereby enabling someone on the employment register to obtain a job with the firm, receives a weekly allowance, substantially higher than unemployment benefit, pending entitlement to retirement pension;[4] and the Job Splitting Scheme which pays grants to employers who divide a full-time job into two part-time jobs, one of which is filled by an unemployed person.[5] But the majority are intended to stimulate the demand for labour, involving typically the subsidising of the cost of employing particularly young people. The most important of these has probably been the Youth Training Scheme under

1 The literature on the subject is immense. Lawyers should find particularly helpful e.g. Hauser and Burrows *The Economics of Unemployment Insurance* (1969); Creedy *The Economics of Unemployment in Britain* (1981); Sinfield *What Unemployment Means* (1981); Creedy and Disney *Social Insurance in Transition* (1985) ch 7.
2 The policy originated in Keynes *The General Theory of Employment, Interest and Money* (1936).
3 See, generally, Metcalf *Alternatives to Unemployment* (1982) and Whiting *A Guide to Unemployment Reduction Measures* (1987).
4 Ibid, ch 7.
5 Ibid, ch 14.

which a grant is made to a relevant employer to cover overheads associated with the training and an allowance is paid to the trainee.[6] In addition to schemes of this kind, there are, of course, the conventional arrangements to encourage mobility of labour, through the provision of information, guidance and retraining.[7] In 1988 the government announced an intention to integrate all training programmes for individuals over 18 into a new Employment Training Scheme.[8]

The extent to which the form and level of financial benefits payable to the unemployed affect their willingness to accept redundancies, to remain unemployed, or to seek employment elsewhere, is a much disputed question.[9] In a much publicised book, Minford argued that the ratio of unemployment benefit (and other social security payments) to post-tax earnings was too high and created strong work disincentives – he thus recommended that benefit be 'capped'.[10] The theoretical basis may be clear, but empirical support for the hypothesis is difficult to find, not the least because of the complexities involved in the analysis.[11]

B History[12]

Prior to the twentieth century, relief from the consequences of unemployment took one of two forms: private schemes of insurance administered by trade unions and friendly societies, or resort to the antiquated and degrading poor law. Once it became widely recognised that unemployment was not, in the great majority of cases, the result of personal moral failing but rather the product of economic forces, there was an obvious case for some form of state protection outside the poor law. The Royal Commission on the Poor Law, reporting in 1909,[13] placed great reliance on the system of labour exchanges (established on a national basis some four years previously), and the redeployment of labour and industry. The Majority recommended the extension of unemployment insurance but felt that it should continue to exist on a voluntary basis and should be administered independently for each trade group.

The most penetrating analysis of unemployment in the early years of this century came from Beveridge.[14] For him, the creation of labour exchanges was only part of a broader approach to unemployment which though influenced by economic policy required residual support in an insurance scheme: the unemployed must be able 'to subsist without demoralisation till they can be reabsorbed again after industrial transformations'.[15] The philosophy was reflected in Part II of the National Insurance Act 1911 which established the first compulsory system of unemployment insurance in a

---

6 Ibid, ch 10.
7 See generally Manpower Services Commission *Review of Services for the Unemployed* (1981).
8 White Paper *Training for Employment* (Cm 316) ch 5.
9 Barr *Economics of the Welfare State* (1987) pp. 199–201, contains a very helpful survey of the considerable literature.
10 Minford *Unemployment: Cause and Cure* (2nd edn).
11 Cf Barr, n.9, above, loc cit.
12 Tillyard *Unemployment Insurance in Great Britain 1911-1948* (1949); Cohen *Unemployment Insurance and Assistance in Britain* (1938) ch 1-3; Harris *Unemployment and Politics, 1886-1914* (1972); *Ogus* pp. 179-186 and 202-205.
13 Cd 4499.
14 *Unemployment: A Problem of Industry* (1909). See also *Harris* ch 6.
15 *Beveridge*, n.14, above, at p. 236.

major industrialised country, with the employee, the employer and the state contributing in equal proportion. However, its experimental nature should not be overlooked. It was restricted to certain industries (notably engineering and shipbuilding) which were liable mainly to seasonal fluctuations and fell midway between those which had a relatively stable employment record, and for which the need was therefore less pressing, and those liable to chronic unemployment and which were therefore difficult to handle. It covered only 2¼ million of a 10 million working population. Moreover, the benefits payable were not generous; they were not intended to provide a substitute for wages but rather a supplement to personal savings to avoid resort to charity or the poor law. In short, it was conceived of as a temporary lifebelt.[16]

Soldiers returning to civilian life after the First World War but unable to find employment were not insured, and were granted a donation or 'dole'.[17] This led to the feeling that those unemployed through no fault of their own were entitled to relief as of right, which, in turn, induced the government to promise a universal insurance scheme. A reform of 1920 went a long way in fulfilling the promise.[18] The scheme now covered all workers except those in agriculture, domestic service and the civil service, the numbers insured rising from 4 to 11 millions.

Unfortunately the burden placed on the scheme became, in times of great economic depression, too heavy to bear. The actuaries in computing the level of contributions and benefits had assumed an unemployment level of 5.32 per cent. Between 1920 and 1940 the figure never fell below 10 per cent, and during some periods was much higher. The result was a debt of £59 million in the insurance fund, and as a concession to extreme political and economic pressure both at home and abroad, in 1932 the government made its notorious cut in benefit of 10 per cent.[19] But there was a second problem, even graver. In the 1920s it became evident that a large proportion of unemployment in Britain was confined to certain industries which were situated in narrow geographical areas. In consequence, in these areas there was chronic and long-term unemployment, against which the scheme gave no protection, for benefit was given only for a limited period. The only method of saving the persons affected from the poor law was to establish an uncovenanted benefit scheme which would run alongside standard insurance. Throughout the interwar years some such system continued to operate, though under different guises. Under the 1920 Act, for example, benefit might be paid in advance of contributions on the assumption that in the long run such contributions would be made.[20] An 'uncovenanted benefit' was introduced in 1921[1] (later known as 'extended' or 'transitional' benefit). This was payable at the discretion of the Minister[2] in the exercise of which he might investigate the personal and financial circumstances of the claimant, a practice of course impossible under the standard insurance scheme. The Blanesburgh Committee, reporting in 1927,[3] found this dual system to be unsatisfactory and recommended that all benefits should be paid as of right. The proposal was enacted but the

16 Royal Commission on Unemployment Insurance, Final Report (1932, Cmd 4185), para 198.
17 Paid under powers conferred on the Board of Trade by NI (Part II) (Munition Workers) Act 1916 s.3(1).
18 UIA 1920.
19 SR & O 1932/814. See Gilbert *British Social Policy 1914–39* (1972) pp. 162–175.
20 UIA 1920, s.8(4).
 1 UIA 1921, s.3.
 2 For a short period in 1924–25 the claimant had a right to such benefit (UIA (No 2) 1924, s.1(1)) but this was soon repealed by UIA 1925, s.1.
 3 Published by Ministry of Labour.

onset of extreme economic difficulties meant that the aim of abolishing uncovenanted benefit was never realised. The 'transitional arrangements' which were intended to be superseded were several times extended. Indeed in 1933 the number of claimants in receipt of transitional benefit exceeded those on insurance benefit.

A major review of the system was undertaken by the Royal Commission on Unemployment Insurance in 1930-32.[4] As implemented by the Unemployment Act of 1934, its recommendations established a pattern which, subject to certain modifications, has remained in force ever since. The basis was a distinction, hitherto only partially recognised, between insurance and relief. The former should continue (and indeed be extended to certain industries as yet excluded, notably agriculture) along traditional lines of covenanted benefit, limited in duration. When the right to benefit had been exhausted special assistance, based on a means test, would be provided and administered by the Unemployment Assistance Board.

Under Beveridge's plan and the subsequent legislation, unemployment was integrated into the general scheme of social insurance and was made compulsory for all employed earners. It was, in fact, Beveridge's intention that the benefit should be of unlimited duration.[5] But the recommendation was not found acceptable: there were fears that it would be an inducement to abuse, and his suggested safeguard – a requirement that an individual undergo training after six months' unemployment – was regarded as impracticable.[6] The only major modification to the scheme subsequent to 1946 was the introduction of the earnings-related supplement in 1966.[7] This was however abolished by the Conservative government in 1982, as part of its programme of economies in the public sector. Ironically, the latter reform took place at a time when unemployment had attained a level not experienced since the 1930s. The consequence has been an ever-growing reliance on means-tested benefits.[8] However, the government has revealed no intention of extending entitlement or raising the amount payable. Indeed, reforms have been directed rather at reducing entitlement to unemployment benefit: the contribution conditions have become more restrictive;[9] the arrangements for ensuring that the claimant is available for employment in appropriate occupations have been tightened;[10] the period of disqualification from benefit for voluntary unemployment and related reasons has been extended;[11] and the rights of students and occupational pensioners have been curtailed.[12]

C Scope and structure

The law governing entitlement to unemployment benefit is complex. The difficulties result partly from the need to adapt the system to changing industrial practices (particularly the shift from six-day to five-day working) and

---

4 Interim Report (1931, Cmd 3872); Final Report (1932, Cmd 4185).
5 Paras 129–130.
6 *Social Insurance* Part I, para 67.
7 For details, see 1st edn of this book, pp. 424–426.
8 In 1984–85, of those registered for employment 29 per cent received unemployment benefit without supplementary benefit, 62 per cent supplementary benefit without unemployment benefit and 9 per cent both benefits: *Green Paper 1985* vol 3, para 5.33.
9 P.66, below.
10 P.92, below.
11 P.109, below.
12 Pp. 71 and 120, below.

partly from the relationship between social security and labour law. The problems have been exacerbated by a reluctance in the DHSS to reformulate traditional concepts, some of which are outmoded, and a tendency instead to prefer patchwork solutions, occasionally implemented by poorly drafted regulations.[13]

Viewed from a very broad level of generality, however, the structure of the system is not difficult to comprehend. Apart from the contribution conditions (Part 2), entitlement rests on two fundamental notions. The first is that the claimant should be unemployed (Part 3). The complexities in this area of the law arise primarily from the fact that benefit may be payable notwithstanding that the contract of employment between the claimant and his employer is still subsisting, viz for periods of lay-off or short-time. The second idea is that the unemployment should be involuntary, that is, must result from external economic factors rather than from the claimant's own conduct or physical condition. If he is physically or psychologically incapable of work he must satisfy the relevant criteria for the disability benefits. The involuntary nature of the unemployment is judged first by the requirement (Part 4) that he is 'available' for work and subsequently by the sanctions of disqualification imposed where the claimant voluntarily leaves his employment, is dismissed for misconduct, or refuses a suitable offer of employment (Part 5). On one view, the notion may also account for the disqualification of those involved in a trade dispute (Part 6). The remainder of the chapter is largely devoted to an account of the rules governing special categories of employment, notably seasonal workers (Part 7), and the duration and amount of benefit (Part 8).

Part 2   Contribution conditions

Only persons who have paid Class 1 contributions can qualify for unemployment benefit.[14] The exclusion of the self-employed has not been controversial:[15] it has generally been regarded as too difficult to ascertain when they are not gainfully occupied. In the words of Beveridge, 'the income of a farmer, a shopkeeper or a business manager may come at any time; how busy or how active he is on a particular day is largely within his own control. It is not practicable to have a general system of maintaining earnings of persons gainfully occupied otherwise than by way of employment, by benefits conditional upon not working or appearing to work on a particular day.'[16]

The contribution conditions for Class 1 contributors were made significantly more onerous in 1988.[17] They are:[18]

(1) the claimant must have paid contributions of that class for either of the two tax years preceding the year in which benefit is claimed, and the earnings factor derived from such contributions must be not less than that year's lower earnings limit multiplied by 25;[19] and

13 Cf Ogus, 4 ILJ 12.
14 SSA 1975, s.13(1): the one exception is share fishermen, p.121, below.
15 Though see Lister and Field *Wasted Labour* (1978) pp. 18, 62–63.
16 Para 122. See also DHSS Discussion Document *The Self-Employed and National Insurance* (1980) paras 44–45.
17 SSA 1988, s.6, on which, see p.55, above.
18 SSA 1975, Sch 3, para 2, as amended.
19 Before the 1988 reform the condition could be satisfied for *any* year before the benefit year.

(2) in each of the last two complete tax years preceding the year in which benefit is claimed, he must have been paid, or (provided he is not a student[20]) been credited with, contributions of that class, the earnings factor from which must be not less than the relevant year's lower earnings limit multiplied by 50.[1]

Part 3 Unemployment

A General

Benefit is payable in respect of 'any day of unemployment which forms part of a period of interruption of employment'.[2] This proposition contains a number of diverse elements. For the purposes of exposition they will be classified as follows. The first question is whether the claimant is 'unemployed' in the sense that he is not engaged in a profitable activity (section B). It is then necessary to show that the day of unemployment in respect of which the claim is made is one recognised by the law as forming part of a period of interruption of employment (section C). In cases of partial unemployment there are additional requirements to be satisfied (section D).

B Whether unemployed

Benefit is not payable for any day in which the claimant 'is engaged in any employment'.[3] 'Employment', as used here, is not limited to the notion of a contract of service, for it includes 'any trade, business, profession, office or vocation'.[4] The general principle is that a claimant is unemployed if he is not engaged in an activity from which he intends to derive remuneration or profit. Such activity can conveniently be considered under four heads.

i Contracts of service

In general, a person engaged to work for remuneration under a contract of service cannot be unemployed. Payments in kind rather than money may constitute remuneration,[5] but not the mere reimbursement of expenses.[6] On the other hand, subject to the special regulations on subsidiary employment,[7]

---

20 SI 1983/1598, reg 22. The modification for students was justified by the argument that they were not in a genuine sense 'available for work' during the academic year and that further evidence of attachment to the labour market was desirable. The reform was carried out in 1979 in the face of criticism by the majority of the National Insurance Advisory Committee that the proposals were unduly discriminatory. See Report on Unemployment Benefit for Students (1979, Cmnd 7613).

1 Before the 1988 reform, this condition was applied only to the last year before the benefit year.

2 SSA 1975, s.14(1)(a).

3 SI 1983/1598, reg 7(1)(g). Older regulations (e.g. SI 1967/330, reg 7(1)) used the term 'occupation', but the change is not thought to be significant: *R(U) 4/77*, para 5; *R(U) 5/81(T)*, para 9.

4 SSA 1975, Sch 20, and see *R(U) 3/77*, para 7 and *R(U) 6/77*.

5 *CU 236/50*; *CWU 42/50*. This may constitute an infringement of the Truck Acts but the claimant cannot rely on the illegality of the contract as the basis for the claim that he was unemployed: *UD 1404/27* (Umpire's decision under the old Unemployment Insurance legislation).

6 Cf *R(U) 6/77*, para 7, and *R(U) 5/83*, para 9.

7 Pp. 79–80, below.

it does not generally assist the claimant to show that the amount of remuneration was small. So, a·disabled person paid what was described as a 'nominal wage' for work in an occupational centre was held to be following a gainful occupation.[8] But the amount may be so small as to indicate that it was intended as a gratuitous payment rather than contractual remuneration;[9] for example, where a person receives for therapeutic work payments 'more in the nature of pocket money given as an incident of rehabilitation treatment'.[10]

The remuneration need not have been actually paid to the claimant on the day or days for which the claim is made.[11] So a person working according to an unexpired contract is employed, notwithstanding that his employer defaults on payment.[12] The same is true of someone who, following a change of jobs, has to work for a certain period before receiving wages.[13] Prima facie, for the purposes of unemployment benefit, a person is 'employed' from the date on which his obligation to work under the contract begins to the date when it is discharged.[14] But there are several important qualifications to this principle.

a *Contract suspended*
The contract may subsist but be suspended where, for example, the employee has been laid-off or put on short-time working. During such periods of inactivity he may claim unemployment benefit, though, as will be seen,[15] he must satisfy certain special rules.

b *No work available*
The fact that on a particular day or period of days an employee is given no work by his employer does not, of course, necessarily mean that he is unemployed. Most importantly, he cannot claim benefit for any period during which, under the terms of the contract, he is bound to make his services available to the employer; when, in short, he is 'on call'.[16] That this principle may lead to harsh consequences is evident from cases concerning part-time professional footballers. The contracts in question contained a clause whereby, in return for the payment of a small weekly sum, the player was to attend for training whenever the club so required. The authorities have found themselves compelled to hold that the claimant was employed for the whole of the week[17] unless it could be found that the attendance clause had been modified or waived in practice.[18] Where, on the other hand, the employment is for a specific job of work and it does not oblige the employee to make himself available to the employer throughout the period of the contract, he may be unemployed when he is not actually engaged on the job in question.[19] In *R(U) 1/73*:

8 *R(U) 4/64.*
9 *R(U) 4/63.*
10 *R(U) 2/67*, para 11.
11 *R(U) 16/64*; *R(U) 6/77*; *CSU 1/81.*
12 *R(U) 5/75.*
13 He may nevertheless be entitled to income support: p. 420, below.
14 *R(U) 3/72*, R J A Temple, Comr.
15 Pp. 77–90, below.
16 *R(U) 5/58*; *R(U) 10/80.*
17 *R(U) 24/53*; *R(U) 23/57*; *R(U) 10/72*; *R(U) 3/84(T).*
18 *R(U) 8/59.*
19 *R(U) 20/51.*

A census enumerator was appointed in March 1971. He was paid a lump sum for the execution of certain specific duties which were to begin on 1 April 1971. R S Lazarus, Commissioner, held that he was gainfully employed only from this latter date.

The decision contrasts with several in which it was held that a census *officer* was employed throughout the period of appointment.[20] In the 1973 case, the Commissioner, though critical of these earlier decisions, felt able to distinguish them on the ground that census officers were given different instructions: they had to attend a training session before the duties commenced.[1] This fact was not regarded as significant in the earlier decisions and *R(U) 1/73* seems to depart from the view apparently held previously that the duration of the occupation is conclusively established by the contract of employment. But the departure does seem to be a proper one. In the words of the Commissioner, 'I find it hard to see the logic of holding that a person follows the occupation of census enumerator on a day on which his employer does not require him to, and he does not, do any part of the specified job for which he is employed'.[2]

The situation in which the employee is instructed to do particular jobs at particular times must be distinguished from that in which the employee is effectively given discretion as to how he allocates the work over time. The Commissioners have consistently held in these cases that the claimant is not unemployed on days when he decides not to work.[3] That the principle can operate harshly is evident from a recent decision in which the claimant, acting as consultant to a firm, was paid on annual basis but for a workload that it was estimated he would be able to discharge in about twelve weeks. It was held that he was continuously employed throughout the year.[4]

c *Contract terminated*

Although the period of employment will end when the employee's contractual obligation to work or be available for work is discharged,[5] it may be difficult to determine when this has taken place. For example, both parties may anticipate and intend that the employment relationship will be resumed after the expiration of a short period. Is the employee unemployed during that period?

Initially, it was held that if the employee received some payment in consideration of which he agreed to return to the employment, there was a contract of employment subsisting throughout the period, and he was not unemployed.[6] A new approach was taken by the Commissioner in 1968.[7] Regard is now had to the extent of the claimant's obligations during the interim period. If he agrees to be at the disposal of the employer when required, he is

---

20 Those reported are *R(U) 16/61* and *R(U) 3/72*. They are confirmed in *R(U) 5/81(T)*.
1 *R(U) 1/73*, para 10, R S Lazarus, Comr.
2 Ibid, at para 14.
3 *R(U) 31/53*; *R(U) 11/60*; *R(U) 5/81(T)*; *R(U) 5/84*.
4 *R(U) 5/84*. The position under employment protection law may be different: see e.g. *Bromsgrove Casting and Machine Ltd v Martin* [1977] 3 All ER 487.
5 The period may in some occupations, such as supply teaching, last only a day: *R(U) 2/87*.
6 *CU 28/48*; *CU 62/48*; *R(U) 38/52*; *R(U) 8/54*. These decisions were made at a time when 'termination' was given a special meaning in unemployment benefit law: see p.84, below.
7 *R(U) 6/68*, H Magnus, Comr. See also *R(U) 7/68(T)*.

properly to be regarded as gainfully employed.[8] But if he is free to do whatever he likes throughout the period, he is not gainfully employed.[9]

As we have already seen,[10] availability to an employer is, indeed, the key to determining whether a claimant is unemployed and the approach adopted since 1968 is consistent with that. However, in recent years, some doubts have arisen regarding its application to cases in which an employee is engaged on a rota system, for example, as has occurred in relation to work on oil-rigs, two weeks on duty, followed by two weeks off duty. Even where the contract of employment purports to cease at the end of the on-duty period, the Commissioner has invariably held that the employee is not unemployed during the off-duty period.[11] In one such case, the employer had the right to recall the claimant during that period, and so the decision was compatible with the general principle.[12] In another, one of the terms of the contract referred to 26 weeks of 'continuous employment', which was held to imply that the claimant had been engaged on an indefinite basis.[13] In two further cases, the Commissioner was content to have regard to 'the consistent pattern of employment' which, he said, rendered the employment more compatible with a 'continuing or running contract'.[14] As has been suggested,[15] there seems to be a strong case for making special provision for this form of employment, where high rates of remuneration are paid for intensive periods of work alternating with substantial periods of rest. This would then not prejudice application of the general principle.

ii Other profitable activity

Other forms of profitable activity will also defeat a claim. But difficulties arise as to determining what is so to be regarded. It seems clear, on the caselaw, that it is the expectation of profits rather than their actual receipt which is decisive.[16] According to the Commissioner, 'a gainful occupation is one in which a person is engaged with the desire, hope and intention of obtaining for himself, directly and personally, remuneration or profit in return for his services and efforts'.[17] So, the claimant may show a net loss during the period in question and still be gainfully employed.[18] As regards the activity, the authorities must assess, on the evidence available, the period of time during which it might reasonably be concluded that the claimant was *personally* active in the enterprise.[19] Regard is had to such factors as the number of hours in which he was so engaged, relative to the amount of work which might reasonably be done.[20] The mere fact that the claimant is the proprietor of, or a partner in, a business is not sufficient by itself to render him gainfully employed,[1] though in practice to succeed in his claim he will have to show that his assumption of responsibilities and management involved only a negligible amount of time.[2]

8 *R(U) 10/80.*
9 *R(U) 6/68*; *R(U) 2/87.*
10 P.68, above.
11 *R(U) 10/80*; *R(U) 14/80*; *R(U) 4/81*; *R(U) 5/81.*
12 *R(U) 10/80*, I O Griffiths, Comr.
13 *R(U) 5/81.*
14 *R(U) 4/81*, para 8, D Reith, Comr; *R(U) 14/80*, I Edward-Jones, Comr.
15 Ibid, para 2.
16 *R(U) 3/88(T)* See also in relation to retirement, pp. 193–195, below, and the nature of earnings, p.376, below.
17 *CU 30/49*, para 5.
18 *R(U) 12/55.*
19 *R(U) 11/57.*
20 *CU 235/50*; *R(U) 8/55.* See also *R(U) 1/67.*
1 *R(U) 11/57.*
2 *R(U) 22/64.*

iii Education and training

During periods of attending full-time courses of education, students cannot claim unemployment benefit.[3] Periods during which a maintenance grant is, or would be, payable and the Christmas and Easter vacations come within this rule.[4] Subject to fulfilling the normal conditions, students may claim benefit during the summer vacation.

In general, those attending training courses and in receipt of some payment are disentitled. If the training is with a scheme, established under section 5 of the Employment and Training Act 1973, for example, the Youth Training Scheme, the Unemployment Benefit Regulations provide that benefit is not payable for any day during a week of such training.[5] The position as regards training schemes not covered by these provisions is somewhat unclear. Where, during the currency of the contract of service, an employer requires an employee to undergo training, he is surely not to be regarded as unemployed.[6] But the case where the training takes place before the contract begins is more problematic. The standard approach taken by the Umpire under the Unemployment Insurance Acts was to determine on the evidence available whether, explicitly or implicity, an employer had undertaken to employ the claimant on his successful completion of the course. If so, whether or not he received remuneration, the claimant was gainfully employed.[7] For several years, this principle was applied to the modern legislation,[8] but in *R(U) 3/67* the Commissioner adopted a quite different perspective. He argued that under the National Insurance legislation then in force a person was employed if he was gainfully occupied in employment, and not employed if he was not so gainfully occupied. Attendance at a training course was neither an 'occupation' nor was it 'gainful'. The wording of the relevant regulation has since been changed – 'occupation' has been replaced by 'employment' – and so the authority of the decision is to that extent reduced. The solution adopted by the Commissioner has the merit of simplicity and also avoids the weakness in the old approach, whereby a trainee without income and not yet engaged under a contract was disentitled. If applied literally, it seems to suggest that a trainee receiving remuneration from a prospective employer might nevertheless qualify for benefit. However, it is very unlikely that the authorities would be drawn to this conclusion, and in any event the trainee would probably fail to satisfy the 'availability' test.[9]

C Periods of unemployment

It will be recalled that title to benefit rests on proof of a 'day of unemployment which forms part of a period of interruption of employment.'[10] It is now necessary to consider the meaning of 'day' and 'period'.

---

3 SI 1983/1598, reg 7(1)(m).
4 Ibid, reg 7(3).
5 Ibid, reg 7(1)(n). Under the Overlapping Benefits Regulations, a training allowance from public funds is, in any event, deducted from any unemployment benefit payable: SI 1979/597, Sch 1 and see pp. 89–90, below.
6 There is no direct authority for this but it appears to be a necessary implication of *R(U) 3/67*, para 9, H Magnus, Comr.
7 *UD 4903*. The undertaking was inferred where the training was made a condition precedent of the employment: *UD 2605/28*.
8 *CU 162/50*; *R(U) 30/51*; *R(U) 4/59*.
9 P.92, below.
10 SSA 1975, s.14(1)(a).

i Day of unemployment

The minimum unit of time recognised for benefit purposes is a day: a claimant cannot be unemployed on part only of a day. If he is employed for more than a token amount[11] on a particular day, it will not constitute a day of unemployment. If this principle were applied universally it would cause hardship to night-workers who might lose a shift but still work for more than a token amount on each calendar day.[12] The Regulations, therefore, allow for an exception to the general rule: where a person works through midnight he is deemed to be employed on that day on which the greater part of his shift falls.[13] For the exception to apply, however, the shift must begin within 24 hours of one calendar day and end within 24 hours of the following day; the general principle applies to longer periods of unemployment. Thus in *R(U) 18/56*

> C was employed as a deckhand on a trawler from 18.00 hours on Monday to 02.00 hours on Wednesday. He claimed benefit for Monday on the ground that the greater part of his shift fell on Tuesday and Wednesday. But it was held that the Night Regulations did not apply.[14]

ii Days of rest

Benefit is payable on the basis of a six-day week. Thus the daily rate is one-sixth of the appropriate weekly rate.[15] If follows that the seventh and rest day of the week is not a day of unemployment.[16] Six-day workers who normally work on Sunday but not on another day may, if unemployed, claim for Sunday but not for that other day.[17] Even if a claimant does not normally work on Sunday, nevertheless if he is available for work on that day and objects on religious grounds to working on another day, that other day is substituted for Sunday.[18]

iii Compensated days

If a person receives money in substitution of wages for a period after the termination of the contract, it is sound policy that for such a period he should not be entitled to unemployment benefit. The principle that compensated days should not rank as days of unemployment has been recognised since 1924,[19] but in modern times its formulation and application have caused considerable difficulties. Today there is a wide variety of severance payments which an employer may, and under legislation must, make. The problem is to what extent these should be covered by the principle and, if so, for what period they should disentitle the recipient. Prior to 1966 a claimant was ineligible for benefit if he continued to receive wages or received compensation

---

11 In *CS 37/53* 15 minutes was disregarded, but in the Northern Ireland decision *2/56 (UB)* 20 minutes was sufficient to defeat the claim. See also *CI 263/49*.

12 See *CS 363/49*, decided when the anomaly existed for sickness benefit.

13 SI 1983/1598, reg 5(1) (which, however, refers to a period of 'unemployment' spanning midnight – presumably a typographical error). Where the shifts are of equal duration he is deemed to be employed the second day: ibid. Where he works through Saturday/Sunday midnight the same rules apply to determine the week in which the shift falls: *R(U) 37/56*.

14 But see *Calvert* p.120, who argues that the decision, though consistent with the policy of the regulation, is not justified by its wording.

15 SSA 1975, s.14(8).

16 Ibid, s.17(1)(e).

17 SI 1983/1598, reg 4(1).

18 Ibid, reg 4(3).

19 See UIA (No 2) 1924, s.1(4).

which was substantially equivalent to the wages lost.[20] This proved to be too restrictive an approach and in 1966 was replaced by the concept of payment in lieu either of notice to terminate or, if the contract was for a term certain, of the remuneration which would have been paid if the contract had not been terminated.[1] This too was thought to be insufficiently broad – in particular it could not apply to employees (e.g. civil servants) whose contract was not for a term certain and who were legally not entitled to notice. The current regulation 7(1)(d), introduced in 1971, provides that

> a day shall not be treated as a day of unemployment if it is a day in respect of which a person receives a payment (whether or not a payment made in pursuance of a legally enforceable obligation) in lieu either of notice or of the remuneration which he would have received for that day had his employment not been terminated. . . .[2]

Finally, in 1976, special provision was made to disentitle the claimant for days for which certain types of compensation (notably for unfair dismissal) were payable under the employment protection legislation.[3]

a *Payments covered*
For the claimant to be caught under the general regulation, the payments in question must have been made in lieu either of notice or of the remuneration which he would have received if the contract had not been terminated. In other words, some nexus must exist between the payment and the period of notice required or the claimant's prospective remuneration for the unexpired portion of the term for which he was engaged.[4] The fact that an employee voluntarily accepts redundancy does not by itself imply the absence of such a nexus,[5] though if the payment which induces the agreement is not calculated by reference to the period of notice or remuneration which would otherwise have been paid the regulation does not apply.[6] The period of notice referred to is that required by the contract or the general law of employment.[7] This does not include the period of 90 days which, under employment protection legislation,[8] must intervene between the consultation of a trade union and the coming into effect of redundancy notices affecting more than 100 employees, since the relevant provision confers no direct rights on individual employees.[9] Nevertheless, if the employer and union agree that employees leaving during that period should receive payments reflecting earnings for the unexpired portion of the period, those payments may still disentitle claimants on the alternative ground stipulated by regulation 7(1)(d) that they were 'in lieu . . . of the remuneration which he would have received . . . had his employment not been terminated'.[10] Cases such as those of Crown servants in which there is no legally enforceable right to notice but where it is customarily given are also covered: that is the import of the passage in parentheses introduced by

20 SI 1948/1277, reg 6(1)(d).
1 SI 1966/1049, reg 7(1).
2 SI 1983/1598, reg 7(1)(d).
3 Now ibid, reg 7(1)(l). See also p.89, below.
4 *R(U) 2/80*, para 16, V G H Hallett, Comr.
5 *R(U) 9/73(T)*, paras 13–14 (majority opinions).
6 *R(U) 2/80*.
7 See on this the standard labour law texts, e.g. Davies and Freedland *Labour Law* (2nd edn) pp. 432–435.
8 Employment Protection Act 1975, s.99.
9 *R(U) 3/83(T)*.
10 Ibid.

the 1971 reform.[11] However ambiguous they may appear, these words were not intended, and should not be construed, to cover payments of a purely gratuitous nature: 'a payment which is made truly *ex gratia* (i.e. out of kindness) by an employer, and not having the characteristic of either a payment in lieu of notice or in lieu of remuneration, would be outside the ambit' of the regulation.[12] Payments representing a reward for past services or simple compensation for the loss of a job are similarly treated; they are not intended to reflect prospective remuneration.[13]

The real difficulty arises where, as in most cases, the payment includes elements both of reward for past service and of the lost prospective earnings. To sever the payment into its constituent elements would be too difficult and is not encouraged.[14] In two Commissioners' decisions of 1968, it was held that a payment was caught by the regulation if it contained *any* element representing future remuneration.[15] As has been pointed out, where the element is insignificant this can lead to the grotesque result that the employee is disentitled to unemployment benefit for what may be a substantial period of notice.[16] The view taken of these decisions by the Court of Appeal in the leading case of *R v National Insurance Comr, ex parte Stratton* was ambivalent.[17] In a subsequent decision, the Commissioner purported to find in the *Stratton* case authority for a different approach, that regard was to be had to 'the true nature of the terminal payment'.[18] Though this is a doubtful interpretation of the judgments in *Stratton*,[19] it provides a fairer and less artificial solution. On this basis, a statutory redundancy payment escapes the regulation as its *main* purpose is to provide compensation for the loss of the proprietary interest in the job,[20] and this is true of analogous payments made to members of the armed forces on redundancy, under the special government scheme.[1] The character of the payment will naturally depend on the intention of the parties to the agreement or scheme under which it is made: the description given to it by them may be some evidence of its character but is by no means conclusive.[2] Payments calculated by reference to future remuneration are normally

11 *R v National Insurance Comr, ex parte Stratton* [1979] QB 361 at 371, per Lord Denning MR. See also *R(U) 8/73(T)*, para 19.
12 *R(U) 7/73(T)*, para 45, and see *R v National Insurance Comr, ex parte Stratton*, n.11, above, per Lord Denning MR at 372.
13 Ibid at 370. See also Templeman LJ at 376.
14 Ibid at 371, per Lord Denning MR, approving *R(U) 3/68*, para 8. See also *R(U) 7/73(T)*, paras 35–37, and *R(U) 4/80*, para 6.
15 *R(U) 2/68*; *R(U) 3/68*.
16 Per Cantley J in *R v National Insurance Comr, ex parte Stratton* [1978] 1 WLR 1041 at 1045, Div Ct, echoed by Bridge LJ on appeal [1979] QB 361 at 373.
17 Lord Denning MR thought that the ruling in *R(U) 3/68* was correct (ibid at 370–371) but this seems to be inconsistent with his ruling that a redundancy payment, which includes elements both of compensation for past services and future remuneration, escaped the regulation. Bridge LJ clearly disliked the principle in *R(U) 3/68*; he conceded that his conclusion might not be reconcilable with that decision, but thought it inappropriate to overrule it (ibid at 374). The attitude of Templeman LJ was obscure.
18 *R(U) 4/80*, para 6, H A Shewan, Comr. But contrast this with *R(U) 1/80*, J G Monroe, Comr, which is consistent with the 1968 decisions.
19 Mesher [1980] JSWL 117, 119.
20 *R(U) 6/73*, para 10a, H Magnus, Comr, approved in *R v National Insurance Comr, ex parte Stratton* [1979] QB 361 at 370, per Lord Denning MR, at 376, per Templeman LJ. Bridge LJ thought that the regulation did not apply for the different reason that such payments are made after employment has been terminated by notice or effluxion of time: ibid at 373.
1 *Ex parte Stratton*, ibid; and see *R(U) 1/80*.
2 *R(U) 7/73(T)*, para 45, and see *R(U) 29/55*; *R(U) 4/56*; *R(U) 10/58*; *R(U) 8/73(T)*; *R(U) 1/80*; *R(U) 7/80*.

regarded as payments in lieu, and this is generally true even if the payment exceeds[3] or falls short of[4] the amount that would have been earned in the period of notice.[5] An award of damages for wrongful dismissal is necessarily so treated[6], and this extends to a settlement made in pursuance of such a claim.[7]

The position of unfair dismissal compensation is mainly governed by special provision. A claimant's right to unemployment benefit for the period between the termination of employment and the date of a tribunal award is unaffected, but the National Insurance Fund may recoup money from the employer.[8] Where a so-called 'compensatory award' for unfair dismissal or for non-compliance with an order of reinstatement or re-engagement includes a sum representing remuneration which the tribunal considers would reasonably have been paid to the employee for future days, those days cannot rank as days of unemployment.[9] However, this applies only if the 'amount is ascertained and cannot be disputed and it is legally due in the sense that court remedies for its recovery are immediately and unconditionally available'.[10] An award calculated without reference to future remuneration (including the so-called 'basic award') does not fall within this provision and *ex hypothesi* there is no ground for treating it as a payment in lieu under regulation 7(1)(d).[11] Settlements of unfair dismissal claims are also not covered by the special provision. Prior to the introduction of the latter in 1976, they were generally treated as payments in lieu[12] and this would seem to be the appropriate characterisation, provided it can be reasonably inferred that the payment included a significant element based on future remuneration.[13] Finally, the claimant is disentitled for days in respect of which there is payable to him remuneration under a protective award, in accordance with the employment protection legislation.[14]

b *Duration of disentitlement*
The Regulations referred to above cannot operate to disentitle a claimant for a period exceeding a year after the termination of the contract. Subject to this maximum, the general rules for determining the duration of the disentitlement, as laid down by the Commissioner,[15] are as follows. Where the contract is for a fixed term (i.e. there is no requirement as to notice), the claimant in

3 *R(U) 7/73(T)*.
4 *R(U) 2/68*; *R(U) 3/68*.
5 *R(U) 1/80*.
6 *R(U) 4/56*, para 10; *R(U) 3/68*, para 6.
7 Ibid.
8 SI 1977/674, Part III, as amended.
9 SI 1983/1598, reg 7(1)(k)(iii). The same principle applies to interim relief payable pending determination of a claim for unfair dismissal: ibid, reg 7(1)(k)(iv). The amount of the award is immaterial for the application of these rules: *R(U) 6/85*.
10 Per M J Goodman, Comr, *R(U) 4/82*, para 12, holding that since the claimant could not enforce the award against a company which had been the subject of a High Court winding-up order he was not disentitled.
11 *R v National Insurance Comr, ex parte Stratton*, n.20, above, per Templeman LJ at 376. Lord Denning MR in the same case (at 370–371) suggests that unfair dismissal awards should be treated as payments in lieu, but he seems to have in mind cases which include both the basic and compensatory awards. Curiously both judges overlooked the special provisions in what is now reg 7(1)(k).
12 *R(U) 5/74*.
13 *CU 2/78*.
14 SI 1983/1598, reg 7(1)(k)(v).
15 *R(U) 37/53*; *R(U) 6/73*; *R(U) 7/73(T)*.

receipt of a relevant payment will be disentitled for the rest of that term. Where he is entitled to notice, he is barred for the period of notice, as determined by the contract (or the general law of employment), whether or not the sum was intended to be limited to that period. As a rule of thumb this has the merit of avoiding detailed investigation into daily rates of pay to ascertain the number of days of remuneration the payment was intended to represent,[16] but as was pointed out by Bridge LJ in the *Stratton* case, it can lead to 'absurd and extravagant results', for example, when a small payment is received in lieu of a substantial period of notice.[17] In a more recent decision the Commissioner has stressed that it is only a general rule.[18] There is authority for treating the payment as being made for less than the full period of notice where it was made without prejudice to any later claim for more;[19] and in one unreported case, the Commissioner held that settlement of an unfair dismissal claim was intended to cover a longer period than that of the notice to which the claimant was entitled.[20] Where, as in the case of Crown servants, the employee is not legally entitled to a period of notice, the authorities may have regard to the period of notice which was in practice given.[1] Failing that, they will have to ascertain as best they can from the circumstances the number of days intended to be covered by the compensatory payment.[2]

iv Waiting-days

In some systems of unemployment insurance, the claimant is eligible for benefit on the first day of unemployment,[3] but the British scheme in common with the majority has always insisted that a waiting-period be served. During the time of greatest unemployment between the wars the period was a week,[4] but in 1937[5] the current rule was adopted that benefit is not available for the first three days of a period of interruption of employment.[6] All the evidence shows that the administrative costs of paying benefit for one or two days is disproportionately large.[7] There is a widespread assumption that an individual is generally able to absorb a few days of earnings loss, and if he is not he may be entitled to income support. Further, in many cases the employer, through a guarantee agreement or otherwise, indemnifies his employees against short spells of unemployment and, under the employment protection legislation, he is bound to provide a limited form of such coverage.[8] These factors were also used to justify the decision in 1971 to abolish the right

---

16　Ibid, paras 38–40.
17　[1979] QB 361 at 373.
18　*R(U) 1/80*, paras 8–9, J G Monroe, Comr.
19　*R(U) 5/72*.
20　*CU 2/78*.
1　*R(U) 8/73(T)*.
2　*R(U) 1/79*, R J A Temple, Chief Comr. The point was not considered in the judgments of the Divisional Court [1978] 1 WLR 1041 and Court of Appeal [1979] QB 361 as in both courts it was held that the payment did not disentitle the claimant.
3　E.g. in W. Germany and France.
4　UIA (No 2) 1921, s.3(3).
5　SR & O 1937/194, reg 2(b).
6　SSA 1975, s.14(3). The days in question must be those which rank as days of unemployment or incapacity for the purposes of unemployment and sickness benefit: ibid, s.17(1)(c). It follows that e.g. days of rest, p.72, above, compensated days, pp. 72–76, above, and (if the claimant is on short-time) 'normal idle days', pp. 83–86, below, cannot count as waiting days.
7　See NIAC Report on Very Short Spells of Unemployment (1955, Cmd 9609).
8　See p.89, below.

hitherto enjoyed by those unemployed for two weeks or more retrospectively to claim for the three days.[9]

v Periods of interruption of employment

Where a claimant is subject to intermittent periods of unemployment (e.g. where he is on short-time) it would clearly be impossibly severe to impose the three waiting-days for each such period. By means of the so-called 'continuity' and 'linking' rules, the legislation therefore enables him to aggregate spells of unemployment, so that he will be disentitled for only the first three days of the aggregate 'period of interruption of employment'. The 'continuity' rule prescribes that a 'period of interruption of employment' exists where he is unemployed for any two days (consecutive or not)[10] within six consecutive days,[11] for example:

> C is unemployed on Monday and Friday within the same week. These two days constitute a single period of interruption of unemployment.

The 'linking' rule then provides that any two such periods not separated by more than eight weeks are treated as one period of interruption of employment.[12]

> If, in the above example, C is unemployed again on the Monday and Friday of the following week, the two periods of interruption of employment are linked so that he will be entitled to benefit for the Friday of week 2 (the waiting-days being the Monday and Friday of week 1 and the Monday of week 2). Subject to the rules to be described in the next section, he will continue to be entitled for each subsequent day of unemployment forming part of a period of interruption of employment (i.e. satisfying the two-in-six continuity rule) which is not separated from the previous such period by more than eight weeks.

D Partial unemployment

i General

The discussion so far has focused on the phenomenon of 'total' unemployment, that is, where the individual has terminated any contractual relationship with an employer and, during the period in question, has no work. But less clear-cut forms of unemployment also exist:

(1) the contract of employment may have been only suspended and the claimant 'laid-off' until work is once more available;
(2) the claimant may have been put on 'short-time', i.e. his regular hours, or days, of work, and therefore also his wages, have been reduced by a certain amount each week;

---

9 SSA 1971, s.7(1) and see Sir K Joseph, Secretary of State, introducing the Second Reading of the Bill, 816 HC Official Report (5th series) cols 61–63.
10 This is deemed to include days (a) of attendance at a training course, and (b) (if aged over 60) of receipt of income support when the claimant does not have to be available for work (see p.422, below): SI 1983/1598, reg 13. Further, if the claimant is a man aged 60–70, or a woman aged 60–65, days of unemployment count notwithstanding that (a) the right to unemployment benefit is exhausted or (b) the contribution conditions are not satisfied or (c) unemployment benefit has been abated to nil through the receipt of an occupational pension (on which, see p.121, below): SI 1983/1598, reg 14.
11 SSA 1975, s.17(1)(d).
12 Ibid, as amended by SSA (No 2) 1980, s.3. Prior to this reform the periods could be separated by 13 weeks.

(3) the contract of employment has been terminated but the claimant has been able to find part-time work.

The cases of 'partial' unemployment give rise to a major policy issue: should the insurance system protect the individual's current (or normal) level of employment; or should compensation be available only when earnings (for part-time, or short-time, work) are insufficient for subsistence needs?[13] In principle, the British scheme adopts the former approach; it is based on *days* of unemployment and the problem is simply to formulate rules which enable the authorities to compare the current pattern of partial unemployment with the previous pattern of full-time employment. During the inter-war period, there was considerable reliance on unemployment insurance to compensate for short-time working, a device much used by employers to deal with reduced demand caused by the economic crisis.[14] Claims were facilitated by the fact that, at that time, benefit was payable for single days of unemployment, once the period of waiting days had been served.

Since the Second World War, doubts have arisen as to the appropriateness of using the conventional unemployment insurance scheme for this purpose.[15] The administrative costs of paying benefits for short and often irregular periods are high, and the employment services are not suited to dealing with persons who already have an employer but who in theory must make themselves available for other work. Moreover, as will emerge from the following pages, it has proved to be most difficult to formulate a set of satisfactory rules for comparing current with previous patterns of work and this has rendered the law both complex and difficult to understand. There is also the economic argument that contributors to the National Insurance Fund should not have to subsidise those industries which regularly have to lay off workers,[16] particularly when, as the evidence reveals,[17] patterns of work are commonly fixed to attract the maximum amount of benefit.

Not surprisingly, therefore, attempts have been made to devise other methods of compensating employees. The most favoured of such methods is for the employer to assume responsibility by agreements guaranteeing a minimum amount of wages or work. In the hope that guarantee agreements would become universal, the Labour government in 1966 sought to discharge the National Insurance Fund from liability for benefit for periods of unemployment of less than a week. The policy was put into effect immediately as regards earnings-related supplement,[18] but for the flat-rate benefit was postponed[19] while employers and unions made the appropriate arrangements. Although ten years later it was estimated that about 80 per cent of workers liable to be put on short-time were covered by some such agreement, the guarantee was usually for considerably less than a week's pay and subject to stringent conditions.[20] Moreover, the guarantee could often be suspended so that employees could still claim unemployment benefit. Rather than remove entitlement to the flat-rate benefit in all cases, the government introduced, in the Employment Protection Act 1975, compulsory guarantee payments,

---

13 Cf Buck [1987] JSWL 23.
14 Bakke *Insurance or Dole* (1935); Szyszczak in Lewis (ed) *Labour Law in Britain* (1986) p.372.
15 See, generally: Ogus 4 ILJ 12; Department of Employment Consultative Document *Compensation for Short-Time Working* (1978); Szyszczak, n.14, above.
16 First Report of the Royal Commission on Unemployment Insurance (1931, Cmd 3872), para 777.
17 Consultative Document, n.15, above.
18 NIA 1966, s.2.
19 Originally only for three years (ibid, s.3(1)) but then indefinitely: NIA 1969, s.12(3).
20 Consultative Document, n.15, above.

though these too were unambitious: only for a maximum of five 'workless' days within a period of three months, and subject to an overall limit of £30 (now £40) for that period.[1]

While the system of guarantee payments remains in force, it has not proved to be an ideal solution both because of the low level of payments and because its interaction with entitlement to unemployment benefit has generated some anomalies.[2] A reversal of policy occurred in the late 1970s, when the arguments for collective responsibility for short-time working were resurrected.[3] The government issued far-reaching proposals under which employers would be obliged to guarantee 75 per cent of normal pay to employees put on short-time which did not involve more than one week's continuous lay-off.[4] A substantial proportion of the payments would be refunded to employers from a new fund, to which employers and the Exchequer would contribute. The proposal was never implemented; instead the government introduced several temporary schemes under powers conferred by the Employment Subsidies Act 1978.[5] The most important of these, the Temporary Short Time Working Scheme, applied to employers who agreed to withdraw a notice of redundancy issued to more than ten workers. Employees placed on short-time, as a consequence, were paid 50 per cent[6] of lost normal pay, which sums were reimbursed by the Exchequer. Until it was terminated in 1984, the scheme completely overshadowed unemployment benefit in importance: for example, in March 1981, it provided compensation for 984,000 employees working short-time, compared with under 20,000 in that category receiving unemployment benefit.[7]

Together with guarantee payments, unemployment benefit currently provides the primary source of compensation for partial unemployment. It is now necessary to consider the special rules applicable.

ii Subsidiary employment

The first rule enables the authorities to disregard certain forms of subsidiary employment and reflects a general policy of encouraging recipients of unemployment benefit to engage in some part-time work, provided that it is consistent with availability for full-time employment and the remuneration is modest.[8] In recent years, the policy has been focused particularly on promoting voluntary and community work and, to implement this, the regulations were amended in 1982.[9] Under current provisions, the onus is on the claimant[10] to satisfy three conditions.[11]

---

1 Employment Protection Act 1975, ss.22–28; now Employment Protection (Consolidation) Act 1978, ss.12–18.
2 Szyszczak, n.14, above, pp. 373–375; and see p.90, below.
3 Consultative Document, n.15, above.
4 Metcalf *Alternatives to Unemployment* (1982) pp. 6–17, 56–60. The schemes were discretionary, and potential applicants could only rely on short descriptions in pamphlets; hence the appellation 'leaflet law': Freedland 9 ILJ 254.
5 75 per cent from 1979 to 1980.
6 Szyszczak, n.14, above, p.377.
7 Ibid.
8 See SSAC Second Annual Report (1983) para 4.18ff.
9 SSAC Report on Draft Amendment Regulations (1982, Cmnd 8486).
10 *R(U) 16/64*; *R(U) 2/67*.
11 SI 1983/1598, reg 7(1)(g). The conditions need not be satisfied if the subsidiary employment is manning (or launching) a lifeboat or performing part-time duties with a fire brigade: ibid, reg 9.

a *Earnings not to exceed £2 per day*
The policy of exempting part-time work from consideration is subject to the important qualification that it must not be too profitable, hence the limit of £2 per day. If the earnings are paid in relation to a longer period than a day, the average daily rate must not exceed that limit.[12] The method of calculating the earnings for the purpose of the rule is described in Chapter 9.[13]

b *Available for full-time employment*
The claimant must be available for full-time employment in an employed earner's employment. This repeats a condition which must in any event be satisfied by anyone claiming unemployment benefit and which is fully considered below.[14]

c *Charitable work or not usual main occupation*
Finally, if the subsidiary employment is employed earner's employment,[15] it must be charitable work organised by a private charity, a local authority or a health authority or it must not be in the claimant's usual main occupation. The first of the alternative conditions dates from the 1982 reform; the second was introduced in 1955[16] to prevent collusion: an employer dismissing the claimant and then re-engaging him at a nominal wage.[17]

iii 'Full extent normal' rule
The second of the special rules applies not only where a contract of employment has been suspended but also where it has been terminated. It involves a comparison of the claimant's current and previous patterns of work. A regulation provides that:

> [A] day shall not be treated as a day of unemployment if on that day a person does no work and is a person who does not ordinarily work on every day in a week (exclusive of Sunday or the day substituted [therefor]) but who is, in the week in which the said day occurs, employed to the full extent normal in his case. . . .[18]

The 'full extent normal' rule, as it has become known, had its origin in case-law under the pre-war unemployment insurance scheme[19] and is designed to disentitle a claimant who though he may be unemployed on one or more days in a week nevertheless, on aggregate, is engaged for an amount of work which, in his case, is 'normal'.[20] For the claimant to be caught by the rule, the adjudication officer must establish both (1) that he does not ordinarily work six days a week – an easy condition to satisfy in modern circumstances[1] – and (2) that the number of hours worked in the week in question is

12 Ibid, reg 7(1)(g)(i) and see *R(U) 3/84(T)*.
13 Pp. 373–379, below.
14 Pp. 92–97, below. The condition is waived for some (e.g. those undertaking duties in an emergency or attending work camps) who cannot, in practice, satisfy it: see SI 1983/1598, regs 10–12, and pp. 96–97, below.
15 On which see p.35, above. The subsidiary employment may thus be self-employed work.
16 SI 1955/143.
17 While recognising the practical importance of this, SSAC nevertheless regard the limitation as harsh: Report, n.9, above, para 8.
18 SI 1983/1598, reg 7(1)(e).
19 See e.g. *UD 4149/38*.
20 *R(U) 3/86(T)*. An alternative view of the purpose of the rule, that it seeks to prevent payment of benefit when days of unemployment are combined with (relatively well-paid) part-time work, derives little support from the authorities: cf Buck [1987] JSWL 23, 33–34.
 1 *R(U) 3/86* para 8. The policy justification for the exclusion of six-days worker is, in any event, obscure: *Calvert* p.78.

'normal' for him.[2] It is irrelevant to the operation of the rule that the employee has lost earnings, giving rise to the anomaly that a claimant working fewer hours but receiving the same pay as previously will probably fall outside it, while another working the number of hours which is 'normal' for him, but for reduced pay, is caught by it.

Real difficulties arise in relation to the interpretation of what is 'normal'.[3] The rule was developed mainly with regard to cases where an employee was temporarily put on 'short-time' by the employer and it was relatively easy to determine what was 'normal' for that employment. In recent years, there would seem to have been some policy change in the application of the rule by the authorities: it has been increasingly used where a contract for full-time employment has been terminated and the claimant has been able to find only part-time work.[4] Is full-time employment 'normal' for such a person? If so, how long does it remain so? Some practical tests have evolved to deal with these questions.[5] The most frequently adopted appears to have been the 'one year before test', according to which the adjudicating authorities would decide that, in general, a pattern of working would be 'normal' only if it was regularly followed in the period of twelve months immediately before the date of claim.[6] Another test – now referred to as the '50 per cent test' – is a refinement on this: regularity during the twelve-months period is to be determined by ascertaining whether the relevant pattern of work was adopted in more than 50 per cent of the weeks in that period.[7] A mechanical application of these tests obviously facilitated routine decisionmaking,[8] but proved to be too rigid to cope with the wide variety of situations that can affect working patterns. Two qualifications to the full extent normal rule were therefore added to the regulations.

First, in applying the 'full extent normal' rule

> no account shall be taken, in determining either the number of days in a week on which he ordinarily works or the full extent of employment in a week which is normal in his case, of any period of short-time working due to adverse industrial conditions.[9]

But the phrase 'adverse industrial conditions' has not been broadly interpreted: to justify looking beyond the twelve-months period the conditions must have been temporary or sporadic.[10] There must be a reduction below the standard level of employment: for the purposes of the regulation a dropping of overtime is not 'short-time'.[11]

The second express exception arises where the claimant's pattern of employment was irregular and casual. Indeed in these circumstances, the 'full

---

2 *R(U) 13/59*; *R(U) 3/86(T)*. The rule has thus been applied to those working 'rotas', for example two weeks on duty, followed by two weeks off-duty: benefit cannot be claimed during off-duty weeks because during each such week the claimant is employed to the full extent normal for him (i.e. no work): *R(U) 2/83*.

3 See, generally, Buck, n.20, above.

4 Cf the observations of Ralph Gibson LJ in *Chief Adjudication Officer v Brunt* [1988] 1 All ER 466 at 476.

5 They are critically discussed by Slade LJ in *Riley v Chief Adjudication Officer* [1988] 1 All ER 457 at 460–461 and by Lord Templeman in *Chief Adjudication Officer v Brunt* [1988] 2 WLR 511 at 515–516.

6 *CU 518/49*.

7 *R(U) 14/59* and see *R(U) 14/60*

8 Cf Ogus in Burrows and Veljanovski (eds) *The Economic Approach to Law* (1981) ch 9.

9 SI 1983/1598, reg 7(1)(e).

10 *R(U) 13/60*.

11 *R(U) 2/73*, H A Shewan, Comr.

extent normal' rule cannot function at all[12] and the regulations provide that the rule shall not apply to a person unless

(a) there is a recognised or customary working week in connection with his employment; or

(b) he regularly works for the same number of days in a week for the same employer or group of employers.[13]

Even with such exceptions, the 'one year before' and '50 per cent' tests have been regarded by some Commissioners in recent years as insufficiently flexible,[14] and, it is argued, should not be applied when the claimant engages in the part-time work only as a 'stop-gap' measure, while full-time employment is being sought.[15] Although it is acknowledged that a subjective inquiry into the intentions or desires of the individual claimant would be inappropriate, nevertheless the 'stop-gap' test has regard to his past employment history, his own working abilities and skills and the nature of the present employment to determine whether it would be reasonable to say of *him* that he was employed to the full extent normal.[16] Perhaps even more significantly, account would also be taken of current economic and social conditions, so that in periods of high unemployment, 'one may more readily accept that part-time work is undertaken as a stop-gap exercise'.[17]

In *Riley v Chief-Adjudication Officer*[18] and *Chief Adjudication Officer v Brunt*[19] these interpretations of the full extent normal rule were reviewed by the Court of Appeal and House of Lords. In the *Riley* case, Slade LJ recognised the importance of considering the personal circumstances of the claimant, in establishing what, in the words of the regulation, is 'normal in his case'. His past employment record is, of course, relevant but only for the purpose of shedding light on what is normal for him at the relevant week of the claim, and, for this purpose, the 'one year before test' provides a 'practicable, but not inviolable, approach'.[20] The 'stop-gap test' may also assist in identifying the normal pattern of work as at the relevant week but should be applied 'only with circumspection'.[1] This attempt to harmonise previously discordant approaches may seem to be uncontroversial but the learned judge then added a new, and arguably impracticable[2] dimension to the inquiry: 'the officer or tribunal concerned should try to look into the future in order to decide how permanent or transitory the present pattern of work is likely to be'.[3]

In the *Brunt* case, a Tribunal of Commissioners had decided that the rule should not be applied to a claimant engaged in part-time work on the MSC Community Programme, primarily because that work was only for a temporary period and, by itself, should not be regarded as 'normal' work for

---

12 *R(U) 32/51*; *R(U) 37/56*.

13 SI 1983/1598, reg 7(2), on which see *R(U) 2/88*.

14 See e.g. *R(U) 1/72*.

15 Esp in *R(U) 2/86* and (by a majority, L Bromley, Chief Comr, dissenting) *R(U) 3/86(T)*, relying on *CU 518/49* para 16.

16 *R(U) 3/86(T)* para 10 (Tribunal majority).

17 Ibid.

18 [1988] 1 All ER 457, [1987] 3 WLR 1224.

19 [1988] 1 All ER 466, [1987] 3 WLR 1200 upheld by the House of Lords [1988] 1 All ER 754, [1988] 2 WLR 511. Both the *Riley* and *Brunt* cases involved part-time work under MSC training schemes. This is now the subject of special provision: p.71, above.

20 N.18, above, at 465.

1 Ibid at 464.

2 Cf Buck [1987] JSWL 23, 31–32.

him.[4] The Court of Appeal, while sympathetic to this approach, held that it was inconsistent with the guidelines laid down in the *Riley* case: the temporary nature of the part-time employment was only one of the factors to be considered and when regard was had both to the claimant's history of employment and to his future prospects, it was reasonable to conclude that, at the relevant week, part-time work had become the 'normal' pattern.[5] At the same time, it was admitted that the policy basis of the rule was obscure and that its application had led to inconsistency and uncertainty.[6] No doubt it was anticipated that an appeal to the House of Lords would help to resolve the difficulties. Unfortunately, such expectations were to be disappointed. The decision that was handed down,[7] and which dismissed the appeal on the same ground as that adopted in the Court of Appeal, contains only one speech – that of Lord Templeman. His Lordship made no serious attempt to grapple with the difficulties of interpretation described above. There is some irony in his recognition that regulation 7(1)(e) 'bristles with ambiguity and doubt' and that 'a radical reappraisal of [its] wording . . . is required',[8] since arguably the law has been rendered more, rather than less, uncertain as a result of his speech. After the Court of Appeal decision in this case, the position appeared to be that, in determining what was 'normal' for the claimant, the adjudicating authorities should have regard to his past working record and to his future prospects and that the 'rules of thumb' ('one year before' test etc) provided some assistance but were in no sense conclusive. While acknowledging that there was a need for 'speed, certainty and simplicity' in this field of law, Lord Templeman clearly regarded the application of those rules as unsatisfactory;[9] however, no substitute was offered which might facilitate decisionmaking. Amendment or clarification of the regulation might seem preferable but governments are not always swift to respond to judicial suggestions of this kind.

iv 'Normal idle day' rule

The second rule designed to test that there has been a genuine reduction in the work available to the claimant applies only where the contract of employment has been suspended. It was rendered necessary by the fact that, while unemployment benefit is payable on the basis of a six-day working week, the great majority of employees are engaged for less than that amount per week. Quite apart from Sunday, there is for such workers at least one other 'normal idle day'. It would clearly be anomalous if a four-day worker losing one day a week could claim both for that day and the two other days when he would not normally work – thus entitling him to 3/6 of weekly benefit – while a five-day worker losing one day could claim for two days – entitling him to 2/6 of weekly benefit. Worse still, a six-day worker losing a single day might not be able to claim even for that day, as he would typically not satisfy the two-in-six continuity rule.[10] Following consideration of the matter by the National

---

3 N.18, above, at 464. No reference is made to the view of the Tribunal majority in *R(U) 3/86* that economic and social conditions may impact on this.
4 *CU/274/1984(T)*.
5 [1988] 1 All ER 466 at 481, 483.
6 Ibid at 476 (Ralph Gibson LJ) and 482–483 (Kerr LJ).
7 [1988] 1 All ER 754, [1988] 2 WLR 511.
8 Ibid at 514 and 516.
9 Ibid at 516.
10 See p.77, above. He would however satisfy the rule if his 'lost' day were altered from week to week.

Insurance Advisory Committee,[11] the government introduced in 1957 a rule disentitling the claimant from benefit for any day on which he would not normally work, unless he were unemployed on all the other days (excluding Sunday or its substitute) of the week.[12] However, like the 'full extent normal' rule, this solution while eliminating some anomalies created others. If, as part of the short-time arrangements, an employee now works a 'normal idle day' instead of a normal working day, he is not prevented from claiming benefit for the latter day and thus will be more favourably treated than an employee who does not switch his working pattern in this way. For example:

> C and D normally work on four days, Monday to Thursday inclusive. During a recession, C works on Monday and Friday. He can claim for three days (Tuesday, Wednesday and Thursday, none of which are 'normal idle days'). But if D works on Monday and Tuesday he can only claim for two days (Wednesday and Thursday – but not Friday which is a 'normal idle day').

Quite apart from this weakness, the indigestible statutory provision which enshrines the rule has given rise to considerable difficulties and necessary modifications. As reenacted in 1975 it prescribes that

> where a person is an employed earner and his employment as such has not been terminated, then in any week a day on which in the normal course that person would not work in that employment or in any other employed earner's employment shall not be treated as a day of unemployment unless each other day in that week [other than Sunday or a substitute therefor] on which in the normal course he would so work is a day of interruption of employment.[13]

a *Employment terminated or treated as terminated*
The rule only applies where the claimant's employment has not been terminated. Clearly if his engagement with the employer has ceased he should receive a full week's benefit even though that week includes days when he would not normally work. But difficulties have been encountered in deciding when, for this purpose, a contract has been terminated. The Commissioner has been faced with a choice between applying the ordinary contractual meaning of termination (viz that the rights and obligations of the parties have ceased[14]) and adopting the special meaning attributed to 'termination' by the Umpire under the old Unemployment Insurance Acts. On the latter view, the contract was not to be regarded as terminated unless the claimant had been 'finally' discharged without any intention of resuming the relationship of employer and employee on the next available opportunity.[15] For a long time, the special meaning prevailed,[16] notwithstanding a 'stream of indignant appellants who could not understand how their employment could be said not to have terminated when their contract of employment no longer subsisted'.[17] The line of decisions upholding this second approach was ques-

11 Report on Very Short Spells of Unemployment (1955, Cmd 9609), and see Ogus 4 ILJ 12, 16–17.
12 NIA 1957, s.4(1).
13 SSA 1975, s.17(1)(b).
14 Cf p.69, above.
15 *UD 16930/31.*
16 E.g. *R(U) 16/59*; *R(U) 11/61*. In N. Ireland one decision went so far as to hold that where in one week C was regularly employed by different employers, (i) the 'employment' was the totality of all employments, and therefore (ii) the termination of contract with one employer did not terminate the 'employment' as a whole: *16/59 (UB)*.
17 *R(U) 7/68(T)*, para 26.

tioned by a single Commissioner in 1967[18] and effectively overruled by a Tribunal of Commissioners in 1968.[19] Hence the general law of contract now applies, though, as we have seen,[20] the construction of the contract is sometimes highly problematical.

There are a number of cases in which the regulations treat the employment as having been terminated, even though in accordance with the general law of contract it has been only suspended. Most of these deal with situations for which the 'normal idle day' rule is inappropriate because the claimant has not established a 'normal' pattern of work – for that reason they are considered below.[1] The single case calling for mention here is that where the claimant's employment has been 'indefinitely suspended'. *Ex hypothesi*, he has not been put on short-time but has been laid-off for an indefinite period and there is therefore every justification for paying him a full week's benefit, even for days when he would not normally work. To invoke this exception to the 'normal idle day' rule, the claimant must show not only that the employment has been 'indefinitely suspended' but also that it has lasted for at least six continuous days.[2]

b *What is normal*

Where the rule does apply, the onus is on the adjudication officer to prove that a day for which benefit is claimed is one on which the claimant would not normally work.[3] If that is satisfied, the claimant can only escape disentitlement if he is able to show that his normal days of work in the week in question[4] are also days of interruption of employment, in other words, that he has been 'laid-off' for the whole of the week in question.[5] While, in general, in determining what is 'normal' for both parts of the rule, the authorities have adopted a similar approach to that used in relation to the 'full extent normal rule', the problems have been less acute because reference can always be made to what is normal under the *current* contract of employment – the 'full extent normal rule', it will be recalled, applies also where the contract has been terminated. The contract may itself provide evidence as to what is 'normal' – for example, where it envisages a rota system of working[6] – but regard is typically had more to the claimant's actual record of work.[7] The twelve-months reference period was adapted to meet the requirements of the new condition: during the period of twelve months immediately preceding the claim, but ignoring holidays and sickness, had the claimant worked on the day in question more often than he had not?[8]

18 *R(U) 4/67*, J S Watson, Comr. It was not necessary to decide which approach was right, as on either view the claimant succeeded.
19 *R(U) 7/68(T)*. It was said that the Umpire had employed the doctrine not to interpret the word 'termination' but rather to decide whether or not the claimant had been 'continuously unemployed', a concept not relevant to modern legislation: ibid, para 20.
20 Pp. 69–70, above.
1 P.86, below.
2 SI 1983/1598, reg 19(2). The period is determined in accordance with SSA 1975, s.17(3)(a) and SI 1983/1598, reg 6: Sundays and days of customary or recognised holiday do not count, but days of incapacity which would otherwise have been days of suspension do count.
3 *R(U) 14/59*, para 11.
4 The work must be in 'employed earner's employment', on which see pp. 35–42, above.
5 A person employed on a rota basis, two weeks of work followed by two weeks of rest, is not assisted by this when claiming for days during a week of rest: he cannot show that one other day in the week is normally a day of work: *R(U) 10/80*; *R(U) 6/81*.
6 *R(U) 10/80*; *R(U) 14/80*; *R(U) 6/81*.
7 *R(U) 19/58*; *R(U) 22/58*.
8 *R(U) 14/59*.

But this practice was no more successful at coping with the varying situations to which it was applied. It was clearly inappropriate where an employee had moved to a new situation or was governed by a new agreement, and whether working on a particular day is 'normal' for him must be judged in the light of the changed circumstances rather than on his record during the last year.[9] Short-time work due to adverse industrial conditions was to be excluded, a principle later recognised in an extraordinarily complex form by the regulations,[10] though given the same interpretation as the parallel provision governing the 'full extent normal' rule.[11]

In cases where the claimant's work pattern has been irregular or not relevant to his current employment, it is impossible to apply any test of 'normality' and so the regulations exclude the 'normal idle day' rule altogether by treating the employment as having been terminated. The cases so governed are as follows.

(a) There is not a recognised or customary week in connection with the employment.[12]
(b) The claimant does not regularly work for the same number of days in a week for the same employer or group of employers.[13]
(c) The claimant works in casual employment.[14] This provision predates[15] and has probably been superseded by cases (a) and (b). When clearly operative, it was given a restrictive interpretation by the Commissioner.[16]
(d) The employer for whom he is working in the week in question is not his usual employer.[17]

v The 'holiday' rule

a *General*

The questions whether, and to what extent, a holiday should affect entitlement to benefit may be viewed from two different perspectives. On the *broader* perspective, payment during a holiday should in principle be excluded. A holiday is in its nature relief provided by the employer so that the employee may 'enjoy rest, recreation or amusement'.[18] The employee is thus estopped from claiming that circumstances have prevented him from pursuing his gainful occupation. But this view cannot be maintained without substantial qualifications. On the one hand, it can hardly be applied to someone whose contract of employment has been terminated. It would be speculative and impracticable for the authorities to make inquiries whether, if he had

---

9   *R(U) 18/62*; *R(U) 14/60*; *R(U) 1/72*.
10 SI 1983/1598, reg 19(3)(d) provides that in any week of short-time due to adverse industrial conditions, the employment is to be treated as if 'terminated' immediately after its commencement, thus excluding from operation the 'normal idle day' rule. But reg 19(5) then stipulates by an equally circumlocutory formula that it shall nevertheless not be treated as a day of unemployment if, quite apart from the short-time, it would still have been a normal idle day. See in general *R(U) 17/60(T)*.
11 The conditions must involve some temporary reductions in the working hours general in the relevant industry (*R(U) 13/60*), thus excluding conditions peculiar to the claimant (*R(U) 14/60*) and general recessions in trade (*R(U) 1/64*).
12 SI 1983/1598, reg 19(6)(a). 'Week' can be read as 'weeks': *R(U) 6/81*.
13 SI 1983/1598, reg 19(6)(b).
14 Ibid, reg 19(3)(a).
15 It was introduced by SI 1957/1319. Cases (a) and (b) were introduced by SI 1966/1049.
16 See especially, *R(U) 16/59* and *R(U) 11/61*.
17 SI 1983/1598, reg 19(3)(b).
18 Per H Magnus, Dep Comr, *R(U) 1/66*, para 22.

been employed in his normal occupation, the claimant would have been on holiday on a certain day or week. At the most, then, the principle can only apply where the contract of employment has been merely suspended. On the other hand, the principle draws no distinction between holidays with pay and holidays without pay, and yet the distinction must be crucial. It is only the employee on holiday *without pay* that has any legitimate claim, and yet on the general principle he is bracketed with another who continues to receive his ordinary wage. This last consideration lies at the heart of the *narrower* perspective. On this view, there is no need for a general principle governing holidays. The legislation should simply be concerned to protect those who are *involuntarily* on holiday *without pay*. Such persons may be ascertained by applying the ordinary rules which refuse to characterise as days of unemployment days for which remuneration is received[19] and disqualify from benefit where employment is left voluntarily.[20] On either view, there is the independent question whether a claimant, who is admittedly unemployed, but who is absent on holiday from his normal place of residence, nevertheless satisfies the ordinary requirement of being 'available' for suitable employment.[1]

On the general question of entitlement during periods of holiday, the history of the British system has been far from consistent. Originally, there were no special provisions,[2] but the Umpire of his own initiative decided that a claimant on holiday was not 'continuously unemployed'.[3] This then hardened into a rule of law[4] and was applied irrespective of whether or not the claimant had received any holiday pay. The modern law has in general maintained this position: if the employment has not been terminated or indefinitely suspended, a day of 'recognised or customary holiday in connection with that employment' is not to be treated as a day of unemployment.[5] The broader perspective was thus explicitly admitted into the system, and with it came all its attendant difficulties: problems in deciding what are customary holidays, distinctions between termination and suspension, and still the need to provide for the man who is forced to take a holiday without pay – a need which was only partially met by a typically complex measure in 1966. By adopting the narrower perspective many systems[6] not only find a more complete solution to this problem, but at the same time avoid the subtle and complex difficulties to which the British approach so unnecessarily gives rise.[7]

b *Recognised and customary holidays*
The first question to be decided is whether the day in question is 'a recognised or customary holiday in connection with that employment'. There must be an agreement, express or implied, between the employer and the employee that

19 Pp. 72–76, above.
20 Pp. 101–104, below.
 1 P.92, below.
 2 UIA 1939, s.1 made statutory provision for the exclusion of holidays from unemployment benefit but owing to the outbreak of war the section never came into force.
 3 *UD 228/12.*
 4 *UD 7712* and see the 'codifying decision' *UD 18284/32.*
 5 SI 1983/1598, reg 7(1)(h).
 6 Including most of those in the USA. Thus, e.g. the Illinois Unemployment Compensation Act does not in principle exclude holidays from the ambit of the fund. A simple provision (§ 440) assimilates 'vacation pay' to 'wages', and a claimant entitled to such 'wages' is ineligible for benefits for any week in which the sums equal or exceed the weekly benefit amount.
 7 As *Calvert* points out (pp. 103–104), it is, however, sometimes difficult to determine whether or not an employee receives holiday pay.

on the day in question the employee is relieved from his working duties for the purposes of rest, recreation or amusement.[8] A mere agreement not to work is insufficient. If it is envisaged that the employee will take a break from his ordinary employment and take work elsewhere he is not 'on holiday'.[9] The existence of an agreement is to be determined according to the facts, regard being had in particular to the length of time during which the alleged holiday was habitually observed,[10] and whether extra payments are made for such work.[11] Although the holiday must be recognised or customary 'in connection with that employment', it need not, it seems, refer to the claimant's individual employment as distinct from the general conditions applying at his factory or place of work. This somewhat surprising proposition results from *R(U) 3/53*.

> For the purposes of their trade cycle, C's employers wished to change the dates of the factory's annual holiday. The large majority of employees agreed and the employers allowed those who wished to abide by the original agreement to take their holiday at the earlier date. It was held, however, that they were not entitled to benefit during the period when the majority took their holiday (and when the factory consequently closed). The minority were subject to the wishes of the majority. A claimant may be on holiday even if he does not wish to be so.[12]

A similar principle operates to disentitle those on casual employment. If a man habitually works in a certain place and that place closes for an agreed holiday, the casual employee is prima facie bound by that agreement unless he can show that it does not apply to him because, for example, he had another source of employment outside the place of work in question.[13] But the existence of an alternative occupation or source of employment creates problems which are not easy to solve. In *R(U) 7/63*

> a professional musician worked partly as a school-teacher and partly as a performer. In his former capacity he generally worked four days a week. During the school's Easter vacation he did not work on these four days and received no holiday pay. It was held that he was entitled to benefit. He was not 'on holiday' from his employment as a whole which included his other occupation as a performing musician.

The same approach was taken by a Tribunal of Commissioners in two later decisions.[14] They concluded that it would have been too artificial and impracticable to hold that a person could be on holiday for part only of a week. It is submitted, with respect, that this is only because the holiday rule is itself artificial and impracticable. The same result in *R(U) 7/63* could have been reached by the simpler route: (i) was the claimant unemployed on the day in question? (ii) did he receive remuneration for that day?

The existence of a special holiday rule is also responsible for another difficulty. Some 'agreed holidays' have their origin in a slack period of trade. It is established law that if there is an agreement that there should be a holiday, the actual reasons for its institution are irrelevant.[15] This means that there will

---

8 *R(U) 1/66(T)*.
9 *R(U) 8/64*.
10 *R(U) 39/53*; *R(U) 27/58*. Cp. *R(U) 11/53* which is hard to reconcile with these decisions. *Semble*, it places too much weight on the requirement of an agreement.
11 *R(U) 11/53*.
12 See also *CU 224/86(T)*.
13 *R(U) 18/54*; *R(U) 31/56*.
14 *R(U) 18/64(T)* and *R(U) 4/88(T)*. *See also R(U) 2/87*.
15 *UD 18284/32*; *R(U) 4/52*.

be an awkward transitional stage between 'short-time working' when benefit will be payable, and an implied 'holiday' when it will not. But the crucial question should surely be not whether there was a 'holiday' but whether the employees were paid when they were not working.

c *Suspension of contract*

If the contract has been either 'terminated' or 'indefinitely suspended', the holiday rule will not apply. As elsewhere,[16] the special meaning attributed to 'termination' by the Umpire under the old Unemployment Insurance Acts was for a long time applied.[17] Following a similar change to the 'normal idle day' rule, a Tribunal of Commissioners in 1968 departed from a long line of authority and held that the ordinary contractual meaning of 'termination' should henceforth prevail.[18] For the purposes of this rule, 'indefinite suspension' is equated with termination and this is construed in accordance with the 1966 provisions on short-time unemployment.[19]

d *Holidays without pay*

It has been seen that one of the defects of the British system is that it draws no general distinction between holidays with and without pay. With this handicap it was faced with an anomaly:[20] a man who changed his employment may not have qualified for holiday pay, and yet he may be unable to work because at the place of employment there is a general holiday shutdown. A simple solution would have been to exclude from the operation of the holiday rule holidays involuntarily taken without pay, but as will have emerged from earlier remarks, such a step would effectively have robbed the holiday rule of any function. A compromise but complex solution was therefore adopted. The regulations effectively provide that if in the same period of 12·months (beginning for this purpose on 1 March) as the holiday in question, the claimant has already been on holiday (under a contract of employment) equalling or exceeding the period of the present holiday in question, the holiday rule shall not apply to disentitle the claimant from benefit for this latter period.[1]

vi Compensated days

The final question arising under this section is how entitlement to benefit for short-term unemployment may be affected by guarantee and other payments. Under the Employment Protection (Consolidation) Act 1978 the employer is *bound* to pay the employee for five 'workless days' within a period of three months, but only to a current maximum of £40 for that period.[2] Regulations then provide that a day on which a sum is payable under the Act is not to be treated as a day of unemployment.[3] The same applies to payments under agreements which have been made the subject of an exemption order by an appropriate Minister,[4] and also to payments arising from a scheme made under the Employment Subsidies Act 1978.[5]

16 Pp. 69 and 85, above.
17 E.g. *R(U) 12/54*; *R(U) 19/54*; *R(U) 1/62*; *R(U) 18/64*; *R(U) 1/66(T)*.
18 *R(U) 8/68(T)*.
19 P.85, above.
20 See NIAC Report on Very Short Spells of Unemployment (1955, Cmd 9609), paras 63–65.
1 SI 1983/1598, reg 7(1)(h).
2 Ss. 12–15; and see Hepple, Partington and Simpson 6 ILJ 54.
3 SI 1983/1598, reg 7(1)(k)(i). For criticisms of these provisions, see Hepple et al, n.2, above, and Dept of Employment Consultative Document *Compensation for Short-Time Working* (1978).
4 Under Employment Protection (Consolidation) Act 1978, s.18.
5 SI 1983/1598, reg 7(1)(l): see p.79, above.

For payments which do not come within any of these categories, the general principles as developed by the Commissioner apply. One crucial question is whether the agreement is construed to confer remuneration on the employee on the day or days when he does not work. The earlier decisions tended to draw a distinction between two classes of agreement: those in which the employer guaranteed a weekly *wage*; and those in which he guaranteed a certain amount of *work*. In the former case it was inferred that the intention was to pay the sum for the *whole* of the week, and that therefore the employee could not be 'unemployed' for any part of that week.[6] The same inference could not be drawn for the 'work' guarantees[7] and not unnaturally, in order that short-time workers should have access to the fund, many employment contracts were modified so that they might be characterised as belonging to this latter type.

In *R(U) 21/56*, however, a Tribunal of Commissioners held that a mere change of wording of an agreement made solely for the purposes of unemployment benefit, and which had no effect industrially, and which did not modify the rights and obligations of the parties could not by itself confer a title to benefit. The emphasis was shifted from the question of what the employer guaranteed to what the employee undertook in consideration of the guarantee. The new approach focused on whether or not, under the agreement, the employee was bound to make himself available to the employer on the days of the alleged unemployment.[8] This involves examining the *legal* consequences of the agreement: the fact that the employer is in practice prepared to regard the employee as available for other employment is irrelevant.[9]

That entitlement to benefit may confer advantages not only on the short-time worker (the benefit may be more valuable than the guaranteed sum) but also on the employer (who may be relieved from paying anything above the limit imposed by the Employment Protection Act) has led to joint efforts to undermine the validity of the guarantee agreement. While an agreement can, subject to the Employment Protection Act, be varied or abrogated, this must be done by mutual agreement: a unilateral decision to this effect or the mere rearrangement of the work timetable will be ineffective.[10] The Commissioner has also held that an agreement cannot be revoked retrospectively.[11]

Part 4   Availability

A   General

The unemployment must be involuntary. The notion is incorporated in various areas of the law. First, there are the administrative requirements that a claim be made in person at an unemployment benefit office,[12] and, if the claimant is under 18, register for work at the Careers Office or Jobcentre.[13] A

6   *R(U) 27/51.*
7   *CWU 49/50; R(U) 13/51; R(U) 23/55.*
8   See further *R(U) 2/58* and *R(U) 15/61.*
9   *R(U) 1/76,* H A Shewan, Comr.
10   *R(U) 10/73(T); R(U) 1/75.*
11   *R(U) 1/76.*
12   P.541, below.
13   The requirement is administrative and, curiously, not imposed by legislation, primary or secondary. Following a recommendation in the Report of Joint DE/DHSS Rayner Scrutiny *Payment of Benefits to Unemployed People* (1980) paras 4.03–4.37, the equivalent obligation for those over 18 has been abandoned.

second rule applies where a claimant fails, within fourteen days and without good cause, to comply with a written notice requesting him to report to an officer of the Department of Employment (or DHSS, Manpower Services Commission, or local education authority) for an interview in connection with employment prospects or the satisfaction of the conditions for unemployment benefit. A failure, without good cause, to comply with a second notice to similar effect will have the consequence that the day specified in the second notice, and all subsequent days until the claimant complies with it, will not constitute a day (or days) of unemployment.[14] Thirdly, there is a condition for unemployment benefit that the claimant be 'available' for suitable employment – the subject matter of this Part. Fourthly, there are various grounds for disqualification where effectively the unemployment results from his own conduct or attitude.[15]

As regards availability, the difficulty has been to formulate a test which provides sufficiently precise guidelines for those administering it and yet is flexible enough to allow for consideration of all the relevant factors, including the claimant's age, qualifications, working capacity and intentions, as well as the general level of unemployment and characteristics of the labour market particular to the locality.[16] Under the National Insurance Act 1911, the claimant had to prove that he was 'capable of work but unable to obtain suitable employment'.[17] Faced with a sudden and dangerous rise in unemployment in the 1920s, the government decided that the conditions of eligibility had to be strengthened and introduced the notorious requirement that the claimant must prove that he was 'genuinely seeking whole-time employment but unable to obtain such employment'.[18] Although regarded by employers as an essential feature of unemployment insurance,[19] it had a serious impact on the workings of the scheme,[20] and was bitterly attacked by the trade union movement.[1] As it was interpreted, the new condition seemed to require that a claimant look around for work where there might be none available. An adverse decision left a stigma which was difficult to remove. On the recommendations of a committee,[2] the condition was repealed in 1930.[3]

Under the 1946 Act, the question was simply whether the claimant was 'available for employment,'[4] and this was construed to mean whether there was a reasonable prospect of his obtaining the work for which he *held* himself available.[5] This resulted in the anomaly that some claimants might place such restrictions on their availability that for all practical purposes they were not available. On the recommendations of the National Insurance Advisory Committee,[6] a regulation was therefore introduced which limited the

14 SI 1983/1598, reg 7(1)(i)–(j).
15 Pp. 97–109, below.
16 *Fisher* para 237, and for economic considerations see Worswick (ed) *The Concept and Measurement of Involuntary Unemployment* (1976).
17 S.86(3).
18 It was applied to claims for uncovenanted benefit by UIA 1921, s.3(3)(b), and extended to covenanted benefit by UIA (No 2) 1924, s.3(1).
19 Report of the Committee on the Procedure and Evidence for the Determination of Claims for Unemployment Insurance Benefit (1929, Cmd 3415) (the Morris Report), para 37.
20 In 1928–29 of approx. 10 million claims, 340,000 were denied benefit for not genuinely seeking work: ibid, at para 36.
1 Ibid, at para 38.
2 Ibid, at para 43.
3 UIA 1930, s.6.
4 S.11(2)(a)(i).
5 See esp. *R(U) 12/52(T)*.
6 Report on the Availability Question (1953, Cmd 8894).

restrictions which an unemployed person might place on his availability.[7] In 1980 the working of this area of law was critically examined by a joint Department of Employment and DHSS team.[8] In its view, the 'availability' condition, as then administered, was inefficient and too imprecise. The vagueness of the statutory criteria led, in the team's view, to too much discretion and it was suggested that more specific rules should be formulated: if, in the first three months of unemployment, the claimant were unwilling to take a job similar to his previous one, he would have to show that vacancies for work of the kind he was seeking existed in the locality; after three months, claimants whose last work was manual would be expected to accept any manual work within their mental and physical abilities and, analogously, non-manual workers would be expected to accept any appropriate non-manual work.[9] In response, the government decided to tighten the administrative arrangements rather than the law, in particular by the completion of questionnaires, both at the time of the claim and after six months' unemployment, which would serve to clarify the terms on which the claimant is prepared to accept work.[10]

The basic principle of availability is contained in section 17(1)(a) of the Social Security Act 1975 which provides that a day shall not be treated as a day of unemployment unless on that day the claimant

> is capable of work and he is, or is deemed in accordance with regulations to be, available to be employed in employed earner's employment.

In addition to the statutory test (discussed in Section B), there are regulations governing restrictions which a claimant may place on availability (Section C) and treating the test as satisfied in defined circumstances (Section D).

B Statutory test

The onus is on the claimant to satisfy the condition in section 17(1)(a).[11] The requirement of capacity for work excludes cases where statutory sick pay, sickness benefit or invalidity benefit is appropriate.[12] The limitation to 'employed earner's employment' means that availability for self-employed or other uninsured work is irrelevant.[13] The Commissioners have traditionally ruled that, to be 'available to be employed', the claimant must prove both (i) that there is a reasonable prospect of his obtaining the relevant employment; and (ii) that he is willing and able at once to accept a suitable offer.

i Reasonable prospect
In determining whether there are reasonable prospects of employing the claimant on his stated terms of availability, the authorities have regard to such factors as his employment history (in particular, whether in the past he

---

7 SI 1955/143.
8 Report, n.13, above.
9 Ibid, paras 4.54–4.55.
10 White Paper *Training for Employment* (1988, Cm 316) para 7.13 ff.
11 *R(U) 12/52(T)*; *R(U) 34/53*. If, however, a doubt has arisen regarding the availability of a claimant already in receipt of unemployment benefit, he is deemed to satisfy the test until the question has been resolved or he fails, within a month, to respond to a request for information, whichever is earlier: SI 1983/1598, reg 12A.
12 See *R(U) 24/51*, and ch 4, below.
13 *R(U) 14/51*. For the meaning of 'employed earner's employment' see pp. 36–42, above.

has succeeded in obtaining employment on these terms),[14] and the attitude of employers.[15] If the stated terms of availability are drawn sufficiently widely, in terms both of type of work and of location, it will not be difficult to satisfy the requirement since the claimant need not show that an actual vacancy consistent with those terms exists: 'the requirement is that the claimant be available for work rather than that work be available for the claimant'.[16] Benefit is more frequently denied on the ground that the stated terms are too narrow, an issue governed by specific regulations and discussed in the next section.

ii Willingness and ability to accept

The general rule is that claimants must be 'prepared to accept at once any offers of suitable employment brought to their notice'.[17] The authorities will normally assume that the claimant is prepared to accept such offers,[18] but the rule may be invoked to disentitle him where his 'statements or actings' suggest the contrary,[19] most obviously where he actually refuses a suitable offer.[20] In some cases, the question turns on whether he is *able* to accept. He cannot be available if, during the relevant period, he cannot lawfully accept an offer of employment, for example, if he is an immigrant without an appropriate work permit[1] or is contractually bound to be at the disposal of another employer.[2] On the other hand, participation in training courses has been generously construed, so that if the claimant can be readily contacted and can take up an offer immediately he will be regarded as available.[3] If he is absent from the locality this will not generally be possible. This is a ground on which the claimant in *R(U) 5/80* could have been disentitled.

> He had been employed abroad for several years, but on losing his job there came to England to set up home. During the period for which he claimed benefit, he was however in England only a few days, mainly for the purpose of arranging his personal affairs.

In holding that he did not satisfy the 'availability' condition, the Commissioner nevertheless stated a general principle which seems to recall the 'genuinely seeking' work test applied in the inter-war years. He said that

> availability implies some active step by the person concerned to draw attention to his availability: it is not a passive state in which a person may be said to be available provided he is sought out and his location is ascertained.[4]

It is not clear what the Commissioner meant by 'active step' and there was little previous authority for such a requirement applying generally to non-itinerant claimants, but the proposition has not been questioned and it must, therefore, be treated as authoritative. Not surprisingly, there is evidence that

---

14 *CU 10/49*; *R(U) 44/53*.
15 *R(U) 6/72*, D Neligan, Comr.
16 Bonner et al *Non-Means Tested Benefits: The Legislation* (1987) p.14.
17 *R(U) 1/53* para 7. Under the 'deeming' regulations, in some cases the claimant is entitled to 24 hours' notice: p.96, below.
18 *R(U) 2/57*.
19 *R(U) 3/65*, para 11, H A Shewan, Dep Comr.
20 *R(U) 4/53*; *R(U) 15/58*.
1 *R(U) 13/57*; *R(U) 1/82(T)*; *Shaukat Ali v Chief Adjudication Officer*, reported as Appendix to *R(U) 1/85*.
2 *R(U) 11/51*; *R(U) 1/53*; *R(U) 1/69*.
3 *CWU 47/49*; *CU 162/50*.
4 *R(U) 5/80*, para 14, J S Watson, Comr.

adjudication officers frequently rely on the dictum to support decisions of disentitlement.[5]

To deal with the situation where the claimant is absent for a holiday, the Umpire in a decision on the pre-war legislation laid down three conditions which in such circumstances are to be satisfied,[6] and these were subsequently adopted by the Commissioner:[7]

(1) the claimant must be ready and willing immediately to return and accept an offer of suitable employment; and
(2) he must have taken reasonable and satisfactory steps to ensure that any such offer would be brought to his notice without delay;[8] and
(3) there was nothing connected with his absence which would have prevented him accepting at once any such offer.

Though this approach may be sound in theory, in practice, as the joint Department of Employment and DHSS team found, it is a 'fiction'.[9] Jobs are not offered to claimants while on holiday. The team recommended that considerable savings on the administrative costs of applying these holiday rules could be made if claimants were given an entitlement to two weeks holiday in any one year during which they would not be required to be available for work.[10]

C Reasonable restrictions test

The question whether restrictions placed by the claimant on his availability are reasonable is the subject of a regulation which, though it does not explicitly govern the availability condition, has been treated as such by the Commissioners.[11] It applies where

> a person places restrictions on the nature, hours, rate of remuneration or locality or other conditions of employment which he is prepared to accept and as a consequence of those restrictions has no reasonable prospects of securing employment. . . .[12]

The essence of the matter is that the lack of reasonable prospects should result from restrictions which the claimant himself *places* on his availability. If the restrictions result from such natural characteristics as age or sex, the regulation does not apply.[13]

If it does apply, the claim for benefit will fail unless one of three conditions is satisfied.

5 Private communication from a SSAT chairman.
6 *UD 7550/35.*
7 *R(U) 3/65* and *R(U) 4/66*, though in the latter case O George, Dep Comr, thought that the conditions might be regarded as more appropriate for the exceptional employment circumstances prevailing at the time they were devised.
8 If he moves from place to place there is a presumption that he cannot satisfy this condition: *R(U) 2/57.*
9 Report of Joint DE/DHSS Rayner Scrutiny, Payment of Benefits to Unemployed People (1980), para 5.36.
10 Ibid, paras 5.39–5.41.
11 *R(U) 4/57(T).*
12 SI 1983/1598, reg 7(1)(a).
13 *CU 3/71*, cited in Mesher *Compensation for Unemployment* (1976) p.45. This was one of the grounds which induced the government to introduce the abatement of benefit payable to occupational pensioners: pp. 120–121, below.

i Adverse but temporary industrial conditions
Under the first the claimant must prove that

> he is prevented from having reasonable prospects of securing employment consistent with those restrictions only as a result of adverse industrial conditions in the locality or localities concerned which may reasonably be regarded as temporary, and having regard to all the circumstances, personal and other, the restrictions which he imposes are reasonable.[14]

The concept of 'adverse industrial conditions' has already been the subject of discussion.[15] The limitation to such conditions as are 'temporary' has been interpreted to connote the idea of abnormality: ordinary seasonal fluctuations, such as those typically prevailing in seaside resorts, are not included.[16] The second limb contains a requirement analogous to that applicable under condition (iii), and may be conveniently considered under that head.

ii Physical condition
Alternatively, the claimant may show that 'the restrictions are nevertheless reasonable in view of his physical condition'.[17] The provision is illustrated by *R(U) 6/72*:

> A technical manager, suffering from a heart condition, on medical advice retired at the age of 62. He claimed benefit but restricted his availability to offers of employment at a minimum salary of £5,500 a year in his home town or its close environs. There was no reasonable prospect of finding such employment and it was held that in the light of his physical condition, the restriction to the locality (but not that as to remuneration) was reasonable.

iii Generally reasonable
The third alternative is the broadest and confers a necessary degree of flexibility on the authorities. The claimant must prove that

> the restrictions are nevertheless reasonable having regard both to the nature of his usual occupation and also to the time which has elapsed since he became unemployed.[18]

The consideration of 'usual occupation' is designed to protect job skills, and the general standard of remuneration to which the claimant is accustomed. On the other hand, the protection cannot last indefinitely, so that after a reasonable time has expired he must be prepared to accept an offer of a less appropriate kind.[19] The restrictions may, in any event, only be 'reasonable' if they relate to the nature of the claimant's occupation. Thus an actor who held himself available only on certain days when he was not required by the BBC was disentitled: the restrictions arose not from his occupation as an actor but from the particular arrangement with the BBC.[20] In other respects, the authorities have a broad discretion in determining reasonableness so that account may be taken of the claimant's general intentions,[1] the way he

---

14 SI 1983/1598, reg 7(1)(a)(i).
15 P.81, above.
16 *R(U) 3/59.*
17 SI 1983/1598, reg 7(1)(a)(ii).
18 Ibid, reg 7(1)(a)(iii).
19 *R(U) 3/59* and see the analogous principle in the disqualification provisions, pp. 105–106, below.
20 *R(U) 1/69*, E R Bowen, Comr.
 1 *R(U) 33/58.*

defines his 'occupation',[2] his domestic circumstances[3] and the state of the labour market in the locality.[4]

D Deemed availability

As has already been seen, the government in recent years has adopted a general policy of encouraging the unemployed to engage in activities which do not constitute ordinary, remunerated employment.[5] A strict application of the 'availability' requirement might disentitle those so engaged because they might not be able to take up 'at once' an offer of suitable employment.[6] The regulations thus treat the availability condition as having been satisfied in appropriate circumstances.[7]

i Dealing with emergencies
Originally this was the only category and it was narrowly confined to those engaged in manning a lifeboat or serving part-time in a fire brigade.[8] In 1982, it was extended to a broader group, namely those 'engaged, during an emergency,[9] in duties for the benefit of others'.[10]

ii Attending work camps
The second category, also added in 1982, covers persons attending a work camp in Great Britain, under the auspices of a charity or local authority 'to provide a service of benefit to the community'; they are deemed to be available for a maximum period (in one calendar year) of 14 days of such attendance, provided that prior notice is given to the unemployment benefit office.[11]

iii Requiring 24 hours' notice of job opportunities
Finally, it was recognised that it might be unreasonable to expect some other claimants to respond forthwith to an appropriate offer of employment. Thus, if:

> on any day a person is engaged, whether by contract or otherwise, in providing a service with or without remuneration and the circumstances are such that it would not be reasonable to require him . . . to make himself available at less than 24 hours' notice

2 *R(U) 3/59; R(U) 1/69.*
3 *R(U) 14/57; R(U) 17/57; R(U) 6/59.*
4 *R(U) 17/57; R(U) 6/72.*
5 Cf p.79, above.
6 Cf *R(U) 1/53*, p.93, above.
7 See, generally, the SSAC Report on the Draft Amendment Regulations (1982, Cmnd 8486).
8 SI 1983/1598, reg 9, which also provides that such persons may qualify for benefit even if they do not satisfy the conditions in reg 7(1)(g), governing subsidiary employment (pp.79–80, above).
9 This includes '(a) a fire, a flood or an explosion; (b) a natural catastrophe; (c) a railway or other accident; (d) a cave or mountain accident; (e) a person being reported missing and the organisation of a search for that purpose': SI 1983/1598, reg 10(3).
10 This covers: '(a) providing assistance to any person whose life may be endangered or who may be exposed to the risk of seriously bodily injury or whose health may be seriously impaired; (b) protecting property of substantial value from imminent risk of serious damage or destruction; or (c) assisting in measures being taken to prevent a serious threat to the health of the people; [and in any one such case] as a member of a group of persons organised wholly or partly for the purpose of providing such assistance or, as the case may be, protection': ibid, reg 10(2).
11 Ibid, reg 11.

he is deemed to be available on that day if he would be ready for suitable employment on 24 hours' notice.[12] The vagueness of the phrase 'providing a service with or without remuneration' is deliberate: it is intended to cover not only voluntary work and remunerated part-time work but also 'some worthwhile activity that might not be defined as work', for example, caring for a sick relative.[13]

Part 5   Disqualification for voluntary unemployment

The idea that unemployment must be involuntary may be seen as justifying not only the condition that a claimant be 'available' for employment, but also the circumstances in which he may be disqualified from benefit for a maximum period of 26 weeks. These may be conveniently grouped under three headings:

(a) losing employment through misconduct;
(b) voluntarily leaving employment without just cause;
(c) without good cause, refusing or failing to take, a reasonable opportunity to secure employment.

Part 5 concludes with an account of the principles determining the period of disqualification.

A Misconduct

The first ground for disqualification arises where the claimant has 'lost his employment as an employed earner through his misconduct'.[14] The rule was to be found in the National Insurance Act of 1911,[15] and has existed effectively in the same form ever since. However, the exact policy considerations on which it is based have never been made entirely explicit,[16] and as a result its interpretation and evolution have not been wholly consistent.[17] Three alternative theories may be invoked to support the disqualification.

a *Punishment* From a moral or social point of view, a worker who has been dismissed for misconduct is unworthy of the support of the fund: he has transgressed the ethical standards of the community.

b *Suitability* The claimant should be disqualified where his own actions reveal him as unsuitable for the job. The fund is intended to cover only those who lose employment through external circumstances, and not those whose lack of skill results in dismissal.

c *Voluntary unemployment* The purpose of the disqualification is to protect the fund against voluntary unemployment. Benefit is therefore to be

---

12 Ibid, reg 12.
13 DHSS Note to SSAC on the scope of the draft regulations: Report, n.7, above, Annexe 2, para 9.
14 SSA 1975, s.20(1)(a).
15 NIA 1911, s.87(2).
16 For an economic appraisal, see Fenn in Burrows and Veljanovski (eds) *The Economic Approach to Law* (1981) ch 13.
17 Lewis [1985] JSWL 145.

denied to a claimant who knew or should have known that his conduct was reasonably likely to incur dismissal.

The first theory has been most explicitly rejected in the United Kingdom.[18] The third theory is more consistent with the general purpose of the legislation,[19] and its influence can be seen in certain decisions,[20] but like most doctrines dependent on mental states, it creates grave problems of proof.[1] The suitability theory, though less attractive on policy grounds, can explain most of the law on this subject. Account is rarely taken of whether the claimant appreciated, or might reasonably have appreciated, that his conduct would lead to dismissal. While, in theory, an objective test of suitability is adopted – whether a reasonable employer would dismiss the employee[2] – it has been alleged that, in practice, the authorities rely on the managerial standards adopted by individual employers.[3] If this is the case and the standards vary according to the economic circumstances (e.g. a stricter standard when there is reduced demand for the firm's output),[4] the employee may be unfairly prejudiced: such circumstances should be irrelevant to the disqualification issue.

i Dismissal caused by misconduct

In principle, the adjudication officer must prove that the claimant was dismissed for an act or omission which constituted 'misconduct'.[5] But the requirement of 'dismissal' and its causal relationship with the alleged misconduct have been broadly construed. The contract of employment need not have been terminated by the employer: it will suffice if, as a result of the misconduct, the contract has been suspended[6] or both parties regard the employment as ended.[7] Nor need the 'dismissal' follow as an immediate consequence of the misconduct. In one case, a bus driver was convicted of a driving offence. He was disqualified even though the immediate cause of his dismissal was the loss of his licence rather than the commission of the offence.[8]

ii Misconduct connected with employment

If an employee were to be disqualified for misconduct committed in any circumstance, in effect the system would be regarding the employer's attitude to the misconduct as conclusive, and would be adopting a punitive approach to the claimant's entitlement. If, however, it requires that the misconduct be related to the employment, it may still question whether the dismissal warrants disqualification, as viewed from the policy dictate of protecting the insurance fund. The Commissioner has adopted this latter stance and ruled

---

18 *CU 190/50*; *R(U) 27/52*; *R(U) 8/74(T)*. Some American jurisdictions prescribe a *further* period of disqualification for those convicted of a criminal offence connected with the employment, while some impose special disqualifications for 'gross misconduct': Packard 17 Villa L Rev 635.
19 Cf Fenn, n.16, above.
20 *CU 190/50*; *R(U) 35/53*; *R(U) 24/55*.
 1 In the US jurisdictions where this theory is favoured, the courts allow a presumption of knowledge in many situations: Packard, n.18, above.
 2 *R(U) 2/77*.
 3 Lewis, n.17, above.
 4 Fenn, n.16, above, p.317.
 5 *R(U) 2/77*, R J A Temple, Chief Comr, and see *R(U) 2/81*, para 9.
 6 *R(U) 10/71*.
 7 *R(U) 17/64*; *R(U) 2/76*.
 8 *R(U) 7/57*.

that the conduct must be 'causally but not necessarily directly connected with the employment'.[9] The test is whether the misconduct, whenever and wherever it occurred, was such that it would induce a reasonable employer to dispense with the services of the claimant on the ground that he was not fit to hold the particular situation.[10] Of course, this will generally depend on the nature both of the misconduct and of the employment. What a man does outside his working hours may be totally irrelevant to his work or his employer's interests. A railway fireman who was dismissed for fighting in a railway carriage on his return from work was not disqualified.[11] But the misconduct may so closely affect his suitability for the job that it will justify disqualification no matter where and when it occurs. Such was the case where a park keeper was convicted of gross indecency with another man.[12]

iii Types of conduct
The use of the unqualified term 'misconduct' is unhelpful in determining the standard of conduct which is to be applied. Indeed, in the early years of the scheme it caused some embarrassment as it had to be explained to many women claimants that it was not intended to refer to their moral behaviour.[13] A Royal Commission, reporting in 1932, felt that the choice of language was unfortunate but was unable to suggest any positive improvement.[14] According to the Commissioner, the conduct must be such that it renders the claimant an unfit person to hold the job[15] and will include

> industrial shortcomings, disobedience, faulty workmanship, idleness, unauthorised absence, some types of carelessness, and conduct . . . connected with the employment adversely affecting the claimant's proper discharge of his duties.[16]

But the refusal to leave[17] or to join a trade union[18] does not constitute misconduct.

iv Blameworthiness
It is generally said that there must be blameworthiness,[19] but exactly what must be proved in terms of mental attitude is far from clear. On occasions, the Commissioner has tended towards a test appropriate to the 'voluntary unemployment' theory and spoken of the necessity of showing 'deliberate' or 'wilful negligence'.[20] The view most popularly held, however, is that a wilful or reckless breach of the appropriate standard is not required. A valuable illustration is provided by *R(U) 8/57*.

---

9 *R(U) 2/77*, para 15, R J A Temple, Chief Comr. See also *R(U) 1/71*.
10 *R(U) 2/77*.
11 *UD 4120*.
12 *R(U) 1/71*, R G Micklethwait, Chief Comr.
13 Tillyard *Unemployment Insurance in Great Britain 1911–48* (1949) pp. 24–25.
14 Final Report (1932, Cmd 4185), para 443. To meet the objection, the ground for disqualification has in practice frequently been called 'industrial misconduct': see esp. *R(U) 24/55* and *R(U) 1/71*.
15 *R(U) 24/55*; *R(U) 7/57*.
16 *R(U) 2/77*, para 15, R J A Temple, Chief Comr.
17 *UD 1528/26*.
18 *R(U) 2/77*.
19 E.g. ibid, at para 15.
20 *R(U) 34/52*, cp 'culpable negligence' (*R(U) 35/53*). Some schemes have attempted to introduce such language into the statutory definition: e.g. the West German Arbeitsförderungsgesetz § 119(1)(i) and the Massachusetts Employment Law, § 25(3)(2).

C, the manager of a branch pharmacy, was dismissed when cash was found to be missing in the shop. He was prosecuted for, but acquitted of, embezzlement. It was held that this was not sufficient to bar disqualification. 'Serious carelessness' only was required, and this might legitimately be inferred from the evidence.

The Commissioner observed, more generally,

Misconduct . . . may be constituted by mere carelessness; but in considering whether a person has been guilty of misconduct it is necessary to discriminate between that type and degree of carelessness which may have to be put up with in human affairs, and the more deliberate or more serious type of carelessness which justifies withholding unemployment benefit because the employee has lost his employment through his own avoidable fault.[1]

v Relevance of other legal proceedings

The situation in which an employee is dismissed for misconduct may have important repercussions in other areas of law. The conduct may constitute a criminal offence. The employee may allege that he was wrongfully dismissed (i.e. his employer acted in breach of contract), or that he was entitled to the statutory remedy for unfair dismissal. The dispute may have been the subject of a court hearing or of an adjudication by an industrial or disciplinary tribunal. In all such situations, the question arises as to the significance for the disqualification issue of the findings of such court or tribunal.

It is evident that in many instances the concept of 'misconduct' will be wider than a criminal offence with which the claimant was charged. In such a case an acquittal by a criminal court will in no sense be conclusive of the disqualification point.[2] Where the claimant has been *convicted*, there is no question of double jeopardy since the object of the disqualification is not to punish him,[3] but there is nevertheless some difficulty as to the weight to be given to the conviction. It clearly has evidentiary value,[4] but despite an earlier Commissioner's decision to the contrary,[5] it now seems clear that it will not be regarded as conclusive proof that the facts which were the basis of the criminal charge and also constituted the alleged misconduct actually occurred. In a more recent sickness benefit case,[6] the Commissioner adopted a compromise position whereby the initial onus lies on the adjudication officer to show that a conviction relates to the benefit issue involved. The onus then passes to the claimant to show that, notwithstanding the conviction, he is nevertheless entitled to the benefit in question.

The position is far from clear as regards the decisions of disciplinary bodies. It would seem to depend on how 'judicial' in character is the tribunal and the nature of the information emanating from its findings. So, in one case, confirmation of dismissal, without detailed reasons, by a hospital management committee afforded little assistance to the Commissioner,[7] but, in another, the more formal 'quasi-judicial' proceedings of a police disciplinary committee, while not 'absolutely conclusive' for social security purposes, were nevertheless treated as 'very cogent evidence'.[8]

1 *R(U) 8/57*, para 6.
2 *R(U) 10/54*; *R(U) 8/57*.
3 *CU 190/50*; *R(U) 27/52*; *R(U) 7/75*.
4 *R(U) 10/54*.
5 *R(U) 24/55*.
6 *R(S) 2/80*, J S Watson, Comr. He applied the principle of the Civil Evidence Act 1968, s.11(2)(a) (on which see *Stupple v Royal Insurance Co Ltd* [1971] 1 QB 50, [1970] 3 All ER 230) even though that Act does not apply to social security tribunals.
7 *R(U) 7/61*.
8 *R(U) 10/67*.

One would have thought that a finding by an industrial tribunal that an employee was entitled to compensation for an unfair dismissal would be almost conclusive that the same employee was not guilty of such misconduct as to be disqualified from unemployment benefit. Certainly it is appropriate for the authorities to take full cognisance of any *evidence* given to the industrial tribunal,[9] but its finding as to whether or not an employee has been unfairly dismissed is in no sense conclusive of the social security issue whether the claimant has been guilty of misconduct.[10] There are different questions of law involved: whether a person has been unfairly dismissed in the main depends on the conduct of the *employer*, whereas for unemployment benefit the main emphasis is on the behaviour of the *employee*.[11] The onus and standard of proof applicable may also differ between the two tribunals.[12]

B Voluntarily leaving without just cause

The second ground for disqualification is that the claimant

> has voluntarily left such employment [as an employed earner] without just cause.[13]

Such a provision is a typical feature of all unemployment insurance schemes, and has existed in the British system since its inception in 1911.[14] On the traditional theory, it may be justified on the ground that here unemployment is caused not by external circumstances but by the claimant himself.[15] In recent times, however, some forms of voluntary redundancy are actively encouraged to promote mobility in the labour market and, in 1985, the legislation was amended to take account of this policy goal.[16] For disqualification to be imposed, three conditions must be satisfied:

(a) the claimant *left* the employment;
(b) the leaving was *voluntary*;
(c) it was *without just cause*.

Following the 1985 amendment, the disqualification will be avoided if (d) the claimant was dismissed *by reason of redundancy*.

i Leaving

The onus is on the adjudication officer to show that the claimant left his employment.[17] 'Leaving' is not confined to terminating the contract of employment, but includes any temporary severing of the employment relationship, including absenteeism.[18]

9 *R(U) 2/74*, para 15, R G Micklethwait, Chief Comr, and see *R(U) 4/78*, para 6, H A Shewan, Comr.
10 *R(U) 2/74*; *R(U) 4/78*; *R(U) 3/79*.
11 *R(U) 2/74*, para 14.
12 *R(U) 4/78*, para 6.
13 SSA 1975, s.20(1)(a).
14 NIA 1911, s.87(2).
15 Cf *R(U) 20/64(T)*, para 8; *Crewe v Social Security Comr* [1982] 2 All ER 745, [1982] 1 WLR 1209, per Donaldson LJ at 750, per Slade LJ at 751.
16 SSA 1985, s.10.
17 *R(U) 20/64(T)*.
18 Ibid, para 7.

ii Voluntary

The onus is also on the adjudication officer to show that such leaving was voluntary.[19] It is this condition which distinguishes the case from dismissal for misconduct,[20] but in some cases it will be of no great significance which of the two is adopted,[1] and the word 'voluntarily' has been broadly construed so that it might extend to cases of termination by the employer which are instigated by the employee but which do not amount to misconduct.[2] In *R(U) 16/52*

> C was engaged as a canteen assistant subject to passing a medical examination. She refused to undergo an X-ray test and was dismissed. She was disqualified for leaving her employment voluntarily without just cause. 'It is an established principle of unemployment insurance', said the Commissioner, 'that, if a person deliberately and knowingly acts in a way which makes it necessary for the employer to dismiss him, he may be regarded as leaving his employment voluntarily'.[3]

But if the dismissal is not the 'natural consequence' of his actions, the leaving will not be voluntary. Thus in *R(U) 9/59*,

> C was dismissed when he refused to join the employer's superannuation scheme. He did not know at the time he entered the contract that he would be expected to join, and therefore his conduct did not 'invite' dismissal.[4]

Subject to the 1985 saving provisions for redundancy, a decision to take early retirement will normally constitute voluntarily leaving and thus attract disqualification,[5] but it has been held that an employee who accedes to a request from his employer to retire does not act 'voluntarily'.[6]

iii Without just cause

Once it has been established that the claimant voluntarily left his employment, the onus passes to him to show that he did so for 'just cause'.[7] The phrase is broad and flexible. Legislation provides no guidance on how it is to be interpreted but according to the Court of Appeal, in the leading case of *Crewe v Social Security Comr*, it has to be interpreted by reference to the insurance character of the scheme: 'the justice which the legislature had in mind was justice as between the employee and the general body of persons underwriting the fund'.[8] The interest of contributors to the National Insurance Fund is to be distinguished from the general public interest. In the instant case, a school teacher who had taken early retirement unsuccessfully argued that the 'public interest' of savings in the education budget or of making way for younger members of the profession constituted 'just cause'.[9] Examples of situations in which the interest of the claimant has been allowed to prevail over that of contributors are:

19 *UD 10841/30.*
20 *R(U) 9/59.*
 1 Cf p.98, above.
 2 *R(U) 5/71*, but see *R(U) 2/77*, para 26, where R J A Temple, Chief Comr, suggests that as the principle is not to be found in the Act itself it should be applied with restraint.
 3 *R(U) 16/52*, para 8; and see *R(U) 7/74.*
 4 See also *R(U) 2/77* (refusal to join trade union).
 5 *R(U) 20/64(T)*; *R(U) 4/70*; *R(U) 2/81*, affirmed without discussion of the point in *Crewe v Social Security Comr*, n.15, above; *R(U) 3/81.*
 6 *R(U) 1/83.*
 7 *R(U) 20/64(T)* para 7.
 8 Per Slade LJ, n.15, above, p.751. To similar effect, see Lord Denning MR at p.749 and Donaldson LJ at p.750. See further, *R(U) 4/87* para 9.
 9 See also *R(U) 4/87*. The decisions may have been superseded by the 1985 legislative amendment discussed at p.103, below.

- reduction in wages,[10] non-compliance by the employer with the contract of employment,[11] lack of confidence in mental or physical ability to perform duties,[12] pressing domestic or personal circumstances,[13] difficulty of travel to work,[14] reluctance to join a trade union,[15] general grievances about working conditions.[16]

But though such circumstances may constitute a good reason for leaving the employment, they may not be sufficient in themselves to avoid disqualification. It is a general principle that a dissatisfied employee should look for an alternative situation before leaving his present job.[17] He need not actually have secured a vacant post,[18] but the prospects of his finding one must be good.[19] The principle has not been rigidly applied. For example, it was not invoked where a wife left her job to join her husband who had been posted elsewhere,[20] nor to a spouse who was not the principal breadwinner and who left to look after a child who would otherwise have remained unattended.[1] Nor was it applied where the current employment did not provide any opportunities for looking for another job,[2] or where the relations between the claimant and his employer or his fellow employees had become so strained that it was in the interest of all that he should quit immediately.[3] As regards grievances about working conditions and other disputes with an employer, there is another general principle, which is again subject to the undue friction exception, that before tendering his notice, a claimant should seek to redress the grievances by making representations to the employer through the proper channels, usually with the assistance of his trade union.[4]

iv Dismissal by reason of redundancy
In consequence of the 1985 amendment,

> a person who has been dismissed by his employer by reason of redundancy within the meaning of section 81(2) of the Employment Protection (Consolidation) Act 1978 after volunteering or agreeing so to be dismissed shall not be deemed to have left his employment voluntarily.[5]

The subsection is unhappily phrased. There are no provisions 'deeming' a claimant to have left his employment voluntarily and so presumably it should

---

10 *R(U) 15/53.*
11 *CU 248/49.*
12 *R(U) 3/73.*
13 *R(U) 31/59.*
14 *R(U) 20/69.*
15 *R(U) 38/53.*
16 *R(U) 33/51.* There may be an overlap here with the criteria applied in deciding whether the claimant had unreasonably refused an offer of suitable employment, pp. 105–108, below.
17 *CU 96/48; R(U) 14/55; R(U) 20/64(T).*
18 *R(U) 4/73.*
19 *R(U) 20/64(T); R(U) 4/70.*
20 *R(U) 19/52:* the decision must be read in the light of SI 1974/2010, reg 8, which provides that for the purposes of the disqualification provisions the test for married women 'shall be determined on the same basis as that applicable to a single woman, but not so as to exclude such consideration of the responsibilities arising from her marriage as is reasonable in the circumstances of the case'.
1 *R(U) 6/59.*
2 *R(U) 25/52.*
3 *UD 5287.*
4 *R(U) 33/51; R 3/65 (UB).* Contrast *R(U) 18/57:* the Commissioner held that such steps were not necessary where the *employer* issued an ultimatum to do additional work, or withdraw.
5 SSA 1975, s.20(3A).

be read as if the wording was 'shall be deemed not to have left . . .'.[6] The requirement that the claimant must previously have volunteered or agreed to the dismissal suggests that 'dismissal' should be given a broad interpretation, analogous to that used in connection with the misconduct disqualification.[7] In contrast, the statutory definition of 'by reason of redundancy' referred to is somewhat circumscribed, covering only cases where:

> the dismissal is attributable wholly or mainly to (a) the fact that [the] employer has ceased, or intends to cease, to carry on [the] business in the place where the employee was . . . employed, or (b) the fact that the requirements of that business for employees to carry out work of a particular kind, or for employees to carry out work of a particular kind in the place where he was so employed, have ceased or diminished or are expected to cease or diminish.[8]

C Unreasonable refusal of suitable offer

The third ground for disqualification directed against voluntary unemployment comprises a number of variations on the same theme: the claimant unreasonably refuses an offer or fails to take the appropriate steps to obtain employment which is suitable for him. Of course, this complements the condition that the claimant is available for suitable employment,[9] and there is inevitably some overlap between the two areas of law[10] – most obviously on the question whether the restrictions the claimant places on his availability are reasonable. But there is an important difference. The availability test is a *general* one: it is concerned with the claimant's attitude to the labour market. The grounds for disqualification to be considered in the section are concerned with the claimant's refusal or failure to follow a *particular* course of conduct, or to accept a *particular* offer of employment.[11]

There are, in fact, four different grounds of disqualification which fall under the general heading of refusal of suitable employment:

(a) refusal or failure to apply for a suitable situation, or refusal to accept that situation when offered;
(b) neglect to take advantage of a reasonable opportunity of suitable employment;
(c) refusal or failure to carry out official recommendations;
(d) refusal or failure to take advantage of a reasonable opportunity of training approved by the Secretary of State.

---

6 Cf p.106, below for a similar problem.
7 P.98, above; and hence not the narrower interpretation applied to 'dismissal' when used in employment protection legislation which excludes cases of termination by mutual consent: *Birch v University of Liverpool* [1985] ICR 470, [1985] IRLR 165.
8 Employment Protection (Consolidation) Act 1978, s.81(2). For these purposes, the business of 'associated employers' is treated as the same business as that of the principal employer: ibid. On these provisions, see Hepple and O'Higgins *Encyclopedia of Labour Relations Law* §2-1888.
9 Pp. 92–96 above. The disqualification provisions were introduced (UIA 1930, s.4) because failure to satisfy the availability condition entailed disentitlement, a less flexible sanction than disqualification: see Report of the Committee on Procedure and Evidence for Determination of Claims for Unemployment Insurance Benefit (1929, Cmd 3415) paras 43–44.
10 See e.g. *R(U) 2/59*.
11 For policy discussion, see Layard *How to Beat Unemployment* (1986) pp. 50–52.

i Refusal of suitable employment

The most widely used, and most frequently contested, of the four grounds arises where

> after a situation in any suitable employment has been properly notified to him as vacant or about to become vacant, he has without good cause refused or failed to apply for that situation or refused to accept that situation when offered to him.[12]

a *Onus of proof*

The burden is first on the adjudication officer to show that a situation, which is prima facie suitable, has been offered or notified to the claimant. It is then for the latter to prove either that employment was not suitable or that he had good cause for refusing it, or failing to apply for it.[13]

b *Notification and refusal*

'Properly notified' in the subsection connotes a communication not only from the Manpower Services Commission or local education authority but also from some other recognised agency, or indeed from an employer seeking to fill a vacancy.[14] The claimant cannot complain that the information provided was insufficiently detailed. So long as the broad nature of the situation is clear, it is his duty to find out further particulars.[15] 'Refusal', too, has been widely construed. An explicit rejection of the offer is unnecessary: it is sufficient if the claimant's conduct was such as positively to discourage the employer from offering him the situation.[16]

c *Suitability of employment*

The real problem in this area is to decide what employment is 'suitable'. The Act does not define the concept, but some guidance is supplied by section 20(4), which provides that

> employment shall not be deemed to be employment suitable in the case of any person if it is either—
> (a) employment in a situation vacant in consequence of a stoppage of work due to a trade dispute; or
> (b) employment in his usual occupation in the district where he was last ordinarily employed at a rate of remuneration lower, or on conditions less favourable, than those which he might reasonably have expected to obtain having regard to those which he habitually obtained in his usual occupation in that district, or would have obtained had he continued to be so employed; or
> (c) employment in his usual occupation in any other district at a rate of remuneration lower, or on conditions less favourable, than those generally observed in that district by agreement between associations of employers and of employees or, failing any such agreement, than those generally recognised in that district by good employers;
> but, after the lapse of such an interval from the date on which he becomes unemployed as in the circumstances of the case is reasonable, employment shall not be deemed to be unsuitable by reason only that it is employment of a kind other than employment in his usual occupation if it is employment at a rate of remuneration not lower, and on conditions not less favourable, than those

---

12 SSA 1975, s.20(1)(b).
13 *R(U) 26/52.*
14 SSA 1975, s.20(5)(a).
15 *R(U) 32/52.*
16 *R(U) 28/55* (claimant presented himself for interview with the prospective employer in a dirty and unshaven state).

generally observed by agreement between associations of employers and of employees or, failing any such agreement, than those generally recognised by good employers.

The provision in section 20(4)(a) was designed to prevent employers from using the threat of disqualification to force individuals to be employed as 'blacking labour'. It has not caused any difficulty, and consistently with its purpose it has been held not to extend to a situation in which a man, himself laid off as a result of a trade dispute, is offered work by another employer.[17] As regards the remainder of the subsection, the intention of the draftsman seems to have been to prescribe two different standards of 'suitability'. During the first period of unemployment, the claimant should be entitled to refuse employment which was not in his usual occupation, and on terms less favourable than he would have enjoyed if he had continued in his former job, or, if in another district, than were generally recognised in the trade. But after the lapse of a reasonable time, he should be less optimistic in his search for work and be prepared to accept work in a different occupation, though on conditions generally prevailing in that trade.

If the parliamentary spokesmen are to be believed,[18] this was indeed the general intention, but the specific provisions are more cautiously worded. Conditions (b) and (c) only apply if the claimant is offered employment in his *usual* occupation, and the import of the subsection is that if the terms offered are less favourable than he might reasonably expect, the situation is not necessarily to be regarded as suitable. This falls short of the apparent intention of the provision in two major respects: first, it has no bearing on the suitability of an offer of employment in a different occupation; secondly, offers on terms less favourable may still, if regard is had to concomitant circumstances, be regarded as suitable. Because the subsection involves a *negative* proposition, that the 'employment shall not be deemed to be . . . suitable' if conditions (a), (b) or (c) are satisfied, it leaves open the possibility that notwithstanding the fulfilment of any one of those conditions, an employment *may* be found to be suitable if regard is had to other circumstances. However, the Chief Commissioner has construed the subsection as if it commenced 'employment *shall* be deemed to be *unsuitable* . . .'.[19] He has thus concluded that if the claimant succeeds in bringing his case within (b) or (c) the authorities cannot (whatever the concomitant circumstances) characterise the employment as suitable. This interpretation is consistent both with common sense and with the apparent object of the provision, but is not justified by its wording.

The proviso for the subsection (beginning 'but after the lapse of such an interval . . .') does accord with the stated intention of prescribing a less exacting standard of suitability than that enshrined in the first half of section 20(4). Literally construed, it provides that after a reasonable lapse of time, an employment will not necessarily be unsuitable merely because it involves a different occupation, though it may be so treated on consideration of other circumstances. This would seem to be both workable and just, but the Chief Commissioner, to achieve consistency with his unorthodox interpretation of the first part of section 20(4), has been forced to give it a strange and

17 *R(U) 1/52.*
18 Mr S Buxton, Pres. Bd. of Trade, introducing the Amendment to NI Bill 1911, cl 62, on which the current provision is based: 31 HC Official Report (5th series) cols 1074–1077.
19 *R(U) 5/68*, R G Micklethwait.

restricted meaning. Notwithstanding the disjunctive 'but', he construes it as providing a solution for a different factual hypothesis, rather than qualifying the first half of section 20(4).[20] If the *only* reason for holding the employment to be unsuitable is that it is different from the claimant's usual occupation, the authorities, if the other conditions are satisfied, are precluded from finding that it is unsuitable. Such a hypothetical situation would be rare indeed, and on the Chief Commissioner's own admission practically robs the provision of any effect. Again his reading involves a misconstruction of the words actually used. This time he has read 'shall not be deemed to be unsuitable' as being 'shall be deemed to be suitable'.

It remains to consider the practical questions arising from the subsection. What is a man's 'usual occupation' is, of course, a question of fact. On the one hand, he must have followed it for some substantial time.[1] On the other hand, what was his usual occupation may have lapsed through continuous unemployment, disability or a change of locality.[2] To determine whether the rate of remuneration or the conditions of employment are 'habitually observed' or 'generally observed in that district' regard is to be had to such collective agreements as have been made. These may however be inconclusive. So in one case, it was held that the claimant was not entitled to refuse an offer on the ground that no tea-break was provided, when some employers in the area permitted a tea-break and others did not.[3] However, in Northern Ireland, a Tribunal of Commissioners faced with an analogous dichotomy (two rates of pay) focused on the reference in the subsection to 'good' employers, and held that the claimant was entitled to hold out for the higher rate.[4]

Subject to the Chief Commissioner's doubtful ruling that in some circumstances the authorities are *bound* to hold an offer suitable or unsuitable, the statutory provisions are not conclusive on the suitability question and regard must be had to other factors. For example, it would be unfair to regard as conclusive the fact that the terms on which the claimant was offered employment in his usual occupation were as favourable as those he enjoyed in his former employment, if the long-term prospects in the situation offered were particularly dim.[5] Further, a claimant may sometimes legitimately claim that to accept an offer of employment of a lower status than that to which he was accustomed would prejudice his future chances of returning to his former occupation.[6] Of course, it will always be sufficient for him to show that the employment offered was beyond his abilities.[7] A typical ground for refusal is that the situation offered was incompatible with the claimant's domestic responsibilities.[8] Mere inconvenience for the family is not sufficient: a claimant must be prepared to make reasonable adjustments to his or her personal

20 Ibid, at para 13.
 1 *UD 7678* suggests that this should normally be three years, but there is no reported decision on the point under modern legislation, and apparently the DHSS have regard to periods of shorter duration: cf the cases on equivalent points under the industrial injury scheme: p.295, below.
 2 *R(U) 15/62.*
 3 *R(U) 9/64.*
 4 *R 16/60 (UB).*
 5 Thus a claimant on short-time is justified in refusing an offer of full-time work in a similar occupation with another firm, if the long-term prospects in that other firm are no better: *R(U) 34/56.* See also *R(U) 10/61.*
 6 Accepted in *R 21/60 (UB),* but not in *R(U) 35/52* where the offer was only for two weeks employment.
 7 *R (U) 26/52*; *R(U) 32/52.*
 8 For married women, see the rule cited at n.20, p.103, above.

circumstances.[9] But the case is different where there are children or other dependent relatives whose needs must be catered for.[10]

d *Without good cause*

The claimant may escape disqualification if the refusal or failure was with 'good cause'. In fact, this adds little to the substantive requirements of the subsection, for if there is good cause to refuse an offer of employment, it will not be an offer of 'suitable employment'. 'Suitability' and 'without good cause' are alternative formulations of the same principle, and the Commissioner has not distinguished between them.[11]

ii Neglect to avail himself of reasonable opportunity of suitable employment

The ground for disqualification considered above arises only when the claimant has failed to apply for a situation, or has refused an offer which was made to him. Of the remaining grounds, the first two are also based on the concept of 'suitable employment' but are not limited to any specific vacancy and therefore are broader in scope. A person may be disqualified if

> he has neglected to avail himself of a reasonable opportunity of suitable employment.[12]

Notwithstanding (or perhaps because of) the breadth of this provision, it is apparently seldom invoked by the authorities[13] and as a result there is little by way of guidance on its meaning.[14] It has been employed in the exceptional situation when a claimant so behaves at or before an interview that he effectively deters a prospective employer from offering him a vacancy.[15] Unlike the other disqualification provisions relating to refusal of suitable employment there is here no defence of 'good cause'. But this is not significant. As seen above, there is, in principle, no distinction between a defence based on good cause, and another claiming that the employment in question was 'unsuitable'. So here the factors which would have been relevant to the finding of good cause are the same as those considered in determining whether the employment was 'suitable' or the opportunity not taken was 'reasonable'.[16]

iii Failure to carry out official recommendations

The claimant will be disqualified if

> he has without good cause refused or failed to carry out any official recommendations given to him with a view to assisting him to find suitable employment, being recommendations which were reasonable having regard to his circumstances and to the means of obtaining that employment usually adopted in the district in which he resides.[17]

---

9 *12/52 (UB)*.

10 E.g. *R(U) 20/60*. NB the existence of such circumstances may render the claimant's prospects of finding employment remote and therefore exclude him from benefit on the ground of unavailability: p.94, above.

11 See e.g. *R(U) 20/60*. According to Slade LJ in *Crewe v Social Security Comr* [1982] 2 All ER 745 at 751, 'without good cause' perhaps means no more than 'without reasonable cause' and, as such, should be distinguished from 'without just cause', which imposes a heavier burden on those seeking to avoid disqualification for 'voluntary leaving': p.102, above.

12 SSA 1975, s.20(1)(c).

13 Private communication from DHSS.

14 For its use under the UIAs, see esp. *UD 11734/34*.

15 *R(U) 28/55*.

16 *R(U) 5/71*, H A Shewan, Comr.

17 SSA 1975, s.20(1)(d).

'Official recommendations' for this purpose are defined as 'recommendations in writing made by an officer of the Manpower Services Commission, a local education authority, or the Secretary of State'.[18]

iv Failure to avail himself of reasonable opportunity of training
Finally, the Act disqualifies a claimant who

> has without good cause refused or failed to avail himself of a reasonable opportunity of receiving training approved by the Secretary of State in his case for the purpose of becoming or keeping fit for entry into, or return to, regular employment.[19]

This used to be treated as merely one instance of a failure to carry out written directions[20] but since 1946 has constituted a separate provision. As a ground for disqualification, it has increased in importance as the government has placed greater emphasis on training, especially for younger claimants.[1] The training scheme in question does not have to be administered by the Department of Employment, but it has to be approved by the Secretary of State for the particular claimant. His determination that the training is suitable is conclusive and cannot be reviewed by the adjudicating authorities.[2] But it is still open to the claimant to contend that he had good cause for the refusal or failure;[3] or that the opportunity given to him was not, in the circumstances, 'reasonable'.

D Period of disqualification

The Conservative government's concern to reduce the level of voluntary unemployment and more generally to discourage abuse of social security provision has led to radical changes in the duration of disqualification. The traditional maximum period, dating from the 1911 Act,[4] was six weeks. The Social Security Act 1986 extended the maximum period to 13 weeks and, at the same time, enabled the Secretary of State to make further amendments to the period by an order to that effect.[5] Such an order was issued in 1988, extending the maximum period to 26 weeks.[6] These reforms must be set alongside a complementary measure[7] which provides that a day of disqualification is not to be treated as a day of entitlement for the purpose of determining a claimant's maximum entitlement to unemployment benefit – 312 days of a period of interruption of employment.[8] Prior to this measure, the effect of the disqualification, at any rate for the long-term unemployed, was only to delay entitlement to unemployment benefit; the deduction of the period of disqualification from the 312 days maximum gives rise to a more substantial penalty.

18 Ibid, s.20(5)(b).
19 Ibid, s.20(1)(e).
20 E.g. *UD 6424/36*.
 1 Cf p.419, below.
 2 *2/57 (UB)*.
 3 See e.g. *R 10/60 (UB)*.
 4 NIA 1911, s.87(2), which, however, imposed a mandatory period of six weeks. Following UIA 1920, s.8(2), the period became discretionary, subject to the statutory maximum.
 5 SSA 1986, s.43(2)–(3).
 6 SI 1988/487.
 7 Ibid, made under SSA 1986, s.18(4), as amended.
 8 See p.125, below.

The severity of the sanction which now may be imposed contrasts sharply with the previous law and may result in hardship for the claimant, particularly when account is taken of consequential reductions in income support entitlement.[9] It remains to be seen whether changes will occur in the way in which the adjudicating authorities (adjudication officer, appeal tribunal, Commissioner) exercise their discretion to impose a period shorter than the maximum. The relevant principle was formulated by a Tribunal of Commissioners in 1974. Rejecting a previously expressed view that the maximum period should be imposed unless special circumstances dictated otherwise,[10] they considered that

> the correct approach is to adhere firmly to the statutory language, regarding each case as one in which a sensible discretion has to be exercised in such manner as the justice of the case requires.[11]

Given the more punitive consequences which now attach to disqualification, as the Commissioner, J.G. Monroe, observed in a recent case, it is 'essential that adjudication officers should abandon their old habit of virtually automatically imposing the maximum'.[12] They should reveal, on the face of the decision, active consideration of the discretion;[13] a failure to do so may constitute an error of law.[14] The situations which, in the past, have been regarded as justifying a period of disqualification less than the maximum seem to fall within three main categories:

(1) where the maximum causes hardship, because of the claimant's domestic circumstances[15] or because he has already been subject to a serious sanction;[16]
(2) where he has come close to justifying his loss of employment (through just or good cause) but has just failed;[17]
(3) where the insurance fund is already sufficiently protected (e.g. because the claimant is no longer unemployed).[18]

Where the ground for disqualification is misconduct or leaving voluntarily the period will run, in general, from the date of discharge:[19] in other cases it will commence on the date when the claimant refused an offer, or failed to take an appropriate step.

Part 6   Trade disputes disqualification

A   Introduction

With the remaining ground for disqualification, we enter into a highly controversial area. The scheme must here grapple with problems of industrial

---

9 Pp. 453–455, below.
10 *R(U) 17/54.*
11 *R(U) 8/74(T)* para 20.
12 *R(U) 4/87* para 11.
13 *R(U) 3/79* para 5.
14 *R(U) 4/87.*
15 *R(U) 27/52.*
16 *R(U) 1/71.*
17 *R(U) 35/52; R(U) 20/64(T).*
18 E.g. *R(U) 20/64(T); R(U) 10/71.*
19 *CU 155/50.* If, however, the claimant continues to receive remuneration (e.g. by payment in lieu of notice) it will run from the date when it is no longer payable: *R(U) 35/52.*

relations,[20] and, needless to say, political opinions are well to the fore in discussions of the substantive law. The general position is that unemployment resulting directly from trade disputes in which the claimant was 'involved' should not give him a title to benefit. There is a widespread assumption that such a limitation must exist, and the principle finds a place in almost every system of unemployment insurance.[1] But the theoretical or policy justifications of the principle are not so obvious as may appear and require some consideration.[2]

In the first place, it is said that this is but another instance of *voluntary* unemployment (like misconduct, leaving, refusal, etc.), and, as such, does not come within the risk of unemployment for which the insurance fund was established. However, at least by itself, this is not a complete justification, for if applied consistently, it would compel the law to distinguish between *strikes* and *lockouts*, and, in general,[3] the distinction is irrelevant. Moreover, the other grounds of disqualification based on voluntary unemployment recognise that in certain circumstances the leaving or refusal of employment may be excused on grounds of 'just' or 'good cause'. Here there are no such qualifications. There is, indeed, a fundamental rule that the authorities should not enter into the merits of the dispute.

Secondly, resort is had to the idea of industrial neutrality:

> the National Insurance Fund, to which both employers and employees contribute, should not become involved in industrial disputes . . . the scheme should not be open to the criticism that it is supporting one side or the other.[4]

While this is, on the face of it, an appealing argument, it leaves open the question as to what constitutes 'neutrality'. It may not be neutral for payments to be made to strikers (and, as will be seen, the same may be said of income support which is paid to the families of strikers[5]), but it is arguable that it is equally not neutral if workers with a legitimate grievance are deterred from taking industrial action because of the refusal to pay benefit.

The neutrality argument appears often to be a gloss on the less compromising stance taken by others, that on economic and political grounds, contributors to the fund should not financially support those who withdraw their labour, particularly as this may encourage industrial stoppages, and therefore losses in productivity.[6] Finally, removal of the disqualification would arouse the hostility of those contributors who are not able effectively to express their grievances by withdrawing their labour. Whether or not such arguments are found acceptable depends, in the last resort, on political attitudes.[7]

Section 19(1) of the Social Security Act 1975, as amended, imposes disqualification on two categories of unemployed claimants:

20 This was the one area of unemployment insurance law to be considered in detail by the Royal Commission on Trade Unions and Employers Associations (the Donovan Commission). See its Report (1968, Cmnd 3623), paras 953–993.
1 Schindler 38 Col LR 858; Hickling *Labour Disputes and Unemployment Insurance in Canada and England* (1975).
2 Cf Lesser 55 Yale LJ 167; Shamir 17 U of Chi LR 294; 2nd Memo of Ministry of Social Security to Royal Commission, Minutes of Evidence, pp. 2310–2318; Gennard *Financing Strikers* (1977). See also on income support, pp. 455–458, below.
3 SSA 1975, s.19(1)(b), introduced by SSA 1986, s.44, does apply the distinction. Cf p.118, below.
4 Memo n.2, above at p.2310.
5 P.457, below.
6 Conservative Political Centre *Financing Strikers* (1974).
7 Cf Ralph Gibson LJ in *Cartlidge v Chief Adjudication Officer* [1986] QB 360 at 376.

(a) an employed earner who has lost employment as an employed earner by reason of a stoppage of work due to a trade dispute at his place of employment . . . unless he proves that he is not directly interested in the dispute
   and
(b) an employed earner who has withdrawn his labour in furtherance of a trade dispute but does not fall within paragraph (a) above. . . .

B Loss of employment due to stoppage of work

The onus is on the adjudication officer[8] to prove that (i) there was a trade dispute; (ii) it was at the claimant's place of employment; (iii) it resulted in a stoppage; (iv) the claimant lost employment as a result of that stoppage. To avoid disqualification, it is then for the claimant to show that (v) he was not directly interested in the dispute.[9] The discussion is divided accordingly.

i Trade dispute
This is statutorily defined as

> any dispute between employers and employees, or between employees and employees, which is connected with the employment or non-employment or the terms of employment or the conditions of employment of any persons, whether employees in the employment of the employer with whom the dispute arises, or not.[10]

This is an interesting example of a statutory definition being lifted from another context in which it served a completely different purpose. It was based on that in the Trade Disputes Act 1906[11] whose object was to create an *immunity* from certain actions in tort.[12] It is not surprising, therefore, that the definition has given rise to some strange decisions. No one would question the application of the term 'trade dispute' to strikes (official or unofficial),[13] lockouts,[14] and demarcation disputes,[15] at least where the dispute arose between a group of employees and their employer or another group of employees.[16] But in *R(U) 1/74*

> in pursuance of a national pay claim, building labourers withdrew their labour on a number of building sites. The site on which C worked was unaffected until pickets from a nearby site came and persuaded C and his fellow employees not to work. R S Lazarus, Commissioner, relying on certain decisions concerned with common law immunities,[17] held that there was a trade dispute between C's employer and the pickets who arrived from other sites, notwithstanding that he was not *their* employer.

Even more doubtful was the decision in *R(U) 2/53*.

> C was prevented from working by the unlawful acts of pickets who threatened him with violence. It was held that C lost his employment as a result of the trade dispute between himself and the pickets!

8 *R(U) 17/52(T)*
9 Per Lord Brandon, *Presho v Department of Health and Social Security* [1984] AC 310 at 315.
10 SSA 1975, s.19(2)(b).
11 S.5(3).
12 See the historical survey in *R(U) 1/74*, paras 12–15, R S Lazarus, Comr.
13 *R(U) 5/59*.
14 *R(U) 17/52(T)*.
15 *R(U) 14/64*.
16 The claimant need not himself be a party to the dispute: *R(U) 3/69*.
17 E.g. *Huntley v Thornton* [1957] 1 All ER 234, [1957] 1 WLR 321.

The necessary connection between the dispute and 'the employment or non-employment or the terms of employment or the conditions of employment' has caused some difficulty.[17a] In *R(U) 26/59* it was held that a dispute as to whether an employee was entitled to an income tax rebate under his contract of employment was not a trade dispute, since it was concerned with the existence of a term, not with whether there *should* be such a term. The distinction is an elusive one and was ignored by the Commissioner in a later case.[18]

Apart from a short period during the 1920s when the claimant could escape disqualification if he could show that the stoppage was due to the employer contravening an agreement,[19] the tradition has been that the authorities should not attempt to adjudicate on the merits of the dispute,[20] and so it is of no avail to claim that there was 'just cause' for the withdrawal of labour. There are persuasive arguments for this approach: it would be very difficult for adjudication officers to reach an objective decision on the merits of a particular dispute, and it would be very costly in terms of time and money.[1] But as a consequence it may penalise employees who have undisputedly legitimate grounds for grievance. So, in one case, a disqualification was imposed on those who had been dismissed by an employer when they had objected to a reduction in wages.[2] The Donovan Commission assumed that the same result would ensue where the substance of the dispute was that the employer had been in breach of contract,[3] and more recently the Divisional Court held that complaints that the employer was in contravention of the health and safety legislation may quite properly be characterised as a 'trade dispute'.[4]

It is not entirely clear when a difference of opinion becomes a dispute but 'a question . . . must reach a certain stage of contention before it may properly be termed a dispute'.[5] While it will usually end by some form of agreement, it will no longer operate to disqualify from benefit if it results in one party totally severing relations with the other.[6]

ii Place of employment

The general rule does not require that the claimant himself be involved in the trade dispute. Subject to the exception on lack of direct interest considered below,[7] it is sufficient if the dispute was located at his place of employment. The traditional justification for what is effectively a presumption of participation or interest in the dispute is that there is 'a common bond of mutual interest and loyalty . . . between workers at one place of employment which enables them to be distinguished from other workers.'[8] In the days of

17a This phrase covers disputes as to the manner in which the employment is carried out: *R(U) 5/87.*

18 *R(U) 3/71*, J S Watson, Comr, and see *Calvert* p.157.

19 UIA (No 2) 1924, s.4(1). It was repealed by UIA 1927, s.6. See generally Gennard n.2, above, pp. 16–19.

20 Sir J Simon Sol. Gen., introducing the trade disputes clause in the 1911 Bill, 31 HC Official Report (5th series), col 1729; Report of the Committee on Unemployment Insurance (Blanesborough Committee) (1927); Donovan Commission Report, n.20, p.111 above, para 994.

1 Ibid.

2 *R(U) 27/56.*

3 (1968, Cmnd 3623), para 994.

4 *R v National Insurance Comr, ex parte Thompson* (1977), published as Appendix to *R(U) 5/77.*

5 *R(U) 21/59*, para 6.

6 *R(U) 17/52.*

7 Pp. 116–118, below.

8 Memo of Ministry of Social Security to Royal Commission, Minutes of Evidence, p.2312.

the small family firm this rationalisation may have been attractive, but in the industrial conditions prevailing today, its appeal is less obvious.

If, in theory, the identification of the dispute with the place of employment is not easy to justify, in practice the application of the test is even more elusive. Section 19(2)(a) of the Social Security Act 1975 defines a claimant's place of employment as 'the factory, workshop, farm or other premises or place at which he was employed . . .'. This still leaves open what is to be considered as 'other premises or place'. It is clear that each case must be decided on its facts, and that some fairly arbitrary lines must be drawn. In one case, it was held that 'the place of employment' of someone loading ships was the whole of the docks,[9] while in another the place of employment of a man working in an engineering shop attached to a group of collieries, but physically separated from them, was not the colliery.[10] To cope with this, section 19(2)(a) continues:

> where separate branches of work which are commonly carried on as separate businesses in separate premises or at separate places are in any case carried on in separate departments on the same premises or at the same place, each of these departments shall . . . be deemed to be a separate factory or workshop or farm or separate premises or a separate place, as the case may be.

The onus of proving certain premises are the claimant's place of employment (the first part of section 19(2)(a)) is on the adjudication officer. The onus of proving that they constitute a separate business (the second part of section 19(2)(a)) is on the claimant.[11] It is a formidable obstacle, for he must satisfy the authorities (i) that there are 'separate branches' of work at his place of employment; and (ii) that typically elsewhere such branches are carried on as 'separate businesses in separate premises or at a separate place', and (iii) that at his place of employment the branches are carried on 'in separate departments'. He will not succeed on (i) if the branch of work in question is 'a step in an integrated process of production'.[12] As regards (ii), much will depend on evidence of the practices of other firms that the claimant is able to adduce.[13] The concepts of 'branches', 'businesses' and 'departments' are none of them terms of art, and all involve questions of degree. Determination by the authorities may be based on somewhat arbitrary classifications of industrial processes, totally unrelated to the policy behind the rule which is based on the alleged mutual interest and loyalty of those working on the same enterprise. Suggestions to modify the provision have, however, as yet gone unheeded.[14]

iii Stoppage due to trade dispute

There may be disqualification only where there has been a cessation of work by a significant number of employees[15] arising from an unwillingness on their

---

9 *R(U) 4/58*; cf *UD 5568* where it was held that a person employed on a barge was not employed in the same place as the dockers at the dock where the barge happened to be.
10 *UD 5145/26.*
11 *R(U) 1/70*, R G Micklethwait, Chief Comr.
12 *R(U) 4/62*, para 7.
13 Ibid, and see: *R(U) 6/51*; *R(U) 24/57*; *R(U) 1/70.*
14 The Donovan Commission rejected, on the 'community of interest' argument, the proposal of the CBI that the definition of 'place of employment' should be extended; and, on the grounds that it would encourage selective strikes, that of the TUC that it should be narrowed: n.3, above, at paras 970–972.
15 *R(U) 7/58.* 'A situation in which operations are being stopped or hindered otherwise than to a negligible extent': *R(U) 1/87* para 7, J J Skinner, Comr.

part to work or from a refusal by the employer to provide work until the dispute is settled.[16] The stoppage must constitute a move, by either side, in the contest, the intention of both parties being eventually to resume normal working.[17] If an employer or the whole group of employees decide categorically that they do not wish the employment relationship to continue on *any* terms, the cessation of work no longer forms part of the trade dispute.[18] The question is then whether persons unemployed as a result should be disqualified on the grounds either of voluntarily leaving or of misconduct. To determine whether an allegedly absolute discharge or withdrawal was intended to be taken seriously may obviously create an acute problem of interpretation for the authorities. A series of Commissioners' decisions shows that many such statements, though formulated in the most categorical terms, are not to be taken at their face value.[19]

The stoppage of work must be 'due to' the trade dispute, but the nature of the causal link involved has given rise to some difficulty where it has been impracticable or impossible to restart work immediately after the settlement of the dispute. For example, in *R v Chief National Insurance Comr, ex parte Dawber*,[20]

> the stoppage had created a risk of damage to the industrial plant. Notwithstanding attempts by the employer to forestall damage, it did in fact occur, and he laid off all employees while repairs were carried out. Both the Chief Commissioner and the Divisional Court held that the employees were disqualified from benefit during the lay-off, as the continued stoppage was due to the original dispute.

For the requisite causal connection to exist, it did not have to be shown that the continuance of the stoppage was an 'inevitable' consequence of the dispute; it is sufficient if it was 'reasonably foreseeable'.[1] Moreover, the fact that the employer might not have adopted the most appropriate method of forestalling damage to the plant did not break the chain of causation. It may have been an error of judgment but it was

> something done not unreasonable or otherwise objectionable. And . . . it does not lie in the mouth of those who put the employers in a position of emergency where they had to take a decision to say that, because that was the wrong decision, it breaks the chain of causation.[2]

iv Loss of employment by reason of stoppage
The claimant must have lost his employment 'by reason of the stoppage' which was itself due to the trade dispute. If the loss of employment results from a fresh, supervening cause, such as the closure of the employer's business when that closure is attributable not to the trade dispute but to other financial pressures, there is no disqualification from benefit.[3] The principles determining this causal relationship should, *mutatis mutandis*, be those described in the previous paragraph. The motives or attitudes of those losing

---

16 *R(U) 19/51.*
17 *R(U) 17/52; R(U) 11/63; R(U) 1/87.*
18 *R(U) 1/65.*
19 *R(U) 17/52; R(U) 19/53; R(U) 36/53; R(U) 27/56; R(U) 11/63; R(U) 1/65.*
20 (1980), published as Appendix to *R(U) 9/80.*
 1 Ibid, at para 10, J G Monroe, Comr; per Forbes J, Appendix, p.10. See also *R(U) 19/51*, para 11.
 2 Per Forbes J, Appendix to *R(U) 9/80*, p.8.
 3 *R(U) 15/80*, R J A Temple, Chief Comr. The question whether, and when, a particular business has closed down is not easy to determine. For guidance, see ibid, at para 17.

employment are irrelevant: 'if enough people stay away for a stoppage of work to result then . . . all those who are caused to lose employment by the event, whether by their own choice or by the actions of others taking part in the event, must be regarded as losing employment by reason of the stoppage'.[4]

Perhaps because of a fear that some unworthy claimants should not be allowed to succeed, the Commissioners have been prepared to find that the causal test has been satisfied in situations where such a result was less than obvious. First, if the period of unemployment begins before the stoppage takes place, it has been held that the stoppage may still have caused the loss of employment, since the claimant may have anticipated what was going to happen and may have attempted to avoid disqualification by this means.[5] Indeed, there was, at one time, a presumption that the employment was lost by reason of the stoppage if the claimant was discharged within 12 working days of the beginning of the stoppage;[6] a harsh approach, the validity of which has been doubted in the most recent Commissioner's decision on the point[7] and which is, apparently, rarely used in practice.[8] Secondly, the authorities have not taken the reference to 'loss' of employment entirely literally. The claimant need not have been employed on the day immediately prior to the date of unemployment in question.[9] The effect of the stoppage may have been to obstruct an employer's intention to re-engage a workman who had been off work for a period.[10]

Thirdly, it has been consistently held that the disqualification cannot be avoided by an allegation that a claimant, losing his employment during a stoppage, would *in any event* have been unemployed for part or all of that period for reasons of redundancy or short-time.[11] In 1985, the Court of Appeal upheld this approach and, albeit with some reluctance, considered it appropriate in a case where the claimant had resumed the employment before it was terminated on grounds of redundancy, rejecting the argument that the resumption had broken the chain of causation between the loss of employment and the stoppage.[12] As will be seen, legislative amendments in 1986 have reversed this decision: disqualification now ceases if either the claimant bona fide resumes the employment and subsequently leaves for reason other than the trade dispute or the employment is terminated by reasons of 'redundancy'.[13] However, 'redundancy' is, for this purpose, given a narrow meaning and the provision does not extend to those claiming that, but for the stoppage, they would have been 'laid-off' or subject to short-time working. It follows that the interpretation upheld by the Court of Appeal continues to apply to some cases.

v Proviso: not directly interested in dispute

The breadth of the general rule is evident. There may be a stoppage at the claimant's place of employment with which his connection is remote and yet

4 Per Ralph Gibson LJ, *Cartlidge v Chief Adjudication Officer* [1986] QB 360 at 369.
5 *R(U) 30/55*.
6 *R(U) 20/57(T)*; *R(U) 31/57*. The rule was originally formulated in *UD 18901/31*.
7 Per H A Shewan, Comr, *R(U) 6/71* para 8.
8 Private communication from DHSS.
9 *R(U) 12/72(T)*, para 12 and *R(U) 13/72*.
10 E.g. *R(U) 19/56*.
11 *R(U) 11/52*; *R(U) 32/55*; *R(U) 17/56*; *R(U) 29/59*; *R(U) 12/61*; all affirmed in *R(U) 12/72(T)*.
12 *Cartlidge v Chief Adjudication Officer*, n.4, above.
13 SSA 1975, s.19(1A), inserted by SSA 1986, s.44, pp. 119–120 below.

his benefit is lost. Since 1924 there has existed an escape clause to provide relief for some so affected, but its content has undergone several fundamental changes. Originally, the claimant had to show that he was neither participating in, financing, or directly interested in the dispute, nor belonged to a grade or class the members of which were participating in, financing or directly interested in the dispute.[14] The provision was, however, soon perceived to give rise to inequities. In the general strike of 1926 members of a class of colliery workers throughout the country were disqualified because other members of the same class in one *particular* district belonged to a union which was financing the dispute. A committee reporting in 1927 doubted whether an entirely satisfactory form of wording could ever be found but recommended that the 'grade or class' should be specifically linked to the claimant's place of employment.[15] This was implemented in 1927,[16] but for many years thereafter the TUC continued to express dissatisfaction, and eventually in 1965 the matter was specifically referred to the Royal Commission on Trade Unions and Employer's Associations.[17] The Commission was highly critical of the law then prevailing. In the first place, it rejected the principle that an individual should be 'involved' in a dispute merely because he was 'financing' it, which had consistently been held to include membership of a union or association which was financially supporting those involved in the dispute. Apart from common membership, the individual might have no other interest in the dispute.[18] Secondly, it recommended abolition of the 'grade or class' limb, regarding as unreliable the traditional justification that there was a 'community of interest' between workers caught by this provision.[19] The proposals of the Commission lay dormant until 1975 when they were implemented by the Employment Protection Act.[20] Finally, in 1986, the 'non participating' alternative was removed.[1] This last change is not, perhaps, a significant one: it is unlikely that a claimant who has been participating in a dispute will be able to show that he has not had a direct interest in it.

For the proviso to operate, then, the current position is that the claimant need only establish that 'he is not directly interested in the dispute'.[2] The phrase is not defined in the legislation but a decision of the House of Lords[3] has done much to clarify its operation. The proviso comes into play where the stoppage results from a dispute in which one group of employees are involved leads to loss of employment for others employed at the same place. In the words of Lord Brandon, for the latter to be disqualified on the ground that they are 'directly interested' in the dispute, two conditions must be satisfied.

> The first condition is that, whatever may be the outcome of the trade dispute, it will be applied by the common employers not only to the group of workers belonging to the one union participating in the dispute, but also to the other groups of workers belonging to the other unions concerned. The second condition is that this applica-

14 UIA (No 2) 1924, s.4(1). For the history see 1st Memo of Ministry of Social Security to Donovan Royal Commission: Minutes of Evidence, pp. 2298–2304.
15 Committee on Unemployment Insurance (1927), para 137.
16 UIA 1927, s.6.
17 1968, Cmnd 3623.
18 Ibid, at para 985.
19 Ibid, at paras 975–976.
20 S.111(1).
 1 SSA 1986, s.44.
 2 SSA 1975, s.19(1)(a).
 3 *Presho v Department of Health and Social Security* [1984] AC 310, [1984] 1 All ER 97.

tion of the outcome "across the board" . . . should come about automatically as a result of one or other of three things: first, a collective agreement which is legally binding; or, secondly, a collective agreement which is not legally binding; or, thirdly, established industrial custom at the place (or possibly places) of work concerned.[4]

The 'across the board' outcome is not necessarily confined to remuneration but may include anything relating to the terms and conditions of employment.[5] The fact that the dispute which caused the stoppage also involved another issue in which the claimant had no direct interest will not assist him, unless he can show that such other issue was *the* cause of the stoppage, in the sense that without that issue there would not in all probability have been that stoppage at that particular time.[6] It is not necessary that the claimant's remuneration or terms of employment should actually have changed as a result of the dispute[7] – of course, the outcome may be such that no concessions are won from the employer. On the other hand, the outcome must potentially affect the claimant and normally it cannot have this effect once the employment relationship is terminated. In such a case, the direct interest (if any) ends at the date of termination.[8]

C Withdrawal of labour

The alternative road to disqualification arises under section 19(1)(b) of the Social Security Act 1975:

> an employed earner who has withdrawn his labour in furtherance of a trade dispute . . . is disqualified for receiving unemployment benefit for any day on which his labour remains withdrawn.

This was introduced in 1986 to plug a gap left by section 19(1)(a). Disqualification under that provision can, of course, only arise if there has been a 'stoppage of work', which, as we have seen, must involve a significant number of employees,[9] and which must have resulted from a trade dispute at the claimant's place of employment. While the new ground for disqualification retains the requirement that there has been a trade dispute,[10] this need not have been at the place of employment. More importantly, by dispensing with the condition that there be a stoppage of work, the subsection catches those whose withdrawal of labour is personal or, at least, is not combined with industrial action by many others.

'Withdrawal of labour' is a new concept in social security law and is bound to give rise to difficult questions of interpretation. Traditionally, in the application of (what is now) section 19(1)(a), the authorities have not had to distinguish between cases of withdrawal of labour and of 'lockouts': it has been sufficient if the employment has been lost as a result of a stoppage of work whether that stoppage resulted, predominantly from action by the employer or the employees. For the purposes of section 19(1)(b), that distinc-

---

4 Ibid at 318. To similar effect, see Lord Emslie P in *Watt v Lord Advocate* 1979 SLT 137, 141; *R(U) 13/71* para 8; *R(U) 8/80* para 17. The view of the Court of Appeal in the *Presho* case ([1983] ICR 595) that there was a crucial distinction between being interested in a trade dispute (which alone would warrant disqualification) and being interested in its *outcome* was discredited. See, generally, Wilton [1984] JSWL 186.
5 *R(U) 5/79* para 12. Thus e.g. safety standards: *R(U) 3/71*; *R(U) 5/77*.
6 *Cartlidge v Chief Adjudication Officer* [1986] QB 360 at 372, per Ralph Gibson LJ.
7 *R(U) 5/59* para 13.
8 *R(U) 5/86(T)*; *R(U) 1/87*.
9 P.114, above.
10 On which, see p.112, above.

tion must now be made and in so doing it is not easy to see how the authorities will be able to avoid being drawn into a consideration of the merits of the dispute.

D Period of disqualification

Unlike the disqualifications for voluntary unemployment, no maximum period is stipulated for trade disputes: under section 19(1)(a), it lasts 'so long as the stoppage continues'; and under section 19(1)(b) it is imposed for each day of withdrawal of labour. In the case of the former provision, however, there are circumstances in which the disqualification will be terminated before the stoppage ceases. As has been seen, this will occur if the stoppage no longer forms part of the trade dispute,[11] or if the claimant's direct interest in the dispute ends because the relationship with the relevant employer has been terminated, thus allowing him to invoke the proviso.[12] In addition, there are three statutory grounds for bringing the disqualification to an end: where the claimant proves that during the stoppage

  (a) he has become bona fide employed elsewhere; or
  (b) his employment has been terminated by reason of redundancy within the meaning of section 81(2) of the Employment Protection (Consolidation) Act 1978; or
  (c) he has bona fide resumed employment with his employer but has subsequently left for a reason other than the trade dispute.[13]

i Bona fide employment elsewhere

Engagement in other employment normally removes the claimant from the ambit of the dispute. But this will not be the case if he takes a temporary job for a very short time solely to requalify for benefit. The onus is then on him to show that the new employment was 'bona fide'.[14] This means both that the employment was genuine and that it was taken up for an honest motive.[15] The mere fact that the employment was of short duration does not, by itself, justify an inference that the employment was not bona fide; but such an inference may be drawn where it is clear from the evidence that the claimant did not intend permanently to sever relations with his original employer.[16]

ii Redundancy

The remaining two statutory grounds were introduced in 1986 to deal with the injustices arising from the *Cartlidge* decision.[17] For the purposes of the first of these, the definition of 'redundancy' is the same as that adopted in the provision conferring relief from disqualification for voluntarily leaving and has been discussed in that context.[18]

iii Bona fide resumption of employment

The aim of this new provision is clear: an employee who breaks the link with the dispute by resuming work and then loses employment for reasons

11 *R(U) 1/65*; p.115, above.
12 *R(U) 5/86(T)*; *R(U) 1/87*.
13 SSA 1975, s.19(1A).
14 *R(U) 39/56*.
15 *R(U) 6/74*, H A Shewan, Comr.
16 Ibid, at para 10.
17 [1986] QB 360, p.116, above.
18 SSA 1975, s.20(3A), p.104, above.

unconnected with the dispute is not to be disqualified during the latter period of employment. 'Bona fide' carries the meaning attributed to it by the Commissioners in interpreting the first of the statutory grounds.[19] In other respects, however, there is some uncertainty as to the scope of the provision. Interpreted literally, it does not cover an employee who at no point during the stoppage ceases to work, but there is no obvious reason why such a person should not enjoy the same protection. 'Has subsequently left for a reason other than the trade dispute' is undefined and vague. Does it cover cases where the claimant does not terminate the employment relationship but, for example, is laid-off or put on short-time work? And if the termination (or suspension) of the employment results indirectly from the trade dispute because the stoppage has reduced the demand for the claimant's labour, will he escape disqualification? In due course, such questions will presumably arise for determination by the Commissioner.

Part 7 Special provisions

A General

The nature of certain occupations makes it difficult to accommodate them within the framework of the ordinary law of unemployment benefit. For such cases, specific provision has been made.

i Students

Students may claim benefit only during the summer vacation and any such claim is subject to a special contribution condition. These rules have already been considered.[20]

ii Armed Forces

A member of the forces may not receive benefit while serving.[1] He does become entitled on leaving, and will not be disqualified under the 'voluntarily leaving' rule if he does so at his own request,[2] though a disqualification will be incurred if he is dismissed for disciplinary reasons.[3]

iii Occupational pensioners

The entitlement to unemployment benefit of those who retire early has been a controversial issue in recent years.[4] In practice, it is typically very difficult for such persons to find alternative employment, so that the requirement of being available for work is an artificial one. Moreover, many early retirers are entitled to an occupational pension and thus have a reduced need for income-maintenance. Government policy has been, on the one hand, to preserve entitlement to unemployment benefit without imposing a special availability condition and, without disqualifying early retirers for 'voluntarily

19 *R(U) 39/56*; *R(U) 6/74*; p.119, above.
20 Pp. 67 and 71, above.
1 SI 1975/493, reg 2.
2 Ibid, reg 3(2).
3 Ibid, reg 3(1).
4 NIAC Report on the Question of Conditions for Unemployment Benefit and Contribution Conditions for Occupational Pensioners (1968, Cmnd 3545). See also the report on Draft Regulations, 1969–70 HC 211.

leaving',[5] but, on the other hand, to take account of the receipt of occupational pensions in determining the amount payable. Two legislative proposals to introduce abatement of benefit failed to secure parliamentary approval but the principle was finally endorsed for those aged 60 to 65 by the Social Security (No 2) Act 1980 and in 1988 was extended to those aged 55 to 60.[6]

Section 5 of the 1980 Act provides for a weekly reduction from unemployment benefit of 10p for each 10p of occupational pension[7] above a prescribed amount (in 1988–89 £35 per week).[8] Sums paid solely as compensation for redundancy and not provided for in the occupational pension scheme are disregarded.[9] There are rules for calculating the weekly value of a pension when it is not paid on a weekly basis,[10] but if a pension is commuted into a lump sum entitlement to unemployment benefit is unaffected[11] – a somewhat anomalous result.[12] It should also be noted that where as a consequence of these rules the occupational pensioner receives nothing by way of unemployment benefit, nevertheless the period in which, but for the reduction, he would have been entitled to unemployment benefit still counts as days of unemployment for the purpose of the provision which limits the duration of unemployment benefit to 312 days.[13]

iv Mariners

Mariners pose problems both because they enjoy substantial periods of paid leave and because when not employed they are sometimes absent from Great Britain. Regulations thus provide:

(1) that days in a period of paid leave are not to be treated as days of unemployment;[14] and
(2) that they are deemed to be available during days of absence from Great Britain.[15]

v Share fishermen

A share fisherman holds a somewhat anomalous position under the social security system. His remuneration takes the form of a share in the profits of the fishing boat and he is not employed under a contract of service.[16] As such he pays Class 2 contributions and yet for the purposes of entitlement to unemployment benefit they are treated as Class 1 contributions.[17] These circumstances necessitate two special conditions.

– A condition is added to the ordinary rule of availability requiring the *claimant* to prove that on the alleged day of unemployment he did no work

5 Pp. 103–104, above.
6 SSA 1988, s.7.
7 For definition, see SSA (No 2) 1980, s.5(3) and *R(U) 2/84*. Account is taken of the gross amount received by way of pension: *R(U) 8/83*.
8 Reduction should be made first from the personal element of the benefit: SSA (No 2) 1980, s.5(1A).
9 SI 1983/1598, reg 25, on which see *R(U) 5/82* and *R(U) 4/85*.
10 SI 1983/1598, reg 27.
11 *R(U) 5/85*.
12 Ibid, at para 10, R F M Heggs, Comr.
13 SI 1983/1598, reg 28 and see p.125, below.
14 SI 1975/529, reg 2, but payment of establishment benefit under the Merchant Navy Scheme does not prevent a day being treated as a day of unemployment: ibid, reg 6(3).
15 Ibid, reg 6(3).
16 See the definition in SI 1975/529, reg 1(2).
17 Ibid, reg 8(1).

as a share fisherman,[18] and had not neglected to avail himself of a reasonable opportunity of employment as a fisherman.[19]

- Secondly, if the claimant is the master or member of the crew of a fishing boat, and either the master or member of the crew of that boat (though not necessarily the claimant himself)[20] is owner or part-owner, he must show that the failure to fish on that day resulted from either (1) the state of the weather;[1] or (2) repairs or maintenance of the boat; or (3) absence of fish in the normal fishing grounds; or (4) 'any other good cause'.[2]

B Seasonal workers: policy

The most important of the special rules apply to seasonal workers. This is a form of labour which is inefficient in that it gives rise to high overhead costs and low productivity, and creates shortages and surpluses of labour at different periods of the year. Better organisation of the labour market and the advance of technology has reduced the amount of seasonal work in industries which are not, in their essence, seasonal. But there are still some occupations which are almost wholly seasonal (e.g. working in holiday resorts), and in 1977 it was estimated that about one million individuals engaged, or intended to engage, in seasonal work.[3] The problem arises how such special circumstances are to be accommodated within the framework of unemployment benefit law. There would seem to be three main solutions. One might simply apply the ordinary principles of eligibility, and impose such restraint on the granting of benefit as might seem desirable by means of the requirement that the claimant must be 'available' for employment. This is the general position in the United States,[4] and prevailed in Britain until 1931.[5] The objection was then taken that seasonal workers were not really attached to the labour market during their off-season. A second view was that a special insurance fund should be established, but this was rejected on the grounds of administrative inconvenience, and that the fund would not have sufficient income to pay benefits at an acceptable level.[6] The third method was that favoured by the Royal Commission on Unemployment Insurance[7] and subsequently adopted by the British system: imposing special conditions on claims made during the off-season. These were that the claimant must have had a record of continuous registration for employment and, in the light of his work record, must have reasonable prospects of finding a substantial amount of employment during the off-season. The National Insurance Advisory Committee which reexamined the problem in 1977 conceded that the law was cumbersome and might sometimes operate harshly but doubted whether a more satisfactory solution could be found.[8] Its only major recom-

18 On which, see *R(U) 9/52*; *R(U) 9/53*; *R(U) 1/81*.
19 SI 1975/529, reg 8(5).
20 *R(U) 6/63*.
 1 See *R(U) 1/81*.
 2 SI 1975/529, reg 8(6). For the interpretation of 'good cause' see e.g. *R(U) 7/55*; *R(U) 17/55*; *R(U) 3/64*.
 3 NIAC Report on Seasonal Workers (1977, Cmnd 6991), para 30.
 4 Corp. Juris. Secundum, vol 81, pp. 411–412.
 5 See e.g. *UD 4720*.
 6 See NIAC Report on Seasonal Workers, 1948–49 HC 202, paras 18–21.
 7 First Report (1931, Cmd 3872), para 125.
 8 N.3, above.

mendation, the abolition of the registration condition, was implemented in 1982.[9]

C Definition of seasonal worker

In terms of policy there seems to be a choice between a narrow and a broad concept of a seasonal worker. On the narrow view the rules should only apply to those persons whose employment is truly 'seasonal', that is their work (e.g. in agriculture or tourism) varies according to climatic conditions. This is the definition preferred by the National Insurance Advisory Committee,[10] and seems to have been the original view taken. Under an amendment in 1935 a seasonal worker must have been employed 'in an occupation or occupations of a seasonal nature'.[11] On a broader view, it extends more generally to persons who are regularly employed for certain portions of the year (e.g. a school-meals attendant). This seems to be the position under the Regulations now in force. A 'seasonal' worker is defined as:

> a person whose normal employment is for a part or parts only of a year in an occupation or occupations of which the availability or extent varies at approximately the same time or times in successive years; or any other person who normally restricts his employment to the same, or substantially the same, part or parts only of the year.[12]

The onus of proving that the claimant is a seasonal worker is on the adjudication officer,[13] though once this has been established it shifts to the claimant to show that the pattern of seasonal work has come to an end.[14] The seasonal nature of the work need not be voluntary: a disabled man may be forced by his handicap to take on only this kind of work.[15] Several more specific points under the statutory definition now arise for discussion.

i Part(s) of a year

The shift of emphasis from the narrower to the broader meaning of seasonal workers can be seen most clearly in the pattern of employment which must be established. The Commissioners originally construed 'part or parts of the year' in accordance with the climatic theory of 'seasonal' to include only those who were substantially unemployed for a period of three months.[16] This was felt to be too lax and, following an amendment in 1952, 'part or parts of a year' may now be of any duration, and may be aggregated, so that, however, the total period of unemployment during the year is not less than seven weeks.[17] There is no *lower* limit to the amount of *employment* necessary to qualify as seasonal, so that a man whose only work during the year was to assist the GPO over Christmas was properly to be regarded as coming within the regulation.[18] The minimum of seven weeks of unemployment may be

9 SI 1982/1105.
10 N.3, above, paras 61–66.
11 SR & O 1935/804, reg 2.
12 SI 1983/1598, reg 21(1).
13 *R(U) 23/53*.
14 *R(U) 14/53*; *R(U) 19/54*.
15 *R(U) 43/52*; *R(U) 4/64*. Also, where no other employment is available: *R(U) 8/81*.
16 *R(U) 5/51*; *R(U) 7/51(T)*.
17 SI 1983/1598, reg 21(1). NIAC proposed that the period be extended to 13 weeks: n.3, above, para 67.
18 *R(U) 3/61*.

spread over the whole year.[19] The only concession to the more traditional concept of 'seasonal' is that the periods of employment must recur at approximately the same times of the year; and this has been given a flexible interpretation. In one case, a variation in the starting dates of employment of ten weeks and in the finishing dates of nine weeks was not regarded as too great.[20]

ii Normal employment

In establishing the pattern, regard is to be had only to the claimant's 'normal employment'. This is a question of fact and is determined in a way similar to that of the analogous issue of a claimant's normal working week.[1] To decide whether or not the normal employment is for part or parts only of the year, the authorities are instructed to concentrate on 'factors inherent in the nature or conditions of the occupation' rather than 'factors abnormal to that occupation . . . notwithstanding that those factors persist for a prolonged period'.[2] Both the objective characteristics of the occupation, as evidenced by the pattern of employment of others engaged in it, and the personal employment record of the claimant are relevant for this purpose.[3] There is a well established convention that three years of work governed by the provision raise a presumption that the claimant is a seasonal worker.[4] But it is 'a yardstick and not a magic wand. It does not solve all cases'.[5] It may be rebutted where sickness renders it difficult to discern a pattern,[6] or where the claimant has moved to a new district.[7]

D Duration of off-season

Once it has been established that the claimant is a seasonal worker it is necessary to calculate the duration of his off-season, for the special condition only applies to a claim during that period. The regulation, not surprisingly, defines the 'off-season' as the part of the year (or aggregate of parts) when the claimant is normally not employed, but then excludes from consideration any period shorter than seven days.[8] The prevailing practice is to take the average periods of non-employment over the last three years, discounting abnormally short periods of work which were irrelevant to the claimant's usual occupation.[9]

E Special condition for seasonal workers

A seasonal worker claiming during his off-season must prove that *either* (1)

in his current off-season he has had a substantial amount of employment

before the date of claim *or* (2)

19 *R(U) 5/64.*
20 *R(U) 8/62.*
 1 Pp. 81–83, above.
 2 SI 1983/1598, reg 21(1). See also *R(U) 8/81* and *R(U) 2/82(T).*
 3 Ibid and *R(U) 3/87.*
 4 *R(U) 3/51,* and see *R(U) 4/75(T).*
 5 Ibid, at para 16.
 6 *R(U) 36/51.*
 7 *R(U) 14/53.*
 8 SI 1983/1598, reg 21(1).
 9 *R(U) 29/51.*

(having regard to all the circumstances of his case, including the nature and extent of his employment (if any) in any past off-seasons and the industrial or other relevant conditions normally obtaining in the district or districts in which he is available to be employed) he can or could reasonably expect to obtain, after that day in his current off-season, employment which, together with his employment (if any) before that day in that off-season, constitutes a substantial amount of employment.[10]

'Substantial amount of employment' is defined in the Regulations as

employment which is equal in duration to not less than one-fourth (or such other fractional part as may, in the circumstances of the particular case, be reasonable) of the current off-season.[11]

The primary calculation, therefore, involves ascertaining the duration of the off-season and seeing whether the amount of employment actually obtained or likely in all the circumstances to be obtained exceeds one-fourth. Under (2), there is inevitably an element of speculation. But resort may be had to the claimant's past employment record, and for this purpose the authorities will adopt much the same approach as was appropriate to determine whether or not the claimant was a 'seasonal worker'.[12]

Even if the claimant fails the one-fourth test, he may yet persuade the authorities to exercise their discretion to accept a smaller amount of employment, though the reported decisions reveal a noticeable reluctance to do this.[13]

Part 8   Duration and amount of benefit

A   Duration

Unemployment benefit is not payable after 312 days (not counting Sunday or a substitute rest day) of one period of interruption of employment.[14] It will be recalled that one period of interruption of employment is linked to another only if it is not separated by more than eight weeks. The consequence is that if a claimant receives benefit for less than 312 days and this is followed by a period of eight weeks which does not constitute a period of interruption of employment, he may subsequently begin a new period of entitlement to a maximum of 312 days. To avoid deliberate attempts to extend receipt of unemployment benefit by such means, the regulations provide that a person who would have been entitled to benefit for any day but for any delay or failure to make or prosecute a claim is treated as having been entitled to benefit for that day.[15] A provision which enabled the claimant to escape the regulation if he could prove that the delay or failure was not intended to avoid the 312 day rule[16] was abolished in 1986.[17] To re-establish title after the 312

---

10 SI 1983/1598, reg 21(2), on which see *R(U) 6/88*.
11 SI 1983/1598, reg 21(1).
12 P.123, above, and see *R(U) 21/55*; *R(U) 14/61*; *R(U) 2/63*.
13 *R(U) 14/61*; cp *R(U) 5/55*.
14 SSA 1975, s.18(1). For 'period of interruption of employment' see p.77, above.
15 SI 1983/1598, reg 16, as amended. The same applies to any day for which, as a result of abatement (see p.121, above), an occupational pensioner receives nothing by way of unemployment benefit: ibid, reg 28.
16 See ibid, reg 16 in its original form, and the difficulties to which it gave rise: *R(U) 6/83* and *R(U) 7/86(T)*.
17 SI 1986/1011.

days the claimant must be in employment as an employed earner[18] for 13 weeks, and in each of those weeks must be so employed for at least 16 hours.[19] For the latter condition, account can be taken only of hours during which he was required by his employer to work.[20]

B Amount

Since the abolition of the earnings-related supplement in 1982, unemployment benefit has been a flat-rate sum, to which may be added an increase for a dependent spouse.[1]

Men aged 65–70, and women aged 60–65, who have not retired, but who would have been entitled to a Category A or B retirement pension if they had retired, are paid at the current rate of the relevant pension.[2]

18 SSA 1975, s.79(4).
19 Ibid, s.18(2), as amended.
20 *R(U) 3/82*, in which a college lecturer unsuccessfully argued that time taken in preparing his lectures (five and a half hours a week) should also be included.
 1 Pp. 341–342, below.
 2 SSA 1975, s.14(6). For details, see ch 5, below.

Chapter 4
Benefits for sickness and disability

Part 1 General

A Scope of chapter

An independent study carried out in 1976–77 concluded that 'the present UK system of benefits for handicapped people is a ragbag of provisions based on differing, sometimes conflicting and anachronistic principles'.[1] Not all these benefits are properly to be described as 'social security', and some which are appropriately so termed are dealt with elsewhere in the book. Excluded from the present chapter are the following.

i *Benefits in kind* There is a wide variety of facilities provided for sick and disabled people under the National Health Service and by such legislative measures as the Chronically Sick and Disabled Persons Act 1970 and the Disabled Persons Act 1981.[2]

ii *Schemes for disability resulting from specific causes* For historical and policy reasons, there are special social security schemes for those disabled as the result of industrial accident or diseases or of service in the armed forces. These will be described in chapters 7 and 8 respectively. In 1979 two new schemes were introduced to remedy deficiencies in the private law. Both are administered by the DHSS but are not primarily seen as social security measures. The Vaccine Damage Payments Act provides for compensation where severe disablement results from vaccination against certain diseases or contact from persons so vaccinated,[3] the Pneumoconiosis etc. (Workers Compensation) Act confers lump sum benefits on those who have suffered from specific lung diseases as a result of their employment but have received no tort compensation because their employer ceased business before the manifestation of the symptoms.[4] Since 1964 there has existed a criminal injury compensation scheme under which payments are made to those sustaining personal injury directly attributable to a crime of violence. The payments were originally ex gratia in character but since the Criminal Justice Act 1988, which placed the scheme on a statutory basis, they have been the

---

1 Simkins and Tickner *Whose Benefit?* p.17.Cf '[t]his dreadful mess is a tribute to the havoc which politicians' over-zealous response to interest group pressures can create': Dilnot, Kay and Morris *The Reform of Social Security* (1984) p.100.
2 See generally Meredith Davies *The Disabled Child and Adult* (1982).
3 See Dworkin [1978–9] JSWL 330.
4 See Carson, ibid, pp. 350–351.

subject of legal entitlement. The scheme is financed from general taxation, but is not administered by the DHSS.[5]

iii *Family fund*[6]   This was set up in 1973 as an immediate response to the thalidomide disaster. It originally conferred benefits in cash and kind on families having the care of a child with a severe congenitial disability, but subsequently all severly handicapped children became eligible. It is financed by government but is administered by the Joseph Rowntree Memorial Trust.

B History[7]

i National health insurance

State involvement in provision for the sick and disabled effectively dates from the National Insurance Act 1911. Prior to that date, there was no 'system' of medical care outside the rudimentary facilities provided by the poor law. Those who could not afford treatment had to rely on charitable assistance or membership of a friendly society. The latter had existed for several centuries, but with nineteenth century industrialisation had come into their own in providing support, particularly in cases of sickness and death, for the more prosperous workman or artisan.[8] In 1905, their total membership amounted to no less than 6 million. Nevertheless, over one half of the working population had no form of sickness insurance.[9] In the words of Lloyd George, the chief architect of national health insurance, there was a perceived need for the state to assist in making 'provisions against the accidents of life which bring so much undeserved poverty to hundreds of thousands of homes, accidents which are quite inevitable such as the death of the breadwinner or his premature breakdown in health'.[10] The conviction was strengthened by the study which he initiated of the German insurance system.[11]

While the case for a national health insurance scheme was a powerful one, the proposal had to face considerable opposition from the friendly societies and the insurance companies who had vested interests in the existing systems and from the medical profession who resisted the notion of a national salaried service and bureaucratic control.[12] The result was a compromise. The provision of medical services was administered by specially created bodies, the Insurance Committees, on which insured persons, medical practitioners, local authorities and central government were represented. But the administration of cash benefits was in the hands of 'Approved Societies', such friendly societies, trade unions, insurance and collecting societies as satisfied two conditions: they were not carried on for profit and they were subject to the absolute control of their members. The individual would enrol with the

5 *Atiyah* ch 13.
6 Bradshaw *The Family Fund* (1980).
7 Harris *National Health Insurance 1911–1946* (1946); Levy *National Health Insurance: a Critical Study* (1944); Eder *National Health Insurance and the Medical Profession in Britain, 1913–1939* (1982).
8 Gosden *The Friendly Societies in England, 1815–1875* (1961), and *Self-Help: Voluntary Associations in the 19th Century* (1973).
9 Bruce *The Coming of the Welfare State* (4th edn) p.214.
10 Quoted in Fraser *The Evolution of the British Welfare State* (1973) p.150.
11 In 1911 the government issued a Memorandum on Sickness and Invalidity Insurance in Germany, Cd 5678.
12 Eder, n.7, above, pp. 31–45.

society of his choice but, within certain statutory limits, the society had power to make rules and regulations governing the payment of benefit, and might decline to accept a person as member (except on the ground of age). The scheme covered initially all manual workers, and non-manual workers earning less than £160 per annum. In return for weekly contributions (4d for men, 3d for women the insured person would, on proof of incapacity for work, be entitled to 10s per week (7s 6d for women) from the fourth day of incapacity for a maximum of 26 weeks. After that period had elapsed, 'disablement benefit' was payable so long as he remained incapable of work, though the amounts in question were half those for sickness benefit. The individual society could, however, pay additional benefits at its discretion and in the manner it thought fit from any surplus in its funds. The result was that benefits varied widely according to the membership and geographical location of the society. No doubt the intention was to preserve the 'private' nature of friendly society insurance, but it seemed hardly to be compatible with a compulsory scheme.[13]

In contrast to unemployment insurance which underwent many changes between 1911 and 1946, the structure of health insurance, at least as regards sickness and disablement benefits, remained more or less intact until the fundamental revision at the end of the Second World War. The number of persons insured was gradually increased. The Royal Commission on Health Insurance, reporting in 1926,[14] recommended certain minor changes in contribution requirements and these were effected two years later. Its most substantial criticisms, however, went largely unheeded until Beveridge's Report in 1942. The scheme, it was said, was too little concerned with health improvement – 'sickness insurance' would have been a more appropriate title than 'health insurance'. The intended democratic nature of the Approved Societies had become a fiction – they were ordinary commercial undertakings in a different guise.[15] Perhaps most important of all, benefit was inadequate in that, unlike unemployment benefit, it did not provide for dependants' allowances. The 1926 Report, then, in some ways looked forward to the substantial reforms proposed by Beveridge and implemented by the government after Second World War.

ii Beveridge and the National Insurance Act 1946
The fundamental achievement of this period was, of course, the establishment of the National Health Service.[16] The provision of medical services and of medicaments was extricated from the insurance scheme and they were made freely available to all. Sickness benefit was brought more into line with unemployment benefit: the rates were assimilated and for the first time sick claimants were paid an allowance for dependants. At the same time, though remaining ineligible for unemployment benefit, the self-employed became entitled to sickness benefit. This was, however, a controversial measure. At first it was thought to be too impracticable to administer and in the original 1946 Bill there was a waiting-period of 24 days for such persons. This was eventually removed, but the price to be paid was an increase of 3d in the contributions demanded of the self-employed. The Approved Societies were

13 *Harris*, n.7, above, pp. 88–93.
14 Cmd 2591,
15 The minority recommended the abolition of the Approved Societies and the transfer of their functions to local authorities.
16 National Health Service Act 1946, implementing proposals in the White Paper (1944, Cmd 6502).

abolished and their functions transferred to the newly created Ministry of National Insurance. Disablement benefit also disappeared and sickness benefit became payable for an unlimited duration provided that the contribution requirements had been satisfied. But the distinction between short-term and long-term incapacity was not entirely eradicated: the contribution conditions became much more stringent after a year's entitlement to benefit.[17] Indeed, the distinction was broadened in 1966 when an earnings-related supplement was introduced only for the first 26 weeks of incapacity.[18]

iii New provision for the disabled

During the 1960s the political background to provision for the disabled had altered significantly. On the one hand, there had emerged some powerful pressure groups,[19] concerned to bring to public attention the plight of the disabled, to conduct inquiries and publish their findings, and to campaign actively for reform. On the other hand, the 'rediscovery' of poverty in the 1960s had brought to light that disability featured prominently among the causes of deprivation and financial hardship.[20] Under the influence of these movements, the government sponsored in 1968–69 a massive survey of handicapped and impaired persons in Great Britain (OPCS Survey).[1] The findings largely confirmed the conjectures of those campaigning for more generous financial support. It was estimated that there were about three million 'impaired' persons, that is those lacking part or all of a limb, or having a defective organ or mechanism of the body, and that about 1,100,000 were 'handicapped' in the sense that they had difficulty in carrying out the normal functions of daily living.[2] Perhaps the most significant finding was that a high proportion of the latter (35–40 per cent) were in receipt of supplementary benefit, thus revealing the inadequacy of national insurance protection.[3]

In response to the problem, the strategy of successive governments has been that of piecemeal improvements by identifying and satisfying specific needs. This was made explicit by the Secretary of State in her 1974 Report on Social Security Provision for Chronically Sick and Disabled People.

> No clear picture emerges of the 'problem of disablement'. There are, in fact, a number of different interlocking problems rather than one single problem. No simple analysis can be made and no single simple solution is appropriate. . . . There must be priorities. The greatest needs must be identified and met first on the basis of a sound programme of cash benefits and services which takes account both

17 NIA 1946, s.12(2).
18 NIA 1966, s.2.
19 The most influential has probably been the Disablement Income Group formed in 1965. There is now a co-ordinating organisation, the Disability Alliance, which lists about 30 associations concerned with the welfare of the disabled. See, generally, on these movements Walker in Jones (ed) *Yearbook of Social Policy in Britain 1975* pp. 204–207.
20 See particularly Abel-Smith and Townsend *The Poor and the Poorest* (1965) p.62.
 1 The Report of the Survey by the Office of Population Censuses and Surveys was published in 3 volumes: Part One, Harris *Handicapped and Impaired in Great Britain* (1971); Part Two, Buckle *Work and Housing of Impaired Persons in Great Britain* (1971); Part Three, Harris, Smith and Head *Income and Entitlement to Supplementary Benefit of Impaired People in Great Britain* (1972).
 2 *Harris*, n.1, above, at p.18.
 3 Report on Social Security Provision for Chronically Sick and Disabled People, 1973–74, HC 276, at paras 8 and 41.

of the practical limitations of detailed assessments of need and of the choices expressed by disabled people themselves.[4]

The OPCS Survey had revealed that poverty was particularly prevalent among the long-term disabled. Paradoxically, as we have seen, the national insurance system conferred less generous support on this group than on those whose incapacity for work lasted for less than six months. The desire to reverse this situation generated a confusing variety of responses. The Labour administration of the late 1960s proposed, as part of its National Superannuation scheme, an earnings-related pension for those incapable of work for more than six months,[5] but the Bill lapsed. The succeeding Conservative government adopted an alternative strategy: the invalidity benefit introduced in 1971[6] comprised a pension (in effect the standard flat-rate sickness benefit) plus a small allowance which varied according to the claimant's age at the onset of incapacity and which was based on the assumed greater loss of those giving up work at an earlier stage in their working life. The emphasis on satisfying needs rather than providing earnings replacement was taken further by certain complementary measures which favoured the receipients of invalidity benefit relative to sickness benefit claimants: there was no reduction for contribution deficiencies; higher increases were paid for dependent children; and there was an easier test of dependency for a working wife. The trend was reinforced when, in 1979, an earnings-related component was added to the invalidity pension, though only on the basis of contributions made to the new pension scheme;[7] and in 1982 the earnings-related supplement to sickness benefit was abolished.[8]

Of course, these reforms could not assist those unable to satisfy the conditions for the contributory benefits: the majority of these had been disabled from birth, but there was also a substantial number who had not worked sufficiently to pay the requisite number of contributions.[9] In 1975 the non-contributory invalidity pension was introduced to cater for this group.[10] It became payable in circumstances similar to those of the contributory invalidity pension but without contribution conditions and (to achieve equity as compared with those who had contributed to the National Insurance Fund) at a lower rate.

Income replacement constituted inadequate financial support for the severely disabled. Government policy then became targetted on categories of particular need. The first group to benefit from this approach comprised those who required assistance to cope with the normal functions of living. An attendance allowance payable to such persons was included in the ill-fated National Superannuation Bill of 1969 and was adopted and enacted by the Conservative administration in 1970.[11] Five years later, it was complemented by a measure designed to assist those who sacrificed their own work opportunities: the non-contributory invalid care allowance.[12] Quite apart from the justice of compensating a group who performed an unattractive and unpaid

---

4 Report on Social Security Provision, n.3, above, at paras 52–53.
5 See White Paper, National Superannuation and Social Insurance (1969, Cmnd 3883) para 88, and the Bill of the same name, cl.12.
6 NIA 1971, s.3.
7 SSPA 1975, s.14.
8 SSA (No 2) 1980, s.4.
9 Report on Social Security Provision, n.3, above, at para 24.
10 SSBA 1975, s.6.
11 NIA 1970, s.4.
12 SSBA 1975, s.7.

task, there was the economic consideration that by so doing they relieved the social services of the burden.

The second category of the disabled identified with a specific financial need was the immobile. Those unable to walk but able to drive had for some time been entitled to invalid carriages or, if they owned a car, to a private car allowance; but the disabled passenger was not assisted and the safety and reliability of the carriage had been subjected to considerable doubt.[13] Rather than switch entitlement to a small car, which would involved a considerable increase in expenditure, the government decided to introduce, as an alternative to the invalid carriage, a cash allowance payable to adults of working age and children aged five and above who were unable, or virtually unable, to walk.[14]

Finally, there were two categories of disabled persons who were excluded from the contributory scheme: housewives not normally engaged in remunerative employment; and children. Consideration of the disabled housewife featured prominently in the campaign conducted by the pressure groups.[15] The OPCS Survey revealed that there were some 225,000 housewives prevented by their disability from doing the household chores,[16] though of these only about one fifth were under pensionable age without entitlement to any personal benefit.[17] Those not engaged in remunerative employment were not, of course, entitled to sickness or invalidity benefit. The solution adopted in 1977 was to extend to this group entitlement to the non-contributory invalidity pension if they were able to show that they were 'incapable of performing normal household duties'.[18] While on the face of it this innovatory measure had much to commend it, it suffered from the serious objection that it was discriminatory:[19] it assumed that only married women were primarily responsible for housework, and to receive benefit they had to satisfy not only the 'household duties' test but also the condition applied to all claimants, that they were incapable of paid work.

The chief difficulty posed by disabled children was that the extent of the problem was largely unknown. The OPCS Survey did not cover persons under sixteen, and such estimates as were made of the number handicapped ranged from 80,000 to 350,000.[20] Moreover, as with the immobile, it was not clear whether the main effort should be directed at improving facilities or granting cash allowances.[1] Attendance allowances had been payable for children aged two or more, and those aged five and over were to become entitled to the mobility allowance. But it was the plight of the thalidomide children which prompted immediate government action. Since 1973 a Family Fund established on a non-statutory basis and administered by the Rowntree Memorial Trust has conferred benefits on severely disabled children. The government, which initially contributed £3 million, and has since continued to finance the scheme, indicated however that this was not intended as com-

13 See the government-sponsored Report by Lady Sharp, Mobility of Physically Disabled People (1974).
14 Introduced by SSPA 1975, s.22.
15 E.g. Disablement Income Group *Creating a National Disability Income* (1972) pp. 19–20.
16 *Harris*, n.1., above, at pp. 63–91.
17 Report on Social Security Provision for Chronically Sick and Disabled People, 1973–74, HC 276, at para 43.
18 SSBA 1975, s.6.
19 See the NIAC Report (1980, Cmnd 7955).
20 See Disability Alliance *Poverty and Disability* (1975) pp. 4–5; *Pearson* para 1514–1520, and *Townsend* ch 21.
 1 Report on Social Security Provision, n.17, above, at para 45.

pensation for disablement, but rather to complement services already provided by statutory and voluntary bodies.[2]

iv Reform in the 1980s

Two policy goals largely explain the reforms carried out by the Conservative
government in the 1980s: reduction in administrative costs; and elimination
of sex discrimination.

Independently of social security entitlement a large majority of
employees – about 90 per cent[3] – have a contractual right to sick pay from
their employers during short spells off work. The overlap with sickness benefit suggested that there would be substantial administrative savings if the burden of income replacement were to be borne exclusively by employers for
such periods.[4] In 1983, therefore, a statutory obligation on employers to pay
prescribed amounts replaced sickness benefit for the first eight weeks of
incapacity but the financial burden remained with the National Insurance
Fund, as employers deducted the cost of such payments from their contributions liability.[5] In 1987, the period of statutory sick pay was extended to six
months,[6] with the consequence that sickness benefit remains only for the self-
employed and the relatively few employees not entitled to statutory sick pay.

Sex discrimination was implicit in two of the non-contributory benefits
introduced in the 1970s: married women and those cohabiting had to satisfy
the additional household duties test to gain entitlement to the non-contributory invalidity pension and were excluded altogether from the invalid care
allowance. The latter provision was held by the European Court of Justice[7] to
be in breach of the EEC Directive on Equal Treatment[8] and was repealed in
1986.[9] After a prolonged review of the former,[10] the government decided to
abolish NCIP altogether and to replace it by a new benefit, the severe disablement allowance, payable to a narrower range of claimants but without sex
discrimination: the favoured groups are those incapable of work since
childhood and those who satisfy certain functional tests of severe
disablement.[11]

The major review of social security provision undertaken in 1984–85 did
not cover disability benefits. However, the government has commissioned a
major new OPCS survey on the numbers, circumstances and needs of disabled persons, the report of which is expected in 1988.[12]

C Determining priorities and defining disability

The dominant trends, to be perceived from the last section, of a major expansion of benefit programmes in the 1970s and some retrenchment thereafter

2 848 HC Official Report (5th series) written answer cols 241–242. See generally Bradshaw *The Family Fund* (1980).
3 13 HC Official Report (6th series) cols 642–643.
4 Green Paper *Income During Initial Sickness* (1980, Cmnd 7864).
5 SSHBA 1982, Part I.
6 SSA 1985, s.18.
7 *Drake v Chief Adjudication Officer* [1987] QB 166, [1986] 3 All ER 65.
8 Dir 79/7, OJ 1979, L6/24, on which see Luckhaus 83 JSWL 325.
9 SSA 1986, s.37.
10 See NIAC Report on the Household Duties Test for Married Women (1980, Cmnd 7955), Equal Opportunities Commission *Behind Closed Doors* (1981) and DHSS Report, Review of the Household Duties Test (1983).
11 HSSA 1984, s.11.
12 *White Paper 1985* paras 5.3–5.6.

have occurred also in other countries.[13] The political dimension is important. Growth in provision for the disabled may be attributed to an increasing public recognition, fostered particularly by pressure group activity, of the moral worthiness of such persons to benefit from redistributive measures.[14] The reluctance to maintain the momentum in the 1980s results from a reassertion of more traditional values which give priority to reward for work over the fulfilment of need, however legitimate. The tension between the rival values is evident not only in the evolution of the current system but also in the prolific debate concerning the future.[15]

As has been observed,

> It would be difficult to find anyone involved in the present disability income system – from politicians through officials, voluntary agencies, academics, lobby groups to individual disabled people – who is not highly critical of the current arrangements.[16]

and yet clearly such dissatisfaction has different sources. In the first place, there is considerable criticism of the complexity of the system.[17] While, in part, this is a consequence of incremental change and a disinclination to engineer radical restructuring, nevertheless, in part, it also results from specific claims of distributional justice. The argument is that different groups of disabled persons *deserve* to be treated differently, even at the price of complexity and high administrative cost. The more generous protection offered to the victims of war, industrial accidents, crimes of violence and torts is often rationalised on this basis – it is argued that the cause of the disability strengthens the case for compensation[18] – and the notion that social security contributors should be more favourably treated than non-contributors can be similarly justified. Naturally, as policymakers quickly discover, there are those with vested interests in each special scheme who will resist simplification, if it involves some loss to those interests.[19]

Perceptions of distributional justice can generate other complexities. The more diverse the need, the greater the pressure on legal and administrative machinery to evaluate it. For example, a much-voiced criticism of the present general system of disability benefits[20] is that it makes no provision for *partial* incapacity for work.[1] The proposals formulated to fill this gap would involve either a detailed medical assessment or an assessment of earnings loss, or both.[2] The same problem would arise if more recognition were given to the

---

13 Stone *The Disabled State* (1985); Copeland 44 Soc Sec Bull 25.
14 Haber and Smith 36 Am Soc Rev 87.
15 *Pearson*, esp chs 10–11; Walker and Townsend *Disability in Britain: A Manifesto of Rights* (1981); Brown *The Disability Income System* (1984); Harris et al *Compensation and Support for Illness and Injury* (1984).
16 Ibid, p.313.
17 Simpkins and Tickner *Whose Benefit?* (1978) pp. 12–17. In 1978, the Royal Commission on Civil Liability referred to 122 DHSS leaflets on benefits for the disabled: *Pearson* para 134. For some empirical evidence on the difficulties posed for claimants, see Harris et al, n.15, above, ch 5.
18 Pp. 253–254, below.
19 *Atiyah* p.554; Brown, n.15, above, pp. 315–316.
20 In contrast to the industrial injuries and war pension schemes, pp. 293–306 and 329, below.
1 Britain is one of the few EEC states with this gap: cf *Pearson* paras 814–821; Economist Intelligence Unit *Benefits for Partial Disability* (1982).
2 Ibid, and SSAC Second Report (1983) pp. 34–36.

needs of other neglected groups of the disabled population such as children[3] and the elderly.[4]

Nor is it to be assumed that there is general agreement on how disability should be defined.[5] Other areas of social security entitlement can adopt criteria which are predominantly objective in character: age, jobless and even 'poor' in the sense that available resources are below a prescribed level. 'Disability', on the other hand, is 'a socially created category rather than an attribute of individuals',[6] and, as such, depends crucially both on policy goals and on those responsible for assessment

In terms of policy goals, we can observe the primacy within the British system of 'incapacity for work' (the definition used for *inter alia* sickness benefit, statutory sick pay and invalidity benefit) because the system focusses traditionally on income replacement for those unable to participate in the labour market. The creation of benefits to meet special needs called for criteria tied to those needs; thus, requiring 'attention' and 'supervision' from another person (attendance allowance) and 'unable or virtually unable to walk' (mobility allowance). Pressure groups and other arguing for more comprehensive provision for the disadvantages suffered by those handicapped or impaired, physically or mentally, have of necessity to propose criteria which involve assessing the degree of such handicap or impairment.[7] This approach was first adopted in the industrial injury and war pension schemes[8] and was recently introduced into the general social security programme to determine entitlement to the severe disablement allowance.

All of these definitions require assessment which, itself, poses practical and theoretical difficulties.[9] Traditionally, most reliance has been a placed on clinical assessment: for most purposes the views of the medical profession, in the form either of medical statements by general practitioners or of examination by specialists, have been regarded as decisive. There has been a recent tendency to reduce the significance of clinical assessment for questions of entitlement[10] and the reasons are not, perhaps difficult to locate.[11] First, clinical tests cannot themselves determine functional incapacity, for example, incapacity for work. Quite apart from the fact that the definition requires a decision on what work it is reasonable for the claimant to perform,[12] there is no objective measurement of physical and mental ability; at the last resort, the ultimate obstacle to work lies in the subjective experience of the claimant and pain, fatigue and so on are not susceptible of measurement.[13] Secondly, unlike administrators concerned with cost constraints, doctors have no motivation to restrict entitlement, particularly if they are general practitioners who wish to preserve good relations with their patients. Also, given

3 Walker and Townsend, n.15, above, ch 6.
4 Ibid, ch 5.
5 Blaxter *The Meaning of Disability* (1967); Duckworth *The Classification and Measurement of Disablement* (1983); Stone, n.13, above.
6 Ibid, p.26.
7 Disability Alliance *Poverty and Disability* (1975) and *Poverty and Disability: Breaking the Link* (1987).
8 Pp. 286–288, below.
9 Duckworth, n.5, above; Mashaw *Bureaucratic Justice: Managing Social Security Disability Claims* (1983).
10 See generally Oglesby *Review of Attendance Allowance and Mobility Allowance Procedures and of Medical Adjudication* (1983).
11 Cf Stone, n.13, above, ch 4.
12 Cf pp.150–152, below.
13 Blaxter, n.5, above, pp. 11–13; Stone, n.13, above, pp. 134–139.

the sometimes high degree of uncertainty involved in diagnosis, they may wish to err on the side of assisting claimants where serious hardship may result from an adverse determination.[14] The apparent shift away from medical assessment has not been accompanied by a greater involvement of other professionals, such as social workers and psychologists, notwithstanding the views of some that the social and emotional consequences of disability are as important as financial consequences.[15]

The distributional dilemma of deciding who should benefit from financial support, involving, as it does, difficult issues of defining disability, is in practice and for the foreseeable future dominated by cost considerations. They explain the hitherto cool official responses to the far-reaching proposals for a National Disability Income advanced by pressure groups representing the disabled.[16] The basic idea is for a single state scheme for all disabled people with uniform criteria of entitlement. It would comprise: an income replacement benefit, on the lines of the existing invalidity pension but without contribution conditions and with a reduced rate for those partially incapable of work; and a disablement costs allowance to cover other losses, payable on a scale according to the degree of disablement. Varying estimates have been made on the cost of these proposals[17] but even the proponents of the scheme recognise (in 1987 terms) that the figure is about £3 billion.[18]

Part 2   Income replacement benefits

A General

The income maintenance of those who are unable to work because they are sick remains one of the cardinal purposes of social security. Its importance may be gauged from the fact that in 1980 there were over 300 million recorded days of incapacity in connection with claims to benefit.[19]

It might have been assumed that the improvement in medical facilities and techniques over past decades, in particular that resulting from the introduction of the National Health Service, would have led to an overall improvement in the health of the community and consequently to a diminishing reliance on benefit.[20] In fact, the contrary has occurred. Absence for sickness has shown a steady increase over a number of years. The inference might be drawn that payment of benefit has encouraged 'absenteeism'. There is a risk here of over-simplification. Statistical analysis has indeed revealed a correlation between the level of benefit and the number of days lost through sick-

14 Ibid, pp. 148–152; Mashaw, n.9, above, pp. 26–29.
15 Townsend *The Disabled In Society* (1967) pp. 5–6; Blaxter, n.5, above, pp. 6–7 and ch 8.
16 See the references cited n.7, above. The Labour Party Manifesto for the 1987 General Election did, however, contain some commitment to a disability income programme.
17 See Brown *The Disability Income System* (1984) pp. 388–389.
18 Disability Alliance (1987), n.7, above.
19 Social Security Statistics 1981, Table 3.70; and the number of total days lost must be considerably higher since the statistics do not record the sickness of those uninsured, nor periods of absence of less than four days. The introduction of SSP has meant that equivalent figures for recent years are unavailable.
20 This formed the basis of one of the arguments used for a National Health Service: Ross *The National Health Service in Great Britain* (1952) p.15.

ness;[1] and the trend towards self-certification of illness in recent years appears to have added to this number.[2] Yet this may indicate only that, as financial support for absence has increased, so those who *should* stay at home have been able to do so.[3] There are other plausible explanations for the phenomenon. Some attribute it to the growing problems of job dissatisfaction,[4] others to changing attitudes in the medical profession: minor incapacities, including mental illness, may now be treated more seriously;[5] and when jobs are scarce medical certification may be a convenient way of reducing the number of marginal and elderly workers on the employment register.[6]

Under the 1946 legislation there was a single benefit payable, whatever the duration of the incapacity. This approach proved to be most inappropriate as it masked fundamental differences between two sections of the population: 90 per cent of those off work whose incapacity lasted no more than six weeks and whose needs were limited to income maintenance during this short period; and the remaining 10 per cent who required a greater degree of financial assistance for much longer periods.[7] The current provisions treat the two groups very differently: statutory sick pay (section B) covers the great majority in the first category, leaving a small minority reliant on sickness benefit (section C); invalidity benefit (section D) and severe disablement allowance (section E) are paid to those in the second category. Section F deals with principles of entitlement common to these benefits.

B Statutory sick pay

Since the Second World War there has been a considerable growth in contractual provision for occupational sick pay; in 1981 it was estimated that some 90 per cent of employees benefited from some such scheme.[8] Entitlement to the state sickness benefit was unaffected, although the employer might, and usually did, take account of social security provision in calculating the amount of sick pay. The processing of two claims for payment seemed wasteful and it was mainly to reduce administrative expenditure that a Government Green Paper in 1980 proposed that employers should be bound to pay sick pay, at a minimum level, for the first eight weeks of incapacity, during which period sickness benefit would not be payable.[9] The proposal provoked considerable opposition,[10] not only from trade unions and poverty pressure groups who argued that it would involve a radical departure from the notion of comprehensive state welfare established since Beveridge and less rhetorically that the suggested flat-rate payment, without dependency additions, would disadvantage families in comparison with sickness benefit,[11] but also

1 Doherty (1979) 89 Econ J 109, but see also Fenn (1981) 91 Econ J 158.
2 Creedy and Disney *Social Insurance in Transition* (1985) pp. 127–128.
3 Whitehead 70 Social Trends, No 2. pp. 13–23; *Kaim-Caudle*, p.105.
4 Taylor 25 Brit J Ind Medicine 106; cf Martin and Morgan *Prolonged Sickness and the Return to Work* (1975) pp. 157–163.
5 Office of Health Economics *Work Lost Through Sickness* (1975) p.27.
6 Stone *The Disabled State* (1984) p.11.
7 Creedy and Disney, n.2, above, p.125.
8 13 HC Official Report (6th series) cols 642–643.
9 Income During Initial Sickness (Cmnd 7864)
10 See Appendix 2 to the Second Report of the Committee on Social Services, 1980–81, HC 113, for a summary of the published responses to the Green Paper.
11 The dependency additions to sickness (and unemployment) benefit were themselves abolished in 1984: p.339, below.

from the CBI who felt that the additional burden on the employer would not be sufficiently compensated by the simple reduction of 0.5–0.6 per cent in social security contributions proposed by the government. This latter point was eventually conceded by the government and the Social Security and Housing Benefits Act 1982 which implemented the scheme made provision for a 100 per cent reimbursement by the National Insurance Fund of statutory sick pay (SSP). Later, in 1985, the Fund also became responsible for paying social security contributions during periods of SSP, notwithstanding the argument that this would leave employers without any financial incentive for verifying the validity of employees' claims. The same legislation extended the scheme to cover 28 weeks of incapacity.

i Persons covered
The scheme broadly covers all those who are treated as employed earners for social security purposes and thus pay Class 1 contributions.[12] Married women with reduced contributions liability are included and there are analogous provisions governing airmen, mariners and workers on the continental shelf.[13] However, the following are not entitled to SSP:[14] employees over pensionable age; those employed for a period of less than three months;[15] those earning less than the lower earnings limit currently in force;[16] and those working for certain foreign employers or international agencies.

ii Period of incapacity for work
The first condition of entitlement is that the day for which SSP is claimed forms part of a period of incapacity for work, that is, a period of four or more consecutive days of incapacity, whether the latter days are normally working days or not.[17] Two such periods may be linked if not separated by more than eight weeks, thus obviating the need to serve again the three 'waiting days'.

iii Period of entitlement
Secondly, the employee must show that the day in question also falls within a 'period of entitlement'.[18] Most importantly, this limits the employer's liability to 28 weeks of incapacity of work,[19] but it may end earlier if:-

(1) as a result of linking periods of incapacity, SSP has been paid over a period of three years by the same employer;[20] or

---

12 SSHBA 1982, s.1(1) and see pp. 35–43, above.
13 SI 1982/1349.
14 SSHBA 1982, Sch 1, para 2 and SI 1982/894, reg 16.
15 Except where the contract has become one for a longer period, or it was preceded by another contract with the same employer and the period linking the two contracts was less than eight weeks: SSHBA 1982, Sch 1, para 3.
16 See p.43, above.
17 SSHBA 1982, s.2. Incapacity during a night-shift is attributed to the day when the shift began: SI 1982/894, reg 2.
18 SSHBA 1982, s.3 and Sch 1.
19 Ibid, s.5(4) as amended
20 SI 1982/894, reg 3(3), as amended. Where a contract of service begins between two such linked periods, the period of entitlement begins with the first day of the second of those periods: SSHBA 1982, s.3(6A).

(2) no work has been done by the employee under the contract of employment, or it has expired;[1] or

(3) the employee is placed in legal custody or leaves the EEC;[2] or

(4) there is a stoppage of work due to a trade dispute at the place of employment.[3]

Moreover, SSP is superseded by statutory maternity pay or maternity allowance when the conditions for those benefits are satisfied,[4] and title to invalidity benefit or maternity allowance is preserved (and SSP is not payable) if the day of incapacity is separated from a prior period of entitlement to either of those benefits by less than eight weeks.[5]

iv Qualifying days

The final condition is that the day of claim is a 'qualifying day'.[6] This is, effectively, a day on which the employee is required to be available for work. Thus, an employee working a four-day week may only be paid SSP for absence on the four specified days, but for each such day he will be entitled to one-fourth of the weekly rate. In some cases, there will be evidence of an agreement as between employer and employee as to qualifying days, but the authorities will not have regard to such agreements made retrospectively or to those which identify 'qualifying days' by reference to actual days of incapacity,[7] practises which have led to abuse.[8] If there is no appropriate agreement on qualifying days, regard is had to those days when the employee is required to work.[9] If, in a particular week, the employee is not expected to work, Wednesday will nevertheless be a qualifying day; if no pattern of normal work can be established, all days of the week except recognised rest days are qualifying days.[10]

v Amount

Occupational sick pay rarely takes account of family size and, in transferring responsibility for short-term income maintenance to the employer, the government considered it appropriate to follow that model, rather than sickness benefit which included additions for dependants. While the rates of SSP are broadly equivalent to that benefit, it nevertheless follows that those with large families receive less under the new system.[11] Also in contrast to sickness

---

1 Ibid, ss.3(2)(c), and Sch 1, para 2(f), though a period of entitlement in relation to one contract of service may form part of a period of entitlement in relation to another such contract: ibid, s.3(4) Further, the employer's liability continues if a contract has been brought to an end solely, or mainly, for the purpose of avoiding SSP liability: SI 1982/894, reg 4.

2 Ibid, reg 2.

3 SSHBA 1982, Sch 1, para 2(g). The employee is disentitled for the whole of the period of incapacity of work even if the stoppage is terminated: *R(SSP) 1/86*. But SSP is payable if he can show that he did not participate, or have a direct interest, in the trade dispute: SSHBA 1982, Sch 1, para 7. The law governing the equivalent disqualification from unemployment benefit applies: pp. 110–120, above.

4 SSHBA 1982, ss.3(2)(d) and 3(8)–(9), and SI 1982/894, reg 3(4).

5 SSHBA 1982, Sch 1, paras 2(d)–(e) and 5.

6 Ibid, s.4.

7 SI 1982/894, reg 3.

8 Harvey *Industrial Relations and Employment Law* I [1360.01].

9 SI 1982/894, reg 5(2)(a), thus not days when the employee is merely 'asked' to work overtime: *R(SSP) 1/85*.

10 SI 1982/894, reg 5(2)(b)–(c).

11 SSP involves considerably less redistribution than the state sickness scheme: Creedy and Disney *Social Insurance in Transition* (1985) p.140.

benefit, two rates are payable;[12] the higher sum is paid to employees whose normal weekly earnings exceed a prescribed amount.

vi Adjudication and enforcement

SSP involves a mixture of private and public law, the state having a major supervisory role primarily to protect the National Insurance Fund. This is reflected in the arrangements for adjudication and enforcement. Questions on the scope of the scheme may be referred to the Secretary of State by employees, employers or DHSS inspectors.[13] His determination follows the procedure established for social security questions.[14] As regards entitlement, either an employee or the Secretary of State may refer a question to the adjudicating authorities (adjudication officer, appeal tribunals, Commissioner).[15] Decisions of these authorities, entitling an employee to SSP, are enforceable by order of the county court (Sheriff Court in Scotland).[16] Where an employer fails to comply with a court order for payment, or in cases of insolvency, liability for payment is transferred to the Secretary of State.[17]

C Sickness benefit

The introduction of SSP and its extension in 1986 to cover the first 28 weeks of incapacity means that today sickness benefit plays only a minor role in the social security system. It is available for the self-employed and the unemployed, as well as those who are employed but not entitled to SSP, because, for example, the contract of employment is for less than three months, the claimant is over pensionable age, or SSP has been paid for 28 weeks and the current period of incapacity is separated from that period of 28 weeks by more than eight weeks.

The rules of entitlement may be briefly stated. First, the claimant must satisfy the following contribution conditions:[18]

(1) during any one tax year he must have paid contributions of Class 1 and/or Class 2, the earnings factor from which is at least 25 times the lower earnings for that year; and
(2) for each of the two tax years immediately preceding the year in which the claim is made, he must have paid, or been credited with, contributions of Class 1 and/or Class 2, the earnings factor for which is at least 52 times the lower earnings limit for that year.

Those whose incapacity results from an industrial accident or a prescribed disease are deemed to have satisfied these conditions.[19]

Secondly, the day for which benefit is claimed must be a day of incapacity for work forming part of a period of interruption of employment.[20] Four or

---

12 Until 1987 there were three rates.
13 SSHBA 1982, s.11; SI 1982/1400, Part II.
14 Pp. 567–570, below.
15 SSHBA 1982, s.12; SI 1982/1400, Part III.
16 SSHBA 1982, s.16. To assist the employee in enforcement, the Secretary of State must advance to him the amount of court fees and any enforcing officer's fees paid or payable, though such advances are to be repaid to the extent that the employee recovers them from the employer: SI 1982/1400, Part IV.
17 SSHBA 1982, s.1(5); SI 1982/894, regs 9A–9B.
18 SSA 1975, Sch 3, Para 1, as amended. For the concepts involved, see pp. 54–56, above.
19 SSA 1975, s.50A. The dispensation is a consequence of the abolition in 1982 of the short-term industrial injury benefit: see pp. 282–283, below.
20 SSA 1975, s.14(1)(b).

more consecutive days of incapacity are required to constitute a period of interruption of employment and two such periods may be linked if not separated by more than eight weeks.[1] The law is similar to that governing SSP but three differences should be noted. For the purposes of sickness benefit:

(1) Sundays, or rest days normally substituted for Sundays, cannot count towards the four consecutive days of incapacity;[2]
(2) night-workers are governed by a different rule developed in relation to unemployment benefit;[3] and
(3) kidney dialysis patients and others requiring regular medical treatment preventing them working for two or three days every week qualify for benefit for those days.[4]

Thirdly, there are rules disqualifying claimants from benefit where, for example, they fail to attend for a medical examination by the Regional Medical Officer. These do not apply to SSP but are shared with invalidity benefit and, as such, are considered below.

Sickness benefit is a flat-rate sum, somewhat less than unemployment benefit to reflect the fact that unlike the latter it is not taxable.[5] The rates for those above pensionable age and the increases for dependants are the same as for unemployment benefit.[6]

D Invalidity benefit

Invalidity benefit constitutes the principal public instrument for the maintenance of the long-term disabled. Its unnecessarily complex character is the result of an historical accumulation of three different components. The first, the *flat-rate pension*, was formally introduced in 1971[7] but was little different in character from that which it replaced, entitlement to sickness benefit for periods of incapacity exceeding six months. Nevertheless, the provisions for dependants were made more generous and in subsequent years the fact that the benefit was called a 'pension' did mean that governments came under pressure to confer more favourable treatment than was considered appropriate for the short-term benefits: currently, the rate of the pension is some 20 per cent higher than that for sickness benefit. The second, the *allowance*, introduced at the same time,[8] reflected the Conservative party's adherence to needs-based, rather than earnings-related, provision. It was described by one commentator as 'a complete novelty and a marked departure from previous thinking about social insurance in this or (so far as I know) any other country'.[9] This supplement to the pension is graded according to the age at which the claimant became incapable of work; the younger he was at the time of disablement, the higher the rate he receives. The explanation for this differential was not only that the younger disabled person would typically have greater

---

1 Ibid, s.17(1)(d), as amended.
2 Ibid, s.17(1)(e).
3 See p.72, above.
4 SI 1983/1598, reg 15.
5 The government's intention to subject it to income tax has not been implemented.
6 P.126, above.
7 NIA 1971, s.3.
8 Ibid.
9 *Walley*, p.238.

financial commitments but also, according to the government of the day,[10] that during normal working life an earner should be able to put something aside for the days of retirement and that a disabled person should be compensated for the inability to do this. The third, *earnings–related* pension was introduced by the Labour government in 1975 as part of its 'Better Pensions' programme.[11] Until 1985, claimants were permitted to accumulate this with any entitlement to the allowance. In that year, the Thatcher government introduced the principle of abatement: henceforth, the allowance was to be set off against entitlement to the earnings-related pension.[12] The case for abatement was that the allowance had been intended for those unable to build up pension entitlements. While historically accurate, this argument fails to take into account the fact that the amount of earnings-related pension paid to invalidity pensioners is typically small. This is not only because entitlement is based exclusively on contributions made to the pension scheme since 1977 (and this scheme does not mature until 1998) but also and more importantly because, unlike retirement pensioners, invalids are rarely able to maintain an adequate contribution record during their working life.

i The basic pension

Broadly speaking, invalidity pension is payable to those who have been incapable of work for 28 weeks. Specifically, the claimant must establish *either* that in respect of a period of interruption of employment he has been entitled to sickness benefit for 168 days, excluding Sundays or equivalent rest days[13] *or* that he is deemed to have been so entitled.[14] The latter alternative will arise where, as in the great majority of cases, he has been in receipt of SSP: he is deemed to have received sickness benefit throughout the period of SSP entitlement.[15] Some claimants will have to rely on periods of both actual and deemed sickness benefit where, for some reason,[16] the maximum SSP is not payable.[17]

In establishing the 168 days of actual or deemed entitlement to sickness benefit in one period of interruption of employment, the claimant may take advantage of the linking rule. Under this, periods of incapacity of work of four or more consecutive days[18] may be linked to constitute one period of interruption of employment, provided that they are not separated by more than eight weeks.[19] By the same rule, spells of unemployment may count towards the same period of interruption of employment. Normally, these must have been days which qualify for unemployment benefit,[20] thus

---

10 Sir K Joseph, Secretary of State, introducing the 1971 Bill: 816 HC Official Report (5th series) col 1015. The assumption has been challenged. See *Walley,* p.234 and Sainbury *Registered as Disabled* (1970) ch 4.

11 (1974, Cmnd 5713), paras 30–32.

12 SSA 1985, s.9.

13 The period may include periods of entitlement to maternity allowance or statutory maternity pay.

14 SSA 1975, ss.15 and 15A.

15 Since sickness benefit entitlement is based on a six-day week, the deemed receipt is, technically, for the first six days in each week of full entitlement to SSP, with a proportionate reduction for weeks of less than full entitlement to SSP: SI 1983/1598, reg 7A.

16 E.g. the contract of employment has been terminated.

17 See SI 1983/1598, reg 7A(3).

18 For those requiring regular weekly treatment by dialysis, radiotherapy or chemotherapy with cytotoxic drugs, the days need not be consecutive: n.4, above.

19 SSA 1975, s.17(1)(d).

20 Ch 3, above.

requiring the claimant to be available for work. However, for those approaching retirement (men aged 60 to 70 and women aged 60 to 65) a special rule enables these days to count towards a period of interruption of employment even if they do not satisfy the rules on unemployment benefit.[1] One of the principal objects of this provision was to enable those whose employment record was, as a result of illness, patchy in the later years of working life to qualify more easily for the invalidity pension.

The pension is payable until a man is 70, or a woman is 65. If the claimant is over pensionable age (65 for men, 60 for women) he must not have retired from regular employment[2] but must have satisfied the contribution conditions for a Category A or Category B retirement pension.[3] Apart from this special rule there are no contribution conditions as such for the basic pension, though the claimant must have satisfied the appropriate conditions for 168 days of sickness benefit;[4] and this applies where he relies on the receipt of SSP and thus is deemed to have received sickness benefit.[5] The basic invalidity pension is a weekly flat-rate sum, to which may be added allowances for certain dependants.[6] Claimants over pensionable age are paid at the same rate as the retirement pension to which otherwise they would have been entitled.[7] In fact, at the time of writing, the basic retirement pension is paid at the same rate as the invalidity pension.

There are special provisions governing widows and widowers. If a widow does not qualify for a widow's pension, because of her age or lack of dependent children, she receives an invalidity pension if she has been incapable of work for 168 days of a period of interruption of employment and she is able to satisfy the contribution conditions for a *widow*'s pension.[8] She is then paid at the rate either of invalidity pension or of widow's pension, whichever is more favourable.[9] There are no benefits specifically for widowers under the general contributory scheme but a special concession is made for those who are invalids. A man who, after 6 April 1979, becomes a widower and who was at the death of his wife, or within 13 weeks thereafter,[10] incapable of work, and remains so incapable for the standard period of 168 days of a period of interruption of employment, is entitled to an invalidity pension, which is based on either his own contributions or those of his deceased wife, whichever gives him the higher rate.[11]

ii The earnings-related pension

The earnings-related pension is derived from contributions paid since April 1978. It is calculated in the same way as the Category A earning-related retirement pension,[12] as described in the next chapter.[13] However, one difference should be noted: the earnings on which the pension is calculated are those

1 SI 1983/1598, reg 14.
2 SSA 1975, s.15(1)(b)(ii), and see pp. 191–199, below.
3 SSA 1975, s.15(2), as amended.
4 Unless the incapacity resulted from an industrial accident or disease: p.283, below.
5 SI 1983/1598, reg 7A(5).
6 Pp. 340–343, below.
7 SSA 1975. s.15(4).
8 SSPA 1975, s.15(1)–(2).
9 Ibid, s.15(3), as qualified by SI 1978/529, reg 3.
10 SI 1978/529, reg 4.
11 SSPA 1975, s.16 and SSA 1979, Sch 1, para 18.
12 SSPA 1975, s.14.
13 Pp. 206–209, below.

referable to each tax year up to and including the last tax year before the invalidity pension became payable (instead of the tax year in which the claimant reached pensionable age).[14]

iii The allowance

The allowance is payable to invalidity pensioners who were under 60 (men) or 55 (women) on the first day of incapacity within the period of interruption of employment in question.[15] The usual linking rule applies in determining the continuity of such a period.[16] Further, regulations provide that in some cases the relevant first day of incapacity of work need not have been a day on which the claimant was entitled to sickness or invalidity benefit: most importantly, this covers a day for which SSP was received.[17]

If the allowance is rationalised as a means of compensating for the inability to save, then the earlier the onset of incapacity, the greater the need. On this basis, three rates are payable: the highest for those under 40 on the date when the period of incapacity began (or where the latter date was before 5 July 1948); the middle rate for those aged 40 to 49 on the relevant date; and the lowest rate for men aged 50 to 59 or women aged 50 to 54 on the relevant date.[18] Once title to the allowance has been established before pensionable age (65 for men, 60 for women), it is paid indefinitely thereafter, and so may be added to a retirement pension. However, the age groups for the two higher rates of the allowance are somewhat less generous for those who reached pensionable aged before 6 April 1979: viz highest rate, under 35 on the relevant date; and the middle rate, 35 to 44 on the relevant date.[19] Finally, following a recent reform, to which reference has been made,[20] amounts received by way of earning-related components or guaranteed minimum pension are deducted from the allowance.[1] The earnings-related component and the allowance are, therefore, now being treated as alternative means of boosting the basic pension.

E Severe disablement allowance

Social insurance cannot provide a comprehensive system of income maintenance for the disabled for the obvious reason that the congenitally disabled and others outside the labour market for considerable periods will have an inadequate contribution record. To fill the gap, the Labour government introduced in 1975 the non-contributory invalidity pension (NCIP), similar in scope to the contributory pension, but less generous in amount and without the additional allowance. The criterion of entitlement, incapacity for work, was the same as that for sickness and invalidity benefit, and it followed that 'work' meant remunerated employment. There was a perceived need to extend NCIP to those primarily engaged in unremunerated work, such as caring for a home and family, conveniently if not always accurately, classi-

14 SSPA 1975, s.14.
15 SSA 1975, s.16(1).
16 P.142, above.
17 SI 1983/1598, reg 8A.
18 SSA 1975, s.16(2), as amended.
19 Ibid.
20 P.142, above.
 1 SSA 1975, s.16(2B)–(2D), but not so as to reduce the amount below that received on 15 September 1985: SSA 1985, s.9(6)–(9).

fied as 'disabled housewives'.[2] Two problems presented themselves: how was this group to be defined? And what test of incapacity should be applied to them? The answers which were eventually forthcoming and which were brought into force in 1977 were crude and discriminatory. The group was defined as comprising married women living with husbands and other women cohabiting with men. For NCIP to be payable, *any* such woman had to satisfy a dual test: that she was incapable of work (the standard condition applicable to remunerated employment) and that she was incapable of performing 'normal household duties'.[3] The latter posed considerable problems for medical assessment and reportedly subjected claimants to distress and humiliation,[4] but the most potent criticism was directed against the sex discrimination involved in the provision.[5] In particular, a majority of married women claimants who had to satisfy the dual test had been recently active in the labour market.

In 1983, the government published a departmental review of the provisions; this endorsed the criticisms and offered several options for reform.[6] The simplest of these would have been to abolish the household duties test and confer NCIP on all those incapable of remunerated work. This was rejected by the government on grounds of cost – an estimated additional £250 million per year. The alternative proposals involved selecting the more deserving cases from those who would not satisfy the contribution conditions for invalidity benefit and eliminating the sex discrimination under the existing law. The most obvious group requiring protection comprised those disabled at birth or in childhood. To select from those disabled when of working age but unable to fulfil the contribution conditions (the vast majority of whom are married women), required some rationing criterion. One possibility was to concentrate on lost earning potential and hence impose some test of recent activity in the labour market. This was regarded as too costly[7] and too difficult to apply in practice. The other proposals adopted a broader, income-maintenance goal but concentrated on the more severely disabled. Understandably, there was little enthusiasm for a revamped and non-discriminatory household duties test. The alternative, and the solution in fact adopted, was to apply an objective measurement of the degree of disablement through methods already used in the industrial injuries and war pension schemes. The new benefit, the severe disablement allowance, replaced NCIP in November 1984.[8] It is a flat-rate benefit, payable at approximately two-thirds of the basic rate for invalidity pension. A similar proportion governs the amount of increases for adult dependants, but child dependency additions are the same as those for the contributory benefit.

2 Report on Social Security Provision for Chronically Sick and Disabled People, 1973-74, HC 276, paras 43-44.
3 SSA 1975, s.36(2).
4 See particularly Equal Opportunities Commission *Behind Closed Doors* (1981) and Glendinning *After Working All These Years* (1980).
5 In addition to the references in n.4, above, see Richards [1978-9] JSWL 66, Loach and Lister *Second Class Disabled* (1978) and NIAC Report on A Question Relating to the Household Duties Test for Non-Contributory Invalidity Pension for Married Women (Cmnd 7955, 1980).
6 Review of the Household Duties Test (1983). The Report contains a valuable comparative account of foreign schemes.
7 Not the least because it would extend potentially to the 3 million working wives who still pay reduced contributions (see p.52, above) and who (arguably) are less deserving because they had made the deliberate decision not to be covered for sickness and invalidity: n.6, above, para 23 and 37.
8 HSSA 1984, s.11.

To gain title to the allowance (SDA), the claimant must (i) be incapable of work *and* (ii) have been so incapable when young *or* (iii) be severely disabled *or* (iv) have previously been entitled to NCIP. These will be considered in turn, followed by (v) other rules of entitlement.

i Incapable of work

The claimant must be incapable of work and have been so incapable for a period of 196 consecutive days.[9] The period of 196 days is in effect the same as the 168 days required for invalidity benefit – the latter, being based on entitlement to sickness benefit, necessarily excludes Sundays (or equivalent rest days) – but there is an important difference. For purposes of invalidity benefit, the claimant may aggregate spells of incapacity within one period of interruption of employment when they are not separated by more than eight weeks. For SDA, on the other hand, the test is 196 *consecutive* days of incapacity. However, once this initial requirement has been satisfied, continuous entitlement is based on a less strict criterion. The condition of 196 days is deemed to have been met for any subsequent days of incapacity within the same period of interruption of employment.[10] Since the 'period of interruption of employment' is construed in accordance with the linking rule,[11] the 196 consecutive waiting days will have to be served again only if the claimant is regarded as capable of work for a period of eight weeks or more.

ii Incapable when young

The first of the alternative routes to SDA is for those incaable of work when young. A claimant in this group has to establish that a period of 196 consecutive days of incapacity began on or before his twentieth birthday.[12] If he remains incapable of work he will normally be entitled immediately that waiting period has been served. However, the government was concerned to encourage young persons with a history of disability to attempt work without risking losing eventual entitlement to the allowance.[13] Thus, if the period of 196 days is followed by a period of capacity for work which does not exceed 182 days, then the claimant may still qualify under this head once a further period of 196 consecutive days of incapacity have been served.[14] The period of 182 days is relevant only if it occurs after the age of 15 years and 24 weeks.

iii Severely disabled

The second route is for the claimant to show that he is, and has been for a period of 196 consecutive days, 'disabled'.[15] A person is 'disabled', for this purpose'

> 'if he suffers from loss of physical or mental faculty such that the assessed extent of the resulting disablement is not less than 80 per cent'.[16]

This criterion adopts a principle and technique of assessment used for many years in the industrial injury and war pension schemes, and reference should

9 SSA 1975, s.36(2)–(3).
10 SI 1984/1303, reg 6.
11 P.141, above.
12 SSA 1975, s.36(2).
13 Mr T Newton, 59 HC Official Report (6th series) col 495.
14 SI 1984/1303, reg 7(3).
15 SSA 1975. s.36(3).
16 Ibid, s.36(5).

be made to the analysis of the relevant provisions in those contexts.[17] Suffice it here to observe that the level of disablement required is severe and would not, for example, cover the loss of a hand for which the prescribed degree of disablement is only 60 per cent.[18]

To satisfy the 80 per cent test, claimants must typically submit themselves for assessment by the medical authorities. However, there are categories of disabled persons who are deemed to have satisfied the test without further examination:[19]

(1) (most obviously) those whose disablement has been assessed at 80 per cent or more under the industrial injury or war pension schemes;

(2) those entitled to an attendance or mobility allowance (or the latter's equivalent under the war pension scheme);[20]

(3) those provided by the DHSS with an invalid tricycle or car or a private car allowance;[1]

(4) those registered as blind or partially sighted;[2]

(5) those who have received a payment under the Vaccine Damage Payments Act 1979.[3]

iv Prior entitlement to NCIP

At the time of the introduction of SDA, it was estimated that it would cover some 20,000 who had not been entitled to NCIP; on the other hand, the new provisions would exclude some 16,000 then entitled to NCIP.[4] In order that the latter should not be disadvantaged, transitional provisions enabled those entitled to NCIP immediately before both 10 September 1984 and 29 November 1984 to receive SDA for the remainder of the period of interruption of employment.[5]

v Other rules of entitlement

The allowance is not paid to those under 16 or in receipt of full-time education.[6] 'Full-time education' in this context applies to those aged 16 to 19 inclusive and must involve courses lasting at least 21 hours a week.[7] However, as a concession to children who require special teaching because of their handicap, a regulation provides that

in calculating the number of hours a week during which claimant attends that course no account shall be taken of any instruction or tuition which is not suitable

---

17 Pp. 286–292, below.

18 SI 1982/1408, Sch 2.

19 SI 1984/1303, reg 10, as amended.

20 See pp. 161–168 and 173–177, below.

1 See p.172, below.

2 Under National Assistance Act 1948, s.29, on which see Meredith Davies *The Disabled Child and Adult* (1982) ch 21.

3 For details, see Dworkin [1978–9] JSWL 330.

4 Written Answer 50 HC Official Report (6th series) col 623.

5 SI 1984/1303, reg 20. In Case 384/85 *Clarke v Chief Adjudication Officer* [1987] 3 CMLR 277, the European Court of Justice ruled that the transitional provisions contravened the principle of equal treatment laid down in EEC Directive 79/7 (OJ 1979, L6/24) since it discriminated against women who, because they could not satify the 'normal household duties' test, had not been entitled to NCIP. The decision, in principle, enabled such women to gain entitlement to SDA by demonstrating that they had been incapable of work for 196 consecutive days before the relevants dates in 1984. It seems, however, that many attempts to do this have been rejected on the ground that a relevant claim to NCIP was not made within the appropriate time limit.

6 SSA 1975, s.36(4).

7 SI 1984/1303, reg 8(1).

for persons of the same age and sex who do not suffer from a physical or mental disability.[8]

In particular, this means that hours during which methods of instruction specially designed for handicapped children are employed may be disregarded.[9]

SDA is paid to those who have reached pensionable age (65 for men, 60 for women) only if they were entitled (or would have been if not barred by the rules on overlapping benefits[10]) immediately before reaching that age.[11] Such persons must, of course, continue to satisfy the conditions of entitlement. Once, however, 'retiring age' is reached (70 for men, 65 for women) this no longer applies and the allowance will be paid until death, provided that it was in payment immediately before the retiring age was attained.[12]

Since SDA is a non-contributory benefit, there are special rules of entitlement to establish a sufficient connection with this country.[13]

(1) The claimant must have been resident in GB for an aggregate of 10 years in the 20 years immediately preceding the date for which the claim is made, or, if he is aged under 20, for an aggregate of 10 years since birth.
(2) Unless an airman, a merchant seaman, a member of the armed forces, or employed on the continental shelf (or a member of a family of such a person), he must be present in GB on that date and have been so present for 168 of the 196 days immediately preceding that date.

Once these conditions have been satisfied, they are deemed to have been satisfied for all subsequent days of incapacity during the same period of interruption of employment.[14]

F Common concepts

In this section we analyze concepts which are common to two or more of the specific benefits considered above. In general, questions concerned with the meaning of incapacity for work, the evidence required by the authorities and the grounds for disqualification as they arise in relation to sickness benefit, invalidity benefit and severe disablement allowance are the subject of identical provisions under the Social Security Act 1975 (and its subordinate legislation) and of common judicial interpretation by the Commissioner and the courts. Statutory sick pay is governed by a separate code. While some of the relevant provisions adopt language identical or similar to those in the social security legislation, the latter is not formally incorporated. Nevertheless, it would be surprising if the authorities who are responsible for determining issues of entitlement to SSP were not to have regard to decisions which they themselves have made on the same concepts in relation to the social security benefits. In this section, therefore, we shall assume a uniformity of interpretation but point to differences as and when necessary.

8 Ibid, reg 8(1)(b).
9 *R(S) 2/87*.
10 SI 1984/1303, reg 4.
11 SSA 1975, s.36(4)(d).
12 SI 1984/1303, reg 5.
13 Ibid, reg 3.
14 Ibid, reg 3(3).

i Some specific disease or bodily or mental disablement

For the purposes of all four benefits, incapacity of work must result from 'some specific disease or bodily or mental disablement'.[15] Whether the claimant's condition may be so determined is a question of fact[16] for which resort must be had to expert medical opinion. A 'disease' has been defined as 'a departure from health capable of identification by its signs and symptoms, an abnormality of some sort'[17] and 'specific' implies that it is of a kind identified by medical science.[18] 'Disablement' involves a state of deprivation or incapacitation of ability measured against the abilities of a 'normal' person.[19] The ordinary condition of pregnancy does not come within these definitions and is, in any event, the subject of specific provision, viz. maternity allowance and statutory maternity pay.[20] During periods of entitlements to either of these, a woman is precluded from claiming an income-maintenance disability benefit.[1] But there is no reason why she should not qualify for the latter outside of such periods on proof of a physical or mental disablement resulting from, but going beyond, the ordinary incidents of pregnancy.[2] There is no reported decision on the question whether damage to a prosthesis, such as an artificial limb, can constitute 'bodily disablement', but for analogous purposes under the industrial injuries scheme it has been held that such damage is to be treated as 'personal injury' where the prosthesis concerned is so intimately linked with the claimant's body as to form part of that body.[3]

As medical science has shown greater awareness of different types of psychological disorder, so there has been a natural tendency to extend the certification for 'mental disablement'. But the legislation must necessarily assume some principle of moral responsibility, or 'work-shy' persons might claim to be mentally disabled. The authorities have attempted to resolve the difficulties by reference to the word 'specific' in the statutory definition which, it is said, qualifies both 'disease' and 'bodily or mental disablement'; so if the alleged condition cannot be identified in the state of current medical knowledge, the claimant may not succeed.[4] Even if the condition is recognised, it may be regarded as a 'defect of personality' rather than a 'disease'. Such was the view taken by a Commissioner in 1959 when denying benefit to a claimant with Munchausen's syndrome, a condition in which a person habitually presents himself at hospital for treatment of a disease from which he does not, in fact, suffer.[5] In a recent case on the point, I.Edward-Jones, Commissioner, drew a distinction between a mental disability, as a result of which the claimant could not work and a voluntary attitude in which the claimant could, but would not, work; however, he went on to suggest that a 'personality disorder' might come within the former category.[6]

The disability (or treatment rendered necessary by it[7]) must be the substan-

15 SSA 1975, s.17(1)(a)(ii) (sickness and invalidity benefit); SI 1984/1303, reg 2(3) (SDA); SSHBA 1982, s.1(3) (SSP).
16 *R(S) 7/53*.
17 *CS 221/49*, para 3.
18 *CS 7/82*, noted at [1982] JSWL 306.
19 Ibid.
20 Ch 6, below.
 1 SSHBA 1982, s.3(2)(d) and s.3(9), as amended; SSA 1986, Sch 4, para 11.
 2 *CS 221/49*.
 3 *R(I) 8/81*, p.258, below.
 4 *CS 1/81*, noted at [1982] JSWL 48.
 5 *R(S) 6/59*.
 6 *CS 7/82*, n.18, above.
 7 *CS 69/50*; *R(S) 24/51*.

tial cause of the incapacity for work, but factors extraneous to the physical or mental condition, such as the personal or domestic circumstances of the claimant, are irrelevant.[8] A person with limited mobility who, as a result of the weather, cannot get to his normal place of work may not draw benefit.[9]

ii Incapable of work

The disease or disablement must render the claimant incapable of work. The work which is relevant for this purpose is 'work which the person can reasonably be expected to do'.[10] In applying this test, the authorities will have regard, first, to the duration of the incapacity. In the large majority of cases, where the incapacity is only temporary, the question is simply whether the claimant is incapable of carrying out his usual work.[11] In relation to SSP, this is reinforced by the legislative provision that the work of which he must be incapable is the work which he can be reasonably expected to do under the contract with the employer who is liable to pay SSP.[12] The same approach will typically be taken in relation to sickness benefit which, it will be recalled, is available for the first six months of a period of interruption of employment. There is, however, no hard and fast rule to this effect. Before the end of the six-month period, it may become clear that the claimant will not be able to resume his normal occupation.[13] The governing principles were stated by the Commissioner in 1978:

> Reasonableness, rather than any specific measure of time, is the crucial matter. It is not normally reasonable, in the case of a short-term incapacity, to expect a claimant to change his occupation. If incapacity is continued, it may become reasonable to do so. Just at what stage must depend on the circumstances of the particular case: not merely age, education, experience and state of health, but other possible factors such as the nature of the claimant's normal occupation, how long he has been engaged in it, whether his incapacity for it is likely to be permanent or long-continued, whether he is likely to be adaptable to a new form of employment, and possibly whether he is due to retire at no distant date.[14]

So, in the instant case, he concluded that a salesman suffering from osteo-arthritis of spine and hypertension could, after five months of benefit, reasonably attempt other kinds of work.[15]

Typically, then, for invalidity benefit and exceptionally also for sickness benefit the claimant's capacity is judged in relation to work other than that in his usual occupation. Such work must be 'remunerative work . . . for which an employer would be willing to pay, or work as a self-employed person in some gainful occupation'.[16] This includes part-time work, but it is not to be

---

8 *R(S) 13/54.*

9 *R(S) 8/53; 2/58 (SB).*

10 SSA 1975, s.17(1)(a); SSHBA 1982, s.1(3). This statutory test was introduced only in 1973 (NISBA 1973, s.5) but was intended to restate an interpretation of the law which had been applied in practice for many years: *R(S) 2/78* para 6.

11 *R(S) 2/82* para 4. Where employed, e.g. under different contracts of employment, on different types of work, the test applies to all such types: *CS 8/79*, noted at [1978–9] JSWL 59.

12 SSHBA 1982, s.1(3).

13 See, e.g. *R(S) 6/85.*

14 *R(S) 2/78*, para 8, H A Shewan, Comr.

15 See also *R(S) 3/81*: unreasonable to hold to an occupation after 18 months merely because pursuit of another occupation would involve the loss of valuable pension rights.

16 *R(S) 11/51(T)* para 5. See also *R(S) 4/79.*

assumed that because a claimant is able to do light (e.g. clerical) work at home he will necessarily come within this principle: there must be evidence that he would be remunerated for such work.[17] In some cases, it will be legitimate for the authorities to conclude, on the basis of medical assessment of the claimant's condition and common knowledge of work opportunities, that there is a range of occupations, or at least one occupation, of which the claimant must be capable; in less obvious cases, more specific evidence, for example, that supplied by Disablement Resettlement Officers, may be required.[18]

As a result of some disability the claimant may have given up remunerated employment and yet have been able to do some housework at home. In 1951 a Tribunal of Commissioners held in such a case that if the claimant was able to do the work of a normal household that was prima facie evidence that she was capable of doing the same work for remuneration.[19] While this decision accords with the principles stated above, it would clearly be discriminatory if applied only to woman. More problematic are the cases of self-employed persons who are capable of doing some form of management or supervision of their own business. A large number of reported decisions have been concerned with this issue,[20] and it is obviously difficult to draw the line between an active manager and a mere onlooker. Perhaps the greatest assistance is to be had from the approach suggested by a Northern Ireland Commissioner.[1] According to him, the question is whether the work which the claimant is capable of doing is of such substance or extent as either (1) would be likely to command remuneration if it was carried out for an outside employer, or (2) materially affected the day-to-day carrying on of the business. To determine these points regard may be had to e.g. the size and ownership of the business, the nature of accounting and drawing of profits, and whether there was a change of personnel consequent on the claimant's disability.

It is in principle irrelevant that there is available in the locality no work for which the claimant is admittedly capable or that the prospects of finding such work are poor;[2] the incapacity is *for* work, not *in obtaining* work.[3] Unemployment benefit is available for those capable of, but unable to find, appropriate work. The degree of mobility expected of claimants for the disability benefits will, nevertheless, vary from case to case and is dependent on such factors as age, health and experience.[4] Thus the test will not be applied strictly to an individual able to work only irregularly because of intermittent disablement,[5] and a claim will not be defeated by evidence that 'he would be capable of working in some exotic employment which was undertaken only by a few workers in some part of Great Britain remote from his established

---

17 *R(S) 3/82* para 13.
18 *R(S) 6/85*. Other social security systems provide for a more systematic and structured approach to issues of vocational capacity: see e.g. Mashaw *Bureaucratic Justice* (1983) pp. 114–123.
19 *R(S) 11/51(T)*. It may be rebutted if the claimant is capable only of 'light' household duties e.g. the purchase and preparation of food: *R 3/60 (SB)*.
20 See, inter alia, *R(S) 5/51; R(S) 22/51; R(S) 2/61; R(S) 4/79; R(S) 10/79*. See also the cases considered pp. 193–195, below.
1 *5/57 (SB)*, para 3.
2 *R(S) 21/51; R(S) 24/51; R(S) 1/79*.
3 *R(S) 2/82(T)* para 11(2).
4 Ibid, para 11(1).
5 *R(S) 9/79*. para 8.

home', or work 'so rarely encountered as to put it outside the limits of practical contemplation'.[6]

iii Evidence of incapacity

The onus of satisfying the incapacity for work test is on the claimant.[7] Where a spell of incapacity lasts for seven days or less, or for the first seven days of a longer spell,[8] the claimant is entitled to rely on self-certification, that is, a declaration in writing that he is unfit for work.[9] If the claim is for SSP, the question of whether a doctor's certificate is required for periods of incapacity longer than a week is determined solely by the relevant employer.[10] The reluctance to impose a legislative obligation to this effect may be attributed partly to cost considerations and partly to a policy of non-interference in employer – employee relationships but it is controversial. Since the National Insurance Fund provides a 100 per cent reimbursement to the employer for SSP, he has little financial incentive to verify the validity of his employees' claims and, in times of slack demand, there is a temptation from him to 'lay off' employees not genuinely sick substantially at the cost to other contributors.

The provision of medical evidence is obligatory for the social security benefits (sickness benefit, invalidity benefit, severe disablement allowance) following the first seven days of incapacity. The prescribed form of evidence is governed by the Medical Evidence Regulations[11] and there is an equivalent instrument for SSP claims where the employer requires medical certification.[12] The regulations provide that evidence of incapacity shall be furnished by the claimant either 'by means of a certificate in the form of a statement in writing given by a doctor' in the manner prescribed by the Regulations, or 'by such other means as may be sufficient in the circumstances of any particular case'.[13] The alternative, unprescribed method is designed to cater for those, particularly Christian Scientists, who on grounds of conscience prefer not to attend for medical treatment,[14] but it is far from clear what sort of evidence will in such circumstances satisfy the authorities. In one case an acknowledgement by an employer of the claimant's incapacity was regarded as insufficient.[15] On the other hand, the fact of hospitalisation will raise a presumption of incapacity and this remains true even where after investigation the claimant is found not to be suffering from the suspected disease.[16]

The normal method involves a statement by a registered medical practi-

---

6 *R(S) 2/82(T)* paras 10(2) and 19.
7 *R(S) 13/52.*
8 The period in question must, however, follow a period of capacity of work: SI 1976/615, reg 5(2).
9 Ibid, reg 5. The system of self-certification for short periods was introduced in 1982 (SI 1982/699) mainly to reduce costs and the burden on general practitioners who have always regarded the work as interfering with the doctor-patient relationship. See SSAC Report on the Draft 1982 Regulations (Cmnd 8560) and more generally *Fisher*.
10 SSHBA 1982, s.17(2).
11 SI 1976/615, as amended.
12 SI 1985/1604.
13 SI 1976/615, reg. 2(1).
14 See Report of the National Insurance Advisory Committee on the draft regulations 1975–76, HC 349, para 32.
15 *R(S) 13/51.*
16 *R(S) 1/58.*

tioner that, as a result of diagnosis of a disorder, he has advised the claimant to refrain from work.[17]

– The statement must contain a diagnosis of the claimant's disorder justifying the advice to refrain from work. Where the doctor is of the opinion that work may be resumed within a period of two weeks, he is to issue a 'closed' statement, that is, one specifying the date when the claimant should be fit to resume. In other cases it will be an 'open' statement, the doctor merely indicating the minimum period during which the patient should abstain from work. This should not be a period greater than six months, unless (for the purposes of invalidity benefit) the claimant has already, on the advice of the doctor, refrained from work for six months. In such a case, if it is his opinion that work should not be resumed for the foreseeable future, the doctor will simply enter 'until further notice'. Where a claimant has been the subject of an 'open' statement but nevertheless becomes fit to resume work, the doctor should issue a 'closed' statement to that effect. In such cases, where there are no longer any clinical signs of the previously disabling disorder, the doctor need not specify a diagnosis.

Normally medical statements in the above form will be regarded by the adjudication officer as sufficient proof of incapacity. But in certan situations, for example, where the period of incapacity has been longer than originally anticipated, or where repeated short-term claims have been received, and where the claimant has been on holiday or on strike, the adjudication officer is likely to take steps to verify the claimant's condition, either by a reference to the Regional Medical Officer, or by an officer visiting the claimant in his home.[18] Social Security Appeal Tribunals and Commissioners may also refer a case to a medical practitioner for examination and report.[19] The usual practice[20] in the former case is to advise the claimant to see his own doctor for an examination, and then to present himself for a further examination by the Medical Officer. The latter's opinion is then communicated to the claimant's doctor who thus has an opportunity to disagree, stating his own views. Should a conflict of opinion remain unresolved, it is the duty of the determining authorities to examine all the evidence and form their own view.[1] They are in no sense bound to prefer the Medical Officer's opinion. Indeed, in several cases, the Commissioner has rejected this evidence.[2] Conversely, the medical statement by the claimant's own doctor is in no sense conclusive, and it may be over-ridden even where the conflicting evidence is of a non-medical character, such as the cases where a claimant allegedly disabled by influenza could not be found at home[3] or another supposed to be suffering

17 SI 1976/615, Sch 1. This replaces the former system under which the doctor 'certified' that the claimant was incapable of work (see SI 1967/520). The new formulation was intended as a more accurate reflection of clinical responsibility towards the patient: see SSAC Report, n.9, above, para 5 and *Fisher* para 187.
18 Ibid, Appendix 7. There is a power to disqualify the claimant should he fail to co-operate: p.157, below.
19 SI 1986/2218, reg 8 and see *R(S) 3/84*.
20 See *R(S) 7/53*.
1 The adjudication officer may decide on this evidence not to renew entitlement to benefit, but he cannot rely on medical evidence alone to review an award already made on the ground that there has been a relevant change of circumstances: *R(S) 6/78*, and see p.585, below.
2 E.g. *R(S) 15/54; 30/58 (SB)*
3 *R(S) 16/54*.

from a sprained ligament was seen cycling.[4] If the authorities are dissatisfied as to the evidence produced by either side they may, if they think it advisable, order a further examination, perhaps by a specialist.[5]

In adverting to all relevant information available, the authorities may take into account the claimant's past medical and employment record. This may reveal a pattern which gives rise to a suspicion of malingering. In several cases, for example, the claimant's record has shown a number of claims for short periods near public holidays.[6] This by itself is not necessarily prejudicial to his case, but if it is supported by other factors which cast doubt on his doctor's statement, it may serve to disentitle him from benefit.[7] Of course, it would be quite wrong to use a long-term record of bad health as evidence *against* the claimant. Unless, therefore, there are additional facts which render the evidence suspect, it may help him to prove that he is incapable of work, especially if there is a seasonal cycle in his record of illness.[8]

iv Deemed incapable
The Regulations[9] allow for a claimant to succeed in four situations where he is not 'incapable of work' within the principles described above.

a *Precautionary or convalescent reasons for not working*
The first has its origin in the way the approved societies administered benefits under the old national health insurance scheme.[10] The idea was that persons who were capable of working but whose doctor advised them on health grounds not to, should be encouraged to follow that advice, without losing benefit. In fact, there has never been a special form of medical certification for this purpose, and in the past doctors and administrators have not been too concerned to distinguish cases of genuine incapacity for work from those where absence of work is regarded as medically desirable.[11] Nevertheless, in strict law, there is a special set of conditions which must be satisfied if the claimant is to be paid benefit in the latter situation. He must prove that

(i)   he is under medical care in respect of a disease or disablement . . . and
(ii) it is certified by a registered medical practitioner that for precautionary or convalescent reasons consequential on such disease or disablement he should abstain from work, and
(iii) he does no work.[12]

For the purposes of (i), 'medical care' is to be broadly construed: it covers all cases where the claimant receives advice from the doctor in relation to the disease or disablement.[13] As regards (ii), it is not necessary for the doctor to use

---

4 *3/59 (SB).*
5 This is particularly true of psychiatric illnesses: e.g. *R(S) 4/56.*
6 *R(S) 16/54; R(S) 5/60; R(S) 1/67; R(S) 15/55.*
7 *R(S) 4/60.*
8 *4/59 (SB); R(S) 1/67.*
9 References in the following paragraphs are to the regulations which govern sickness and invalidity benefit (SI 1983/1598). There are explicitly applied to SDA by SI 1984/1303, reg 7(1) and are similar in all material respects to those governing SSP (SI 1982/894, reg 2) except that the latter does not cover therapeutic work, p.155, below, a situation which cannot realistically arise on a SSP claim.
10 See *R(S) 1/79* para 11.
11 *R(S) 2/79* para 15.
12 SI 1983/1598, reg 3(1)(a).
13 *R(S) 8/61; R(S) 1/72; R(S) 1/79.* The narrower interpretation in *R(S) 24/25* has been discredited.

any particular form or language: 'a letter or other informal document would suffice, provided that the advice can be taken to be a certificate and includes reasons that can be recognised as precautionary or convalescent'.[14] Such advice is a necessary, but not a sufficient, condition for entitlement:[15] the adjudication officer is to take account of all the circumstances, including the medical evidence, to determine whether there is some medical reason why the claimant should have abstained from work.[16]

b *Carrier of infectious disease*
This covers the case where the claimant though capable of work represents a risk to others at his place of employment. But here the mere advice of a doctor is insufficient; he must show that

> he is excluded from work on the certificate of a Medical Officer for Environmental Health and is under medical observation by reason of his being a carrier, or having been in contact with a case, of infectious disease.[17]

c *Incapacity for part of day*
Where the claimant is incapable of work for only a part of the day, he is nevertheless deemed to have been incapable for the whole of the day, provided that he does no work on that day.[18]

d *Therapeutic work*
The fact that a claimant does some work is, of course, prima facie evidence that he is capable of such work, and thus, not entitled to benefit. But the work in question must be of a type for which he would be remunerated as an employed person or would constitute the gainful occupation of a self-employed person.[19] Work carried out primarily for therapeutic purposes for little reward would not typically come within this definition, but a special regulation governs the matter though, unfortunately, not without ambiguity.

> A person who is suffering from some specific disease or bodily or mental disablement but who, by reason only of the fact that he has done some work while so suffering, is found not to be incapable of work by reason thereof, may be deemed to be so incapable if that work is–
> (i) work which is undertaken under medical supervision as part of his treatment while he is a patient in or of a hospital or similar institution, or
> (ii) work which is not so undertaken and which he has good cause for doing, and from which, in either case, his earnings do not ordinarily exceed £26.00 in the week in which that work is performed.[20]

The Court of Appeal has held[1] that the phrase 'by reason only . . . suffering' is not to be treated as a pre-condition to the application of the remainder of

14 *R(S) 2/79 (T)* para 19.
15 *R v National Insurance Comr, ex parte Department of Health and Social Security,* Smith J dissenting, quashing *R(S) 1/79,* reported as Appendix to that decision. See also *R(S) 2/79* paras 9–11.
16 Per Wien J, *R v National Insurance Comr, ex parte Department of Health and Social Security,* n.15, above.
17 SI 1983/1598, reg 3(1)(b) and see *R(S) 1/72* para 14, D Neligan, Comr.
18 SI 1983/1584, reg 3(2).
19 P.70, above.
20 SI 1983/1598, reg 3(3), as amended. The 'earnings rule' incorporates an amendment (SI 1987/688) designed to deal with problems of intermittent earnings arising in *R(S) 6/86(T)*: see p.377, below.
 1 *Hunt v Chief Adjudication Officer, Merriman v Insurance Officer,* reported in *R(S) 3/86.*

the regulation. Therefore, the discretion to treat the claimant as incapable of work arises if he can satisfy either (i) or (ii), provided that any earnings do not exceed the prescribed amount. This interpretation may have the merit of simplicity but it seems to override the clear literal meaning of the provision, previously attributed by the Commissioner[2] that if the adjudication officer denies benefit on a ground other than the fact of working, for example, a medical opinion that the claimant was capable of work, the regulation cannot apply.[3]

The first category of excepted work is not broad. The claimant must be a patient of the institution in question, though he need not be a resident. Thus in *R(S) 3/52,*

> C, suffering from tuberculosis, was engaged for two-and-a-half days a week in a factory specially operated for the rehabilitation of tuberculosis victims. He attended hospital as an out-patient once every two months. It was held that he was a patient 'of' (though not 'in') a hospital.

The rule on hospitalisation, at least as interpreted, is a very artificial one. If, in the last case, the claimant had been under the supervision of a specialist without attending a hospital he would not have succeeded.[4]

The second and alternative category of excusable work is much vaguer. It used to apply only to work undertaken as a 'non-employed' person,[5] but this limitation no longer obtains. Nor need the claimant show that the work was undertaken under medical supervision, but 'good cause' for doing the work must be proved. The meaning of the phrase in this context has received little attention from the Commissioner, but it seems clear that medical (i.e. therapeutic) reasons will suffice.[6]

v Disqualification

There are certain grounds on which the claimant may be disqualified from benefit for a maximum period of six weeks.[7] The underlying purposes of these provisions are threefold: to protect the fund against fraudulent claims; to exclude from benefit those who are incapacitated or remain incapacitated as a result of their own deliberate conduct; and to reinforce the machinery for the control and administration of the system. There are, however, no equivalent provisions governing SSP. Control is here left in the hands of the individual employer, though there is a residual power in the Secretary of State of ensure that the system for controlling sickness absence is adequate.[8]

a *Misconduct*

The first ground is where the claimant has 'become incapable of work through his own misconduct'.[9] Under the old National Health Insurance

---

2 In the *Hunt* and *Merriman* cases, *CS 491/82* and *CWS 23/83* respectively.
3 Kerr LJ, n.1, above, at pp. 7–8, argued that if the Commissioner's interpretation were followed the provision would be self-defeating because in almost all cases there would be medical evidence that work in (i) or (ii) would be within the claimant's capacity. See, generally, Mesher [1986] JSWL 53.
4 See *R(S) 5/52.*
5 Cf SI 1967/330, reg 7(h).
6 *R(S) 4/79* para 11, V G H Hallett, Comr. An intention merely to earn some money is insufficient: *CS 8/79*, noted [1978–79] JSWL 443.
7 The provisions which extended the maximum period of disqualification for unemployment benefit (p.109, above) do not apply to disability benefits.
8 SSHBA 1982, s.19, incorporating relevant provisions in SSA 1975, ss.144–145.
9 SSA 1975, s.20(2)(a); SI 1983/1598, reg 17(1)(a).

Acts, an approved society might, in accordance with its own rules and subject to the approval of the Minister, suspend an insured person from benefit for misconduct.[10] The principle was derived from and analogous to[11] the defence of 'serious and wilful misconduct' under the Workmen's Compensation Act.[12] The rules of some societies spelt out in greater detail the types of misconduct which would entitle them to disqualify the sick person. Thus, according to one,[13] benefit might be refused if the condition was 'wilfully incurred' by 'fighting, wrestling, using weapons (except in self-defence), drunkenness, indecent or disorderly conduct, venereal disease'. The modern provision does not limit the misconduct to 'serious' or 'wilful', and it is possible to argue that it extends to reckless disregard of precautions ordered or recommended by, for example, an employer or a doctor.[14] The only reported decision, however, carries the implication that the conduct must be wilful.[15] The incapacity was due to alcoholism and it was held that the claimant could only rebut the inference of misconduct if he could show that his will-power had been so impaired that he was unable to moderate his drinking. There are two explicit situations in which disqualification is not to be imposed: where the incapacity is due to venereal disease or to pregnancy.[16]

b *Examination*
Disqualification may be incurred if the claimant

> fails without good cause to comply with a notice in writing given by or on behalf of the Secretary of State requiring him to attend for and submit himself to medical or other examination on a date not earlier than the third day after the day on which the notice was sent and at a time and place specified in that notice. . . . [17]

It will be recalled that the adjudication officer may wish to verify a claimant's alleged disability by requiring him to submit to an examination by the Regional Medical Officer. Not surprisingly, the requirement is reinforced by a sanction, hence the above regulation. Of course illness or physical disability preventing the claimant attending for examination will constitute good cause.[18] What of those who on grounds of religious conviction or otherwise object to medical examination? The question was considered in *R(S) 9/51*. It was held that a Christian Scientist who satisfied the authorities on the conviction of her beliefs should not be disqualified. The onus of proof was on her, and it was not sufficient to show that she was a member of a church whose tenets forbade her submission to treatment or examination. The crux of the matter was her *personal* attitude, and this must be based on a firm conviction that her religious beliefs required her to refuse.

10 See the Model Rules issued by the Ministry, esp. No 13(1).
11 See Reported Decision on Appeals and Applications under NHIA 1936, s.163, No CIII.
12 WCA 1897, s.1(2)(c).
13 N.11, above, Decision XIII.
14 Potter and Stansfield *National Insurance* (2nd edn) p.111.
15 *R(S) 2/53*.
16 SI 1983/1598, reg 17(1)(a).
17 Ibid, reg 17(1)(b); 'medical . . . examination' includes 'bacteriological and radiographical tests and similar investigations': SSA 1975, Sch 20. The three days following the notice may include a Sunday (SI 1983/1598, reg 17(2)) but the requirements as to notice must be strictly complied with: *R(S) 1/87*.
18 But the test is an objective one: it will be insufficient if the claimant merely 'thinks' that he is not well enough to attend: n.11, above, Decision XXXVIII.

c *Treatment*
The third ground of disqualification arises where the claimant

> fails without good cause to attend for, or to submit himself to, medical or other
> treatment.[19]

The rationale here is similar to that justifying the misconduct rule. The
incapacity must not be voluntarily incurred. Consequently the claimant must
take reasonable steps to regain his capacity to work. As regards 'good cause',
there is little to add to what was said under 'examination'. But difficult questions arise as to the steps in recovery which might reasonably be required of
an individual. Should he be compelled to undergo an operation for which he
has a morbid fear? The matter was very fully discussed at the Committee
stage of the 1911 Bill.[20] On the one hand, it was argued that to compel a person to be vaccinated or to undergo an operation interfered with a fundamental liberty, and in many cases would involve a risk greater than that
inherent in avoiding the treatment.[1] The opposing view was that the contributors to the fund ought not to support for a number of years a man who
refused to undergo on wholly inadequate grounds an operation which was
necessary for his health and which could not possibly endanger his life.[2] A
compromise solution was reached, and the amendment so formulated has
been incorporated in the legislation ever since. In its present form it provides
that the

> disqualification shall not apply to any failure to attend for or to submit to vacci-
> nation or inoculation of any kind or to a surgical operation, unless the failure is a
> failure to attend for or submit to a surgical operation of a minor character, and is
> unreasonable.[3]

As with the other grounds of disqualification, little guidance is to be found
in the Commissioners' decisions on what might be regarded as 'unreasonable' failure, and how a distinction is to be drawn between 'major' and
'minor' operations. On the latter point, however, both the policy inherent in
the provision, and the currency of medical usage,[4] suggest that a 'minor'
operation is one which, in ordinary circumstances, does not involve a risk
to life.

d *Rules of behaviour*
Under the old National Health Insurance Acts an approved society might,
subject to the approval of the Minister, make rules governing the behaviour
of the insured person during sickness or disability. The Model Rules prepared
by the Minister, and in practice adopted by most societies,[5] prescribed certain
standards of conduct. After 1946 these were incorporated in the draft
Unemployment and Sickness Benefit Regulations, but, following recommendations of the National Insurance Advisory Committee,[6] were significantly
amended before they were brought into effect. Under the Regulations now in

---

19 SI 1983/1598, reg 17(1)(c); 'medical . . . treatment' means 'medical, surgical or rehabilitative treatment (including any course of diet or other regimen)': SSA 1975, Sch 20.
20 29 HC Official Report (5th series) cols 330–342.
 1 See e.g. Mr D Lloyd-George ibid, at col 333.
 2 See e.g. Mr A Chamberlain, ibid, at cols 334–335.
 3 SI 1983/1598, reg 17(1)(c).
 4 See Dorland *Medical Dictionary* (26th edn) at p.927.
 5 The 1938 version of the Rules are set out in Lesser *The Law of National Health Insurance*
   (1939) pp. 1108–1109.
 6 1947–48, HC 162, para 26.

force, disqualification may be imposed if the claimant fails without good cause to observe any one of three rules.

(1) to refrain from behaviour calculated to retard his recovery, and to answer any reasonable enquiries . . . by the Secretary of State or his officers directed to ascertaining whether he is doing so.[7]

This, together with the 'misconduct' provision, constitute the statutory safeguards against voluntary disability. The latter ground governs cases where the voluntary conduct causes the incapacity; the behaviour provision applies throughout the period of disability. The word 'calculated' is not to be taken too literally. The test is an objective one: was the behaviour likely to retard recovery?[8] On the other hand, there has been a limited interpretation of the 'recovery' which has been retarded. It must be from a disease or disablement: it cannot be invoked against a claimant who declines to continue rehabilitative treatment which was having no effect on his physical condition.[9] There are few reported instances of this ground for disqualification. In *R(S) 21/52* it was held to have been rightly imposed on a claimant who, suffering from influenzal bronchitis, nevertheless undertook a motoring expedition 60 miles away and was there taken ill.

The requirement as to the answering of enquiries is regarded as an essential part of the control mechanism, but the provision expressly excludes 'enquires relating to medical examination, treatment or advice'.[10] This resulted from the National Insurance Advisory Committee's dislike of the approved society rules of which it was one.[11] It was thought to be too much of an intrusion into the privacy of the relationship between the medical practitioner and his patient.

(2) Not to be absent from his place of residence without leaving word where he may be found.[12]

The purpose of this rule is to provide a safeguard against deliberate and persistent avoidance of the DHSS visiting officers. Paradoxically in the light of this aim, it has been held that it cannot be invoked to disqualify a claimant who, at the relevant time, had no place of residence.[13] The pre-war rules tended to be more rigorous, not only stipulating certain times when the claimant must be at home, but also restraining him from leaving his locality at any time without either just cause or the consent of the Society. The present form of the rule has been considered unnecessarily restrictive by some,[14] but in practice it will not be invoked by the Department unless visits by officers have already proved to be ineffective[15] and it is, in any case, subject to the defence of good cause.[16]

(3) To do no work for which remuneration is, or would ordinarily be, payable. . . .[17]

7 SI 1983/1548, reg 17(1)(d)(i).
8 *R(S) 21/52*.
9 *R(S) 3/57*.
10 SI 1983/1598, reg 17(1)(d)(i).
11 N.6, above.
12 SI 1983/1598, reg 17(1)(d)(ii).
13 *R(S) 7/83*.
14 NIAC Report, n.6, above.
15 *Fisher* para 181.
16 Cf *R(S) 6/55*.
17 SI 1983/1598, reg 17(1)(d)(iii).

A person who works may be disentitled from benefit on the ground that it is prima facie evidence that he is not incapable of such work.[18] The provision quoted above is different in two respects. First, it gives rise to disqualification for a maximum period of six weeks; it does not disentitle the claimant altogether. Secondly, unlike the ground for disentitlement, it is not confined to 'work which the person can reasonably be expected to do'.[19] In other words, a claimant may be disqualified, but not disentitled, if during a period when he is incapable of work which is regarded as suitable for him (for the first six months, generally his normal occupation[20]), he does another kind of work 'for which remuneration is, or would ordinarily be, payable'.[1] However, it is provided that this should not include work of a therapeutic nature.[2] The conditions which the claimant must satisfy to obtain relief from disqualification on this ground have been described in a previous section.[3]

e *Good cause*
The claimant may avoid disqualification if he is able to show 'good cause'. Mere ignorance of rules of conduct will not suffice.[4] The following of medical advice, if unambiguous and specific, that the claimant should do a little work,[5] or should absent himself from his residence for a few days, has been held to constitute good cause.[6]

f *Relevance of other legal proceedings*
The circumstances relied on to justify disqualification may also have been the subject of other legal proceedings, for example a criminal prosecution for making false representations to obtain benefit. A finding of fact made in such proceedings is not regarded as conclusive for social security purposes, but may nevertheless be used as evidence by the adjudicating authorities.[7] The Commissioners has held that a conviction for an offence relating to the same benefit for the same period as is in issue should shift the onus of proof onto the claimant to show that, notwithstanding the conviction, he is entitled to benefit.[8]

g *Period of disqualification*
The maximum period of disqualification under the Act is six weeks. As with unemployment benefit,[9] the adjudicating authorities have a discretion as to the appropriate period for the particular case and the factors considered in that context apply equally here.

18 Cf p.150, above.
19 Cf SSA 1975, s.17(1)(a). and p.150 above.
20 P.150, above.
 1 On which see p.70, above.
 2 SI 1983/1598, reg 17(1)(d)(iii).
 3 P.155, above.
 4 *R(S) 21/52.*
 5 *R(S) 10/60.*
 6 *R(S) 6/55.*
 7 See also, on unemployment benefit, pp. 100–101, above.
 8 *R(S) 2/80*, J S Watson, Comr, applying by analogy the principle contained in the Civil Evidence Act 1968, s.11(2)(a) – on which see *Stupple v Royal Insurance Co Ltd* [1971] 1 QB 50 – even though that Act does not apply to social security determinations. Cf *R(S) 10/79* where it was held that when the evidence on which the convictions was based is not made available to the adjudicating authorities and the evidence that it available is plainly inconsistent with any grounds upon which the conviction could have been based, the fact of criminal conviction should be ignored.
 9 P.110, above.

Part 3 Benefits for specific needs

A Attendance allowance

i General

The new concern for the disabled manifested in the 1960s was directed in particular to a major group insufficiently protected under existing schemes, comprising those who those who needed substantial personal assistance from another in matters of self-care. The attendance allowance was proposed in 1969 as part of the Labour government's National Superannuation plan,[10] and was adopted by the Conservative government immediately on assuming power in 1970. Provision was made for a single flat-rate benefit payable to a person requiring either 'frequent attention throughout the day and prolonged or repeated attention during the night; or . . . continual supervision from another person in order to avoid substantial danger to himself or others'.[11] The joint test on the first of the alternative conditions excluded many potential claimants, and in 1973 a lower rate of allowance became payable to those who required the necessary attention either during the day or during the night.[12] The question of what degree of attendance should be required during the night proved to be troublesome. An authoritative interpretation of the statutory provisions by the Court of Appeal in 1987[13] appeared to resolve the matter but the government considered this to be too generous and the criteria of entitlement were narrowed by the Social Security Act 1988.

Decisions on the medical criteria are formally made by the Attendance Allowance Board. In practice, an examination is carried out by one doctor selected by the Board and the report is scrutinised by another doctor who has delegated authority from the Board to determine eligibility. A claimant dissatisfied with an adverse decision can apply for a review which will be carried out by another doctor whose report will be the subject of a provisional determination by a committee of delegated medical practitioners. If the claimant disagrees with this, further evidence may be communicated to the Board which itself may sometimes make the final decision. Thereafter, the claimant has a right of appeal to the Commissioner, but only on a question of law.

The system of medical assessment and adjudication has given rise to much criticism.[14] While the average delay in reaching a decision is 12½ weeks, some cases have taken over six months to clear.[15] There is evidence which suggests that, perhaps because of the complexities of assessment, take-up is low.[16] In 1979–80 some 75 per cent of reviews resulted in a more favourable decision for the claimant,[17] suggesting that the quality of decisionmaking at first examination is low, an impression confirmed in a report on the process

---

10 See White Paper, National Superannuation and Social Insurance (1969, Cmnd 3883), para 90–91.
11 NIA 1970, s.4(2).
12 NIA 1972, s.2(1).
13 *Moran v Secretary of State for Social Services* (1987) Times, 14 March.
14 Smith (1981) 48 Poverty 9; Brown *The Disability Income System* (1984) pp. 249–253; and especially Oglesby *Review of Attendance and Mobility Allowance Procedures and of Medical Adjudication* (1983); study commissioned by the Secretary of State.
15 Oglesby, ibid, paras 15–16.
16 It is reviewed in Brown, n.14, above, pp. 252–253. See also Baldwin in Jones (ed) *Yearbook of Social Policy in Britain 1975* (1975) p.180.
17 Brown, n.14, above, p.250.

commissioned by the Secretary of State.[18] The report recommended some fundamental reforms, though at the time of writing none of the proposals has yet been implemented. The Attendance Allowance Board should be relieved of its adjudicatory functions and should become a wholly advisory body. Initial decisions should be made, as with other disability benefits, by adjudication officers on medical evidence which in many cases could be supplied by the claimant's own doctor. A right of appeal on the merits should lie to a social security appeal tribunal, but specially constituted to include a doctor and a person experienced in giving attendance (e.g. a nurse) as members.

ii Medical criteria

The OPCS Survey used very detailed criteria to determine the number of persons who required substantial personal assistance from others in matters of self-care.[19] For the purposes of the attendance allowance it was decided not to adopt such precise tools, but rather to allow the decision-making authority (in this case the Attendance Allowance Board) considerable discretion. The Social Security Act 1975, as amended, lays down two conditions both of which must be satisfied for the higher rate of allowance, but the fulfilment of either is sufficient for the lower rate. The 'day' condition is that the claimant

> is so severely disabled physically or mentally that, by day, he requires from another person either –
> (i)   frequent attention throughout the day in connection with his bodily functions, or
> (ii) continual supervision throughout the day in order to avoid substantial danger to himself or others.[20]

The 'night' condition is that:

> he is so severely disabled physically or mentally that, at night, –
> (i)   he requires from another person prolonged or repeated attention in connection with his bodily functions, or
> (ii) in order to avoid substantial danger to himself or others he requires another person to be awake for a prolonged period or at frequent intervals for the purpose of watching over him.[1]

a *Nature of tests*

The first issue that arises under this provision is whether the two tests raise questions of law, and thereby come within the jurisdiction of the Commissioners (and eventually the ordinary courts), or are rather questions of fact on which the medical decisions are final. The issue is part of the general nature of decision-making and is treated as such in another chapter.[2] It is necessary here to see what implications the general principles have for entitlement to this specific benefit. On the one hand, the tendency has been for the courts to treat the question as to whether 'the words of the statute do or do not as a matter of ordinary usage of the English language cover or apply to the facts

18 Oglesby, n.14, above, paras 81–84.
19 These are set out in Appendix D of Harris *Handicapped and Impaired in Great Britain* (1971).
20 SSA 1975, s.35(1)(a).
 1 Ibid, s.35(1)(b), as amended.
 2 Pp. 578–579, below.

which have been proved' as a question not of law but of fact.[3] It follows that the fulfilment of the above conditions is regarded primarily as a medical question to be decided by the Board.[4] Where a word is capable of different shades of meaning, decisions as to the correct shade of meaning in a given statute are a matter of construction and therefore of law.[5] In some cases, however, it will be difficult to show that a finding by the Board was a consequence of an incorrect interpretation. For example, in *R v Secretary of State of Social Services, ex parte Connolly*,[6] the Board, having regard to a number of factors, concluded that a claimant did not require constant supervision at night. The Court of Appeal held that an error of law might have been made only if the Board had considered itself bound to reach that decision because of the existence of those factors. As it stood, the decision was only one on all the facts. Moreover, the House of Lords has recently stressed the importance of considering the language of the statutory provision as a whole, rather than analysing each work or phrase separately,[7] a view which suggests some restraint in the identification of errors of law.

b *Severely disabled*
The invalid must be 'severely disabled physically or mentally'. There is no reported decision in which a claimant has failed to satisfy this criterion, and it would seem to be no obstacle that the disability is attributable solely to age.[8]

c *Requires*
It is important to observe that the attention or supervision referred to in the statutory conditions must be 'required' rather than 'provided'. In other words, the test is based on the objective existence of the need rather than on the actual provision of a service.[9] As such it must be 'reasonably required',[10] but that does not necessarily imply for medical reasons: the physical comfort of the claimant may be sufficient.[11]

d *Night and day*
The first condition applies to day time attention; the second to night time. The distinction is crucial, since the claimant seeking a higher rate of benefit must satisfy both conditions, but 'night' is not defined in the Act. To resolve a conflict of different interpretations of this word, the Divisional Court in 1974 ruled that it meant

---

3 Per Lord Reid, *Brutus v Cozens* [1973] AC 854 at 861: applied by the Divisional Court in *R v National Insurance Comr, ex parte Secretary of State for Social Services* [1974] 3 All ER 522 at 526 and by R G Micklethwait, Chief Comr, in *R(S) 3/74*.
4 Per R G Micklethwait, Chief Comr, *R(S) 1/73* para 13.
5 Per Lord Widgery CJ, *R v National Insurance Comr*, n.3, above, at 526.
6 [1986] 1 All ER 998, [1986] 1 WLR 421.
7 *Woodling v Secretary of State for Social Services* [1984] 1 All ER 593 at 596, per Lord Bridge.
8 See e.g. *R(S) 2/80*, where the claimant was senile, (the Court of Appeal in *R v National Insurance Comr, ex parte Secretary of State of Social Services* [1981] 2 All ER 738, [1981] 1 WLR 1017 quashed the decision allowing her claim, but on other grounds).
9 *R(A) 1/72; R(A) 1/73; R(A)3/74; R(A) 1/75*.
10 *CA 26/79*, quoted with approval by Slade LJ in *R v Secretary of State, ex parte Connolly*, n.6, above, at 1001.
11 *R(A) 3/86*.

that period of inactivity, or that principal period of inactivity through which each household goes in the dark hours, and the . . . beginning of the night (could be measured) from the time at which the household, as it were, closed down for the night.[12]

This definition was adopted because it had clearly been the intention of Parliament to treat as more onerous on members of the household attention provided during the night as opposed to during the day: this will occur if the attendant has to interrupt his normal period of repose to deal with the invalid. It follows that the definition applies equally where the latter is a child, even though its sleeping hours are more prolonged.[13]

e *Attention in connection with bodily functions*
This is relevant for the purposes of both the day and night conditions, though in relation to the former the attention must be 'frequent', which means 'several times, not once or twice',[14] while for the latter it must be 'prolonged', that is, lasting for 'some little time',[15] or 'repeated', which means at least twice.[16] The common condition of 'attention in connection with bodily functions' has caused some difficulty. The notion of 'attention' is not controversial. It is broader than the notion of dealing with a specific health risk.[17] According to Dunn LJ in *R v National Insurance Comr, ex parte Secretary of State for Social Services* (the *Packer* case),[18] attention

> indicates something more than personal service, something involving care, consideration and vigilance for the person being attended . . . a service of a close and intimate nature.[19]

But what of 'bodily functions'? This might literally include, as Forbes J in the *Packer* case suggested, 'every mode of action of which the fit body is capable at the dictate of the normal brain'.[20] As such, it would cover functions of which the invalid is capable, and those quite irrelevant to his circumstances and needs – which would surely be inconsistent with the purpose of the provision. According to the House of Lords, 'bodily functions' is a 'restricted and precise' phrase narrower than 'bodily needs'.[1] More helpful, perhaps, is the dictum of Lord Denning MR in the *Packer* case that the words:

> include breathing, hearing, seeing, eating, drinking, walking, sleeping, getting in and out of bed, dressing, undressing, eliminating waste products, and the like, all of which an ordinary person, who is not suffering from any disability, does for himself. But they do not include cooking, shopping or any of the other things which a wife or daughter does as part of her domestic duties, or generally which one of the household normally does for the rest of the family.[2]

---

12 *R v National Insurance Comr, ex parte Secretary of State for Social Services* [1974] 3 All ER 522 at 527. See also CA 15/81, noted at [1983] JSWL 311.
13 *R(A) 1/78.*
14 Per Lord Denning MR, *R v National Insurance Comr, ex parte Secretary of State for Social Services* (the *Packer* case) [1981] 2 All ER 738 at 741.
15 Ibid. See also *R 1/72 (AA)*, para 22.
16 Per Lord Denning MR, *Packer* case, n.14, above, at 741.
17 *R(A) 3/78,* R J A Temple, Chief Comr.
18 N.14, above, at 742. The dictum was approved by the House of Lords in *Woodling's* case, n.7, above, at 596.
19 See to similar effect: Lord Denning MR, n.14, above, at 741; *R(A) 3/74,* para 11; *R(A) 3/80,* para 8.
20 Quoted at [1981] 2 All ER 738 at 740. See also Dunn LJ, ibid, at 742.
 1 N.7, above, at 596.
 2 [1981] 2 All ER 738 at 741. See also *R(A) 3/78* para 12. The list of functions is not, of course,

Finally, the attention must be 'in connection with' the bodily functions. This involves a test of remoteness or proximity, as to which there has again been a diversity of opinion.[3] The Court of Appeal held in the *Packer* case that ordinary domestic duties such as shopping and cooking (including the preparation of a special diet) are too remote.[4] These were to be distinguished from

> duties that are out of the ordinary, doing for the disabled person what a normal person would do for himself, such as cutting up food, lifting the cup to the mouth, helping to dress and undress or at the toilet.[5]

f *Continual supervision to avoid substantial danger*

This is the alternative requirement for the day condition. According to a Tribunal of Commissioner,[6] it contains four elements. First, 'the claimant's medical condition must be such that it may give rise to a substantial danger either to himself or to someone else'. It has been suggested that the phrase, though incapable of precise definition, should not be narrowly construed – the risk of harm could result not only from a fall but also from exposure, neglect 'and a good many other things'.[7] 'Substantial danger . . . to himself or to someone else' includes not only the risk of injury caused to the claimant or others *by himself*, but also such a risk where caused *by others*.[8] Care must be taken to assess this risk in relation to the individual claimant and not to the general class of persons suffering from the condition or handicap.[9]

Secondly, 'the substantial danger must not be too remote a possibility'.[10] The fact that it may take the form of an isolated incident does not necessarily make it too remote: the question is whether or not it is likely to occur.[11]

Thirdly, supervision by a third party must be necessary to avoid the danger. In comparison with 'attention', 'supervision' is a passive concept, perhaps of only a precautionary or anticipatory nature, being prepared to intervene if necessary in emergencies.[12]

Fourthly, the supervision must be 'continual'. This will generally involve overseeing or watching,[13] as would be expected of a childminder in care of young children. In *R(A) 1/83*, a Tribunal of Commissioners held that epileptics capable of looking after themselves between attacks are unlikely to establish the need for continual supervision unless the attacks are very frequent. This approach was criticised by the Court of Appeal in *Moran v Secretary of*

---

exhaustive. In *R v Social Security Comr, ex parte Butler* [1984] Legal Action 117, the Divisional Court quashed the decision of a delegated medical practitioner that a claim based solely on the need for a mother to act as interpreter for a profoundly deaf child could not constitute 'attention . . . in connection with . . . bodily functions'.

3 See the authorities reviewed in *R(A) 2/80*, paras 9–17. The latter confirmed a new trend which commenced in *CA 2/79*, and included *R(A) 1/80*, that cooking for the invalid was a relevant factor. But the decision in *R(A) 2/80* was quashed by the Court of Appeal, n.14, above.

4 Ibid, per Lord Denning MR at 741, per Dunn LJ at 744, per O'Connor LJ at 745.

5 Per Lord Denning MR, ibid, at 741–742.

6 *R(A) 1/83(T)* paras 5–8.

7 *R(A) 1/73* para 17, R.G.Micklethwait, Chief Comr.

8 *R(A) 5/81*.

9 *R(A) 2/83*.

10 On which see also McNeill J, *Morris v Social Security Comr,* reported as Appendix to *R(A) 5/83*.

11 *R(A) 1/83(T)* para 5. See also *R(A) 5/81*.

12 *Moran v Secretary of State for Social Services* (1987) Times, 14 March; *R(A) 2/75* para 9.

13 *R(A) 2/75*.

State for Social Services;[14] in its view, the need for supervision might arise even between attacks, particularly if they could occur without warning. The position might, however, be different if the sufferer had the opportunity, and was able, to summon help.

g *Another person awake to avoid substantial danger*
Originally the wording of the alternative night condition was identical to that of the alternative day condition. As a consequence of the *Moran* decision, it was considered that 'constant' supervision could be provided while the carer was asleep, so long as he or she could respond when the danger arose. The new version of the condition, which applies only to claims made after 15 March 1988, eliminates this possibility since, to avoid the danger, the carer must now be required to 'be awake for a prolonged period or at frequent intervals for the purpose of watching over' the disabled person.[15]

h *Intermittent needs*
The phrases 'by day . . . throughout the day . . . at night . . . during the night' do not indicate on how many days (or nights) during the week the need must occur. It is clear that the conditions do not have to be satisfied on each and every day (or night),[16] but apart from this ruling the Commissioners have generally left it to the discretion of the medical authorities to reach a decision on the frequency and pattern of the need.[17] In 1977 the Attendance Allowances Board advised its delegated medical practitioners that, subject to each case being considered individually, a person suffering from renal failure should require at least three sessions a week on a kidney machine if he is to qualify. The Chief Commissioner held in *R(A) 4/78* that this did not amount to an error of law. Following that decision, the government made special provision for this group of claimants. A person receiving dialysis treatment for two or more sessions a week is deemed to satisfy either the day or the night condition, and thus is entitled to the allowance at the lower rate; if, however, he is an out-patient at an NHS hospital, the treatment must not be provided by a member of the staff of that hospital.[18]

iii Period
The Attendance Allowance Board must be satisfied that the conditions of entitlement have been fulfilled for a period of six months,[19] though a claim may be made before that period has clapsed.[20] The allowance is then payable for such period as the Board considers that the invalid is likely to continue to fulfil the conditions.[1] The period of six months need not be served again if he recovers but subsequently suffers a relapse and again satisfies the requirement within two years from the beginning of the last six months period.[2]

14 N.12, above.
15 SSA 1975, s.35(1)(b)(ii), as amended. Presumably the interpretation of 'for a prolonged period or at frequent intervals' will be influenced by the decisions on the analogous phrases used for 'attention in connection with bodily functions': p.164, above.
16 See esp. *R(A) 3/74* and *R(A) 4/78*.
17 Ibid, para 28.
18 SSA 1975, s.35(2A), and SI 1975/598, regs 5B and 5C, as amended.
19 SSA 1975, s.35(2)(b).
20 Ibid, s.35(4)(a).
 1 Ibid, s.35(2)(a).
 2 SI 1975/598, reg 5A.

iv Residence

– The invalid must be ordinarily resident in GB, present in GB on every day for which the attendance allowance is claimed, and have been present in GB for an aggregate of not less than 26 weeks in the year immediately preceding the date of the claim.[3] For the purpose of the latter two conditions, however, he is deemed to be present in GB (i) if an absence is for a temporary purpose and has not lasted for more than six months; or (ii) where the absence is temporary and for the specific purpose of being treated for an incapacity from which he suffered before he left GB, and the Secretary of State certifies that it is consistent with the proper administration of the Act that he should be treated as though he were present in GB.[4] There is also relief for airmen, mariners, persons employed on the continental shelf and members of the armed forces and their families.[5]

v Exclusions

The Act stipulates that 'a person' is entitled to attendance allowance.[6] In *R(A) 3/75,* Dr Barnardo's, the well known charity, a body corporate, sought to argue that the phrase incuded legal as well as natural persons. The claim was rightly rejected. The conditions to be satisfied for the benefit can hardly be applied to someone other than the individual himself, let alone an institution.

Explicit exclusions apply to those who are already in receipt of state subsidy for their accommodation.[7] More precisely, the Regulations provide that it shall be a condition for receipt of the allowance that a person aged 16 or over is not maintained free of charge while undergoing medical treatment as an in-patient in either an NHS hospital or another hospital or similar institution in pursuance of arrangements made with the Secretary of State.[8] The exclusion also applies where such a person is living in accommodation (I) provided under the National Assistance Act 1948, the National Health Service Act 1977 (or their Scottish equivalents) or (II) in which the cost of accommodation is borne wholly or partly out of public funds, in pursuance of a scheduled enactment.[9] To encourage local authorities in particular to assume the financial burden, the latter exclusion extends to (III) accommodation the costs of which may be borne out of public funds, in pursuance of the enactments.[10] The Court of Appeal has construed (III) literally to disentitle a claimant where there existed a relevant power to subsidise the accommodation even though the power had not been exercised[11] Given the extensive powers contained in the scheduled enactments, this has potentially grave implications for claimants. (III) does not, however, apply where the person is living in temporary accommodation provided for the homeless, and there is a residual discretion in the Secretary of State to exclude its operation in other

3 Ibid, reg 2(1)(a)–(c).
4 Ibid, reg 2(2)(d)–(e).
5 Ibid, reg 2(2)(a)–(c).
6 SSA 1975, s.35(1).
7 Ibid, s.35(6).
8 SI 1975/598, reg 3. A person is only to be regarded as 'not being maintained' free of charge if he pays charges which are intended to cover the whole cost of accommodattion and services (excluding the cost of treatment): ibid, and see *R(A) 3/75.*
9 SI 1975/598, reg 4 (1)(a)–(b). Where accommodation is so provided it is irrelevant that the claimant himself contributes to the cost: *R(A) 2/79.*
10 SI 1975/598, reg 4(1)(c).
11 *Jones v Department of Health and Social Security*, reported as Appendix to *R(A) 3/83.*

cases.[12] (I) to (III) may not operate to exclude a person under 18 accommodated in a private house under the National Health Service Act 1977[13] and for the purpose of these rules, the Regulations list ancillary matters which are not to be regarded as 'costs of accommodation'.[14] Finally, a claimant already in receipt of the allowance remains entitled for the first four weeks of treatment or accommodation excluded under the rules.[15]

There are also special rules for children (i.e. those under 16 years). Allowances are not paid to those under two years,[16] and in other cases the attention or supervision etc required must be 'substantially in excess of that normally required by a child of the same age and sex'.[17] The person entitled to receive the allowance on behalf of the child is determined according to rules of priority:

– First, a mother living with the child; failing that, a father living with the child; failing that any other person living with the child, or a mother, father, grandparent, brother or sister not living with the child but contributing to the cost of providing for him.[18] Of course, only one person is entitled to an allowance in respect of one child for any one period of time, and if more than one person satisfies the rules it is payable to the individual nominated under the discretion conferred on the Secretary of State.[19]

The exclusions regarding treatment or accommodation at public expense are broadly similar to those applied to adults.[20]

B Invalid care allowance

i General

A household in which a severely disabled person requires attendance may suffer from financial hardship not only directly through the needs of the invalid, but also from the sacrifices made by other members of the household in looking after him. In a study carried out by Sainsbury,[1] it emerged that about two-thirds of disabled persons requiring care received it from relatives, and frequently this would involve a complete or partial interference with the relative's own earnings potential. Quite apart from the social justice of compensating such persons, the granting of state financial support also makes economic sense. In many cases, the care supplied voluntarily by the individual involves a saving on public facilities which would otherwise have been necessary. In addition, an estimated 11,500 persons were in receipt of supplementary benefit substantially because they had forsaken gainful employment to care for an elderly or disabled relative,[2] and there was pressure to transfer

12 SI 1975/598, reg 4(3). It is not clear how this discretion is exercised.
13 Ibid, reg 4(2).
14 See ibid, reg 1(2A).
15 Ibid, reg 5. Periods of less than four weeks may be aggregated provided they are not separated by more than 28 days. The enables arrangement to be made for 'respite care' (i.e. carer given respite from attendance duties) without loss of benefit.
16 Ibid, reg 6(2)(a).
17 SI 1975/598, reg 6(2)(c)–(d), as amended.
18 Ibid, reg 6(4), and see SI 1977/1361, reg 4.
19 SI 1975/598, reg 6(5).
20 For details, see ibid, reg 7.
 1 *Registered as Disabled* (1970) p.135.
 2 Report on Social Security Provision for Chronically Sick and Disabled Persons 1973–74, HC 276, para 61.

such persons to a non-means tested benefit. The arguments apply not only to the care of severely disabled persons but also to that of small children, those temporarily sick and elderly persons. The government was not, however, prepared to introduce a general 'home care' allowance.[3] The non-contributory invalid care allowance (ICA) was introduced by legislation in 1975.[4] Initially entitlement was limited to a prescribed category of relatives of the invalid.[5] This had no obvious justification apart from saving on public expenditure and it led to some arbitrary distinctions. The limitation was abolished in 1981,[6] but there was greater government resistance to reform of a more important, and discriminatory, exclusion, that of women living with a husband or a cohabitee. Criticism within Britain[7] failed to provoke a response and it required a decision of the European Court of Justice[8] that the exclusion was contrary to the principle of equal treatment enshrined in the EEC Directive of 1979[9] to force a repeal of the provision.[10]

ii Persons for the care of whom ICA is payable

As indicated above, the category of persons for the care of whom the allowance was made payable was not intended to be wide. The Act limits it to 'a severely disabled person',[11] and this is defined[12] as a person in receipt of attendance allowance (or its equivalents under the industrial injuries and war pensions schemes). This definition has the merit of avoiding the addition of yet another concept of disability to those already existing in the law. But it does mean that where the conditions of entitlement to the attendance allowance are satisfied, perhaps only marginally, the household will effectively benefit from the two allowances, while a marginal decision that the conditions have not been satisfied results in neither being payable.[13]

iii Persons entitled to ICA

There are two substantive conditions which the claimant must satisfy:

(a) he is regularly and substantially engaged in caring for that person; and
(b) he is not gainfully employed.[14]

---

3 Ibid, at para 60.
4 SSBA 1975, s.7.
5 See the first edition of this book. pp. 181–182.
6 SI 1981/655, following NIAC Report on Extension of Title to Invalid Care Allowance to Non-Relatives (1980, Cmnd 7905).
7 NIAC, in its Report on Non-Relatives, ibid, exceeded its terms of reference to attack the provision. See also Equal Opportunities Commission *Behind Closed Doors* (1981) pp. 14–23, *Dear SSAC,* CPAG Poverty Pamphlet 49 (1980) and the First Annual Report of SSAC (1983, Cmnd 8993) para 75.
8 *Drake v Chief Adjudication Officer* [1987] QB 166, [1986] 3 All ER 65.
9 Dir 79/7 (OJ 1979, L6/24). In the light of the ECJ ruling, L Bromley, Chief Comr, held that the terms of the Directive were of direct legal effect, enabling an individual to invoke them: *R(G) 2/86.* By 31 August 1987, 126,000 backdated claims to ICA were made by married or cohabiting women. Some of these were caught by the 12-month time limit on claims (SSA 1975, s.165A), on which see, p.545 below. The government, recognising that this was due to its own mistaken view of the legality of the exclusion, granted 'extra statutory payments' to meet such claims. See generally 82 Welfare Rights Bull 1.
10 SSA 1986, s.37.
11 SSA 1975, s.37(1).
12 SI 1976/409, reg 3.
13 Cf Brown *The Disability Income System* (1984) p.264.
14 SSA 1975, s.37(1).

a *Nature of care*
The linking of the ICA with attendance allowance is sufficient in itself to establish that the severely disabled person is in substantial need of care, but it was
still necessary to provide more guidelines for the requirement of 'regularly
and substantially engaged in caring. . .'. It was decided that the best
approach was to set a minimum number of hours' care which was consistent
with the notion of it being a full-time occupation for the claimant, but yet
which was not 'so high as to cause the claimant to have to examine in detail
what among her activities constituted "caring" and whether the minimum
had been met'.[15] The result was the creation of the '35 hours' rule formulated
in the following regulation:

> a person shall be treated as engaged and as regularly and substantially engaged in
> caring for a severely disabled person on every day in a week if, and shall not be
> treated as engaged or regularly and substantially engaged in caring for a severely
> disabled person on any day in a week unless, as at that week he is, or is likely to be,
> engaged and regularly engaged for at least 35 hours a week in caring for that
> severely disabled person.[16]

The reason for the rather circuitous form of this provision is that the base
period of the claim is for 'any day' of care, but the 35 hour criterion of course
applies to a calender week. It is not, however, clear that the rule as formulated has achieved the stated objective of relieving the authorities of deciding what constitutes 'caring', or how 'regular' it is to be. Is it to be assumed
that the mere presence of the claimant in the premises of the disabled person
will be sufficient, or is some more active role required? As yet, there is no
reported decision which provides guidance on these matters.

The care provided may be temporarily interrupted by, for example, a short
period of respite for the carer or the invalid's need to enter hospital. To
achieve flexibility, and to reduce the administrative expenses of frequent
investigation, the '35 hours' rule is relaxed in certain circumstances. The
Regulations provide that the rule is deemed to have been satisfied if

- (1) the claimant has only temporarily ceased to satisfy the conditions; and
  (2) he has satisfied them for an aggregate period of 14 or more weeks in
  the immediately preceding six months; and (3) he would have satisfied
  them for at least 22 weeks in such a period but for the fact that he or the
  disabled person was undergoing treatment as an in-patient in a hospital or
  similar institution.[17]

b *Gainful employment*
The intention being to confer benefit only on those engaged full-time in the
care of the invalid, it was thought appropriate to have some form of earnings
rule. Indeed, the Department appears at one stage to have considered the
argument that in principle all earnings should be taken into account.[18] However, the fact that the majority of persons benefiting from the new allowance
were previously in receipt of supplementary benefit, to which an earnings disregard applied, induced the proposal that a similar disregard should apply to
the ICA. There has been no up-rating of the disregard (currently £12) since
1982. This limit must not be exceeded in the week immediately preceding that

15 NIAC Report on Draft Regulations, 1975–76, HC 271, para 12.
16 SI 1976/409, reg 4(1).
17 Ibid, reg 4(2).
18 See NIAC Report, n.15, above, at para 18.

in which ICA is claimed, and all subsequent weeks of entitlement.[19] The ordinary rules for the computation of earnings apply to this provision,[20] but the claimant is entitled to have disregarded any earnings during a week in which he temporarily ceases to satisfy the 'caring' provisions, or during a week in which he was, with the authority of his employer, absent from employment.[1]

iv Age

ICA is not payable to those under 16 or in receipt of full-time education.[2] The rules governing entitlement of those over pensionable age (60 women, 65 men) and 'retiring' age (65 women, 70 men) are identical to those applicable to SDA.[3]

v Residence and presence

The requirements as to residence and presence[4] are substantially equivalent to those which must be satisfied by a severely disabled person claiming an attendance allowance.[5]

vi Amount

ICA is a flat-rate benefit equivalent in amount to the SDA and the increases for dependants also follow that benefit.[6] Of course, not more than one person can claim the allowance for the same period,[7] and two or more who satisfy the conditions may elect, by sending an appropriate notice to the Secretary of State, which is to benefit; in default of such election, entitlement is determined at the discretion of the Secretary of State.[8]

C Mobility allowance

i General

The new policy towards the disabled of isolating particular needs and providing income on a flat-rate, non-contributory basis, inevitably became directed to the question of mobility. This was not an easy subject to treat, because help in this area had existed for a considerable period of time primarily in the form of kind rather than money.[9] Since 1921 invalid vehicles, generally a single-seat three-wheeler, were supplied to war pensioners. After the Second World War, however, those receiving a war pension at 20 per cent or more might opt instead for a small car, which might be driven by a 'nominated' driver if the pensioner so preferred.[10] The provision for other disabled persons was not so generous. Under the National Health Service

19 SI 1976/409, reg 8(1).
20 Pp. 373–379, below.
 1 SI 1976/409, reg 8(2).
 2 SSA 1975, s.37(3).
 3 Ibid, s.37(5)–(6) and see p.148, above.
 4 SI 1976/409, reg 9.
 5 P.167, above.
 6 SI 1976/409, regs 12, 13. See pp. 340–343, below.
 7 SSA 1975, s.37(7).
 8 SI 1976/409, reg 7.
 9 See the government-sponsored report by Lady Sharp, *Mobility of Physically Disabled People* (1974).
10 Ibid, para 11.

legislation, the three-wheeler was made available to some categories of severely disabled persons, basically those unable to walk or those with some limited walking ability but needing personal transport to get to and from work.[11] In 1964 the government decided to extend to a small category of persons the facility of a small car, as already granted to war pensioners. The category of benefit was selected according to social rather than physical circumstances: the claimant had either to be living with a relative, who was himself eligible for a three-wheeler or was blind, or to be for a substantial part of the day in sole charge of a young child.[12] In 1972 haemophiliacs were added to this group, but in all cases the claimant had to be capable of driving himself, and no one else was allowed to drive the car. Alongside these provisions, certain cash allowances were made available. Those entitled to the three-wheeler or car were exempt from road vehicle excise duty; and, in response to the mounting pressure for the issue of cars rather than three-wheelers, from 1972 those qualifying for a three-wheeler might be allowed, as an alternative, a tax free sum of £100 per annum to help them run and maintain their own car.[13] The latter was seen as a temporary holding measure, while the whole structure of mobility benefits was examined. The appropriate report, on a study undertaken by Lady Sharp, was published in 1974,[14] and its findings were critical of the prevailing system. First, existing facilities were distributed inequitably – in particular, they were limited to invalids who themselves were able to drive. Secondly, the three-wheeler itself was unsatisfactory – it was dangerous, noisy, uncomfortable, liable to break down, and could not carry a passenger. The recommendation was that is should be replaced by a small car as soon as this became economically feasible, but with a narrower range of individuals retaining the right to elect instead for a cash allowance to help maintain and run the car.

The provision of cars would indeed have been too expensive, and the Labour government resisted Lady Sharp's proposal as it would have reduced the range of disabled persons entitled to assistance. Instead it was decided to provide as an alternative to the three-wheeler a flat-rate, non-contributory mobility allowance. This solution, implemented by the Social Security Pensions Act 1975, did not, however, prove to be entirely satisfactory. On the one hand, there was continuing concern for the safety of the three-wheeler; on the other hand, the allowance was insufficient for many of those without a vehicle of any kind to finance the necessary means of locomotion.[15] As regards the first of these problems, the government decided to phase out production of the vehicle and to allow those already in possession of one to qualify automatically for the mobility allowance, as and when they gave up use of it.[16] Secondly, the 'Motability' scheme was established to help immobile persons to get maximum value for their resources, and in particular to enable them to lease or obtain on hire purchase a car on favourable terms.[17] A number of other measures had also been taken to reduce the costs of motoring, including exemption from hire-purchase restrictions on standard cars, exemptions from VAT when buying Motability cars, or car adapta-

---

11 For the precise criteria see Sharp, n.9, above, Appendix D, para 1.
12 Ibid, para 5.
13 Ibid, para 7.
14 N.9, above.
15 Cf DHSS Research Report No 7 *The Impact of Mobility Allowance* (1981).
16 SS(MP)A 1977, s.13.
17 For details of the scheme, see DHSS Booklet *Non-Contributory Benefits for Disabled People* (1984) pp. 45–47.

tions, rate rebates on garages, driving licences at the age of 16 and free medical examination for exemption from the requirement to wear seat belts.[18]

ii Entitlement

a *Inability to walk*
The basic statutory test of entitlement is that the claimant is 'suffering from physical disablement such that he is either unable to walk or virtually unable to walk'.[19] The Regulations then prescribe more specifically the conditions which must be satisfied.

> A person shall only be treated . . . as suffering from physical disablement such that he is either unable to walk or virtually unable to do so, if his physical condition as a whole is such that, without having regard to circumstances peculiar to that person as to place of residence or as to place of, or nature of, employment, –
> (a) he is unable to walk; or
> (b) his ability to walk out of doors is so limited, as regards the distance over which or the speed at which or the length of time for which or the manner in which he can make progress on foot without severe discomfort, that he is virtually unable to walk; or
> (c) the exertion required to walk would constitute a danger to his life or would be likely to lead to a serious deterioration in his health.[20]

The claimant must, therefore, fulfil one of the three conditions (a), (b) or (c). Before these are examined, it is necessary to consider factors which are common to all three.

b *Factors common to alternative conditions*
(i) *Physical disablement* A controversial feature of the mobility allowance,[1] and one which distinguishes it from other disability benefits, is its restriction to physical disablement, thus excluding cases such as agoraphobia where the inability to walk results solely from mental disablement.[2] Nevertheless, the distinction between the two types of disablement is not always easy to draw and has given rise to a substantial and not wholly consistent case-law.[3] In a case decided on a version of the Regulations previously in force, the Chief Commissioner indicated that the weight to be attached to physical and mental disablement where both factors were present was for the medical adjudicating authorities to determine.[4] It would seem that one purpose of the amendment of the Regulations, which now refer to the claimant's 'physical condition as a whole', was to clarify the issue by concentrating on the effect of a disabling condition, rather than its causation.[5] Nevertheless, in the leading House of Lords decision of *Lees v Secretary of State for Social Services*, it was held that impairment of the capacity for spatial orientation is not sufficient to render the claimant unable (or virtually unable) to walk

18 Ibid, p.44.
19 SSA 1975, s.37A(1).
20 SI 1975/1573, reg 3(1), as amended.
1 Cf *Pearson* para 534.
2 *R(M) 1/80*.
3 For commentary, se Richards [1985] JSWL 16, Wilton [1985] JSWL 299 and Mesher [1986] JSWL 62.
4 *R(M) 2/78*.
5 See NIAC Report on Draft Amendment Regulations (1979, Cmnd 7491), para 6.

unless it *results* from a physical disablement.[6] So if the claimant has the ability physically to control the movement of the feet so as to move in an intended direction he does not qualify for the allowance even though he needs the assistance of another to steer him in the right direction.

The application of this principle to the facts in *Lees* itself may have been relatively unproblematic – the claimant was blind but capable of putting one foot in front of the other – but how far it extends to more complex behavioural limitations on mobility is unclear. As one Commissioner has observed

> It may be that in the last analysis all mental disablement can be ascribed to physical causes. But if so, it is obvious that the Act on drawing the distinction between physical and mental disablement did not mean this last analysis to be resorted to.[7]

In another case, a Tribunal of Commissioners indicated that the criterion was 'whether the claimant *could* not walk, as distinct from *would* not walk'.[8] Manifestly, all attempts such as this to devise verbal formulae to address what are essentially medical questions, to be determined by the medical authorities, are flawed; inevitably, decisions by those authorities will remain difficult to predict.

(ii) *Personal circumstances*   Circumstances relating to the physical condition of the claimant are, of course, crucial, but the Regulations provide that the authorities should ignore where he lives and the place and nature of his employment. In other words, the extent of mobility is to be determined by a mechanical test, not by reference to the purpose of the locomotion.[9] No doubt, in social policy terms, it might be desirable to link the criterion to what was reasonably necessary for the claimant to participate in the minimal essential activities of life, or to reach, for example, his place of employment,[10] but in legal and administrative terms this would be difficult to formulate and might lead to inequitable treatment between different claimants.

(iii) *Use of prostheses etc*   Ability to walk is to be judged having regard to a prosthesis or artificial aid which the claimant habitually wears or uses.[11] So if such an appliance enables him to walk, when he might otherwise not do so, he is not entitled. Of course, a claimant still unable (or virtually unable) to walk with the appliance will succeed.[12]

(iv) *Ability to benefit from locomotion*   The allowance is not available to all severely disabled persons. Legislation provides that it is payable only where the invalid's condition is 'such as permits him from time to time to benefit from enhanced facilities for locomotion'.[13] This excludes human vegetables, those whom it is unsafe to move and persons so severely mentally deranged that a high degree of supervision and restraint is required to prevent

---

6 [1985] AC 930, [1985] 2 All ER 203, effectively overruling the more generous interpretation suggested in *R(M) 1/83(T)*: see *R(M) 3/86(T)* para 6.
7 J G Monroe, Comr, quoted with approval by the Lloyd LJ in *Harrison v Secretary of State for Social Services* (1987) *Independent*, 18 May.
8 *R(M) 3/86(T)* para 8.
9 *R(M) 3/78* para 9–12, J S Watson, Comr.
10 Douglas, (1980) 48 Poverty 7.
11 SI 1975/1573, reg 3(2).
12 NIAC Report, n.5, above, para 13.
13 SSA 1975, s.37A(2)(b).

them injuring themselves or other.[14] Only a few of the remainder will not benefit from an occasional sortie and the authorities have been slow to apply the exclusion. This has resulted in awards accumulating for some hospital patients unable to spend them.[15] A proposal has been made (at the time of writing not yet implemented) that when the balance standing to a patient's credit exceeds £1,000, the Hospital Management Team might certify that it was not likely to be used for the claimant's benefit and, in consequence, the adjudication officer should be empowered to withdraw the allowance.[16]

c *The alternative conditions*
Subject to these general considerations, the claimant must satisfy one of the following conditions.

(i) *Total inability to walk* This condition almost speaks for itself. 'Walk' means 'to move by means of a person's legs and feet or a combination of them'.[17]

(ii) *Virtual inability to walk* The present wording of the second, crucial, condition results from amendments made in 1979.[18] It requires the medical authorities to ascertain qualitatively and quantitively the limits of the claimant's ability to walk outdoors without severe discomfort, having regard to distance, speed, length of time of manner; they are to ignore 'any extended outdoor walking accomplishment which the claimant could or might attain only with severe discomfort'.[19] In considering what the claimant is able to do with, and without, severe discomfort, the authorities are to have regard only to the discomfort which arises from the exertion of moving, not from external factors, such as the risk of encountering obstacles or stepping in front of traffic.[20]

(iii) *Exertion constituting risk to life or health* It is important, for this condition, to establish a connection or a relationship between the 'exertion required to walk' and the danger to life or a risk of serious deterioration in health. So, for example, a person advised medically not to walk because he might, in the process, be subject to an epileptic fit is not entitled on this ground alone, for there is no causal relationship between the exertion of walking and the risk of a fit.[1]

d *Determination of medical questions*
On submission of a claim, the adjudication officer normally refers 'medical questions', effectively the criteria considered above, for report by a specialised medical practitioner[2] and then makes a decision in the light of all the medical evidence, including that supplied by the claimant or his doctor; if in doubt, he may refer the decision to a medical board.[3] If denied the allowance

14 *R(M) 2/83*.
15 Oglesby *Review of Attendance Allowance and Mobility Allowance Procedures* (1983) para 161.
16 Ibid, para 162.
17 *R(M) 3/78*, para 10, J S Watson, Comr; but also an intended direction: *R(M) 2/81*.
18 On which see NIAC Report. n.5, above.
19 *R(M) 1/81* para 9, I Edward-Jones, Comr.
20 *R(M) 1/83(T)*.
 1 *R(M) 3/78*.
 2 SI 1986/2218, reg 56.
 3 Ibid, reg 57.

on medical grounds, the claimant may appeal to the medical board, or, if already examined by that body, to the medical appeal tribunal.[4] From the decision of the latter, there is an appeal on matters of law only to the Commissioner.[5] A review of these processes, commissioned by the government in 1983, concluded that the legal and medical questions were too closely interrelated to justify the special adjudicatory procedures for the latter.[6] It suggested that the ordinary tribunals should, therefore, determine appeals with, if necessary, doctors as members or assessors. The proposal has not been implemented.

e *Prior entitlement to mobility assistance*

As indicated above, the government decided to phase out the supply of invalid vehicles. A person entitled to such a vehicle may not in addition receive mobility allowance, but if (I) he elects no longer to use it, or (II) he has acquired a private car or (III) he intends, with the help of the allowance, to acquire one and also to learn to drive it the allowance becomes payable.[7] For this purpose, he is deemed to satisfy the medical criteria, provided that his physical condition has not improved.[8]

f *Exclusions*

In exercise of a power conferred under the overlapping benefits provisions, the Secretary of State has reduced or excluded the entitlement of those receiving a grant, or receiving any payment by way of grant under the National Health Service Act 1977 towards the cost of running a private car, or any payment out of public funds which he regards an analogous thereto.[9] The regulation apportions the payments over the various weeks of entitlement, and the weekly amounts so apportioned are deducted from the claimant's mobility allowance.

g *Period*

The allowance is payable for any period throughout which the claimant satisfies the criteria stated above, but it must also be established that the 'inability or virtual inability to walk is likely to persist for at least 12 months from the time when a claim for the allowance is received by the Secretary of State'.[10]

iii Age

Under the 1975 Act, the allowance was not payable to persons over pensionable age.[11] The Social Security Act 1979 extended entitlement to those under 75. Persons between 65 and 75 must, however, have been entitled on reaching the age of 65 or, in certain circumstances, 66.[12] The provision marked another, if minor, step in the equal treatment of men and women: by adopting 65 rather than pensionable age as the date by which title must have

4 Ibid, regs 59–60 and see pp. 576–578, below.
5 SSA 1975, s.112, and see pp. 580–581, below.
6 Oglesby, n.15, above, pp. 30–33. It also recommended that the claimant's own doctor should play a more significant role: ibid, pp. 19–20.
7 SI 1975/1573, reg 8.
8 SS(MP)A 1977, s.13(1) and SI 1977/1229.
9 SI 1975/1573, reg 8.
10 SSA, s.37A(2)(a).
11 Ibid, s.37A(5)(a).
12 Amending SSA 1975, s.37A(5)(a).

been established, Parliament allowed women another five years in which to qualify.

The allowance is not payable for children under five.[13] In the case of other children (aged 5 to 15 inclusive) the benefit is payable to an adult, appointed according to typical rules of priority to receive the allowance.[14] This is an interesting provision, for it appears to be the first time that a benefit intended to assist a child 'follows' that child whereever he may be living, whether, for example, with a foster parent, in hospital, or in residential care. It is to this end that the Regulation insists that the recipient of the allowance must give an undertaking to use it for the child's benefit.[15]

iv Residence and presence

In the ordinary case three conditions must be satisfied.[16]

– During the period for which benefit is claimed the invalid must be (i) ordinarily resident in GB; (ii) present in GB; and (iii) he must have been present there for an aggregate of 52 weeks in the 18 months immediately preceding that period. Temporary absences not lasting for more than a continuous period of 26 weeks, and those for the special purposes of treating the incapacity, are disregarded.[17] There are the usual special provisions for airmen, mariners, those employed on the continental shelf, and members of the forces and their families.[18]

v Disqualifications and other rules

Broadly speaking, the benefit is administered in the same way as the sickness and invalidity benefits, so that the 'rules of behaviour' and the disqualifications for misconduct, failing to attend for examination or treatment formulated for those benefits, apply also here.[19]

vi Amount

A flat-rate sum is payable which, like attendance allowance, is disregarded in the assessment of the income-related benefits.[20] It is also exempt from income tax.[1]

---

13 Ibid. The Pearson Commission recommended that entitlement be extended to children aged two or more: para 1533.
14 Viz mother or father living with the child, or failing that, such person as the Secretary of State may determine: SI 1975/1573, reg 21.
15 Ibid, reg 21(3).
16 Ibid, reg 2. The conditions must be satisfied on a continuing basis, throughout the period of entitlement: *Insurance Officer v Hemmant* [1984] 2 All ER 533, [1984] 1 WLR 857.
17 SI 1975/1573, reg 2(3)(b)–(c).
18 Ibid, reg 2(3)(a).
19 Ibid, reg 7: see pp. 156–160, above.
20 SSA 1975, s.37A(8).
 1 Finance (No 2) Act 1979, Sch 2, para 3.

Chapter 5

Retirement pensions

Part 1 Introduction

A General

In terms both of the number of recipients and of total expenditure, retirement pensions are the most important benefit provided by the British social security system. In 1988–89 about 9¾ million people are in receipt of them. The expenditure on pensions is about £19,300 million, out of total social security benefit expenditure of some £51,100 million.[1] The number of people of pensionable age (60 for women, 65 for men) is set to increase dramatically in the first three decades of the twenty-first century, rising from about 10.1 million in 2005–06 to over 12.3 million in 2025–26, though the size of the working population is expected to remain at roughly its present level.[2] Both the rising numbers of elderly people and the resulting increase in the cost of pensions are bound to keep pensions high on the political agenda.

The state does not have a monopoly in pension provision. In particular, there was a rapid growth in occupational pension schemes in the 1950s and 1960s. About half the working population – 11 million people – are now covered by such schemes.[3] Since the mid-1960s, there has been little change in the numbers but major changes in the schemes themselves, especially in the private sector. A renewed growth of private pension provision is expected to result from the Social Security Act 1986, partly in the form of personal rather than occupational pension schemes.

When the present system of flat-rate retirement pensions was introduced in 1946, it was envisaged that the pension would eventually be adequate for subsistence needs in most cases and that supplementation from other sources would not be required. However, despite the fact that the flat-rate pension has generally at least kept pace with the rises in prices and, for much of the period, with average earnings, it has never been high enough to remove the dependence of large numbers of pensioners on means-tested assistance. In 1986, just under 2 million (including pensioner wives) were dependent on supplementary benefit,[4] and the numbers receiving income support from

1 The Government's Expenditure Plans 1988–89 to 1990–91 (1988, Cm 288), Vol II, Tables 15.1 and 15.6.
2 Government Actuary's Department, 'Population and Pension Costs', Reform of Social Security (1985, Cmnd 9519), Vol 3, Background Papers, p.46, Table 1.
3 Green Paper 1985 Vol 1, p.21.
4 Social Security Statistics 1987, Tables 34.31 and 34.77.

April 1988 will not be significantly different. The fact is that the flat-rate state pension, which is still all that many pensioners receive, has never provided a standard of living above the official poverty line – the level of disposable income (after meeting housing costs) prescribed as a minimum in the supplementary benefit and income support regulations. The political debate over the past 30 years has been largely concerned with competing proposals for the provision of additional pension rights to close this income gap and thus reduce dependence on means-testing.

Throughout this debate and the legislative changes which have resulted from it, the main conditions of eligibility for a retirement pension, laid down in 1946, have remained largely unaltered. They are the subject of Part 2 of this chapter. There is then a short discussion of graduated benefit, followed by a more extended exposition, in Part 4, of the scheme for additional earnings-related pensions established by the 1975 legislation, including the provisions for 'contracting-out'. Parts 5 and 6 deal with the increments payable to those claiming pensions after the minimum pensionable age and other increases to the retirement pension. The chapter concludes with an account of the two categories of non-contributory retirement pensions.

B History

i The Old Age Pensions Act 1908[5]
Pressure for the introduction of state old age pensions began in the 1870s. The pamphlets of an Anglican clergyman, the Rev William Blackley, and of Charles Booth first drew attention to the acute poverty of many old people and the inadequacy of the poor law to deal with it. The call was taken up by the trades union movement and the new Labour Party. It also attracted a few Liberals, notably Joseph Chamberlain.[6] It was resisted, however, by the Charity Organisation Society, which constantly emphasised the virtues of self-help, and by the friendly societies, worried that a contributory scheme such as that introduced in Bismarck's Germany in 1889 would hamper their recruitment of members.

The introduction in 1899 of a non-contributory pensions scheme in New Zealand increased interest in proposals for a state pension. The following year a Parliamentary Select Committee recommended the introduction of a means-tested scheme. Even the friendly societies were gradually won over to support non-contributory pensions financed by taxation; and in 1906 Asquith, then Chancellor of the Exchequer, promised to introduce old age pensions on this basis as soon as there was a budget surplus. The Old Age Pensions Act 1908 provided for a means-tested pension at a maximum of five shillings a week.[7] This was payable to anyone aged 70 on an annual income of less than £21, with a reduced pension on a sliding scale to persons with less than £31 a year. Those in receipt of poor relief at any time in the previous two years were at first not entitled, nor were those recently in prison or who had failed to maintain themselves and their dependants. At a time when it was more common than now to draw a distinction between the deserving and

5 See in particular the very full account in Gilbert *The Evolution of National Insurance in Great Britain* (1966) ch IV. Also see Bruce *The Coming of the Welfare State* (4th edn) pp. 173–181; Fraser *The Evolution of the British Welfare State* (2nd edn, 1984) pp. 150–154.
6 In 1895, Chamberlain joined the Conservative government; his interest in pensions waned over the years, but he continued to support a voluntary, contributory scheme.
7 Ss.1–3, and Schedule. See *Harris* pp. 99–103.

undeserving poor, these qualifications did not seem surprising. Payment was made, as it still is, through local post offices, but the administration was in the hands of local authority committees, assisted, where investigation of facts was necessary, by the Board of Customs and Excise.[8] Although many aspects of the scheme now appear archaic, at least the principle was established that in certain circumstances anyone over seventy was entitled to support from the state.

ii The establishment of contributory pensions[9]

The Old Age Pensions Act 1919 relaxed the means test a little and, more importantly, enabled a person on poor relief to receive a pension.[10] But more radical reform soon followed. The increasing number of pensioners imposed a large burden on the Treasury at a time when the government wished to reduce taxation.[11] Another factor which induced change was the acceptance of the contributory principle after its successful use in the health and unemployment insurance schemes.

The Widows', Orphans' and Old Age Contributory Pensions Act 1925,[12] for which Neville Chamberlain, then Minister of Health, was largely responsible, introduced contributory pensions for those between 65 and 70 who were covered by the health insurance scheme.[13] The additional contributions were shared equally between employer and employee. The old age pension was payable irrespective of means and the other restrictive conditions existing under the 1908 Act. At 70, the pensioner received his pension under the old non-contributory scheme, without the application of a means test, which therefore applied only to those already in receipt of the pension. Criticism from the Labour benches focused on the low level of the Exchequer contribution to the insurance fund.[14] But, generally, the reform was welcomed as completing the structure of insurance benefits started by the pre-war Liberal government.

iii Pensions reform and the Beveridge Report

Under the 1925 Act pensions were only payable at the married couple rate when *both* spouses were over 65. Husbands with dependent wives under 65 only received a single person's pension. This created an anomaly if, immediately before he reached 65, the husband had been in receipt of unemployment benefit, because then he would also have received an additional payment for his dependent wife. The couple would thus become worse off when the husband reached pensionable age unless his wife was also 65. In response to pressure, particularly from women's organisations, the Old Age and Widows' Pensions Act 1940 reduced the pensionable age for women from 65 to 60.[15] This applied whether the claim was brought by an insured woman in

---

8 The Board retained its functions with regard to the administration of non-contributory pensions until 1947: see *Bruce* n.5, above, at p.181. For administration of benefits, see ch 15, p.531, below.
9 *Bruce*, n.5, above, at pp. 246–254; Gilbert *British Social Policy 1914–1939* (1970) pp. 235–254; *Fraser* n.5, above, at p.204.
10 S.3(1).
11 See *Bruce*, n.14, above, at p.246.
12 Ss.1(1)(c) and 7–8.
13 This had been introduced by NIA 1911: see ch 4, p.128, above.
14 See *Bruce*, n.5, above, at pp. 252–253.
15 S.1(1)

her own right or for the wife of an insured pensioner. The change was in accordance with the position in a number of the Dominions, such as Australia and New Zealand,[16] and it increased from 28 per cent to 63 per cent the proportion of cases in which the married couple pension rate was payable on the husband attaining pensionable age.[17] The discrepancy between the relevant ages for men and women is now widely regarded as indefensible; in an attempt to remove one anomaly, the 1940 Act created another.

The other change during the Second World War which should be mentioned is the availability from 1940 of supplementary pensions administered by the Assistance Board.[18] Pensioners whose means did not equal their basic requirements could supplement their pensions from the Board's funds rather than have recourse to the poor law authorities. The numbers applying for the new form of assistance showed how inadequate their pensions were.[19]

But the most important aspect of this period was the discussion in the Beveridge Report and the adoption (for the most part) of its recommendations in the National Insurance Act 1946. The Report drew attention to the reasons why old age pensions present particular difficulties; first, old age far exceeds in importance all other causes of inability to earn and to maintain a reasonable standard of living; secondly, the economic and social consequences of old age vary considerably from person to person.[20] Thus, although the frequent recourse to supplementary pensions showed that for many the pension was inadequate, the facts that, at the start of the war, about one-third of all persons over 65 did not receive either a state pension or any form of public assistance revealed that some could manage on their own resources.

Beveridge argued that it would be prohibitively expensive for the state to pay everyone on reaching 65 (or 60) a subsistence income sufficient to remove the necessity to apply for assistance. For this reason, he recommended that the payment of pensions should be made conditional on retirement from regular employment. The TUC had suggested the retirement condition as a way of encouraging older workers to leave the labour market, making jobs available for younger people. Beveridge, however, as his biographer José Harris has noted, 'strongly rejected the view that the elderly should be *kept out* of the labour market, but adopted the retirement condition (in conjunction with higher pensions for deferred retirement) as a means of *keeping them in*.[1] It was envisaged that more people over 65 would remain at work, though this expectation has not been fulfilled.[2] Beveridge also proposed that full pensions should not be payable immediately, but should be phased in gradually over a 20-year period to allow the National Insurance Fund to accumulate.[3]

Instead, the new Labour government decided to introduce the full rate immediately and to allow people who had not been insured before 1948 and were then within ten years of pensionable age to receive a full pension from July 1958. These decision dramatically increased the cost and led to the reforms of the late 1950s.[4]

---

16 357 HC Official Report (5th series) col 2148.
17 Ibid, col 1198.
18 See ch 11, p.413, below, for a discussion of this aspect of the history of means-tested benefits.
19 *Bruce*, n.5, above, at p.294.
20 Paras 233–235.
 1 Para 244; *Harris* pp. 394, 412.
 2 Para 255; see p.190, below.
 3 Para 241; *Harris* pp. 411–412.
 4 Shenfield *Social Policies for Old Age* (1957) p.98.

The National Insurance Act 1946 adopted the Beveridge scheme of retirement pensions and increments for postponed retirement, supported by an earnings rule designed to prevent evasion of the retirement condition.[5] There were two other respects in which the Act was more generous than either the previous law or Beveridge's proposals. First, a pensioner with a wife under 60 was now entitled to claim a dependant's allowance for her; this had the effect of equating his pension to that payable on a husband's insurance to a married couple both of pensionable age, but it greatly weakened one of the arguments put forward for lowering women's pensionable age in 1940.[6] Secondly, the retirement condition was not to be applied to men over 70 or women over 65, who were thus entitled to full pension no matter to what extent they worked, a modification urged by a number of small traders.[7]

iv The move towards earnings-related pensions

Under the Beveridge proposals, retirement pensions, like the other contributory benefits, were to be flat-rate. This principle was maintained until the late 1950s. In 1958 the government proposed a graduated pensions scheme, under which earnings-related contributions and benefit would be paid in addition to the flat-rate provisions.[8] The main purpose of the scheme was to supplement through graduated contributions the National Insurance Fund which was seriously in deficit.[9] To avoid competing with occupational pension schemes, the additional benefits were set at a low level and contracting-out was allowed on condition that the employee (but not necessarily his widow) enjoyed rights under his occupational scheme broadly equivalent to the maximum available under the state graduated scheme. In practice it was mainly higher paid employees who were contracted out.[10] A major disadvantage of the new scheme was that there was no suggestion that the graduated pension would be inflation-proofed. Any such suggestion would have had serious repercussions because it was assumed that the contracting-out provisions would have had to require occupational schemes to provide similar protection against inflation.

When earnings-related supplements to short-term benefits were introduced by the Labour government in 1966, there was no demand for contracting-out and the option was not offered. All employees had to pay the additional graduated contributions, which also counted towards their graduated pension entitlement.[11] Three years later, the government published proposals for radical reform, in particular the introduction of earnings-related pensions at 42½ per cent of earnings for the average single male earner.[12] Lower paid employees' pensions would be a higher percentage of their earnings, so the proposals involved a substantial element of redistribution. Most importantly, the scheme based pensions on average lifetime earnings, revalued in line with changes in national earnings, so that the pension was in

5 The reasons for these particular rules are considered in more detail at pp. 189–90 below.
6 P.180, above.
7 Mr J Griffiths, Minister of Pensions and NI, 418 HC Official Report (5th series) cols 1733 ff.
8 Provision for Old Age: The Future Development of the National Insurance Scheme (1958, Cmnd 638): see p.33, above, for the history of contributions.
9 For a discussion of graduated pensions, see pp. 205–206, below.
10 For a criticism of the graduated pensions scheme, see *Walley* ch XI, *passim*.
11 NIA 1966, ss.1–4.
12 White Paper, National Superannuation and Social Insurance: Proposals for Earnings-Related Social Security (1969, Cmnd 3883).

effect not only inflation-proof but geared to rising living standards. Contracting-out from part of the superannuation scheme was to be permitted. However, before the Bill became law, the government was defeated at the 1970 election, and it became the Conservatives' turn to attempt reform of retirement pensions.

Their proposals at least reached the statute book, but were never implemented. The distinctive characteristic of this scheme, embodied in the Social Security Act 1973, was the emphasis on the role of occupational pension schemes in supplementing the basic state pension.[13] The basic pension was to be financed by earnings-related contributions from employee (collected through PAYE) and employer, the latter being required to pay more than the former.[14] The Exchequer contribution was to remain at about 18 per cent of the total employee and employer contributions. In most other respects, the provision for a basic retirement pension did not differ from that which had been made since 1946. Occupational pension schemes had to satisfy a new administrative body, the Occupational Pensions Board, on various matters. The main conditions related to the level of benefits – a weekly pension of not less than 1 per cent of total earnings in each year of pensionable employment and some protection of its value against inflation.[15] There was to be a state reserve scheme for employees not covered by a recognised occupational scheme.[16] Some critics thought the reserve scheme might be sufficiently attractive to discourage younger people from joining occupational schemes. On the other hand, older contributors would have fared poorly in the reserve scheme. Partly for this reason and partly because of the absence of guaranteed inflation-proofing, the Labour government, which took office in 1974, decided not to use the Conservative state reserve scheme as the basis for its own plans for an earnings-related pension.

The Labour scheme, which replaced the provisions embodied in the Social Security Act 1973,[17] was introduced in the White Paper 'Better Pensions',[18] enacted in the Social Security Pensions Act 1975, and came into operation in April 1978. This reversed the relationship between the state and occupational schemes in the previous government's legislation. Now occupational schemes must follow for the most part the standards set by the state scheme for contracting-out to be allowed. But it was still thought to be impracticable to require private schemes to provide inflation-proofing after retirement. Contracting-out was therefore allowed on the basis that the occupational pension, once in payment, would continue at the same rate, any additions required to compensate for inflation being provided by the state scheme at the same level as if the employee had not been contracted out.

Details of the scheme as amended by the Social Security Act 1986 are considered later in this chapter.[19] In its original form, it offered earnings-related pensions of 25 per cent of earnings between the upper and lower earnings limits for payment of contributions, as an addition to the flat-rate basic

---

13 See the White Paper, Strategy for Pensions (1971, Cmnd 4755), esp. paras 23–28.
14 The employer's contribution was 7.25 per cent of the employee's PAYE earnings, the employee's contribution being 5.25 per cent.
15 See Cmnd 4755, paras 57–62, for the conditions of recognition by the Occupational Pensions Board.
16 Ibid, at para 73.
17 The relevant provisions of the 1973 Act were repealed by the Social Security (Consequential Provisions) Act 1975, s.3.
18 (1974), Cmnd 5713.
19 Pp. 206–222, below.

pension (in this it differed from the previous Labour government's proposals for a wholly earnings-related pension). The pension was to be based on the individual employee's earnings for the best twenty years of his or her working life from 1978–79 onwards. This meant that those retiring at the end of the century would get a full pension after only 20 years' contributions to the scheme. In calculating the pension, each year's earnings were to be revalued in line with the increase in average earnings up to the year before pension age, to give a pension related to living standards at the time of retirement. In case of invalidity or death before pension age, the earnings-related pension based on earnings up to then was to be added to the flat-rate invalidity or widow's benefit.

Although the 1975 Act was passed with all-party support, it was not long before the 1979 Conservative government was considering ways of reducing the cost of the new scheme or even abolishing it entirely.[20] This was not simply part of the government's continuing quest for cuts in social security expenditure. It was also a response to growing concern about the cost of the scheme in the next century, when the rising proportion of elderly people in the population would add to the emerging cost of pensions as the scheme approached maturity. At the same time, reducing the level of benefits offered by the state scheme would make room for the private alternatives favoured by the government: occupational and personal pension schemes operating on a 'money purchase' basis.

Accordingly, the Social Security Act 1986 not only modified the earnings-related pension formula to provide pensions of 20 instead of 25 per cent of earnings and abolished the 'best 20 years' provision, but also widened the scope for contracting out to include money purchase schemes, whether provided by an employer or negotiated on an individual basis between the employee and an insurance company, bank or other financial institution.[1] The essence of a money purchase scheme is that the pension is not fixed in advance, either in money terms or as a proportion of earnings, but depends on the value of the fund built up by investing the contributions to the scheme. For the first time, therefore, contracting out is now permitted without any guarantee that the employee will get as good a pension as he or she would have received from the state scheme.

Part 2   Entitlement to a retirement pension

In this Part of the chapter the conditions of entitlement to a retirement pension, laid down now in the Social Security Act 1975 as amended, are set out. Generally, they have not been altered by subsequent reforms of the pension system except for the contribution requirements, where major changes have been made, in particular in their application to married women.[2] Most of these conditions, therefore, apply to eligibility for both the flat-rate basic contributory pension and the earnings-related additional pension introduced by the 1975 reforms; the special rules relating to the latter are set out in Part 4 of the chapter.

20 *Green Paper 1985* Vol 1, ch 7.
 1 *White Paper 1985* ch 2.
 2 See p.201, below.

A Components of a contributory retirement pension

A contributory retirement pension can be made up of all or some of the following components:

(a) Basic (flat-rate) pension;
(b) additional (earnings-related) pension, based on contributions paid since April 1978;[3]
(c) graduated pension, based on earnings-related contributions paid between 1961 and 1975;[4]
(d) increases for dependents;[5]
(e) invalidity addition;[6]
(f) increments for deferred retirement;[7]
(g) age addition (80 or over).[8]

The basic and/or additional pension can be based either on the pensioner's own contribution record (a Category A pension) or on the contributions of the pensioner's husband or wife (a Category B pension). In some circumstances, the husband's or wife's contribution record can be taken into account in calculating a Category A pension, either by substituting it for the pensioner's own contribution record or by combining them to produce a 'composite' pension.

B Pensionable age

i Policy
The first condition of eligibility for a retirement pension (Category A or B) is that the claimant has attained pensionable age.[9] 'Pensionable age' is 60 for women and 65 for men.[10] The lower age for women dates from 1940, when the war-time government made the change under pressure from women's organisations. The principal object was to enable the typical married couple, where the husband was 65 and the wife a few years younger, to draw the full married couple's pension.[11]

If the object of retirement pensions were simply to provide an income for those no longer able to earn their living because of the effects of old age, there would, in principle, be no need to specify a particular age from which the pension should be payable. Provided that the basic condition of loss of earning capacity was satisfied, the pension could be paid from any age. In fact, however, retirement pensions serve the wider purpose of enabling people to retire from paid work before they are compelled to do so by failing powers or loss of relevant skills. More controversially, at a time of high unemployment, pensions make it possible for older workers to retire so that their jobs can be taken by younger people who might otherwise be unemployed. To achieve these wider aims, it is necessary to fix a minimum age at which the pension can be claimed.

3 See pp. 206–209, below.
4 See pp. 205–206, below.
5 See pp. 338–349, below.
6 See pp. 224–225, below.
7 See pp. 222–224, below.
8 See p.225, below.
9 SSA 1975, ss.28, 29.
10 Ibid, s.27(1),
11 See pp. 180–181, above.

Whatever age is chosen must be to some extent arbitrary. The obvious course is to choose the age at which most people would wish to retire and at which it would generally be considered reasonable that they should do so. In practice, however, views about retirement age are themselves largely determined by the age at which a pension is available. This is particularly true where, as in Britain, a large proportion of the working population is covered by occupational pension schemes which typically adopt the same pension ages as the state scheme. Once fixed, therefore, pensionable ages become entrenched in retirement practices. It is this fact, more than anything else, that explains why the present pensionable ages have remained unchanged for nearly half a century.

When pensionable ages have been changed, it has been in a downwards direction: first by the provision of pensions at 65 instead of 70 under the 1925 Contributory Pensions Act, and then by the reduction of women's pensionable age to 60. Any further reduction, however, would have large cost implications, both for the state scheme and for occupational schemes, and is likely to be strongly resisted on those grounds. Proposals to raise pensionable ages, on the other hand, encounter the objection that established rights, on which people have based their retirement plans, would be removed.

Most of the discussion of this subject in recent years has been concerned with the difference between pensionable ages for men and women. While EEC Directive 79/7 on equal treatment for men and women in social security has led to the removal of most other forms of discrimination between the sexes, the Directive specifically allows member states to exclude from its scope 'the determination of pensionable age for the purposes of granting old-age and retirement pensions and the possible consequences thereof for other benefits'.[12] Nevertheless, it is generally agreed that the difference is anomalous and that equal pension ages for men and women are a desirable policy aim. The most thorough exploration of the subject is to be found in the House of Commons Social Services Committee's report published in October 1982.[13] The committee noted the trend towards earlier retirement, especially since the mid-1970s, and quoted a DHSS estimate that, while about 600,000 men aged 60–64 were in employment, a number 'perhaps approaching half a million' were effectively retired, including those who were sick or disabled, long-term unemployed, retired under the Job Release Scheme, or occupational pensioners. Simply reducing pensionable age for men to 60, however, would be 'massively expensive'.[14] Instead, the committee proposed a 'flexible' pension age: both men and women would be allowed to claim an abated pension at 60, the full pension being available at a 'notional common pension age' of 63. Implementation of the change, they suggested, should be deferred so that women already near retirement would not lose their right to a full pension at 60, and to allow pension rights under the 1975 Pensions Act to build up to a level at which most people claiming an abated pension would still have an adequate income. For the minority who would not, a new form of means-tested benefit – a 'minimum personal income guarantee' – was proposed.

12 OJ 1979, L6/24.
13 House of Commons Social Services Committe, 3rd report, Session 1981–82, Vol I *Age of Retirement* (1982, HC 26–I).
14 The most recent official estimate of the net cost to public funds of reducing men's pensionable age to 60 is over £3,000 million, if two-thirds of the resulting job vacancies were filled and 75 per cent of those filling them were on the unemployment register; or about £2,000 million if all the vacancies were filled by unemployed people (Written answer, 25 April 1988, 132 HC Official Report (6th series) col *36*).

Despite the loss of pension rights that would have resulted for women retiring under the age of 63, the committee's proposals were estimated to cost about £500 million a year for the state scheme alone. The Green Paper *Reform of Social Security*, therefore, did not endorse the proposals but put forward the idea of a 'decade of retirement' between 60 and 70. Within these limits, earlier retirement would give entitlement to a reduced pension and later retirement to an enhanced pension. The Green Paper did not suggest that this would result in equal treatment of men and women but only that 'it would also be possible . . . to bring the rights of men and women closer together'. Instead of the select committee's minimum income guarantee, the Green Paper proposed that those wishing to retire early should have to demonstrate that they would not be dependent on means-tested benefits to supplement the abated pension.[15] The White Paper that followed six months later took the idea no further, merely recording that, while many of those responding to the Green Paper favoured greater flexibility, none suggested a way of introducing the 'decade of retirement' without substantial initial costs.[16]

Towards the end of 1987, a new draft EEC Directive 'completing the implementation of the principle of equal treatment for men and women in statutory and occupational social security schemes' was issued. The draft proposed the gradual elimination of differences of pensionable age between the sexes. While not requiring the adoption of a particular means of achieving this aim, it proposed that the principle should be deemed to have been complied with where, within prescribed limits, choice of pension age was left to the beneficiaries; or where entitlement to pension depended solely on completion of a given number of contribution years, thus eliminating the age condition.[17] The British Government, however, is understood to have been unenthusiastic about this proposal, presumably for the same reasons of cost which motivated its rejection of the Social Services Committee's proposals.

There, for the present, the matter rests. The issue will remain a live one, but no solution acceptable to the government is in sight. It should be noted, however, that a degree of flexibility of pension age already exists, in the form of increments to the basic pension for those deferring their retirement for up to five years from the minimum pensionable age of 60 or 65,[18] and also in a variety of provisions which treat unemployed people under pensionable age as effectively retired. These include the award of a 'pensioner premium' to income support claimants of either sex from the age of 60,[19] the exemption of such persons from the requirement to be available for employment,[20] and the Job Release Scheme under which allowances are paid to people approaching pensionable age who retire or reduce their working hours to provide work for an unemployed person.

ii The law

Section 27 of the Social Security Act 1975, in effect, lays down two pensionable ages for each sex. Subsection (1) defines pensionable age as 65 for a man and 60 for a woman. At those ages, however, it is a condition of entitlement

15 *Green Paper 1985* Vol 1, paras 7.24–7.26.
16 *White Paper 1985* para 2.59.
17 Proposal for a Council Directive, COM(87) 494.
18 See pp. 222–224, below.
19 See p.430, below.
20 See pp. 423–424, below.

to a retirement pension that the person has (or is treated as having) retired from regular employment. Five years later, at age 70 for a man or 65 for a woman, a person who has not retired is deemed to have done so. The pension thus becomes an 'old age pension' (the term used in the legisation before the introduction of the retirement condition, and still often used in practice, though it does not appear in the Act).

The age conditions, whatever else may be said of them, are simple and pose few legal problems. Generally the claimant will prove his age by reference to his birth certificate, though a population census has been accepted as providing satisfactory evidence.[1] In a case where the claimant was a Pakistani immigrant from a district where there had been at the relevant time no register of births, it was held that documentary evidence is not the only method of proof of age; medical evidence is admissible.[2]

Since pensionable age depends on the sex of the claimant, difficulties can arise where a person claims to have changed his or her sex. Two such cases have been reported. In the first,[3] the claimant argued that, though born a male, she had been issued with a woman's national insurance card in her adopted female name after medical treatment and had thus been led to believe she would be treated as a woman for pension purposes. The Chief Commissioner, however, concluded that as she remained biologically male, no pension could be paid until the age of 65; the issue of a woman's national insurance card could not raise an estoppel binding the statutory authorities.[4] In the second case, the claimant contended that under section 27 what was important was the person's social rather than biological role, since as a woman she would be expected to retire at 60 and therefore the award of a pension would then be appropriate. This contention was also rejected on the grounds, first, that the relevant sections of the 1975 Act indicate that a 'woman' is someone capable of forming a valid marriage with a husband,[5] and secondly, that there was no evidence that Parliament ever intended to make more favourable provision for women because in practice they retired earlier than men.

It might seem that the pension should be payable as soon as the age and, where appropriate, retirement conditions are satisfied. Section 28 of the 1975 Act certainly states that a person is entitled to retirement pension if he is over pensionable age and has retired from regular employment, and that the pension shall commence from the date of retirement. But the Claims and Payments Regulations provide that a pension or other benefit is to be payable on a specified day of the week – normally Monday in the case of a new retirement pensioner – unless the Secretary of State arranges for it to be payable on a different day, and that benefit is to commence on that day.[6] The result is that entitlement to pension starts on the appropriate pay day following the claimant's birthday, rather than on the day when the claimant reaches pensionable age, unless the two days coincide. In *R(P) 2/73* it was regarded as far-fetched to argue that the similar regulation then in force was unreason-

1 *CP 11/49.*
2 *R(P) 1/75* R J A Temple, Comr.
3 *R(P) 1/80.*
4 The Chief Comr, R J A Temple, doubted the use of the estoppel doctrine in *Robertson v Minister of Pensions* [1949] 1 KB 227, [1948] 2 All ER 767: see p.549, below.
5 SSA 1975, ss.28–9.
6 SI 1987/1968, regs 16(1) and (3), 22(3) and Sch 6. Payment days are discussed in the chapter on administration of benefits, p.555, below.

able and, therefore, ultra vires in that it discriminated against certain claimants in respect of the date of their birth.[7]

C The retirement condition and the earnings rule

i Policy

The second condition for entitlement to a pension for a woman aged between 60 and 65 or a man between 65 and 70 is that he or she has retired from regular employment. The retirement condition was introduced by the 1946 legislation, following the recommendations of the Beveridge Report. As explained earlier, the object was to reduce the cost of providing an adequate pension by limiting entitlement to those 'past work'. Those who were able to carry on working were to be encouraged to do so by the prospect of an increment to their pension when it was eventually paid – in practice not later than age 65 for a woman or 70 for a man, when the retirement condition ceases. But it was also recognised that a person who had retired and was receiving a retirement pension might wish to continue working to a limited extent and that such work was not necessarily inconsistent with retirement. Retirement, Beveridge explained, meant 'giving up regular earnings, not being idle 100 per cent of one's time'. There was therefore to be an earnings rule, under which a pensioner would be allowed to have a limited amount of earnings without any reduction of pension, earnings above the limit being deducted wholly or in part from the pension.[8]

The three elements – retirement as a condition of entitlement to a pension during the first five years after pensionable age, increments for deferred retirement, and an earnings rule to limit the amount of paid work regarded as consistent with retirement – have survived the numerous changes in the legislation since 1946. The most important change was introduced by the National Insurance Act 1960, which provided that a person whose earnings were not expected to exceed the earnings rule limit (currently £75 per week) was to be treated as retired. This provision is now to be found in section 27(3) of the Social Security Act 1975. Its practical effect is that retirement is now defined, for pension purposes, mainly in terms of earnings. As a result, much of the pre-1960 case law on the circumstances in which a person has or is to be treated as having retired is now of little importance.[9]

The connection between the earnings rule and the retirement condition explains why it is only 'earnings' and not other sources of income that affect pension entitlement. In the context of the pensioner's needs, it is not obvious why someone earning more than £75 a week should suffer a reduction while someone with a much higher income from shares or other sources does not. The answer is that the pension is intended to replace earnings, not other income. Although the distinction between earnings and other income may sometimes be a fine one, its erosion could lead to the replacement of the present system by a means-tested basic pension – a radical development which few people would advocate.

The retirement condition itself has attracted comparatively little criticism. One reason for this is the general move towards earlier retirement. After 1946 the pensionable ages of 60 and 65 were increasingly adopted as normal retire-

7 Per H A Shewan, Comr. See also *R(P) 16/52*.
8 Cmd 6404, 1942, pp. 95–7.
9 For a fuller account of the Commissioners' decisions on this subject, see the 2nd edition of this book, pp. 200–207.

ment ages for a wide range of occupations, and this trend was reinforced by the adoption of the same pension ages in occupational schemes. The high levels of unemployment in the 1970s and 1980s not only increased the pressure on older workers to retire as soon as they could claim a pension but forced many into premature retirement before reaching pensionable age. The House of Commons Social Services Committee was told that the number of men and women of pensionable age deferring claiming their pensions had fallen from a quarter of a million in 1971 to 100,000 in 1980.[10]

The trend towards earlier retirement has also diminished the importance of the system of increments for those deferring retirement. This may explain why there has been little criticism of the way in which increments have operated over the period since 1948.[11] The earnings rule has proved to be more controversial. As explained above, the rule was presented by Beveridge as a mitigation of the retirement condition, allowing people to draw a pension while continuing to do a limited amount of paid work. But it was also a means of enforcing the retirement condition, preventing a person of pensionable age from retiring for the purpose of claiming a pension and then resuming full-time employment without loss of pension. At whatever level the earnings limit is set, it is bound to be criticised as preventing people from working up to their full capacity and thereby making a useful contribution to the economy; and it is bound to seem unfair to those whose pensions, earned by a life-time of contributions, are reduced or withdrawn as a result of it. They are unlikely to be impressed by the argument that what they have contributed for is not an *old age* pension but a *retirement* pension. Criticism of the rule was reflected in the 1979 Conservative election manifesto: 'It is wrong to discourage people who wish to work after retirement age, and we will phase out the "earnings rule" during the next Parliament'.[12] Section 4(1) of the Social Security Act 1979 paved the way by giving the Secretary of State power to shorten the five-year period for which the rule operates (age 60–64 for women, 65–69 for men); but the power has not been used. The 1983 Conservative manifesto reaffirmed 'our intention to continue raising the limit and to abolish this earnings rule as soon as we can', but the 1987 manifesto did not mention the subject. The limit *has* been raised, though by less than the rate of inflation, but abolition is no longer on the agenda.

The fact is that it would be virtually impossible to abolish the earnings rule without also abolishing the retirement condition. It is difficult to assess the probable effects of doing so. The number of pensioners actually affected by the earnings rule is not large. A 'Retirement Survey' conducted in 1977 for the DHSS showed that only about 5,000 pensioners, about 4 per cent of those pensioners with earnings, were having their pension reduced because of the rule. Many more were limiting their earnings owing to its existence, but it was found that half of these pensioners did so under a misconception as to the amount of 'permitted' earnings. It is possible, on the other hand, that the rule actually keeps some people working full-time, who would otherwise rely on the pension to supplement their part-time earnings. On the basis of the 1977 survey it was thought likely that about 40 per cent of those then deferring retirement would continue to do so if the earnings rule and retirement condition were abolished. Paying pensions to the rest would have entailed a net additional cost of about £64 million.[13] As noted above, the numbers deferring

10 HC 26–1, 1982, p.xi.
11 See pp. 222–224, below.
12 Conservative Manifesto 1979, p.27.
13 1977–78 HC 697.

retirement have fallen rapidly, while the numbers receiving pensions which are reduced by the earnings rule may be even smaller than in 1977. The cost of abolishing the retirement condition and the earnings rule would therefore be relatively small. Even so, paying full pensions to people earning more than £75 a week would hardly be regarded as a high priority at a time when public expenditure is under severe pressure.

In the case of dependent wives' earnings, the 1978 report on the earnings rule concluded that it provided a useful test of dependency and that there would be much to be said for its retention here, even if it were eventually abolished for retirement pensioners themselves.[14] In 1985, using similar arguments, the government introduced a far more stringent earnings rule for dependency additions. An addition for a dependent wife, unless entitlement commenced before 16 September 1985, is no longer paid if she earns more than the unemployment benefit rate for a single person;[15] before that date the same earnings rule applied to wives as to pensioners.

The earnings rule in its original form provided for the pension to be reduced by one shilling for every shilling earned over the limit. In 1956 the National Insurance Advisory Committee recommended that there should be a band within which only half the excess earnings should be deducted (the 'proportionate band'), and this was implemented by the National Insurance Act 1956. The effect was to modify the confiscatory impact of the earnings rule; instead of only £2, pensioners were allowed to earn £2.50 a week without any loss of pension, while half the next £1 was deducted. But the proportionate band has not been increased in line with the basic limit, and is now only £4, compared with the basic earnings limit of £75 a week. At this level it is merely an unnecessary complication, serving no useful purpose.

The effect of the earnings rule has been modified in another respect. When it was first introduced, the national insurance scheme provided only a flat-rate pension, the whole of which was lost if the pensioner's earnings were far enough above the earnings limit. With the introduction of earnings-related pensions, first under the National Insurance Act 1959 (the 'graduated' pension scheme) and then under the Social Security Pensions Act 1975, the principle of deductions for excess earnings was not extended to the earnings-related element which will represent an increasing proportion of the total pension. Thus, although entitlement to an earnings-related retirement pension depends on retirement or being treated as retired, in the same way as entitlement to the basic pension, it is not affected by subsequent earnings as long as the retirement condition is still satisfied.

ii The law – 'Retired from regular employment'

The legal requirement of 'retirement', enacted by sections 28(1) and 29 of the Social Security Act 1975, is that the person 'has retired from regular employment'. The term 'retired' is not defined in the legislation, but section 27(3) sets out certain circumstances in which a person is to be *treated* as retired:

> . . . a person may . . . be treated as having retired from regular employment at any time after he has attained pensionable age –
> (a) whether or not he has previously been an earner;
> (b) notwithstanding that he is, or intends to be, an earner, if –
>   (i) he is or intends to be so only occasionally or to an inconsiderable extent, or otherwise in circumstances not inconsistent with retirement, or

14 Ibid, ch 5. And see pp. 341–342, below.
15 SI 1977/343, reg 8, as amended.

(ii) his earnings can be expected not to exceed, or only occasionally to exceed, the amount any excess over which would, under section 30(1) below (earnings rule), involve a reduction of the weekly rate of his pension; . . ..

It will be seen that a person may be treated as retired, despite the fact that he is earning or intends to be earning in employment, if one of the conditions of section 27(3)(b) is satisfied. In practice, the question whether someone has in fact retired is seldom a source of difficulty since, in a borderline case, it can usually be circumvented by reference to the treating provisions. The circumstances in which a person may be treated as retired will therefore be considered before the interesting but practically less important question of the meaning of 'has retired from regular employment'.

iii 'Treated as retired'
The notion of 'retirement' strongly suggests that the claimant must have been employed and then have given up work. However, section 27(3)(a) of the 1975 Act makes it clear that a person can be treated as retired whether there has been a previous history of employment or not. In particular, a married woman claiming a pension on her husband's contributions need not have been employed or even have paid contributions at any time before her 'retirement'. Similarly, a person who had never worked could qualify for a retirement pension by virtue of having paid voluntary class 3 contributions.[16]

Section 27(3)(b) provides that a claimant may be treated as retired if any one of four conditions is satisfied. The first three – that he or she is or intends to be an earner 'only occasionally', 'to an inconsiderable extent' or 'in circumstances not inconsistent with retirement' – have existed since the 1946 legislation, unamended except that the 1946 Act referred to a person being 'engaged in a gainful occupation'. These words were replaced by 'an earner' by the National Insurance Act 1973 as part of a series of changes aimed at harmonising the contribution and income tax systems. The fourth condition, known as the 'earnings condition', was added by the National Insurance Act 1960 and is the most easily satisfied: provided that earnings are not expected generally to exceed the amount disregarded under the earnings rule (now £75 per week), the person will be treated as retired. As a result, the first condition is now redundant and the second and third affect relatively few claimants. Indeed, many of the Commissioners' decisions on the first three conditions relate to questions which would not have arisen after the enactment of the earnings condition.

a *The first condition: An earner 'only occasionally'*
Since 1960, this condition has been effectively replaced by the earnings condition, under which a person whose earnings are expected to exceed the earnings limit 'only occasionally' can be treated as having retired.

b *The second condition: An earner 'to an inconsiderable extent'*
The reported cases relating to this condition pre-date the change of wording from 'engaged in a gainful occupation' to 'an earner' and are concerned with the amount of work done or expected to be done rather than with the amount earned. In *CP 33/49*, where a school meals attendant worked 12½ hours a week, the Commissioner upheld the '12-hour rule' formulated by the Umpire

16 See p.48, above.

in construing an identical provision in the earlier Contributory Pensions Regulations of 1946.[17] This rule stated that the claimant was engaged in a gainful occupation 'to an inconsiderable extent' if he was working for not more than 12 hours a week, or (if more) less than one-quarter of the normal weekly working hours for the relevant occupation. It was further decided that the hours would have to be considered in relation to the normal working months of the trade in question: it was, therefore, wrong to contend that, averaged over the whole year, her working week was less than 12 hours. She was accordingly not treated as retired.

Although the 12-hour rule pre-dates the earnings condition of section 27(3)(b)(ii), there will still be cases where a person earning more than the present limit of £75 week, who therefore does not satisfy the earnings condition, would fall to be treated as retired under the 12-hour rule. But the change of wording in 1975 from 'engaged in a gainful occupation' to 'an earner' might be thought to throw some doubt on the continued applicability of the rule. A person who works for 12 hours a week or less but earns more than £75 may be 'engaged in a gainful employment to an inconsiderable extent', but it is by no means self-evident that he is also 'an earner to an inconsiderable extent'. The definition in section 3(1) of the 1975 Act:

> In this Act 'earnings' includes any remuneration or profit derived from an employment; and 'earner' shall be construed accordingly.

suggests that the amount of the remuneration may be a more important consideration than the hours worked. The guidance issued to adjudication officers implies that the 12-hour rule is still operative,[18] but if the question arose on appeal to a Commissioner, it is possible that a different view would now be taken.

c *The third condition: an earner 'otherwise in circumstances not inconsistent with retirement'*

This condition produced a large number of cases until the early 1960s when the earnings condition was introduced. The use of the word 'otherwise', following the first and second conditions, implies that, if the circumstances are not inconsistent with retirement, a person may be treated as retired though still being, or intending to be, an earner more than occasionally and to more than an inconsiderable extent. Nevertheless, the Commissioners' view is that the frequency and regularity of the work are material, though not conclusive, factors in determining whether this condition is satisfied.

The leading case is the Tribunal decision in *R(P) 8/54*:

> The claimant, who had been employed in the school meals service since 1943, gave notice of retirement but stated that she intended to continue in the same employment, working 12½ hours a week. The Tribunal held that this would not be inconsistent with retirement, as it was the type of work which someone who had retired from regular employment might well perform.

Two points may be emphasised. First, the hours of work exceeded the maximum allowed under the '12-hour rule' for the purpose of satisfying the 'inconsiderable extent' condition. Secondly, it was decided that a claimant need not show any specific circumstance causing a change of occupation, or an alteration in the terms of her employment, for the work to be consistent

---

17 Reported Decision *UP 4/47*, construing SR & O 1946/1508, reg 10(1).
18 AOG, para 80567.

with retirement.[19] In another case, *R(P) 8/56*, it was emphasised that it is the present scale of the claimant's activity, rather than whether there has been a reduction in his working hours, which is important; while in *R(P) 1/54*, where there had been a reduction from 45 to 20 hours a week, this was not enough for the claimant to be treated as retired. A change of circumstances may, however, influence the Commissioners in treating the claimant as retired.

> In *R(P) 6/54*, a railway porter intended to retire from his regular employment and immediately to start part-time work for 20 hours a week as an outside porter. He was to work for tips, and not regular wages. The Commissioner ruled that the change in the nature of his employment enabled him to be treated as retired; it was unlikely that he would in fact work for the full 20 hours, though he would be in attendance for that time.

Although there is no absolute limit, comparable to the 12-hour rule, it seems to be the Commissioners' view that beyond a certain number of hours' work it is virtually impossible to contend that the work is not inconsistent with retirement. There have been very few cases where more than 18 hours' work a week has been held not inconsistent with retirement.[20]

In a number of cases it has been emphasised that there must be some aspect of the part-time work which is particularly charactertic of occupations followed by elderly people who have given up their regular employment. The nature of the work, the claimant's freedom to choose his hours, the pressure (or lack of it) under which he works, and whether it is done as a hobby or is still pursued as a substantial source of livelihood are all relevant factors.[1] In an interesting and more recent case, the Chief Commissioner, R J A Temple, rejected the argument that the work of a city councillor presented special features which were characteristic of the occupations followed by retired people; in view of the number of hours (generally 30) which the claimant spent weekly on council business, it could not be said that his work was not inconsistent with retirement.[2]

In *R(P) 11/55* it was suggested that the claimant must point to a special feature charactertic of post-retirement occupation. However, in *R(P) 13/55* where a Methodist minister had retired from full-time work and later took up duties as a part-time supernumerary minister, the test was formulated in a way slightly more favourable to the claimant:[3]

> Having regard to the rather inconclusive nature of the inferences falling to be drawn, in this case, from the size of congregation, hours of work involved, and amount of remuneration, I am not prepared to say that there is any feature in the occupation which would render it unreasonable to speak of a person engaged in it as having retired from regular employment.

19 On this point the Tribunal overruled *R(P) 15/52*.
20 *R(P) 10/55* and *R(P) 2/59* are two such cases. In rather more cases 18 hours' work has been held inconsistent with retirement: *R(P) 4/57; R(P) 5/57; R(P) 6/55; R(P) 11/55; R 1/60(P); R(P) 2/76*.
1 See *R(P) 6/55* and *R(P) 11/55*.
2 *R(P) 2/76*. The case incidentally shows that the third condition may still be important despite the introduction of the earnings condition. The attendance allowances claimed by the applicant precluded any reliance on that condition.
3 The Commissioner followed *R(P) 9/54* (Baptist minister with similar duties) and not *R(P) 11/52* where the Methodist minister's duties seem to have been lighter than those in *R(P) 13/55; R(P) 11/52* may now be regarded as wrongly decided.

But the Commissioners do not seem to be wedded to one version of the test rather than the other.[4]

The position of self-employed persons may present particular difficulties.

In *R(P) 12/55*, the woman gave up employment as a school meals attendant on reaching pensionable age, and then kept a small sweet shop in her house, open for 13 hours a day. Although this occupation was found to be characteristic of those pursued by retired people, it was held that she could not be treated as retired because the number of hours for which the shop was open made the manner of its pursuit inconsistent with retirement.[5]

In another case, however, where a claimant worked 20 hours a week in his own off-licence business, where trade was light, it was held that his occupation was not inconsistent with retirement.[6] His freedom to organise his own hours was emphasised as a crucial factor. But it was not decisive in *R(P) 1/60* where a writer was not treated as retired under this condition because he set no specific limit to the number of hours devoted to his writing.

In summary, the Commissioners appear concerned in applying this condition to see whether there is some feature which is characteristic of the work generally done by elderly people. In determining this, the hours of work are extremely relevant, the level of earnings less so.[7] Some of the decisions are hard to reconcile, as is perhaps inevitable where the Commissioner are asked to interpret such a vague and imprecise requirement.

d *The fourth condition: earnings*
The retirement condition, strictly applied, would have the odd result that a man who abandoned work at 65 (or a woman at 60) would be entitled to a retirement pension, even though he might subsequently change his mind and resume work, while another man, out of work at 65 but prepared to resume work if a job became available, would not be so entitled. The effect was mitigated to some extent by the relatively liberal interpretation of the first three conditions for being treated as retired: that, if a person intended to continue working, it must be 'only occasionally or to an inconsiderable extent, or otherwise in circumstances not inconsistent with retirement'. But, generally speaking, the level of the claimant's earnings was not a crucial factor in deciding whether these conditions were satisfied. This was particularly hard on lower-paid workers such as women in textile factories,[8] who worked long hours and were therefore unable to satisfy any of the three conditions. For this reason, the earnings condition was introduced by the National Insurance Act 1960. Its effect was well summarised by Mr Douglas Houghton, the opposition spokesman, during the uncontentious committee stage:[9]

It will mean that they can go to the limit of the earnings rule irrespective of the number of hours worked without finding themselves questioned as to whether what they are doing is inconsistent with retirement.

Under the earnings condition, the claimant will be treated as retired if his earnings are expected not to exceed, or only occasionally to exceed, the

4 E.g. in *R(P) 4/57*, the test in *R(P) 11/55* was applied, while in R(P) 5/57 the test in *R(P) 13/55* was followed.
5 The Commissioner followed *R(P) 12/53* (sub-postmistress keeping office open for 44 hours a week was not treated as retired, even though the business was very slight).
6 *R(P) 2/59*.
7 *R(P) 16/56*.
8 630 HC Official Report (5th series) col 220.
9 Ibid, col 1096.

amount above which a deduction from the pension would be made under the earnings rule. Thus, if the claimant's anticipated earnings are £75 or less, he will be treated as retired under this fourth condition, while if his earnings are likely to exceed £75, he must satisfy one of the first three conditions. The calculation of earnings for this purpose raises general problems common to many social security benefits, and is therefore dealt with in chapter 9.[10]

In its original form, the earnings condition did not apply in a small minority of cases where the claimant was entitled only to an earnings-related or graduated pension (which are not subject to reduction under the earnings rule) and had no entitlement to a basic pension. This gap was closed by the Social Security Act 1980,[11] and a person with no basic pension entitlement can now be treated as retired under the earnings condition in the same way as any other pensioner.

iv Actual retirement

The retirement condition may be satisfied either by virtue of the treating provisions of section 27(3) of the 1975 Act or by having actually retired from regular employment. For practical purposes, the four conditions of section 27(3) can generally be regarded as separating those who have actually retired from those who have neither retired nor can be treated as having done so. Thus, a person of pensionable age who is not and does not intend to be an earner even to the limited extent permitted by section 27(3)(b) is, in practice, assumed to have retired from regular employment; while a person who is or intends to be an earner to an extent that exceeds all the limits set by the four conditions is assumed not to have retired. It is not entirely clear whether the words 'whether or not he has previously been an earner' in section 27(3)(a) apply only to a person who is now or intends to be an earner (i.e. who satisfies one of the conditions of section 27(3)(b)) but in practice they are assumed to apply also to a person who has no such intention. For example, a married woman of pensionable age who has never been, is not and does not intend to be a earner is treated as having retired and the question of actual retirement does not arise.

One type of case where the question of actual retirement may arise is where the claimant's income exceeds the £75 earnings limit but the activity from which it is derived is of such a nature that he can nevertheless be regarded as having retired from regular employment. In Schedule 20 to the 1975 Act, 'employment' is defined to include 'any trade, business, profession or vocation'.[12] It includes employment under a contract for services, as in the case of a claimant who continued after pension age to live with an old friend as a paid companion and was held not to have retired.[13] In a more recent case the Chief Commissioner held that a city councillor whose duties, for which he received attendance allowances, occupied him for about 30 hours a week, was pursuing a gainful occupation and, therefore, had not retired, even though he was not employed under a contract of service or for services.[14] But in a case where a former coal dealer let out four properties at a substantial rent but performed no work in connection with the lettings, his income did not preclude a holding that he had retired.[15] Similarly, where a woman let rooms but did not

10 See pp. 373–379, below.
11 SSA 1980, s.3(2), amending SSPA 1975, s.11.
12 See on this pp. 35–42, above.
13 *CP 21/49.*
14 *R(P) 2/76.*
15 *CP 129/50.*

provide service or board, it was held that she was not engaged in a gainful occupation and could be accepted as retired.[16] In *R(P) 19/56*, however, where the claimant was a partner with his son in a dairy farm but performed only light duties after pensionable age, he was held not to have retired. The Commissioner said:

> In determining whether the claimant was at the relevant time retired, I therefore take into account not only the evidence as to his activities, but also the circumstance that he was a partner, and the circumstance that his financial return from the venture in which he was a partner was a substantial one.

It appears that both the financial return and the nature of the work done are relevant in determining whether a person has retired.

The mere fact that the claimant is not working at the time of the claim is not by itself enough to show that he has retired from regular employment. Retirement must be final and intended to be permanent.[17] An illusory intention to resume work will not, however, preclude a finding of retirement: thus, when a miner entertained hopes of working again, though this was impossible because of his injuries, it was held that he had retired.[18]

v Notice of retirement

Under the Act, the claimant must give notice of retirement in order to be treated as retired.[19] This requirement must be distinguished from that of a claim for a pension, which is discussed in chapter 15.[20] The Claims and Payments Regulations require that the notice be given in writing, specifying the date of retirement. This date must not be earlier than pensionable age, nor later than four months after the giving of the notice (if the date given is before pensionable age, it is treated as notice of retirement at pensionable age).[1] The date of retirement specified may antedate that of the notice by up to twelve months.[2] The requirement of notice does not apply to a women over 65 or a man over 70, as they are deemed to retire on reaching that age.[3]

There is some case-law on what constitutes a valid notice of retirement. Notice is normally given on the pension claim form, but a recorded note of a conversation with a claimant may amount to such notice,[4] as may a notice of appeal.[5] In one case, a British subject gave notice of his retirement to the Sécurité Sociale in Paris on his 65th birthday. The Commissioner held that the Sécurité Sociale, under the reciprocal arrangements in force between the United Kingdom and France for the payment of pensions, could be regarded as agents of the Ministry of Pensions and, therefore, the notice was valid.[6] For EEC countries the point is now covered by regulations providing that a declaration which should have been submitted to one Member State may be admissible if submitted to another.[7]

16 *R(P) 5/55*.
17 See *141/49(P)* where there is a full treatment of this point by the Northern Ireland Commissioner.
18 *CP 49/49*.
19 SSA 1975, s.27(4).
20 R(P) 3/59; see pp. 540–547, below.
 1 SI 1987/1968, reg 15(2) and (3).
 2 Ibid, reg 15(4).
 3 SSA 1975, s.27(5).
 4 *R(P) 4/53*.
 5 *R(P) 8/51*.
 6 *R(P) 14/55*.
 7 Reg 2003/83, art.86.

vi Cancelling retirement
The decision to retire, or to be treated as retired, and claim a retirement pension is not irreversible. The National Insurance Act 1957 introduced a procedure by which a retirement pensioner under 60 (for a woman) or 65 (for a man) could elect to be treated as not having retired – a procedure known in the departmental jargon as 'de-retirement'. A former pensioner could thus resume full-time work, earning increments to the pension payable on retiring again or at 65 (for a woman) or 70 (for a man). The term 'de-retirement' can be misleading. A person who is *treated* as having retired from regular employment, or a widow whose Category B pension is not subject to the retirement condition, can also invoke this provision. It is now in section 30(3) of the Social Security Act 1975.

A person can only elect to de-retire once.[8] Because de-retirement is regarded as a serious step, leading to loss of entitlement to pension and any dependants' increases, notice of an election to cancel retirement must be in writing,[9] and a document should not be construed as notice unless it is clearly intended as such.[10] Unlike a retirement notice, it may not take effect before the date on which it is given.[11] In the case of a widow who has become entitled to a Category B pension on her husband's death after she reached pensionable age, however, if she elects to de-retire, her entitlement to earn increments to her pension is back-dated to the date of her widowhood.[12]

A husband whose wife is entitled to a Category B pension on his contributions or a 'composite' Category A pension based in part on his contributions[13] may not elect to de-retire without the wife's consent, unless that consent is 'unreasonably withheld'.[14] In the only reported case on this provision (a Northern Ireland case, *R 6/60 (P)*), the Commissioner held that it was not unreasonable for a wife to refuse consent becasue of the substantial financial detriment she would suffer. It was for the husband to show that the wife had acted unreasonably, for example through pique, spite or a desire just to stand in his way.[15]

vii The earnings rule
Section 30 of the Social Security Act 1975 provides that, where the earnings of a retirement pensioner (Category A or B) for the previous week.[16] exceed the earnings limit (currently £75), the pension is to be reduced by half the first £4 of excess earnings and the whole of any earnings above that level. The reduction is applied to the basic pension, including the increase for a dependent wife or husband and any increment for deferred retirement, but not to the additional pension and increments to it, nor to any graduated pension under the pre-1975 scheme.[17] The earnings rule does not apply to the pension

---

8 SI 1979/642, reg 2(2)(a).
9 Ibid, reg 2(3).
10 *R(P) 1/61*.
11 SI 1979/642, reg 2(4).
12 Ibid, reg 2(6).
13 See pp. 201–202, below.
14 SSA 1975, s.30(4).
15 The Commissioner followed with approval the approach taken in cases where consent is refused to the assignment of a lease: *Shanly v Ward* (1913) 29 TLR 714, CA. Compare the objective approach now taken in the consent to adoption cases: Cretney *Principles of Family Law* (4th edn) pp. 448–455.
16 A 'week', for this purpose, ends on Saturday: SSA 1975, Sch 20.
17 SSPA 1975, s.11, as amended.

payable for the first week after retirement – in other words, the fact that the pensioner's earnings for the last week of employment exceeded the earnings limit will not affect the first pension payment.

The increase for a dependent adult is liable to reduction on account of the dependant's earnings as well as the claimant's.[18] Where the dependant is the claimant's wife or a woman looking after his child and entitlement to the increase commenced before 16 September 1985, the increase is reduced by half the dependant's earnings between £45 and £49 per week and the whole of any earnings over £49 (the earnings limits which applied immediately before that date). In other cases, the earnings limit is £32.75 a week and the increase is not payable at all if the dependant earns more than that. The dependant's earnings, however, do not affect the rest of the pension.[19]

There is a considerable amount of case-law, in addition to the Computation of Earnings Regulations,[20] concerning what income is to be regarded as 'earnings' and how it is to be assessed. The rules are relevant to a number of benefits, apart from retirement pensions, and are, therefore, discussed in chapter 9.[1]

D Contribution conditions

The third requirement for entitlement to a Category A or B basic retirement pension is that the contribution conditions are satisfied. A person may claim a Category A pension, normally based on his (or her) *own* contributions, or a Category B pension based on a husband's or deceased wife's contributions. The same person cannot receive both a Category A and a Category B pension, even though the contribution conditions for each may be met; he is entitled to whichever is more favourable to him.

The position of married women, widows, widowers and divorced men and women, and the basis of entitlement to the additional earnings-related pension, are discussed later in this chapter. In this section we are concerned with the general contribution requirements for the basic Category A pension. Unlike the retirement condition, which affects pension entitlement only for the five years until the person is deemed to have retired,[2] a deficient contribution record may render him permanently ineligible for a basic pension.[3]

The contribution conditions are set out in paragraph 5 of Schedule 3 to the Social Security Act 1975, as amended by section 19 of the Pensions Act 1975. The amended conditions are:

(a) the claimant must have paid, in at least one year, contributions of the relevant class on earnings of at least 52 times the lower earnings limit;[4] and

---

18 In this respect a married couple will be more favourably placed if the wife is entitled to a Category B retirement pension: this is her pension, not part of her husband's, and is not affected by his earnings: see p.201, below.
19 SI 1977/343, reg 8, as amended.
20 SI 1987/1698.
1 Pp. 373–379, below.
2 P.189, above.
3 The claimant may be eligible for a non-contributory retirement pension: pp. 225–226, below.
4 The condition is expressed in terms of earnings factors (see p.54, above), enabling class 2 (self-employed) and class 3 (voluntary) contributions to be taken into account as well as earnings-related class 1 contributions. It can be satisfied by having paid 50 flat-rate contributions at any time (not necessarily in one year) before 6 April 1975 (SI 1979/643, reg. 6(1)), or contributions on earnings of at least 50 times the lower earnings limit for one of the years 1975–76, 1976–77 or 1977–78.

(b) the claimant must have paid or been credited with contributions equivalent to that sum for nine-tenths of his working life (if that is not a whole number of years, it is rounded down to the nearest whole number).[5]

The effect of this second contribution condition – the continuing contributions condition – is that, where the claimant's working life is of 41 years or more, up to five years' contributions may be missed.

The continuing contributions condition is, however, modified in respect of anyone who was over 16 when the post-war national insurance scheme commenced on 5 July 1948. If he had been insured for pension purposes under earlier legislation, his working life is taken to have started at the beginning of the tax year in which he last entered insurance under that legislation, but not before 6 April 1936, and contributions for the period prior to 5 July 1948 are taken into account accordingly. If he was not insured under the pre-1948 legislation, his working life is taken as having started on 6 April 1948.[6]

The second contribution condition is further modified to provide 'home responsibilities protection' for persons who have been out of the employment field for considerable periods (generally, though not necessarily, married women). It is enough for a claimant to have complied with the condition for half the required years (i.e. half of nine-tenths of her working life), or at least 20 years if that is less, provided she (or he) can establish that for all the other years she was 'precluded from regular employment by responsibilities at home'.[7] Regulations define the meaning of this phrase. The claimant will be regarded as satisfying the requirement if throughout any year after April 1978 (a) she receives child benefit for any child under 16, (b) she is regularly engaged in caring for a person aged 16 or over in receipt of the attendance allowance or of a constant attendance allowance under the war pensions or industrial injuries scheme, or (c) she is in receipt of supplementary benefit or (since April 1988) income support and exempted from the requirement to be available for work because looking after an elderly or incapacitated person. But a woman who, at the beginning of the tax year, has elected for reduced contribution liability cannot claim home responsibilities protection for that year.[8]

A retirement pension (Category A or B) may be paid at a reduced rate to a person who does not fully satisfy the second contribution condition.[9] This rate is the proportion of those years of contributions liability (nine-tenths of the claimant's working life) in which contributions of the required amount were in fact paid or credited. No benefit is payable unless this proportion is more than 24 per cent.

E Married women

A married woman who has reached pensionable age may be entitled to a Category A pension on the basis of her own contributions. Alternatively, she may be entitled to a Category B pension on her husband's contributions. She

5 The total number of flat-rate contributions paid or credited before 6 April 1975 is divided by 50 and the result rounded up to the nearest whole number, to arrive at the number of reckonable years for that part of a person's career (SI 1979/643, reg 7(2)).
6 Ibid, reg 7.
7 SSA 1975, Sch 3, para 5(6): see p.56, above. Also see Atkins [1980] JSWL 33.
8 SI 1978/508, reg 2, as amended. For reduced contribution liability, see pp. 51–52, above.
9 SI 1979/642, reg 6.

cannot claim both but she may be able to use her Category B entitlement to enhance the value of her Category A pension.

i Claim by a married woman on her own contributions (Category A pension)

Until 1979 a married woman was not entitled to a Category A pension unless (in addition to the other conditions) either her marriage occurred after she was 55 or, alternatively, she satisfied the second contribution condition for a least half the years between her marriage and pensionable age (the 'half test').[10] However, the 1975 Pensions Act removed these additional requirements for women reaching pensionable age on or after 6 April 1979, and the Social Security Act 1985 abolished them entirely with effect from 22 December 1984.[11] A married woman, therefore, now has the same rights as a single woman to a Category A pension on her own contributions. The position of married women has been further improved by the 'home responsibilities protection' provisions of the Pension Act.[12]

ii Claim on a husband's contributions (Category B pension)

A married woman can claim a Category B basic pension at the lower rate[13] by virtue of her husband's contribution record if they have both reached pensionable age and have (or are treated as having) retired.[14] If he has not fully satisfied the second contribution test, the Category B pension is proportionately reduced, in the same way as the Category A pension.[15] While the husband is alive it does not generally make any difference to their joint income that his wife is entitled to a Category B pension, since in most circumstances (whether she is under or over pensionable age) he would receive a dependant's allowance in respect of her[16] at the same rate as the Category B pension. The dependency allowance, however, is an increase of the husband's pension and may be reduced under the earnings rule because of his earnings as well as hers. The Category B pension is paid directly to the wife and is subject to reduction only if her earnings exceed the limit.

It should be noted that the United Kingdom is the only EEC country, apart from Gibraltar, where a separate pension is paid to a wife by virtue of her husband's contributions.[17] The trend of policy in recent years (as in the abolition of the 'half test', the introduction of 'home responsibilities protection', and the phasing out of the married woman's option to pay reduced contributions[18]) has been towards enabling wives to qualify for a full pension on their own contributions, thus reducing dependence on their husbands' contributions.

iii Composite pension (Category A)

If a married woman is entitled to a Category A pension on her own contributions, but her Category A basic pension is less than the standard lower rate of Category B pension (or her Category A pension consists only of an additional

10 SSA 1975, s.28(2).
11 SSPA 1975, s.19(4), as amended, and SSA 1985 s.11.
12 See p.200, above.
13 Approximately 60 percent of the Category A basic pension rate.
14 SSA 1975, s.29(2) and (3).
15 SI 1979/642, reg 6: see p.200, above.
16 See pp. 341–342, below.
17 133 HC Official Report (6th series) col 593.
18 See pp. 51–52, above.

pension with no basic pension entitlement), it can be increased by either the whole of the Category B pension derived from her husband's contributions or as much of it as is necessary to raise the Category A basic pension to the level of the lower-rate Category B pension, whichever is less. The resulting 'composite' pension is a Category A pension, even if most of it is payable by virtue of the husband's contributions. The two pension entitlements can be combined in this way only if the wife became entitled to a Category B pension on or after 6 April 1979.[19]

F Widows

A widow who has reached pensionable age can benefit from her late husband's contribution record in a number of ways, depending in part on whether he died before or after she reached pensionable age.

i Widow under 60 on husband's death

Under section 20 of the 1975 Pensions Act, for the purpose of calculating the Category A basic pension entitlement of a widow whose husband died before she reached pensionable age and who did not remarry before that age, where for any year up to that of her husband's death her own contributions do not satisfy the contribution conditions, the husband's contribution record can be substituted for hers, either for the period of the marriage or for the whole of her working life up to his death.[20]

A widow who was under 60 on her husband's death may be entitled to a Category B pension (basic and additional) on his contributions, but only if she has retired and was entitled to a widow's pension (or, in certain circumstances, is treated as having been so entitled) immediately before her sixtieth birthday. The Category B pension is paid at the same rate as the widow's pension.[1] If she has not retired, she can instead continue to receive her widow's pension until she is 65, when the retirement pension will become payable without a retirement condition.[2] It should be noted, however, that these provisions do not apply to a woman who is widowed under pensionable age and who does not qualify for a widow's pension because she was under 45 on her husband's death or when her widowed mother's allowance ceased. She may be able to use her husband's contribution record to help her qualify for a full basic retirement pension at 60, as explained in the preceding paragraph, but she cannot inherit any of his additional pension entitlement.

Like a married woman, a widow cannot receive both a Category A and a Category B pension; but if her husband died on or after 6 April 1979 and her own contribution record does not entitle her to a full Category A basic pension she can receive a 'composite' pension, using all or part of her Category B basic pension entitlement to raise the Category A basic pension to the full standard basic pension rate.[3] Similarly, her Category B additional earnings-related pension entitlement will be added to her Category A additional pension, but not so as to raise it above the maximum additional pension that she

19 SSPA 1975, s.10, as amended.
20 SI 1979/642, reg 8 and Sch 1: SSA 1975, s.28(3) made similar provision for widows who reached pensionable age before 6 April 1979.
 1 SSA 1975, s.29(5), and SI 1979/642, reg 7. For the widow's pension and the reduction in the widow's additional pension where the husband dies after 5 April 2000, see pp. 242–243, below.
 2 See p.189, above.
 3 SSPA 1975, s.9(2).

would have earned as a single person.[4] So far as the basic pension is concerned, however, this is an alternative to the provision explained above, under which a widow can substitute her husband's contribution record for part of her own: she cannot do this and also receive a composite basic pension, thus taking advantage of her husband's contributions twice over.[5]

The effect of these provisions is that a widow aged between 60 and 65 may be faced with a choice between three courses of action. She can claim a retirement pension (Category A or B, whichever is more favourable), subject to the retirement condition; retain her widow's pension until she is 65; or give up her widow's pension and go on working and earning increments to the retirement pension payable when she retires or reaches age 65.[6] Which option is best will depend on the circumstances of the individual case.

ii Widow aged 60 or over on husband's death

A widow who was 60 or over when her husband died can claim a Category B pension (basic and additional) at the same rate as the Category A pension that he was receiving or (if he was under pensionable age or had not retired) would have received. In this case there is no retirement condition. This is because, if the husband had died before the widow reached pensionable age, she would have been entitled to a widow's pension which is not dependent on retirement.[7] If the husband's death occurred after 10 April 1988 and resulted from an industrial injury or disease, the Category B basic pension will be calculated as if he had fully satisfied the contribution conditions, even if he had not.[8] As one of the economy measures enacted by the Social Security Act 1986, the widow's category B additional pension will be reduced to half that of her husband if he dies after 5 April 2000.[9]

If the widow is entitled to a Category A pension on her own contributions, it can be topped up by her Category B entitlement to the same extent as if she had been widowed before pensionable age: the composite additional pension, in this case, cannot exceed the maximum to which a single person could have been entitled on reaching pensionable age at the date of the husband's death.[10] The alternative of substituting her husband's contribution record for her own is not available to a woman who is over pensionable age when her husband dies.

G Widowers

The 1975 Pensions Act extended to a widower the possibility of substituting his wife's contribution record for his own, either for the duration of the marriage or for the whole of his working life up to the wife's death, provided that he did not remarry before reaching pensionable age. This mirrors the entitlement of a widow to substitute her late husband's contribution for her own. It applies only where either the wife's death or the widower's sixty-fifth

---

4 Ibid, s.9(3) and SI 1978/949.
5 SI 1979/642, reg 8(5).
6 For the rules regarding increments, see pp. 223–224, below.
7 SSA 1975, s.29(4).
8 SSA 1986, Sch 3, para 10, as amended.
9 Ibid, s.19(1).
10 SSPA 1975, s.9(2) and (3).

birthday occurred on or after 6 April 1979 and one of them was under pensionable age when she died.[11]

The Pensions Act also extended entitlement to a Category B pension to a widower whose wife died on or after 6 April 1979 when they were both over pensionable age. The widower inherits his wife's entitlement to both basic and additional pension. Like widows, widowers will receive only half their partner's additional pension if she dies after 5 April 2000.[12] Widowers' Category B pensions, however, differ from those of widows in two respects: the Category B retirement pension of a widow over pensionable age on her spouse's death is subject to the retirement condition while a widower's is not; and a widower cannot qualify for a Category B pension at all if his wife died before he reached pensionable age.[13]

The rule that a person cannot receive both a Category A pension and a Category B pension applies to widowers in the same way as to widows; and so does the provision enabling the Category B pension entitlement to be used to top up the Category A pension. The provisions regarding 'composite' pensions are exactly the same for widowers as for widows.[14] In the case of a widower, however, Category B entitlement and, therefore, the possibility of a composite pension arises only if he and his wife were both over pensionable age on her death.

These provisions go some way to achieving a degree of equalisation of widows' and widowers' rights, but the law may still be considered to discriminate against widowers. Further changes may follow the proposed EEC Directive on equal treatment for men and women in social security.[15] Full equality of treatment, however, would involve more fundamental reforms in the field of widows' and widowers' benefits as such.[16]

H   Divorced persons

For the purpose of calculating a divorced person's Category A basic pension, the former spouse's contribution record can be substituted for his or her own, in the same way as for a widow or widower, either for the period of the marriage or for the whole working life up to the termination of the marriage, provided that he or she has not remarried before reaching pensionable age. This provision does not apply to a person who, on 6 April 1979, was over pensionable age and already divorced; but, with that exception, divorced persons, unlike widows and widowers, can take advantage of it regardless of the age of either partner when the marriage ended.[17]

A divorced person, on the other hand, cannot add the former spouse's pension rights to his or her own in order to obtain a composite pension, since the relevant provisions of the Pensions Act (sections 9 and 10) apply only to married women, widows and widowers. This means that there is no way in which a divorced person can benefit from a former spouse's entitlement to an additional earnings-related pension.

11 SSPA 1975, s.20(1), SSA 1979, Sch 1, para 20, and SI 1979/642, reg 8 and Sch 1.
12 SSA 1986, s.19(1)(b).
13 SSPA 1975, s.8, and SSA 1979, Sch 1, para 14.
14 SSPA 1975, s.9. See pp. 202–203, above.
15 Proposal for a Council Directive, COM(87) 494.
16 See ch 6, pp. 234–238, below.
17 SSPA 1975, s.20(1), SSA 1979, Sch 1, para 20, and SI 1979/642, reg 8 and Sch 1.

Part 3 Graduated retirement benefit

Graduated retirement benefit[18] was introduced by the National Insurance Act 1959, marking the first departure from the principle of flat-rate contributions and benefits. Under the National Insurance Act 1965[19] the benefit is an increase in the weekly rate of retirement pension, originally calculated as 2½p for each unit of graduated contributions paid by an employee (the scheme did not cover the self employed) between April 1961 and April 1975.[20] A unit is £7.50 for a man and £9 for a woman; and a fraction of a unit, if a half or more, is treated as a complete unit.[1] There was at first no provision for up-rating the 2½p pension 'bricks', a weakness of the scheme which was strongly criticised since it meant that the benefits were not protected against inflation. Regulations made under the 1975 Pensions Act now apply the up-rating provisions of the Social Security Act 1986[2] both to the graduated pension rights of future pensioners and to graduated pensions already in payment. Accordingly, the amount of graduated pension payable for each unit of contributions was increased to 5.39 pence for 1988–89.[3]

Although described as an increase in the claimant's retirement pension rate, a graduated pension can be paid to a person over pension age and retired from regular employment, but who is not otherwise entitled to a retirement pension, for example because he does not satisfy the contribution conditions or his basic pension entitlement is eliminated by the earnings rule.[4] A married woman, similarly, can claim a graduated pension on her own contributions at 60, subject to the retirement condition, even if she cannot yet claim a Category B pension on her husband's insurance because he is under 65 or has not retired. A widow is entitled to the graduated pension earned by her own contributions *and* half that earned by her husband. A widower can add half his deceased wife's graduated pension to his own provided that they were both of pensionable age at the time of her death.[5]

The National Insurance Act 1959 broke new ground not only by adding an earnings-related element to the flat-rate retirement pension but also by allowing employers whose occupational pension schemes satisfied certain minimum standards to 'contract out' of the graduated pension scheme. The basic condition for contracting out was that the employer's scheme must offer pensions at least equivalent to the maximum graduated pension, which was itself extremely modest (widows' benefits equivalent to those of the graduated scheme were not required). The new graduated contributions were not payable in respect of contracted-out employees; instead, they were required to pay a higher flat-rate contribution, in recognition of the first of the scheme's declared aims, which was 'to place the National Insurance Scheme on a sound financial basis'.[6]

Contributions payable since April 1975 have not earned entitlement to graduated pension, even though entitlement to the additional pension under the

18 The legislation uses the term 'benefit', though the DSS leaflets refer to graduated pension, and the two words are used interchangeably here.
19 Ss.36, 37 (the sections are kept in force in a modified form by SI 1978/393, made under the Social Security (Consequential Provisions) Act 1975).
20 NIA 1965, s.36(1).
1 Ibid, s.36(2), (3).
2 See p.380, below.
3 NIA 1965, s.36(1), kept in force, as amended, by SI 1978/393, Sch 1.
4 Ibid, s.36(7).
5 Ibid, s.37.
6 White Paper, *Provision for Old Age* (1958, Cmnd 538) p.13.

Pensions Act 1975, which replaced the graduated pension scheme, did not begin to accrue until April 1978. Payment of graduated pensions will, however, continue for many years to come. In 1986, 67 per cent of all pensioners and 90 per cent of recently retired male pensioners were receiving graduated pensions, but the average amount was only £1.23 a week and more than half were getting less than £1 a week.[7]

Part 4   The Social Security Pensions Act 1975[8]

A brief account of the main provisions of the 1975 Pensions Act and the modifications introduced by the Social Security Act 1986 has been given in the introductory section of this chapter. The main purpose of the Pensions Act was to add a new earnings-related element to the flat-rate basic pension. The resulting combined weekly benefit was conceived as a single pension, consisting of a 'basic component' and an 'additional component'.[9] The baisc component was regarded as replacing pre-retirement earnings in full up to that level (roughly a fifth of average earnings), while the additional component was to replace about a quarter of the individual's earnings above that level and up to the higher earnings limit for payment of contributions. The 1986 Act, however, substituted the terms 'basic pension' and 'additional pension' for 'basic component' and 'additional component', wherever they occurred in the legislation.[10] This was more than a change in terminology. It reflected a different approach to pension provision, in which only the provision of a basic flat-rate pension is seen as a necessary function of the social security system, while additional pensions may be provided in a variety of ways and through a variety of financial institutions of which social security is only one and, in the view of the Conservative government, not the most desirable. Even before the Pensions Act was amended, however, the 'additional component' was already commonly referred to as a separate scheme: the State earnings-related pension scheme, or 'SERPS'. In the following pages, therefore, the term 'additional pension' will be used, whether in reference to the original provisions of the Pensions Act or to the Act as now amended.

The provisions of the Pensions Act relating to the additional pension were never simple, but their complexity was increased by the 1986 amendments. The reason for this is that the revised pension formula designed to reduce the cost of the scheme is to be phased in over a long period, in order to provide some protection for pension rights based on contributions payable prior to 6 April 1988 and for employees already near retirement age, and also to avoid dramatic differences in pension rights between people reaching pensionable age on successive days. The method of calculating the additional pension will therefore vary according to whether contributions were paid prior to the tax year 1988–89 and whether the contributor reaches pensionable age before 6 April 1999, between then and 5 April 2009, or after the latter date.

A   The basis of calculation

In principle, the additional pension is calculated as a percentage of a person's earnings above the lower earnings limit, after adjusting each year's earnings

7 Social Security Statistics 1987, Tables 13.45 and 13.46.
8 See Mesher 39 MLR 321 for an admirable summary of the Act in its original form.
9 SSPA 1975, s.6(1).
10 SSA 1986, s.18(1).

to take account of increases in average earnings during the remainder of that person's working life. In this way, the pension, though based on earnings between 1978 and the year before pensionable age, is related to the general standard of living at the time when it becomes payable.

The method of calculation is set out in section 6 of the Pensions Act, as amended by the 1986 Act. It involves, first, ascertaining the person's earnings factors[11] for each tax year, starting from 1978–79 or the year in which his sixteenth birthday occurred (whichever is later) and ending with the year before he reached pensionable age – the 'relevant years'.[12] The earnings factor for each year (representing, in broad terms, the person's earnings between the lower and upper earnings limits; i.e. between, approximately, the basic pension rate for that year and about seven times that level) is revalued in line with the increase in average earnings up to the year before pensionable age. For this purpose, the Secretary of State is required, in each tax year, to review the general level of earnings in Great Britain, estimated in such manner as he thinks fit, and to make an order increasing the value of earnings factors from 1978–79 onwards by the amount necessary to restore their value in relation to the general level of earnings.[13]

The next stage in the calculation is to work out the 'surplus' in the earnings factor for each year:[14] the amount, if any, by which the earnings factor for that year, revalued as above, exceeds the 'qualifying earnings factor', which is 52 times the lower earnings limit for the year before pensionable age.[15] These surpluses represent the amounts of earnings on which the additional pension is calculated as a percentage. There is no other contribution condition. Provided that there is a surplus for at least one year of a person's working life, this is enough to confer entitlement to an additional pension, even if the contribution conditions for a basic pension are not satisfied. The way in which the surpluses are translated into weekly pension entitlement, however, depends on the year in which pensionable age is reached.

i Persons reaching pensionable age before 6 April 1999
In the case of a man reaching age 65 or a woman reaching age 60 before 6 April 1999, the additional pension is calculated by means of the formula laid down in section 6 of the Pensions Act in its unamended form. The surpluses in the claimant's earnings factors for the relevant years are added together, and the weekly additional pension is 1¼ per cent of the total, divided by 52.[16]

ii Persons reaching pensionable age between 6 April 1999 and 5 April 2009
Under the original formula described above, the additional pension accrued at the rate of 1¼ per cent of earnings between the lower and upper earnings limits for up to 20 years, producing an additional pension of about 25 per cent of pre-retirement earnings. In a case where there were earnings factor surpluses for more than 20 years, the pension would have been based on the 'best' 20 years, other years being ignored.[17] The effect of the new formula enacted by section 18(3) of the Social Security Act 1986, which applies only to

11 See p.54, above.
12 SSPA 1975, s.6(6).
13 Ibid, s.21.
14 Ibid, s.6(4).
15 Ibid, s.5(3).
16 Ibid, s.6(2) and (3), as amended.
17 Ibid, s.6(2).

those reaching retirement age on or after 6 April 1999, is to take into account the surpluses for the whole of a person's working life from 1978 on, instead of for a maximum of 20 years. The pension accrual rate is, however, reduced so that the formula will normally produce an additional pension of 20 rather than 25 per cent of pre-retirement earnings. An important implication of the new formula is that, since no-one reaching pensionable age before 6 April 1999 will have contributed to the scheme for more than 20 years, the 'best 20 years' provision of the Pensions Act will never take effect.

For those reaching pensionable age during the transitional period from 6 April 1999 to 5 April 2009, the additional pension will be calculated in two parts, the first relating to the part of their working life between 1978–79 and 1987–88 inclusive, and the second to the part falling between 1988–89 and the tax year before they reach pensionable age. The pension based on surpluses for the years up to 1987–88 will be 25 per cent of those surpluses divided by the total number of relevant years, while surpluses for the years from 1988–89 to 2007–08 will produce a pension based on a lower percentage, between 20 and 25, depending on the year in which pensionable age in reached: 25 per cent for those reaching pensionable age in 1999–2000, 24½ per cent in 2000–01, 24 per cent in 2001–02, and so on, diminishing by a half per cent per year until, for those reaching pensionable age in 2009–10, the 20 per cent rate is reached.[18]

The way in which this transitional formula will operate can be illustrated by an example: a man aged 39 in April 1978, who reaches the age of 65 in the tax year 2003–04, with a surplus in his earnings factor for each of the 25 years up to 2002–03 (his last 'relevant year'). If the surpluses amount to £60,000 for the ten years up to 1987–88 and £100,000 for the fifteen years from 1988–89 to 2002–03, his additional pension will be calculated as follows:-

$$25 \text{ per cent of } £60,000 \div 25 \quad = \quad £600$$
$$23 \text{ per cent of } £100,000 \div 25 \quad = \quad £920$$

$$£1,520 \quad \div \quad 52 \quad = \quad £29.23 \text{ per week}$$

iii Persons reaching pensionable age on or after 6 April 2009

For those reaching pensionable age in the tax year 2009–10 or later, a similar two-part calculation will be needed if any of their relevant years were earlier than 1988–89. The percentage to be applied to surpluses for the years from 1988–89 on, however, will in these cases always be 20 per cent.[19] Eventually, assuming no further changes in the legislation, all additional pensions will be calculated at the 20 per cent rate; but men reaching age 65 as late as the year 2036–37 will still have part of their pension calculated at the 25 per cent rate, and many such pensions will remain in payment well into the 2060s.

iv Protected years

The 'best 20 years' provision of the 1975 Pensions Act would have been highly advantageous to people reaching pensionable age in the twenty-first century whose working lives had been interrupted, whether by family responsibilities or by sickness, unemployment or other causes. It would also have helped those whose earnings for part of their working lives were particularly low, including mothers returning to work part-time, people whose

18 Ibid, s.6(2A) and (2B).
19 Ibid, s.6(2A)(b)(i).

earning capacity was reduced by disabilities, young people in low-paid apprenticeships, and heavy manual workers whose earnings tend to fall off in the years preceding retirement. The decision to base the additional pension on a person's earnings averaged over the whole working life (except any years before 1978–79) meant that other arrangements would have to be made to protect at least some of those with fluctuating or interrupted earnings, who would have benefited from the best 20 years' formula.

The solution adopted in the Social Security Act 1986 was to exclude certain years of a person's working life from the number of 'relevant years' over which his or her earnings factor surpluses would be averaged; but not so as to reduce it below 20 years. These protected years are those in which the pensioner was credited with earnings or Class 2 or 3 contributions to help towards meeting the contribution conditions for any benefit; years in which he or she was precluded from regular employment by home responsibilities; or years which, in circumstances prescribed by regulations, would have been treated as being in one of these categories. Such years, however, are to be excluded from the calculation only in certain cases or classes of cases, which are also to be prescribed by regulations.[20] These regulations, which will only affect persons reaching pensionable age after 5 April 1999, had not been made when the 1986 amendments to the Pensions Act came into force in April 1988. The Government's stated intention, however, was that the years to be excluded would be those in which the person was entitled either to home responsibilities protection[1] or to contribution credits[2] due to incapacity or while receiving invalid care allowance, and years which, although these conditions were not satisfied, it would be unfair to treat differently (e.g. where a person was incapable of work for most of the year but earned just enough in the remainder of the year to satisfy the contribution condition for basic pension and therefore did not need credits).[3]

An obvious gap in these provisions is that, while a year of sickness will not affect a person's additional pension because it will be excluded from the number of years over which his earnings will be averaged, no similar protection is to be given for years of unemployment. Compared with the 'best 20 years' provision, they have the further disadvantage that only years in which a person has no earnings factor surplus or almost none will be excluded. A year of greatly diminished earnings, therefore, may still have the effect of reducing the person's average surplus and thus the amount of additional pension they can expect to receive. To a mother considering whether to resume work on a part-time basis, or a man or woman facing the prospect of returning to work at a reduced level of earnings after a long illness, the fact that by working and paying contributions they will reduce their pension entitlement may seem unfair and could act as a disincentive.

B Occupational pensions and contracting out

i Types of contracted-out schemes
The most complicated parts of the legislation discussed in this chapter are concerned with occupational and 'personal' pension schemes and their

---

20 Ibid, SSPA 1975, s.6(2B).
 1 See p.200, above.
 2 See p.57, above.
 3 Social Security Bill 1986: House of Commons Notes on Clauses, p.29.

relationship to the state earnings-related additional pension. It was a fundamental principle of the 1975 Pensions Act that a person's employment could
be contracted out if he or she was a member of an occupational pension
scheme providing pensions of a specified standard and the appropriate consents had been given by the Occupational Pensions Board.[4] Among other
conditions, the occupational scheme had to guarantee a minimum pension,
the amount of which was to be deducted from the state pension that would
otherwise have been payable.[5] Contracted-out employees could thus be confident of receiving at least the same total pension as they would otherwise
have received from the state scheme alone. Occupational schemes of this kind
are now known as 'defined benefit' or 'salary-related' schemes.

The Social Security Act 1986, however, extended the contracting out provisions of the 1975 Act to cover occupational schemes providing 'money purchase' benefits, defined as 'benefits the rate or amount of which is calculated
by reference to a payment or payments made by a member of the scheme or
by any other person in respect of a member. . .' .[6] In a money purchase
scheme, the pension is not fixed in advance as a percentage of earnings or of
contributions paid; instead, its amount depends on the outcome, over the
pensioner's working life, of the investment of his or her contributions. It may
turn out to be either more or less than the additional pension forgone in the
state scheme. There can be no 'guaranteed minimum pension' in a money
purchase scheme, but the Category A or B pension derived from the contributions of a person who has been contracted out in such a scheme will nevertheless be reduced by a notional 'GMP'.[7] The extension of contracting out to
money purchase schemes, therefore, represents a radical departure from the
principle that no-one should risk losing part of their pension as a result of
their employer's decision to contract out.

Another innovation under the 1986 Act is that individual employees can
now elect to contract out by contributing to a personal pension scheme. A
personal pension scheme used for this purpose *must* provide money purchase
benefits.[8] The Act does not use the term 'contracted-out' in this connection,
but the effect is similar: the Category A or B additional pension is reduced by
a notional GMP, whether this turns out to be more or less than the pension
produced by the personal scheme. The provisions of the 1986 Act relating to
personal pension schemes are considered separately below.[9]

ii Contracting out certificates

Section 30 of the Pensions Act 1975, as amended by the 1986 Act, defines
'contracted-out employment' as employment of an earner under pensionable
age where either the employment qualifies him for a GMP provided by a contracted-out occupational scheme or the employer makes minimum payments
to a money purchase contracted-out scheme, and in either case a 'contracting-out certificate' issued by the Occupational Pensions Board (OPB) is
in force.[10] The application for a certificate must be made by the employer.[11] If
he wants his employees, or some of them, to be contracted out, or to cease

4 SSPA 1975, s.30.
5 Ibid, ss.26 and 29.
6 Ibid, ss.30(1)(a) and 66(1) as amended.
7 Ibid, s.29(2A).
8 SSA 1986, Sch 1, para 5.
9 See pp. 220–222, below.
10 SSPA 1975, s.30(1), as amended.
11 Ibid, s.31(3).

to be contracted out, he must first give at least three months' notice to the other parties concerned: the employees (including any in the employment in question who are not to be contracted out), the trustees (if any) and administrator of the scheme, the insurance company or friendly society if the GMPs are secured by an insurance policy or annuity contract, and any independent trade unions (the period of notice can be reduced to one month with the consent of all the unions concerned).[12] The employer is also obliged to consult with the unions on the proposal to contract out.[13] Having done this and given the required notice, he must send a formal election to the OPB.[14] The OPB then decides whether the employment should be treated as contracted-out by reference to the scheme and, if so, issues a contracting-out certificate specifying the employments (or the categories of earners in those employments) to which it relates.[15] The OPB may also cancel or vary a certificate if it has reason to suppose that any employment covered by it should not continue to be contracted out.[16]

Any interested party may ask the OPB to review its determination on a contracting out question,[17] and it may hold an oral hearing on request or if it considers it desirable.[18] Any person aggrieved by the OPB's decision on a review, or a refusal to review, can appeal on a point of law to the High Court, the Court of Session or the Northern Ireland Court of Appeal; and the OPB may itself refer any such question of law to the Court for decision.[19]

iii The effect of contracting out on the state pension
It is important to note that contracting out does not mean that an employee is totally excluded from the additional pension of the state scheme. A contracted-out scheme does not have to match the state scheme fully in regard to the inflation-proofing of pensions, protection of the rights of 'early leavers', or provision of widows', widowers' and invalidity pensions. Even in a salary related scheme, which is required to provide a GMP as a condition of contracting out, the pension may fall short of the standards of the state scheme, if not when first awarded, then subsequently as its value is reduced by inflation or when the pensioner dies. For this reason, in calculating the state pension, the whole of the additional pension based on the person's earnings factor surpluses (including upratings after pensionable age) is taken into account and the GMP is then deducted in respect of any period when he was contracted out.[20]

iv The contracted-out contribution rebate
Section 26 of the Pensions Act establishes the principle that, where an earner's employment is contracted out, the social security contributions payable and the Category A or B pension based on those contributions are both to be reduced. Section 27(1) specifies that the lower contracted-out contribution rate is to be payable only on earnings between the lower and upper earnings

12 SI 1984/380, reg 3, as amended.
13 Ibid, reg 4.
14 Ibid, reg 2(1).
15 Ibid, reg 8.
16 SI 1976/185, reg 4(1).
17 SSA 1973, s.67(2), as amended.
18 SI 1973/1776, reg 3.
19 SSA 1973, s.86, as amended.
20 SSPA 1975, s.29.

limits.[1] The Secretary of State is required to lay before Parliament, at intervals of not more than five years, a report by the Government Actuary on the contracted-out contribution rates and any changes in the cost to occupational schemes of providing GMPs. The contracted-out rebate (the difference between the normal and contracted-out contribution rates) is fixed on the basis of that report.[2] From 1988–89 on, the rebate is 5.8 per cent, of which 3.8 per cent is deducted from the normal rate of employers' contributions and 2 per cent from employees'.[3] It is expected that the rebate will remain at this level for the five years 1988–93. It reflects the estimated cost to salary related schemes of providing GMPs, including an allowance for contingencies (intended in part to encourage contracting out) and an additional 0.4 per cent 'to provde a further cushion against any additional costs arising from the implementation of the 1986 Act'.[4]

v Incentive payments to contracted-out and personal pension schemes
The White Paper of 1985 announced that, in order to 'give employees without their own pension and their employers a good incentive to start saving for their own pension', an 'extra rebate' of 2 per cent of earnings would be allowed until the end of 1992–93 for all personal pension schemes and for occupational schemes becoming contracted-out for the first time.[5] This was a controversial proposal. Doubts were expressed as to the propriety of using public funds to encourage the growth of private pension provision at the expense of the state scheme (the expression 'their own pension' in the White Paper meant a pension from a personal or occupational scheme, not from the state scheme), especially as the cost was to be borne by the National Insurance Fund though most contributors could derive no benefit from it. There were also fears that members of existing occupational schemes might be tempted to transfer to personal schemes and claim the extra rebate, with adverse effects on the finances of the occupational schemes. To allay these fears, the Government agreed that the extra rebate would not be available to a personal pension scheme in the case of an employee voluntarily leaving a contracted-out occupational scheme of which he had been a member for two years or more, without changing his employment.[6]

The 2 per cent incentive takes the form of a payment by the DSS to the occupational or personal scheme, rather than a contribution rebate as such. It is calculated on earnings between the lower and upper earnings limits, in the same way as the contracting-out rebate. A minimum payment of £1 per week is made where 2 per cent of earnings would be less than this.[7] In the case of an occupational scheme, incentive payments can be made for up to five years from 1988–89 to 1992–93 inclusive, but only if neither the scheme nor the particular earner's employment had previously been contracted out at any time since 1 January 1986.[8] The payments can be made to a personal pension scheme for up to six years from 1987–88 to 1992–93.[9]

1 Cf p.43, above.
2 SSPA 1975, s.28.
3 Ibid, s.27(2), as amended.
4 Report by the Government Actuary, *Occupational pension schemes: review of certain contracting-out terms* (1987 Cm 110), para 50.
5 Paras 2.30–2.32.
6 SSA 1986, s.3(2): SI 1987/1115, reg 2.
7 SSA 1986, s.3(1)(b).
8 Ibid, s.7(1).
9 Although the option to 'contract out' by means of a personal pension scheme did not begin

vi Contracting out: salary related schemes

Occupational schemes of the 'salary related' type have to comply with a number of conditions in order to qualify for a contracting-out certificate and, once contracted out, are subject to the supervision of the OPB to a greater extent than the 'money purchase' schemes allowed to contract out since April 1988. This is understandable because a salary related scheme has to provide for the payment of pensions in the distant future, of unpredictable amount but calculated according to a predetermined formula, while money purchase schemes involve no such obligation.

a *Guaranteed minimum pension*

Section 33 of the Pensions Act 1975, as originally enacted, required an occupational scheme, as a condition of contracting-out, to provide a pension, at pensionable age (60 for a woman, 65 for a man), which satisfied two criteria. The first, now repealed by the Social Security Act 1986, was that the pension must be not less than 1¼ per cent of either his average annual salary throughout his service in contracted-out employment (each year's earnings being revalued as with earnings factors for the state additional pension) or his final salary, multiplied in either case by his years of service up to 40.[10]

The second requirement, which remains in force, is that the weekly pension, however calculated, will not be less than the GMP.[11] The GMP is calculated by taking the earnings factors derived from Class 1 contributions paid on earnings between the lower and upper earnings limits, and revaluing each year's earnings factors as in the state scheme. The GMP is a percentage of the total revalued earnings factors: 1¼ per cent for a person who was within 20 years of pensionable age on 6 April 1978; for a younger person, 25 per cent divided by the number of years of his working life from 6 April 1978.[12] For a working life of 20 years or more in the same contracted-out employment, therefore, the GMP will be one-quarter of the person's average revalued earnings between the two earnings limits – broadly equivalent to the additional pension that would otherwise be payable by the state scheme. The scheme must also provide a GMP for the earner's widow or widower, of half the amount of the earner's GMP. The requirement to provide a widower's GMP, however, was added by the 1986 Act and applies only where the wife dies on or after 6 April 1989, the widower's GMP being based only on her earnings factors for 1988–89 and subsequent years.[13] The widow's GMP must be payable for periods when she is entitled to a state benefit on her husband's contributions (widowed mother's allowance, widow's pension or retirement pension);[14] and the widower's pension is payable in comparable circumstances (for example, if he is 45 or over or has a dependent child when his wife dies), even if he is not entitled to a state benefit in those circumstances.[15]

The GMP derived from earnings factors for the years prior to 1988–89 is not subject to any subsequent adjustment to take account of increases in prices or average earnings; it is fixed at pensionable age or at the date of death, any increases from then on being provided as part of the normal

---

until July 1988, if it was exercised by 5 April 1989 it could be backdated to April 1987 (SI 1988/137, reg 12(2)), in which case the incentive payments also became payable from then.
10 SSPA 1975, ss.33(1)(a) and 34, repealed by SSA 1986, Sch 11.
11 SSPA 1975, s.33(1)(b).
12 Ibid, s.35.
13 Ibid, s.36, as amended.
14 Ibid, s.36(6).
15 SI 1984/380, reg 33B.

uprating of the state scheme additional pension. The Social Security Act 1986, however, inserted a new section 37A in the 1975 Pensions Act, providing for annual increases in GMPs derived from earnings factors for 1988–89 and subsequent years. The annual increase will be prescribed in an order following a review by the Secretary of State in each year from 1989–90 on (presumably as part of the annual benefits uprating exercise), and will be either the percentage increase in prices since the previous review or 3 per cent, whichever is less. The increase will take effect at the beginning of the following tax year.[16] Salary related contracted-out schemes will, therefore, have to provide at least partial inflation-proofing of GMPs after award, instead of being allowed to leave this entirely to the state scheme.

b *Early leavers*
The accrued occupational pension rights of an employee who leaves the employment before pensionable age are protected by the preservation requirements of the Social Security Act 1973, as amended, and the revaluation requirements of Schedule 1A to the 1975 Pensions Act. These provisions are outside the scope of this book. It is, however, necessary to consider here the ways in which the GMP is protected in these circumstances. There are three possibilities: the scheme can retain the liability for payment of the GMP when the employee reaches pensionable age or dies; the liability can be 'bought out', normally with the member's consent, by means of an insurance policy or annuity contract[17] or transferred to another contracted-out occupational scheme (including a money purchase scheme) or to a personal pension scheme;[18] or it can be transferred back to the state scheme.

If the scheme retains the liability, arrangements must be made to revalue the GMP between the date of leaving and the time when the pension becomes payable. The scheme may continue to revalue the GMP in accordance with the orders made annually by the Secretary of State under section 21 of the Pensions Act,[19] as if the contracted-out employment had not terminated. Alternatively, the scheme's rules may provide for either 'limited revaluation' or 'fixed rate revaluation'. The effect of limited revaluation is that, from the year after the date of leaving to the year before pensionable age, the scheme revalues the GMP by 5 per cent compound or in accordance with section 21 orders, whichever is less taking the period as a whole.[20] Since this is likely to result in increased cost to the state scheme (the smaller the GMP, the larger the additional pension payable by the state scheme), the contracted-out scheme is required to pay the Secretary of State a 'limited revaluation premium' representing the difference between the cost of limited and full (section 21) revaluation.[1] Fixed rate revaluation, on the other hand, involves revaluing the GMP by 7½ per cent compound (8½ per cent if the contracted-out employment terminated before 6 April 1988), whether this turns out to be more or less than the revaluation required under section 21. If this option is chosen, no premium is payable.[2]

16 SSPA 1975, s.37A: the Secretary of State's review in the first year, 1989–90, will be of price levels over a period of 12 months commencing in 1988–89.
17 SSPA 1975, s.52C, as amended.
18 Ibid, s.38(1), as amended: SI 1985/1323, as amended.
19 See p.207, above.
20 This is similar to the general requirement, in Sch 1A to SSPA 1975, to revalue preserved 'final salary' benefits of pension scheme members leaving pensionable service on or after 1 January 1986, whether contracted-out or not.
 1 SSPA 1975, s.45, as amended: the premium is calculated on the basis of actuarial tables in SI 1987/657.
 2 SSPA 1975, s.45(1)(b): SI 1984/380, reg 22, as amended.

Where an employee left contracted-out employment before 1 January 1985, it is possible, in effect, to evade the requirement to revalue the GMP by a practice known as 'franking'. This involves using pension rights in excess of the GMP to offset the GMP revaluation: thus, as GMP rights increase with revaluation, the person's other preserved rights in the scheme diminish. Sections 41A–41E of the Pensions Act, added in 1984, now impose restrictions on franking where contracted-out employment ceased on or after 1 January 1985. Under these provisions, the pension increases resulting from revaluation of the GMP must be paid in addition to the pension rights required to be preserved on leaving employment before pension age. Similarly, where the occupational pension is payable before pensionable age in the state scheme and contracted-out employment ceases for that reason, subsequent increases in the value of the GMP must be paid in addition. The provisions are complicated and still leave some room for franking.[3]

Where a person's rights are 'bought out' or transferred to another salary related occupational scheme, the effect is to preserve entitlement to the GMP. Where the transfer is to a contracted-out money purchase scheme or to a personal pension scheme, a transfer payment must be made, at least equal to the cash value of the GMP rights, calculated on actuarial principles, and the transfer payment must be used to provided money purchase benefits, which may or may not prove as valuable as the GMP would have been.[4] A transfer payment may be made to an overseas occupational scheme if the employee is moving to employment outside the United Kingdom; but only with the approval of the OPB, which may impose conditions.[5]

The possibility of transferring GMP liability back to the state scheme arises in two types of case. The first is where the employee leaves or dies after less than two years' pensionable service and does not qualify for preservation of pension rights under the provisions of the Social Security Act 1983 as amended. If these conditions are satisfied, a 'contributions equivalent premium' can be paid to the state scheme, equivalent to the additional amount of contributions that would have been payable if the employment had not been contracted out.[6] The employee's share can be recovered from any refund of occupational scheme contributions due to him.[7] With limited exceptions,[8] in deciding whether to pay contributions equivalent premiums, the trustees of the scheme may not discriminate between members of the scheme on grounds other than length of service.[9]

The second case in which the liability for GMPs can be transferred back to the state scheme is where a person's accrued rights in excess of the GMP are transferred with his consent to a non-contracted-out scheme and the conditions for paying a 'contributions equivalent' premium are not satisfied. In these circumstances, the trustees can dispose of their GMP liability by paying a 'transfer premium', calculated on a similar basis to an 'accrued rights premium'.[10]

---

3 SSPA 1975, ss.41A–41E, as amended.
4 SI 1985/1323, reg 2B and Sch 2A.
5 SI 1985/1323, reg 2(3) and Sch 1, para 4, as amended.
6 SSPA 1975, ss.42–43, as amended. The qualifying period of service was reduced from less than five to less than two years by SSA 1986, Sch 10, para 21, with effect from 6 April 1988.
7 SSPA 1975, s.47.
8 SI 1984/380, reg 19(1).
9 SSPA 1975, s.43(4), as amended.
10 SSPA 1975, s.44A, as amended: SI 1984/380, reg 18A: SI 1987/657, reg 4. For accrued rights premiums, see p.216, below.

The procedures described above for protecting the rights of early leavers depend on the provisions of the occupational scheme's rules or the discretion of the trustees. In addition, a member of an occupational scheme whose pensionable service terminates on or after 1 January 1986 has the right, at any time one year or more before normal pension age (or before age 60 if normal pension age is earlier[11]), to take the actuarial 'cash equivalent' (generally referred to as the 'transfer value') of his accrued benefits (including the GMP) under the scheme, which must either be transferred to another scheme or invested in an insurance policy or annuity contract on his behalf.[12] If the member has left the scheme voluntarily while remaining in the same employment, the scheme may restrict the transfer payment to the cash equivalent of the rights accrued from 6 April 1988 onwards.[13]

c *Scheme ceasing to be contracted-out*

A salary related scheme may cease to be contracted-out, either on cancellation or surrender of the contracting-out certificate or because, even though a certificate remains in issue, the scheme no longer provides the benefits required as a condition of contracting out. The OPB has the power to cancel a certificate under a number of sections of the Pensions Act, some of which are very widely drafted: for example, section 32(4) under which a certificate may be cancelled 'if the Board consider that there are circumstances which make it inexpedient that the employment should be or, as the case may be, continue to be, contracted-out employment by reference to the scheme.'[14]

On a scheme ceasing to be contracted-out, the GMP rights of members, past early leavers and pensioners must be protected either by arrangements approved by the OPB for their preservation or transfer[15] or by payment of a state scheme premium representing the cost of providing the GMP.[16] A premium paid in respect of the rights of future pensioners is known as an 'accrued rights premium'; if it is in respect of existing pensioners, it is a 'pensioner's rights premium'. The effect of the premium, in either case, is to extinguish the accrued rights to a GMP under the scheme.[17] Instead, the persons concerned become entitled to additional pension under the state scheme as if they had not been contracted out. Whichever alternative is adopted – an approved arrangement or payment of state scheme premiums – the trustees of the scheme are given the option of having the last five years' earnings factors revalued at 12 per cent per annum compound, instead of at the normal rates of revaluation prescribed in section 21 orders.[18] The object of this is that pension scheme trustees should know in advance what will be the limit of their liability for GMPs if the scheme should cease to be contracted-out.

---

11 SI 1985/1931, reg 5.
12 SSPA 1975, Sch 1A, pt II, as amended. 'Normal pension age' here has the meaning ascribed to it by SSA 1973, Sch 16, para 4: the earliest age at which the member is entitled to benefits from the scheme on retirement other than through ill-health.
13 SI 1985/1931, reg 2A.
14 SSPA 1975, s.32(4), as amended. See also SSPA 1975, ss.31(2), (4) and (6), 32(3), 41(2), 41(5), 43(4) and 51A(5).
15 The conditions imposed by the OPB for approval of such arrangements are set out in Memorandum No 74 issued by the OPB (September 1982, with subsequent amendments).
16 The premium is calculated on the basis of actuarial tables in SI 1987/657, regs 3 and 6.
17 SSPA 1975, s.44(2),(3),(9).
18 Ibid, s.44(6), as amended.

vii Contracting out: money purchase schemes

Before 6 April 1988, the definition of contracted-out employment, in section 30 of the Pensions Act, required that it should qualify the earner for a GMP provided by an occupational pension scheme. From that date, the GMP condition does not apply if, instead, the employer makes 'minimum payments' to a 'money purchase contracted-out scheme'.[19] A money purchase contracted-out scheme (generally known as a 'COMP scheme'; this term will be used in the following pages) is defined as a scheme which is contracted-out by virtue of satisfying section 32(2A) of the Pensions Act;[20] and that subsection specifies (a) that the requirements of Schedule 1 to the 1986 Act relating to personal pension schemes, as modified by section 32(2B) of the Pensions Act, must be satisfied; (b) that, as with salary related schemes, the employer must contribute to the cost; and (c) that the rules of the scheme relating to 'protected rights' must comply with any regulations and with any conditions imposed by the OPB.[1] The essential distinction between COMP schemes and salary related schemes, however, is that the latter must provide a minimum pension while the former must receive minimum contributions but are not required to guarantee a pension of any particular amount.

a *Minimum payments*

The minimum payment which the employer is required to make to a COMP scheme is the amount of the contracted-out contribution rebate.[2] The employer can recover the employee's share of the contracted-out rebate by deduction from his earnings, but he is not obliged to do so.[3] Since the value of the benefits produced by a money purchase scheme depends in part on the investment return on the contributions, it is important that contributions should be paid promptly. The employer is therefore required to make minimum payments to the scheme within 14 days of the end of each 'tax month'.[4] Failure to do so could result in cancellation of the contracting-out certificate.[5]

b *Investments*

A COMP scheme's powers of investment may be limited either by regulations or by directions issued by the OPB. Regulations have been made specifying the types of investment that are permitted and, for certain types of investment, the maximum percentage of the scheme's resources that can be held in that form.[6]

c *Benefits*

The minimum payments made to the scheme, together with the 2 per cent incentive payments, must be used to provide money purchase benefits,[7] except to the extent that they are used for administrative expenses and commission; and the Secretary of State has power to limit by regulations the pro-

---

19 Ibid, s.30(1)(a), as amended.
20 Ibid, s.66(1), as amended.
 1 Ibid, s.32(2A).
 2 Ibid, s.30(1A): for the contracted-out contribution rebate, see pp. 211–212, above.
 3 Ibid, s.30(1C)(b): SI 1987/1101, reg 3.
 4 Ibid, reg 4(1).
 5 OPB Memo 93, para 25.
 6 SI 1987/1101, reg 2.
 7 For the meaning of 'money purchase benefits', see p.210, above.

portion of the scheme's resources that can be devoted to administration, commission or other non-benefit expenditure.[8] Rights to money purchase benefits derived from minimum payments and incentive payments are known as 'protected rights' and, unless the scheme's rules provide otherwise, a person's protected rights also include his or her rights to any other money purchase benefits under the scheme.[9] If they do not, the value of the protected rights must be calculated in a way no less favourable than the calculation of the value of other rights under the scheme.[10]

The scheme must give effect to a member's protected rights by payment of a pension, either directly or through an insurance company or friendly society, by a transfer payment to another occupational or personal scheme, or in certain cases by payment of a lump sum.[11] A lump sum must be paid where the member dies before the pension commences and leaves no widow or widower entitled to a pension, or where the widow or widower also dies before effect has been given to the protected rights;[12] and a pension of £104 a year or less may be commuted to a lump sum.[13]

If a pension is provided, it must commence at pensionable age (60 for a woman, 65 for a man) or at a later date agreed by the member and must be payable for life. If the pensioner dies leaving a widow or widower over 45 or with a dependent child (a 'qualifying' widow or widower), half the pension must continue in payment to the widow or widower.[14] If the scheme member dies before receiving a pension, however, and leaves a qualifying widow or widower, the whole of the protected rights must be used to provide the widow's or widower's pension.[15] This is at first sight more generous than the half-rate pension payable by a salary related contracted-out scheme,[16] but the other side of the coin is that, if a COMP scheme member dies before reaching pensionable age, the whole of his or her notional GMP, not just half of it, is deducted from the state scheme benefits payable to the widow or widower.[17]

The pension payable by a COMP scheme, whether directly or by purchase of an annuity, must satisfy a number of other requirements. The rate of the pension or annuity must be determined without regard to the sex or marital status of the scheme member.[18] Thus it is not permissible to pay smaller pensions to women because of their longer expectation of life, though in practice women's pensions will be smaller than men's because of the five years difference in pensionable ages. Once in payment, the pension must be increased annually by at least the percentage prescribed for GMPs under section 37A of the Pensions Act: the rate of prices inflation or 3 per cent, whichever is less.[19] The scheme's rules may provide for pension increases of up to, but not more than, 3 per cent to be awarded even when the rate of inflation is less.[20] If the pension is to take the form of a purchased annuity, the member

8 SSA 1986, Sch 1, paras 4 and 5; SSPA 1975, s.32(2B).
9 SSA 1986, Sch 1, para 7(1) and (2).
10 Ibid, para 7(4).
11 Ibid, para 9.
12 Ibid, para 9(4): SI 1987/1117, reg 10(2).
13 SSA 1986, Sch 1, para 9(3) and (4): SSPA 1975, s.32(2B): SI 1987/1117, regs 6 and 10(3).
14 SSA 1986, Sch 1, para 9(7): SSPA 1975, s.32(2B).
15 SSA 1986, Sch 1, para 9(4): SI 1987/1117, reg 10(4).
16 See p.213, above.
17 SSPA 1975, s.29(2A)(b)(ii): SI 1987/1113, reg 5(1)(b).
18 SI 1987/1117, reg 4(2), 9 and 12.
19 See p.214, above.
20 SI 1987/1117, reg 4(3),(6), 10(6),(8).

or, where the member dies before receiving a pension, the widow or widower has the right to choose the insurance company or friendly society which is to provide it. If this right is not exercised by the member at least one month before the pension is due to commence (or by such later date as the rules of the scheme may allow), or by the widow or widower within three months of being notified of the right, the trustees or managers of the scheme can make the choice.[1]

d *Early leavers*
The range of options available for protecting the pension rights of an employee leaving a COMP scheme before pension age is more limited than for those leaving salary related contracted-out schemes.[2] There is no possibility of 'buying out' the scheme's liability through an insurance policy or annuity contract, or of reinstating the employee's rights in the state scheme by paying a 'contributions equivalent premium'. The protected rights must either be retained in the scheme or transferred to another scheme which is or has been contracted-out or to an overseas occupational scheme. The absence of any requirement to provide a GMP, on the other hand, greatly simplifies the protection of early leavers' rights. If the protected rights are retained in the scheme, to provide benefits at pensionable age or on death, all that is required is that the employer should notify the DSS of the termination of contracted-out employment.[3] There is no need for regulations stipulating the basis on which protected rights should be revalued between the date of leaving and the date of award of a pension, since under the provisions of Schedule 1A to the 1975 Pensions Act preserved pension rights in a money purchase scheme, whether contracted-out or not, must benefit from the investment yield of the scheme in the same way as the rights of current scheme members.[4]

If protected rights are to be transferred to another scheme, the member's consent must be obtained,[5] and the transfer payment must be at least equal to the value of the protected rights that are being transferred.[6] If the payment is made to a personal pension or COMP scheme, or a money purchase scheme that was formerly contracted-out and is still subject to OPB supervision, it must be used by the receiving scheme to provide money puchase benefits.[7] Transfer payments from COMP to salary related schemes, whether contracted-out or formerly contracted-out, cannot be made before 6 April 1990,[8] and it is a condition of making such a payment that the receiving scheme provides a GMP in respect of the period of employment to which the protected rights relate, equal to the notional GMP deductible from the state pension.[9] If the member is moving to employment outside the United Kingdom, the protected rights can be transferred to an overseas occupational pension scheme which is not contracted-out, subject to any conditions imposed by the OPB.[10]

1 SSA 1986, Sch 1, para 9(8)(c),(9): SI 1987/1117, reg 8(12),(13).
2 See pp. 214–216, above.
3 SI 1984/380, reg 43(1).
4 SSPA 1975, Sch 1A, para 5.
5 SI 1987/1118, reg 2 and Sch 1, para 1.
6 Ibid, reg 2 and Sch 2, para 1.
7 Ibid, reg 3(a) and Sch 3, para 1.
8 Ibid, reg 2(5),(6), and Sch 1, para 5.
9 Ibid, reg 3(b) and Sch 3, para 2.
10 Ibid, reg 2(7) and Sch 2, para 2.

In addition to the arrangements described above for transferring protected rights in a COMP scheme, any member of a money purchase occupational scheme, whether contracted-out or not, whose pensionable service ended on or after 1 January 1986 can claim a 'transfer value' in the same way as a member of a salary related scheme.[11]

e Scheme ceasing to be contracted out

As with salary related schemes, a COMP scheme which ceases to be contracted-out, for whatever reason, must either make arrangements approved by the OPB to secure the rights of its members and pensioners or pay a state scheme premium known as a 'contracted-out protected rights premium' (COPRP or 'PROP') in respect of those rights.[12] Arrangements which may be approved by the OPB are the retention of the protected rights of members in the scheme, transfer to another contracted-out or personal pension scheme (but transfers to salary related schemes are not permitted before 6 April 1990), or the purchase of annuities for members already receiving pensions.[13]

The PROP is the cash equivalent of the member's protected rights in the scheme, calculated on actuarial principles,[14] and it may or may not be enough to make good the whole of the notional GMP which would otherwise have been deducted from the member's state pension in respect of the period of contracted-out employment. If it is more than enough, the excess will be lost, since the PROP cannot do more than eliminate the GMP deduction. If the PROP is insufficient to buy back the whole of the GMP, the member can elect to have it supplemented by the cash equivalent of any other rights he may have under the scheme; and voluntary contributions from any other source can also be added to the PROP. The total amount paid to the DSS is compared with the cost (based on actuarial tables) of providing the GMP, to arrive at the percentage of the deduction that can be made good.[15] For example, if the PROP, with any additions, amounts to 90 per cent of the cost of providing the GMP, 90 per cent of the deduction from the state pension will be eliminated.

viii Contracting out: personal pension schemes

The Social Security Act 1986 introduced the concept of personal pension schemes as an alternative to full participation in the state scheme. The term 'contracting-out' is not applied to these schemes in the Act since, unlike contracted-out occupational schemes, they do not depend on a decision by the employer; nor do they affect the rate of national insurance contributions payable by either the employer or the employee. Both pay the normal contracted-in rate, but the equivalent of the contracted-out contribution rebate is passed on to the personal scheme by the DSS, together with the 2 per cent incentive payment where appropriate[16] and tax relief on the employee's share,[17] without the employer being involved in the transaction. The rules of

---

11 See p.216, above.
12 SSA 1986, Sch 1, para 9(6): SSPA 1975, ss.32(2B) and 44ZA.
13 DHSS, Employer's guide to procedures on termination of contracted-out employment, NP 29, April 1988, para 130.
14 SSPA 1975, s.44ZA(7): SI 1987/1103, reg 2.
15 SSPA 1975, s.44ZA(8)–(11): SI 1987/657, regs 7–9.
16 See p.212, above.
17 Income and Corporation Taxes Act 1988, s.649.

the scheme may, however, provide for the payment of additional contributions direct to the scheme by employee, employer or both.

The end result is very similar to that achieved by contracting-out through a COMP scheme, and much of the detailed legislation relating to personal pensions, in Schedule 1 to the 1986 Act, applies to COMP schemes too, with only minor modifications.[18] In particular, the payments made by the DHSS to the scheme, known as 'minimum contributions', must be used, after deductions for administrative expenses and commission, to provide money purchase benefits.[19] These benefits and (unless the rules of the scheme provide otherwise) any other money purchase benefits provided by the scheme constitute the member's 'protected rights',[20] to which effect may be given in the same ways as to protected rights in a COMP scheme,[1] with one exception: the option to commute a pension of £104 a year or less to a lump sum is not permitted.[2] The member's state pension is reduced by a notional GMP in respect of any period for which minimum contributions are paid to a personal pension scheme, in the same way as if he had been a member of a COMP scheme; and the effect on a widow's or widower's state pension is also the same.[3]

To receive minimum contributions from the DSS, the scheme must be an 'appropriate personal scheme' chosen by the earner in question.[4] It can take a number of forms: an arrangement for issuing insurance policies or annuity contracts; a unit trust scheme authorised under the Financial Services Act 1986; or an arrangement for investing in a bank account or building society shares or deposits.[5] An 'appropriate' scheme is one for which an 'appropriate scheme certificate' issued by the OPB is currently in force[6] and which satisfies the requirements of Schedule 1 to the 1986 Act and regulations made under that schedule.[7] Even if these requirements are satisfied, the OPB may withhold or cancel a certificate on the grounds that there are circumstances which make it inexpedient that the scheme should be, or continue to be, an appropriate scheme.[8] Any question as to whether and for what period a scheme is or was 'appropriate' is to be determined by the OPB,[9] subject to the same provisions as to review and appeal as apply to a determination on a contracting-out question.[10] The OPB was empowered to issue certificates from 1 July 1988. A certificate can have effect from the beginning of the tax year in which the application is received. As a transitional measure, if the application is received before 6 April 1989, the certificate can be backdated to either 6 April 1988 or 6 April 1987.[11]

18 Sch 1 to SSA 1986 sets out the requirements for personal pension schemes. SSPA 1975, s.32(2B) modifies these requirements in relation to COMP schemes.
19 SSA 1986, Sch 1, para 5.
20 Ibid, para 7(1),(2).
 1 See p.218, above.
 2 SI 1987/1117, reg 6, 10(3)(c). Apart from this difference, and the fact that Schedule 1 to SSA 1986 applies to personal pension schemes without modification, personal pension scheme benefits are governed by the same statutory provisions as COMP scheme benefits.
 3 SSA 1986, s.4: SI 1987/1113, reg 3(1)(b).
 4 SSA 1986, s.1(1)(c).
 5 SI 1988/137, reg 2.
 6 SSA 1986, s.1(8).
 7 Ibid, s.2(2).
 8 Ibid, s.2(3).
 9 SI 1988/137, reg 11.
10 See p.211, above.
11 SI 1988/137, reg 5.

For a scheme to be a member's 'chosen scheme', thus qualifying for payment of minimum contributions, the member and the trustees or managers of the scheme must jointly give notice to that effect to the DSS, with effect from 6 April in the same or the following tax year, or from 6 April 1987 if the notice is received before 6 April 1989; but if the member's previous chosen scheme ceases to be an appropriate scheme, the choice of another scheme can take effect on the same date, even if it is not 6 April, and the second scheme will receive the whole of the minimum contributions for that tax year. Although a person can contribute to more than one personal scheme, only one can be his 'chosen scheme' at any time and the DSS can only pay minimum contributions to one scheme in any tax year.[12] Notice that a scheme is no longer the member's chosen scheme must also take effect on the previous or following 6 April.[13]

When contributions to a personal pension scheme cease before pensionable age, the protected rights can be left in the scheme where they will continue to appreciate, under the revaluation provisions of Schedule 1A to the Pensions Act.[14] Alternatively, the member has a right to a transfer payment on similar terms to a member of a COMP scheme.[15] It should be noted, however, that one of the advantages of personal pension schemes is their 'portability': an employee who changes jobs can simply continue to have minimum contributions paid to his chosen personal scheme. If a personal scheme ceases to be 'appropriate', however, a state scheme premium, known as a 'personal pension protected rights premium', is payable unless other arrangements are made, with the approval of the OPB, for the preservation or transfer of protected rights. The calculation of the premium and its effect in buying back the notional GMP that would otherwise be deducted from the state pension are precisely the same as in the case of a contracted-out protected rights premium (PROP) payable when a COMP scheme ceases to be contracted-out.[16]

Part 5   Increments for deferred retirement

Although the retirement condition inevitably encourages some people to give up full-time work at pensionable age, Beveridge hoped and expected that those able to continue working would do so.[17] They were to be encouraged by the prospect of increments to their pensions on retirement or at the age (65 for women, 70 for men) when the retirement condition would no longer apply. Increments can be earned not only by deferring retirement but also by cancelling retirement and temporarily forgoing the pension.[18]

Doubts were expressed at an early stage as to the effectiveness of increments. The Phillips Committee in 1953 found no evidence that they encouraged people to stay on at work: 'a small prospective increase in the pension later on, though welcome when it comes, can seldom affect the decision'.[19]

12 SSA 1986, s.1(9): SI 1988/137, regs 12, 14(4).
13 SSA 1986, s.1(10): SI 1988/137, reg 13.
14 SSPA 1975, Sch 1A, Part I: SI 1987/1116, Sch 4, paras 1–6.
15 SI 1987/1118: SSPA 1975, Sch 1A, Part II: SI 1987/1116, Sch 4, paras 7–16. See pp. 219–220, above.
16 SSA 1986, s.5: SI 1987/1111, reg 2. For contracted-out protected rights premiums, see p.220, above.
17 Beveridge Report, paras 244 ff.
18 See p.198, above.
19 The Phillips Committee Report (Cmd 9333), paras 200–201.

Since then, social and economic pressures inducing early retirement have been far more potent than the system of increments as a reward for later retirement. We have already noted, in relation to the retirement condition, the dramatic fall during the 1970s in the number of people of pensionable age deferring claiming their pensions.[20] This trend is strikingly confirmed by a comparison of the proportions of pensioners in different age groups who receive increments to their pensions. In September 1986, 32 percent of pensioners aged 80 and over received increments, but only 15 per cent of those aged 70–74. Among male pensioners the difference was even more marked: 37 per cent of those aged 80 and over but only 14 per cent of those aged 70–74 received increments. The average increment was then only £3.26 per week.[1]

Entitlement to increments is now governed by Schedule 1 to the Pensions Act. A pensioner can claim an increment for each 'incremental period', consisting of six consecutive 'days of increment', assessed as 1/7 per cent of the weekly rate of the relevant pension (Category A or B).[2] But the minimum increment is 1 per cent of that rate, so there must be at least 42 days, or seven weeks (Sundays are not counted),[3] of deferment of retirement to earn any increment (42 days, at 1/7 per cent for every six days, equals 1 per cent). Days of increment do not include days for which the claimant received other social security benefits such as unemployment, sickness, invalidity or widows' benefits, severe disablement allowance or invalid care allowance.[4] Increments are calculated as a percentage of the whole of the Category A or B pension except any increase for an adult or child dependant. This includes the earnings-related additional pension, after deducting the guaranteed minimum pension (GMP) in respect of any period for which contributions were paid to a contracted-out or personal scheme.[5] It also includes any pension uprating that has taken place during the period of deferment.[6] There is separate but similar provision for increments to graduated retirement benefit.[7]

A married woman can earn increments to a Category A pension (based on her own contributions) in the normal way, by deferring her retirement. She can also earn increments to a Category B pension (on her husband's contributions) by virture of either her husband's deferred retirement or her own. The effect is that she will earn an increment to the Category B pension for each 'incremental period' from the time when they have both reached pensionable age, until they have both retired or are deemed to have done so five years after pensionable age. Days for which she herself receives another social security benefit or her husband receives a dependency addition to such a benefit in respect of her do not count as days of increment for this purpose.[8]

A widow can inherit the whole of the increments to which her husband was entitled, or would have been entitled had he retired immediately before his death. Similarly, a widower can inherit his wife's increments, provided he was over pensionable age on her death. The inherited increments, uprated as appropriate, will be paid in addition to any that the survivor may have earned

20 See p.190, above.
1 Social Security Statistics 1987, Table 13.43.
2 SSPA 1975, Sch 1, paras 1–2.
3 SI 1979/642, reg 4(1).
4 Ibid, reg 4(1)(b).
5 SSPA 1975, Sch 1, para 1(4). For the GMP deduction, see pp. 210–211, above.
6 SSPA 1975, Sch 1, para 1(5).
7 SI 1978/393, Sch 2.
8 SSPA 1975, Sch 1, para 5.

through postponing retirement.[9] But a widow loses the inherited increments if she remarries before pensionable age; she must then look to her new husband for any pension rights based on a spouse's contributions. Remarriage after pension age does not affect entitlement to increments inherited from the former spouse.[10]

Members of contracted-out occupational pension schemes of the salary-related type can also earn increments. The rules of the scheme may provide for payment of the guaranteed minimum pension (GMP) to be postponed if a person continues in employment after pensionable age, but his consent is required for any postponement if the employment does not relate to the scheme concerned or if the postponement continues more than five years after pensionable age (i.e. beyond age 65 for a woman or 70 for a man).[11] The GMP must be increased in the same way as the state pension, by 1/7 per cent for each week of deferment, provided that the pension is deferred for at least seven weeks. Unlike the state pension, however, the GMP can be deferred for more than five years after pensionable age, in which case increments continue to accrue at the same rate.[12] There are no similar requirements for contracted-out money purchase (COMP) schemes or personal pension schemes to provide increments of any defined amount for deferred retirement. Schedule 1 to the Social Security Act 1986 merely requires that the pension should commence at pensionable age or such later date as has been agreed by the member.[13] The value of the member's protected rights will automatically be increased by the investment returns during the period of deferment.

Part 6   Other additions to retirement pension

A Invalidity addition

A person who was receiving invalidity benefit before becoming entitled to a Category A retirement pension and whose invalidity benefit included an invalidity allowance (the addition to invalidity benefit payable where incapacity commenced at least five years before pensionable age)[14] may qualify for an invalidity addition to the retirement pension, at the same rate as the invalidity allowance increased by any subsequent upratings. The object of the addition is to ensure that the person's benefit income is not reduced on retirement. The basic condition is that he or she was entitled to a invalidity allowance at some time in the period of eight weeks and one day before reaching pensionable age, whether the retirement pension was actually paid from that age or up to five years later. Once the condition is satisfied, entitlement to the invalidity addition is not lost even if entitlement to invalidity benefit ceases between pensionable age and the date of retirement. It is payable for life as an integral part of the retirement pension and, as such, is included in the rate of pension on which increments for deferred retirement are calculated, and subject to reduction under the earnings rule.[15]

 9 Ibid, para 4, as amended.
10 SI 1974/2010, reg 3A.
11 SSPA 1975, s.33(3).
12 Ibid, s.35(6), as amended.
13 SSA 1986, Sch 1, para 7(7)(a).
14 See p.144, above.
15 SSA 1975, s.28(7) and (8) as amended.

From 16 September 1985, entitlement to an invalidity addition was restricted in the same way as entitlement to the invalidity allowance, subject to transitional protection of existing beneficiaries. The addition is reduced or eliminated by the amount of any additional pension or guaranteed minimum pension under the Pensions Act (excluding increments for deferred retirement).[16]

B Age addition

The National Insurance Act 1971 introduced an additional payment of 25p per week, known as the 'age addition', for pensioners of all categories over 80.[17] As Sir Keith Joseph said during the Second Reading in the House of Commons, 'this age addition recognises, albeit in a small way, the special claims of very elderly people, who on the whole need help rather more than others'.[18] In fact the measure now appears as an insignificant gesture since its value has not been increased since its introduction. A person in receipt of certain other prescribed benefits, and who would be entitled to a retirement pension if he were to claim it instead, is also entitled to the addition.[19] It need not be claimed, and is therefore paid automatically.[20]

Part 7   Non-contributory retirement pension (Categories C and D)

Category C retirement pensions were introduced by the National Insurance Act 1970 and Category D pensions a year later by the National Insurance Act 1971. The relevant provisions are now in section 39 of the Social Security Act 1975. Category C pensions were a response to political pressure to help those who were uninsured under the pre-1948 schemes and, being over pensionable age when the 1946 Act came into effect, had not had the chance to establish eligibility to a pension under this legislation. They were to receive a non-contributory flat-rate pension of 60 per cent of the basic contributory pension, with the exception of married women who were to get a similar proportion of the contributory pension for a dependent wife. It was considered inappropriate to pay the same amount as to those who had contributed fully to the National Insurance Fund.[1]

Contrary to general expectation, the introduction of Category C pensions still left a number of elderly people without pension entitlement, and Category D pensions were therefore introduced to provide for those over 80 who were in this situation or whose basic pension was less than the Category C rate. Originally Category D pensions were payable at the same rates as Category C, including the lower rate for married women, but the lower Category D rate was abolished by the Social Security Act 1985.[2] All Category D pensions, therefore, are now paid at the higher Category C rate. The lower rate

16 Ibid, s.28(7A)–(7C): transitional protection is provided by SSA 1985, s.9(6)–(9).
17 The provision is now in SSA 1975, s.40(1).
18 816 HC Official Report (5th series) col 1019.
19 SSA 1975, s.40(2): see SI 1979/642, reg 17, which prescribes these other benefits.
20 SI 1987/1968, reg 3(c): see p.540, below (claims and payments).
 1 Mr P Dean, Under-Secretary of State, 803 HC Official Report (5th series) col 1551.
 2 SSA 1985, s.12, amending SSA 1975, s.39 and Sch 4.

remains in operation for the wife of a Category C pensioner who is over pensionable age and retired.

Both Category C and Category D pensions are subject to a residence test. The Category D test, which is easier to satisfy, is that the person was resident in Great Britain for ten years in any period of 20 years ending on his eightieth birthday or later and was ordinarily resident in Great Britain on his eightieth birthday or on the date of his claim if later.[3]

The Category C pension is of little importance, since nearly all those entitled to it would otherwise be entitled to a Category D pension. Moreover, given that entitlement depends on the claimant, or the claimant's husband, having been over pensionable age in 1948, it is now virtually confined to widows, very few of whom are still under 80 and therefore dependent on Category C (their husbands would have been 105 or over in July 1988). The number of pensions in payment in the two categories combined fell from 132,000 in December 1971 to 41,000 in September 1983 but has fallen only slightly since then.[4] There will always be some people whose contribution record is deficient, in particular immigrants and British citizens returning from abroad who have not paid contributions throughout their working lives. Category D remains as a residual provision for them when they reach the age of 80.

3 SI 1979/642, reg 9–10, as amended. The residence conditions are discussed in *Re an Italian Widow* [1982] 2 CMLR 128. For the concepts of 'residence' and 'ordinary residence', see pp. 362–364, below.
4 Social Security Statistics, 1987, Table 13.35.

Chapter 6
Benefits for birth and death

Part 1 Maternity benefits
A General

Social security provision in Britain for maternity has a long, if also unstable, history.[1] There are two principal explanations for the lack of continuity in the legislative arrangements. In the first place, different weight has been attributed at different times to two independent policy objectives: on the one hand, the need to protect the health of the mother and child by alleviating financial hardship; and, on the other, to provide a measure of income maintenance for women who, temporarily or permanently, give up paid employment to have children, thus indirectly advancing the social and economic status of women, in particular by consolidating their participation in the labour market. Secondly, there have been major shifts of opinion on the appropriate method of financing and targetting the benefits, themselves reflecting changes in the social and economic structure. Maternity may be perceived as a risk appropriate for inclusion in a social insurance scheme. As such, does the risk attach to the mother who, therefore, must satisfy contribution conditions, or to the family, in which case the father's contribution record will be relevant? The public interest in the healthy production of children might suggest that benefits should be financed from general taxation. If so, should those benefits be universal (and non-contributory) or rather targetted on those who can demonstrate financial need? Finally, at least as regards the income-maintenance goal, there are arguments for employers assuming responsibility and the question then arises whether protection should be mandatory or optional. As will be seen, at various times, each of these solutions, or more typically a combination of them, has been adopted.

B Assistance with maternity expenses

Under the National Health Insurance scheme of 1911, a lump sum benefit was payable to a mother if she was either insured herself or the wife of an insured person.[2] In practice, it was used to pay for medical and nursing care.[3] After the Second World War these were available free of charge under the National Health Service. The inclusion of the maternity grant in the 1946

1 Brown and Small *Maternity Benefits* (1985).
2 NIA 1911, s.8(1)(e).
3 Brown and Small, n.1, above, pp. 7–9.

national insurance scheme was then rationalised on the need to cover non-medical expenses[4] even though, according to Beveridge, it was not 'intended to cover the whole cost of maternity, which has a reasonable and natural claim upon the husband's earnings'.[5] Nevertheless, following a review of the provision in 1952, the National Insurance Advisory Committee found that the sums paid were inadequate, particularly in relation to the expenses arising on home confinement.[6] A home confinement grant was introduced in 1953 to supplement the existing grant but was abolished in 1964 on the ground that mothers were being discharged from hospital more rapidly and so the difference in costs of a hospital and home birth was no longer substantial.

Although there was no explicit acknowledgement of this, it is clear that from the end of the 1960s the policymakers' concern to assist with maternity expenses diminished.[7] Throughout the period of high inflation in the 1970s, the grant remained at £25, the sum payable in 1969. Faced with increasing criticism,[8] the Conservative government responded by reclassifying the grant as a non-contributory benefit, thereby enabling some additional 60,000 mothers a year to qualify. Enacted in 1980,[9] this was only an interim measure, pending a resolution of the major policy questions thrown up by a review of all of the social security provisions for maternity.[10] In the 1985 Green Paper, the government recognised that, at its current value, the grant was 'hopelessly inadequate' for the job of meeting the immediate costs associated with birth.[11] Given the high cost of restoring it to its 1969 value (estimated at over £70 million),[12] the preferred solution was to abolish the grant as a universal benefit and to provide help with maternity costs on a more realistic basis for those in genuine need. This was to be effected through the new social fund and, indeed, in 1987 was (with funeral expenses) the first part of that system to be brought into operation.[13] The arrangements are fully discussed in Chapter 14.[14]

C Income maintenance: general

Social security provision for income maintenance was introduced by the National Insurance Act 1946. The maternity allowance was payable for 13 weeks spanning the period of confinement. Unlike the grant, entitlement to the allowance was based on the woman's own contributions[15] – those of her husband did not count for this purpose. The explicit aim of the benefit, to remove from the mother the economic pressure to continue at work for as long as possible,[16] was reconcilable with traditional concerns for the health of

---

4 Mothers not in receipt of maternity allowance, the income-replacement benefit were also entitled to an 'attendance allowance', designed to pay for domestic help. In 1953, the allowance was subsumed in the maternity grant, the amount payable being increased accordingly.
5 Para 341.
6 Report on Maternity Benefits (1952, Cmd 8446).
7 Cf Brown and Small, n.1, above, pp. 33–36.
8 See e.g. SSAC Report on Draft Maternity Grant Regulations (1981, Cmnd 8336), para 10.
9 SSA 1980, s.5.
10 DHSS Discussion Document *A Fresh Look at Maternity Benefits* (1980).
11 Vol 1, para 10.6.
12 *Green Paper 1985* vol 2, para 5.17.
13 SI 1986/2173.
14 Pp. 527–528, below.
15 Until 1953, married women who had exercised the option not to contribute were credited with the appropriate number of contributions: SI 1948/1470.
16 *Beveridge* para 341.

the mother. In time, this was complemented by the notion that, in the light of the increasing number of mothers in paid employment, it was necessary to enable them to *maintain* a role within the labour market.[17] As such, it was to rank alongside other measures such as the right to resume work with a particular employer and the provision of child care facilities.[18]

The movement towards equal opportunities in employment, while not, as in Sweden,[19] extending to the introduction of a 'parental' benefit, payable to either a mother or a father who temporarily gives up work to care for young children, also stimulated the growth of occupational maternity pay, especially in the public sector.[20] Developments in the private sector were slower but the position was radically altered by the Employment Protection Act 1975, which introduced a statutory right to maternity pay for women who had been continuously employed with the same employer for two years. For the period of six weeks' entitlement, the mother received nine-tenths of her gross weekly pay, less the amount of the maternity allowance, whether or not she actually received the latter benefit. The employer was entitled to a rebate from the Maternity Pay Fund, financed by a levy on all employers.

The coincidence of different sources of income maintenance – the maternity allowance, statutory maternity pay, extended in some cases by contractual provision – created confusion and unnecessary administrative expense. In 1980, the government issued a consultative document, with several alternative proposals for rationalisation.[1] There was consensus in favour of none of these and the reform process was temporarily halted. Four years later, the government undertook another review, the critical new factor being the introduction in 1983 of the statutory sick pay scheme which had furnished a solution to the analogous problem of overlap between social security and occupational provision for short periods of sickness.[2] Not surprisingly, in the 1985 White Paper,[3] the government declared its intention of copying the sick pay model: the responsibility for administering income maintenance payments should, in the large majority of cases, be assumed wholly by the employer.[4] In consequence, statutory maternity pay (SMP) which was introduced by the Social Security Act 1986 and which supersedes the maternity pay provisions under the Employment Protection Act is now the primary instrument for income maintenance. The maternity allowance – now referred to as the state maternity allowance (SMA) – remains available only for some women not entitled to SMP.

D Income maintenance: statutory maternity pay

i Persons entitled

SMP is payable to an employee who satisfies four conditions.[5]

(1) She has been continuously employed in an employed earner's employ-

17 See generally Creighton *Working Women and the Law* (1979), esp pp. 37–51.
18 See, generally, Terry [1978–79] JSWL 389.
19 Agell in Samuels (ed) *Social Security and Family Law* (1979) pp. 173–174.
20 Brown and Small, n.1, above, pp. 39–43.
 1 N.10, above, and for commentary, see Dalley [1981] JSWL 329.
 2 Pp. 137–140, above.
 3 Though not in the Green Paper which contained less radical proposals: vol 1, paras 10.4–10.5.
 4 Paras 5.20–5.22.
 5 SSA 1986, s.46(1).

ment[6] for 26 weeks up to the 15th week – the 'qualifying week' (QW) – before the expected week of confinement (EWC). The regulations provide for certain periods of absences from work, e.g. for sickness, to be disregarded in establishing the continuity of employment.[7]

(2) Her average weekly earnings in the eight weeks before QW exceeded the lower earnings limit[8] used for contribution purposes.[9] No contribution conditions are, however, exacted so that a married woman who (prior to 1977) had opted for reduced liability[10] may qualify even though she would not be entitled to the maternity allowance.

(3) She is pregnant at the eleventh week before EWC or has been confined by that time.[11]

(4) She has ceased to work 'wholly or partly because of pregnancy or confinement'.

An employer who has terminated a contract of employment 'solely or mainly' to avoid SMP liability cannot rely on a failure by the claimant to fulfil these conditions, provided that the claimant had been continuously employed by him for eight weeks.[12] If the termination is on the ground that, because of pregnancy, she cannot adequately do the work she is employed to do (and for that reason the dismissal is not treated as 'unfair' under the employment protection legislation),[13] SMP is payable, provided that previously she was continuously employed by him for eight weeks, she satisfies condition (2) in relation to those eight weeks and, but for the dismissal, she would have satisfied condition (1).[14]

ii Meaning of 'confinement' and 'pregnancy'

For the purpose of these rules, 'confinement' means 'labour resulting in the issue of a living child, or labour after 28 weeks of pregnancy resulting in the issue of a child whether alive or dead'; and where labour begins on one day and birth takes place the following day, the latter is the day of confinement.[15] It follows that if a six months' pregnancy terminates without the issue of a live child the woman is not entitled.[16] Difficulties may arise where there is a miscarriage following a number of weeks' pregnancy, for it then has to be determined whether the period of pregnancy amounted to 28 weeks. The approach of the Commissioner, confronted with this question under the maternity allowance provisions, has been to estimate the period by counting back from the expected date of confinement, using 273 days as the conven-

---

6 For 'employed earner's employment, see pp. 35–43, above, and SI 1986/1960, reg 17. For the exceptional cases where a change of such employment will not affect entitlement, see ibid, reg 14.

7 SI 1986/1960, regs 11–13.

8 Cf p.43, above.

9 SSA 1986, s.50(3). On the calculation of average weekly earnings, see SI 1986/1690, regs 20–21.

10 Cf p.52, above.

11 An early confinement will affect the application of conditions (1) and (2): see SI 1986/1960, reg 4(2). If the interpretation of the equivalent SMA provisions is relied on, reference to the EWC is not affected by the fact that confinement actually takes place in another week: *R(G) 8/55*; *R(G) 2/61*.

12 SI 1986/1960, reg 3.

13 Employment Protection (Consolidation) Act 1978, s.60(1), on which see *Elegbede v Wellcome Foundation Ltd* [1977] IRLR 383.

14 SI 1986/1960, reg 4(1).

15 SSA 1986, s.50(1).

16 *CWG 1/49*. See also *CG 3/49* (delivery of a 'hydatidiform mole').

tional gestation period,[17] or, where this is not possible, to take expert medical opinion.[18]

The term 'pregnancy' is not defined in the legislation. This omission enabled a Commissioner in Northern Ireland to hold that a woman was 'confined' when she produced, two months before the expected date of confinement, a foetus which had ceased developing three months after conception.[19]

iii Liability for SMP

SMP is payable by the employer or employers liable to pay secondary class 1 contributions for the employee;[20] in the case of two or more employers, liability is apportioned as they may agree, or failing such agreement, proportionately according to earnings paid by them to the employee.[1] All SMP payments, and social security contributions payable on SMP, are reimbursed; in practice by appropriate deductions being made from the employer's secondary class 1 contributions.[2]

iv Notice

The employee must give notice of absence for pregnancy or confinement to the liable employer at least 21 days before such absence or, if that is not reasonably practicable, as soon as is reasonably practicable.[3] The latter alternative covers cases of premature labour[4] but may also apply where the employee was unaware of the notice requirement.[5]

v Duration of SMP

SMP is payable for a maximum of 18 weeks.[6] To enable women to exercise some choice as to when to stop work, there is some flexibility as to when this period begins and ends. 13 of the 18 weekly payments will normally be made in the period beginning with the sixth week before EWC and the employee can choose whether the remaining five weekly payments are taken before or after that period, or partly before and partly after that period.[7] In the case of a confinement before that sixth week, the 18-week period will begin with the week after the week of confinement.[8] SMP is not payable for periods when the employee works for a liable employer, works (after confinement) for another employer, is absent abroad or is detained in legal custody.[9]

vi Rates of SMP

There are two rates payable. The higher rate, designed to reflect payments previously made under the employment protection legislation, is 90 per cent

17 *R(G) 4/56.*
18 *R(G) 12/59.*
19 *R 1/64 (MB).*
20 SSA 1986, ss.46(3) and 50(1).
1 SI 1986/1960, reg 18(2).
2 SSA 1986, Sch 4, Part I and SI 1987/413.
3 SSA 1986, s.46(4).
4 See SI 1986/1960, reg 23.
5 See *Nu-Swift International Ltd v Mallison* [1979] ICR 157, interpreting an equivalent provision under the employment protection legislation.
6 SSA 1986, s.47(1).
7 SI 1986/1960, reg 2.
8 Ibid, reg 2(3).
9 SSA 1986, s.57(4),(6), SI 1986/1960, regs 8,9 and SI 1987/418.

of the average weekly earnings in the eight weeks preceding QW.[10] This rate is payable only for the first six weeks and only to an employee who has been employed by the liable employer, for at least 16 hours per week, during a continous period of two years immediately preceding QW, or, if employed for at least eight hours per week, then during a continous period of five years immediately preceding QW.[11] The lower rate, a flat-rate sum equivalent to the lower rate of statutory sick pay, is paid to those who do not qualify for the higher rate and for the remaining twelve weeks of entitlement of those who do.[12]

vii Adjudication and enforcement

The arrangements are identicial to those adopted for statutory sick pay, an account of which is given in Chapter 4.[13]

E Income maintenance: state maternity allowance

i Contribution and employment conditions

SMA, which replaces the former maternity allowance, is, like its predecessor, a contributory benefit payable under the (amended) Social Security Act 1975. It is, however, available only to those not entitled to SMP, typically because they are self-employed or unable to satisfy the test of 'continuous' employment. To facilitate entitlement for the latter, the contribution condition has been significantly relaxed. The claimant must have actually paid class 1 or class 2 contributions for 26 of the 52 weeks ending in QW; but contributions paid at the reduced rate because the claimant had in 1977 exercised the married woman's option do not count for this purpose.[14]. She must also have been engaged in employment as an employed or self-employed earner for 26 of those 52 weeks.[15]

ii Entitlement to SMA

In the normal circumstances SMA will be claimed before confinement when the woman gives up work. The principles of entitlement largely follow those of SMP: thus, the claimant must be pregnant at the eleventh week before EWC or have been confined by that time;[16] and the period of payment is the same as that for SMP.[17] However, there is provision for an alternative claim for SMA to be made when the woman has actually been confined.[18] The maximum period of entitlement, in such a case, is 18 weeks, if she was engaged in employment (or self-employment) at the beginning of the eleventh week before EWC, or six weeks, if she was not so engaged. Payment normally commences in the week following that in which she was confined. Exceptionally, if she can show that she had good cause for her failure to make

---

10 SSA 1986, s.48(2) and for details governing this calculation, see SI 1986/1960, regs 20–21.
11 SSA 1986, s.48(4)–(5). For the disregard of periods of absence, see n.9, above.
12 SSA 1986, s.48(7)–(8).
13 P.140 above.
14 SSA 1975, Sch 3, Part I, para 3, as amended.
15 Ibid, s.22(1)(b).
16 Ibid, s.22(1)(a) (as amended), incorporating SSA 1986, s.46(2)(c).
17 SSA 1975, s.22(2), and SI 1987/416, reg 3. See p.231, above.
18 SI 1987/416, reg 13.

a claim in expectation of confinement,[19] the period of entitlement may begin earlier, up to 11 weeks before EWC, provided that she does no work within that period.

iii Disqualification

There are three grounds of disqualification.[20]

(1) A woman doing any work in employment, whether as an employee or self-employed, during the SMA period may be disqualified for such part of that period (not less than the number of days worked) as is reasonable.

The reference to 'work in employment; is to make it clear that a woman who does housework cannot be disqualified. In contrast to equivalent provisions governing the disability benefits,[1] there is no saving for 'good cause'.

(2) If, during the SMA period, the claimant fails without good cause to take due care of her health and answer reasonable inquiries concerning it, she may similarly be disqualified for a reasonable period.
(3) If she fails without good cause to attend a medical examination, she may be disqualified for a reasonable period. But if the confinement occurs after the failure to attend, she cannot be disqualified for the days of, and after, confinement.

iv Amount

The weekly amount of SMA is less than the lower rate of SMP, but is higher than that of sickness benefit. Increases for dependent children are no longer payable, but where a husband is being maintained by the claimant and he earns less than the amount of such maintenance, she may claim an addition for him.[2]

Part 2 Benefits on death

A Introduction

i General

While, sadly, death is a contingency to which all must succumb, nevertheless its occurrence generates social and economic consequences which have always been thought to justify some form of social protection. A 'rational' social welfare policy in relation to death has not been easy to formulate, primarily because emotional responses, and the political considerations to which they give rise, play a significant role. A pure needs-based approach to social security would, for example, find it difficult to explain why, at least until recently, the meeting of funeral expenses should assume such priority or why a widow should be treated so generously in comparison to a woman whose marriage has been ended for another reason, such as divorce.[3] It is not surprising, therefore, that the law and policy on death benefits have been subject to frequent change and that it is not easy to locate coherent principles.

19 On which, see *R(G) 3/83*.
20 SI 1987/416, reg 2.
 1 Pp. 159–160, above.
 2 Pp. 341–342, below.
 3 Cf Richardson *Widows Benefits* (1984) pp. 107–108; Masson [1986] JSWL 343.

ii Funeral expenses

The desire to avoid imposing on relatives the humiliation of a pauper's funeral was an important cultural phenomenon of the industrial revolution and accounts in part for the rapid expansion of friendly and burial societies, but particularly industrial assurance companies, in the nineteenth century.[4] Fierce competition between the companies resulted in much sharp practice and exploitation. A series of committees investigated the matter and their recommendations, as implemented by legislation, did much to control abuse,[5] but when Beveridge again surveyed the problem,[6] he found that there was a strong case for drastic reform, not least because the cost of funeral insurance constituted a substantial drain on the resources of lower-income groups.[7]

As a result of his proposals, a lump sum death grant was included in the 1946 national insurance scheme, payable on the death of a contributor, or member of his family. The rates set varied according to the age of the deceased but were based on pre-war funeral costs. Like the maternity grant,[8] the death grant was neglected by successive governments and the maximum rate remained at £30 from 1967 onwards. By 1982, when the government reviewed the grant, it covered only about 10 per cent of the cost of a simple funeral and the administrative costs consumed about one-half of the amount paid out.[9] The government's proposal to target assistance on those with demonstrated need was reinforced by a survey which showed that very few families had difficulty in meeting funeral costs from their own resources.[10] The grant was abolished in 1986, leaving those with inadequate resources to claim from the newly established social fund.[11]

iii Income maintenance: widows

It has been written of the history of British provision for widowhood that 'no part of our social security has shown such a consistent pattern of political failure as this',[12] and the phenomenon is not peculiar to this country. The author of a comparative survey has observed that,

> the variety of responses [to the problems of widowhood] is due to his-torical circumstances and the unequal strength of the pressure groups influen-cing public opinion and the public authorities. It seldom follows any logical pattern.[13]

The major problem has been to find a satisfactory compromise between two conflicting principles: that of providing universal income maintenance for a widow irrespective of age, family circumstances and attachment to the labour market, and that of guaranteeing an income to a widow only when she is deemed to be unlikely to obtain the necessary income support for herself.[14]

4 Wilson and Levy *Industrial Assurance* (1937); Gosden *Self-Help: Voluntary Associations in Nineteenth-Century Britain* (1973) pp. 115–132.
5 See Wilson and Levy, n.4, above, for an historical survey.
6 Paras 157–160 and Appendix D.
7 Ibid, paras 79–80.
8 Cf p.228, above.
9 DHSS Consultative Document *The Death Grant* paras 5–6.
10 Hennessy *Families, Funerals and Finances* (1980).
11 Pp. 528–529, below.
12 *Walley* p.249.
13 Laroque 106 Int Lab Rev 1, 7. See also Tamburi in (1973) 5 ISSA Studies and Research *Women and Social Security* 128ff.
14 Cf Richardson, n.3, above, ch 8.

Overlaying the problem has been an awareness of the public sympathy aroused by widowhood with its important political implications.

These difficulties were manifest from the very beginning. In the early 1920s, there was a vigorous campaign, particularly by womens' associations, to extend national insurance to widowed mothers and orphans, following Lloyd George's earlier failure, as a result of pressure from the insurance lobby, to carry through this idea.[15] Yet what emerged in the Baldwin government's proposal was the surprising notion of a pension of 10 shillings per week payable for life or until remarriage to *all* widows, regardless of means or family commitments. Payment to childless widows was by no means a popular move[16] but Churchill, influenced by the difficulties of providing a more selective scheme and by the naive assumption that, if the husband had paid his contributions, the insurance principle required that benefit could not be refused to the widow, steered the measure through Parliament as part of the Widows', Orphans' and Old Age Contributory Pensions Act 1925.

The rashness of this decision had long-term harmful effects on the future of widows' benefits. For a widow with a family, the flat-rate universal scheme was not always adequate, while for childless recipients it was relatively generous and created a vested interest which it was subsequently difficult to remove. The hostility of Beveridge to the scheme is evident from the incisive terms in which he criticised it:

> there is no reason why a childless widow should get a pension for life; if she is able to work, she should work.[17]

Under his plan, the abolition of long-term entitlement of childless widows or those able to work was to be accompanied by more generous treatment of widows with children. He proposed a short-term benefit payable to all widows for 13 weeks, to allow them to adjust to the new circumstances, and a pension payable only for so long as there were dependent children.[18] The government, while accepting these two basic principles, was also impressed by an argument which he had rejected, that a pension equal to a retirement pension should be paid to a widow who, at her husband's death or when her youngest child ceased to be dependent on her, had reached an age at which she would find it hard to take up paid work.[19] Under the 1946 legislation, therefore, there was payable a widow's allowance (WA), for the first 13 weeks, a widowed mother's allowance (WMA), if there were dependent children, and a widow's pension (WP), if the claimant was widowed over the age of 50 or was over 40 when entitlement to the WMA ceased.[20]

The policy inherent in this approach has been maintained throughout much of the post-war period[1] but the legislative arrangements have been subject to frequent amendments. Some of these reflected the increased participation of married women in the labour market and thus changes in expectations of a widow's earning potential: for example, in 1956 the qualifying age for WP for those previously entitled to WMA was raised to 50 (though from 1970, a reduced WP has been payable to those widowed or

---

15 Gilbert *The Evolution of National Insurance in Great Britain* (1966) pp. 326–343.
16 *Walley* pp. 63–64.
17 Para 153.
18 Para 346.
19 *Social Insurance* Part I, para 121.
20 If the husband had died before 1948 the entitlement of childless widows to the 'ten shillings' pension was preserved.
 1 See esp NIAC Report on Question of Widow's Benefits (1956, Cmd 9684).

ceasing to receive WMA between the ages of 40 and 49); and in 1964 the rule which provided for the reduction in benefit if earnings exceeded a certain amount was abolished. Other reforms aimed at more generous protection for those assumed to be in need: in 1956 additions became available for all dependent children; in 1966 the period of WA was extended to 26 weeks and could be supplemented by an allowance based on the husband's recent earnings; and, finally, under the 1975 pension scheme, earnings-related components, derived from the husband's contributions, became payable to those entitled to WMA or WP.

A change of direction is evident in the most recent reforms. Abolition of the earnings-related supplement to WA and substantial reductions in increases payable for dependent children fall in line with other, general social security economizing measures.[2] More specifically, the Conservative government has argued that the situation of widows has altered substantially since 1946.[3] This arises not only from increased participation in the labour market – in 1985 it was estimated that two-thirds of all married women with children over school age and over 50 per cent. of widows between 40 and 60 go to work, if only part-time[4] – but also from more extensive protection by occupational pension schemes.[5] The aim has been to 'give greater emphasis to providing for widows of working age who have children to support, and for older widows less able to establish themselves in work'.[6] In pursuance of this aim, the Social Security Act 1986 implemented three reform proposals: WA has been abolished and replaced by 'widow's payment', a tax-free lump sum of £1,000, payable immediately after the husband's death; payment of WMA or WP, if the widow is so entitled, starts from the same date, instead of 26 weeks later, as previously; and the age threshold for full entitlement to WP has been increased to 55, with reduced rates for widows between 45 and 55 when the husband dies or when entitlement to WMA ceases.

iv Income maintenance: children

In the typical case where the dependent children of the deceased live with their mother who is the contributor's widow, provision for them takes the form of a dependency increase to the benefits payable to her. Today it is only in the war pension scheme that allowances for surviving children are independent of the widow's benefits.[7] To deal with cases where the mother, or other person, caring for the child, is not the deceased's widow, two special benefits have been made available.

The first, the child's special allowance, was introduced in 1957, following a recommendation of the Royal Commission on Marriage and Divorce that the death of a man who had been making payments to a former spouse for the maintenance of their child or children should entitle her to some allowance to compensate for the loss of that maintenance[8] – of course, because of the

---

2 Cf p.339, below.
3 *Green Paper 1985* Vol 1, paras 10.8–10.13; Vol 2, paras 5.38–5.55.
4 Ibid, vol 1, para 10.9.
5 In 1983 93 per cent of occupational schemes covered widows, compared with 60 per cent in 1975: ibid, vol 2, para 5.47. See, further, Richardson *Widows Benefits* (1984) pp. 97–100 and Brown and Small *Occupational Benefits as Social Security* (1985) ch 10.
6 *Green Paper 1985* vol 1, para 10.9.
7 P.333, below. The same applied to the industrial injuries scheme before such allowances were abolished by SSA 1986, s.39.
8 1956, Cmd 9678, paras 714–716. See also NIAC Report on Question of Dependency Provisions (1956, Cmd 9855), paras 72–73.

divorce, she had no entitlement to a widow's benefit. Notwithstanding a substantial increase in the divorce rate, the number of claims to this allowance was always small and in 1985 only about one thousand families received this benefit.[9] The government argued that, given the additional help available for single parents, as regards both the one-parent benefit and the means-tested benefits, there was no case for continuing with the allowance.[10] It was abolished by the Social Security Act 1986.

The guardian's allowance (GA), broadly payable to a person looking after a child, both of whose parents are dead, was introduced in 1946 to replace the orphan's pension for which provision had been made in the Widows', Orphans' and Old Age Contributory Pensions Act 1925. The allowance differs in two significant respects from the pension: first, it is a non-contributory benefit (entitlement to the pension depended on one of the deceased parents having satisfied contribution conditions); secondly, the death of *both* parents need not be established – it is sufficient if the whereabouts of one of them is unknown. The relaxation of the requirement that the child be an orphan, in the strict sense of that term, raises a difficult question as to the rationale or principle justifying payment of the allowance. Is it designed primarily to 'compensate' the child for the loss of his parents or, on the other hand, to provide some state assistance to encourage a person to look after a child who for some reason lacks parental support? As will be seen, the question is not a purely theoretical one, since those, notably the Commissioners, responsible for interpreting the statutory conditions have found it difficult to do so in the absence of a clearly perceived policy goal.[11] The present compromise position appears to be that while the allowance has departed from a principle of orphanhood, it still falls short of providing assistance merely because a parent cannot be found or, if found, cannot be induced to contribute towards the child's maintenance.[12]

The uncertainties regarding the function of GA have not been resolved by the recent major reviews and reforms of social security. Indeed, while government policy has been to concentrate child support on child benefit and the mean-tested benefits and has abolished the child special allowance and the increases to short-term contributory benefits for children, entitlement to GA, which can be accumulated with child benefit, has been preserved[13] – although the amount payable has been frozen at the 1985 level.

v Income maintenance: widowers and other surviving adult dependants
Social security provision for widowers, divorced spouses, unmarried partners and other surviving dependent adults has always been very limited. Under the war pensions scheme, pensions are payable to widowers, parents and others adults who were dependent on the deceased, but they must in general be 'in pecuniary need' and incapable of self-support.[14] Equivalent provisions in the industrial injury scheme were abolished in 1986.[15] In marked

9 *Green Paper 1985* vol 3, Table 5.2.
10 Ibid, vol 2, para 4.52.
11 See especially *R(G) 2/83*, *R(G) 4/83(T)* and *Secretary of State for Social Services v S* [1983] 3 All ER 173, [1983] 1 WLR 1110.
12 *R(G) 2/83*, para 16, J G Monroe, Comr, declining to follow the more generous approach taken by Commissioners in Northern Ireland: *R 3/74 (P)*; *R 3/75(P)(T)*. See also NIAC Report 1948, HC 165, paras 8–13.
13 Cf *Green Paper 1985* vol 1, ch 8.
14 Pp. 333–334, below.
15 P.310, below.

contrast to the situation in some other countries,[16] the general British social security scheme confers income maintenance only on widows. The absence of a widower's pension may be regarded as a blatant example of sex discrimination[17] and not simply against men: especially in the light of their increasing role in relation to family incomes, women may legitimately complain that the present law provides them with an unfairly reduced return on their contributions. This inability to provide through the state scheme may discourage decisions on role reversal within the family or involve extra expenditure on life assurance.[18] In both the United States of America[19] and the Federal Republic of Germany[20] there have been important judicial decisions declaring unconstitutional social security legislation which confers death benefits only on the widow. In Britain, reform has concentrated on occupational pensions. For such a pension scheme to be 'contracted-out', with consequential reduced contributions to the state scheme, it must now provide for a widower's pension payable broadly where the widower receives child benefit for a dependent child, or is over 45 when the wife dies or when entitlement to the relevant child benefit ceases.[1] The single concession granted to widowers for the purposes of the state scheme enables a husband to rely, in certain circumstances, on his deceased wife's contributions for the purposes of his invalidity or retirement pension.[2] A similar facility applies to a divorced wife[3] who otherwise gains no benefit on the death of her former husband who was contributing to her maintenance.

B Widow's benefits

i Widowhood

A woman claiming a widow's benefit must, of course, prove that she 'has been widowed'. This involves two elements: she was lawfully married to the man on whose contributions she relies and, while so married, he died. The first will be considered in Chapter 9;[3] the second calls for treatment here. The primary method of proof is by a certificate issued by the Registrar General for social security purposes only.[4] But other less formal means will suffice, it being necessary to satisfy the adjudicating authorities on the balance of probabilities that the husband is dead.[5] The real problem arises where he has been absent for some years and nothing has been heard of him.

In Scotland since 1977 legislation has provided that if, on a balance of probabilities, it is determined that a missing person has not been known to alive for a period of at least seven years, a decree may be granted declaring that that person died seven years after the date on which he was last known to

---

16 Eg other EEC member states: see the Commission's *Comparative Tables of the Social Security Schemes* (14th edn) Table VIII.
17 Survivors' pensions are excluded from the 1979 EEC Directive on Equal Treatment in Social Security: OJ 1979 L6/24, Art 3(a).
18 Masson [1985] JSWL 319, 331.
19 *Weinberger v Wiesenfeld* (1975) 95 S Ct 1225, noted in 44 Ford L Rev 170.
20 Decision of Federal Constitutional Court 12 March 1975 BVerfGE 39, 169. See generally Ruland in Gitter, Thieme and Zacher (eds) *Im Dienst des Sozialrechts* (1981) 391–429.
 1 SSPA 1975, s.36(7A), inserted by SSA 1986, s.9 and SI 1984/380, reg 33B, inserted by SI 1987/1100.
 2 SSPA 1975, ss.8 and 16: see pp. 143 and 202, above.
 3 Pp. 349–353, below.
 4 SSA 1975, s.160 and SI 1987/250.
 5 *R(G) 4/57*.

be alive.[6] It has been decided that the social security adjudicating authorities are competent to apply this criterion for benefit purposes.[7] In England, on the other hand, while a similar presumption exists for several specific areas of law,[8] social security is not one of them, and efforts have consequently been made to find something equivalent in the common law. The reported decisions of the Commissioner on the point suggest that no such general presumption exists. In *R(G) 1/62* it was held that at common law a man is presumed to live his normal span, and that the onus is on the claimant to rebut the presumption by evidence that, for example, the husband was last seen setting out on a dangerous mission, or was known to be at the site of a calamity. Such evidence had been available in an earlier case when a claim succeeded ten months after the hat and jacket of the missing spouse had been found at the landing stage of a port.[9] In the 1962 case no equivalent circumstances could be invoked and, despite the fact that nothing had been heard of the husband for 25 years, the claim failed. It may be, however, that it is open to the adjudicating authorities to take a different approach. The 1962 decision purported only to apply pre-1977 Scots law and the English decision of *Chard v Chard*[10] was not cited. In that case Sachs J, having carefully reviewed the relevant authorities, advanced a proposition to cover the situation where legislation had not intervened and where there was no acceptable affirmative evidence that the missing person was alive at some time during a continuous period of seven years or more. It was to the effect that,

> if it can be proved first, that there are persons who would be likely to have heard of him over that period, secondly that those persons have not heard of him, and thirdly that all due inquiries have been made appropriate to the circumstances,

the missing person will be presumed to have died at some time within that period.[11] Whether this dictum should be applied to social security law remains an open question. *Chard v Chard* was concerned with the validity of a subsequent marriage. The policy considerations relevant to a benefit intended as a replacement for the husband's maintenance which, *ex hypothesi*, is not paid in cases of prolonged absence, may point to a different conclusion. But it does seem undesirable that English and Scots law should differ, a situation which is hardly compatible with the British basis of social security law.

ii Remarriage and cohabitation

Entitlement to widowed mother's allowance (WMA) and widow's pension (WP) is lost on remarriage and payment is suspended during a period in which she is living with a man as his wife[12] (the latter concept is discussed in Chapter 9[13]). Remarriage cannot affect entitlement to the lump-sum widow's payment, but it is not payable if the widow was cohabiting with another man at the time of her husband's death.[14]

6 Presumption of Death (Scotland) Act 1977, s.2(1)(b).
7 *R(G) 1/80.*
8 E.g. Offences against the Person Act 1861, s.57 (as a defence to bigamy); Matrimonial Causes Act 1973, s.19(3) (dissolution of marriage).
9 *R(G) 4/57.*
10 [1956] P. 259, [1955] 3 All ER 721.
11 Ibid, at 272.
12 SSA 1975, ss.25(3), 26(3).
13 Pp. 354–357, below.
14 SSA 1975, s.24(2), as amended.

iii Widow's payment

The widow's payment, a lump-sum of £1,000, was introduced by the Social Security Act 1986 and replaces the widow's allowance, a weekly benefit period paid for the first six months following the death. The provision is independent of income-maintenance, the need for which is met either by the other widow's benefits (WMA or WP) or by the widow's earnings (or benefit in default of such earnings, such as unemployment benefit or a disability benefit). As such, it may be rationalised as compensation for the non-pecuniary losses involved in bereavement, or as providing immediate assistance with the financial adjustments necessitated by the death.[15] However, it is not payable if the widow was over pensionable age at the date of death (unless the deceased was not then entitled to a Category A retirement pension)[16] and presumably the bereavement of women in these circumstances is not significantly different in its impact.

The contribution condition is easily satisfied:

– in any one year before the date on which he attained pensionable age or died, the husband must have paid Class 1 contributions on earnings amounting to at least 25 times the weekly lower earnings limit for that year, or 25 Class 2 or 3 contributions.[17]

iv Widowed mother's allowance

For Beveridge, care of a family constituted the principal reason for making long-term provision for widows.[18] To determine the circumstances in which such care might be presumed, the legislation imposes conditions similar to those employed where an increase to a personal benefit for a child dependant is claimed.[19] It may, however, be questioned whether the two situations are entirely analogous: WMA is based on the idea that family responsibilities prevent a widow working, which implies that the child or children should be living with the widow; the increases to personal benefit are rather meant to assist the claimant with *financial* obligations.

The necessary relationship between the widow and child or children is, for the most part, governed by the principles of child benefit. The claimant must prove either that she is pregnant by her late husband or that she is entitled to child benefit[20] in respect of a child who is either

(a) a son or daughter of the woman and her late husband; *or*
(b) a child in respect of whom her late husband was immediately before his death entitled to child benefit;[1] *or*
(c) if the woman and her late husband were residing together immediately before his death, a child in respect of whom she was then entitled to child benefit.[2]

---

15 Cf *Green Paper 1985* vol 2, para 5.51. In any event, it would not have been politically viable to have abolished the allowance without any kind of substitute.
16 SSA 1975, s.24(1)(a).
17 Ibid, Sch 1, para 4.
18 Para 153, where he uses the term 'guardian's allowance'.
19 Cf pp. 340–341, below.
20 See ch 10, below.
1 This is deemed to include a child of the widow's previous marriage if the husband of *that* marriage was immediately before *his* death entitled to child benefit for that child and the woman was entitled to child benefit at the time of the death giving rise to the present entitlement to WMA: SI 1979/642, reg 16(2).
2 SSA 1975, s.25(1)–(2), as amended.

As will be seen, child benefit is generally payable only for children present in Great Britain and, if aged between 16 and 19, if they are engaged in full-time education. The traditional test of dependency for WMA was not so limited. To preserve the broader base for the allowance, those 'entitled to child benefit' in the rules cited above are deemed to include those who would have been so entitled if the child in question had been present in Great Britain.[3] However, the equivalent regulation conferring entitlement in relation to children not engaged in full time education was revoked in 1987.[4]

The contribution conditions[5] are different from those applicable to the widow's payment, resembling instead those imposed for retirement pensions.

(1) In any year before that in which the husband died or reached pensionable age, he must have paid Class 1 contributions on earnings amounting to at least 52 times the weekly lower earnings limit for that year, or 52 Class 2 or Class 3 contributions. The condition is deemed to be satisfied if he was entitled to invalidity pension at any time during the year in which he attained pensionable age or died, or the year immediately preceding that year.

(2) For each year of his working life, less one year for each ten years' working life, the deceased husband must have paid, or been credited with, Class 1 contributions on earnings amounting to at least 52 times the weekly lower earnings limit for that year, or 52 Class 2 or Class 3 contributions. This condition is deemed to be satisfied if the husband had fulfilled the condition for at least half the number of years (or 20 of them if that is less than half) and in the remaining years he was precluded from regular employment by responsibilities at home.

The amount of WMA, now payable from the date of the husband's death, is equivalent to the basic component in the retirement pension and is increased by an amount for each child dependant.[6] Originally, as with retirement pensions,[7] the WMA was reduced for earnings above a prescribed level. This was an extremely unpopular rule and there was continual pressure for its removal.[8] After a number of concessions had been made, the rule was finally abolished in 1964.[9]

v Widow's pension

Provision for widows without dependent children has been the subject of greatest dispute and the most frequent changes. Under the 1946 Act, a pension was payable to those aged 50 or over when the husband died, or 40 or over when entitlement to WMA ceased. In either case, it was felt necessary to establish evidence of prolonged dependence on the husband by requiring proof that they had been married for at least ten years, though if the widow was incapable of self-support, the pension was payable irrespective of the duration of the marriage or her age at her husband's death or when WMA

3 SI 1979/642, reg 16(1), as amended.
4 SI 1987/1854, reg 2(6).
5 SSA 1975, Sch 3, para 5, as amended.
6 Cf pp. 340–341, below.
7 Cf pp. 195–196, above.
8 NIAC, while remaining committed to the principle underlying the earnings rule, had found great difficulties in its application: see its Report on the Earnings Rule (1955, Cmd 9752). A proposal for its abolition played a leading role for several years in the Labour Party Manifesto. See, generally, Richardson *Widows Benefits* (1984) pp. 28–29.
9 NIA 1964, s.1(5).

ceased. In 1956, this concession was revoked but at the same time the duration of the marriage test for all widows was reduced to three years[10] and subsequently, in 1970, was abolished altogether.[11]

As regards the age condition, the distinction between those who had, and
those who had not, been entitled to WMA was an eleventh hour political concession made before the 1946 Bill was passed, and was difficult to justify
except on sentimental grounds. In 1956, following the National Insurance
Advisory Committee's recommendations,[12] the preferential treatment for
widowed mothers was removed and henceforth the '50 year' age test was to
apply to all. This, in turn, proved to be politically unacceptable: the main
objection was the all-or-nothing distinction which depended on the widow's
exact age when her husband died or when entitlement to WMA ceased.
Accordingly, as part of its National Superannuation plan, the Labour
government proposed to introduce a sliding scale of pensions for those aged
between 40 and 50 at the relevant date. The proposal was resurrected by the
succeeding Conservative government and was implemented in 1970.[13] The
final modification was enacted in 1986, following the conclusion reached in
the Fowler review that, given the greater involvement or women (and widows
in particular) in the labour market, as well as the expansion of occupational
schemes, the state system should concentrate on older widows.[14] The current
position is that, to receive a pension, the widow must have been over 45 at the
date of the husband's death, or when she ceased to be entitled to WMA.[15] If,
at that date, she was under 55, the weekly rate of pension is reduced by 7 per
cent for each year of age less than 55 (any fractions of a year counting as one
whole year).[16] (For example, the pension payable to a widow aged 52 at her
husband's death is reduced by 21 per cent and if aged 46 by 63 per cent.) Transitional provisions protect the entitlement and rates of pension of those who
qualified under the age rules operative before the 1986 reform.[17]

WP is payable until the widow reaches pensionable age. The contribution
conditions are the same as those for WMA,[18] and, as with that benefit, no
earnings rule is applied.

vi Earnings-related additions

The 1975 pensions scheme, described in detail in Chapter 5, may have been
primarily directed at providing an adequate income during old age but it was
also designed to have a considerable impact on widows' rights.[19] Under the
Social Security Pensions Act 1975, those widowed after 5 April 1979 and
entitled to WMA or WP may augment those benefits with an additional component, calculated on the basis of the earnings-related contributions made by
the deceased husband. As originally formulated, and as will apply to those
widowed before 5 April 2000, the entitlement under the SERPS scheme is to

10 FANIA 1956, s.2, following a NIAC recommendation: Report on the Question of Widow's
Benefits (1956, Cmd 9684).
11 NIA 1970, s.3, which however conferred a power by regulations to exclude or reduce the pension where the husband had attained pensionable age before marriage and had died within a
year. The power was never exercised and was abolished by SSA 1973, Sch 28.
12 N.10, above, para 45.
13 NIA 1970, s.2.
14 *Green Paper 1985* vol 1, para 10.9; *White Paper 1985* para 5.14.
15 SSA 1975, s.26(1), as amended.
16 Ibid, s.26(2), as amended.
17 SI 1987/1692.
18 SSA 1975, Sch 3, para 5, as amended; p.241, above.
19 See White Paper *Better Pensions* (1974, Cmnd 5713), pp. iii–iv.

what the husband himself would have received, as an addition to the Category A retirement pension, if he had reached pensionable age and had retired on the day he died.[20] The review of the scheme published in 1985 suggested that such provision was over-generous in the light of the anticipated future burden on contributors and in comparison to what was required for contracted-out occupational schemes.[1] In consequence, the 1986 legislation has prospectively reduced the rights of those widowed after 5 April 2000: they will be entitled to one-half of what would have been paid to the deceased as an addition to his Category A retirement pension.[2]

The additional component is payable even if, because of deficiencies in the contribution record, the widow is not in receipt of the full basic rate of WMA or WP or the husband, at the time of his death, was not paid the full basic rate of retirement pension.[3] On the other hand, and perhaps inconsistently, the rule which provides for a reduction in the amount of WP where entitlement to this commences between the age of 45 and 55 operates also to reduce the amount of additional component payable: by 7 per cent for each year of age less than 55.[4]

If the husband had been a member of a contracted-out scheme, the arrangements are analogous to those which operate in relation to retirement pensions and which have been discussed in detail in Chapter 5.[5] The entitlement of the widow under the scheme will vary but during periods when she receives a WMA or WP it must provide (1) a guaranteed minimum pension (GMP) equal to one half of what the husband would have received if he had survived and had retired and (2) a pension calculated on the basis of 0.625 per cent of the husband's final or average annual salary in the contracted-out employment.[6] The widow is then paid (1) or (2), whichever confers the higher amount. The widow is also entitled under the SERPS scheme to the difference between the additional component, payable if the husband had not contracted-out, and her GMP. As with retirement pensions, the object of this provision is for the state to provide some protection against inflation. In accordance with the Social Security Act 1986, however, the GMP must now be revised to cover annual inflation rates of up to 3 per cent,[7] and the impact of the provision is correspondingly reduced. The legislation requires that widowers be offered the same protection as widows, but only where the death of the wife occurs on or after 6 April 1989.[8]

vii Old cases

In order to protect those with vested interests under pre-war legislation, equivalents to WMA and the flat-rate WP are payable to widows of persons over pensionable age on 5 June 1948.[9]

viii Other benefits

The benefits described in the previous paragraphs are paid only until the age of 60. When the widow attains that age, she will normally be entitled to a

20 SSPA 1975, s.13, and see pp. 207–209, above.
 1 *White Paper 1985* para 2.15.
 2 SSA 1986, s.19(1).
 3 SI 1979/642, reg 6(1).
 4 SSPA 1975, s.13(3), as amended.
 5 Pp. 209–222, above.
 6 SSPA 1975, s.36.
 7 Ibid, s.37A, inserted by SSA 1986, s.9(7).
 8 Ibid, s.9(3)–(6), making appropriate amendements to SSPA 1975. See also SI 1987/1100.
 9 SI 1979/642, regs 13–15.

retirement pension, and the same applies if she is over 60 when the husband dies. The special provisions facilitating her entitlement in these circumstances have already been described.[10] A widow under 60 may have difficulty in qualifying for other contributory benefits because of an incomplete contribution record, and two special rules deal with this situation.

(1) As regards the short-term benefits for sickness, unemployment and maternity, once entitlement to WMA has ceased, she is deemed to satisfy the first contribution condition and is granted credits sufficient to satisfy the second condition.[11]
(2) A widow may claim invalidity benefit after 168 days of incapacity even though she does not satisfy the normal requirement that sickness benefit or statutory sick pay has been received during this period.[12] The additional component of the invalidity pension is calculated on the basis either of her own contributions or of those of her deceased husband, whichever is more favourable to her.[13] The same applies *mutatis mutandis* to widowers,[14] one of the few concessions made to this category of social security claimant.

C Guardian's allowance

i Orphanhood

Guardian's allowance, as has already been seen,[15] has the character of a compromise – somewhere between a benefit for orphans and a benefit for children who lack parental support. This is reflected in the three alternative conditions which form the basis of entitlement.

a *Both parents dead*

The first alternative relates to the conventional meaning of orphanhood: both of the child's parents are dead.[16] Proof of death is governed by the same principles as have been considered in relation to widowhood.[17]

b *One parent dead and the other missing*

The second alternative is

> that one of the child's parents is dead and the person claiming a guardian's allowance shows that he was at the date of the death unaware of, and has failed after all reasonable efforts to discover, the whereabouts of the other parent.[18]

The claimant must show that *one* of the child's parents is dead by the normal means of proof.[19] He will not succeed if he can merely show that he is unaware of (or has failed after all reasonable efforts to discover) the whereabout of both parents. Although it can be argued that the normal parent-

10 Pp. 202–203, above.
11 SI 1974/2010, reg 3(1).
12 SSPA 1975, s.15(2).
13 Ibid, s.15(3).
14 Ibid, s.16(3).
15 P.237, above.
16 SSA 1975, s.38(2)(a).
17 Pp. 238–239, above and see *R(G) 11/52(T)* (presumption of death after seven years' absence can be relied on for GA claims).
18 SSA 1975, s.38(2)(b).
19 Cf n.17, above.

child relationship is as much absent here as it is if one is dead and the other's whereabouts cannot be discovered, for the claim so to succeed would involve a total departure from the orphanhood principle.

Under the 1946 Act the rule was that GA could be paid if one parent was dead and the other 'cannot be traced'.[20] Perhaps surprisingly,[1] a Tribunal of Commissioners interpreted this as requiring the claimant to demonstrate that there was no evidence indicating whether the second parent was alive or dead;[2] the claim would thus be defeated if there was *any* evidence that the second parent was still alive. On the recommendation of the National Insurance Committee,[3] the rule was changed to the present formulation, now contained in section 38(2)(b).[4] Its interpretation has, however, given rise to some conflict of opinion. Influenced by the orphanhood principle, the Commissioner in *R(G) 3/68*[5] was not prepared to give the new formulation a wide ambit. He held that 'whereabouts' does not imply a specific place of residence: since the basis of GA remained the entire non-existence of the parent-child relationship (the orphanhood principle), it is not payable if the second parent is known to be alive. This has been regarded, both in Northern Ireland, by a single Commissioner and a Tribunal of Commissioners,[6] and by the British Commissioner in the most recently reported decision on the issue,[7] as unduly restrictive; it involves reading the statutory words '. . . to discover the whereabouts' as if they had been drafted '. . . to discover whether he is still alive'. On this view, 'whereabouts' means 'a place identifiable with some particularity'[8] and hence mere knowledge that the second parent is still alive somewhere will not suffice to defeat a claim.

Other points emerging from the Commissioners' decisions are less contentious. It seems clear that, in applying the statutory test, the adjudicating authorities should take account of facts which have come to light since the date of the claim, notably that the whereabouts of the second parent have been discovered.[9] Once the whereabouts have been discovered, the condition cannot be met and the claim will not be assisted by the subsequent disappearance of that parent.[10] Further, to defeat a claim to GA, knowledge of the whereabouts of the second parent need not result from the claimant's own efforts but might be gleaned from another source.[11] Indeed, if exhaustive inquiries have already been made by another source, for example the DSS, it may be reasonable for the claimant not to repeat them; but the mere fact that the Department has been unable to trace the missing person will not by itself suffice.[12] The onus is on the claimant to show that he has made 'all reasonable efforts'[13] to discover the whereabouts of the second parent

20 NIA 1946, s.19(1).
1 Cf the criticism of J G Monroe, Comr, in *R(G) 2/83* para 10.
2 *R(G) 11/52(T)*.
3 NIAC Report on Question of Dependency Provisions (1956, Cmd 9855), para 88.
4 The revised test was originally in regulations; it was incorporated in parliamentary legislation by SSA 1973, s.22(2). In the opinion of J G Monroe, Comr, this latter step was of significance since it revealed that the statutory principles themselves were no longer exclusively concerned with orphanhood: *R(G) 2/83* para 16.
5 See also the decision of the same Comr (R S Lazarus) in *CG 1/75*.
6 *R 3/74(P)*; *R 3/75(P)(T)*
7 *R(G) 2/83*.
8 *R 3/74 (P)* para 7, F A Reid, Comr.
9 *R(G) 3/68*; *R 3/75 (P)(T)*.
10 *R(G) 2/83*.
11 *R(G) 3/68*; *R 3/74 (P)*.
12 *R(G) 2/83* para 21.
13 *R 2/61 (P)*.

(including during the period after the death of the first parent[14]) and this means 'efforts that would be reasonably expected to be made by a person who wanted to find [the missing] person'.[15] It is irrelevant that it is thought not to be in the interests of the child that the parent be found because, for example, it is assumed that the latter would be unable or unwilling to contribute to the child's maintenance.[16] This last principle may create a dilemma for the claimant who fears that contacting the missing parent might result in a contest about custody but who knows that a failure to attempt such contact will disentitle him to the allowance.[17]

c *One parent dead and the other in prison*
The third situation giving rise to entitlement is where 'one of the child's parents is dead and the other is in prison',[18] and a person is to be treated as being in prison if

> he is serving a sentence of imprisonment of not less than five years or of imprisonment for life, or is in legal custody as a person sentenced or ordered to be kept in custody during Her Majesty's pleasure or until the directions of Her Majesty are known.[19]

In assessing the five years for this purpose, no account is taken, inter alia, of any period of the sentence served before the first parent's death.[20] Detention in 'legal custody' here covers orders for an accused to be detained following a finding that he is unfit to plead or not guilty of a criminal charge on the ground of insanity,[1] but perhaps surprisingly has been held not to apply where the parent was detained in Broadmoor following a conviction of manslaughter by reason of diminished responsibility.[2]

Where the condition is satisfied, the amount of GA is reduced by any contribution made by the parent in prison or custody to the cost of providing for the child.[3] This suggests that, in this case at least, the rationale for payment of the allowance is 'compensation' not for loss of the normal parent-child relationship but for loss of the financial support usually provided by parents.

ii Meaning of 'parents'
There are a number of rules governing who are to be treated as 'parents' for the purpose of the statutory provisions considered above and also the stipulation in section 38(6) of the Social Security Act 1975, that 'no person shall be entitled to a guardian's allowance in respect of a child of which he or she is the parent'.

a *Step-parents*
Following a legislative change in 1957,[4] a step-parent is not considered to be equivalent to a natural parent, so the fact that one step-parent is alive does

14 *R(G) 10/55*; *R 1/73 (P)*.
15 *R(G) 2/83* para 21, J G Monroe, Comr.
16 Ibid, thus rejecting the so-called 'maintenance principle'.
17 Ibid, para 20.
18 SSA 1975, s.38(2)(c).
19 SI 1975/515, reg 5(1).
20 Ibid, reg 5(2)(a).
 1 *R(G) 4/65* and *R(G) 2/80* para 12.
 2 The relevant provision of the Mental Health Act which allowed for release by the Secretary of State was regarded as being inconsistent with the notion of 'custody during Her Majesty's pleasure. . .'.
 3 SI 1975/515, reg 5(6).
 4 NIA 1957, s.6.

not disentitle the person looking after the child from GA. It follows too that a step-parent may himself claim the allowance, since section 38(6) does not apply.

b *Adopting parents*
Where a valid adoption order has been made in favour of two spouses jointly, they (and not the natural parents) are treated as the child's parents for GA purposes.[5] Therefore, for the allowance to be awarded, either both adopting parents must be dead, or one of them must be dead and the other's whereabouts cannot be discovered, etc. An exception to this has been created by the Social Security Act 1986:[6] an adoptive parent may retain the allowance where he was entitled to it immediately before the adoption.[7] Where a child has been adopted by one person, GA is payable on his death.[8] The Court of Appeal has held that on the death of the adoptive parent(s) a natural parent may become entitled, notwithstanding section 38(6).[9] It did so on the ground that the latter subsection must be interpreted in the light of the Children Act 1975 which provides that, subject to any contrary intention in other enactments or instruments, an adopted child is in law treated as if he were not the child of any person other than the adopter.[10] Contrary to the view taken by the majority of a Tribunal of Commissioners,[11] the Court of Appeal decided that section 38(6) did not display a 'contrary intention'; the general intention of section 38 was to confer title to GA on an individual who assumes care of the child after the death of the person previously caring for the child, whether such person was the natural or adoptive parent of the child.

c *Parents of illegitimate children*
In the case of an illegitimate child, where

(a) a person has been found by a court of competent jurisdiction to be the father of the child, or
(b) . . . in the opinion of the determining authority the paternity of the child has been admitted or established,

the mother and father (so determined) of the child are regarded as its parents for GA purposes.[12] For the allowance to be payable, therefore, unless the child has been adopted *either* both the natural father and mother must have died, *or* one of them must be dead and the other missing, or in prison. Moreover, for the provision to be invoked there must be determinations as to both the illegitimacy of the child and its paternity. As regards the first of these conditions, there is a common law presumption that a child born during the subsistence of a marriage is legitimate.[13] The Commissioner has held that the Family Law Reform Act 1969, section 26, applies to determinations under social security legislation,[14] so that the presumption may be rebutted 'by evidence which shows that it is more probable than not' that the child is illegitimate. As regards paternity, this is deemed to be 'admitted' by the entry of the

5 SI 1975/515, reg 2(2)(a).
6 SSA 1986, s.45.
7 Now SSA 1975, s.38(7). To the same effect, see SI 1975/515, reg 2(3).
8 Ibid, reg 2(2)(b).
9 *Secretary of State for Social Services v S* [1983] 3 All ER 173, [1983] 1 WLR 1110.
10 Children Act 1975, Sch 1, para 3.
11 *R(G) 4/83(T)*.
12 SI 1975/515, reg 3(1).
13 *Banbury Peerage Case* (1811) 1 Sm & St 153.
14 *R(G) 2/81* paras 16–17, M J Goodman, Comr.

father's name on the birth certificate.[15] But an order by a district registrar of the High Court under section 41 of the Matrimonial Causes Act 1973 is not regarded as a finding of paternity by a 'court of competent jurisdiction' and is therefore not conclusive of the issue.[16]

d *Divorced parents*

If the child's parents have been divorced and on the death of one of those parents,

> the child was not in the custody of, or being maintained by, the other parent and there was no order of a court granting custody of the child to that other parent or imposing any liability on him for the child's maintenance

then entitlement arises on the death of the first parent.[17] In this case the parent-child relationship has already been severed with the other parent, so there is every justification for modifying the usual requirement for both parents to have died. However, the fact that a court order has been made against the surviving spouse means that the parent-child relationship has not been destroyed and GA is not payable; it is irrelevant that no money has actually been paid under the order.[18]

e *Parent connected with Great Britain*

As with all non-contributory benefits, there is a need to show a sufficient connection with Great Britain. In relation to GA, this is met, as will be seen, by the requirement that the *claimant* be entitled to child benefit (which is subject to conditions of residence) but also by the rule that one of the child's parents must either have been born in the United Kingdom or by the date of the death of the parent whose death give rise to the GA claim must have been present in Great Britain for at least 52 weeks in any period of two years after attaining the age of 16.[19]

iii Conditions imposed on claimant

The conditions of entitlement already described relate primarily to the circumstances of the child's parents or previous maintainors. There are, in addition, two conditions which have to be satisfied by the claimant, designed to ensure that an equivalent to a parent-child relationship exists. It should be noted, however, that the claimant need not have the legal status of 'guardian', as that expression is formally used in family law.[20]

(1) The claimant must be entitled (or treated under regulations as entitled) to child benefit for the child for whom GA is claimed.[1]

(2) The claimant (or his spouse) must *either* be contributing to the cost of maintaining the child[2] by an amount at least equivalent to the rate of GA

---

15 *R(G) 15/52*; *R(G) 4/59*.

16 *R(G) 2/81*.

17 SI 1975/515, reg 4. This applies also to the annulment of a void marriage: ibid, reg 4(3).

18 See *R(G) 10/52*.

19 SI 1975/515, reg 6, as amended. For the meaning of 'present', see p.362. Periods spent abroad serving in the armed forces or working on the continental shelf are treated as periods of presence in GB.

20 Cf Cretney *Principles of Family Law* (4th edn) p.297.

1 SSA 1975, s.38(1), as amended. See ch 10, below.

2 On which, see pp. 346–349, below.

currently payable *or* be treated for the purposes of the Child Benefit Act[3] as having the child living with him.[4]

iv Payment and amount

GA is a weekly allowance, equivalent in amount to the child dependency addition paid to pensioners and, of course, may be aggregated with child benefit. Where a husband and wife are residing together and both satisfy the conditions specified in the previous paragraph, title to GA is conferred on the wife,[5] but payment may be made to either, unless she elects that it is not to be made to her husband.[6]

3 On which, see p.398, below.
4 SSA 1975, s.43, as amended.
5 Ibid, s.38(5), as amended.
6 SI 1975/515, reg 6A.

Chapter 7

Industrial injury

Part 1   Introduction

A History

Provision for the consequences of industrial accidents and diseases has always taken a prominent position among social welfare systems. Typically it manifests four characteristics:

> It is the oldest branch of social security, it provides the most generous benefits, it is a pace-setter for other social security provisions and it is administered as a separate entity.[1]

The surge of legislation at the end of the nineteenth century in the industrialised countries was quite remarkable in its coincidence.[2] The movement may be attributed to a number of causes:[3] the increasing power of the trades unions; the inadequacies of the tort system as a means of compensation; social concern at the high accident rate in industry; the need for an incentive to industrial safety and the rehabilitation of disabled members of the labour force.

The British Workmen's Compensation Act 1897, in certain respects, bore traces of the traditional common law liability, but in more important respects foreshadowed a system of social insurance. Liability was imposed on the employer himself, but compensation was payable for all accidents 'arising out of and in the course of employment', irrespective of proof of negligence.[4] Loss was effectively shared between employer and the employee, for the latter might claim at most only one half of his average earnings,[5] and that subject to a statutory maximum.[6] Short-term claims were excluded by a waiting period of three weeks.[7] The principle of individual employer's liability led naturally to an adversarial method of adjudicating claims, and, though provision might be made for less formal arbitration, proceedings would typi-

---

1 *Kaim-Caudle* p.65.
2 1883, Italy; 1884, Germany; 1894, Norway; 1897, UK; 1898, France and Denmark.
3 Köhler and Zacher (ed) *A Century of Social Insurance* (1982) pp. 18–19, 112–114, 166–175; Bartrip and Burman *The Wounded Soldiers of Industry* (1983); Wilson and Levy *Workmen's Compensation* (1939) vol 1, ch 1.
4 In 1897 £1.00 per week (WCA 1897, Sch 1, para 1(b)). The WCA 1923, s.4(1) raised the maximum to £1.50.
5 WCA 1897, s.1(1).
6 Ibid, Sch 1, para 1(b). Under WCA 1923, s.4(2), for workmen earning less than £2.50 per week, the proportion was fixed on a scale varying from 50 per cent–75 per cent.
7 WCA 1897, s.1(2)(a), reduced to one week by WCA 1906, s.1(2)(a) and three days by WCA 1923, s.5.

cally be taken in the county courts and often, on appeal, to the higher courts.[8] Apart from cases of death, for which a lump sum of three years' annual earnings, to a maximum of £300, was payable to dependants,[9] compensation would normally take the form of weekly payments. However, the concept of a 'private right' was used to support the idea that an individual might compromise his claim for a lump sum settlement. Indeed, after six months of payments, an employer had the *right* to redeem the continuing obligation by a lump sum, provided only that it was registered with, and obtained the approval of, a county court judge.[10]

Originally the Act was confined in its scope to certain dangerous trades. In 1906, it was extended to cover all manual occupations, and those non-manual workers earning less than £250 a year.[11] Employment-related illnesses had been a major source of hardship, and in the same year, compensation became payable to those suffering from certain specified diseases which were attributable to the nature of the employment.[12] The only other substantial reform before the scheme was abolished in 1946 was the introduction of increases for dependants.[13]

The brevity of this account should not be allowed to disguise the complexity of the scheme's operation, the frequency of government reviews and legislative changes, and the general contention and dissatisfaction which it engendered. The criticism reached its height in the late 1930s with the publication by Wilson and Levy of their massive sociological and comparative treatise on the subject.[14] A Royal Commission established in 1938 curtailed its inquiries on the outbreak of war and its task was assumed by Beveridge as part of his overall survey of social security. His own dislike of the scheme is immediately apparent: 'the pioneer system of social security in Britain was based on a wrong principle and has been dominated by a wrong outlook'.[15] From his exposition of the weaknesses of workmen's compensation the following may be highlighted: the adversarial nature of adjudication which was disruptive of good industrial relations and which created problems of adequate representation for the workman;[16] the lack of any obligation on employers to insure against liability with the consequent lack of security for accident victims;[17] the ability to compromise a claim for a lump sum settlement, which presupposed equality of bargaining power and under which a claimant was tempted to accept less than his due;[18] the high administrative costs of the scheme, resulting in part from the inefficiencies of the private insurance market[19] and in part from excessive resort to litigation.[20]

8 See *Wilson and Levy* n.3, above, vol 3, at pp. 255–262.
9 WCA 1897, Sch 1, para 1(a)(i).
10 Ibid, s.1(3)–(4).
11 WCA 1906, s.13.
12 Ibid, s.8.
13 For cases of death by WCA 1923, s.2 and in other cases by WC (Supplementary Allowances) Act 1940, s.1(1).
14 Wilson and Levy *Workmen's Compensation* (1939).
15 Para 80.
16 Para 79(i)–(ii); *Wilson and Levy*, n.14, above, vol 2, ch 15. The point was also stressed in *Social Insurance* Part II, para 23.
17 Para 79(iii). If the defendant was insured, the worker's position was more secure. The Employers' Liability Insurance Companies Act 1907 required a deposit of £20,000 with the Board of Trade.
18 Para 79(iv); *Wilson and Levy*, n.14, above, vol 2, ch 7.
19 Para 79(vii). Appendix E of the Report revealed that the proportion of administrative costs to premiums paid was, for some insurance companies, 46 per cent.
20 In 1938 alone 75 appeals had gone to the Court of Appeal: Potter and Stansfield *National Insurance (Industrial Injuries)* (2nd edn) p.8.

Beveridge's plan to unify responsibility and administration of industrial injuries compensation under a national insurance scheme, and at the same time to afford more generous benefits than those available for unemployment and sickness,[1] and without contribution requirements, was accepted. The exact form and level of benefits remained, however, a matter for considerable dispute. The proposal to pay a rate of benefit which would, only after a period of thirteen weeks' incapacity, be higher than that for sickness,[2] was rejected: preferential treatment was to be provided throughout.[3] Conversely, the government was not prepared to depart from the general principle of flat-rate benefits in favour of an earnings-related pension,[4] as Beveridge had recommended.[5] It proposed, for long-term cases, the tariff method of compensation, derived from the war pensions scheme and based on the degree of disablement.[6] This idea of basing benefits on need rather than earnings-potential proved to be unacceptable politically, and there ensued an unsatisfactory compromise combining the tariff benefit with the so-called 'special hardship allowance' which compensated for impaired earning capacity.

Apart from the introduction in 1966 of a new allowance for the very seriously disabled, the substance of the law governing industrial injury benefits remained during the period until 1982 largely unaltered. Administratively, however, there was a gradual process of integrating the scheme within the general structure of social security. In 1973–75 the high point of this process was reached by the abolition of the separate Industrial Injuries Fund,[7] and by the inclusion of both the general national insurance and the industrial injury schemes in the Social Security Acts.

These developments took place against the background of a marked improvement in the general social security provision for the disabled,[8] a decline in the real value of the preferential treatment offered under the industrial injury scheme,[9] and also a reduction in the number of work-related accidents.[10] Not surprisingly, therefore, the scheme has been subject to critical scrutiny and major reform in the last decade or so. The Pearson Royal Commission on Civil Liability and Compensation for Personal Injury concluded that the scheme 'had stood the test of time'[11] and argued for its extension,[12] though it also found several respects in which it could be improved.[13] A more radical stance was taken by a DHSS team in a study consequential on

1 Paras 97–105. The idea of a state insurance system dates back to the turn of the century: see Departmental Committee on Workmen's Compensation (1904), p.123.
2 Para 332.
3 *Social Insurance* Part II, paras 26–27.
4 Ibid, at paras 28–29.
5 Para 332.
6 *Social Insurance* Part II, para 29; and see pp. 282–286, below.
7 SSA 1973, s.94. It may not have been irrelevant that, at the time, the Industrial Injuries Fund, unlike the non-industrial fund, was showing a healthy surplus; cf Brown *Industrial Injuries* (1982) p.86.
8 Pp. 130–133, above.
9 As a result of inflation, in 1982 injury benefit was only 12 per cent higher than sickness benefit and the death benefit payable to widows only 55p per week more than that available under the general scheme. See, further, *Lewis* pp. 16–17.
10 A consequence of improved safety but also of a reduction in the number employed in manual work and dangerous industries: Brown, n.7 above, p.67.
11 Para 283.
12 To cover e.g. the self-employed, commuting accidents and a wider range of industrially-caused diseases: see ch 17. The proposed scheme for road accidents would be modelled on industrial injuries: ch 18.

the Pearson Report and published as a discussion document in 1980.[14] They focused, in particular, on the high cost of administering a system[15] which in practice offered to most of its beneficiaries a relatively small material advantage over the general social security provisions. The government accepted the force of this criticism and in a White Paper, published in 1981,[16] indicated a general commitment to restructure the scheme so as to concentrate resources on the more seriously disabled. The first step, taken in 1982, was to abolish injury benefit; henceforth, the short-term consequences of an industrial injury or disease were to be met through the standard provisions for statutory sick pay and sickness benefit.[17] Following yet another policy document,[18] the government in 1986 abolished industrial death benefit and some of the special allowances payable with the disablement benefit.[19] The latter was, itself, only to be granted to those with a significant handicap. Finally, the special hardship allowance was replaced by the reduced earnings allowance for those still at work and by the less generous retirement allowance for those above pensionable age who have retired.

These reforms may be rationalised primarily as economy measures – they will save an estimated £50 million a year[20] – but the government portrays them as 'a sensible further step towards a more coherent system of benefits for sick and disabled people'.[1] The focus on provision for the more seriously disabled may, indeed, point the way forward for the disability programme as a whole. It is, perhaps, for this reason that, while the reforms met considerable opposition from the trade union movement and the Industrial Injuries Advisory Council,[2] criticism by the pressure groups representing all the disabled was somewhat muted.[3] On the other hand, it is not to be assumed that the industrial scheme will continue to decline in importance. Technological change is creating new risks in the workplace and, at the same time, medical research is uncovering new links between the working environment and conditions, such as cancer, mental illness and heart disease which, in the past, have not typically be seen as occupational hazards.[4]

B Industrial preference

Fundamental to the recent debate on the future of the industrial injuries scheme has been the question whether the industrial preference, that is, the

---

13 E.g. increases to short-term benefit and an advanced entitlement to full payment of the earnings-related element in the invalidity pension.
14 *Industrial Injuries Compensation*.
15 13.3 per cent of benefit expenditure, compared with 4.2 per cent for the general contributory scheme: ibid, para 1.1.
16 *Reform of the Industrial Injuries Scheme*.
17 SSHBA 1982, s.39.
18 Consultation Paper *Industrial Injuries Scheme* (1985).
19 SSA 1986, s.39 and Sch 3. Details are provided below, pp. 306–307. A proposal to integrate the constant attendance allowance with the attendance allowance available under the general scheme has been postponed.
20 Standing Committee B Debates on the 1986 Bill, col 1825.
 1 Mr T Newton, Minister for Social Security, in the introduction to the Consultation Paper, n.18, above, p.1.
 2 Lewis 15 ILJ 256, 258.
 3 Cf Disability Alliance *Reforming the Industrial Injuries Scheme: The Wrong Priorities* (1982). The speed with which the government executed the reform did, however, stifle debate and discussion: Lewis, n.2, above, pp. 258–259.
 4 *Lewis* pp. 19–20.

more favourable treatment given to the victims of industrial accidents and diseases over those disabled by other causes, can still be justified.[5] The classic arguments for the preference are to be found in a famous passage in the Beveridge Report.[6] Having conceded that, 'a complete solution is to be found only in a completely unified scheme for disability without demarcation by the cause of disability', he nevertheless submitted three grounds for maintaining a differential.

> First, many industries vital to the community are also specially dangerous. It is essential that men should enter them and desirable, therefore, that they should be able to do so with the assurance of special provision against their risks. . . . Second, a man disabled during the course of his employment has been disabled while working under orders. This is not true generally of other accidents or of sickness. Third, only if special provision is made for the results of industrial accident and disease, irrespective of negligence, would it appear possible . . . to limit the employer's liability at Common Law to the results of actions for which he is responsible morally and in fact, not simply by virtue of some principle of legal liability.

The main difficulty with the first argument is that it confuses the source of the injury – the environmental condition of working – with its consequences. The fact that an individual may be subjected to a greater hazard at work than elsewhere does not mean that his need will be greater if the risks materialise. If there is a case for discrimination between various groups of disabled persons it must surely be made according to the gravity of the consequences to the individual and his family rather than to the cause of the injury. The argument based on the need to pay more compensation to those encountering higher risks in special occupations would carry more force if there were evidence that current wage rates were insufficiently high to attract individuals to the workforce.[7]

Beveridge himself conceded that the second and third arguments were less convincing than the first and they are less persuasive than they were at the time of his report.[8] The notion of working 'under orders' is certainly artificial and arbitrary: why should a risk arising from employment be treated differently from one generated by self-employment?[9] As regards the third argument, ironically tort liability for industrial injuries has expanded rather than retracted. What remains is the political fact that it is difficult to remove an advantage once it has been conferred on a group with significant voting power.[10]

C Financing

When workmen's compensation, with its notion of individual employer liability, was replaced by social insurance the question arose whether all risks

5 There is a wealth of literature on the subject. See, especially: Higucha 102 Int Lab Rev 109; *Industrial Injuries Compensation* pp. 1–12; Walker 15 Soc Pol and Admin 54; Brown, n.7, above, pp. 277–295.
6 Paras 80–86.
7 *Industrial Injuries Compensation* para 1.10.
8 Ibid, paras 1.11–1.15; *Pearson* para 290.
9 Hence the recommendation in the Pearson Report that the scheme should be extended to this group: para 853.
10 In Australia the National Compensation Bill encountered strong opposition from the trade unions on the ground that it would abolish advantages hitherto enjoyed under the workmen's compensation scheme: Ibid, vol 3, para 812.

should be pooled, as for unemployment and sickness, or whether each industry should continue to bear at least a part of its own accident costs, by, for example, varying the contribution on the basis of the industry's accident record.[11] There are two main arguments for relating the financial responsibility of the industry or firm to the risks created by its activities. The first is that it acts as an incentive to safety and the prevention of injuries.[12] Secondly, it avoids the price distortion which results from a low-risk industry subsidising a high-risk industry: for example, the accident record of the mining industry is high, and it has been calculated that if the industrial injury scheme were risk-related, the 'fair' price of coal (in 1969) would have been higher by 15p per ton.[13] Such distortion, it is argued, leads to over-employment in dangerous industries and insufficient expenditure on accident prevention.[14] Opponents of the differential approach doubt the force of the incentive argument for which, in any event, there is a lack of compelling empirical evidence. Risk-rating cannot be applied to small firms whose accident record is too limited for statistical purposes.[15] It is always based on past experience which may be unreliable as a guide for future contingencies, particularly in relation to diseases for which there is a long latency period.[16] The price-distortion argument is countered by the principle of social interdependence. No industry works in isolation from others. Coal, for example, is used in the production of many other goods. Finally, even if the differential approach may be more equitable it is certainly much more expensive to administer.[17] In the light of such considerations, Beveridge formulated a compromise solution: a general pooling of responsibility with a special charge on certain high-risk industries.[18] The proposal did not win the approval of the government[19] and the National Insurance (Industrial Injuries) Act 1946 created a fund based on flat-rate contributions (five-twelfths each from the employer and employee, the remaining one-sixth being paid by the Exchequer). In 1975 the Industrial Injuries Fund was abolished, and since then the scheme has been financed by the general National Insurance Fund. Despite a recommendation of the Robens Committee on Safety and Health at Work to reopen the issue of risk-rating,[20] and a greater readiness in foreign systems to apply this method,[1] the principle of uniform contributions has remained unchanged. The Pearson Commission, with one dissenter (significantly an economist),[2] reaffirmed the principle, mainly on the ground that risk-relating contributions for each employer, or industry, would involve substantial administrative costs which would outweigh any benefits in terms of increased safety.[3]

11 Report of the Royal Commission of Inquiry on Compensation for Personal Injury in New Zealand (The Woodhouse Report) (1967), at paras 328–336; Report of the Committee on Safety and Health at Work (1972, Cmnd 5034) (Robens Report), paras 428–430; Atiyah 4 ILJ 1, 89; Phillips 5 ILJ 148; *Pearson* paras 898–904.
12 Calabresi *The Cost of Accidents* (1970).
13 *Kaim-Caudle* p.71.
14 Phillips, n.11, above, at pp. 150–151.
15 In the USA, the rating system is only fully operative for firms employing over 2,500; in the U.K. over 90 per cent of firms employ less than 500: *Atiyah* p.504.
16 Barth 13 J Legal Stud 569, 582.
17 See e.g. the very complex French system of differentials: *Saint-Jours Traité de Sécurité Sociale* (1980) pp. 281–283.
18 Paras 88–92.
19 *Social Insurance* Part II, para 31.
20 N.11, above, at para 447.
 1 *Kaim-Caudle* pp. 69–75.
 2 Paras 940–948.
 3 Paras 898–904.

D Plan of chapter

Claims under the industrial injuries scheme must satisfy two conditions:

(a) that the person injured or killed was an employed earner (Part 2); *and*
(b) that the injury or death was caused by 'accident arising out of and in the course of his employment' (Part 3) or resulted from a disease prescribed in relation to that employment (Part 4).

The principal instrument of compensation is the disablement benefit (Part 5). The reduced earnings allowance (Part 6) may be payable whether or not there is entitlement to this benefit. The chapter concludes with discussion of other allowances (Part 7) and miscellaneous matters (Part 8).

Part 2   Persons covered

The Workmen's Compensation Act 1897 covered only specified dangerous employments,[4] but in 1906 was extended to all persons working under a contract of service or apprenticeship, with a few exceptions, the most important of which were non-manual workers earning more than £250 (subsequently £420) a year.[5] The 1946 state scheme covered the same categories, but included also all non-manual employees irrespective of income, and did not permit contracting-out which had been possible under workmen's compensation. In general, the categories of insured persons were the same as those regarded as 'employed persons' for the purposes of the non-industrial national insurance schemes. However, there were reasons for creating distinctions between the scope of the two schemes: first, 'employment' in the non-industrial scheme was confined to those working a minimum number of hours a week, a limitation which had not existed under the Workmen's Compensation Act and which was therefore considered inappropriate for the industrial scheme; secondly, the non-industrial benefits were, in general, payable only on the fulfilment of certain contribution conditions, whereas under the industrial scheme, as with its predecessor, the employee was covered as from the first day of employment, irrespective of contributions. The present position is, then, that the scheme covers those who are 'employed earners', as the term is interpreted for the contribution provisions of the Social Security Act 1975.[6] But the claimant for industrial injury benefit need not have paid, or be liable for, Class 1 contributions; he may, for example, be exempt from such contributions on the ground of low earnings,[7] and still be covered by the scheme.[8] Moreover, the Secretary of State has power to extend or exclude, by regulation, categories of employed earners for the purposes of the scheme.[9] The more important categories so regulated may be summarised as follows.

(1) Included are apprentices,[10] members of fire brigades and other rescue services, mine inspectors, certain taxi drivers and special constables.[11]

4 WCA 1897, s.7.
5 WCA 1906, ss.1, 13.
6 SSA 1975, ss.2(1)(a) and 50(1). See generally, pp. 35–43, above.
7 P.43, above.
8 Married women with reduced liability (p.52, above) are also covered.
9 SSA 1975, s.51(1)–(2) and SI 1975/467, as amended.
10 Trainees working under the Youth Training Scheme are not covered but in practice the Manpower Services Commission makes appropriate payments: *Lewis* p.32.
11 SI 1975/467, Sch 1, Part I.

(2) Excluded is employment (i) by a relative or spouse where not for the purpose of trade or business,[12] and (ii) as a military or civilian member of a visiting force or as a member of an international headquarters or defence organisation unless, in either case, the civilian pays Class 1 contributions.[13]

(3) Those employed abroad are covered if they pay either Class 1 contributions or, as voluntary development workers, Class 2 contributions.[14]

As with analogous questions arising under the non-industrial schemes, disputes as to classification are determined not by the adjudicating authorities but by the Secretary of State.[15] He is also given power to direct that where a contract of service is rendered void or unlawful as a result of non-compliance with any statutory requirement passed for the protection of employed persons, the employment is nevertheless, for the purposes of industrial injury benefits, to be treated as an employed earner's employment.[16]

The most important economically active group outside the scheme is the self-employed. The government has resisted a proposal by the Pearson Commission[17] to cover them, on the grounds, first, that there did not seem to be a demand from the self-employed for such protection and, secondly, that coverage would create difficulties in determining the scope of the employment.[18] The latter point overlooks the fact that several European schemes offer the protection, apparently without undue problems.[19]

Part 3 Industrial injury

Entitlement to the various industrial benefits is fundamentally based on proof that the 'employed earner suffers personal injury caused . . . by accident arising out of and in the course of his employment'.[20] This contains three different elements:[1]

(a) a personal injury,
(b) caused by an accident,
(c) arising out of and in the course of employment.

The discussion will be divided accordingly.

A Personal injury

This means a 'hurt to body or mind'.[2] Thus it includes a nervous disorder or nervous shock.[3] Even a trivial hurt which is ephemeral, like the watering of an

---

12 Where employed by a spouse for the purposes of business, the claimant must also be a Class I contributor.
13 SI 1975/467, Sch 1, Part II, as amended.
14 SI 1975/563, reg 10C, as amended in 1986. For discussion of the reform, see *Industrial Injuries Compensation* pp. 57–60.
15 SSA 1975, s.93(1)(d) and *R(I) 2/75*. See generally, pp. 567–570, below.
16 SSA 1975, s.156.
17 Paras 851–857.
18 *Reform of the Industrial Injuries Scheme* paras 63–65.
19 Though usually only on a voluntary basis: *Pearson* vol 3.
20 SSA 1975, s.50(1).
1 Cf Lord Denning MR in *Re Dowling* [1967] 1 QB 202 at 217.
2 Per Lord Simon, *Jones v Secretary of State for Social Services* [1972] AC 944 at 1020.
3 *R(I) 49/52*; *R(I) 22/59*.

eye,[4] will qualify, though, as will be seen, the claimant must establish a loss of faculty. Real difficulty arises where there is damage to a prosthesis, such as an artificial limb. In *R(I) 7/56* it was ruled that there had to be an injury to the living body of a human being. This was decided at a time when replacement surgery was in its infancy and in *R(I) 8/81* the Commissioner was prepared to give 'personal injury' a broader interpretation. On his view, the test was 'whether or not the prosthesis has become so intimately linked with the body that on any realistic assessment of the situation it can be said to have become part of that body'.[5] On this definition, there is no doubt that where the prosthesis damaged is a living tissue or synthetic material inserted into the body, the claimant has sustained a 'personal injury'. In cases of external appliances it is a question of fact and degree. The Commissioner suggested that the 'intimate link with the body' might be regarded as broken by the detachability of the appliance. A claimant would succeed where damage is inflicted on an artificial limb permanently attached to the body but not, for example, where the appliance in question is a pair of spectacles[6], a hearing-aid or a crutch.

B Accident

The personal injury must be caused 'by accident'.[7] This indicates the preference granted by the system – itself, of course, a preferential system – to traumatically caused disability. As will be seen, sickness and disease are covered, but only within carefully prescribed limits. The preference is deeply rooted in most legal systems[8] and it is not difficult to locate the reasons for this. Industrial injury schemes replaced systems of individual responsibility which in practice, if not theory, attached to accidents rather than processes. This reflected an assumption that, while diseases were natural hazards, accidents were typically 'man made'; in its turn, the assumption underpinned the deterrence function of the compensation process. The assumption is manifestly false,[9] but pragmatically it is certainly easier to prove the causal relationship between an accident and working conditions.[10] Although some systems have abandoned the requirement of an 'accident',[11] it is retained in the great majority, not the least because of cost constraints.[12] Paradoxically, there is empirical evidence which suggests that victims of illness are more likely than accident victims to suffer residual incapacity and to incur serious medical needs.[13]

i Meaning of 'accident'
The starting point must be Lord Macnaghten's famous dictum in 1903:[14]

> The expression 'accident' is used in the popular and ordinary sense of the word as

4 *R 5/60 (II)*.
5 Para 14, D G Rice, Comr.
6 *R(I) 1/82*.
7 SSA 1975, s.50(5).
8 Barta *Kausalität in Sozialrecht* (1983), esp chs 17, 18, 65.
9 Stapleton *Disease and the Compensation Debate* (1986) ch 1.
10 Ibid, ch 3, and see Report of the Departmental Committee on Disease Provisions of the National Insurance (Industrial Injuries) Act (1955, Cmd 9548), para 55.
11 For USA, see Horovitz 12 Law Soc Jo 465, 494 and for Australia Luntz 40 ALJ 179.
12 Cf the Australian proposals for a general compensation scheme which would have covered both accidents and sickness, analyzed in Luntz *Compensation and Rehabilitation* (1975).
13 Harris et al *Compensation and Support for Illness and Injury* (1984) pp. 242, 323.
14 *Fenton v J Thorley & Co Ltd* [1903] AC 443 at 448.

denoting an unlooked-for mishap or an untoward event which is not expected or designed.

But 'popular' meanings are notoriously unreliable and, as critics have pointed out,[15] nowhere more so than in this context. It soon became clear that Lord Macnaghten's definition was neither accurate nor sufficient. In the first place, while it was construed to exclude deliberate acts by the injured party himself, it has been held to include a deliberate, even unlawful, act of a third party. The point was decided in *Trim Joint District School v Kelly*,[16] in which pupils assaulted and killed a schoolmaster responsible for discipline. Secondly, the phrase 'not expected' could not be taken seriously. An event need not be unforeseeable or exceptional to constitute an 'accident'.[17] To take a frequently encountered example, a man incapacitating himself by heavy exertions does not have to prove that the strain was violent or exceptional for his job.[18]

As the case-law on the statutory principle developed, it became crucial to distinguish an 'event' from a 'process', thereby ensuring that the scheme retained its character as one concerned with traumatic work injuries. However, a generous interpretation initially by the courts and then by the Commissioner of what constituted an 'event' created logical and practical difficulties. First, in 1905, the House of Lords held that unobservable infection of bacteria could constitute an 'injury by accident'.[19] Secondly, it was held, again by the House of Lords, that while an 'accident' does not include the growth of incapacity by a continuous progress, nevertheless the employee would succeed if he was able to point to 'an incident *or series of incidents* . . . which caused or contributed to the origin or progress of the disease'.[20] The distinction is neither logical nor recognised in medical usage.[1] As a result, decisionmaking in this area has been somewhat arbitrary.[2] Reference to a few of the decisions should be sufficient to illustrate the point.

> Strain to chest muscles caused by the daily lifting of heavy weights is not covered,[3] but a claimant, who, when lifting heavy equipment on a particular day, felt severe pains in the chest and subsequently suffered from coronary thrombosis, was entitled to succeed. He had experienced a physiological change at that particular time.[4]

> A worker who developed a psychoneurotic condition having worked near a machine which produced explosive reports at irregular intervals recovered. Each explosion was 'an accident' and thus the condition was the result of a 'series of accidents'. The interval between each such explosion was not so short that the series was to be regarded as a single

15 See *Trim Joint District School Board of Management v Kelly* [1914] AC 667 at 681, per Lord Loreburn; *Re Dowling* [1967] 1 AC 725 at 759, per Lord Wilberforce; *Jones v Secretary of State for Social Services* [1972] AC 944 at 1009, per Lord Diplock. See also Bohlen 25 Harv L Rev 378.
16 N.15, above. See also *CI 51/49* and *R(I) 30/58*.
17 *Clover Clayton v Hughes* [1910] AC 242; *CWI 6/49*; but the 'abnormality' of an event may be relevant in proving the causal link between the injury and the accident: p.260, below.
18 *CI 5/49*.
19 *Brinton's Ltd v Turvey* [1905] AC 230.
20 Per Lord Porter, *Roberts v Dorothea Slate Quarries* [1948] 2 All ER 201 at 205–206, adopted by a Tribunal of Commissioners in *CS 257/49(T)* para 11.
1 Stapleton, n.9, above, pp. 50–51.
2 See the decisions collected in *Lewis* pp. 39–42.
3 *R(I) 42/51*.
4 *R(I) 54/53*.

continuous process.[5] On the other hand, a claimant who became sick on inhaling gas which leaked from the vehicle he used from time to time did not succeed: the illness was caused by the taking of breath on an infinite number of occasions, and these did not constitute separate incidents.[6]

Apart from the somewhat arbitrary nature of some of these distinctions, it is apparent from other decisions that certain illogicalities may ensue. A claimant will be fortunate if the condition, though developing gradually, manifests itself on a particular occasion. Thus in *R(I) 18/54* the claimant had been using a pad for three months, the buckle of which rubbed against a nerve. One day, he felt a numbness in his leg, and he was allowed to recover on the basis that this constituted a particular incident.[7] Even more anomalously, a person who encounters an employment risk only once will be in a better position than one who is exposed to it regularly. Hence, a nurse who had come into contact with, and was infected by, a child with poliomyelitis succeeded,[8] but a doctor who was attending a large number of patients infected with tuberculosis and subsequently contracted the disease was refused benefit. It was assumed that he must have been infected by the regular penetration of bacteria into his system.[9] It must be noted, however, that once the claimant has succeeded in establishing, on the balance of probabilities, that the injury resulted from an event or a series of events,[10] his claim will not be jeopardised by his failure to identify the specific occasion when the condition began or was aggravated: for procedural purposes the earliest probable date will be taken.[11]

ii Causal link between accident and injury

The claimant must also prove,[12] on the balance of probabilities, that the accident 'caused' the injury.[13] This does not mean that it has to be the sole cause of the injury; it is sufficient if it is a contributory cause, in combination with, for example, a condition from which the claimant already suffered.[14] It is irrelevant that the previous condition rendered the claimant more susceptible to the later event.[15] But, at the same time, the accident must have been 'an efficient cause (*causa causans*) and not a mere condition (*causa sine qua non*)' in which the earlier cause operated.[16] Thus in *R(I) 4/58*,

> The claimant suffered from burns when his clothing, which had been soaked in inflammable liquid in a work accident, caught fire when coming into contact with a cigarette which he was lighting at home. It was held that the *causa causans* of the injury was the lighting of the cigarette, and not the accidental soaking.

5 *R(I) 43/55*.

6 *R(I) 32/60*. See also *Fraser v Secretary of State for Social Services* 1986 SLT 386.

7 The case should be compared with *R(I) 11/74* in which the claimant was unable to advert to a specific date.

8 *CI 159/50*.

9 *CI 83/50*.

10 See *R(I) 8/66*.

11 *CI 49/49*; *CI 196/50*.

12 In contrast to the war pension scheme, where the burden of proof of the causal link between service and the disability generally favours the claimant: p.323, below.

13 For a detailed analysis of the case-law, see *Lewis* pp. 45–49.

14 *R(I) 19/63*.

15 *CI 147/50*.

16 *R(I) 14/51* para 6. See also *R(I) 12/58* para 5.

iii Critique

It will be apparent from the analysis above that the requirement of an 'accident' has produced severe difficulties and that quite apart from being an elusive criterion for distinguishing between injuries and sickness, it is not conclusive of the issue. On the one hand, a claimant will succeed if he can show that an illness (not an injury) was attributable to an event rather than to a process. On the other hand, as will be seen, he is entitled to benefit if he suffers from a prescribed disease, provided that it was contracted in the appropriate prescribed employment. One alternative, then, would be to link the two concepts and allow recovery for any injury or disease which was work-caused. The possibility is considered later in connection with prescribed diseases.[17] An alternative, less radical, is that proposed by Sir Owen Woodhouse as part of his recommendations for new schemes in both New Zealand[18] and Australia.[19] The idea is to incorporate in legislation a list of all possible forms of accident to be made the subject of compensation, and for such a purpose it might be possible to adopt a classification of injuries and external causes of injury prepared by the World Health Organisation.[20] Of course, like all attempts at exhaustive listing, this could not be a perfect solution and would have to be supplemented by some residual general clause. But it might serve to remove some of the doubt and uncertainty which the case-law on the more traditional approach reveals.

C Employment risk

i General

It is of the essence of an industrial injuries insurance scheme that the accident must be connected with the employment. In 1897, the Workmen's Compensation Act contained a test which was adopted by English speaking jurisdictions throughout the world, and remains the basis of the current scheme: personal injury by accident 'arising out of and in the course of employment'.[1] This classic formulation, perhaps the most notorious in the whole of social security law, has been responsible for vast amounts of disputed claims and complex litigation. In 1920, Lord Wrenbury was moved to remark that:

> The language of the Act and the decisions upon it are such that I have long since abandoned the hope of deciding any case upon the words 'out of and in the course of' upon grounds satisfactory to myself or convincing to others;[2]

and two years later a Departmental Committee reported that:

> No other form of words has ever given rise to such a body of litigation.[3]

The original Act sought to delimit the connection with the employment more precisely by requiring that the accident should occur, 'on, in or about' the

17 P.278 below.
18 Report of Royal Commission of Injury into Compensation for Personal Injuries in New Zealand (1967), para 289(c).
19 Report of National Committee of Injury into Compensation and Rehabilitation in Australia (1974), para 350.
20 The relevant parts are conveniently published in a Schedule to the draft Bill at the end of the Australian report.
1 WCA 1897, s.1.
2 *Armstrong, Whitworth & Co v Redford* [1920] AC 757 at 780.
3 Departmental Committee Report on Workmen's Compensation (Holman Gregory Report) (1920, Cmd 816), para 29.

employer's premises,[4] but this condition was soon abandoned.[5] Most obviously it discriminated against employees whose work took them away from the employer's premises. Other common law jurisdictions have attempted to mitigate the rigours of the statutory test by amending the formula. Thus, in some systems, the workman need only show that the accident arose '*in* the course of employment',[6] while in others he is given the alternative of proving that it happened 'out of *or* in the course of employment'.[7] But no formula adopted (and this includes non-English speaking jurisdictions[8]) has managed to alleviate problems involved in establishing the connection between the work and the accident.[9] As Atiyah has observed:

> The difficulty is inherent in the system; it has nothing to do with the 'meaning' of . . . words. . . . The difficulty is inherent in the concept of insurance against special 'employment' risks.[10]

The most significant reforms, therefore, both in Britain and elsewhere, have not been through a modification of the basic formula, but rather by specific extensions of the scheme to cover contingencies which might not otherwise have been regarded as employment risks. As will be seen, the most important developments in this respect have been the coverage of certain accidents occurring on a journey to or from work, or caused by a natural event or the conduct of a third party.

ii The statutory test

It has long been a subject of debate whether the formula 'out of and in the course of employment'[11] involves two different principles or only a single test. It has sometimes been said that the authorities should treat the phrase as a combined whole.[12] The more generally accepted view is that the 'in the course of' criterion delimits the time, place and activity of the work, while the 'out of' criterion concerns itself with the cause or connection between the accident and the work.[13] In the simple case, the distinction is obvious. A man working at his bench inadvertently spikes himself with a pin which he had earlier put in his trouser pocket. The accident arises 'in the course of' his employment but not 'out of' it. But there are other situations where there is an inevitable overlap between the two tests. If, for example, an employee injures himself through horseplay on his employer's premises and during the normal hours of duty, it might be said either that the accident did not arise out of the employment because the risk was not caused by his work, or that it did not arise in the course of employment, because the claimant's activity at the time interfered with and diverged from his ordinary working duties. For the sake of clarity of exposition, the traditional distinction has been followed

---

4 WCA 1897, s.7(1).
5 WCA 1906, s.1(1).
6 E.g. in the USA: N. Dakota, Pennsylvania, Texas and Washington.
7 E.g. in Australia, New South Wales.
8 See e.g. *Dupeyroux* pp. 476–493.
9 Cf *Pearson* para 896.
10 *Atiyah* p.328.
11 It should be noted that since the scheme covers 'office-holders' as well as 'employed earners', the appropriate test for those in the former category would seem to be whether the accident arose out of an in the course of the office: see *CI 6/78* and Partington 7 ILJ 251, 8 ILJ 64. It is not, however, clear whether this test requires any modification to the principles expounded in this section.
12 See e.g. *CSI 63/49*; *R(I) 62/51*.
13 E.g. per Lord Wright, *Dover Navigation v Craig* [1940] AC 190 at 199; *R(I) 10/52*; *R(I) 2/63*.

in this work, and the overlap recognised at appropriate points in the discussion.

The exposition of the law which follows is, of course, primarily based on judicial and Commissioners' decisions under the Workmen's Compensation and modern legislation respectively.[14] While such decisions are undoubtedly authoritative, the Court of Appeal has, in the recent case of *Nancollas v Insurance Officer*,[15] suggested that they should not be treated as binding precedents, in the commonly accepted meaning of that term.

> [T]he reality is that none of the authorities purports to lay down any conclusive test and none propounds any proposition of law which, as such, binds other courts. They do indeed approve an approach which requires the courts to have regard to and weigh in the balance every factor which can be said in any way to point towards or away from a finding that the claimant was in the course of his employment.[16]

Adjudication officers should aim at an aggregate picture from each set of facts and should then approach questions regarding the employment risk as if they were jury questions. As yet, the impact of the suggestion on the practice of adjudication is unclear. However, it is by no means obvious that the more impressionistic approach favoured by the Court of Appeal will improve the quality of decision-making: the traditional approach has the merits of (relative) certainty and consistency, and therefore also of horizontal equity between claimants.[17] It is, perhaps, not without significance that the Pearson Commission rejected a proposed change in the statutory formula precisely because 'a considerable body of case law has been developed around the existing definition and we should be reluctant to change the definition after such a long period of use'.[18]

iii In the course of employment

a *General principles*
According to the classic formulation of Lord Loreburn,

> An accident befalls a man 'in the course of' his employment if it occurs while he is doing what a man so employed may reasonably do within a time during which he is employed, and at a place where he may reasonably be during that time to do that thing.[19]

From this, it will be seen that the limits to the course of employment are determined by three different criteria: place, time and activity. A claimant will set up a prima facie case if he is able to show that the accident occurred at his normal *place* of work during his normal *hours* of work. His *activity* at the time of the accident may be relevant in two different respects. It may serve to defeat a prima facie case by showing that the claimant interrupted the time element in the work or deviated from the spatial element for reasons unconnected with his employment. Or it may serve to extend the 'course of employment' to cover hours or places not normally considered as within its ambit. The discussion will proceed accordingly.

It must also be observed that the notion of employment covers functions

14 For a more comprehensive analysis, see *Lewis* pp. 50–89.
15 [1985] 1 All ER 833.
16 Per Sir John Donaldson MR, ibid at 836.
17 Cf Mesher [1986] JSWL 244.
18 Para 896.
19 *Moore v Manchester Liners Ltd* [1910] AC 498 at 500–501.

and objectives which are regarded as reasonably incidental to the actual work process. The contract of employment is rarely relevant or helpful in determining what is to be so regarded. Obviously this varies enormously according to the nature of the work and the status of the claimant but the case-law reveals that resort is usually had to two different but related notions. Under the first (supervision test) the question is whether the accident happened while the claimant was under the authority, supervision or control of his employer.[20] The alternative and complementary criterion (public zone test) is concerned to ascertain whether the activities of the claimant at the time of the accident were such as to distinguish him from an ordinary member of the public.[1]

b *Fixed place and hours of work*
Most employees have fixed places and hours of work. The task, here, is to determine what, for the purposes of benefit, are to be regarded as the limits of the employment, though this is not always easy. The mere fact that during a period when not actually working an employee must remain available to be summoned by his employer – in other words, when he is 'on call' – is not sufficient by itself to bring that period within the course of employment.[2] But if his freedom of movement is limited or his activities controlled by the employer, then, in accordance with the 'supervision test', he may be covered.[3] This seems to be the best explanation of the perhaps surprising decision in *R v National Insurance Comr, ex parte Reed*.[4]

> A police sergeant was permitted to take lunch at home during his period on duty, but throughout he remained on call. He was injured while travelling back to the police station and the Divisional Court held that he was entitled to benefit. Woolf J stressed that his choice as to where refreshment could be taken was limited and while at home he was still responsible for performing his duties.[5]

The limits of work, as defined by the contract, are not rigidly applied. The law allows the claimant a certain amount of time and space to 'prepare himself for, or to disengage himself from', his employment.[6] As regards time, the course of employment includes a reasonable period at either end of his official hours of duty.[7] What this amounts to may depend on the nature of the job and the character of the claimant. Arriving early the more properly to equip oneself for work will be generously treated,[8] but not if the intention is instead to fit in a game of billiards.[9]

As regards place, the extract area is difficult to locate. It generally includes the premises in which the claimant is about to work, has just worked, and the access to them.[10] The 'public zone' test will usually be conclusive in deter-

---

20 See particularly *R(I) 84/51*.
 1 See particularly *R(I) 61/51*.
 2 *R(I) 10/52* para 8; *R(I) 11/55* para 6; *R(I) 5/81*.
 3 *R(I) 49/51*; *R(I) 11/55*.
 4 (1980) reported as Appendix to *R(I) 7/80*, and see *R(I) 5/81* paras 11–14.
 5 Cf J G Monroe, Comr, who drew a distinction between being employed to stand by, and being given leave of absence on condition that the employee stands by: *R(I) 7/80* para 8.
 6 *Gane v Norton Hill Colliery* [1909] 2 KB 539; *R(I) 61/51*; *R(I) 3/72*.
 7 *R v National Insurance Comr, ex parte East* [1976] ICR 206.
 8 Ibid, and to similar effort: *R(I) 22/51*; *R(I) 72/54*; and *R(I) 3/62*.
 9 *R(I) 1/59*.
10 *R(I) 7/52*; *R(I) 5/67*.

mining the necessary limits. The claimant must be within an area excluded from public access,[11] but this is to be decided according to existing practice rather than legal rights.[12] The question is whether the members of the public make substantial use of that part of the land.[13] Equally, the mere fact that the land on which the accident occurs is owned by the employer is rarely conclusive.[14] Some industrial enterprises own vast areas of land, and the claimant may be on a part of it miles from his place of work.[15] Conversely, a social worker injured while descending a staircase common to several households may recover, though her business took her to only one.[16] The authorities must determine the part of the land on which the claimant normally works, and this may be particularly difficult in agricultural cases.[17] It is not possible to reconcile all the decisions.[18] In some cases the authorities are apparently prepared to show some indulgence, and avoid nice distinctions which would have the effect of depriving the claimant of benefit. They may then admit a claim on the vague basis that the claimant had 'so nearly approached the means of access as to make it reasonable to hold that he had returned to the sphere in which his employment operated'.[19]

c *Extensions for authorised or incidental purposes*

The spatial and temporal boundaries may be extended for purposes which are reasonably necessary for, or incidental to, the employment.[20] In *R v National Insurance Comr, ex parte Michael*, the Court of Appeal stressed that the 'reasonably incidental' test is not part of the statutory formula and should not be applied without careful consideration: 'if the injury is not suffered in the actual course of the work which the employee is engaged to do, it must have at least been suffered by reason of some event incidental to *that work*'.[1] Obviously this covers, primarily, situations where the employer directly or indirectly authorises the employee to perform his duties outside normal hours, or his usual locality, e.g. where a bus conductor was required by her employer to make a cup of tea for herself and the driver at the end of each journey.[2] But it seems that 'employer' in this context must be strictly construed. An unauthorised request from an immediate superior will not bring the resulting activity within the scheme.[3] This may operate harshly, for the employee may find it difficult to refuse the request and feel that his prospects of promotion will otherwise suffer. But the test should be a subjective one: if *he* has reasonable grounds to think that the request has the implied authority

11 Even if the claimant's duties sometimes take him into the 'public zone': *R(I) 72/51*; *R(I) 7/62*. See also *R(I) 7/52*; *R(I) 23/55*; *R(I) 70/57*. 'Access' here means qua member of the public – not, of course, for business purposes: *R(I) 41/57*.
12 *R(I) 43/51*; *R(I) 1/68*.
13 Per Lord Macmillan, *Northumbrian Shipping Co Ltd v McCullum* (1932) 25 BWCC 284.
14 *CI 65/49*; *R(I) 67/52*; *R(I) 43/51*.
15 *CI 69/49*; *R(I) 67/52*.
16 *R(I) 3/72*.
17 See *R(I) 7/52* and *R(I) 42/56*.
18 Cf *R(I) 42/56* para 11.
19 *R(I) 3/53* para 4; cf *R(I) 10/81*.
20 *Armstrong, Whitworth & Co v Redford* [1920] AC 757 at 777, 779, 780; *R v Industrial Injuries Comr, ex parte Amalgamated Engineering Union (No 2)* [1966] 2 QB 31 at 48, 50, 51.
1 Per Roskill J, [1977] 2 All ER 420 at 427. See also Lord Denning MR at 423–424.
2 *R(I) 21/53*; cf *R(I) 5/77*. See also the cases where the employee is obliged to participate in physical education, competition or other 'outside' activities e.g. *CI 228/50*; *R(I) 4/51*; *R(I) 80/52*; *R(I) 66/53*; *R(I) 39/56*.
3 *R(I) 36/55*; *R(I) 8/61*.

of the employer, he should succeed.[4] Where the claimant is under no obligation to carry out the activity, but is merely permitted to, the case is more difficult. Clearly mere knowledge of, or acquiescence by, the employer is insufficient. The issue becomes whether or not the activity in question is sufficiently connected with the employment. There are obvious cases like working overtime,[5] collecting equipment or clothing necessary for work,[6] or taking a bath after duty in a mine.[7] The receipt of wages comes within the scope of employment but not the cashing of a money order representing them: the processes of employment are complete when the money order is received by the employee.[8] Participants in a trade union meeting are also covered, provided that it is directly concerned with the terms and conditions of employment with the particular employer.[9]

The status of recreational activities is problematic. In the leading case of *R v Industrial Injuries Comr, ex parte Michael*, the Court of Appeal held that a police constable injured when playing football for his force was not covered by the statutory formula.[10] The court was not impressed by the argument, which had been regarded as sufficient by some Commissioners,[11] that such activity improved the fitness and morale of the force and therefore was in pursuance of the employment. At the same time, the view held by one Commissioner,[12] that recreation can never come within the course of employment, was rejected.[13] Clearly, a claimant will succeed if he can show that he was required by his employer to participate in the activity,[14] and it is doubtful whether the *Michael* ruling has affected the authority of previous decisions entitling a claimant injured while engaged in physical exercises as part of a training course authorised by the employer,[15] or in games which were regarded as therapeutically valuable to patients at the hospital where he was employed.[16]

Injuries incurred while meeting an emergency may be covered even if the incident occurred away from the employee's place of work or outside his normal working hours.[17] It is, however, necessary that the action can be construed as being in some way in the employer's interests (e.g. the protection of his property[18]) and was reasonable in the circumstances.[19]

d *Accidents while travelling*
Accidents to the claimant while travelling have always posed special problems for industrial injury schemes, and they have been the subject of much

---

4 In *R(I) 36/55* paras 7, 8, the Commissioner speaks of acting under the 'ostensible' authority of the employer.
5 *R(I) 52/52*.
6 *R(I) 72/54*; *R(I) 20/58*.
7 *CI 22/49*.
8 *R(I) 34/53*. In W. Germany the legislation expressly extends the protection to cover such activity: Reichsversicherungsordnung ξ 548(1).
9 *R(I) 63/55*; *R(I) 9/57*; *R(I) 46/59*; *R(I) 10/80*.
10 N.1, above. See also *R(I) 2/80* and *R(I) 4/81*.
11 *R(I) 13/66*; *CI 7/73*.
12 *R(I) 5/75* para 21, J S Watson, Comr.
13 N.7, above, per Roskill LJ at 426, per Lawton LJ at 431.
14 See e.g. *R(I) 3/81*.
15 *R(I) 31/53*; *R(I) 66/53*; *R(I) 2/68*, and see *Ex parte Michael*, n.1, above, per Lawton LJ at 430–431.
16 *R(I) 3/57*.
17 *R(I) 63/54(T)*. See also p.277, below.
18 *R(I) 63/54(T)*; cp *R(I) 6/63*.
19 *R(I) 32/54*.

dispute both general and specific. For the purposes of discussion it is necessary to distinguish between three types of case.[20]

(1) The employee is required to make a journey for purposes necessary or incidental to his employment.
(2) The employee's work is peripatetic: that is, the employment consists of travelling from place to place.
(3) The employee merely travels to and from his work.

(1) This is merely an instance of the situation discussed in the preceding section. The employee's place and hours of work are defined but he is required by his employer, expressly or impliedly, to make a journey for purposes connected with the employment.[1] Thus, an employee instructed to proceed at a specified time from one working place to another is protected.[2] Travel from home to work does not, in general, come within this category even if the claimant is paid for travelling time or for expenses incurred.[3] The traditionally stated distinction is between a journey *to* duty and a journey *on* duty.[4] The latter may, however, be given a liberal construction, as can be observed from a Court of Appeal decision[5] which involved an application of the vague, impressionistic test which it had, itself, formulated in the *Nancollas* case.[6] The decision went in favour of a policeman injured while travelling from home to work. The approach, it will be recalled, requires consideration to be taken of all of the facts of the case. It may be inferred that some or all of the special facts here – the destination was not the normal place of work, the claimant had first telephoned his station to report for duty, his travel expenses were reimbursed – were instrumental to the decision but the lack of explicit principle means that its impact on the law is very uncertain. In contrast, previous cases, allowing recovery can be rationalised on the basis of the supervision principle: an employee obliged by his employer to travel to work by a specific mode of transport;[7] an employee called out from home by his employer for a specific purpose (e.g. an emergency) and under a duty, expressly or impliedly, to arrive by the shortest practical route and as quickly as possible.[8] The suggestion has also been made that the exclusion of journeys to and from work should be confined to cases involving 'reasonable daily travelling distance or commuter distance', and that different considerations apply where the journey involves longer distances.[9] But the suggestion was rejected by a Commissioner who decided that a civil servant injured during the journey from his home to a temporary place of employment some 100 miles away was not entitled.[10] Nor does it make any difference if the employee is carrying with him tools or essential equipment for his work:[11] to

---

20 Cf Ogus 4 ILJ 188. For another classification, see Lewis [1986] JSWL 193.
 1 See generally, *R v National Industrial Injury Benefits Tribunal, ex parte Fieldhouse* (1974) 17 KIR 63; *Vandyke v Fender* [1970] 2 QB 292, [1970] 2 All ER 335; *R(I) 5/77*: and *R(I) 14/81*.
 2 *R(I) 11/57*; *R(I) 4/59*; *R(I) 39/59*.
 3 *R(I) 9/51*; *R(I) 34/57*; *R(I) 3/71*.
 4 *R(I) 45/52* para 3; *R(I) 14/81* para 7.
 5 *Ball v Insurance Officer* [1985] 1 All ER 833.
 6 Ibid, on which see, p.263, n.17, above.
 7 *R(I) 8/51*; *R(I) 17/51*; *R(I) 3/81*.
 8 *R(I) 21/51*; *R(I) 27/56*: the mere fact that the employee is required to report for duty earlier than normal is not sufficient – his employer is not concerned with the mode or speed of his journey.
 9 *CI 21/68*.
10 *R(I) 3/71*, J S Watson, Comr.
11 *R(I) 48/52*; *R(I) 78/53*; *R(I) 16/58*.

succeed he must show that he had to make some special and required journey to deliver or collect such equipment.[12] The question whether an employee injured while staying away from home during the course of his travels may succeed is resolved along similar lines. If the employee is required by his employer to stay at a particular place,[13] or is in some way supervised by his employer there,[14] benefit is payable. If he is free to stay where he likes, he is not covered during the passage to, or while at, the chosen accommodation.[15]

(2) Certain types of employment are peripatetic: they necessarily involve frequent journeys. Obvious examples of such situations are sales representatives,[16] insurance agents,[17] journalists[18] and home helps.[19] In such cases, benefit is payable for accidents occurring during travel for the purposes of the work. But in defining the limits of the course of the employment, an important distinction has to be drawn.[20] A person who has no fixed hours and no precisely definable place of work may be protected against injuries while travelling to or from home.[1] Conversely, a person whose work requires him to be at particular places at particular times is treated no differently from other employees who have fixed places of work. His employment does not begin until he arrives at his first call, unless his employer specifies a particular route or mode of transport.[2] To decide into which of the two categories a particular case falls involves consideration of the circumstances of the job.

(3) If the journey comes within neither category described above, it is difficult to regard it as creating an 'employment risk'. In terms of the 'public zone' principle, the commuting employee is in a position no different from other members of the public, and, as regards the 'supervision' principle, the employer generally exercises no control over the journey. Yet there has been considerable political pressure to extend industrial injury schemes to cover commuting accidents and in several foreign jurisdictions special provision has been made for them,[3] notwithstanding the blurring of the concept of employment risk which is involved, and the practical problems of definition and administration to which it gives rise.[4] The Pearson Commission found the arguments to be very finely balanced but by a bare majority of one recommended that accidents to and from work should be covered.[5] The government, on the other hand, considered the objections, both of principle and of practice, to be significantly greater and therefore rejected the proposal.[6]

The current legislation in Britain offers only very limited coverage for commuting accidents, such as would be justifiable on the 'supervision' principle. Section 53(1) of the Social Security Act 1975 provides that:

12 *R(I) 34/59.*
13 *R(I) 30/57.*
14 *CI 347/50.*
15 *R(I) 22/54*; *R(I) 4/81.*
16 *R(I) 38/53.*
17 *CSI 63/49.*
18 *R(I) 55/53.*
19 *R(I) 2/67.*
20 Ibid, at para 10.
1 *Nancollas v Insurance Officer* [1985] 1 All ER 833; *R(I) 4/70.*
2 *R(I) 19/57*; *R(I) 2/67*; *R(I) 12/75.*
3 E.g. Australia, France, W. Germany and Sweden: *Pearson* vol 3, paras 384, 471, 600, 717. See also International Labour Organisation's Recommendation 121 (1964).
4 Cf *Industrial Injuries Compensation* paras 6.38–6.43. For the difficulties arising in France, see Saint-Jours *Traité de Sécurité Sociale* (1980) pp. 304–313.
5 Paras 858–867.
6 *Reform of the Industrial Injuries Scheme* paras 66–67.

An accident happening while an employed earner is, with the express or implied permission of his employer, travelling as a passenger by any vehicle to or from his place of work shall, notwithstanding that he is under no obligation to his employer to travel by that vehicle, be deemed to arise out of and in the course of his employment if—

(a) the accident would have been deemed so to have arisen had he been under such an obligation; and

(b) at the time of the accident, the vehicle—

    (i) is being operated by or on behalf of his employer or some other person by whom it is provided in pursuance of arrangements made with his employer; and

    (ii) is not being operated in the ordinary course of a public transport service.

The requirement in the opening paragraph that travel in the vehicle be permitted by the employer might seem to be otiose when regard is had to the condition in (b) that the vehicle be operated by him or by another under an arrangement with him. But the Commissioner has held that they are independent conditions, both of which must be satisfied.[7] The first envisages permission given prior to the event, though exceptionally subsequent permission may be acceptable provided that it is express.[8] As regards the second condition, the employer need not initiate the arrangement, and need not himself own or provide the vehicle,[9] but there must be something more than a mere undertaking by a third party to provide a vehicle for the use of the employees. The employer must be involved in some way in the running of the service:[10] an unauthorised conveyance of the employee, even for the employer's purposes, will not suffice.[11] The 'public zone' principle features in the exclusion of vehicles 'operating in the ordinary course of a public transport service'. But the words do not imply that the vehicle must be provided by a private company. The question is whether members of the public may and do habitually use the service.[12] On this point, the authorities have regard to such factors as whether the service is advertised in the ordinary timetable, whether it connects directly with the employer's premises, whether it ceases during closure of the factory.[13] A claimant cannot be a 'passenger' if he is also driving the vehicle.[14] A 'vehicle' includes 'a ship, vessel, hovercraft, aircraft'[15] and, perhaps surprisingly, need not be designed to carry a passenger (e.g. a tractor).[16] The accident must happen while the claimant is 'travelling as a passenger', so that walking to meet the vehicle, or between two vehicles, is not included.[17]

e *Interruptions and deviations*

The 'course of employment' includes not only the objective elements of time and space but also the subjective one of the claimant's activity.[18] The

7 *R(I) 5/80*, R S Lazarus, Comr.

8 Ibid, para 7.

9 *R(I) 49/53*.

10 *R(I) 5/60*.

11 *R(I) 5/80*.

12 *R(I) 67/51*: a claim does not fail merely because the public is entitled to use the service (though ordinarily this will be the case) if there is evidence that it rarely does so.

13 *R(I) 15/57*.

14 *CI 49/49*; *R(I) 9/59*.

15 SSA 1975, s.53(2).

16 *R(I) 42/56*.

17 *R(I) 67/52*; *R(I) 48/54*.

18 See especially Lord Finley LC in *Davidson & Co v M'Robb* [1918] AC 304 at 314–315.

traditional criterion is that of performing a duty for the employer,[19] but the tendency has been to mitigate the rigours of this notion and to concentrate instead on what is 'reasonably incidental to' the employment: 'if the man is doing something for his own purposes which is reasonably incidental to his employment, he is still acting in the course of his employment'.[20] Only *material* interruptions of the working pattern destroy the connection with the employment:[1] trifling or inadvertent departures are disregarded.[2] Of course, what is reasonably incidental to a man's employment is a question very much for individual judgment, but the case-law has established a pattern of activities and events which are normally to be regarded as coming within or outside the course of employment.

i *Deviation from journey*   Most obviously, an employee who deviates from a journey for purposes unconnected with his work, e.g. to visit a public house, will not succeed.[3] But stopping to take a meal en route is covered.[4] The position of an employee whose duties are peripatetic will, of course, be more flexible, as, *ex hypothesi*, he has no fixed hours or places of work. Thus a salesman returning home after entertaining a business associate succeeded.[5] But a point may be reached in his travels where he steps beyond the boundaries of his employment. Generally the employee will have discretion where he stays overnight so the course of employment will be broken from the point at which his journey ends.[6] An apparent deviation may, however, be covered where the employee had no reasonable alternative. Thus in one case,[7] the widow of an employee succeeded when her husband, a passenger in his employer's van, had departed from the prescribed route to enable a fellow employee to visit a doctor: it would have been unreasonable to expect the deceased to have left the van during the deviation.

ii *Breaks between spells of duty*   There is a large number of cases involving accidents to employees in breaks between spells of duty, and it is impossible to reconcile all of them. Certainly, as one Commissioner remarked,[8] some fine distinctions are necessary (though undesirable) if decisions are to be based on logical principles. But the 'logical principle' involved is a vague one of the supervision and control of the employer, which does not make the prediction of decisions easy. Lunch and tea breaks, if spent on the employer's premises, are usually protected,[9] but not if the employee is off the premises and free to do what he likes,[10] nor, or course, if he exceeds the time

---

19 See e.g. *St Helens Colliery Co Ltd v Hewitson* [1924] AC 59.
20 Per Salmon LJ, *R v Industrial Injuries Comr, ex parte Amalgamated Engineering Union (No 2)* [1966] 2 QB 31 at 51. See also *R(I) 1/77* (putting up Christmas decorations).
1 *R(I) 4/73*, per H A Shewan, Comr, at para 5.
2 Per Salmon LJ, *R v Industrial Injuries Comr, ex parte Amalgamated Engineering Union, (No 2)* n.20, above; per O'Connor J, *R v National Insurance Comr, ex parte East* [1976] ICR 206 at 208.
3 *R(I) 40/55*.
4 *CI 148/49*.
5 *R(I) 38/53*.
6 *R(I) 22/51; R(I) 51/61; R(I) 22/54*; cf where the employee is bound, in practice if not by the terms of his employment, to stay at a particular place: *CI 374/50; R(I) 30/57*.
7 *R(I) 40/56*.
8 *R(I) 11/55* para 5.
9 *R(I) 11/53*, but not at the beginning or end of a day's work (*CI 120/49; R(I) 11/54*) unless the meal or refreshment is regarded as part of the employee's remuneration (*R(I) 15/55*).
10 *R(I) 84/52; R(I) 24/53; R(I) 4/79; R(I) 10/81*. See also *R(I) 6/76* where the employee was forced to vacate the premises as the result of a bomb scare. If, however, the claimant con-

allocated.[11] Quite apart from formal breaks, many occupations involve lulls in the working effort. A distinction is drawn between voluntary idleness which will interrupt the course of employment,[12] and a lull imposed by the pattern of work. If, in the latter case, an employee, to fill in time, does something not unreasonable, not prohibited by his employer, and which does not interrupt someone else's work, he will succeed.[13] But this will not be so if he removes himself completely from his sphere of operations so that he is no longer under the supervision of his employer.[14]

iii *Non-working activities* Even though a claimant may have been at his place of work during his normal working hours, what he was doing at the time of the accident may have been so far removed from his duties that he is regarded as having been outside the course of employment. The widow of an employee killed while taking a nap during night duty could not recover.[15] The interruption of work to achieve something entirely for personal purposes is similarly treated: a level-crossing keeper fetching milk from the garden;[16] a factory worker leaving work without permission to accompany a fellow employee to the work stores.[17] As regards physical activities not incidental to work, there has been a significant change of attitude within recent years marked, in particular, by the decision of the Court of Appeal in *R v Industrial Injuries Comr, ex parte Amalgamated Engineering Union (No 2)*.[18] Lord Denning MR said:

> In the ordinary way, if a man while at his place of work, during his hours of work, is injured by a risk incidental to his employment, then the right conclusion usually is that it is an injury which arises out of and in the course of the employment, even though he may not be doing his actual work but chatting to a friend or smoking or doing something of that kind.[19]

The course of employment is not broken merely because, at the time, the employee was doing something for his own purposes. The question is, first, whether the interruption was a natural one and, secondly, whether it was a reasonable use of the employee's time. A decision of 1973 reveals the impact of the new approach.[20]

> C, a factory worker, was acting as agent for a football pools firm. While being handed a coupon by a fellow employee he was injured. It was held that though strictly speaking he was not, at the time, doing something he was employed to do, nevertheless it did not involve a *material* interruption of his employment.

iv Out of the employment

a *General causal test*
The second element in the statutory test requires that the accident arises 'out

---

tinues to perform an employment duty during the break he is covered: *R(I) 20/61*; *R v National Insurance Comr, ex parte Reed* (1980) reported as Appendix to *R(I) 7/80*.
11 *R(I) 49/57*; *Ex parte AEU*, n.20, above.
12 *Ex parte AEU*, ibid.
13 *R(I) 46/53*; *R(I) 13/66*; *R(I) 13/68*.
14 *R(I) 1/58*.
15 *R(I) 68/54*; cf where sleeping is involuntary: *R(I) 36/59*.
16 *R(I) 9/59*.
17 *R(I) 1/58*.
18 [1966] 2 QB 31.
19 Ibid, at 49.
20 *R(I) 4/73*.

of (the) . . . employment'.[1] It is not sufficient that the accident happens within the temporal and spatial limits of the employment: it must be causally linked to it.[2] For example, a man may suffer from a heart attack while he is working, but benefit is not payable unless, in some way, the condition resulted from his work. The courts and tribunals have been wary of precise formulations on this point.[3] Some have generalised in terms of employment being the 'proximate' cause of the accident;[4] others have stipulated that it be the *causa causans*, rather than the *causa sine qua non*, of the accident.[5] In a decision of 1963, a Tribunal of Commissioners attempted to be more specific.[6] Basing their view on some prominent House of Lords decisions under the Workmen's Compensation Acts,[7] the Commissioners argued that the crucial question is whether the claimant's own act (or by implication an 'external cause') creates a risk which is different from that created by the employment. Once the *sine qua non* test is satisfied, i.e. it is established that the accident would not have happened but for the employment, then it will generally be held to have arisen out of that employment, unless the claimant (or another) added or created 'a different risk . . . and this different risk was the real cause of the accident'.[8] But like all similar tests of causation, it is of limited utility. The authorities will always have to form their own decision on the facts of a given case,[9] guided only by the general orientation of the test, which in this instance implies that the requirement of a causal link should be liberally construed.

b *Statutory presumption*

Under the Workmen's Compensation Acts, the onus of proving that the accident arose both out of and in the course of employment lay on the claimant. In 1946, it was felt that some of the difficulties of establishing the causal link might be mitigated if the burden was on the authorities to prove that the accident did *not* arise out of the employment. The statutory presumption in its present form provides that:

> an accident arising in the course of an employed earner's employment shall be deemed, in the absence of evidence to the contrary, also to have arisen out of that employment.[10]

Its introduction was greeted by some as a revolutionary measure which would lead to a great improvement in the claimant's position.[11] They were to be disappointed. No major change did result and it is not difficult to see why. For the presumption to apply, not only must the claimant prove that the accident occurred in the course of the employment,[12] but also there must be no 'evi-

---

1 SSA, 1975, s.50(1).
2 *Dover Navigation Co Ltd v Craig* [1940] AC 190, [1939] 4 All ER 558; *R(I) 16/61*; *R(I) 2/63*.
3 See e.g. *Dover Navigation* case, n.2, above, per Viscount Maugham at 193 and Lord Wright at 199; *R(I) 2/63* para 20.
4 E.g. *R(I) 8/54*; *R(I) 75/54*; *R(I) 27/60*.
5 E.g. *R(I) 13/65*; *R(I) 26/59*.
6 *R(I) 2/63*.
7 Notably *Thom v Sinclair* [1917] AC 127; *Upton v Great Central Rly Co* [1924] AC 302; *Harris v Associated Portland Cement Manufacturers Ltd* [1939] AC 71; and *Cadzow Coal Co Ltd v Price* [1934] 1 All ER 54.
8 *R(I) 2/63* para 26.
9 Ibid, at para 16.
10 SSA 1975, s.50(3).
11 See Mr R Prentice, Standing Committee B Debates on the Family Allowances and National Insurance Bill 1961, cols 51–52.
12 *CI 47/49*.

dence to the contrary'. In fact, in almost every disputed case, there is *some* evidence to the contrary. The approach taken by the Commissioners is that the presumption applies only if there is *nothing* in the known circumstances from which it might reasonably be inferred that the accident did not arise out of the employment.[13] Thus an epileptic found injured at the foot of a staircase could not invoke the principle: the fact of his epilepsy was 'evidence to the contrary'.[14] The first sign of a more generous interpretation of the provision came in 1964.[15]

> C, a post office engineer, was repairing a fault in a phone booth when a young man opened the door apparently to make a call. C remembered nothing more until he arrived home bleeding from a head wound. The Commissioner discounted the possibly that C might have provoked an assault as being too 'speculative' and thus not constituting contrary evidence. The presumption therefore applied and C was awarded benefit.

c Pre-existing conditions

A major problem that arises in applying the general causation principles concerns the effect of pre-existing conditions. An employee may have a latent physical disability (e.g. a heart condition) unconnected with his work. Should the disability manifest itself during the course of the employment, the authorities must decide whether the accident arose 'out of' that employment. The problem is resolved on principles analogous to those already described concerning the causal link between the 'accident' and the 'injury'.[16] If the employment provides merely the background or setting for the event, the claimant will not succeed.[17] The work must contribute in a material degree to the risk.[18] Once that is established, the fact that the prior condition rendered him more liable to sustain an accident will be irrelevant. So in *R(I) 11/80*

> C, who suffered from postural hypotension, fell during his course of work at a factory, and was rendered unconscious when his head struck the floor. The Commissioner, J G Monroe, held that he could succeed on the alternative grounds: (i) that he fainted as a result of changing his posture, which he did for the purpose of his employment; or (ii) that, in any event, the fact that he came into physical contact with the employer's premises was sufficient to associate the accident with the employment.[19]

d Common risks

The causation test implicit in the requirement that the accident arises out of the employment carries with it the assumption that the employment creates a risk for the claimant which is greater than, or at least different from, that to which he would have been subject as a member of the public. Should the assumption not be justified, the employment may not be the substantial cause

---

13 *CI 3/49*, approved in *R v National Insurance (Industrial Injuries) Comr, ex parte Richardson* [1958] 2 All ER 689, [1958] 1 WLR 851. See also *R(I) 41/55* and *R(I) 30/60*.
14 *CI 68/49*.
15 *R(I) 1/64*.
16 P.260, above.
17 *R(I) 12/52*.
18 *R(I) 73/51*.
19 Applying a dictum of Lord Atkin in *Brooker v Thomas Borthwick & Sons (Australia) Ltd* [1933] AC 669 at 677. See also *CI 82/49* and *R(I) 6/82*.

of the accident. In principle, then, an employee struck by lightning,[20] or bitten by an animal,[1] while working should not succeed. The employment has not exposed him to a risk greater than that to which an ordinary member of the public is subject. On the other hand, if the 'accident has occurred to the workman by reason of the employment bringing about his presence at the particular spot and so exposing him to a danger . . .', he will be entitled.[2] So a seaman suffering from heat exhaustion while working aboard a vessel in the Arabian sea was clearly covered, and it was irrelevant that other persons living in tropical climates are exposed to the same risk.[3] Here the employment took the claimant to a locality to which he would otherwise not have gone. While the theoretical distinction between these cases may be clearly recognised, there is a large shady area between them which cannot easily be divided according to any precise criterion. As a consequence, the authorities tended to approach the problem causistically, declining to justify their decisions in terms of principle. The resulting unpredictability may be gauged from comparing two, unhappily typical, cases:

> A foreign body struck the eye of a lorry driver while on the road. He was not entitled: 'I do not think that a person driving a lorry is thereby exposed to any greater risk of getting something in his eye than anyone else'.[4]

> A piece of grit entered the eye of a police motorcyclist when on patrol duty. He succeeded: 'a man who is employed to drive a motor-bicycle about the streets of a city is exposed by his employment to a greater risk of getting something in his eye than a person not so employed'.[5]

The confusion created by such decisions led to dissatisfaction with the statutory formula. The reaction of some Commissioners was to aid the injured person by broadening the category of 'locality risks'. They were prepared to hold, more often than was perhaps justifiable, that the employment had taken the claimant to the particular spot where he encountered the hazard. It was so decided in the case of a bus driver stung by a wasp[6] and that of an agricultural worker struck by lightning.[7] Another device was to find an intermediate agent which intervened between the original hazard and the injury and so to regard it, rather than the original hazard, as the 'proximate cause' of the injury. Thus when an employee, riding a bicycle on her employer's business, was blown off by a freak gust of wind, the Commissioner felt able to decide in her favour on the somewhat artificial ground that 'the proximate cause was that she fell from her bicycle while travelling on duty, and it does not seem to me to be necessary to consider any remoter cause'.[8]

Such generous approaches were by no means universal. In 1958, the Divisional Court held that a bus conductor, attacked while on duty by a gang of youths, could not succeed because his position was no different from that of

20 *R(I) 7/60.*
 1 *CI 101/50; R(I) 89/52.*
 2 Per Russell LJ, *Lawrence v George Matthews (1924) Ltd* [1929] 1 KB 1 at 20.
 3 *R(I) 4/61,* following *Dover Navigation Co Ltd v Craig* [1940] AC 190, [1939] 4 All ER 558.
 4 *R(I) 62/53* para 3.
 5 *R(I) 67/53* para 5. See also *R(I) 71/53.*
 6 *R(I) 5/56.*
 7 *R(I) 23/58.*
 8 *R(I) 27/60,* following a similar idea in *R(I) 46/54.*

any other person on the bus.[9] The decision created consternation among the trade unions, and there was immediate pressure for legislative reform.[10] It was forthcoming in 1961, the method chosen being to extend the coverage of the scheme to certain specified risks.[11] The provision, as re-enacted in 1975, is that:

> an accident shall be treated . . . as arising out of an employed earner's employment if–
> (a) the accident arises in the course of the employment; and
> (b) the accident either is caused by another person's misconduct, skylarking or negligence, or by steps taken in consequence of any such misconduct, skylarking or negligence, or by the behaviour or presence of an animal (including a bird, fish or insect), or is caused by or consists in the employed earner being struck by any object or by lightning; and
> (c) the employed earner did not directly or indirectly induce or contribute to the happening of the accident by his conduct outside the employment or by any act not incidental to the employment.[12]

The risks selected for special protection manifestly reflect particular situations in which claimants had previously encountered difficulty in recovering benefit, and there is no obvious common principle to which they all relate.[13] The cumulative effect of this provision, and the Commissioners' decisions previously referred to, reduces the significance of the 'out' requirement, provoking one commentator to the conclusion that

> we appear to have got very close to a point where an accident arising in the course of employment will almost inevitably fall within the system.[14]

But, so far at least, successive governments have refused to abandon the 'out' requirement. To do so, it is argued, would make nonsense of the existence of the special scheme for work-caused accidents.[15] The argument is obviously sound, but it seems hard to reconcile with the policy behind the 1961 reform.

e *Claimant's conduct*
The third condition of the 1961 provision quoted above, that the claimant should not contribute to the accident by conduct outside the employment, restates a principle existing in the case-law prior to the enactment and falls now for consideration. It is clear, in the first place, that the mere negligence or carelessness of the claimant is not by itself sufficient to bar entitlement to benefit:[16] the legislation has not incorporated the common law doctrine of contributory negligence. Rather the conduct of an employee will defeat his claim only if (1) he 'added or created a different risk' to or from that arising from the employment and (2) 'this different risk was the real cause of the accident'.[17] In the case in which this test was propounded,

> C, attempting to light a cigarette, as permitted by his employer, ignited gas which was escaping from an unlit blow-pipe. He was awarded

9 *Ex parte Richardson*, n.13, above.
10 See General Council Report of the TUC (1960).
11 FANIA 1961, s.2.
12 SSA 1975, s.55(1).
13 See the Standing Committee B Debates on the 1961 Bill.
14 *Atiyah* p.329.
15 Mr J Boyd Carpenter, Minister of Pensions and NI, in the Standing Committee B Debates on the 1961 Bill, cols 59–60.
16 *Harris v Associated Portland Cement Manufacturers Ltd* [1939] AC 71; *R(I) 36/59*.
17 *R(I) 2/63*; *R(I) 3/63*.

benefit. C's act converted a potential risk into an actual explosion. 'It did not make it a different danger or create a fresh one'.[18]

In contrast in another case,

> In an effort to warm himself, C poured petrol onto a fire and was burned by the conflagration. Fires were prohibited on the site, but in terms of causation C's act had added or created a different risk from that inherent in the circumstances of the employment.[19]

It is convenient here to consider the relevance of the fact that the claimant's conduct was prohibited by his employer or by the law generally. In the early years of the Workmen's Compensation Act, employers were frequently able to rely on the existence of such a prohibition as a defence.[20] The position was altered in 1923,[1] when the legislature provided that an act would be

> deemed to have arisen out of and in the course of employment, notwithstanding that the workman was . . . acting in contravention of any statutory or other regulation . . . or of any orders given by or on behalf of his employer, or that he was acting without instructions from his employer, if such act was done by the workman for the purposes of and in connection with his employer's trade or business.

It was optimistically argued by some that this effectively overruled the 'out' requirement. Such an interpretation, though perhaps feasible on a literal view of the phrase 'acting without instructions', was obviously unintended: it would place disobedient employees in a better position than obedient ones. The argument was quickly denounced by the House of Lords.[2] 'Acting without instructions' was equated with an implied prohibition. More importantly, the provision left open the possibility that the employee was, in any event, acting outside the scope of his employment. If so, he failed. The effect of the 1923 reform was merely to prevent a certain class of evidence being sufficient of itself to oust the right to compensation.[3] It did not operate to extend the scope of the employment. The point was confirmed by legislative amendment when the provision was incorporated into the national insurance scheme. A new condition was added. For the fiction to apply, the claimant must now show that:

> (a) the accident would have been deemed so to have arisen had the act not been done in contravention of any such regulations or orders, or without such instructions as the case may be; and
> (b) the act is done for the purposes of and in connection with the employer's trade or business.[4]

On condition (a), the claimant must show that apart from the contravention the accident arose out of and in the course of employment. Thus, if he is doing something quite different from that which he was employed to do, he

---

18 *R(I) 2/63* para 29.
19 *R(I) 24/51*.
20 See e.g. *Lowe v Pearson* [1899] 1 QB 261.
 1 WCA 1923, s.7.
 2 *Kerr v James Dunlop & Co* [1926] AC 377.
 3 Per Viscount Dunedin, ibid, at 386.
 4 SSA 1975, s.52.

cannot benefit from the provision.[5] For example, in *R v D'Albuqerque, ex parte Bresnahan*[6]

> D, a dock labourer engaged in loading a ship, attempted to move an obstacle with a fork lift truck which had been left unattended by its driver. He fell into the dock with it and was drowned. His widow failed. It was not within the scope of his employment to use a fork life truck and therefore condition (a) was not satisfied.

Whether the act is 'done for the purposes of and in connection with the employer's trade or business' has been given a generous interpretation in the recent cases. Thus, it was held to be in the interests of both the employer and the employee (though prohibited by the former) that a locomotive driver should take a short cut on his way from the railway shed to a station.[7]

f *Emergencies*

It is an obvious principle that the causal link with the employment is not broken if the accident occurs through the employee responding to an emergency. To this end, section 54 of the Social Security Act 1975 provides that

> An accident happening to an employed earner in or about any premises at which he is for the time being employed for the purposes of his employer's trade or business shall be deemed to arise out of and in the course of his employment if it happens while he is taking steps, on an actual or supposed emergency at those premises, to rescue, succour or protect persons who are, or are thought to be or possibly to be, injured or imperilled, or to avert or minimise serious damage to property.

The provision does not cover all possible emergencies; in particular, the emergency must have occurred 'in or about' premises where the employee is working.[8] But it is complemented by a case-law doctrine which holds that the act of meeting an emergency arises out of the employment if it can be construed as being in some way in the interests of the employer and was reasonable in the circumstances.[9]

v Special cases

Finally, mention should be made of rules which deem that accidents occurring to special categories of employee arise out of and in the course of employment.

(a) Airmen and mariners are covered if the accident occurs when returning from work abroad at the employer's expense.[10]

(b) An airman travelling to his work in an aircraft is deemed to have the permission of his employer, for the purpose of section 53(1),[11] and to like effect a mariner travelling to his work in a vessel need not show that this was under an arrangement with his employee.[12]

(c) A mariner employed on a vessel as a pilot is covered for accidents while on board, while embarking or disembarking, or while returning (without

5 *CI 11/49; R(I) 77/54; R(I) 7/55; R(I) 41/56; R(I) 12/61.*
6 [1966] 1 Lloyds Rep 69.
7 *R(I) 5/67.*
8 On which, see *R(I) 6/63.*
9 *CI 280/49; R(I) 63/54; R(I) 46/60.*
10 SI 1975/469, reg 3(a); SI 1975/470, reg 3(a).
11 SI 1975/469, reg 3(c).
12 SI 1975/470, reg 3(c).

undue delay) to a port other than that from which he normally plies his trade.[13]

Part 4   Industrial diseases

A   General

Soon after the passing of the first Workmen's Compensation Act, it became clear that the 'personal injury by accident' formula was inadequate to cope with sickness or disease resulting from employment. It has already been seen that in principle an incapacity resulting from a 'process' as opposed to an 'event' is not caught by the general provisions. Granted that protection should be afforded in these cases, there would appear to be two basic possibilities:[14] (1) to provide a general definition of occupational disease as an alternative to the 'accident' formula, the claimant having to satisfy the authorities (with or without the aid of a presumption) that the disease was contracted as a result of his employment; (2) to create a list of specified diseases which experience and medical expertise have shown to be typical risks for certain specified categories of employment. Generally with the aid of a presumption, the claimant would then have to show that he contracted a prescribed disease as a result of working in the prescribed occupation. Persuasive arguments can be made out for either approach.[15] (1) has the great advantage that its scope is wider (those suffering from non-prescribed diseases in (2) are without remedy) and it is more flexible: legislatures, it is claimed, cannot keep pace with new and changing industrial risks. The advantages claimed for (2) tend to be more incidental to the policy of providing compensation for those suffering from industrial diseases. Thus it is said that the requirement of prescription encourages more detailed and intensive study of the problems, which in turn contributes to safety and rehabilitation systems. The more general coverage in (1) creates difficulties of proof (particularly of causation) and thereby greater uncertainty and, it is claimed, is thereby more costly and more conducive to false claims and abuse.

Most countries including Britian have adopted the more restrictive approach in (2).[16] But recommendations have been made both by the EEC[17] and the International Labour Organisation[18] for a so-called 'mixed system' which effectively combines the two approaches: the claimant benefits from a presumption that he incurred a scheduled disease from employment in a relevant occupation; but if he is suffering from a non-scheduled disease, the onus is on him to establish the causal link with the employment. Such a system operates in Denmark and the Federal Republic of Germany and was urged on the British government by the Pearson Commission.[19] The matter was fully considered by the Industrial Injuries Advisory Council (IIAC) in a report published in 1981.[20] While acknowledging the merits of the individual proof method, and recommending that in general it should be available, it consi-

13 Ibid, reg 4.
14 Cf Riesenfeld 52 Calif L Rev 531, 542–543.
15 Sears and Groves 31 Rocky Mountain L Rev 462; Angerstein 18, ibid, 240.
16 See generally IIAC Report on Industrial Diseases (1981, Cmnd 8393), paras 6–32.
17 Recommendation 2188/62.
18 Recommendation No 121 (1964).
19 Paras 880–887.
20 N.16, above, and see Wilson 11 ILJ 141 and Lewis [1983] JSWL 10.

dered nevertheless that some diseases, such as lung cancer, strokes, coronary diseases and mental diseases, should be excluded because, though often thought to be connected with certain types of employment, they would give rise to considerable difficulty. The medical opinion would differ as to their aetiology, thus leading to a lack of uniformity in decisions on entitlement, and claimants might have inappropriately high expectations of success.[1] Even this limited proposal proved to be unacceptable to the Conservative government,[2] and thus the British system remains wedded to protection against prescribed diseases.

The system of prescribed diseases was introduced by the Workmen's Compensation Act of 1906.[3] A Departmental Committee set up shortly after the passing of the Act felt that a new disease should be included only if it were so specific to the prescribed employment that in individual cases the causal link with the employment could be established without difficulty, or, in other words, that the claimant would be unlikely to contract it outside his work.[4] Thus bronchitis was not added since 'it would attract endless litigation, as no one knows whether the sufferer has contracted it from dust irritation, or would have contracted it anyway, as hundreds of other people in the locality do'.[5] Notwithstanding severe criticism of the approach by trade unions, on the ground that it was too restrictive,[6] the principle of inclusion is still law, section 76(2) of the Social Security Act 1975 providing that:

(a) [the disease] ought to be treated, having regard to its causes and incidence and any other relevant considerations, as a risk of their occupations and not as a risk common to all persons; and

(b) it is such that, in the absence of special circumstances, the attribution of particular cases to the nature of the employment can be established or presumed with reasonable certainty.

Although the principle has remained unaltered, it is clear that its application, now primarily the responsibility of the IIAC,[7] has in practice shifted significantly.[8] In the early days, the emphasis was on showing that the disease was peculiar to the specified employment, and not to others. Later, the crux became whether the employment created a vulnerability to the disease greater than that of the general public, even though other employments were equally susceptible. While proviso (b) remains a serious obstacle to the admission of some diseases, there is apparently a tendency to attach less importance to it. So in 1974 occupational deafness was added, notwithstanding the finding of the IIAC that loss of hearing is a common affliction and has 'a number of different causes'.[9]

Naturally, the current approach still gives rise to considerable dissatisfaction. The IIAC has made some organisational changes to meet complaints that the prescription process was too slow.[10] It remains to be seen whether the

1 IIAC Report, n.16, above, at paras 144–149.
2 In 1984: 52 HC Official Report (6th series) Written Answer, col 327.
3 S.8, following proposals of a Departmental Committee (1904, Cd 2208).
4 Report of the Departmental Committee on Compensation for Industrial Diseases (Gladstone Committee) (1907, Cd 3495).
5 Ibid, at para 25.
6 Considered in the Report of the Departmental Committee on Compensation for Industrial Diseases (Holman Gregory Committee) (1920, Cmd 816) and the Report of the Departmental Committee on Compensation for Industrial Diseases (1932).
7 *Lewis* pp. 95–97, and pp. 537–538, below.
8 Young *Industrial Injuries Insurance* (1964) p.26.
9 Report on Occupational Deafness (1973, Cmnd 5461), para 45.
10 *Lewis* p.132.

new structure will be able to cope adequately with the growth of occupational hazards resulting from the introduction of new toxic hazards in the workplace, but it cannot meet the more fundamental criticism that the system offers no protection against diseases which occur generally in the community and yet in particular cases may be employment-related. So long as the individual proof proposal remains unimplemented, unequal treatment between the victims of occupational disease will, therefore, persist. On the other hand, there are inherent limits to the ability to connect some hazards to working conditions:

> the only conclusion that can be drawn is that no-one knows how much industrial disease exists and whether it is increasing or decreasing.[11]

B Proof of prescribed disease

Proof that the claimant is suffering from a prescribed disease or injury 'due to the nature of (his) employment' is an alternative basis of entitlement to that provided by 'a personal injury caused by accident arising out of and in the course of employment'.[12] Inconvenient overlaps between the two criteria are prevented by the provision that

> a person shall not be entitled to benefit in respect of a disease as being an injury by accident arising out of and in the course of any employment if at the time of the accident the disease is in relation to him a prescribed disease by virtue of . . . that employment.[13]

To establish entitlement on the basis of a prescribed disease the claimant must satisfy three conditions:

(a) he suffers from a prescribed disease;
(b) that disease is prescribed in relation to his occupation;
(c) the disease developed as a result of employment in that occupation.

i Suffering from prescribed disease
A Schedule to the Prescribed Diseases Regulations lists descriptions of conditions covered by the scheme.[14] The claimant must prove that he is suffering from or has suffered from[15] one such condition which resulted in loss of faculty on which title to benefit is based. Evidence is normally supplied through doctors specialising in the relevant diseases.[16] A decision is then made by the adjudication officer in the light of that evidence. He may refer the question, or an appeal may be brought against his decision, to an adjudicating medical authority, and from that body to a medical appeal tribunal.[17]

11 Brown *Industrial Injuries* (1982) p.145. See also Stapleton *Disease and the Compensation Debate* (1986) who refers (p.54) to the 'essential dilemma . . . that the more generous the scheduling guidelines and the more available is the device of individual proof, the more non-occupational claims will be admitted to the scheme, calling into doubt its preferential basis itself'.
12 SSA 1975, s.76(1).
13 Ibid, s.76(5).
14 SI 1985/576, Sch 1, Part I. The conditions are classified according to whether the cause is a physical, biological, chemical or other agent.
15 Thus the condition from which the claimant is currently suffering may be a sequela (after-effect) of a prescribed disease: see ibid, reg 3.
16 Details of typical symptoms and after-effects of prescribed diseases are given in the DHSS booklet *Notes on the Diagnosis of Occupational Diseases* (rev edn, 1983).
17 SI 1986/2218, regs 41–50., and see further pp. 576–578, below.

Because of the expertise required, there are special boards constituted for 11 of the prescribed diseases, most of them affecting lungs.[18]

ii Disease prescribed for claimant's occupation

Against the description of each disease, there is listed in the Schedule the occupation or occupations for which the disease is prescribed. The claimant's task is to prove that he has been employed in the relevant occupation on or after 5 July 1948.[19] It is important to appreciate that the scheduled description is not a legal categorisation of the type of occupation but a factual account of work actually undertaken.[20] It follows that though a claimant's employment may in theory include work in the prescribed activity, in practice he may not be engaged at all on it, or only for a trivial amount of time. In such circumstances he will not be entitled to benefit.[1] The scheduled descriptions of the occupation vary from the very vague[2] to the highly specific.[3] There is a considerable case-law on some of these but consideration of it lies beyond the scope of this work.[4]

iii Causal link between occupation and disease

Finally the claimant must establish the causal link between employment in the prescribed occupation and the prescribed disease. In the ordinary case, there is a presumption that the disease was due to the nature of the relevant occupation if he was employed in it at any time within one month preceding the date on which he is treated as having developed the disease,[5] normally the date on which he first suffers the relevant loss of faculty.[6] There are, however, special conditions for the presumption to apply to the important diseases of pneumoconiosis, byssinosis, tuberculosis and occupational deafness,[7] and it does not apply at all to two diseases: inflammation of the nose, throat or mouth and non-infective dermatitis.

To rebut the presumption, where it exists, the adjudication officer must prove on the balance of probabilities that the disease was not due to the nature of the relevant occupation.[8] In some cases, he will seek to show that it was caused by employment in an occupation not prescribed.[9] In others, the disease may allegedly arise from activities or contacts outside his employment[10] or from a condition pre-existing in the claimant before the commencement of the occupation.[11] In all cases, the question is not whether the

18 SI 1986/2218, reg 50.
19 SI 1985/967, reg 2(a). For older cases, see p.312, below. In relation to occupational deafness, the claimant must have been employed for a minimum aggregate of ten years in one or more of the prescribed occupations and the claim must be made within five years of his last work in such an occupation: SI 1985/576, regs 2(c) and 25.
20 Therefore it is not sufficient for the claimant to establish that he was contractually bound to undertake such work. The question is whether he actually *did* the work (*CI 59/49*; *R(I) 3/78*) which depends on the individual circumstances of the case: *R(I) 2/77*.
1 E.g. *CI 265/49*; *R(I) 40/57*.
2 E.g. Prescribed Diseases Nos 22 and 35: 'work in or about a mine'.
3 E.g. Prescribed Disease No 39.
4 Reference should be made to *Lewis*, ch 4.
5 SI 1985/967, reg 4(1).
6 Ibid, reg 6, though earlier if there has been a recrudescence of the disease previously suffered: ibid, reg 7(3) and see p.282, below.
7 SI 1985/967, reg 4(2)–(5).
8 *R(I) 37/52*.
9 E.g. *R(I) 9/53*.
10 E.g. *R(I) 20/52*.
11 E.g. *R(I) 37/52*; *R(I) 38/52*.

employment was the sole cause of the disease: it is sufficient if it was the real and substantial cause.[12]

C Recrudescence and fresh attacks

A claimant may have been awarded disablement benefit for a particular disease and then have recovered wholly or partly. If he subsequently suffers a further attack, this may be diagnosed as a 'recrudescence', that is, continuation of the old disease. In such a case, the conditions of entitlement do not have to be satisfied again and the claimant gains immediate entitlement to benefit.[13] Conversely, if it is diagnosed as the contraction of a new disease, the conditions must be satisfied afresh. If the further attack occurs during the period covered by an existing assessment of disablement, there is a rebuttable presumption that it is a recrudescence of the earlier disease, but if it occurs after the end of such a period, it is always treated as the contraction of a new disease.[14] Decisions as between recrudescence and fresh attack are made by those bodies which determine diagnosis questions.

Part 5   Disablement benefit

A General

From 1948 until 1982, provision was made in the industrial scheme both for short-term incapacity for work – injury benefit, payable for a maximum period of six months – and for residual disability, whether or not accompanied by incapacity for work – disablement benefit, payable when entitlement to injury benefit had expired. The existence of the flat-rate injury benefit had its origin in pressure on the post-war government to offer a higher level of compensation to those off work as the result of an industrial accident or disease than they would obtain under the non-industrial sickness benefit.[15] However, the real value of the difference between the injury and sickness benefits declined over the years as successive governments became sensitive to criticisms of the industrial preference, at least with regard to short-term consequences.[16] The 1980 departmental study of the industrial scheme produced an almost unanswerable argument for rationalisation: 'considerable administrative cost is . . . incurred to deal with hundreds of thousands of cases in most of which little extra benefit is at stake'.[17] A suggestion to abolish injury benefit was accepted forthwith by the government[18] and implemented in 1982.[19] The very great majority of those who would have received injury benefit would, of course, be entitled to sickness benefit, or statutory sick pay which, in 1986, became available for the first six months of incapacity. To

12 *R(I) 10/53*.
13 SI 1985/576, reg 7(1). The regulation does not apply to certain diseases full recovery from which is rarely obtained.
14 Ibid.
15 Brown *Industrial Injuries* (1982) p.30. Beveridge had recommended that the injured employee should rely on sickness benefit for the first 13 weeks: para 100.
16 P.253, above.
17 *Industrial Injuries Compensation* para 2.7. The difference between injury and sickness benefit was, at the time, £2.73 per week.
18 *Reform of the Industrial Injuries Scheme* ch 2.
19 SSHBA 1982, s.39(1).

protect the few who would not be so entitled, the legislation now provides that a person incapable of work as a result of an industrial accident or prescribed disease is treated as having satisfied the contribution conditions for sickness benefit.[20]

The method of compensating long-term disability was a much disputed question during the Second World War and immediately thereafter.[1] First, should provision be made for those who were only partially disabled, that is, whose earning capacity had been reduced rather than eliminated altogether? Such persons had been covered by the workmen's compensation legislation, and the principle of compensation applicable there, both to totally and to partially disabled, had been that of 50 per cent (and for lower paid workers 75 per cent) of lost earnings, though subject to a statutory maximum.[2] Beveridge preferred to retain this mode of compensation, but on the level of two-thirds of lost earnings, to bring the scheme in line with the more generous protection offered by European and American systems.[3] The post-war government was not, however, prepared to accept this recommendation. It was seen as conflicting with the then generally held dogma of social insurance that any differential in benefit should be based on need, typically according to the extent of family responsibility, rather than on earnings.[4] Further, it was felt that one of the main weaknesses of the workmen's compensation scheme had been the difficulty of calculating the earnings-based award: predictions had to be made not only on the future earnings of the claimant in the light of his reduced capacity, but also on those which he would have received if he had not been injured. The government proposed what was described as 'an entirely new approach' (though it had formed the basis of the war pensions scheme for some time[5]): benefit payable according to the degree of disablement, irrespective of actual earnings loss. The rates would be assessed on the claimant's assumed needs, and therefore might include increases for family responsibilities and for any additional care and attention necessary.

As the following pages will reveal, the principles of assessment and modes of payment have continued to be the subject of considerable debate and substantial reform. Nevertheless, the principle of providing *basic* compensation according to the severity of disablement has remained unaltered and uncontroversial.[6] Indeed, it has served as a model for those arguing for a universal system of disability income, not confined to industrial cases.[7]

B Loss of faculty

To gain title to disablement benefit, the claimant must show that 'he suffers as the result of the relevant accident from loss of physical or mental faculty . . .'.[8] The legislation does not define 'loss of faculty'. It is one link in the statutory chain of causation

$$\left. \begin{array}{l} \text{accident} - \text{injury} \\ \text{prescribed disease} \end{array} \right\} - \text{loss of faculty} - \text{disablement}$$

20 Ibid, s.39(4), inserting s.50A in SSA 1975.
1 Brown, n.15, above, pp. 213–218.
2 WCA 1925, s.9(2).
3 Paras 99–100.
4 *Social Insurance* Part II, paras 28–29.
5 Cf p.315, below.
6 Cf *Pearson* paras 822–824; *Industrial Injuries Compensation* para 3.11.
7 P.136, above.
8 SSA 1975, s.57(1).

and its meaning, therefore, must be understood in the light of those other elements.[9] Whereas 'injury' covers all the adverse physical or mental consequences of the accident,[10] 'loss of faculty' connotes 'impairment of the proper functioning of part of the body or mind',[11] and this is 'a cause of disabilities to do things which in sum constitute the disablement' which is the subject of the assessment.[12] If this seems to be very complicated, its practical importance is small. Though the medical authorities are expected, in theory, to make separate decisions on loss of faculty and disablement respectively, because of the possibility that either might not exist[13], in practice this rarely occurs.[14] In any event, the Act provides that 'there shall be deemed not to be any relevant loss of faculty where the extent of the resulting disablement, if so assessed, would not amount to 1 per cent'.[15]

What amounts to an 'impairment of the proper functioning' may sometimes cause difficulties. In one case, the malfunctioning of one kidney was regarded as a loss of faculty, even though the claimant could survive by using the other kidney.[16] For some time there was doubt as to whether disfigurement constituted a loss of faculty, on the ground that a person does not put his appearance to any use. The traditional view that it was covered is confirmed by the Social Security Act 1975 which provides that 'references to loss of physical faculty include disfigurement, whether or not accompanied by any actual loss of faculty'.[17] This oddly-worded provision does imply, however, by using the contradistinction of '*actual*' loss of faculty, that were it not for the Act, disfigurement would not be regarded as a loss of faculty.[18]

C Causal link with relevant accident

The next task is to establish that the loss of faculty resulted from the industrial accident or prescribed disease. The onus of proof is on the claimant and the standard is the balance of probabilities.[19] The ordinary principles of causation apply,[20] so the claimant need not show that the accident was the sole or even *the* effective cause – it is sufficient if it was *a* real and effective cause.[1] The major problem here has been the question of competence to make a binding decision on the point. One of the disablement questions to be resolved by the medical authorities is 'whether the relevant accident has resulted in a loss of faculty'.[2] But the prior question that the claimant had sustained an injury by accident arising out of and in the course of employment is determined by the ordinary adjudicating authorities (viz adjudication officer, SSAT and

---

9 *Jones v Secretary of State for Social Services* [1972] AC 944, per Lord Diplock at 1009–1010 and Lord Simon at 1019.
10 Per Lord Diplock, ibid, at 1010; 'hurt to body or mind': Lord Simon, ibid, at 1020.
11 Per Lord Simon, ibid, cf 'loss of power or function of an organ of the body': Lord Diplock, ibid, at 1010.
12 Per Lord Diplock, ibid.
13 *R(I) 5/84(T)*.
14 *Lewis* pp. 138–139. The fact that now the assessment of disablement must, in general, be at least 14 per cent renders the distinction of even less importance.
15 SSA 1975, s.57(3).
16 *R(I) 14/66*.
17 SSA 1975, Sch 20.
18 But see *R(I) 39/60*.
19 *R(I) 12/62*.
20 Cf p.260, above.
 1 *R(I) 3/66(T)*.
 2 SSA 1975, s.108(1)(a).

Commissioner). In interpreting legislation previously in force, the House of Lords held that a decision by the adjudicating authorities that the claimant had suffered an injury by accident precluded the medical authorities from making a subsequent decision that a loss of faculty did not result from the accident.[3] The DHSS had always taken the view that the medical authorities had the superior expertise to decide issues of this kind and the ruling was reversed by statute.[4] In its reenacted form, the legislation provides that a decision by the adjudicating authorities that the claimant sustained an injury by an industrial accident is not 'to be taken as importing a decision as to the origin of any injury or disability suffered by the claimant, whether or not there is an event identifiable as an accident apart from any injury that may have been received'.[5] The point of the last clause is to cover cases where the accident and the injury appear to be the same, such as a cardiac condition caused by exertion at work.[6]

D Degree of disablement

The 1946 legislation did not confer benefit in all cases of disablement: the claimant had to show that the loss of faculty, resulting from the industrial accident, was likely to be permanent or substantial, the latter meaning an assessment of 20 per cent or more.[7] There was soon pressure to extend entitlement to less serious cases and in 1953 the threshold was reduced to 1 per cent, thus excluding only trivial handicaps.[8] Those benefiting from the reform, because their disablement was assessed between 1 and 20 per cent, received a lump-sum 'gratuity', rather than a pension.[9]

The DHSS team which reviewed the scheme in 1980 saw no reason to question the appropriateness of these arrangements. Indeed, they remarked on the popularity of gratuities with claimants and on the medical opinion that, in comparison with pensions, lump sum awards had a positive effect on rehabilitation.[10] The government White Paper, published eighteen months later, took quite a different line. In accordance with the policy that the industrial preference should concentrate on more serious cases, it argued for a threshold similar to that prevailing before 1953: a 10 per cent assessment where the disablement was not likely to be permanent.[11] In the event, the reform effected in 1986 went even further: the threshold is raised to 14 per cent, at which point the pension is payable; and the gratuity was abolished.[12] An exception is made for three lung diseases – byssinosis, diffuse mesothelisma and pneumoconiosis – for which benefit is still payable on assessments of 1–13 per cent.[13] Many other diseases, however, typically attract only low

---

3 *Minister of Social Security v Amalgamated Engineering Union* [1967] 1 AC 725, [1967] 1 All ER 210; *Jones v Secretary of State for Social Services*; *Hudson v same* [1972] AC 944, [1972] 1 All ER 145. The latter two cases were heard *en banc*.
4 NIA 1972, s.5, against determined opposition: cf Mrs B Castle who characterised the reform as 'designed to establish the victory of unimaginative bureaucracy' (Standing Committee D Debates on the Bill, col 373).
5 SSA 1975, s.117(3).
6 E.g. *CI 5/49*.
7 NI(II)A 1946, s.12(1)(a).
8 NI(II)A 1953, s.3.
9 For details, see the second edition of this book, pp. 308–309.
10 *Industrial Injuries Compensation* para 3.25.
11 *Reform of the Industrial Injuries Scheme* ch 3.
12 Sch 3, para 3, following the consultation paper of December 1985, paras 2.1–2.4.
13 SI 1985/967, reg 20(1), substituted by SI 1986/1561.

assessments and their continued existence in the schedule of prescribed diseases has become largely symbolical.[14] Moreover, as regards the whole field of industrial accidents and diseases, it has been estimated that abolition of the gratuity will eliminate about 90 per cent of all new awards.[15]

E Assessment of disablement

i General

The general principle of assessment is to take into account all disabilities incurred as a result of the loss of faculty

> to which the claimant may be expected, having regard to his physical and mental condition at the date of the assessment, to be subject during the period taken into account by the assessment as compared with a person of the same age and sex whose physical and mental condition is normal.[16]

With the exception of the factors mentioned in this provision, measurement is objective: 'the assessment shall be made without reference to the particular circumstances of the claimant other than age, sex and physical and mental condition'.[17] It follows that not only is the effect of the disability on the claimant's earning capacity irrelevant,[18] but personal and social circumstances are also ignored,[19] and, unlike the system of common law damages, there is no attempt to compare the claimant's condition before and after the injury.[20]

The objective approach, though found to be satisfactory by a departmental committee reporting in 1965,[1] has been criticised by many, particularly sociologists,[2] who feel that insufficient regard has been paid to the considerable amount of research which has taken place on the functional, social and psychological effects of disability.[3] It has, therefore, been proposed that the assessment should be based on the ability to perform normal everyday activities and that decision-making power should be conferred on social workers.[4] Some foreign systems have developed not only tariffs of disablement more detailed and sophisticated[5] than their British counterparts

14 Lewis 15 ILJ 256, 259.
15 Ibid at 260. Cf approximately 3,400 a year, with an assessment of 14–19 per cent, now receive a pension instead of a gratuity: ibid. Account must also be taken of the extension of the reduced earnings allowance: p.295, below.
16 SSA 1975, Sch 8, para 1(a).
17 Ibid, para 1(c).
18 *R(I) 3/61*; *Murrell v Secretary of State for Social Services* (1984), reported as Appendix to *R(I) 3/84*.
19 In *R(I) 6/75* C sought to have his assessment of disability reduced from 20 per cent to 19 per cent on the ground that the consequent award of a lump sum gratuity instead of a pension would enable him to purchase a small business. The reduction was quashed by the Commissioner.
20 A suggestion that the comparison should be attempted was rejected in *Industrial Injuries Compensation* para 3.16.
 1 Report of the Committee on the Assessment of Disablement (McCorquodale Committee) (Cmnd 2847).
 2 See esp. Townsend *The Disabled in Society* (1967).
 3 See the references cited in *Townsend* and Blaxter *The Meaning of Disability* (1976).
 4 Lewis and Latta 4 J Soc Pol 25; Disability Alliance *The Case for Reforming the Industrial Injuries Scheme* (1980).
 5 E.g. France: Mayet et Rey *Barème des Accidents du Travail* (1975); USA: American Medical Association Committee on Rating Medical and Physical Impairment *Guidelines to the Evaluation of Permanent Impairment* (1971).

but also criteria more functional in character.[6] A statement in the 1980 discussion document that 'the department . . . has no evidence that the present schedule is outmoded'[7] is surprising in the circumstances,[8] but it is characteristic of the generally negative government response to suggestions for reform in this area.

ii Assessment for prescribed conditions

Schedule 2 of the General Benefit Regulations[9] contains a tariff of the prescribed degrees of disablement. The first column sets out descriptions of the injury and the second column the degree of disablement, expressed as a percentage of total disablement (e.g. loss of a hand and a foot, 100 per cent; loss of thumb, 30 per cent etc.). For each specified condition, then, the prima facie assessment is the prescribed degree of disablement, but the medical authorities are not tied to this figure; it is subject

> to such increase or reduction . . . as may be reasonable in the circumstances of the case where, having regard to the [statutory provisions and regulations] . . . that degree of disablement does not provide a reasonable assessment of the extent of disablement resulting from the relevant loss of faculty.[10]

The conditions specified in the tariff must, it seems, be construed literally. Thus, for example, reference to the loss of the phalanx of a finger does not cover loss of *part* of the phalanx of a finger.[11] Although the Act specifically entitles the Secretary of State to make special provision for the difference between injuries to the hand and arm of right- and left-handed persons,[12] he has not done so. But it may be a suitable case for the medical authorities to increase or reduce assessment in the exercise of their discretion referred to above.

A problem arises if, as a result of the accident, the claimant suffers from two of the conditions specified in the tariff. The regulations provide that assessment at the prescribed degree of disablement should be made only where the condition in question is 'the sole injury which a claimant suffers as a result of the relevant accident . . . whether or not such injury incorporates one or more other injuries' as specified.[13] In other words, if one injury is incorporated into another, the assessment should be made according to the prescribed degree of the more serious disability. Where the accident results in two separate injuries, there is no automatic assessment under the tariff, and the principles next to be described apply.

iii Assessment for non-prescribed conditions

For conditions not specified in the Schedule, assessment is at large. It is a question of fact, and the decision of the medical authorities will generally be

6 E.g. France: Rousseau in Van Steenberge and Geerts (eds) *Le Dommage Humain* (1981) ch 4; USA: Howards, Brehm and Nagi *Disability: From Social Problem to Federal Program* (1980) ch 5.
7 *Industrial Injuries Compensation* para 3.19.
8 The document did, admittedly, precede the comprehensive report published by the DHSS: Duckworth *The Classification and Measurement of Disablement* (1982).
9 SI 1982/1408.
10 Ibid, reg 11(6).
11 *R(I) 22/63*.
12 SSA 1975, Sch 8, para 2.
13 SI 1982/1408, reg 11(6). The regulation was made in 1970 to deal with uncertainty in the case-law, especially *R(I) 39/61* and *R v Industrial Injuries Comr, ex parte Cable* [1968] 1 QB 729, [1967] 1 All ER 9.

regarded as conclusive, though they 'may have such regard as may be appropriate to the prescribed degrees of disablement' of the injuries specified in the Schedule.[14] The prescribed degrees of disablement, then, provide a guideline for the appropriate assessment, but no more. In one case,[15] the claimant suffering from a condition of the finger which was more severe than one prescribed finger condition but less severe than another prescribed finger condition sought to argue that as a matter of *law* medical authorities were bound to assess at a figure between the two prescribed degrees of disablement. The argument was rejected. The discretion of the medical authorities was not to be fettered by thus enlarging the Schedule. In cases where the claimant has sustained multiple (and separate) injuries, and there is no composite disability for which the Schedule prescribes an assessment, the medical authorities must form their own judgment on the total disablement resulting from the various injuries.[16] They may compare this total condition with those giving rise to the prescribed degrees of disablement and select an appropriate figure.

iv Successive industrial accidents

Where successive accidents (or diseases) are covered by the scheme and give rise to separate conditions, the claimant is entitled to an assessment based on the aggregate of the respective degrees of disablement.[17] This principle is, however, subject to two qualifications. First, if the condition caused by the first accident gave rise to a lump sum gratuity payment, it cannot count towards the aggregate[18] – the claimant has already been compensated in full for the condition. Secondly, the aggregate cannot exceed 100 per cent.[19]

v Reductions for disability resulting from extraneous causes[20]

The fact that the claimant's condition results in part from an extraneous cause, that is, one not arising from an industrial accident, in principle justifies a reduction in the assessment of the disability. It is felt that the Fund should not be charged with the burden of such disabilities as the claimant would have suffered if he had not been injured in the industrial accident. The policy is a simple one to understand, but the provisions implementing it have caused great difficulties. The chief concern has been to see that generous treatment should be given to an employee who sustains two disabilities, only one of which is caused by an industrial accident, but which are in some way connected, so that the total disability resulting is greater than the sum of the two disabilities taken separately. A simple example will illustrate the point.

14 SI 1982/1408, reg 11(7). There are, however, some non-statutory guidelines which are used in practice: see *Lewis* pp. 146/147.
15 *R(I) 23/63.*
16 *Ex parte Cable*, n.13, above, and see *Murrell v Secretary of State for Social Services*, reported as Appendix to *R(I) 3/84.*
17 SSA 1975, ss. 57(1A) and 77(4).
18 Ibid, and SI 1982/1408, reg 38.
19 SSA 1975, s.91(1). Regulations made under s.91(1)(b) provide that the principle should not affect entitlement to dependency additions or the allowances for constant attendance and exceptionally severe disablement, though, of course, the claimant cannot receive more than one of each such addition or allowance: SI 1982/1408, reg 39. These provisions do not govern the reduced earnings allowance (REA) and in *R(I) 3/73* it was held that its predecessor, the special hardship allowance (SHA), did count towards the 100 per cent maximum. However, unlike SHA, REA may be paid independently of entitlement to the disablement pension and this fact might justify a different approach: *Lewis* p.148.
20 Lewis 43 MLR 514.

Under the tariff, the loss of vision in one eye, the other being normal, is 30 per cent, but the loss of sight 'to such an extent as to render the claimant unable to perform any work for which eyesight is essential' is assessed at 100 per cent.[1] Thus a claimant, already blind in one eye, who loses the sight of the other eye in an industrial accident under the ordinary principle unmodified would be entitled to only 30 per cent but the effect of the accident has been to increase disablement from 30 per cent to 100 per cent.[2]

The solution originally adopted was the so-called 'paired-organs' rule. Where the claimant sustained an injury to one of a pair of similar organs, whose functions were interchangeable or complementary, and the other had already been incapacitated – in an industrial accident or otherwise – the total disablement was treated as resulting from an industrial injury.[3] Application of the doctrine, however, produced difficulties and anomalies,[4] and in 1969–70 it was replaced by a new set of rules.[5]

a *Total disablement*
The medical authorities should first assess the total disablement resulting from the relevant loss of faculty, whether or not it was derived in part from another cause.[6] In so doing, they should not merely arbitrate between two opposing views (those of the claimant and those of the Department) but rather obtain all the information which they regard as relevant, and assess the disablement resulting from the relevant loss of faculty on the balance of probabilities.[7] They may then, for the purpose of making a reduction from the first assessment, only take account of causes other than the relevant accident to the extent allowed by the General Benefit Regulations 11(3) and 11(4).[8] These apply to disabilities from other causes suffered, respectively, before and after the industrial accident. But for there to be a 'disability' for this purpose, there must have been some inability to perform a bodily or mental process which manifested itself; a constitutional or latent condition which simply renders the sufferer more prone to such an inability cannot be invoked as a ground for reducing benefit.[9]

b *Other disability preceding industrial accident*
Regulation 11(3) provides that where the disability, defined as above, preceded the industrial accident, the medical authorities must assess what degree of disablement would have resulted from that disability if the industrial accident had not occurred and deduct it from the total disablement.

E.g. C has suffered an amputation to one foot. In the industrial accident he suffers an amputation to the other foot. Total disablement is 90

1 SI 1982/1408, Sch 2, items 32 and 4 respectively.
2 Cf *R(I) 1/79*.
3 SI 1964/504, reg 2(4).
4 See *R v Medical Appeal Tribunal, ex parte Burpitt* [1957] 2 QB 584; see also Report of the Industrial Injuries Advisory Council on the Rules Governing the Assessment of Disablement (1956, Cmd 9827); and Micklethwait 37 Medico-Legal Jo 172, 185.
5 NIA 1969 s.7(1)(a); SI 1970/1551.
6 SI 1982/1408, reg 11(2).
7 *R v Industrial Injuries Comr, ex parte Cable*, n.13, above; *R v National Insurance Comr, ex parte Viscusi* [1974] 2 All ER 724, [1974] 1 WLR 646.
8 SI 1982/1408.
9 *R(I) 13/75*; *R(I) 3/76*; *R(I) 1/81*.

per cent. If there had been no industrial accident he would have been disabled to the extent of 30 per cent. Benefit is then payable on an assessment of 90 per cent – 30 per cent = 60 per cent.

c *Industrial accident preceding other disability*

In the converse case where the industrial accident precedes the other disability, the solution is not so simple. On the ordinary principles of causation, it is arguable that no account should be taken of the fact that the subsequent event has exacerbated the claimant's condition, since it has superseded the effect of the industrial accident. This was indeed the position prevailing before the 1970 reform, and yet it created an apparent inequality of treatment according to the sequence of events.[10] The Committee which reviewed the issue in 1956[11] was divided on the issue. The minority opinion was that the assessment should take account of the greater incapacity caused by the non-industrial accident (as in regulation 11(3)), but the majority found no justification for such a 'radical' departure from the ordinary rules of causation. Aware, presumably, of the political repercussions of strict adherence to the ordinary rules, however, they suggested the compromise solution of taking into account 50 per cent of the increase in disability. A compromise solution was in fact adopted by the Department in 1970, but not that proposed by the Committee. It was decided to take into account the *whole* of the increase for those more seriously injured, but to ignore it altogether for those less seriously injured. The dividing line was arbitrarily made at an 11 per cent disablement. Regulation 11(4), which now incorporates the solution, lays down two rules.

(1) The authorities should only take into account the disablement which would have resulted if the non-industrial accident had not occurred.

E.g. C loses the whole of a ring finger in an industrial accident. As a result of a later non-industrial accident, the hand containing that finger is rendered useless. The relevant assessment for the disability of the ring finger = 7 per cent.

(2) Where the assessment made under the first rule is 11 per cent or more, a solution analogous to that in regulation 11(3) is adopted. From the assessment of total disablement is deducted the degree of disablement resulting solely from the non-industrial accident (i.e. if the industrial accident had not occurred).

E.g. in an industrial accident, C is amputated through the left foot. He is subsequently amputated through the right foot. Amputation of a foot is 30 per cent, thus the second rule applies. Total disablement is 90 per cent from which is deducted 30 per cent for the right foot. Benefit is payable for 60 per cent.

d *Where 100 per cent disablement*

A special rule operates where the total assessment of disablement is 100 per cent. In such circumstances the medical authorities are given power *not* to reduce for the fact that some of the disablement has been caused by a non-

---

10 Cf at common law *Baker v Willoughby* [1970] AC 467, [1969] 3 All ER 1528; *Jobling v Associated Dairies Ltd* [1982] AC 794.
11 N.4, above.

industrial event, if they are satisfied that, 'in the circumstances of the case, 100 per cent is a reasonable assessment of the extent of disablement resulting from the loss of faculty'.[12] This is designed to cover cases where the disability caused by the industrial accident itself, without the addition of disability arising from an extraneous event, would amount to 100 per cent. It would obviously be unjust to make a deduction merely because the non-industrial event has made the claimant's condition even worse. The anomaly arises because the tariff knows no degree of assessment higher than 100 per cent.

vi Rounding modifications
When the total assessment of disablement has been reached in accordance with the principles described above, the percentage figure must be expressed in a multiple of 10.[13]

> Assessments 14 per cent–19 per cent inclusive are rounded up to 20 per cent; those which are multiplies of 5 are rounded up to the next multiple of 10; others are rounded up or down to the nearest multiple of 10. Thus, e.g., assessments of 25 per cent and 28 per cent become 30 per cent, while 24 per cent becomes 20 per cent.

The most significant consequence of these modifications, effected by the Social Security Act 1986, is that those whose disablement is assessed between 14 and 19 per cent, previously entitled only to a gratuity, now receive a pension.

vii Period of assessment
The assessment is made for the period 'during which the claimant has suffered and may be expected to continue to suffer from the relevant loss of faculty', beginning not earlier than 90 days (not counting Sundays, thus 15 weeks) after the accident or onset of the prescribed disease.[14] It will in any event terminate on the claimant's death,[15] but it may be limited to an earlier day, if the disability is expected to end by that date. If the assessment is less than 14 per cent, the period must last for so long as the prognosis suggests that disablement of at least 1 per cent will persist.[16] This may be important for entitlement to the reduced earnings allowance, for which that latter figure is the threshold. Determination of the period is either 'provisional' or 'final'. A final assessment is appropriate where the medical authorities are reasonably certain in their prognosis; it may be modified only by a review – to be considered in the next paragraph. A provisional assessment is to be made where 'the condition of the claimant is not such, having regard to the possibility of changes therein (whether predictable or not) as to allow of a final assessment'.[17] The claimant's condition must be examined again before the end of the period for which the assessment was made, and the new assessment (either provisional or final) will apply from that time.[18] A provisional assessment is

12 SI 1982/1408, reg 11(6).
13 SSA 1975, s.57(1B). The rounding modification applies only to the aggregate assessment, not to any component forming part of an aggregate: ibid, s.57(1C).
14 Ibid, s.57(4) and SI 1985/967, reg 6.
15 SSA 1975, Sch 8, para 4(1).
16 Ibid, para 4(2).
17 Ibid, para 4(1).
18 SSA 1975, s.108(4) and Sch 8, para 4(1).

in no sense binding on a subsequent assessment, and the medical authorities determining the latter may come to a different view on whether a condition which was also the subject of the previous assessment resulted from the relevant accident.[19] On the other hand, a subsequent assessment cannot modify the benefit for the earlier period.[20]

F Review

The adjudicating and medical authorities have a general power to review a decision where satisfied that it was given in ignorance of, or was based on a mistake as to, some material fact. This is considered in chapter 15.[1] But what of changes taking place in the claimant's condition *since* the time of the original hearing? The principle has always been that once a final (not a provisional) decision has been made, the receipt of benefit should not be affected by an amelioration in the claimant's condition: the assumption is that the prospect of a reduction in benefit might inhibit recovery.[2] Even though the result is asymmetrical, the assessment of disablement may be increased for subsequent deterioration. Under the 1946 legislation the claimant had to show an unforeseen aggravation to his condition which was *substantial*, and even then the medical authorities would have power to review only if to refuse him a revision would create 'substantial injustice'.[3] These harsh limitations provoked strong criticism, and they were revised in 1953.[4] Since that date, it has been sufficient if the medical board is satisfied

> that since the making of the assessment there has been an unforeseen aggravation of the results of the relevant injury,[5]

though if the original assessment was made, confirmed or varied by a medical appeal tribunal, then the leave of that body must be obtained.[6] The aggravation must be 'unforeseen' in the sense that it was not taken into account in the earlier assessment, and, of course, it must have been substantially caused by the relevant injury – the principles of causation applied are the same as those governing the injury/loss of faculty connection.[7]

The 1953 reform also plugged another gap. Where unforeseen aggravation is shown, the medical authorities may now alter a previous finding that no loss of faculty had resulted from the relevant accident.[8]

G Benefit

Since the gratuity was abolished in 1986, disablement benefit is payable only in the form of a pension, a weekly sum proportionate to the degree of disable-

19 *R v Industrial Injuries Comr, ex parte Howarth* (1968) 4 KIR 621; *R v National Insurance Comr, ex parte Viscusi*, n.7, above.
20 *R(I) 8/69*.
 1 Pp. 584–585, below.
 2 Cf Luntz *Compensation and Rehabilitation* (1975) pp. 75–76.
 3 NI(II)A 1946, s.40(2).
 4 NI(II)A 1953, Sch 1.
 5 SSA 1975, s.110(2).
 6 Ibid, s.110(5). The granting of leave is discretionary and the adjudicating authorities have no jurisdiction to overturn it: *R(I) 15/68*.
 7 *R(I) 18/61(T)*, *R(I) 18/62* and p.284, above.
 8 Now SSA 1975, s.110(3).

ment (after rounding modifications).[9] For example, in 1988–89, the relevant rates for 100 per cent and 50 per cent are £67.20 and £33.60 respectively. Beneficiaries under 18 and not entitled to an increase for dependants are paid less, about 60 per cent of the general rate.[10] As part of its policy to confer preferential treatment on more seriously disabled beneficiaries, the government has proposed some revision of the amounts payable so that, for example, a 30 per cent assessment would give rise to payment of 25 per cent of the maximum pension, and an 80 per cent assessment would lead to an 85 per cent pension.[11] A decision on this has been deferred until the general survey of the disabled which it has commissioned[12] has been published.[13]

Part 6   Reduced earnings allowance

A   General

From the earliest, there was confusion as to the role and nature of disablement benefit: the effect of the accident on earning capacity was irrelevant and the benefit could be drawn while the claimant worked or was in receipt of another social security benefit, for example, sickness benefit; and yet the government felt that it was, at the same time, an instrument for income replacement.[14] It was believed that for most injured workers it would provide compensation at a higher level than a wage-related benefit.[15] The original Industrial Injuries Bill, therefore, made no provision for lost earnings. During the passage of the Bill, the criticism was made that this would offer insufficient protection to workers who suffered a relatively minor disablement which, nevertheless, prevented them pursuing their regular occupation.[16] 'The House [of Commons] wanted it both ways and in the end got what they wanted . . .':[17] a so-called special hardship allowance (SHA) which enabled the authorities to supplement the disablement benefit with a sum for lost earnings, up to a prescribed maximum, if the claimant was able to show that he was no longer capable of following his regular occupation or one which would give him remuneration of an equivalent standard.[18]

In the years that followed, SHA generated more difficulties and criticism than any other aspect of the industrial injuries scheme and has been the subject of repeated investigation and reform proposals.[19] Its very title was a

---

9 SSA 1975, s.57(6). For the rules on calculating the pension for the three diseases for which the threshold remains at 1 per cent, see SI 1986/1561, reg 3.
10 SSA 1975, Sch 4, Part V, para 3.
11 *Reform of the Industrial Injuries Scheme* para 22. For the heavier 'weighting' in favour of more serious cases in France, see *Dupeyroux* p.526.
12 P.133, above.
13 DHSS Consultation Paper *Industrial Injuries Scheme* (1985) para 7.1.
14 See the Commons' debate on *Social Insurance Part II* 404 HC Official Report (5th series) cols 1396–1397.
15 *Social Insurance Part II*, p.17.
16 413 HC Official Report (5th series), cols 1589–1590.
17 Brown *Industrial Injuries* (1982) p.218.
18 NI(II)A 1946, s.14. The method of calculating the sum was altered from increasing the assessment of disablement by 25 per cent (Second Reading of the Bill) to a flat-rate addition of 11s 3d (Committee Stage) to, finally, attributed lost earnings up to a prescribed limit (NI(II)A 1948, s.1).
19 Fourth Report of the Ministry of National Insurance (1953, Cmd 8882), pp. 28–30; *Pearson* pp. 176–178 and Annex 6; *Industrial Injuries Compensation* pp. 29–42; *Reform of the Industrial Injuries Scheme* ch 4; and see Brown, n.17, above, ch 11.

misnomer: far from being confined to cases of 'special hardship', in 1978 it was being paid to 38.5 per cent of those in receipt of disablement pension.[20] And, presumably, it fell short of providing adequate compensation for the loss of earnings since 90 per cent of SHA recipients were being paid the maximum rate.[1] Ironically, the higher the degree of disablement, the lower the compensation for reduced earnings, for the legislation provided that the aggregate of disablement benefit and SHA should not exceed the rate paid for 100 per cent disablement pension.[2] The formulation of the law, in terms of different standards of remuneration for categories of occupation or employment created great complexity and uncertainty. In turn, this meant that, on the one hand, claimants were disadvantaged because they rarely had access to the evidence required for the issues of entitlement and calculation and, on the other, high administrative costs were incurred by the DHSS in ascertaining, on a periodical basis, not only the claimant's current pattern of earnings but also what he would have earned if still employed in his regular occupation – which might no longer exist.

The DHSS review team in the 1980 discussion document recognised the many unsatisfactory features of SHA and put forward several alternative strategies, some of a radical nature: for example, that SHA should be abolished and the resources used for a general increase in disablement benefit; or that it should revert to the role for which it was originally designed and thus be available for cases of 'special hardship', notably where the wage loss was disproportionate to disability.[3] In the White Paper which followed, the government revealed a preference for a more cautious approach.[4] In relation to the reduced earnings allowance (REA), as it would now be called, it was prepared (I) to increase the maximum rate and (II) to make entitlement wholly independent of disablement pension. On the other hand, a manifest concern for work incentives led to the proposals, (III) that no more than 50 per cent of lost earnings should be replaced, and (IV) where the industrial injury prevents work of any kind, the receipt of sickness benefit, invalidity benefit or sick pay should be taken into account, as should actual earnings. In addition, (V) REA would no longer be paid after retirement, and (VI) the method of calculating earnings loss on a continuing basis would be simplified. Proposals (II), (V) and (VI) were implemented by the Social Security Act 1986, and in 1988 a new retirement allowance was introduced for those no longer at work, payable at 25 per cent of the REA to which they were entitled prior to retirement.[5] Decisions on (I), (III) and (IV) have been deferred until the findings of the disablement survey are available.[6]

Pending these final links in the chain of reforms, it would be premature to judge the package as a whole, but this does seem to be another example of piecemeal reform to deal with specific anomalies, as opposed to a radical restructuring of the system of compensation for the long-term consequences of industrial injuries. That would necessarily have entailed confronting the fundamental issues of the level and purposes of the allowance and of disablement benefit, in particular, to what extent income replacement, or rather compensation on a more general basis, is the goal. Nor, as the following

20 *Industrial Injuries Compensation* para 3.1.
 1 Ibid, para 3.43.
 2 SSA 1975, s.60(1).
 3 *Industrial Injuries Compensation* pp. 34–35.
 4 *Reform of the Industrial Injuries Scheme* paras 30–38.
 5 SSA 1988, s.2.
 6 N.13, above.

pages should reveal, is it to be assumed that REA will be much simpler in its application than SHA. It is to be regretted that, given the time spent on the various reform proposals, such little effort was made to investigate how foreign legal systems deal with the same problems. The typical European scheme combines a scale of disablement with a multiplicand based on the claimant's earning potential.[7] Thus, for 100 per cent disablement there is an effective indemnity (subject to an appropriate ceiling) of total earning capacity and for lesser degrees of disablement the figure is reduced on a proportionate basis, so that, for example, for 30 per cent disablement, the injured worker receives a pension based on 30 per cent of his pre-accident earning capacity. The failure to consider models of this kind is all the more reprehensible given that the Pearson Commission, in its appraisal of the SHA problems, specifically urged the government to undertake this very exercise.[8]

The basic conditions for entitlement to REA are set out in section 59A(1) of the 1975 Act. The claimant must be:

(a) . . . entitled to a disablement pension or would be so entitled if that pension were payable where disablement is assessed at not less than 1 per cent; and

(b) as a result of the relevant loss of faculty, he is *either* –
   (i) incapable, and likely to remain permanently incapable, of following his regular occupation; *and*
   (ii) incapable of following employment of an equivalent standard which is suitable in his case,

or is and has at all times since the end of the period of 90 days . . . been, incapable of following that occupation or any such employment.

B Relationship to disablement pension

As the wording of section 59A(1)(a) indicates, entitlement to disablement pension is no longer required, since REA is payable on assessments of disablement between 1 and 13 per cent. However, the conditions of entitlement to the pension, apart from that of a 14 per cent assessment, must still be satisfied; so, in particular, there must be a finding that, as a result of the relevant accident or disease, the claimant suffered a loss of physical or mental faculty.[9]

C Regular occupation

In essence, section 59A(1)(b) involves a comparison of the claimant's earning capacity before and after the accident (or disease). For the purposes of such comparison, the concept of 'regular occupation' is used as an indicator of his pre-accident employment and level of earnings. Identification of the claimant's 'regular occupation' is a question of fact, determinable on consideration of all the relevant evidence: the label given to the employment by the employer, or employees and employers generally, or trade union rules and agreements, is not thought to be particularly helpful.[10] Consistently with this,

7 *Pearson* vol 3, paras 387 (France), 475 (Federal Republic of Germany), 539 (Netherlands), and 603 (Sweden), though invariably a more complex formula is used to provide higher rates for the more seriously disabled: cf n.11 above.

8 Para 820. The proposal extended beyond the industrial injuries scheme which, perhaps, helps to explain the government's failure to respond.

9 P.283, above.

10 *R(I) 28/51*; *R(I) 66/51*; *R(I) 11/65*; *R(I) 6/75*.

though surprisingly given the overall policy of the legislation, a Tribunal of Commissioners has held that the regular occupation need not be in an 'employed earner's employment' (i.e. one covered by the industrial scheme).[11]

The date when the regular occupation must be considered is that of the accident, or, in the case of a prescribed disease, the formally attributed date of onset.[12] An absence of a regular pattern of work at that date will, in principle, mean that the claimant is unable to come within the subsection.[13] However, case-law and legislative provision have mitigated the harshness of the principle. First, the Commissioners have shown great readiness to find 'regularity' even where the duration of employment is very limited.[14] Secondly,

> The Secretary of State may by regulations provide that in prescribed circumstances employed earner's employment in which a claimant was engaged when the relevant accident took place but which was not his regular occupation is to be treated as if it had been his regular occupation.[15]

A regulation made under this power provides, in effect, that if the claimant was engaged in part-time work in employed earner's employment while pursuing a course of full-time education that employment is to be treated as his regular occupation.[16] Thirdly, to meet the problem that the victim of a prescribed disease may have suffered from some of the symptoms before the formally ascribed date of onset and, as a result, abandoned an occupation before that date, another regulation provides that, for the purpose of REA entitlement,

> Any occupation he has so abandoned may be treated as his regular occupation . . . if it would have been so treated had the date of development . . . fallen immediately before he so abandoned it.[17]

Other difficulties may be encountered where, though in regular employment in the period before the accident, the claimant has moved from one type of employment to another, with consequent changes in his pattern of earnings. The general principle applied is that the authorities should have regard to the whole employment history rather than to an isolated period before, or at the time of, the accident (or date of onset).[18] They will be primarily concerned with the claimant's own intentions. If he voluntarily transfers from one type of employment to another he may rapidly establish the new 'regular occupation'.[19] But if the change was necessitated by his state of health, and he hoped eventually to return to his former occupation, the latter may still be treated as his 'regular occupation'.[20] If, at the time of the accident, he has

---

11 *R(I) 15/56(T)*. The Act expressly requires that 'employment of an equivalent standard' for the purposes of the post-accident occupation shall include only employed earners' employment but makes no corresponding limitation as regards the pre-accident regular occupation. The Commissioners inferred that the omission was deliberate.

12 *CI 440/50(T)*.

13 *R(I) 3/60; R(I) 18/60*.

14 E.g. *R(I) 1/63* (employment for ten weeks as a trainee, when such employment was bound to end four weeks later).

15 SSA 1975, s.59A(2), inserted by SSA 1986, Sch 3, para 5(1), in response to the particular case of *CI 188/83: Lewis* pp. 183–184.

16 SI 1986/1561, reg 2.

17 SI 1975/1537, reg 19. The causal connection between the abandonment and the relevant disease may, however, be difficult to prove. See *R(I) 8/58; R(I) 13/58;* and *R(I) 31/58*.

18 *CI 80/49; R(I) 5/52*.

19 *R(I) 65/54*.

20 *CI 80/49; R(I) 5/52*.

been engaged in an occupation for a substantial period of time, there is a presumption that that has now become the relevant occupation,[1] though this may still be rebutted, as in *R(I) 44/52*.

> C changed from bus-driving to store-keeping to earn more money. At the time of the accident he was not yet earning more. It was held that bus-driving was still his regular occupation, as he would have returned to it if he were unable to secure the hoped-for increase of earnings.

The non-technical interpretation of 'regular occupation' has also led to the conclusion that more than one occupation can be included, so that the earnings therefrom can be aggregated.[2] However, the Act explicitly provides that 'references to a person's regular occupation are to be taken as not including any subsidiary occupation'.[3] It seems evident that the draftsman of the original provision had not contemplated the varieties of activities and earnings which claimants would argue came within their 'regular occupation'. The efforts of the Commissioner to exclude casual work and yet include normal overtime pay, to exclude subsidiary occupations, and yet include co-equal occupations, has challenged his ingenuity and created some nice and perhaps arbitrary distinctions. Voluntary work done for the employer outside the normal activities (e.g. the work's fire brigade[4]) is 'subsidiary', but work which is, in some way, contemplated by the contract of employment, without being obligatory under it, may be included (e.g. a colliery repairer working regular weekends on overtime as a shaftsman[5]). A combination of two or more activities with the same employer or for different employers will be covered,[6] but not if one of those activities is clearly subordinate to the other(s), typically where a full-time employee engages in private contract or other work in his spare time.[7] The dividing line between these various distinctions is obscure and some of the decisions are impossible to reconcile.[8] In principle it is difficult to see why regular overtime payments should be included but regular subsidiary work for an external source excluded.

Equity suggests that account should be taken of normal prospects of promotion or advancement to a better-paid occupation, but it has not been easy to formulate an appropriate legal principle. The provision currently in force, dating from 1961,[9] treats as included in regular occupation

> employment in the capacities to which the persons in that occupation (or a class or description of them to which he belonged at the time of the relevant accident) are in the normal course advanced, and to which, if he had continued to follow that occupation without having suffered the relevant loss of faculty, he would have had at least the normal prospects of advancement.[10]

1 *R(I) 22/52*: three years.
2 *R(I) 43/52*; *R(I) 33/58*; *R(I) 6/75*.
3 SSA 1975, s.59A(3)(a). But this does not apply to part-time work undertaken by those in full-time education: ibid and SI 1986/1561, reg 2.
4 *R(I) 58/54* and see *R(I) 13/62*.
5 *R(I) 24/55* and see *R(I) 10/65*.
6 *R(I) 43/52*; *R(I) 16/54*; *R(I) 11/65*; *R(I) 6/75* (same employer); *R(I) 33/58* (different employers).
7 *CWI 30/50*; *R(I) 54/54*; *R(I) 9/61*. The fact that C receives payment from an external source for work carried out primarily for his employer will not disentitle him: *R(I) 60/52*.
8 E.g. *R(I) 24/55* and *R(I) 2/70*.
9 FANIA 1961, s.3(1). It was previously necessary to show that the prospects of advancement existed within a particular occupation, which naturally led to invidious distinctions between 'grades' and 'occupations': see, e.g., *R(I) 29/55*.
10 SSA 1975, s.59A(4).

To invoke this provision, the claimant must first show that the position which he would have obtained would have constituted an 'advancement'.[11] Typically this will arise through promotion, though it also covers cases where greater earnings are payable as a result of seniority, as with many appointments in the public sector which provide for annual salary increments. But 'the mere transfer from a lower paid to a higher paid job does not necessarily constitute advancement', since the higher pay may be intended to compensate for certain less attractive features of the new situation.[12] Once 'advancement' in the sense described has been established, the onus is on the claimant to satisfy two further conditions:[13] first, objectively, he must show that advancement to the alleged occupation or grade was normal for persons in his occupation; and secondly, subjectively, that he possessed the personal qualities and employment record to justify advancement according to this normal pattern. The existence of the first, objective, test will debar the abnormally gifted or industrious worker from reaping the benefits of these qualities,[14] and to that extent still leaves room for improvement.

D The 'permanent' condition

The first of the two alternative conditions requires the claimant to prove that he '(a) is incapable, and likely to remain permanently incapable, of following his regular occupation; and (b) is incapable of following employment of an equivalent standard which is suitable in his case'.[15]

i Incapacity for regular occupation

After the accident the claimant may have returned to his pre-accident employment, and yet his capacity for the work may have been adversely affected. The question thus arises whether for the purpose of limb (a) of the first condition he is thereby rendered incapable of following his regular occupation. According to a Tribunal of Commissioners, the test is whether 'he is unable to fulfil all the ordinary requirements of employers in that field of labour'.[16] The mere fact that the claimant has been unable to earn as much as before by itself is not sufficient but 'if a person obtains employment in his old job only through charity or because he has an exceptional employer, he should be regarded as incapable of following his regular occupation'.[17] As for the analogous purpose of determining what was his regular occupation, not much significance is to be attributed to labels attached to the work: regard must be had to the nature of the activity.[18] An employee unable to perform the normal incidents of his regular occupation (e.g. a miner compelled to work in dust-free conditions[19] or a stevedore incapable of lifting heavy cargo[20]) will satisfy the condition. Traditionally, the view has been taken that

11 *R(I) 12/81.*
12 Ibid, para 9, D G Rice, Comr.
13 *R(I) 8/67.*
14 See *R(I) 8/73* and *R(I) 8/80.*
15 SSA 1975, s.60(1).
16 *CI 443/50* para 11.
17 Ibid para 12.
18 *R(I) 28/51.*
19 *R v Industrial Injuries Comr, ex parte Langley* [1976] ICR 36; *R v National Insurance Comr, ex parte Steel* [1978] 3 All ER 78.
20 *R(I) 28/51.* See also *CI 201/50* and *R(I) 39/55.*

a mere reduction in productivity (e.g. the loss of overtime) is not sufficient,[1] though a claimant has succeeded where he could work only part-time, instead of full-time,[2] and where he had to rely substantially on his workmates to maintain the previous output.[3] In 1977, the Commissioner, J G Monroe, considered that the traditional approach was unsatisfactory and refused to apply it to a pieceworker whose speed of work had been reduced.[4] In relation to such a worker he held that the test should be whether the claimant is 'incapable of attaining the standard of remuneration . . . of his regular occupation'.[5] There is, however, no evidence of this more generous approach being applied to other types of employment.

ii Incapacity for suitable employment of equivalent standard

Of course, if the claimant is able to earn as much as he would have done in his regular occupation, he should not be entitled to the REA. Hence, the second limb requires proof of incapacity to follow also suitable employment of an equivalent standard. The employment in question must be one covered by the industrial scheme, i.e. 'an employed earner's employment'.[6] What is 'suitable' is judged according to the claimant's 'personal qualifications, including his mental and physical capacity'.[7] In general, family and domestic circumstances are irrelevant;[8] the question is, given his physical and psychological condition, his training, experience and general aptitude, was he capable of that kind of employment?[9]

The fact that the claimant has worked in the 'suitable' employment constitutes, of course, persuasive evidence of his capacity for such employment,[10] but the authorities may have regard to job opportunities which exist and which the claimant has not pursued.[11] On the other hand, care must be taken to avoid attributing to the claimant an earnings potential which he has, in practice, little chance of realising. Thus the employment in question must be a recognised occupation, not having an 'exceptional' character, such as sheltered employment, since the latter is not indicative of the claimant's earning capacity in the open labour market.[12]

The question then arises whether the employment of which the claimant is capable, and which is suitable, is of an 'equivalent' standard to the regular occupation. The test is objective and impersonal: the normal earnings of persons employed in the suitable employment are compared with the normal earnings of those employed in the regular occupation.[13] The pattern of

---

1 *CI 443/50(T)*; *CI 447/50(T)*; *CI 448/50(T)*.
2 *CI 444/50(T)*.
3 *R(I) 39/52*; *R(I) 5/55*; cf *R(I) 29/52*.
4 *R(I) 4/77*.
5 Ibid, para 10, applying the principle propounded in *R v National Insurance Comr, ex parte Mellors* [1971] 2 QB 401, [1971] 1 All ER 740, p.304, below.
6 SSA 1975, s.59A(3)(b).
7 *R v Industrial Injuries Comrs, ex parte Humphreys* [1966] 2 QB 1 at 18–19.
8 Ibid at 15–16 and 18.
9 *R(I) 4/76(T)* para 22 (decision upheld by the Divisional Court without discussion of the point: *Ex parte Steel*, n.19, above).
10 *R(I) 29/52(T)*; *R(I) 27/57*; *R(I) 42/61*.
11 *R(I) 29/53*.
12 *R(I) 6/77*, following earlier decisions in *R(I) 42/52*; *R(I) 73/52*; *R(I) 7/58*.
13 *R(I) 6/68(T)*; *R(I) 7/68(T)*. If both types of employment exist in the place where the claimant lives, then regard must be had to the respective rates of pay there: *Ex parte Humphreys*, n.7, above, per Davies LJ at 17, per Salmon LJ at 20. Lord Denning MR, at 13, considered such an approach appropriate only for the purpose of quantifying the award, p.303, below.

earnings in both occupations must be assessed over a relatively long period (e.g. 12 months),[14] earnings here including bonuses,[15] overtime (if normal)[16] and benefits in kind,[17] but not the reimbursement of expenses.[18]

iii Permanent incapacity

The incapacity to follow the regular occupation (first limb) but not the incapacity to follow employment of an equivalent standard (second limb) must be shown to be permanent. This poses a severe obstacle for a claimant who, though at present unable to work in his regular occupation, nevertheless cannot prove that this is likely to continue for the indefinite future. The onus of proof is on him[19] and it is not sufficient to show that the loss of faculty, as opposed to incapacity for work, is likely to be permanent.[20] Even more critically, the rule penalises a claimant who, in an effort to rehabilitate himself, returns to his regular occupation and tries to cope, perhaps only for a trial period. Prior to 1953 the difficulty was alleviated only for victims of pneumoconiosis. A regulation creates a rebuttable presumption that such a person satisfies the 'permanent' condition if he has received advice from a special medical board that he should not follow his regular occupation except under special conditions (e.g. that the environment is dust-free).[1] It also provides that, for the purposes of the condition, any work in the regular occupation or in a suitable employment of equivalent standard which he carried out 'between the date of onset of the disease and the date of the current assessment of his disablement, or for a reasonable period of trial thereafter, shall be disregarded'.[2]

E 'The continuing condition'

The limited assistance given to pneumoconiosis victims did little to help the large number of other industrially disabled persons who, having courageously gone back to their regular occupations after the accident, found that they were for ever barred from the allowance. The defect was remedied in 1953, and the claimant may now satisfy the alternative condition that he 'is, and has at all times since the end of the period of 90 days [after the accident or onset of the disease], been incapable of following his regular occupation or suitable employment of an equivalent standard'.[3] This has considerably eased the claimant's burden. If, since the time of the accident or development of the disease, he has continuously been incapable of the relevant occupation

---

14 *R(I) 31/59*; *R(I) 5/62*.
15 *CWI 30/50*; *R(I) 66/51*.
16 *R(I) 7/51*; *R(I) 1/72*.
17 *R(I) 7/51*; *R(I) 47/52*; *R(I) 47/54*.
18 *R(I) 1/54*. Expenses necessarily incurred in the employment are deducted from gross earnings: *R(I) 79/52*.
19 *R(I) 7/53*.
20 *R(I) 86/52*.
 1 Now SI 1985/987, reg 23(a) and see *R(I) 34/60*; *R(I) 35/60*; *R v National Insurance Comr, ex parte Steel*, [1978] 3 All ER 78. The fact that at the time the 'advice' was received the claimant was already working under the approved conditions does not prevent his relying on the regulation. The provision is based on his 'receiving' the advice, not following it: *R(I) 69/54*.
 2 SI 1985/987, reg 23(b). For the 'date of onset' see p.281, above; for the 'date of current assessment' see esp. *R(I) 74/54*; and for 'reasonable period of trial' see *R(I) 44/54* and *R(I) 74/54*.
 3 SSA 1975, s.59A(1).

or suitable employment[4] there is no longer a need to make predictions as to whether the condition will persist indefinitely. On the other hand, taken by itself, the 'continuing' condition is not able to remedy the plight of a claimant who, unwisely or otherwise, returns to work in the hope that he is fit to carry out his duties but eventually succumbs to the effects of his indisposition. To meet the problem, regulations provide that work in the regular occupation or suitable employment should be disregarded in two sets of circumstances.

(1) The first arises where the claimant has worked in the relevant occupation or employment 'for the purpose of rehabilitation or training or of ascertaining whether he had recovered from the effects of the relevant injury'.[5] Obviously this covers cases where there is some uncertainty as to the effect of the disability on the claimant's capacity and he returns to the employment to see whether he has in fact recovered sufficiently to enable him successfully to carry out the normal working activities.[6] But it frequently happens that, with or without medical advice, the injured employee returns to work under the belief that he is fit to do so, though perhaps subject to certain restrictions (e.g. avoiding the heavier aspects of his normal duties). It then transpires that he cannot cope, and he withdraws. After some initial doubts,[7] it is now clear that such work will be disregarded, even though there may be no direct evidence that the work was undertaken for the purpose of rehabilitation, training or ascertaining whether the claimant has recovered.[8] The period to be disregarded under this regulation is *any* period during which he so works with the approval of the Secretary of State or on the advice of a medical practitioner, and any other period up to six months without such approval or advice.[9]

(2) Secondly, the authorities should disregard work in the relevant occupation or employment 'before obtaining surgical treatment for the effects' of the injury,[10] that is

> any period during which he worked thereat and throughout which it is shown that having obtained the advice of a medical practitioner to submit himself to such surgical treatment he was waiting to undergo the said treatment in accordance therewith, *and* any other period during which he worked thereat and throughout which it is shown that he was in process of obtaining such advice.[11]

'Surgical treatment' in this context does not necessarily involve the use of the surgeon's knife – 'manipulative' treatment will suffice[12] – but it is important that throughout the period for which the disregard is claimed, he should be waiting to obtain the treatment. A doctor should have given a definite opinion that surgical treatment was desirable and that it should be carried out as soon as could conveniently be arranged. The claimant must have accepted the advice and intended to give up work as soon as the arrangement has been made.[13] A substantial period of waiting will raise the presumption that the

---

4 An assessment of disablement of at least 1 per cent must be in force throughout the period: *R(I) 25/57*, as modified by SSA 1975, s.59A(1)(a).
5 SI 1982/1408, reg 17(1)(a).
6 *R(I) 1/69*.
7 *R(I) 81/53*.
8 *R(I) 13/61*; *R(I) 1/69*.
9 SI 1982/1408, reg 17(2)(a).
10 Ibid, reg 17(1)(b).
11 Ibid, reg 17(2)(b).
12 *R(I) 13/56*.
13 *R(I) 81/53*.

claimant did not use reasonable zeal and expedition in trying to secure the necessary surgical treatment, and will disentitle him.[14]

F   Incapacity

Both of the conditions in section 59A(1) are based on proof of an incapacity which results from the relevant loss of faculty. The onus of proving this causal connection is on the claimant,[15] though, in certain circumstances pneumoconiosis victims benefit from a presumption to that effect.[16] While the existence and extent of the loss of faculty are for determination by the medical authorities, the causal link between that loss and the incapacity comes within the jurisdiction of the ordinary adjudicating authorities.[17] The latter may, then, take a view different from that of the medical authorities on the consequences of the loss of faculty; they cannot, however, treat an incapacity as resulting from a relevant loss of faculty if it arises from a condition which the medical authorities did not characterise as part of that loss of faculty.[18] On the general causation issue there is little to add to the now familiar principle that the loss of faculty need not be the sole or even primary cause of the incapacity: it is sufficient if it is a substantial cause.[19] The test has been applied typically where the claimant has left the relevant occupation or employment and it is alleged that the incapacity was caused by his age,[20] or by a pre-existing disability,[1] rather than by the loss of faculty resulting from the industrial accident.

Greater difficulties have arisen where objectively the claimant is regarded as fit for his work, but his apprehensions for the consequences of another accident have led to a refusal to continue. Initially the authorities adopted a strict approach: this was not to be regarded as a disability.[2] In one case, a Tribunal of Commissioners was prepared to make special concessions for a worker who had lost the sight of one eye and who feared that another accident would result in total blindness.[3] This exception is of very limited application and its legal basis is obscure.[4] Fortunately, a more fruitful line of reasoning has been found. In *R(I) 15/74* it was held that if by reason of his physical condition the claimant could not work in his regular occupation without danger to himself or others he should be regarded as incapable of following that occupation.[5] In other words, the accident has placed him or others at greater risk than would otherwise be the case. But this does not cover the situation where the accident renders the employee unwilling to continue out of fear that the accident will be repeated, when objectively there is

14 *R(I) 35/57*, where the period was four and a half years.
15 *R(I) 56/51*.
16 The same circumstances in which the presumption described above, p.300, operates: SI 1985/967, reg 23a. For the effect of the presumption, see e.g. *R(I) 35/50, R v Industrial Injuries Comr, ex parte Langley* [1976] ICR 36, and *R v National Insurance Comr, ex parte Steel* [1978] 3 All ER 78.
17 *R v Industrial Injuries Comr, ex parte Ward* [1965] 2 QB 112 at 128–129.
18 *R(I) 5/84(T)*.
19 *R(I) 17/59*.
20 *R(I) 29/51*; *R(I) 37/51*; *R(I) 67/53*.
 1 *R(I) 64/52*; *R(I) 49/54*.
 2 *R(I) 61/52*; *R(I) 44/54*.
 3 *R(I) 85/52*, and see *R(I) 8/56, R(I) 6/59*.
 4 It has been followed in only one reported case (*R(I) 32/59*) and there was an alternative ground for the decision. For criticism, see *R(I) 12/80* para 14, R S Lazarus, Comr.
 5 See also *R(I) 2/81*.

no increase in the risk. To succeed here, he must show that his apprehensions themselves constituted a medical condition which was part of his loss of faculty and, as was seen in the last paragraph, this is a question for the medical, not the ordinary adjudicating, authorities.[6]

G Duration of allowance

REA is payable 'for such period as may be determined at the time of the award; and . . . if at the end of that period the beneficiary submits a fresh claim for the allowance, for such further period as may be determined'.[7]

Although the authorities have, in consequence, a discretion as to the duration of the allowance, it has been suggested that it should generally be for a substantial period (e.g. 12 months) unless there are special circumstances, most importantly where changes are anticipated in the standard of remuneration either in the claimant's regular occupation or in his post-accident occupation.[8] As the quoted provision indicates, at the end of the period, it is for the beneficiary to apply for a fresh award; there is no obligation on the Department to initiate the process.[9]

Entitlement to REA is, in any event, limited to the period taken into account by the medical authorities in the assessment of disablement.[10] Until the recent reforms, the principle was that payment could continue after the date of retirement – an odd feature for an allowance intended to replace lost earnings and one that made for administrative difficulties.[11] The principle now holds only for those who on 10 April 1988 were entitled to REA, had reached pensionable age and had retired from regular employment; such persons are entitled to the REA for life, though the amount is frozen at the rate payable on 10 April 1988.[12] Other persons over pensionable age and retired cannot be paid REA,[13] though, as will be seen, a special allowance, at a reduced rate, has been introduced for them.[14]

H Amount

Section 59A(8) prescribes that the amount of the allowance is to be determined,

> by reference to the beneficiary's probable standard of remuneration during the period for which it is granted in the employed earner's employments, if any, which are suitable in his case and which he is likely to be capable of following as compared with that in his regular occupation. . . .[15]

i General principles
The wording of the subsection is very similar to that in section 59A(1) which, as we have seen, resolves the question of entitlement to REA by means of an

6 *R(I) 12/80.*
7 SSA 1975, s.59A(6).
8 *CI 81/49,* though it is undesirable that the period be for less than three months: *CI 330/50.*
9 Cf *R(I) 6/62.*
10 SSA 1975, s.59A(7).
11 See *Industrial Injuries Compensation* paras 3.62–3.67 and *Reform of the Industrial Injuries Scheme* paras 36–38.
12 SSA 1988, s.2(4)–(5).
13 Ibid, s.2(8).
14 P.307, below.
15 SSA 1975, s.59A(8).

objective, impersonal comparison of normal earnings of those employed in respectively the claimant's regular occupation and the 'suitable' employment of which he is now capable.[16] The traditional interpretation of the *quantification* provision, reenacted as section 59A(8), is of a subjective, personal comparison of the claimant's standard of earnings in the regular occupation and the relevant post-accident employment, respectively.[17] Thus in calculating the difference for the latter purpose, the authorities would have regard to the claimant's ability (as evidenced by regular practice[18]) to earn overtime[19] or bonus payments,[20] to any history of absenteeism[1] or to the fact that he was a seasonal worker[2] – whether these incidents of work attached to his pre-accident or to his post-accident employment. At the same time, since the comparison has reference to the 'probable standard of remuneration', the earnings may be entirely hypothetical.[3] This may be the case as regards the post-accident employment for the claimant may be capable of, but not actually engaged in, such work. It is necessarily the case for the regular occupation, for here the authorities must speculate on what would have been the claimant's standard of earnings if he had not been injured and had continued to follow that employment.[4]

Nevertheless, when there is evidence of the claimant's actual work experience it would seem to be appropriate, on the traditional subjective approach, to take account of it. The question arose before the Court of Appeal in 1971.[5]

> In his regular occupation as a coal miner, C would have earned £28 1s 9d for working 36¼ hours, no overtime being available. In his post-accident employment as a lorry driver, for a considerably longer period of working (which included overtime), his average earnings were £27 6s 2d.

The claimant argued that the rate for one hour's work should be taken as the basis of the comparison which could then be multiplied by the number of hours worked in the regular occupation.[6] This more refined approach won the support of only a dissenting judgment in the Divisional Court[7] and was repudiated by the Court of Appeal. If taken to its logical conclusion this form of calculation would involve comparing not only the duration of work in the two relevant occupations but also the domestic advantages or disadvantages, the amount of leisure within the working period, and the relative hazards, strains and inconveniences of the work. The right approach was to compare the level of remuneration which would have probably been received in a normal working week in the regular occupation with the level of remuneration which the claimant was capable of receiving in a normal week's work, even though he now works longer hours than in the pre-accident occupation.[8] The approach of the Court of Appeal may have the practical advantage

16 P.295, above.
17 *CWI 17/49; R(I) 10/55; R(I) 6/68.*
18 Thus not where earned only sporadically: *CI 81/49; R(I) 54/54.*
19 *CI 81/49; R(I) 27/57.*
20 *R(I) 66/51; R(I) 47/54.*
 1 *R(I) 23/51; R(I) 61/52.*
 2 *R(I) 76/52; R(I) 5/53; R(I) 56/53.*
 3 *R(I) 11/65; R(I) 1/68.*
 4 *R(I) 14/57; R(I) 1/63.*
 5 *R v National Insurance Comr, ex parte Mellors* [1971] 2 QB 401, [1971] 1 All ER 740.
 6 An approach taken by R G Micklethwait, Chief Comr, in two unreported decisions: *CI 18/68* and *CI 29/68.*
 7 Donaldson J, [1971] 2 QB 401, 413–415.
 8 See also *R(I) 9/80.*

claimed for it, but it undermines what had emerged as a clear distinction between the objective and subjective standards applied to the entitlement and quantum issues respectively and by ignoring the genuine loss that occurs through having to work much harder for the same pay is arguably unjust.[9] That the failure to take account of the claimant's own working pattern prior to the accident will cause problems was impliedly recognised by the judges in the Court of Appeal, for they thought that some special exception would have to be made for part-time workers.[10] The Commissioner has followed the suggestion,[11] but it is not clear whether the exception will be extended to other patterns of work which are significantly different from normal full-time employment, for example, seasonal work.

ii Index linking of subsequent awards

While calculation of the initial award clearly poses considerable difficulties – and it is to be regretted that no attempt to simplify the process was included in the recent reforms – the difficulties multiply on each subsequent renewal.[12] Inquiries have to be made regarding not only the current earnings potential of the claimant but also what he would have earned if he had been able to work in the pre-accident regular occupation, an hypothesis which becomes increasingly artificial as time passes – the occupation in question may no longer exist. The task was manageable when the provisions governing SHA were in force because the maximum rate was paid to some 90 per cent of the beneficiaries and for whom, therefore, detailed inquiries were unnecessary.[13] As will be seen, the 1986 Act did raise the maximum rate for the more seriously disabled and it is envisaged that the limit for other beneficiaries will be increased by future legislation. Simplification of the continuing assessment process was thus seen to be an administrative necessity. The method adopted is, in appropriate cases, to index-link the amounts selected in previous awards to represent the probable standard of remuneration in both pre-accident and post-accident occupations to indices of earnings in the relevant industries.[14]

The rules are set out in the REA Regulations.[15]

(1) The index-linked calculation applies only to third and subsequent awards where one of the following alternative conditions is satisfied: either (a) the previous award was at the maximum rate,[16] or (b) (if the previous award was at less than the maximum rate) either (I) the claimant's regular occupation no longer exists[17] or (II) the claimant is not employed in 'suitable' employment.[18] It does not apply in either

9 Cf Micklethwait *The National Insurance Commissioner* (1976) p.108.
10 N.5, above, per Lord Denning MR at 421, per Sachs LJ at 424, per Buckley LJ at 426.
11 *R(I) 3/83*.
12 *Pearson* Annex 6, paras 32–38.
13 *Pearson* para 817. Even so, over 200,000 inquiries to employers were being made annually: Consultation Paper on Industrial Injuries Scheme (1985), para 3.5.
14 SSA 1975, s.59A(10). This goes further than the proposals in the White Paper which envisaged index-linking only earnings in the regular occupation and using one general index for all earnings increases: *Reform of the Industrial Injuries Scheme* para 33.
15 SI 1987/415.
16 Or would have been at the maximum rate if the post-retirement freezing rule had not applied.
17 This is where (a) the 'former employer has ceased to trade in the locality' or (b) the work done 'at the former place of employment no longer exists or has changed to such a degree that the work amounts to a different occupation' and (in either case) there is in the claimant's 'locality no employer providing work similar to that in which he was engaged': SI 1987/415, reg 2(8).
18 On which, see p.299, above.

(a) or (b) if there has been a relevant change in the claimant's circumstances, for example, where his capacity for work has altered and other types of employment have become suitable for him.

(2) Where the conditions in (1) are satisfied, a percentage increase is applied to the amounts in the previous award which represented the probable standard of remuneration in the claimant's pre-accident regular occupation and post-accident suitable employment respectively. This increase is derived from indices published by the Department of Employment relating to movements in the average gross weekly earnings of full-time adult employees[19] in occupational groups which are *nearest* to the regular occupation and suitable employment, respectively. The increases, so derived, for one year are applied to awards of REA made from the first Wednesday in February in the following year.

(3) For the purpose of these rules, account is taken of SHA awards made prior to October 1986, so that the new calculation can be used in appropriate cases, for the first REA award made in 1987, if there were two or more SHA awards made previously. However, an award which follows a relevant change of circumstances – see (1) – is treated as a first award.

iii Maximum awards

The maximum payable for an award of SHA was a flat-rate sum, traditionally 40 per cent of the current rate of disablement pension or the amount by which the rate of the claimant's disablement pension (excluding any allowances for dependants, constant attendance or exceptionally severe disablement) fell short of that payable for a 100 per cent assessment, whichever was the less.[20] The 1986 reform raised the latter limit to 140 per cent.[1] At the same time, it fixed the rate payable to those who have reached pensionable age and have retired to the amount they received immediately before retirement and from that sum must be deducted any invalidity allowance or earnings-related additional pension to which they are entitled.[2] The reform proposals affecting the maximum award still to be implemented involve a compromise between a recognition that REA typically provides a low measure of compensation for lost earnings and the fear that too generous an award would create work disincentives.[3] The compromise would involve increasing the ceiling on REA itself from 40 per cent to 100 per cent of the disablement pension rate but allowing recovery for no more than one half of lost earnings, taking account also of social security payments (or SSP) for sickness and invalidity.

Part 7   Other allowances

A General

The Social Security Act 1986 abolished two allowances which had always been available to supplement a disablement pension. The unemployability supplement had been paid to a small number ineligible for invalidity benefit because they could not satisfy the contribution conditions.[4] Since 1982, the contribution conditions for that benefit have been waived for the victims of

19 Ignoring rates affected by absence from work.
20 SSA 1975, Sch 4, Part V, para 6.
 1 Ibid, s.59A(8).
 2 Ibid, s.59A(11) and SSA 1986, Sch 3, paras 5(3)–(8).
 3 *Reform of the Industrial Injuries Scheme* paras 31, 34–35.
 4 SSA 1975, s.58.

industrial accidents and diseases,[5] and so the need for the supplement disappeared. The hospital treatment allowance enabled those receiving medical treatment for the relevant injury or loss of faculty in a hospital or similar institution to be paid at the rate of a 100 per cent disablement pension, whatever the assessed degree of disablement.[6] The idea, borrowed from the war pensions scheme (which had provided the basic model for disablement benefit) was to encourage pensioners to obtain hospital treatment by providing additional financial support.[7] Elsewhere in the social security system, the fact that a beneficiary is obliged to stay in hospital is a ground for reducing, rather than increasing, benefit, to reflect the assumed savings on living expenses.[8] The allowance was thus considered to be anachronistic and its abolition was not opposed.[9] There are three other allowances on the statute book: retirement allowance; constant attendance allowance; and exceptionally severe disablement allowance.

B Retirement allowance

This was introduced by the Social Security Act 1988, following the decision to withdraw entitlement to the reduced earnings allowance (REA) from persons who are retired.[10] The conditions of entitlement are that the claimant is over pensionable age (65 men, 60 women), has retired from regular employment[11] and was entitled to REA on the day before retirement.[12] The amount of retirement allowance is *either* 25 per cent of the REA he was paid immediately before retiring *or* 10 per cent of the maximum rate of disablement pension, whichever is less.[13] It is payable for life.[14]

C Constant attendance allowance

The constant attendance allowance, as part of the 1946 industrial injuries scheme, was introduced before the non-contributory attendance allowance became available to the general population in 1971.[15] The Pearson Commission considered that the maintenance of separate provision was not justified: it felt that 'at these extremes of disablement, cause is less important than effect, and that on grounds of both principle and administrative expediency the two types of attendance allowance should be rationalised'.[16] The government accepts this view and has proposed to abolish constant attendance allowance, leaving industrial injury victims to rely on the allowance payable under the main scheme.[17] At the time of writing, this

5 P.140, above.
6 SSA 1975, s.62.
7 *Industrial Injuries Compensation* para 4.16.
8 Pp. 364–367, below.
9 *Reform of the Industrial Injuries Scheme* para 45.
10 Cf p.306, above.
11 The rules governing retirement pension apply here: ch 5, above.
12 SSA 1975, s.59B(1).
13 Ibid, s.59B(5).
14 Ibid, s.59B(3), though payment will cease if he elects to deretire (cf p.198, above): SSA 1975, s.59B(4).
15 Cf pp. 161–168, above.
16 Para 831.
17 *Reform of the Industrial Injuries Scheme*, paras 46–47. See also *Industrial Injuries Compensation* paras 4.7–4.14.

proposal is receiving further consideration, but the Social Security Act 1986 confers on the Secretary of State powers to implement it by statutory instrument.[18]

Under the existing legislative structure, questions of entitlement, duration and quantum are determined not by the adjudicating authorities but by the Secretary of State.[19] The result is that in terms of legal principle much concerning this area of the social security system is shrouded in secrecy.[20] Apparently, internal guidelines for interpretation are circulated within the Department, but their contents have been jealously guarded.[1]

The Act provides that where disablement pension is payable at 100 per cent, and as a result of the relevant loss of faculty the claimant 'requires constant attendance', the pension is to be increased by an amount determinable in accordance with regulations and not exceeding the legislatively prescribed amount.[2] The regulations effectively lay down four different standards by which the need for attendance is to be judged and for which different rates of increase are to be payable.[3]

(1) Where the claimant is 'to a substantial extent dependent on [constant] attendance for the necessities of life and is likely to remain so dependent for a prolonged period',[4] the lower of the two fixed rates is payable.
(2) If, however, the attendance required for (1) is 'part-time only' then 'such sum as may be reasonable in the circumstances' is payable.
(3) Alternatively, when 'the extent of such attendance is greater by reason of the beneficiary's exceptionally severe disablement', a sum up to 150 per cent of the fixed rate in (1) is payable.
(4) The higher of the two fixed rates is payable where the claimant is 'so exceptionally severely disabled as to be entirely, or almost entirely, dependent on such attendance for the necessities of life,[5] and is likely to remain so dependent for a prolonged period and the attendance so required is whole-time'.

The attendance in question may be provided by anyone; it is not necessary to prove that he came in from outside.[6] But if the claimant is a hospital in-patient, he is entitled only if the treatment he receives there is not provided free.[7] It is unnecessary to show that the claimant actually *receives* the attendance; the statutory criterion is based on need.[8]

---

18 SSA 1986, Sch 3, para 6.
19 SSA 1975, s.95(1)(b).
20 See the pertinent criticism of Carson 126 NLJ 59.
 1 But there are a few guidelines in DHSS *Industrial Injuries Handbook for Adjudicating Medical Authorities* (3rd edn): referred to in *Lewis* p.160.
 2 SSA 1975, s.61.
 3 SI 1982/1408, reg 19.
 4 'Prolonged period' is generally interpreted to mean at least six months: *Lewis* p.160.
 5 The interpretation of this is not dissimilar to that attributed by the Commissioner and the courts to the criterion of 'attention . . . in connection with . . . bodily functions' used for the non-industrial attendance allowance (SSA 1975, s.35(1) and pp. 164–165, above): *Lewis* p.160.
 6 Mr J Griffiths, Minister of NI, introducing the 2nd Reading of the 1946 Bill in the House of Commons, 414 HC Official Report (5th series) col 278.
 7 SI 1975/559, reg 13(1), though if he was entitled to disablement pension in the period immediately before the date he entered the hospital for treatment, the requirement does not apply for the first four weeks: ibid, reg 13(2).
 8 Potter and Stansfield *National Insurance (Industrial Injuries)* (2nd edn) p.95.

D Exceptionally severe disablement allowance

The exceptionally severe disablement allowance was introduced in 1966[9] following the recommendations of the McCorquodale Committee on the Assessment of Disablement.[10] It felt that the system then prevailing gave insufficient assistance to some of those in receipt of 100 per cent disablement pension. The 100 per cent assessment contained a wide range of physical conditions, and recipients differed considerably, from those who were completely helpless to others substantially short of that condition. Rather than a modification or extension to the tariff, as had been suggested, the Committee proposed the introduction of a flat-rate allowance. Under the current legislation, this is payable to a claimant who is in receipt of 100 per cent disablement pension together with a constant attendance allowance under categories (3) or (4) above, and 'his need for constant attendance of an extent and nature qualifying him for such an increase' of those standards 'is likely to be permanent'.[11] As with the constant attendance allowance, this condition is determined by the Secretary of State, from whose decision there is no appeal.

The Pearson Commission considered the justification for this allowance to be no different from that of the constant attendance allowance and recommended its abolition.[12] The government, on the other hand, felt that 'there is a continuing case for such a special allowance as an extra provision for a small number of beneficiaries who are worst affected by their industrial injury'.[13] It proposed, therefore, to retain it but to revise the conditions of eligibility so as to link them to receipt of the higher rate of the non-industrial attendance allowance.

Part 8　Miscellaneous

It is appropriate now to consider three miscellaneous matters related to compensation for the consequences of industrial accidents and diseases.

A Death

The Workmen's Compensation Act 1897 made provision for those wholly or partly dependent on the victim of a fatal industrial accident. It took the form of a lump sum, based on the deceased's earnings but subject to a statutory maximum,[14] and, after 1923, a children's allowance.[15] In devising the new scheme in 1944, the government accepted the arguments for industrial death benefit but was not attracted by the lump sum method of compensation.[16] It therefore proposed, and subsequently introduced, a pension analogous to that payable to non-industrial widows: an initial high flat-rate benefit for the first six months, which would then fall to one level if the widow had children

---

9 NIA 1966, s.6.
10 1965, Cmnd 2847.
11 SSA 1975, s.63(7).
12 Para 833.
13 *Reform of the Industrial Injuries Scheme* para 48.
14 WCA 1897, Sch 1, para 1(a)(i).
15 WCA 1923, s.2(a).
16 *Social Insurance Part II* para 30; cf *Beveridge* para 34 (proposal for a lump sum grant to supplement benefits paid under the non-industrial scheme).

to care for or was otherwise deemed incapable of joining the labour market, and another, lower level if she did not come within either of these categories.[17] However, the industrial death benefit was more generous than the general national insurance provisions in a number of respects:[18] the standard widow's pension was paid at a higher rate; a small permanent pension was payable to a childless widow under 40; benefit was paid for children independently of the widow's entitlement (and thus could continue after she had remarried) and also, under highly restrictive conditions,[19] to widowers and other dependants; and a widow could accumulate her pension with income maintenance benefits (e.g. sickness or unemployment benefit).

Support for these particular features of the industrial preference was, however, never strong and successive governments allowed the real value of many of the advantages to be eroded by inflation so that, for example, when the Pearson Commission reviewed the matter in 1978, the standard industrial widow's pension was only 55p higher than that payable under the general scheme. The Commission felt that financial provision for dependants should not vary according to the cause of death and recommended that industrial death benefit be abolished.[20] The government, mindful of the high cost of administering the benefit relative to the marginal advantages it conferred, agreed[1] and the proposal was implemented by the 1986 Act.[2]

Transitional provisions, of course, protect those entitled on the date of abolition (10 April 1988).[3] Moreover, the fact that a death after that date resulted from an industrial accident or disease may still be relevant in a few cases since, in such circumstances, a widow will gain entitlement to appropriate benefits under the general scheme, notwithstanding an insufficient contribution record.[4]

B Conduct of the claimant

The legislation lays down rules governing the conduct of a claimant for two independent purposes. First, as a direct instrument of social policy, it attempts to encourage greater personal safety by refusing benefit should the disability have been incurred in certain circumstances, e.g. through the exclusive fault of the injured person. Secondly, to prevent fraud and abuse, it requires the claimant to satisfy certain standards of conduct after the disability has been incurred.

i Conduct at time of accident
Compensation systems have varied considerably in their willingness to treat certain forms of conduct as a ground for disentitling a claimant from benefit.

---

17 NI(II)A 1946, ss.19–24, reenacted as SSA 1975, ss.67–75, on which see the second edition of this book, pp. 331–336.

18 Though the non-industrial scheme was more generous in its 'scaling' of benefit rates for those widowed between 40 and 50: cf p.242, above.

19 So restrictive that in 1980 only one widower's pension was being paid: *Industrial Injuries Compensation* para 5.26.

20 Paras 835–844. However, somewhat inconsistently, it also suggested that entitlement to the full earnings-related component in the general scheme (p.242, above) should be accelerated for industrial widows. For criticism, see Ogus, Corfield and Harris 7 ILJ 143, 150–151.

1 *Reform of the Industrial Injuries Scheme* ch. 6, following the review in *Industrial Injuries Compensation* ch. 5.

2 SSA 1986, Sch 3, paras 8, 11.

3 Ibid, paras 11, 12, and SSA 1988, Sch 1.

4 SSA 1986 Sch 3, para 10, and SSA 1988, Sch 1.

Under the Workmen's Compensation Acts, the employer would escape liability if the injury was caused by the employee's 'serious and wilful default'.[5] After 1906, however, the doctrine was excluded in cases of serious and permanent disablement.[6] In France, benefit may be reduced for the 'inexcusable fault' of the accident victim.[7] In Germany, it may be reduced or withheld altogether for injuries caused by criminal acts.[8] In most systems there are exclusions for intentional self-injuries.[9] In Britain, there is no explicit rule comparable to these provisions, but, as has been seen, an intentionally inflicted injury will generally not be regarded as an 'accident'.[10] The lack of sanction for other degrees of faulty conduct has not been controversial. The general opinion is that the prospect of a reduced benefit is unlikely to operate as an effective deterrent.[11]

ii Post-accident conduct

The Social Security Act 1975 and regulations made under it impose two sets of obligations relating to conduct after the accident. To facilitate decisions on whether an accident arose 'out of and in the course of employment', as well as, of course, to assist in the administration of health and safety at work legislation, the victim, or someone acting on his behalf, must give notice of the accident 'as soon as is practicable after the happening thereof' to the employer, foreman or safety officer.[12] Secondly, claimants for, and recipients of, disablement benefit must, on receipt of the appropriate notice, submit themselves to a medical examination by the medical authorities or to such medical treatment as is considered appropriate by the medical practitioner in charge of the case or the medical authority which carried out the examination.[13] In the event of non-compliance without reasonable cause with any of these obligations, or if 'the claimant or beneficiary wilfully obstructs, or is guilty of other misconduct in connection with' medical examination or treatment, the adjudication officer may disqualify him from benefit for a period up to a maximum of six weeks.[14] But disqualification cannot be imposed 'for refusal to undergo a surgical operation not being one of a minor character'.[15]

C Workmen's compensation cases

The industrial injuries scheme applies only to accidents occurring or diseases developing on or after 5 July 1948; earlier cases were governed by the Workmen's Compensation Acts. In order, however, to maintain approximate

---

5 WCA 1897, s.1(2)(c).
6 WCA 1906, s.1(2)(c).
7 *Dupeyroux* pp. 535–539.
8 Reichsversicherungsordnung, § 554(1).
9 E.g. New Zealand Accident Compensation Act 1972, s.137; France, Codes des Sécurités Sociales, art 467; Germany, n.8, above, § 503. Cp Report of the National Committee of Inquiry into Compensation and Rehabilitation in Australia (1974), which regarded deliberate self-injury as manifesting mental illness and should not therefore lead to disqualification from benefit (para 351(b)).
10 P.275, above. For the purpose of death benefit, suicide severed the link between the accident and the employment (*R(I) 42/59*) unless the state of mind conducive to the suicidal act was itself the result of the industrial accident or disease: *R(I) 2/57*.
11 *Atiyah* pp. 498–499.
12 SI 1979/628, reg 24.
13 Ibid, reg 26.
14 SI 1982/1408, reg 40(3).
15 Ibid, reg 40(6), and see p.158, above.

equality between beneficiaries under the two schemes, state benefits are available to those with rights of compensation under the old legislation. The numbers involved are small, and, of course, are declining.[16]

i   *Basic allowance*   Under the workmen's compensation legislation, those injured after 1923 were more favourably treated.[17] It was therefore felt desirable to provide a more generous supplement for earlier invalids. For such persons, a small allowance (maximum £2 per week) is payable if on or after 21 March 1951 a claimant is entitled to weekly payments of compensation under the WCAs and he is totally or partially incapacitated for work.[18]

ii   *Major incapacity allowance*   To qualify for this allowance the claimant must be entitled, at any time since 5 July 1956, to the basic allowance or to weekly payments of compensation under WCAs for accidents or diseases occurring after 1923. In addition, as a result of the accident or disease, the claimant must be totally incapable of work and likely to remain so for at least 13 weeks.[19] The amount payable is equivalent to the weekly industrial disablement pension for those assessed at 100 per cent less the weekly amount of any WCA compensation and the basic allowance (if any).[20]

iii   *Lesser incapacity allowance*   This is payable to those who are not entitled to a major incapacity allowance but who are partially or totally incapacitated and who, since 1 March 1966, have been entitled to weekly payments of compensation under WCA for lost earnings.[1] The amount payable is a proportionate part of the lost earnings to a maximum prescribed.

iv   *Additional payments*   The major incapacity allowance only brings WCA recipients up to the level of disablement pensions. Those entitled to WCA payments on or after 5 July 1948 and who are, as a result of the relevant injury or disease, incapable of work and likely to remain so incapable are treated by the legislation as if they were covered by the industrial injuries scheme, for the purposes of entitlement to the allowances which may supplement a disablement pension.[2]

v   *Diseases resulting from pre-1948 employment* . Special provision is also made for those who subsequently became disabled through an industrial disease, but were employed in the prescribed occupation only before 1948.[3] However, the provisions do not extend to all prescribed diseases, but are restricted to those which generally take some considerable time to manifest themselves.[4] The benefits payable are similar to the major and lesser incapacity allowances,[5] to which may be added, in appropriate cases, the supplements and allowances referred to in the previous paragraph.[6]

16 In 1985, 2,613 supplementary allowances were being paid: DHSS Social Security Statistics 1986, Table 23.37.
17 In particular, the Act raised the maximum weekly payment from £1 to £1.50: WCA 1923, s.4(1).
18 IIDA 1975, ss.2(1), 2(3)(a) and 2(3), (7).
19 Ibid, ss.2(1), 2(3)(b), 2(7), 14(4)(a).
20 Ibid, s.2(6)(b).
 1 Ibid, s.2(4).
 2 SSA 1975, s.159 and SI 1982/1408, regs 42–45.
 3 IIDA 1975, s.5.
 4 Ibid, s.5(2), (3).
 5 Ibid, s.7(2).
 6 Ibid, s.7(3).

Chapter 8

War pensions

Part 1 Introduction

A General

War pensions are almost certainly the most ancient type of state benefit. It is said that they existed in classical Greek times,[1] and in Britain their history has been traced back to the days of King Alfred.[2] The first statutory provisions, for payment of benefit to soldiers and sailors from the local rates, can be found in measures at the end of the sixteenth century.[3] Even if attention is confined to the origins of the present system of disability pensions, the story must be started during the nineteenth rather than the twentieth century. The explanation for this rich heritage is not hard to discover: it has generally been thought right to make special provision for those injured, and also for the relatives of those killed, in the service of their country. War pensions are as old as patriotism itself.

In terms of critical analysis and policy discussion, the war pension scheme is the most neglected area of social security law.[4] In recent years, the analogous scheme for industrial injuries has been the subject of a major scrutiny and substantial reform. In 1981, the government indicated that a similar review would be undertaken of war pensions,[5] but this does not appear to have taken place. The unwillingness to disturb the status quo may be due in part to the comparative absence of armed conflict since 1945 and a consequent reduction in the number of pensioners.[6] A second explanation may lie in the peculiarly emotive character of the subject – until recently the special position and privileges of those maimed or killed in the service of their country has not been questioned.[7] Thirdly, it was only in 1978 that the scheme was regulated by statutory instrument and thus became subject to parliamentary scrutiny; traditionally, as part of the Royal Prerogative, it was

1 See the reference to Solon's observation in Plutarch's *Lives* made by Mr J Manders, 401 HC Official Report (5th series) col 1519.
2 39 Halsbury's Laws of England (3rd edn), p.153, n.(d).
3 E.g. 35 Eliz 1 c. 4 (1592–93); 39 Eliz 1 c. 21 (1597–98); 43 Eliz 1 c. 3 (1601).
4 It was ignored in both *Pearson* and the Report on Social Security Provision for Chronically Sick and Disabled People, 1973–74, HC 276.
5 *Reform of the Industrial Injuries Scheme* para 8.
6 In 1986, 275,000 pensions were in payment, compared with over one million in 1950: DHSS *Social Security Statistics 1987* Table 36.30. However, the scheme does cover members of the armed forces injured or killed in the Falklands War and the Ulster 'troubles'.
7 Cf Standing Committee B Debates on the Social Security Benefits Bill 1975, col 145. Cp the extensive literature on the 'industrial preference': n.5, p.254, above.

legally exclusively within the control of the Crown and thus in practice a matter for executive or administrative decision.

In this introductory part of the chapter, there is an outline of the modern history of war pensions and an examination of the reasons for their special position in the social security system. Parts 2 and 3 are respectively concerned with the rules regarding entitlement to, and the assessment of, war pensions. Part 4 deals with those payable on the death of a member of the forces, and Part 5 with some miscellaneous rules. Part 6 discusses very shortly other comparable schemes providing pensions for persons outside the regular forces. Administrative and adjudicatory aspects are dealt with in chapters 15 and 16 respectively.

B History

During the early nineteenth century, the Commissioners of the Chelsea Hospital were responsible for the award of disability pensions to soldiers wounded in combat. From 1846 payment of pensions was made by the Secretary of State for War. There was no provision at this time for widows and children; the first move in this direction was the institution of the Patriotic Fund by voluntary subscription in 1854, under which small pensions might be paid to them.[8] During the later part of the century entitlement to pensions was regulated by the terms of the Royal Warrants in the case of soldiers, and by Orders in Council in the case of navy personnel and marines. The Boer War was responsible for a further development: for the first time, disease attributable to war service was compensated in the same way as physical injury.[9]

War pensions became a crucial problem in the course of the First World War. Many changes were made in the rules concerning entitlement to pensions, and also, and perhaps more importantly, with regard to their administration. In this latter respect these changes have for the most part survived the last 50 years, so that despite the improvements to the system during the Second World War, the years 1914–18 were perhaps the most influential in the development of war pensions.

In 1914, pensions were administered by four authorities: the Chelsea Commissioners, the War Office, the Admiralty Commissioners (for navy pensions) and the Royal Patriotic Fund Corporation.[10] Considerable disquiet was expressed at this dispersal of authority and there was criticism that decisions on entitlement were not subject to any appeal and that no Minister was answerable for them. The mischief suggested its own remedy. Responsibility was transferred to a new Ministry of Pensions.[11] From that time, decisions were taken in the name of the Minister, and shortly afterwards an appeal tribunal was formally constituted.[12] Legislation passed at the end of the First World War established a legal right to receive a war pension, once it had been awarded by the Minister.[13] Before this payments had been discretionary. (It

---

8 The Patriotic Fund was put on a statutory basis by the Patriotic Fund Reorganisation Act 1903.

9 Compare the more cautious treatment of disease in the industrial injuries system, pp. 278–282, above.

10 At this time the Patriotic Fund enjoyed Royal patronage and title, a fact which emphasised the importance of war pensions in popular feeling.

11 Ministry of Pensions Act 1916, s.2.

12 War Pensions (Administrative Provisions) Act 1919, s.8.

13 Ibid, s.7; War Pensions Act 1920, s.8. See also Pensions Appeal Tribunals Act 1943, s.11.

has, however, never been clear whether there is a legal right to the pension, prior to the Minister's decision.) With regard to the conditions of entitlement, the major changes were: a disability aggravated by war service (as distinct from one attributable to service) attracted a full pension instead of the previous four-fifths award; a claim could be made by a widow in respect of the death of her husband which was not in itself attributable to war service, provided that he was then in receipt of a pension.[14] The principal alteration in the rules of assessment made during the same period was that pensions were from then on to be assessed with regard to the degree of *physical disability itself* rather than the loss of earning capacity. This remains the basis of their assessment. Alternative pensions, as they were then known, could be awarded to compensate for the claimant's loss of earning capacity.

Claims for a disability pension in respect of service after 30 September 1921 were transferred back to the Chelsea Commissioners and the other authorities which had administered them in 1914.[15] The outbreak of the Second World War, and the consequent increase in claims, necessitated the retransfer of administration to the Ministry of Pensions, which with its departmental successors (now the DSS) has ever since then remained responsible for war pensions.

From 1939 criticism of the entitlement rules mounted and several changes were made in response. By far the most important was the imposition in some cases of the burden of proof on the Ministry to show that the disablement was neither attributable to, nor aggravated by, service.[16] The claimant was given the benefit of any doubt on this question. It is interesting that a similar relaxation of the law occurred at much the same time in the United States of America.[17] This strong presumption in favour of the claimant is without parallel in the British social security system. Another change enabled claims to be made more than seven years after the termination of the service, though here the claimant has to satisfy an initial evidential burden.[18]

The Royal Warrants issued during this war limited entitlement to injuries due to *war* service. By the Warrant of 1949 pensions could be awarded for disablement occasioned in peace-time service, and, with some qualifications, service in the Territorial and Reserve Forces.[19] Another major development has been the provision of additional benefits for seriously injured servicemen and their dependants. For the most part, these mirrored provisions in the industrial injury scheme but the substantial amendments to that scheme enacted in 1986, including the abolition of lump-sum payments for minor handicaps,[20] have not been followed by equivalent changes in the war pensions scheme. The only significant reform to the latter in recent years took place in 1978. The scheme regulating the benefits for the three services was consolidated in a single Order in Council;[1] and this (together with any amendment) is now issued as a statutory instrument, which must be laid before Parliament.

14 The changes were introduced by the Royal Warrant 1917.
15 War Pensions Act 1920, s.1.
16 Pp. 323–326, below.
17 See Fitzgibbons 31 Iowa L Rev 1 at 13–16.
18 Royal Warrant (RW) 1964 (Cmnd 2467), art 5.
19 RW 1949 (Cmd 6499).
20 P.285, above.
 1 SI 1978/1525.

C Policy

Mention has been made of the privileged position of war pensioners. Not only is there the strong presumption in certain cases that a serviceman suffering from a disability is entitled to a pension, but the level and range of awards is wider than that afforded by other benefits for people suffering from similar disabilities. The most obvious analogy is industrial disablement benefit, which also compensates for mere disability, not necessarily related to loss of earning capacity. War pensions compare favourably with this benefit, however, in the matters of burden of proof, the absence of any requirement that the injury be attributable to an 'accident' as distinct from a continuous process of events,[2] the concept of 'war' or 'service risk' which is wider than that of 'course of employment',[3] and the range of allowances which supplement the basic disablement benefit in the two cases. While the death benefits paid to widows and other dependants under the industrial injury scheme have been abolished, they have been retained at a generous level in the war scheme.

War pensioners also enjoy other advantages. Widow's pensions are exempt from income tax[4] and the estates of those who have died from wounds inflicted during active service are exempt from capital transfer tax.[5] Those leaving the service, and those widowed, after 1973 may derive additional benefits under the Armed Forces Pension scheme introduced in that year.[6] As regards those injured or killed in the Falklands campaign, charitable donations are available from the South Atlantic Fund.[7] Moreover, the system of cash benefits is complemented by a welfare service to help war pensioners and widows with problems. This reflects a general policy of care and concern which is not matched elsewhere in the social security system and which is epitomised in the following statement, made in 1950.

> The award of a pension by the Department entitles the individual to more than merely the payment of a sum of money. It gives him a passport to the goodwill of a large Government Service, to the benefit of a sympathetic interest in his affairs and to such help as may be given or obtained for him in the solving of his problems. It entitles him to believe that nothing which should be his is held back. . . .[8]

Two explanations may be adduced for the traditional preferences given to war pensioners. In the first place, the force of popular sentiment cannot be overestimated. It is this which was responsible for the frequency of parliamentary debates and questions in both wars. In the First World War the facts that the numbers involved were so large, and that frequently the wounded or killed would be conscripts, reinforced the general feeling that those disabled and their families should be generously treated.[9] This political factor has been reinforced by the pressure exerted by the British Legion (now the Royal British Legion) and other ex-servicemen's organisations.

2 Cf for industrial injuries, pp. 258–260, above.
3 Cf pp. 261–278, above.
4 Finance (No 2) Act 1979, s.9.
5 Finance Act 1975, Sch 7, para 7.
6 Brown *The Disability Income System* (1984) p.65; Richardson *Widows Benefits* (1984) pp. 69–70.
7 The 138 women widowed as a result of the campaign each received an average of £40,000 in addition to their war pensions: ibid, pp. 71–72.
8 Annual Report 1949–50 of Ministry of Pensions (1950), p.1, quoted in Brown, n.6, above, p.48.
9 Nothing else would have been compatible with Lloyd George's pledge in 1918 to make 'a fit country for heroes to live in'. For a modern restatement, see Mr R Whitney, Under-Secretary of State for Heath and Social Security, 80 HC Official Report (6th series) col 1118.

The second argument is based on the fact that, as a result of the Crown Proceedings Act 1947, servicemen had, in general, no rights of action in tort against the Crown for injuries sustained during the course of that service,[10] and thus their position was distinguishable from that of employees injured in an industrial accident who might have a tort claim against the employer. The provision has now been repealed,[11] though without retrospective effect, so that only a small number of war pensioners will be able to benefit. Nevertheless, the argument does not seem convincing. It is not obvious why greater state provision should be made for those whose common law rights of action are excluded by special defences, whether statutory or common law, than for those who never have any right at all.

Part 2 Entitlement

A General

The fundamental principle is that under the Service Pensions Order 1983, war pension 'awards may be made where the disablement or death of a member of the armed forces is due to service'.[12] The use of the permissive '*may*' is deliberate and reflects the origins of the scheme in the Royal Prerogative: strictly speaking, and rather anachronistically, the Secretary of State is under no obligation to carry out the provisions of the Order beyond the duty he owes to the Sovereign.[13] However, once an award has been made the claimant has a statutory right to receive it.[14]

There must be some causal connection between the disablement or death and service; it is not enough that either occurred *during* service. The principle was defended by the wartime government on the ground that to treat indiscriminately all disablement arising during service would be to do less than justice to those whose injury or illness was genuinely due to the dangers and risks of service.[15] Given, as we shall see, the more generous criteria of eligibility introduced towards the end of the war and their interpretation by the relevant authorities, the principle is no longer controversial.

Article 4 of the Service Pensions Order sets out the basic conditions for entitlement to a pension on a claim in respect of disablement brought within seven years of the end of the member's service; or when the death of a member occurs within that period, whenever the claim is brought:

> Where, not later than 7 years after the termination of the service of a member of the military forces, a claim is made in respect of a disablement of that member, or the death occurs of that member and a claim is made (at any time) in respect of that death, such disablement or death, as the case may be, shall be accepted as due to service . . . provided it is certified that –
> (a) the disablement is due to an injury which –
>   (i) is attributable to service; or
>   (ii) existed before or arose during service and has been and remains aggravated thereby; or

10 S.10, on which see *Pearce v Secretary of State for Defence* [1988] 2 All ER 348, [1988] 2 WLR 144.
11 Crown Proceedings (Armed Forces) Act 1987, s.1.
12 SI 1983/883, art 3.
13 *Griffin v Lord Advocate* 1950 SC 448 at 450, per Lord Sorn.
14 Pensions Appeal Tribunals Act 1943, s.11.
15 White Paper *Changes in War Pensions* (1943, Cmd 6459).

(b) the death was due to or hastened by –
   (i) an injury which was attributable to service; or
   (ii) the aggravation by service of an injury which existed before or arose during service.

Article 5 is concerned with entitlement when the claim for disablement is brought, or the death occurs, more than seven years after termination of service. The principles governing the issue of a certificate are the same as those in article 4 except in three important respects. The first relates to the burden of proof: for claims under article 5, the onus of proving that the disablement or death was due to service is initially on the serviceman, while under article 4 it is for the Secretary of State to rebut the presumption of this causal link.[16] Secondly, for the purposes of article 5 it must be certified that 'the death was due to or *substantially* hastened by' an injury attributable to or aggravated by service.[17] Thirdly, while both articles cover only cases of disablement attributable to, or aggravated by, service since 2 September 1939,[18] article 5 provides that an award may be made in respect of death more than seven years after the end of service, irrespective of the date of that service.

B Disablement

'Disablement' means physical or mental injury or damage, or the loss of physical or mental capacity.[19] A successful claim may, therefore, be made for acute hysteria or neurosis, provided, of course, that it is attributable to, or aggravated by, service.[20] 'Injury' is defined as including 'wound or disease'.[1] There is virtually no limit, therefore, to the quality or type of impairment which may entitle the claimant to a war pension, though many difficult cases naturally concern claims in respect of illness and disease where the causation issue is complex. As a consequence of the alternative definition of 'disablement', it has been held that a claimant may be entitled in respect of his injury, even though he has not suffered any loss of capacity for work or the enjoyment of life.[2] In this case, however, a nil assessment will be made until the time when the injury causes a loss of flexibility or movement in the injured limb, or some other handicap.

Occasionally the question arises whether a particular disease is a separate phenomenon from another injury or illness for which a claim has already been made.[3] If an acute anxiety state is brought about by worry over a disease, in respect of which a pension is already being paid, the appropriate course is to apply for an increase in the assessment for the first disease, not to make an entirely new claim.[4] The test would appear to be whether the further

16 Pp. 323–325, below.
17 P.325, below.
18 Claims for disablement in the 1914–1918 war, of which there are very few, are brought under the Royal Warrants of 1919 (Cmd 457), and 1920 (Cmd 811).
19 SI 1983/883, Sch 4, Item 22.
20 Cf the more restrictive position under the civilians' scheme, where recovery is limited to personal injuries, p.337, below.
1 SI 1983/883, Sch 4, Item 27.
2 *Harris v Minister of Pensions* [1948] 1 KB 222, [1948] 1 All ER 191.
3 E.g. *Secretary of State for Social Services v Yates* (1969) 5 WPAR 765. (The War Pensions Appeal Reports (WPAR) are available for consultation at the DHSS, though they are not published.)
4 *Goodman JA v Minister of Pensions* (1951) 5 WPAR 13. See 5th Report of the PCA, 1972–73 HC 406, Case No C33/T.

condition is a separate disease rather than part of the accepted illness or injury.

C 'Attributable to service'

i General principles

A war pension will be awarded if it is certified that the disablement or death is due to an injury attributable to service. Before the changes introduced by the Royal Warrant of December 1943, the injury had to be *'directly* attributable to service'; the removal of the qualifying adverb was one of the relaxations introduced by the coalition government to ease the conditions for entitlement under the war pensions schemes.[5] The question whether the injury is attributable to service is one of fact, but the nominated judge will allow an appeal by either the claimant or the Secretary of State if the appeal tribunal has applied the wrong principles of law in arriving at its decision.[6] A tribunal makes a mistake of law if it holds that a particular injury or type of disease cannot be attributable to war service merely because a previous decision of the judge in another case was to the effect that that injury or disease was not then attributable to service.[7] In each case the Secretary of State (or medical board) and, on appeal the tribunal, must consider all the circumstances, and must not be bound by previous decisions regarding the same type of injury.

The court's attitude on questions of attributability has been shown clearly in the 'pre-existing disposition' cases. The particular issue there was whether it should be held that a disease or neurosis was attributable to service when the soldier's pre-existing temperament or disposition made him especially vulnerable to it. The court has consistently held that where service brought on a disease, which did not exist before, it was attributable to the service; only if the soldier's condition before service actually amounted to the illness in question, albeit a latent illness, could it be held that the service merely aggravated the injury.[8] Denning J stated the principle to be as follows:

> The task of the Minister and of the tribunal is to ascertain what are the causes of the arising of the disease, not to assess their relative potency. If one of the causes is war service the disease is attributable to war service, even though there may be other causes and, it may be, more powerful causes, operating, and to which it is also attributable.[9]

The court's refusal to evaluate the relative weight of service and other factors in bringing about the disablement, coupled with the fact that the onus of proof is on the Secretary of State in those cases where the claim is brought, or the death occurs, within seven years of the end of service, has meant that in practice the criteria for entitlement are generous. On the other hand, the court has been aware that the law does not embody the maxim, 'fit for service, fit for pension', so that in a number of circumstances a pension has been

---

5 See the White Paper, n.15, above.

6 *Horsfall v Minister of Pensions* (1944) 1 WPAR 7. Cf pp. 589–590, below.

7 See *Freeman v Minister of Pensions and National Insurance* [1966] 2 All ER 40, [1966] 1 WLR 456 (suicide); *Kincaid v Minister of Pensions* (1948) 2 WPAR 1423 (leukaemia).

8 E.g. *Baird v Minister of Pensions* (1946) 1 WPAR 169; *O'Neill v Minister of Pensions* (1947) 1 WPAR 839. Similar principles have been employed in industrial injuries cases in determining whether an accident caused an injury, to which the claimant's previous condition rendered him more susceptible, p.260, above.

9 *Marshall v Minister of Pensions* [1948] 1 KB 106, 109.

refused although the disability arose during the claimant's period of service. Three types of cases have proved particularly difficult.

ii Anxiety states

In the first, the question has been whether an acute anxiety state was attributable to service. In one decision it was held that the strain of hard training, followed by the worry induced by orders for foreign service, might well be the precipitating cause of the claimant's acute neurosis, although there was medical evidence to the effect that he had an unstable personality.[10] On the other hand, in two cases, the nominated judge, Denning J, held that the claimant's worry about his wife's relations with other men while he was in the army, leading in both cases to acute neurosis, could not be held attributable on the facts to service.[11] The husband's enforced separation from his wife was not the cause, but only the circumstance in which the real cause of the illness, the wife's conduct, operated. It is not easy to reconcile these cases, and the latter two decisions may be thought wrongly decided in the light of Denning J's principle set out earlier.

iii Suicide etc.

The second difficult question is whether suicide can ever be said to be caused by service in the forces. In *XY v Minister of Pensions*,[12]

> the deceased's fiancée attempted to persuade him to marry her while he was on embarkation leave. He refused, and shortly after his return to service, she wrote calling off the engagement; he then shot himself. Denning J held that the tribunal was right not to attribute the death to service.

However, in a more recent decision,[13] it was held that the suicide was so attributable; the deceased took his life because of the pain and anxiety resulting from a disability which was itself due to service. Edmund Davies J emphasised that each case should be decided on its own facts, and that there is no rule of law prohibiting a suicide's dependants claiming a war pension.[14]

iv Claimant on leave, etc.

The third line of cases where causation presents particular problems occurs when the serviceman is injured or killed when on leave, or temporarily away from camp.[15] This has been the topic of political debate as well as legal argument. The 1943 White Paper[16] stated that the Ministry of Pensions would relax its attitude to claims in respect of accidents occasioned outside the

10 *Hollorn v Minister of Pensions* [1947] 1 All ER 124.
11 *W v Minister of Pensions* [1946] 2 All ER 501; *R J v Minister of Pensions* (1947) 1 WPAR 351.
12 [1947] 1 All ER 38, followed in *Miers v Minister of Pensions* (1964) 5 WPAR 673. See also *Wedderspoon v Minister of Pensions* [1947] KB 562 and *Monaghan v Minister of Pensions* (1947) 1 WPAR 971.
13 *Freeman v Minister of Pensions and National Insurance* [1966] 2 All ER 40, [1966] 1 WLR 456.
14 Cf *Jones v Minister of Pensions* [1946] 1 All ER 312, where it was held that the mere fact that the claimant adopted a course of action within his own control – failure to report sick – did not mean that service was not a cause of his illness.
15 There are analogous problems in the industrial injuries scheme, when the accident occurs while the employee is travelling, pp. 266–271, above.
16 Changes in War Pensions (Cmd 6459).

serviceman's place of duty; it would in future treat accidents sustained in the soldier's spare time, or while he was travelling to and from home on short leave, or when he was travelling between his place of duty and privately arranged accommodation (if he were allowed to live out) as attributable to war service. But an injury or illness arising during a period of full leave would not be treated as so attributable. The nominated judge, however, has pointed out that question of attributability must be decided solely on the facts in the light of the legal provisions. Thus, a bicycling accident suffered on the claimant's day-off,[17] and an accident at the claimant's home where, owing to a lack of room in the barracks, he was billetted,[18] have both been held not to be attributable to service. On the other hand, in two cases the judge held that an injury while on full leave was so attributable. In the first,[19] Denning J held that the injury suffered by a soldier who shot himself in the left foot while cleaning his rifle on embarkation leave was attributable to war service; in the second,[20] Ormerod J decided that the appellant shot in the back with a blank cartridge by some cadets on shooting practice was entitled to a pension, although the incident occurred while he was on leave; the decisive fact was that he was required to wear uniform which may have created the impression in the cadets' minds that he was involved in their exercise!

v Miscellaneous cases
The court has had less difficulty in other situations. Injuries occasioned by playing a game for the serviceman's own amusement are not attributable to service,[1] nor are injuries resulting from private fights between soldiers[2] or from assaults by third parties entirely unrelated to the military character of the victim.[3] But even if the initial injury is not attributable to service, negligent treatment in hospital will enable the claimant to be considered for a pension, if he went to that particular hospital because he was a serviceman, rather than merely because it was the nearest available.[4]

vi Critique
It is difficult to detect any clear principle or policy running through these decisions, despite the attempt by the nominated judges, particularly Denning J, to formulate one. On the one hand, they have been concerned to award a pension when the service has any real causal connection with the injury or disease, but on the other hand, they have carefully refrained from holding a claimant entitled merely because the service was a cause (*causa sine qua non*) of the disablement. The case-law sometimes resembles in its apparent inconsistency the decisions of the Commissioners interpreting the 'out of and in the course of employment' test for entitlement to industrial injuries benefit.[5] The absence of such a two-limbed test in the war pensions provisions makes the

---

17 *Standen v Minister of Pensions* (1947) 1 WPAR 905.
18 *Ridley v Minister of Pensions* [1947] 2 All ER 437.
19 *Williams v Minister of Pensions* [1947] 2 All ER 564.
20 *Giles v Minister of Pensions* (1955) 5 WPAR 445.
1 *Horsfall v Minister of Pensions*, n.6 above; cf, on industrial injuries, p.266, above.
2 *Richards v Minister of Pensions* (1956) 5 WPAR 631.
3 *Gaffney v Minister of Pensions* (1952) 5 WPAR 97.
4 *Minister of Pensions v Horsey* [1949] 2 KB 526, [1949] 2 All ER 314. See also *Buxton v Minister of Pensions* (1948) 1 WPAR 1121.
5 See pp. 261–278, above.

reasoning less complex than in the Commissioner's rulings, but the results are often as hard to understand. For example, it is difficult to see why a claimant cleaning his rifle on leave should succeed,[6] while a claimant suffering neurosis about his absent wife when he was actually in service failed.[7] In the last resort the decision will depend on the court's judgment how closely related the injury is to the incidents of service life.

D Aggravated by service

The issue whether the claimant is entitled to a pension because service has aggravated an injury, which is primarily attributable to other causes, only arises if it is first found that his injury was not attributable to service conditions.[8] The difference between an award on the basis of attributability and an award on the basis of aggravation is that in the former case the pension is paid as long as the disability continues, while in the latter, it is payable only so long as the disability remains aggravated by the service conditions.[9]

It must be certified that the disablement is due to an injury which 'has been *and remains aggravated*' by service.[10] The construction of this part of Article 4 was considered in the leading case, *Shipp v Minister of Pensions*.[11] Denning J held that it did not mean that the disablement must be found to be aggravated by service at the time the claim was made, or at the date of the Minister's decision. Such a construction would penalise those who made late claims or whose claims were handled slowly by the Ministry; the words must be read as meaning, 'and remains aggravated or remained aggravated during the period of disablement'.[12] A claim may, therefore, be made in respect of a past disablement. However, where a claim in respect of a disablement is brought under article 5 more than seven years after the end of service, the aggravation must remain at the time the claim is made, though it need not subsist after that date.[13] In this case it is reasonable to require the aggravation to remain at this time in view of the long period which has passed since discharge from service. In all cases the tribunal is entitled to consider whether the aggravation remains at the date of the hearing before it, provided the claimant has been told that the question will be raised.[14]

The judge has held that the Secretary of State and tribunal should be reluctant to conclude that the injury is no longer aggravated by service unless the evidence is quite clear.[15] The reason is that once an award on this basis has been terminated, it cannot be revived. The award should only be terminated if the claimant is in no worse a condition than he was in before the service, or if the disease has progressed to the same extent as it would have done if the man had not been in service.[16] The tribunal may take into account the fact that the claimant is working full-time in coming to its conclusion whether the injury remains aggravated by service.[17]

6 *Williams v Minister of Pensions*, n.19, above.
7 *W v Minister of Pensions*, n.11, above.
8 E.g. *Baird v Minister of Pensions* (1946) 1 WPAR 1121.
9 See Denning J in *Marshall v Minister of Pensions*, n.9, above, at 108.
10 SI 1983/883, art 4(1)(a)(ii).
11 [1946] 1 KB 386.
12 Ibid, at 390.
13 SI 1983/883, art 5(3).
14 *Ansell v Minister of Pensions* (1948) 2 WPAR 2237.
15 *Sanders v Minister of Pensions* (1948) 4 WPAR 31.
16 *Whitt v Minister of Pensions* (1947) 1 WPAR 343.
17 *Collicott v Minister of Pensions* (1948) 3 WPAR 1715.

Rather oddly, aggravation by service may occur before the onset of a disease. Thus, where the serving-man was so weakened by his period of service that he was unable to resist typhoid contracted on leave, his widow was awarded a pension.[18] The reasoning is that the disease, though not attributable to service, was more acute because of his weakened condition. A difficult question arose in *Sullivan v Secretary of State for Social Services*:[19]

> C was discharged in 1962 on the ground of a gastric ulcer attributable to service in respect of which he was awarded a pension. Six years later he claimed a further award on the ground of his anxiety state which arose when he gave up the French horn because of the ulcer. The Secretary of State and tribunal rejected this claim. Willis J concluded it could reasonably be held that C's anxiety state was not attributable to service; but on the alternative argument based on aggravation, the tribunal was wrong to hold that the service factors must cause a deterioration of a condition *before discharge* for an aggravation claim to be made. The aggravation, as in this case, could arise subsequently to the discharge.

As in attributability cases, the problem sometimes arises whether the serviceman's own responsibility for the course of action which leads to the disablement or death precludes a finding that service aggravated the injury. In *Jones v Minister of Pensions*,[20] a hardworking officer with a strong sense of duty refused to report sick. About eighteen months later he died from cancer. Denning J held that the officer's conduct was a reasonable response to the pressures of war service, which was, therefore, responsible for aggravating the disease and so hastening his death.

E Burden of proof

Before 1943 the burden of proof was on the serviceman. The imposition of the burden on the Minister in those cases governed by article 4, where the claim is brought within seven years of the end of service, so that it is for him to show the absence of any connection between service and the injury, was the most important of the reforms made in that year. However, under article 5 an initial burden of proof is on the applicant, so this provision must be considered separately. One point, however, is common to both articles: it is for the applicant to prove that there is a disablement.[1] It is only after this is shown that the cause of the disablement must be considered.

i Claims under article 4
The relevant provisions of article 4 are:

> (2) . . . in no case shall there be an onus on any claimant under this article to prove the fulfilment of the conditions set out in paragraph (1)[2] and the benefit of any reasonable doubt shall be given to the claimant.
>
> (3) . . . where an injury which has led to a member's discharge or death during service was not noted in a medical report made on that member on the commencement of his service, a certificate under paragraph (1) shall be given

18 *Bridge v Minister of Pensions* (1946) 1 WPAR 139.
19 (1971) 5 WPAR 799.
20 [1946] 1 All ER 312.
 1 *Royston v Minister of Pensions* [1948] 1 All ER 778.
 2 See pp. 317–318, above.

unless the evidence shows that the conditions set out in that paragraph are not fulfilled.

a *Article 4(2)*

The judical interpretation of this article has undergone several vicissitudes. The question is whether it imposes on the Secretary of State the general civil burden of proof – to make out his case on the balance of probabilities – or whether it imposes the stricter criminal burden of proof – to show beyond reasonable doubt that the injury was not attributable to, nor aggravated by, service. On a literal construction the latter seems the correct answer, but, as the court has observed,[3] the problem has been complicated by the connected question of the relationship between article 4(2) and article 4(3).

At first both the High Court in England[4] and the Court of Session in Scotland[5] took the view that the burden of proof under article 4(2) was the criminal one. The one difference between article 4(2) and 4(3) was said to be that under the former the issue was to be decided by weighing the evidence adduced by the Minister and the applicant, while under the latter the applicant could rely merely on the presumption.[6] But in *Miller v Minister of Pensions*[7] Denning J held that the burden imposed by article 4(2) was only the ordinary civil one, that is the Minister had to show on a balance of probabilities that injury was not caused by service conditions. In contrast, the judge said that article 4(3) imposed the criminal burden of proof.

The previous position, however, was restored by Edmund Davies J in *Judd v Minister of Pensions*.[8] He stated that the opening words of article 4(2) imposed at least the ordinary civil burden on the Minister, and that the concluding words of the paragraph would be redundant if the burden were no higher than that.

A perennial problem has been the application of the principles of proof where the aetiology of the disease concerned is unknown, and surmises about the part played by service conditions are necessarily conjectural. During the Second World War the Ministry had a list of diseases which, according to the weight of medical opinion, could not be held attributable to war service.[9] It was revised from time to time, and was used as a guide rather than as a determinant of particular applications. Nevertheless, its use was criticised in Parliament, and certainly its employment was outside the legal provisions. The nominated judge has consistently ruled that the evidence must show that it is improbable that the service played any part.[10] The leading authority now is *Coe v Minister of Pensions and National Insurance*.[11]

> C claimed a pension when symptoms of Behcet's syndrome (a disease causing blindness) appeared 14 months after he had left the navy. The claim was rejected by the Minister as the aetiology of the disease was not known, and it seemed improbable that any service factors could have

3 See Edmund Davies J in *Judd v Minister of Pensions* [1966] 2 QB 580 at 591.
4 *Starr v Minister of Pensions* [1946] 1 KB 345, [1946] 1 All ER 400; *Rowing v Minister of Pensions* [1946] 1 All ER 664.
5 *Irving v Minister of Pensions* 1945 SC 21.
6 Denning J, in *Starr v Minister of Pensions*, n.4, above, at 350.
7 [1947] 2 All ER 372.
8 N.3, above.
9 Sir W Wormersley, Minister of Pensions, 391 HC Official Report (5th series) cols 796–798.
10 *Smith AS v Minister of Pensions* (1947) 1 WPAR 495; *Donovan v Minister of Pensions* (1947) 1 WPAR 609.
11 [1967] 1 QB 238, [1966] 3 All ER 172.

been responsible. The appeal tribunal dismissed C's appeal, but Edmund Davies J allowed it on the ground that the approach adopted by the Ministry and tribunal imposed an onus on the applicant.

Three rules were laid down to assist the Minister and tribunals in determining such claims.

(1) If the medical evidence is that nothing at all is known about the aetiology of the disease, then neither the presumption in article 4(2), nor that in article 4(3), is rebutted.
(2) If there is evidence before the tribunal to the effect that the disease is one which arises and progresses independently of service factors, then the presumption is rebuttable even if the precise origins are not known.
(3) It is not enough for the Ministry to argue that there is no evidence suggesting any connection between the onset of the disease and service conditions.

As attributability is a question of fact, there is nothing to prevent tribunals coming to different conclusions on the attributability to service of a particular disease of unknown origin; but they must apply the correct test with regard to the onus of proof.[12]

b *'The compelling presumption' under article 4(3)*
The presumption applies whenever the serviceman is discharged, or dies, because of an injury not noted in the medical report which was made on him at the start of his service. Its effect is that the pension will be awarded, unless it is shown beyond reasonable doubt that the injury was not attributable to, or aggravated by, service.[13] The serviceman who is invalided has the advantage that his case is automatically considered by the Department.[14] There is no need for him (or his dependants if he is killed) formally to apply for a pension. In cases under article 4(3) the nominated judge has held that the tribunal should look at all the facts[15] and it is not bound to accept that the diagnosis which led to the man's discharge was correct.[16]

ii **Claims under article 5**
Paragraph (2) of this article provides that where a claim is brought, or the death occurs, more than seven years after the end of service, the disablement or death shall only be certified as due to, or substantially hastened by, service if 'it is shown that the conditions' set out in the article are fulfilled. Paragraph (4) states that where on reliable evidence a reasonable doubt exists whether they are fulfilled, the benefit of that doubt should be given to the claimant. The leading case is *Dickinson v Minister of Pensions*[17] construing the identical provisions in the 1949 Royal Warrant.

A widow claimed that her husband's death from a coronary was substantially hastened by worry brought on by neurasthenia which in its turn had been aggravated by war service. The Ministry and tribunal dismissed her claim as she had not produced sufficient reliable evidence in its support. Ormerod J upheld the tribunal's approach.

12 Ibid, at 243.
13 *Birchenough v Minister of Pensions* (1949) 3 WPAR 635.
14 See Ministerial Statement, 401 HC Official Report (5th series) col 970.
15 *Trroughear v Minister of Pensions* (1947) 1 WPAR 569.
16 *Hayden v Minister of Pensions* (1947) 1 WPAR 775.
17 *Dickinson v Minister of Pensions* [1953] 1 QB 228, [1952] 2 All ER 1031.

The clear words of article 5(2) supported the general principle that it is for an applicant to make out his claim. Only when a tribunal has found that enough reliable evidence has been adduced in support of the application, is it bound under article 5(4) to give the benefit of any reasonable doubt to the claimant. This decision has been followed in England by the nominated judge in a case[18] arising under the equivalent provisions in the civilians' scheme and in a Scottish case on the services' scheme[19] The *Dickinson* case seems correct as a matter of interpretation of the provisions in the Pensions Order. It is also, it is submitted, right that where a claim is brought (or the death occurs) as long as seven years after the termination of the service, the claimant should be required to adduce some evidence that the disablement or death was connected with service in the forces.

F Serious negligence or misconduct

Article 6 provides that the Secretary of State may withhold, cancel or reduce an award on the ground that the injury or death 'was caused or contributed to, by the serious negligence or misconduct' of the serviceman. There is surprisingly little case-law on this provision, nor is there any indication how the responsible minister has applied his discretionary power. The two leading cases are both decisions of Ormerod J. In the first,[20] 'serious negligence' was defined 'as negligence of a quality that would certainly call for some criminal action if it were done in civil life'. However, shortly afterwards the judge said this remark was only obiter, and should be related to the particular facts of this case, in which the alleged 'serious negligence or misconduct' consisted in the careless riding of a motor-cycle. In the second case,[1] he, therefore, allowed the Minister's appeal and ruled that the applicant was guilty of serious negligence or misconduct in disobeying an order not to handle enemy ammunition.

It is possible to infer from the comparative dearth of reported decisions that article 6 has rarely been invoked; this may be because the view is taken that it should only apply in extreme circumstances. As in the industrial injuries system, it is clear that the common law test of contributory negligence has no place in the war pensions scheme. But the latter differs from industrial injuries in providing that 'serious negligence or misconduct' may as such debar recovery.[2] In both systems wrongful conduct may lead to a ruling that the injury was not due to the employment or service.[3] Outside the situation where there is deliberate disobedience to orders it is hard to think of circumstances where the application of article 6 is necessary or appropriate.

18 *Cadney v Minister of Pensions and National Insurance* [1965] 3 All ER 809, [1966] 1 WLR 80.
19 *Minister of Social Security v Connolly* 1967 SLT 121.
20 *Robertson v Minister of Pensions* (1952) 5 WPAR 245, 266.
 1 *Minister of Pensions v Griscti* (1955) 5 WPAR 457. This approach is consonant with that of Denning J in *Williams v Minister of Pensions* [1947] 2 All ER 564, where the case was sent back to the tribunal to consider whether the applicant, in shooting himself in the foot, had been guilty of serious negligence or misconduct.
 2 It has been suggested that inclusion of the 'serious negligence or misconduct' rule in the war pensions scheme may reflect the higher value placed on discipline in the armed services: Brown *The Disability Income System* (1984) p.51.
 3 Pp. 275–321, above.

Part 3   Awards for disablement

War pensions for disablement are payable only after the termination of service.[4] They consist of a basic award, assessed according to the degree of disablement, and a variety of allowances covering dependants, losses to earning capacity of, and the needs of, the more seriously disabled. Without parallel in the social security system, there are differences of treatment according to the rank of the serviceman.[5] Some of these are purely formal: pensions payable to officers are described as 'retired pay'; and this and other allowances for officers are expressed in annual sums and paid either monthly or quarterly, while those for other ranks are expressed and paid weekly. However, more substantially, a component in the basic award is also varied according to rank and this is not intended to reflect earning differentials for which, as has been mentioned, there is separate provision. In the light of current social values, these aspects of the scheme must appear to be anachronistic and it is no doubt for this reason that successive governments have not increased the component since 1964.

A The basic award

The principles for assessing the basic award are in almost all material respects identical to those adopted by the industrial scheme; these have been fully analysed in chapter 7.[6] The degree of disablement is determined by comparing the condition of the disabled person with 'the condition of a normal healthy person of the same age and sex, without taking into account the earning capacity of the member in his disabled condition in his own or any other specific trade or occupation, and without taking into account the effect of any individual factors or extraneous circumstances'.[7] This is then expressed as a percentage, total disablement being represented by 100 per cent. A schedule to the Pensions Order sets out assessments for some particular injuries in the same form as is adopted for the industrial injuries scheme;[8] in other cases, the appropriate percentage is determined by the Secretary of State (in practice a medical officer or board of officers appointed by him) or on appeal by a pensions appeal tribunal.[9] Where the serviceman's condition has not stabilised, the assessment is made on an interim basis,[10] and may be revised where there is a subsequent change in the degree of disablement due to service.[11] A final assessment may be increased, but not reduced, in similar circumstances.[12]

A pension is payable for degrees of disablement between 100 per cent and 20 per cent inclusive.[13] Awards for disablement of less than 20 per cent are paid as lump-sum gratuities.[14] These provisions are different from those now

4 SI 1983/883, art 8(2). In the case of an officer it is payable when he ceases to be on the Active List.
5 The complex rules for determining the relevant rank of a member of the forces for war pension purposes are set out ibid, art 7.
6 Pp. 286–291, above.
7 SI 1983/883, art 9(2)(a).
8 Ibid, Sch 1, Parts III, V, as amended.
9 Pensions Appeal Tribunals Act 1943, Sch, para 3.
10 SI 1983/883, art 9(2)(d).
11 Ibid, art 67.
12 Ibid.
13 Ibid, art 10.
14 Ibid, art 11.

applicable to the industrial injuries scheme under which the gratuity has been abolished and pensions are payable on assessments of 14 per cent and above.[15] The basic war pension awards are supplemented by the rank additions: e.g. for a 100 per cent pension, a Rear-Admiral receives an additional annual sum of £270 and a corporal the weekly sum of £0.17.

B Increases and additions

A variety of supplementary allowances may be paid with the basic award. While these are in many respects similar to those available under the industrial injury scheme, there are significant differences, especially following the recent legislative amendments to the latter.

i Allowances for member of the claimant's family

a *General allowance for dependants*
The payment of dependency allowances irrespective of the claimant's earning capacity and of general social security entitlement is now regarded as anomalous and the sums awarded for a spouse, partner or eldest child are derisory: a proportionate part of £0.60 per week, according to the degree of the claimant's disablement.[16] A more detailed account seems therefore to be unnecessary.[17]

b *Education allowance*
This may be paid subject to certain prescribed conditions, most importantly, that the child must be at least five, that the circumstances of the family must be such as to require the extra payment, and that the Secretary of State is satisfied that the type of education concerned is suitable.[18] The amount of the supplement is determined by him, subject to a maximum.

ii Reduced earning capacity allowances

This second group of supplementary payments is designed to compensate the war pensioner for the reduced opportunities for earning which he suffers owing to his disabilities. To some extent, they counterbalance the inflexibility of the basic award, which, does not take into account loss of, or reduced, earning capacity.[19]

a *Unemployability allowance*
This provides an equivalent to the general social security invalidity pension for a claimant who does not qualify for that benefit but whose disablement is 'so serious as to make him unemployable'.[20] He may be deemed unemployable even though he has earnings below a prescribed threshold.[1] If over pensionable age, the claimant must show that, on reaching that age, he was unemployable by reason of pensioned disablement and, in any event, the

15 Pp. 285–286, above.
16 SI 1983/883, art 12.
17 Cf the second edition of this book, p.354.
18 SI 1983/883, art 13.
19 For a further discussion of this point, see pp. 293–294, above, in the context of industrial injuries.
20 SI 1983/883, art 18(1).
 1 Ibid, art 18(2).

allowance may not be accumulated with the basic component of a retirement pension.[2] In addition to the personal allowance, increases may also be payable for one adult dependant and any child dependants.[3]

b *Invalidity allowance*
Those entitled to the unemployability allowance may also receive a further payment equivalent to the invalidity allowance, payable under the general social security scheme.[4] The principles of entitlement and the amounts payable are identical and reference should be made to the account given in chapter 4.[5]

c *Allowance for lowered standard of occupation*
This allowance, is equivalent to the reduced earnings allowance available under the industrial injuries scheme.[6] The grounds of entitlement are virtually identical,[7] though in the case of a war pensioner his present earning capacity is generally compared with his regular occupation before he entered military service.[8] The allowance, when combined with the pension, may not exceed that payable for 100 per cent disablement,[9] and is in any event subject to a prescribed maximum. Those over pensionable age must have satisfied the relevant conditions on the date when that age was reached.[10]

iii Serious disablement allowances
This third group comprises a variety of further allowances which may be conferred in cases of serious disablement.

a *Constant attendance allowance*
This may be awarded in respect of a pensioned disablement, the degree of which is not less than 80 per cent, if it is shown to the Secretary of State's satisfaction that constant attendance is necessary because of the disablement.[11] There are two rates at which the allowance may be paid, compared with four in the similar provision in the industrial injuries scheme.[12]

b *Severe disablement occupational allowance*
Article 16 provides that a pensioner in receipt of the higher rate of constant attendance allowance may also receive this further allowance, 'for any period during which he is . . . ordinarily employed in a gainful occupation'. The object of this provision appears to be to compensate the exceptionally severely disabled pensioner who nevertheless is able to pursue an occupation. There is no parallel benefit in the industrial injuries system.

---

2 Ibid, art 18(2A)–(3).
3 Ibid, art 18(5).
4 Ibid, art 9.
5 P.144, above.
6 Pp. 293–306, above.
7 SI 1983/883, art 21, as amended by SI 1985/1201, which, however, does not provide for the alternative 'continuing condition' described at pp. 300–302, nor for the index-linking assessment principle (p.305).
8 SI 1983/883, art 21(2)(c), as amended.
9 Ibid, art 21(1). Cf the industrial scheme where the maximum has been raised to 140 per cent: p.306, above.
10 SI 1983/883, art 21(1A).
11 Ibid, art 14.
12 Pp. 307–308, above.

c *Exceptionally severe disablement allowance*

This was introduced, as was the equivalent provision in the industrial injuries system,[13] following the recommendations of the McCorquodale Committee on Assessment of Disablement.[14] It will be paid when the disablement is, and is in the Secretary of State's view likely to remain, one for which the higher rate of constant attendance allowance is payable, or would be if the serviceman were not in a hospital or other institution.[15] As with the industrial injuries supplement, entitlement is, therefore, geared to eligibility for the constant attendance allowance; however, it does not appear to depend on the pensioner's receipt of a 100 per cent disablement benefit.[16]

d *Treatment allowances*

A pensioner receiving medical treatment may claim an allowance equal to the 100 per cent disablement pension, but in lieu of the pension (at whatever rate) payable to him.[17] 'Treatment' is defined as 'a course of medical, surgical or rehabilitative treatment', which the Secretary of State is satisfied the pensioner should receive.[18] It excludes treatment which involves only an occasional interruption in the pensioner's normal work, or, in the case of an unemployed pensioner, would have had such consequences if he had been normally employed. In these situations a part-time treatment allowance is payable.[19] In certain cases, increases may be paid for an adult dependant,[20] or where the pensioner has reached 65.[1] The allowance itself may be paid for a discretionary period when treatment as an in-patient at a hospital has been completed but the pensioner is still incapable of work.[2] Finally, the Secretary of State has a broad discretion to indemnify the claimant for 'any necessary expenses in respect of the medical, surgical or rehabilitative treatment . . . and of appropriate aids and adaptations for disabled living' where these are not provided under any other legislative scheme.[3]

e *Mobility supplement*

The general policy issues regarding assistance for disabled persons with limited mobility have been discussed in chapter 4.[4] In 1983, it was decided to introduce a special allowance for war pensioners which might complement that available under general social security provisions. Entitlement is based on proof that the disablement for which the pension is payable satisfies one of three alternative conditions:[5]

(1) it results from amputation of both legs (and in the case of one leg, through or above the knee);
    or
(2) it results from another injury which is wholly or mainly responsible for

    (i)   rendering him unable to walk, or

13 P.309, above.
14 Committee on the Assessment of Disablement (1965, Cmnd 2647), para 9.
15 SI 1983/883, art 15.
16 Cf p.308, above.
17 SI 1983/883, art 23(1)–(4).
18 Ibid, art 23(6).
19 Ibid, arts 23(6)–(6A) and 25.
20 Ibid, art 23(4).
 1 Ibid, art 23(3).
 2 Ibid, art 24, provided he is not in receipt of an unemployability supplement.
 3 Ibid, art 26.
 4 Pp. 171–173, above.
 5 SI 1983/883, art 26A, as amended.

(ii) restricting his leg movements to such an extent that his ability to walk without severe discomfort is of little or no practical use to him, or

(iii) restricting by physical pain or breathlessness his ability to walk to such an extent that it is of little or no practical use to him, or

(iv) rendering the exertion required to walk a danger to his life or a likely cause of serious deterioration in his health;[6]

or

(3) immediately prior to the date of claim, it had been such as to entitle him to the use of an invalid carriage, a grant towards the cost of running a private car (or analogous payment), or a mobility allowance payable under the Social Security Act 1975.

A pensioner may accumulate a mobility supplement with a mobility allowance payable under the general scheme, but the supplement is not paid during periods when the pensioner makes use of an invalid carriage.[7]

f *Comforts allowance*

This supplement, like the following two, is without an equivalent in the industrial injuries and general social security schemes. It may be awarded where the claimant is in receipt of a constant attendance allowance, and *either* an employability allowance *or* a 100 per cent basic award from multiple injuries which, in the Secretary of State's view, are so serious as to justify the award of a comforts allowances.[8] A lower rate of comforts allowance is payable to a pensioner who is in receipt of either the constant attendance allowance or the unemployability allowance.[9]

g *Allowance for wear and tear of clothing*

This is generally awarded to a pensioner who regularly wears an artificial limb.[10] Where one artificial limb is worn, the allowance is paid at a lower rate. A higher rate is payable where more than one such limb is worn, or the Secretary of State is satisfied that the wear and tear on the pensioner's clothing as a result of the disablement is exceptional.

h *Age allowance*

A supplement is paid to pensioners over 65 with a disablement assessed at 40 per cent or over.[11] This is paid at four different rates for degrees of pensioned disablement of, respectively, 40–50 per cent, 50–70 per cent, 70–90 per cent, and 90–100 per cent.

Part 4   Awards in respect of death

A General

Awards may be made in respect of a death of a member of the forces which is due to service.[12] As with claims by disabled members of the forces, the

---

6 These criteria are similar, but not identical, to those used for the mobility allowance payable under SSA 1975, s.37A: see pp. 173–175, above.
7 SI 1983/883, art 26A(3), as amended.
8 Ibid, art 20(1)(a).
9 Ibid, art 20(1)(b).
10 Ibid, art 17(1)(a).
11 Ibid, art 22.
12 Ibid, art 27(1).

conditions of entitlement depend on the date of the material event; in this case, however, they vary according to whether the *death* (rather than the claim in respect of that death) occurs less or more than seven years after the termination of service. If the death occurs not later than seven years after this, the death is to be accepted as due to service, provided it is certified that it was 'due to or hastened by *either* an injury attributable to service, *or* the aggravation by service of an injury which existed before or arose during service'.[13] Where the death occurs more than seven years after service, it must be certified that it was due to, or *substantially* hastened by, an injury attributable to, or aggravated by, service.[14]

The general condition that death must be due to service is more restrictive than the approach which obtained in the First World War. Then a widow might receive what was termed a 'modified pension' (half the husband's pension) if he was in receipt of a war pension at the date of his death, even though the death itself was not caused by his war service. This provision seems to have been unique to the British war pensions scheme.[15] Awards of this type were not made after 1921. But there have been two modifications to the general position, though in the first case only for the benefit of widows, and not for all dependants. Since 1966 a temporary allowance has been payable for 26 weeks to the widow, or unmarried dependant who has lived as the wife of a severely disabled pensioner, whatever the cause of his death.[16] It is payable whenever the member of the forces was in receipt of a constant attendance or an unemployability allowance, or in a case where though eligible for the latter, he was in fact in receipt of the lowered standard of occupation allowance.[17] Additional allowances may be paid for this period for the serviceman's children. The second change provides that the death of a member of the forces in receipt of a constant attendance allowance (or one who would have been in receipt of this allowance if he had not been in hospital) is to be treated as due to service for the purposes of awards on his death.[18]

B Widows

There are two basic rates for widows' pensions. The higher rate is paid where the widow is not expected to join or rejoin the labour market: where she is over 40, or is in receipt of an allowance for the child of the deceased, or is incapable of self-support.[19] In other cases, the lower rate is paid.[20] As with disablement pensions, there are additions based on the deceased's rank,[1] but here the status differentials are taken even further, for the widows of the highest ranking officers (in the army, Lieutenant-Colonel and above) are always paid at the higher rate, whatever their age and family commitments.

---

13 Ibid, art 4(1)(b). See pp. 314–323, above, for 'attributable to' and 'aggravated by' service.
14 SI 1983/883, art 5(1)(b).
15 See Comparative Tables of War Pension Rates in Allied Countries and Germany during Great War (1920, Cmd 474).
16 SI 1983/883, art 33.
17 A person in receipt of the allowance for lowered standard of occupation may prefer not to apply for the unemployability allowance because of the loss of concurrent social security benefits.
18 SI 1983/883, art 27(3).
19 Ibid, art 29(1)(a). Cf the age threshold and reduced rates applied to widow's pensions under the general social security scheme: pp. 241–242, above.
20 SI 1983/883, art 29(1)(b).
 1 Ibid, Sch 2, Part II, Tables 2 and 4, as amended.

Clearly it is regarded as socially inappropriate for such widows to earn their livelihood!

A widow was formerly only entitled if she was living with the deceased at the date of his death or if the Secretary of State took the view that the separation was attributable to the soldier's mental instability. But this restriction was removed by the Royal Warrant of 1974.[2] A frequent source of controversy during the Second World War was the question whether pensions should only be paid to widows who had married the deceased before his disability arose. It was not until 1946 that the present position was reached that the date of marriage is irrelevant.[3]

An unmarried dependant who has been living as a wife of the member of the forces[4] may be awarded a pension on his death, as long as she has in her charge his child and is in receipt of a child allowance.[5] The amount of this pension is at the discretion of the Secretary of State, subject to a prescribed maximum. A supplementary rent allowance may be paid to a widow, or an unmarried dependant, who has lived as a wife, provided the household includes a child. A further allowance is paid to some widows of 65, and then at a higher level when they reach 70.[6]

These benefits cease on the remarriage or cohabitation of the widow (or other recipient).[7] Another feature of the status differential between officers and other ranks emerges at this point. On remarriage, the Secretary of State may award to widows of the latter a gratuity equal to one year's pension.[8] There is no such provision for officers' widows, but they may be more favourably placed in that on the death of the husband of the remarriage, the Secretary may at his discretion restore the lost pension. The Secretary of State has discretion to restore the widow's pension on termination of a period of cohabitation.[9]

C Widowers

A widower may be awarded a pension, where he was dependent on a female member of the armed forces, and is in pecuniary need and incapable of self-support.[10] The rate is at the discretion of the Secretary of State, subject to a prescribed maximum.

D Children

An allowance is payable for a child of the deceased if he is under 16, or an apprentice, or in full-time education, or incapable of self-support by reason of an infirmity which arose before he attained 16.[11] The amount is increased if

2 Cmnd 5670, art 4.
3 RW 1946 (Cmd 6799).
4 See SI 1983/883, Sch 3, Item 51.
5 Ibid, art 30.
6 Ibid, art 32.
7 Ibid, art 42.
8 Ibid, art 42(4).
9 Ibid, art 42(3). Widows' benefits under the Social Security Act 1975 are automatically paid on the termination of cohabitation, for they are only suspended when this begins: p.239, above.
10 SI 1983/883, art 34.
11 Ibid, arts 35, 37.

the child is under 16 and is not under the control of the surviving parent.[12] Further, an education allowance may be payable in the same circumstances, and subject to the same maximum, as those which obtain when a disabled serviceman claims this benefit.[13]

E Parents and other relatives

Allowances for parents were paid as a matter of course for deaths occurring during the First World War. Despite constant pressure in the House of Commons for equivalent provision,[14] the instruments governing military service during the Second World War and afterwards have imposed very restrictive conditions on entitlement to such awards, in particular that the parent must be 'in pecuniary need by reason of having reached the age of not less than 65 years in the case of a man, or 60 years in the case of a woman, or of infirmity or other adverse condition which is not merely of a temporary character'.[15] Moreover, the sums payable, between £0.25 and £1.00 per week, have not been altered since 1949.

Awards to other relatives are also now only trivial (a maximum of £1.00 per week for one adult and £0.30 per week for children under 16). The relative must have been dependent on the deceased, in pecuniary need and incapable of self-support.[16]

Part 5   General miscellaneous provisions

A Overlap provisions

The object of these provisions is to prevent over compensation from public funds or from a combination of these funds and a damages award. Article 55 provides that the Secretary of State may take into account any other compensation which is, or may be, awarded a claimant and may withhold or reduce the pension or gratuity accordingly. Compensation which might have been obtained but for the unreasonable act or omission of the claimant may also be taken into account for this purpose. 'Compensation' means any periodical or lump sum payment in respect of death or disability for which provision is made under any statute, ordinance, regulation or scheme, or any sum recoverable as damages at common law.[17] A similar rule applies to children who are provided for from public funds.[18] Another overlap measure enables a deduction to be made from a pension or gratuity where the claimant is being cared for in an institution which is supported by public funds, though this does not apply where he has entered it for the purpose of receiving medical or surgical treatment.[19] The pensions of servicemen entering Chelsea Hospital are terminated, but may be restored on departure from it.[20]

---

12 Ibid, arts 35(3), 36.
13 Ibid, art 38; see p.328, above.
14 387 HC Official Report (5th series) col 1511; 391, ibid, col 764; 433 ibid, col 159. See 1st Report of the PCA for 1975–76, HC 37, Case No C 291/V.
15 SI 1983/883, art 40(1).
16 Ibid, art 41.
17 Ibid, art 55(3).
18 Ibid, art 58.
19 For the position where the pensioner is receiving medical treatment, see p.330, above.
20 SI 1983/883, art 57.

B Forfeiture provisions

The Secretary of State may withhold, or direct the forfeiture of, a pension on the ground that the person to, or in respect of whom, it has been awarded is serving a term of imprisonment or detention after a court order, or is deported from or required to leave the United Kingdom.[1] A forfeited pension may be restored upon terms imposed by the Secretary of State. The rule discussed in Part 4 under which a widow's pension may be terminated on remarriage or cohabitation is, of course, tantamount to a forfeiture provision.[2]

There are two other provisions analogous to forfeiture rules. Under the first, the Secretary of State may reduce a pension by not more than half, if the claimant refuses unreasonably to undergo medical, surgical or rehabilitative treatment.[3] Secondly, an award may be cancelled if a pension is not drawn for a continuous period of a year or more.[4]

C Commencing date of awards

The general principle is that awards are payable only from the date of claim.[5] However, in recent years, provision has been made for back payments in certain circumstances. First, payments can be made from the day after the termination of service if this was due to invaliding and it occurred not more than six months before the claim; where the termination does not result from invaliding, this earlier date applies only if the claim is brought within three months.[6] Secondly, where a successful application has been made for review of a decision (e.g. that a particular disablement did not result from military service), awards may be backdated for a maximum period of six years prior to that application.[7] More generally, the Secretary of State has power to direct an earlier payment 'to any particular case or class of case'. His policy has generally been to do this only where there is substantial evidence that the serviceman was prevented from claiming earlier because of mental or physical disability, or it is clear that there has been some error in processing the claim.[8] In one situation, consequent upon a special report by the Parliamentary Commissioner, the DHSS made a direction back-dating awards in a class of cases not covered by this general rule. After the *Judd* decision,[9] the Department decided it would review any claim which had previously been rejected on the basis of the earlier rules with regard to the burden of proof. The DHSS accepted the Parliamentary Commissioner's recommendation that where a claim was accepted, payments should be made from 4 October 1965 (the date of the *Judd* judgment) rather than from the date when the revision was made.[10] Otherwise, the date of payment would have depended arbitrarily on the order in which the DHSS reviewed the claims.

1 Ibid, art 62; cf under SSA 1975, pp. 368–370, below.
2 See p.333, above.
3 SI 1983/883, art 63: cf p.158, above.
4 SI 1983/883, art 64.
5 Ibid, Sch 3, para 1(a)(iii).
6 Ibid, para 1(a)(i)–(ii).
7 Ibid, paras 2–3.
8 See Parliamentary Commissioner Case No C5 36/L, Annual Report for 1970, 1970–71 HC 261. See also his 4th Report for 1977–78, HC 312, where he is highly critical of the DHSS 'deceitfully withholding' arrears of an element in the pension which through error had not been paid.
9 P.324, above.
10 2nd Report of the PCA for 1970, 1970–71 HC, 507 (Report on Captain Horsley's Claim).

Part 6   Other war pension and civilian schemes

There are a number of schemes similar to the war pensions scheme providing pensions for those outside the regular armed forces who are injured in war service. The conditions of entitlement are on the whole more restrictive in these schemes, due to the fact that for members of the forces pensionable disablement can result from any aspect of service, whereas for civilians the disablement must be related specifically to the effects of war. They have been less liberally construed by the nominated judge than the equivalent requirements in the Service Pensions Order. One reason for this was that often the effect of allowing a claim by a merchant mariner or civilian for a pension was to debar him from pursuing his remedy under the workmen's compensation legislation or at common law.[11] In other respects, for example, on the questions of causation and burden of proof, authorities on the construction of these schemes have followed cases on the armed forces provisions[12] and in their turn they have been cited in war pensions cases.[13] There are two principal types of scheme, neither of which is of much practical importance now.

i   Schemes for mariners and other seafaring persons

Under the Pensions (Navy, Army, Air Force and Mercantile Marine) Act 1939, as amended by the Pensions (Mercantile Marine) Act 1942, the Secretary of State may make schemes for the benefit of merchant marines and other seafaring persons who have suffered war injuries, war risk injuries, or have incurred disabilities from certain other specified causes. There are a number of such schemes,[14] administered in much the same way as war pensions; there is a right of appeal from the initial decision in the DSS to a pensions appeal tribunal.[15] The concepts of 'war injury' and 'war risk injury' have been more narrowly developed than the notion of 'injury attributable to service' in the Pensions Order: for example, a merchant mariner injured by equipment which was not normally kept on board ship during peace-time was held not to have incurred a 'war risk injury'.[16]

ii   Civilian Injuries' Scheme

Under the Personal Injuries (Civilians) Scheme 1983,[17] made under the Personal Injuries (Emergency Provisions) Act 1939, a civilian may receive a pension for disablement or incapacity due to a 'war injury', or in the case of a civil defence volunteer a 'war service injury', in both cases sustained between 3 September 1939 and 19 March 1946. 'War service injury' and 'war injury' are both defined in the 1939 Act, the latter being accorded the same definition as in the Pensions (Navy, Army, Air Force and Mercantile Marine) Act of 1939. An appeal lies from the Secretary of State's decision to a pensions

11 See Tucker J in *Re Kemp* [1945] 1 All ER 571, discussing Personal Injuries (Emergency Provisions) Act 1939, s.3.

12 E.g. *Cadney v Minister of Pensions and National Insurance* [1965] 3 All ER 809, [1966] 1 WLR 80; see p.326, above.

13 *Minister of Pensions v Chennell* [1947] KB 250 has been an influential authority on problems of causation in the war pensions area.

14 E.g. the War Pensions (Naval Auxiliary Personnel) Scheme 1946 (SI 1964/1985); the War Pensions (Mercantile Marine) Scheme 1964 (SI 1964/2058).

15 See Pensions Appeal Tribunals Act 1943, s.2.

16 *Douglass v Minister of Pensions* (1952) 5 WPAR 85; also see *Cook v Minister of Pensions* (1948) 1 WPAR 1223.

17 SI 1983/686, as amended.

appeal tribunal.[18] The nominated judge seems to have adopted a restrictive approach when the claimant has suffered mental shock or hysteria at the sight of war damage. The definitions in the 1939 Act of both 'war injury' and 'war service injury' refer to '*physical* injury', and Tucker J has held that this excludes mental shock, in contradistinction to the position under the armed forces' scheme where 'disablement' is defined to mean 'physical or mental injury or damage'.[19]

A 'war service injury' must have arisen out of and in the course of the performance by the volunteer of his civil defence duties and, therefore, an injury sustained while bicycling to his place of duty did not entitle a defence worker to recover a pension.[20] In an important ruling, often followed in cases under the services' scheme, it was held that a 'war injury' was caused by the discharge of a missile, even though it was a few days before it was carelessly picked up and tampered with by a small boy, resulting in injury to the claimant.[1] The discharge of the missile was not too remote for it to be regarded as the cause of the injury and so a pension was awarded.

18 Pensions Appeal Tribunals Act 1943, s.3.
19 *Young v Minister of Pensions* [1944] 2 All ER 308 ('war injury'); *Ex parte Haines* [1945] KB 183, [1945] 1 All ER 349, and *Re Drake* [1945] 1 All ER 576 ('war service injury'): see p.318, above.
20 *Davis v Minister of Pensions* [1951] 2 All ER 318.
 1 *Minister of Pensions v Chennell*, n.13, above.

Chapter 9

General provisions

In this chapter we consider a number of issues and concepts which are common to several or all of the benefits payable under the Social Security Act 1975 (viz those discussed in chapters 3 to 7). The principles to be described are themselves primarily drawn from that Act and, as a matter of law, do not govern war pensions, child benefit, family credit, income support, housing benefit and the social fund unless, and to the extent that, they are specifically adopted in the legislation concerned with the latter schemes. In practice, however, where there is no reason to adopt a different interpretation, the provisions of the Social Security Act, as developed by the Commissioners' decisions, may properly act as guidelines for the administration of those areas of social security law which are not governed by that Act. This applies particularly to the meaning attributed to such concepts as 'marriage', 'living together as husband and wife', 'residence', 'presence', 'imprisonment' and 'detention in legal custody'.

Part 1   Increases for dependants

A   General

The principle that special allowance should be made for persons dependent on the claimant was, of course, recognised from the beginning as regards benefits which were means-tested. Family support is without doubt the most significant differential in assessing an individual's need. For those benefits governed wholly or partly by the contributory principle such provision is not so obvious but is readily acceptable. If the benefit is intended to provide a minimum standard of living for the claimant, then regard should be had to his family needs, even though, in the absence of a family-weighted contribution, this will mean that those without family obligations will be subsidising those with them. Such a policy has occupied a central position in the British tradition of social security because of its reluctance to be committed to an earnings-related principle of income maintenance. Nevertheless, in recent years, the policy has been undermined by the government's concern for work disincentives which it considers may arise if the level of family support for those without gainful employment is too high.[1]

---

1 This is sometimes expressed in terms of being 'even-handed' to those in and out of work: cf Mr N Fowler, Secretary of State, 44 HC Official Report (6th series) col 167.

Indeed, in general, the history of dependency provision has been far from consistent. Before the Second World War, it was incorporated in various benefit schemes only gradually and somewhat haphazardly. It was added to the unemployment insurance scheme in 1921 on a temporary basis to relieve 'winter hardships',[2] but in the next year was made permanent.[3] Remarkably, additions for dependants were never included in the national health insurance scheme, and the reasons for the distinction remain far from obvious. They were belatedly added to workmen's compensation in 1940,[4] as a result of continuous complaints that the ceiling to earnings-related compensation was too low for those with heavy family responsibilities. Beveridge in his restatement of the social insurance principle, based as it was on a system of flat-rate benefit, was content to see the increase payable to all recipients of insurance benefit.[5] The contemporaneous introduction of family allowances necessitated a technical modification of the rules, though in no fundamental way interfered with them.

By the time earnings-related supplements were introduced for short-term benefits in 1966, the principle of increases for dependants was already firmly entrenched, and there was no serious attempt to argue that it should be discontinued.[6] But the reform prompted the decision to pay the increase on a higher scale to long-term beneficiaries who were not entitled to the supplement. Paradoxically, this more favourable treatment of pensioners was not affected by the introduction of the earnings-related component under the 1975 scheme, nor by the abolition of the earnings-related supplements for short-term beneficiaries. Indeed, the position of the latter has deteriorated further as a result of other reforms. First, statutory sick pay which replaced sickness benefit for most employed claimants does not include an allowance for dependants.[7] Secondly, the consolidation of child endowment through the child benefit scheme was rationalised as the first step of a new policy to reduce differences in the level of family support between short-term beneficiaries and those in employment.[8] As a result, the value of the child dependency increases payable with short-term benefits was frozen and subsequently they were abolished altogether.[9] While concern for work disincentives may have motivated these changes, it does not explain a later decision not to up-rate, in line with inflation, the child dependency increases paid to long-term beneficiaries (and those over pensionable age).

The traditional rules on dependency allowances assumed stereotyped family relationships in which the husband/father is the primary or only breadwinner, while the wife/mother assumes domestic responsibilities and her earnings, if any, are inessential additions to the family income. The EEC Directive on Equal Treatment for Men and Women in Social Security[10] prompted the government to make fundamental changes so that, for

2 Unemployed Workers Dependants' (Temporary Provisions) Act 1921.
3 UIA 1922.
4 WC (Supplementary Allowances) Act 1940.
5 Paras 311 and 325.
6 Cf *Walley* p. 206.
7 Cf p.139, above.
8 Cf n.1, above. See also Brown *Children in Social Security* (1984) pp. 116–121.
9 HSSA 1984, s.13. The reforms were tolerated politically so long as compensating adjustments were made to child benefit: First Report of Social Security Advisory Committee (1982), pp. 30–32. However, the real value of this benefit has also been allowed to decline: p.392, below.
10 Dir 79/7, OJ 1979, L6/24.

example, the rules governing a husband's entitlement to claim for a wife and a wife's entitlement to claim for a husband have been largely harmonised.[11]

B Persons for whom increase payable

i Children

Increases for child dependants may be added to the following benefits payable under the Social Security Act 1975:

> unemployment and sickness benefits, but only where the beneficiary is over pensionable age; invalidity and Category A, B or C retirement pensions; widowed mother's, invalid care and severe disablement allowances.[12]

To qualify for the increase, the beneficiary must satisfy three conditions, the first referring to his relationship with the child, the second to the state of the latter's dependence on him and the third to the earnings (if any) of his spouse or unmarried partner.

a *Sufficient relationship*

The first general rule for the increase simply incorporates the law on child benefit: it is payable where the beneficiary is 'entitled to child benefit in respect of a child or children'.[13] On this test, therefore, reference should be made to the discussion in chapter 10.

In certain respects, however, the traditional rules on increases covered a wider range of relationships than those acknowledged under the child benefit scheme. To ensure that the entitlement of this broader group is preserved, a regulation sets out circumstances in which for the purpose of the increase a person is treated as if he were entitled to child benefit.[14]

(1) The beneficiary is *either* a parent of the child *or* is wholly or mainly maintaining him, *and* he resides with a parent of the child to whom child benefit has been awarded and with whom the child is living.
(2) The beneficiary or his spouse would have been entitled to child benefit for the child if the latter had been born at the end of the week before that in which the birth in fact occurred.[15]
(3) The beneficiary is entitled to a family benefit in respect of that child payable by the government of a country outside the UK.

Conversely, there is a situation where child benefit is payable but the increase is excluded.[16]

– The claimant of the increase (who is entitled to child benefit) is not a parent of the child and someone who is his parent is treated, under section 3(1)(a) of the Child Benefit Act 1975,[17] as responsible for the child. Never-

---

11 SSA 1980, Sch 1, Part I, on which see Atkins [1980] JSWL 16.
12 SSA 1975, ss. 41(2), (4) and 49.
13 Ibid, s.41, as amended. It is sufficient if a claim for child benefit has been made for the relevant period: *R(S) 3/80.*
14 SI 1977/343, reg 4A. For the meaning of parent in these rules, see CBA 1975, s.24(a), *R(S) 4/81* and *R(S)9/83.*
15 This reflects the rule that CB entitlement is determined weekly by reference to facts existing at the end of the previous week.
16 SI 1977/343, reg 4B.
17 See p.397, below.

theless, the claimant remains entitled to the increase if, under the same provision, he is also treated as responsible for the child and he is wholly or mainly maintaining him.

b *Dependence*

The second condition is that the beneficiary must prove *either* that the child in question is living with him *or* that he is contributing to the cost of providing for the child at a weekly rate of not less than the amount of the increase, over and above the amount (if any) received by way of child benefit.[18]

c *Earnings of spouse or partner*

The 'equal treatment' reform of 1983 abolished the discriminatory rule that a married woman residing with her husband could be paid a child dependency increase only if the husband was 'incapable of self support'. The current provisions nevertheless reflect a similar policy, that the earnings of a partner should affect entitlement to the increase. So, where the beneficiary is a member of a married or unmarried couple residing together, and the partner earns £85 or more per week, no increase is payable for a first or only child; each complete £10 in excess of £85 precludes an increase for a further child.[19]

ii **Husband or wife**

An increase for a spouse may supplement short-term, as well as long-term, benefits, and hence may be claimed in respect of the following:

> unemployment and sickness benefits, invalidity and category A, B or C retirement pensions, and maternity, invalid care and severe disablement allowances.[20]

The marriage must be one recognised by law and sufficiently proved.[1] The usual test of dependency applies: the beneficiary must either be residing with the spouse[2] or contributing to his/her maintenance at not less than the amount of the increase.[3] While much of the sex discrimination previously existing in this area[4] has been eliminated, nevertheless a woman claiming a dependency increase to a category A retirement pension for a husband has to satisfy an additional condition: immediately prior to entitlement to that pension she was in receipt of a dependency increase for him as an addition to unemployment benefit, sickness benefit or invalidity pension.[5] In a recent Commissioner's decision,[6] it was held that this requirement, though clearly discriminatory, was not in breach of the EEC Directive on Equal Treatment, since the latter explicitly excluded from its provisions increases to an old age benefit for a dependent spouse.[7]

The possibility of the beneficiary's spouse being an earner raises an important policy question: presumably, the increase should be paid if its object is to

---

18 SSA 1975, s.43(1)-(2), as amended.
19 Ibid, s.43(2A)-(2B). For this purpose 'earnings' include occupational pension payments: SSA 1988, s.10.
20 SSA 1975, ss.44, 45, 45A and 49.
1 Pp. 349-357, below.
2 Pp. 343-345, below.
3 SSA 1975, s.44(1)(a), 45(2) and 45A(2). But for the invalid care allowance, the claimant must prove residence – there is no maintenance alternative: SI 1977/343, Sch 2, para 7.
4 See the second edition of this book, pp.367-369.
5 SSA 1975, s.45A(1).
6 *R(P) 3/88*.
7 Dir 79/7, OJ 1979, L 6/24, art 7(1)(d).

provide compensation for the loss of actual support but not if it is instead to satisfy the need for support. Quite apart from this, there is the question of incentive, whether the wife, assuming she is capable of doing so, should be encouraged to work. While the government appears unequivocally to adopt the 'needs' approach,[8] the various statutory provisions are not uniformly consistent with it. Certainly it is adopted in the case of short-term benefits (viz those for unemployment, sickness and maternity); the increase is not payable if the spouse's weekly earnings exceed the amount of that increase.[9] The same also applies to long-term benefits (retirement and invalidity pensions) where the spouse is not residing with the beneficiary, i.e. where the alternative maintenance test has to be satisfied.[10] If the spouses do reside together, no increase to the long-term benefits is payable if the dependent spouse's earnings exceed the standard rate of unemployment benefit.[11]

Just as the earnings rule differs according to the nature of the benefit, so also does the amount of increase which is payable for adult dependants. Broadly speaking, the highest increase is paid with contributory retirement and invalidity pensions, the lowest increase with non-contributory benefits and there is a middle rate for increases to the short-term contributory benefits.

iii Other adult dependants

The British social security system has never been generous in its support of dependants who are not members of the nuclear family. Provisions allowing for increases for certain adult relatives were abolished in 1980.[12] While unmarried partners are treated as spouses for the purposes of the income-related benefits,[13] their position with regard to benefits payable under the Social Security Act 1975 is less favourable. Except for a short period of 'entitlement' under the Unemployment Insurance Acts,[14] dependency increases have not been payable for cohabitees as such. They are, however, payable for a dependant who cares for a child of the beneficiary and, since 1983, following the 'equal treatment' reforms, such person can be male or female.[15]

The claimant must be entitled to child benefit[16] – or treated as so entitled[17] – for the child who is the subject of the care. As regards the latter, the Commissioner has held that the necessary care will be shown if the alleged carer 'to a substantial extent performs those duties for a child, with which a child needs assistance because he or she is a child, or exercises that supervision over a child which is one of the needs of childhood'.[18] It does not con-

---

8 Report of Secretary of State on the Earnings Rule for Retirement Pensioners and the Wives of Retirement and Invalidity Pensioners 1977–78, HC 697, para 5.6. the same policy does not apply to earnings of the retirement pensioner himself: p.198, above.
9 SSA 1975, s.44(1)(b); SI 1977/343, reg 8(1).
10 SSA 1975, ss.45(2)(b) and 45A(2)(b).
11 SI 1977/343, reg 8A. For this purpose, 'earnings' include occupational pension payments: SSA 1988, s.10.
12 SSA 1980, Sch 1, para 3. On the repealed provisions, see the NIAC Report on the Question of Dependency Provisions (Cmd 9855, 1956).
13 P. 425, below.
14 UIA 1922, s.1(1), repealed by UIA 1927, s.4(2).
15 In the case of Category A and C retirement pensions, however, the carer must be a woman: SI 1977/343, reg 10(f).
16 SSA 1975, ss.44(3)(c) and 46(2).
17 SI 1977/343, reg 4A.
18 *CS 726/49* para 11.

note exclusive care[19] or even a greater amount of care than that provided by the claimant himself.[20] But the mere distant supervision of a child's needs while he is at boarding school does not qualify.[1]

This firm emphasis on the care of a child carries no necessary implication of a sexual relationship with the beneficiary. The carer can be of the same sex as, and need not reside with, the beneficiary.[2] Indeed, the increase may be paid for a carer where the beneficiary is living with a spouse, provided that the latter is in full-time work and is not substantially involved in the care of the child.[3] The short-term benefits which may be supplemented by the increase are those for maternity, sickness and unemployment.[4] The long-term benefits are invalidity and Category A and C retirement pensions, severe disablement and invalid care allowance.[5]

To qualify for any of these increases the child carer must either be residing with the beneficiary or be maintained by him at not less than the standard rate of the increase, or employed by him for consideration of not less than that amount.[6] No increase is payable where the carer earns more than the amount of the increase but the amounts (if any) which the beneficiary pays the child carer are, of course, ignored, and the exclusion does not apply at all to those employed by the beneficiary and not residing with him.[7] There are, moreover, some further limitations which do not apply to spouses.

– The child carer must not be imprisoned or detained in legal custody[8] or absent from GB.[9] Finally, an increase to invalidity pension is not payable if the beneficiary has a wife who is entitled to a Category B or C retirement pension.[10]

C 'Residing with' or 'living with' the beneficiary

The principle that a beneficiary should be either maintaining the dependant or residing (or living) with him is not difficult to rationalise. If the beneficiary shares a home with another, and is an earner, it is a reasonable assumption that he is contributing to that other's maintenance. The different formulation for adult dependants ('residing with') and children ('living with') is deliberate. The latter concept was that used in the family allowances, and subsequently the child benefit, legislation and was explicitly incorporated into the national insurance scheme in 1957.[11] As the Commissioner has consistently held, 'living with' does not carry the same meaning as 'residing

---

19 *UD 10914/31.*
20 *CS 726/49* paras 9, 10.
 1 *R(S) 17/54.*
 2 *CS 726/49*, unless an increase is claimed for an invalid care allowance: p.341, n.3, above. A non-residing child carer must, however, be maintained by the beneficiary.
 3 *R(S) 20/54.*
 4 SSA 1975, ss.44(2)–(3).
 5 Ibid, ss.46(1); SI 1977/343, reg 1(3).
 6 Ibid, reg 10(2)(b). For the invalid care allowance, residence must be proved, p.341, n.3, above.
 7 SI 1977/343, reg 10(2)(e).
 8 Ibid, reg 10(2)(d).
 9 Unless he is residing with the beneficiary who himself is not disqualified: ibid, reg 10(2)(c) and (3).
10 SSA 1975, s.46(3), presumably because this is analogous to an increase for a wife, and a beneficiary may not claim increases for both a wife and a resident child carer.
11 NIA 1957, s.6(4).

with'.[12] It seems clear, therefore, that the intention of Parliament was to apply to child dependency increases the interpretation given to the phrase in child benefit law; this is fully discussed in chapter 10.[13] It thus remains to consider the concept of 'residing with' which qualifies the relationship with adult dependants.

The term is not defined in the Social Security Act and guidance is to be had only from the case-law.[14] The basic idea is that the two people concerned should be living under the same roof.[15] This does not mean either that one of them should be the owner or tenant of the property[16] or that, in the case of spouses, they are sleeping in the same bed or otherwise maintaining the normal relationship of husband and wife.[17] But there must be an element of continuity and permanence in the co-residence.[18] In some cases, it will be necessary for the claimant to prove that he has acquired a new 'co-resident'. It will be more difficult to establish that living in a hotel, lodgings or the home of relatives constitutes co-residence than the entering into a tenancy agreement or setting up home with a woman as his wife.[19] More often, the question is whether an admitted co-residence has in fact ceased. On this the legislation is more helpful. Regulations made under the Social Security (Miscellaneous Provisions) Act 1977 lay down three rules.

i Temporary absence
Under the fist rule:

> two persons shall not be treated as having ceased to reside together by reason of any temporary absence the one from the other.[20]

This reinforces the notion that 'residing with' implies a permanent rather than a temporary conditon, but it is naturally difficult to draw the line between the two. Some authorities, applying an equivalent rule under regulations previously in force, held that the test depends primarily on the parties' state of mind: did they intend to resume co-residence when the period of separation had ceased? Or has the separation been so long that, on reasonable inference, it was likely to be permanent?[1] On this view, the purpose of the absence becomes important. Thus the acquisition of accommodation removed from the family but near the claimant's employment will not generally be regarded as indicative of 'temporary' absence,[2] but it may be so categorised if the claimant is merely looking for work and intends that the family should join him when he finds it,[3] or lodges near the work but returns home at weekends and for holidays.[4] Other authorities have regarded the

---

12 *R(I) 10/51; R(U) 11/62; R(F) 2/79.*
13 Pp. 398–399, below.
14 The expression also has been used in the Rent Acts (see e.g. *Morgan v Murch* [1970] 2 All ER 100, [1970] 1 WLR 778) and in the law of family maintenance (see e.g. *Curtin v Curtin* [1952] 2 QB 552).
15 Per Lord Goddard CJ, ibid, at 556; *R(P) 15/56.*
16 *CU 201/50.*
17 *Curtin v Curtin*, n.14, above; *R(S) 14/52*: though cp *Hopes v Hopes* [1949] P 227, [1948] 2 All ER 920 and the child benefit decision *R(F) 3/81.*
18 *CS 3/48.* See also SI 1977/956, reg 2(3), p.345, below.
19 *R(P) 4/54, R(F) 1/62.*
20 SI 1977/956, reg 2(4).
1 See e.g. *CS 3/48; CS 6/48; R(S) 1/51.*
2 *UD 4053/28; UD 5131/29; R(S) 10/55; R(I) 37/55.*
3 *R(S) 14/58.*
4 *UD 6702/29; UD 15405/32.*

intention of the claimant as too elusive a criterion and have concentrated more on the duration of the absence. In the early 1950s the Commissioner devised a rule of thumb that:

> a period of absence which has lasted for more than a year, and of which there is no reasonable prospect of its coming to an end, cannot . . . be spoken of as 'temporary'.[5]

This was then combined with another.rule of thumb that the 'reasonable prospect of its coming to an end' should be judged within a period of six months from the date of application.[6] The two tests were regularly applied[7] but they were not regarded as hard and fast rules, and might be ousted by special circumstances.[8] In 1962, a Tribunal of Commissioners reported on a tendency to take a 'much shorter term view of residence', and implied that it would be better to regard the matter as one of degree in each case, rather than argue it in terms of legal presumption.[9]

ii Widows

In relation to widow's benefit the position of persons under 19 who may be engaged in full-time education or training away from home has caused some difficulties.[10] The regulations thus prescribe that:

> in the case of a woman who has been widowed, she shall not be treated as having ceased to reside with a child or person under the age of nineteen by reason of any absence the one from the other which is not likely to be permanent.[11]

iii Hospital in-patients

The application of the 'residing with' criterion to cases where the beneficiary or the dependant is in hospital has been equally problematical. The National Insurance Advisory Committee reviewed the matter in 1955 and concluded that special provision should be made for spouses.[12] Under the current rule:

> two spouses shall not be treated as having ceased to reside together by reason only of the fact that either of them is, or they both are, undergoing medical or other treatment as an in-patient in a hospital or similar institution, whether such absence is temporary or not.[13]

Where the treatment of a dependant is free under the National Health Service, the need of the beneficiary to support him or her is obviously reduced. For this reason, as will be seen later in this chapter, there are rules for adjusting the rates of the increases.[14] In that context, too, the meaning of 'medical or other treatment as an in-patient in a hospital or similar institution' will be considered.

---

5 *CP 84/50* unreported, but cited in *R(P) 7/53* para 8.
6 *R(P) 7/53*.
7 See e.g. *R(U) 15/54; R(S) 7/55; R(U) 14/58*.
8 See e.g. *R(S) 14/55*.
9 *R(U) 11/62*.
10 Cf *Fox v Stirk and Bristol Electoral Registration Officer* [1970] 2 QB 467, [1970] 3 All ER (on franchise qualifications).
11 SI 1977/956, reg 2(3).
12 Report on the Question of Dependency Provisions (Cmd 9855).
13 SI 1977/956, reg 2(2)(b).
14 Pp. 364–367, below.

D Maintenance by beneficiary

In some cases, the beneficiary may prove as an alternative to 'residence' that he was 'maintaining' the dependant. In others, he must prove both 'residence' and 'maintenance'. To establish the required degree of maintenance, the beneficiary must contribute to the cost of providing for the dependant at a weekly rate of not less than the amount of the increase claimed.[15]

i Mode and time of payments

The maintenance question is one of fact and not of legal liability. The mere existence of an obligation to maintain, even if the result of a court order, will not be sufficient to establish title to the increase.[16] The claimant must therefore prove that he has actually been making the appropriate payments during the relevant period, though in the case of an increase for a child the condition is satisfied if the beneficiary gives an undertaking in writing to make such payment and he makes the payment when he receives the increase.[17] In no case does he have to show that the maintenance payments were actually received or consumed by the dependant, for example, the money might be held by the clerk of a court[18] or diverted to the DSS.[19] The fact that the prescribed amount of maintenance is expressed in terms of weekly payments does not, of course, mean that the actual payments must be made weekly. They must be, however, regular payments and hence a payment of an occasional lump sum cannot be treated as regular maintenance and apportioned to weekly payments.[20] Interruptions in payments cannot be ignored,[1] so that if the claimant falls in arrears, he may not count against current payments any payments made to clear arrears.[2] To hold otherwise would unduly benefit those who accumulated arrears.[3]

ii Payment in kind

It has long been recognised that maintenance need not necessarily take the form of a monetary payment. Account may be taken of the regular provision of food, clothing, fuel and other items necessary for sustenance and welfare.[4] So also if the claimant conveys to the dependant his beneficial interest in the matrimonial home.[5] The calculation of maintenance will then proceed on the basis of the rateable value, or interest on the capital value, of the property transferred.[6] In another case, the same principle was applied to the transfer

---

15 E.g. SSA 1975, ss.43(2)(a) and 44(1)(a).
16 *R(U) 25/59*; *R(U) 1/77*.
17 SI 1977/343, reg 5(1). For the origins of this regulation, see NIAC Report (1966, Cmnd 2959). It cannot be invoked to support entitlement for a period longer than a week before the undertaking was made: *R(U) 3/78*; cf *R(U) 6/79*, where the undertaking confirmed one that had been made earlier.
18 *CS 638/49*.
19 Cf p.462, below. There is no reported case on the point but the proposition in the text should be accepted as a matter of principle.
20 *R(U) 14/62*.
 1 Compare child benefit, p.400, below, where the rule is perhaps more generous.
 2 *R(U) 11/62*.
 3 *R(U) 25/58* para 7. In *R(S) 3/74* R G Micklethwait, Chief Comr, refused to apply the 'allocation' regulation, (p.347, below) to assist in cases of regular but inadequate payments.
 4 *CI 111/50*; *R(I) 10/51*.
 5 *R(U) 3/66*, though J S Watson, Dep. Comr, reserved his opinion on whether the position would have been the same if the dependant has sold or let the property in question. In *R(S) 6/52* it was held that such a sale would not affect the claimant's rights.
 6 *R(U) 3/66*.

of a business share: the interest obtained on the purchase-money of the share sold was deemed to be a regular contribution to maintenance.[7]

iii Joint maintenors

A regulation deals with the situation, presumably not of frequent occurrence, where a dependant is being maintained by two or more beneficiaries. If the aggregate amount of such maintenance equals or exceeds the rate necessary for any one of them to claim the increase, such increase is payable notwithstanding that no one individual himself is able to satisfy the criterion.[8] The recipient will be the person who makes the largest contributions, or, if there is no such person, then either the eldest member of the group or one designated by the majority in a written notice sent to the Secretary of State.[9]

iv Allocation principle

Sometimes maintenance payments are explicitly allocated as between spouse (or ex-spouse) and children; sometimes they are not. It would be invidious if the exact classification of the payments were to be decisive in determining whether one or other dependant would qualify for the increase. So long as a marriage is subsisting,[10] the system assumes a principle of non-discrimination between a beneficiary's spouse and the children. Where a payment is made to a spouse or children or both, the authorities are given discretion to apportion the maintenance in such a way as will entitle the claimant to the largest payment by way of increase.[11] A typical exercise of this power would be as follows:

> C, in receipt of invalidity benefit, is paying by way of maintenance every week £24.00 for his wife and £8.00 for each of two children. If the apparent apportionment were to be binding, C could claim no increase since the currently prescribed amount of maintenance is for an adult dependant £24.75, and for a child £8.40. By notionally apportioning the aggregate of £40.00 into £25.00 for the wife, £9.00 for the first child and £6.00 for the second child, the authorities will be able to confer on C title to an increase for the wife and for the first child.

v Family fund[12]

The technique used for calculating individual dependency in the typical situation where money from various sources is used to support a number of individuals is a judicial creation and owes nothing to legislative prescription. It was originally conceived by judges deciding dependency issues under the Workmen's Compensation Acts,[13] and subsequently adopted by the Umpire adjudicating unemployment insurance claims.[14] There being nothing in the postwar legislation to discourage its continued application, it has been accepted by Commissioners as part of modern social security law.[15]

---

7 *R(I) 37/54.*
8 SI 1977/343, reg 2(2).
9 Ibid, reg 2(2)(b).
10 Cf *R(S) 9/61.*
11 SI 1977/343, reg 3.
12 See generally, Kahn-Freund 16 MLR 148, 164–173.
13 See esp. *Main Colliery Co v Davies* [1900] AC 358, and *Hodgson v West Stanley Colliery* [1910] AC 229.
14 See esp. *UD 1838/31.*
15 *CSI 59/49*, affirmed in *R(I) 1/57 (T)* and *R(I) 20/60(T)*. For a valuable recent exposition of the principles, see *R(S) 12/83.*

The fundamental principle is that the authorities should have regard to the normal phenomena of family support rather than to strict legal obligations to maintain.[16] Thus if a woman is in fact supported by her brother, a cousin or a son, it is irrelevant that she is in law wholly dependent on her husband. The technique proceeds by calculating the 'unit cost' of each family member. For this, the total family income[17] is divided by the number of individuals (counting two children under 14 as one adult).

> In a family group of three adults (H, the husband, W, his wife and B, his brother) and two children (K and L) there will be 4 units. If the total family income is £120.00 (H contributing £70.00, W £10.00 and B £40.00) per week, the unit cost of one adult is £ $\frac{120}{4}$ = £30.00 and of one child £15.00.

Each individual then has a surplus or deficit of contribution over cost.

> H has a surplus of £40.00, B a surplus of £10.00, W a deficit of £20.00, and K and L each a deficit of £15.00.

To assess the degree of dependency of an individual with a deficit on an individual with a surplus, one divides the amount of the deficit proportionally between those providing a surplus.

> H is providing $\frac{4}{5}$ of the total surplus and B $\frac{1}{5}$. Thus the extent of W's dependency on H is $\frac{4}{5} \times 20$ = £16.00, and the extent of K's (or L's) dependency on H is $\frac{4}{5} \times 15$ = £12.00.

The calculation is to be applied to the family circumstances existing at the time immediately prior to the event (e.g. sickness, unemployment, retirement) for which the benefit is payable: subsequent changes in the composition of the group or financial contributions are to be ignored,[18] and the average or normal contributions of individuals are to be assessed as at that date.[19]

If the method is one of simple arithmetic, it nevertheless raises some delicate issues when applied to actual family situations. It is sometimes argued that the method does not accord with the reality of how a particular family organises its household budget. The answer to this is that it is a convenient and less expensive method of calculating typical expenditure. Complete accuracy is neither obtainable nor (presumably) desirable. The method should be departed from only in wholly exceptional cases where there is clear evidence that it substantially conflicts with the actual circumstances, or where the relevant facts cannot be determined.[20] It may be that an individual member consumes more or less than the attributed 'unit cost', e.g. because he is aged or disabled, but it has always been held that no account is to be taken of the actual way in which money is spent.[1] Forms of income other than earnings, for example, social security benefits, raise greater difficulties: (I) are they to be regarded as contributions by one or more family members, or are they provided by an 'outsider'? (II) should they be regarded as part of the

16 See particularly the speech of Lord Loreburn LC in *Hodgson v West Stanley Colliery*, n.13, above at 232.
17 Typically, earnings after deductions for tax and social security, plus any social security benefits and/or maintenance payments: *R(S) 12/83* para 10(a).
18 *CS 52/50*.
19 *R(I) 10/51*; *R(S) 12/83*.
20 *R(I) 46/52*; *R(U) 37/52*; *R(I) 20/60*; *R(S) 12/83*.
 1 *CS 52/50*; *R(I) 1/57*; *R(I)20/60*.

aggregate household resources, or rather earmarked for a particular person, or persons? As regards (I), while a contributory benefit is regarded as a resource provided by the person on whose contributions the benefit is payable,[2] non-contributory benefits are normally treated as income fron an 'outsider'.[3] The possibility of earmarking some income, for the purposes of (II), and thus excluding it from the calculations, has been admitted by some authorities, (e.g. where there are maintenance payments for children[4] or an attendance allowance has been used to pay a non-family carer[5]) but some have regarded this as an unnecessary complication.[6] In any event, child benefit and the income-related benefits are normally integrated into the household fund.[7]

E Trade disputes

As part of its general programme to limit the social security entitlement of strikers and their families,[8] the government in 1986 introduced a provision to disentitle a beneficiary from receiving an increase for any dependant who has been disqualified from unemployment benefit under section 19 of the Social Security Act 1975,[9] or would have been so disqualified if he had claimed that benefit.[10]

Part 2 Marriage

A General

While it may be the case that a significant proportion of social welfare provision is concerned with remedying the lack of the traditional family structure, nevertheless much of the social security legislation, particularly that part concerned with contributory benefits, focuses on the unit of the family as defined by the general law. References in the legislation to 'marriage', 'wife', 'husband', 'widow' and 'widower' have all been construed to require the existence of a marriage which is recognised in the United Kingdom,[11] and which was subsisting at the time of the claim or the event which gave rise to entitlement.[12] What is legally recognised as a valid marriage is determined according to the general law of England (or Scotland), including as it does the principles of private international law when, for example, the validity of foreign marriages, or divorces, is in question. There is no space here to describe such rules in detail.[13] Instead a brief outline will be provided, together

---

2 *CP 96/50*; *R(S) 12/83*.
3 *R(S) 2/85*; *R(S) 12/83*, though J G Monroe, Comr, left open the question whether child benefit might not be treated as a contribution by the person entitled to it: ibid, para 14.
4 *CU 544/50*.
5 *R(I) 1/57(T)*, para 19, *obiter*.
6 *UD 12616/31*; *R(S) 12/83*.
7 *R(I) 8/65*; *R(S) 12/83*.
8 Cf pp. 110–111, above, and pp. 455–458, below.
9 See pp. 112–120, above.
10 SSA 1975, s.49A, inserted by SSA 1986, s.44.
11 *CG 3/49*; *R(S) 4/59*. Thus under Scots law if the claim is made in Scotland.
12 *R(G) 1/52*; *R(P) 14/56*; *R(G) 2/73*.
13 For the English family law see Bromley *Family Law* (7th edn) ch 2, and Cretney *Principles of Family Law* (4th edn) chs 1–2, for Scots family law see Clive *Law of Husband and Wife in Scotland* (2nd edn) chs 3–4 and for the relevant principles of private international law, Dicey and Morris *The Conflict of Laws* (11th edn) ch 7.

with such principles as have been developed within the framework of the social security legislation.

B Marriages celebrated in the United Kingdom

A marriage celebrated in England and Wales must have satisfied the rules regarding formalities, which include the necessary preliminaries as well as due solemnisation, whether by civil or religious proceedings.[14] Production of the marriage certificate[15] will constitute prima facie evidence that the marriage has been duly celebrated,[16] but the absence of such a certificate will not be fatal. Provided that the parties can establish with sufficient reliability that a ceremony in due form took place[17] and that it was followed by prolonged cohabitation as husband and wife, a valid marriage will be presumed.[18] The presumption will be rebutted by proof as to the invalidity of the marriage[19] but the standard of proof required is uncertain. One authority suggests that 'clear proof' will be sufficient,[20] but perhaps the better view is that the invalidity must be proved beyond reasonable doubt.[1] Scots law, in contrast to English law, recognises a marriage 'by habit and repute', but the doctrine is narrowly confined.[2] There must have been a substantial period of cohabitation,[3] the bulk of which was in Scotland,[4] and the parties must have been free to marry[5] and consented, as between themselves, to a state of marriage.[6]

C Marriages celebrated abroad

In general a foreign marriage will be recognised as valid by English and Scots law if it satisfied the formalities of the law of that jurisdiction where the marriage took place,[7] and if each party had capacity according to the law of his domicile at the time of the alleged marriage.[8] The large number of immigrants, particularly from India and Pakistan, has caused considerable difficulties here. The problem is that sometimes expert evidence on the foreign law in question is required but it will not always be readily available to an adjudication

14 *Bromley* n.13, above, at pp. 34–55; *Cretney* n.13, above, at pp. 9–34.
15 SSA 1975, s.160 makes provision for the obtaining of copies of the certificate for this purpose.
16 *CG 203/49*.
17 See *38/49 (P)*; *R(P) 4/60*; *R(G) 2/70*.
18 *CG 53/50*.
19 *R(G) 1/51*.
20 Per Harman LJ, *Re Taylor* [1961] 1 All ER 55 at 63.
 1 Per Sir Jocelyn Simon P, *Mahadervan v Mahadervan* [1964] P 233 at 244–246, adopted (obiter) by R J A Temple, Comr, in *R(G) 2/70* para 17.
 2 See *Low v Gorman* 1970 SLT 356, and generally *Clive*, n.13, above. The law appears not to have been affected by the Marriage (Scotland) Act 1977.
 3 'Years' rather than 'months': *R(G) 8/56* para 11.
 4 *R(G) 1/71*.
 5 *R(P) 1/51*; *R(I) 37/61*; *R(G) 2/82*; *R(G) 7/56* which regarded an impediment to marry as fatal only if known to the parties. The period during which the parties are free to marry need only be short relative to their period of cohabitation: *R(G) 5/83(T)*.
 6 *R(G) 8/56*; *R(P) 1/58*; *R(G) 1/71*; *R(G) 2/82*. A deliberate rejection of the institution of marriage is sufficient to rebut a presumption, arising from prolonged cohabitation, that there has been tacit consent: *R(G) 4/84*.
 7 *R(U) 1/68* and see *Dicey and Morris*, n.13, above, at pp. 599–622.
 8 *R(G) 3/75* and see *Dicey and Morris*, n.13, above, at pp. 622–642.

officer or appeal tribunal.[9] Decisions on the domicile of an individual, at different stages of his life, are also fraught with difficulties, depending as they do on a considerable amount of background information on family circumstances at some remote time or place.[10]

D Effects of marriages void or voidable or terminated by divorce

A marriage which is void[11] because, for example, it is bigamous[12] or within the prohibited degrees[13] has no effect at law and cannot be relied on for the purposes of entitlement to benefit. On the other hand, the fact that a marriage is void may revive an entitlement to widow's benefit from a 'previous' marriage if it had ceased to be payable on the alleged remarriage.[14] The widow may not, of course, claim for any period during which she was cohabiting with the second 'husband' and she will in any event be subject to the rules on time-limits.[15] A marriage which is terminated by divorce is treated as valid until the decree is made absolute, but from that date it is no longer effective to ground entitlement. Though there is no direct decision on the point, it is assumed that a previous entitlement to widow's benefit is not revived by dissolution of a subsequent marriage[16] – in this respect it is different from a marriage held to be void. The problems to which divorced marriages give rise are concerned mainly with whether a foreign decree should be recognised; this is determined by the rules of private international law.[17]

Between void marriages and those terminated by divorce comes the third and problematic category of voidable marriages[18] (e.g. those which have not been consummated). Prior to 1971, for most legal purposes, such a marriage was regarded as valid and subsisting until the time of the decree of nullity, but the securing of such a decree would operate to invalidate the marriage retrospectively.[19] Under a legislative reform of 1956,[20] power was given to the Minister to provide by regulations that, for specified purposes, a voidable marriage was to be treated as a marriage terminated by divorce. This power was exercised as regards questions of entitlement to guardian's allowance and

---

9 See the remarks of R S Lazarus, Comr, in *R(G) 2/71* paras 4 and 8.
10 See e.g. *R(P) 1/57*; *R(G) 2/71* and *R(G) 3/75*.
11 See generally *Bromley* n.13, above, at pp. 77–82.
12 *R(G) 2/63*.
13 *R(G) 10/53*.
14 *CG 28/53*, cited in *R(G) 1/73(T)*.
15 P. 547, below.
16 See *R(G) 1/73* para 14 (Tribunal majority).
17 Much of the law on recognition of foreign divorces is governed by the Recognition of Judicial Divorces and Legal Separations Act 1971, as modified by the Domicile and Matrimonial Proceedings Act 1973. See, in general, Dicey and Morris *The Conflict of Laws* (11th edn) pp. 686–717. The Commissioner has in several instances been faced with the problem of customary divorces by 'talaq'. In *R(G) 2/71* and *R(G) 4/74* such a divorce was recognised because, on the expert evidence available, it was found that on the balance of probabilities the divorce would have been recognised by the law of domicile even though there was no direct judicial authority in the particular jurisdiction (cf *R(G) 1/70*), though it was important to ascertain whether the correct procedure had been adopted (see *R(G) 5/74*). The Domicile and Matrimonial Proceedings Act 1973, s.16, provided that from 1 January 1974, and subject to certain exceptions, such divorces if obtained in the British Isles would no longer be recognised. Divorces obtained before that date or abroad are unaffected by this provision.
18 See generally Bromley *Family Law* (7th edn) pp. 82–99.
19 Ibid, at p.98.
20 NIA 1957, s. 9(1)(c).

the now obsolete child's special allowance.[1] The principles governing other benefits under social security legislation were unclear. In particular, there were conflicting decisions on whether a widow who lost benefit on entering a voidable marriage was entitled to claim for all periods except those during which she was cohabiting with the second 'husband'.[2] The process of retrospectively invalidating a marriage caused grave problems in other areas of the law and in 1971, following the recommendations of the Law Commission,[3] the Nullity of Marriage Act was passed. As reenacted by section 16 of the Matrimonial Causes Act 1973, this provides that:

> a decree of nullity granted . . . on the ground that a marriage is voidable shall operate to annul the marriage only as respects any time after the decree had been made absolute, and the marriage shall, notwithstanding the decree, be treated as if it had existed up to that time.

Some consequences of this provision are undisputed. For the purpose of claiming benefit based on the marriage, it is, during its subsistence to the time of the decree of nullity, to be regarded as valid. It is also clear that a widow cannot claim benefit on a previous marriage for any period before the decree.[4] The problem is, however, whether such a claim is valid for the period *after* the decree: in other words, is the woman's status as a widow revived by the annulment of the second marriage? The arguments are evenly balanced. If attention is focused on the first part of section 16 (down to the words 'after the decree had been made absolute'), it might be said that, for the period after the decree, the marriage is annulled and therefore to be regarded as if it had never existed. If, conversely, attention is focused on the last limb of section 16 ('and the marriage shall, notwithstanding the decree, be treated as if it had existed up to that time'), it might be said that even for purposes subsequent to the decree the marriage is to be treated as having existed at some time, and thus the woman's status as a widow is forever lost. A Tribunal of Commissioners, having taken into account the Law Commission's report on which proposals the measure was passed, preferred the second interpretation.[5]

E Polygamous marriages

The extent to which a polygamous marriage should be recognised in this country has always been a difficult issue,[6] and entitlement to social security benefits features not least among the problems to which it has given rise.[7] Originally, only marriages celebrated in a monogamous form were recognised as valid for the purpose of entitlement to benefits under the National Insurance legislation – a harsh interpretation since it excluded not only an actual polygamous marriage but also any marriage celebrated under a law which permitted polygamy, whether or not it had at all times been in fact monogamous.[8] There is no apparent policy justification for denying social

1 SI 1957/1392. See now SI 1975/497, reg 3 and SI 1975/515, reg 4(3).
2 In *R(G) 3/72*, following unreported decisions in *CG 2/70, CG 1/71* and *CG 2/71*, J S Watson, Comr, held that a widow was not so entitled. In *R(G) 1/53* it had been held that she was entitled.
3 Report No 33, 1970–71 HC 164.
4 *R(G) 1/73(T)* para 14.
5 *R(G) 1/73* paras 18–20 and 25; *R(G) 2/73*. Cf the discussions in *Bromley* n.18, above, at pp. 98–99 and Cretney *Principles of Family Law* (4th edn) pp. 90–92.
6 See Law Commission Reports Nos 42 (1970–71, HC 227) and 146 (Cmnd 9595, 1985).
7 Pearl [1978–79] JSWL 24.
8 *R(G) 6/51; R(G) 18/52(T); R(G) 11/53; R(G) 3/55; R(G) 7/55*; and see Webb 19 MLR 687.

security entitlement to parties to a marriage which is in fact monogamous and, following reforms enacted in 1956[9] and 1971[10], the position is now that

> a polygamous marriage shall . . . be treated as having the same consequences as a monogamous marriage for any day, but only for any day, throughout which the polygamous marriage is in fact monogamous.[11]

There are also special rules enabling a woman to claim retirement pension on her husband's contributions as from any date on which the marriage was in fact monogamous, and in such cases the rate of pension payable is that which would have been payable in the case of a monogamous marriage whether or not, prior to the date in question, the marriage had been polygamous.[12]

It should be noted, however, that these provisions only apply to a polygamous marriage which 'was celebrated under a law which, as it applies to the particular ceremony and to the parties thereto, permits polygamy'.[13] As regards English law, marriages celebrated after 31 July 1971[14] in a polygamous form are void if at the time either party was domiciled in England.[15] There seems to be no obvious reason why contributory benefits should be denied to a party of such a marriage when it in fact remains monogamous.[16]

The position of persons who at the time of the claim (or in the case of widow's benefit at the time of the contributor's death) are actually polygamously married is more delicate. The fact that there are relatively few actual polygamous families (i.e. where a man has two or more dependent wives) present in this country no doubt helps to explain why the decision to grant them entitlement under the income-related benefit schemes, the conditions for which include presence in Great Britain, has not been controversial.[17] The position as regards contributory benefits is different since payments can be made for persons, particularly pensioners, abroad. Actual polygamous marriages are not recognised for the purpose of these benefits, notwithstanding the objection that it is unfair on a party to such a marriage who has duly paid his contributions. The Law Commission has studied the problem in depth but felt unable to recommend on grounds of administrative feasibility or acceptability by the general public a number of proposed solutions.[18] These included: full entitlement for each wife (with or without increased contributions); a sharing of normal benefit by the wives; nomination by the husband (or the Secretary of State) of one wife for full benefit; full benefit for a wife living in Britain. This last suggestion would seem to be the most attractive and the objection raised to it, that it would be inequitable to the wife (or wives) living abroad, does not seem very persuasive.[19]

9 FANIA 1956, s.3, implementing proposals in NIAC Report on the Question of Widow's Benefit (Cmd 9684, 1955).
10 NIA 1971, s.16(3).
11 SI 1975/561, reg 2(1). For equivalent provisions under CBA 1975, see SI 1976/965, reg 12.
12 SI 1975/561, reg 3.
13 Ibid, reg 1(2).
14 For marriages before this date see the controversial decision in *Radwan v Radwan (No 2)* [1973] Fam 35, [1972] 3 All ER 1026, where it was held that the common law permitted a person presently domiciled in England to contract a valid potentially polygamous marriage if the intention of the parties at the time of celebration was to set up a home in a country permitting polygamy.
15 Matrimonial Causes Act 1973, s. 11(d).
16 A view taken by the Law Commission in Report No. 146, n.6, above.
17 Cf p.427, n.18, below.
18 Law Commission Published Working Paper No 21, paras 61–66. The Report which followed (No 42) took the matter no further: n.6, above.
19 See also Pearl, n.7, above, at 29.

Part 3   Living together as husband and wife

A   General

For certain purposes social security legislation treats an unmarried couple living together as husband and wife as if they were married. One important consequence is that a widow in this situation may lose entitlement to a widow's benefit;[20] another is that the couple are treated as a family unit for the purposes of the income-related benefits.[1] The 'cohabitation rule', as it is often referred to, was included in the national insurance widow's scheme introduced in 1925[2] but, perhaps surprisingly, was not expressly contained in the National Assistance Act 1948. If a woman cohabiting with a man claimed assistance, the National Assistance Board was compelled to use its discretionary powers to refuse an award. In 1966, when supplementary benefits replaced national assistance, the rule was embodied in the legislation and has remained a constant, if controversial, feature of both the contributory and the means-tested schemes.

There has been a lively debate on the legal consequences of cohabitation in general and the merits of the social security rule in particular.[3] The main justification for the latter is that:

> . . . it would be wrong in principle to treat the women who have the support of a partner both as if they had not such support and better than if they were married. It would not be right, and we believe public opinion would not accept, that the unmarried 'wife' should be able to claim benefit denied to a married woman.[4]

To counter this, notions of individual autonomy are urged. It is said that, in deciding not to marry, the parties are, by implication at least, declaring an intention that the legal consequences of marriage should not apply to them;[5] since an unmarried woman is not legally entitled to support from the man with whom she is living, it is wrong for the state to assume that such support is provided.[6] The argument may be persuasive more for private law than public law consequences and (because of the analogy with private insurance) more for contributory than for income-related benefits: if state assistance is invoked to meet actual need it can hardly be right to ignore the *de facto* meeting of that need by another party.[7]

While the theoretical arguments for the rule have been widely accepted, it has nevertheless been contended that the problems of applying it, in particular the intrusion of privacy necessarily involved, on balance impair its legitimacy.[8] There is no obvious answer to this contention since much depends on departmental practice. The level of complaints against DHSS inquiry agents seems to have dropped since the late 1960s and 1970s.

20 SSA 1975, ss. 25(3) and 26(3).
1 P.425, below.
2 WOOCPA 1925, s.2(1).
3 Lister *As Man and Wife* (1970); SBC Report *Cohabitation* (1971); SBC Report *Living Together as Husband and Wife* (1976); Deech 29 ICLQ 480; Pearl in Eekelaar and Katz *Marriage and Cohabitation in Contemporary Societies* (1980) 335; Freeman and Lyon *Cohabitation Without Marriage* (1983).
4 *Cohabitation* Report, n.3, above, para 7; and see *Finer* para 5.269.
5 Deech, n.3, above.
6 The argument was regarded as crucial by the US Supreme Court in holding invalid a cohabitation regulation introduced in Alabama: *Smith v King* 88 S Ct 2128 (1968); see also *Van Lare v Hurley* 95 S Ct 1741 (1975).
7 Cf *Living Together as Man and Wife*, n.3, above, para 22.
8 Lister, n.3, above.

B The meaning of 'living together'

The term 'cohabiting' was never defined in the social security legislation. This was criticised by the Fisher Committee Report on Abuse of Social Security Benefits,[9] arguing that individuals should not be left in such uncertainty as to what will lead to forfeiture of benefit. But the view has always been taken that precise statutory definition is impossible.[10] Indeed, in one case Lord Widgery CJ said that the phrase 'cohabiting as man and wife', then in force, was 'so well known that nothing I could say about it could possibly assist in its interpretation'.[11] In 1977, the term 'cohabiting' was replaced by 'living together',[12] largely on the ground that the former had acquired a pejorative meaning,[13] but it is clear that no different interpretation was intended.[14]

'Living together as husband and wife' is a ground for forfeiture from both income-related benefits and those payable under the Social Security Act 1975. The intention is clearly that a uniform interpretation should govern these various provisions.[15] It is therefore proposed to consider together such guidelines on the meaning as emerge from Commissioners' and court decisions, and also statements of Departmental policy which were formulated for the supplementary benefit scheme[16] and which have been described judicially as 'admirable signposts'.[17] Most of these authorities point to a number of factors whose absence or presence may assist in deciding the issue; but none is to be regarded as conclusive.[18]

i Members of same household

It is a necessary condition for the application of the rule to the income-related benefits,[19] and an obvious assumption for its application to the contributory benefits,[20] that the man and woman should be members of the same household, i.e. residing together under the same roof.[1] If, for example, he spends much of his time at another house, it will be difficult to infer that the two parties are living together.[2] A finding that they live in the same household is not by itself sufficient: the relationship might be commercial (e.g. landlady and lodger)[3] or to provide mutual aid and support in relation to disability.[4] In *Butterworth v Supplementary Benefits Commission*,[5] Woolf J said that the

9 Para 330(b).
10 N.7, above, at paras 49–51.
11 *R v South West London Supplementary Benefits Appeals Tribunal, ex parte Barnett* (1973) SB Dec 28 (Decision SB4).
12 SS(MP)A 1977, ss. 14(7) and 22(2)–(4).
13 N. 7, above, at para 52.
14 *R(SB) 17/81* para 9, D G Rice, Comr.
15 Ibid, para 4; and *R(G) 3/81*.
16 In a revised form, they are now contained in the DSS *Guide to Income Support* (1988) pp. 70–71
17 Woolf J, *Crake v Supplementary Benefits Commission* [1982] 1 All ER 498 at 505. See also *Campbell v Secretary of State for Social Services* (1983) 4 FLR 138.
18 *Crake*'s case, n.17, above. See also: *R(G) 3/71* para 5; *R(G) 1/79* para 8; *R(SB) 17/81* para 11.
19 SSA 1986, s.20(11).
20 See e.g. *R(G) 11/55*.
1 On 'residing together', see pp. 343–345, above.
2 *Guide to Income Support*, n.16, above, p.70. A person can be a member of only one household at a time: *R(SB) 8/85*.
3 *R(G) 3/71*.
4 *Robson v Secretary of Social Services* [1981] LAG Bull 238; *R(SB) 35/85*.
5 [1982] 1 All ER 498 at 502.

crucial issue was *why* they did so; it was thus a question of whether they intended to establish a marriage-like relationship.[6] If the intentions of the parties are clear, this is no doubt an appropriate test,[7] but in many cases a subjective inquiry of this kind will prove to be elusive and some authorities have preferred an objective approach which has regard primarily to the conduct of the parties.[8]

ii Duration
The duration and stability of the cohabitation is clearly an important factor.[9] Where there is no evidence as to continuity of co-residence or where its existence remains uncertain, benefit should not be refused, though once it has been established that the required relationship exists, it is much easier to show that it continues.[10] The suggestion that a couple should be allowed to live together for a number of months without entitlement being affected has, however, been rejected.[11]

iii Financial support
While the financial support by one party of the other would seem to be an important factor – it is the existence of that support which primarily explains why public funds should not be used – it is less reliable than might be supposed: in the first place, financial payments might be attributed to a commercial relationship;[12] secondly, evidence of regular financial support might be difficult to obtain; and thirdly, undue emphasis on this factor might encourage a man not to support a woman, in order to improve her chance of receiving benefit.[13] Financial support is, therefore, not required for a finding of cohabitation[14] but where there is evidence that the parties do pool their resources, this will be taken into account as one relevant factor.[15]

iv Sexual relationship
In the light of criticisms of intrusions of privacy and of forming judgments on the basis of sexual morals, the DSS now places much less emphasis on this factor and, indeed, has instructed its staff not to question claimants about their sexual relationships and not to inspect sleeping arrangements.[16] However, where claimants choose to make statements about this matter, they may help to determine whether a marriage-like relationship exists. In particular, if a couple have never had a sexual relationship, it is most unlikely that they will be regarded as living together as husband and wife.[17]

---

6 An intention to *marry* need not be shown: *R(SB) 17/81*.
7 *Robson*'s case, n.4, above, per Webster J, who, however, suggested that 'purpose' was more apposite than 'intention'.
8 *R(G) 3/81* para 8, D G Rice, Comr.
9 *R(P) 6/52*.
10 *Crake*'s case, n.17, above, at 502.
11 SBC Report, *Living Together as Husband and Wife* (1976) para 55(2).
12 *R(G) 3/71* para 7.
13 N. 11, above, para 55(3).
14 *R(G) 2/64* para 7.
15 *R(G) 2/72; R(G) 1/79; Amarjit Kaur Dhanjal v Secretary of State for Social Services* (1981) unreported, noted at [1981] JSWL 372 at 375.
16 *Guide to Income Support* n.16, above, p.71.
17 *R(SB) 35/85* para 9(3).

v Children

There will be a strong presumption that a man and woman are living together as husband and wife if they are looking after their own children.[18]

vi Public acknowledgement

A public acknowledgement by a woman that she is living with someone as his wife by taking his surname is compelling evidence of cohabitation.[19] On the other hand, little significance is to be attached to a refusal to acknowledge the relationship in public.[20]

Part 4   Residence and presence

A General

The geographical boundaries of the social security system may not seem to raise policy issues of the dimension encountered elsewhere but it has long been an area the difficulties of which have provided a fruitful supply of problems for lawyers. Under the poor law perhaps the question giving rise to most litigation was that concerned with the 'settlement' of paupers, the condition of residence on which the responsibility of parishes was based.[1] Happily, the centralisation of social security obviated the need to distinguish between parts of the country, but the increased facilities for foreign travel, the growth of multinational enterprises and the emergence of the 'migrant worker' underline the continued importance and difficulty of the topic. To some extent the problems have been solved by reciprocal agreements with other national systems and by the 'co-ordinating' Regulations of the European Economic Community. These instruments are described in chapter 17. The discussion in the present chapter is concerned with the limits imposed by the British social security legislation independently of the facilities available under the intruments. The rules emerging will thus indicate the circumstances in which an individual must resort to the additional facilities described in chapter 17.

B The framework

In general, the relationship with Great Britain, as expressed in such concepts as 'residence', 'presence', or (in a very few instances) 'nationality', is relevant for four different purposes.

i Participation in the contributory scheme

There are rules to determine who is compelled (or in the case of non-employed persons and certain self-employed persons who is entitled) to contribute to the scheme. These have been set out in chapter 2.[2]

---

18 *CG 214/50*; *R(G) 3/64*; *R(G) 3/71*; *R(G) 2/72*.
19 *R(G) 5/68*; *R(G) 1/79*.
20 *CP 97/49*; *R(P) 6/52*.
 1 Blackstone *Commentaries* vol 1, p.362, refers to the 'infinity of expensive law-suits between contending neighbourhoods'. See, generally, Holdsworth *History of English Law* (1938) vol X, pp. 257–269. See also pp. 411–412, below.
 2 Pp. 43, 45, 47 and 50, above.

ii Alternatives to contribution conditions

For those benefits the entitlement to which depends on the fulfilment of contribution conditions there is no *positive* requirement as to residence. Participation in the scheme for the requisite number of years is prima facie sufficient to justify the conferring of benefit. Indeed, to a limited extent, the system is prepared to make concessions to those whose work abroad has prevented them from making the requisite contributions. The rules designed to implement this policy were also mentioned in chapter 2.[3]

iii Disqualifications for absence

The Social Security Act 1975 lays down as a general ground for disqualification for contributory benefits absence (whether of the claimant himself or a dependant for whom an increase is claimed) from Great Britain.[4] This principle, as elaborated and modified in the Regulations, is described in this Part.

iv Requirements for non-contributory benefits

For benefits entitlement to which does not depend on fulfilment of contribution conditions, the need to impose limits on the scheme, according to an individual's connection with Great Britain, is more obvious and important. For each such benefit there is, therefore, a combination of rules generally requiring 'residence', 'ordinary residence', or at least 'presence' in Great Britain. The rules are stated in the appropriate chapters; here it will be necessary only to give an account of the interpretation of the general concepts employed.

C Absence as a ground of disqualification from contributory benefits

The principles applicable proceed according to consistent but sometimes controversial policy dictates. Except for EEC instruments,[5] there is no relief for absent persons claiming unemployment benefit, it being felt desirable to maintain unequivocally the claimant's attachment to the labour market in this country (or the EEC). Those entitled by reason of their incapacity or confinement are given some concessions, notably for temporary absences. The most generous provision is for those whose entitlement in no way rests on their inability to work, because, for example, they have reached pensionable age or are caring for dependent children. Here the disqualification is often removed altogether. The general rule is then that a person is disqualified from receiving benefit (or an increase in benefit for a dependant) during a period during which the person (or the dependant) is absent from Great Britain.[6] The modifications to the rule are as follows.

i Benefits for incapacity

For the purposes of sickness benefit, invalidity benefit, severe disablement allowance, and maternity allowance a temporary absence is disregarded if:

3 P.53, above.
4 SSA 1975, s.82(5)(a).
5 Pp. 597–612, below.
6 SSA 1975, s.82(5)(a).

(a) the Secretary of State has certified that it is consistent with the proper administration of the Act that the disqualification should not apply, *and either*

(b) the absence is for the specific purpose of being treated for incapacity which commenced before the claimant left Great Britain, *or*

(c) the absence is for the specific purpose of being treated for an industrial injury, *or*

(d) when the absence began he was, and had for six months continuously been, incapable of work and when benefit is claimed he has remained continuously so incapable since the absence began.[7]

The claimant must first establish that the absence is only temporary. No guidance is given for the interpretation of this and the Commissioner has held that there is no universal period to which reference may be made in determining whether an absence is temporary or not: the particular circumstances of the case are crucial.[8] A finding that the absence is 'permanent' or 'indefinite' precludes it being 'temporary', but the fact that it is not permanent does not necessarily mean that it is to be regarded as 'temporary'.[9] The stated intentions of the claimant are not decisive[10] but are clearly relevant. A vague hope to return to Great Britain sometime in the future, or when health permits, will not normally render the absence temporary.[11] If there is an unequivocal intention to return when the claimant is fit to do so, the issue will turn on the duration of the absence; only, it seems, in exceptional circumstances will periods of over 12 months be disregarded under the rule.[12] A seasonal worker, absent for the period of his off-season, cannot escape disqualification during that period.[13]

Condition (a) was orginally introduced in 1975 to solve some of the difficulties, described below, arising from the other conditions. It conferred a discretion on the Secretary of State to determine what was 'reasonable in all the circumstances of the case, having regard in particular . . . to the nature of the person's incapacity and to his location'.[14] In 1976 the Commissioner held that the Regulation was ultra vires.[15] The concept of consistency with the proper administration of the Act was inserted by an amendment in 1977 and the Court of Appeal has held that the present form of the Regulation is valid.[16] It is to be anticipated, however, that the Secretary of State will continue to have regard to the considerations mentioned under the 1975 Regulation.

According to the majority in a recent Tribunal of Commissioners decision, there are, in effect, three conditions to be satisfied under (b):[17]

(1) Immediately prior to his departure, the claimant must have been incapable of work, as that expression is interpreted in relation to entitlement to

---

7 SI 1975/563, reg 2(1), as amended.
8 *R(S) 1/85* para 19. In the event of an appeal, account may be taken of events occurring since the initial decision: *R(S) 10/83* para 9.
9 *R(S) 1/85* para 20.
10 *R(S) 10/83*.
11 *R(S) 3/58*; *R(S) 5/59*; *R(S) 9/59*.
12 *R(S) 9/55*. The actual decision in this case, enabling an absence of nearly four years to be disregarded, was doubted in *R(S) 1/85*.
13 *R(I) 14/51*; *R(I) 73/54*.
14 SI 1975/563, reg 2(1).
15 *CS 5/76*.
16 *Bhatia v Birmingham (Insurance Officer)* (1985), reported as Appendix to *R(S) 8/83*.
17 *R(S) 2/86(T)*.

benefit,[18] viz some specific disease or bodily or mental disablement, and hence not including pregnancy.[19]

(2) The absence abroad is for the specific purpose of having treatment for that condition. While it remains clear that the treatment need not be the sole objective of the absence – it may rank alongside social or pleasurable purposes[20] – the Tribunal majority cast doubt on the generous interpretation of this condition evident in earlier Commissioners' decisions, notably that the intention to be treated need not be formed before the claimant leaves this country.[1] As regards the meaning of 'treatment', there is general agreement that some activity by a person other than the claimant must be involved,[2] but there is little uniformity on what form is envisaged. Some decisions imply that medical supervision or care is required;[3] others do not regard this as necessary.[4] In cases of mental illness, the authorities scrutinise the nature of the 'treatment' with particular care,[5] but in one case a claimant with psychological problems avoided disqualification when he was assisted in the solving of his spiritual problems by a Doctor of Divinity.[6] On one major issue there is, however, no disagreement: it has repeatedly been held that to go abroad merely to convalesce, for a change of environment, air or food, or to obtain freedom from anxiety, even if undertaken according to medical advice, does not amount to 'being treated'.[7]

(3) The condition for which treatment abroad is sought can be identified with the incapacity from which the claimant was suffering immediately prior to departure. The Tribunal majority left open the question whether the latter incapacity must continue without interruption from the date of departure to the date of the claim but obiter considered that this was not necessary.[8]

Alternative condition (c) was introduced in 1983 to accommodate the slightly more generous rule previously applied to recipients of industrial injury benefit, which was abolished in that year. Condition (d) dates from 1967 and is designed to assist the long-term incapacitated. In these cases, proximity to the labour market is obviously of less importance. On the other hand, the absence must still be temporary, and therefore the number likely to succeed on this ground must be relatively small.

ii Long-term benefits immune from disqualification

When the benefit in question is paid irrespective of the working capacity of the claimant, supervision of the claim is less important and, arguably, he should receive the return on the contributions paid irrespective of where he chooses to live. The disqualification does not, therefore, apply to retirement

18 Pp. 149–150, above.
19 *R(G) 5/53*; *R(S) 1/75*.
20 *R(S) 6/61*.
 1 See *CS 317/49*; *R(S) 1/57*; *R(S) 1/75*; *R(S)1/77*.
 2 *CSS 71/49*; *CS 474/50*;. *R(S) 10/51*.
 3 *R(S) 16/51*; *R(S) 5/61*; *R(S) 2/69*.
 4 *R(S) 10/51*; *R(S) 2/51*.
 5 See *R(S) 5/61*.
 6 *R(S) 1/65*.
 7 *R v National Insurance Comr, ex parte Mcmenemy* (1966), reported as Appendix to *R(S) 2/69*; *R(S) 16/51*; *R(S) 10/52*; *R(S) 25/52*; *R(S) 5/61*; *R(S) 3/68*; *R(S) 1/69*; *R(S) 4/80*; *R(S) 6/81*.
 8 J N B Penny, Comr, dissented on this point.

pensions, widow's[9] and industrial disablement benefits, guardian's, attendance, invalid care and mobility allowances.[10] On the other hand, those
claiming widow's benefit, or retirement pension[11] may not be entitled to an
increase resulting from an up-rating of benefit unless they satisfy certain residence conditions.[12] The disqualification is not, however, automatic and it is
for the Secretary of State to determine, when issuing the up-rating order,
whether or not these special conditions are to apply.[13] The discretion has
invariably been exercised to exclude from the increases beneficiaries abroad,
the arguments being that the contributions on which entitlement to the benefits was based were not actuarially related to the increases and that it would be
inequitable for the other contributors to the fund, effectively paying for the
increases, to assist those living abroad.[14] In practice, however, relatively few
beneficiaries are disadvantaged as they are entitled to the increases under
EEC law and reciprocal arrangements with other countries.[15]

iii Dependants

It is part of the general rule that a claimant may not receive an increase for an
absent dependant. In some cases, this caused hardship, for a person resident
in Great Britain might, while abroad, have married a person who had never
set foot in this country. The foreign spouse would not, as a result of the
marriage, 'acquire' the residence of the claimant (as for example under the
old rules whereby a woman on marriage acquired the domicile of her husband) and the increase would not be payable.[16] The general rule is therefore
modified so that:

> a husband or wife shall not be disqualified for receiving any increase (where pay-
> able) of benefit in respect of his or her spouse by reason of the spouse's being
> absent from Great Britain, provided that the spouse is residing with the husband or
> wife, as the case may be.[17]

As regards increases for child dependants, these are generally linked to
entitlement to child benefit. The residence and presence requirements of the
latter are generally stricter than those applied previously to child dependency
increases and so regulations exist to preserve the broader base of entitlement:
in general, the increase is payable if the beneficiary or the child is only temporarily absent from Great Britain.[18]

D Some common concepts

It remains to provide an account of the meaning of concepts which are common to the various rules on residence and absence.

9 In the case of widow's payment, however, the widow or her late husband must have been in
   GB at the time of the death, or she must have returned to GB within four weeks of that death,
   or the contributions for widowed mother's allowance or widow's pension must have been
   satisfied: SI 1975/563, reg 4(2A).
10 Ibid, regs 4(1), 9(3), 10, 10A, 10B.
11 This includes the guaranteed minimum pension, payable as part of an occupational pension.
12 Normally 'ordinary residence' in GB: SI 1975/563, reg 5. See p.364, below, and *R(P) 1/78.*
13 SI 1975/563, reg 5(1).
14 See the remarks of Mr P Dean, Under-Secretary of State, in Standing Committee E Debates
   on Social Security Bill 1973, col 783.
15 Cf ch 17, below.
16 See e.g. *CG 32/49* and *55/50 (MB).*
17 SI 1975/563, reg 13.
18 Ibid, reg 13A.

i 'United Kingdom' and 'Great Britain'

For some purposes the geographical unit is the 'United Kingdom', but for the majority it is 'Great Britain'. The former means 'Great Britain and Northern Ireland',[19] the latter, England, Wales and Scotland.[20] Territorial waters are included[1] but, notwithstanding the fact that British courts may exercise criminal jurisdiction over British ships, aircraft and embassies, they are not regarded as part of the territory for purposes of the residence requirements.[2] The same is true of the Continental Shelf but special provisions render persons employed there immune from disqualification.[3]

ii Presence and absence

The two concepts are mutually exclusive.[4] To be 'absent' from Great Britain does not necessarily imply that the person concerned must have been present at some time in the past – it simply means not present.[5] Both presence and absence are questions of fact dependent on physical circumstances and concerned in no way with intention, or external events. Thus in a case where a claimant would have arrived in England but for technical problems in the mode of transport, it was to no avail for her to argue that she would but for another's fault have been present in Great Britain.[6]

iii 'Residence'

This is the term most widely used to represent the necessary connection with Great Britain. Its use has not of course been confined to social security legislation. There are many other areas, notably taxation,[7] insolvency[8] and matrimonial causes,[9] where it features prominently. Although the Commissioner has pointed out the danger of relying on decisions made in quite a different context,[10] nevertheless he has drawn freely from them for ideas in elucidating the term.[11]

The burden of proof is normally on the claimant to show that he is 'resident' in Great Britain at the relevant time.[12] The question is one of fact and degree[13] and does not lend itself easily to definition but reference has been made to the word's ordinary meaning, formulated in the Oxford English Dictionary as 'to dwell permanently or for a considerable time, to have one's

---

19 Royal and Parliamentary Titles Act 1927, s.2(2).
20 Union with Scotland Act 1706, preamble, art 1; and Wales and Berwick Act 1746, s.3. Northern Ireland, the Isle of Man and the Channel Islands are thus excluded. However, as a result of the relevant reciprocal agreements, the various schemes are almost wholly integrated.
1 SSHBA 1982, s.44, rendered necessary by the decision in *Earl of Lonsdale v A-G* [1982] 3 All ER 579, [1982] 1 WLR 887.
2 *CSG 2/48; CP 93/49; R(S) 8/59; R(I) 44/61; R(P) 8/61.*
3 SI 1975/563, reg 11.
4 *R(U) 18/60.*
5 *R(U) 16/62.*
6 *R(S) 8/59.* See also *R(S) 6/81.*
7 E.g. Income and Corporation Taxes Act 1970, ss. 49–51.
8 E.g. Insolvency Act 1985, s.119(2)(c).
9 E.g. Matrimonial Causes Act 1973, s.35(1).
10 E.g. *R(G) 2/51; R(P) 4/54; R(P) 1/72; R(P) 1/78.*
11 A prime example is *R(F) 1/62(T).*
12 *R(G) 2/51(T).*
13 *R 5/62 (UB); R(P) 2/67.* See also *Levene v IRC* [1928] AC 217, 222, *IRC v Lysaght* [1928] AC 234, 241, 243 and *Hipperson v Newbury District Electoral Registration Officer* [1985] QB 1060, [1985] 2 All ER 456.

settled or usual abode'.[14] Though the claimant need not be physically present at any one particular time, there must be a sufficient amount of physical presence in the place on which the residence may be grounded: a theory of 'constructive residence' is not recognised.[15] Conversely, the degree of permanence necessary need not be such as to render the place in question the claimant's domicile,[16] he may, consequently, be resident in more than one place or country at any one time.[17] But a person who has his matrimonial home in one country is not normally to be treated as resident in another while he is residing at the matrimonial home.[18]

Within these broad outlines there are a number of factors to be taken into account. Perhaps the most important is the intention of the claimant himself. If he intends to settle in one place, he is likely to reside there.[19] In *R(P) 6/58*:

> C returned from Rhodesia where he had been living for nine years in the hope that he would benefit under the will of a relative. Eleven months later, when his expectations were not fully realised, he went back to Rhodesia. It was held that during these eleven months he was 'resident' in GB, as it had been, at the time, his intention permanently to stay there.

Conversely, a person taking a job abroad may still be resident in Britain if he intends to return immediately on its completion.[20] But in this situation the authorities are likely to have regard to the nature of the employment: if it is of a finite nature, e.g. a fixed term contract, the intention to return will prevail;[1] if, however, it is of indeterminate length, the mere expression of hope to return at sometime in the future will generally be insufficient.[2] Of course, the amount of time actually spent in Britain (or abroad) may be significant – in *Fox v Stirk*[3], Lord Denning MR spoke of a stay amounting to residence when it involves 'a considerable degree of permanence' – but if the intention is unequivocal, even a short time may be sufficient.[4] Another very important factor in practice is the nature of arrangements made for living while the individual is in Britain. It is not necessary that he should own or rent his own accommodation, but if he stays throughout in a hotel or with relatives, he must be able to show that he made his 'home' there.[5] If he leaves furniture and other personal effects in one place, this will help to show that he is still resident there even if he has lived for a considerable period elsewhere.[6] In any

---

14 Quoted in *Levene v IRC*, n.13, above, at 222, *Fox v Stirk and Bristol Electoral Registration Officer* [1970] 2 QB 463 s.475, 477, and *CG 32/49*.

15 *CG 32/49; 55/50 (MB); R 5/62 (UB); R(P) 1/72*. For the theory as applied to the poor law see *R v Glossop* (1866) LR 1 QB 227 and *West Ham Union v Cardiff Union* [1895] 1 QB 766.

16 *R(F) 1/62(T), R 1/71 (P)*. For the concept of domicile generally, see Dicey and Morris *Conflict of Laws* (11th edn) ch 7.

17 *R(G) 2/51; R(P) 2/67*. See also *Re Norris, ex parte Reynolds* (1888) 4 TLR 452, *Levene v IRC*, n.13, above, *IRC v Lysaght*, n.13, above, and *Fox v Stirk and Bristol Electoral Registration Officer*, n.14, above.

18 *R(P) 1/78* para 7, H Magnus, Comr.

19 See esp. the dictum of Somervell LJ in *Macrae v Macrae* [1949] P 397, 403.

20 *CG 204/49*.

1 *R(G) 2/51*.

2 CG 165/50; *R(G) 5/52*. See also *Lewis v Lewis*]1956] 1 All ER 375, [1956] 1 WLR 200.

3 [1970] 2 QB 463, 475.

4 *R(F) 1/62* and see *Macrae v Macrae*, n.19, above.

5 *R(P) 4/54; R(F) 1/62; R(P) 1/72*; and see: *Re Norris, ex parte Reynolds*, n.17, above; *Re Erskine, ex parte Erskine* (1893) 10 TLR 32; *Levene v IRC*, n.13, above and *Re Brauch, ex parte Brittanic Securities and Investments Ltd* [1978] Ch 316, [1978] 1 All ER 1004.

6 *R(G) 2/51; R(F) 1/62; R(P) 2/67*. See also *Hopkins v Hopkins* [1951] P 116, [1950] 2 All ER 1035, *Stransky v Stransky* [1954] P 428 and *Lewis v Lewis*, n.2, above.

event, it is easier to prove a continued residence in one place than a change to another country.[7]

iv 'Ordinarily resident'

Social security law employs the term 'ordinarily resident' less frequently than 'resident'. Where it is used it connotes the idea of residence with 'some degree of continuity'.[8] Its object is to exclude from entitlement persons who live mostly abroad but who come to reside in Great Britain intermittently without wishing to settle here.[9] According to the House of Lords, interpreting the same expression in relation to eligibility for an education grant, it means 'that the person must be habitually and normally resident here, apart from temporary occasional absences of long or short duration'.[10] 'Habitually' implies that the residence should be adopted both voluntarily and for settled purposes, for example, education, business employment or health, but it does not require an intention to live in a place permanently or indefinitely.[11]

v Days of residence and absence

A person bearing the burden of proving that he was resident, or absent, on a day or period, must establish that he was resident or absent *throughout* that day or period.[12]

Part 5   Hospital in-patients

A   General

Where the claimant, on a dependant for whom he is entitled to an increase, is a long-term hospital in-patient, enjoying free maintenance there under the National Health Service, the amount payable is reduced. The policy is an obvious one, and may be seen as part of the provisions for overlapping benefits,[13] to the extent that a person's primary living needs are being supplied by services financed by public funds full benefit is inappropriate.[14] Notwithstanding opposition from the Social Security Advisory Committee,[15] some major amendments to the rules were made in 1987, the majority of which further reduced the entitlement of beneficiaries.[16] The government justified the reforms on the grounds that the rules needed to be simplified[17] and to be

---

7 *R(F) 1/62; Macrae v Macrae*, n.19, above.
8 *R(P) 1/78* paras 7–8, adopting a dictum of Viscount Cave LC in *Levene v IRC*, n.13, above, at 225. See also *Stransky v Stransky* n.6, above, at 437, per Karminski J.
9 *R(P) 1/78* para 9.
10 Per Lord Scarman, *Shah v Barnet London Borough Council* [1983] 2 AC 309 at 342, adopting a dictum of Lord Denning MR in the same case: [1982] QB 688, 720.
11 Per Lord Scarman, loc cit, at 343–344.
12 *R(S) 1/66* and *Re a Farm Manager* [1979] 1 CMLR 445 at 446, in preference to an earlier interpretation that the state of affairs at the beginning of a day should be treated as persisting throughout that day: *CU 54/48*.
13 Cf pp. 381–386, below.
14 See NIAC Reports on Draft Hospital In-Patient Regulations 1948–49, HC 241, on the Question of Long-Term Hospital Patients (1960, Cmnd 464) and SSAC Report on Draft Hospital In-Patient Amendment Regulations 1987 (Cm 215).
15 Ibid.
16 SI 1987/1883.
17 More specifically to integrate the contributory benefit rules with the income support rules – on the latter, see pp. 465–466, below.

brought into line with what it assumed to be changing patterns in hospitalisation practices and domestic expenditure.[18]

B Adjustments to personal benefit

No adjustment is made for the first six weeks of free in-patient treatment. It is assumed that expenditure will continue to be incurred during short stays: in particular, it is unlikely that a person will discontinue his occupation of premises, and thus he will remain liable for rent or mortgage repayments. Once, however, this period has elapsed, it is assumed that his living expenses will be significantly reduced, though if he has dependants the family home will still have to be maintained. The rules are classified, therefore, according to the length of stay in hospital, and the existence or non-existence of dependants; they incorporate references to the current standard rate of a Category A retirement pension.[19]

i   *From 7–52 weeks*   If the claimant has a dependant for whom an increase is, or would but for the rules to be described in the next paragraph be, payable, benefit is reduced by 20 per cent of the standard rate; if he has no such dependant it is reduced by 40 per cent; but the reduction in any case is not to leave him with less than 20 per cent of the standard rate.[20]

ii   *After 52 weeks*   After a year, the principle is modified so that the claimant himself, while in receipt of treatment, never receives more than 20 per cent of the standard rate – often referred to as 'pocket-money' benefit. The next 40 per cent is not payable, but if he has a dependant, and has made an appropriate application to the Secretary of State, any excess remaining is paid to that dependant.[1] A spouse who has also received free in-patient treatment for a year or more is not regarded as a dependant for this purpose. The provisions which enabled a claimant without a dependant to accumulate the excess and receive it in the form of a 'resettlement benefit' on discharge from hospital have been abrogated.[2]

C Adjustment to increases for dependants

There are analogous rules governing the adjustment of increases for dependants.[3]

i   *Dependent spouse in-patient*   Where a dependent spouse has been an in-patient for a period of six weeks, the increase payable for that person is reduced by 20 per cent of the standard pension rate, though not so as to reduce it to less than 20 per cent of that rate. After 52 weeks, if the dependent in-patient is a spouse and is still regarded as 'residing with' the beneficiary,[4] the reduced increase is not payable at all unless the latter is regularly incurring expenditure, or causing some payments to be made, on the spouse's behalf.

18 See the Secretary of State's statement which precedes the SSAC Report, n.14, above.
19 SI 1975/555, Part II, as amended.
20 For the meaning of 'dependant' see ibid, reg 2(3).
 1 The excess may, alternatively, be paid to another person who satisfies the Secretary of State that he will apply the sum for the benefit of the dependant.
 2 The policy is to target resources on those in need at this time through the social fund: SSAC Report, n.14, above, p.2, and see pp. 522–525, below.
 3 SI 1975/555, Part III, as amended.
 4 Cf pp. 343–345, above.

ii *Both beneficiary and dependent spouse in-patients* Where both have been in-patients for a period of six weeks, the increase is reduced by 20 per cent of the standard pension rate (though not so as to reduce it to less than 20 per cent of that rate). After 52 weeks, the increase can never exceed 20 per cent of the standard pension rate; the next 20 per cent is not payable, and any part of the remaining increase exceeding 40 per cent of the standard pension rate is payable for the benefit of a child of the beneficiary's family to some other person undertaking to use it for that purpose or to the dependant (if he/she leaves hospital).

iii *Child dependant in-patient* Where a child dependant has been an in-patient for a period of 12 weeks the increase is payable only if the beneficiary is regularly incurring expenditure on his behalf, or causing some such payment to be made for his benefit.

D Incapacity to enjoy proceeds

The condition of some long-term patients is such that there is little personal use to which the 'pocket-money' benefit (20 per cent of the standard pension rate) can be put. The Regulations therefore provide that where a single claimant has been an in-patient for over a year and a medical officer treating him issues a certificate to the effect that no sum, or only a specified weekly sum (less than that to which he could otherwise be entitled) can be applied for the 'personal comfort or enjoyment' of the patient, his weekly entitlement is reduced to that sum (if any).[5]

E Free in-patient treatment

Adjustments are made only for periods of 'free in-patient treatment'. The regulations provide that:

– 'a person shall be regarded as receiving or having received free in-patient treatment for any period for which he is or has been maintained free of charge while undergoing medical or other treatment as an in-patient' in a 'hospital or similar institution' maintained or administered under the National Health Service or by the Secretary of State (or Defence Council) or in such an institution 'pursuant to arrangements made by the Secretary of State or by anybody in exercise of functions' on his behalf.[6]

It is clear, in the first place, that the word 'treatment' is a misnomer. The object of these regulations is to avoid overpayments to persons being maintained free of charge in hospitals and similar state-financed institutions, and the nature of the treatment offered there is not crucial. Hence the Chief Commissioner has ruled that the phrase should not be the subject of refined distinctions: the mere fact that a person is an in-patient in a hospital is strong prima facie evidence that he is undergoing 'medical or other treatment'.[7] In any event, the receipt of nursing services will be sufficient.[8] In the light of these policy objectives, the finding that he is an 'in-patient' is obviously very

---

5 SI 1975/555, reg 16, as amended.

6 Ibid, reg 2(2), as amended. For the institutions covered, see *R(S) 4/53* and *R(S) 2/54*.

7 *R(P) 1/67* para 14 (R G Micklethwait).

8 Ibid, at para 13, and see *Minister of Health v General Committee of Royal Midland Countries Home for Incurables at Leamington Spa* [1954] Ch 530, 541, 547, 549–550.

important; and the phrase has been consistently interpreted to mean 'housed overnight' at the relevant institution.[9] Thus a person living at home because there are not sufficient beds available at the hospital, even though in all other respects he is treated as an in-patient, is not an 'in-patient' for the purposes of these regulations.[10]

While a private patient in a hospital or equivalent institution is not subject to the reduction rules, the onus is on him[11] to show that he (or a third party, but not a public fund[12]) is paying charges designed to cover the whole cost of accommodation and services other than treatment.[13]

F Calculation of periods

The periods of in-patient treatment referred to must in principle be continuous, but this is modified by the regulations to take account of the possibilities both of time spent in other accommodation maintained at public expense, and of short interruptions to the free treatment.

i Residence in other accommodation

The period of in-patient treatment is deemed to include any period of prior residence in 'prescribed accommodation' which, broadly speaking, covers publicly financed caring or residential accommodation.[14] If it has been decided by the appropriate authority that residence in such accommodation is not temporary, it is deemed, for purposes of the rules on adjustment, to have lasted for 52 weeks.[15]

ii Linking of periods

Any two or more periods of free in-patient treatment (or residence in prescribed accommodation) separated by intervals not exceeding 28 days may be linked,[16] though the aggregate period thus taken into account does not include the intervals themselves.[17]

G Benefit to be adjusted

The benefit to be reduced is, with one exception,[18] that which is payable after the Overlapping Regulations have taken effect.[19] The age addition is not affected, however, unless the beneficiary has been an in-patient for more than 52 weeks and he has no spouse or child 'residing' with him.[20]

---

9 *CS 65/49*; *R(S) 8/51*; *R(I) 14/56*. But if the patient only sleeps in the institution and is responsible for his own maintenance during the day, he is not covered by the rules: *R(S) 4/84*.
10 *R(I) 27/59*.
11 *CS 59/49*.
12 *R(S) 4/53*.
13 SI 1975/555, reg 2(2), as amended, incorporating a reference to National Health Service Act 1977, s.65. See also *R(P) 13/52*.
14 SI 1975/555, reg 17(6) and see: *R(S) 26/54*; *R(S) 15/55*; and *R(S) 6/58*.
15 SI 1975/555, reg 17(2). For the meaning of 'residence' see *R(P) 17/55*; *R(P) 1/67* and pp. 362–364, above.
16 SI 1975/555, reg 17(4).
17 See *R(S) 8/51*. On parts of a day see *CS 131/49*; *R(S) 8/51, R(S) 9/52* and *R(S) 4/84*.
18 See SI 1975/555, reg 18(2).
19 Ibid, reg 18.
20 Ibid, reg 19.

Part 6   Imprisonment and detention in legal custody

A   General

The disqualification from benefit (or a dependant's increase) during periods when a person is 'undergoing imprisonment or detention in legal custody'[1] has always existed in social security law,[2] and yet its policy basis remains ambiguous. It may be seen simply as a penal provision to apply to persons who have forfeited their natural rights as citizens.[3] If this were so, it would be appropriate to confine the disqualification to those imprisoned or detained in connection with a criminal offence. As will appear, this is in practice how the provision has been interpreted, though its wording is not so limited. The alternative policy basis is identical to that encountered in relation to hospital in-patients: the detainee is being maintained at public expense and thus has no need of income maintenance. This may indeed be the case but it is to be observed that in comparison with the hospital in-patients rules, those on detention are much stricter: there is no period of six weeks to adapt to new circumstances; and there is no provision for 'pocket-money' benefit.

B   Scope of disqualification

A person shall be disqualified for receiving any benefit, and an increase of benefit shall not be payable in respect of any person as the beneficiary's wife or husband, for any period during which that person is undergoing imprisonment or detention in legal custody.[4]

i   Benefits affected
Except for guardian's allowance[5] and industrial disablement benefit,[6] this disqualification applies to all benefits, including the additions and increases to the disablement benefit.

ii   Connection with criminal offence
A literal reading of the regulation quoted above indicates that it should cover all cases where the claimant is lawfully detained in custody, in other words, where a court would legitimately refuse an order of habeas corpus. This was, indeed, the interpretation suggested by the Divisional Court in 1955,[7] notwithstanding a stream of earlier Commissioners' decisions which held that the detention must be connected with criminal proceedings or a criminal act.[8] The National Insurance Advisory Committee, when it examined the matter in 1960, manifestly preferred the narrower interpretation.[9] But the amending regulations, consequential on its Report, failed fully to implement this

1 SSA 1975, s.82(5).
2 Cf NIA 1911, s.87(3).
3 Per Widgery, arguendo, *R v National Insurance Comr, ex parte Timmis* [1955] 1 QB 139 at 145.
4 SI 1982/1408, reg 2.
5 Ibid, reg 2(5). The allowance is payable to a person appointed by the Secretary of State to receive and deal with it on behalf of the beneficiary: ibid, reg 3(3).
6 Ibid, reg 2(6). Payment of the disablement benefit is, however, suspended: p.370, below.
7 Per Lord Goddard CJ, *R v National Insurance Comr, ex parte Timmis*, n.3, above, at 149.
8 *R(S) 20/53*; *R(S) 21/52*; *R(P) 10/54*; *R(S) 3/55*; *R(S) 4/55*; *1/55 (SB)*.
9 Report on the Question of Long-Term Hospital Patients (1960, Cmnd 964).

view.[10] They provided that there will be no disqualification for a period of imprisonment or detention in legal custody which arises from criminal proceedings unless a penalty is imposed at the conclusion of the proceedings.[11] This does not make criminal proceedings a condition of the disqualification; it only adds a further condition – that of a penalty – where the detention is connected with criminal proceedings. Thus in strict law the position is that someone, for example, remanded in custody in respect of a criminal charge from which he is later acquitted, does not lose benefit, but those detained for civil contempt are disqualified. However, the adjudicating authorities are not, it seems, prepared to tolerate such a result. In 1974 the High Court of Northern Ireland reiterated the traditional view that the detention had to be connected with a criminal offence,[12] and in *R(S) 8/79* the British Commissioner held that a beneficiary who was committed to prison for failing to carry out a maintenance order was not to be disqualified. He admitted that if the point has been raised for the first time, he would have preferred the literal interpretation suggested by the Divisional Court, but he considered himself bound by the authorities adopting the narrower view.[13]

iii Mentally abnormal offenders

If this narrower view be maintained, those detained under the Mental Health legislation but who have not been the subject of criminal proceedings escape disqualification. Understandably, the Natinal Insurance Advisory Committee considered that it was, however, appropriate to disqualify an individual who was transferred from a prison (or analogous institution) to a mental hospital during the currency of a penal sentence.[14] The regulations thus provide[15] that a person shall not be disqualified for a period of:

> detention in legal custody after the conclusion of criminal proceedings[16] if it is a period during which he is liable to be detained in a hospital or a similar institution[17] in Great Britain as a person suffering from mental disorder[18] unless
> (a) pursuant to any sentence or order for detention made by the court at the conclusion of those proceedings, he has undergone detention by way of penalty in a prison, a detention centre, a borstal institution or a young offenders' institution; *and*
> (b) he was removed to the hospital or similar institution while liable to be detained as a result of that sentence or order, and, in the case of a person who is liable to be detained [under the Mental Health Act 1983] . . . a direction restricting his discharge has been given.

10 SI 1960/1283, now SI 1982/1408, reg 2(2).
11 For the definition of 'penalty', see ibid, reg 2(8)(c).
12 *R(O'Neill) v National Insurance Comrs* [1974] NI 76, approving *R 1/76 (P)(T)*.
13 See also *R(S) 1/81* para 4. In considering an application to quash this decision, the Divisional Court refers without comment to the fact that the narrower view has been 'accepted by all concerned': *R v National Insurance Comr, ex parte Warry* [1981] 1 All ER 229, 231.
14 N.9, above, at para 19.
15 SI 1982/1402, reg 2(3).
16 'Criminal proceedings against any person shall be deemed to be concluded upon his being found insane in those proceedings so that he cannot be tried or his trial cannot proceed': ibid, reg 2(8)(g).
17 This means any place (other than prison or analogous institution) in which 'persons suffering from mental disorder are or may be received for care or treatment': ibid, reg 2(8)(b). For 'mental disorder' see n.18, below.
18 The reference to 'mental disorder' is to be construed as including references to any mental disorder within the meaning of the Mental Health Act 1983: SI 1982/1402, reg 2(8)(f), as amended.

Thus, a person transferred from a prison, detention centre, borstal or young offenders' institution may be disqualified but only for the period of his original sentence[19] and for this purpose the Home Secretary, or Secretary of State for Scotland, will issue a certificate stating the earliest date on which the person would have been expected to be discharged.[20] Of course, any other period of detention may well be subject to the rule on hospital in-patients.

iv Detention abroad

As a matter of construction, it has been held, after protracted litigation, that the provisions apply to periods of detention abroad.[1] To meet the objection that they are in consequence discriminatory under EEC law, because the exceptions considered in the previous paragraphs have reference only to British legislation,[2] the regulations have been amended, so that a claimant is not disqualified if he is detained in circumstances similar to those which if they had existed in Britain would have excepted him from the disqualification.[3] A final problem, as yet unresolved, is whether a criminal conviction abroad is to be treated as conclusive for British social security purposes. A conviction in Britain is certainly conclusive; but the Commissioner and the courts have left it open whether they might go behind a foreign conviction on the ground that it offends British notions of justice.[4]

C Suspension of benefit

It follows from the previous discussion that there are circumstances in which persons undergoing imprisonment or detention in legal custody are not disqualified from benefit. Those transferred to mental hospitals are entitled to receive the benefit themselves,[5] in other cases payment is suspended until their release.[6]

Part 7   Forfeiture

A General

The social security legislation contains a number of provisions which deny benefit to a claimant on grounds which to a greater or lesser extent include considerations of public policy: for example, he is disqualified from sickness and unemployment benefit if the contingency occured through his own misconduct.[7] In *R v National Insurance Comr, ex parte Connor*, the question

---

19 See e.g. *R(P) 2/57*.
20 SI 1982/1408, reg 2(4).
 1 *R(S) 2/81*, following *Ex parte Warry*, n.13, above, and *Kenny v Insurance Officer* [1978] ECR 1489.
 2 *Ex parte Warry*, n.13, above, and p.602, below.
 3 SI 1982/1408, reg 2(a)–(10).
 4 *R(S) 1/81* para 5, J G Monroe, Comr, referring to *R v Brixton Prison Governor, ex parte Caborn-Waterfield* [1960] 2 QB 498, [1960] 2 All ER 178. The Divisional Court in *Ex parte Warry*, n.13, above, did not consider this suggestion.
 5 SI 1982/1408, reg 3(2).
 6 Ibid, reg 3(1); for guardian's allowance, however, see n.5, p.368, above.
 7 [1981] QB 758 [1981] 1 All ER 769, upholding *R(G) 2/79*, R J A Temple, Chief Comr. The decision was followed in Scotland: *R(G) 1/83*, upheld by the Court of Session in *Burns v Secretary of State for Social Services* 1985 SLT 351.

arose, apparently for the first time in this context, whether there are general principles of public policy not incorporated in the legislation but which might be invoked by the authorities to deny benefit in appropriate circumstances. In the instant case a woman had been convicted of the manslaughter of her husband. The Chief Commissioner decided that since her status as a widow directly resulted from the unlawful act of manslaughter she had properly been denied benefit; and the Divisional Court upheld this decision.[8] Although the social security legislation was, in effect, a code, it was not exhaustive of the principles to be applied and it was to be assumed that the draftsman formulated its content against the background of the general law.

B Adjudication

Shortly after the *Connor* case, the Forfeiture Act 1982 was passed.[9] In the context of social security, it is mainly concerned to determine which authorities are to decide questions of forfeiture and not how they are to exercise their discretion in that regard. Section 4 provides that the question whether benefit has been forfeited as the result of any unlawful killing is to be determined by a Commissioner.[10] The jurisdiction is one of first-instance and differs from that given by section 2 to the courts in relation to property cases in that there is no power to *modify* the effects of the forfeiture rule when the justice of the case so requires; it is, therefore, a question simply whether or not the rule should be applied.[11] The justification for the special jurisdiction is, presumably, that, given the rarity of the issue and the probability that each case will have its own individual aspects, it is thought desirable to concentrate the discretionary decision in the hands of a single authority at a senior level.

C Application of rule

The scope of the rule is still somewhat uncertain. So far, it seems only to have been applied in cases of unlawful killing, though arguably it could be extended to assaults giving rise to a disability as a result of which the assailant receives some benefit, for example a dependant's increase. In any event, receipt of the relevant benefit (most obviously widow's benefit but also, for example, retirement pension where the claimant bases entitlement on a deceased spouse's contributions[12]) must directly result from the unlawful act.

A conviction of murder will invariably lead to forfeiture.[13] But lesser degrees of homicide will not always have this consequence. According to Lord Lane CJ in the *Connor* case, 'it is not the label which the law applies to the crime which has been committed but the nature of the crime itself which in the end will dictate whether public policy demands the court to drive the

8 Applying by analogy the principles developed in the law of succession (e.g. *Re Giles, Giles v Giles* [1972] Ch 544, [1971] 3 All ER 1141) and private insurance (e.g. *Beresford v Royal Insurance Co Ltd*]1938] AC 586, [1938] 2 All ER 602; *Gray v Barr* [1970] 2 QB 626, [1970] 2 All ER 702).
9 See generally Matthews [1983] JSWL 141.
10 For rules of procedure, see SI 1984/451, Part VI. In *R(G) 2/84(T)*, the Commissioners considered that it made no difference whether the rule disentitled the claimant or merely prevented enforcement of entitlement; cf *R(G) 1/83* para 10.
11 *R(G) 1/84(T); R(G) 2/84(T)*.
12 *R(P) 1/84*.
13 This seems to be a necessary implication of Forfeiture Act 1982, s.5. See also *R(G) 1/84(T)*.

applicant from the seat of justice'.[14] In subsequent cases, the Court of Session in Scotland[15] and the Commissioners[16] have invoked judicial dicta from other contexts which suggest that the requisite moral culpability must be established by acts which are deliberate or intentional.[17] As such, the rule has been applied to disentitle a widow convicted of manslaughter (or the Scottish equivalent, culpable homicide) where provocation was involved[18] but not where the killing resulted from a mental disorder.[19] As yet, there has been little discussion of wider policy considerations; for example, the problem of double penalties, the protection of the public purse (or social security contributors) and financial hardship to the claimant.[20]

Part 8   Christmas bonus

A   General

The origin of this curious, and far from commendable, feature of British social security is to be located in the political and economic circumstances of 1972. The Conservative government was, at the time, planning a major offensive against inflation, mainly through centralised controls on wages and prices. It was acknowledged that certain groups within the community, notably pensioners, were particularly in need of protection against rising prices and while the possibility of introducing statutory obligations for uprating benefits was being considered, the government decided to make a single lump-sum payment of £10 at Christmas time to long-term social security beneficiaries,[1] as an 'earnest of their good intentions'.[2] Apart from one minor hitch – under the original Act it was not paid to those deprived of a pension by the earnings rule and a new Act had to be swiftly passed to remedy this defect[3] – the measure proved to be politically popular. It was therefore repeated in 1973 and 1974. The Labour government was not initially enthusiastic, preferring to concentrate attention on the major reforms of 1975 but the practice was renewed in 1977 and 1978. The Conservative Party Manifesto for the General Election of 1979 included a commitment that the Christmas bonus would continue. Consequently the Pensioners' Payments and Social Security Act of that year established the payment as a permanent feature of the social security system. In social policy terms, it serves little obvious purpose except that of courting political popularity,[4] but its importance is no doubt sufficient to justify a short description of the principles governing payment, as reenacted in the Social Security Act 1986.

14 [1981] QB 758, 765.
15 *Burns'* case, n.7, above.
16 *R(G) 1/83; R(G) 2/84(T); R(G) 3/84.*
17 Notably, *Hardy v Motor Insurers' Bureau* [1964] 2 QB 745 at 760, 762, 766–767; *Gray v Barr* [1970] 2 QB 626 at 640, on appeal [1971] 2 QB 554 at 568.
18 *R(G) 2/84(T); Burns'* case, n.7, above.
19 *R(G) 3/84.*
20 Cf Robilliard 44 MLR 718, 720. These issues were raised during parliamentary discussions of the 1982 Bill: see Matthews, n.9, above, at 147.
 1 Pensioners and Family Income Supplement Payments Act 1972.
 2 Sir K Joseph, Secretary of State, 846 HC Official Report (5th series) col 971.
 3 Pensioners' Payments and National Insurance Contributions Act 1972.
 4 Cf Slack 7 Jo Soc Pol 201.

B Persons entitled

To receive payment, an individual must be entitled (or treated as entitled) to one of the following benefits for a period which includes a day in a prescribed week in December:[5]

> retirement, invalidity, or widow's pension; widowed mother's, severe disablement, attendance or invalid care allowance; war pension; income support (if over pensionable age).

The claimant is treated as being so entitled if the non-receipt is the result of some other payment from public funds or from an employer, or the operation of the earnings rule; so also if his earnings or those of his spouse render him ineligible for income support.[6]

C Residence

The claimant must be present or ordinarily resident in the United Kingdom or any other EEC member state at any time during the prescribed week.[7]

D Amount

The amount payable (£10) has remained the same since 1972, though the Secretary of State has the power to increase this by an appropriate order.[8] A beneficiary may receive a second payment for his spouse if they are both over pensionable age and he is entitled (or treated as entitled) to an increase to the qualifying benefit for that person.[9] The same applies in relation to an unmarried couple, living together as husband and wife, one of whom is entitled to income support. These payments are tax free, and are disregarded for the purposes of any income-related benefit.[10]

E Adjudication

Questions of entitlement are determined by the Secretary of State, from whose decision no appeal lies.[11]

Part 9 Earnings

A General

There are a number of rules arising under the Social Security Act 1975 in connection with entitlement to, or assessment of, benefit which refer to the weekly earnings of a person either before benefit was payable or during a period of entitlement. They are for the following purposes:

---

5 SSA 1986, Sch 6, paras 1(1) and 2(1).
6 Ibid, para 3(2)–(3).
7 Ibid, para 2(1)(a).
8 Ibid, para 2(3)(b).
9 Ibid, para 2(2)(b). Entitlement is deemed in circumstances analogous to those of the personal benefit, n.6, above.
10 SSA 1986, Sch 6, para 3(6).
11 Ibid, para 4.

(1) to calculate the reduced earnings allowance payable under the industrial injuries scheme;[12]

(2) to disregard casual or subsidiary work, the earnings from which are below a specified level, where entitlement to benefit is based on incapacity for work, unemployment or retirement – such rules apply to sickness and invalidity benefits,[13] severe disablement[14] and invalid care allowance,[15] unemployment benefit[16] and retirement pension;[17]

(3) to determine whether the earnings of a spouse or child carer disentitle a claimant to a dependant's increase for such a person;[18]

(4) to assess the amount to be deducted from retirement pension for earnings received during the period of entitlement.[19]

The law governing the calculation of earnings for these purposes is primarily to be found in the Computation of Earnings Regulations[20] and the Commissioners' decisions. It has recently been held that 'earnings' in the present context has the same meaning as when used in the legislation governing family income supplement (now family credit)[1]; further guidance may, therefore, be acquired from the case-law on that benefit.[2] On the other hand, the law governing the assessment of contribution liabilities is significantly different since it reflects more closely the rules on income tax.[3]

B What are 'earnings'?

The Social Security Act 1975 provides that ' "earnings" includes any remuneration or profit derived from an employment', the latter term being defined to include 'any trade, business, profession, office or vocation'.[4] These definitions show that a line is to be drawn between earnings, including profits, which are derived from an occupation, and payments which vest in the recipient in some other capacity, e.g. shareholder.[5] The Regulations state more narrowly that ' "earnings" means earnings derived from a gainful employment'.[6] It is clear, however, that the term is not confined to the salary or profits drawn from employment or business, and may include, for example, an allowance paid to the holder of an office.[7]

The claimant need not have actually worked[8] during the period to which the earnings relate – being available to the employer will be sufficient.[9] The

12 Pp. 293–306, above.
13 P.155, above.
14 P.155, above.
15 P.170, above.
16 P.79, above.
17 P.196, above.
18 Pp. 341–343, above.
19 Pp. 198–199, above.
20 SI 1978/1698.
 1 *R(P) 1/87*, para 13, M.J. Goodman, Comr.
 2 Pp. 481–482, below.
 3 Pp. 43–44 and 50–51, above.
 4 SSA 1975, s.3(1), and Sch 20.
 5 *R(P) 22/64*.
 6 SI 1978/1698, reg 1(2).
 7 See *R(P) 2/76*, in which an allowance for attendance paid to a city councillor was held to be 'earnings'. See also *R(U) 8/83* and *R(S) 6/86 (T)*.
 8 Nor have actually received payments: p.376, n.6, below.
 9 Cf *R(P) 7/61(T)* in which the claimant received sick pay, now governed by specific regulations: p.376, below.

fact that payments are described as ex gratia is not conclusive;[10] nor is it relevant that the claimant's motive in carrying out work was not one of financial gain.[11] A difficult case on the other side of the line is *R(P) 4/67:*

> C, a former partner in a firm of accountants, was paid £1,000 at the end of his first year of retirement for advisory services rendered to the firm. At no time during this year when the claimant gave advice was it suggested that a payment would be made.

The Commissioner, H Magnus, held that the payment did not constitute earnings, as there was no contractual obligation on either party, and the claimant never expected or even hoped to be paid. It was suggested, however, that any further payment for advisory services would be so construed. The suggestion was borne out by the later case *R(P) 1/69*, where a similar payment made the following year to this claimant was held to constitute 'earnings'.[12] The Commissioner, D Neligan, laid particular emphasis on the fact that the claimant had been awarded earned income tax relief on the £1,000.[13] Other situations where it may be difficult to determine whether payments constitute 'earnings' can now conveniently be discussed under a number of specific headings.

i Director's fees and partnership profits
A director's fees will constitute earnings from employment, even though the duties – attendance at an annual general meeting – are very slight.[14] The fact that he has considerable financial power is enough to make a directorship a gainful employment. In a Northern Ireland case, it was held that a woman who owned a farm (worked by her son) and enjoyed the profits from it was in an analogous position to a director; therefore, the income was treated as earnings, and not as interest on an investment.[15] Partnership profits are clearly earnings for social security purposes, while dividends from a limited liability company are not.[16] Nor is trust income.[17]

ii Payments for assisting in spouse's business
Some nice questions arise when one spouse assists in a business, typically a retail shop, owned and conducted by the other. The approach taken by the Commissioner is that if, say, the wife does appreciable work and brings money into the business, she is to be treated as gainfully employed, and a proportion of the profits will be regarded as her earnings.[18] This principle will not be applied if the amount of work is trivial, or if the wife organises her husband's business while he is temporarily unable to work.[19] On the other hand,

---

10 *R(P) 7/61(T)*.
11 *R(P) 1/65* (following *Benjamin v Minister of Pensions and National Insurance* [1960] 2 QB 519, [1960] 2 All ER 851). See also *R(P) 2/76* and *R(S) 6/86(T)*.
12 See also *R(G) 1/60*.
13 The attitude of the tax authorities is relevant, but not decisive: see *R(P) 1/65* para 10, (G Glover, Dep. Comr).
14 *R(P) 9/55*; *R(G) 14/56*.
15 *2/57 (P)* Compare the cases on the 'retirement condition', where there appears to be more emphasis on the work done by the claimant: pp. 196–197, above.
16 *R(P) 9/56*; *R(U) 22/64*.
17 *R(G) 9/55*.
18 *R(P) 7/51*; *R(S) 17/52*.
19 *R(S) 8/56*; *R(U) 11/57*.

the fact that no money passes between the spouses does not preclude a finding that one spouse draws 'earnings' from the other's business.[20]

iii Payments in kind and other miscellaneous payments
The Computation of Earnings Regulations provide that the following shall not count as earnings:[1]

(a)   the value of luncheon vouchers (up to 15p a day);
(b)   the value of meals provided at the place of work;
(c)   the value of accommodation in which the employee is required to live as a condition of his employment;[2]
(d)   the value of food or produce provided for his needs and those of his household;
(e)   (for the purpose only of disregarding subsidiary work in relation at an unemployment benefit claim) certain payments made to members of a territorial or reserve force;
(f)   sums (or remuneration in kind) provided by the employer in December as a Christmas bonus, up to £10.

The implication of this last rule is that other bonuses are to be taken into account.[3] Other remuneration in kind, e.g. board and lodging (not disregarded under the regulations), is to be included and its value is the actual worth of the services, not the amount the claimant has saved by receiving them.[4]

iv Payments assigned or not received by the claimant
The fact that the claimant immediately assigns his or her salary to a third party has been held by a Northern Ireland Commissioner to be irrelevant.[5] So also is the fact that the earnings are not actually received in the week in question.[6] This ruling has been followed with striking effect:

> C claimed an increase of pension for his wife, thinking that the profits from her business in Italy did not amount to earnings, because they were not transmitted to this country. But the earnings rule was applied and the increase refused.[7]

v Other payments to employees and occupational pensions
Legislation provides that statutory maternity pay is to be treated as earnings,[8] and the same applies to any sickness payments 'to or for the benefit of the employed earner' made by an employer.[9] This covers both statutory and contractual sick pay. A power, by regulation, to disregard any part of these payments attributable to contributions made by the employee[10] has not been exercised. While payments under occupational pension schemes do not, in

20 *R(P) 6/57* para 3.
 1 SI 1978/1698, reg 3.
 2 See *R 2/72 (P)*.
 3 See *R(G) 7/59*.
 4 *CP 1/48; R 5/61 (P)*.
 5 *2/59 (P)*.
 6 *R(P) 5/53; R(S) 6/86 (T)*.
 7 *R(P) 1/70*.
 8 SSA 1986, Sch 4, para 10.
 9 SSA 1975, s.3(1A).
10 Ibid, s.3(1B).

general, count as earnings, they are treated as such for the purpose of all rules governing increases for dependants.[11]

C Earnings which cannot be immediately ascertained

Special problems are posed by earners whose employment, generally self-employment, produces earnings which are not immediately ascertainable. The various rules on earnings normally refer to a weekly or daily amount and the problems arise, typically in connection with self-employment, where money is not received on this basis. For the purpose of dealing with such cases, the regulations distinguish between two categories of claim.

The first arises where the earner is a retirement pensioner or an adult dependant of a retirement or invalidity pensioner. If 'a return or statement of the emoluments or the profits or gains from the employment' has been or will be delivered to the Inland Revenue, the earnings are to be calculated by dividing the profits or gains by the number of weeks in the relevant assessment period during which he was employed.[12] This is the current income tax year,[13] or, in the case of self-employed claimants, the accounting period, whether or not this is a full year.[14] Pending the delivery of such a statement, the Secretary of State may suspend payment of the pension or dependant's increase and make an interim award instead. When the assessment is finally determined, any excessive interim payments may be recovered from the beneficiary.[15]

In all other cases, regulations direct the authorities to calculate the earnings 'as best they may', taking into account available information and 'the probabilities of the case'.[16] A Tribunal of Commissioners has recently provided some helpful guidelines on the application of this vague principle.[17] A reference period should be adopted (13 weeks unless that is inappropriate)[18] and then it should be determined whether the weekly earnings exceed the specified amount in more than half of the weeks in the selected period. However, the latter period should not include weeks in which the claimant earns nothing.

D Deductions from earnings

The question next arises as to what deduction may be made from gross profits, wages or salary. The frequency with which retirement pensioners (or the adult dependants of retirement or invalidity pensioners) take in boarders or lodgers made it convenient to formuate a special rule for these cases. Where full board and lodgings is provided, half the amount paid in excess of £6.00 per week is treated as earnings;[19] where less is provided, the authorities should have regard to half the amount of such smaller sum as they consider to be

---

11 SSA 1988, s.10.
12 SI 1978/1698, reg 5. It was held in *R(S) 1/82* that a P60 form was not such a 'return or statement'; it therefore follows that this regulation cannot apply to the vast majority of employed earners who make no other income tax return. See also *R(S) 3/83*.
13 *R(P) 1/73* para 33, per R G Micklethwait, Chief Comr.
14 *R 2/75 (P)*.
15 SI 1978/1698, reg 6(3) and see *R(S) 3/83*.
16 SI 1978/1698 reg 2(3).
17 *R(S) 6/86(T)*; see also *R(U) 3/88(T)*.
18 Cf *R(P) 4/56* and *R(P) 1/62*.
19 SI 1978/1698, reg 7(a).

reasonable in the circumstances.[20] In all other cases, the regulations provide an exhaustive list of such deductions as may be made.[1]

(a) social security contributions;
(b) 'expenses reasonably incurred . . . without reimbursement in respect of – '
  (i)   travel between home and work, and in connection with and for the purpose of work;
  (ii) premises (other than those in which he normally resides), tools and equipment for the claimant's work;
  (iii) protective clothing;
  (iv) trade union or professional association subscriptions;
  (v)   reasonable provision for the care of another member of the claimant's household, because of his necessary absence from home;
  (vi) the cost (up to 15p) of a meal during hours of work, for which no voucher is given.
(c) 'any other expenses (not being sums the deduction of which from wages or salary is authorised by or under any enactment) reasonably incurred by him without reimbursement in connection with and for the purposes of that employment.'

Income tax, whether paid through PAYE or after assessment, is not deductible,[2] nor are contributions payable to occupational pension schemes.[3]

The major legal difficulty arises from the inconsistent interpretation by the Commissioners of the phrase 'in connection with that employment'. In some older cases, this was construed to mean 'in consequence of' the employment; on that approach the expense would be deducted if it was incurred as a result of the work done by the claimant.[4] In at least three more recent reported decisions, the Commissioner has taken the view that this is a gloss on the ordinary meaning of the phrase, and that the expenses must be reasonably connected with the employment.[5] It does not appear, however, that this change in approach would affect previous rulings disallowing deductions for insurance premiums,[6] household rent,[7] subscriptions to a sick fund,[8] and the costs of sending a child to boarding-school even though this was the very reason why the claimant went to work.[9]

Whether an expense is reasonable for the purpose of the deduction provisions is to be determined by reference to the level of the claimant's earnings and the particular facts of the case.[10] The test is 'whether the expenses can be regarded as being incurred in respect of the performance of the duty that carries the right to the earnings in question'.[11] Among the miscellaneous expenses held to have been reasonably incurred in connection wth the clai-

20 Ibid, reg 7(b).
 1 Ibid, reg 4.
 2 Ibid, reg 4(c), abrogating the previous position whereby PAYE payments were deducted: *R(P) 3/56; R(P) 3/62*. The change followed a recommendation of NIAC (1966, Cmnd 3170), paras 41–47.
 3 *R(P) 2/75*.
 4 *CG 114/49; R(P) 2/54*.
 5 *R(P) 2/56; R(P) 1/64; R(P) 1/66*.
 6 *R(G) 7/52*.
 7 *CP 2/48*.
 8 *R(G) 7/52* and see SSA 1975, s.3(1B) (n.10, above).
 9 *R(G) 7/53*; cf *R(G) 9/51*.
10 *R(G) 1/56; R(G) 7/62*.
11 *R(U) 5/83* para 13, J G Monroe, Comr.

mant's employment have been: the costs of domestic assistance in the home;[12] commission paid to an employment agency;[13] and 15 per cent of the cost of new fixtures and installations for a business, and of the legal expenses incurred in acquiring them.[14] In a Northern Ireland case, the Commissioner ruled that the expenses (in the case, travelling expenses to a holiday camp) should be averaged over the whole of the earning period during which they were incurred.[15]

Allowances recognised by the Inland Revenue for income tax purposes, for example, those for heating and lighting a place of work, will usually be deductible.[16] But the fact that the tax authorities do not allow a certain item of expenditure is not conclusive in the present context, since it is clear that, in several respects, such as the cost of meals and of travel to and from work, the Computation of Earnings Regulations are more generous than income tax law and practice.[17]

Part 10　Up-rating of benefits

A　General

The problem of maintaining the value of benefits in relation to rising prices and wages and the various solutions available were considered in chapter 1.[18] It remains here to describe the methods currently adopted under the social security legislation. Prior to 1973 there were no legislative obligations to ensure that benefits kept pace with inflation, and the real value of some, notably family allowances, declined considerably. The sharp increase in the rates of inflation in the early 1970s and the desire to confer on contributors the security that benefits would retain their value prompted the Conservative government to introduce in 1973 for the most important contributory benefits a mechanism for annual 'up-rating'[19] – a word which one judge has described as 'a recruit to the English language which does not notably enrich it'.[20] As a result of a later amendment, the annual review of long-term benefits was to take account of rises in prices *or* earnings whichever would be more advantageous to beneficiaries.[1]

In retrospect, 1975 may be regarded as the year in which the legal obligations to maintain the value of social security benefits were at their most powerful. In the subsequent period, there has been an almost continual tendency to impair their efficacy, a consequence predominantly of the Conservative government's aim to reduce public expenditure.[2] The relevant measures included: the linking of long-term benefits to increases in prices (rather than prices *or* earnings, whichever was more favourable to beneficiaries); an up-rating of short-term benefits for 1980–81 at 5 per cent *less*

---

12 *R(G) 7/62.*

13 *R(G) 6/54.*

14 *R(P) 3/57* (but no sum could be deducted for 'depreciated' goodwill).

15 *R 2/72(P)*; cf *R(U) 5/83* (travelling expenses deducted from particular days of earnings).

16 *R(P) 1/87.*

17 Cf NIAC Report (1966, Cmnd 3170), para 81.

18 P.20, above.

19 SSA 1973, ss. 7–8.

20 Per Megarry VC, *Metzger v Department of Health and Social Security* [1977] 3 All ER 444 at 445.

1 NIA 1974, s.5; SSBA 1975, ss. 3–4.

2 See generally Lynes *Maintaining the Value of Benefits* (1985).

than the increase in prices (though the cut was later restored when the relevant benefits became taxable); postponement by two weeks of the coming into force of the up-rating order; release from the obligation to maintain the value of the earnings limits placed on retirement pensioners and the dependants of beneficiaries.

To analyse the current principles, it is necessary to distinguish between the Secretary of State's duty to review the value of benefits, a consequential duty to up-rate certain benefits in the light of that review, and a power to up-rate others.

B Duty to review value of benefits

The Secretary of State is under a legislative duty to review annually almost all benefits, but not the income-related benefits, to determine whether 'they have retained their value in relation to the general level of prices obtaining in Great Britain'.[3] The latter is to be 'estimated in such manner as the Secretary of State thinks fit'.[4]

C Duty to up-rate certain benefits

Where, as a result of the review, the Secretary of State finds that there has been an increase in the general level of prices, he must lay before Parliament a draft order up-rating the amounts payable for certain benefits by the same percentage increase.[5] It follows that the value of these benefits must keep pace with price inflation only on an historical basis; the Secretary of State is not required to predict the future rate of inflation, something which understandably created great difficulties under previous legislation.[6] The benefits protected by these provisions are, broadly speaking, all contributory and non-contributory benefits payable under the Social Security Act 1975 (as well as statutory sick and maternity pay) except mobility allowance and the age addition.[7] It will be noted that, significantly, the duty to up-rate does not apply to child benefit or to the income-related benefits. In addition, the duty as applied to certain payments made for children, for example a dependency increase or guardian's allowance, is in effect weakened by the power conferred on the Secretary of State by the Child Benefit Act 1975[8] to reduce those payments in the light of the rate of child benefit currently payable.[9]

D Power to up-rate other benefits

The Secretary of State has a broad discretion as regards benefits subject to the duty of review but not to the duty to up-rate (notably child benefit and mobility allowance). If 'he considers it appropriate, having regard to the

---

3 SSA 1986, s.63(1). For child benefit, account must be taken of 'increases in the Retail Price Index and other relevant external factors': SSA 1988, s.5.
4 SSA 1986, s.63(1).
5 Ibid, s.63(2)(a). The duty does not apply where the amount of the increase would be 'inconsiderable': ibid, s.63(4). The draft order must be accompanied by a report of the Government Actuary on the likely impact of the increases on the National Insurance Fund: ibid, s.63(11).
6 See the second edition of this book, p.412 and Lynes, n.2, above, pp. 17–19.
7 SSA 1986, s.63(2)–(3).
8 S.17.
9 See SSA 1986, s.63(6).

national economic situation and any other matters which he considers relevant' he may increase the relevant payments 'by such percentages or percentages as he thinks fit'.[10] Finally, there is a power, the exercise of which is not constrained in any way, to include in the draft of any up-rating order provision for increases to the income-related benefits.[11]

Part 11   Overlapping benefits

A General

Any broadly based system of social welfare encounters the problem arising from the availability of two or more benefits to cover the same, or an essentially similar, risk. The problem has two dimensions. The first is concerned with overlaps in the social security system itself; an obvious example is unemployment benefit and invalid care allowance. The general principle to be applied has never been in doubt: 'double provision should not be made for the same contingency'.[12] The principle may be stated thus easily but its implementation is more difficult as it begs the question of what benefits are intended to cover the same contingency: for example, does a war pension deal with the same risk as invalidity benefit? Moreover, even where it is conceded that two benefits are concerned with the same risk, the intention may be to allow the beneficiary to accumulate them: one obvious example is child benefit and increases to a personal benefit for dependent children. Finally there is the problem of deciding what are the limits of the social welfare system for the purpose of applying the principle: are local authority benefits included? Most of these questions receive a solution, explicit or implicit, within the social security legislation itself. An account of these rules forms the subject matter of sections B to E. The second dimension poses even greater difficulties. In many cases there is an overlap between public welfare benefits and private provision, e.g. occupational schemes. There is no consistent policy on this issue, partly because there has never been an overall view of the relationship between the public and private sector, partly because the policy issues themselves are so difficult. They include deciding whether benefits are payable 'as of right' as under a private insurance contract, or are payable rather 'according to need'. In section F a brief summary will be given of the various measures taken, most of them discussed in detail in other parts of the book.

B Recipients of benefits payable under SSA 1975

i Income-maintenance benefits
The principle that double payments should not be made for the same contingency finds its first and most obvious application with regard to benefit intended as basic income maintenance. Thus adjustment is made to those in receipt of two or more of the following non-industrial, personal benefits:[13] unemployment and sickness benefit, widow's, retirement and invalidity

---

10 Ibid, s.63(2)(b).
11 Ibid, s.63(10).
12 NIAC Report on Draft Overlapping Regulations 1948–49, HC 36, para 9. The principle had been stated both by *Beveridge* para 321 and in *Social Insurance* Part I, para 147.
13 SI 1979/597, reg 4(1).

pension,[14] maternity, widowed mother's, invalid care and severe disablement allowance. Entitlement to benefits not intended for income maintenance (attendance and mobility allowance) is not affected, nor, of course, is entitlement to the earnings-related additional component in pensions, or the graduated retirement benefit.[15] The latter are treated as part of the principal benefit which they supplement.[16]

Any adjustment is made according to the following rules.[17]

(1) A non-contributory benefit is deducted from a contributory benefit.

(2) Unless an alternative arrangement has been made, a proportionate part of a benefit paid weekly is deducted from one paid on a daily basis.

(3) In all other cases, the claimant receives the higher or highest of the benefits to which he is entitled.

There are analogous rules for adjustment where entitlement to a personal income maintenace benefit under the Social Security Act 1975 overlaps with entitlement to a similar benefit under other publicly financed schemes, notably a training allowance[18] or an unemployability supplement payable under the war pensions scheme.[19] However, entitlement to the basic pensions awarded for disablement under the war pension and industrial injury schemes is not affected since these are available irrespective of working capacity and are intended more as 'compensation' for the injury itself.[20] The adjustment rules do not apply to the receipt of statutory sick pay or statutory maternity pay for the simple reason that the relevant legislative provisions preclude any overlap of entitlement with the corresponding benefits (sickness benefit and maternity allowance) payable under the Social Security Act.[1]

ii Benefits for special needs

The case for adjusting benefits intended to remedy specific needs arises only as regards overlap between the different schemes for disability. Thus the attendance allowance, invalidity allowance and the mobility allowance may not be accumulated with their equivalents in other schemes.[2]

iii Dependency benefits

Dependency benefits payable under the general social security provisions, the industrial injury and war pension schemes and government training allowance schemes for the same dependant for the same period may not be accumulated.[3] There are two exceptions to this: both a war pension allowance for a child's education and a dependency benefit which is part of a war dis-

---

14 An invalidity pension may be paid with widowed mother's allowance or widow's pension, but the sum of the two basic components should not exceed the standard rate for the invalidity pension: ibid, reg 3. Invalidity allowance may be accumulated with retirement pension.

15 Ibid, reg 4(2).

16 Ibid, reg 4(4).

17 Ibid, reg 4(5).

18 Grants for full-time education and teacher training are, however, treated as 'training allowances' for this purpose: ibid, reg 2(1) and see *R(U) 38/56* and *R 1/68(P)*.

19 SI 1979/597, reg 6 and Sch 1.

20 Cf pp. 283 and 327 above. This does not apply to a war widow's pension which cannot be accumulated with a corresponding benefit under the general scheme: SI 1979/597, reg 6 and Sch 1.

1 SSHBA 1982, Sch 2, para 1 and SSA 1986, Sch 4, Part II.

2 SI 1979/597, Sch 1, paras 6, 7, 10.

3 Ibid, regs 7, 9–10.

ablement pension (not being payable as an increase to unemployability supplement) are disregarded.[4] The former may be rationalised on the ground that it covers a special need, and the latter in that it is really part of the 'compensation' for the injury.

C Child benefit

The traditional view has been that child benefit, which is payable to all families as a general redistributive device, is distinguishable from child dependency increases which are primarily intended to cope with the additional financial problems arising when the main source of income is lost. The legal position remains that in general they may be aggregated but this principle has been undermined by government policy in recent years: the increase payable with long-term benefits has diminished in value and that payable with short-term benefits abolished altogether.[5] In addition, there is a rule that dependency increases may not be aggregated with the increase to child benefit paid to single parents.[6]

D Income-related benefits

The income-related benefits are designed to raise the income of an individual or family to specified levels. In the light of this aim, the general principle is that all other social security benefits are treated as 'income' and thus, effectively, deducted from the amount otherwise payable.[7] There are, nevertheless, some exceptions: in particular, child benefit may be accumulated with family credit and any amounts received by way of mobility allowance or attendance allowance (or their equivalents under other schemes) are disregarded in computing entitlement under that and the other income-related benefit schemes.[8]

E Recipients of National Health Service facilities

To the extent that a social security beneficiary is being maintained free of charge at a hospital or other institution his need for financial support is reduced, and if the maintenance is financed from public funds, there is a strong argument for reducing the amount of benefit. There are special rules governing this subject which have been fully discussed in Part 5 of this chapter.

F Social security benefits and private rights

In many situations, a person subject to a hazard covered by the contributory or non-contributory schemes will be entitled to benefit from another source

---

4 SI 1979/597, reg 7(3).
5 P.339, above.
6 SI 1979/597, reg 8.
7 There is a special rule to cover the contingency where income support is not so reduced (often because it is paid earlier than the other social security benefit): the authority administering the other social security benefit is given power to deduct the amount of overpayment of income support (SSA 1986, s.27).
8 P.446, below.

directed towards the same hazard but arising by way of private law, for example through an occupational scheme. Indeed, in the Beveridge scheme such arrangements were to form an important part of the general welfare system: while the state was to provide the minimum security for each kind of hazard, 'it should leave room and encouragement for voluntary action by each individual to provide more than that minimum for himself and his family'.[9] The argument logically leads to a principle that a person prudent enough to avail himself of facilities elsewhere should be entitled to reap the reward of his prescience and aggregate the public with the private benefit. Unfortunately, the matter is much more complex. In the first place, it is no longer the policy that the state benefit should provide merely the minimum. The unreality of the Beveridge laissez-faire thesis has emerged through the huge reliance on means-tested benefits, and the introduction of earnings-related pensions. Secondly, the insurance basis of the social security scheme has become increasingly undermined as is evident in the shift to earnings-related contributions and the introduction of non-contributory benefits. Thirdly, in those fields where occupational schemes are widespread, it is illusory to regard them as resulting from the 'voluntary' action of individuals. Most frequently they result from collective bargains between trade unions and employers.

In the light of these considerations, we may briefly survey the position reached in the most important areas of overlap between public and private provision. Because no general principle exists, different rules prevail in different areas, and these have generally been described in the sections of the book devoted to the specific benefits in question. The purpose here is to provide, by way of summary, an outline of the various approaches adopted.

i Private insurance
Life insurance is very common; accident or sickness insurance is comparatively rare and, for practical purposes, private insurance against unemployment (as opposed to redundancy schemes) is non-existent. Where private insurance does exist, it fits neatly into Beveridge's prototype and it has never been doubted that the income so obtained might be fully accumulated with the non-means tested benefits.

ii Redundancy payments and compensation for wrongful or unfair dismissal
The state redundancy payments scheme is intended to provide compensation for the loss of a job, the employee having been deprived of his proprietary interest in the employment; the social security benefit is intended as a partial replacement of income lost as the result of the redundancy. Entitlement to one benefit is not affected by receipt of another. Other categories of redundancy payments are similarly treated to the extent that they are regarded as compensation for the loss of a job; but if intended as a substitute for the wages which would otherwise be paid, their receipt disentitles the claimant from unemployment benefit.[10]

On general common law principles, unemployment benefit and/or income support is deductible from an award of damages for wrongful dismissal.[11] The same principle in effect applies to awards of compensation for unfair dis-

9 Para 9.
10 P.73, above.
11 *Parsons v BNM Laboratories* [1964] 1 QB 95, [1963] 2 All ER 658.

missal[12] but in this case the employee receives the unabated award and the amount of unemployment benefit (and/or income support) is recouped from the liable employer.[13]

iii Guarantee payments
Insofar as an employer agrees, or is bound, to maintain a certain degree of remuneration for periods when an employee is laid-off or put on short-time, the employee is to that extent not regarded as unemployed. The guarantee payments are treated as wages and will disentitle him from benefit.[14]

iv Sick pay and maternity pay
Short-term income maintenance for those incapable of work through sickness or maternity is now provided primarily by an employer under the statutory sick pay and statutory maternity pay schemes.[15] Since, where payable, these replace entitlement to sickness benefit and maternity allowance, respectively, no overlap arises. However, the employer may be contractually bound to make payments which exceed in length or amount those prescribed under the statutory schemes. Such additional payments will not affect any social security entitlement (other than that to an income-related benefit) and the question whether the employee should account to the employer for the value of a social security benefit (for example, invalidity benefit) is a matter which is left to the contract of employment.

v Occupational and personal pension schemes
The relationship between state and occupational or personal pensions is complex and has been fully discussed in chapter 5. Broadly speaking, all claimants who satisfy the relevant conditions are entitled to the basic state pension to which may be added *either* a state earnings-related pension *or* an equivalent under an approved occupational or personal scheme.[16] Apart from this, private pension payments may, in general, be accumulated with social security benefits. There are, however, two important exceptions. First, and most obviously, such payments are treated as 'income' for the purpose of the income-related benefits and are thus, in effect, deducted from the amounts otherwise payable. Secondly, and more controversially, since 1980 there has been a pound for pound reduction of unemployment benefit in respect of proceeds of an occupational pension in excess of a prescribed sum. As we have seen,[17] this was to deal with an alleged anomaly whereby those in receipt of such a pension had claimed unemployment benefit without any real expectation that suitable work would be available for them.

vi Tort claims
The overlap between tort claims for personal injury or death and social security provision has been an area of great difficulty and much discussion.[18]

---

12 But not to settlements of unfair dismissal claims.
13 P.75, above.
14 Pp. 89–90, above.
15 Pp. 137–140 and 229–232, above.
16 Though, for inflation-proofing purposes, some entitlement to SERPS remains: p.211, above.
17 P.120, above.
18 See esp. *Pearson* ch 13; *Atiyah* ch 18.

Beveridge had assumed that some adjustment was necessary.[19] The Monckton Committee, examining the question in 1946, agreed but sensibly concluded that it would be wrong to disturb full entitlement to the social security benefit.[20] The latter was payable almost immediately and was not subject to problems of proof of fault, or quantum of damages. It recommended instead that the damages award should take account of the benefit paid or payable,[1] a proposal which in its entirety proved to be politically unacceptable, and resulted in an unsatisfactory compromise: a deduction of one half of any sums paid or payable within five years from the time when the cause of action accrued for sickness or invalidity, industrial disablement benefit and severe disablement allowance.[2] No deduction is made from a damages award under the Fatal Accidents Act for any social security benefit.[3] Legislation is silent on the effect of other social security benefits on personal injury claims, and it has been left to judges to apply general common law principles, though their decisions have not been entirely consistent. It would appear that deductions are to be made for unemployment benefit,[4] income support,[5] family credit[6] and statutory sick pay[7] but curiously not for attendance or mobility allowance.[8]

The Pearson Royal Commission on Civil Liability and Compensation for Personal Injuries made proposals for substantial reform of these matters; they argued that the full value of social security benefits payable to an injured person or the dependants of a deceased person should be deducted.[9] In 1981, the government declared its intention of implementing these recommendations,[10] but, at the time of writing, no legislative proposal has yet emerged.

---

19 Para 260.
20 Final Report of Departmental Committee on Alternative Remedies (1946, Cmd 6860), paras 41–43.
1 Ibid, at paras 48, 92, 96, 98.
2 Law Reform (Personal Injuries) Act 1948 s.2(1), as amended. For details and the case-law see McGregor *Damages* (15th edn) paras 1490–1496.
3 Fatal Accidents Act 1976, s.4(1).
4 *Nabi v British Leyland (UK) Ltd* [1980] 1 All ER 667, [1980] 1 WLR 529.
5 *Plummer v P W Wilkins & Son Ltd* [1981] 1 All ER 91, [1981] 1 WLR 831; *Lincoln v Hayman* [1982] 1 WLR 488.
6 *Gaskill v Preston* [1981] 3 All ER 427.
7 *Palfrey v Greater London Council* [1985] ICR 437.
8 *Bowker v Rose* (1978) 122 Sol Jo 147; *Gohery v Durham County Council* (1978) unreported, Kemp and Kemp *The Quantum of Damages* (4th edn) para 5–323.
9 Paras 467–498.
10 *Reform of the Industrial Injuries Scheme* ch 8.

Chapter 10

Child benefit

Part 1 Introduction

A General

Family provision has frequently been treated as the poor relation of the British social security system. Family allowances, introduced only in 1945, were rarely up-rated with rising living standards and did not appear to be regarded as significant benefits. In 1975 they were replaced by child benefit in a new scheme, which integrated the social security benefit and the more valuable income tax allowances for children. Lower income families, not paying tax, had of course not been able to take advantage of the latter. So the change effected by the Child Benefit Act 1975 was designed to provide a more generous benefit for all families with children, while the tax allowances, which had disproportionately benefited higher income groups were withdrawn. Benefit is paid at a flat rate for all children, though there is a further one-parent benefit for single parents.

For a short period the reform was generally regarded as a significant improvement; child benefit has certainly proved popular and has a very high take-up rate. One important feature is that it, like the family allowance, is paid in the normal course of events to the child's mother. (Income tax allowances in contrast usually benefited the father.) However, in its recent review of the social security system the Conservative government decided that, while the benefit should be retained on its present basis as a universal provision, more resources should be devoted to those on low incomes through means-tested benefits. As a result the level of child benefit has not recently kept pace with inflation, and indeed was not increased at all in the up-rating of April 1988. The benefit seems to have assumed the Cinderella[1] status of its predecessor. The government has persistently resisted calls for significant increases in its level, made by its own backbenchers, the Opposition and pressure groups, some of which emphasise the particular importance of the benefit to women.[2]

In this Part of the chapter, there is first a short outline of the history of family allowances, and then an examination of the reasons which led to their replacement by child benefit. The principal policy questions concerning the

---

1 The term is used by *Kaim-Caudle* p.264.
2 See for example 81 HC Official Report (6th series) cols 1098–1129, and 99 HC Official Report (6th series) col 1078; *Faith in the City*, Report of Archbishop of Canterbury's Commission on Urban Priorty Areas (1985), para 9.91.

child benefits scheme are discussed. In Part 2 of the chapter, the legal conditions for entitlement to the benefit are analysed.

B The history of family allowances[3]

The first proposal to introduce a special allowance for the benefit of children was made in 1796 by William Pitt, then Chancellor of the Exchequer. His enlightened attitude is exemplified by his peroration, often quoted in modern debates: 'Let us make relief, in cases where there are a number of children, a matter of right and an honour, instead of a ground for opprobrium and contempt.'[4] But the Bill never became law, because of the pressure of other business. It seems that the issue was not discussed widely again until after the First World War, when Eleanor Rathbone founded the Family Endowment Society, an important pressure group in the inter-war years. In her book, *The Disinherited Family*, published in 1924, she argued that it was in the interest of society as a whole to ensure that children were well clothed and fed, and that a state allowance should be paid to make this possible. The case for such a payment took on additional strength from the fact that in 1921 and 1922 dependants' allowances were introduced for the unemployed. The absence of any comparable provision when the man was in work might have been viewed as a disincentive to employment. But, unlike other European countries, there was no move at this time to introduce family allowances in Britain.[5]

The introduction of the Family Allowances Bill in 1945, during the last months of the war-time Coalition government, was largely influenced by the Beveridge Report. This adduced three principal arguments for the payment of family allowances. First, the only way of guaranteeing a reasonable subsistence income for all families, whether the head of the family was in work or not, was to pay an allowance for children; this object could not be secured by wages, as they did not take account of the size of a man's family.[6] Secondly, 'it is dangerous to allow benefit during unemployment or disability to equal or exceed earnings during work. But, without allowances for children, during earning and not earning alike, this danger cannot be avoided.'[7] The third argument seems surprising these days: the provision of family allowances was thought conducive to a higher birth rate.[8] The Beveridge Report further argued that payments should be financed by general taxation, so that the whole community should share in the task of maintaining children. But parents were not to be relieved of their entire responsibility, and for this reason it was recommended that nothing should be paid for the first child in a family.[9] Lastly, the Report rejected the argument that the allowance for each child should be reduced as the size of the family increased; there were no real

---

3 See *Walley* pp. 16–20, 54–55, 70–73; Land in (1966) 2 Poverty 13; Hall, Land, Parker and Webb *Change, Choice and Conflict in Social Policy* (1975) ch 9; *Harris* pp. 341–346; Macnicol *The Movement for Family Allowances 1918–45* (1980); Brown, *Children in Social Security* (1985), PSI, Studies of the Social Security System No 3, at pp. 27–38.
4 Quoted by Sir W Jowitt, introducing the debate on *Social Insurance*, Part I 404 HC Official Report (5th series) col 988.
5 In the inter-war years family allowances were introduced in France, Germany and the Netherlands. New Zealand had been the first country to introduce such a scheme – in 1926.
6 Para 411.
7 Para 412.
8 Para 15 and 413. Churchill gave particular emphasis to this point when he announced the Coalition government's acceptance of Beveridge's proposals in a broadcast in 1943.
9 Para 417. See *Harris* p.412.

economies of scale when this occurred. A flat rate payment of 8s (40p) was proposed, though Beveridge indicated that at some future time consideration should be given to grading allowances according to the children's age.[10]

The government modified the scheme proposed by Beveridge in some minor respects. The most important change was that a substantial part of the allowance was to be paid in kind through the provision of free school meals and milk. This reduced the cash payment to 5s (25p) a week, which the government proposed should belong to the father. But on a free vote Miss Rathbone's amendment to make allowances the property of the mother was passed. As the title of the Act and the name of the benefit suggested, the allowance was to be paid to families 'for the benefit of the family as a whole'.[11] The claimant was required to show that the family contained at least two children.

The rate of payment was only twice increased between 1948 and 1967. One development of note was that from 1956 a higher amount was paid for third and subsequent children; this is often a feature of family benefit systems.[12] The 1956 legislation also made the allowance payable for children beyond the general age limit of 16, if they were receiving full-time education or in an apprenticeship. It could be paid for these groups until the age of 18, and after a further amendment in 1964, until the age of 19.[13] There is no obvious reason why family allowances were so neglected throughout this period. It has been suggested that to some extent they suffered because they were the first benefit introduced after the Beveridge Report: the 1945 Act was passed before the Attlee Labour government assumed office and, therefore, the role of family allowances in combating poverty was not discussed during the late 1940s.[14] A second reason is perhaps that the demographic argument for their payment was no longer taken seriously.[15] In fact, there seems very little evidence that the availability of family provision affects population trends.[16] But the belief that it does may have been partly responsible for government reluctance to increase the level of payments. Thirdly, it appears that the allowances were at that time, in contrast to modern attitutes to child benefit, among the least 'popular' of the welfare benefits.[17]

The Labour government did increase the allowance twice in 1968, but only for the benefit of those too poor to pay any income tax. In order to prevent taxpayers benefiting from the increases, an equivalent sum was 'clawed back' from them by a reduction in the value of their children's tax allowances.[18] The device had originally been suggested in the Beveridge Report, and signalled the new approach which led to the Child Benefit Act 1975.

C The change to child benefit

Before the 1975 legislation is discussed, something should be said about child income tax allowances, because their abolition was a crucial aspect of the new

---

10 Para 421. The argument on the appropriate rates for paying benefit still continues: see pp. 390–391, below.
11 FAA 1945, s.1, repeated in FAA 1965, s.1.
12 See *Comparative Tables of Social Security Schemes in Member-States of the European Communities* (13th edn, 1984).
13 FANIA 1964, s.1.
14 The point is made by *Walley* p.182.
15 Ibid, at pp 186–187. See Brown, *Children in Social Security* (1985) PSI Studies of the Social Security System No 3, at pp. 50–51.
16 See Schorr in (1967) 2 Poverty 8.
17 See Bull, (ed) *Family Poverty* (1972) pp. 167–168.
18 For the 'claw-back', see Kincaid *Poverty and Equality in Great Britain* (1973) pp. 69–73.

scheme. They were first introduced by William Pitt two years after his unsuccessful attempt to provide a family benefit. But they were abolished in 1806, and were not reintroduced until 1909. From 1957 their value was graduated according to the child's age, a significant difference from family allowances. Unlike the latter, child tax allowances (CTA) could be claimed in respect of the first child. Two further points may be made. First, CTA benefited high earners proportionately more than those on an average income, because it reduced taxable income, and so enabled the former group to pay tax at a lower rate. Secondly, since tax is normally deducted by PAYE at source, CTA typically benefited the male wage-earner rather than the child's mother.

Towards the end of the 1960s a number of schemes were suggested for integrating family allowances and tax allowances.[19] The Labour party put forward proposals in 1969; then the Conservative government, which took office the following year, recommended their integration as part of a tax credit system.[20] Although the 1974 Labour government was not in favour of this radical reform, it did support a child endowment scheme which had much in common with the tax credit proposal so far as it applied to children. Thus the Child Benefit Bill, introduced in May 1975, enjoyed all party support, and the opposition was only concerned to amend the measure in detail. Its purpose was well summarised by Mrs Castle, the Secretary of State for Social Services:

> It achieves a long overdue merger between child tax allowances and family allowances into a new universal, non-means tested, tax-free cash benefit for all children, including the first, payable to the mother. In this way it ensures that the nation's provision for family support is concentrated first and foremost where it is needed most – on the poorest families; and that it goes to the person responsible for caring for the children and managing the budget for their food, clothing and other necessities.[1]

Child benefit has at least in theory two major advantages over its predecessors. First, it can be paid at a generous level to all families, while families not in receipt of taxable income had not been able to take advantage of CTA. Secondly, unlike the allowance, it is payable for the first child. One important feature is that the benefit is tax free, in this respect differing from the tax credits for children proposed then by the Conservatives and from family allowances. Another is that the benefit is paid to the mother. This had also been the case with the allowance, but some of the tax credit proposals would have entailed award of the credit to the father.[2]

Two further aspects of the legislation should be explored before we look at recent controversies. Child benefit is paid at a flat-rate for each child. There is no variation according to the age of the children or their number in the family. There is in fact considerable evidence that the costs of providing for children vary considerably with their age, older children requiring much greater expenditure on food and clothing.[3] The graduated income tax

19 See *George* pp. 196–197; *Walley* pp. 193–194, Brown, n.3, above, at pp 52–62.
20 P.29, above.
1 892 HC Offficial Report (5th series) col 330.
2 E.g. the Conservative government's Green Paper, Proposals for a Tax-Credit System, Cmnd.5116.
3 See Piachaud *The Cost of a Child* (1979, CPAG), Poverty Pamphlet No 43; Field *What Price a Child?* (1985), PSI Studies of the Social Security System No 8, chs 6 and 7.

allowances had recognised this, as did the supplementary benefit scale rates. However, the government in 1975, while approving of differential rates in principle, took the view that more research should be done before they could be implemented in practice. In particular, not enough in its opinion was known about the costs of the first child (which will include the costs of items such as clothes which can be used for subsequent children) and whether marginal costs are affected by the size of a family.[4] Further, against the evidence of the higher costs of older children, there is the argument that the poorest families are those with young children below school age where the mother is unable or unwilling to go out to work.[5]

The practice in many other countries in the EEC is often to pay higher allowances for second and third children, etc. Thus in 1983 West Germany paid DM 50 a month for the first child, DM 100 for the second, DM 220 for the third, and DM 240 for the fourth and subsequent children.[6] Other countries have more complex provisions under which different payments are made, depending on both the child's age and the number in the family; for example, in Holland a certain amount is paid for a child aged 6–11 if there are two children in the family and a little more for a child of the same age if there are three, and so on.[7] In theory there is much to be said for such systems, but they lack simplicity, an attractive feature of the present British system, and they are naturally a little more expensive to administer.

At all events, the Child Benefit Act 1975 does contain powers for the government to prescribe different rates in relation to different cases, either by reference to the child's age or to other factors.[8] But so far they have only been used to prescribe a higher rate for single parent families, now the one-parent benefit. In the last few years there have been calls for the government to investigate the costs of looking after children and to base the level of child benefit on those figures.[9] But they have not been heeded, for the present administration intends child benefit only to be a basic universal provision to assist all families, irrespective of their need and their actual weekly expenditure on children. Varied rates are most unlikely to be introduced in the immediate future.

The second provision in the 1975 Act of general policy interest concerns the up-rating of the benefit a matter which has continued to create difficulty. While resisting attempts to link the value of the benefit to price movements, the government did insert an amendment to the 1975 Bill which required the Secretary of State to *consider* annually whether the rates should be increased.[10] This weak duty was repealed by the Conservative government in 1986. However, following the outcry at its failure to increase the rate of benefit for 1988, the government accepted an obligation to review its level each April, 'taking account of increases in the Retail Price Index and other

---

4 Standing Committee A Debates, cols 99–100. But the Beveridge Report, para 417, and an unpublished DHSS Report by McClements suggest there is no evidence for economies of scale as family size increases: Standing Committee A Debates, col 81.
5 See Bradshaw (1980) 45 Poverty 15.
6 Brooke Ross and Zacher *Social Legislation in the Federal Republic of Germany* (1982) pp. 33–4.
7 *Comparative Tables of Social Security Schemes in Member-States of the European Community* (13th edn, 1984).
8 CBA 1975, s.5.
9 See (1984–5) 59 Poverty 27–30.
10 CBA 1975, s. 5(5).

relevant external factors.[11] But in contrast to many other benefits, there is no duty to up-rate child benefit, even when there has been a sharp increase in the cost of living.[12]

D Child benefit from 1975

Child benefit has been payable from 1977, and the new scheme finally became effective in 1980 with the end of the CTA, which had been phased out gradually over the three preceding years. Almost from the start there have been criticisms that the level of benefit is too low, and that there is now less financial support for those families with two or more children who had been in receipt of both family and child tax allowances. The Conservative government in 1980 did commit itself to maintaining the value of the benefit in line with inflation,[13] but this pledge has not been honoured. The increases in 1985 and 1986 were below those necessary to keep pace with inflation. Further and most significantly, there was no increase at all to standard (as distinct from one-parent) benefit in 1988, a decision which attracted the fury of the opposition parties and many Conservatives.[14] They argued in particular that the benefit should be up-rated as much as income tax allowances. In fact in the period since the Thatcher government first took office, the real value of child benefit has declined, while in contrast the value of the married man's tax allowance has gone up by 18 per cent.[15]

The reason for this relative decline in the benefit's value is that the government has decided to target financial assistance to help families with low incomes. At first this was brought about by the award of higher amounts of family income supplement for older children and of more generous needs allowances for children under the housing benefits scheme. The Green Paper, *Reform of Social Security*,[16] then proposed the introduction of the new family credit system, which came into effect in April 1988, as the most effective method of achieving the aim. It rejected the alternative solution of reforming child benefit. Three principal possibilities were canvassed. The first, that favoured by many pressure groups, in particular the CPAG, was a substantial increase in the level of the benefit. It was rejected because of its expense, and further because assistance would also be provided for many families who would not need it. This consequence would not occur under the second alternative: the taxation of child benefit, coupled with its more generous provision. A variant on this proposal would be to abolish the married man's tax allowance and radically increases the level of benefit, a change which would benefit women at the expense of men.[17] These ideas, however, run counter to the government's general commitment to reduction in the level of income tax, and it is not surprising that they were robustly rejected. Finally the Green Paper considered whether it would be better to

11 SSA 1988, s. 5. See 129 HC Official Report (6th series) cols 866–962 for the Commons debate on the Lords' amendment imposing the obligation.
12 See pp. 379–380, above.
13 989 HC Official Report (5th series) col 1063.
14 121 HC Official Report (6th series) cols 179ff.
15 98 HC Official Report (6th series) cols 317–8.
16 See Vol 2, Cmnd 9518, paras 4.28–4.44.
17 See *The Structure of Personal Income Taxation and Income Support* 3rd Special Report of the Treasury and Civil Service Committee for 1982-3, HC 386, ch 12; Berthoud and Ermisch *Reshaping Benefits: The Political Arithmetic* (1985) PSI Studies of the Social Security System No 10 pp. 96–105; Brown *Child Benefit: Investing in the Future* (1988, CPAG), pp. 64–5.

adopt a different structure for the benefit, perhaps along the lines followed in some other European countries, where more is paid for older children or larger families. The solution was dismissed, almost certainly rightly, as an ineffective and administratively expensive method for steering help where it was most needed.

The government's perspective, as revealed in the Green Paper, is that the primary function of child benefit is to recognise, and provide some help towards meeting, the costs of bringing up children. Its purpose is not to assist the needy or, in alliance with the tax system, to act as a general redistributive device. One or two bodies, such as the Institute of Directors and the Institute of Fiscal Studies, have questioned whether the benefit has any place in a social security system which, in their view, should be directed entirely to meet the needs of those with low or no income.[18] This crude perspective ignores the existence of other non-means tested benefits, such as retirement pensions, and other aspects of the child benefit scheme. To a limited extent child benefit does act as a redistributive device: from families without children to those with, and from men to women. For some commentators, for example, feminists, these are central features of the scheme.[19] Although the government has not lent any clear support to these views, it is probable that they are considered sufficiently weighty to make abolition of the benefit relatively unlikely. On the other hand, they have not been taken sufficiently seriously by the Thatcher government to persuade it to increase the benefit to a level where it meets the costs of bringing up children. The scheme, therefore, wholly unaffected in its structure by the 1986 reforms, remains a compromise. It does not satisfy those who advocate means testing for all benefits, or those who favour effective redistribution through the social security system. Yet, as the government found in its 1985 review, child benefit is well understood and liked.[20]

Part 2 Entitlement to child benefits

Under section 1 of the Child Benefit Act 1975:

> a person who is responsible for one or more children in any week . . . shall be entitled to a benefit . . . for that week in respect of the child or each of the children for whom he is responsible.

There are two major issues in the determination of entitlement to child benefit: first, whether the child is one in respect of whom benefit is payable, and secondly, whether the claimant is to be treated 'as responsible for a child'. Since two or more persons may concurrently be responsible for the same child, difficult questions as to priority of title to the benefit may arise if there is more than one claim; these are discussed at the end of the second section. The third section is concerned with the residence qualifications which have to be satisfied by both the child and the person responsible for him, and the fourth with the benefit paid to one-parent families.

---

18 (1984–5) 59 Poverty 28 & 39, and see also Dilnot, Kay and Morris *The Reform of Social Security* (Institute for Fiscal Studies, 1984) 122–3.
19 See essay by David and Land in H Glennester (ed) *Sex and Social Policy* in *The Future of the Welfare State* (1983); Brown, n.17, above, at p.53.
20 N.16, above, para 4.44. Also see Walsh and Lister *Mother's Life-line* (1985, CPAG).

A The child

Section 2(1) of the Act provides that:

> a person shall be treated as a child for any week in which –
> (a)   he is under the age of 16; or
> (aa)   he is under the age of 18 and not receiving full-time education and prescribed conditions are satisfied in relation to him; or
> (b)   he is under the age of 19 and receiving full-time education either by attendance at a recognised educational establishment or, if the education is recognised by the Secretary of State, elsewhere.

There is, therefore, a normal age limit under the 1975 Act of 16, with an upper age limit in some circumstances of 18 or 19.

i The normal age limit

The normal age limit of 16 provoked comparatively little discussion during the passage of the Bill. It seems that the government chose this age, because after a person became 16, he might at that time have been entitled to supplementary benefit.[1] Under the previous family allowances scheme, the normal limit was defined by reference to the school leaving age;[2] but as that had been raised to 16, it was practicable to frame the general rule in terms of that age. This normal age limit is quite common in other countries: it is 16 in New Zealand, Australia, Canada, Belgium, Holland and Germany. But in some countries, it is higher: 17 in France, 18 in Italy, Greece, Denmark, and Luxembourg.

In practice the normal age limit has now been modified by regulations made under the amended 1975 Act.[3] The government was anxious to reduce supplementary benefits expenditure on school leavers, so regulations first made in 1980 (and subsequently amended in detail) provide that a school leaver shall continue to be treated as a child for benefit purposes from the date he leaves school (if then 16) or from his sixteenth birthday until the 'terminal date', that is, a date prescribed in the regulations, broadly speaking a day at the end of the school holidays following the date on which the person left school.[4] For this period the child is ineligible for means-tested benefits in his own right. Child benefit under these regulations cannot however be paid for a child who is over 19, nor for a child who is in full-time work. Further, a separate regulation provides that no benefit is payable for any week in which training is provided for the child under the youth training scheme and for which an allowance *may* be paid under that scheme. Under an amendment to the regulations made in 1987, a child whose name has been entered as a candidate for an external examination before he left school shall continue to be treated as a child for benefit purposes until the first 'terminal date' after the conclusion of his examinations (or after his nineteenth birthday).[6]

ii The further age limit of 18

The Social Security Act 1988 provided that child benefit may be paid for a child under 18, who is not receiving full-time education (and not therefore falling in the third category of beneficiary discussed below).[6a] The conditions

1   Standing Committee A Debates, col 10.
2   FAA 1965, s.2(1) and (2)(a).
3   CBA 1975, s.2(3).
4   SI 1976/965, reg 7, amended by SI 1987/357, reg 5.
5   SI 1976/965, reg 7B.
6   Ibid, reg 7(4)–(6), and see Report of SSAC, Cm 106, paras 5–28. The change followed a ruling of a Tribunal of Commissioners in *R(F) 2/85*, which had held that normally a return to sit an examination was not a return to full-time education, so that child benefit would not

are set out in regulations.[6b] The child must be registered for work or for training under the youth training scheme, and must not actually be in employment. Further, he will be treated as a child eligible for benefit only for a limited 'extension period', in effect until he has a place on a training scheme. He is ineligible for child benefit under these provisions if he is in receipt of income support or is already engaged in training.[6c] Finally the person responsible for him must make a written request for payment during the extension period.

iii The further age limit of 19

Under the legislation benefit may be paid for a child under 19 if he is receiving full-time education. There was some criticism of the failure to extend benefit to children over 16 suffering from a physical handicap. This is a common provision in other European countries,[7] but, as was mentioned in the Committee proceedings,[8] in Britain a handicapped child over 16 is eligible for non-contributory disablement benefits, and to award child benefit would create an unnecessary overlap.[9]

The upper limit of 19 is very low in comparison with other EEC countries, almost all of which extend the provision of family benefit beyond the normal age limit for children receiving vocational training or further education.[10] Thus, in France benefit in either circumstance may be extended for children up to 20, while in Germany and Holland there is a high upper limit in these circumstances of 27. In Italy benefit may be extended to 21 for a child in receipt of vocational training and 26 for one in receipt of further education. The British position also seems odd, because the CTA abolished when child benefit was introduced did not have an upper age limit for dependent children, and there was some anxiety at the time of the reform that parents with children at college or university would suffer as its result. But changes were then made to the level of student grant to improve their position. In fact it is difficult to draw satisfactory comparisons between different countries without taking into account the availability and level of student grants, training allowances and other benefits available for young people not fully integrated in the labour market. Nevertheless the limit of 19 does seem low and somewhat arbitrary, there apparently being no reason for its choice, apart from the argument that this also was the limit in the family allowances system.[11]

iv 'Receiving full-time education . . .'

Under the original 1975 Act benefit could only be paid for a child in receipt of full-time education until he was 19, if that education was received 'by attendance at a recognised educational establishment'. By an amendment to that legislation made by the Social Security Act 1986, section 70(1), benefit may also be paid for a child educated elsewhere, perhaps at home, where this is recognised by the Secretary of State. But in the normal case, the child must be in attendance at a school, college or other institution recognised as comparable.[12] Education is regarded under the regulations as 'full-time' if the time spent receiving instruction and undertaking supervised study, etc., is more

6b SI 1976/965, reg 7D, inserted by SI 1988/1227, reg 6.
6c For the limited availability of income support for children between 16 and 18, see pp. 418–420, below.
7 *Kaim-Caudle* ch 8.
8 Standing Committee A Debates, cols 39–40.
9 For disablement allowance, see ch 4, above.
10 See *Comparative Tables of Social Security Schemes in Member-States of the European Communities* (13th edn, 1984).

than 12 hours a week, no account being taken of meal breaks or unsupervised study.[13] A reasonable interruption of up to six months, or even longer where this is attributable to illness or disability, is allowed, provided the period of interruption is not likely to be followed, or actually followed, by a period in which the child receives financial support under the youth training scheme or receives education by virtue of his employment.[14] Some of the case law, interpreting the equivalent provisions in the family allowances scheme, may still be of some help in determining what constitutes a reasonable interruption; for example, it was held that school holidays and leaving one school for the purpose of removal to another would be treated as reasonable interruptions to full-time education.[15] Education received by virtue of the child's work, unless it is part of a course for which he receives no financial support, does not count as full-time education for benefit purposes; the object of these provisions is clearly to prevent an overlap of benefit and wages or other compensation received from an employer. However, a reimbursement of the cost of books, equipment, examination and travelling expenses does not count as financial support in the context.[16]

No benefit is payable for a child between 16 and 19 who is in receipt of 'advanced education'. This is now defined as full-time education for the purposes of a degree, a diploma of higher education, various national diplomas (of a standard above ordinary national diploma), a teaching qualification or any other course above GCE 'A' level and its Scottish equivalents.[17] The purpose of this rule is clearly to prevent benefit being paid for someone eligible for a student grant or other educational maintenance allowance, though the patchy award of these latter benefits may mean that it sometimes operates harshly.

v Married children

There has been some discussion whether child benefit could ever be obtained in respect of a married child:[18] this would, of course, generally be applicable to a child over 16 with regard to whom it is payable under section 2(1)(aa) or (b).[19] The government's intention was that benefit should be awarded in respect of a married child if he has left the other spouse and is in receipt of full-time education. This is covered by the General Regulations:[20]

– A person may be entitled to benefit in respect of a married child, provided that person is not the child's spouse, *and* that either the child is not residing with his spouse or that, if he is, the latter is receiving full-time education.[1]

Interesting possibilities occur if the married child is a mother. She will herself be entitled to benefit in respect of her infant merely on the ground that it is living with her.[2] Further, her own mother (or other person with whom she is

13 SI 1976/965, reg 5.
14 Ibid, reg 6.
15 *R(F) 4/60, R(F) 1/68.*
16 SI 1976/965, reg 8.
17 Ibid, reg 1(2) (definition amended by SI 1987/357).
18 Standing Committee A Debates, cols 19–22.
19 In a few cases a child under 16 will lawfully be married under a foreign legal system and the marriage will be recognised in England if neither spouse is domiciled there: Morris *The Conflict of Laws* (3rd edn) p.165.
20 SI 1976/965, reg 10.
 1 Ibid, reg 11, prescribes the circumstances in which persons are not to be treated as having ceased to reside together: p.403, below.
 2 CBA 1975, s.3(1)(a).

living) will also entitled to benefit in respect of her. This odd situation could have occurred under the family allowances scheme, though the young mother under nineteen would have to have had two children in order to receive family allowances![3] It does seem, however, that one local tribunal was persuaded that a schoolgirl could not be both a mother and child for family allowances purposes.[4]

vi Disqualified children

Benefit is not payable in respect of certain children under Schedule 1 to the Act. First there are disqualifications if the child in the particular week is 'undergoing imprisonment or detention in legal custody', or is in the care of a local authority in various prescribed circumstances. The disqualification only applies if the child has been in detention, care, etc., for more than eight weeks; and it does not apply after that period for a week in which the child lives with a person otherwise entitled, or if that person establishes that as at that week the child ordinarily lives with him throughout at least one day in each week.[5] The regulations have been amended to reverse a Court of Appeal ruling that someone with whom a child had been placed for adoption by a local authority could receive child benefit in addition to the boarding out allowance paid him by that authority.[6] There is also a disqualification if the person otherwise entitled to benefit or his spouse (if they are residing together) is in receipt of any income exempt from UK income tax, e.g. because he is a member of visiting forces or works in an embassy or consulate.[7] This provision is understandable in view of the connection between the tax and child benefit systems, but it works rather harshly for someone whose exempt earnings are considerably lower than his total earnings, the greater part of which is liable to tax here.[8]

B 'Person responsible for the child'

Under section 1, it is the person responsible for a child who is entitled to the benefit in respect of him. This term is primarily defined in section 3(1):

> a person shall be treated as responsible for a child in any week if –
> (a) he has the child living with him in that week; *or*
> (b) he is contributing to the cost of providing for the child at a weekly rate which is not less than the weekly rate of child benefit payable in respect of the child for that week.

The claimant must, therefore, comply with one of these two conditions in order to establish entitlement. In many cases more than one person will satisfy them, and there are, therefore, rules in the Second Schedule to the Act determining which claimant has priority of title to the benefit. These rules are discussed in detail later, but it is perhaps useful to indicate at the outset that generally a person claiming it as 'responsible for a child' under section 3(1)(a) will have priority over a person claiming under section 3(1)(b); in other words, normally the person with whom the child is actually living will be entitled to benefit.[9]

---

3 This, of course, was because family allowances were not payable in respect of the first child of a family.
4 (1975) 31 Poverty 50.
5 SI 1976/965, reg 16(6).
6 Ibid, reg 16(9), added by SI 1987/357 and reversing *DHSS v Simpson*, reported as Appendix to *R(F) 1/85.*
7 SI 1976/965, reg 9.
8 There used to be an exception for such claimants, but this was removed by SI 1984/337.
9 CBA 1975, Sch 2, para 2: pp. 401–405, below, for discussion of the priority rules.

These rules contrast sharply with the equivalent conditions for entitlement to family allowances.[10] As has been mentioned previously, they were paid for every family with two or more children, 'and for the benefit of the family as a whole'.[11] In the typical case eligibility was dependent on proof that the child was 'issue'[12] of the claimant and, therefore, a member of his family. Another person might apply in respect of a child whom he was maintaining, but that claim would always rank lower in priority to one made by the parent(s). The provisions in the Child Benefit Act are in contrast designed to secure that benefit is paid to the person who prima facie most needs it.[13] No special privileges are conferred on a parent as such, though, of course, in normal circumstances it will be (s)he who will receive it.

i 'Child living with him in that week'

a *General*
The Act does not define 'living with', but it would seem generally to mean living in the same place, under the same roof or in the same residence. The term was used in the family allowances legislation,[14] where it was construed by the Commissioner to mean no more than that the claimant and the child must be living together; it did not necessarily imply a requirement of financial support.[15] On the other hand in an earlier case it had been ruled that the relationship between a parent and a child might be so tenuous that the former could not be said to be 'living with' the latter, even though they both resided in the same premises.[16]

It seems that the Commissioner in construing the term in the Child Benefit legislation has adopted a similar, pragmatic approach. The issue arose in *R(F) 2/79*, where the children of divorced parents spent part of their school holidays with each parent. Both claimed child benefit, and an important question was whether the sons were 'living with' their father when they stayed with him.[17] V G H Hallett ruled that the phrase was not synonymous with 'residing together', nor did it necessarily require the exercise of de facto care and control, though where this did exist it would be an important factor in the argument that the child was living with the person concerned. The issue must be decided on all the relevant evidence. In the circumstances, where the facts were that the father looked after the children while they were with him, paid for their education and was generally responsible for them, they were to be regarded as 'living with' him.[18] In another case it has been emphasised that it is not enough for the child only to spend a small part of the week with his parent.[19]

10 See Calvert *Social Security Law* (1st edn) pp. 259–270.
11 FAA 1965, s.1
12 Under FAA 1965, s.19, 'issue' meant issue of the first generation.
13 Mrs B Castle, Secretary of State, 892 HC Official Report (5th series) col 337.
14 FAA 1965, s.3: it was also used in the National Insurance legislation for the purposes of dependants' allowances: p.343, above.
15 *R(F) 1/74*. J S Watson, Comr, pointed out that there was a separate provision enabling a person providing for a child to claim benefit, as is the case under the 1975 Act.
16 *R(F) 1/71*. This decision has been mentioned with approval in *R(F) 2/81* para 12.
17 It was agreed that the children were 'living with' their mother.
18 Where, as in this case, two parents are living with the child, entitlement is determined under the priority rules: see pp. 401–405, below.
19 *R(F) 2/81*.

b *Temporary absence*[20]
Entirely different problems occur when a child and the person responsible for
him (usually his mother) are temporarily apart, perhaps because the former is
away at school or is in hospital or because for some reason he is staying with
other relatives. An absence of 56 days or less during the 16 weeks preceding
the claim is to be disregarded.[1] Thus, where a mother boards her child out
with a relative for up to eight weeks, she continues to be entitled to benefit as
she is to be treated as having her child living with her for that time. Only then
(or after cumulative periods totalling 56 days within 16 weeks) would she lose
her entitlement on the basis of section 3(1)(a), so that the relative with whom
the child is physically living would, if he made a claim, become entitled to
benefit in priority to the mother.[2]

In some cases, a longer absence is disregarded in determining whether a
person is to be treated as having a child living with him in the particular week.
A separation which is attributable solely to the child's 'receiving full-time
education by attendance at a recognised educational establishment' is wholly
disregarded.[3] If, however, the child is away from the claimant's home for reasons additional to attendance at a school, the latter will not be entitled on a
'living with' basis.[4] Secondly, absence attributable to the child's undergoing
medical or other treatment as an in-patient in a hospital or similar institution', or being in residential accommodation under the National Health Service Act 1977 (or the National Health Service (Scotland) Act 1978) is to be
disregarded for up to 84 consecutive days.[5] In these circumstances an
unlimited period of absence (beyond the 84 days) may be ignored if 'the person claiming to be responsible for the child regularly incurs expenditure in
respect of the child'.[6] Regulations may be made prescribing the circumstances in which this condition is satisfied[7] but none have been issued.

The purpose of these provisions is clearly to enable a person (generally,
though not necessarily, a parent) to receive benefit for a child *normally* living
with him. This is reasonable as a parent will often spend money on clothes
and other articles for a child, even when the latter is away at school or in hospital. In the second situation there may also be the expense of paying frequent
hospital visits. But where the child is in hospital for longer than 84 days, it is
justifiable to require the claimant to show that he is regularly incurring
expenditure.

c *The right to benefit of a voluntary organisation*
A voluntary organisation may be regarded as a person with whom the child is
living for any week he is residing in premises managed by that body or is
boarded out by it.[8] Very similar provisions to those described in the previous
section cover the temporary absence of the child from the voluntary organisation, so that the latter may continue to be entitled to receive benefit, even

20 See pp. 344–45, above, for equivalent rules for the contributory benefits.
1 CBA 1975, s.3(2).
2 Before this period, the relative might claim under s.3(1)(a), but the parent would have the
prior entitlement: Sch 2, para 4: p.403, below.
3 CBA 1975, s.3(3)(a).
4 See *Hill v Minister of Pensions and National Insurance* [1955] 2 All ER 890, [1955] 1 WLR
899, where a mother was refused family allowances in respect of children taken into care
under the Children Act 1948, s.1 and put by the authority into a residential school.
5 CBA 1975, ss.3(3)(b)–(c), and 3(4); SI 1975/966, reg 4.
6 CBA 1975, s.3(4).
7 Ibid, s.3(5).
8 SI 1976/965, reg 17(1).

though the child is not in fact living in its premises.[9] The eligibility of an organisation for benefit here seems to be unique in the social security system;[10] there is no clear reason why it was decided to depart from the general rule that only natural persons are entitled. It should be noted, however, that an organisation is not entitled to child benefit on the alternative basis that it is contributing to the cost of providing for him.

ii 'Contributing to the cost of providing for the child'

The second way in which a person may be treated as 'responsible for a child' is when:

> he is contributing to the cost of providing for the child at a weekly rate which is not less than the weekly rate of child benefit payable in respect of the child for that week.[11]

An application on this alternative basis will not succeed, because of the priority rules, if a claim has also been made by a person who has the child living with him. The main purpose, therefore, of this second head of eligibility is to cover the case where the parent of a child arranges for it to be boarded with a relative or friend, and it is agreed that the parent should receive the benefit to cover the costs of the child's maintenance to which he is contributing.[12] If, however, the relative or friend himself claims in this situation, then he, and not the parent, would be entitled to the benefit.

Neither the Child Benefit Act nor the Regulations made under it define 'providing for' the child. This might seem odd because the family allowances legislation had defined this phrase.[13] It is, however, also used in the Social Security Act 1975 for the purposes of entitlement to an increase of benefit for a dependent child,[14] and there are a number of Commissioners' decisions interpreting it in this context. In some respects it seems that this legislation was the model for the concepts used in the Child Benefit Act and, therefore, the discussion in chapter 9 would appear to be relevant here.[15]

A problem which occurred under the family allowances legislation, and which may be of importance under the Child Benefit Act, is how periodic, but not weekly, payments made by the claimant to the person actually maintaining the child are to be treated for the purpose of determining the former's entitlement. The point is important because the claimant must contribute at a weekly rate not less than the weekly rate of benefit payable in respect of the child. The principles of 'spreading', as it is known, were set out in *R(F) 8/61*.[16] The period the payments relate to is a question of fact, the determination of which should take into account the payer's intentions. Regular periodic payments may be intended to cover a future period, and then they will be averaged over the number weeks in this period. But if he has fallen behind with his payments, and then makes a large payment, this may be attributed to arrears.

The only regulations made under the Child Benefit Act in this context provide that where two or more persons make weekly contributions, which

9 Ibid, reg 17(2).
10 Cf the refusal by the Commissioner to allow Dr Barnardo's to claim attendance allowance: *R(A) 3/75*, p.167, above.
11 CBA 1975, s.3(1)(b).
12 Standing Committee A Debates, cols 44–45.
13 FAA 1965, s.18.
14 SSA 1975, s.43(1)(b).
15 Pp. 346–349, above.
16 See also *R(F) 1/73*.

individually do not, but together do, equal the amount of the benefit, the aggregate amount is to be treated as paid by one of them or, if they cannot agree on this, by that person nominated by the Secretary of State.[17] But after the week in which benefit is first paid under this arrangement, the recipient must contribute the full amount to retain his entitlement. It is further provided that where two spouses are residing together, a contribution made by one of them shall by their agreement, or (in default of that) at the discretion of the Secretary of State, be treated as contributed by the other.[18] It is not entirely clear what is the purpose of this provision, which applies whether the spouses concerned are parents of the child or not. Their ability to 'transfer' benefit to the non-contributing spouse may give a sensible measure of flexibility in some cases. But it is less easy to see the justification for the power of the Secretary of State to treat the non-contributing spouse as the contributor.[19] It appears to enable him in this situation to vary the provision which gives priority, as between a husband and a wife residing together, to the latter.[20] Fortunately, the situation will rarely arise, as the claim of either spouse will have lower priority than a claim by the person with whom the child is living.

iii Priority between persons entitled

It has already been mentioned that one of the principal features of the scheme is the priority given to a claimant with whom the child is living, over other claimants, who might include the child's parents. The Child Benefit Act sets out the relevant rules in Schedule 2. The exposition in this section follows the order of priority laid down there – with some examples to make it clearer. Two important preliminary points should be made. First, entitlement to child benefit is dependent on the making of a claim in the prescribed manner,[1] so if a person with a prior right under these rules has not in fact made a valid claim, they do not come into operation. Secondly, the right conferred by any of the priority rules (except, of course, the first one) only vests if nobody is entitled under one of the previous provisions.

a *Person with prior award*

A person with an existing award of child benefit for a certain week is entitled to priority over anyone else who claims benefit in respect of the same child for that period. But this rule does not apply where the claim is made *for* a week later than the third week after that *in* which it is made.[2] The effect of these provisions is that, whatever the circumstances, a person with an existing award is entitled to priority over all other claimants for up to four weeks.[3]

---

17 SI 1976/965, reg 2.
18 Ibid, reg 2(3).
19 Under the family allowances legislation (FAA 1965, Sch para 3) the Secretary of State had power to determine whether a child was to be included in his father's or his mother's family, in the absence of agreement between them. But this conflict could only arise if the child was provided for by *both* parents, was living with *both* of them, or was living with one and provided for by the other (see Calvert *Social Security Law* (1st edn) p.267). The power under the 1975 Act seems wider in that the Secretary of State is able to award benefit in effect to a spouse who does not live with the child or even provide for him.
20 CBA 1975, Sch 2, para 3.
 1 CBA 1975, s.6(1).
 2 Ibid, Sch 2, para 1. Claims may be made three months before the claimant is entitled to benefit: SI 1987/1968, reg 13.
 3 If it is subsequently decided that the person with the existing award was not entitled to benefit and he has been required to repay it, then the second claimant may be awarded it for that week: SI 1976/965, reg 14A, modifying CBA 1975, s.6(3).

Thus:

> A is paying contributions to the cost of providing for the child and has
> been awarded benefit in respect of him. B, with whom the child is living,
> claims benefit. A is entitled under the prior award rule for at least the week
> in which B claims, and may be entitled for the next three weeks.

This rule allows payments to continue, while the authorities investigate the
facts to determine whether the new claimant should be awarded benefit.

b *Person having the child living with him*

Any person entitled to benefit by virtue of having the child living with him is
entitled to priority over anyone entitled on the alternative basis that he is contributing to the cost of maintenance.[4] This important departure from the
rules applicable under the family allowances system represents one of the
main advantages of the child benefit scheme. The reason for the change is
that generally it is the person with whom the child is living who is primarily
responsible for its care, and he should be entitled to priority.

c *Husband and wife*

Subject to the application of the previous rules, if a husband and wife, who
are residing together, both claim child benefit, the wife is entitled in priority
to her husband.[5] Thus,

> where A and Mrs A live with their children (and nobody has a prior award
> under the first rule). Mrs A is entitled to the benefit; on the other hand,
> where they live together, but the child lives with B, it is B who has the prior
> entitlement and Mrs A will only secure payment if B does not claim or
> waives his priority.

The government retained the principle of the family allowances legislation,
under which the benefit went to the mother. In the debates on the Bill, there
was a move to provide for equal entitlement, where both spouses were in
agreement on this course.[6] But this was resisted. It is surely right for the
mother to receive the benefit, for it is still usually she who is responsible for
the day-to-day feeding and clothing of children. There has been general
agreement on this principle since then, and indeed it is seen as one of the benefit's chief merits that it steers some money towards the mother. The Social
Security Advisory Committee considered it as a powerful argument for the
universal character of the benefit, for even in well-off families the mother
herself might have insufficient funds of her own to look after the children.[7]
The criticism which followed the present government's original intention to
pay the new family credit through the wage packet rather than directly to the
mother further shows the support for the principle.[8]

If the husband does claim he may be awarded the benefit, though he may
be required to submit a written statement signed by his wife that she does not
wish to claim it.[9] Further, he may receive payment of the benefit on behalf of

4 CBA 1975, Sch 2, para 2.
5 Ibid, para 3.
6 Sir G Young, Standing Committee A Debates, cols 57ff, arguing that in some European
   countries childrens' benefits are paid to the father.
7 3rd Report of the Social Security Advisory Committee, 1984, para 6.12. Also see Brown
   Child Benefit: Investing in the Future (1988, CPAG), pp. 51–53.
8 See pp. 474–475, below.
9 SI 1987/1968, reg 7(2).

his wife;[10] this will often be appropriate where, for example, the wife is too ill or handicapped to visit the post office to collect the benefit.

These provisions only apply when the husband and wife are residing together. If they are residing apart, the spouse with whom the child is living has priority under the rule described above. Under the General Regulations, the spouses are treated as residing together for any period of absence from each other until either there is a formal separation or they have been apart for 91 consecutive days, and even after those dates they are to be regarded as residing together where the absence is not likely to be permanent.[11] In *Grove v Haydon (Insurance Officer)*[12] the Court of Appeal held that two spouses may be regarded as 'residing together', even though they have never in fact lived together, as they married when the husband was in prison; the absence was clearly not permanent. And they are to be regarded as residing together if one, or both, of them is receiving treatment in hospital, whether this is temporary or not.[13] The consequence of these provisions may be illustrated by the following example:

> Mrs A leaves her husband and her child, in respect of whom she is in receipt of benefit. Unless there has been a formal separation, the spouses are to be treated under the Regulations as residing together until they have been apart for at least 91 days and, therefore (subject to the other priority rules), Mrs A retains her prior entitlement to benefit. It does not seem that A can claim priority over his wife under the previous priority rule for 56 days. This is because under section 3(2) of the Act, Mrs A is still to be treated as living with her child, despite their absence from one another for 56 days. Until that period is over, A cannot claim to be entitled on the ground that he is living with the child, and his wife is not.[14]

This result seems difficult to defend, as for a considerable period Mrs A has 'abandoned' her child, and Mr A has been looking after it without any support.

d *Parents*

The fourth priority rule is that, as between a parent and someone who is not a parent, the former is to have priority.[15] 'Parent' for this purpose includes natural parents, step-parents and adoptive parents.[16] The priority is, of course, subject to the previous rules: this can be illustrated by the following two examples.

> Miss A lives with her young child and B, not his father. Each is equally entitled as a person who has the child living with him. Miss A is awarded the benefit because she is a parent, and B is not.
>
> Miss A does not live with her young child; he lives with her brother, B, though Miss A sends B a weekly sum towards the cost of providing for

10 Ibid, reg 36: see Mr B O'Malley, Minister of State, Standing Committee A Debates, col 71.

11 SI 1976/965, reg 11. Spouses can be treated as separated if they are living under the same roof, but not living as one household: *R(F) 3/81*.

12 Reported is Appendix to *R(F) 4/85*.

13 SI 1976/965 reg 11(2).

14 It is possible that before then payment could be made to the husband on the wife's behalf under the power to divert payments conferred on the Secretary of State by SI 1987/1968, reg 34.

15 CBA 1975, Sch 2, para 4(1).

16 Ibid, s.24(3). The status of step-parent continues after the termination of the relevant marriage by death *(R(F) 1/79)* or by divorce *(R(S) 4/81)*, and it does not depend on whether the child was the legitimate child of a previous marriage or was illegitimate *(R(S) 9/83)*.

her child. Miss A does not have priority as a parent because B has priority under the earlier rule, which accords entitlement to the person with whom the child is living.

Where two unmarried parents are residing together, the mother enjoys priority;[17] this is comparable to the priority a wife has under the previous rule. Regulations provide that two unmarried parents are to be treated as residing together during a period of 'temporary absence',[18] but there is no specific rule (as there is for husband and wife) explaining the meaning of this phrase. The consequences of the Regulations may be illustrated by the following example:

> Miss A who has been residing with B and is in receipt of benefit in respect of their illegitimate child, leaves that child with B. Under section 3(2) she is to be treated as having the child living with her for 56 days of absence. During this period, she will continue to have priority over B, provided it is held that she is still residing with B, notwithstanding her departure. But if it is decided that the absence is permanent, the rule conferring priority on her as the mother does not apply. It seems in that event that for the period of 56 days priority is to be determined under the rule discussed below, covering priority in other cases, where no previous rule applies. Under this *either* Miss A and B elect which of them is to be entitled *or* priority is decided by the Secretary of State. After 56 days B enjoys priority because he has the child living with him, and Miss A does not.

e *Other cases*

Finally, if none of the other priority rules determines entitlement, benefit is awarded to the person elected jointly by those eligible to claim it, or in default of election, the person chosen by the Secretary of State.[19] An election must be made in writing on the appropriate form; it is not permanently binding, and may subsequently be changed.[20] An example of the possible application of this provision was given in the previous paragraph, but a more typical case might be the following:

> A and Miss B (a brother and sister living together) look after the young child of Mrs C (their deceased sister). Neither has priority under any of the earlier rules, so they may elect which of them is to receive child benefit. If it subsequently becomes more appropriate for the other to receive it (Miss B who has been in receipt of it may become infirm), another election may be made and entitlement varied.

In *R(F) 2/79*, where the two claimants were parents of the child, but were not married and were not residing together, the Commissioner ruled that the child was 'living with' them both. In this circumstance, none of the previous priority rules applied and, as they were unwilling to make a joint election, the issue was referred to the Secretary of State. He decided the child's mother was entitled for the relevant weeks, and this was binding on the Commissioner.[1]

17 CBA 1975, Sch 2, para 4(2).
18 SI 1976/965, reg 11(3).
19 CBA 1975, Sch 2. para 5.
20 SI 1976/965, reg 13.
 1 SI 1986/2218, reg 23.
 2 CBA 1975, Sch 2, para 6.
 3 SI 1976/965, reg 14.

f *Waiver of prior entitlement*

A person with a prior entitlement under these provisions may waive it.[2] The procedure for this step is set out in the regulations.[3]

– Thus, when a claim is made by A, a person (B) with prior entitlement, who is in receipt of the benefit,[4] may give the Secretary of State notice in writing at a Department office that he does not wish to have priority. In that case the provisions are ousted, and the claimant A is awarded the benefit (provided, of course, that he is otherwise entitled to it).

But the person who has waived his prior entitlement may subsequently make a further claim, and then the priority provisions in the Schedule take effect to give him title to the benefit.[5]

C Residence qualifications

The Child Benefit Act 1975, as modified by regulations made under it,[6] set out a number of detailed provisions concerning residence qualifications. They concern both the residence, or more accurately, the presence in Great Britain of the child, in respect of whom benefit is claimed and the presence there of the claimant.[7] The law is extremely complex, largely because the government attempted to formulate rules which would combine the presence requirements for family allowances with the more generous conditions for tax allowances. Modifications applying to certain classes of persons were introduced by regulations,[8] but they do not cover immigrants to Britain who are supporting children overseas.[9]

This section first discusses the general requirements concerning the presence of the child, secondly, those concerning the presence of the claimant and thirdly, the special relaxing provisions, applicable to certain categories of persons, in the Residence and Persons Abroad Regulations 1976.

i Presence of child in Great Britain

Section 13(2) provides that:

> Subject to any regulations . . . no child benefit shall be payable in respect of a child for any week unless –
> (a) he is in Great Britain in that week; *and*
> (b) either he or at least one of his parents has been in Great Britain for more than one hundred and eighty-two days in the fifty-two weeks preceding that week.

Both these requirements have been modified by regulations made under section 13(1).

(a) The absence of a child from Great Britain for a particular week will not be material if three conditions are satisfied:[10]

---

4 The problem only arises when the person with the prior entitlement is actually in receipt of the benefit, since under s.6(1) of the Act, no person is entitled to the benefit unless he has claimed it.

5 SI 1976/965, reg 14(2).

6 SI 1976/963.

7 The usual requirements in social security law of 'residence' and/or 'ordinary residence' for which, see pp. 362–364, above, are not exacted in this area.

8 SI 1976/963, Part II.

9 See the criticism of the law in *Divide and Deprive,* a report by the Joint Council for the Welfare of Immigrants and the Child Poverty Action Group.

10 SI 1976/963, reg 2(2). It follows that the regulation is of no help where the child has *never* been in GB: *R(F) 1/88.*

(1) A person must be entitled to benefit for the week immediately before the first week of the child's absence from GB.
(2) The child's absence is both initially and throughout intended to be temporary.[11]
(3) The child must not be absent from GB for more than 8 weeks, or more than 156 weeks if the absence is solely attributable to receiving full-time education, *or* for more than such extended period as the Secretary of State allows if the absence is for the purpose of treatment for an illness, etc. which began before the period of absence.

(b) The purpose of the general requirement that either the child or one of his parents must have been present for more than half the year preceding the week for which benefit is claimed is to ensure that it is payable only for those children who have more than a transitory connection with Great Britain. This requirement is modified in certain ways by the regulations,[12] the principal relaxation being that benefit may be payable if the child is in Britain and (though not residing with his parent(s)) is living with another person with whom he is likely to continue to live permanently, and that person satisfies the requirements exacted by section 13(3)(b) of the Act, i.e. has been in Britain for more than 182 days in the year preceding the relevant week. The result is that benefit is payable for a child who has recently been left in Britain with a person who has been resident there for at least half the year preceding the week for which he claims.

ii Presence of claimant in Great Britain

There is a general requirement that the claimant is present in Britain, and has been present there for some time. Subject to regulations, the claimant must be there for the week for which he claims benefit, and must have been there for more than 182 days in the 52 preceding weeks.[13] Both these requirements have been modified to cover the cases where the claimant is, or has been, temporarily absent from the country, but still has sufficient connection with it to justify entitlement to benefit.

(a) The absence of the claimant from Britain for the relevant week is not material if three conditions are satisfied:[14]

(1) That person must have been entitled to benefit for the week immediately before the first week of his absence from GB.
(2) The claimant's absence is both initially and throughout intended to be temporary.
(3) The absence must not be longer than 8 weeks.

A person's absence for a week is also immaterial with regard to a child born to a mother within 8 weeks of her departure for a temporary absence – so that the claimant (usually the mother) may be entitled to benefit for the 8 weeks following the *mother's* departure from Britain.[15] This enables a mother to be entitled in respect of a child born abroad, perhaps because she wished to join her husband for the birth, even though she has been outside

11 For the meaning of 'temporary absence', see p.344, above.
12 SI 1976/963, reg 3.
13 CBA 1975, s.13(3).
14 SI 1976/963, reg 4(2).
15 Ibid, reg 4(3).

Great Britain for more than 26 weeks, so that she could not otherwise take advantage of the regulations.

(b) The general requirement that the claimant must have been present for the six months preceding the week for which benefit is claimed has been modified substantially.[16] In particular, the general condition is not to apply if the person is in fact in Great Britain and is responsible for a child who satisfies the presence requirements of section 13(2). This appreciably reduces the significance of the six months' presence requirement.

iii Special relaxing provisions

The general requirements, together with these modifications in the Regulations, may be further relaxed with regard to certain categories of persons by the rules in Part II of the Residence and Persons Abroad Regulations. These additional provisions were a response to the anxiety that the presence requirements for child benefit appeared from the draft Bill to be more onerous than those applicable to the child tax allowance.

– Part II applies to civil servants (other than those recruited outside the United Kingdom for service abroad), serving members of the forces,[17] and people temporarily absent from Britain, by reason only of employment abroad, for an income tax year in which at least half the earnings are liable to United Kingdom income tax.[18] It also applies to spouses of such people.[19]

Any week in which a person to whom Part II applies is away from Britain in connection with his employment is to be treated for the purposes of the presence requirements as one in which he is present there; moreover, a child's absence is to be disregarded entirely if he is living with a person to whom Part II applies, and that person is either a parent or someone who before the week in question was entitled to benefit in respect of him.[20] Days of separation of a child and such a person, which are attributable to the latter being abroad, are to be wholly disregarded under the 1975 Act for the purposes of determining whether he has the child living with him. Thus, a civil servant serving in a foreign embassy may be entitled to child benefit in respect of a child for whom he is responsible, even if the child spends the whole year in Britain, both school-terms and holidays. It seems that he would also be entitled if the child is being educated in and spends his holidays in another country, not the one in which the civil servant is working.[1]

D One-parent benefit

From the scheme's inception there has been more generous treatment of single parent families. Even before the full introduction of child benefit in 1977, an interim benefit was paid in the preceding year for the children of an

16 Ibid, reg 5.
17 Defined by SI 1975/492, reg 1(2).
18 SI 1976/963, reg 6(1)(a)–(c).
19 Ibid, reg 6(1)(d).
20 Ibid, reg 7(1), (2).
 1 Ibid, reg 7(3). The Secretary of State, however, may refuse in his discretion to apply this disregard of days of absence in any case.

unmarried or separated parent, not living with another person as his (or her) spouse.[2] When the benefit became payable to all persons responsible for a child, a single parent received an extra 50p a week for his only, or eldest, child, and this differential became £1 in the following year, 1978.[3] This preferential treatment was almost certainly a response to the Finer Committee on One-Parent Families, which had recommended the introduction of a guaranteed maintenance allowance for lone mothers with young children.[4] Their needs have also been recognised in the more generous disregard of earnings for lone parents claiming supplementary benefit, and more recently by their treatment in the income support scheme.[5]

In order to encourage its take-up, the government renamed 'child-benefit increase' in 1980 as 'one-parent benefit', though curiously this nomenclature is found only in government leaflets and not in the regulations. The benefit is a hybrid, sharing the entitlement rules for the principal benefit discussed in this chapter, and enjoying further requirements of its own, set out in the next paragraph. The extra amount paid for one-parent children is now quite significant, at least in relation to the value of child benefit: in 1980 it was £3.00, and now one-parent benefit is £4.90, about two-thirds the value of the latter. The benefit has not been affected by the changes made in 1986, and indeed its role was scarcely discussed in the Green and White Papers.[6]

There has been one interesting legal development in the special conditions for entitlement to one-parent benefit. Initially the claimant had to be a *parent* of the child in question, but this condition was removed in 1980: any person may qualify, provided he is not residing with a parent of the child.[7] This amendment to the regulations followed a decision of the Chief Commissioner, R J A Temple, holding that a step-father was eligible for the increase after the child's mother's death.[8] The other conditions are that the claimant must be living with the child (i.e. he cannot claim under section 3(1)(b) of the Act), must either be unmarried or not residing with his spouse, and must not be living with anyone else as his spouse.[9] The benefit is only paid for an only, or eldest, child; ordinary child benefit is paid for the others in the family. Moreover, one-parent benefit is not paid if the claimant is in receipt of a variety of allowances set out in the regulations, e.g. guardian's allowance, or a dependant's increase for a child paid with a widow's benefit or retirement pension.[10] In these cases the claimant is in a less vulnerable position.

---

2 CBA 1975, s.16, now repealed.
3 See SI 1976/1267, reg 2 and SI 1977/1328, reg 2.
4 The Finer Committee's principal recommendations are briefly discussed in ch 11, p.464, below.
5 See p.429, below.
6 See *Green Paper* Vol 1, para 8.9, where it is mentioned that no changes are proposed, though the government will consider whether help to lone parent families should be rationalised through the tax and benefit systems.
7 SI 1976/1267, reg 2(2A), inserted by SI 1980/110.
8 *R(F) 1/79*.
9 SI 1976/1267, reg 2(2): for the meaning of 'living with' and 'residing with', see p.398 and p.403, above.
10 Ibid, reg 2(4)–(5).

Chapter 11

Income support

Part 1   Introduction

A   General

i   The role of income support

Most social security systems provide some form of public assistance for people in need who are not, for one reason or another, able to maintain themselves from other resources. In Britain, there are two means-tested (or, as they are now referred to legislatively, 'income-related') benefits which are designed to guarantee a sufficient income to meet regular needs, other than housing. Broadly speaking, while family credit is available to families which contain a low-paid earner, income support is paid to individuals or families without an income from employment. Income support, which was introduced by the Social Security Act 1986 and came into force in April 1988, replaces supplementary benefit which itself had succeeded national assistance as the principal means-tested benefit.

On the assumption that the coverage and level of national insurance benefits would be adequate, Beveridge had envisaged only a residual role for national assistance.[1] However, his expectations were to be disappointed: the level of insurance benefits never exceeded the minimum income guaranteed by the means-tested benefits and so the latter became in practice the primary instrument of welfare for the large numbers of individuals and families who had no other resources. Indeed, there has been a steady growth in the number of recipients. At the end of 1979, supplementary benefit was paid to nearly three million claimants, compared to approximately one million in receipt of national assistance in 1948.[2] By 1986, the figure had increased to five million and, given that the payments were intended to support members of the claimant's family, this meant that 8.29 million individuals were dependent on supplementary benefit.[3] While, no doubt, this figure will diminish if the level of unemployment is reduced and as the proportion of pensioners with a substantial entitlement to an earnings-related addition under the 1975 scheme rises, nevertheless, given the Conservative government's fundamental policy of targetting public resources on cases of demonstrated need, it is to be assumed that income support will continue to serve as the primary instrument for maintaining the income of the poorest sections of the community for the foreseeable future.

1 Para 369.
2 SBC Annual Report 1979 (Cmnd 8033), paras 8.1–8.33.
3 DHSS *Social Security Statistics 1987* Tables 34.30 and 34.31.

ii Benefits and poverty

Definitions of 'poverty' and therefore also the principles for determining the levels of income maintenance have always given rise to debate and controversy.[4] It seems that in 1948 the assistance rates were fixed at a level just above the subsistence standard set by Beveridge for single adults and married couples, but a little below that for a family with children.[5] This standard was itself lower than that arrived at by Rowntree in his studies shortly before the Second World War.[6] Both calculations had proceeded on the assumption that it was possible to measure 'poverty' by reference to absolute standards: a certain amount of money is needed for food, housing and clothing, and then a margin may be added for other expenditure and to allow for inefficiency.[7] There is no reason why weekly payments of public assistance could not be calculated in this way. It is very likely that initially such assessments played some part in the determination of weekly benefit rates but, on this 'absolute standards' approach, it would be plausible to expect poverty to disappear over the years with continued economic growth, and that correspondingly the numbers of people relying on assistance would decline.[8] In fact, as has just been mentioned, the opposite has occurred.

It is now more common to measure poverty, not by the absolute approach of a minimum standard of living, but as relative to the general or average quality of life in the country.[9] In his major study, Townsend defined the 'poverty line' as the point at which a person's or family's withdrawal from participation in social activities increases disproportionately in relation to declining resources.[10] On this approach those with an income below, say, 40 per cent of the average industrial wage may be characterised as poor, even though they may have adequate resources to feed and house themselves, and so would not fall beneath the poverty line on the more traditional 'subsistence' definition. The difficulty with the concept of 'relative poverty' is arguably that it confuses poverty with inequality.[11]

Government policy has been ambivalent with regard to the relative poverty criterion. A White Paper published in 1959 acknowledged that those in receipt of assistance should have a 'share in increasing national prosperity'[12] and for some time the scale rates of benefits rose more than increases in the Retail Prices Index and indeed improved relative to the average net earnings of manual workers.[13] The policy of the Conservative administrations since 1979 has been to prioritise economic growth as a precondition of social security spending and one consequence has been that benefits have been up-rated by reference to prices, rather than earnings. Nevertheless, some acknowledgement of the influence of the relative concept may be inferred from a statement in the Green Paper of 1985, that '[f]amilies whose needs are

---

4 Deacon and Bradshaw *Reserved for the Poor* (1983).
5 Fiegehen, Lansley and Smith *Poverty and Progress in Britain 1953-1973* (1977), p.13; *Townsend* pp. 242-243.
6 *Human Needs of Labour* (1937).
7 It is this further margin which identified people living in what Rowntree described as 'secondary poverty': 'primary poverty' refers to the situation where the people, however carefully they marshal their resources, cannot afford the necessities of life. See *Harris* pp. 393-394.
8 Fiegehen et al, n.5, above, pp. 13-14.
9 Ibid, pp. 14-15. See also pp. 18-19, above.
10 *Townsend* pp. 57, 248-262. This approach won the support of the Supplementary Benefits Commission: SBC Annual Report 1978 (Cmnd 7725), paras 1.4 and 3.13; see also Donnison *The Politics of Poverty* (1982) pp. 148-151.
11 Robson *Welfare State and Welfare Society* (1976) pp. 142-143; but see *Townsend* p.57.
12 *Improvements in National Assistance* (Cmnd 782) para 3.
13 See, e.g., SBC Annual Report for 1976 (Cmnd 6910), paras 9.14-9.20.

likely to be greatest may be defined as those falling in the bottom 20 per cent of the national distribution of income'.[14]

Income support rates may be said, therefore, to reflect an uncertain compromise between the absolute and relative concepts of poverty. The standards of eligibility for benefit are also sometimes used to measure the extent of poverty in British society.[15] It is obviously outside the scope of this book to pursue these questions in detail, but some reservations to this test should be stated. First, if income support rates are increased relative to earnings and other income, so more people are defined as having a standard of living below the official 'poverty' line. This odd consequence – the more the government attempts to help the poor, the more 'poor' there are – is perhaps inevitable if this relative (and perhaps also tautologous) concept of poverty is adopted. Secondly, the number of recipients of benefit is an unreliable guide to the extent of poverty insofar as otherwise eligible people are disentitled to assistance by the legislation. Persons in full-time work, however low their earnings, may not claim income support, though if responsible for a family with at least one child, they may be entitled to family credit. Claimants may also be disqualified because of their participation in a trade dispute, or because they are not genuinely looking for work.[16] Finally, an important group, living below the official poverty line but not receiving benefit, are those who for one reason or another do not claim it. It has been officially estimated that the take-up rate for supplementary benefit in 1986 was 72 per cent, indicating that some 1.6 million eligible individuals did not claim it.[17]

B History of Public Assistance

i Early history of the poor law[18]

The first statutes encouraging parishes to assist the deserving poor (the old, sick and infirm) were passed in 1531 and 1536. The Acts, and subsequent legislation, were consolidated in the famous Poor Relief Act of 1601. Under this, overseers were appointed in each parish under the general supervision of the Justices of the Peace to give relief to the deserving poor and to raise local taxes for this purpose. The able-bodied were to be given work. Section 6 imposed a duty on a person's father, grandfather, mother, grandmother and child to maintain him, an assertion of family responsibility which was not repealed until 1948. Although the parish might provide relief to someone neglected by his relatives, it could recover this from the defaulters. Thus, two important features of the poor law regime were established from the outset: local administration, which led to inconsistent provision in different parts of the country, and the emphasis on family responsibility.

Inevitably, there were many changes in the administration of the poor law in the two centuries before the major reform of 1834. The most important resulted from the 1662 Act of Settlement the object of which was to prevent paupers wandering from their home to impose themselves as charges on other

14 Vol 1, para 4.7.
15 Atkinson *Poverty in Britain and the Reform of Social Security* (1969) and in Weddeburn (ed) *Poverty, Inequality and Class Structure* (1974) p.48. *Townsend* pp. 241–247, is very critical of this approach.
16 Pp. 452 and 455, below.
17 Written answer, 103 HC Official Report (6th series), cols 231, 234. See also Beltram *Testing the Safety-Net* (1984) Appendix J.
18 De Schweinitz *England's Road to Social Security* (1949) ch 1; Bruce *The Coming of the Welfare State* (4th edn) ch 2; Checkland (ed) *The Poor Law Report of 1834* (1974) editors' introduction; Cranston *Legal Foundations of the Welfare State* (1985) ch 2.

parishes. Any person without property or other means of support could be removed to his parish 'of settlement', generally his place of birth. In effect, a pauper had to look to his own parish for relief, a restriction which naturally hindered freedom of movement.

The eighteenth century saw the first workhouses which the able-bodied were required to enter as a condition of securing relief.[19] But the experiment was halted towards the end of the century. The poverty of agricultural workers at this time led to the use of poor law relief to supplement wages in the famous 'Speenhamland system'.[20] This, in its turn, became one of the reasons for the disquiet responsible for the institution of the Poor Law Commission in 1832. Many felt that relief for the employed merely subsidised low wages, an argument since deployed against family income supplement (now family credit).[1]

ii Poor law reform: 1834–1930[2]

The Poor Law Commission found that provision for those able to work was corrupting for the recipients; in future, they were only to be given relief in the workhouses. Under the notorious principle of 'less eligibility', conditions there were to be less attractive than those of the poorest worker outside.[3] Thus, the familiar distinction was drawn between the deserving poor, who might benefit from allowances paid outside the workhouse ('outdoor relief') and the less deserving, who in practice would be able to secure relief only in conditions of destitution. The objective of more efficient administration was achieved, first, by the merging for poor law purposes of parishes into unions, with elected Boards of Guardians, and, secondly, by the institution of a central Board of three Commissioners, responsible for the making of regulations and the national administration of the poor law.

Though well intentioned, the remedy was perhaps worse than the disease. The horrors of the workhouse, with their degrading treatment of the inmates and enforced separation of husband and wife, are well-known from the novels of Dickens. The sick and the old were often, for reasons of economy, housed with the unemployed. Eventually a Royal Commission was appointed in 1905. All its members were agreed that the 1834 reforms had been misconceived, that the workhouses should be abolished and the administrative structure changed.[4] But it was divided in its proposals for specific solutions; partly because of this and partly because other events dominated political discussion, there was no immediate attempt at reform.

During the 1920s unemployment increased, exposing the weaknesses of the poor laws. With the workhouses quite unable to cope, many unions used their power to afford outdoor relief for the able-bodied in cases of 'urgent necessity'. But they were not all so generous, with the result that provision varied widely from area to area. Naturally those with the heaviest unemployment were the least able to afford the costs of relief. The inherent weakness of local administration and financing became widely recognised. But even then, the solution of national administration was not immediately adopted. Instead by

19 Bruce, n.18, above, pp. 54–55.
20 Cf p.471, below.
 1 P.472, below.
 2 Rose *The English Poor Law 1780–1930* (1971); Rose *The Relief of Poverty 1834–1914* (1972); Bruce, n.18, above, chs 4, 5; Fraser *The Evolution of the British Welfare State* (2nd edn) pp. 48–55.
 3 Ibid, pp. 96–97.
 4 Report of the Royal Commission on the Poor Law (1909, Cd 4499).

the Local Government Act 1929, the functions of the poor law guardians and unions were transferred to the local authorities to be discharged largely by their public assistance committees. In the following year, the last Poor Law Act, a consolidation measure, was passed.[5] A more significant event was the repeal of the Regulation which had made entry into the workhouse a condition of relief to the able-bodied.[6]

iii Unemployment assistance and the end of the poor law 1930–1948[7]

Governments in this period were troubled by the problems of the unemployed who were unable to claim contributory benefit.[8] In 1931 the National Government introduced means-tested transitional allowances for people out of work for more than 26 weeks. These were funded nationally, but administered by the local authority public assistance committees. When it became clear that there was inconsistency in their administration of the allowances, the demand for a national scheme could no longer be resisted. The Unemployment Assistance Act 1934 instituted a Board to administer public assistance for the unemployed.

In a number of respects the 1934 scheme is interesting as a forerunner of the modern law. Assistance was calculated by reference to the applicant's requirement, based on weekly scale rates, with a deduction for his resources. Extra lump sum payments could be made for exceptional needs and the regular weekly payments could be increased in special circumstances. An adjustment could be made for particularly high or low rents. An important feature of the scheme was the 'household means' test: the resources of all members of the applicant's household were taken into account before determining that he was in need of assistance.

During the war years, the functions of the Unemployment Assistance Board were extended to cover administration of the means-tested supplementary pensions payable to widows and the elderly under the Old Age and Widows' Pensions Act 1940.[9] A further significant development was the virtual abolition of the 'household means' test by the Determination of Needs Act 1941. In future, where the applicant was a householder, only the resources of his wife and dependants were to be added to his own, in assessing need.[10]

It was the Beveridge Report which heralded the final demise of the poor law. He pointed to the anomalies necessarily entailed by the co-existence of a number of tests for different groups, administered by different authorities.[11] The 'existing poor law' was repealed by the National Assistance Act 1948. The provision of public financial assistance became exclusively the function of central government, acting through the National Assistance Board (NAB), as it was now called. Many of the features of the poor law went: there was no law of settlement, so that it no longer mattered where the applicant resided; the requirement that able-bodied applicants be set to work was replaced by a discretionary requirement to register for employment; and relief by way of loan, a common provision under the poor law, was abolished as a normal form of assistance.

5 The Act is exhaustively analysed in Jennings *The Poor Law Code* (2nd edn).
6 SR & O 1930/186, art 6.
7 Deacon and Bradshaw *Reserved for the Poor* (1983) chs 2–3.
8 Cf p.64, above.
9 Cf p.181, above.
10 The 'household means' test survived in vestigial form for non-householders until 1948.
11 Para 372.

iv The reforms of 1966[12]

In 1948, it was thought right to keep the administration of means-tested assistance entirely separate from that of the insurance benefits; the NAB was, therefore, an independent government department.[13] However, it gradually became apparent that national assistance was playing a more important role than had been envisaged and that some potential applicants were discouraged from applying because of the wide area of discretion accorded to officials under the 1948 Act. The Labour government decided, therefore, in 1966 to make some changes to the scheme, from that time to be known as supplementary benefit.[14] The major alteration was to confer a *right* to benefit in the circumstances set out in the legislation; another was the automatic provision of higher benefit rates for pensioners and those who had been in receipt of the benefit for two years – both reduced the amount of discretion in the system. The principal administrative change was that the NAB was dissolved and its functions transferred to the Ministry of Social Security[15] and to the Supplementary Benefits Commission (SBC), though the latter was not a separate department.[16] The object of these changes was to merge the administration of contributory and means-tested benefits and thereby remove the stigma associated with claiming the latter.[17]

v The reforms of 1980[18]

Change in the structure of the supplementary benefits scheme had been urged by the SBC in its annual reports, and in 1976 a team of DHSS officials was formed to take a thorough look at it. Their report, *Social Assistance*, published two years later,[19] broadly recommended that the scheme should be simplified to make it more intelligible and less costly. In particular, awards of discretionary additions to benefit had radically increased in the 1970s and these were making the scheme both expensive to administer and unfair in its application, since it was difficult to ensure equal and uniform allocation of such payments throughout the country.

Within six months of assuming office, Mrs Thatcher's first administration decided to proceed on the basis of the report and amending legislation followed in 1980.[20] The main reform was to incorporate in a voluminous set of regulations detailed rules of entitlement, most of which had previously existed only as internal instructions to officials for the exercise of discretion. The balance between regulation-based rights and discretion in the supplementary benefits scheme had been a subject of much debate in the 1970s.[1] The primary effect of the 1980 reforms was to increase 'legalisation' and

12 Webb in Hall et al *Change, Choice and Conflict in Social Policy* (1975) ch 14.
13 Cf p.531, below.
14 The changes were made by the Ministry of Social Security Act 1966, later renamed the Supplementary Benefit Act 1966.
15 Its functions were later transferred to the Secretary of State for Social Services: p.532, below.
16 P.532, below.
17 Miss M Herbison, Minister of Pensions and National Insurance, 729 HC Official Report (5th series), cols 355 ff.
18 Walker in Jones and Stevenson (eds) *The Yearbook of Social Policy in Britain 1982* (1983) ch 8.
19 For the background to, and comments on, the report, see Donnison *The Politics of Poverty* (1982) chs 5–6.
20 See White Paper *Reform of the Supplementary Benefits Scheme* (1979, Cmnd 7773) and SSA 1980.
 1 See, esp: Titmuss 42 Political Q 113; Adler and Bradley *Justice, Discretion and Poverty* (1975); Bull [1980] JSWL 65.

reduce the role of discretion: the discretionary weekly 'exceptional circum-stances additions' and lump-sum 'exceptional needs payments' were replaced by detailed regulation on, respectively, 'additional requirements' and 'single payments'.[2] The claimant had only to meet the prescribed criteria in the regulations to gain entitlement to these additions to the basic benefit, though some residual discretion was retained.

The revised legal structure was reflected in changes made to administrative and adjudicative institutions. There was no longer any need for the SBC to formulate informal rules and policies for the exercise of discretion. Its advi-sory role was, therefore, transferred to the new Social Security Advisory Committee (SSAC), which was concerned with advice on almost all social security matters.[3] The adjudicative arrangements were also, by stages, integrated: first, a right of appeal on questions of law was introduced from decisions of supplementary benefits appeal tribunals (SBATs) to the Commissioner; subsequently, adjudication officers (AOs) became responsi-ble for first instance decisions on almost all social security claims (including those for supplementary benefit) and SBATs were merged with national insurance local tribunals to form the new social security appeal tribunal (SSAT).[4]

C The Fowler Reviews and income support

i General
In 1984, Norman Fowler, then Secretary of State for Social Services, announced that a major review of social security policy and provision would be undertaken, its main objective being to examine whether the system could be made simpler and financially more secure and whether resources could be targetted more effectively on those in need. One of the four review teams was charged specifically with the task of scrutinising the supplementary benefits scheme. In June 1985 the reviews were published in a Green Paper; a White Paper followed in December 1985, the main proposals of which were imple-mented in the Social Security Act 1986.

ii Perceived defects in the supplementary benefit scheme[5]
Complexity was the main defect identified by the review team.[6] The detail of the 500 or so pages of published regulations was intimidating; the rules on single payments alone ran to over 1,000 printed lines and one regulation con-tained 20 separate categories of essential furniture and household equipment. The regulations were themselves subject to interpretation by the adjudicating authorities and a substantial case-law had emerged. For the purpose of deter-mining the basic weekly rates, distinctions not always easy to apply were drawn between 'householders' and 'non-householders' and a further set of complex rules were used to define categories of claimants entitled to the 'long-term' rate. The regular weekly additions to cover such items as heating, diet, and laundry had become an integral part of the scheme – over 90 per

2 For details, see the second edition of this book, pp. 477–480, 487–493.
3 Pp. 535–537, below.
4 Pp. 571–576, below.
5 Rowell and Wilton [1986] JSWL 16.
6 *Green Paper 1985* vol 2, para 2.27 et seq. In a Gallup poll commissioned by the review team, 31 per cent of supplementary benefit claimants reported difficulties in understanding how their payments were calculated: ibid, vol 3, para 4.49.

cent of pensioners received at least one such addition[7] – but many applications required considerable investigation of the claimant's circumstances, which could be unduly intrusive.[8] The most stringent criticism was, however, reserved for the system of 'single payments' designed to meet one-off needs. The 'labyrinth' of rules and the very large number of appeals to which their application gave rise involved a disproportionately heavy administrative burden and cost and was a significant cause of friction between claimants and staff.[9]

Another set of problems arose from the relationship between supplementary benefit and the other means-tested schemes, family income supplement and housing benefit. Different criteria of need had developed as had different methods of assessing income and capital.[10] Not only did this create confusion among claimants and a sense of unfairness, but it also hindered the development of a coherent strategy to deal with the problems of work incentives and the 'poverty trap' – the situation in which efforts to increase income result in a withdrawal of benefit and thus to a net loss.[11]

iii The reform strategy

The strategy for reform published in the Green Paper of 1985 evolved from the perception that the core problem was structural.[12] The supplementary benefit system was being over-extended in attempting to fulfil two separate roles: the provision of weekly income, its basic purpose; and help with special needs, a complementary function which was designed to take account of particular exceptional pressures faced by a minority of claimants but which had grown to unmanageable proportions. 'The result is that the efficient delivery of a regular weekly income for claimants is prejudiced by the attempt to incorporate in the main structure the detailed consideration of special needs'.[13] It was necessary to separate the two roles. 'Income support' would replace weekly supplementary benefit by fulfilling its basic purpose of providing regular income. While need would obviously vary according to the situation of each claimant, individual circumstances should not be investigated in detail; rather, in addition to standard personal allowances, there would be 'premiums' for different 'client' groups, for example, families, the elderly, disabled people and lone parents. The complexities of the 'householder' and 'non-householder' categories, the 'long-term' rates and the weekly additional requirements would be abolished. The system of single payments and urgent needs would be replaced by the new 'social fund' which would operate quite independently of income support and would be administered on a discretionary basis and subject to budgetary limits. (For further details of the social fund proposals and their implementation, reference should be made to chapter 14.)

7 Ibid, vol 2, para 2.55.
8 The age-related heating addition did not require investigation of the claimant's circumstances but for this reason was criticised for being poorly targetted: ibid, para 2.57.
9 Ibid, para 2.63. 21 per cent of all appeals to SSATs involved single payment claims.
10 The classic example arose from discrepancies between housing benefit and supplementary benefit which resulted in a net loss for those who switched from the latter to the former. This necessitated the introduction of the complex 'housing benefit supplement' to make up the difference: see McGurk and Raynsford *Guide to Housing Benefit* (1987/88 edn) pp. 69–77.
11 *White Paper 1985* para 3.3.
12 *Green Paper 1985* vol 2, para 2.30.
13 Ibid.

iv Implementation of reform proposals

A period of only three months was allowed for responses to the Green Paper, which also of course contained far-reaching proposals on other areas of social security, notably pensions. Not surprisingly, therefore, comment tended to concentrate more on the Conservative government's general policy of targetting existing resources more efficiently and on its reinforcement of the means-tested approach than on the specific proposals.[14] It was pointed out by the Social Security Advisory Committee (SSAC), among others, that the lack of published illustrative benefit levels in the Green Paper hampered the task of making informed comment.[15] This was remedied by the publication of a Technical Annex to the White Paper in which estimates of the impact of the proposed changes were made.[16] While SSAC in general approved the structural changes *within* the income support system (personal allowances plus premiums for particular client groups), there was some concern that an appropriate balance between a 'broad brush' approach and an investigation of individual needs had not been struck:[17] unless the new benefit was set at levels adequate to meet the everyday expenses of most claimants, there would be an 'intolerable pressure' on the social fund which would threaten the viability of the reform.[18]

The White Paper substantially endorsed the Green Paper proposals. Some important recommendations were brought into force under the existing supplementary benefit legislation; for example, a significant reduction in entitlement both to single payments[19] and to the meeting of mortgage interest payments.[20] The main reforms were effected by the Social Security Act 1986, which provided for the new income support scheme to be introduced in April 1988. Complex transitional arrangements were made to protect existing supplementary benefit claimants against losses that might otherwise result from the changes.[1] Finally, as a consequence of the government's new policy towards the employment training of young people, the Social Security Act 1988 narrowed the entitlement of this group to income support.

Part 2   General conditions of entitlement to income support

The principal conditions of entitlement to income support are set out in the Social Security Act 1986. Broadly speaking, the claimant:

(1) must be present in Great Britain;
(2) must be over the age of 18 (though some aged 16–17 may be entitled);
(3) must be not engaged in remunerative work or full-time (non-advanced) education;
(4) (subject to important exceptions) must be available for employment;
(5) must not have income exceeding the 'applicable amount'; and
(6) must not have more than a prescribed amount of capital.

14 E.g. CPAG *Burying Beveridge* (1985); Labour Research Department *Social Insecurity* (1986); Alcock *Poverty and State Support* (1987).
15 Fourth Report (1985) para 1.2.
16 *Reform of Social Security: Technical Annex to the White Paper* (Cmnd 9691).
17 N. 15 above, para 1.4.
18 Ibid, para 3.5.
19 SI 1986/1961 and 1987/38.
20 SI 1987/17.
1 SI 1987/1969. For a detailed account, see CPAG *National Welfare Benefits Handbook* (18th edn) pp. 139–147.

Conditions (1) to (4) will be discussed in this Part; the mode of assessing the 'applicable' amount will be considered in Part 4, and the principles governing the determination of income and capital in Part 5.

Most of these conditions of entitlement apply not only to the claimant but also to the partner (if any) and the income and capital of other members of the family unit may also be relevant. The rules for determining the membership of the family unit for these purposes are described in Part 3.

A   Presence in Great Britain

There is no general condition that only a British national or resident may be entitled to income support. Mere presence in Great Britain is in principle enough[2] and a period of up to four weeks' temporary absence may be ignored, provided that the absence is unlikely to last for a year and the claimant satisfies *one* of the following conditions:[3]

(1)   he is in Northern Ireland;
(2)   he is not required to be available for work (for reasons other than incapacity for work);[4]
(3)   he is incapable of work and the sole purpose of the absence is to receive treatment for that incapacity;[5]
(4)   he has been continuously incapable of work for 28 weeks; or
(5)   he has a partner abroad for whom a pensioner premium, a higher pensioner premium, or a disability premium is payable.[6]

Nevertheless, although not excluded from the scheme, some foreign visitors are not eligible for the ordinary weekly payments and may therefore have to rely on the much reduced amounts payable to 'urgent cases'.[7] Full entitlement is denied to those who under immigration law:[8] are illegal entrants; are subject to a deportation order or have exceeded the period of limited leave; have been granted only temporary admission to the UK; or are awaiting a decision on immigration status.[9] Most importantly, this also applies to foreign visitors whose leave to stay is conditional on them making no recourse to public funds. An immigrant may be allowed into this country under a sponsorship agreement, whereby the sponsor, generally a relative, undertakes to maintain him. In such a case, the immigrant is normally able to obtain income support if the sponsor is unable, or refuses to meet the undertaking.[10]

B   Age

Section 20(3) of the 1986 Act originally provided that the claimant must be at least 16, a lower age limit which has existed in the public assistance schemes

---

2   For the meaning of 'presence', see p.362, above.
3   SI 1987/1967, reg 4, as amended.
4   Pp. 422–424, below. However, if the exemption from the requirement arises because the claimant is in full-time education, a discharged prisoner or a person from abroad, the condition is not satisfied and if because he has been incapable of work, condition (3) and (4) must be satisfied.
5   Cf p.150, above.
6   Cf pp. 428–431, below.
7   P.450, below.
8   Primarily under the Immigration Act 1971, on which see Macdonald *Immigration Law and Practice* (2nd edn).
9   SI 1987/1967, reg 21(3) and Sch 7, para 17.
10   P.451, below.

since at least 1948. As is explained below, young persons above this age cannot claim income support in their own right if they remain at school; in these circumstances, parents are paid child benefit for such persons and may claim allowances for them in their claim for income support. However, in the period following the passing of the 1986 Act, the Conservative administration resolved to narrow the entitlement of young persons aged 16–17 who leave school and are unemployed, specifically to encourage them to participate in employment training schemes and, more generally, to discourage them from leaving home and establishing a dependence on social security.[11] Notwithstanding objections from the Opposition that the measure would lead to compulsory 'workfare',[12] the Social Security Act 1988 amended section 20(3), so that now it is only claimants of 18 and above who are entitled on satisfying the ordinary conditions. Those between 16 and 18 must *either* satisfy special conditions prescribed in the regulations *or* persuade the Secretary of State to issue a direction that 'severe hardship will result . . . unless income support is payable'.[13]

i Prescribed conditions

The first group of young persons covered by the regulations[14] are those who are following an approved training course (and thus are in receipt of a training allowance) or who have been temporarily laid off employment and are available to be re-engaged in that employment. In addition, they extend to a number of other categories of young persons who, because of their circumstances, cannot reasonably be expected to undergo training, viz:

> lone parents and members of a couple with children, those incapable of work and training (and such incapacity is unlikely to end within 12 months), or who are registered blind, women during the period of confinement, persons caring for a sick or elderly relative, refugees and some other persons from abroad.

In all cases in this first group, the normal rules of entitlement to income support apply throughout the period before the claimant reaches the age of 18. In a second group of cases, they may apply for a shorter period:[15]

(1) if a claimant's incapacity for work and training is likely to last for less than 12 months, for the duration of such incapacity;
(2) if the claimant is a student (i.e. pursuing a course in advanced education), normally only for the summer vacations;[16]
(3) if the claimant is a discharged prisoner (unless he comes within the first group) normally only for the first eight weeks after discharge;
(4) if the claimant does not fall within the first group and, because he is married, is without parents, or living away from the parental home for reasons of, for example, safety or health, no child benefit is paid for him, only for the period for which child benefit would have been paid if he had been living with his parent(s).[17]

11 The 1987 Conservative party election manifesto had included a pledge that young persons who chose to be unemployed would be denied benefit. See further on the reform the Sixth Report of SSAC (1988), ch 2.
12 121 HC Official Report (6th series), col 665.
13 SSA 1986, s.20(4A), inserted by SSA 1988, s.4(2).
14 SI 1987/1967, reg 13A and Sch 1A, Part I.
15 Ibid, reg 13A(4)–(7) and Sch 1A, Part II.
16 Cf pp. 467–469, below.
17 Cf p.421, below.

ii Special hardship

The residual category of 'special hardship' is not defined in the legislation and it is to be observed that the question whether a direction is to be issued is one for decision by the Secretary of State and not an adjudication officer. In consequence, there is no right of appeal to the adjudicating authorities from any such decision; and the only recourse available is to apply to the Divisional Court for a judicial review.

C Exclusion of persons engaged in remunerative work

With the exception of the Speenhamland system introduced in 1795,[18] public assistance was not used to supplement low earnings until the introduction of family income supplement (FIS) in 1970. Supplementary benefit was, therefore, not available if the claimant (or partner) was engaged in 'remunerative full-time work',[19] which normally denoted work amounting to 30 hours or more a week. Under current legislation, the term 'full-time' has been dropped[20] and the concept of 'remunerative work' which marks the boundary between income support and the family credit scheme (the successor to FIS) is now defined as:

> work in which a person is engaged, or, where his hours of work fluctuate, he is engaged on average, for not less than 24 hours a week being work for which payment is made or which is done in expectation of payment.[1]

The regulations provide methods to assist in a determination of the average number of hours worked per week.[2] Where there is a 'recognisable cycle' of work, hours will be averaged over that cycle. Where the hours of work fluctuate but there is no such cycle, the adjudication officer should derive an average from the period of five weeks preceding the date of claim, or such other period as, in the circumstances of the case, may enable him to determine the average more accurately. For the purpose of these rules, a person is treated as being engaged in 'remunerative work' during periods of absence from work which in other respects satisfies the definition, if the absence is for holiday or 'without good cause', and the same applies during the first seven days of a stoppage of work due to a trade dispute.[3]

On the other hand, there are a number of situations in which the claimant (or partner) is treated as if he were *not* engaged in 'remunerative work', where:[4]

(1) his earning capacity has been reduced by 25 per cent or more as a result of mental or physical disablement;
(2) he is engaged in childminding at home or regularly and substantially engaged in caring for a severely disabled person who is entitled to an attendance allowance;
(3) he is engaged in charitable or voluntary work for which the only payment is the reimbursement of expenses;
(4) he is in receipt of a training allowance;[5]

18 P.412, above.
19 SBA 1976, s.6(1).
20 SSA 1986, s.20(3)(c).
 1 SI 1987/1967, reg 5(1).
 2 Ibid, reg 5(2).
 3 Ibid, reg 5(3)–(4).
 4 Ibid, reg 6.
 5 Paid by a government department or the MSC for following an approved training scheme, but not for full-time education or a teacher training course: ibid, reg 2.

(5) he is without work as a result of a stoppage due to a trade dispute and that stoppage has lasted for more than seven days.[6]

D Exclusion of persons in, or having recently left, full-time education

We have already seen that there are severe limits to the ability of young persons under 18 to claim income support. In a later part of the chapter, we shall examine the special rules which restrict the entitlement of students following courses in advanced education.[7] Here we are concerned with the principle that, in general, excludes the entitlement of a child or young person who is in receipt of, or who has recently left, 'relevant education'. The intention is to ensure that provision interlocks with child benefit, so that, in general, if a parent is able to claim child benefit in respect of the young person (and indeed include him in the family unit for the purposes of any entitlement to income support), the young person is himself not entitled to income support.

Under section 20(3) of the Social Security Act 1986, except in prescribed circumstances, a person 'receiving relevant education' is not entitled to income support. For this purpose, a child or young person is treated as 'receiving relevant education' in two alternative situations: first, where he is engaged in full-time non-advanced education, that is GCE 'A' Level or below; or, secondly, where he is treated as a 'child' under the Child Benefit Act 1975.[8] The latter alternative is fully discussed in chapter 10,[9] but it is important to observe here that, following modifications to the arrangements for young persons aged 16–17 made in 1988, it now covers a short period after such a person has left school and is unemployed but during which he is registered for work or training under the youth training scheme. The period in question is, for summer school leavers, 16 weeks, and, for those leaving school at Christmas or Easter, 12 weeks.

It remains to consider the prescribed circumstances in which a young person in receipt of 'relevant education' may nevertheless be entitled to income support.[10] The exclusion does not apply if he is a parent of, and responsible for, a child, if he is unlikely to be able to obtain work because of a handicap, or if he is an orphan or living away from and estranged from his parents or guardian. Moreover, a young person attending a course of education or training for up to 21 hours[11] a week will not be disentitled if he is prepared immediately to end that course once suitable employment becomes available.[12] However, to invoke the '21 hour rule', for the three months immediately preceding the start of the course,[13] the claimant must have been in receipt of unemployment benefit, sickness benefit, or income support, or have been engaged on a Youth Training Scheme course.[14]

6 See, further, p.455, below.
7 Pp. 467–469.
8 SI 1987/1967, reg 12.
9 P.394, above.
10 SI 1987/1967, reg 13.
11 This does not include meal breaks or periods of unsupervised study.
12 Ibid, regs 13(2)(f) and 9, on which see Harris [1988] JSWL 21.
13 Or for an aggregate of three months in the six months immediately preceding the start of the course and for the remaining part of those six months was earning too much to qualify for benefit.
14 SI 1987/1967, reg 9(1)(c) and (2). For the difficulties encountered under previous versions of the rule, see Harris, n.12, above.

D Condition of availability for employment

i General rule

The general rule is that the claimant must be 'available for employment'.[15] The condition is similar to that imposed on claimants for unemployment benefit[16] and may be justified on the same basis, that if the claimant is of an appropriate age, and fit and able to work, the unemployment must be involuntary. For the purposes of the rule, 'employment' means 'employed earner's employment' (that is, working under a contract of employment rather than as a self-employed person[17]):

(a)   which the claimant can reasonably be expected to do;

(b)   for which payment is made or which is done in expectation of payment; and

(c)   for which he would normally be engaged for not less than 24 hours a week, or, if he is mentally or physically disabled, such lesser number of hours as, having regard to his disability, he is usually capable of working.[18]

Generally he will be regarded as available if he satisfies the equivalent test for unemployment benefit, though he may be treated as available for income support purposes if he is attending a course of education or training for up to 21 hours a week and is prepared to terminate the course immediately a suitable vacancy occurs.[19]

The availability condition is fulfilled in practice by the claimant satisfactorily responding to certain questions on the claim form and attending in person to 'sign on' at the unemployment benefit office, as required under administrative arrangements.[20] However, at any time during the currency of the claim he may be summoned for an interview at that office by a claimant adviser, to ensure that the condition is still being satisfied. These procedures are to be distinguished from the requirement to 'register' for work at a Jobcentre or careers office of a local education authority which, prior to 1982, was imposed on most unemployed claimants. A joint Department of Employment and DHSS scrutiny team, reviewing the arrangements in 1981, found no evidence that the requirement led to the speedy filling of employment vacancies or discouraged the 'work-shy' from avoiding work.[1] Consequently, registration, with the Manpower Services Commission (since 1987 responsible for Jobcentres) or a local education authority, is now compulsory only for claimants under 18 who are required to be available for work.[2]

ii Persons not treated as available for employment

To complement the general rule, the Income Support Regulations provide for circumstances in which a claimant is not to be treated as available for employment; if they apply, the claimant becomes ineligible for income support. These provisions, together with the 40 per cent deduction rule discussed in Part 7 of this chapter, now form the principal method by which allegedly

15 SSA 1986, s.20(3)(d)(i).
16 Pp. 90–97, above.
17 Cf pp. 36–41, above.
18 SI 1987/1967, reg 7.
19 Ibid, reg 9. For details of the '21-hour rule', see p.421, above.
20 SI 1987/1968, reg 8(1).
1 DE/DHSS Rayner Scrutiny Team *Payments of Benefit to Unemployed People* (1981).
2 SSA 1986, s.20(4) and SI 1987/1967, reg 11(3).

'work-shy' claimants are induced to find employment.[3] In outline, a claimant will be treated as unavailable:[4]

(1) if he has without good cause refused to apply for, or accept an offer of, suitable employment when he has been properly notified of the vacancy; or

(2) if has placed unreasonable restrictions on the employment he is prepared to accept;[5] or

(3) if, aged 18 to 45, with no dependants and not living with a partner over 45, and neither partner is pregnant or mentally or physically disabled, he fails to avail himself of a reasonable opportunity of short-term work available in the area where he lives; or

(4) if after two notices he fails to report to the appropriate authorities for an interview in connection with his prospects of employment.

In (1) and (3), the determination of non-availability is not to apply for more than 26 weeks[6] or the period during which the situation or opportunity is still available, whichever is the shorter; and (3) can be applied only after the claimant is given 14 days' written notice.

Finally, a student is treated as unavailable during periods when he is attending a course or is engaged on a programme of studies.[7] In effect, this means that a student will normally be eligible for income support only during the long vacation (see Part 9).

iii Exemption from availability for employment

There are clearly important categories of claimant who cannot reasonably be expected to display attachment to the labour market as a condition of benefit. The regulations exempt the following from the obligation to be available for employment:[8]

(1) lone parents, single parents looking after foster children, persons responsible for a child while their partner is temporarily abroad or temporarily caring for a child or a relative who is ill, and those engaged full-time in caring for a seriously disabled person;

(2) persons who are registered as blind, are incapable of work,[9] or whose earning capacity has been reduced by 25 per cent;

(3) Open University students attending a residential course, persons in receipt of a training allowance or an allowance under the Job Release Act 1977 and those in full-time education who, because for example they are parents, seriously handicapped, or estranged from their parents[10] are not excluded from income support;

---

3 Until 1980 there were discretionary powers to withhold benefit: see the first edition of this book, pp. 536–538.

4 SI 1987/1967, reg 10.

5 Both (1) and (2) incorporate principles developed in unemployment benefit law: pp. 92–96, above.

6 This was originally six weeks; it was changed to 13 weeks in 1987 and 26 weeks in 1988; cf p.109, above.

7 SI 1987/1967, reg 10(1)(h).

8 Ibid, reg 8 and Sch 1, as amended.

9 Also where the adjudication officer has determined, contrary to a doctor's opinion, that the claimant is not incapable of work, and the claimant has appealed against the decision: ibid, reg 8(2).

10 See p.421, above.

(4) persons over 60, or within 10 years of pensionable age, and who have been out of work for the last ten years during which time they are not required to be available for work;

(5) refugees undertaking a course in English, persons from abroad entitled to an urgent cases payment,[11] discharged prisoners (for seven days), persons in custody, persons required to attend court (for more than two days) and those subject to a trade disputes disqualification.[12]

Finally, there is a residual discretion conferred on the adjudication officer to dispense with the availability requirement in cases where he is satisfied that 'unless income support is paid, the claimant or a member of his family (if any) will suffer hardship.[13]

Part 3　The 'family' for income support purposes
A　General

Obviously persons living alone can claim income support for themselves, but only one member of a 'family' can claim benefit at any one time.[14] The scheme, recognising the economies of scale involved in family life, in general treats a couple living together (whether married or not) and their children as one unit for the purposes both of determining whose needs are relevant to the claim and whose resources should be taken into account in determining the amount payable.[15] The statutory definition of a 'family'[16] may be considered under three heads: married couples; unmarried couples; children and young persons. Where both members of a couple qualify for income support, either can make the appropriate claim[17] but care is necessary in exercising the choice since in some circumstances consequences vary according to which member is the 'claimant' and which is the 'partner'.[18]

B　Married couples

A married[19] couple who are 'members of the same household' are treated as a family unit. The term 'members of the same household' is not defined so recourse must be had to general principles.[20] In divorce law, where it is commonly an issue whether spouses are living separately, the test seems to be whether cohabitation and forms of common life have ceased. If they have not, the courts will generally rule, at least if the parties are under the same

11 P.451, below.
12 Pp. 455–458, below.
13 SI 1987/1967, reg 8(3), which, in general, does not apply to students. The regulation differs significantly from its equivalent under the SB scheme where the discretion was exercisable in circumstances 'analogous' to those listed and where it was 'unreasonable' to require the claimant to be available for employment. See on this, esp, *R(SB) 5/87(T)* and *R(SB) 16/87*.
14 SSA 1986, s.20(9).
15 Ibid, s.22(5).
16 Ibid, s.20(11).
17 SI 1987/1968, reg 4(3), a refreshingly simple rule which replaces the 'nominated bread-winner' provisions applied to the SB legislation, on which see Luckhaus [1983] JSWL 325.
18 Notably where a disability premium is applicable (p.429, below).
19 For 'marriage', see pp. 349–353, above. Polygamous marriages are covered but there are special rules applying to them: n.18, below.
20 It is not clear that the SB case-law (e.g. *R(SB)13/82* and *R(SB) 4/83*) interpreting this phrase to determine whether the claimant came within the now defunct 'householder' status should be applied here.

roof, that they are still living in the same household.[1] This seems to be the appropriate approach here. The fact that a husband is not giving his wife any financial support does not in itself prevent them from being regarded as 'members of the same household'.

Regulations provide that generally a couple will be treated as members of the same household notwithstanding a temporary absence of one of them from the home.[2] However, this will only be the case where the absentee intends to return home, the part of the home occupied by that person has not been let, and the period of absence is unlikely to exceed 52 weeks (or in exceptional circumstances unlikely 'substantially' to exceed that period).[3] In any event, a couple will not be treated as sharing the same household where either of them is in custody, is detained in hospital under the mental health legislation, is living permanently[4] in residential accommodation, or has been abroad for more than four weeks.[5] The position of separated and divorced partners is treated separately in Part 8 of this chapter.

C Unmarried couples

'A man and a woman who are not married to each other but are living together as husband and wife' are treated as if they were married and living in the same household.[6] The concept of 'living together as husband and wife' is used elsewhere in social security legislation and, as such, has been the subject of critical discussion in chapter 9.[7]

D Children and young persons

The general position is that a child (under 16) or a young person (aged 16 to 19 and in receipt of full-time education) who is a member of the same household as the claimant is treated as part of the family unit for income support purposes, provided that the claimant (or the claimant's partner, in the case of a couple who are members of the same household) is 'responsible' for the child or young person.[8]

i 'Responsible' for child or young person
'A person shall be treated as responsible for a child or young person for whom he has primary responsibility'.[9] Clearly, this cannot apply to those young persons who can themselves claim income support under rules which have already been considered,[10] nor does it apply to children being fostered under statutory provisions or while awaiting an adoption order.[11] In other situations, 'primary responsibility' is determined largely by reference to

1 E.g. *Hopes v Hopes* [1949] P 227, [1948] 2 All ER 920. See Bromley and Lowe *Bromley's Family Law* (7th edn) pp. 189–190, 201.
2 SI 1987/1967, reg 16(1), as amended.
3 Ibid, reg 16(2) and Sch 3, para 4(8).
4 Or temporarily and the couple is not entitled to income support (see p.466, below) and cannot afford to pay for that accommodation.
5 SI 1987/1967, reg 16(3).
6 SSA 1986, s.20(11).
7 Pp. 354–357, above.
8 SSA 1986, s.20(11).
9 SI 1987/1967, reg 15(1).
10 Ibid, reg 14 and see pp. 418–420, above.
11 SI 1987/1967, reg 16(4).

entitlement to child benefit. Thus, a child (or young person) whose time is split between different households is regarded as being the primary responsibility of the person who receives child benefit in respect of him.[12] A person making a *claim* for such benefit is so regarded, provided that it is the only claim; in other cases, the adjudication officer has a discretion to determine primary responsibility.[13]

ii Member of same household

The second condition is that the child (or young person) should be a member of the same household as the claimant. While the general principles regarding the interpretation of this phrase and the disregard of temporary absences which we have examined in relation to couples apply equally here, there is a special set of rules. A child (or young person) is treated as *not* being a member of the claimant's household where:[14]

(1) he has been abroad for more than four weeks;
(2) he has been in hospital or residential accommodation for more than 12 weeks and has not been in regular contact with the claimant or members of the claimant's household;
(3) he has been placed for adoption elsewhere, or is boarding with someone prior to adoption; or
(4) he is in custody or in the care of a local authority.

Part 4   Assessment of the applicable amount

A General

A claimant's needs might be met in three alternative ways. He might be provided with assistance in kind, at least where this was practicable. If there was a need for clothing or toilet articles, he would be provided with them (or a voucher for their purpose) on proof that he was unable to afford them. This approach is still used in the United States, for example by the distribution of 'food stamps',[15] but has been relatively uncommon in this country. Secondly, cash payments might be awarded for the purposes of purchasing the specific goods or services required by the applicant. Traditionally this method has been used in British means-tested systems, notably under the supplementary benefit legislation in the form of 'single payments'. While this kind of relief is still available under the social fund, most such payments are made by way of loan. The third method is the one most widely adopted in Britain: cash payments are made to cover the applicant's assumed needs, which are calculated according to formulae set out in legislation (or regulations made under it).

The advantage of paying benefit according to a standard scale rate is that it gives the recipient some discretion how to spend it. Thus, in one week a claimant may pay a little more for food than usual, while in the next week money may be spent on a hobby or some recreation. Different claimants have varying needs, particularly with regard to clothes and amenities, and the scale rates are fixed so as to enable them to exercise choice. Since the late 1950s, it has been generally agreed that those in receipt of assistance should share in

12 Ibid, reg 15(2)(a).
13 Ibid, reg 15(2)(b).
14 Ibid, reg 15(5).
15 Myers *Social Security* (2nd edn) pp. 606–607.

increasing national prosperity and in consequence the payments are designed, in theory, to be high enough to cover some amenities as well as the goods necessary to carry on a subsistence existence.

Under the supplementary benefit scheme, a person's needs were assessed by aggregating 'normal', 'additional' and 'housing' requirements. 'Normal' requirements were intended to cover 'items of normal expenditure on day-to-day living apart from housing costs', for example food, household fuel, clothing, normal travel and laundry costs, miscellaneous household expenses and leisure amenities.[16] To reflect an assumed higher cost of living, the scale rates varied according to whether the claimant was a 'householder' or a 'non-householder'; larger payments were also made to pensioners and those in receipt of benefit for over a year who were not required to be available for employment (the 'long term' rate).[17] 'Additional requirements', which had replaced the discretionary 'exceptional circumstances additions', enabled the weekly payments to be increased to cover regularly occurring expenditures, such as heating, laundry and diet, resulting from the individual circumstances of the claimant or the family unit. Finally, 'housing requirements' were to deal with housing costs though, given the availability of housing benefit also for this purpose, in the latter years of the supplementary benefit scheme they principally covered only mortgage interest payments, water rates and the maintenance and insurance of property.

The structure of the income support scheme is significantly different. While the 'personal' allowances are, broadly speaking, the equivalent of 'normal requirements', the 'additional requirements', the 'long-term rate' and the distinction between 'householder' and 'non-householder' have all been abolished. Instead, the varying needs of different client groups (families, lone parents, the disabled and the elderly) are met by a system of premiums. For some claimants an element of housing costs may still be included, provided that they are not met by housing benefit.

The income support scheme thus attributes to each claimant an 'applicable amount' which is the aggregate of the relevant personal allowances (Section B), premiums (Section C) and housing costs (Section D). There are special rules governing the applicable amount for those living in board and lodging accommodation (Section E). Benefit is calculated by subtracting the relevant income of the claimant (discussed in Part 5) from the applicable amount.

B Personal allowances

The rates of personal allowances vary according to age and whether the claimant is single or living with a partner. There are three rates for single claimants (aged, respectively, under 18, 18 to 24, and 25 and above); two rates for lone parents (under 18, and over 18); and two rates for couples (both partners under 18, one or both over 18).[18] If, however, one member of a couple is not eligible for income support under the special rules for claimants

---

16 Supplementary Benefits Handbook (1984), para 3.13 and see SI 1983/1399, reg 2, which lists the main items included.
17 See the second edition of this book, pp. 466–472.
18 SI 1987/1967, reg 17(a) and Sch 2, para 1, as amended. In the case of a polygamous marriage (cf p.352, above) the higher couple rate is applicable to the claimant and one partner, and the difference between that rate and the highest rate for a single claimant is applied to each other partner: ibid, reg 18.

aged 16–17 discussed in Part 2,[19] the amount payable for the couple is that for a single person at the rate appropriate for the age of that member's partner. The normal under-18 couple rate nevertheless applies if at least one of the couple is responsible for a child or each of them is either registered for work or training under the youth training scheme or is exempt for that requirement because of, for example, disability or pregnancy.[20]

The different treatment of single claimants (without children) aged under, and over 25, respectively, has been a matter of some controversy. It is intended to reflect an assumption that most single claimants under 25 do not have full household responsibilities and thus, in effect, replaces the house-holder/non-householder distinction the application of which generated considerable administrative difficulties.[1] Originally, the government proposed that the same age split should apply to couples but this was withdrawn in the light of criticism, particularly from the Social Security Advisory Committee,[2] that it failed to take account of the trend to establish households at increasingly younger ages.[3] However, no equivalent protection was offered to the 20 per cent of single supplementary benefit claimants in the 18 to 24 age group who had been paid at the householder rate.[4]

As we have seen,[5] the 'family' for income support purposes does not include adult dependants (other than partners). Consequently the only dependants for whom personal allowances are available are children and young persons (under 19). There are four age bands: under 11, 11 to 15, 16 to 17, and 18 and over.[6] Considerable attention has been given in recent years to the impact of age differences on the cost of bringing up children.[7] The Green Paper of 1985 sought views on the possible restructuring of the age bands, with the dividing lines at 8 and 13, rather than 11 and 16.[8] The proposal received support but the government eventually concluded that it could not be implemented without making available additional resources.[9]

C Premiums

The system of premiums for different 'client groups' represents the government's attempt to resolve the tension between the concern to simplify the means-testing process and the recognition that there are wide divergencies of need according to individual circumstances. The groups designated for such premiums are: families, lone parents, pensioners (two rates – ordinary and higher), the disabled, the severely disabled and disabled children. Whether the new structure adequately compensates claimants for the loss of the 'additional requirements' and 'long-term' rates, previously available under the

19 Pp. 418–420, above.
20 For the complete list, see SI 1987/1967, Sch 1A, Part I.
 1 *Green Paper 1985* vol 2, para 2.34.
 2 Fourth Report (1985), para 3.6.
 3 Cf *White Paper 1985* paras 3.10–3.11.
 4 It was argued that the reform released resources for older people: ibid, para 3.13.
 5 P.424, above.
 6 SI 1987/1967, reg 17(b) and Sch 2, para 2.
 7 Field *What Price A Child?* (1985). The contrast between the social security rates and those prescribed by the National Foster Care Association, based on the Family Expenditure Survey, was the subject of comment during discussion of the 1986 Bill: Mr M Meacher, Standing Committee B Debates, col 698.
 8 Vol 2, para 2.77.
 9 *White Paper 1985* para 3.16.

supplementary benefit scheme, has been much debated.[10] Criticism has focussed, in particular, on the provisions for the disabled.[11] The problem is that, as will be seen, application of the premiums typically requires the claimant (or the disabled member of the family) to satisfy the conditions for other social security disability benefits, whereas under the more flexible supplementary benefit system additions were available for a broader range of health and disability problems.[12]

i Family premium
This applies where at least one member of the family is a child or young person.[13] The idea is to provide additional help to families which had previously been largely dependent on the ordinary rates of supplementary benefit.[14] Only one such premium is payable, however many children in the family.

ii Lone parent premium
Lone parents only qualified for the 'long-term' rate of supplementary benefit after 52 weeks; the premium is applied immediately. The simple condition is that the claimant 'is a member of a family but has no partner'.[15]

iii Disability and severe disability premiums
As indicated above, the income support provision for disabled persons has given rise to some controversy. The current approach includes not only the two premiums discussed here but also, for the purpose of computing the claimant's income, the total disregard of attendance and mobility allowance and the partial disregard of earnings.[16] The government has indicated that it will review the level of support when the major survey it has commissioned of the numbers, needs and circumstances of the disabled is published.[17] In defence of its existing strategy, it has adverted to the fact that the disability and severe disability premiums are applied as soon as the conditions for them are fulfilled, whereas the 'long-term' supplementary benefit rate was in general only paid after one year's incapacity for work.[18] The government suffered a defeat in the House of Lords when this part of the Social Security Bill 1986 was being considered[19] and, to pacify critics, introduced what is now section 22(3) of the 1986 Act. This stipulates that 'the applicable amount for a severely disabled person shall include an amount in respect of his being a severely disabled person' – a curious provision, since there is no explicit reference in the parliamentary legislation to other 'client groups', or to the premiums applicable to them.

---

10 See, esp, SSAC Fourth Report (1985), paras 3.13–3.21 and Seventh Report of Commons Select Committee on Social Services, 1984–85 HC 451.
11 SSAC Report, n.10, above, para 3.18; Disability Alliance *Reform of Social Security: Response* (1985).
12 See Rowell and Wilton *The Law of Supplementary Benefits* pp. 54–55, 61–63.
13 SI 1987/1967, reg 17(c) and Sch 2, para 3. For definitions, see pp. 424–426, above.
14 *White Paper 1985* para 3.15.
15 SI 1987/1967, Sch 2, para 8.
16 Pp. 443 and 446, below.
17 *White Paper 1985* para 3.23.
18 Though, as the White Paper acknowledges (ibid) some of the conditions are based on entitlement to disability benefits which require a six-month waiting period.
19 477 HL Official Report (5th series), cols 12–24.

The disability premium applies to persons under 60. Where the claimant is single (or a lone parent) he must[20] *either*

(1) be registered as a blind person; *or*
(2) receive an attendance,[1] mobility or severe disablement allowance, an invalidity pension, or a mobility supplement, or be provided with an invalid carriage or a DSS grant towards the cost of maintaining a car; *or*
(3) have been treated as incapable of work (for the purposes of the Social Security Act 1975[2]) for a continuous period of 28 weeks.[3]

In the case of a couple, the claimant must satisfy one of these three conditions *or* the partner must satisfy (1) or (2).[4]

To qualify for a severe disability premium, a single claimant (or lone parent) must satisfy three conditions: he must be in receipt of an attendance allowance;[5] there are no non-dependants aged 18 or over in the same household;[6] and no-one is in receipt of the invalid care allowance for looking after the claimant.[7] However, where someone comes to the household to care for the invalid, an existing entitlement to a severe disability premium will continue for 12 weeks. If the claimant is one of a couple, the same conditions broadly apply[8] but both partners must be in receipt of the attendance allowance.[9]

iv Pensioner and higher pensioner premiums

The 'long-term' rate of supplementary benefit was automatically awarded where the claimant (or partner) was aged 60 or over. The new system consolidates this provision. There are, however, two different premiums. The 'ordinary' pensioner premium is applicable where the claimant, or partner, is aged 60 to 79.[10] There is automatic entitlement to the higher pensioner premium if the claimant, or partner, is aged 80 or over; those aged 60 to 79 receive the higher award if one of two conditions relating to disability is fulfilled:[11]

(a) The claimant or partner is over 60 and satisfies conditions (1) or (2) for the disability premium, specified above. The condition is treated as satisfied if entitlement to a mobility allowance or invalidity pension ceased solely because the relevant person reached the maximum age for these

20 SI 1987/1967, Sch 2, para 11(a).
1 Or would have satisfied the conditions for this benefit but for the fact that he was in hospital or other publicly-funded accommodation: see p.167, above.
2 Cf pp. 150–152, above.
3 The waiting period of 28 weeks need not be served again if an intervening period of less than 8 weeks occurs between two spells of incapacity for work.
4 SI 1987/1967, para 11(b).
5 Though see n.1, above.
6 The following are not treated as 'non-dependants' and thus their presence can be ignored: members of the claimant's family; joint occupiers of the dwelling; tenants and lodgers; persons caring for, and paid by, the claimant (or partner) under arrangements with a voluntary organisation; persons in receipt of attendance allowance. See SI 1987/1967, reg 3(3) and Sch 2, para 13(3).
7 Ibid, para 13(2)(a).
8 Except that invalid care allowance might be payable in respect of one member of the couple.
9 SI 1987/1967, Sch 2, para 13(2)(b).
10 Ibid, para 9.
11 Ibid, para 10, as amended.

benefits, provided that income support has been continuously paid since that date.[12]

(b) The claimant was entitled to income support, including a disability premium, in respect of a benefit week within eight weeks of his sixtieth birthday and has remained continuously entitled to income support since reaching that age.[12]

Condition (b) will be of relatively minor significance for the next few years since it cannot assist those aged 61 or over when the income support system first came into force.

v Disabled child premium

The introduction of this premium constituted a response by the government to the criticism that its original proposals took insufficient account of the needs of disabled children.[13] It is applicable for each child or young person who is a member of the family unit[14] is either blind or in receipt of attendance allowance[15] *and* does not have capital exceeding £3,000.[16]

vi Accumulation of premiums

The family premium and the disabled child premium may be accumulated with any other premium.[17]

— For example, a single parent with three children, two of whom were disabled, would qualify for a family premium + lone parent premium + two disabled child premiums.

The general principle is that only one of the other premiums is applicable to a family at any one time and therefore if the claimant satisfies the conditions for more than one of these, the higher or highest applies.[18] The single exception to this is the severe disability premium which may be accumulated with either a disability premium or a higher pensioner premium.[19]

D Housing costs

i Policy

A feature of social assistance schemes since 1935 has been the payment of separate allowances to cover housing costs. Two arguments in particular have been used to justify them.[20] First, there are significant variations in such costs, and these cannot easily be covered by standard scale rates; this is not really the case for any other goods or services. Secondly, while a claimant can adjust expenditure on, say, food or clothing, this is impossible with housing costs. They have to be paid regularly and it is unreasonable to expect someone

---

12 A gap in entitlement to income support not exceeding eight weeks and which spans the claimant's sixtieth birthday is disregarded for this purpose.
13 *White Paper 1985* para 3.22 See also p.429, above.
14 See pp. 425–426, above.
15 Though see n.1, above.
16 SI 1987/1967, Sch 2, para 14. On the capital condition, see pp. 447–450, below.
17 SI 1987/1967, reg 17(c) and Sch 2, para 6(2).
18 Ibid, para 5.
19 Ibid, para 6(1).
20 Cf *George* pp. 214 et seq.

to move to cheaper accommodation every time he is ill or unemployed, and has to rely on benefit.

Until 1983, housing costs formed a very significant portion of total supplementary benefit expenditure and indeed many claimants only qualified for that benefit because of their expenditure on rent or other housing costs.[1] The system was, however, expensive to administer and the rules added considerably to the overall complexity of the scheme. Another drawback was that there was often overlap between the rent element of supplementary benefit and the rent rebates and allowances, and rate rebates, available from local authorities. The problem was partly resolved by the Social Security and Housing Benefits Act 1982 which introduced a unified housing benefit scheme, administered by local authorities. Nevertheless, mortgage interest payments, water rates and some other miscellaneous housing costs, such as additions for insurance and maintenance, continued to be administered by the DHSS under the supplementary benefit scheme.

The Fowler Reviews examined afresh the arrangements for dealing with housing costs. While most of the recommendations related to housing benefit and, as such, are described in chapter 13, the role of income support was not ignored. Indeed, one of the most discussed issues was whether the latter system could adequately cope with the consequences of the controversial proposal that, to ensure political accountability for local authority spending, no household should be able to recover more than 80 per cent of chargeable rates.[2] The prospect of income support not supplying any recompense for the 20 per cent loss in rate rebates was the subject of critical comments by the Social Security Advisory Committee,[3] among others, but these did not lead to any significant change in government policy.[4] As regards those housing costs met by the supplementary benefit scheme, the government made two main proposals. The first was that water rates and certain residual housing costs, such as insurance and minor building repairs, should no longer be separately covered, since the amounts were small and the administrative cost of dealing with them was high; rather, they should be subsumed under the general system of personal allowances.[5] Though widely criticised,[6] this proposal was implemented in the Social Security Act 1986. Secondly, it was suggested that the meeting of mortgage interest payments in full led to work disincentive problems and to unfairness between those in and out of work.[7] Partly in response to objections that these arguments were hardly applicable to, for example, the elderly and the disabled and a reduction in this form of assistance would discriminate unfairly between tenants and owner-occupiers,[8] the decision was made to limit the entitlement only of those of working age in receipt of benefit for less than 16 weeks. This reform was applied to the supplementary benefit legislation and was subsequently carried over into the new income support scheme.

---

1 In its Annual Report for 1979 (Cmnd 8033), para 4.2, the Supplementary Benefits Commission estimated that there were 0.3 million such claimants.
2 *Green Paper 1985* vol 1, para 9.20.
3 Fourth Report (1985), para 3.33.
4 Cf *White Paper 1985* para 3.56.
5 *Green Paper 1985* vol 2, para 2.49.
6 The government considered that such criticisms had 'exaggerated the effect on claimants and under-estimated the gains from this simplification for local office staff': *White Paper 1985* para 3.42.
7 *Green Paper 1985* vol 2, para 2.48.
8 Fourth Report of SSAC (1985), para 3.39.

ii Conditions of entitlement

For housing costs to be added to the applicable amount, two conditions must be satisfied.

a *Responsibility for housing costs* The claimant, or any other member of the family unit, must under the Income Support Regulations be 'treated as responsible' for the expenditure to which the housing cost relates.[9] This does not necessarily mean 'legal' responsibility in the strict sense[10] and so will arise not only where the claimant or partner is liable to meet the costs[11] but also where a person so liable does not in fact meet them and it is therefore necessary to attribute the expenditure to another. This will commonly arise where spouses have separated and the spouse who has left was legally responsible for the mortgage payments. Another situation is where a person in practice shares the costs with someone other than a partner or a close relative;[12] such a person will be treated as having a shared responsibility, particularly where the expenditure is similarly shared for the purpose of the housing benefit regulations.[13] Where some but not all members of a family are involved in a trade dispute, the housing costs are treated as those of the members not so involved.

b *Dwelling occupied as the home* The second condition is that the housing cost for which the relevant person is responsible must be in respect of a dwelling which the claimant, or a member of his family, occupies as his home.[14] This means:

> the dwelling together with any garage, garden and outbuildings, normally occupied by the claimant as his home including any premises not so occupied which it is impracticable or unreasonable to sell separately, in particular, in Scotland any croft land on which the dwelling is situated.[15]

Generally a person is treated as occupying only the dwelling in which he normally lives.[16] But the regulations provide for exceptions to this rule.[17] Costs for two dwellings may be allowed where a person has moved from one house to another through fear of violence or where one member of a couple is a student or on a training course and the occupation of two dwellings is 'unavoidable'. The same applies where the claimant moves to a new dwelling, though the costs of both the old and the new home will be met only for a maximum of four weeks and the provision does not apply where the move is only a temporary one, undertaken so that repairs are carried out on the normal home. In some circumstances, a person is treated as occupying a dwelling for a period of up to four weeks before he actually moves in (e.g. because a member of the family is disabled and adaptations have to be made to the house or because the move cannot be undertaken until a decision on a social fund application for removal expenses has been made). Finally, there are

---

9 SI 1987/1967, Sch 3, paras 2–3.
10 *CSB 213/1987* and see the analogous test used for housing benefit: p.492, below.
11 Provided that this is not to a member of the same household.
12 For the meaning of 'close relative', see SI 1987/1967, reg 2(1); also *CSB 209/1986* and *CSB 1149/1986*.
13 Cf p.492, below.
14 SI 1987/1967, Sch 3, para 2.
15 Ibid, reg 2(1).
16 Ibid, Sch 3, para 4(1).
17 Ibid, para 4(2)–(8).

provisions allowing for the disregard of temporary absences, up to 52 weeks, from the home. The conditions are that: the relevant person intends to return to occupy the dwelling as a home; the part of the premises normally occupied by him is not let (or sub-let); and the period of absence is unlikely to exceed 52 weeks.[18]

iii Assessable housing costs

a *Mortgage interest payments*   The principal type of housing cost met under the income support scheme is that of mortgage interest payments. Traditionally, systems of social assistance have not covered capital repayments. The argument is presumably that public money should not be used to allow individuals to acquire capital assets, though the provision of home improvement grants and concessions to house purchase by council tenants is difficult to reconcile with it. On the other hand, income tax relief is only allowed on the interest part of mortgage repayments. A mortgagor who claims income support should therefore attempt to persuade the building society to accept interest payments only and defer repayment of capital. It would also appear possible for a claimant who lets the premises to arrange for the tenant to make payments, reflecting the capital element, directly to the building society. Under the regulations, such a payment would not be treated as part of the claimant's income.[19]

Subject to the 50 per cent rule, which may apply to the first 16 weeks of a claim (see below), assessable housing costs include payments of interest on a loan taken out for the purpose of 'acquiring an interest in the dwelling occupied as a home',[20] or a second loan taken out to pay off a first loan, provided that the latter itself related to acquiring an interest in the home.[1] There is only one situation in which a loan secured against a dwelling *not* for the purpose acquiring an interest in the home can be an assessable housing cost. This is where the loan was taken out by a former partner who has left the claimant and cannot, or will not, continue the interest payments. The claimant's payments of interest will be covered, provided that they are necessary to continue to live in the home.[2] Interest on arrears of interest cannot be met unless they have accrued as a result of the 50 per cent rule, now to be considered.[3]

b *The '50 per cent' rule*   The origins of this rule have already been described.[4] Its effect is that where the claimant (and partner, if any) is under 60, for the first 16 weeks of income support only 50 per cent of the mortgage interest repayments is treated as an assessable housing cost.[5] As we have also seen, its severity is mitigated by the fact that, after the 16 weeks have been served, there is entitlement to interest on the arrears of interest which have built up during this period.[6] Naturally, this creates a powerful incentive for

---

18 Students absent from their term-time home during the summer vacation cannot invoke this rule: ibid, para 4(4).
19 Ibid, reg 42(a)(ii).
20 On which, see *R(SB) 21/85*.
 1 SI 1987/1967, Sch 3, para 7(3).
 2 Ibid, para 7(7). It follows that e.g. insurance premiums paid under an endowment mortgage are not covered: cf *R(SB) 46/83*.
 3 SI 1987/1967, Sch 3, para 7(6) and see *CSB 467/1983*.
 4 P.432, above.
 5 SI 1987/1967, Sch 3, para 7(1).
 6 Ibid, para 7(6).

claimants to remain entitled to income support for 16 weeks – an ironical effect for a rule which was itself created to counter work disincentives. As a partial solution to the problem, the regulations provide that gaps in entitlement to income support of not more than eight weeks should be disregarded in counting the 16-week period,[7] thus allowing the claimant to take on work of a short duration without having to serve the 16 weeks again. There are also rules to prevent the continuity of this period being affected by a change in the composition of the family unit, for example, separation from, or acquisition of, a partner.[8]

The application of the 50 per cent rule will, in some cases, lead to the claimant losing entitlement to *any* income support, because it will reduce the applicable amount to a level below his relevant income. To prevent such a claimant being permanently disentitled, the regulations provide in effect that if the application of the 50 per cent rule was the sole reason for the refusal of a claim, the claimant will become entitled on the making of a second claim 16 weeks (but no later than 20 weeks) after the first, and the assessable housing costs will then include the full interest payments.[9] Interest on arrears of interest may also be included but only to a maximum of 50 per cent of the interest that otherwise would have been treated as an assessable housing cost during the 16-week period.[10]

c *Interest on loans for repairs and improvements*   Assessable housing costs may include interest payable on a loan taken out for the purpose of carrying out repairs or improvements to the home, or for repaying a second loan entered into to pay the interest on a first loan taken out for the same purposes.[11] 'Repairs and improvements' are defined in the regulations as 'major repairs necessary to maintain the fabric of the dwelling' but also are taken to include a number of measures (e.g. damp-proofing, installation of bath or shower, sink or lavatory) 'undertaken with a view to improving its fitness for occupation'.[12]

The amount is calculated in the same way as for interest on a loan for a house purchase and is, therefore, also subject to the 50 per cent rule. However, a special 'capital threshold' applies here: any excess of relevant capital[13] over £500 will be deducted from the amount of the loan, and it is only interest on the remainder which will be treated as an assessable housing cost.[14]

d *Miscellaneous housing costs*   The scheme covers a number of miscellaneous housing costs which are to some degree analogous to those already considered but which are not covered in the housing benefit scheme. These include ground rents relating to long tenancies, (in Scotland) feu duty, service charges, site charges for tents and payments under a co-ownership scheme or

---

7 Ibid, para 7(9)(a) which also enables the claimant to include in the 16-week period for which it was subsequently held, on appeal or review, that he was entitled to income support.
8 Ibid, para 7(9)(c)–(e).
9 Ibid, para 7(2)(b).
10 Ibid, para 7(6)(b).
11 Ibid, para 8(1).
12 Ibid, para 8(3).
13 On this, see p.447, below, though not all the items there mentioned are disregarded for the purposes of the £500 rule stated in the text. For details, see SI 1987/1967, Sch 3, para 8(4) and Sch 10.
14 Ibid, Sch 3, para 8(2).

relating to a Crown tenancy, but deductions will be made for heating, water and electricity charges if they are included in the payments.[15]

iv Restrictions and deductions

a *Housing benefit expenditure*   There is an overriding principle that assessable housing costs may not include anything in respect of housing benefit expenditure, to avoid overlap with that scheme.[16]

b *House purchases by tenants*   If, while in receipt of income support, a claimant with security of tenure purchases property from a private landlord or exercises the 'right to buy' option available to public sector tenants the assessable housing costs will be limited to the amount of 'eligible rent' – the figure used for calculating housing benefit[17] – immediately before the purchase.[18] However, any subsequent increase in housing expenditure (e.g. interest on a loan taken out to effect repairs) will be covered. Moreover, the restriction does not apply where 'its application becomes inappropriate by reason of any major change in the circumstances of the family affecting their ability to meet expenditure on housing costs'; and it will cease to apply once there has been a break of entitlement to income support of at least eight weeks.[19] Depending on the age of the claimant, the '50 per cent rule' may apply in the latter situation. Curiously, a tenant who has a break in entitlement to income support of less than eight weeks and that period straddles the date of the house purchase will, on renewal of his claim, be caught by neither the 'eligible rent' rule nor the '50 per cent rule', provided that the aggregate period of entitlement, before and after the break, exceeds 16 weeks.

c *Excessive housing costs*   An adjudication officer may disallow housing costs to the extent that they are 'excessive'.[20] They will be so regarded where the dwelling is 'larger than is required . . . having regard, in particular, to suitable alternative accommodation occupied by a household of the same size', or where there is suitable accommodation available in a less expensive area.[1] However, the existence of certain 'relevant factors' may make it unreasonable to expect the claimant to seek alternative accommodation, in which case the costs will be allowed in full. 'Relevant factors' are defined in the regulations as 'the availability of suitable accommodation and the level of housing costs in the area' and 'the circumstances of the family including in particular the age and state of health of its members, the employment prospects of the claimant and, where a change in accommodation is likely to result in a change of school, the effect on the education of any child or young person' in the family.[2] If there are no such relevant factors, the restriction does not apply for the first six months of a claim, and this may be extended by a further period of six months if, and so long as, the claimant 'uses his best endeavours to obtain cheaper accommodation'.[3] These relaxations only apply if the claimant was able to meet the housing costs when he first entered

---

15 Ibid, paras 1 and 9.
16 Ibid, para 5(a).
17 Pp. 494–496, below.
18 SI 1987/1967, Sch 3, para 10(1).
19 Ibid, para 10(2).
20 Ibid, para 10(3).
 1 Ibid, para 10(4).
 2 Ibid, para 10(7).
 3 Ibid, para 10(6).

the accommodation – clearly an anti-abuse provision, to prevent claimants using the social security system to 'move up' the housing market.[4]

d *Non-dependants sharing housing costs* There are provisions to reduce the amount of assessable housing costs where part of them are met, or deemed to be met, by other persons. We have already seen[5] that there are situations in which the costs are shared between the claimant and someone other than a partner or a close relative. In such a case, it is the proportionate part of those costs for which the claimant is responsible which are allowed.[6] Analogously, where the local rating authority treats the claimant's premises as a mixed hereditament, for example, because part of it is used to take in boarders, the allowable amount is the proportion of the mortgage interest attributable to that part of the premises in which the claimant (and family, if any) lives.[7] A reduction is also made where a non-dependant normally resides with the claimant, because that person is deemed to contribute to housing expenditure.[8] 'Resides with' here means sharing any room (e.g. kitchen) except a bathroom, toilet or common access area.[9] Clearly, a member of the claimant's family unit[10] is not a 'non-dependant'; the expression also does not cover:[11]

(1) a child or young person living with the claimant, or
(2) a joint occupier (since that will be treated as a case of shared responsibility (above)), or
(3) a tenant (since the rent payable will normally be treated as part of the claimant's income),[12] or
(4) a person engaged by a charitable or voluntary body to care for the claimant (or partner) and who is paid by the claimant (or partner).

There are two rates of deduction: the higher applies to non-dependants who are in remunerative work or who are boarders, the lower to those not engaged in such work or whose gross weekly income is less than a prescribed amount.[13] Only one deduction (the higher one) can be made in respect of a couple. Where the claimant is a joint occupier, the deduction will be apportioned in accordance with the proportion of housing costs attributed to him.[14] Finally, no deduction is made if the claimant (or partner) is blind or in receipt of attendance allowance, nor if the non-dependant is a full time student, a YTS trainee, or under 25 and in receipt of income support.[15]

E Applicable amount for boarders

i General
As under the supplementary benefits scheme, there are special rules for calculating the needs of boarders. Some highly controversial changes were

4 Cf the comparable provisions in the housing benefit scheme, p.507 below, and *Housing Benefit Review* paras 3.7–3.9.
5 P.433, above.
6 SI 1987/1967, Sch 3, para 6(2).
7 Ibid, para 6(1).
8 Ibid, para 11.
9 Ibid, reg 3(3), but not rooms of common use in sheltered accommodation (ibid, reg 3(4)).
10 P.424, above.
11 SI 1987/1967, reg 3(2).
12 P.447, below.
13 SI 1987/1967, Sch 3, para 11(1)–(2).
14 Ibid, para 11(5).
15 Unless, in any of these cases, he is a boarder: ibid, para 11(6)–(7).

made to them in April 1985 as a response to the escalating costs of meeting boarding charges and the allegations that there was extensive abuse of the system, particularly by young unemployed people living in accommodation in holiday resorts.[16] The amendments to the supplementary benefit regulations introduced cost ceilings for designated 'board and lodging areas' and time limits for the meeting of such costs. In addition, fraud teams were employed specifically to deal with board and lodging abuse.[17] The new rules were extensively challenged in the tribunals and in the courts and the success of at least one of these actions,[18] as well as political pressure and problems of drafting, resulted in a series of further amendments.[19] Eventually, a form of regulations was devised which satisfied the courts[20] and these were effectively adopted in the Income Support Regulations. However, at the same time, the government was actively considering proposals to transfer board and lodging charges to the housing benefit scheme, leaving income support to cover only the personal expenses of boarders.[1] The proposed reform will take effect in April 1989.[1a] The provisions now to be explained operate until then.

ii Who are 'boarders'?

The special rules apply to claimants living in 'board and lodging accommodation or a hostel'[2] but not if the accommodation and meals (if any) are provided in whole or in part by a close relative, or 'other than on a commercial basis'[3] – an exclusion intended to avoid the risk of abuse through collusive arrangements. Others excluded from the definition are: young persons in local authority care (unless someone other than the local authority is paid for the accommodation); persons on holiday and absent from their normal residence for a period of up to 13 weeks; and those who can be shown to have entered board and lodging accommodation for the specific purpose of obtaining the special rate of income support.[4] In addition, as will be seen, certain young persons are not treated as boarders after a prescribed time period has elapsed.

iii Applicable amount

A boarder's applicable amount combines sums for 'personal expenses' with an allowance for the accommodation; if the accommodation is only temporary, it may also include the assessable housing costs of the claimant's normal home.[5] There are sums for the personal expenses of each member of the

16 See generally Stewart, Lee and Stewart 13 J Law and Soc 371.
17 See 73 Welfare Rights Bull 6.
18 The use of discretion in the regulations to impose maximum amounts and time limits for payment was held to be *ultra vires* in *R v Secretary of State for Social Services, ex parte Cotton and Waite* (1985) Times, 14 December.
19 According to Stewart et al, n.16, above, at 372, during the parliamentary session 1985–86, the board and lodging regulations were the subject of at least eight actual or attempted amendments, 163 parliamentary questions and 25 debates in the House of Commons.
20 *R v Secretary of State for Social Services, ex parte London Borough of Camden* [1987] 2 All ER 560, [1987] 1 WLR 819. See also *R v Secretary of State for Social Services, ex parte Elkington* and *Kiburn v Chief Adjudication Officer*, both reported in (1987) Independent, 18 March.
1   See DHSS *Consultation Paper: Help with Board and Lodging Charges for People on Low Incomes* (1986) and the comments of SSAC: Fifth Report (1986–87), para 5.26.
1a For details, see SI 1988/1445.
2   SI 1987/1967, reg 20(1); for definitions, see ibid, reg 20(2).
3   Ibid, Sch 5, para 12, as amended. For the definition of 'close relative', see ibid, reg 2(1).
4   Ibid, Sch 5, paras 13–15.
5   Ibid, Sch 5, para 1, as amended.

family unit, other than those of a partner who is under 18 and who is ineligible for income support under the special rules applicable to such persons.[6] The rates for children and young persons are divided into age bands (under 11, 11–15, 16–17, above 18).[7] Adults receive a higher sum if they have a child or they would have qualified for one of the premiums (except the family premium) if they had not been boarders.[8]

The allowance for accommodation is prima facie the amount charged, though if this is not inclusive of meals, it is increased in respect of each family member by the actual cost of such meals if provided on the premises, or otherwise by standard rates for each meal.[9] Most importantly, there is a maximum accommodation allowance prescribed for each geographical area.[10] In the normal cases, this sets the limit on what can be claimed for each adult, or child over 11, and a lower amount is added for each child under 11.[11] Nevertheless, where the actual accommodation charges exceed these ceilings, the regulations allow for an increase, up to a prescribed amount, for certain cases, notably where a single claimant is over pensionable age, where one of a couple is over 65, or where a member of the family is disabled.[12] Further, the full amount of the accommodation charge will be applicable, even though it exceeds the maximum, for a period of up to 13 weeks where (1) the claimant has lived in the same accommodation for at least a year, (2) he could afford the charges when he first lived there, (3) having regard to alternative accommodation available, as well as to personal circumstances, it is reasonably necessary to live there for this period, and (4) the claimant is seeking alternative accommodation.[13] This concession does not, however, apply to claimants living in accommodation provided by local authorities for the homeless.

iv Special restriction for young boarders
Boarders who are under 25 will, in general, only qualify for the applicable amount for an initial period, which varies between two and eight weeks, in any one designated 'board and lodging area'.[14] This restriction only applies for six months and so once that period has elapsed, the claimant may again qualify for another 'initial period'. And there is nothing to prevent a young boarder completing the initial period in one area and then moving to, and qualifying in, another area. It is this aspect of the scheme which has given rise to criticisms that the provisions create a new class of itinerant poor.[15]

The restriction does not apply to young persons who are not required to be available for employment and the regulations provide a long list of other exempting circumstances.[16] Broadly speaking, they are equivalent to the situations in which young persons aged 16–17 may claim income support in

---

6 P.419, above.
7 Though no sums are payable for children or young persons with capital exceeding £3,000: cf p.450, below.
8 SI 1987/1967, Sch 5, para 11.
9 Ibid, para 2.
10 These are set out in elaborate detail, ibid, Sch 6. There is a national maximum for hostels.
11 Ibid, Sch 5, para 5.
12 Ibid, paras 7–9.
13 Ibid, para 10.
14 Ibid, Sch 5 and for the specific areas, Sch 6. Coastal resorts tend to have the shortest periods and inner city areas the longest.
15 Stewart et al, n.16, above, at 388–389.
16 SI 1987/1967, Sch 5, para 16.

their own right[17] and, as in that context, there is a residual discretionary exemption (where to impose the restriction would create 'exceptional hardship' to the claimant, or partner) which is subject to determination by the Secretary of State, and not the adjudicating authorities.

Part 5   The assessment of income

A   Introduction

i   General

In order to calculate the weekly benefit, a claimant's income is deducted from the applicable amount (the aggregate of personal allowances, premiums and housing costs), as assessed under the rules discussed in Part 4. Here we are concerned with the rules used to assess income. Sometimes, of course, the claimant will be completely destitute and have no resources of any sort; in that case, benefit is calculated simply in terms of the applicable amount. In many cases, however, he will have some savings and will also, or alternatively, be in receipt of other social security benefits or part-time earnings, some or all of which may be deducted from the applicable amount to arrive at the sum payable.

In principle it might seem right to take account of all the claimant's resources but under the various social assistance schemes it has always been the case that some of them have been wholly or partially ignored, or 'disregarded' to use the term employed in the regulations. The effect of these 'disregards' is to raise the poverty line, for those people with some capital or income, above the weekly scale rates of benefit, and it is partly for this reason that these rates prove to be a misleading guide to the true extent of poverty in the country.[18] Moreover, the disregards, like the premiums, can be used to discriminate between different categories of claimant. The DHSS review of the supplementary benefits scheme published in 1978 justified the system of disregards on the basis that, in the case of capital, it encouraged saving and, as regards earnings, it encouraged self-help.[19] The review team considered that a balance had to be struck between these principles and the general policy that assistance should be directed to those who needed it most and not to those who enjoyed substantial resources of their own.

More recent policy discussions, notably those emanating from the Fowler Reviews, have concentrated on how this balance should best be struck. On capital, the government concluded that the rule which deprived a claimant with assets over £3,000 of any entitlement to benefit reduced the incentive to save.[20] A proposal to raise that limit to £6,000 and to ignore capital below £3,000 was implemented under the income support legislation. Concern was also expressed that the rules under which only a small amount of earnings was disregarded discouraged people, particularly those who had received benefit for some time, to regain contact with the labour market.[1] The result was a substantial increase in the earnings disregard applied to lone parents, the disabled and some of the long-term unemployed.

17 P.419, above.
18 *Townsend* p.244.
19 *Social Assistance* paras 8.9–8.10.
20 *Green Paper 1985* vol 2, para 2.41.
 1 Ibid, para 2.43.

Since the National Assistance Act 1948, only the applicant's resources and those of his partner and dependants have been taken into account. The ability of any other relatives to maintain him was,[2] and remains,[3] wholly irrelevant to the computation of relevant 'resources' (now 'income').

ii The distinction between income and capital

It is important for this distinction to be drawn for, as will be seen, virtually all income payments are taken into account but capital below £3,000 is wholly ignored and different rules apply to more specific disregards. There is a general power in the Social Security Act 1986 enabling income to be treated as capital and capital to be treated as income in prescribed circumstances[4] and under this a number of specific regulations have been made. But the legislation follows income tax law[5] in not drawing a *general* distinction between the two concepts. In consequence, it is sometimes for the adjudicating authorities (and the courts) to determine whether a particular resource is to be regarded as income or capital. It has been held that the essence of income is an element of 'periodic recurrence',[6] but the nature of the obligation giving rise to the payment must also be taken into account. Thus, a capital payment may be made in instalments and yet, subject to regulations,[7] still be treated as capital.[8]

Special rules govern irregular charitable and other voluntary payments, whether derived from one or more sources: in a period of 52 weeks beginning in the first week of entitlement, the first £250 of any such payments is treated as capital and the remainder (if any) as income.[9]

iii Time periods for income

Income, whether from earnings or other sources or that deemed to arise from capital between £3,000 and £6,000, is calculated on a weekly basis. The regulations prescribe methods for converting income received at other intervals to weekly sums.[10] Where the amount of income fluctuates, an average is derived from a work cycle, if that exists, and, if not, normally over a period of five weeks.[11] Once a weekly figure has been arrived at, it may be important to determine the week to which it relates; for example, if it is attributed to a week before that for which a claim is made, it can normally be ignored. The general rule is that the payment will be taken into account from the date on which it was *due to be paid*, rather than that on which it was actually paid.[12] While undoubtedly this may be justified on grounds of administrative

2 See *R v West London Supplementary Benefits Appeal Tribunal, ex parte Clarke* [1975] 3 All ER 513, [1975] 1 WLR 1396 where the claimant had been denied benefit on the ground that she had resources calculated by reference to her son-in-law's undertaking to the immigration authorities to support her. The Court of Appeal held that the son-in-law (and her son with whom she subsequently lived) did not have any obligation to look after her and therefore that their resources were irrelevant.
3 See SSA 1986, s.22(5).
4 S.22(9)(c)–(d).
5 Tiley *Revenue Law* (3rd edn) paras 2.31–2.33.
6 *R v Supplementary Benefits Commission, ex parte Singer* [1973] 2 All ER 931, [1973] 1 WLR 713.
7 Pp. 443–444, below.
8 *Lillystone v Supplementary Benefits Commission* (1982) 3 FLR 52.
9 SI 1987/1967, reg 24.
10 Ibid, regs 32–34.
11 Ibid, reg 32(6).
12 Ibid, reg 31 and see *R(SB) 33/83*.

convenience, it can give rise to budgeting problems and sometimes hardship where payments are late.[13]

B Earnings

The general principle is that, subject to certain disregards, the earnings of the claimant and partner (if any) count as income.

i Employed earners

For those working under a contract of employment, regard is had to the amount of 'net earnings', that is, gross earnings less income tax, social security contributions and one-half of any contributions to an occupational or personal pension scheme;[14] no deductions are, however, made for expenses incurred, such as travel and childminding costs. 'Earnings', for these purposes, include:[15]

— bonuses, commission, retainer payments, holiday pay (unless payable 4 weeks after the termination of employment), payments in lieu of remuneration or notice,[16] expenses paid by the employer 'not wholly, exclusively and necessarily incurred in the performance of the duties of employment', awards of compensation for unfair dismissal and analogous payments ordered by an industrial tribunal

but not maternity or sick pay (which are treated as 'other' income), nor[17]

— payments in kind, occupational pension payments, and redundancy payments (except to the extent that they represent loss of income).

ii Self-employed earners

The assessable income of a self-employed earner is the 'net profit' from the employment, calculated in the following way.[18] From gross receipts (which include any MSC allowance) are deducted any expenses 'wholly and exclusively defrayed' for the purpose of the employment,[19] income tax, social security contributions and one-half of a premium or contribution payable under an annuity contract and giving rise to tax relief. The calculations are normally made on the basis of a period of a year and then converted into a weekly average.[20]

iii Disregards

The system of disregards, which applies both to employed, and self-employed, earners attempts to strike a balance between the desire to encou-

13 If as a result of a late payment, two payments of the same kind are received in the same week, the claimant is entitled to apply a relevant disregard to each: SI 1987/1967, reg 32(5).
14 Ibid, reg 36.
15 Ibid, reg 35(1).
16 For details, see ibid, reg 35(1)(b)–(c).
17 Ibid, reg 35(2).
18 Ibid, regs 38–39.
19 This *includes* interest on a business loan, income spent or repayment of capital on a loan for repairs to a business asset (unless covered by an insurance policy) and repayment of capital on a loan for replacement of equipment but *excludes* the repayment of capital on other business loans as well as capital expenditure and depreciation: ibid, reg 38(5), (6), (8). In the case of childminders, two-thirds of gross receipts are effectively attributed to expenses: ibid, reg 38(9).
20 Ibid, reg 30(1).

rage recipients to undertake part-time work and a concern that there should be adequate incentives for those of an appropriate age and capacity to relinquish dependence on income support by engaging in full-time employment.[1] As such, the weekly amount of the disregard varies according to the claimant's circumstances. In the standard case, the first £5 of weekly earnings are disregarded.[2] Where both members of a couple earn, each is entitled to the £5 disregard[3] (special rules apply to dependent children and young persons – see below[4]). A higher disregard of £15 is applicable where presumptively it will not constitute a disincentive for full-time employment, thus where:[5]

(1) a lone parent premium or a disability premium is applicable (or would have been if the claimant had not been a boarder or living in a residential care home or equivalent accommodation); *or*

(2) a higher pensioner premium is applicable *and* from immediately before reaching 60 the claimant (or partner) has been continuously doing work *and* since that time a disability premium has been (or would have been if he had not been a boarder or living in a residential care home or equivalent accommodation) applicable;[6] *or*

(3) in the case of a couple, both are under 60 *and* there has been continuous entitlement to income support for two years[7] *and* neither has been in full-time work or full-time education for a period of more than eight consecutive weeks during those two years; *or*

(4) the claimant is a part-time firefighter, member of a lifeboat crew, belongs to the Territorial Army or is an auxiliary coastguard, though only from his earnings in these occupations.

Only one £15 disregard can be claimed by a couple or a single claimant.

C Other income

Subject to disregards, all other income is taken into account. This includes payments specifically excluded from the definition of earnings,[8] social security benefits, charitable or voluntary payments, capital which under the regulations is treated as income, maintenance payments and 'notional income' (e.g. where the claimant had deliberately deprived himself of income). The last three of these call for special discussion.

i Capital treated as income
As will be seen in the next paragraph, most lump sum maintenance payments are considered to be income. The regulations provide for three other situations in which capital is treated as income.[9] The first arises where capital is owed to the claimant in instalments: if one or more outstanding instalments

---

1 *White Paper 1985* para 3.39.
2 SI 1987/1967, Sch 8, para 9. Nb foreign earnings which cannot be transferred to the UK are wholly disregarded: ibid, para 11.
3 The regulation (ibid) is ambiguous but the text reflects DSS practice: see *Guide to Income Support* (1988 edn) p.94.
4 P.449.
5 SI 1987/1967, Sch 8, paras 4–8.
6 Gaps of up to eight weeks in the continuity of work or of the application of a disability premium are ignored.
7 Gaps of eight weeks in entitlement are ignored.
8 SI 1987/1967, reg 40(4).
9 Ibid, reg 41.

would take him over the £6,000 capital threshold and thereby disentitle him from income support, such instalments are treated as income. The second applies to payments received under an annuity and the third to welfare payments made under the Child Care Act 1980 to families affected by a trade dispute.

ii Maintenance payments

Any periodic payment (including arrears paid periodically) made by a liable relative (usually, parent or former spouse), whether by court order or agreement, is taken into account in full as income.[10] Lump sum payments are also normally treated as income and there is a complex formula to determine the number of weeks it is deemed to cover.[11] Broadly, if the maintenance is paid for the claimant (and not for her children only) the lump sum is divided by a figure consisting of an aggregate of £2 and the amount of income support that would otherwise be paid. The number obtained will then constitute the period of weeks to which the lump sum is attributable. There is a similar formula for determining the weeks to which a lump sum payable only for children is to be attributed. If the claimant receives a lump sum in addition to periodic payments, and it is equal to or more than the amount of income support to which otherwise she would be entitled, it is treated as capital.[12] Payments to an immigrant by his sponsor are treated in the same way as maintenance payments.[13]

iii Notional income

In certain cases account is taken of notional income in addition to, or instead of, actual income.[14] The following rules are designed primarily to deal with problems of abuse or collusive behaviour.

(1) The claimant is treated as 'possessing income of which he has deprived himself for the purpose of securing entitlement to income support or increasing the amount of that benefit'.[15] In interpreting the equivalent provision in the supplementary benefit regulations, the Commissioner held that the desire to obtain (or increase the amount of) benefit must have been a significant, though not necessarily the sole, motive for disposing of resources; mere carelessness in looking after the resources is insufficient.[16]

(2) Income which would have been available to the claimant if he had applied for it is treated as being possessed by him from the date when it would have been paid to him.[17] The impact of this provision is somewhat unclear. In theory, it could cover a wide range of public and private sources of funds to which the claimant potentially had access. At any rate, it does not apply to income which could have been obtained from a

10 Ibid, reg 55.
11 Ibid, reg 57.
12 Ibid, reg 60.
13 SSA 1986, s.26(3)(c) and SI 1987/1967, reg 54.
14 The attribution of notional income is mandatory where the conditions in the regulations are satisfied; this contrasts with the position under supplementary benefit law where the use of the term 'may' indicated that the adjudicating officer had an overriding discretion: e.g. SI 1981/1527, reg 4.
15 SI 1987/1967, reg 42(1).
16 *R(SB) 35/85; R(SB) 40/85.*
17 SI 1987/1967, reg 42(2).

discretionary trust, a trust set up to provide compensation for personal injury, nor to one-parent benefit or unemployment benefit payable to someone who, exceptionally, is not required to be available for employment.

(3) Where the claimant performs a service for another person and the latter either makes no payment or else pays less remuneration than is typically earned for that work in the locality, he is treated as receiving such earnings as are reasonable for that employment.[18] Work for a voluntary or charitable organisation is excluded from this if it is reasonable for the claimant to provide services free of charge, as are cases where the 'employer' has insufficient means to pay (or pay more) for the work.[19]

(4) Payments made, by for example a relative, to a third party in respect of the food, clothing, fuel or housing costs of the claimant (and family, if any) are treated as the claimant's income.[20]

Another set of rules attributing notional income exists more for reasons of administrative convenience, where it would be difficult to determine the claimant's actual income or prove actual receipt.

(1) The apparently harsh rule that payments due but not in fact received are treated as income[1] may be justified on this basis; in any event it does not apply to income from a discretionary trust or a trust for personal injury compensation, nor to late payments of certain specified social security benefits.[2]

(2) Claimants whose earnings cannot be ascertained at the time of the claim are deemed to receive 'such earnings as is reasonable in the circumstances of the case having regard to the number of hours worked and the earnings paid for comparable employment in the area'.[3]

(3) There are rules attributing notional weekly earnings to seasonal workers during their 'off-season'.[4] Broadly, if the net weekly earnings of such persons during their periods of seasonal employment exceed three times the personal allowances applicable to them (during the off-season), such excess is divided by the number of weeks in the off-season and the resulting figure is treated as earnings in each of those weeks.

iv. Disregards

Some of the disregards applied to income other than earnings are designed specifically to confer on the claimant a higher level of support than would otherwise be the case, and thus may be regarded as justified on 'public interest' grounds; others exist predominantly for administrative purposes, for example, to avoid double counting. The list is divided accordingly.

a *'Public interest' disregards* A first group reflects recognition of patriotic or community efforts.

---

18 Ibid, reg 42(6).
19 See *R(SB) 13/86*.
20 SI 1987/1967, reg 42(4). This does not apply to payments in kind unless the claimant is involved in a trade dispute.
1 Ibid, reg 42(3).
2 These are set out in SI 1987/491, regs 9–10.
3 SI 1987/1967, reg 42(5).
4 Ibid, reg 43. For the definition of 'seasonal worker' and 'off-season', see pp. 123–124, above.

— Sums payable to holders of the Victoria or George Cross and analogous payments are wholly disregarded, as are the first £5 of weekly war pensions.[5]

Secondly, there are disregards intended to promote child welfare. These include:

— Adoption allowances and custodian payments to the extent that they exceed the personal allowance (and disabled child premium, if any) for the relevant child and fostering allowances paid under the Child Care Act 1980.[6]

The third group serves to encourage young persons in particular to seek training or further education, thus:

— Travelling expenses, 'living away from home' allowances and training premiums received in connection with an employment training scheme are disregarded, as are job start allowances and educational maintenance allowances payable for children staying on at school beyond 16 or studying or pursuing non-advanced courses at colleges of further education.[7]

A fourth group exists so that the generosity of third parties should not be nullified.

— Any payment from the Macfarlane Trust or the Independent Living Fund and the first £5 per week of regular charitable and other voluntary payments (other than a payment made by a person for the maintenance of a member of his family, or former family).[8]

Finally, there are a number of disregards which offer some assistance to a miscellaneous group of vulnerable people:

— The pensioners' Christmas bonus, mobility and attendance allowance, mobility supplement, a proportion of income from certain annuities purchased with a loan by persons over 65, resettlement benefits paid to certain hospital patients and (unless the claimant is involved in a trade dispute) any income in kind.[9]

b *Administrative disregards*   To avoid the double counting of the same amount, or so as not to defeat the effect of concessions made elsewhere, the following are disregarded:

— Tax paid on unearned income, social fund payments, housing benefit, income from most capital assets,[10] any contribution made by a member of the claimant's household towards living and accommodation costs (where there is no contractual liability for such contribution), the first £4 of equivalent payments made by a joint occupier and any payments made to the claimant which are intended as a contribution to mortgage

5 SI 1987/1967, Sch 9, paras 10, 16.
6 Ibid, paras 25–26.
7 Ibid, paras 11, 13, 14.
8 Ibid, paras 15, 39, as amended.
9 Ibid, paras 6–9, 17, 21, 33, 38, as amended.
10 Though, a 'tariff income' is derived from some assets, p.447 below; actual income from such assets is treated as capital, p.447, below. Income from property which the claimant owns but does not live in is only disregarded in some circumstances: see SI 1987/1967, Sch 9, para 22 and Sch 10, paras 1, 2, 4.

interest, capital repayment or other housing costs which are not assessable housing costs under the regulations.[11]

Special rules apply to those who take in boarders, or sub-let premises. Money received in this capacity is regarded as income rather than self-employed earnings and is thus not calculated on a 'net profit' basis. To make some allowance for the expenses incurred, the regulations therefore provide for the disregard of £35 of the weekly charge paid by boarders and £4 (£10.70 if heating costs are not included in the charge) of that paid by tenants, sub-tenants or licensees.[12]

D Capital

i General
It will be recalled that there is no entitlement to income support if the capital of the claimant (and partner, if any) exceeds an upper threshold (currently £6,000).[13] Capital below this amount but above a lower threshold (currently £3,000) is deemed to give rise to a 'tariff income' of £1 per week for each complete £250 (or part thereof) exceeding that threshold[14] – so, for example, capital of £5,760 is treated as giving rise to weekly income of £12. The tariff income is then aggregated with assessable earnings and/or other income. There are three potential components in capital: ordinary capital such as savings or property, income which is treated as capital and 'notional capital'; these are subject to important disregards.

ii Ordinary capital
All capital[15] that is not disregarded or, under the regulations, is treated as income,[16] is valued at its current market or surrender value, less 10 per cent, if expenses would be incurred on sale, and the amount of any incumbrance (such as a mortgage) secured on the asset.[17]

iii Income treated as capital
Under the regulations, certain forms of income are treated as capital:[18]

(1) income tax refunds;
(2) holiday pay which is not treated as earnings because it is paid more than four weeks after the termination of employment;
(3) an advance or loan from an employer;[19]
(4) arrears of custodianship payments;
(5) discharge payments received on release from prison;
(6) any annual bounty or lump sum paid in relation to certain employments

---

11 Ibid, Sch 9, paras 1, 5, 18–19, 22, 30–31.
12 Ibid, paras 19–20.
13 SSA 1986, s.22(6) and SI 1987/1967, reg 45.
14 Ibid, reg 53.
15 For the distinction between 'income' and 'capital', see p.441, above.
16 P.443, above.
17 SI 1987/1967, reg 49. For the valuation of land, see *R(SB) 6/84*, of shares, *R(SB) 18/83*, and of National Savings Certificates, SI 1987/1967, reg 49(b).
18 Ibid, reg 48.
19 Except during the currency of a trade dispute in which the claimant is involved and for the first 15 days of employment thereafter.

(e.g. part-time firefighting) which attract the higher earnings disregard;[20]

(7) actual income derived from savings or investments.

iv Notional capital

There are provisions analogous to those on 'notional income'[1] to deal with possible abuse or collusive behaviour. Thus a claimant is treated as possessing capital representing: assets of which he has deprived himself for the purpose of obtaining benefit; assets which would have been available if he had applied for them; and capital payments to a third party used for purchasing food, clothing, fuel or housing expenditure.[2] In addition, if the claimant does not work for, but is effectively the sole owner of, or partner in, a company, whatever the value of his actual holding in the company he is treated as possessing the capital of the company, or (if a partner) the relevant share in the capital.[3]

v Disregards

As with income, these may be categorised into public interest and administrative disregards.

a *Public interest disregards*   The most important group of disregards protects personal possessions (unless they have been acquired to gain entitlement to, or increase the amount of, benefit)[4] and the claimant's home.[5] In addition to the value of one dwelling occupied as a home, this covers:

— Other premises acquired which the claimant intends to occupy, the proceeds of the sale of a home which are intended to be used for the purchase of another home, sums received, and intended to be used, for repairs, replacements, or improvements to the home (in all such cases, the relevant intention must relate to the period of six months following the receipt of the capital or such longer period as is reasonable in the circumstances); also sums deposited with a housing association as a condition of occupying premises as a home and refunds of tax deductions for mortgage interest repayments.

A number of disregards are intended to protect vulnerable groups or promote the welfare of children:[6]

— Arrears of benefits which are disregarded in calculating income (for a maximum of 12 months after their payment), the value of premises wholly or partly occupied by a dependant or relative who is over 60 or incapacitated, rights under a trust set up to compensate for personal injury, payments under section 1 of the Child Care Act 1980 (unless the claimant is involved in a trade dispute), and payments from the McFarlane Trust or Independent Living Fund.

20 P.443, above.
1 P.444, above.
2 SI 1987/1967, reg 51.
3 Ibid, reg 51(4)–(5).
4 Ibid, Sch 10, para 10.
5 Ibid, paras 1–3, 5, 8–9. The proceeds of the sale of a house which the claimant did not occupy as a home were, in some circumstances, disregarded under the supplementary benefit scheme. Under transitional provisions (SI 1987/1969, as amended) such a disregard may continue to apply to an income support claim.
6 SI 1987/1967, Sch 10, paras 4, 7(a), 12, 17, 22.

A third group serves to encourage thrift:[7]

— The surrender value of a life insurance policy, an occupational pension or annuity, reversionary or life interests in property and the value of a right to receive rent.

Finally, so as not to hinder movement in business assets, after the claimant has ceased to work as a self-employed person in a business, the value of his interest in the business is disregarded but only for such time as is reasonable for him to dispose of those assets.[8]

b *Administrative disregards* For administrative convenience or to provide coherence and/or equity between income support and other systems, the following are disregarded:[9]

— Social fund payments and arrears of income-related benefits (for a maximum of 12 months after their payment), the capital value of the right to receive income of a kind which is disregarded, and capital which is treated as income (including, where the claimant's capital exceeds £6,000, outstanding instalments of capital).

E The income and capital of children and young persons

For the purpose of the rules described above, the income and capital of the claimant and partner are aggregated. One important modification to this arises in the case of a couple, where one or both members are under 18 and, because one of them is ineligible for income support under the special rules for young persons,[10] the personal allowance for the couple is that normally applicable to a single claimant.[11] In this situation, it is only the amount (if any) by which the income of the partner exceeds the difference between the relevant personal allowance for a single person and a couple, respectively, which is taken into account.[12] The treatment of resources belonging to members of the family unit[13] who are dependent children or young persons (hereafter 'child' includes 'young person') is even more complex.

i Income

The general principle is that the income of a child is aggregated with that of the claimant.[14] Where the child attends a residential school, payments by a third party to the school for his maintenance are treated, for this purpose, as the child's income.[15] The general principle is modified in the following circumstances. First, the earnings of a child still at school are wholly disregarded.[16] Secondly, if the child has left school but is pursuing a course in

---

7 Ibid, paras 5–6, 13–16, 23–24.
8 Ibid, para 6.
9 Ibid, paras 7(b), 16, 18, 20–21.
10 Pp. 418–420, above.
11 P.427, above.
12 SI 1987/1967, reg 23(4).
13 Cf p.424, above.
14 SSA 1986, s.22(5).
15 But only for periods when the child is present at the school: SI 1987/1967, reg 44(2). Where he is maintained there by a local authority, the income is calculated by a special formula: see ibid, reg 44(3).
16 SI 1987/1967, Sch 8, para 14.

full-time, non advanced education (i.e. up to and including 'A' Level), while subject to the disregards[17] any earnings are taken into account, they are wholly ignored if the child's earning capacity has been reduced by 25 per cent or more as the result of a disability.[18] Thirdly, if any such earnings and/or income exceed the personal allowance applied to that child (as part of the claimant's applicable amount), the excess is ignored.[19] Finally, if the child's *capital* exceeds £3,000, as will be seen, income support cannot be claimed for him; as a corollary, any income of such a child is not aggregated with that of the claimant.[20]

ii Capital

Capital belonging to a child is *not* aggregated with that of the claimant.[1] Nevertheless, if that capital exceeds the lower threshold (currently £3,000) no personal allowance for that child can form part of the claimant's applicable amount.[2] If the child's capital is payable in instalments, any outstanding instalments (at the date of application for income support) which, when added to the child's capital, exceed £3,000 are treated as the child's *income*.[3]

Part 6   Urgent cases

A Background

Until 1980, the now defunct Supplementary Benefits Commission had a discretion to make urgent needs payments to persons not entitled to ordinary supplementary benefit in circumstances where the need was 'urgent, sudden and unforeseeable'.[4] In that year, as part of the general retreat from discretion, many of the circumstances in which such payments could be made (and these included some cases where ordinary benefit was payable) were prescribed by regulations,[5] but a residual discretion was retained for cases where the payment was 'the only means by which serious damage or serious risk to the health or safety' of the family could be prevented.[6] The Urgent Cases Regulations were aptly described as the 'long-stop' of the supplementary benefit scheme;[7] as such, and not surprisingly, the Fowler review team recommended return to the discretionary approach which was to be adopted more generally for one-off needs.[8] The proposal was implemented in the 1986 reforms and much of the function of the Urgent Cases Regulations was taken over by the social fund. As will be seen in chapter 14, the latter makes provision for emergency relief in the form of 'crisis loans'[9] and several principles

17 P.442, above. The £15 disregard applies where a disabled child premium is applicable.
18 SI 1987/1967, Sch 8, paras 14–15.
19 Ibid, reg 44(4).
20 Ibid, reg 44(5).
 1 Ibid, reg 47. Any attempt by the claimant to exploit this rule by transferring his own capital to the child will be thwarted by the 'notional capital' regulation, p.448, above.
 2 SI 1987/1967, reg 17(b).
 3 Ibid, reg 44(1).
 4 SBA 1976, s.4.
 5 Subsequently consolidated in SI 1981/1529.
 6 Ibid, reg 24.
 7 Mesher CPAG's *Supplementary Benefit and Family Income Supplement: The Legislation* (4th edn) p.187.
 8 *Green Paper 1985* vol 2, para 2.67.
 9 P.517, below.

of the Urgent Cases Regulations have been adopted, for example, that a need should be regarded as urgent only if it cannot be met from other sources. Nevertheless, the overriding discretionary character of the social fund means that some claimants who would have obtained an urgent needs payment under the old law may now receive nothing or else only a reduced amount.

There remains within the income support system three relatively narrow categories of urgent cases, where the circumstances are such that claimants cannot meet the ordinary conditions for benefit, but have a need for recurrent payments which are not available from the social fund.

B The categories of urgent cases

The first of the three categories to which the urgent cases regulations apply covers certain persons from abroad. It will be recalled from an earlier section of this chapter[10] that some foreign visitors are not entitled to the standard amounts of income support. Of these, the following may claim an urgent cases payment (UCP):[11]

(1) persons whose leave to stay was conditional on having no recourse to public funds but whose support from abroad has been temporarily interrupted;
(2) persons awaiting a decision on immigration status, on an application to vary the terms of leave, or on an appeal under the Immigration Act 1971;
(3) persons who have exceeded the terms of leave, or who for other reasons have no right to stay here, but whose removal from the UK has been deferred.

The other two categories comprise cases where notional income is attributed to a seasonal worker during his 'off-season'[12] and those where it is attributed to others who are due to receive certain payments.[13] A UCP may be paid in such cases if the notional income is not in fact available *and* the amount of UCP payable (see below) is higher than what would be paid under the ordinary income support rules *and* the adjudication officer is satisfied that the claimant or his family will 'suffer hardship' if a UCP is not awarded.[14]

C Applicable amounts

In general, the applicable amount in urgent cases is the aggregate of 90 per cent[15] of the personal allowances for the claimant and partner (if any), the full personal allowance for any children and any assessable housing costs; the only premiums which may be included are the pensioner and higher pensioner premiums.[16] For boarders and persons in residential accommodation, the applicable amount is 90 per cent of the lower rate of personal expenses which

10 P.418, above.
11 SI 1987/1967, reg 70(3). In some of the cases there is a prescribed maximum period of entitlement to a UCP.
12 P.445, above.
13 P.444, above.
14 SI 1987/1967, reg 70(2),(4).
15 Where the '40 per cent deduction rule' applies (cases of voluntary unemployment, pp. 452–455, below), the 90 per cent formula is applied after the relevant deduction has been made.
16 SI 1987/1967, reg 71(1)(a), as amended.

they can normally claim[17] plus the accommodation charge and, where appropriate, a meals allowance.[18]

D Assessment of income and capital

The means-test applied to UCP applicants is more severe than that to which ordinary income support claimants are subjected. All income, except 'tariff' income from capital,[19] is deducted from the applicable amount and, apart from payments from the Macfarlane Trust or Independent Living Fund, there are no disregards.[20] The treatment of capital is even more different. No 'tariff' income is deemed to arise from it; rather, available capital is itself deducted from the applicable amount. In other words, claimants are expected to use up all available capital before relying on a UCP. For this purpose, capital is assessed in accordance with the rules described above[1] but with the following modifications. The liquid assets of a business, arrears of social security benefits, and the proceeds of the sale of a home which are intended to be used for the purchase of another home are all taken into account.[2] Most importantly, there is no disregard of the first £3,000 capital.

Part 7   Work incentive rules

In this Part of the chapter, two sets of circumstances are discussed in which benefit may be reduced or withheld altogether in order to encourage claimants to work rather than rely on income support. The first category concerns the 'voluntarily unemployed', those who do not, or are thought not to, make any real effort to stay in work or find employment when out of it. Secondly, the special rules concerning strikers and other persons affected by trade disputes are explained. There are, of course, other rules in the income support system which may be characterised as work incentive rules: for example, the condition that a claimant be available for work. But this is a requirement for entitlement to benefit in the first place, and has therefore been treated together with other similar rules in Part 2 of the chapter.

A The voluntarily unemployed

i General

In any society where the 'work ethic' is important, it is inevitable that there will be reluctance to extend assistance to those who are capable of supporting themselves by work, but refuse to obtain it.[3] The 'work-shy' or 'scroungers', as they are often called, understandably arouse the resentment of the taxpaying public. Nevertheless, it is important to understand the real nature of the

17 Cf p.438, above and p.466, below.
18 SI 1987/1967, reg 71(1)(b).
19 Notional income attributed where a claimant is due to receive payments (n.13, above) is also excluded.
20 SI 1987/1967, reg 72(1).
 1 Pp. 447–449.
 2 SI 1987/1967, reg 72(2).
 3 For general discussion, see SBC Annual Report 1979 (Cmnd 8033), chs 4–5, Sinfield *What Unemployment Means* (1981) and Alcock *Poverty and State Support* (1987) ch 9.

problems involved; this is particularly true at a time when unemployment is high and work is hard to find. Medical, psychological and various social factors may bring about unresponsive attitudes to work; for example, a person unable to find a job after searching for several months may be inclined to become lethargic and abandon any real attempt to secure suitable employment.[4] While there may be cases where the system is exploited by those who prefer to live off welfare payments, it is difficult to distinguish them from the almost certainly larger number who are genuinely unable to find work.[5] The difficulty is reflected in the fact that disqualifications or deductions from benefit on the ground of voluntary unemployment are frequently the subject of appeals to the Social Security Appeal Tribunals.[6] It has been estimated that a significant proportion of such appeals are eventually decided in the claimant's favour.[7]

Not only is there uncertainty about the precise nature of the problem, there is also, as might be expected, doubt about its scale. During the passage of the Social Security Bill 1986, it was said that every year there are about 300,000 persons voluntarily unemployed,[8] but it is not clear how this figure was arrived at. In 1973 the Fisher Committee thought it reasonable to assume that a large proportion of the younger men out of work for long periods were in this position through no fault of their own, and this was even more the case with older claimants.[9] Now that unemployment rates are considerably higher, this proposition seems incontrovertible.

Before examining the detailed rules applied to discourage the work-shy, something should be said here about the work of Claimant Advisors, who in 1986 assumed the role previously taken by Unemployment Review Officers. Their function in relation to both unemployment benefit and income support is to ensure that claimants are genuinely available for work, to give them advice on how to find work and, particularly under the 'Restart scheme', to encourage attendance at a training course.[10] Under the supplementary benefit legislation a claimant could, in extreme cases, be required to attend a re-establishment centre or training course.[11] Primarily because they were duplicating services run by the Manpower Services Commission, these centres were phased out in 1985 and the relevant legal powers to require attendance were repealed in 1986.

ii The 40 per cent rule

In general, the rule affects only claimants who, to establish entitlement to income support, must be available for work.[12] It incorporates unemployment benefit law and applies if the claimant has been disqualified from receiving

---

4 Sinfield, n.3, above, pp. 89–96; Allen and Waton in Allen et al *The Experience of Unemployment* (1986) ch 1.
5 *Fisher*; Franey *Poor Law: The Mass Arrest of Homeless Claimants in Oxford* (1983).
6 In 1985, there were about 400,000 such cases: Standing Committee B Debates on Social Security Bill 1986, col 1869.
7 Ibid, col 1833.
8 Ibid, cols 1840, 1870.
9 *Fisher* para 246.
10 See also pp. 90–92, above.
11 SBA 1976, s.10 and Sch 5, para 1.
12 SI 1987/1967, reg 22(4)(b) and see p.422, above. It may also apply where: (i) an appeal has been lodged on the claimant's capacity to work, and, pending its outcome, he is not required to be available for work; or (ii) a decision that the claimant should not be available was made on the residual discretionary ground (see p.424 above) that otherwise he (or his family) would suffer hardship (SI 1987/1967, reg 22(5)).

that benefit for misconduct, leaving work voluntarily or refusing suitable employment without good cause[13] or if he would be so disqualified (in the adjudication officer's view) if and when a claim for such benefit is made and determined.[14]

In the case of a single claimant, the effect of the rule is that 40 per cent is deducted from his personal allowance. In the case of a couple, the amount deducted is, if both are under 18, 40 per cent of the rate of personal allowance for a single claimant aged under 18; and, if either is over 18, it is 40 per cent of the highest rate of such allowance.[15] For boarders and persons in residential accommodation, 40 per cent of the appropriate amount of personal expenses is deducted.[16]

Before 1980 the Supplementary Benefits Commission issued guidelines for reducing the normal 40 per cent deduction in cases of hardship which included sickness, pregnancy, high housing costs, children in the family and a history of low-paid employment. The reforms of that year consolidated these guidelines in regulations under which a deduction of only 20 per cent was made where one of the hardship grounds existed and the claimant's capital did not exceed a certain amount.[17] The result was an increase in the number of cases attracting the lower deduction[18] and in 1983 the government decided to limit its application to cases where a member of the family is seriously ill[19] or pregnant.[20] This provision, together with the rule that the claimant's capital should not exceed £200, is incorporated in the Income Support Regulations.[1]

iii The period of deduction

Since 1971 the *maximum* period of deduction has followed that adopted for the equivalent disqualification for unemployment benefit.[2] In October 1986, this was extended from six to thirteen weeks and, in April 1988, to 26 weeks. Given that a claimant may potentially be subject to determinations under both benefit systems, there are some complex provisions which serve to avoid inconsistency between them.[3] If a decision has already made on unemployment benefit disqualification, the income support deduction will last for the period of that disqualification. If, however, the claim for unemployment benefit has not yet been determined but the adjudication officer considers there is a possible case for disqualification, a deduction must be made for 26 weeks, and then if later the disqualification is for a shorter period, or no disqualification is imposed, an adjustment is made to the income support deduction and, where appropriate, amounts wrongly deducted are recoverable. Finally, where no claim for unemployment benefit has been made, the deduction is made for such period as would have been imposed in relation to an unemployment benefit disqualification.

13 See pp. 97–104, above.
14 SI 1987/1967, reg 22(4)(c).
15 Ibid, reg 22(1)(a).
16 Ibid, reg 22(1)(b).
17 See the second edition of this book, p.499.
18 The proportion of 20 per cent deductions rose from 2 per cent before the reforms to 34 per cent in 1981: Mesher CPAG's *Supplementary Benefit and Family Income Supplement: The Legislation* (4th edn) p.148.
19 For the meaning of this term, see *R(SB) 14/83*.
20 SI 1983/1240, for criticism of which, see the SSAC Report on the Draft Amendment Regulations (Cmnd 8978).
 1 ·SI 1987/1967, reg 22(2).
 2 Pp. 109–110, above.
 3 SI 1987/1967, reg 22(6).

The principle that the period of income support deduction should coincide with the period of unemployment benefit disqualification is not beyond criticism. Unlike the contributory benefit, income support is designed to provide a floor of minimum resources to meet the claimant's needs and clearly any reduced payment may cause hardship. Given the recent extensions of the maximum period of deduction from six to 26 weeks, the question has become one of considerable importance.

iv Criminal prosecution

An alternative, if seldom used, method of dealing with voluntary unemployment is available under the criminal law. A person who persistently refuses to maintain himself or any other person whom he is liable to maintain, as a result of which income support is payable, is guilty of a summary offence.[4] The sanction for this is three months' imprisonment and/or a level 4 fine. There is, however, no offence if such conduct is committed in the context of a trade dispute.[5] The relevant obligation to maintain is owed to partners and children, including illegitimate children, and also covers sponsorship agreements made on or since 23 May 1980 under the Immigration Act 1971.[6] Prosecutions are rare, especially in relation to a claimant's failure to maintain himself.[7]

B Persons affected by trade disputes

i General

The extent to which a social assistance scheme should support strikers and their families has always been a highly controversial question and was the subject of much public attention during the Miners' Strike of 1984-85.[8] Many of the issues on which views sharply differ – for example, whether the availability of benefit encourages strikes and whether it is legitimate to deter them by withdrawing benefit – are to some extent peripheral to the principal concerns of a social assistance scheme. It may be for this reason that there has been relatively little discussion of these questions in the major policy documents, such as the Fowler Reviews. Nevertheless, the legal position has remained remarkably constant. Under the poor law, the striker himself could not lawfully be maintained out of rates, unless completely destitute, though his wife and children could be so supported.[9] Now the position broadly is that a single striker is not entitled to income support, though he may be able to claim a social fund payment; but income support is available in respect of other members of his family, subject to some special rules discussed below.

The arguments[10] against supporting strikers and their dependants are first, that it is wrong for people withholding their labour, usually to 'induce' their employers to pay them higher wages, to be supported by the general

---

4 SSA 1986, s.26(1).
5 Ibid, s.26(2).
6 Ibid, s.26(3)–(4).
7 There have been no such prosecutions since 1981 (Standing Committee B Debates on Social Security Bill 1986, col 924); in 1985, there were about 200 prosecutions for failure to maintain others (ibid, col 926).
8 See generally Mesher 14 ILJ 191; Booth and Smith 12 J Law and Society 365.
9 *A–G v Merthyr Tydfil Union* [1900] 1 Ch 516.
10 See also discussion of the analogous arguments used in relation to unemployment benefit: pp. 110–112, above.

taxpaying public, an argument which is perhaps reinforced by the point that some low-income taxpayers could be said to be subsidising the bargaining strength of groups with more industrial weight than they themselves can command. Secondly, the existence of welfare payments is widely believed to encourage a larger number, and the longer duration, of disputes. The first argument may have some merit with regard to the strikers themselves: they are not the 'deserving poor' and should not expect militancy to be subsidised.[11] It is less attractive when applied to their dependants; the further proposition must then be argued that it is for the strikers themselves, and their unions, to support their families. In any case, it can be replied that for the state not to support people in need because of the particular cause of their privation is to depart from the principle of neutrality, and in the context to take sides in an industrial dispute. Furthermore, the disqualification provision, as will be seen shortly, applies to persons who would not conventionally be defined as 'strikers', although this term is used throughout for reasons of convenience. It applies to persons locked out of work, or laid off because of a dispute at their place of work. The second argument was strongly voiced, particularly by members of the Conservative party, in the 1970s, and led to the 1980 reform which, effectively, reduced the payments. which could be made for a striker's family. But the view that the availability of benefit does encourage industrial unrest has been strongly challenged by commentators,[12] and was implicitly rejected by the Supplementary Benefits Commission in its last Annual Report.[13]

ii Strikers without families

The rules apply to a person other than a child or young person:

(a) who is disqualified under section 19 of the Social Security Act 1975 for receiving unemployment benefit; or

(b) who would be so disqualified if otherwise entitled to that benefit
except during any period shown by the person to be a period of incapacity for work by reason of disease or bodily or mental disablement or to be within the maternity period.[14]

Section 19 (as amended) imposes the disqualification on those who have lost employment by reason of a stoppage of work at their place of employment due to a trade dispute (unless they are not 'directly interested' in the dispute) and those who have withdrawn their labour in furtherance of a trade dispute. There is a considerable body of case-law on this provision and reference should be made to chapter 3 for a full discussion of the relevant legal principles.[15]

For the purposes of the first exception, 'incapacity for work etc' has the meaning attributed to it in the context of the disability benefits.[16] The second exception relates to a period beginning six weeks before the expected week of confinement and ending seven weeks after confinement.[17] If these excepting

---

11 For a particularly robust assertion of this view, see Page in Boyson (ed) *Down with the Poor* (1971).

12 E.g. Duncan and McCarthy [1974] Br J Industrial Relations 26. A more cautious view is expressed by Hunter, ibid at 438.

13 Annual Report 1979 (Cmnd 8033), para 10.46.

14 SSA 1986, s.23(1), as amended.

15 Pp. 112–119, above.

16 Pp. 149–152, above.

17 SSA 1986, s.23(2). The exception was introduced during the Committee stage of the 1986 Bill: Standing Committee B Debates, col 903.

circumstances fall within the period of a trade dispute, normal benefit will be paid for as long as those circumstances last.

A claimant without a family who is involved in a trade dispute, in accordance with the definition above, is not entitled to income support and the same applies where both members of a couple are so involved and have no children.[18]

iii Strikers' families

A striker (i.e. a person who comes within the statutory definition quoted above) who has a partner, who is not himself/herself on strike, or children, may claim income support but only after a period of seven days following the start of the stoppage or the withdrawal of labour.[19] After that period has elapsed, the applicable amount will be as follows:[20]

(1) for a couple without children, one half of the personal allowance for a couple, plus any premium for the partner not on strike;
(2) for a couple with a child or children, as (1) plus the personal allowance(s) for the child(ren) and any disabled child premium;
(3) for a single parent with a child or children, the personal allowance(s) for the child(ren), plus the family premium, the lone parent premium and any disabled child premium;

and assessable housing costs may be added in any of these cases.[1]

Some important modifications are made to the rules on assessment of income and capital which therefore significantly affect the amount of income support payable. Tax refunds and any advance of earnings or a loan made by an employer are treated as income, rather than capital.[2] The usual disregards for payments in kind, payments under section 1 of the Child Care Act 1980 and charitable or voluntary payments do not apply (unless they are from the MacFarlane Trust or the Independent Living Fund) and thus are fully taken into account as income.[3]

The regulations also provide that any payment (up to a specified maximum – currently £17.70[4]) which the striker receives, or is entitled to receive, from a trade union because of the dispute is to be *disregarded* in assessing income.[5] This disregard can only be understood in the light of section 23 of the Social Security Act 1986, which reenacts a controversial and bitterly opposed reform made in 1980.[6] Section 23 provides in effect that any income support payable for the family of a striker is subject to a deduction of a prescribed amount equal to the specified maximum disregard (£17.70), referred to above. The combined purpose of the deduction rule and the disregard is to encourage trade unions to assume responsibility for providing for the needs of families affected by labour disputes. This can be illustrated by the following example.

18 SSA 1986, s.23(3)(a) and (d)(i).
19 During this period, strikers are treated as in full-time work: SI 1987/1967, reg 5(4).
20 SSA 1986, s.23(3).
 1 They are attributed to a member of the family not involved in the trade dispute: SI 1987/1967, Sch 3, para 3(2).
 2 SSA 1986, s.23(5)(a)(ii) and SI 1987/1967, reg 48(6).
 3 Ibid, Sch 9, paras 15, 21, 28, 39.
 4 This figure must be increased in line with the percentage increases to benefit made by up-rating orders: SSA 1986, s.63.
 5 SI 1987/1967, Sch 9, para 34 and SSA 1986, s.23(6), incorporating a reference to SSA (No 2) 1980, s.6(1)(b).
 6 Ibid. Previously only the claimant's actual income, subject to a £4 disregard, was taken into account: see generally on this Gennard and Lasko [1974] Br J Industrial Relations 1.

Suppose the applicable amount for a family affected by a dispute is £42.60 and the striker receives £17.70 from his union. This latter sum is disregarded but, because of the deduction rule, the family is only entitled to £24.90 weekly benefit. This in effect tops up the basic provision made by the union. If, however, no strike pay was received, he would still be entitled only to £24.90.

As revealed in this example, an obvious consequence of the rule is that where a union cannot make the appropriate payment, hardship may be suffered by the family. Such a situation arose during the Miners' Strike of 1984–85 when the sequestration of the NUM's funds precluded any possibility of strike pay.[7]

iv The position after return to work

A claimant resuming work after a trade dispute is entitled to claim benefit for the first 15 days after his return, subject to the condition that, in the case of a couple, his partner is not engaged in remunerative, full-time work.[8] The benefit payable includes amounts in respect of the person resuming work after the strike but in most cases is effectively a loan as certain sums are recoverable from the employer (or, where this is not practicable, from the claimant) by the Secretary of State.[9] The adjudication officer determines a level of 'protected earnings' below which no recovery may be made. This is assessed as the claimant's applicable amount, excluding housing costs, *plus* a prescribed sum (which is reduced in the case of a boarder or a person in residential accommodation and is thus effectively a fixed rate for housing costs), *less* any child benefit payable.[10] A notice is then served on the employer to deduct one-half of any excess of the beneficiary's 'available earnings'[11] over his 'protected earnings'.[12]

v Social fund payments

Under supplementary benefit law, urgent needs payments could, in rigourously prescribed circumstances, be claimed by strikers for themselves or their families in relation to emergency relief and other urgent needs.[13] Most of these situations are now covered by the social fund and are dealt with in chapter 14.[14]

Part 8   Income support and maintenance

A Introduction

This Part is concerned with the award of benefit to separated and divorced spouses and to unmarried mothers, and its relationship to maintenance payments. Problems arise because the social security legislation imposes a duty on spouses to maintain each other and their children, and similarly a duty on a mother and a man adjudged to be a putative father to maintain illegitimate

7 See the references cited in n.8, above.
8 SSA 1986, s.23A.
9 SI 1988/664, Part VIII.
10 Ibid, reg 19.
11 For definition, see ibid, reg 18(2).
12 Ibid, reg 22.
13 See Rowell and Wilton *The Law of Supplementary Benefits* (1982) pp. 163–164.
14 Pp. 517–520, below.

children.[15] Thus, a separated wife is entitled to look to her husband as well as the DSS for support if she and her children are in need, and this raises a number of questions, in particular whether she should be expected to exhaust her maintenance remedies against her husband before relying on benefit. The recent social security reforms left this area substantially unchanged but developments in family law introduced by the Family Law Reform Act 1987 have significant implications, and these are discussed in Section D. Some consideration is also given in Section E to reforms enacted in 1980 whereby a sponsor is liable to maintain an immigrant.

The area has been relatively little regulated by statutory instrument and in practice used to be governed by policies formulated by the Supplementary Benefits Commission and published in its Handbook. The discretion formerly vested in the Commission is now exercised by the Secretary of State and applied by adjudication officers under his guidance. Some statement on these policies is contained in the DSS Guide to Income Support[16] but this is not very detailed. Another source of information is the Finer Report on One-Parent Families, though this is now rather dated.[17]

B Evolution of the present law[18]

The position of deserted wives and children was not specifically covered by the Poor Law Amendment Act 1834. The practice of poor law guardians varied widely; some refused relief on the ground that payment of assistance might encourage collusive desertion and fraudulent claims.[19] Those who did provide outdoor relief could, after the Poor Law Amendment Act 1868, apply to a summary court requiring the woman's husband to reimburse them.

The antecedents of the present law with regard to unmarried mothers can be seen even earlier in the nineteenth century.[20] The 1834 Act enabled parishes to recover from the putative father any money spent on the relief of illegitimate children. Amending legislation in 1844 temporarily took matters out of the hands of the poor law guardians, and introduced a direct civil action by the mother against the putative father – the precursor of modern affiliation proceedings. But in 1868 the poor law authorities regained their power to recover from him when a mother and her child became a charge on the parish.

These principles were substantially reflected in the National Assistance Act 1948. This removed the obligation of grandparents and children to maintain destitute relatives, which had existed since 1601; but spouses remained under a duty to maintain each other and parents, including the putative father, owed the same obligation to their children. These 'liable relative' provisions, as they are known, have been re-enacted in the present legislation and the Secretary of State (referred to subsequently for convenience as the DSS) has a right to recover sums paid in benefit from those with obligations of maintenance.

While there are reciprocal duties of maintenance between spouses, in the large majority of cases it is the wife's claim to income support which is

---

15 SSA 1986, s.26(3)–(4).
16 (1988 edn), pp. 72–74.
17 See also Cretney *Principles of Family Law* (4th edn) ch 29.
18 See *Finer* Appendix 5, section 5; Brown 18 MLR 113; and the judgment of Lord Goddard CJ in *National Assistance Board v Wilkinson* [1952] 2 QB 648, [1952] 2 All ER 255.
19 *Finer* Appendix 5, para 69.
20 Ibid, paras 55–65.

principally affected by the liable relative provisions. To facilitate exposition, therefore, it will be assumed that the claimant is a woman.

C Separated wives

i General[1]

A separated wife has an autonomous entitlement to income support (i.e. the aggregation provisions do not apply), provided that she and her husband are no longer considered to be members of the same household.[2] The husband's income and capital are irrelevant to the assessment of her benefit but, as we have already seen,[3] subject to certain exceptions, maintenance paid to her is fully taken into account when assessing her income. A separated wife will be asked about the circumstances of her separation and her husband's whereabouts. This is to enable the DSS to contact him as soon as posssible in order to induce him to pay maintenance and reduce the burden on the state. However, the Department will not usually approach him if maintenance is being paid regularly under a court order, or if she has already started proceedings. If the amount paid or offered by the husband equals (or exceeds) the wife's benefit entitlement, this is accepted, and provided payments are made, that is the end of the matter.[4]

However, much more often than not, the husband will have taken on other commitments since the separation, for example by living with another woman, and he will be unable, or unwilling, to pay very much. The Finer Committee, reviewing this situation in 1974, found that in the vast majority of cases he was unable to afford as much as the supplementary benefit scale rates,[5] and concluded that:

> The overwhelming majority of one-parent families on supplementary benefit are better off with the scale rates of benefit which they receive than they would be on maintenance orders paid regularly and in full.[6]

It is in these situations that policy was controversial, and difficult questions still arise whether a woman should be expected to take maintenance proceedings and, if so, how much her husband should be required to pay in the context of his new responsibilities.

Of course, a robust attitude here may be influenced by a suspicion that, when an application for benefit is made by a deserted wife, the case is really one of fictitious desertion and the husband is still supporting her.[7] However, in some instances it may be that an apparent attempt to abuse the social security system masks a welfare problem which requires sympathetic treatment.[8]

ii The liable relative's contribution

DSS practice is to accept an offer by the husband falling short of the benefit which the claimant is entitled to receive if it is as much as he can reasonably

---

1 For a (now dated) comparison of the position in Britain and Germany, see Müller-Fembeck and Ogus 25 ICLQ 382, 400–402.
2 On which, see p.424, above.
3 P.444, above.
4 N.16, above, p.73.
5 Appendix 7, Table 60.
6 Para 4.185.
7 Cf *Fisher* paras 346–347.
8 Stevenson *Claimant or Client?* (1973) p.138.

afford.[9] For the purposes of supplementary benefit, a formula was devised to decide this issue, by reference to his needs and those of his new dependants, if any.[10] If the formula is still used under the new system, a weekly 'protected' income is calculated by reference to what would have been the applicable amount, if he had claimed income support, including any premiums and eligible housing costs, plus one-quarter of his net earnings[11] (that is, after deducting tax and social security contributions). It is only the sum left after deducting this protected income from his resources which is to be regarded as available for meeting his wife's needs. In this way, it is recognised that priority will be given to the family actually living with, and dependent on, the husband.

What is particularly interesting is that this formula may be more generous to the husband and his 'second family' than that adopted by the courts when they are confronted with a maintenance application by his wife (or former wife). In principle they do not take account of the fact that she is receiving benefit when deciding whether to award maintenance,[12] an approach which can perhaps be justified in the context of a system which puts the emphasis on individual rather than collective responsibility for the financial consequences of marital breakdown. There is also the practical point that an award of maintenance will continue even if the wife ceases to receive benefit, perhaps because she takes on full-time work.

However, state benefits are not entirely excluded from the court's calculation and it is probably fair to say that, while the availability of benefit is not in itself a persuasive factor against an award of maintenance, their financial impact will often be considered in determining what level of award should be made. In the words of Russell LJ, 'the existence of . . . benefits enables the court in effect to deal with a larger purse than would otherwise be available'.[13] Although, in general,[14] the courts accept that the maintenance order should not reduce the husband's resources below subsistence level, they do not adopt the DSS formula in determining that level; in particular, 25 per cent of net earnings is not protected.[15] There is clearly still some force in Finer J.'s observation that:

> there is something radically unsatisfactory in a state of the law . . . which allows two authorities . . . when dealing with precisely the same people in the identical human predicament to make different determinations, each acting in ignorance of what the other is doing and applying rules which only tangentially meet each other.[16]

iii DSS policy with regard to maintenance applications
If the husband is not paying any maintenance when his wife claims benefit and is not persuaded to make a contribution when contacted by the DSS, the question arises whether she should be encouraged in any way to make a

---

9 N.16, above, p.73.
10 See DHSS *Supplementary Benefits Handbook* (1983 edn) para 13.10.
11 This is intended to cover expenses, such as fares to work and hire purchase payments.
12 *Barnes v Barnes* [1972] 3 All ER 872.
13 Ibid, at 876.
14 But see *Tovey v Tovey* (1978) 8 Fam Law 80.
15 Cf *Shallow v Shallow* [1979] Fam 1. The more recent decision in *Allen v Allen* [1986] 2 FLR 265 suggests that account will be taken of the husband's applicable amount if he were entitled to income support.
16 *Williams v Williams* [1974] Fam 55 at 61.

maintenance application, the effect of which (if successful) would be to transfer part of the burden of supporting her from the state to the husband. Following the recommendations of the Finer Committee,[17] DSS policy is now only to discuss the possibility with the wife but to make it clear that the choice is entirely hers; full entitlement to income support is preserved, whatever she decides.[18]

In principle this policy seems reasonable. But it is questionable whether there are often substantial advantages to the initiation of maintenance proceedings. It is very rare for the sum awarded on such an application to be larger than benefit. It is true that a maintenance award will not lapse when benefit is no longer payable, but this may only be of academic interest in the typical case where a woman is left to look after children and there is no realistic prospect of her finding work.

iv The 'diversion procedure'

Under an administrative arrangement made with the co-operation of the Home Office and justices' clerks, maintenance payments may be 'diverted' to the DSS while the full income support is paid weekly to the woman.[19] This procedure saves her the anxiety occasioned by irregular maintenance payments and the resulting necessity to visit the DSS office to obtain benefit to meet the deficit. It may always be used where the maintenance award is lower than the income support to which she is entitled; in the very rare cases where it is equal to or higher than her benefit, the procedure is only used if it becomes clear after a few weeks that there will be repeated failures to comply with the court order. It may also be employed for the benefit of divorced women, though the court order must then be registered in the magistrates' court, so that periodic payments are made to the justices' clerk.

In 1979 nearly 80 per cent of maintenance orders in favour of women in receipt of supplementary benefit were subject to this procedure.[20] It would, however, no longer be necessary if the radical reform proposals mentioned later were to be implemented.

v Enforcement by the DSS

The Department may take *criminal* proceedings under section 26 of the Social Security Act 1986 for a persistent failure to maintain a spouse or dependant. Such proceedings are taken only as a last resort and typically where there is consistent and unjustifiable refusal to maintain, or where the defaulter has disappeared without making arrangements for payment.[1] The Finer Committee was not in favour of this method of enforcement[2] and, in fact, there has been some decline in its use in recent years.[3] Much more important would appear to be the DSS power to take civil proceedings against the defaulting spouse under section 24, though the evidence suggests that this has been used little more frequently than criminal prosecution.[4] The magistrates' court considering the application 'shall have regard to all the circumstances

17 Paras 4.199–4.202.
18 DHSS *Guide to Income Support* (1988 edn) p.72.
19 N.10, above, paras 13.20–13.22.
20 973 HC Official Report (5th series) col 785.
 1 N.10, above, para 13.25.
 2 Para 4.211.
 3 Standing Committee B Debates on Social Security Bill 1986, col 926.
 4 SBC Annual Report 1979 (Cmnd 8033), para 8.30.

and, in particular, to the income of the liable person'.[5] Apart from this, there is nothing in the legislation which limits the circumstances in which a contribution may be recovered from the liable relative. The Divisional Court did once hold that the wife's adultery or desertion might provide the husband with a defence,[6] but later cases explained that such conduct is only a factor to be taken into consideration together with other relevant circumstances.[7] It is clear that a husband may be liable to make payments to the Department even though a condition of the separation from his wife was that she would not claim maintenance,[8] and it has been held that the husband's statutory obligation is not discharged by the making of a consent order under which he transferred the former matrimonial home to his ex-spouse.[9]

vi Divorced wives

For income support purposes, the position of a divorced wife is very similar to that of woman separated from her husband. Thus, she may claim benefit in her own right and the amount of maintenance paid by her former husband is included in her income. The only significant difference is that a former spouse is not a 'liable relative' under the legislation and so the DSS has no power to recover payments from one spouse for benefit paid to the other. However, as a parent he (or she) is liable to maintain the children and the DSS may take proceedings to secure performance of this obligation.

D Single mothers

In many respects the entitlement of a single (i.e. unmarried) mother is the same as that of a separated wife but, as the law stands at the moment, there are two significant differences. First, the child's father is not liable to maintain the mother. Secondly, the father is only liable to maintain their child if he has been made the subject of an affiliation order.[10] The latter distinction has been abolished by the Family Law Reform Act 1987[11] and when the relevant provisions are brought into force the unmarried father will be in the same position as the married father (and indeed as the unmarried mother) as far as financial responsibility for the child is concerned.

The woman is entitled to claim income support for herself and her children, though of course any money actually paid to her by the natural father, whether for herself or the child and whether under a voluntary agreement or (in the case of payments for the child) under an affiliation order, must be taken into account as part of her income.[12] As with separated wives, if no voluntary agreement has been made, the DSS officer discusses with the mother the possibility of taking affiliation proceedings.[13] Many single mothers are understandably reluctant to name the father of the child and her entitlement does not depend on her willingness to disclose this information, or to take proceedings.

5 SSA 1986, s.24(4).
6 *National Assistance Board v Wilkinson* [1952] 2 QB 648, [1952] 2 All ER 255.
7 *National Assistance Board v Prisk* [1954] 1 All ER 400, [1954] 1 WLR 443; *National Assistance Board v Parkes* [1955] 2 QB 506, [1955] 3 All ER 1.
8 Ibid.
9 *Hulley v Thompson* [1981] 1 All ER 1128, [1981] 1 WLR 159.
10 SSA 1986, s.24(4).
11 Sch 2, para 91.
12 SI 1987/1967, reg 54.
13 N.18, above, p.74.

The Department may itself take affiliation proceedings under section 25 of the 1986 Act. Such proceedings will be abolished when the Family Law Reform Act 1987 is fully in force and the Department will then be able to apply for an order against the putative father, as though he were the married father.[14] The mother will, of course, still be able herself to take proceedings for the maintenance of the child under the amended Guardianship of Minors Act 1971.[15]

E Reform of the law

The Finer Committee recommended a new scheme to regulate the relationship between benefit payments and maintenance from liable relatives.[16] A lone mother would receive benefit in the normal way and no advice (or encouragement) would be given to her on possible proceedings against the husband, or father. Instead the Department would determine what he should pay as a contribution and this would be enforced by the issue of an 'administrative order'. There would be an appeal to a tribunal on questions of quantum, while on legal issues (for example, the paternity of a child) the husband/father could appeal to a court. The woman would only be motivated to take proceedings herself if she thought there was a real chance of obtaining more by such means than she would in benefit.

These proposals were entirely separate from the principal recommendation in the Report for a new, non-contributory benefit for single parent families, the 'guaranteed maintenance allowance'.[17] Even if this new benefit were introduced, there would still be a role for income support here, particularly during the first three months of separation when the allowance would not be payable. While these proposals would avoid some of the problems of the present system, it may be argued that in principle it is objectionable to require a liable relative to contribute without a court hearing. In any case, it is difficult to believe that the proposals will be implemented in the present political and economic climate.

F Sponsored immigrants

An immigrant's sponsor (under the Immigration Act 1971) is liable to maintain him,[18] and this duty may be enforced by the DSS in the same way as it enforces the obligations of liable relatives.[19] In effect, this restores the position to that which used to exist before 1975; until then, the Supplementary Benefits Commission used to withhold benefit from an immigrant if his sponsor was able to support him. The practice was ruled illegal by the Divisional Court, as it was improper to take into account an undertaking to support, rather than actual support, in assessing the claimant's resources.[20] The principle established by this ruling has not been affected by the legislative reforms: the immigrant will be fully entitled to benefit, but this may then be recovered from his sponsor.

14 SSA 1986, s.24(7), as amended.
15 Family Law Reform Act 1987, s.12.
16 *Finer* Part 4, sections 11–12.
17 Ibid, Part 5, sections 5–7, and see Eekelaar [1976] Public Law 64.
18 SSA 1986, s.26(3)(c).
19 Ibid, s.24(4). The DSS may recover sums which it has paid in benefit.
20 *R v West London Supplementary Benefits Appeal Tribunal, ex parte Clarke* [1975] 3 All ER 513, [1975] 1 WLR 1396.

Part 9 Special cases

In this Part there is a short summary of the principal rules governing the award of benefit to some special categories of claimant. These mostly entail modifications to the normal rules for assessing the applicable amount.

A Hospital patients[1]

The amount of benefit paid to patients in hospital depends on a number of factors, principally whether the claimant is a member of a couple or single and the duration of his stay. The general aim of the provisions is to ensure that the claimant (and his family) have enough to meet continuing commitments while he is in hospital and to pay for some personal expenses during that period. On the other hand, there will generally be a reduction in the benefit payable to take account of diminished costs.[2]

During the first six weeks of a stay in hospital, benefit is generally unaffected.[3] The position thereafter may be summarised in outline under the following heads.[4]

(1) *Adults in hospital 6–52 weeks* For each adult in hospital there is a special rate of personal allowance, sometimes called 'hospital pocket money' (HPM),[5] to which may be added (where appropriate) the ordinary personal allowances for other members of the family, and the family, lone parent, and disabled child premiums, and housing costs. The calculation is different where one member of a couple is in hospital: the normal benefit is then payable *minus* HPM.

(2) *Children in hospital for a period exceeding 12 weeks* The personal allowance for the child is reduced to HPM but any premium in respect of the child remains payable.

(3) *Adults in hospital over 52 weeks* Adults remaining in hospital for a period exceeding 52 weeks are treated as single claimants, whatever their family circumstances,[6] and will be entitled only to HPM.[7] An exception to this was created by a late amendment to the regulations:[8] lone parents even if they have been in hospital for 52 weeks can continue to claim for dependent children. A lesser sum is payable if the patient is unable to act for himself and a medical practitioner certifies that he cannot make personal use of all or any of the HPM. If the patient is a member of a couple, the other partner (if not himself in hospital) becomes entitled to income support as a single person or lone parent (if there are dependent children) and the standard rules for assessing the applicable amount, including premiums and housing costs, as appropriate, prevail.

(4) *Boarders etc. in hospital* There is a set of complex rules which determine the entitlement of those who prior to being a hospital patient were

1 For the similar rules for contributory benefits, see pp. 364–367, above.
2 For policy discussion, see SSAC Report on Draft Hospital In-Patient Amendment Regulations 1987 (Cm 215).
3 But if the claimant was previously a boarder or in residential accommodation, only if he continues to pay the relevant accommodation charge: SI 1987/1967, Sch 7, para 18.
4 Ibid, paras 1–3, 18.
5 It is equivalent to 20% of the standard retirement pension.
6 Because they are treated under the regulations as no longer being a member of the same household as, e.g. a partner: SI 1987/1967, reg 16(2).
7 It is assumed that such persons are no longer liable for housing costs.
8 SI 1988/663, reg 8.

boarders or living in residential care, nursing homes or hostels. In general, such a person is entitled to HPM plus any part of the accommodation charge for which he remains liable.

For the purpose of these rules, periods in hospital which are not separated by more than 28 days are aggregated and treated as conditions.[9]

B Persons in residential accommodation

There are several categories of claimant who are housed in special accommodation, and who because of the range of services provided under these arrangements, have unusual, often reduced, needs. It may in some cases be important to distinguish these groups from boarders who pay board and lodging charges on a commercial basis: the method of assessing their applicable amount has already been discussed.[10]

i Residential homes for the elderly and disabled

Under section 21 of the National Assistance Act 1948, as amended, local authorities are empowered, and may be directed by the Secretary of State for Social Services, to provide:

> residential accommodation for persons who by reason of age, infirmity or any other circumstances are in need of care and attention which is not otherwise available to them.

This responsibility may be discharged either by local authorities providing their own homes or by arrangements with private hostels and old people's homes. In either case, the applicable amount is calculated as follows.[11]

— If a single claimant is only temporarily in such accommodation, the standard rules for assessment apply. In all other cases, the applicable amount comprises, for each adult in the accommodation, a sum equal to the basic rate of retirement pension, 80 per cent of which is taken to cover accommodation and meals and 20 per cent 'pocket money'. If the resident is a member of a couple, the partner who is not in the accommodation is treated as a single claimant (or lone parent) and the applicable amount is assessed accordingly.

ii Residential care and nursing homes

Broadly speaking, persons in residential care homes and nursing homes[12] are treated as if they were boarders,[13] that is, the applicable amount includes the special rates of personal allowances for each member of the family in the accommodation and the weekly accommodation charge, plus the cost of meals not included in that charge.[14] However, some differences should be noted. First, if separate charges are made for heating, diet, extra baths, laundry or attendance needs, they are added to the applicable amount.[15] Secondly, there are upper limits to the allowable accommodation charges and

9 SI 1987/1967, reg 21(2).
10 Pp. 437–440, above.
11 SI 1987/1967, Sch 7, paras 10A, 10B, 13.
12 For definitions, see ibid, reg 19(3).
13 See pp. 438–439, above.
14 SI 1987/1967, Sch 4, paras 1, 2(2).
15 Ibid, para 2(1).

these vary according to the circumstances of the resident (e.g. if he is disabled) and the type of accommodation.[16] If the actual charge exceeds the relevant limit, the local authority may make up the difference and normally income support is unaffected.[17] Alternatively, where the person concerned has been in the home since 29 April 1985 and at that date was able to pay the charges himself, the whole or part of the excess may be included in the applicable amount.[18]

C Temporary separation of couples

As we have seen, where a couple is temporarily separated because one partner is in residential accommodation, the partner who remains at home is treated as a single claimant (or lone parent). Analogously, where the temporary separation is the result of one partner being in a nursing or residential care home, a rehabilitation unit (for drug or alcohol addiction), a probation or bail hostel or is attending a residential MSC training course, each partner is treated as a single claimant (or lone parent) if the aggregate of the two claims exceeds what would have been paid to them as a couple.[19] Finally, where one partner is temporarily absent abroad, the standard rules for assessment apply during the first four weeks of such absence; thereafter the applicable amount of the remaining partner is assessed as if he were a single claimant (or lone parent).[20]

D Prisoners

No benefit is payable to a prisoner, defined as a person detained in custody pending trial or sentence or under a sentence imposed by a court.[1] The single exception to this is that housing costs such as mortgage interest payments will be covered during periods of custody in remand or committals for trial or sentence.[2] The aggregation rules do not apply to a prisoner's family, since a prisoner is not treated as a member of the same household as his partner.[3] The latter may, therefore, make an independent claim for income support. On final discharge, the prisoner is entitled to income support in the usual way, but any discharge grant will be taken into account as income.[4] In addition, he will not be required to meet the availability condition for the first seven days after discharge.[5]

E Students

i General

In the 1970s the number of student claims for supplementary benefit during their vacations steadily grew. Adjustments to the rules in 1977 made it more

---

16 For details, see ibid, paras 6–11.
17 Ibid, reg 21(4).
18 Ibid, Sch 4, para 12.
19 Ibid, Sch 7, para 9.
20 Ibid, para 11.
 1 Ibid, reg 21(3). Persons detained under the Mental Health Act 1983 are specifically excluded from the definition.
 2 SI 1987/1967, Sch 7, para 8(b).
 3 Ibid, reg 16(3)(b).
 4 Ibid, reg 40.
 5 Ibid, Sch 1, para 18.

difficult for such claims to be made in the short vacation periods for Easter and Christmas.[6] The reforms did not, however, stop there; the government considered that it was wrong in principle for the social security system to support grant-aided students[7] and the administrative cost of payments was very high.[8] Further adjustments were therefore made to the rules of entitlement in 1986[9] and these were incorporated into the income support regulations.

For the purposes of the rules, a student is a person under 19 attending a full-time course of advanced education (i.e. above GCE 'A'-level) or over 19 (but under pensionable age) and pursuing a full-time course of study[10] at an educational establishment.[11]

ii Availability for work

Control on claims made during the academic year (i.e. including the Easter and Christmas vacations but not the summer vacation) is achieved by means of the availability for work requirement. In general, students are deemed not to be available during this period and cannot, therefore, be entitled to income support.[12] However, lone parents, disabled persons and foreign students who are temporarily without funds[13] are exempt from this requirement[14] and thus, subject to fulfilling other conditions, may claim income support throughout the calendar year.

iii Educational grants and covenants

Claims made by students during the summer vacation (or in the case of those not required to be available for work, at other times) are subject to the ordinary rules, but some discussion of the treatment of educational grants and covenants is called for. Subject to certain disregards, educational grants including any parental contribution (whether or not it is actually paid[15]) are fully taken into account as income for the period they are intended to cover,[16] normally the whole of the academic year but not the summer vacation.[17] The list of disregards includes: tuition and examination fees, book and equipment grants and travelling expenses.[18]

The treatment of covenant income, from a parent or partner, depends on whether the student also receives a grant and whether the covenantor has been assessed for a contribution.

---

6 See Harris [1987] JSWL 348 and the first edition of this book, p.551.
7 *Green Paper 1985* vol 1, para 9.28.
8 In 1985, there was an estimated administrative cost of £1 for each 65p of supplementary benefit paid to students during the short vacations: Harris, n.6, above, p.354, n.55.
9 SI 1986/1010 and SI 1986/1283.
10 On which see *R(SB) 40/83* and *R(SB) 41/83*. These decisions emphasise the need to look at the nature of the course rather than merely the number of hours of study; the description of the course by the educational institution is relevant but not conclusive.
11 SI 1987/1967, reg 61(1).
12 Ibid, reg 10(1)(h).
13 Such foreign students will normally only be entitled to an urgent cases payment: above, p.451.
14 SI 1987/1967, reg 10(1)(h) and Sch 1, paras 1, 2, 7, 20.
15 Though if the claimant is a lone parent or disabled only if it is paid: ibid, reg 61.
16 Ibid, reg 62(1), (3).
17 For some, e.g. postgraduate students, it may cover the summer vacation. The same applies to maintenance allowances for dependants and mature students: ibid, reg 62(3A). For sandwich courses, see ibid, reg 62(4).
18 Ibid, reg 62(3).

(1) *Grant and contribution* The annual value of the covenant minus the contribution is apportioned over 52 weeks but subject to a £5 weekly disregard.[19]

(2) *No grant* Subject to the disregards mentioned above, income equivalent to the standard maintenance grant is attributed to the period of the course (i.e. normally the academic year but not the summer vacation); any balance is apportioned over 52 weeks with a £5 per week disregard.[20]

(3) *Grant but no contribution* As (2) except that the amount to be apportioned over the period of study is the difference between the standard maintenance grant and the student's actual grant.[1]

Part 10 Deductions and payment to third parties

There is provision for certain deductions to be made from the weekly amount of income support. This may occur where the claimant has received an overpayment of this, or any other social security benefit,[2] or where he is required to repay a social fund loan.[3] Here we are concerned with the powers under the Claims and Payments Regulations[4] to withhold certain sums in order that payment may be made directly to a third party to whom the claimant is in debt. Equivalent measures were taken under the supplementary benefit legislation, the policy being to help those claimants who showed themselves, perhaps only temporarily, incapable of budgeting for their own needs. The number of cases to which they applied was not inconsiderable. In 1986, housing costs were being paid directly to the landlord in some 124,000 cases[5] and fuel costs directly to the utilities in over 300,000 cases.[6] While this type of intervention in a claimant's financial affairs arguably undermines individual responsibility and self-reliance, nevertheless a prudent use of the powers can be used to prevent a crisis of eviction or fuel disconnection which might otherwise arise.

Under the supplementary benefit legislation, adjudication officers also had power to postpone payment of part of the weekly benefit where he considered that the claimant had failed to budget for items the need for which arose at irregular intervals. Payment would then be made, when the relevant need arose.[7] Effectively, this was a compulsory form of saving, the need for which has been overtaken by provision for budgeting loans under the social fund.[8]

Under the income support system, the powers to make payments to third parties arise where the debts have been incurred by the claimant (or partner) in relation to housing costs, board and lodging and other accommodation charges, gas, electricity and water charges.[9] Unlike the equivalent provisions in the supplementary benefit legislation, it is no longer a formal condition for

19 Ibid, reg 63. There may be a further deduction for travel expenses.
20 Ibid, reg 64(1).
 1 Ibid, reg 64(2).
 2 See generally, pp. 557–562, below.
 3 Pp. 520–522, below.
 4 SI 1987/1968.
 5 A fall from 171,000 cases in 1982, no doubt the result of the introduction of housing benefit.
 6 DHSS *Social Security Statistics 1987* Tables 34.66 and 34.68.
 7 See the second edition of this book, p.519.
 8 Pp. 514–517, below.
 9 SI 1987/1968, Sch 9, para 2. See also on housing benefit, p.509, below.

the exercise of these powers that the claimant should have failed to budget for the item in question. The payments to the third party creditor are made at intervals determined by the Secretary of State and they may continue even after the initial debt has been discharged. But the decision to make a direct payment can only be made if it is in the interests of the claimant's family. Normally, this is done only where substantial arrears have accrued, for example, in respect of mortgage interest payments only where there are more than four weeks' arrears due from a 12-week period and, as regards other housing costs, only where half the annual amount is owing.[10]

— The regulations further prescribe the normal sum which may be deducted from the benefit paid to the claimant and made over to the third party: this is the sum of a weekly amount equal to 5 per cent (in the case of fuel debts, 10 per cent) of the personal allowance for a single claimant over 25 *and* the weekly cost (actual or estimated) of the items in question.[11] But a complex set of rules then sets out various maximum limits to the sums which may be deducted in this way, and other qualifications to the formula.[12]

It may well be that a claimant has accumulated debts under more than one of the relevant heads, so there are rules for determining priority between them.[13] Thus, housing costs are to be met before fuel and water costs and, as between different items of housing costs, mortgage payments enjoy priority.

10 SI 1987/1968, para 3(4)(a).
11 Ibid, paras 3(2), 6(2) and 7(3).
12 Ibid, paras 6(5) and 8.
13 Ibid, para 9.

Chapter 12

Family credit

Part 1 Introduction

A General

Family credit is one of the three main 'income-related' benefits. As with income support and housing benefit, the scheme was introduced by the Social Security Act 1986 and came into force in April 1988. In broad terms, it is designed to provide some assistance for low-paid working individuals who have responsibilities for children. Like the other two income-related benefits, it is financed by general taxation.

Family credit (FC) takes over the area of welfare legislation previously covered by family income supplement (FIS) but, unlike its predecessor (which was introduced in 1970 as a temporary measure), it has been conceived as a permanent part of the benefit systems developed by the Fowler reviews. In addition, the provision is intended to be both more generous and more extensive.[1]

B Background

i The 'Speenhamland' system

Clearly, a wage that is sufficient to support a single person may be totally inadequate for a family. When William Pitt first proposed income tax in 1798 it was recognised that the system should take account of the wage earner's family commitments. A few years before this, the magistrates at Speenhamland in Berkshire declared that the parish could supplement the wages of local farm workers. They conducted a survey into the price of bread as a basis of setting 'out-door' relief, to bring the income of workers up to a prescribed level.[2] There were always legal doubts about this system of wage supplementation and it was swept away by the Poor Law Amendment Act 1834. Although such historical parallels must be treated with some caution, British policymakers have shown in recent times a marked preference for dealing with the problem of low wages by means of the social security system rather than by a direct regulation of the wages system.[3] When attention was

1 With an annual expenditure of £400 million, compared with £130 million for FIS in 1984–85 (at 1984 prices): *Green Paper 1985* vol 2, paras 4.25–4.26.
2 Bruce *The Coming of the Welfare State* (4th edn) pp. 55–56, 91–92; Fraser *The Evolution of the British Welfare State* (1975) pp. 34–39.
3 Brown *Family Income Supplement* (1983) p.48.

focussed on the problem in the 1960s,[4] there was discussion of the desirability of introducing a minimum wage[5] but the option had receded into the background as a realistic policy choice by the time the Conservative party was returned to office in 1970.

ii Family income supplement

The Conservative party had promised to ameliorate the problems of family poverty by raising family allowances, but this commitment was reconsidered and the means-tested family income supplement scheme introduced instead.[6] Sir Keith Joseph explained that the extension of family allowances to cover families with only one child would have been too costly.[7] Moreover, the lowering of the tax threshold in the previous few years made the raising of the allowances, with their 'claw-back' through the reduction in child tax allowance, a less efficient way of helping the poor.[8] The merit of FIS, it was claimed, was that it directed help where it was most needed and, for the first time, conferred assistance on a family with a wage-earner and only one child.[9] Those in receipt of FIS could also be 'passported' to a number of other welfare benefits.

The temporary nature of FIS was reflected in its simplicity. Thus the scheme contained very few discretionary elements and, in particular, there was no provision initially for varying the amount according to the age, (as distinct from the *number*) of children; nor, unlike the supplementary benefit scheme, was any account taken of housing costs.

In the form in which FIS stood immediately prior to its replacement by FC, it could be claimed by any person engaged in 'remunerative full-time work', defined as 30 hours per week (or 24 hours in the case of a single parent) and responsible for at least one child. The calculation was a simple set-off between the family's normal gross income and a 'prescribed amount'. The shortfall of earnings below this amount was halved and, subject to appropriate maximum limits for different sized families, this figure was the claimant's entitlement. The maximum limits were thought necessary both to preserve the work-incentives of employees and to deal with the risks that employers might pay artificially low wages, knowing that any shortfall below the market rate would be met in full by the government, and that self-employed persons might falsify their incomes.[10] From November 1985, the flat-rate allowances for children gave way to three age bands (under 11, 11 to 15, and 16 and over) which mirrored the variables used in the supplementary benefit scheme. At the same time, the real value of FIS payments was increased, in contrast to that of child benefit which did not keep pace with inflation. Arguably, these initiatives were paving the way for the introduction of family credit.

4   E.g. Abel-Smith and Townsend *The Poor and the Poorest* (1965).
5   E.g. Department of Employment and Productivity *A National Minimum Wage: An Inquiry* (1969). The option of a national minimum wage has been adopted in many European countries: cf Walker, Lawson and Townsend (eds) *Responses to Poverty: Lessons from Europe* (1984) pp. 112–117, 121–122.
6   FISA 1970.
7   806 HC Official Report (5th series) cols 217ff. This was accomplished some years later by the introduction of child benefit: ch 10, above.
8   Cf Brown, n.3, above, pp. 52–55.
9   Family allowances only catered for second and subsequent children.
10   For criticism, see Brown, n.3, above, pp. 119, 135.

C Reform

The policy concerns that shaped family credit derived in part from specific criticisms of FIS and in part from the wider aim of reforming and harmonising all three means-tested benefits.[11] The proposals in the Green Paper of 1985 set out several policy objectives:[12] low wage earners should not suffer an overall reduction in income by earning more (the 'poverty trap'); individuals with families should not be worse off in work than out of work (the 'unemployment trap'); help should be provided in the form of income from work rather than separate benefit payments; and, finally, to preserve choice, the form of assistance should be cash rather than kind (welfare foods, etc.) The ensuing debate focused on these and other issues.

i Policy options

Of the three policy options discussed in the 1960s, minimum wages, increasing universal family endowment and wage supplementation, only the last two were being considered seriously at the time of the Fowler reviews. It had been repeatedly argued that the best way to reduce dependence on FIS would be to increase radically the level of child benefit.[13] The government, though conceding that doubling the rate of child benefit would eliminate the poverty and unemployment traps, estimated the cost at some £4 billion and therefore 'unsupportable' on economic grounds. In addition, such a strategy would have been inconsistent with the overall policy of targetting resources on those in need.[14]

ii Poverty trap

The poverty trap refers to the situation where a recipient of one or more means-tested welfare benefits finds it difficult to improve his financial position by increasing his wages, because he then loses entitlement to those benefits; to put it another way, he faces a very high marginal tax rate. The problem could be acute under the FIS scheme. If a claimant received a wage increase, FIS entitlement was calculated by reference to the difference between the new wage and the amount prescribed in the legislation. Prior to the increase, the claimant would have received 50 per cent of the difference between the wage level and the prescribed amount, so that half of the wage increase would be lost through reduction in FIS entitlement. The disincentive to earn that increase might be magnified by two other factors: first, since FIS assessments were based on *gross*, rather than *net* income, the net benefit to those claimants – the great majority[15] – who paid tax and social security contributions on their earnings would be even smaller; secondly, the increase might have taken the claimant above the threshold of entitlement to housing benefit and resulted in the loss of one or more of the 'passported' benefits.[16]

11 See generally Brown, n.3, above, pp. 116–119.
12 Vol 2, para 4.46.
13 E.g. SBC Annual Report for 1979 (Cmnd 8033), para 17.16.
14 *White Paper 1985* para 3.67.
15 Brown, n.3, above, p.89.
16 These effects may have been mitigated to some extent by the facts: (i) that FIS awards were for 12 months; and (ii) that many FIS claimants did not take advantage of the 'passported' benefits – though (ii) can hardly be used as a justification of the system (SBC Annual Report for 1979 (Cmnd 8033), para 17.8).

Some of the most important features of the FC scheme are designed to combat the poverty trap. The withdrawal of entitlement to some of the other welfare benefits furnishes one example. Perhaps more significantly, the assessed income is now net of tax and social security contributions and the new method of calculating entitlement, which involves no withdrawal of benefit until an income threshold is reached, will clearly reduce work disincentives for low earners. However, the poverty trap cannot be totally eliminated, since the very nature of a means-testing principle assumes that benefit will be taken away as income rises.[17] Indeed, the fact that the withdrawal rate on income above the threshold is 70 per cent, compared with 50 per cent under FIS, may have largely offset the effect of basing the calculation on net, instead of gross, income.

iii Unemployment trap

The unemployment trap differs from the poverty trap in that it creates major disincentives for the claimant to engage in *any* employment, typically because earnings from a job will not increase income significantly. FIS failed to deal with this problem in the sense that, for some families, particularly those with older children, it was not sufficiently generous in comparison with supplementary benefit. Measures were taken to deal with the problem in two stages. First, the FIS rules, under which rates did not vary according to the age of children, were amended in 1985 to incorporate the age-related bands used in the supplementary benefit system. Secondly, when FC replaced FIS, the prescribed amounts for children within those bands were set at a significantly higher level than the equivalent rates under the income support system (which replaced supplementary benefits).

iv The 'passport' principle

Entitlement to FIS was an automatic 'passport' to certain other welfare benefits, notably free school meals, milk and vitamins, free NHS prescriptions, dental treatment and spectacles, the refund of fares to and from hospital and free legal advice and assistance. Under the new scheme, automatic entitlement arises in relation only to free NHS prescriptions, dental treatment, assistance with the cost of spectacles and fares to and from hospital. The reform reflects, in part, the policy of 'cash rather than kind' – FC payments will normally be higher than FIS payments – and, in part, as we have seen, the concern that the broader FIS 'passport' principle had increased the 'poverty trap' effects of that benefit.[18]

v Pay packet or separate payment

Both the Green and White Papers of 1985 proposed that FC be paid by employers in the claimant's paypacket as an offset of tax and social security contributions or, if appropriate, as an addition to gross pay. The reimbursement of employers was to be modelled on the statutory sick pay scheme.[19] The proposal was motivated by a desire to reduce administrative costs and to

17 It was estimated that in some cases the marginal tax rate would still be as high as 93 per cent and that the proportion of households with marginal rates over 80 per cent would increase from 3 to 9 per cent: Institute of Fiscal Studies *The Benefit Reviews: The Figures* (1985).
18 *White Paper 1985* para 3.86. For criticism, see Social Security Consortium *Of Little Benefit: An Update* (1987) p.25.
19 P.137, above.

achieve a greater integration between the tax and social security systems but it encountered some fierce resistance, principally on the ground that a benefit intended to relieve family or child poverty should go into the 'handbag' rather than the 'wallet'.[20] Opposition from the poverty lobby was joined by groups representing small businesses, for employers were reluctant to assume an additional administrative burden. By the time the Social Security Bill reached the House of Lords, the government had announced that the proposal would be abandoned.

vi Single parents and part-time employment

FIS was considered to be a primary instrument for dealing with single-parent family poverty and single parents normally formed the majority among FIS recipients. Following a recommendation of the Finer Committee,[1] the definition of 'full-time' employment was, for this group, reduced in 1979 from 30 hours to 24 hours a week, to accommodate their special needs and work opportunities. Under the FC scheme, the requirement of 'full-time' employment has been abandoned and, in the case of two-parent families, it is now sufficient if either works 24 hours per week. The aim is to accommodate changing practices in the labour market, particularly in relation to women, and to enlarge the scope of the scheme.

vii Manipulation

Assessment of income under the FIS scheme was typically based on the period of five weeks immediately preceding the claim. Claimants could increase their FIS entitlement, which would last for 12 months irrespective of any change in circumstances, by artificially depressing their earnings during the five-week period, for example, by not working overtime. After considering several alternatives,[2] the government decided that the most cost-effective way to deal with the possibility of 'manipulating' entitlement was to reduce the period of entitlement to six months.

viii Take-up

In the first years of its operation, FIS was subject to a low take-up rate of only about 50 per cent.[3] Notwithstanding extensive publicity,[4] the take-up rate did not appear to improve significantly in subsequent years.[5] A number of explanations have been offered for this – stigma, difficulties attaching to the claiming process, lack of incentive to claim small amounts and instability of circumstances – but it would seem that absence of knowledge was still a major factor. A Gallup survey commissioned by the Fowler review team found that only 32 per cent of all respondents and 49 per cent of respondents with children knew about the benefit.[6] Statements by the present government that the take-up of FC will be better than that of FIS[7] should, perhaps, be treated with caution, particularly as the expectations were based in part at

---

20 Cf Sir B Rhys Williams, Standing Committee B Debates on Social Security Bill 1986, col 936.
 1 Para 5.279.
 2 Cf *Green Paper 1985* para 4.50, which proposed an assessment period of 13 weeks.
 3 DHSS *Social Security Statistics 1976* Table 32.15.
 4 In 1973–74, about £920,000 was spent on advertising FIS: 886 HC Official Report (5th series), Written Answers, cols 1–2.
 5 Corden *Taking Up a Means-Tested Benefit* (1983); Stanton 5 Policy and Politics 27.
 6 *Green Paper 1985* vol 3, para 4.61.
 7 See Standing Committee B Debates on Social Security Bill 1986, col 964.

least on the subsequently discarded proposal for payments in the wage-packet.

Part 2   Entitlement to family credit

The conditions of entitlement to FC may be considered under five heads: (i) presence and residence in Great Britain; (ii) remunerative work; (iii) responsibility for a child; (iv) capital, and (v) income.

A   Presence and residence in Great Britain

Under the FIS scheme, the connection with Great Britain was established by a residence condition imposed on the *family*. To avoid difficulties inherent in this concept, the new provisions distinguish between different members of the family:[8]

(1) the claimant must be present and ordinarily resident in GB;[9] *and*
(2) the partner (if any) must be ordinarily resident in the UK; *and*
(3) at least part of the earnings of the claimant and part of those (if any) of the partner must derive from remunerative work in the UK.

These conditions must be satisfied on the date of the claim; it would not seem to matter if, shortly after an award, the claimant leaves the country. There are no presence or residence conditions for the children of the family but since, as will be seen,[10] a child is treated for FC purposes as being a member of the family only if he 'is normally living' with the claimant (or partner),[11] it would be rare in practice for an adult member of the family to be ordinarily resident without the relevant children also satisfying that condition.

B   Engaged in remunerative work

The claimant, or his partner, must be 'engaged and normally engaged in remunerative work'.[12]

i Remunerative work – the '24-hour rule'
'Remunerative work' is defined in the Regulations as:

> work in which a person is engaged, or where his hours of work fluctuate, is engaged, on average, for not less than 24 hours a week, being work for which payment is made or which is done in expectation of payment.[13]

Charitable or voluntary work for which only expenses are paid is explicitly excluded.[14] These provisions are identical to those used to *exclude* entitlement to income support and have been discussed in chapter 11.[15] Of particular

8 SI 1987/1973, reg 3(1).
9 On these concepts, see pp. 362–364, above.
10 P.478, below.
11 SI 1987/1973, reg 7(1).
12 SSA 1986, s.20(5)(b).
13 SI 1987/1973, reg 4(1).
14 Ibid, reg 5(3).
15 Pp. 420–421, above.

importance in the present context is the question of what hours count for those engaged in self-employed work. Under the FIS legislation, it was held that time spent in activities which were 'essential' to the employment, that is, were carried out with the desire, hope and intention of deriving some reward or profit, was properly to be regarded as time engaged in remunerative work, even though the time was not 'costed' for accounting purposes.[16]

ii Engaged and normally engaged in remunerative work

The requirement that the claimant (or partner) must be both engaged and normally engaged in remumerative work has regard, in effect, to two time periods. He can only be treated as *engaged* in remunerative work if 'he carries out'[17] activities in the course of his work for not less than 24 hours in the week of the claim or (provided he remains employed up to the date of the claim) either of the two weeks preceding that week.[18] '*Normally engaged*' is not defined and in consequence the adjudicating authorities have been given a broad power of interpretation. In construing an equivalent provision under the FIS legislation, the Commissioners held that normality should not be judged by reference to some arbitrary period (for example, six months preceding the claim). Rather, regard should be had to the circumstances of each individual case as they appear at the time of the claim, including future prospects as well as the past employment record.[19] Further, the standard of normality is personal to the claimant (or partner); what is 'normal' for other persons in his occupation or similarly so employed is irrelevant.

If the case-law on FIS is to be followed,[20] it would seem that to be 'engaged' must involve some positive work effort. It was held that the claimant must be actually engaged 'at' work, rather than being 'in' work.[1] Thus, the mere receipt of remuneration calculated by reference to the number of hours actively available for work did not amount to 'undertaking activities' in the course of remunerative work.[2] In particular, this meant that days for which an employer was unable to provide work but for which he nevertheless made payments could not count,[3] and the same must apply to absences for sickness. However, the Regulations specifically provide that a person shall be treated as engaged in work during absences for a 'recognised, customary or other holiday'.[4]

---

16 *R(FIS) 6/85*.
17 Cf 'undertakes' used in the FIS regulations – the change reinforces the idea of *active* engagement.
18 SI 1987/1973, reg 5(1).
19 *R(FIS) 1/83(T); R(FIS) 6/83; R(FIS) 1/84*. There are obvious parallels with the test of 'normality' applied to some unemployment benefit entitlement rules: pp. 80–86, above. In *R(FIS) 1/83(T)*, a Tribunal of Commissioners indicated that where short-time working had recently begun it would be appropriate to make 'a short award', i.e. one for less than the normal period of 12 months. It should be noted that the power to make such an award does not exist under the FC scheme but that the period of award has, in any event, been reduced to 26 weeks.
20 The wording of the Regulations would suggest that it should be: cf n.17, above.
1 *R v Ebbw Vale and Merthyr Tydfil Supplementary Benefits Appeal Tribunal, ex parte Lewis* [1981] 1 WLR 131.
2 Cf *R(U) 10/80*.
3 *R(FIS) 2/82; R(FIS) 2/81*.
4 SI 1987/1973, reg 4(3); and see pp. 87–89, above.

C Responsibility for child or young person in same household

The family unit for the purpose of FC entitlement comprises: *either*

(1) a single person responsible for at least one child (or young person) living in the same household and that child or those children; *or*
(2) a couple (married or unmarried) one member of which is responsible for at least one child (or young person) living in the same household and that child or those children.[5]

In this context, a 'child' must be under 16 and a 'young person' must be aged between 16 and 19 and receiving full-time education.[6]

The concepts of 'responsibility' for a child (or young person) and 'membership of the same household' are common to the income-related benefits and have been fully explained in chapter 11.[7]

D Capital

A major departure from the principles governing FIS, is that account is taken of the capital resources of the claimant (and/or partner). Where the relevant capital exceeds a prescribed threshold, currently £6,000, FC is not payable.[8] The rules for calculating relevant capital follow almost completely those used for the purposes of income support and have been fully described in chapter 11.[9]

E Income

The fifth, and last, condition of entitlement relates to the income of the family, which includes the 'tariff' income assumed to be derived from part of any capital below the £6,000 threshold. The statutory provision is, unfortunately, complex as it incorporates references to the principles governing assessment of FC entitlement and cannot, therefore, be fully comprehended until those principles have been explained (see Part 3). Suffice it, at this stage, to indicate that the claimant must establish that the relevant income of the family (see Part 4) *either*:

(1) does not exceed the 'applicable amount', a figure prescribed by regulations every year; *or*
(2) exceeds the 'applicable amount' by no more than an amount which will leave some entitlement to family credit.[10]

The circuitous formula in (2) thus means that the claimant's entitlement may depend on what he would be awarded if he were entitled!

Part 3 Calculating entitlement

A General

To understand the principles for calculating FC entitlement, it is first necessary to explore the general strategy underlying the scheme and to contrast it

5 SSA 1986, s.20(5).
6 Ibid, s.20(11) and SI 1987/1973, reg 6(1). For 'full-time education', see p.468, above.
7 Pp. 425–426, above.
8 SSA 1986, s.22(6) and SI 1987/1973, reg 28.
9 Pp. 447–449, above.
10 SSA 1986, s.20(5)(a)(i)–(ii).

with the family income supplement system. Under the latter, as we have seen, the claimant was paid one half of the difference between a prescribed amount (which was variable according to the size of the family) and gross income, up to a statutory maximum (which also depended on family size). The 'withdrawal rate' of 50 per cent, which applied throughout the income scale, as we have also seen, was unsatisfactory in that, when combined with other factors, it often led to a very high marginal tax rate. To avoid these problems, the design of the FC system is different. Until income reaches a certain threshold (known as the 'applicable amount'), there is no withdrawal of benefit and the claimant receives in full sums, known as 'maximum family credits', which reflect the size of the family and the age of children. It is only when income exceeds the threshold that deductions are made from the credits; such deductions are calculated by applying a prescribed percentage 'taper' to the excess income.

i Maximum family credits

There is one credit for adults and four child or young person credits, categorised according to the following age-bands: under 11, 11 to 15, 16 to 17, and 18 to 19.[11] Only one adult credit may be awarded, whether the claimant is single or a member of a couple,[12] the intention being to offer a high degree of protection to single parents. The adult credit may be accumulated with credits for each child (or young person) for whom the claimant (or partner) is responsible, except where the child (or young person) has capital exceeding £3,000.[13]

ii Applicable amount

The lower threshold, the 'applicable amount', applies whatever the composition of the family[14] and, at the time of writing, is equivalent to the rate in the income support scheme for a couple where one of the partners is over 18. However, this does not mean that both schemes aim at the same level of protection: under the FC scheme, child benefit and family credits are added in full to income below the applicable amount; for the purposes of income support, the applicable amount includes personal allowances for children, as well as a family premium.

iii Prescribed percentage taper

The legislation provides that the percentage of any excess of income over the applicable amount to be deducted from maximum family credits is to be prescribed by regulation.[15] This contrasts with the statutory (and uniform) 50 per cent deduction rule under the FIS system and, no doubt, reflects the government's concern to retain some flexibility in determining levels of marginal tax rates in the light of fiscal and other policies. At the time of writing, the prescribed percentage is 70 per cent.[16] For the purposes of comparison with the FIS withdrawal rate, it should be recalled that the relevant FC amounts are net of income tax and social security contributions.

11 SI 1987/1973, reg 46(1) and Sch 4.
12 In the case of a polygamous marriage, the credit for a second or subsequent spouse is equivalent to the highest young person credit or that for ages 16 to 17, if the age of the spouse comes within that band: ibid, reg 46(2).
13 Ibid, reg 46(4).
14 Ibid, reg 47.
15 SSA 1986, s.20(5)(a).
16 SI 1987/1973, reg 48.

B   Amounts payable

On the basis of the principles outlined above, the methods of calculating the amounts payable may now be restated, together with arithmetical examples.

i   Income below applicable amount

Where the income to be taken into account falls below the applicable amount, the claimant is entitled to the aggregate of the maximum family credits appropriate to the composition of the family unit.[17] A simple example, using 1988–89 figures, would be as follows:

> H & W, a married couple, live with their children L (aged 8), M (aged 12) and N (aged 14). The net relevant income is £49, which is less than the applicable amount (£51.45). The FC entitlement is:

1 adult credit	£32.10
1 child credit (under 11)	£6.05
2 child credits (11–16)	£22.80
Total payable	£60.95

ii   Income above applicable amount

Where the relevant income exceeds the applicable amount, the claimant is entitled to:

$$\text{MAX FC} - 0.7 \times (I - AA)$$

where MAX FC is the aggregate of appropriate maximum family credits, I is the net relevant income and AA is the applicable amount.[18]

> As in the above example, but the net relevant income of the family is £85.45. The FC entitlement is:

$$£60.95 - 0.7 \times (85.45 - 51.45)$$
$$£60.95 - £23.80$$
$$= £37.15$$

Part 4   Assessment of income

A   General

For the purposes of the fifth condition of entitlement to FC, the claimant's income is calculated on a weekly basis by ascertaining his 'normal weekly income' (and, with certain exceptions, that of other members of the family), and adding to it the 'tariff' income which is assumed to be derived from capital.

B   Periods of assessment

i   General

The Family Credit Regulations contain detailed provisions governing the appropriate periods for the assessment of income. Their object is to identify those periods which can provide a reference for the claimant's 'normal'

17 SSA 1986, s.21(2).
18 Ibid, s.21(3).

weekly income, and thus they relate predominantly to patterns of work. To some extent, the specific rules which prescribe the appropriate periods address problems previously encountered under the FIS scheme, particularly in relation to the self-employed and to employees with a history of short-time working. But not all such difficulties can be resolved by these means and there is a broad residual discretion conferred on the adjudication officer which enables him to select a non-prescribed period where that will provide a more 'accurate' determination of normal weekly income.

ii Employed earners

The standard periods prescribed for employed earners are five weeks for those paid weekly and two months for those paid monthly.[19] In the normal case reference is made to the five weeks (or two months) immediately preceding the week of the claim but if there has been a trade dispute[20] or period of short-time working the relevant period is that immediately preceding the start of the dispute or period of short-time working.[1] For this purpose, a 'period of short-time working' is defined as 'a continuous period not exceeding 13 weeks during which the claimant is not required by his employer to be available to work the full number of hours normal in his case under the terms of his employment'.[2]

There are three exceptions to these rules. First, where a claimant has not yet been employed for five weeks (or two months) either because he has begun work or else resumed work after a continuous period of interruption of 13 weeks or more, the earnings obtained during such period as he has been employed will form the basis of calculation, provided that they are 'likely to represent his weekly earnings from that employment'.[3] If the latter condition is not satisfied, the employer may be required to provide an estimate of earnings for five weeks (or two months) or regard may be had to another period, if that will enable the adjudication officer to determine normal weekly earnings 'more accurately'.[4] Secondly, the same general discretion to have regard to another period applies where a claimant's earnings fluctuate, or are not representative of weekly earnings for some other reason.[5] Thirdly, there is in any event an overriding rule that periods within the assessment period during which earnings are 'irregular or unusual' should be disregarded; calculations are then based exclusively on the remaining part of the assessment period.[6]

iii Self-employed earners

The standard period of assessment for self-employed earners is the 26 weeks immediately preceding the week of the claim.[7] However, if the accounts of

19 SI 1987/1973, reg 14(1)(a). The same periods were used under the FIS scheme and the proposals to lengthen them were abandoned: cf p.475, n.2, above.
20 The rule reflects the approach taken by the Court of Appeal in *Lowe v Rigby* [1985] 2 All ER 903, [1985] 1 WLR 1108 in dealing with a FIS claim. The question was there left open whether the appropriate period should be that before the start of a strike or before the start of an overtime ban which preceded the strike. Since 'trade dispute' covers both strikes and overtime bans, it would seem that the latter solution applies to FC claims.
1 SI 1987/1973, reg 14(1)(a).
2 Ibid, reg 14(4). Cf *R(FIS) 2/83(T)*, para 15(2), where the adoption of 13 weeks as a rule of practice was regarded by a Tribunal of Commissioners as 'wholly inapt'.
3 SI 1987/1973, reg 14(2)(a).
4 Ibid, reg 14(2)(b).
5 Ibid, reg 14(1)(b). On the exercise of the analogous discretion under the FIS scheme, see *R(FIS) 2/83(T)*.
6 SI 1987/1973, reg 17(a).
7 Ibid, reg 15(1)(a).

the employment are audited, the relevant period is the one year accounting period, provided that this ends within the 26 weeks before the week of the claim.[8] If the self-employment has been for less than 26 weeks, reference is made to earnings already acquired as well as to an *estimate* of likely earnings in the remainder of the 26 weeks.[9] Parts of the assessment period during which no business activities have been carried out are disregarded[10] and, as with employed earners, there is a general discretion to refer to a non-prescribed period where that would enable normal weekly earnings to be determined more accurately.[11]

iv Other income

The standard period for assessing other income is also the 26 weeks before the claim and it is again subject to the general residual discretion.[12] Maintenance payments made, or due to be made, at 'regular intervals' are assessed by reference to the normal weekly amount of such payments; if they are not made regularly, regard is had to the average weekly amount received in the 13 weeks preceding the week of the claim.[13]

C Assessment of earnings and other income

A major feature of the 1986 reforms was the broad harmonisation of the principles governing the assessment of earnings and other income for the purpose of the income-related benefits. Since an account of the detailed rules has been provided in chapter 11,[14] we shall concentrate here on general principles and on those rules which are peculiar to family credit.

i Earnings from employment

The earnings relevant for FC purposes are net earnings, that is, after deduction of income tax, social security contributions and half of any contributions to an occupational or personal pension scheme.[15] The definition of 'earnings' is the same as that used for income support except that:

(1) statutory sick pay and maternity pay are treated as earnings[16] (they are treated as 'other income' under the income support scheme); and
(2) notional earnings (normally of £12 per week[17]) are attributed to persons provided by an employer with free accommodation.[18]

ii Earnings from self-employment

As regards the self-employed, the relevant amount is the net profits, that is, the gross receipts from the employment during the period of assessment, less

8   Ibid, reg 15(1)(b).
9   Ibid, reg 15(2), confirming the approach taken in *R(FIS) 1/82(T)*.
10 SI 1987/1973, reg 17(b).
11 Ibid, reg 15(1)(c).
12 Ibid, reg 16(1).
13 Ibid, reg 16(2).
14 Pp. 440–450, above.
15 SI 1987/1973, reg 20.
16 Ibid, reg 19.
17 A reduced amount may be attributed where the claimant satisfies the AO that the weekly value of the accommodation is less than £12.
18 SI 1987/1973, reg 19(3).

(a) expenses 'wholly and exclusively defrayed in that period for the purposes of that employment' and (b) income tax, social security contributions and half of pension contributions.[19]

iii Tariff income from capital

As we have seen, FC is not payable where the capital of the claimant (and/or of the partner) exceeds a prescribed amount (currently £6,000). Relevant capital[20] below that amount but above a lower threshold (currently £3,000) is treated as producing a weekly 'tariff' income: this is £1 for each £250 of capital, or part thereof.[1] Any income actually derived from capital of £6,000 or less is ignored as *income* but is nevertheless added to, and treated as part of, the capital.[2]

iv Other income of claimant or partner

The general principle is that all other income[3] is taken into account.[4] There are, however, a large number of items which are disregarded. The list corresponds broadly to that already described in relation to income support.[5] In addition, income from the following sources is disregarded for FC purposes:[6]

(1) child benefit;
(2) housing benefit and income support;
(3) payments from members of the claimant's household towards living or accommodation expenses.[7]

v Income of children and young persons

Any earnings of a child or young person are totally disregarded,[8] a provision which is generous in comparison with that applicable to income support under which a school-leaver's earnings are taken into account, subject to a £5 per week disregard.[9] In general, all other income is aggregated with that of the claimant,[10] but this is subject to some important exceptions.[11]

(1) Sums which would have been disregarded if they were part of an adult's income are ignored.
(2) If the child or young person has capital exceeding the lower threshold (£3,000) *or* has income exceeding the amount of family credit appropriate for his age[12] no such credit is payable for him and any income, unless it is in the form of maintenance payments,[13] is ignored.

19 Ibid, regs 21–22.
20 Pp. 447–449, above.
 1 SI 1987/1973, reg 36.
 2 Ibid, reg 31(4).
 3 This includes 20 per cent of payments received by way of board and lodging charge: ibid, reg 24(3). However, if such payments form 'a major part' of the claimant's income, they are, subject to the deduction of expenses, fully taken into account as self-employed earnings: ibid, reg 21(2).
 4 Ibid, reg 24(1).
 5 Pp. 445–447, above.
 6 SI 1987/1973, Sch 2, as amended.
 7 Unless this is treated as self-employed earnings: n.3, above.
 8 SI 1987/1973, Sch 1, para 3.
 9 P.449, above.
10 SI 1987/1973, reg 10(1).
11 Ibid, reg 27.
12 Cf p.479, above.
13 Whether the maintenance obligation results from a court order or not; a modification of the equivalent FIS rule (SI 1980/1437, reg 2(6)).

(3) If the child or young person receives capital by instalments and, at the date of the FC claim, an instalment is due which would take the capital above the lower threshold (£3,000), payment of that instalment will be treated as the claimant's income, thus preventing loss of entitlement to the appropriate credit under (2).

Part 5   Duration of award

The policy inherent in the FIS scheme, that administrative costs should be minimised by avoiding frequent changes to the amount payable, has been retained. Although the period of the award has been reduced from 52 to 26 weeks,[14] there is no longer a power to make 'short awards' where there is uncertainty about the rate payable.[15] Section 20(6) of the Social Security Act 1986 provides that:

> subject to regulations, an award of family credit and the rate at which it is payable shall not be affected by any change of circumstances

during the period of 26 weeks. Exceptions are made by the regulations in only two situations:[16]

(1) the death of the claimant (though if he is survived by a partner, the award is transferred to the latter);
(2) a child or young person, for whom a credit is payable, leaves the claimant's household, becomes a member of a different household, and FC or income support is payable in respect of him there.

---

14 SSA 1986, s.20(6).
15 Cf SI 1980/1437, reg 3(1). The provision had created difficulties and the Commissioners had striven to give it a narrow interpretation: *R(FIS) 1/81; R(FIS) 1/82(T); R(FIS) 2/83(T); R(FIS) 2/85(T)*.
16 SI 1987/1973, Part VI.

Chapter 13

Housing benefit

Part 1　Introduction

A　General

The fundamental importance of good housing to social welfare has long been reflected in government economic and social policy.[1] In general, such policy has two main aims: to secure an adequate supply of good quality homes; and to ensure an equitable distribution of that supply.[2] The cost of housing is relevant to both objectives and it has been a feature of government intervention since at least 1915 to provide assistance with such costs. Initially, at a time when the large majority lived in privately rented accommodation, the assistance took the form of controls on rent.[3] While rent control still exists, the private rented sector now constitutes only a minor part of the housing market[4] and two other forms of intervention have assumed central importance. First, there is the subsidisation of both the private and public sectors through tax relief for owner occupiers and the complex system of public housing finance for local authority and other public sector tenants. The device of subsidy may be seen to be concerned with the supply objective although, in the case of tax relief, the evidence for this is not strong.[5] Secondly, pursuit of the distributional objective has led to the development of a means-tested benefit system to meet housing costs, so that those on low incomes can afford housing which the market would otherwise place beyond their means.

B　The evolution of housing benefit

i　Rent rebates

The early history of housing benefit may be located in the introduction of rent rebates for local authority tenants in the 1930s, as part of a programme

---

1　Rasmussen *Urban Economics* (1973) p.83.
2　Lansley *Housing and Public Policy* (1979) p.18; Ermisch *Housing Finance: Who Gains?* (1984) p.9.
3　Increase of Rent and Mortgage Interest (War Restrictions) Act 1915.
4　MacLennan *Housing Economics* (1982) ch 8. In 1914, 90 per cent of housing stock was privately rented accommodation. By 1982 this had fallen to 12 per cent, with owner-occupation accounting for 61 per cent and local authority/New Town accommodation 27 per cent: Ermisch, n.2, above, p.9.
5　Lansley, n.2 above, ch 1.

to encourage slum clearance and public sector re-housing.[6] The need for the rebates occurred because, not surprisingly, the re-housed slum dwellers could not often afford the rent for their new homes. In 1930, local authorities were given financial incentives in connection with slum clearance and encouraged to adopt localised rent rebate schemes for those displaced.[7] Six years later the arrangements were extended to allow rebates schemes covering all tenants.[8] The schemes were not popular, apparently because tenants objected to the resulting differentials in rents.[9] The permissive rather than mandatory nature of these schemes, together with their strictly local application, was an enduring aspect of rent rebate legislation.

Changes in 1956 to reduce the subsidy of local authority housing had the long-term effect of raising rent levels and the Conservative government encouraged the use of rebates, leading to a large rise in the number of schemes.[10] This encouragement was sustained by a subsequent Labour administration which issued a circular containing a model local scheme. By 1970, over 60 per cent of local authorities operated some kind of scheme[11] but, since no compulsory standards applied, there was a wide divergence between them.

In the early 1970s, in order to reduce public expenditure, the Conservative government reduced subsidies to local authorities and extended 'fair rent' controls to public sector tenancies. The introduction in 1972 of the first national system of rent rebates for council tenants[12] was, in part, intended to mitigate the impact of this new 'fair rents' policy. Reflecting a concern for the equitable distribution of assistance with rents, the scheme also provided for rent allowances for private and housing association tenants. In partnership with family income supplement (FIS), it was seen as an 'important new weapon against family poverty'.[13] Again, for reasons of equity, assistance was deliberately made available to some tenants who were not entitled to supplementary benefit. This was considered to be necessary in view of the projected increases in public sector rents[14] but in consequence there now existed, alongside supplementary benefit and FIS, a third major means-tested system, with different rules of assessment.

ii Rate rebates

The expansion of local authority services in the 1960s resulted in significant increases in local rates and there was concern about the impact of this growing burden on ratepayers with low incomes.[15] The Rating Act 1966 introduced a national rate rebate scheme as a temporary measure, pending attempts to devise a more radical reform of the rating system in the light of the findings of a Royal Commission on Local Government.[16] The rebate scheme involved a comparison of 'reckonable rates', broadly those in respect

6 See generally Deacon and Bradshaw *Reserved for the Poor* (1983) pp. 11–14.
7 Housing Act 1930.
8 Housing Act 1936.
9 Ravetz *Model Estate* (1974) pp. 37–38.
10 From 1956 to 1965 the proportion of local authorities with schemes rose from 15 per cent to 39 per cent: Parker *The Rents of Council Houses* (1967) p.47.
11 Deacon and Bradshaw, n.6, above, p.70.
12 Housing Finance Act 1972.
13 White Paper *Fair Deal for Housing* (1971, Cmnd 4728) para 42.
14 Ibid, para 5.
15 See *Report of the Committee of Inquiry into the Impact of Rates on Households* (1965, Cmnd 2582).
16 (1966, Cmnd 2923).

of the dwelling in which the applicant lived less a deduction for non-dependants, with 'reckonable income', determined under the Act and set at about the supplementary benefit level. The scheme suffered from low take-up and at certain income levels the tapering of assistance worked unfairly.[17] In 1975, a new scheme, modelled on the rent rebate scheme, was introduced with dramatically improved results in terms of both coverage and the level of assistance offered.[18]

iii General schemes for income maintenance and housing costs

Quite apart from the specific programmes designed to assist with rent and rates, the role of general income maintenance benefits should not be overlooked. Although the poor law made no allowance for, and indeed normally prohibited, relief payments to meet rent,[19] this item was an established component in determining needs under the unemployment assistance scheme, and was retained in the national assistance scheme proposed by Beveridge.[20] Regulations made under the National Assistance Act 1948 defined 'net rent' as including not only the actual rent but also rates, an allowance towards repairs and insurance and, where appropriate, mortgage interest payments.[1] This definition was retained when supplementary benefit replaced national assistance in 1966 and continued to apply until the housing benefit reform in 1983.

iv The 1983 reform

The picture emerging from the historical survey to this point is of a complex, fragmented approach to the payment of benefit for housing costs. By 1975, the national rent and rebate schemes were fully operative and were administered by local authorities which were, in turn, subject to regulation by the Department of the Environment. At the same time, the Supplementary Benefits Commission (SBC) was making payments for rent and rates to those entitled under its scheme. The Labour government's Green Paper on Housing Policy in 1977 included an undertaking to review the overlap,[2] but the main impetus to reform was given by the SBC in its Annual Reports from 1976 to 1979.[3] The Commission took as its focus the 'better off' problem, described as the confusion of, and actual loss to, some householders caused by the overlap. Because of the different means-tests and allowances, it was difficult to estimate whether a person not in full-time work should claim supplementary benefit or rebates. The SBC proposed a single housing benefit to replace rent and rates rebates, rent allowances and the rent and mortgage interest element of supplementary benefit. In addition to clarifying the entitlement issue, it was argued that since the new benefit would be available to those with low earnings, as well as the unemployed, it would not involve work disincentives. The Commission proposed that income tax relief on

17 Meacher *Rate Rebates: A Study of the Effectiveness of Means Tests* (1973) pp. 1–4.
18 The scheme was set out in the Rate Rebate Act 1973. The reform more than doubled the number of households receiving assistance and by 1976 take-up had reached an estimated 65–70 per cent: Deacon and Bradshaw, n.6, above, p.91.
19 General Outdoor Relief Regulation Order 1852.
20 Para 206.
1 SI 1948/1344, Sch 1.
2 *Housing Policy Review* (Cmnd 6851) para 12.09.
3 See, esp, Annual Report for 1977 (Cmnd 7392), ch 8 and Annual Report for 1979 (Cmnd 8033), ch 4. See also Donnison *The Politics of Poverty* (1982) pp. 184–193.

mortage interest payments should also be rationalised within the framework
of a unified scheme; this would allow a reallocation of resources which would
help both to simplify the scheme and to redress inequities in the prevailing
systems of housing support. Finally, there would be manifest administrative
advantages if responsibility for the unified scheme were to be conferred on
the local authorities. The new Conservative administration of 1979 was
attracted by the prospect of savings in the civil service establishment but
concerned at the cost of a comprehensive scheme for all low income households.[4] Moreover, it was clear that radical reform extending, for example, to
the system of tax relief on mortgage interest was not on the government's
agenda.

The housing benefit reform which was enacted in 1982[5] and brought into
force in 1983 proceeded on a 'nil-cost' basis and effectively achieved the
unification of the existing means-tested schemes for assisting tenants with
their housing costs. Owner-occupiers were included in the new system only so
far as general rates were concerned. Thus, mortgage interest payments
continued to be met by the supplementary benefit scheme alone[6] and the
system of tax relief on such interest was unaffected.[7] The legislation followed
the pattern set by the existing rent and rebate schemes and, accordingly,
administrative responsibility was placed on the local authorities. Those in
receipt of supplementary benefit (except boarders) generally qualified for full
assistance with rent and rebates (subject to deductions for non-dependants
living in the premises). These were referred to as 'certificated cases' since, if
the householder was entitled to supplementary benefit, the DHSS would
issue a certificate to the local authority which would then meet the eligible
housing costs. In cases where there was no entitlement to supplementary
benefit (known as 'standard cases'), a 'needs allowance' for the household
was compared with gross income. If that income was less than or equal to the
allowance, 60 per cent of the rent and rates were met. Income exceeding the
allowance gave rise to deductions from the 60 per cent amount, according to a
complex system of six tapers which varied as between rent rebates (or
allowances) and rate rebates and between pensioners and non-pensioners.[8]

The partial simplification of the previous schemes, together with the 'nil-
cost' policy, resulted in a large number of householders sustaining a net loss
in benefit.[9] This number was reduced by the awkward device of a housing
benefit supplement (HBS).[10] The need for this arose in cases where a householder could not claim supplementary benefit because his income exceeded
the relevant threshold by a small amount. In respect of the housing benefit
claim, the application of the tapers might result in the householder's *unmet*
housing costs exceeding that small amount; in consequence such a person
would be worse off overall than an applicant categorised as a 'certificated
case'. HBS was available to make up this difference but, to compound the
complexity of the arrangements, though it was added to the housing benefit
paid by the local authority, it was formally part of supplementary benefit.[11]

4 Consultative Document *Assistance with Housing Costs* (1981), and see Donnison, n.3,
   above, ch 7.
5 SSHBA 1982.
6 P.434, above.
7 For comment, see Donnison, n.3, above, p.188.
8 For details, see McGurk and Raynsford *Guide to Housing Benefit* (1987/88 edn) ch 4.
9 Cf Hill 13 J Soc Pol 297.
10 See McGurk and Raynsford, n.8, above, pp. 69–77.
11 SI 1983/1399, reg 16(b).

Identifying those entitled to HBS was a major difficulty because of the divided responsibility between the local authorities and the DHSS.[12]

Additional dimensions to the 1983 housing benefit system could be provided by individual local authorities. An authority could seek the approval of the Secretary of State to operate a high rent scheme where the average rents in the area exceeded the national average by 30 per cent or more. If such approval was given, the figure of 60 per cent of eligible rent used in the initial calculation could be raised to 80 or 90 per cent. A local authority could in addition, and at its own cost, increase expenditure on standard cases by up to 10 per cent by paying more to individuals subject to 'exceptional circumstances' or to classes of individuals (such as war pensioners) under so-called 'local schemes'.

Subject to this last qualification, local authorities were subsidised by central government in relation both to housing benefit and to the cost of its administration. Some authorities raised rent by various stratagems and, in so doing, used the subsidy arrangements to increase their own income.[13] Various amendments to the subsidy orders had to be made to halt manipulation of this kind.[14]

v Further reform
Shortly after the implementation of the 1983 reforms, the government announced a programme of economies in housing benefit which were to be achieved by adjusting the tapers for both rents and rates. This reflected concern at the substantial rise in expenditure due, at least in part, to growth in unemployment coinciding with increases in local authority rent and rates.[15] Even more important was the decision to set up an independent review of the scheme, the findings of which were published in 1985,[16] at the same time as the Green Paper on the reform of social security generally. Three main problems were identified.[17] First, the housing benefit scheme had not succeeded in removing inequities as between households with similar needs and income; in particular between those entitled and those not entitled to supplementary benefit – the advantages obtained by those in the former category might substantially weaken work incentives. Secondly, the scheme was far too complex, the provision of housing benefit supplement being an obvious example. Thirdly, and perhaps most significantly, the view was formed that, in comparison with other countries with similar economies and social security systems, housing benefit which reached about one third of all households was too widely available.

The suggested restructuring of the other means-tested benefits[18] created the opportunity to address these problems and, at the same time, to achieve some degree of integration with those systems. Thus, the White Paper of 1985 proposed that the rules for the new income support scheme should be used to assess entitlement to housing benefit.[19] This would considerably simplify the law and would provide uniform support for all claimants with income at or

12 Hill, n.9, above, p.314.
13 See e.g. *R v Secretary of State for Health and Social Security, ex parte City of Sheffield* (1985) 18 HLR 6.
14 See, further, pp. 507–509, below.
15 SSAC Fifth Report (1986–87), para 2.4.4.
16 *Housing Benefit Review.*
17 Cf *Green Paper 1985* vol 1, paras 9.14–9.16.
18 Pp. 415–417 and 473–476, above.
19 Para 3.45.

below the appropriate 'poverty' level, whether or not they were in work. It would also avoid the complexities of the housing benefit supplement and the 'high rent' schemes. There would be just two tapers (for rent and rates, respectively) and these would be set against net, rather than gross income, which would help to deal with the 'poverty trap' problem arising from the withdrawal of benefit as income increased.[20]

In fact this strategy proved to be somewhat too bold. Housing benefit had never taken account of the householder's capital. Harmonisation with income support assessment, as effected in the Social Security Act 1986, meant that there would be no entitlement to housing benefit if the claimant's relevant capital exceeded £6,000 and capital between £3,000 and £6,000 would be treated as generating assessable income. It was estimated that these changes would cause substantial losses and disentitle some 375,000 households from housing benefit.[1] Considerable political pressure at the time that the new scheme came into effect[2] led to a 'thirteenth hour' modification: the upper capital threshold was raised to £8,000.[3] In contrast, no compromise was made to another controversial aspect of the scheme, that in order to enhance the accountability of local authorities, all households, whatever their resources, should make a minimum contribution of 20 per cent to domestic rates.[4]

Mention should also be made of other policy developments which affect (or will affect) the housing benefit scheme. It has recently been announced that in April 1989 responsibility for meeting board and lodging charges will be transferred from the income support scheme[5] to housing benefit.[6] Under the Local Government Finance Act 1988, the community charge will replace the rating system: some groups of householders will be exempt; others will be eligible for rebates up to 80 per cent. Finally, if the Housing Bill 1988 is enacted in its present form, rent officers will acquire the new functions of assessing reasonable (i.e. market) rents for the purpose of calculating the extent of a local authority's entitlement to central government subsidy and themselves assisting in the determination of whether the claimant's accommodation is unduly large or expensive for his (and his family's) circumstances.[7]

C Harmonisation with income support

For reasons given above, many of the concepts and rules employed in the housing benefit provisions are identical with, or substantially similar to, those used in the income support system and hence there will be frequent reference to the exposition in chapter 11. An important example of this concerns the composition of the claimant's household. As will be seen, a number of rules, notably those which govern the assessment of needs (Part 3), are applied to members of the claimant's 'family' which, as explained in

---

20 Cf p.473, above.
 1 SHAC *Housing Benefit: is this the promised end?* (1985) p.6.
 2 131 HC Official Report (6th series) cols 173–216; 132 ibid, cols 351–394.
 3 SI 1988/909. SSAC in its Fourth Report (1985), para 4.16, had recommended that it be raised to £12,000.
 4 *Green Paper 1985* vol 1, para 9.20; *White Paper 1985*, para 3.56.
 5 Pp. 437–440, above.
 6 Consultation Paper *Help with Board and Lodging Charges for People on Low Incomes* (1986). For details of the reform, see SI 1988/1445.
 7 See generally Consultation Paper *Deregulation of the Private Sector: Implications for Housing Benefit* (1987).

chapter 11[8] comprises a partner (married or unmarried) and/or dependent children under 19, provided in either case they are 'members of the same household' as the claimant.

Part 2   Entitlement to housing benefit

There are three basic conditions of entitlement for housing benefit: (i) the claimant must be liable to make payments in respect of a dwelling in Great Britain; (ii) he must occupy that dwelling as a home; and (iii) his capital and income must not exceed prescribed amounts. The discussion will be divided accordingly.

A Liability to make payments in respect of a dwelling

i Dwelling
'Dwelling' for the purposes of housing benefit means:

> any residential accommodation, whether or not consisting of the whole of part of a building and whether or not comprising separate or self-contained premises[9]

and which is located in Great Britain.[10] It follows that accommodation used for business purposes is excluded and the same would seem to apply to holiday accommodation.[11]

ii Payments
Broadly speaking, housing benefit may consist of a rent allowance or a rent rebate, payable to private sector and public sector tenants respectively and a rate rebate, payable to those, including owner-occupiers, liable for rates. 'Rent' is generously interpreted; it includes:[12]

— payments as a licensee; informal payments for the occupation of a dwelling; mooring charges for a houseboat or site payments for a caravan; rental purchase agreement payments; contributions by the resident of an almshouse to the relevant housing association or charity; and service charge payments (provided that occupation is conditional on them).

It also covers charges for board and lodging accommodation, if the boarder is not entitled to income support.[13] However, a boarder under 25 who has exhausted his entitlement to income support under the special rules applied to such persons, and described in chapter 11,[14] cannot claim housing benefit in respect of the relevant accommodation charge.[15] Other payments

---

8 Pp. 424–426, above.
9 SSA 1986, s.84(1).
10 Ibid, s.20(7)(a).
11 *Housing Benefit Guidance Manual* para 3.16.
12 SI 1987/1971, reg 10(1).
13 Ibid, reg 8(2)(a). Though a boarder in receipt of housing benefit who subsequently becomes entitled to income support will continue to receive the former for four weeks, with an adjustment made to his income support assessment: ibid, reg 8(3) and SI 1987/1967, Sch 5, para 3.
14 Pp 439–440, above.
15 SI 1987/1971, reg 8(2)(c).

excluded – e.g. those by co-owners, long leaseholders, Crown tenants, and charges for a local authority old persons' home or other 'Part III' residential accommodation[16] – are also designed to prevent overlap with income support and the same applies, of course, to mortgage payments and ground rent paid by owner-occupiers.[17]

'Rates' refers to the general domestic rates levied by local authorities.[18] Water rates are not included.[19]

iii Liability for payments

In most cases, the claimant will be the person who is legally liable to make the rent or rates payment in respect of the dwelling. However, the regulations also treat as 'liable':[20]

(1)   the partner of the person liable;
(2)   a person who has to make payments to continue to live in the home because the liable person has failed to do so (provided that the former was the latter's partner or the authority considers it reasonable to treat the former as liable);
(3)   a tenant whose landlord has waived liability as compensation for repair or redecoration work (to a maximum of eight weeks in respect of any one waiver);
(4)   a person who has actually met his liabilities before claiming.

Conversely, there are situations in which certain persons are treated as if they were not liable for the payments and cannot themselves, therefore, claim housing benefit. These rules are intended primarily to deal with cases of collusive agreement and abuse, thus where:[1]

(1)   the claimant resides with[2] the person to whom the payment is made, and that person is a close relative[3] of the claimant (or partner) or the agreement was not on a commercial basis;
(2)   the liability appears to the authority to have been created to take advantage of the housing benefit scheme (but not if at any time during the eight weeks before the relevant agreement the claimant was genuinely liable for payments for the same dwelling);
(3)   in the eight weeks before the creation of a joint tenancy, the claimant was a non-dependant of one of the other joint tenants (unless the authority is satisfied that the tenancy was not created to take advantage of the benefit scheme).

B   Occupation of dwelling as a home

It is only the housing costs of a single dwelling 'normally' occupied by the claimant (and his family) which are covered by housing benefit.[4] The

---

16   Ibid, reg 8(2)(b).
17   SSA 1986, s.20(8).
18   Ibid, s.84(1), incorporating the definition in the General Rating Act 1967.
19   They used to be treated as a separate item of housing costs under the supplementary benefit scheme but a similar provision has not been made in relation to income support: p.432, above.
20   SI 1987/1971, reg 6(1)–(2).
 1   Ibid, reg 7.
 2   I.e. lives under the same roof: see *R v Sutton London Borough Council, ex parte Dadson* 20 November 1987, Lexis transcript, a decision under the former housing benefit legislation.
 3   I.e. parent, parent-in-law, step-parent, step-son, step-daughter, brother, sister, or the spouse or partner of any of these; SI 1987/1971, reg 2(1).
 4   Ibid, reg 5(1).

exceptions to this and the rules governing absences from the home are almost identical to those applied to housing costs under the income support scheme and which are set out in chapter 11.[5]

C Capital and income

A major departure from the principles governing the former housing benefit scheme is that account is now taken of the capital resources of the claimant (and/or partner). Where the relevant capital (see Part 4) exceeds a prescribed threshold, housing benefit is not payable.[6] As explained above, there was originally a common threshold set for the three income-related benefits (£6,000) but the government subsequently raised that applicable to housing benefit to £8,000.[7] The change was given retrospective effect (to the date when the new scheme came into force), compensatory payments being made by the DHSS and not the local authorities.[8]

The claimant must also establish that his relevant income, which includes 'tariff income' assumed to be derived from capital between £3,000 and £8,000, does not exceed the 'applicable amount', a figure prescribed by regulations every year, or by no more than remains after applying the 'tapers'.[9] This condition can best be understood in the context of the method of calculating benefit and will therefore be explained in Part 3. The assessment of income is discussed in Part 4.

Part 3 Calculating entitlement

A General

Under the 1983 housing benefit scheme, a claimant in a 'certificated' case, that is, where he was in receipt of supplementary benefit, would receive, subject to some deductions, 100 per cent of eligible housing costs. In a 'standard case', where supplementary benefit was not payable, the starting point was 60 per cent of eligible rent and/or rates. This amount would be modified according to whether the claimant's gross income was more or less than a prescribed 'needs allowance'. If it was less than the allowance, an addition was made to the 60 per cent by the application of a percentage taper to the shortfall (e.g. in relation to rent, an addition of 25p for each £1 shortfall); if it was more than the allowance, a deduction was made from the 60 per cent by the application of an analogous taper to the excess (e.g. in relation to rent, a deduction of 29p for each £1 excess). Different tapers were used for claimants over pensionable age.

As has been explained, the major defect of this scheme was the use of two different means tests which resulted in different entitlements for similar households with similar income. The new scheme is designed to avoid these problems. Claimants are now entitled to what is known as the 'maximum housing benefit', which covers 100 per cent of eligible rent and 80 per cent of eligible rates, if their income from whatever source is equal to or less than the 'applicable amount'. Unlike the needs allowance, the equivalent threshold

5 P.433, above. The HB regulations allow benefit to be paid in one situation not covered by the IS regulations, where a family is so large that it is housed by a local authority in two separate dwellings: SI 1987/1971, reg 5(5) (c).
6 SSA 1986, s.22(6).
7 SI 1987/1971, reg 37, as amended.
8 SI 1988/458. For other transitional arrangements, see p.499, below.
9 SSA 1986, s.20(7)(c).

under the 1983 scheme, the applicable amount is, subject to some minor modifications, the same as that used for income support. If the claimant's income exceeds the applicable amount, a deduction is made from the maximum housing benefit, calculated by applying percentage tapers to the excess income.

B Maximum housing benefit

The claimant's maximum housing benefit is a weekly amount comprising 100 per cent of his eligible rent and 80 per cent of his eligible rates, less any deductions for non-dependants who share, or are deemed to share, these costs.[10]

i Eligible rent and rates

Prima facie, the eligible rent and rates are those payments for which the claimant must be liable to establish entitlement to housing benefit and which have been described in Part 2 of this chapter.[11] However, in many cases the whole of such payments will not be met, because either (a) they include components not covered by the scheme, or (b) the amount paid or the size of the accommodation in question is regarded as unreasonable.

a *Apportionment of payments*   Given that the maximum housing benefit covers only 80 per cent of eligible rates, it is important to separate the rate element from the rent element in any composite payment; the local authority will apportion any such payment accordingly.[12] As we have seen, only residential accommodation comes within the scheme. Hence, if rent and/or rates payments are for premises which consist partly of business accommodation, a proportion of the payments referrable to the latter will be deducted.[13] There will be analogous apportionments where more than one person is liable for the payments[14] and, in the case of rent, where the payments include ineligible service or fuel charges.[15] An ineligible service charge is one which does not have to be paid as a condition of occupying the dwelling or is excessive in relation to the service provided or is specified as ineligible in the regulations, notably charges in respect of:[16]

— meals; personal laundry services;[17] cleaning (other than of communal areas) except where no member of the household is able to do this; medical and nursing care; furniture and household equipment which will become the claimant's property; and other living expenses or leisure items 'not connected with the provision of adequate accommodation'.

Fuel charges are not eligible unless they are for communal areas.[18] Some fixed fuel costs were met in certificated cases under the 1983 scheme and there are,

10 SI 1987/1971, reg 61.
11 Pp. 491–492, above.
12 SI 1987/1971, reg 10(3)(a).
13 Ibid, regs 9(4) and 10(4).
14 Ibid, regs 9(5) and 10(5).
15 Ibid, reg 10(3) and Sch 1, para 2. There is a formula for deducting fuel charges where these cannot be easily identified: ibid, para 5(2).
16 Ibid, Sch 1, Part I.
17 Charges for laundry premises and equipment are eligible costs.
18 SI 1987/1971, Sch 1, para 4. For definition, see ibid, para 7.

therefore, relevant transitional provisions to protect housing benefit claimants also in receipt of income support.[19]

b *Restrictions on unreasonable rent or rates payments*   Eligible rent cannot exceed the 'fair' or 'reasonable' rent which has been registered by a rent officer (or rent assessment committee or rent tribunal) under the provisions of the Rent Act 1977.[20] Independently of this, the local authority[1] may reduce the eligible rent or rates 'by such amount as it considers appropriate having regard in particular to the cost of suitable alternative accommodation elsewhere' if it considers:

(a) that a claimant occupies a dwelling larger than is reasonably required by him and others who occupy that dwelling . . . having regard in particular to suitable alternative accommodation occupied by a household of the same size; or

(b) that the rates payable . . . are unreasonably high by comparison with the rates payable in respect of suitable alternative accommodation elsewhere; or

(c) that the rent payable . . . is unreasonably high by comparison with the rent payable in respect of suitable alternative accommodation elsewhere.[2]

A common feature of these provisions is the comparison with 'suitable alternative accommodation elsewhere'. In determining suitability, account must be taken of the nature of such accommodation and the facilities provided, in the light of the age and state of health of the claimant (and family).[3] Moreover, if the claimant enjoys security of tenure, other accommodation will be regarded as suitable only if it affords security which is reasonably equivalent.[4] Under the 1983 scheme, unreasonably high rents were judged by reference to the rent payable for equivalent accommodation in the same area.[5] The regulation quoted above is not so qualified; nevertheless the guidance manual issued by the DSS suggests that authorities should not make comparisons with areas where the costs of accommodation are different from those applying locally.[6]

These provisions confer a discretion on the local authorities; even where they consider that the accommodation is unreasonably large, or that the rent or rates are unreasonably high, they may decide not to make a deduction. And the regulations themselves provide relief in certain circumstances. No deduction can be made for the first 13 weeks of a claim if the authority is satisfied that the claimant (or another member of the household) was able to meet the eligible housing costs when he first moved into the premises;[7] though this does not apply if he was entitled to housing benefit at some time during a period of one year before the claim.[8] Further, no deduction can be made if the claimant or a member of the family is over 60 or incapable of work or if the family includes a child or young person (under 19), unless:

19 Ibid, para 5(4).
20 Ibid, reg 11(1).
1 If the Housing Bill 1988 is enacted in its present form, regulations may provide for determinations by the rent officer to be used for this purpose.
2 SI 1987/1971, reg 11(2).
3 Ibid, reg 11(6)(a).
4 Ibid.
5 SI 1982/1124, reg 17(1)(c).
6 *Housing Benefits Guidance Manual* para 4.66(ii).
7 SI 1987/1971, reg 11(4).
8 Ibid, reg 11(5).

suitable cheaper alternative accommodation is available and the authority considers that, taking into account the relevant factors, it is reasonable to expect the claimant to move from his present accommodation.[9]

It will be noted that, in contrast to the general rule, the emphasis here is on (1) the availability of alternative accommodation and (2) whether a move is reasonable. As regards (1), the authority must produce some evidence on availability but need not identify specific accommodation so available.[10] Also 'availability' should be interpreted in the broad sense of whether or not the claimant could in practice obtain the accommodation; this might not be the case, for example, if he is required to pay a large deposit.[11] For (2), the 'relevant factors' referred to are the effects of the move on the claimant's prospects of retaining employment and the education of any children in the household.[12]

An eligible rent will normally include any increases made to it but the authority has an equivalent power not to meet all or some of such an increase if it is considered unreasonably high or, when it takes place within a year of the last increase, 'unreasonable having regard to the length of time since that previous increase'.[13] Again, for the purposes of comparison, reference is made to the level of increases for suitable alternative accommodation. The DSS Guidance Manual suggests that account should also be taken of any improvements to the accommodation which may justify the increase.[14]

ii Deductions for non-dependants

The attribution of part of the housing costs to non-dependent members of the household has been an important feature of all the recent housing benefit schemes.[15] The principle that such persons should help to meet the costs if they are able to do so would seem to be unchallengeable[16] but the problem of determining how much they should contribute is a delicate one. If the amount of contribution is disproportionately high relative to the non-dependant's income and the quality of his accommodation, this will reduce the likelihood that contributions will in fact be paid and indeed may encourage the non-dependant to move to accommodation elsewhere.[17] Arguments such as these appear to have had some influence on government policy for the levels of deduction set under the new scheme are somewhat lower than those which previously applied. Nevertheless, criticism can be made of the fact that the assumed contributions are still not related in any way to the claimant's actual housing costs – the amount of deduction is the same whether the eligible rent is £50 or £30 per week.[18] Not only does this seem to be inequitable as between non-dependants whose accommodation differs significantly in quality; it also means that in some cases the notional contribution will bear little relation to the actual contribution.

a *Who are non-dependants?*

The categories of persons who are deemed to contribute to housing costs and for whom a deduction will be made are the

9 Ibid, reg 11(3).
10 Cf *R v Housing Benefit Review Board of South Herefordshire District Council, ex parte Smith* (1987) 19 HLR 217.
11 DHSS Circular HB (87)4, section 3, para 7.
12 SI 1987/1971, reg 11(6)(b).
13 Ibid, reg 12.
14 Para 4.78.
15 In 1985, it was estimated to apply to some 850,000 households in receipt of housing benefit: *Green Paper 1985* para 3.22.
16 Cf *Housing Benefit Review*, para 4.12 and SSAC Fourth Report (1985), para 4.47.
17 Ibid, para 4.52. See also SHAC *Housing Benefit: is this the promised end?* (1985) pp. 17–19.
18 Ibid, p.19.

subject of a definition common to income support and housing benefit – this has been examined in chapter 11.[19]

b *Cases exempt from deduction* The circumstances of either the claimant (or partner) or the non-dependant may justify exemption from the normal deductions. Thus, no deduction is made:[20]

(1) if the claimant (or partner) is blind or in receipt of attendance allowance; or
(2) if the non-dependant although residing with the claimant has his normal home elsewhere or (not being a boarder) is a YTS trainee or a full-time student.

Also if a deduction is made for one member of a couple, none is made for the partner.[1]

c *Deductions from rent rebates and allowances* No deduction is made if the non-dependant is single, under 25 and in receipt of income support (unless he is a boarder).[2] Two levels of deduction apply to other non-dependants: the higher rate to those in remunerative work (i.e. normally at least 24 hours per week)[3] and those who are boarders; the lower rate to those not engaged in such work, or whose earnings do not exceed a prescribed amount.[4]

d *Deductions from rate rebates* Rather anomalously, a uniform sum is deducted from rate rebates, whatever the resources of the non-dependant.[5] However, that sum is currently smaller than the lower of the two rent deductions.

C Applicable amount

As explained above, the 'poverty' thresholds in the income support and housing benefit schemes have been aligned. The applicable amount is therefore made up of the same structure of personal allowances and premiums applied to different client groups (e.g. pensioners, and the disabled) as that used to in relation to income support and which is fully discussed in chapter 11.[6] There are, nevertheless, two important differences between the schemes. First, and most obviously, housing costs are not included in the applicable amount for housing benefit purposes – those included in the income support system comprise costs (notably mortgage interest payments) which are not covered by housing benefit. Secondly, the premium applied to lone parents is somewhat higher under the housing benefit scheme. The explanation for the difference lies in the contrasting functions of the two schemes.[7] Income support is designed to meet the claimant's non-housing needs for food, clothing, fuel and so on; a lone parent would not expect to pay as much on these as a couple. However, to some degree at least, housing costs are independent of the size of the family and the housing needs of lone parents resemble those of a two-parent family,

19 P. 437, above.
20 SI 1987/1971, reg 63(6)–(7).
 1 Ibid, reg 63(3).
 2 Ibid, reg 63(8).
 3 See p.420, above.
 4 SI 1987/1971, reg 63(1).
 5 Ibid.
 6 Pp. 428–431, above.
 7 Cf SSAC Fourth Report (1985), para 4.21.

rather than those of a childless single person. The higher premium in the housing benefit scheme represents a compromise between the situation which would have prevailed if the income support level had been adopted and the more favourable treatment accorded to couples.[8]

D Deductions for income and the prescribed percentage tapers

The method devised for taking account of income, in relation to the applicable amount, is identical to that used for family credit[9] and like that scheme is concerned to preserve work incentives, particularly for persons with low incomes.[10] Until income reaches the level of the applicable amount, or if the claimant is entitled to income support, there is no withdrawal of housing benefit and the claimant is entitled to the appropriate maximum housing benefit (MHB) – subject to a deduction for non-dependants. When income exceeds the applicable amount, a prescribed percentage of the excess is deducted from MHB.[11] At present the prescribed percentages are 65 per cent, in calculating a rent rebate or allowance, and 20 per cent in relation to a rate rebate.[12]

E Amounts payable

On the basis of the principles discussed above, the methods of calculating the amount payable may now be restated, together with arithmetical examples, using 1988–89 figures.

i Income below applicable amount

If the claimant is in receipt of income support, or his relevant net income is less than the appropriate applicable amount, calculation is simple: he is paid the maximum housing benefit (MHB). Because rent rebates/allowances and rate rebates are governed by different tapers and deductions for non-dependants, it will generally be helpful to calculate them separately; thus MHB is the aggregate of the maximum rent rebate/allowance (MRN) and the maximum rate rebate (MRT). MRN is 100 per cent of eligible rents (ERN) less any appropriate deduction for non-dependants (NDD) and MRT is 80 per cent of eligible rates (ERT) less any deduction for non-dependants (NDD).

(1) C and Mrs C live with their child L, aged 10, and a non-dependant M, aged 20 and earning £55 per week. C pays weekly £40 rent and £10 rates and also receives income support.

$$\text{MRN} = \text{ERN} - \text{NDD}$$
$$= £40 - 8.20$$
$$= £31.80$$

$$\text{MRT} = (0.8 \times \text{ERT}) - \text{NDD}$$
$$= £8 - 3$$
$$- £5$$

$$\text{MHB} = \text{MRN} + \text{MRT}$$
$$= £36.80 = \text{amount payable.}$$

8 See Standing Committee B Debates on the Social Security Bill 1986, cols 692–695.
9 Pp. 480–484, above.
10 Cf *White Paper 1985* para 9.25.
11 SSA 1986, s.21(5).
12 SI 1987/1971, reg 62.

ii Income above applicable amount

If the claimant's relevant net income (I) exceeds the appropriate applicable amount (AA), he is paid as a *rent rebate/allowance*:

$$MRN - 0.65 \times (I - AA)$$

and as a *rate rebate*:

$$MRT - 0.2 \times (I - AA)$$

(2) As in (1) above, but C has net earnings of £58.45 per week and Mrs C receives child benefit for L (£7.25); thus I = £65.70. AA for the family is: personal allowance for C and Mrs C (£38.80) + personal allowance for L (£10.75) + family premium (£6.15) = £55.70. The rent rebate/allowance payable is:

$$£31.80 - 0.65 \times (£65.70 - 55.70) = £25.30$$

and the rate rebate payable is:

$$£5 - 0.2 \times (£65.70 - 55.70) = £3$$

F Duration of awards and transitional protection

Awards of the amounts, calculated in accordance with the rules described above, are payable for the 'benefit period' which is at the discretion of the local authority but which cannot exceed 60 weeks.[13] In exercising that discretion, the authority should take account of when a change of circumstances which will affect entitlement is likely to occur.[14] If, nevertheless, such a change of circumstances occurs during a benefit period, the amount can be modified or entitlement can be terminated, normally as from the date of the change, or in the week following.[15]

There are the usual set of regulations to provide transitional protection for those adversely affected by the reforms which were implemented in April 1988.[16] They do not, however, cover losses resulting from the 20 per cent reduction in rate rebates which, as we have seen,[17] was designed to increase the political accountability of local authorities.

Part 4 Assessment of income

A General

The income and capital of claimants already entitled to income support will have been assessed by the DSS in accordance with the rules prescribed for that system and, in their case, no further assessment is required. In other cases, the assessment is carried out by the local authority under the rules contained in the Housing Benefit (General) Regulations.[18] These have been largely harmonized with the equivalent income support rules and, since a detailed account of the latter has been provided in chapter 11,[19] we shall concentrate here on general principles and on those rules which are peculiar to housing benefit.

13 Ibid, reg 66.
14 Ibid, reg 66(2).
15 Ibid, regs 67–68.
16 SI 1987/1972.
17 P.490, above.
18 SI 1987/1971, Part VI, as amended.
19 Pp. 440–450, above.

B   Periods of assessment

Since housing benefit is awarded on a weekly basis, an estimate must be made of average weekly income for the whole of the benefit period.[20]

i   Employed earners

In the case of employed earners, the average is derived from a period of five weeks immediately preceding the benefit period, if the claimant is paid weekly, or a period of two months, if he is paid monthly.[1] If the earnings fluctuate, the authority may have regard to another period, if that will enable the determination to be made more accurately; and if they change *during* the benefit period, the new average will be applied for the remainder of that period.[2] If the claimant has been employed for less than the standard period of five weeks (or two months), assessment is made on any earnings paid, provided that these are likely to be representative of his future earnings.[3]

ii   Self-employed earners

The authority has a discretion in selecting the period for assessing earnings from self-employment but it must not exceed 52 weeks.[4] The DSS Guidance Manual suggests that the last year's trading account should normally be selected, though a shorter, and more recent, period (e.g. of three months) may be preferable if that is more representative of the claimant's trading position.[5]

iii   Other income

Income from other social security benefits is attributed to, and averaged over, the period for which such benefits are payable.[6] The period of assessment for all other income is at the discretion of the authority, but must not exceed 52 weeks.[7]

B   Assessment of earnings and other income

The general principle is that all income of the claimant (and partner), including 'tariff' income assumed to be derived from capital between £3,000 and £8,000, is taken into account. This is, however, subject to several important qualifications and special rules apply to the income (and capital) of children and young persons.

i   Earnings from employment

The earnings relevant for housing benefit purposes are now net earnings, that is, after the deduction of income tax, social security contributions and half of any contributions to an occupational or personal pension scheme.[8] The

---

20 SI 1987/1971, reg 21. For the 'benefit period', see p.499, above.
  1 SI 1987/1971, reg 22(1).
  2 Ibid, reg 22(1)(b), (3).
  3 Ibid, reg 22(2).
  4 Ibid, reg 23(1).
  5 *Housing Benefit Guidance Manual* para 7.36.
  6 SI 1987/1971, reg 24(2).
  7 Ibid, reg 24(1).
  8 Ibid, reg 29(3).

definition of 'earnings' is the same as that used for income support,[9] except that it covers statutory sick pay and maternity pay (these are treated as 'other income' under the income support scheme).

As with income support,[10] there are provisions which allow for the first £5 (and in some cases the first £15) of earnings to be disregarded.[11] However, there is one important difference between the two schemes: if one member of a couple is employed, the housing benefit disregard is normally £10;[12] in relation to income support, both have to be employed for this amount to be disregarded.

ii Earnings from self-employment

As regards the self-employed, the relevant amount of earnings is net profits, that is, the gross receipts from the employment during the period of assessment, less (a) expenses 'wholly and exclusively defrayed in that period for the purposes of that employment', and (b) income tax, social security contributions and half of pension contributions.[13] This is subject to the same disregards as those described in relation to employed earners.[14]

iii Tariff income from capital

As we saw in Part 2, housing benefit is not payable where the relevant capital (on which, see chapter 11[15]) of the claimant (and/or partner) exceeds a prescribed amount – currently £8,000. Capital below that amount but above a lower threshold (currently £3,000) is treated as producing a weekly 'tariff' income: this is £1 for each £250, or part thereof.[16] Any income actually derived from capital of £8,000 or less is ignored as *income* but is nevertheless treated as, and added to, the claimant's capital.[17]

iv Other income of claimant or partner

In general, all other income is taken into account.[18] There are, however, a large number of items which are disregarded.[19] The list broadly corresponds to that described in relation to income support;[20] in addition, the following items are disregarded:[1]

(1) parental contributions made by the claimant to a student grant and contributions to the maintenance of a student under 25 who is not in receipt of a standard grant;
(2) maintenance paid by the claimant to a former partner or for children who are not members of his household;

9 Pp. 442–443, above. If the case-law on the previous scheme is to be followed, this does not include strike pay, which should be treated as 'other income': *R v Housing Benefits Review Board of the London Borough of Ealing, ex parte Saville* (1986) 18 HLR 349.
10 Pp. 442–443, above.
11 SI 1987/1971, Sch 3, paras 1–11.
12 Ibid, para 5. The £15 disregard will apply in appropriate cases.
13 SI 1987/1971, reg 31(3).
14 Ibid, reg 31(2).
15 Pp. 447–449, above.
16 SI 1987/1971, reg 45, as amended.
17 Ibid, reg 40(4).
18 Ibid, reg 33(1).
19 Ibid, Sch 4, as amended.
20 Pp. 445–447, above.
 1 SI 1987/1971, Sch 4, paras 17–19, 27.

(3) payments made to the claimant by a child, young person or non-dependant.

v Income of children and young persons

As with the other income-related benefits, the general rule is that capital belonging to a child or young person (hereafter, for the sake of convenience, 'child') is not aggregated with the claimant's capital,[2] but if the child's capital exceeds £3,000 the claimant's applicable amount cannot include a personal allowance in respect of him.[3] Since, in the latter case, the child's needs are effectively ignored, it follows that his income is also disregarded.[4] Even where an allowance for the child is included in the applicable amount, any earnings received while still at school are not taken into account.[5] If the child leaves school and gets a job (but is still counted as the claimant's dependant because the terminal date for child benefit purposes has not been reached[6]) the net earnings, subject to the appropriate disregard, will be added to the claimant's income, as will any other income of a child which is not disregarded.[7] However, if the aggregate of such earnings and income exceeds the personal allowance for the child (plus the disabled child premium, if applicable), the excess is ignored.[8]

Part 5   Special cases

A Hospital patients

Periods spent in hospital do not normally affect liability for housing costs unless they are prolonged; on the other hand, if the hospital in question provides free treatment and accommodation, the patient's other needs may be reduced. The rules have been designed accordingly.

Entitlement to housing benefit ceases after the claimant has been in hospital for more than 52 weeks, because he is then not treated as occupying his dwelling as a home.[9] Of course, if he has a partner who continues to live in the dwelling, who is liable for the housing costs and who satisfies the other conditions, she will be entitled to benefit. Benefit is not affected if the period spent in hospital is six weeks or less, though for this purpose (and for the other rules described in this section), two or more periods in hospital not separated by intervals exceeding 28 days are aggregated to form one period.[10]

If the claimant or partner is in hospital for a period between six and 52 weeks, the applicable amount, which represents the assumed income needs other than housing costs, is modified.[11] The rules are identical to those used for income support and described in Chapter 11.[12] However, in contrast to that system, no modifications are made for children in hospital, unless the

2 Ibid, reg 39.
3 Ibid, reg 16(b).
4 Ibid, reg 36(2).
5 Ibid, Sch 3, para 13.
6 Cf p.394 above.
7 SI 1987/1971, reg 19(1) and Sch 3, para 14.
8 Ibid, reg 36(1).
9 Ibid, reg 5(8).
10 Ibid, reg 18(3).
11 Ibid, reg 18(1).
12 P.465, above.

stay exceeds 52 weeks – after such a period of absence, the child ceases to be a member of the claimant's household and no personal allowance for him is applicable.[13]

B Students

i General

Claims made by students to housing benefit under the 1983 system created major administrative difficulties. Such claims could be made as many as six times per year – at the beginning and end of each vacation – and the students' circumstances might change frequently. The Housing Benefit Review team envisaged the eventual exclusion of students from the scheme but, recognising that this would require a major restructuring of the grant system, they recommended a compromise solution, that entitlement should be reduced to the period of the summer vacation.[14] The government endorsed the general approach of the Review team but opted for a somewhat modified short-term compromise, which was brought into force in September 1986, alongside analogous modifications to the rules governing students' entitlement to unemployment benefit and supplementary benefit. Housing benefit could no longer be paid during the academic year for accommodation owned by an educational establishment, nor, during the summer vacation, for periods of absence from that or other accommodation exceeding a week. These reforms have been incorporated into the new scheme. Notwithstanding the Review team's view that the rules should be simplified,[15] they remain complex, partly because they interlock with provision for housing costs in the student grant. Here we provide a summary of the principal rules.[16]

ii Students subject to special rules

For the purpose of these rules, a 'student' is 'a person who is attending a course of study at an educational establishment'.[17] The latter phrase is not defined but the DSS Guidance Manual suggests that it includes private institutions, as well as state schools, colleges and universities.[18] A 'course of study' covers any full-time, part-time or sandwich course, irrespective of whether a grant is paid for attendance; this should be distinguished from a 'period of study' which, for most students, runs from the beginning of the first term to the end of the final term, and thus includes the Christmas and Easter vacations but not the summer vacation.[19] In the case of students (e.g. postgraduates and clinical medical students) who receive a grant for the whole of the academic year, it covers this period. With some exceptions, the special rules also apply to a claimant whose partner is a student.[20]

---

13 SI 1987/1971, reg 15(2).
14 *Housing Benefit Review* paras 4.6–4.9.
15 Ibid, paras 1.14–1.15.
16 For a more detailed account, see Ward and Zebedee *Guide to Housing Benefit* (1988–89) ch 17.
17 SI 1987/1971, reg 46. An overseas student may claim housing benefit if he is entitled to income support or if, under immigration law, he has leave to stay in Britain which is not conditional on him making no recourse to public funds: ibid, reg 49.
18 *Housing Benefit Guidance Manual* para 12.01.
19 SI 1987/1971, reg 46.
20 Ibid, reg 52.

iii Modifications to general rules of entitlement

Outside the 'period of study' full-time[1] students are not entitled to housing benefit for any week of absence.[2] However, this does not affect a claim made by the student's partner, nor does it apply if the absence was for treatment in hospital or if the main purpose of the occupation *during* the period of study was not to facilitate attendance at the course – in other words, there were family or other reasons for occupying the dwelling.[3] Students, whether full-time or part-time, cannot generally count as eligible housing costs payments made to their educational establishment for accommodation during the period of study.[4] Rent payable to a third party is not affected unless the arrangement was made by the educational establishment in order to attract housing benefit payments.[5]

iv Modifications to rules governing income and amounts payable

The amount of housing benefit payable to a student who (or whose partner) is in receipt of income support remains unaffected by the special housing benefit regulations.[6] In other cases modifications are made to the rules governing eligible rent and the assessment of income.

a *Reduction of eligible rent* During the period of study, the eligible rent of a full-time student is normally reduced by an amount which correlates with the 'housing' element in the standard maintenance grant.[7] To avoid hardship in some cases, the regulations provide that no deduction should be made where the student is a lone parent *or* has a partner who is not a full-time student *or* the applicable amount includes a disability premium[8] *and* the student's relevant income for housing benefit purposes is less than the aggregate of his applicable amount and the amount of the deduction.[9]

b *Income* Broadly speaking, the special rules used to assess a student's income follow those adopted under the income support system and which have been described in chapter 11.[10] Subject to some important disregards, maintenance grants (including parental contributions, whether paid or not) are treated as income for the period they are intended to cover,[11] and there are complex provisions for taking into account covenant income received from parents.[12]

---

1 Apart from the statement that it includes sandwich courses, this is not defined in the regulations. In cases of doubt, local authorities are expected to consult the relevant educational institution: *Housing Benefit Guidance Manual* para 12.2.
2 SI 1987/1971, reg 48.
3 E.g. because the student was living there before the course began or needs the accommodation to house children: cf *Housing Benefit Guidance Manual* paras 12.10–12.12.
4 SI 1987/1971, reg 50(1). This does not apply if the educational establishment itself pays rent to a third party, unless the premises are held under a long tenancy or the third party was an educational authority providing the accommodation in exercise of its functions as such an authority: ibid, reg 50(2).
5 Ibid, reg 50(3).
6 Ibid, reg 51(2), Sch 3, para 10, Sch 4, para 4, and Sch 5, para 5.
7 Ibid, reg 51(1): a larger deduction is made for students attending courses in London.
8 Cf. p.429, above.
9 SI 1987/1971, reg 51(2)(c).
10 P.468, above.
11 SI 1987/1971, reg 53.
12 Ibid, regs 54–56.

Part 6   Discretion and controls of abuse and expenditure

In this Part we discuss the background to, and rules governing, the discretionary features in the housing benefit system, the anti-abuse provisions and the subsidy arrangements which enable central government to control expenditure.

A Discretion

i General

As we have already seen, the incorporation of local discretion into the national housing benefit scheme was a significant feature of its development; indeed, the ability to tailor the national scheme to local needs was part of the original rationale for conferring administrative responsibility on the local authorities. Under the 1983 arrangements, the calculation of benefit for standard cases (i.e. where there was no concurrent entitlement to supplementary benefit) formulated by legislation for the national model housing benefit scheme could be modified in three different ways. First, under a so-called 'local scheme', benefit for all, or particular groups of, claimants could be increased provided that expenditure on such a scheme did not exceed 10 per cent of the total cost of benefit payments for standard cases. These powers were widely exercised to increase payments to war pensioners but, on occasion, were also used by some authorities to mitigate the cuts in housing benefit imposed by central government.[13] The local authority would have to bear the costs of any local scheme but assistance was available through the Rate Support Grant. Secondly, local authorities might apply to the Secretary of State for permission to establish a 'high rent scheme' by showing that rents in its area were 30 per cent or more above the national average. If rents in both the private and public sector fell into this category, an authority was under a duty to make such application. Thirdly, there was power to confer a higher benefit on individual claimants who were subject to 'exceptional circumstances', a phrase which was left undefined and which therefore involved a very broad discretion.

The changes in the method of housing benefit calculation, in particular, the fact that maximum housing benefit comprises 100 per cent of eligible rent, obviated the need to preserve 'high rent schemes'. The Review team recommended the abolition of the power to make 'local schemes' on the grounds that these were inconsistent with the overriding aim of simplification and unification, they created inequities between householders in different areas and they hindered national initiatives to promote or administer the scheme more effectively.[14] While endorsing this view, the government was prepared to meet the concern expressed by, among others, the Social Security Advisory Committee,[15] that this would result in significant losses to war pensioners[16] and the power to provide special treatment for this group has been explicitly conferred on local authorities by the 1986 legislation. There was a broad consensus of opinion that the power to grant extra benefit to individual claimants in exceptional circumstances should be retained and, under the new scheme, this covers all cases, including those where the claimant is also entitled to income support.

13 McGurk and Raynsford *Guide to Housing Benefit* (1987–88 edn) p.66.
14 *Housing Benefit Review* para 4.21.
15 Fourth Report (1985), para 4.56.
16 *White Paper 1985* para 3.63.

ii Local schemes: disregard of war pensions
Section 28(6) of the Social Security Act 1986 which honours the government's undertaking to maintain a local discretion in relation to war pensioners is not, however, so narrowly confined: it confers a power on authorities to modify any part of the housing benefit scheme:

(a) so as to provide for disregarding, in determining a person's income . . . the whole or part of any war disablement pension or war widow's pension payable to that person;
(b) to such extent in other respects as may be prescribed.

Nothing has so far been prescribed under (b). While the government has apparently no plans to extend the discretion by this means, the provision does create the possibility for this to be done at some future date without the need for primary legislation. Section 28(6)(a) enables local authorities to provide for a more generous disregard of war pensions than the £5 stipulated in the national scheme.[17] Although the subsection requires that a discretionary modification should be adopted by a resolution of the authority, the condition is waived if the authority operated a local scheme containing such modification before April 1988.[18]

iii Discretionary increases for individuals in exceptional circumstances
The most important remaining discretionary power is conferred by the regulations:[19]

[t]he appropriate authority may, if a claimant's circumstances are exceptional, increase the weekly amount of any housing benefit . . . but only where such an increase is in respect of costs which are eligible housing costs.

As with the 1983 scheme, there is no guidance on when circumstances are to be considered 'exceptional'. While hardship to the claimant and his family is an obvious factor, the Court of Appeal ruled, in interpreting an equivalent provision in the supplementary benefit scheme, that this was not the only test of 'exceptional need'.[20] The DSS Guidance Manual emphasises the importance of having regard to the possibility of obtaining assistance from other sources, notably from the social fund.[1]

The proviso in the regulation indicates that the increase cannot enable the claimant to receive by way of total housing benefit a payment which exceeds his eligible housing costs. In consequence, the maximum increase comprises: 20 per cent of eligible rates (since, following the 1986 reform, only 80 per cent of these are normally covered), plus any deficit from the meeting of eligible costs resulting from the operation of the tapers, plus any deduction made for a non-dependant. It might be thought that this presents an invitation to local authorities to counter the spirit of the 1986 reform and regularly use the power to make up the 20 per cent loss in rates' coverage. However, such an approach might well constitute an unlawful exercise of the discretion which requires a finding of exceptional circumstances in *individual* cases.[2]

17 SI 1987/1971, Sch 4, para 14.
18 SI 1987/1972, reg 10.
19 SI 1987/1971, reg 69(8).
20 *Supplementary Benefits Officer v Howell*, reported as Appendix to *R(SB) 21/84*.
 1 *Housing Benefit Guidance Manual* paras 2.16–2.23.
 2 A DHSS Circular Letter of 2 October 1987 sent to local authorities supports this view.

There are two other factors which serve to constrain the award of discretionary increases. First, as we shall see, central government subsidies cannot be used to finance their payment. Secondly, there is a prescribed limit to what can be spent on the increases:[3] at present this is set at 0.1 per cent of total housing benefit expenditure.[4]

B Abuse

While fraud and other forms of abuse are problems common to most social security benefits,[5] their incidence in relation to housing benefit has been a matter of particular concern to the government, because of the decentralised administration of the system. The control policy of local authorities varies considerably[6] and, as we have seen, it has not been unknown for some authorities themselves to exploit the system by, for example, attempting to use the subsidy arrangements to increase their own income.[7]

As we have also seen,[8] the scheme contains provisions for dealing with collusive arrangements designed to attract benefit, such as a tenancy created between the claimant and a close relative. In relation to tenants and landlords, the Review team and the Green Paper identified two other risks of abuse which might result from the introduction of total coverage of rent for claimants entitled to income support (and others with equivalent low incomes).[9] First, the insulation of households from increases in rent might encourage what is known as the 'up-marketing' effect, when claimants move to more expensive accommodation on the assumption that the additional housing costs will be met by the scheme.[10] Secondly, landlords might respond by setting higher rents in the knowledge that their tenants would be unlikely to object, given the protection offered by the scheme. These problems were potentially controllable through the powers to reduce or withhold benefit where the accommodation was unreasonably large or expensive[11] and to refer cases of unreasonable rent to the rent officer under the provisions of the Rent Act 1977. Nevertheless, the conclusion was reached that local authorities had not used the existing powers sufficiently to check abuse, primarily because there were inadequate incentives on them to do so.[12] The government therefore sought to impose additional safeguards, first, by means of the subsidy arrangements (see below) and, secondly, by provision in the Housing Bill 1988 for the direct involvement of rent officers in the determination of eligible rents.[13]

3 SSA 1986, s.28(9).
4 SI 1988/471.
5 Cf pp. 000-000 below.
6 Loveland [1987] JSWL 228 and see *Housing Benefit Review* para 5.44 for proposals to enhance uniformity of prosecution policy between authorities and to establish a closer liaison with the DHSS machinery used in relation to other social security benefits.
7 P.489, above, *Housing Benefit Review* para 3.10 and *Green Paper 1985* vol 2, para 3.64.
8 P.492, above.
9 *Housing Benefit Review* paras 3.9–3.15; *Green Paper 1985* vol 2, paras 3.61–3.67.
10 As the Review team itself acknowledged (loc cit), the risk might be exaggerated, since 'up-marketing' was unlikely to occur in the public sector where the policy was to match the needs of tenants to suitable accommodation and, in the private sector, there was often little choice in accommodation – the cost of moving also acted as a disincentive.
11 P.495, above.
12 *Green Paper 1985* vol 2, para 3.64.
13 P.495, n.1, above.

C Subsidy arrangements

i General

Under the 1983 scheme, a central government subsidy was paid to local authorities for 100.6 per cent of housing benefit expenditure on 'certificated cases'[14] and 90 per cent of expenditure on 'standard cases'. Where permission to run a 'high rent' scheme was issued, this also qualified for a subsidy. 'Local schemes' were not so eligible though expenditure on them, as well as on the 10 per cent deficit from 'standard case' costs, counted as grant related expenditure for Rate Support Grant purposes. Approximately 60 per cent of administrative costs were directly subsidised.

The concern of the government to create incentives for local authorities to monitor and control housing benefit costs[15] has led to some important changes in these arrangements. While the subsidy on ordinary housing benefit payments remains at about the level operating under the 1983 scheme,[16] a new formula has been adopted for meeting administrative costs and substantial penalties are imposed in relation to expenditure on unreasonably high rents or increases.

ii Subsidies for benefit payments

The Social Security Act 1986 confers powers on the Secretary of State to pay subsidies to local authorities, calculated by reference to a subsidy order.[17] This is subject to an important complementary power which enables him to deduct 'any amount which [he] considers it unreasonable to meet'.[18] If the Housing Bill 1988 is enacted in its present form, the Secretary of State will be able to exercise his discretion as to what is 'unreasonable' in relation to private sector rents by reference to determinations made by rent officers. Currently, the subsidy is normally 97 per cent of benefit payments,[19] though this does not cover any discretionary additions for war pensioners or individuals in 'exceptional circumstances'.

iii Subsidies for administrative costs

A sum of £25 million has been made available to meet the costs of implementing the new scheme.[20] As regards regular administrative costs, in the short-term the subsidy is based primarily on a proportion (currently 60 per cent) of recent actual benefit expenditure.[1] This will, however, gradually be replaced by a new 'workload' formula which takes account, inter alia, of the number of claims processed.

iv Penalties

To encourage control over excessive expenditure, the subsidy is reduced in certain situations. Most importantly, there is a subsidy of only 25 per cent for

14 The additional 0.6 per cent was to provide compensation for additional benefit paid to some claimants who, as a result of the 1983 reforms, lost entitlement to supplementary benefit and thus were treated as 'standard cases' for which the local authority received a subsidy of only 90 per cent: McGurk and Raynsford *Guide to Housing Benefit* (1987–88 edn) p.110.
15 *Green Paper 1985* vol 2, para 3.65.
16 The government had initially proposed that it would cover only 80 per cent of benefit expenditure: ibid, para 3.66.
17 S.30(1)–(2).
18 SSA 1986, s.30(2)(b).
19 *Housing Benefit Guidance Manual* para 19.05.
20 SI 1987/1910.
 1 *Housing Benefit Guidance Manual* para 19.37

any disproportionate increase in rent rebate expenditure,[2] that is, where the average increase in council tenants' rents covered by housing benefit exceeds that of other council tenants' rents within the local authority's area. This is, of course, to prevent authorities using the subsidy system to generate more income. An equivalent reduction is made for expenditure on unreasonably high rent or unreasonable rent increases in the private sector.[3] The comparator here is based on the average registered rent (or increase in such rent) in the relevant registration area of the authority.

The penalties incurred in relation to overpayments mean that a subsidy of only 25 per cent is paid if the mistake has been made by the local authority or the claimant; however, understandably, there is no reduction in the subsidy if the overpayment is due to a DSS error.[4] Finally, so as to discourage local authorities from accumulating arrears of liability, only a 25 per cent subsidy is payable on backdated awards.[5]

Part 7 Direct payment to the landlord

The amounts awarded by way of rent and rate rebates are deducted from the claimant's liability to the local authority. A rent allowance is normally paid to the claimant but, as with income support,[6] there are prescribed circumstances in which the local authority may, or must, withhold benefit and make payment directly to the third-party landlord.

The authority *must* pay the rent allowance directly to the landlord where the DSS is, under equivalent powers, paying some part of the claimant's (or partner's) income support to that person.[7] The same applies where arrears of eight or more weeks' rent have accumulated, unless the authority decides 'that it is in the overriding interest of the claimant' that this should not be done[8] – if such a decision is made, the authority will nevertheless withhold payment.[9] As has been pointed out,[10] the withholding of payment in such circumstances might actually be in the interests of the tenant if he has a dispute with his landlord and payment of rent would undermine his bargaining position.[11]

There is a discretion to make direct payment to the landlord in three other situations, where:[12] the claimant requests or consents to such payment; it is determined to be 'in the interest of the claimant and his family'; the claimant has moved and there are arrears of rent.

2 Ibid, para 19.16.
3 Ibid, para 19.22.
4 Ibid, paras 19.09–19.13.
5 Ibid, para 19.07.
6 Pp. 469–470, above.
7 SI 1987/1971, reg 93(a).
8 Ibid, reg 93(b).
9 Ibid, reg 95(1).
10 Ward and Zebedee *Guide to Housing Benefit* (1988–89 edn) p.145.
11 See, e.g., *Berg v Markhill* (1985) 17 HLR 455.
12 SI 1987/1971, reg 94.

Chapter 14

The social fund

Part 1   Introduction

A   General[1]

The origins of the social fund were explored in chapter 11.[2] As is explained there, some of the most forthright criticisms of the supplementary benefit scheme made in the Fowler Reviews were directed against the system of single payments, designed to meet one-off needs. The growth in these payments since 1980[3] had added substantially to social security expenditure,[4] and had increased pressure on the appeals system[5] and on the processing of claims. The highly detailed rules were little understood by claimants and led to undue legalism. Similar criticisms were raised against the system of urgent needs payments which provided emergency relief for some claimants, including those otherwise not entitled to supplementary benefit.[6] In the government's view, the high degree of 'fine-tuning' required for single (and urgent needs) payments obscured and hindered the main purpose of supplementary benefit, which was the provision of regular weekly income.[7] While there would always be some people who would face particular difficulties and special needs which could not be met by normal weekly payments, a new system should be devised to cope with them: through employing specialist officers to make discretionary decisions with the minimum of formality, and coordinating with social services, health authorities and voluntary agencies, this would offer greater flexibility in responding to individual financial problems and adapting to changes in need.[8] Concern that the system should operate quickly and effectively on the basis of knowledge and experience of local circumstances, combined with a desire to avoid legalism, led to a further proposal that the formal system of external adjudication and review used for other areas of social security should not apply.[9] Finally, in the absence of

1 See, generally: Berthoud 8 Policy Studies 8; Family Policy Studies *The Social Fund: A Briefing* (1986); Bradshaw in Brenton and Ungerson (eds) *Yearbook of Social Policy 1986–87* (1987).
2 Pp. 415–417, above.
3 From 0.8 million in 1981 to almost 3 million in 1984: *Green Paper 1985* vol 2, para 2.26.
4 Their cost rose from £44 million in 1981 to over £200 million in 1984: ibid.
5 In 1985, 21 per cent of appeals to SSATs involved single payment claims: ibid, para 2.63.
6 Ibid, para 2.67, and see p.450, above.
7 *Green Paper 1985* vol 1, para 9.3; *White Paper 1985* paras 4.4–4.5.
8 Ibid, paras 4.9–4.11.
9 *Green Paper 1985* vol 1, para 2.110; *White Paper 1985* para 4.50.

detailed rules to help control expenditure, there should be a fixed budget so that spending might be monitored and decisions taken on priorities within available resources.[10] Financial constraint would be facilitated by the fact that apart from the meeting of maternity and funeral expenses and grants to support community care, payments would normally take the form of repayable loans[11] – under the supplementary benefit system, this method of assistance had normally been used only for urgent need cases.[12]

Not surprisingly, the proposals generated a considerable amount of hostile criticism.[13] The breadth of discretion would make it very uncertain what could be claimed and what evidence of need would be required; and it would be difficult to avoid diversity of treatment between local offices, particularly when account was taken of cash limits. The very existence of the latter was considered to be inconsistent with general principles of social welfare, and it was unclear what would happen if a local office were to reach its limit with a number of claims still outstanding. The system of loans would create budgetting difficulties and also hardship if the level of income support, from which repayment would typically be made, was insufficiently high. And the aim of coordinating with other agencies might be unrealistic, given the lack of enthusiasm manifested by organisations representing social workers and others.[14] 'Official' bodies, such as the Social Security Advisory Committee[15] and the Council on Tribunals[16] protested vigorously against the plan to dispense with the independent review of decisions.[17]

Prior to, and during, the passage of the Social Security Bill 1986, the government attempted to meet some of these criticisms. A draft Social Fund Manual was published, indicating in detail how the system would work.[18] There would be a system of internal review by social fund inspectors who would be appointed by an independent social fund Commissioner. The function of the latter would be in no way equivalent to that of the Social Security Commissioners since it would be confined to general guidance of decision-making and the training of inspectors – it would not be involved with individual decisions.[19] Subsequently, the operation of the budgetary system was clarified:[20] it would be based partly on previous expenditure on single payments in the area and partly on other estimates of need; and information on each office's budget would be made publicly available. Further, there would be a reserve fund to meet exceptional circumstances, such as a local emergency.

The legislative framework for the social fund was contained in the Social

10 Ibid, para 4.38.
11 Ibid, para 4.25.
12 See the second edition of this book, p.497.
13 In addition to the references in n.1 above, see e.g: CPAG *Burying Beveridge* (1985); Disability Alliance *Reform of Social Security: Response* (1985); Labour Research Department *Social Insecurity* (1985); Land and Ward *Women Won't Benefit* (1986).
14 Cf Bateman 17 Social Work Today (No 11), pp. 17–18; Stewart and Stewart *Boundary Changes: Social Work and Social Security* (1986).
15 Fourth Report (1985), p.83.
16 *Social Security: Abolition of Independent Appeals under the proposed Social Fund* (1986, Cmnd 9722).
17 See also Smith 135 NLJ 947.
18 Cf Lister and Lakhani *A Great Retreat in Fairness: a critique of the draft social fund manual* (1987).
19 'The Commissioner is no more than fig-leaf, inserted into the Bill at the last minute to present the inspectors as in some sense independent and thereby head off demands for a proper independent right of appeal': Social Security Consortium *Of Little Benefit* (1986) p.14.
20 Written Answer 122 HC Official Report (6th series), col 443.

Security Act 1986. Its least controversial element, the provisions to meet maternity and funeral expenses which, as we shall see, base entitlement on non-discretionary regulations and for which traditional social security adjudication is preserved, was brought into force in April 1987; the remaining parts became operative in April 1988. The Social Security Act 1988 conferred powers to add cold weather payments to the non-discretionary provisions.

B The structure of the social fund

It is important at the outset to draw a distinction between two sharply contrasting parts of the social fund. The non-discretionary regulation-based part, which governs maternity, funeral and cold weather payments, follows the pattern of provision for single payments under the supplementary benefit system. It confers entitlement on those who satisfy the conditions laid down in the detailed regulations and decisions are made by the social security adjudicating authorities (adjudication officer, social security appeal tribunals and Social Security Commissioners).[1] As regards the discretionary part of the social fund, on the other hand, decisions whether to make an award and, if so how much, are made by social fund officers (SFOs)[2] and are subject only to an internal administrative review by the same, or another, SFO and, following a further application by the claimant, a social fund inspector.[3] Apart from the prospect of any such review, there are three principal constraints on the SFO's exercise of discretion:[4] first, the legislation specifies certain factors to which regard must be had; secondly, determinations must be in accordance with any general directions issued by the Secretary of State; and thirdly they must take account of any general guidance issued by him or by an SFO nominated by him to provide general guidance for a particular area. In other words, *directions* of the Secretary of State are legally binding on SFOs (and inspectors) but though *guidance* should assist in making most decisions, it is not intended to provide a conclusive solution for every contingency; 'ultimately [SFOs] must use their own judgment in the application of discretion to each case, according to the particular circumstances'.[5] The Secretary of State's directions and guidance are both contained in the Social Fund Manual (hereafter referred to as the Manual), which is revised from time to time and published by HMSO.

As regards the type of payment from the discretionary fund, the legislation indicates only that an SFO may determine that an award is to be repayable.[6] The Secretary of State has directed that non-repayable payments are to be made only by way of community care grants, that is, to help people re-establish themselves in the community, to avoid institutional care, to ease exceptional pressure on families, or to reimburse certain travel expenses.[7] The directions provide for two types of loan: to meet important intermittent expenses for which it may be difficult to budget ('budgeting loans'); and to meet expenses arising from an emergency or disaster ('crisis loans').[8]

1 SSA 1986, s.52(6), and see pp. 570–576 and 580–584, below.
2 SSA 1986, ss. 32(2), (8)–(9), and 33.
3 Ibid, s.34. The possibility of an application to the courts for judicial review is considered at p.587, below.
4 SSA 1986, ss. 33(9)–(10), as amended.
5 *Social Fund Manual* para 1027.
6 SSA 1986, s.32(4).
7 Directive 4.
8 Directives 2–3.

C The social fund budget

i General

Payments into the social fund are determined by the Secretary of State with the approval of the Treasury from money voted by Parliament.[9] For the financial year beginning in April 1988, the discretionary fund was allocated £203 million, of which £140 million was for loans and £60 million for community care grants and the remainder for non-discretionary awards.[10] In addition, there is a contingency fund, which is carried over from one year to the next, to allow for totally unexpected increases in expenditure.[11] As yet the social fund has not formally been cash limited, though the intention is to do this when expenditure levels have become clearer.[12]

ii Local office budgets

Allocations from the annual national budget are made for, respectively, community care grants and loans, in relation to each local office.[13] These may be reviewed only if there have been unforeseen or unforeseeable demands, such as those resulting from a local flood.[14] In total, the allocations will be greater than the voted national budget, as they are expressed as 'gross amounts', which allow for the repayment of loans. The overriding principle of local budgetary management stated in the Manual is that 'the total cost of payments made by [a local office] in a financial year must not exceed its budget allocations for that financial year'.[15] Since this is guidance, rather than a direction, strictly speaking it is not mandatory and the legislation only requires that an SFO in determining individual claims must 'have regard to' the allocations made by the Secretary of State to the local office.[16] The same applies to the complementary proposition that payments 'should approach the year's budget as closely as possible without exceeding it'.[17] As no separate allocation is made for budgeting loans and crisis loans, it is the SFO's responsibility, in processing claims, to determine priority as between them (crisis loans should normally take priority), to maintain consistency with other decisions made in the local office in the same year, as well, of course, as to ensure that the claim can be met from the budget.[18]

Part 2   The discretionary social fund

A General

The discretionary social fund covers in principle all needs except those for which special (and non-discretionary) provision is made, namely maternity

---

9 SSA 1986, ss. 32(6) and 85(1)(b).
10 Written Answer 126 HC Official Report (6th series), cols 762–764. This figure must be compared with £346 million spent on single payments in 1985–86: 127 HC Official Report (6th series), col 1202.
11 *Social Fund Manual* Annex 2, para 4.
12 Ibid, para 9.
13 SSA 1986, s.32(8A)–(8C). For the 1988–89 allocations, see Written Answer 124 HC Official Report (6th series), cols 764–771.
14 *Social Fund Manual* Annex 2, para 13.
15 *Social Fund Manual* para 2016.
16 SSA 1986, s.33(9)(e), as amended.
17 *Social Fund Manual* para 2017.
18 Ibid, paras 2018, 2021.

expenses, funeral expenses, and cold weather heating expenses.[19] In determining whether to make a discretionary award and the amount or value of any such award, the SFO is under a legislative duty to have regard 'to all the circumstances of the case and, in particular-

(a) the nature, extent and urgency of the need;
(b) the existence of resources for which the need may be met;
(c) the possibility that some other person or body may wholly or partly meet it;
(d) where the payment is repayable, the likelihood of repayment and the time within which repayment is likely;
(e) any relevant allocation under section 32(8A) to (8D)'.[20]

The reference in (e) is to allocations made by the Secretary of State to local offices and thus effectively means that cash limits directly impinge on the exercise of discretion. It is not made clear whose 'resources' are relevant for the purposes of (b), but since the fund itself is covered by (e), and third parties by (c), the expression should be taken as referring to the income and capital of the applicant and (subject to some exceptions) of a partner or children. Consideration (d), which has been reinforced by a legally binding direction that 'no budgeting loan may be awarded in excess of the amount which the applicant is likely to be able to repay',[1] has been much criticised[2] since it appears to lead to the paradoxical result that some requests for loans will be rejected on the ground that the applicants are too poor to repay them; systems of public assistance were originally designed to help people such as these.

As we have seen, in making determinations SFOs are also bound to implement the directions made by the Secretary of State.[3] At the time of writing, 39 directions have been issued and they are contained in an Annex to the Manual. Directions 13, 24, and 30 deal with claims and payments and have been effectively superseded by the Social Fund (Applications) Regulations[4] – these are discussed in chapter 15.[5] Directions 31 to 39 are concerned with the system of reviewing SFO decisions which is considered in chapter 16.[6] The remainder specify the needs which may be met by discretionary social fund payments, the conditions which must be satisfied by applicants and the maximum and minimum awards which may be made. The payments are categorised into budgeting loans (Section B), crisis loans (Section C) and community care grants (Section E). Discretion, subject to guidance rather than directions, governs the repayment and rescheduling of loans (Section D).

B Budgeting loans

i General
The purpose of a budgeting loan, as defined in a direction, is 'to assist an eligible person to meet important intermittent expenses . . . for which it may

19 SSA 1986, s.32(2)(b).
20 Ibid, s.33(9), as amended.
 1 Direction 11, as amended. Under the original version, the maximum loan was to be determined in accordance with what the applicant was '*likely*' to repay.
 2 E.g. Lister and Lakhani *A Great Retreat in Fairness: A Critique of the Draft Social Fund Manual* (1987).
 3 SSA 1986, s.33(10).
 4 SI 1988/524.
 5 P.548, below.
 6 Pp. 585–586, below.

be difficult to budget'.[7] In other words, though help is to be provided for some one-off needs which used to be the subject of single payment awards under the supplementary benefit system, it is now assumed that these are in principle capable of being met from the applicant's normal weekly income support. The additional assistance is, therefore, intended to help the applicant manage his budget more effectively and hence takes the form of a loan, rather than a grant.[8]

ii Persons eligible

Under Direction 8, as amended, an applicant is eligible for a budgeting loan if, at the date of the award, he is in receipt of income support and he (or his partner) has received that benefit[9] throughout the last 26 weeks (a single gap of entitlement of up to two weeks is ignored). Payments cannot, however, be made during periods when the applicant (or partner) is disqualified from unemployment benefit because of a trade dispute,[10] or would have been so disqualified if otherwise entitled to that benefit.

iii Items and services excluded

Once a loan has been refused, a second application in relation to the same item or service made within 26 weeks of the refusal will not be entertained unless there has been a change in the applicant's circumstances.[11] Further, Direction 12 contains a long list of items and services for which a budgeting loan cannot be made:

— needs arising abroad, educational or training needs (including clothes and tools), distinctive school uniform or sports clothes or equipment, travelling expenses to or from school, school meals, expenses in connection with court proceedings, removal charges where the applicant is permanently rehoused and for which assistance is normally available from another agency (e.g. local authority), domestic assistance or respite care (i.e. when someone caring for another needs a break or a disabled or elderly person requires some relief from household duties),[12] repairs to public sector housing, medical items or services, work-related expenses, debts to government departments,[13] investments, the cost of mains fuel consumption, housing costs (apart from rent in advance to a private landlord and intermittent housing costs not met by the housing benefit and income support systems).

Many of these items and services are excluded because relief or assistance is provided by another agency, a consideration which ought to influence the interpretation of the Direction.[14] Thus, for example, the Manual suggests that the exclusion of medical items and services should not necessarily extend to some items which though they are needed for medical reasons are nevertheless in everyday use (and may not be obtainable through the NHS or the social services), such as cotton sheets for someone with an allergy.[15] The

7 Direction 2. Any award must include a determination that it is repayable: Direction 3.
8 *Social Fund Manual* para 3001.
9 Entitlement to supplementary benefit counts for this purpose.
10 Cf pp. 110–120, above.
11 Direction 7. The ability to satisfy one of the conditions of eligibility may constitute such a change.
12 *Social Fund Manual* para 3099.
13 This includes arrears on social security contributions and income tax liabilities: ibid, para 3109.
14 The Manual advises SFOs to refer the applicant to such other agency: para 3110.
15 Ibid, para 3105.

regulations governing the award of single payments under the supplementary benefit system contained a similar list of exclusions.[16] There were a number of reported Commissioners' decisions interpreting those provisions[17] but, given the aim of 'delegalising' this area of social security law, it is unlikely that they will have much impact on the application of the Direction.

iv Determining priorities

An applicant who is eligible for a budgetary loan in relation to an item or service which is not excluded must still persuade the SFO to exercise discretion in making a payment. As we have seen, there are a number of factors of which he must take account and, in weighing these, he will naturally form judgments on the relative priority to be accorded to different claims. To assist him in this task, the Manual provides a non-exhaustive list of items which normally may be considered to be of high, medium and low priority, respectively.[18] High priority should be given to applications the refusal of which 'could cause hardship, or damage or risk the health or safety of the applicant or the family'.[19] The Manual indicates in the light of its suggested criterion that the following items will normally be of high priority:

— essential items of furniture and household equipment, bedclothes, essential home repairs and maintenance (for owner occupiers), removal charges (where the move is essential and provided that it is not an excluded item under Direction 12), fuel meter installation and reconnection charges, non-mains fuels costs (e.g. oil).

In contrast, suggested medium priority items are:

— non-essential items of furniture and household equipment, redecoration, HP and other debts, clothing.

Low priority should be given, for example, to removal charges or rent in advance, where the move is not essential, and to leisure items.

Of course, it would be wrong to apply these suggestions without taking account of the applicant's particular circumstances which may justify a higher than normal ranking of priority.[20] Such might be the case where a single pensioner living alone requests a loan to acquire a television[1] or a family with young children or a disabled person needs a washing machine.

v Amount

Discretion also largely determines the amount that should be awarded. There is unexceptionable guidance to the effect that the cost of the item in question must be reasonable; the Manual suggests that in practice the claimant's estimate should normally be accepted.[2] More controversially, as we have seen, the SFO is not permitted to award a sum which exceeds what the applicant is likely to be able to repay[3] and, in general, is expected to take

---

16 SI 1981/1528.
17 See Mesher *CPAG's Supplementary Benefit and Family Income Supplement: The Legislation* (4th edn) pp. 283–285.
18 *Social Fund Manual* paras 3017–3020.
19 Ibid, para 3017.
20 Ibid, para 3021.
 1 This was an excluded item under the SB single payments regulations: SI 1981/1528, reg 6(2)(h).
 2 *Social Fund Manual* para 3143.
 3 Direction 11.

account of the total debt owed by the applicant to the social fund as well as any obligations to third parties.[4] Under Direction 10, the maximum that can be awarded is the difference between £1,000 and any sum already repayable to the social fund by the applicant and his partner; for reasons of adminis- trative cost, it also imposes a minimum limit of £30 per application (though this can be for more than one item[5]).

The SFO is bound to set off against the amount of a budgeting loan any capital possessed by the applicant (or partner) exceeding £500.[6] Guidance in the Manual suggests that the income support rules for assessing capital[7] should be used for this purpose.[8]

C Crisis loans

i General

Broadly speaking, crisis loans replace the provision under supplementary benefit law for urgent cases payments.[9] As under that system, it is intended to help those who have encountered a financial crisis but who are not necessarily dependent on public funds for their basic needs and thus may not be in receipt of income support.

Direction 3 specifies that the purpose of the loan is 'to assist an eligible person to meet expenses . . . in an emergency, or as a consequence of a disaster'. Further, the provision of such assistance must be:

> the only means by which serious damage or serious risk to the health or safety of that person, or to a member of his family, may be prevented.

The one exception to this latter condition is where the applicant's need is for rent in advance. A crisis loan may be available for this purpose if the applicant is leaving institutional or residential care and receives a community care grant to enable him to return to the community.[10]

The concepts of 'emergency', 'disaster' and 'serious damage or serious risk to health or safety' are familiar from the urgent cases regulations governing supplementary benefit payments[11] and were the subject of an important case-law, emanating from the Social Security Commissioners.[12] How- ever, as is evident from the Manual, the intention is that these expressions should not be given a precise objective meaning; rather, they should be inter- preted broadly to take account of the applicant's personal circum- stances, 'because individual people may be affected differently by the same situation'.[13]

The reference to 'expenses' in Direction 3 implies that assistance is to be provided for immediate short-term needs and not longer-term financial consequences. Guidance in the Manual suggests that such needs will generally

---

4 *Social Fund Manual* paras 3143–3147.
5 Ibid, para 3141.
6 Direction 9.
7 Pp. 447–449, above.
8 Paras 3138–3140.
9 See the second edition of this book, pp. 493–497. The provision for urgent cases in the income support system is to cover the basic needs of three categories of claimant, not otherwise entitled to the weekly benefit: pp. 450–452, above.
10 Direction 3(b) and on the community care grant, see p.522, below.
11 SI 1981/1529.
12 See Mesher, n.17, above, pp. 385–425.
13 *Social Fund Manual* para 4003.

be for a specific item or service or for immediate living expenses for a short period not exceeding 14 days.[14]

ii Persons eligible

In contrast to budgeting loans, crisis loans are, in general, available to persons not in receipt of income support. However, just as that latter system denies or reduces benefit for certain groups of individuals whose needs are met in whole or in part by others, so the conditions of eligibility for crisis loans have been formulated to exclude or limit claims from those who will not have to cope with financial crises. Thus, an applicant must be aged 16 or over[15] and Direction 15 specifies that crisis loans cannot be paid to:

(1) a hospital in-patient, or someone in 'Part III' accommodation, a nursing home or a residential care home, unless it is planned that the person will be discharged within the following two weeks;
(2) a prisoner or a person lawfully detained;
(3) a member of a religious order who is fully maintained by that order;
(4) a person engaged in full-time 'non-advanced' education who for that reason cannot claim income support.[16]

Further, unless the claim is made during the long vacation or he is in receipt of income support, a full-time student is only eligible for a loan 'to alleviate the consequences of a disaster'[17] and so the existence of an 'emergency' will not suffice. The same applies to persons from abroad not entitled to income support[18] and those involved in a trade dispute, though in the latter case the loan may extend to items required for cooking or space heating.[19]

iii Resources

Given the availability of crisis loans to some persons not entitled to income support, some means-test is evidently required. Direction 14 imposes a condition that the applicant must be 'without sufficient resources to meet the immediate short-term needs of himself and his family[20] at the date when the application is determined'. The Secretary of State has not, however, issued a direction on how resources are to be assessed. Rather, by way of guidance, he suggests that regard should be had to all income and capital of the family, except those resources which the SFO considers reasonable to disregard in the circumstances.[1] This vague advice is nevertheless complemented by a list of items which might normally be disregarded. These are:[2]

— housing benefit; other social fund payments; the value of a home which is occupied by the applicant or will be so occupied within six months; the value of premises occupied by a relative or former partner; the value of a reversionary interest; personal possessions; business assets owned by the applicant; sums received because of damage to, or loss of, the home or

---

14 Ibid, para 4002.
15 Direction 14.
16 Cf p.421, above.
17 Direction 16.
18 Cf p.418, above. Where an asylum seeker or refugee is entitled to IS, the Manual suggests that particular attention should be given to clothing needs: para 4080.
19 Direction 17.
20 'Family' has the meaning attributed to it by SSA 1986, s.20(11) for the purpose of the income-related benefits: see pp. 424–426, above.
 1 *Social Fund Manual* paras 4051, 4055.
 2 Ibid, para 4055.

personal possessions and other sums acquired for essential repairs or improvements to the home; payments under section 1 of the Child Care Act 1980 (unless made for the same need as the crisis loan application); payments from the MacFarlane Trust or the Independent Living Fund.

An applicant with substantial capital assets which are not immediately realisable will normally be expected to raise money against them.[3] But it is also suggested that resources available on credit should only be taken into account if the applicant is not in receipt of income support and is likely to be able to afford the required repayments.[4]

As with other social fund payments, regard must be had to 'the possibility that some other person or body may wholly or partly meet' the need.[5] But guidance in the Manual indicates that there should be a realistic expectation that such assistance would be available when the applicant needs it; moreover, 'SFOs should not routinely refer applicants to employers, relatives or close friends unless there is reason to believe that an offer of help will be forthcoming'.[6]

iv Situations and needs

As has been observed above, the policy inherent in the arrangements for the social fund is to avoid 'legalistic' definitions and so the SFO has a very broad discretion in determining what constitutes an 'emergency' or the more serious phenomenon of a 'disaster'. The Manual stresses that he must consider the individual circumstances of each case[7] and guidance is limited to a listing of examples of situations where a crisis loan would normally be appropriate.[8]

— A fire or flood resulting in significant damage, loss or destruction will typically constitute a 'disaster'. Examples of 'emergencies' are: being stranded away from home without access to means of support; loss of money; the inability to meet living expenses from normal income because of misfortune or mismanagement;[9] hardship due to the payment of benefit in arrears or employers imposing compulsory unpaid holidays.

In accordance with Direction 23, a crisis loan cannot be made for certain items. These are the same as those excluded by Direction 12 from a budgeting loan[10] except that: a crisis loan *may* be made for board and lodging charges and the cost of mains fuel consumption but may *not* be made for television or radio costs, telephone charges, mobility needs, holidays, and the costs of running a motor vehicle (except in relation to an application for emergency travelling expenses). The rule on repeat applications is identical to that imposed in relation to budgetary loans.[11]

v Determining priorities

Although the SFO is bound to have regard to budgetary considerations before authorising payment of a crisis loan, he will not normally have a

3 Ibid, para 4162.
4 Ibid, para 4053.
5 SSA 1986, s.33(9)(c).
6 *Social Fund Manual* para 4058.
7 Ibid, para 4151.
8 Ibid, paras 4153–4161.
9 It is suggested that normally payment should cover only two weeks' expenses: ibid, para 4159.
10 P.515, above.
11 P.515, above.

problem in determining a priority for it. This is because, as indicated in the Manual, the majority of crisis loans will have highest priority.[12]

vi Amount

There is some overlap with the principles and practice governing the amount of a budgetary loan. There are directions to the effect that no award may exceed what the applicant is likely to be able to repay or the difference between any sum already repayable to the social fund and £1,000,[13] and guidance that the amount requested must be reasonable for the item or service in question.[14] In general, it will be the smallest sum necessary to tide the applicant over the period of need or remove the crisis.[15]

There are a number of more specific rules. Direction 21 stipulates that the maximum to be awarded for an item or service is, where the item can be repaired, the cost of repair (or cost of replacement, if that is lower) or the reasonable cost of purchasing the item (or service).[16] As regards loans for living expenses, there is a standard maximum amount of 75 per cent of the appropriate personal allowance applicable under the income support system for the applicant and partner, plus for each child, of whatever age, 100 per cent of the income support personal allowance applicable to children under 11.[17] Special maxima are imposed in two types of case the treatment of which is influenced by policy considerations applying to income support claims arising in similar circumstances. First, those deemed to be 'voluntarily unemployed' for the purposes of an income support claim cannot be paid more than the applicable amount which would apply to them in relation to such a claim.[18] Secondly, the maximum which may be awarded to those seeking assistance with board and lodging charges is the amount of that charge (but not exceeding the limit imposed under the income support system), plus 75 per cent of the appropriate income support rate of personal expenses applicable to such claimants, if meals are not included in the board and lodging charge.[19] Also, if the applicant is a young boarder whose income support does not include reimbursement of the charge because of the special time limits applicable to such persons,[20] it cannot be covered by a crisis loan and the maximum award will be that applicable to the voluntarily unemployed.[1]

D Repayment and rescheduling of loans

i General

An award of a budgeting or crisis loan must include a determination by the SFO that it is repayable,[2] and the terms and conditions of repayment must be

12 *Social Fund Manual* para 4022.
13 Directions 21–22.
14 *Social Fund Manual* para 4105.
15 Ibid, para 4092.
16 Direction 21.
17 Direction 18. See pp. 427–428, above, for discussion of income support personal allowances.
18 Direction 20. See pp. 452–455, above for the relevant income support rules.
19 Direction 19. See pp. 437–440, above, for relevant provisions under the income support system.
20 Cf p.439, above.
 1 Direction 19.
 2 Direction 5.

notified to the applicant before the award is paid.[3] These terms and conditions are a matter for decision by a local officer (LO), acting on behalf of the Secretary of State, and not an SFO.[4] The Secretary of State has a statutory power to recover the award from the person to, or for the benefit of whom, the payment was made, that person's partner, and someone liable to maintain[5] that person.[6] Guidance in the Manual suggests that repayment should normally be made by the applicant and it is only if he cannot do this that resort should be had to another party;[7] recovery from a partner should in any event cease if the couple have permanently separated.[8] There is a concomitant power to make appropriate deductions from prescribed social security benefits.[9] These include income support, family credit, the contributory benefits, industrial injury benefits, war pensions, severe disablement allowance and invalid care allowance, but not housing benefit, child benefit, attendance allowance or mobility allowance.[10] Deductions will normally be made from income support if that is being paid to the relevant person.[11]

ii Terms of repayment

The discretion exercisable by the LO covers the period and rate of repayment. As regards the former, the guidance suggests that loans should be repaid in the shortest possible time, though naturally this will depend on the circumstances of the person liable to repay (for the sake of convenience hereafter referred to as the applicant).[12] The maximum period should not normally exceed 78 weeks, though exceptionally this may be extended to 104 weeks for additional or rescheduled loans. In the typical case where deduction is made from the applicant's income support, the rate of repayment should take account of the applicable amount (excluding any housing costs) assessed for that benefit,[13] any continuing commitments at the time of application and the possibility of further commitments during the repayment period.[14] Three normal rates of repayment are suggested accordingly:[15] if there are no existing commitments, 15 per cent of the relevant applicable amount (excluding housing costs);[16] if there are existing commitments, 10 per cent or 5 per cent of that amount, depending on the size of the commitments. Exceptionally, the rate may be reduced below 5 per cent if, for example, high deductions are being made from the benefit for fuel and amenity charges and

3 SSA 1986, s.33(4A).

4 *Social Fund Manual* para 5000.

5 As determined by SSA 1986, s.26(3)–(6), thus a 'liable relative' or a sponsor, on which see pp. 460–464, above.

6 SSA 1986, s.33(7).

7 *Social Fund Manual*, para 5102. Only exceptionally should repayment be made from more than one income: para 5103.

8 Ibid, para 5252.

9 SSA 1986, s.33(6).

10 SI 1988/35.

11 *Social Fund Manual* para 5102.

12 Ibid, para 5002.

13 Cf pp. 427–431, above.

14 *Social Fund Manual* para 5005. If the applicant is not in receipt of income support, equivalent rates are suggested but these may be set at a higher level if the applicant agrees and the LO is satisfied that he can budget accordingly: ibid, para 5031.

15 Ibid, paras 5021–5025.

16 If the applicant is in a residential care or nursing home, it is that proportion of the personal allowance granted to such a person and, if a boarder, of the personal allowance plus any amount allowed for meals (cf pp. 438 and 466, above).

if the applicable is accorded high priority.[17] Conversely, the rate may be varied up to 'an absolute maximum' of 25 per cent where the applicant is already repaying one loan at 15 per cent and seeks a further loan of high priority.[18] However, guidance in the Manual suggests that normally applicants should not make repayments on more than one loan at any one time, and that repayment of a second loan should be deferred until the first is paid off.[19]

iii Rescheduling loans

Rescheduling a loan is possible if the applicant can show that the loan might be repaid more quickly or that hardship could result if repayment continues at the original rate because, for example, other deductions from benefit are increased to a high level.[20]

E Community care grants

i General

Community care grants (CCGs) constitute a novel feature of the social fund. Their origin lies in the health and social services policy developed by Conservative governments in the last decade to encourage people to enter or remain in the community rather than be reliant on institutional care.[1] The Green Paper of 1985 contained the observation that:

> [a]t present, the social security system can either be seen as an automatic paymaster, as in the case of residential care, or as a barrier to the most sensible mix of cash and services. What we should be aiming for is a more effective and responsive system which can bring social security resources and those of local authority personal social services and health authorities together in a cost-effective way to meet social and financial needs.[2]

The idea of linking a cash grant to health and social service provision was welcomed by the Social Security Advisory Committee, though they cautioned that 'it would require a great deal of careful development'.[3] Other commentators expressed concern at proposed changes to the boundaries between the social security system and the traditional domain of the social work professions, particularly when there had been inadequate consultation of the latter.[4]

Direction 4 specifies that a CCG may be awarded 'to promote community care:

> (a) by assisting an eligible person with expenses . . . where such assistance will –
>   (i) help that person, or a member of his family, to re-establish himself in the community following a stay in institutional or residential care; or
>   (ii) help that person, or a member of his family, to remain in the community rather than enter institutional or residential care; or
>   (iii) ease exceptional pressure on that person and his family; or

17 *Social Fund Manual* para 5026.
18 Ibid, para 5027.
19 Ibid, para 5033.
20 Ibid, paras 5051, 5053.
 1 DHSS *Care in the Community: A consultative document on moving resources for care in England* (1981).
 2 Vol 1, para 9.9.
 3 Fourth Report (1985), paras 3.61–3.62.
 4 Stewart and Stewart *Boundary Changes: Social Work and Social Security* (1986).

(b) by assisting an eligible person, or a member of his family, with expenses of travel within the United Kingdom in order to . . . visit someone who is ill . . . attend a relative's funeral . . . ease a domestic crisis . . . visit a child who is with the other parent pending a custody decision . . . or . . . move to suitable accommodation.

ii Persons eligible

The applicant must be in receipt of income support at the date of application, though if it is to help him re-establish himself in the community, under Direction 4(a)(i), it is sufficient if it is planned that he will be discharged from the relevant institution within six weeks and in the opinion of the SFO is likely to receive income support on such discharge.[5] Persons involved in a trade dispute can only apply for a CCG under Direction 4(b) and then only in limited circumstances.[6]

iii Situations and expenses for which CCGs may be awarded

The general guidance in the Manual on how the SFO should exercise discretion in relation to the situations and expenses for which CCGs may be paid has three dimensions.[7] First, CCGs should be accommodated to the national policy on community care which is to enable vulnerable groups of the population to maintain themselves in the community, and retain links with family, friends and local life. Secondly, account should be taken of local factors, for which purpose coordination with local social services departments is important. To this end, the SFO is advised to maintain close links with the local authority social services.[8] Little information is, however, given on how the work of the two agencies should be coordinated, presumably because at the time the relevant sections of the Manual were drafted the relevant arrangements had still to be made. Thirdly, particular attention should be given to the needs of certain 'client groups', notably the elderly, the disabled, victims of alcohol or drug abuse, ex-prisoners and others requiring resettlement, families under stress and young people leaving local authority care. Within this broad framework, the Manual provides specific advice in some detail. It is proposed here to consider this in outline, under the heads specified in Direction 4.

a *Re-establishment in the community* To qualify under this head, the applicant must normally have been in an institution for at least three months and intend, on leaving it, to set up home in the community and be responsible for rent and furniture – payment may, however, also be made if the intention is to live permanently with friends or relatives.[9] Priority is to be given to persons who are elderly, disabled, or the victims of alcohol or drug abuse and, where the institution is a prison or youth centre, young persons unable to live with their parents.[10] Those who move house to look after persons discharged from an institution may also be paid a CCG.[11]

---

5 Direction 25. Applicants will normally be asked to sign a form agreeing to repay the grant if it subsequently transpires that they are not entitled to income support: cf Direction 6.
6 For details, see Direction 26.
7 *Social Fund Manual* paras 6023–6026.
8 Ibid, para 6453.
9 Ibid, para 6204.
10 Ibid, paras 6251, 6302.
11 Ibid, para 6321.

An eligible applicant leaving an institution is typically paid a 'start up grant' to cover items of furniture and household equipment, though the amount will be reduced if accommodation is shared or the items are already available.[12] In addition, awards may be made for clothing, removal and travel expenses, and connection charges.[13]

b *Remaining in the community*   Applications under this head will typically be for expenses incurred in moving to more suitable accommodation or in making improvements to existing living conditions. In either case, the SFO must be satisfied that the decision was made to avoid institutional or residential care but the Manual provides no guidance on what sort of evidence should be required for this purpose. Priority is again to be accorded to the elderly and disabled. Grants made to those moving cover items similar to those for which payment is made to applicants setting up home after leaving an institution, though obviously account will be taken of furniture and household equipment which can be transferred from the previous home.[14] As regards improvements to the existing home, CCGs may provide help with minor structural repairs and maintenance, internal redecoration, reconnection of fuel supply laundry equipment, furniture and clothing.[15] Awards are in no sense automatic; rather, in relation to each item the applicant has to establish some causal connection between the expenditure and the risk of resort to institutional care.

c *Exceptional pressure on families*   'Families' here means either couples or single parents with at least one child.[16] The Manual draws a distinction between 'stress' which is regarded as insufficient by itself to justify a CCG and 'exceptional pressure' which arises when there has been (1) a breakdown of an established family relationship, (2) a deterioration in the home, making it unsuitable for the family to live in, or (3) the beginning or continuing existence of persistent disability or chronic sickness.[17] As regards (1), the need may arise not only when a couple split up but also if (and when) they are reconciled,[18] though it is only in the first of these situations that the applicant will normally obtain a 'start up grant'. If the family needs to move and the housing authority is not under a duty to rehouse it, a grant for removal expenses, essential items of furniture and connection charges may be made under (2).[19] For the purposes of (3), priority is to be given to applications from families with a child who is mentally handicapped or mentally ill and whose condition gives rise to behavioural problems.[20] It follows that in such a case the CCG can cover the repair or replacement of items damaged as a result of such a problem.

d *Travelling expenses*   While not obviously related directly to community care, help with travelling expenses is conveniently accommodated in this part of the social fund arrangements, since it would be impracticable to treat the

12 Ibid, paras 6210–6211.
13 Ibid, paras 6214–6222.
14 Ibid, para 6345.
15 Ibid, paras 6376–6392.
16 Ibid, para 6452.
17 Ibid, para 6451. See further on these, paras 6461–6463, 6496, 6501.
18 Ibid, para 6481.
19 Ibid, paras 6496–6498.
20 Ibid, para 6501.

sums awarded as loans.[1] As we have seen, in accordance with Direction 4, CCGs are only available to enable the applicant to 'visit someone who is ill . . . attend a relative's funeral . . . ease a domestic crisis . . . visit a child who is with the other parent pending a custody decision . . . or . . . move to suitable accommodation'. The guidance in the Manual elaborates on some of these situations. Thus, the person visited should normally be a close relative and in hospital or institutional care or, if at home, critically ill.[2] An example of a journey rendered necessary by the consequences of a family crisis would be where a friend or close relative is looking after a dependent child.[3] A grant for a 'move to suitable accommodation' might be made not only where it was necessary to avoid institutional or residential care but also to help a single, homeless person in receipt of income support.[4]

e *Excluded items* The list of items for which, in accordance with Direction 29, a CCG may not be awarded is identical to that excluded from budgetary loans.[5] In addition, it may not cover telephone charges nor any expenses which a local authority has a statutory duty to meet.

iv Amount

The amount to be awarded is largely a matter of discretion, particularly in relation to what is reasonable in the circumstances. In this context, of course, account need not be taken of what the applicant will be able to repay. But the £500 capital rule which governs the award of budgeting loans[6] applies also to CCGs. There is a minimum limit of £30 which applies to all applications other than those for travel expenses.[7] There are suggested maxima specified in the Manual for 'start up grants', clothing grants and minor structural repairs and an indication that no CCG should exceed £500.[8]

F Money advice

Although under no statutory duty to do so, SFOs are expected by the Secretary of State to offer money advice in the course of carrying out their functions.[9] It seems, however, that such advice will normally be given only to those claiming, or in receipt of, income support and that other applicants will be referred to a Citizens' Advice Bureau or a social services department.[10] The advice facility is considered to be particularly important where there is evidence of severe and persistent financial problems, for example, where there has been a request for a further loan in addition to a loan which is near the maximum that can be awarded, or for the rescheduling of an existing loan. In giving the advice, SFOs are assisted by very detailed guidance in the Manual.[11] The latter itself makes it clear that none of this should be regarded

---

1 On the equivalent provision under the supplementary benefit system, see Rowell and Wilton *The Law of Supplementary Benefits* (1982) pp. 125–126.
2 *Social Fund Manual* paras 6551–6553, 6561.
3 Ibid, para 6576.
4 Ibid, paras 6601–6602.
5 P.515, above.
6 P.517, above.
7 Direction 28.
8 *Social Fund Manual* para 6103 and Annex 4.
9 Ibid, para 9004.
10 Ibid, para 9014.
11 Ibid, Part 9.

as 'guidance' which SFOs are, by statute, bound to take into account when determining applications for social fund payments.[12]

Part 3   The non-discretionary social fund

A   General

The provisions governing the award of maternity expenses, funeral expenses and cold weather payments contrast markedly with the arrangements for other parts of the social fund. Regulations made in statutory instruments[13] confer entitlement on claimants who satisfy the prescribed conditions and discretion is reduced to a minimum. Further, claims are determined by adjudication officers, not SFOs, and appeals against such decisions may be made to the social security appeal tribunals and the Social Security Commissioners. The reasons for preserving a more 'legalistic' approach are partly historical and partly pragmatic. Until 1987, non means-tested grants for maternity and funeral expenses used to be widely available to those able to satisfy lenient contribution conditions. As was explained in Chapter 6,[14] the value of these grants declined substantially in the 1960s and 1970s and could be used to reimburse only a small proportion of the actual expenses incurred. In consequence, those with inadequate resources had to claim single payments under the supplementary benefit scheme. The administrative cost of paying the grants was very high. As part of its targetting policy, the government therefore resolved to abolish them and to make available more generous assistance to low income families under the social fund arrangements. The fact that the replaced benefits had not been means-tested, combined with the certainty of the event giving rise to the need and concern that, at least in the case of death, intrusive questioning would be insensitive,[15] no doubt influenced the decision that, unlike other social fund payments, they should not be made the subject of discretionary determinations.[16] The relevant provisions of the Social Security Act 1986 were brought into force in April 1987, one year in advance of the rest of the social fund.

Assistance with heating costs during spells of particularly cold weather falls into another category. Since severe climatic conditions cannot be planned for, it is impracticable to expect that the ordinary weekly amounts of the income-related benefits should cover these costs.[17] Moreover, since the same increased need affects all recipients of those benefits experiencing the conditions it is clearly inappropriate to require them to provide evidence of need in the way usually required for discretionary decisions. Cold weather payments were added to the non-discretionary social fund by the Social Security Act 1988 – at the time of writing, regulations governing entitlement to these have not yet been issued.

12 Ibid, para 9002.
13 SI 1987/481, as amended.
14 Pp. 228 and 234, above.
15 Cf SSAC Fourth Report (1985), para 3.79.
16 The proposals to this effect in the *White Paper 1985* paras 4.18 and 4.20, should be contrasted with those in the *Green Paper 1985* vol 1, para 10.6.
17 See the SSAC Report on the Draft Supplementary Benefit (Single Payments) Amendment Regulations 1986 (Cm 18).

B Maternity expenses

i Conditions of entitlement

The regulations lay down three principal conditions of entitlement:[18]

(1) at the date of claim, the claimant (or partner) is receiving income support or family credit; *and*
(2) the claimant (or a member of the claimant's family) is pregnant or has given birth to a child or the claimant (or partner) has adopted a child who is not older than 12 months at the date of claim;[19] *and*
(3) the claim is made within a period beginning 11 weeks before the expected week of confinement and ending three months after the actual date of confinement[20] (or the date of the adoption order).[1]

Condition (2) enables a maternity payment to be claimed for a member of the family other than the claimant (or partner) but 'family' for this purpose is defined to include only children under 16, and not young persons aged 16 to 19.[2] It follows that a pregnant member of a family above 16 is only able to receive the payment if she is entitled to income support or family credit in her own right.[3] It should also be noted that a single woman under 25 expecting her first child and in receipt of the state maternity allowance[4] is unlikely to be eligible for the social fund payment before confinement, because receipt of the allowance will normally take her above the income threshold for income support. However, once the baby is born, her applicable amount for income support purposes will include both a family premium and a lone parent premium[5] which should be sufficient for her to establish entitlement to income support, and hence also to the social fund payment.

The impact of a trade dispute disqualification[6] on entitlement depends on whether the claimant (or partner) is in receipt of income support or family credit. If the former, the maternity payment cannot be made during the first six weeks of the dispute; if the latter, it can only be made if family credit was claimed before the beginning of the dispute.[7]

ii Amount payable and treatment of capital

The amount currently payable (£85 per child) is approximately equivalent to the aggregate of the former contributory maternity grant and the average single payment made under the supplementary benefit system for maternity needs. It still falls well below typical maternity costs.[8] Since the Social

---

18 SI 1987/481, reg 5, as amended.
19 The claim can be made by the adoptive parent even though the natural parent received a payment on the birth of the child: ibid, reg 4(2).
20 'Confinement' here includes not only labour resulting in the issue of a living child but also labour after 28 weeks' pregnancy resulting in the birth of a stillborn child: ibid, reg 3(1).
1 Incorporating a reference to SI 1987/1968, reg 19 and Sch 4, para 8. The period can be extended for continuous 'good cause' (cf p.548, below) but only to a maximum of 12 months: SI 1987/1968, reg 19(2), (4).
2 SI 1987/481, reg 3(1), which thus contrasts with the definition of family used for income support purposes: p.424, above.
3 Cf pp. 418–420, above.
4 Cf pp. 232–233, above.
5 Cf p.429, above.
6 P.455, above.
7 SI 1987/481, reg 6, as amended.
8 For a first child, estimated at £250: Brown and Small *Maternity Benefits* (1985) p.135.

Security Act 1986 provides for payments for maternity expenses to be made in *prescribed* circumstances and that payments from the discretionary fund are for 'other needs',[9] it would seem that the latter cannot be used to meet the deficit.

Any relevant capital over £500 possessed by the claimant or partner will be set off against the award.[10] Relevant capital is that assessed for income support purposes[11] though in the present context widow's payment is disregarded.

C Funeral expenses

i Conditions of entitlement
There are four conditions of entitlement:[12]

(1) at the date of claim, the claimant (or partner) is receiving income support, family credit or housing benefit;[13] *and*
(2) the claimant, or a member of his family, takes responsibility for the costs of a funeral;[14] *and*
(3) the funeral takes place in the UK; *and*
(4) the claim is made within three months of the date of the funeral.

The existence of a trade dispute does not affect entitlement to a funeral payment. As regards condition (2), the person responsible for the costs need not show any particular relationship with the deceased. If the case-law on the equivalent provision in the supplementary benefits regulations is to be followed, nor need he bear sole responsibility for the costs.[15]

ii Amount payable and treatment of capital
The amount payable is not specified in the regulations; rather, subject to certain deductions, the claimant is entitled to such a sum as will be sufficient to meet any or all of the following expenses for which he is responsible:[16]

— the cost of necessary documentation; the cost of an ordinary coffin;[17] the cost of transport for the coffin and bearers and one additional car; the reasonable cost of flowers provided by the claimant; undertaker's fees and gratuities, chaplain's, organist's and cemetary or crematorium fees; additional expenses (up to £75) arising from the religious faith of the deceased; (if the death occurred away from the deceased's home) the cost of transporting the body within the UK; reasonable travelling costs for one return journey incurred by the claimant in connection with arrangement of, or attendance at, the funeral.

---

9 S.32(2)(a)–(b).
10 SI 1987/481, reg 9(1).
11 Ibid, regs 9(2), 10 and see pp. 447–449, above.
12 SI 1987/481, reg 7, as amended.
13 Since housing benefit is not administered by the DHSS, evidence of entitlement is normally required: *Social Fund Manual* para 12106.
14 I.e. burial or cremation: SI 1987/481, reg 3(1). Other, e.g. family, ceremonies are not included.
15 *R(SB) 13/85*.
16 SI 1987/481, reg 7(2).
17 Cf *R(SB) 46/84* for the meaning of a 'plain' coffin under the SB regulations.

The following amounts are then deducted from the expenses:[18]

(1) the value of any of the deceased's assets available to the claimant without probate or letters of administration having been granted;
(2) lump sums due to the claimant on the death of the deceased under an insurance policy, an occupational pension scheme, a burial club or analogous arrangement;
(3) any surplus remaining from payments by a charity or relative to meet expenses other than those listed above;
(4) a war pensioner's funeral grant.

In addition, capital possessed by the claimant (or partner) is taken into account to the same extent as in relation to maternity payments, except that: a sum acquired specifically to be used for funeral expenses is disregarded; and payments from capital assets actually made to cover funeral expenses (including those not covered by the regulations) are, for the purpose of assessing capital, assumed not to have been made.[19]

iii Recovery
The Secretary of State has power to recover funeral payments from the estate of the deceased.[20] This takes priority over other liabilities, but personal possessions left to relatives and the value of a home occupied by a surviving partner are disregarded.[1]

D Cold weather payments

As indicated above, the relevant regulations have not (at the time of writing) yet been published. It thus remains to be seen whether the government will adopt, as a model, the provisions used most recently in the supplementary benefit system.[2] These conferred a payment of £5 for each week designated as a period of 'exceptionally cold weather', i.e. when the average mean daily temperature did not exceed 1.5° Celsius (subsequently lowered to 0° Celsius), on claimants responsible for heating costs, if a member of the household was chronically sick, mentally or physically disabled, or aged less than 2 or more than 65. The evident weakness in this approach was that claimants did not know until after the event whether the temperature was cold enough to trigger entitlement, and thus might be disinclined to incur additional heating costs.

---

18 SI 1987/481, reg 8.
19 Ibid, regs 9(2) and 10, as amended.
20 SSA 1986, s.32(4).
 1 *Social Fund Manual* para 12281.
 2 SI 1981/1528 reg 26A, on which see the SSAC Report (1986, Cm 18).

Chapter 15

Administration of benefits

This chapter deals with some aspects of the administration of social security benefits. The government department responsible for their administration is now the Department of Social Security (DSS), and its organisation is briefly described in Part 1 of the chapter. The standing advisory bodies which have always been a feature of the social security schemes, ensuring some degree of non-official participation in policy formulation, are then discussed in Part 2. The largest section of this chapter (Part 3) is concerned with the rules relating to claims for and payment of benefits. Sometimes benefit is overpaid by the DSS, perhaps through its own carelessness, perhaps because the claimant has misrepresented or failed to disclose some pertinent facts. The rules about recovery of overpayments and prosecutions for fraud and other offences are treated in Part 4 of the chapter.

Part 1   The Department of Social Security

From 1968 to 1988 the administration of social security benefits was the responsibility of the Secretary of State for Social Services, who presided over the Department of Health and Social Security (DHSS).[1] The survey of the Department's history and organisation here is necessarily brief; a fuller treatment will be found in books on the machinery of government and social administration.[2] In July 1988 this Department was split into two smaller Ministries, one of which, the Department of Social Security, is responsible for social security benefits.

A History

Before the reforms of 1946 heralded by the Beveridge Report, the administration of social security benefits was undertaken in a number of different departments. The only Ministry with sole responsibility for a benefit was the Ministry of Pensions, which had been set up in 1916, and was responsible for the award of war pensions for death or disability suffered in the Great War and the Second World War.[3] Administration of health insurance (the precursor of sickness benefit) and contributory pensions was shared by the

---

1 As is usual in British government, the legal powers are vested in the Secretary of State, rather than in the department for which he is responsible: see SI 1968/1699. For general comment, see de Smith *Constitutional and Administrative Law* (5th edn) p.203.
2 See e.g. Willson *The Organisation of British Central Government, 1914–1964* (1967) pp. 143–174; Brown *The Management of Welfare* (1975), esp. chs 3–5.
3 See ch 8, above, for the history of war pensions.

Ministry of Health and the Approved Societies.[4] The Ministry of Labour was responsible for contributory unemployment insurance, which was paid at its labour exchanges. The administration of non-contributory old age pensions paid under the 1908 Act was rather anomalously in the hands of the Commissioners of Customs and Excise.[5]

Beveridge proposed the creation of a Ministry of Social Security under a Minister with a seat in the Cabinet. It would be responsible for both social insurance and means-tested national assistance previously administered by an Assistance Board. The Report also urged consideration of an eventual merger of the new Ministry and the Ministry of Pensions.[6] The war-time government accepted these proposals only in part. The suggestion of a Ministry of Social Security, responsible for *all* welfare benefits, was rejected. Insurance and other universal benefits, such as family allowances, were to be the responsibility of a new Ministry, but public assistance was to be separately administered by the National Assistance Board. The new Ministry of National Insurance was instituted by an Act of 1944, and became responsible for the administration of family allowances, benefits payable under the National Insurance Act 1946, and industrial injuries benefits.[7] However, unemployment benefit was paid at offices of the Ministry of Labour, and, since 1970, of the Department of Employment. A new central office was set up in Newcastle to keep insurance records and superintend the administration and payment of long-term benefits and family allowances.[8] In line with the Beveridge proposals, the Ministry worked through regional and local offices.[9]

There was no move at this time to take further Beveridge's suggestion that there might be a merger of the new Ministry of National Insurance and the older Ministry of Pensions. Such a step would have been bitterly resented by the servicemen's organisations and would have run counter to the popular sentiment that war pensioners should have separate and privileged treatment. However, by the early 1950s there was a steady decline of war pensions awarded, and consequently of the staff and special hospitals required to deal with pensioners' problems.[10] Despite fierce opposition the two Ministries were merged in 1953.[11] In one respect the position of war pensioners was much improved as a result. They had access to the 900 local offices of the Ministry of National Insurance, instead of the 80 to 90 local Pensions offices. War pensions continued to be administered (as they are now) under a central office at Blackpool.[12]

For the next 12 years there were relatively few changes in the structure of the new Ministry.[13] The next fundamental reform came in 1966, when at last

4 See ch 4, above, for the history of sickness benefit. The role of the Approved Societies in the administration of health insurance is discussed by Gilbert *The Evolution of National Insurance in Great Britain* (1966), esp. pp. 423–428.
5 Ch 5 (history of retirement pensions) pp. 179–181, above.
6 Paras 385–387. See *Harris* pp. 395–396.
7 Workmen's compensation had been subject to the general control of the Home Office: see *Willson*, n.2, above, at p.145.
8 1st Report of the Ministry of National Insurance (1949, Cmd 7955), paras 19 and 64–80.
9 Ibid, at paras 81–96.
10 28th Report of the Ministry of Pensions, 1952–53 HC 271, paras 116–120.
11 517 HC Official Report (5th series) col 267: the Address was only carried by 226–212 votes.
12 Report of the Ministry of Pensions and National Insurance for 1953 (Cmd 9159), paras 242–244.
13 For the definitive account of the structure and work of the Ministry, see King *The Ministry of Pensions and National Insurance* (1958). (Sir Geoffrey King had been a Permanent Secretary at the Ministry.)

Beveridge's wish for an integrated Ministry of Social Security was fulfilled. The Ministry of Social Security Act of that year had the effect of merging the administration of insurance and means-tested benefits and hence abolished the National Assistance Board. It was considered desirable both from the perspective of policy co-ordination and from the claimants' point of view to have an integrated Ministry. But within it there was a separate body, the Supplementary Benefits Commission, with responsibilities for the formulation of policy on means-tested benefits. Two years later the government took the further step of integrating the Ministries of Health and of Social Security into the DHSS. The title of Secretary of State for Social Services, given to the Minister responsible for this mega-department, emphasised his role as co-ordinator of the whole range of social services.[14]

Another development occurred in 1980 when the Supplementary Benefits Commission was abolished, and the DHSS assumed total responsibility for policy-making and the administration of means-tested benefits. The Commission which had superseded the National Assistance Board had been given a measure of independence by the Labour government; in 1975 it had been asked to submit a separate annual report, in which it could indicate priorities in policy development. With many members experienced in social services work, it was able to criticise government policy from an informed position.[15] The Conservative government, perhaps discomforted by these criticisms, took the view that there was no place for the Commission when the supplementary benefits scheme was radically reformed in 1980; its advisory role is now performed by the Social Security Advisory Committee, discussed in Part 2. There was some criticism of the size of the DHSS, and recently the government has separated the Departments responsible for health and for Social Security.

B The structure and organisation of DSS

i Department headquarters
The Secretary of State for Social Security, a Cabinet Minister, is assisted at the political level by a Minister for Social Security and a Parliamentary Under-Secretary. At the top of the civil service structure is the Permanent Secretary; under him the Department is divided into two 'commands', each headed by a deputy secretary. One is responsible for social security policy, the other, the Director of Social Security Operations (DSSO), for its administration. The DSSO is responsible for the two central offices in Newcastle and North Fylde, mentioned below, and for the regional organisation of the DSS in a network of regional and local offices. Most work at the headquarters is concerned with policy formulation and is discharged by about 1,400 staff, a small fraction of the total 115,000 civil servants engaged in social security work.[16]

ii The regional organisation
There are six regional offices in England and Wales, and a central office in Scotland. They serve as a link between the headquarters and the local offices,

14 Mr R Crossman, Secretary of State, 770 HC Official Report (5th series), cols 1609ff.
15 The work of the Commission is discussed by its chairman from 1975–80, David Donnison in his book, *The Politics of Poverty* (1982).
16 The figures in this and the following paragraphs are taken from DHSS *Facts and Figures* (HMSO, 1987).

and provide special support services for the latter, e.g. reviewing difficult cases, controlling local accounts. The head of the regional office, the Regional Controller, is responsible to the Regional Directorate set up in 1972 at headquarters under the DSSO.[17]

iii Local offices

In mid-1987 there were about 490 local offices, each under a manager, who in the larger offices has a senior executive officer as a deputy. The offices vary considerably in size, but the typical one has about 140 staff. Their work is organised in sections, dealing with various types of benefit, contributions and fraud, under the supervision of local officers I (or executive officers), officials who may also do specialist work in regional or local offices. Local officers II (or administrative officers) process claims, and assist the public. It is from this rank that most adjudication officers are appointed. Finally, there are administrative assistants to perform routine tasks such as filing and writing giro cheques.

Mr J Griffiths, then Minister of National Insurance, said when introducing the 1946 Bill, that local offices should be 'centres where people will not be afraid to go, where they will be welcome, and where they will not only get benefits, but advice'.[18] In the 1970s in particular there was some anxiety about the difficulties caused by rapid staff turnover; this particularly affected the administration of supplementary benefits where there was so much personal contact between applicants and the Department's staff, and led to frequent complaints, particularly in London, about the delay in processing claims.[19] A safeguard against incompetence is that a sample of awards is checked by senior executive officers or the office manager to ensure that the correct payments are made.[20] Since the 1970s there has been increased emphasis on staff training which is given at various regional centres.[1]

iv The central office at Newcastle

In addition to policy headquarters in London, there are two central offices. The first, at Newcastle upon Tyne, was set up in 1946, and now employs over 9,800 staff.[2] The contribution records are kept there, so every claim for benefit, where entitlement depends on a contributions' record, is referred to Newcastle. It is also from there that books are issued and renewed for the long-term benefits, such as retirement and widows' pensions. An office nearby at Washington in County Durham administers the child benefit scheme.

v The central office at North Fylde

The North Fylde central office processes claims for war pensions, attendance allowance, mobility allowance, invalid care allowance and family credit.[3] The office at Norcross has been responsible for the central administration of war pensions since the 1920s. Together the offices employ over 3,300 staff.

17 DHSS Annual Report 1972 (Cmnd. 5352), para 17.10.
18 418 HC Official Report (5th series) col 1754.
19 SBC Report 1978 (Cmnd 7725), paras 7.18–7.20; SBC Report 1979, (Cmnd 8033), paras 14.11–14.13.
20 *Fisher* paras 49–52; also see Annual Report of the Chief Adjudication Officer for 1984/85, paras 2.2–2.3.
 1 See DHSS Annual Report 1972, n.6, above, at para 17.16 and SBC Report 1975, (Cmnd 6615), para 15.6.
 2 See DHSS Facts and Figures (HMSO). For a general treatment and description of the work at the Newcastle office, see Brown, *The Management of Welfare* (1975) pp. 81–86.
 3 See DHSS Annual Report 1975 (Cmnd 6565), paras 2.21. and 8.33.

vi Specialist officers

The work of a number of specialist officers in the DSS should be briefly mentioned. Some of them perform a welfare role, principally in the regional offices, to which cases of claimants wholly unable to look after their financial arrangements are referred.[4] Unemployment review officers used to interview claimants who had been on supplementary or unemployment benefit for a substantial time, and to give them expert advice on employment opportunities. To a considerable extent they performed an anti-fraud or abuse function, since an interview or its prospect often led to the withdrawal of a claim by someone who was probably in work. These officers were replaced in 1987 by claimant advisers who discharge similar functions.[5]

Liable relative officers, of whom there are now about 1,900, interview women, separated from their husbands, and single parents, to discuss with them the possibility of taking maintenance or affiliation proceedings, so that they are less reliant on the DSS.[6] Perhaps the most important groups of specialist officers, and certainly the most controversial, are those concerned to investigate fraud: local offices employ specialist fraud officers, and there are also special investigators, who may work outside office hours, e.g. following or watching claimants, and across local office boundaries. Recently the government has radically increased the numbers of fraud officers, a step which some have seen as showing an excessive concern with the abuse of social security.[7]

Part 2   Standing advisory bodies[8]

Government departments have often made use of advisory bodies in the administration of the various social security schemes, the first of these committees being set up soon after the end of the First World War for war pensions.[9] Advisory bodies may either be national organisations or local committees. To a large extent their functions will differ according to this categorisation. Central advisory bodies will tend to be employed to give advice on matters of general policy, and to comment on the drafting of regulations made by the Secretary of State in the exercise of his delegated legislative powers. They are not suited to handling complaints from claimants, or to dealing with detailed questions concerning the administration of benefits in the regions. On the other hand, local bodies, which now exist only for war pensions, would be able to perform these functions, though, of course, they may also be competent to give advice on broader questions.

A second general point concerns the attitude to be adopted by the advisory committees to the government Department on the one hand, and to social security claimants on the other. The question is whether these committees regard themselves primarily as experts consulted to give disinterested advice

---

4 Stevenson *Claimant or Client?* (1973) p.68.
5 See the Report of National Association for the Care and Resettlement of Offenders (NACRO), *Enforcement of the law relating to social security* (1986) paras 8.5–8.8.
6 Ibid, paras 8.9–8.11.
7 Ibid, paras 6.14–6.19 and 11.4–11.5. Also for an earlier official review of the work of special investigators, see *Fisher* paras 408–417.
8 This discussion does not cover the work of the Royal Commissions and ad hoc Departmental Committees, which have also obviously played an important part in the development of social security law and policy.
9 War Pensions Act 1921: see pp. 539–540, below.

on the formation of policy, or whether they see themselves as mainly concerned to 'represent' the public as consumers of welfare benefits. In this second case, there will inevitably be some tensions between the Department and its advisory committee. In its Report for 1986/7 the Social Security Advisory Committee itself stated it was independent of both the government and social security pressure groups, but it tried 'not to lose the confidence of either party.'[10] Perhaps inevitably during a period when the government has been anxious not to increase social security expenditure, the Committee has tended to be critical of its proposals, drawing attention to any resulting hardship, and examining them in the context of other changes.

Recent governments do not appear well disposed to advisory committees. Not only has the role of the Social Security Advisory Committee been reduced, as discussed later, but the local social security advisory committees which used to advise DHSS office managers were abolished in 1971.[11] There have been suggestions for the institution of local user consultative committees, which would enable representative claimants to discuss matters of social security administration with Department officials, but these have not been taken up by the government.[12]

A The Social Security Advisory Committee

i General

This Committee was set up by the Social Security Act 1980 to assume the functions previously performed by the National Insurance Advisory Committee and (as has already been mentioned) the Supplementary Benefits Commission.[13] The National Insurance Advisory Committee (NIAC) had two precise functions: first, to prepare reports on general matters submitted to it by the Minister (now, the Secretary of State) and secondly, to consider regulations submitted to it in draft. In its initial years NIAC was extremely busy: by the end of 1950 it had submitted nearly 50 reports on draft regulations,[14] and in the following decade it made a major contribution to the development of social security through the publication of general reports, e.g. on maternity benefits,[15] the death grant[16] and widows' benefits.[17] These often contained the best published discussion of the policies underlying the law, and the reasons for subsequent legislative change.

ii Composition and powers of the Social Security Advisory Committee

Under the 1980 Act the Committee (SSAC) consists of a chairman, now Mr P M Barclay and between 8 and 11 other members.[18] One member is to be appointed after consultation with employers' organisations, one after consultation with the TUC and a third after consultation with the head of the

10 5th Report of the Social Security Advisory Committee 1986/87 (HMSO), para 1.4.
11 SSA 1971, s.9. See the second edition of this book, pp. 551–552.
12 See the National Consumer Council discussion paper *Means Tested Benefits* (1976) pp. 63–64 and *Social Security Users – Local Consultative Groups* (Supp. Benefits Comm. Admin. Paper No. 8, 1978).
13 SSA 1980, s.9.
14 See 1st Report of the Ministry of National Insurance (1949, Cmd 7955), para 61, and the 2nd Report (1951, Cmd 8412), para 112.
15 1951, Cmd 8466.
16 1956, Cmnd 33.
17 1956, Cmd 9684.
18 SSA 1980, Sch 3

Northern Ireland Health and Social Services Department. In addition the SSAC must include 'at least one person with experience of work among, and of the needs of, the chronically sick and disabled', and in selecting a member regard is to be had to the desirability of having a sick or disabled person on the Committee. In these respects the provisions closely follow those which governed the composition of NIAC.

Broadly the Committee's task is to give advice to the Secretary of State on social security matters, including means-tested benefits, but excluding industrial injuries benefits, war pensions and occupational pensions for which there are separate advisory bodies. Thus, it is a body which is able to look at the structure of social security benefits and consider the relationship between them. Under this wide rubric, it is possible to identify four more precise functions discharged by the Committee. First, it must advise the Secretary of State on any general questions concerning the working of the relevant social security legislation which he refers to it[19]; under this provision it has been asked, for example, to review the time-limits for claiming benefits. Secondly, it may give its views on proposals by the Department, whether it is specifically invited to comment on them or not.[20] The third function is perhaps potentially the most interesting and important. The SSAC is empowered to give the government advice on its own initiative, a role never enjoyed by NIAC, but of course frequently performed by the Supplementary Benefits Commission.[1] The Committee undertook to look at three major areas of social security where its ability to look at the whole range of benefits is crucial: provision for the long-term unemployed, benefits for the disabled, and family support. Progress on these and other functions of the Committee is reported in Annual Reports, which are published by HMSO.

The fourth function of the SSAC is that of commenting on regulations. As under the earlier legislation, proposals for regulations, 'in the form of draft regulations or otherwise,' must be sent to the Committee for it to comment on, unless it appears to the Secretary of State 'that by reason of the urgency of the matter it is inexpedient so to refer' them.[2] And regulations need not now be referred where the Committee itself has agreed to this:[3] this would cover technical amendments which raise no issue of principle. The Social Security Act 1986 has further weakened the obligations to consult SSAC (and the Industrial Injuries Advisory Council and the Occupational Pensions Board). Even after referring draft regulations to the relevant body, the Secretary of State may make them before receiving its report or advice, if this course appears appropriate because of the urgency of the matter.[4] (But a subsequent report of SSAC or the Board must be laid before the Houses of Parliament, with a statement of how far the government proposes to give effect to its recommendations.[5]) Secondly, the 1986 Act exempts from the consultation requirements any regulations made under that Act or any earlier enactment within a period of 12 months from the commencement date of the relevant provision, and there is a similar exemption for regulations made under later

19 SSA 1980, s.9(3).
20 Ibid, s.9(1)(a).
 1 Ibid.
 2 SSA 1980, ss. 10(1) and (2)(a). There are some specific exceptions: ibid, Sch 3, Part II.
 3 Ibid, s.10(2)(b).
 4 SSA 1986, s.61(3).
 5 Ibid, s.61(4).

social security legislation, provided that they are made within six months of the parent enactment.[6]

When SSAC is asked to comment on draft regulations, it almost always conducts a public consultation exercise before submitting its report, thereby giving an opportunity for members of the public and pressure groups to contribute to policy development. There is often a tension here between the government's timetable and the period required for adequate consultation.[7] The Secretary of State is required to table the SSAC report with the regulations and to explain when appropriate why the government has not followed its proposals.[8]

The duty to consult SSAC and other advisory bodies is probably mandatory, so that a total failure to honour the obligation would mean that the regulations in question are void.[9] In *R v Secretary of State for Social Services, ex p Cotton*,[10] members of the Court of Appeal expressed a variety of views on whether the Secretary of State had discharged his duty when he referred proposals for changes to regulations in general terms, without a detailed draft. Only Sir John Donaldson MR was of the opinion that this was inadequate and that the SSAC was entitled to see precise proposals. In any case the Secretary of State has a broad discretion not to refer in cases of urgency, and it is unlikely that its exercise could be challenged successfully.[11] It is important that the consultation requirements not be weakened further, for the reports of the SSAC and the other advisory bodies are invaluable aids to the construction of the regulations, as Commissioners have frequently affirmed.[12]

B The Industrial Injuries Advisory Council[13]

The Industrial Injuries Advisory Council (IIAC) was set up by the 1946 legislation to act as an advisory body to the Minister of National Insurance on industrial injuries matters. It has always been a larger body than NIAC or the Social Security Advisory Committee, and its procedure less formal. It consists of a chairman and an unspecified number of other members to be determined, and appointed by, the Secretary of State.[14] After consultation with various outside organisations four of the members must be appointed to

---

6 Ibid, s.61(5) and (6). Originally the government proposed that the 12 months' 'quarantine' period should apply to all regulations, but after critical representations by the SSAC, the period was reduced to six months for regulations made under later enactments: see 5th Report of SSAC, para 3.6.

7 Ibid, paras 3.2–3.3.

8 SSA 1980, s.10(4).

9 This seems to have been accepted by counsel for the DHSS in *R v Secretary of State for Social Services, ex p Cotton* (1985) Times, 14 December. For other relevant authority, see *Agricultural, Horticultural and Forestry Industry Training Board v Aylesbury Mushrooms Ltd* [1972] 1 All ER 280, [1972] 1 WLR 190.

10 (1985) Times, 14 December, CA.

11 In principle a ministerial decision could be challenged by judicial review on grounds of unreasonableness, but there is no authority suggesting that the courts would be prepared to intervene in this situation.

12 In *R(SB) 6/86*, J G Monroe, Comr, affirmed the view that SSAC reports (but not DHSS leaflets) could be used as an aid to construction. Also see *R(I) 2/85* for the use of IIAC reports.

13 See *Lewis* pp. 95–7.

14 SSA 1975, Sch 16, para 1.

represent employers, and four to represent employed earners.[15] The Council must also include at least one person experienced in the needs of the chronically sick and disabled, and as with SSAC, in choosing this person the desirability of having a disabled person as a member should be taken into account.[16] The difficult medical questions involved in determining whether there is a case for prescribing a disease as an 'industrial disease' under section 76 of the Social Security Act 1975 are normally referred for examination to an Industrial Diseases Sub-Committee.[17] Its views are considered by the full Council, and then embodied in a report to the Secretary of State.

The Council has two functions under the legislation.[18] First, it considers draft regulations relating to industrial injuries referred to it by the Secretary of State. He is under a duty to refer such regulations unless it appears inexpedient to do this because of urgency or the Council has agreed that this need not be done. The Secretary of State is not required, as he is with reports of the SSAC and the Occupational Pensions Board, to lay before Parliament the Council's report, or to state why he does not propose to follow its conclusions. IIAC publishes reports on regulations infrequently, and in general it would seem that its contribution in this context has not been particularly important.

The second function of the Council is to advise on general questions relating to industrial injuries benefits. It now has the power to give advice on subjects of its own choosing.[19] In fact the overwhelming majority of the IIAC's work has been on the prescription of particular industrial diseases, though it has also submitted general reports on time-limits and reform of compensation for industrial diseases.[20] There are indications that the Council now plays a more active role, in, for example, gathering evidence that a disease should be prescribed.[1]

C The Attendance Allowance Board

The Attendance Allowance Board was set up in 1970.[2] It consists of a chairman and between four and nine other members, appointed by the Secretary of State. All except two of them must be medical practitioners, and of the other two, one or both may be a medical practitioner.[3]

In addition to its primary function to adjudicate on claims to an attendance allowance,[4] the Board also has an advisory role, imposed by section 140 of the Social Security Act 1975. It advises the Secretary of State on matters which he refers to it, and may recommend changes in the attendance allowance provisions.[5] It may also be asked to give advice to him on the exercise of his powers in relation to the scheme.[6] For the purpose of exercising these advisory functions only, additional members (not necessarily medical practi-

15 SSA 1975, Sch 16, para 1(2).
16 Chronically Sick and Disabled Persons Act 1970, s.12.
17 See ch 7 on industrial injuries, pp. 278–281, above.
18 SSA 1975, s.141, as amended by SSA 1981, Sch 2, para 2.
19 SSA 1975, s.141(4), inserted by SSAHBA 1982, Sch 4, para 16.
20 (1952) Cmd 8511; (1981) Cmnd 8393, discussed in ch 7, p.278, above.
 1 *Lewis* p.96.
 2 The relevant legislation was named as NIA 1970 by NIA 1972, s.8(4).
 3 SSA 1975, Sch 11, para 1(1).
 4 Ibid, s.105: see ch 16, pp. 578–579, below.
 5 Ibid, s.140(1)(a).
 6 Ibid, s.140(1)(b).

tioners) may be appointed to the Board.[7] These powers are certainly as broad as those of IIAC, though the Board has not published any report in the exercise of these functions, notwithstanding that regulations have been referred to it under section 140. What is particularly interesting is the combination in one body of adjudicatory and advisory roles. The Ogelsby Report, which reviewed the adjudication of attendance and mobility allowances, considered that its adjudicatory role inhibited the Board from freely advising the Department, and partly for that reason recommended relieving it of the former responsibilities.[8] If true, this seems a pity, because adjudicators such as the Board and perhaps the Commissioners and tribunal chairmen might well have valuable comments to make on social security administration.

D The Occupational Pensions Board

The Board was instituted in 1973, and is one of the few survivals of the Act of that year.[9] It has a chairman, deputy chairman and between 8 and 12 other members, one of whom must be appointed after consultation with employers' organisations and one after consultation with trades unions. The Secretary of State must consult it on a number of regulations, in particular those made under the Pensions Act 1975,[10] and here the same principles apply as govern consultation of the SSAC. The Board also has a number of important administrative functions in connection with occupational and now personal pension schemes, among which are the certification of 'contracted-out schemes' and the approval of personal pensions arrangements.[11]

E The Central Advisory Committee on War Pensions[12]

The Central Advisory Committee was set up by the War Pensions Act 1921.[13] It is a large body consisting of about 30 members, with the Secretary of State as chairman. Under the Chronically Sick and Disabled Persons Act 1970, it must include at least 12 local war pensions committee chairmen and one war disabled pensioner.[14] It is required to meet at least once a year: in practice it does not meet more frequently. Its role is essentially to give advice to the Secretary of State on questions concerning entitlement to, and the administration of, war pensions.

F War Pensions Committees

These committees, often known as local war pensions committees, were set up by the War Pensions Act 1921[15] to give advice to pensioners on benefits they might be entitled to and to give general welfare assistance. With the decline in the number of pensioners in the last few years, several committees have been disbanded or amalgamated with others. Although one of their

7 Ibid, Sch 11, para 1(2).
8 Para 108.
9 SSA 1973, s.68.
10 SSPA 1975, s.61(2).
11 See for the former, SSPA 1975, s.30 and for the latter, SSA 1986, s.1(8).
12 See King *The Ministry of Pensions and National Insurance* (1958) pp. 33–34; *George* p.92.
13 S.3.
14 S.9(1).
15 S.2.

functions is to advise the Secretary of State on the local administration of war pensions, it seems that the committees' principal role is to help the pensioners themselves. This general 'welfare' role is now unique in the social security system, and shows the particularly favourable treatment often accorded to war pensioners.

Part 3 Claims and payments

A Claims: general rules

i When a claim is necessary

It is almost always a necessary condition for entitlement to benefit that a claim is made in the manner prescribed under the legislation. This had always been assumed to be the position, but the House of Lords in 1984 held that a valid claim was not a pre-condition of entitlement, as opposed to the right to payment.[16] However, the original position was restored by amendments to the social security legislation, and it is now clear that a timely claim made in the prescribed manner is necessary to ground entitlement unless regulations state otherwise.[17]

Regulations have now been made under the Social Security Act 1986, establishing common rules for claims to and payment of all social security benefits, as well as making provisions for particular benefits.[18] The regulations cover almost all the new benefits instituted by that Act in addition to established social security benefits, so that of the benefits covered in this book, only war pensions, housing benefit and social fund payments fall outside them.

A claim is not necessary in the following cases:[19]

– a Category A or B retirement pension, where the beneficiary is a woman over 65 on her ceasing to be entitled to widowed mother's allowance, or where she is a woman under 65 in receipt of widow's pension on her reaching 65; in some circumstances a Category C or D pension; age addition.

An increase of benefit for a dependant and the one-parent increase to child benefit must be the subject of separate claims.[20]

Although the requirement of a valid claim may occasionally work hardship on someone who has omitted to claim (or claim in time), a system of automatic entitlement to social security benefits would generally be unworkable. There are perhaps some exceptions, where the conditions of eligibility are very easy for the DSS to ascertain, such as the retirement pensions mentioned in the previous paragraph, but in the vast majority of cases it is reasonable for the claimant to be responsible for drawing the Department's attention to the circumstances which make the payment of benefit appropriate.[1]

A claim may be amended or withdrawn at any time before a determination has been made on it, by giving notice at a DSS office.[2] But after a ruling, it is too late to withdraw the claim.[3]

16 *Insurance Officer v McCaffrey* [1985] 1 All ER 5, [1984] 1 WLR 1353.
17 SSA 1975, s.165A, inserted by SSA 1985, s.17.
18 SI 1987/1968.
19 Ibid, reg 3.
20 Ibid, reg 2(3).
1 See *R(I) 6/62 (T)* para 15.
2 SI 1987/1968, reg 5.
3 *R(U) 2/79*, D Reith, Comr.

ii A claim must be made in writing on an appropriate form

Every claim must be submitted in writing on the form approved by the Secretary of State, or in any other manner in writing, which he is prepared to accept as sufficient in the circumstances.[4] Claim forms must be supplied without charge,[5] and every claim must be delivered or sent to an office of the DSS (or in the case of unemployment benefit the Department of Employment).[6] If the claim is defective or has not been made on the appropriate form, it may be referred to the applicant, and if it is then returned properly completed within a month (or a reasonable longer period), it may be treated as if it had been properly made in the first place.[7]

There are nice questions concerning the powers of the Secretary of State and the ordinary adjudicating authorities in this context. It is for the former to determine whether a written claim should be accepted as an alternative to one made on the proper form, but the question whether the documents constitute a valid claim is for the adjudication officer, tribunal, etc.[8] In practice the requirement that the claim be made on a particular form is applied with some flexibility.[9]

iii Information to be given when claiming

A claimant is required to provide within a month (or such longer period as is reasonable) the certificates, documents, information and evidence in connection with his claim, as the Secretary of State may require.[10] The Secretary of State may also require the partner of a claimant, where the former's circumstances may affect entitlement to or the amount of benefit, or in a family credit case the claimant's employer, to provide documents, information, etc.[11] Insofar as these provisions impose requirements as to the evidence, etc., to be produced by *particular* claimants, they are of doubtful validity.[12] The Act would appear only to authorise regulations which set out *general* requirements in various types of case; further it is for the adjudicating authorities to decide whether the claimant has proved his entitlement, and what evidence is in the circumstances necessary for that proof. An example of appropriate general regulations are the Medical Evidence Regulations, which lay down the certificates that are required for entitlement to sickness benefit or state maternity allowance.[13]

A claimant may also be directed by the Secretary of State to attend any office or place for the purpose of providing documents, information, etc.[14] It is doubtful whether this authorises a medical examination.[15]

iv Interchange with claims for other benefits

In certain circumstances a claim for one benefit may be treated alternatively or additionally as a claim for another benefit to which the applicant is

4 SI 1987/1968, reg 4(1).
5 Ibid, reg 4(5).
6 Ibid, reg 4(6).
7 Ibid, reg 4(7).
8 *R(U) 9/60.*
9 *R(SB) 6/81* paras 8–9, per J Mitchell, Comr.
10 SI 1987/1968, reg 7(1).
11 Ibid, reg 7(2) and (3).
12 The Chief Commissioner in Northern Ireland has raised this point: see *R 1/75(P)*, T A Blair.
13 SI 1976/615: see ch 4, p.152, above.
14 SI 1987/1968, reg 8(2).
15 But see the view of the Parliamentary Commissioner for Administration, 3rd Report for 1974–5, HC 241, Case No C 156/1.

entitled.[16] This rule assists a person who has claimed one allowance, and then discovers he is entitled to another; if his application for the latter was treated as made at the subsequent date (and not when the original claim was made) he might be out of time to claim it. The Regulations set out the detailed provisions in a Schedule. Thus, a claim for sickness benefit may be treated as a claim for invalidity benefit or severe disablement allowance, a claim for a retirement pension of any category may be treated as a claim for a pension of another category, and a claim for income support may be treated as a claim for attendance allowance or invalid care allowance. Also, a claimant for one-parent benefit may be treated as claiming child benefit, but not vice versa.

The decision whether to accept a claim for one benefit as a claim, either additionally or alternatively, for another is a matter for the Secretary of State.[17] In principle it should be a question for the adjudicating authorities, for (as mentioned earlier) they have jurisdiction to decide whether there is a valid claim.

v The date of claim

The date on which a claim is made is crucial for determining the relevant time-limit. Before the 1986 reforms, postal claims were generally treated as made on the day of posting; provided the claimant could show he had posted a claim, the risk of non-delivery was on the Department.[18] However, the new regulations made under the 1986 statute (which itself contains no provision on the matter) provide that a claim is made on the date on which it is received in the appropriate office, a rule which used to apply only for child benefit, supplementary benefit and FIS.[19] There is no obvious justification for this change. The new rule, like some others in the 1987 regulations, is a little harsher on the claimant.

vi Time-limits: general principles

The most important aspect of the Claims and Payments Regulations is the imposition of time-limits for claiming the various benefits. If the claim is not made within the time prescribed for the particular benefit, then the claimant is disqualified from receiving it, either absolutely or in respect of the period specified in the Regulations.[20] The reasons which may justify the imposition of time-limits are largely those which support limitation periods in all civil proceedings: the desire to achieve certainty and avoid adjudicating claims on stale evidence. The absence of time-limits would, moreover, make administration more costly and the financing of social security less predictable. These arguments are persuasive with regard to certain benefits, such as those for sickness and unemployment, where it may well be difficult to decide a late claim because of the unreliability of the evidence. On the other hand, it is more difficult to defend the existence of a time-limit for claiming a retirement pension, when the applicant would probably have little trouble in substantia-

---

16 SI 1987/1968, reg 9. The benefits which may be claimed alternatively or additionally to others are set out in Sch 1 to these regulations.
17 Ibid, reg 9. The question has a complex history (see the second edition of this book, pp. 555–56), and a Northern Ireland Tribunal of Commissioners has held that the matter is one for the statutory, now the adjudicating authorities: *R 2/69 (II)*.
18 SSA 1975, s.79(6).
19 SI 1987/1968, reg 6. For the earlier regulations, see second edition of this book, p.556.
20 SI 1987/1968, reg 19. For a general study of the time-limit rules, see Partington *Claim in Time* (1978).

ting a claim brought months or years after he attained pensionable age and became entitled. Both the NIAC and the IIAC emphasised that a balance had to be struck between the need of the Department to be protected against stale claims and that of the individual to have a reasonable time within which to claim.[1] The matter has now been fully considered by the Social Security Advisory Committee on a reference by the Secretary of State.[2] While approving the general principles stated by its predecessor, the SSAC proposed several modifications to the rules, and its recommendations have for the most part been incorporated in the new regulations. The SSAC favoured liberalisation of the time-limits so far as possible, though it rejected the superficially attractive view that there should be a common time-limit of 12 months for all benefits.[3] The greater difficulty in investigating a late claim for some benefits, e.g. sickness or unemployment benefit, as opposed to others, warranted differences in the relevant time-limits.

The Committee also considered to what extent an extension of the time-limits should continue to be allowed where the claimant showed 'good cause' for his failure to apply within the prescribed period. The possibility of extension allows justice to be done in an individual case, where, for example, the applicant was misled by incorrect official advice and so delayed his claim, but the 'good cause' provision is expensive to administer.[4] So the SSAC recommended an extension of the time-limits for some benefits, in particular, retirement pension and widows' benefits, with the abolition of the 'good cause' provision for those benefits; on the other hand, it should be retained for others, such as unemployment and sickness benefit, invalidity pension and severe disablement allowance, where the time-limits remain relatively short. These proposals were accepted by the government, and are now implemented in the Claims and Payments Regulations.

Another matter considered by the SSAC was the desirability of the absolute time-limit of 12 months, beyond which there can be no extension even for good cause. This bar applies to all benefits, save for disablement benefit and reduced earnings allowance; the former benefit at least involves some element of compensation for injury so that an absolute bar would be inappropriate. The Committee concluded that for practical reasons an absolute cut-off was necessary 'to avoid considerable administrative disruption and doubt'.[5] This is surely right, except for cases where an official has misled the claimant, when an extra-statutory payment is usually made.[6] The bar is imposed by statute,[7] though the regulations further provide that for income support, family credit and social fund payments for maternity and funeral expenses, the time for claiming cannot be extended for good cause to give entitlement in respect of any birth, adoption or funeral occurring more than 12 months before the claim.[8]

---

1 Report of NIAC on Time-Limits (1952, Cmd 8483); Report of IIAC on Time-Limits for claiming industrial injury benefits (1952, Cmd 8511); Report of NIAC on Time-Limits (1968, Cmnd 3597), paras 6–7.
2 *Time limits for claiming benefits* (1987, Cm 100).
3 Ibid, para 12.
4 Ibid, paras 16–17. It is also one of the most common grounds of appeal to SSATs, particularly in unemployment benefit cases.
5 Ibid, paras 18–19.
6 Ibid, para 20.
7 SSA 1975, s.165A(2), inserted by SSA 1985, s.17, and replacing SSA 1975, s.82(2). Until 1969, there was an absolute bar after six months.
8 SI 1987/1968, reg 19(4).

B The time-limits and other rules for particular benefits

i Unemployment benefit

In addition to submitting a written claim, a person applying for unemployment benefit is usually required to attend in person at an unemployment benefit office of the Department of Employment.[9] Unemployment benefit is thus the only contributory benefit for which an application is not normally made by post. At the benefit office, the claimant is interviewed and his claim processed, his contribution record being checked by reference to the central office in Newcastle. He is told that he must return to the benefit office fortnightly, at a particular time on a particular day of the week, to state that he is still unemployed and looking for work – the procedure known as 'signing on'.[10] Until 1982 the claimant also had to register for work at a separate employment office or job centre, but this requirement was removed following the recommendations of the Rayner scrutiny team, which was concerned to reduce the administrative costs of processing unemployment benefit claims.[11]

A claim for unemployment benefit must be made on the day for which it is made, though after the initial claim it is normally enough that subsequent applications are made on the day specified in a notice given the applicant by the unemployment benefit office.[12] In effect this means that the requirement of an immediate claim applies at the start of any period of unemployment. This strict rule is justified on the ground that unemployment benefit is paid on a daily basis and that otherwise it might be difficult to determine whether the claimant was really available for work at the particular time. Recently the Social Security Advisory Committee considered whether the rule might be unduly harsh and indeed would have liked to recommend an initial time limit of seven days, but its terms of reference precluded it from proposing changes which entailed increased costs.[13]

The rule is buttressed by a regulation stipulating that, in the case of an initial claim, no benefit is to be awarded for any period after its date, thus requiring the applicant to renew his claim on the day specified in the notice given him.[14] But when subsequent claims are made during the same spell of unemployment, an award may be made for seven days or, where the Secretary of State has certified that there are or are likely to be circumstances making the normal requirements impracticable, for a period up to 26 weeks (or the period of the certificate where shorter).[15] This latter modification to the general rule is useful where long-term unemployment may be anticipated in a particular area, or where it is difficult for the claimant regularly to attend a benefit office to renew his claim. There are further modifications to the general claims and awards provisions where the claim is made in periods before public holidays, when the offices of the Department are closed.[16]

An important rule frequently applied by the adjudicating authorities enables them to disallow any prospective claims for unemployment benefit for a specified period or while the grounds for the original refusal of benefit

9 SI 1987/1968, reg 8. Unemployment benefit is administered by the Department of Employment, subject to the policy directions of the DSS.
10 There is an excellent summary of the procedures in the Report of the Joint DE/DHSS Rayner Scrutiny, *Payment of Benefits to Unemployed People* (1980) Annex II, ch 2.
11 Ibid, para 11.
12 SI 1987/1968, Schs 4 and 5.
13 Cm 100, paras 48–51.
14 SI 1987/1968, reg 17(2).
15 Ibid, reg 17(2)(b).
16 Ibid, reg 17(5) and Sch 2.

continue to subsist.[17] There must be a continuing feature in the grounds of the initial refusal to justify the application of the provision; for example, benefit may have been refused because the applicant had not shown availability for work, and a forward disallowance will be appropriate if the adjudicating authority takes the view that this state of affairs will continue for some time.[18] Where the claims fails because the claimant has not satisfied the contribution conditions, all subsequent claims are treated as disallowed until these conditions are met.[19]

ii Sickness benefit, invalidity pension and severe disablement allowance
For these benefits the time-limit varies according to whether the claim is an original claim, the first claim in a period of sickness or disability, or a continuation claim. In all cases it may be extended up to 12 months if the claimant shows there was good cause for his delay. There are also special rules where these benefits are claimed after notification that the applicant is not entitled to statutory sick pay (SSP). Under these rules a claim for the state benefit is treated as made on the day accepted by the employer as the first day of incapacity, provided the claim is made within the period stated in the Schedule from the day when the claimant was told he was not entitled to SSP.[20] The other rules will apply when the claimant has not applied for SSP or when his entitlement to that is exhausted.

a *Original claim*
This is a claim where the claimant has at no time made a claim for sickness benefit or severe disablement allowance, or a claim which has been treated as a claim for one of those benefits.[1] For these claims the generous time limit of one month is allowed, a limitation period increased from 21 days by regulations in 1982. Recently the SSAC has repeated the doubts of its predecessor, NIAC, whether this generous time limit was necessary; most people, even those who have never claimed it, are familiar with the existence at least of sickness benefit.[2]

b *First claim in a spell of illness or disability*
In this case the limitation period is six days, that is, the claim must be made within six days from the earliest day in respect of which benefit is claimed; but after 1982 the Secretary of State has had power to extend this period to one month, when he considers this is consistent with the proper administration of the Act.[3] In practice it seems an extension will be granted unless there is some indication that the claim might be abusive, for example, where the claimant has repeatedly made claims for short periods of sickness.[4] Even then it is open for the claimant to argue that he had good cause for delay in not claiming within the six days period. The SSAC thought these rules satisfactory, and found there was little evidence of a large number of abusive claims, even in the context of the procedures for self-certification for the first week of a spell of illness introduced in 1982.[5]

17 Ibid, reg 18(3).
18 See *R(U) 1/78*.
19 SI 1987/1968, reg 18(1).
20 Ibid, reg 10.
 1 Ibid, Sch 4.
 2 Cmnd 2400, paras 22–23, and Cm 100, para 62.
 3 SI 1987/1968, reg 19(3) and Sch 4.
 4 See the Report of the Social Security Advisory Committee, Cm 100, paras 55–56.
 5 Ibid, para 57. (For the self-certification procedure, see ch 4, p.152, above.)

c *Continuation claim*

Any other claim is known as a continuation claim and must be brought within ten days of the start of the period for which it was made.[6] Again the Secretary of State may extend this period to one month in appropriate cases. Where a first (or original) claim has been disallowed on the basis of a failure to satisfy the contribution conditions, later continuation claims are treated as disallowed until these conditions have been met.[7]

The new regulations issued in 1987 provide that sickness benefit and severe disablement allowance, like most other social security benefits (though not unemployment benefit and family credit) may be awarded for an indefinite period, unless this would be inappropriate, because, for example, an imminent change of circumstances is expected.[8] Previously an award could be made for the period stated in the medical certificate, up to a maximum of 13 weeks. The requirement of a medical certificate and other special features of claims for sickness and disability benefits are discussed in chapter 4 of this book.

iii Child benefit, guardian's allowance and increases for dependents

The time-limit for claiming these benefits is now six months, and in these cases there is no extension for good cause.[9] Previous to the 1987 regulations, the positions varied. For child benefit there was a generous time-limit of 12 months, for guardian's allowance the period was three months, but it could be extended to 12 with good cause, and dependant's increases were subject to a one month limit for increases to short-term benefits (in those cases where they were still payable) and to a three month limit for increases to long-term benefits – in both cases subject to extension in the event of good cause for delay. The SSAC recommended the harmonisation of the limitation period for child benefit (including one parent benefit) and dependant's increases at six months, since there was no good reason for the previous generous rule for the former and it was sensible to align the dependency additions.[10] These recommendations were accepted, but the government rejected the SSAC proposal that the little known guardian's allowance should have a more generous time-limit, on the ground that this benefit is usually claimed at the same time as child benefit.

iv Maternity allowance

The time-limit for claiming the residual state maternity allowance is now 12 months from the date of entitlement, that is the date of confinement.[11] There is no extension for good cause. The change follows the recommendation of the SSAC, which pointed out that there is rarely any need to guard against abusive claims, in view of the ease with which the facts can be established for this benefit, and that therefore a longer period than the previous three weeks limitation period was appropriate.[12] The regulations further provide that a claim for maternity allowance in expectation of confinement may be made not earlier than 14 weeks before the expected week of confinement.[13] The

6 Ibid, Sch 4.
7 Ibid, reg 18(1).
8 Ibid, reg 17.
9 Ibid, reg 19(6)(a).
10 Cm 100, paras 71–80 and 82–83.
11 SI 1987/1968, reg 19(6)(b).
12 Cm 100, para 68.
13 SI 1987/1968, reg 14.

state benefit is now subsidiary to the scheme for statutory maternity pay (SMP); if a woman has given notice of her imminent absence of work in order to establish title to SMP, but her employer has told her she is not so entitled, the day on which she gave notice is treated as the date of claim to the state benefit, provided she does claim the latter within a month.[14]

v Retirement pension, widow's benefit and invalid care allowance

Under the 1987 regulations, the time-limit for claiming these benefits has been extended from 3 to 12 months, but there is no extension for good cause.[15] The change was recommended by the SSAC, which thought there should be a more generous limitation period in view of the value of the benefit and (sometimes) the difficulty a claimant may have in appreciating his entitlement; further the removal of the good cause provision would save considerable administrative costs.[16] The Department does write to people approaching pensionable age of their prospective entitlement, but some claimants do not receive this notification because, for example, they have changed address. The government, however, did not accept the SSAC recommendation that the requirement of a separate notice of retirement should be dispensed with. The notice, like the claim, must be given within 12 months of the date of retirement, and both may be made up to four months in advance of the date on which the claimant becomes entitled to a pension.[17]

vi Attendance and mobility allowance

Neither of these benefits can normally be paid for any period prior to the date of claim, and in the case of mobility allowance the legislation clearly indicates that the relevant date is that on which the claim is *received* by the Secretary of State.[18] There can be no extension for good cause. However, renewal claims made within six months of the expiry of an earlier award of the allowances can be backdated to that expiry date to avoid a gap in entitlement.[19] The SSAC in its recent report considered the limits and the absence of a good cause provision unjustified in principle, particularly in view of the difficulty many claimants and their family may have in appreciating their entitlement; further, it was not impressed by the government's argument that it would often be difficult to determine eligibility at a date earlier than the date of claim, since attendance allowance in any case requires that the need has existed for six months (which may precede the date of claim.)[20] But the Committee's inability to make recommendations which would increase costs precluded it from making any definite proposals. The government has indicated in response that it will make greater efforts to publicise the benefits to encourage claims, and it is certainly clear that the number of claims for both allowances has increased in the last few years.[1]

Under the regulations, forward claims for mobility allowance may be made three months in advance of the entitlement date, including in the case of

14 Ibid, reg 10(3) and (4).
15 Ibid, reg 19(6)(b).
16 See Cm 100, paras 24–33, for discussion by the SSAC of the various options for reform.
17 SI 1987/1968, reg 15. For the requirement of notice of retirement, see ch 5, p.197, above.
18 SSA 1975, s.37A; SI 1987/1968, reg 39.
19 For attendance allowance, see SI 1975/598, reg 5D; for mobility allowance, see SI 1987/1968, reg 40.
20 Cm 100, paras 38–43.
 1 See the response of the Secretary of State for Social Services to the SSAC Report, Annex to Cm 100.

a child his fifth birthday.[2] The regulations also provide that the claimant may be required to have a medical examination, or to undergo medical treatment.[3]

vii Disablement benefit including increases

For these benefits the limitation period is three months from the date on which the claimant is entitled to disablement benefit or, where an increase is claimed, to the particular increase, such as constant attendance, exceptionally severe disablement or reduced earnings allowance.[4] If the claim is made after that period, the claimant may still succeed if he can show good cause for his delay, but (save for disablement benefit and reduced earnings allowance) only up to the general 12 months' limitation period. These rules were outside the scope of the recent inquiry by the SSAC.

viii Income support and family credit

Both these new means-tested benefits must normally be claimed on the first day of the period for which the benefit is claimed.[5] But for family credit, there is a separate rule where credit has previously been claimed and awarded; further credit should be claimed within the period from 28 days before to 14 days after the final day of the earlier award.[6] In the case of both benefits, the new regulations apply the sickness benefit rule, that the limitation period may be extended to one month, where the Secretary of State certifies this would be consistent with the proper administration of the Act.[7] And if the claimant can show good cause for delay, the limitation period may be extended to 12 months from the date on which the claim is treated as made.

The regulations also provide time-limits for claiming the social fund payments for maternity and funeral expenses: they must be claimed within three months of the date of confinement or the funeral, as the case may be, and the former type of payment may be claimed within the period starting 11 weeks before the expected date of confinement.[8]

A person claiming income support, subject to the requirement of availability for work, may be directed to attend an unemployment benefit office.[9]

ix Social fund payments

Applications for social fund payments (apart from payments for maternity and funeral expenses, discussed in the preceding paragraph) must be made in writing, either on the official form or on some other document which the Secretary of State is prepared to accept as sufficient in the circumstances.[10] The skeletal regulations on applications for social fund payments are supplemented in the Social Fund Manual, which explain the procedure when a 'claim' is made over the telephone: the officer should tell the claimant that his application must be made in writing, and where appropriate arrange an interview at the local office. The date of the application is the date on which it is received at the DSS office. Since under the Secretary of State's directions

2 SI 1987/1968, reg 39.
3 Ibid, reg 41.
4 Ibid, Sch 4.
5 Ibid.
6 Ibid.
7 Ibid, reg 19(3).
8 Ibid, Sch 4.
9 Ibid, reg 8(1).
10 SI 1988/524, reg 2.

eligibility for budgeting and crisis loans is determined at the date of the award, the precise date of application will not generally be of great importance, and there are no provisions for the acceptance of delayed claims.[11]

x Housing benefit

The procedure for claiming this benefit is covered by the separate Housing Benefit Regulations. A claim must be made in writing on the form approved by the authority (or one which it will accept as sufficient) and delivered to the office it has designated for this purpose.[12] Alternatively it may be delivered to the appropriate DSS office, when the claimant is also claiming income support, and that office must then forward it to the local authority within two days of its receipt or the determination of the income support claim, whichever is the later. A claim for a further grant of benefit may be made from 13 weeks before the expiry of a benefit period until four weeks after that period has ended.[13] Further, a late claim will be accepted if the claimant shows there was good cause for the delay, subject to the 12 months' absolute bar.[14] Other provisions regarding the evidence and information to be produced with the claim are similar to the requirements in the social security regulations.[15]

xi War pensions

There are no prescribed claim forms or procedures, though a document is usually completed and sent to the DSS central office at Blackpool, where claims are handled. An interesting issue of general significance arose in *Robertson v Minister of Pensions*.[16]

> C wrote in 1941 to the War Office concerning his disability, and a month later received a reply to the effect that it was accepted as attributable to war service. The War Office had not consulted the Minister of Pensions, to whom responsibility for the award of pensions had been transferred from September 1939. Relying on this reply C refrained from obtaining an independent medical opinion and destroyed some relevant evidence. The Minister of Pensions later held that C was not entitled to a pension as his injury was not attributable to war service.

On appeal, Denning J held the Crown was bound by the War Office's representation on which Robertson had reasonably relied and, therefore, the Minister was bound by the assurance. The decisive fact would seem to have been that between October 1921 and September 1939 the War Office had dealt with pension claims, so that an applicant could reasonably believe it to be the appropriate department for handling them.[17]

There is no time-limit for claiming a war pension, though the burden of proof shifts to the applicant if he claims more than seven years after leaving service.[18]

11 See ch 14, pp. 514–520, above.
12 SI 1987/1971, reg 72.
13 Ibid, reg 72(12) and (13).
14 Ibid, reg 71(15).
15 Ibid, regs 73–74. See p.541, above.
16 [1949] 1 KB 227, [1948] 2 All ER 767.
17 The decision is a controversial one in the application of estoppel to public authorities: for further discussion, see Treitel [1957] PL 321 at 325–329.
18 Pp. 323–326, above.

C   Extension of time-limits for 'good cause'

i The law on 'good cause'

The 'good cause' principle applies to many of the benefits covered by the Social Security Claims and Payments Regulations. Subject to the absolute time-limit of 12 months, the prescribed time for claiming these benefits will be extended if the claimant shows that there was good cause for the delay in presenting his claim. Under the new regulations good cause must be shown *throughout* the period from the end of the time prescribed for claiming the particular benefit to the date the claim is made.[19] Previously a claimant could also take advantage of the principle, if there was good cause for his delay for the part of the period immediately before the date on which the claim was eventually made (though not for the whole of the time after the expiry of the usual time limit).[20] The provision in the 1987 regulations seems therefore somewhat stricter in this respect.

a *General principles in determining 'good cause'*

These principles are the same for all benefits, though, of course, their application will vary according to the facts.[1] They were stated in *CS 371/49*:

> It will be observed that the expression used is 'good cause', not 'a good excuse'. 'Good cause' means, in my opinion, some fact which, having regard to all the circumstances (including the claimant's state of health and the information which he had received and that which he might have obtained) would probably have caused a reasonable person of his age and experience to act (or fail to act) as the claimant did.

It was also emphasised that the burden of proof is on the claimant. These principles were approved by both NIAC and IIAC,[2] and followed in later decisions of the Commissioner.[3] NIAC did briefly contemplate the formulation of a provision which would allow extension in cases of 'excusable ignorance', though it was persuaded that this was neither necessary nor practicable.[4] Both NIAC and now the SSAC concluded that there has been a continual trend towards a more liberal interpretation of the 'good cause' provision.[5] The latter body in its recent review of time-limits thought the definition of 'good cause' needed to be amended to take account of the difficulties experienced by many claimants in the face of an increasingly complex system. But it made no concrete recommendations, beyond suggesting more emphasis by the Department on the provision of accurate advice and information.[6]

A familiar source of difficulty is whether a claimant, who has not claimed benefit because he did not realise he was entitled to it, has good cause for his failure to claim within the prescribed time. This issue arose before a Tribunal of Commissioners in *R(S) 2/63*:

> C did not claim sickness benefit while he had reasonable grounds for believing, and did believe, that he would be paid wages in full during his

19 SI 1987/1968, reg 19(2).
20 See the second edition of this book, p.565.
1 See T A Blair, Chief Comr, in *R 1/70 (MB)*.
2 See Report of NIAC on Time-Limits (1952, Cmd 8483); Report of IIAC on Time-Limits for claiming Industrial Injury Benefits (1952, Cmd 8511).
3 See esp. *R(S) 2/63 (T)*.
4 Cmd 8483, paras 19–22.
5 Cmnd 2400, para 27; Cm 100, para 15.
6 Cm 100, paras 21–23.

period of sickness, and that this would preclude him from claiming benefit. Both beliefs were wrong. The Tribunal held that he had good cause for his failure to claim, while he suffered from this misapprehension.

It was emphasised that 'over the years there has been a gradual, but appreciable relaxation of the strictness with which problems of good and reasonable cause have been approached'; this was particularly true of sickness benefit claims where the applicant might not act promptly because of his ill-health. In determining how a reasonable person should behave, it is permissible to take account of the conduct of other claimants, as revealed in the cases which come before the Commissioners.[7]

Generally, however, ignorance of entitlement has not been held to afford a good cause for delay in claiming. For example, the Commissioners have not been sympathetic to late claims for sickness benefit by the self-employed, who had believed wrongly that they were not entitled to claim this benefit.[8] In other circumstances, where there have been particularly good reasons for a claimant's ignorance of his entitlement, the Commissioner has been prepared to be more generous.[9] It seems that much will depend on the particular facts of the case, for example, the extent to which the benefit entitlement was publicised, whether the claimant has applied for the benefit on an earlier occasion and other factors, some of which are discussed below.[10] On the other hand, in a recent case it has been held that the question whether there is good cause is one of law, a ruling which enables the Commissioner to exercise appellate jurisdiction over tribunal decisions on the point.[11]

A deliberate decision not to claim a benefit on the required day, because of some false expectation, e.g. that the period of unemployment will be brief, will not constitute good cause.[12] But the applicant may have a good reason for not claiming on a particular day, and the Commissioner has respected this on occasion.[13]

b *Relying on other people's opinion as to entitlement*
Good cause is not generally shown if the claimant has relied on another person's view that he is not entitled to claim.[14] This is true even if the advice has come from a doctor in a sickness benefit case.[15] It is otherwise if it has come from a solicitor, since it is reasonable for an applicant to rely on his opinion.[16]

> In an unemployment benefit case, *R(U) 9/74*, J S Watson, Commissioner, ruled that there was good cause when the claimant had been incorrectly advised by the local Citizens Advice Bureau that he should take his insurance card to the unemployment benefit office, and he had, therefore, waited until it was returned by his former employer.

7 See the statement of general principle in *CS 371/49*, and by the Chief Comr in Northern Ireland, T A Blair, in *R 1/70 (MB)*.
8 *R(S) 1/73, R(S) 8/81*.
9 *R(G) 2/74; R(P) 1/79; R(S) 3/79*.
10 See, for example, *R(I) 10/74*.
11 *R(SB) 39/85*.
12 *R(U) 34/51*.
13 See for example *R(U) 20/56*, (claimant attending meeting at request of his union in hope of being reinstated); *R(U) 33/58*, (Rabbi did not claim benefit on days of Passover).
14 *CSG 9/49; R(U) 35/56*.
15 *R(S) 5/56*; cf *R(I) 40/59*.
16 *CS 50/50; CSI 10/50*.

c *Acting on inadequate information given by the Department office*
Perhaps the most frequent type of case where good cause is shown by the
claimant is where he has delayed in reliance on inadequate or misleading
information given at a local office or in a DSS leaflet.[17] This may occur even if
the leaflet refers to another one where accurate information is obtainable.[18]
In some circumstances there may be good cause if the officials culpably fail to
tell the applicant that he has a claim.[19] In any case it seems that the DSS is prepared to make extra-statutory payments, even beyond the absolute 12
months' limit, where there has been an official error.[20]

d *Claimants outside the country*
In *R(G) 3/53*, the Commissioner ruled that a liberal view should be taken of
any delay attributable to the fact that the claimant was abroad at the time she
made inquiries concerning her rights. A similar approach was taken where a
claimant had emigrated to the United States of America before the present
system of retirement pensions was introduced, and only claimed 18 months
after her entitlement arose, when she read an article about pensions in an
American weekly paper.[1]

e *The claimant's state of health*
The fact that the claimant has been under some physical pain or emotional
distress may persuade the statutory authorities to find good cause.

> Thus, a young girl under nervous strain on her confinement,[2] a war
> veteran who developed a phobia of seeing doctors,[3] and an employee
> who developed a neurotic condition as a result of explosions at work[4] all
> benefitted from an extension of time.

f *Educational limitations*
Allowance may be made for the fact that the claimant is of limited intelligence.[5] Lack of familiarity with the English language or illiteracy is not in
itself likely to constitute good cause, though it might lead to the conclusion
that there was such a failure of communication between the officer and the
claimant that there was good cause.

g *Delegation by the claimant to another person*
The Commissioner has recently summarised the principles to be applied when
the claimant has relied on another person to make his claim.[6] If the claimant
has good reason to delegate the making of his claim, e.g. because he was ill or
(in some circumstances) because he entrusted the matter to his solicitor, he
may have good cause for a delay, even though the agent could not himself
show good cause. But the claimant would normally be expected to follow the
matter up, rather than leave things entirely in the hands of the delegate. These

17 *R(S) 14/54*; *CP 30/50*; *R(U) 3/70*, *R(U) 7/83*; cf *R(G) 15/56*, where the claimant's failure to
    understand the leaflets was her fault. This is also a frequent ground of complaint to the
    Parliamentary Commissioner. Also see F Bates [1987] JSWL 109, 113–119.
18 *R(G) 4/68*; *R(I) 25/61*.
19 *R(I) 10/74*; see also *R(U) 3/60*.
20 See Report of SSAC, Cm 100, para 20.
 1 *R(P) 5/58*.
 2 *R 1/73 (MB)*.
 3 *R(S) 7/61*.
 4 *R(I) 43/55*.
 5 *R(P) 10/59*.
 6 *R(P) 2/85*. Also see *CG 1/50* and *R(S) 25/52*.

cases must be distinguished from those where the claimant has entirely entrusted his affairs to another, perhaps because he is no longer competent to act. In that event, the acts of the delegate will be imputed to the claimant, so the relevant issue is whether the former can show good cause for the delay.[7]

h *Hospital in-patients*
There is deemed to be 'good cause' for certain late claims by hospital in-patients for sickness or invalidity benefit or severe disablement allowance.[8]

D Payments

i General
A full exposition of the rules and practices governing payment of social security benefits would be very complicated, and here the emphasis is placed on general principles. Traditionally the principal methods of payment have been by books of serial orders, cashable at post offices, and by girocheque sent to the recipient's home address. Long-term benefits, child benefit and the means-tested benefits have usually been paid by the former method, while payments of the short-term benefits have been made by cheque. The Conservative government in the last few years, following the recommendations of a DHSS review team working with Sir Derek Rayner,[9] has encouraged beneficiaries to receive payments by direct transfer to their bank accounts. Payment by the traditional methods is administratively expensive, and it may reflect an outdated paternalist view that recipients could not budget properly, particularly where cash payments are made weekly. On the other hand, weekly cash payments are popular with a large number of social security beneficiaries, who value the regular trip to the local post office, and removal of this business from many sub-post offices might endanger their survival. Therefore, the present position represents a compromise.

The regulations make provision for direct credit transfer to the claimant's bank or other account of any social security benefit, but the system only comes into operation, if the beneficiary applies for this method of payment and indicates in writing that he understands its conditions, and the Secretary of State consents.[10] In this event payment is to be made within seven days of the period of entitlement specified in the application, which might be monthly or quarterly. If this option is not taken up, the traditional methods remain operative.

The government's desire to achieve administrative economies has also been implemented in the changes made in 1982 to the payment of child benefit.[11] Previously paid weekly in all cases, the normal method of payment is now monthly in arrears. But recipients of benefit before March 1982 could choose to continue with weekly payments or may revert to that system within six months of the normal arrangements being initiated. Further, any beneficiary

---

7 See *R(S) 2/51* (delay of prioress in making claim for nun who had withdrawn from the world imputed to the latter).
8 SI 1987/1968, Sch 5, para 2.
9 Annex II to the Reply to the First Report from the Social Services Committee on Arrangements for paying Social Security Benefits (1980, Cmnd 8106). The publication contains a comprehensive description of the traditional methods of payment, and this section of the chapter is much indebted to it.
10 SI 1987/1968, reg 21. It is important that the beneficiary understands that overpayments may be recovered from his accounts: see p.560, below.
11 This change is now found in SI 1987/1968, reg 23.

may move to weekly payments if he becomes a lone parent, or if he (or his partner) is in receipt of income support or family credit. Finally, weekly payments may be made if the normal arrangements are leading to hardship.[12]

A factor which used to give rise to complications for both staff and beneficiaries is that while some benefits, such as retirement pension and the former supplementary benefit, are (or were) paid in advance, others, such as unemployment benefit, were paid generally in arrears.[13] This caused considerable confusion when a claimant was in receipt of two benefits at the same time, most commonly supplementary benefit and unemployment benefit. The difficulties have been reduced under the 1987 regulations, in that the new income support is to be paid in arrears, unless the claimant is in receipt of (inter alia) a retirement pension or a widow's benefit.[14]

The Social Security Claims and Payments Regulations draw a distinction between short-term and various other benefits on the one hand, and long-term benefits on the other, so the discussion below follows this. The special rules relevant to income support, family credit, housing benefit and war pensions are then mentioned.

ii Short-term and other benefits
These comprise the following:

- unemployment, sickness or invalidity benefit, maternity and severe disablement allowance.

They are to be paid as soon as reasonably practicable after the award has been made, and in practice are usually paid by girocheque. For example, sickness benefit is paid weekly by cheque posted to the beneficiary, though for longer illnesses payment may be made fortnightly. Until 1979 unemployment benefit was paid weekly, but then after experiments in certain areas over the previous two years the general rule became to pay it fortnightly, and this is now covered by the regulations.[15] A joint Department of Employment and DHSS team reviewing the payments procedures for unemployment benefit recommended that those claimants who have been paid salaries monthly should have the option of being paid benefit monthly in order to reduce costs, and this was accepted.[16]

iii Long-term benefits paid under SSA 1975
These comprise the following:

- widow's benefit, retirement pension of any category, guardian's, mobility and attendance allowances, any allowance for industrial injuries, and invalid care allowance.[17]

With the exception of mobility allowance, which is to be paid at four-weekly intervals, these benefits are to be paid weekly in advance by order books, though the regulations do enable payment to be made by other means; under this provision, some retirement pensioners do choose to be paid by monthly

---

12 Ibid, reg 23(3). The changes were widely criticised, inter alia, by the Social Security Advisory Committee, Cmnd 8453.
13 Reply to the First Report, n.9, above, at paras 2.7–2.8. And see the DE/DHSS Rayner Scrutiny, *Payments of Benefits to Unemployed People* paras 3.15–3.18.
14 SI 1987/1968, Sch 7.
15 SI 1987/1968 reg 24(1).
16 DE/DHSS Rayner Scrutiny *Payments of Benefits to Unemployed People*, paras 5.46–5.50.
17 SI 1987/1968, reg 22, and see Ibid, reg 2 for the definition of 'long-term benefits'.

or quarterly payable orders which can be paid into bank accounts. There are specific rules for the day on which each benefit is to be paid: for example, a retirement pension is generally paid on Mondays, though if the beneficiary has been in receipt of a widow's pension, it is paid (like the widow's benefit itself) on a Tuesday.[18]

iv Income support

Income support is paid in arrears, either by serial orders cashable at post offices or by cheque.[19] The latter method would be used where the claimant is also in receipt of a short-term benefit, such as unemployment or sickness benefit. Indeed, when the beneficiary is also entitled to another 'relevant social security benefit', income support is to be paid together with that other benefit, so that he would receive one cheque or cash one order at the post office.[20] Thus, income support will be paid in advance when the beneficiary is also in receipt of a retirement pension or widow's benefit. Otherwise, entitlement commences normally on the date of claim, and payment is made weekly on the day determined by the Secretary of State.[1]

v Family credit

Payment of the credit, like its predecessor, FIS, will be paid by means of an order book (unless the Secretary of State otherwise directs) cashable on the Tuesday following the week in respect of which the credit is payable.[2] If the entitlement is less than 50p a week, that amount is not payable.[3] A regulation provides that arrangements may be made to pay the credit to the partner of a person entitled to it on his (or more probably her) behalf.[4]

vi Housing benefit

A number of rules are set out in the separate Housing Benefit Regulations. The authority pays the benefit at the times and in the manner it thinks appropriate in the light of the times when payments of rent or rates have to be made and the needs of the beneficiary.[5] When paid in the form of a rent allowance, it must be paid at intervals of two or four weeks, or every month, or at greater intervals with the beneficiary's consent. But in some cases, for example, where the beneficiary is required to pay rent weekly, it may be paid at weekly intervals.[6] The authority is entitled to withhold payments in exceptional circumstances, particularly where it is satisfied that the recipient is not using them to pay his rent.[7]

vii War pensions

Officers' pensions are paid monthly or quarterly (at the option of the recipient) by payable order, while other ranks are paid weekly by order book or

18 Ibid, Sch 6.
19 Ibid, Sch 7, para 1.
20 Ibid, Sch 7, para 3. The term 'relevant social security benefit' means unemployment, sickness or invalidity benefit, severe disablement allowance, retirement pension or widow's benefit.
 1 Ibid.
 2 Ibid, reg 27(1).
 3 Ibid, reg 27(2).
 4 Ibid, reg 36.
 5 SI 1987/1971, reg 88.
 6 Ibid, reg 90.
 7 Ibid, reg 95.

quarterly by payable order. Payment by monthly credit transfer is encouraged, but weekly payments are available in cases of hardship.

viii Extinguishment of right to sums payable by way of benefit

If payment is not obtained within 12 months from the date on which the right is treated as having arisen, then the right is extinguished.[8] The reason for this time-limit on encashment of benefits is said to be that the administrative costs (e.g. of storing copies of instruments of payment and cash instruments) necessary to check late requests for payment, and so prevent abuse, could be very heavy.[9] The right to payment under the Social Security Claims and Payments Regulations is to be treated as having arisen in the following circumstances:

(1) in relation to a sum contained in an instrument of payment sent to the beneficiary, or to an approved place for collection by him, whether or not he has received or collected it – *on the date of the instrument*;
(2) where notice has been given or sent that the sum contained in it is available for collection – *on the date of notice*;
(3) in relation to sums to which the preceding sub-paragraphs do not apply – *on the date determined by the Secretary of State*.[10]

It seems that, with the exception of cases under (3), the relevant date is to be determined by the statutory authorities.[11] It may be noted that the recipient takes the risk of the notification not being delivered in the ordinary course of post.

There used to be provision for an extension of the 12 months' period where the beneficiary gave notice requesting payment and there had been good cause for not giving this notice earlier throughout the 12 months until the date he did give notice;[12] but this provision has not been repeated in the 1987 regulations, in order, it seems, to cut out the costs of investigating some difficult cases.

The extinguishment provisions do not apply to the payment of industrial injuries gratuities (if paid as a single sum and not by instalments) or a sum paid in satisfaction of a right to graduated retirement pension.[13]

E Miscellaneous

i Persons unable to act

A regulation covers the case where the person alleged to be entitled to a benefit, or to whom a benefit is payable, is unable for the time being to act for himself.[14] The rule is:

– unless a receiver has been appointed by the Court of Protection with power to claim benefit, etc.[15] the Secretary of State may, on written application to him by a person over 18, appoint that person to exercise, on

---

8 SI 1987/1968, reg 38.
9 NIAC Report (1968, Cmnd 3591), paras 18–26.
10 *See R(I) 1/84.*
11 This follows recommendations of NIAC in 1952 (Cmd 8483), para 54 and of IIAC in the same year (Cmd 8511), para 28.
12 See the 2nd edition of this book, p.574.
13 SI 1987/1968, reg 38(5).
14 Ibid, reg 33.
15 There is a similar rule for Scotland: Ibid, reg 33(1)(d).

behalf of the person unable to act, all his rights and to receive benefit to which he is entitled. There are provisions for the revocation of, or resignation from, this appointment.

ii Payments on death

When a claimant dies, the Secretary of State may appoint a person of his choice to proceed with the claim.[16] If written application is then made for the sums payable by way of benefit within 12 months (or such longer period as the Secretary of State may determine) the following consequences ensue:

– any sum payable may be paid or distributed among persons over 16 claiming as personal representatives, legatees, next of kin or creditors of the deceased, at the discretion of the Secretary of State; he may pay this to some person on behalf of another under 16. The same rules apply to a sum payable to the deceased before his death, but not obtained by him.

iii Payment to a third party

There is a general power to pay any benefit to another person on the beneficiary's behalf, if the Secretary of State considers this necessary for protecting the latter's interests or those of any child or other dependant for whom the benefit is payable.[17] Further there is a specific power under the regulations to make deductions from payments of income support (whether payable on its own or together with another social security benefit) to pay the sums deducted to third parties on the beneficiary's behalf, e.g. in respect of his liability for housing or fuel costs.[18]

iv Benefit to be inalienable

It is a standard provision that any assignment or charge on, or agreement to assign or charge, the benefit is void.[19] It does not pass to the trustee, or any other person acting on the creditors' behalf, on the bankruptcy of the person entitled. There are obvious policy reasons why it is undesirable to allow a beneficiary to give up or put at risk benefits designed to ensure a minimum standard of living for himself and his family.

Part 4   Overpayments and criminal offences

A   Recovery of overpaid benefit

i General

It frequently happens that benefit is paid, or too high an award is made, in circumstances where either the claimant was not entitled at all or was only entitled to a lower award. In some cases this may be attributable to a misrepresentation of some kind by the claimant, or perhaps more commonly by a failure on his part to disclose some relevant facts which affect his entitlement, either at the time of claiming or subsequently when circumstances change; but the overpayment may be the consequence of some error or omission on the part of the DSS, and of course in some cases both the Department and

16 Ibid, reg 30.
17 SI 1987/1968, reg 34.
18 Ibid, reg 35, and Sch 9. See pp. 469–470, above.
19 SSA 1975, s.87; CBA 1975, s.12.

the claimant may have made mistakes. It is not easy to determine when it is right in principle for the DSS to recover overpaid benefit. On the one hand, it would seem right for it to do so, when the claimant has deliberately or recklessly misrepresented his position or concealed relevant facts. And a broader right of recovery can be justified on the argument that otherwise public money is awarded to people who have no justifiable claim on these resources; in the context of a limited social security budget, it can be said that not to recover overpaid benefit is unfair to those claimants for whom better provision could be made with more resources. On the other hand, it is harsh to order recovery from a beneficiary who has not been at fault at any stage, and who may be in no position to repay the overpaid benefit.[20]

Until 1987 there were broadly two main rules reflecting the balance between these arguments. In the case of social security (and child) benefits, recovery would be ordered unless the beneficiary (and any person acting for him) could show that throughout he had used 'due care and diligence', a rule which had superseded an earlier test enabling a beneficiary to avoid repayment if he showed that he had acted in good faith.[1] In contrast, the position for the means-tested benefits was stricter, and in general terms enabled the Secretary of State to obtain recovery whenever the claimant had fraudulently or otherwise misrepresented or failed to disclose a material fact.[2] This formulation has been the subject of frequent interpretation by the Commissioners, not all of whose rulings seem consistent. But it was clear that under this test recovery could be ordered from a claimant who had misstated a relevant fact, albeit in all innocence, which would not have been the case under the other rule.

In its recent reform of social security the government sensibly decided to adopt a common rule for benefits paid under the legislation of 1975–1986 (apart from housing benefit), but more controversially chose the stricter supplementary benefit test. It resisted attempts during the passage of the Bill to incorporate the more liberal 'due care and diligence' provision.[3] Further, it should be noted that the rule for housing benefit is particularly strict: any overpayment is recoverable, except one attributable to an official error, where the beneficiary could not reasonably have been expected to realise that there was an overpayment.[4] The new common test is not quite as severe as that, but it may be thought somewhat unsatisfactory in view of the uncertainties of its interpretation, now to be discussed.

ii The present law concerning recovery

The common provision for recovery of overpayments is set out in section 53(1) of the Social Security Act 1986:

> Where it is determined that, whether, fraudulently or otherwise, any person has misrepresented, or failed to disclose, any material fact and in consequence of the misrepresentation or failure –. . . .

payment has been made of any social security benefit, the Secretary of State is entitled to recover any payment which would not have been made in the absence of that misstatement or failure to disclose. The decision to recover is

---

20 For an admirable discussion of these policy issues, see the Report of the National Association for the Care and Resettlement of Offenders (NACRO) Working Party, *Enforcement of the Law Relating to Social Security* (1986) paras 9.1–9.18.
1 See the discussion in the 2nd edition of this book, pp. 576–7.
2 SBA 1976, s.20.
3 98 HC Official Report (6th series) Cols 238–249.
4 SI 1987/1971, reg 99. (Also see SSA 1988, s.4.)

taken by the Secretary of State, but it seems that, as under the previous law, it is for the adjudicating authorities to determine whether recoverable over-payments have been made and their amount. Generally, a decision to recover can only be taken after the decision under which the payments was made has been reversed on appeal or revised on review.[5]

The principal legal problem for resolution by the adjudicating authorities is whether the overpayments have resulted from the misrepresentation of, or failure to disclose, a material fact. The claimant himself need not be respon-sible, for recovery to be appropriate, but in all cases the sum overpaid is to be recovered from the person who made the misrepresentation or failed to dis-close the fact.[6] The Commissioners have interpreted the equivalent provision in the earlier supplementary benefits legislation to cover all types of positive misstatement, whether fraudulent, negligent, or purely innocent.[7] But they were less clear whether a non-culpable failure to disclose a fact, the materia-lity of which may not have been appreciated by the claimant (or any other person whose information might be relevant to the success of the claim), fell under the provision.[8] Where the beneficiary has kept quiet about a fact, which the order book clearly states should be communicated to the Depart-ment, there is obviously non-disclosure. Moreover, the obligation to disclose is a continuing one; regulations specifically require claimants to notify the DSS in writing of any change of circumstances which they might reasonably be expected to know might affect their entitlement.[9] The greatest difficulties have arisen where it is argued that some branch of the Department, albeit not the one dealing with the relevant benefit, is already aware of the facts concerning the claimant's entitlement, and so there is no duty to 'disclose' what is already known. The issues have recently been considered by a Tribunal of Commissioners;[10] it ruled that normally the duty should be fulfilled by disclosure to the local office dealing with the claim, but that it can be satisfied by giving information to another branch of the DSS (or in some cases the local unemployment benefit office), if the claimant reasonably believes the information will be passed on to the appropriate local office.[11] The Tribunal also emphasised that the claimant must usually himself dis-charge the onus of disclosure, and cannot rely on casual disclosure of the relevant facts by some person connected with him.[12] Clearly in applying these principles there is some room for the exercise of judgement by social security tribunals. Finally it should be borne in mind that it is for the adjudication officer to prove that a recoverable payment has been made, rather than for the beneficiary to show that the provision is inapplicable.[13]

iii Methods of recovery

The adjudication officer, or on appeal the tribunal, has the responsibility of calculating the sum which is recoverable.[14] In difficult cases, it is permissible

5 SSA 1986, s.53(4). But SI 1987/491, reg 13 provides that this need not be so, where the facts and circumstances of the misrepresentation, etc. do not provide a basis for review of the decision.
6 SSA 1986, s.53(2).
7 *R(SB) 21/82.*
8 Cf *R(SB) 28/83* and *R(SB) 54/83*. It is clear that the beneficiary may disclose material facts orally: see *R(SB) 12/84.*
9 SI 1987/1968, reg 32. See *R(SB) 54/83.*
10 *R(SB) 15/87(T).*
11 Ibid, para 28. See also the decisions in *R(SB) 54/83*, *R(SB) 36/84* and *R(SB) 10/85.*
12 *R(SB) 15/87(T)*, para 29.
13 *R(SB) 34/83* and *R(SB) 10/85.*
14 *R(SB) 9/85.*

for a tribunal to refer a question of assessment back to the officer, though it should indicate that the matter should be restored to it for final resolution if the officer and claimant do not agree.[15] But it is for the DSS subject to various constraints to decide how the payments are to be recovered. Under regulations they may be recovered by deductions from social security benefits in payment to the person concerned, though there are limits on the amounts that may be deducted from weekly payments of income support.[16] In practice this method of recovery is by far the most common; according to the report of a recent NACRO working party nearly two-thirds of recoveries are effected in this way.[17] Overpayments of income support or family credit may be recovered from the payments of those benefits to either member of a married or unmarried couple.[18] Since 1982 recovery may be enforced by a court order of a county court in England or a Sheriff Court in Scotland.[19]

Special rules apply where the overpayments have been made by crediting the beneficiary's bank or other account. The overpayment may be recovered, but only where the Secretary of State has certified that it was 'materially due' to the arrangements for direct credit transfer, and secondly, that notice of the effect of the recovery arrangements was given to the beneficiary when he agreed to this method of benefit payment.[20]

Subject to these rules it is for the Department to decide when to seek recovery or whether to waive it. The NACRO report thought its policy could be more generous in a number of respects.[1] In particular, it should not recover (except in case of fraud) overpayments which occurred more than two years before their discovery, a proposal which has much to commend it, as under the present practice an innocent beneficiary may find himself called on to repay a debt of thousands of pounds. Secondly, the DSS should be more prepared to waive recovery when the beneficiary has little capital or in other ways faces considerable hardship.

B Offences

A variety of specific offences are created by the social security legislation, though a person who obtains benefit by deliberate deception may also be prosecuted under the general law, e.g. for obtaining property by deception under the Theft Act 1968.[2]

i Obtaining benefit by false statements, etc.

It is an offence punishable on summary conviction by a fine of £2,000 or imprisonment for three months, or both, if a person:

for the purpose of obtaining any benefit or other payment under any of the benefit Acts, whether for himself or some other person, or for any other purpose connected with any of those Acts–
(i)   makes a statement or representation which he knows to be false; or

---

15 *R(SB) 11/86.*
16 SI 1988/664, regs 15 and 16.
17 See n.20, above, para 9.4.
18 SI 1988/664, reg 17.
19 See now SSA 1986, s.53(9).
20 SI 1988/664, reg 11.
 1 See Report of the NACRO Working Party, paras 9.5–9.18.
 2 S.15. See Smith and Hogan *Criminal Law* (6th edn) pp. 543–558.

(ii) produces or furnishes, or knowingly causes or knowingly allows to be produced or furnished, any document or information which he knows to be false in an material particular.[2a]

It is now clear that for these offences to be committed it is enough that the defendant knowingly made a false statement; it is immaterial that he did not intend to obtain the benefit by fraud, but lied for some other reason.[3]

A defendant will also be guilty of the offence if he makes an untrue representation when accepting *payment* of the benefit.[4] It does not matter that the decision to pay it has been taken before the false statement. On the other hand, if a beneficiary honestly presents an order for payment at a post office and then *subsequently* adopts a course of action which disqualifies him for entitlement to the relevant benefit (e.g. he works on days for which he has received sickness benefit), it seems that he is only guilty of the offence of failing to inform the authorities of a relevant change of circumstances.[5]

ii Other offences
Other offences under the social security legislation are less important.

(1) It is an offence under the Social Security Act 1986 to delay or obstruct wilfully an inspector in the exercise of his powers, or to refuse either to answer questions or to provide documents and information.[6]

(2) There are some offences with regard to non-payment of contributions and misuse of contribution cards under section 146 of the Social Security Act 1975. (Failure to pay Class 4 contributions, recoverable by the Inland Revenue, may be prosecuted under the Taxes Management Act 1970.)[7]

(3) Under the 1986 Act, regulations may be issued imposing criminal penalties for breach of any requirements imposed under the social security legislation.[8] It is too soon to see how this power will be exercised; but the provision is unacceptably wide, for it would appear to enable the government to make it a criminal offence, say, not to provide the required information when making a claim.

iii Critique
The present government's determination to stamp out fraud and abuse, discussed in the next section, does not necessarily entail an increase in the number of presecutions. There were an increasing number of proceedings in the late 1970s, but this decade has seen a change in policy and a reduction in their number.[9] The DHSS found that a prosecution policy was not cost-effective. The NACRO Working Party, which in 1984–6 considered at length the enforcement of social security law, welcomed this change, and called for a further reduction in the number of offences prosecuted.[10] It is still the case,

2a SSA 1986, s.55(1).
3 *Clear v Smith* [1981] 1 WLR 399; *Barrass v Reeve* [1980] 3 All ER 705, [1981] 1 WLR 408, in which the earlier decision in *Moore v Branton* (1974) 118 Sol Jo 405 was disapproved on this point.
4 *Tolfree v Florence* [1971] 1 All ER 125, [1971] 1 WLR 141.
5 See SI 1979/628, reg 31 and SI 1987/1968, reg 32.
6 See SSA 1986, s.58.
7 Ss.93–107.
8 SSA 1986, s.54.
9 See the Report of the NACRO Working Party, para 10.6.
10 Ibid, para 10.11.

for example, that social security fraud is prosecuted much more readily than revenue offences, though the existence of other sanctions for the latter may provide some explanation.

In the large majority of cases where a conviction for social security fraud is obtained, a non-custodial sentence is imposed. However, in a small number of instances the offender is imprisoned, and the NACRO Working Party expressed concern that sometimes this was done inappropriately and that the sentence seemed severe. Probation or community service orders, and in some cases moderate fines, were more appropriate. It also urged that compensation orders (under the Powers of the Criminal Courts Act 1975) should not be made in social security cases; magistrates' courts were not a suitable forum to decide whether benefit had been overpaid.[11] To some extent these views have now been reflected in the guidelines laid down by the Court of Appeal in 1987 for sentencing in fraud cases.[12] The Court stressed that deterrence should not play a significant part in sentencing, and that prison sentences of two and a half years or more were only appropriate for carefully organised frauds on a large scale. If an immediate rather than a suspended sentence is necessary, normally 9–12 months would be sufficient. On the other hand, it thought that compensation orders were often of value, though they should generally only be imposed when the defendant was in work.

C The control of fraud and abuse

In the last few years there has been considerable public concern about suspected widespread abuse of the social security system, and governments have responded by increasing the numbers of staff deployed to investigate possible cases of fraud and so reduce its incidence. Unfortunately nobody really knows the extent of the problem, and rational discussion is made difficult by exaggerated claims on both sides of the argument: there are those who are willing to believe that the majority of claimants are dishonest 'scroungers', while others appear to contend that any attempt to investigate the scope of fraud and general abuse necessarily constitutes an attack on the welfare state. In 1971 a Committee was set up under the chairmanship of Sir Henry Fisher to review the adequacy of the measures taken to counteract abuse and recommend changes in these procedures. The Committee concluded that there was not enough information to show the scale of the problem, and more thorough steps should be taken to acquire it.[13] In particular detailed surveys should be made on sample claims, chosen at random. The government, however, rejected this as likely to lead to intrusion into the lives of wholly innocent claimants.

The Conservative government in the 1980s has made enormous efforts to eradicate social security fraud and abuse, on several occasions employing more specialist staff in both the DHSS and the Department of Employment to investigate suspected abuses. In 1986, for example, 1,200 extra staff were allocated to this work, a step which the NACRO working party considered unjustifiable, in view of the shortage of staff in many local offices and the time taken to process claims.[14] It was also critical of the organisation at regional level of teams of specialist fraud officers in the two departments;

11 Ibid, paras 10.21–10.22.
12 *R v Stewart* [1987] 2 All ER 383, [1987] 1 WLR 559.
13 Paras 487–490.
14 See n.9, above, para 6.22.

though it seems that the Specialist Claims Control unit of officers in the DHSS which had aroused considerable controvery through its use of indiscriminate checks has been disbanded.[15] There is a danger that specialist officers, entirely divorced from the local office work of processing claims, will develop an attitude of hostility to claimants, and of course their work is not subject to much public scrutiny. A published Code of Practice, of the kind which governs the police under the Police and Criminal Evidence Act 1984, would be a useful step to control of investigate activity.

Few would deny that there is considerable abuse of the social security system and that it should so far as possible be stopped. But it is possible that the present government, fuelled by fits of popular indignation, does not see the problem in proper perspective. There is some indication from a recent report of the National Audit Office that there is considerable underpayment of benefit to claimants entitled to it, which may exceed the cost of overpayments.[16] The solution to both difficulties might be the more careful initial scrutiny of claims, which would admittedly require the employment of more staff in hard-pressed local offices.

15 Ibid, paras 7.1–7.5
16 *Department of Health and Social Security and Department of Employment: Incorrect Payments of Social Security Benefits* (HC 319).

Chapter 16

Adjudication

Part 1 General

A Scope of chapter

Two issues have dominated the history of social security adjudication. First, there is the question how far there should be specialist tribunals to decide entitlement to particular benefits or resolve particular issues relevant to the claim. While there is a case for a degree of specialisation, especially in the context of medical questions, there are perhaps more powerful arguments against an undue plethora of tribunals, as the Council on Tribunals has consistently contended: it creates jurisdictional problems and varieties of procedure which baffle claimants and their representatives.[1] The second issue concerns the role of the ordinary courts of law. Granted that they are unsuitable fora for deciding claims and hearing run of the mill appeals, whether on fact or law, should they play any part in resolving the more complex questions of principle that arise from time to time?

In the last few years answers have been given to both these questions. There is now an integrated system of adjudication for contributory, non-contributory (and child) benefits and means-tested benefits, though this is more complete at the appellate tribunal level than at the officer level where original decisions are taken. Some questions relevant to disablement benefit are however still reserved for separate medical authorities, and the Attendance Allowance Board (AAB) retains jurisdiction over that allowance. But all these bodies are now subject to certain common procedural rules; their composition, jurisdiction and procedure are discussed in Part 2 of this chapter. At the apex of the tribunal systems, with appellate jurisdiction over social security appeal tribunals (SSATs), medical tribunals and the AAB, stand the Social Security Commissioners, whose reported decisions constitute the principal case law in this area; they are the subject of Part 3.

Decisions at all levels, that is, whether they are taken by officers, tribunals or Commissioners, may be subject to review on certain grounds, a procedure which is less formal and certainly cheaper than the exercise of a right of appeal. This process of review is discussed in Part 4 of this chapter, as is the role of the courts. There may now be an appeal with leave on a point of law from the Commissioner to the Court of Appeal (and thence to the House of

---

1 See the Annual Report of the Council on Tribunals 1969-70, para 44, and its Annual Report for 1982-3, para 3.32. Also see Wraith and Hutchesson *Administrative Tribunals* (1973) 289-92.

Lords), so that the specialist tribunals are subject to the ordinary courts. The final two Parts of this chapter concern relatively peripheral topics: Part 5 briefly describes adjudication of war pension claims, which remains entirely separate from the integrated tribunal system, and Part 6 discusses references to the European Court of Justice in social security cases.

B History

From the beginning of the modern social security system before the First World War, powers of adjudication have been vested in special tribunals or other bodies.[2] The decision not to confer jurisdiction on the courts was largely attributable to an understandable fear that their procedure would be too formal and expensive. The 1906 Liberal government was also influenced by the successful use in Germany of special tribunals in this area. Thus, claims for the unemployment benefit introduced by the National Insurance Act 1911 were decided in the first instance by Board of Trade insurance officers. Appeal then lay to a court of referees, a three member tribunal, with a chairman, one member drawn from an 'employer's panel' and the other drawn from a 'workmen's panel'. A further appeal could be made to an Umpire, a lawyer of standing appointed by the Crown.[3] This became the model for the system introduced by the National Insurance Act 1946.

Another pattern of adjudication was established when contributory pensions were introduced in 1925.[4] A claim for an old age or widow's pension would be made in the first place to the Minister; if he rejected it, an appeal lay to an independent Referee, a senior lawyer. His decisions, unlike those of the Umpire under the unemployment insurance legislation, were not publicly reported.[5] This system was adopted in 1945 for the adjudication of disputed claims to family allowances; the Referee could state a case on a point of law for the High Court, though this was done very rarely.[6]

The Beveridge Report recommended a right of appeal to a local tribunal, analogous to the court of referees, and then to the Umpire, whose decisions would be final.[7] This was accepted in principle by the government. The National Insurance Act 1946 provided that claims should initially be determined by the insurance officer, with a right of appeal to a national insurance local tribunal, and then to the National Insurance Commissioner or one of the Deputy Commissioners.[8] Certain questions, however, particularly on contributions, were reserved for the Minister, with an appeal only on a point of law to the High Court. A similar system was instituted under the industrial injuries legislation. An appeal lay to a local appeal tribunal, and from it to the Industrial Injuries Commissioner or a Deputy

2 See Wraith and Hutchesson *Administrative Tribunals* (1973) pp. 33–38; Robson *Justice and Administrative Law* (3rd edn) pp. 188–198; Fulbrook *Administrative Justice and the Unemployed* (1978) ch 6.
3 For a full discussion of this system, see the Committee on Procedure and Evidence for the Determination of Claims for Unemployment Insurance Benefit (the Morris Committee) (1929, Cmd 3415).
4 For the history of pensions, see ch 5, pp. 179–184, above.
5 Safford 17 MLR 197 at 201 (the author was a Deputy Insurance Commissioner).
6 In 596 HC Official Report (5th series) col 713, Mr D Freeth, introducing the 2nd Reading of the Family Allowances and National Insurance Bill 1959, said that only four references to the High Court had been made by the Referee.
7 Paras 394–395.
8 Under NIA 1966, the National Insurance Commissioner was retitled the Chief National Insurance Commissioner, and the Deputy Commissioners became full Commissioners.

Commissioner. But certain questions concerning entitlement to, and the assessment of, disablement benefit were entrusted to medical boards, with an appeal to medical appeal tribunals.

Some of the developments in the thirty years after the Second World War should be mentioned before the more recent reforms are discussed.[9] First, following a recommendation of the Franks Committee on Tribunals and Enquiries,[10] the adjudication of claims to family allowances (subsequently, child benefit) was transferred in 1959 to the insurance officers and on appeal the local tribunal and the National Insurance Commissioner.[11] Secondly, the 1959 legislation also conferred a right of appeal on a point of law from the medical appeal tribunals to the Commissioner. This interesting development reflected the general confidence in the Commissioners and enhanced their position at the apex of the tribunal system.[12] Thirdly, the National Insurance Act 1966 merged the systems of adjudication under the national insurance and the industrial injuries legislation, so that industrial injury cases (apart from those referred to the medical authorities) are determined by the ordinary adjudicating authorities.[13] In 1970, the Attendance Allowance Board was set up to adjudicate claims to the allowance[14] with an appeal from its decisions on a point of law to the Commissioner.[15]

At the same time as these developments, there were changes in the system of tribunals which heard appeals against a refusal of means-tested benefits. The national assistance tribunals (NATs) set up in 1948 had been modelled on earlier bodies which had heard appeals from decisions of the Unemployment Assistance Board.[16] There was no further appeal from the decision of a NAT, a factor which highlighted their informal character. This feature was indeed recognised by the Franks Committee, which saw the work of this tribunal as that of 'an assessment or case committee, taking a further look at the facts and in some cases arriving at a fresh decision on the extent of need.'[17] When national assistance was replaced by supplementary benefits in 1966, the tribunals' structure was unaffected, though they were renamed supplementary benefit appeal tribunals (SBATs).

A SBAT, like its predecessors, had three members, but in contrast to the national insurance tribunals, its chairman was not usually a lawyer. Of the two other members, one was appointed from persons who had knowledge or experience of conditions in the area and of the problems of those on low incomes, while the second was drawn from a panel 'appearing to the Secretary of State to represent work-people.'[18] There was considerable

---

9 For a full discussion, see Sir R Micklethwait *The National Insurance Commissioners* (Hamlyn Lectures, 1976) ch 2.
10 (1957, Cmnd 218), para 184.
11 FANIA 1959, s.1; see now SSA 1986, s.52.
12 FANIA 1959, s.2: see 596 HC Official Report (5th series) cols 714–715.
13 S.8. The term 'statutory authorities' was frequently used to refer to the insurance officer, local tribunal and the Commissioner, though its origin is shrouded in mystery: see *Micklethwait*, n.9 above, p.18, n.4. The term now most often used to refer to officers and tribunals (social security and medical) is 'adjudicating authorities': see S1 1986/2218, reg 1(2).
14 See ch 4, pp. 161–168, above.
15 See pp. 580–583, below.
16 For the history of these tribunals, see Fulbrook *Administrative Justice and the Unemployed* (1978) esp. chs 8–10, and Lynes and Bradley in Adler and Bradley (ed.) *Justice, Discretion and Poverty* (1976) chs II and III.
17 Report of the Committee on Administrative Tribunals and Enquiries (1957, Cmnd. 218), para 182.
18 This quaint phrase was used in SBA 1976, Sch 4, para 1, now repealed. For further discussion, see second edition of this book, pp. 607–8.

disquiet with the performance of SBATs, the major criticisms being that they too frequently relied on the advice of the clerk (an official of the DHSS) and that they gave no or inadequate reasons for their decisions.[19] Despite these failings, their jurisdiction was expanded in 1970 to hear appeals from refusal of family income supplement; admittedly this was a means-tested benefit, but decisions on entitlement to it rarely involved the exercise of the discretion which used to characterise decisions on supplementary benefits.

In 1979 a first step to strengthen the tribunal system in this area was taken with the appointment of some Senior Chairmen to oversee the working of the tribunals and to assist in the appointment of chairmen – a development which heralded the 'presidential system' which is now one of the features of the integrated social security tribunals. A second change was the institution in 1980 of a right of appeal on a point of law to the Commissioners, whose expanded jurisdiction was marked by their restyling as Social Security Commissioners.[20]

The major reform was brought about in 1983 with the merger of the local insurance tribunals and SBATs into integrated social security appeal tribunals.[1] Under the same legislation there was also merger at the officer level where original decisions are taken, insurance, benefit and supplement officers being replaced by adjudication officers; in practice, however, integration has proceeded less rapidly here than with the appellate tribunals. There are now common procedural rules set out in the Adjudication Regulations, many of which also govern the still separate medical boards and tribunals. Exposition of this area of social security law is therefore somewhat easier than it was in the first two editions of the book.

Part 2   The adjudication system

A Questions for the Secretary of State

i General

Under the Social Security Act 1975[2] certain matters are reserved for decision by the Secretary of State. These include the following:

(a) whether a person is an earner and, if so, in which category of earners (employed or self-employed) he is to be included;

(b) whether the contribution conditions for any benefit have been satisfied and any question 'relating to a person's contributions or his earnings factor';[3]

(c) whether a person is, or was, employed in employed earner's employment for the purposes of industrial injuries benefits;

(d) whether a person was under the relevant regulations precluded from regular employment by home responsibilities;

19 Ibid, pp. 608 and 612. Also see Bell *Research Study of Supplementary Benefit Appeal Tribunals, Review of Main Findings: Conclusions: Recommendations* published by DHSS (1975), a report which influenced the changes made in 1979–83.
20 SSA 1980, s.12. See Part 3 below for further discussion.
 1 HASSASSA 1983, s.25 and Sch 8.
 2 Ss.93, as amended by CBA 1975, Sch 4, paras 30 and 31, SSPA 1975, s.60, SS(MP)A 1977, s.22(5), and SSA 1986, s.52 and Sch 5.
 3 SSA 1975, s.93(1)(b): see pp. 54–61, above, for contributions requirements. But other issues, relevant to contributions, may be left to the ordinary adjudicatory authorities: *Re Work in Germany (No 2)* [1979] 1 CMLR 267. Also see *R(G) 1/82 (T)*, where it was held it is for the ordinary authorities to determine the relevant years for contribution purposes.

(e) whether a constant attendance allowance or an exceptionally severe disablement allowance should be awarded or renewed and, if so, how it is to be assessed;[4]

(f) whether a person is, or was, an employee or employer of another person for the purposes of statutory sick or maternity pay;[5]

(g) whether an employer is entitled to make any deductions from his contributions payments under the sick or maternity pay schemes (and other questions arising under those schemes);[6]

(h) questions in connection with minimum contributions to personal pensions schemes or in connection with payments by the Secretary of State to trustees of contracted-out occupational pension schemes.[7]

These questions are entirely outside the jurisdiction of the ordinary authorities, i.e. the adjudication officer, tribunal and Commissioner.[8] It is not enough for them to rely on an informal opinion from an official of the DHSS; there should be a formal referral to the Secretary of State for the matter to be decided by him.[9]

It would appear that a question for the decision of the Secretary of State will only arise if a claimant has formally applied to him,[10] or if it is raised before the ordinary authorities. If, however, the issue is not disputed by the claimant, the latter may determine a matter which, if disputed, would have to be referred to the Secretary of State. This is the clear implication of the Adjudication Regulations which provide that an insurance officer may issue a decision where he:

> has decided any claim or question on an assumption of facts as to which there appeared to him to be no dispute, but concerning which, had a question arisen, that question would have fallen for determination by the Secretary of State. . . .[11]

However, if the claimant is dissatisfied with the decision on the basis of this assumption, he may require the Secretary of State to resolve the question.

ii Procedure on determination by the Secretary of State

When a question is to be determined by the Secretary of State under section 93, he must take reasonable steps to notify persons interested in the issue, e.g. employers, and he may appoint a person to hold an inquiry into and report on it.[12] The inquiry is generally held by a member of the DHSS Solicitor's Office; the procedure may be oral, and the inspector may require persons to attend the inquiry to give evidence or to produce documents. The Secretary of State must notify interested persons of his decision and, if requested, give reasons.[13] Decisions have not been published since 1960.[14] This procedure is frequently invoked in cases concerning liability to pay

4 See pp. 307–309, above.
5 SSHBA 1982, s.11(1)(a); SSA 1986, Sch 5 Pt II.
6 SSHBA, s.11(1)(a)–(e); SSA 1986, Sch 5, Pt II.
7 Ibid, s.52(2) and Sch 5, Pt II.
8 *R(G) 1/61*.
9 *R(I) 2/75*, J S Watson, Comr.
10 SI 1986/2218, reg 14.
11 Ibid, reg 21.
12 SSA 1975, s.93(3); see SI 1986/2218, reg 15.
13 Ibid, reg 16.
14 See ch 2, p.35, above.

contributions, where the correct categorisation of the person concerned may raise difficult questions of law and fact.[15]

iii Reference and appeal to the High Court

A question of law arising in connection with the determination by the Secretary of State of any question under section 93 may be referred by him to the High Court (or in Scotland, the Court of Session).[16] Alternatively, there may be an appeal on a point of law by 'any person aggrieved' with his decision.[17] The appeal is heard by a judge sitting alone, and there is (unusually) no further appeal.[18] Most appeals are brought on the question whether a person is properly to be regarded as employed or self-employed for the purpose of liability to pay contributions, and judicial decisions have substantially shaped the development of this area of law.

The precise grounds on which the judge will entertain an appeal were fully considered by Lord Widgery CJ in *Global Plant Ltd v Secretary of State for Social Services*.[19] He concluded that the court would only allow it:

(1) if the decision contained a false proposition of law ex facie;
(2) if the decision was one supported by no evidence; or
(3) if the decision reached was one which no person acting judicially and properly instructed as to the relevant law could have come to.

It is an open question whether these grounds might be widened in view of developments in the scope of judicial review, in particular to allow an appeal if the facts found leave out of account relevant evidence.[20] As will be seen, the approach of Lord Widgery has been followed by the Commissioner in determining the grounds of appeal to him from decisions of medical appeal tribunals and of the Attendance Allowance Board.

iv Critique

There has never been any substantial argument for allocating these decisions to the Secretary of State, rather than the ordinary adjudicating authorities. It may be that there are some practical reasons as regards decisions on whether a claimant has satisfied the relevant contribution conditions. But it is not clear why the usual authorities should not decide the related question whether a claimant should contribute as an employed or self-employed person. This involves difficult issues of law and fact which are suitable for a tribunal. Broader policy decisions in this area can, of course, be taken by the Secretary of State under his power to make regulations concerning the categorisation of earners.[1] Nor is there any obvious reason why entitlement to the constant attendance and exceptionally severe disablement allowances should be decided by him, while the ordinary adjudicating authorities determine claims to other allowances.

The Labour government in 1969–70 did indeed propose that 'Minister's

---

15 Ch 2, pp. 35–41, above.
16 SSA 1975, s.94.
17 Ibid, s.94(3). 'Person aggrieved' here means any person with a financial interest in the decision, e.g. an employer in a case concerning the classification of a contributor.
18 Ibid, s.94(7).
19 [1972] 1 QB 139, [1971] 3 All ER 385.
20 See in particular Scarman LJ, and Lord Wilberforce in *Secretary of State for Education v Tameside Metropolitan Borough Council* [1977] AC 1014 at 1030, and 1047.
1 See pp. 41–42, above.

questions' should be determined by a new 'special tribunal' with a right of appeal to the High Court on a point of law.[2] The Council on Tribunals argued that they should be decided by the existing statutory authorities with a final appeal to the Commissioner, but this was rejected, apparently on the ground that the matters were too complicated for local tribunals.[3] The Bill lapsed when the 1970 General Election was called.

B Adjudication officers

i General

All claims and questions are initially submitted to an adjudication officer for determination, except for certain questions relating to disablement benefit or an attendance allowance.[4] They are appointed by the Secretary of State for Social Security, and (in the case of unemployment benefit) may include officers of the Department of Employment appointed in consultation with the Secretary of State of the department. In the DSS, about 13,000 officers, generally of Executive Officer rank, decide claims in local offices, monitored when resources permit by Higher Executive Officers. The pattern is different in the Department of Employment, where initial decisions are taken by full-time officers grouped in area adjudication sections. Decisions on entitlement to some benefits is taken by officers at the central branches in Newcastle and North Fylde. Specialist adjudication officers deal with the preparation and presentation of appeals before tribunals.[5]

The 1983 reforms also provided for the appointment of a Chief Adjudication Officer (CAO), whose statutory duties include advising adjudication officers and keeping their work under review.[6] He is also required to report annually to the Secretary of State on adjudication standards; these reports have been rather critical, in particular of the standard of monitoring by senior officers. The CAO also decides whether an officer should appeal from a tribunal to the Commissioner, and whether the latter's decisions should be appealed to the Court of Appeal. In his first Annual Report he recommended the integration of DHSS and Department of Employment officers into common offices, but this step has apparently been postponed until after the substantive reforms brought about by the 1986 legislation have taken effect.[7]

ii Procedure for determining claims

An adjudication officer decides the application entirely on the documents sent to him by the claimant and branches of the Department. He does not interview the claimant or witnesses, though on rare occasions he may obtain statements through a Department inspector.[8] His duties have been characterised as 'administrative' in that he is not adjudicating between the contentions of the claimant and those of the Department or any other party.[9] When he finds it impossible to determine a complex case, he may refer it to a

2 National Superannuation and Social Insurance Bill 1969, cl 78.
3 See the Annual Report of the Council on Tribunals for 1969–1970, para 47 and Appendix B.
4 S.98.
5 This information is drawn from the Annual Reports of the CAO for 1984/85 and for 1985/86 on Adjudication Standards.
6 SSA 1975, s.97(1A)–(1E), inserted by HASSASSA 1983, Sch 8.
7 Annual Report for 1985/86, paras 8.5–8.6.
8 Street *Justice in the Welfare State* (2nd edn) p.13.
9 See Diplock LJ in *R v Deputy Industrial Injuries Comr, ex parte Moore* [1965] 1 QB 456 at 486, and *Jones v Department of Employment* [1988] 1 All ER 725, [1988] 2 WLR 493 at 502–3. But he may be a 'tribunal' for statutory purposes: *R(G) 1/80*.

SSAT for initial decision, with notification of the reference in writing to the claimant.[10]

The officer should decide the application so far as practicable within 14 days after its submission to him.[11] This is often impossible, particularly where, in an unemployment benefit case, written evidence has to be obtained from the claimant's employer. It has been held recently that there is not even an enforceable duty to decide straightforward claims within the 14-day period; this could not be done without the appointment of many more officers, and the court refused to make an order which would in effect compel such appointment.[11a] The case must be decided in accordance with Commissioners' decisions, but the officer is not bound to follow his own previous decision on a prior claim.[12] The claimant must be told in writing of any adverse decision with its reasons, and also of his right to appeal to the local tribunal.[13] However, where the claim has been decided by the officer on an assumption of facts, which if challenged would have raised a question for the Secretary of State, it is enough for the claimant to be told that, if he is dissatisfied with the decision, he can reply to that effect.[14] The claimant is only to be told of his right of appeal if he remains dissatisfied after the appropriate investigations have been made, or the Secretary of State has decided the relevant question.[15]

An adjudication officer is not liable in negligence for a wrong decision (which had been reversed by a social security tribunal). The Court of Appeal held that he was under no common law duty of care to a claimant and that the latter only had public law remedies, that is, judicial review or the statutory right of appeal to a SSAT.[15a]

C Social Security appeal tribunals

i Organisation and membership

These tribunals, the first tier of the appeal system, were formed by the merger of the national insurance local tribunals and supplementary benefit appeal tribunals in 1983. Social Security Appeal Tribunals (SSATs) are organised in seven regions (including one for Scotland and one for Wales and the South West), each under the administrative control of a Regional Chairman, responsible for the organisation and training of tribunal chairmen, members and clerks. At the head of the system is a President (at present, Judge Byrt QC), who assists in the appointment of chairmen and appoints the panels of the other members of tribunals. The President himself, Regional and other chairmen are all appointed by the Lord Chancellor.[16] These provisions are designed to ensure the tribunals' independence; ordinary members of their

10 SA 1975, s.99(3). The claimant cannot waive the requirement of notice in writing: *R(S) 5/86 (T)*.

11 SSA 1975, s.99(1). See *R(S) 6/78*, where the Commissioner deprecated the practice of delaying a decision, until an appeal on an earlier claim connected with the same complaint had been disposed of.

11a *R v Secretary of State for Social Services, ex parte Child Poverty Action Group* (1988) Times, 15 February.

12 *CI 440/50*. The subject of precedent in social security law is considered at pp. 583–584, below.

13 SSA 1975, s.100(2) and SI 1986/2218 regs 20 and 63. In *R(U) 7/81*, a Tribunal of Commissioners ruled that failure to notify the claimant does not invalidate the decision.

14 SI 1986/2218, reg 21(1).

15 Ibid, reg 21(2).

15a *Jones v Department of Employment* [1988] 1 All ER 725, [1988] 2 WLR 493.

16 For the appointment of the President, Regional and other full-time chairmen, see SSA 1975, Sch 10, para 1A, inserted by HASSASSA 1983, Sch 8, and for the appointment of other part-time chairmen, see Tribunals and Inquiries Act 1971, s.7.

predecessors – to take just one point of contrast – had been chosen by the Secretary of State.

The chairman of a tribunal must be a barrister or solicitor of at least five years' standing, though a transitional provision enables those non-legally qualified persons, who were chairmen of a tribunal before the 1983 reforms came into effect, to continue in office for the purposes of appeals concerning means-tested benefits until April 1989.[17] It is obviously desirable that a tribunal which has so much complex law to interpret and apply should be chaired by a lawyer, though some commentators would argue that academic lawyers without a professional qualification should also be eligible. In addition to presiding over the hearing, the chairman has a number of specific duties under the Adjudication Regulations, in particular deciding whether to grant a postponement of the hearing, recording the reasons for the tribunal's decision, and granting leave to appeal to a Commissioner.[18] Chairmen are expected to sit more often than the other members, at least once every two or three weeks, and thus have the opportunity to develop considerable expertise in social security law and practice.

The other two members of the tribunal are now drawn from a single panel composed of 'persons appearing to the President to have knowledge or experience of conditions in the area and to be representative of persons living or working' there.[19] Thus, unlike the position with the previous insurance and supplementary benefit tribunals, there are no longer the two panels, one representing (broadly) employers and the self-employed, the other working-people. The Council on Tribunals expressed a little unease with this change, but it seems that the President will consider nominations from a wide range of bodies, and has drawn up guidelines for the Regional Chairmen to select representative tribunals.[20] The only legal requirement for the selection of particular tribunals is that so far as practicable one member should be of the same sex as the claimant,[1] a requirement which is not regarded by the Commissioner as trivial;[1a] if a SSAT does not have a member of the same sex as the claimant, there is a presumption that it was not properly constituted and an appeal will be allowed. A chairman or member must stand down if otherwise there might be an infringement of the rule against bias, for example, if he is related to or knows the appellant very well. If a member stands down, the case may be heard by a two person tribunal, provided the appellant consents to this course. In this situation, the chairman has a casting vote.[2]

There used to be considerable disquiet with the role of the lay members of social security tribunals; it was felt that they too often left all the questioning to the chairman, and gave the impression of not fully participating in the process.[3] These charges now seem to be rarely made. The guide to procedure produced by the President and Regional Chairmen emphasises that members should play an active role in the hearing and the deliberative process leading

---

17   SSA 1975, s. 97(2E), and for the transitional regulation, see SI 1986/2218, reg 74.
18   Ibid, reg 5(1) (postponement), reg 25(2) (recording reasons for decisions) and reg 26 (leave to appeal to the Commissioner).
19   SSA 1975, Sch 10, para 1(2), substituted by HASSA 1984.
20   See Annual Report of Council on Tribunals 1983–4, paras 3.57–58.
1   SSA 1975, Sch 10, para 1(8).
1a   *R (SB) 2/88*.
2   SI 1986/2218, regs 24(2) and 25(1). For appeals to the Commissioner on the basis of infringement of the rule against bias, see *R(I) 26/54* and *R(I) 51/56*. Also see *Social Security Appeal Tribunals – a guide to procedure* (HMSO, 1988) para 50.
3   See Bell, Collison, Turner and Webber (1974) 3 Jo Soc Pol 289 and (1974) Jo Soc Pol 1, 9. But see Street *Justice in the Welfare State* (2nd edn) p.16.

to the decision.[4] Further, members are present while the chairman sets out the reasons for the tribunal's decision.

Administrative arrangements used to be made by the clerk, an employee of the DSS, who was sometimes considered to exercise an undue influence over tribunal hearings and deliberations, particularly in supplementary benefits cases. The clerk is now appointed by the President, and while the tribunal is sitting he acts under the chairman's direction.[5] In practice the arrangements before the hearing are made by staff at the Regional Chairman's office. In these respects also the reforms made in 1983 appear to have removed complaints. One matter concerning the tribunals' independence does however still give a little cause for concern: the premises where tribunals are held. It has not proved possible to find independent premises for all SSATs, and some continue to sit in DSS buildings, though the tribunal rooms are segregated from the local office.

ii Jurisdiction and powers

SSATs exercise the jurisdiction of the former insurance tribunals and supplementary benefit appeal tribunals, that is, their primary function is to hear appeals against the refusal of a benefit, contributory or means-tested, by an adjudication officer. They also have inherited the appellate jurisdiction to determine whether overpaid benefit is recoverable. Adjudication officers may refer questions to the appeal tribunal for it to make an original decision, a course frequently taken in the more complex unemployment benefit cases, where there is a question of disqualification for misconduct or voluntarily leaving employment without just cause.[6]

The scope of an appeal used to vary according to the nature of the benefit. Under the Social Security Act 1975 a tribunal (or the Commissioner) may determine any question, even though it has not been considered by the officer; this power is to be exercised broadly, although the parties should have an opportunity to comment on the new issues.[7] The provision did not apply to supplementary benefit cases, so a tribunal could not consider the award of a single payment for an item for which no claim had been brought before the officer.[8] Now the 1986 Act applies the general rule to a range of benefits other than those payable under the 1975 legislation and in particular to the new income support and family credit benefits.[9] However, there is to be no general right of appeal at all from social fund decisions, an extremely controversial decision, criticised by, among others, the Council on Tribunals. It described the step as 'the most substantial abolition of a right of appeal to an independent tribunal' since its institution in 1958.[10] There will be a right of appeal to SSATs from decisions on payments to meet maternity and funeral expenses, but from other social fund decisions there may only be a review by social fund officers and inspectors.[11] Since single payment appeals had formed a significant part of the SSATs' work, and further they enjoyed here some 'discretion', the change will clearly reduce the contribution made by people independent of the Department.

4 *Social Security Appeal Tribunals* n 2 above, paras 14, 47, 71.
5 Ibid, para 15. See SSA 1975, Sch 10, para 1B for the assignment of clerks to tribunals by the President.
6 SSA 1975, s.99(2)(3) sets out the power to refer.
7 See *R(I) 4/75*, construing SSA 1975, s.102.
8 *R (SB) 14/82, R(SB) 42/83 (T)*.
9 SSA 1986, s.52(3) and (6).
10 *Social Security – Abolition of independent appeals under the proposed Social Fund* Cmnd. 9722, para 12.
11 SSA 1986, s. 34 (review of social fund decisions) and s.52(6) (limited rights of appeal to SSATs). For the possibility of judicial review, see p.587, below.

iii Notice of appeal and of the hearing

Under the Adjudication Regulations notice of appeal to the SSAT must be given at a local office within three months of the date when notice of the officer's decision was given.[12] (Similar provisions apply to medical appeals, discussed later.) One might have expected that now notice would be given directly to the Regional Chairman's office, but the present arrangement enables the case to be reviewed at the local office before the papers are forwarded (unless the decision has been revised) to the former office for it to set the appeal process in motion. The time-limit of three months, introduced by the 1986 regulations, compares favourably with the previous limitation period of 28 days. The chairman may extend the time for special reasons; there is no appeal against his decision, whether to grant or refuse an extension of time, and further an application for extension may not be renewed.[13]

The Regional SSAT office notifies the appellant of the date and place of the tribunal hearing, enclosing the adjudication officer's submissions and other relevant papers. At least ten days' notice must be given; otherwise the hearing can only take place if the appellant consents.[14] If notice has been sent to his (last known) address, and he does not answer or attend the hearing, the tribunal may proceed with the case in his absence, and it will generally do this, unless there is some good explanation for non-attendance.[15] If it subsequently emerges that the appellant did not in fact receive the papers, or that his wish to attend the hearing at a later date had not been communicated to the tribunal, its decision may be set aside, either by the SSAT or on appeal by the Commissioner.[16]

iv The hearing

The Adjudication Regulations set out a few common provisions for oral hearings before the adjudicating authorities, that is, adjudication officers, SSATs, medical adjudicating authorities and the Attendance Allowance Board; as all appeals and references before SSATs are to be determined after an oral hearing,[17] the provisions are particularly pertinent here. One important rule is that the hearing must be in public, except where the claimant requests a private hearing or the chairman decides that intimate personal or financial circumstances may have to be disclosed or there are considerations of public security.[18] Parties, namely, the appellant, adjudication officer, and any other person appearing to the tribunal to be interested in the proceedings, and their representatives, have a right to attend and be heard.[19] Other persons, in particular, the President, any full-time chairman, and any trainee chairman or member, are entitled to be present at the hearing, whether or not it is otherwise conducted in private.[20]

Subject to these and one or two other common provisions, the procedure is for the chairman to determine. Naturally this will vary a little from one tribunal to another, but the guide to procedure issued to all tribunal members

12 SI 1986/2218, reg 3 and Sch 2.
13 Ibid, reg 3(3) and (4). (See *R(I) 44/59* for a ruling that there is no appeal against the chairman's decision.)
14 Ibid, reg 4(2).
15 Ibid, reg 4(3). If the clerk cannot show that the appellent has been notified, e.g. where the papers have been returned with a note that he was not known at the address, the SSAT should adjourn: *R(SB) 19/83*.
16 For setting aside of decisions, see SI 1986/2218, reg 11.
17 Ibid, reg 24.
18 Ibid, reg 4(4).
19 Ibid, regs 4(5) and 2(1)(b).
20 Ibid, reg 4(6).

sets out some general principles. It is crucial for the appellant to be put at ease, and so the chairman should first introduce the members of the tribunal and emphasise its independence from the government department concerned. In some cases it is appropriate for the appellant to begin by outlining his case, with the adjudication officer's submissions following, but especially where the appellant is unrepresented it is frequently better for the tribunal to ask the officer to start. This gives the appellant time to settle down and see what are the pertinent points in the appeal. The Court of Appeal and the Commissioner have stressed that a tribunal has investigatory functions, so the chairman and other members are expected to determine the facts themselves through questioning the officer and the appellant;[1] they are not restricted to the precise contentions made by the parties. The adjudication officer, whose role has been characterised as that of an *amicus curiae*, is expected to bring out those points favourable to the claimant.[2] It is normal to conclude proceedings by giving the appellant the last word, and then asking the parties to withdraw while the tribunal deliberates.

SSATs, and other adjudicating bodies, are not bound by the law of evidence. Thus, hearsay evidence is admissible, though it should be considered with caution.[3] Nor is there any requirement that the claimant's own evidence must be corroborated for it to be accepted.[4] But natural justice requires that tribunal decisions be based on probative material.[5] Thus, an adjudication officer should produce evidence to support his contentions by, for example, calling a visiting officer as witness, or at least by submitting himself to questions.[6] Sometimes the tribunal should consider adjourning the case where a party wishes to have more time to produce evidence or to call witnesses, though this course should not be taken if there has been ample opportunity to do this before the hearing. Generally tribunals should be reluctant to adjourn in view of the expense and delay that will result; one factor is that where the tribunal is differently constituted after an adjournment, there must be a complete rehearing of the case.[7] Finally where a SSAT has to consider medical evidence, the chairman may invite a medical practitioner to sit as assessor. He acts strictly in an advisory capacity, and is not to be treated as a witness, cross-examined or allowed to examine the claimant.[8]

Studies of the insurance and supplementary benefit tribunals in the 1970s showed that only about 40–50 per cent of appellants attended the hearing, and 20 per cent of them were represented.[9] Appellants who did turn up, and still more those who were represented, had a higher rate of success. This latter fact is not surprising, for an appellant who attends is able to challenge the officer's summary of the facts or the evidence on which he has relied. There are a variety of explanations for the low attendance rate: perhaps many

1 *R v Deputy Industrial Injuries Comr, ex parte Moore* [1965] 1 QB 456 at 486; *R(S) 4/82 (T)*, *R(S) 1/87*.
2 *R v Deputy Industrial Injuries Comr, ex parte Moore* [1965] 1 QB 456 at 486.
3 *R(SB) 5/82* For a general discussion of the rules of evidence in social security tribunals, see Yates [1980] JSWL 273.
4 *R(SB) 33/85*.
5 *R(S) 1/87*.
6 *R(SB) 10/86*.
7 See SI 1986/2218, reg 24(3) for the rehearing rule, and *R (V) 3/88 (T)*, where the Commissioners gave guidance on the procedure to be followed at the rehearing. *Social Security Appeal Tribunals – a guide to procedure* (HMSO, 1988), paras 65–6 offers guidelines when a tribunal should adjourn.
8 SI 1986/2218, reg 24(4) and (5). The assessor's role was considered in *R(I) 14/51* and *R(I) 14/57*.
9 Bell, Collison, Turner and Webber (1974) Jo Soc Pol 289 and (1975) Jo Soc Pol 1. Also see Lawrence, 5 Br J Law & Soc 246.

frivolous appeals are not pursued, perhaps appellants are nervous of attending or are unduly pessimistic of their chances of success. Legal aid is not available for representation before social security tribunals, but this may not matter; the participation of lawyers often leads to undue formality, and there is some evidence that they are less successful than skilled lay representatives.[10] Moreover, there are now many local welfare rights centres and Citizens' Advice Bureaux, who are willing to assist claimants.

v The decision
When the hearing is over, everyone (except the clerk, the President of the social security tribunals, a full-time chairman and, with the leave of the chairman, any trainee chairman or member) must withdraw during the tribunal's deliberations.[11] Its decisions may be unanimous or by a majority, though the latter is very rare; a dissent and its reasons should be recorded. It is the chairman's responsibility to record the tribunal's decision, stating its findings on material issues of fact and its legal reasons in sufficient detail to enable the Commissioner to see the basis on which the case had been determined.[12] There used to be considerate disquiet with this aspect of the tribunal process, particularly in the case of supplementary benefit tribunals, but this is now less often voiced. The practice encouraged by Regional Chairmen is generally for the chairman to inform the parties verbally immediately after the SSAT has come to its decision, and then dictate the reasons into a casette recorder; a typed form is then sent to the parties as soon as practicable, with notification of their right of appeal to the Commissioner.[13]

D Medical Adjudication

i General
Under the Social Security Act 1975 certain questions, in particular 'disablement questions', are referred to separate medical authorities for them to adjudicate.[14] It is not entirely clear whether this course is justified. On one view such questions could be left to the ordinary authorities, sitting where necessary with expert medical assessors, or perhaps members. On the other hand, some of the questions with regard to disablement benefit, compensation for industrial diseases and mobility allowance may be so complex that they should be reserved for expert medical tribunals. But whatever its merits in principle, the division of functions between the different adjudicating authorities has led to complex legal problems, which have twice been before the House of Lords.[15]

The general character of the medical authorities' jurisdiction has been summarized by Diplock J. (as he then was):

> As an expert investigating body it is the right and duty of the medical board to use their own expertise in deciding the medical questions referred to them. They may, if they think fit, make their own examination of the claimant and consider any

10 The proposal of the Royal Commission on Legal Services (1979, Cmnd. 7648) that legal aid should in appropriate cases be extended to cover representation before all tribunals has been summarily rejected by the government: Response of the Government to the Royal Commission (1983, Cmnd. 9077).
11 SI 1986/2218, reg 2(2).
12 Ibid, reg 25(2). For relevant Commissioners' decisions, see *R(U) 3/80, R(S) 2/83, R(S) 1/87.*
13 SI 1986/2218, reg 25(3).
14 S.108 defines 'disablement questions'. Also see SSA 1975, s.113 for adjudication on industrial diseases, and see ch 7, pp. 280 and 284, above.
15 *Ministry of Social Security v Amalgamated Engineering Union* [1967] 1 AC 725, [1967] 1 All ER 210, and *Jones v Secretary of State for Social Services* [1972] AC 944.

other facts and material to enable them to reach their expert conclusion as doctors do in diagnosis and prognosis of the case of an ordinary patient.[16]

These observations are also applicable to the appellate medical tribunals. There is no doubt that these tribunals, like the SSATs, are inquisitorial in their procedure.[17]

Before 1983 medical boards, composed generally of two medical practitioners, exercised original jurisdiction over disablement questions and appellate jurisdiction from (at that time insurance) officer decisions on the diagnosis of prescribed industrial diseases and the medical issues relevant to mobility allowance.[18] Now there is a complex variety of 'adjudicating medical authorities' which exercise (for the most part) original jurisdiction. Medical appeal tribunals (MATs) continue to hear appeals from these medical authorities; they are now organised in the same presidential system as the SSATs.

ii Adjudicating medical authorities
In the usual case where a disablement question has to be resolved the authority is a medical practitioner appointed by the Secretary of State to act for an assigned area.[19] Certain other questions, referred to as 'diagnosis' and 'recrudescence' questions, arising in the context of a sickness or disablement benefit claim, may be referred for report to a medical practitioner, and in the case of certain specified diseases that practitioner is to be a 'specially qualified adjudicating medical practitioner', also appointed by the Secretary of State.[20] Other questions, for example, on claims for benefit in respect of a prescribed disease, or the medical questions arising in connection with claims for mobility allowance may be determined by a medical board or special medical board.[1] The boards may consist of two medical (or specially qualified) practitioners, though where they disagree, the reference is withdrawn and the case sent to a three-member board.[2] Medical boards also enjoy some appellate jurisdiction from the decisions of adjudication officers, where the latter have themselves decided diagnosis or recrudescence questions or medical questions in mobility allowance claims.[3]

The hearings of medical authorities are not treated as oral hearings for the purposes of the Adjudication Regulations so the common provisions discussed in the context of SSATs do not apply; only the claimant is entitled to be present, though with his consent, the authority may allow any other person to attend, if that is conducive to the expedition of the case.[4] But the authority is required to record their decision, including a summary of the findings of fact and the reasons for any dissent, and this is communicated to the claimant.[5]

iii Medical appeal tribunals
The tribunals consist of three members. The chairman must be a lawyer of

16 *R v Medical Appeal Tribunal, ex parte Hubble* [1958] 2 QB 228 at 240–241. Also see *R(I) 7/81*.
17 *R v National Insurance Comr, ex parte Viscusi* [1974] 2 All ER 724, [1974] 1 WLR 646, CA.
18 See the second edition of this book, pp. 597–8, and Smith *Industrial Injuries Benefits* (1978) at pp. 133–35.
19 SI 1986/2218, reg 28.
20 Ibid, reg 42.
 1 Ibid, reg 29. (See pp. 171–177, above for mobility allowance.)
 2 Ibid, regs 27 and 29(5).
 3 Ibid, regs 45(2) and 58(2).
 4 Ibid, reg 29(9).
 5 Ibid, reg 30.

seven years' standing, and is appointed by the Lord Chancellor, while the two other members are medical practitioners, appointed by the Secretary of State in consultation with academic medical bodies.[6] The President and Regional Chairmen of the SSATs and MATs organise meetings and training for chairmen and members, so that as with social security tribunals their independence and competence is ensured. Under the regulations, a person who has taken any part in the case as a medical assessor or who has medically examined the claimant regularly, etc., is disqualified from acting as a member of a MAT or as a medical adjudicating authority.[7]

A MAT is required to hold an oral hearing, so the common provisions in the Adjudication Regulations apply to its procedure.[8] Thus, an appellant has three months from the date of the medical adjudicating authority's decision within which to lodge an appeal. And it is for the chairman to determine the order of proceedings. The tribunals' specialist character is important; thus, it is usual for the medical members to examine the appellant, although this is not required.[9] Further, the courts and the Commissioners have stressed the ability of the MATs to use their own expertise, albeit subject to the requirements of natural justice.[10] So the tribunals may call for a specialist's report, but fairness requires that a copy be shown to the claimant.[11]

A MAT has jurisdiction to decide the issues before it *de novo* and is not limited to those considered by the lower authority.[12] In some cases it may be appropriate to return the case to another board or authority for it to decide.[13] Rather oddly, the provisions for recording the tribunals' decisions differ markedly from those applicable to SSATs. The chairman is not given responsibility for this task, and there is no provision for recording a dissent or its grounds.[14] In a number of cases the Commissioner has emphasized the importance of stating reasons fully; in particular the MAT should make clear why they rejected specific contentions of a party and also when appropriate the grounds on which they departed from the board's decision.[15]

E The Attendance Allowance Board

i General

The Attendance Allowance Board (AAB), in addition to its advisory functions, determines whether the medical conditions for an award of the allowance have been satisfied.[16] Other questions, for example, whether the claimant is eligible for the allowance by satisfying the age and residence requirements, are determined by the ordinary adjudicating authorities. In all but a handful of cases the Board delegates its adjudicatory functions to a delegated medical practitioner(DMP), to whom it may properly issue general

6 SSA 1975, Sch 12, para 2, substituted by HASSASSA 1983, Sch 8, introducing the requirement that the chairman must be a lawyer.
7 SI 1986/2218, reg 33.
8 Ibid, reg 31(1).
9 See Hodge (1974) LAG Bulletin 13 (January), and *R(I) 35/61*, which establishes that a medical examination is not a requirement.
10 E.g., *R v Medical Appeal Tribunal, ex parte Carrarini* [1966] 1 WLR 883, *R v National Insurance Comm, ex parte Viscusi* [1974] 2 All ER 724, [1974] 1 WLR 646, *R(I) 29/61 (T)*, *R(M) 2/80*.
11 See *R(I) 35/61*, *R(I) 6/67*, *R(I) 13/74*.
12 See Diplock J in *R v Medical Appeal Tribunal, ex parte Hubble* [1958] 2 QB 228 at 241.
13 *R(I) 7/75*.
14 See SI 1986/2218, reg 31.
15 *R(M) 1/83*, *R(M) 2/83*, but see *R(M) 5/86*, where the Commissioner and the Court of Appeal emphasized that there were limits on the details tribunals could be expected to record.
16 SSA 1975, s.105(3).

guidance on their discharge.[17] Further the AAB may revoke this delegation at any time before a final decision is made.[18] There are no procedural rules governing determinations by the Board or the DMP, nor it seems need reasons be given for an initial decision. The DMP is either a full-time medical officer of the Department, or doctor doing this work on a full or part-time basis. His decision is based on a medical report made by an examining officer and other reports which he may decide to call for.[19]

Either the claimant or Secretary of State may apply in writing for a review of the decision within three months *on any ground*, or at any time on certain limited grounds: that there has been a change of circumstances since the original decision or that it was reached in ignorance of, or a mistake as to a material fact.[20] The first type of review is analogous to an appeal, while the second is the usual review procedure discussed in Part 4 of this chapter. Leave of the AAB is required for a further review within 12 months.[1] Again there are no procedural rules for reviews, but if the Board (or the DMP) does not intend to revise the decision in the claimant's favour, the practice is to allow him to comment on its provisional opinion.[2] Further the reasons for the determination on review (or a refusal to review) must be notified, unless one of the parties does not want this.[3] They must also be notified of their right of appeal on a point of law to the Commissioner.

It is clear from Commissioners' decisions that, although there are no procedural rules governing DMP determinations, the requirements of natural justice must be observed. There is a breach of the rules if no attempt is made to contact the claimant's doctor (as implicitly requested) or to tell the claimant to produce the medical evidence himself.[4] Further, adequate reasons must be given, particularly when on review a DMP removes an existing award of attendance allowance.[5]

ii Critique

In its first years the AAB attracted some criticism, partly because its procedures were not then revealed.[6] The absence of any procedural rules suggests that it is to be regarded as an informal case committee rather than a quasi-judicial tribunal. On the other hand, the duty to give reasons and the right of appeal to the Commissioner assimilate it to the other adjudicating authorities. The Ogelsby Report in 1983 recommended that the AAB should be relieved of its adjudicatory functions, which should be given to the ordinary authorities, with a specially constituted SSAT.[7] There is much to be said for this proposal for it would reduce the proliferation of tribunals; it is also unsatisfactory that decisions be taken in practice by departmental medical officers without any right of appeal on the merits to an independent body. But this recommendation has not been accepted. In the last few years the AAB has produced an annual report on its adjudicatory functions, and this may have dispelled some of the anxieties about its work.

17 *R(A) 4/78*. The guidance is now to be published: see Annual Report of the AAB for 1986.
18 *R(A) 1/81*.
19 See the Annual Report of the AAB for 1984, pp. 7–9.
20 SSA 1975, s.106(1) and SI 1986/2218, regs 38–9.
 1 Ibid, reg 38(4).
 2 Annual Report of AAB for 1984, p.8.
 3 SI 1986/2218, reg 39(3).
 4 *CA 3/78* and see *R 2/75 (AA)*.
 5 See *R(A) 1/72. R(A) 1/73*, and *R(A) 1/84*.
 6 Carson (1975) LAG Bulletin 67 and Smith (1981) 48 Poverty 9.
 7 Paras 96–110.

Part 3   Social Security Commissioners

A   The Commissioners and their jurisdiction

At the apex of the social security tribunal system sit the Social Security Commissioners, of whom there are now 13, including the Chief Social Security Commissioner, L Bromley QC who sit full-time. There is also one part-time Commissioner. They must be barristers (in Scotland, advocates) or solicitors of ten years' standing, and are appointed by the Crown, in practice by the Lord Chancellor, in consultation where appropriate with the Lord Advocate.[8] Since the start of 1985, the Lord Chancellor has been responsible for the payment and administrative requirements of the Commissioners, and the procedural regulations governing their proceedings are now made by his office.[9] This change, perhaps more of form than real substance, denotes the Commissioners' status and independence. The Chief Social Security Commissioner has statutory responsibility for convening a Tribunal of three Commissioners to hear an appeal which involves a legal question of special difficulty.[10] This course is adopted more frequently than it used to be ten years ago, probably because there are now more complex cases and also more Commissioners, with the consequent risk of disagreement between them. Separate concurring opinions and dissents in Tribunal cases are also more common. The Chief Commissioner has a number of administrative duties, of which the most important is selecting which cases should be reported. Subject to the higher status of Tribunal decisions, the authority of each Commissioner is the same. They are appointed to hear appeals in Great Britain, and not for particular areas of the country. However, two of them sit in Edinburgh and hear appeals largely from Scottish tribunals, while another travels to Cardiff to hear cases from Wales. The others sit in London.

Commissioners exercise appellate jurisdiction from SSATs, MATs and the Attendance Allowance Board. (They also exercise original jurisdiction to determine whether a person who has unlawfully killed another should forfeit entitlement to benefit.[11]) Until recently there used to be significant differences in the extent of rights of appeal, with an appeal from a SSAT (formerly an insurance tribunal) on both law and fact in the case of contributory and child benefits, while there was only an appeal on a point of law for means-tested benefits and from decisions of medical appeal tribunals and the AAB. Other differences related to the leave requirements: for means-tested benefits, leave of the chairman of the tribunal or the Commissioner always had to be obtained, while from 1980 this was a requirement in the case of contributory benefits, etc. when the tribunal's decision was unanimous. Now the position is that the appellant must always obtain leave either from the chairman of the SSAT (or medical tribunal) or the Commissioner.[12] This change is presumably designed to ensure that only appeals involving real points of substance reach the Commissioner. Further, whatever the nature of the benefit, the only ground of an appeal from a SSAT to the Commissioner is on a point of law. The distinction between fact and law is notoriously hard to draw with precision, but in his appellate jurisdiction over medical appeal and social security tribunals (in supplementary benefit cases) the Commissioner has laid down some relevant principles. In a leading case from

8 SSA 1975, s.97(3), amended by SSA 1979, s.9.
9 SI 1984/1818.
10 SSA 1975, s.116. See *R(V) 4/88 (T)*.
11 Forfeiture Act 1982, s.4, amended by SSA 1986, s.76.
12 SSA 1975, s.101(5A), inserted by SSA 1986, Sch 5. An adjudication officer may appeal against a tribunal decision adverse to the claimant: *R(V) 6/88*.

a MAT, he ruled that an appeal will be allowed on a point of law if there has been a breach of the natural justice rules, if the tribunal failed to state the facts and reasons for its decision adequately, if the ruling contained an *ex facie* false proposition of law or if the findings of fact were unsupported by any evidence.[13] These principles were applied to supplementary benefit cases and in appeals on a point of law from the AAB, and there is every reason to believe they will be adopted now for SSATs generally. In practice much the most important ground of appeal is the failure by a tribunal to state the reasons for its decision adequately.

B Procedure for appeals to the Commissioner

i Pre-hearing procedure

The appellant must first obtain the leave of the chairman of the SSAT or of the Commissioner. Leave of the former may be applied for either orally after the tribunal has announced its decision or by written notice within three months of notification of the decision.[14] Applications for leave to appeal from a MAT may only be made by the latter course,[15] and in the case of attendance allowance, the Commissioner's leave must be obtained; there is not the alternative avenue of leave from the Board or the DMP. Where the tribunal chairman has refused leave, the appellant may then apply to the Commissioner within 42 days of the date when notice of the refusal was given him.[16] The Commissioner may, however, consider an application for leave made outside this period, or even if no application at all has been made to the tribunal chairman, if he considers there are special reasons. The appellant must then state grounds for acceptance of his application, despite the delay, etc., in addition to the substantive grounds of appeal. The grounds of appeal need not however be stated in great detail.[17]

The Commissioner must make a written decision on the application for leave but he is under no obligation under the procedural regulations to give reasons.[18] The Court of Appeal has recently rejected the view that in some special cases natural justice requires the Commissioner to give reasons for refusing leave.[19] A Commissioner is always free to give reasons, but it was not appropriate to impose a duty, even in special cases, which would be hard in practice to differentiate from the ordinary run of the mill appeal. This is surely right. Appellate courts are not required to give reasons for refusing leave to appeal, nor is it their normal practice to do so. There is no appeal against a refusal of leave, though there may in exceptional circumstances be a judicial review.[20]

If leave is granted by the Commissioner, notice of appeal is then deemed to be given by the appellant; but where leave had been granted by the tribunal chairman, notice of appeal must be served within 42 days.[1] The Commissioners' office, now responsible for the introductory process, then notifies the respondent (the adjudication officer or claimant), who may

13 *R(I) 14/75.* Also see *R(A) 1/73, R(SB) 6/81.*
14 SI 1986/2218, reg 26.
15 Ibid, reg 32.
16 SI 1987/214, reg 3(3).
17 Ibid, reg 6. For case law on earlier regulations, see *R(I) 15/53* and *R/F 1/70.*
18 See SI 1987/214, reg 22(1).
19 *R v Secretary of State for Social Services, ex parte Connolly* [1986] 1 All ER 998. [1986] 1 WLR 421, rejecting the view of Woolf J. in *R v Social Security Comr, ex parte Sewell* (1985) Times, 2 January.
20 *Bland v Chief Supplementary Benefit Officer* [1983] 1 All ER 537, [1983] 1 WLR 262.
1 SI 1987/214, regs 5(2) and 7.

submit written observations within 30 days. Observations may be sent in reply. The Commissioner himself may direct further particulars to be supplied by any party, and may direct the AAB or MAT in appropriate cases to submit a statement of the facts.[2] There is no automatic oral hearing. But if one is requested by any party in any proceedings (including it would seem an application for leave) it will be granted, unless the Commissioner is satisfied that the case can be determined on the papers.[3] He can himself at any stage decide to hold an oral hearing, whether it has been requested or not. In practice many cases are decided without one. At least ten days' notice of a hearing must be granted, and the Commissioner has the same power to proceed in the absence of a party as a SSAT.[4]

One factor which has length of troubled the Council on Tribunals is the time before appeals are heard. There is no obvious reason for this, though the complex nature of the cases and the periods allowed for written submissions may provide the explanation. At all events the Council has noted an improvement; applications for leave to appeal are now generally heard within 6 weeks of lodgement of the application. The waiting time for oral hearings after submissions have been exchanged is now about eight to ten weeks.[5]

ii The hearing
A number of persons have a right to attend and be heard at an oral hearing, including the appellant, the claimant (if not the appellant), the Secretary of State and an adjudication officer.[6] The public hearing rule applies with the same qualifications as obtain for SSAT hearings.[7] The Commissioner's permission is necessary for a party to give evidence or call or question witnesses, a rule which bears out the point that appeals at this stage are not primarily concerned with reviewing the facts.[8] The Commissioner himself has power to summon a person to attend as a witness to answer questions or produce documents.[9] Apart from these few specific rules, he is free to adopt the procedure he thinks fit, subject to the rules of natural justice.

Like SSATs, the Commissioner is not bound by the issues raised before the adjudication officer.[10] On appeals from SSATs, though not from MATs and the AAB, he may refer any question to a medical practioner for him to prepare a report, which must be given to the parties for their comments.[11] He also has a statutory power where an appeal 'involves a question of fact of special difficulty' to enlist the assistance of a qualified assessor.[12] This facility has not been extensively used, and presumably is of relatively little importance, now that Commissioners only hear appeals on points of law.

iii The decision
The Commissioner's decision must be reasoned and sent to the parties, but he may, and often does, tell them at the conclusion of the hearing.[13] If he holds

---

2 Ibid, regs 10–12.
3 Ibid, reg 15(2).
4 Ibid, reg 17.
5 See the Annual Report of the Council for 1969–70, para 29, for 1981–2, para 3.57, and for 1982–3, para 3.40.
6 SI 1987/214, reg 17(5). For a general discussion, see Micklethwait, *The National Insurance Commissioners* (1976) pp. 48–53.
7 SI 1987/214, reg 17(4).
8 Ibid, reg 17(6).
9 Ibid, reg 18.
10 *R(I) 4/75.*
11 SSA 1975, s.101(7) (and SI 1987/214, reg 13).
12 Ibid, s.101(6). *Micklethwait*, n.6, above, at pp. 60–61 is critical of the restrictions on the use of assessors.

may, and often does, tell them at the conclusion of the hearing.[13] If he holds the tribunal decision wrong in law, he may decide the case himself, if necessary after finding fresh or further facts, or may send the case back to a tribunal, which will be differently constituted from the one which took the original decision.[14] In practice, the Commissioners are reluctant to resolve issues of fact, and so, unless the tribunal's error was purely one of law and there is no doubt about the facts, they are inclined to refer the case back. This course sometimes appears circuitous and productive of delay.

The Commissioner's decision is final, though this statement should be qualified. Quite apart from the right of appeal to the ordinary courts instituted in 1980, his decision may be reviewed by adjudication officers on certain grounds and the Commissioner may himself set aside his decision in circumstances set out in regulations: that relevant documents were not received in time, or that a party was absent from an oral hearing, or 'the interests of justice so require.'[15]

C Precedent and the reporting of decisions

The Commissioners decide about 2,000 cases a year. The vast majority do not raise any points of legal principle or importance, and therefore are not reported, the decisions being circulated only to the parties. But if a Commissioner thinks a decision should be reported, it is sent to his colleagues for them to look at. In the light of their comments and any representations made by the parties to the case and their legal advisers, the Chief Commissioner decides whether it should be reported. These decisions must deal with questions of legal principle and command the assent of the majority of Commissioners. The category of numbered decisions, available for inspection at DHSS regional offices, has been discontinued since 1982, when the Chief Commissioner's Practice Direction inaugurated the new system of reporting.[16] Since then the practice has been for rather more decisions to be reported than had hitherto been the case, a trend which was particularly evident in supplementary benefit cases.

Reporting is important because of the system of precedent. In the leading case, *R(I) 12/75*, a Tribunal of Commissioners set out a number of rules: Commissioners' decisions must be followed by tribunals and officers, and where they conflict a decision of a Tribunal must be followed in preference to the ruling of a single Commissioner and reported decisions given more weight than unreported ones. (Unreported decisions are binding on tribunals, and therefore when an adjudication officer relies on one, a copy should be given the claimant.[17]) Commissioners themselves should follow a Tribunal decision unless there are compelling reasons for not doing this, and generally should follow the previous decision of another Commissioner. Nor is a Tribunal

13 SI 1987/214, reg. 22.
14 SSA 1975, s.101(5), substituted by SSA 1986, Sch 5.
15 SI 1987/214, reg 25. It would appear that this power encompasses the implied power exercised by the Commissioner to set aside decisions for breach of the rules of natural justice: *R(S) 6/83*.
16 The Practice Direction is set out in the bound volume of Social Security Commissioner decisions 1980–2, published by HMSO. For comment on the system, see Annual Report of the Council on Tribunals for 1981–2, paras 3.58–3.63.
17 For the status of unreported decisions, see *R(SB) 22/86*.

absolutely bound to follow a previous Tribunal ruling.[17a] So the strict doctrine of *stare decisis* has not been adopted by the Commissioners.[18].

Part 4 Review and judicial control
A Review of social security decisions
i General

A decision taken by an adjudicating authority, including for this purpose the Commissioner and a medical authority, may be reviewed if it was based on a mistake of fact or law, or there has been a subsequent change of circumstances.[19] This affords a simple method of revising a determination, which was either at the time, or later has become, wrong, without requiring the claimant to make a fresh claim or to make a formal appeal. Review by medical practitioners and boards has been discussed in the chapter on industrial injuries.[20], and review by the AAB has been already been briefly touched on in this chapter; but for the most part the principles on which they review are the same as those applicable to the ordinary adjudicating authorities, so the discussion here is relevant to those bodies. Further the principal rules now apply equally to the review of any decision by an adjudication officer, SSAT or the Commissioner, whatever the character of the benefit in issue. The main provision is section 104(1) of the Social Security Act 1975:

> Any decision under this Act of an adjudication officer, a social security appeal tribunal or a Commissioner may be reviewed at any time by an adjudication officer, or, on a reference by an adjudication officer, by a social security appeal tribunal, if –
> (a) the officer or tribunal is satisfied that the decision was given in ignorance of, or was based on a mistake as to, some material fact; or
> (b) there has been any relevant change of circumstances since the decision was given. . . .

An adjudication officer's decision may also be reviewed for mistake of law.[1] A review may be requested by a written application to an officer, though this is not necessary, and indeed in some circumstances a claim may be treated as an application for review.[2] In fact an adjudication officer automatically reviews a case, when an appeal to the SSAT is lodged at a local office. The decision is not automatically revised merely because one of the grounds set out in section 104 are satisfied; the officer (or SSAT) must decide it is right to revise it, and regulations set out detailed rules prescribing the earliest date from which the revised decision may take effect.[3]

ii Ignorance of, or mistake as to, a material fact
Review will only be permitted if the mistake was as to a primary, specific fact, and not if it lay in a mistaken assessment of the facts or of the issue, on the

17a *R(V) 4/88 (T)*.
18 See *Micklethwait*, n.6, above, at pp. 74 and 129. Decisions of the Northern Ireland Commissioners are of only persuasive authority in Britain, though they may be followed in preference to decisions of the British Commissioner: *R(I) 14/63*.
19 SSA 1975, s.104(1), substituted by SSA 1986, Sch 5. For review of Secretary of State's decisions, see SSA 1975, s.96 and SI 1986/2218, regs 17 and 19.
20 See ch 7, p.292, above.
1 SSA 1975, s.104(1A), inserted by HASSASSA 1983, Sch 8, para 3.
2 *R(I) 50/56*. This may enable the applicant to surmount the time-limits for making claims: ch 15, pp. 544–549, above.
3 SI 1986/2218, regs 65–72. Normally the revision takes effect from the date of the application for review, though in some cases it may be backdated for a period of up to 12 months before that date.

outcome of which the award was made or refused.[4] So there can be no review if an officer changes his mind about the claimant's capacity for work because of a new medical opinion.[5] The position used to be that Commissioners' decisions could only be reviewed if there was fresh evidence to show that the original determination was wrong; this requirement has been removed from section 104, but the provision does enable regulations to be made requiring fresh evidence for a review at any level on this basis.[6]

iii Relevant change of circumstances
This may be brought about in a variety of ways: by a change in the claimant's condition, evidenced perhaps by a fresh medical report,[7] by a subsequent ruling of a MAT[8] or the Commissioner,[9] which undermines the basis of the original determination, or by a retrospective change in the legislation.[10] The Court of Appeal has held that a permanent alteration of the claimant's residence may constitute a 'relevant change of circumstances' to justify review of an award of mobility allowance.[11] Regulations may now prescribe what are or are not such a change.

iv Mistake of law
The power to review the decisions of *officers* was introduced by the 1983 legislative reforms. It is a valuable extension of the review powers, which enables simple errors of law to be corrected without resort by the claimant to the formal appeal process; obviously it would be inappropriate to extend this to tribunals or the Commissioner, when the appellant has already embarked on this process.

v Officer review of social fund decisions
In the absence of any right of appeal to a SSAT, the procedure for internal review of discretionary social fund payments assumes great importance. A social fund officer must review any decision made by him or any other officer on an application from the claimant (or anyone acting on his behalf with his written consent) within 28 days of notification of the decision.[11a] Specific grounds must be given for the application. Further, an officer may review a determination at his discretion, though this is limited by directions and guidance issued by the Secretary of State. Under one direction a review must be made in the same circumstances that govern review of social security decisions, viz., that there was a mistake of law or fact, or there has been a relevant change of circumstances since the decision was made.[11b] A further ground is that the decision was based on a mistake as to the directions. Under other directions a claimant has a right to attend an interview, with a friend or

4 *R(I) 3/75*, cf *R(G) 8/55*.
5 *R(M) 5/86*.
6 SSA 1975, s.104. For the meaning of 'fresh evidence' see the second edition of this book, pp. 604–5.
7 *R(S) 6/78; R(M) 5/86*.
8 *R(M) 1/86*.
9 *R(I) 25/63*.
10 *R(G) 3/58 (T); R(A) 4/81*.
11 *Insurance Officer v Hemmant*, reported as Appendix to *R(M) 2/84*. But the fact that a claimant obtained a higher amount of earnings than that *estimated* by the officer does not constitute a change of circumstances to justify a revision of an award of special hardship allowance: see *R(I) 3/87*.
11a SSA 1986, s.34(1) and (2). The time-limit and other requirements are imposed by SI 1988/34.
11b Direction 31.

representative, before a final determination is made, and must be given the reasons for the original decision against which he is complaining.[11c]

A claimant dissatisfied with the review may then apply for a further review by a social fund inspector.[11d] This application is subject to the same time-limit and other procedural requirements as the initial review. An inspector may confirm the original decision, make any decision which the social fund officer could have made or remit the matter to the officer for him to decide.[11e] As already indicated, this is in no sense an independent review, for the inspectors are appointed and their training directed by the social fund Commissioner, himself an appointee of the Secretary of State.[11f] Moreover, they, like officers, are subject to the guidance and directions issued by the Secretary of State.

B Control by the courts

i History

As has been said at the start of this chapter, disputes concerning social security benefits have been kept away from the ordinary courts. So there was no provision for an appeal to them from decisions of the Commissioners and other adjudicating authorities in the 1946 legislation or in the national assistance and later the 1966 supplementary benefits legislation. The position was approved by the Franks Committee, who regarded it as important that final decisions be reached quickly.[12] However, it became clear in the 1950s and 1960s that medical appeal tribunals (before the institution of an appeal to the Commissioner) and the Commissioners were subject to judicial review by the prerogative orders.[13] On the whole this development was welcome. Not only is it important in principle for the courts to have the last word on questions of law, but resort to them would on occasion be the only way in which a disagreement between the Commissioners could be resolved. A Tribunal of three Commissioners can be convened for this purpose, but when the number of Commissioners increased to nine or ten, the approach of a Tribunal could no longer be taken as representing an absolutely settled view of the law. The prerogative orders were also available to review the decisions of the supplementary benefit appeal tribunals (SBATs).

The courts were, however, reluctant to exercise their powers of review, deferring on occasion to the expertise of the Commissioners.[14] Further, the Court of Appeal expressed reluctance to question SBAT decisions, a cautious approach hard to support in view of the lack of legal expertise in these tribunals.[15] Dissatisfaction with this perspective led to the institution in 1978 of a right of appeal to the High Court, a temporary step superseded two years later by the right of appeal on points of law to the renamed Social Security Commissioner.

11c Directions 33 and 34.
11d SSA 1986, s.34(3).
11e Ibid, s.34(4).
11f See p.511, above.
12 Franks Committee on Administrative Tribunals and Enquiries (1957, Cmnd. 218), para 108.
13 The leading case was *R v Medical Appeal Tribunal, ex parte Gilmore* [1957] 1 QB 574, [1957] 1 All ER 796. For a full discussion of these developments, see the first edition of this book, pp. 644–46.
14 See for example *R v Industrial Injuries Comr, ex parte Amalgamated Engineering Union (No 2)* [1966] 2 QB 31, [1966] 1 All ER 97; *R v National Insurance Comr, ex parte Michael* [1977] All ER 420, [1977] 1 WLR 109, CA.
15 *R v Preston Supplementary Benefits Appeal Tribunal, ex parte Moore* [1975] 2 All ER 807, [1975] 1 WLR 624.

The position was radically altered in 1980 with the provision of a right of appeal on a point of law from any decision of a Social Security Commissioner on any benefit to the Court of Appeal, or in Scotland the Court of Session.[16] The Divisional Court, which had heard applications for the prerogative orders, was therefore by-passed altogether. This development reflects perhaps the standing of the Commissioners, for their position is in this sense equivalent to that of High Court judges.

ii Appeal to the Court of Appeal

Leave of the Commissioner or the Court of Appeal (or Session) is necessary; an application should be made to the Commissioner who took the decision within three months of its notification.[17] If it is impracticable or would cause delay for the matter to be dealt with by him, then the Chief Commissioner may determine the application himself or select a colleague to do this.[18] The time-limit of three months may be extended at the discretion of the Commissioner; there is no right of appeal to the Court of Appeal against a refusal to extend time, though it is conceivable that a perverse refusal might be the subject of an application for judicial review.[19]

Now that appeal has replaced judicial review as the means of control, there is room for more intervention by the courts. They do not need to find that there has been an error of law on the face of the record or a jurisdictional error of law; they can in principle reverse any error of law, no matter how trivial or technical. But the judicial approach has not changed fundamentally. In three leading unemployment benefit cases,[20] the courts approved the cautious stance adopted by Lord Denning MR in a judicial review case:[1] that the courts should treat as binding a Commissioner's decision that has not been challenged and should only intervene in exceptional circumstances, such as where there is a division of opinion between the Commissioners. While there is something to be said for weight being given to the latters' expertise, too great a deference on the courts' part would render pointless the existence of the right of appeal. On the other hand, intervention by the ordinary courts has not always been particularly helpful,[2] and the House of Lords in particular has been unwilling to probe deeply into the subleties of social security law.[3] The courts would certainly step in if there has been a breach of the rules of natural justice, but such cases are likely to be rare.[4]

It goes without saying that decisions of the Court of Appeal are binding on the Commissioners and *a fortiori* tribunals and officers. But a Tribunal of Commissioners has obiter stated that Divisional Court rulings on applications for judicial review from the old SBATs are of only persuasive authority for the Commissioner, since the latter's jurisdiction has replaced

16 SSA 1980, s.14.
17 SI 1987/214, reg 31(1).
18 Ibid, reg 31(2).
19 *White v Chief Adjudication Officer* [1986] 2 All ER 905.
20 *Crewe v Social Security Comr* [1982] 2 All ER 745, [1982] 1 WLR 1209; *Presho v Department of Health and Social Security* [1984] AC 310, [1984] 1 All ER 97; *Cartlidge v Chief Adjudication Officer* [1986] QB 360, [1986] 2 All ER 1.
1 *R v National Insurance Comr, ex parte Stratton* [1979] QB 361, [1979] 2 All ER 278, CA.
2 See in particular *Nancollas v Insurance Officer* [1985] 1 All ER 833, C A discussed at p.263, above.
3 E.g., *Presho v Insurance Officer*, n.20, above, and *Chief Adjudication Officer v Brunt* [1988] 1 All ER 754, [1988] 2 WLR 511, HL.
4 For two cases on natural justice, in the former of which the Divisional Court quashed a decision, when medical evidence was received after the hearing, see *R v Deputy Industrial Injuries Comr, ex parte Jones* [1962] 2 QB 677, [1962] 2 All ER 430, and *R v Deputy Industrial Injuries Comr, ex parte Moore* [1965] 1 QB 456, [1965] 1 All ER 81.

and is co-ordinate with that Court's.[5] The Court of Appeal, while appearing to take a different view of the supervisory authority of the Divisional Court, has held that decisions of High Court judges exercising appellate jurisdiction (from 1978–80) in means-tested benefit cases are not binding on Commissioners.[6]

iii Judicial review of Social Fund decisions

With some exceptions there is no right of appeal from social fund decisions to the ordinary adjudicating authorities and *a fortiori* from them to the courts. In principle, however, the remedy of judicial review would be open to a claimant dissatisfied with a determination by a social fund officer, or more pertinently with a review by a social fund inspector.[6a] English administrative law is reluctant to countenance unreviewable discretionary decisions, except perhaps in matters of high policy. Therefore, although the clear intention of the government was to insulate the scheme from control outside the Department, there seems no reason why the courts should not intervene in appropriate cases. It might be argued, for example, that the decision to refuse a payment was in breach of a binding direction issued by the Secretary of State, or that it was reached in disregard of relevant circumstances stipulated in the legislation or the guidance set out in the Social Fund Manual. There might also be an argument that the inspector weighed the circumstances in an improper way and therefore came to the wrong conclusion.[6b] However, it is doubtful whether in practice the Divisional Court (to which applications for review are made) will be very ready to intervene. Certainly the courts' reluctance to control supplementary benefit decisions suggests they are hesitant in this sort of case. A successful application is most likely to be made, it is suggested, in the following types of case: a plain breach of a direction by the Secretary of State, a total failure by the inspector to give any explanation of his refusal to review, and a gross abuse of discretion.

Part 5   Pensions appeal tribunals

A Composition and structure

Pensions appeal tribunals (PATs) were first set up in 1919; they did not, however, have jurisdiction over claims in respect of service after 1921.[7] Two different types of tribunal were established by the Pensions Appeal Tribunals Act 1943. The first deals with appeals on *entitlement*, where the issue is whether the Secretary of State was right to reject the claim. The hearing is *de novo* and there is no onus on the appellant to show that the decision was wrong.[8] Both medical and legal issues come before these tribunals, and this is reflected in their composition. The chairman is a lawyer, and one of the other two members is a doctor. Both these persons must be of seven years' standing in their profession. The third member is a retired or demobilised officer or

5   *R(SB) 52/83 (T)*.
6   *Chief Supplementary Benefit Officer v Leary* [1985] 1 All ER 1061, [1985] 1 WLR 84, CA.
6a The courts might require an applicant to exhaust internal administrative remedies and apply for review by an inspector before coming before them, as they have on occasion required an applicant to exhaust his right of appeal; see *R v Home Secretary, ex parte Swati* [1986] 1 All ER 717, CA.
6b There is a full discussion of these and other principles of review for abuse of discretion in de Smith *Judicial Review of Administrative Action* (1980) ch 6, see esp. pp. 286–298, and in Wade *Administrative Law* (1982), ch.12.
7   Ch 8, Part 1, above, for the history of war pensions.
8   *Barratt v Minister of Pensions* (1946) 1 WPAR 1225. The rules concerning the burden of proof discussed in ch 8, pp. 323–326, above, therefore, apply.

serviceman of the same sex and rank as the person in respect of whose disability the claim is made.[9] The second type of tribunal entertains appeals from the *assessment* of disabilities.[10] It has two medical members, both doctors of more than seven years' standing, one of whom is appointed to act as chairman of the tribunal.[11] The third member is an ex-serviceman or officer of the same status and rank as the claimant.

Members and chairmen are appointed by the Lord Chancellor, who is also responsible for providing the tribunals' staff. The PATs are organised on the presidential system, which more recently has been adopted for SSATs.[12] In addition to sitting himself as a chairman, the President has general administrative responsibilities for the tribunals and a number of specific procedural powers: for example, he may order the disclosure to the claimant of official documents and may make arrangements where an infirm appellant is unable to attend the hearing.[13] Although the tribunals are national in terms of their administration and jurisdiction, they sit in regional centres as well as in London.

B Procedure

The detailed procedural rules governing appeals to PATs, compared with the provisions concerning other social security tribunals, are often favourable to the appellant.

(1) The appellant has a year within which to appeal against a decision on entitlement or a final assessment, or three months in the case of an interim assessment.[14]

(2) On receipt of the notice of appeal (which need not state its grounds), it is for the Secretary of State to prepare a Statement of Case, containing the relevant facts and the reasons for the decision. This is sent to the claimant for him to submit, if he wishes, an answer; the Statement of Case, the claimant's answer and the Secretary's comments on this (if any) are sent to the Pensions Appeal Office.[15]

(3) The appellant may apply to the President of the PATs for disclosure of official documents which are likely to be relevant to his case.[16]

(4) It is the duty of the tribunal to assist any appellant who appears unable to make the best of his case, and further the chairman may examine an unrepresented appellant's witnesses, if he requests.[17]

(5) Though the tribunal may obtain the opinion of a medical specialist or other technical expert, it must be sent to the parties for them to comment on, and either may request a further hearing.[18]

The appellant's interests are particularly safeguarded by the provision that the appeal is not to be heard in his absence, without his request; even then the tribunal has discretion not to hear the case.[19] The President may make

9 Pensions Appeal Tribunals Act 1943, Sch, para 3.
10 See ch 8, pp. 327–328 above, for the rules regarding assessment.
11 Pensions Appeal Tribunals Act 1943, Sch, para 3.
12 See Wraith and Hutchesson, *Administrative Tribunals* (1973) at pp. 85–86. For the presidential system for SSATs and MATs, see Part 2 of this chapter.
13 SI 1980/1120, rr. 6 and 10. (These rules govern PATs in England and Wales; the comparable rules for Scotland are to be found in SI 1981/500.)
14 Pensions Appeal Tribunals Act 1943, s.8.
15 SI 1980/1120, r. 5.
16 Ibid, r. 6.
17 Ibid, rr. 11(3), 13(1).
18 Ibid, r. 15.
19 Ibid, r. 20.

arrangements, inter alia, for the appellant to be interviewed at home by one or more members of the tribunal, if he is too infirm to attend, and the incapacity is likely to be of a long duration.[20] If for some reason an appeal is not prosecuted, e.g. the appellant simply fails to attend without explanation, it may be put on the deferred list.[1] An application may then be made within the next year for the case to be heard,[2] and this will be granted unless the President is satisfied 'that the appellant's failure to prosecute the appeal was due to his wilful default'.[3] After the lapse of a year, an appeal still on the deferred list will be struck out and may not be brought again without the President's leave.[4]

The PAT may itself summon expert or other witnesses,[5] as well as taking into account the evidence produced by the parties; evidence is not to be refused merely on the ground that it would be inadmissible in a court of law.[6] Rule 18 specifically provides that the tribunal's decision may be announced immediately after the hearing, or within seven days; but only a short indication of reasons need be given. It is surprising that there is no requirement to state them more fully.[7] It is even more surprising that there is no provision at all concerning majority decisions. The nominated judge on appeal has, therefore, ruled that the decision of a tribunal must be unanimous and, if the members cannot agree, the case must be referred to another tribunal.[8]

Like medical appeal tribunals. PATs may use the expertise of their medical member (or in assessment cases, members) in assessing the claimant's condition.[9] The medical member may conduct an examination of the appellant with his consent.[10] But the member's views are not to be taken as evidence which is itself capable of rebutting the presumption that the injury was attributable to service.[11] If the medical member is inclined to doubt the appellant's case, an independent medical specialist should be consulted and his advice given to the claimant for comment.[12]

C Appeal to the nominated judge

From decisions on entitlement (but not on assessment) there is a further right of appeal on a point of law to a High Court judge nominated by the Lord Chancellor to hear such appeals (hence the phrase, 'the nominated judge').[13] Leave of either the tribunal or the judge himself must first be obtained; this should be granted whenever there is any reasonable doubt as to the

20 Ibid, r. 21.
 1 Ibid, r. 10.
 2 Ibid, r. 26(3).
 3 Ibid, r. 26(4).
 4 Ibid, r. 26(5)(b).
 5 Ibid, r. 12(4).
 6 Ibid, r. 12(5).
 7 See p.576 above, for SSATs.
 8 *Brain v Minister of Pensions* [1947] KB 625, [1947] 1 All ER 892 (PAT disallow claimant's appeal by a majority); *Minister of Pensions v Horsey* [1949] 2 KB 526 (majority allow appeal by claimant).
 9 For medical appeal tribunals, see pp. 576–578, above.
10 SI 1980/1120, r. 17.
11 *Moxon v Minister of Pensions* [1945] KB 490.
12 *Diamond v Minister of Pensions* (1947) 1 WPAR 313 at 317. For the correct procedure when an independent medical specialist's advice is sought, see *Harris v Minister of Pensions* (1948) 4 WPAR 82.
13 Pensions Appeal Tribunals Act 1943, s.6(2): for the distinction between an appeal to the High Court and to a nominated judge, see Wraith and Hutchesson *Administrative Tribunals*, (1973) p.160. In Scotland appeal lies to the Court of Session.

correctness of the tribunal decision.[14] Quite exceptionally in the social security system, a claimant's legal expenses may be paid where a successful application for leave is made, either by him or the Secretary of State, or where the latter makes an unsuccessful application for leave.[15] The grounds on which an appeal may be made were fully considered by Denning J (as he then was) in *Armstrong v Minister of Pensions*:[16] they include a wrong direction on law, incorrect admission or exclusion of evidence and breach of the procedural rules or the rules of natural justice. Unless all the facts are before the judge, the correct course is for him to remit the case for the PAT to reconsider.

There is no further appeal to the Court of Appeal.[17] This may afford some justification for the view expressed in two cases by Denning J, that the doctrine of *stare decisis* does not apply in its full rigour in war pension cases.[18] Decisions of the judge are binding on PATs, but need not be followed by the judge in another case if there is a strong reason for taking a different view. There are now very few appeals to the nominated judge.[19] The explanation for this may be the availability since 1970 of an alternative procedure: the claimant and the Secretary of State may present a joint application to the President of the PATs for him to direct that the tribunal's decision be treated as set aside, either on the ground that additional evidence is available or because of some error of law, and that the appeal be heard again by the tribunal.[20]

Part 6   Reference to the European Court of Justice

The significance of European Economic Community law for particular social security benefits is fully discussed in the next chapter. The EEC Social Security Regulations[1] are directly applicable; they must, therefore, be implemented by the British courts and adjudicating authorities.[2] In most cases it will be for the national courts to interpret Community regulations but, in order that there may be uniformity of interpretation in the member states, there is a procedure under which a point of difficulty may be referred to the European Court of Justice in Luxembourg (ECJ) for it to give a preliminary ruling.[3] Article 177 of the Treaty of Rome provides that the Court of Justice has jurisdiction to give preliminary rulings on the interpretation of the Treaty

14 *Atkinson v Minister of Pensions* (1947) 1 WPAR 981.

15 SI 1980/1120, r. 28.

16 (1948) 3 WPAR 1449.

17 Pensions Appeal Tribunals Act, s.6(2). There is also no right of appeal to the Court of Appeal from a decision of the nominated judge refusing leave to appeal: see *Ex parte Aronsohn* [1946] 2 All ER 544, CA.

18 *James v Minister of Pensions* [1947] KB 867, [1947] 2 All ER 432; *Minister of Pensions v Higham* [1948] 2 KB 153 at 155.

19 In 1981, there were four applications for leave, of which two were granted: Report on War Pensions for 1981.

20 Pensions Appeal Tribunals Act 1943, s.6(2A), added by the Chronically Sick and Disabled Persons Act 1970, s.23. For a case in which it was unsuccessfully argued that there was maladministration in the Department's decision not to agree to a joint application to the President, see Fourth Report of the PCA 1970–71, HC 490, Case No C214/73.

 1 Reg 1408/71 (as amended) now consolidated in reg 2001/83.

 2 For the direct applicability of EEC law, see Hartley *The Foundations of European Community Law* (2nd edn), ch 7. The directly applicable effect of the EEC Social Security Regulation was recognised by the Commissioner, J G Monroe, in *Re a Holiday in Italy* [1975] 1 CMLR 184 *(R(S) 4/74* para 7); *Re Medical Expenses incurred in France* [1977] 2 CMLR 317.

 3 *Hartley*, n.2, ch 9, above, Jacobs and Durand *References to the European Court: Practice and Procedure* (1975), *passim*.

and the validity and interpretation of Community legal acts, e.g. regulations and directives. It further provides in paragraphs 2 and 3:

Where such a question is raised before any court of tribunal of a Member State, that court or tribunal may, if it considers that a decision on the question is necessary to enable it to give judgment, request the Court of Justice to give a ruling thereon.

Where any such question is raised in a case pending before a court or a tribunal of a Member State, against whose decisions there is no judicial remedy under national law, that court or tribunal shall bring the matter before the Court of Justice.

A The discretion to refer

i 'Court or tribunal'
Under the second paragraph of article 177, a question may be referred for a preliminary ruling by a 'court or tribunal'. This enables any part of the Supreme Court of Judicature to ask for a preliminary ruling in a suitable case.[4] The Social Security Commissioner clearly is entitled to refer, and it seems that a SSAT could do so. It is possible that the adjudicating authorities could refer some contributions questions to the European Court;[5] this step might not contravene the requirement in the Social Security Act 1975 that a contributions question must be determined by the Secretary of State.[6] In any event it is not clear that the Secretary of State himself could make a reference, since he may not constitute a 'tribunal' for the purpose of article 177.[7]

ii The decision must be 'necessary'
A question may only be referred to the European Court if a decision on it is 'necessary' for the national court or tribunal to give judgment. In the leading English case, *H P Bulmer Ltd v J Bollinger SA*, Lord Denning MR, took the narrow view that a court should only refer a point, if a decision on it would be *conclusive* of the case.[8] The Commissioner, however, has followed the broader approach of Stephenson LJ in the *Bulmer* case,[9] and ruled that a reference is permissible if a case cannot be determined without a decision on the point referred to the European Court.[10] This seems the better view, and is consistent with that adopted by English judges in other cases.[11]

iii Factors relevant to the exercise of the discretion
The factors to be taken into account in deciding whether to refer were discussed at length by the Court of Appeal in the *Bulmer* case.[12] The desirability of ensuring uniform interpretation of Community law must be balanced against the costs and delay entailed by a reference. The more important and difficult the point of law, the more inclined the judge should

---

4 The Divisional Court asked for a preliminary ruling in *R v National Insurance Comr, ex parte Warry* [1977] 2 CMLR 783 and in *Re Stanley, Browning v National Insurance Comr* [1984] 3 CMLR 192.

5 In Case 150/82 *Coppola* [1984] 1 CMLR 406, J G Monroe, Comr, referred the question whether Italian Social Security Contributions can be counted for sickness benefit purposes to the ECJ.

6 See Part 2, above.

7 The ECJ which may give a preliminary ruling on the interpretation of art 177 itself has interpreted 'tribunal' broadly: see *Hartley*, n.2 above, at pp. 254–258.

8 [1974] Ch 401, [1974] 2 All ER 1226, CA.

9 Ibid, at p. 428 and 1240.

10 *Re an Illness in France* [1976] 1 CMLR 243; *Kenny v Insurance Officer* [1978] 1 CMLR 181.

11 See Graham J in *Lowenbrau München v Grünhalle Lager International* [1974] 1 CMLR 1 at 9; Pennycuick VC in *Van Duyn v Home Office* [1974] 1 WLR 1107, 1115–1116.

12 N.8, above, at 423–425, 429–430 and 1235–1236, 1241–1242.

be to refer it to the Luxembourg Court.[13] The Commissioner has generally decided questions of European law himself, and in only a few reported cases has he discussed at length whether to request a preliminary ruling. In one, *Re an Illness in France*,[14] the Commissioner decided to refer a question on the invitation of the DHSS. It was emphasised that the claimant welcomed this step. The issue – the meaning of 'worker' for the purposes of the EEC Regulation – was one which had been previously ruled on by the Commissioner, and it was clear that an authoritative interpretation from the ECJ was desirable.[15] In *Re a Visit to Italy*,[16] however, the Commissioner refused to refer, largely because of the delay involved and the fact that the claimant might not be paid benefit for the interim period. A reference will not be made if the sum in question is very small.[17]

B The duty to refer

In the circumstances covered by its third paragraph quoted above, article 177 imposes a duty to refer. Which British courts or tribunals deciding issues of social security law are under this duty, because 'there is no judicial remedy' against their decision? In *Re a Holiday in Italy*,[18] the Commissioner, J G Monroe, decided that he was not bound to refer, as the prerogative order of certiorari was then available to quash his decision for an error of law, including a wrong interpretation of the EEC Regulation; it did not matter that leave had to be obtained from the Divisional Court before the order could be applied for. This decision was criticised on the ground that it assumed that leave to apply for certiorari is granted as a matter of course, where a point of Community law is involved.[19] Now that there is an appeal to the Court of Appeal, admittedly only with leave, there is a somewhat stronger argument for holding that the Social Security Commissioner is never bound to refer to the ECJ.

A High Court judge entertaining an appeal on a contributions question is almost certainly bound to refer under article 177(3), since there is no appeal from his decision. A more difficult question is whether the Court of Appeal is similarly bound, on the argument that leave of either the Court of Appeal or the House of Lords is required for an appeal to the latter. There are dicta to the effect that the Court of Appeal is never bound to refer,[20] but the point was left open by Stephenson LJ in the *Bulmer* case[1] and it is possible to construe some remarks by Buckley LJ in a later case to support the view that a reference should be made if leave to appeal cannot be obtained.[2] There is no authority on this point in a social security case.

---

13 Ibid, at 430 and 1241, per Stephenson LJ.
14 N.10, above.
15 The earlier decision of the Commissioner in *Re an Ex-Civil Servant* [1976] 1 CMLR 257 did not satisfy the DHSS.
16 [1976] 1 CMLR 506, *(R(I) 1/75)*.
17 *Re Search for Work in Ireland* [1978] 2 CMLR 174.
18 [1975] 1 CMLR 184 *(R(S) 4/74* para 8).
19 See Bridge 1 European L Rev 13 at 19; Jacobs 2 European L Rev 119.
20 N.8 above at p.420, per Lord Denning MR, and more recently, *Pickstone v Freemans* [1987] 3 WLR 811 at 827, [1987] 2 CMLR 572 at 591 per Purchas LJ.
 1 N.8, above at p.430.
 2 *Hagen v Fratelli D and G Moretti SNC and Molnar Machinery Ltd* [1980] 3 CMLR 253 at 255. Also see Collins *European Community Law in the United Kingdom* (3rd edn) at pp. 112–115.

Chapter 17

International and European law

Part 1 General

International collaboration and coordination in the social security field has been a widespread phenomenon in the second half of the twentieth century. In part it is associated with the general movement on human rights;[1] in part it results from an increase in the mobility of labour,[2] a consequence not only of individual initiative but also of governmental stimulus, notably within the European Communities.[3] The legal instruments directed towards these ends may be divided into three groups.

A Minimum standards

In the first place, there are multilateral instruments imposing obligations on those states which ratify them to conform to certain minimum standards. At a comprehensive, but necessarily vague, level there is the Universal Declaration of Human Rights conferring on an individual the right to 'security in the event of unemployment, sickness, disability, widowhood, old age or other lack of livelihood in circumstances beyond his control'.[4] More specifically there is the work of the International Labour Organisation (ILO) established after the First World War,[5] but reconstituted as an agency of the United Nations in 1946.[6] Among its manifold activities, this body through its assembly, comprising not only governments but also representatives of employers and employees, enacts conventions which once ratified by individual states are binding on them as norms of international law.[7] There

1 See e.g. Jenks *Human Rights and International Labour Standards* (1960) ch 7; Watson 6 Jo Soc Pol 31.
2 See generally Lyon-Caen *Droit Social International et Européen* (5th edn) pp. 6–17; Bohning *The Migration of Workers in the United Kingdom and the European Community* (1972); International Labour Organisation *Social Security for Migrant Workers* (1977).
3 Treaty of Rome, arts 48–51, on which see: Wyatt and Dashwood *The Substantive Law of the EEC* (1987) chs 14–15; *Lyon-Caen*, n.2, above, at pp. 198–250; Collins *The European Communities – The Social Policy of the First Phase* (1975) vol 2, ch 4.
4 (1948) UN Doc. A/811, art 25. Also see the International Covenant on Economic, Social and Cultural Rights 1966, Art 9 of which requires the parties to the Convention to recognise the right of everyone to social security, including social assistance.
5 By Part XIII of the Treaty of Versailles 1914. See on the early history, Lowe *International Protection of Labour* (1921).
6 By the International Labour Conference, Montreal.
7 See generally Johnston *The International Labour Organisation* (1970) esp. ch 17; Lawly *The Effectiveness of International Supervision* (1966).

have been a number of such conventions in the field of social security but the most important is that which lays down minimum standards to deal with the social hazards of illness, invalidity, unemployment, old age, maternity, death and industrial accidents.[8] The original plan was to prescribe both minimum and maximum standards, but the latter aim was abandoned in 1952 and even the former appears in a muted form: a state ratifying the convention need only conform to the standard of three of the nine risks specifically dealt with.[9] The standards under the ILO Convention had to be of a nature that would be feasible for states of widely differing economic development. Moreover, it applied only for the protection of employed workers. Within the ambit of Western European industrialised states, it was hoped to improve on the standards, and work to this end has been undertaken by the Council of Europe.[10] The first result of its labour was the European Social Charter of 1961, which required participating states to establish or maintain a social security system at least at the level required for ratification of the ILO Convention, and which further required them to endeavour to raise their systems to a higher level.[11] Three years later there emerged the European Code of Social Security.[12] This was in fact not so much a code in the usual sense of the term, but a convention like that of the ILO, open to ratification by member states. Similar in scope to the ILO Convention and prepared in consultation with that body, it nevertheless was a little more exacting as regards both the standards to be achieved for individual social hazards and the extent of commitment vis-à-vis the range of those hazards – the Code contains twelve points[13] and the ratifying state is to conform to at least six of these.[14] Despite the fact that the majority of member states has been slow to ratify the Code (though the United Kingdom has done so), steps were taken to reach even higher standards in a Protocol which was annexed to it.[15]

B Equality of treatment and aggregation of entitlement

It is obvious that with the growth of migrant labour, the rise of multinational enterprises and increased foreign travel possibilities, problems would be caused for migrants covered by social security systems based entirely on residence and/or contribution conditions. While the need of a state to protect its own workers temporarily employed abroad has always been recognised and to a large extent catered for by its own internal rules, there was naturally a reluctance to extend the provisions of a system to foreigners, at the cost to national contributors or taxpayers, without there being a reciprocal arrangement in the foreigner's own system. Until recently, therefore, the typical solution to the problem was found in bilateral reciprocal treaties. Most obviously this occurred at an early stage in the history of British national

8 Convention nos 102, 210 UNTS 131; Holloway *Social Policy Harmonisation in the European Community* (1981) pp. 12–14; *Johnston*, n.7, above, pp. 198–201; *Lyon-Caen*, n.2, above, at pp. 70–73.
9 Art 2(a).
10 *Lyon-Caen*, n.2, above, at pp. 90–97.
11 Art 12. The Charter was complementary to the better known European Convention on Human Rights and Fundamental Freedoms, 1950.
12 European Treaty Series, No. 48. See also Explanatory Reports on the Code (1961), Council of Europe.
13 In fact provision for old age covers three points, and that of medical care two points: art 241.
14 But in some cases only three hazards need be specified.
15 The Protocol forms part of the same Treaty as the Code. At the time of writing it has still not been ratified by the UK.

insurance in relation to the Republic of Ireland.[16] The Social Security Act 1975[17] explicitly provides that to give effect to any such agreement the Crown may by Order in Council modify or alter the Act, and there are over 30 such Orders currently in force.[18] Within the Western European context, the Council of Europe has introduced a convention based on a principle of multi-lateral reciprocity.[19] If and when ratified, this will replace bilateral agreements between member states.

By far and away the most important international coordination in this field has been that achieved by the European Economic Community. One of the pillars of the Treaty of Rome, as expressed in article 3(c), is the 'abolition . . . of obstacles to freedom of movement for persons'. The implications of this objective for social security legislation are spelled out in article 51:

> the Council shall . . . adopt such measures in the field of social security as are necessary to provide freedom of movement for workers; to this end, it shall make arrangements to secure for migrant workers and their dependants:
> (a) aggregation, for the purpose of acquiring and retaining the right to benefit and of calculating the amount of benefit, of all periods taken into account under the laws of the several countries;
> (b) payment of benefits to persons resident in the territories of Member States.

The direction was quickly implemented by a Council Regulation of 1958,[20] borrowed substantially from the Coal and Steel Community.[1] While the principles underlying the 1958 Regulation were clear – equal treatment for all workers of member states, aggregation of insurance periods served while working in different member states, exporting of benefits from one state to another – the rules themselves posed grave difficulties of interpretation. Moreover, the rulings of the European Court of Justice (ECJ) produced a body of law not always anticipated by the draftsmen of the Regulation. In the light of these difficulties, the 1958 Regulation was replaced in 1971.[2] The new Regulation was formulated without any regard to the social security systems of the members (including the United Kingdom) admitted to the Community in 1972.[3] However, there is no doubt that the 1971 Regulation, as amended, is incorporated into British law,[4] and forms an important part of the social security system. As such, it is the subject matter of the bulk of this chapter; its effect on the adjudication of claims was discussed in chapter 16.[5]

---

16 The power to give effect to reciprocal arrangements on unemployment income was conferred by the Irish Free State (Consequential Provisions) Act 1922, s.6(1)(c).
17 S.143, as amended by SSA 1981, s.6.
18 They are listed in a note to SSA 1975, s.143 in 45 Halsbury Statutes (3rd edn) 1241.
19 European Convention on Social Security 1972, European Treaty Series No 78. At the time of writing this has been ratified by seven countries, but not by the UK. See *Holloway*, n.8, above, at pp. 116–134 for the history of, and problems associated with, international coordination treaties.
20 Reg 3/58, OJ 1958, 561.
1 European Convention on Social Security for Migrant Workers 1957.
2 Reg 1408/71, OJ 1971 L149, supplemented by the implementing reg 574/72, OJ 1972 L74. These regulations, as amended, have now been reissued as Annexes to Reg 2001/83, OJ 1983 L230.
3 See the observations of the ECJ in *Brack* [1976] 2 CMLR 592 at 616.
4 Under art 189 of the Treaty of Rome regulations are directly applicable in all member states, and this principle is applied in British law by the European Communities Act 1972, s.2(1). See *Re Medical Expenses incurred in France* [1977] 2 CMLR 317.
5 Pp. 590–593, above.

B Harmonisation

None of these measures affected the huge differences between the systems of the member states as regards their structure, their range of benefits, the rates payable and the mode of financing them.[6] An economic argument for harmonisation, based on the theory that different rates and systems of contributions for firms distort competition, has been doubted: contributions are only one element of the employer's total labour cost and higher social security charges may be offset by lower wages.[7] More common these days are the arguments based on reducing the complexity and administrative costs involved in resolving conflicts of rules and of achieving greater social justice for workers who have been employed in different states.[8] Whatever the merits of the policy, it was envisaged as a goal by the draftsmen of the Rome Treaty:

> Member States agree upon the need to promote improved working conditions and an improved standard of living for workers, so as to make possible their harmonisation while the improvement is being maintained.[9]

In fact, progress in this field has been almost non-existent. The obstacles were fully expressed at a Conference convened by the Commission in 1962: the goal of harmonisation was a very vague one; the enormous differences between the systems of member states in terms both of structure and of level of support posed political as well as technical difficulties; the Commission lacked the power to achieve the goal; and national governments were unwilling to commit themselves.[10] The single, and not very important, achievement has been some standardisation in the area of industrial diseases.[11]

Part 2 Scope of EEC Regulation

A Introduction

It is important to appreciate that the purpose of the EEC Regulation is not to create a common European scheme of social security, but rather for the most part to coordinate the national systems.[12] A migrant who is covered by the Regulation will still claim benefit from a particular national institution

6 For accounts of the major differences between the national systems see: Lawson and Reed *Social Security in the European Community* (1975); van Langendonck 2 ILJ 17; *Kaim-Caudle*; and the EEC Commission Comparative Tables of the Social Security Systems in the Member States, published periodically.

7 See *Holloway*, n.8, above, at pp. 44–49; Wedel 102 Int Lab Rev 591, 592–605; van Langendonck, n.6, above, at p.24.

8 Collins *The European Communities – The Social Policy of the First Phase* (1975) vol 2, ch 6; van Langendonck, n.6, above, at pp. 24–27.

9 Art 117. It is still unclear whether the Commission has legal power to propose harmonisation measures or whether the task is reserved for the member states: see Holloway *Social Policy Harmonisation in the European Community* (1981) ch 2.

10 See EEC, *Conférence Européenne sur la Sécurité Sociale* (1964).

11 Resulting from the Commission Recommendations of 23 July 1962, OJ 2188/62 and 66/462/CEE, OJ 2696/66.

12 See Holloway *Social Policy Harmonisation in the European Community* (1981) Part II; Watson *Social Security Law of the European Communities* (1980) chs 3 and 4. For recent statements of principle by the ECJ, see *Gravina* [1981] 1 CMLR 529 at 543 and Case 242/83 *Patteri*: [1984] ECR 3171, but see *Testa* [1981] 2 CMLR 552 at 575, pointing out that in some respects the Regulation is more than a coordinating measure: p.611, below.

because of an entitlement either under that state's law alone or under that law supplemented by Community provisions. He is not to be prejudiced by the fact that at some stage during his working life he has moved from one member state to another. This guiding principle, enshrined in article 51 of the Treaty of Rome,[13] is implemented by more specific rules (discussed in Part 4 of this chapter), which are designed to alleviate the problems of the migrant worker. Thus, he is not to be excluded from entitlement to benefit on the ground of his nationality. More importantly, he may keep social security entitlements which he has earned under the law of the country he has left; this is signficant because many national systems are essentially territorial and rights may be lost when a beneficiary leaves the country.[14] And under a third principle he may conserve rights which he is in the process of acquiring in one state by aggregating the relevant contributions or residence periods with those paid or served in the state to which he moves.

The application of the very complex law is in the hands of the courts and tribunals of the member states, but difficult points may be referred to the European Court of Justice.[15] The Court has frequently emphasised that the concepts in the Regulations are to be given a common Community meaning – otherwise the uniform application of the coordinating rules would be endangered. Examples of this approach will be found in the rest of this Part of the chapter. The other major contribution of the ECJ is its consistent ruling that the purpose of the Regulation in the light of article 51 is to protect the rights of migrants, and that, therefore, a worker moving from one country to another is not to lose rights which he would enjoy under national law alone.[16] As will be seen later, this principle has considerable repercussions for the scope of the overlap provisions in the Community Regulation. At this stage, it is perhaps useful to point out that this insistence by the Court on preserving the full rights enjoyed under national law necessarily means that perfect coordination is not achieved. Coordination is applied to the advantage, but never to the detriment, of the migrant.[17]

A final introductory point is that article 6 of the Regulation replaces bilateral and multilateral conventions to which the member states are parties, even if the migrant worker would be better placed to claim under the particular convention.[18] It has, however, been argued in some recent cases that this provision is invalid insofar as it deprives a migrant of a benefit which he would otherwise enjoy under a reciprocal convention – an argument strikingly similar to that accepted by the ECJ in other contexts – but hitherto the Court had refrained from ruling on this issue.[19]

B Legislation

Regulation 1408/71 governs national legislation concerned with benefits[20] for unemployment, sickness, invalidity,[1] old age, industrial injuries and

---

13 P.596, above.

14 See pp. 357–361, above, for the relevant British rules.

15 See ch 16, pp. 590–593, above.

16 The *Petroni* principle, as it is usually called now, is discussed at pp. 606–607, below.

17 See Holloway, n.12, above, at pp. 151–157.

18 *Walder* [1973] ECR 599.

19 See *Giulani* [1977] ECR 1857 and *Galinsky* [1981] 3 CMLR 361. Watson, n.12, above, at pp. 198–201 suggests that the ECJ should reject the argument. Also see *R(S) 6/81* paras 16–17.

20 I.e. payments in cash or in kind, including up-rating increases and supplementary allowances: reg 1408/71, art 1(t). Lump sums granted in lieu of a pension (e.g. to a widow on remarriage: *Vandeweghe* [1974] 1 CMLR 499) are also included, but not payments intended for purposes unconnected with the hazard, e.g. to finance contributions: *Dekker* [1966] CMLR 503.

1 This is deemed to include the British attendance allowance: see *Re a Road Accident in Ireland* [1976] 1 CMLR 522 (*R(A) 4/75*).

diseases, and survivors, as well as death grant and family benefits.[2] The legislation referred to includes regulations and other implementing instruments and even private law agreements provided that they serve to establish a scheme under such legislation and are the subject of a declaration by a member state.[3] All instruments so governed by Regulation 1408/71 are to be specified by the member states.[4] However, a failure to do this is not conclusive, for in a case under the 1958 Regulation the ECJ held that it applied both to present and future legislation, irrespective of notification.[5] Apart from war pension and civil services schemes,[6] all social security benefits, whether contributory or non-contributory, dealing with the hazards listed above are included. The characterisation of the benefit for the purposes of the Regulation is a matter of Community, not national, law.[7]

'Social assistance' is explicitly not covered by the coordination Regulation.[8] This is not surprising, for the extent of its provision varies very considerably in the member states; further, its level is generally fixed by reference to the cost of living in a particular area, so it would be difficult to justify its export when the beneficiary moved from one country to another. There would also be objections to payments of these benefits to persons abroad, when they are financed by general taxation rather than linked in any way to the beneficiary's contributions.[9] Since no definition of the terms 'social assistance' and 'social security' is provided in the Regulation itself, it has been for the ECJ to distinguish them, a matter which it has not always found easy. Its approach now is that a benefit paid universally on the basis of the claimant's need, rather than on the basis of one of the contingencies expressly set out in the Regulation is to be treated as 'assistance'; it is immaterial whether it is paid as of right rather than at the discretion of the authorities.[10] On the other hand, a measure of assistance paid to people in particular categories to supplement a social security benefit has been treated as 'social security.'[11] It is probable on this basis that the British mean-tested benefits would fall outside its scope, though there must be some doubt about the status of income support insofar as it is paid as a supplement to disability or retirement pensions.[12]

The fact that assistance falls outside the social security Regulation does not, however, mean that it is unaffected by EEC law. In a number of cases the Court has held that entitlement to it is a 'social advantage' for the purposes of the EEC Regulation on free movement of workers.[13] It is therefore impermissible for national authorities to impose residence requirements for entitlement to social assistance on EEC workers or members of their families.

C Persons

The 1971 Regulation now applies:

> to employed or self-employed persons who are or have been subject to the legislation of one or more Member States and who are nationals of one of

2 Reg 1408/71, art 4(1).
3 Ibid, art 1(j); and see *Vaassen-Göbbels* [1966] CMLR 508.
4 Reg 1408/71, art 5. See OJ 1973 C43 for the UK legislation so specified. Positive specification of a scheme is conclusive: *Beerens* [1977] ECR 2249.
5 *Dingemans* [1965] CMLR 144.
6 Reg 1408/71, art 4(4). See *Even* [1979] ECR 2019; *Lohmann* [1979] 3 CMLR 618; cf. *Vigier* [1982] 2 CMLR 709.
7 *Jordens-Vosters* [1980] 3 CMLR 412.
8 Reg 1408/71, art 4(4).
9 See the excellent discussion in *Watson*, n.12, above, at pp. 110–111.
10 See Case 249/83 *Hoeckx* [1985] ECR 973 and Case 122/84 *Scrivner* [1985] ECR 1027.
11 Case 139/82 *Piscitello* [1984] 1 CMLR 108; Case 379–381/85 and 93/86. *Giletti* [1988] 1 CMLR 740
12 Neither the legislation on supplementary benefits nor that on family income supplement was specified as being governed by the Regulation.
13 In addition to the cases cited in n.10 above, see *Inzirillo* [1976] ECR 2057.

the Member States or who are stateless persons or refugees residing[14] within the territory of one of the Member States, as also to the members of their families[15] and their survivors.[16]

Nationals of non-member states are excluded, but a person who is a national at the time of the payment of contributions, and hence at the acquisition of the relevant rights, is covered; it does not matter that he is no longer a national at the date of claim.[17] Under the 1958 Regulation only 'workers' were covered,[18] though this was interpreted by the Court to include people who were resident or present in another member state for reasons other than employment there and so were not migrant workers stricto sensu.[19] The 1971 Regulation originally broadened the range of persons covered to include anyone compulsorily insured under a general social security scheme where he could be identified as an employed person because of the way in which the scheme was administered or financed: in other words, the test was one of affiliation to the social security system as an employee rather than one of labour law.[20]

In 1978 the Commission formulated proposals to extend the Regulation to the self-employed, and also (after a suggestion by the European Parliament) to the insured non-employed. After considerable delay the Council of Ministers accepted the extension to the former group and the Regulation was amended in 1981.[1] Legally this was done under articles 52–66 of the Treaty of Rome which set out the freedom of establishment and the freedom to provide services across national frontiers. In contrast, it is difficult to see any adequate legal basis for extending coordination of social security to the non-employed – they do not enjoy freedom of movement under the Treaty.[2] Some people are, therefore, still excluded from the coverage of the Regulation: students are outside the scheme,[3] while an 'au pair' girl is included if she has been required to pay contributions.[4] It should be noted that young or old persons, not themselves covered by the Regulation, are only covered as 'members of [a worker's] family' in respect of certain derived benefits; they cannot use the Regulation to establish entitlement to, say, unemployment benefit, which is payable on the basis of their own situation of unemployment.[5]

---

14 'Residence' means 'habitual residence': reg 1408/71, art 1(h); see further, *Angenieux* [1973] ECR 935; *Di Paolo* [1977] ECR 315.
15 In general, the members of the family included are determined by the law under which the benefit is provided; but if that law regards as members only persons living under the same roof as the relevant person, this condition is regarded as satisfied if such persons are 'mainly dependent' on him: reg 1408/71, art 1(f).
16 Ibid, art 2(1). 'Survivors' are determined in a way similar to 'members of the family' but survivors who are themselves nationals of a member state or are resident stateless persons or refugees are included irrespective of the nationality of the deceased person; reg 1408/71, art 2(2). Also see *Laumann* [1978] 3 CMLR 201.
17 *Belbouab* [1979] 2 CMLR 23, noted 4 European L Rev 106.
18 Reg 3/58, art 4(1).
19 See *Unger* [1964] CMLR 319; *Hessische Knappschaft* [1966] CMLR 82. There is no reason why the same principle should not apply to the new term, 'employed or self-employed persons'.
20 Reg 1408/71, art 1(a): see the first edition of this book, pp. 671–672.
1 The ECJ has adopted a broad interpretation of 'self-employed person': see *Roosmalen*, Judgement of 3 October, 1986, (unreported).
2 Watson 6 European L Rev 290 at 292.
3 Case 66/77 *Kuyken* [1978] 2 CMLR 304; Case 238/83 *Meade* [1984] ECR 2631.
4 Case 84/77 *Tessier* [1979] 1 CMLR 249.
5 Case 94/84 *Deak* [1985] ECR 1873. For relevant Commissioners' decisions, see *R(S) 5/83* and *R(S) 1/84*.

Part 3 Choice of competent legislation

The first substantive issue determined by Community law is the resolution of the conflict of legislative systems which might potentially govern a migrant. Article 13(1) of the 1971 Regulation prescribes that a migrant employed or self-employed person '. . . shall be subject to the legislation of a single Member State only'. The meaning of this provision, which had no exact equivalent in the 1958 Regulation, used to be thought a little uncertain.[6] At one time the general view was that the reference to the exclusive jurisdiction of one state applied only for the purpose of *liabilities*, most importantly that of paying contributions, and that subject to the overlapping rules there was nothing to preclude a worker being covered by two states' legislation for the purpose of entitlement to benefit.[7] However, two recent rulings of the ECJ appear to hold that the Regulation imposes a complete set of conflict provisions, so it is no longer open to a state other than the competent one to determine who is entitled to benefit under its social security system.[8] It is hard to reconcile this approach with the *Petroni* overlapping principle discussed later.[9]

Article 13(2) then lays down rules determining the member state to whose legislation the relevant person is subject. In general this is the state where his place of work is situated even if he is normally resident in another member state or the enterprise employing him has its place of business in another state.[10] But the general rule is subject to the following exceptions in the case of employed persons:

(1) The first and most important exception is that of 'posting' abroad. Whether the worker employed in one member state by an undertaking to which he is normally attached is posted by the employer to work in another member state, he remains subject to the legislation of the first state if the anticipated duration of the work in the second state does not exceed 12 months, and even for longer if the prolongation of the period was due to unforeseen circumstances and the authority of the second state has given its consent.[11] The policy is to avoid the administrative inconvenience of changes in insurability for short periods. The rule applies to cases where the 'undertaking' is merely an employment agency,[12] and less obviously it was held in *Angenieux*[13] to apply to an agent on commission from his employers who worked for nine months every year in another member state.

6 See the discussions in Lipstein *Law of the European Communities* (1974) pp. 96–99 and in Jacobs (ed) *European Law and the Individual* (1974) ch 4; Tantaroudas 8 Rev Trim Dr Eur 36.
7 See *Moebs* [1964] CMLR 338, and the discussion in Wyatt and Dashwood *The Substantive Law of the EEC* (1987) pp. 247–249.
8 See Case 302/84 *Ten Holder* [1987] 2 CMLR 208 and *Vermoolen*, Judgment of 7 July, 1986, unreported.
9 See pp. 606–607, below, and see *Wyatt and Dashwood*, n.7, above.
10 Art 13(2)(a) and (b). For this purpose, mariners are regarded as employed in the state whose flag is flown by the vessel in which they serve: art 13(2)(c). Civil servants and members of the armed forces are regarded as employed in the state to whose administration or force they belong: art 13(2)(d)–(e). In Case 19/67 *Van der Vecht* [1968] CMLR 151 it was held that the whole of a journey (in transport provided by the employer) from the place of the worker's residence across the frontier to the place of work was subject to the law of the place of work. The 'employment' involved in the journey was regarded as inseparable from the employment on the site.
11 Reg 1408/71, art 14(1).
12 *Manpower* [1971] CMLR 222.
13 [1973] ECR 935.

(2) An employee of an international transport undertaking whose work takes him to more than one member state is subject to the law of the place where the undertaking has its registered office or place of business.[14] But if the undertaking has a branch in another member state, an employee working for that branch is governed by the law of that state.[15] Finally, if the worker is employed principally in the territory of the member state in which he resides, the law of that state will prevail, notwithstanding that the undertaking has no place of business or branch there.[16]

(3) A worker, other than (2), who pursues his employment in two or more member states is governed by the law of the state where he resides if it is one of those where he works;[17] if it is not, then by the law of the state where his employer has his registered office or place of business.[18]

(4) There are special rules for frontier workers and mariners.[19]

There are comparable rules for the self-employed. For example, someone normally self-employed in one state who performs work in another remains subject to the former's legislation if the anticipated duration of that work is not more than 12 months.[20] And a person normally self-employed in two or more member states is subject to the law of the state where he resides, provided he does some of his work there.[1] Where a person is simultaneously employed in one state and self-employed in another, the law of the former state is applicable, subject to the qualifications specified with regard to particular activities in Annex VII to the Regulation.[2]

Part 4   General principles

The rules described in Part 3 determine the legislation applicable to a given individual – they indicate what will be referred to in the remainder of this chapter as the 'competent legislation', or, where more appropriate, the 'competent state'. It remains to consider the principles of Community law to which that legislation is subject.

A Non-discrimination

It is enunciated in the Regulation that subject to special provisions:

> Persons resident in the territory of one of the Member States . . . shall be subject to the same obligations and enjoy the same benefits under the legislation of any Member State as the nationals of that State.[3]

The principle of equality of treatment for nationals of member states is the least original: it has been a regular feature of international instruments.[4] It

---

14 Reg 1408/71, art 14(2)(a).
15 Ibid, art 14(2)(a)(i).
16 Ibid, art 14(2)(a)(ii).
17 Ibid, art 14(2)(b)(i); see *Kuijpers* [1982] ECR 3027.
18 Reg 1408/71, art 14(2)(b)(ii).
19 Ibid, arts 14(3) and 14b.
20 Ibid, art 14a(1)(a).
 1 Ibid, art 14a(2).
 2 Ibid, art 14c.
 3 Ibid, art 3.
 4 E.g. European Code on Social Security, European Treaty Series, No 48, art 73, ILO Convention No 102, 210 UNTS, art 68.

governs both obligations of the individual, most importantly the payment of contributions, and rights to benefit. It also applies as regards periods of residence in another territory. Thus, in *Hirardin*:[5]

> A Belgian national working in France, and affiliated to the insurance scheme there, sought to have taken into account in the computation of his benefit periods of employment in Algeria. The ECJ held that the French authorities could not rely on a *loi* of 1964 which purported to restrict the aggregation of such periods to French citizens.

Further it is now well established that covert discrimination, e.g. discrimination against those not born or resident in the competent state, is equally prohibited.[6] However, in *Kenny* the Court ruled that the competent institution of a state was not required always to treat facts occurring in another member state – in that case imprisonment in Ireland – as equivalent to facts occurring in the former state (there Britain) which constitute a ground for loss or suspension of the right to a benefit.[7] It was therefore left open whether the Regulation equally precludes reverse discrimination, that is, discrimination against one's own nationals, which would have required the British tribunal to treat imprisonment in another member state as equivalent to detention in the UK.

More recently the ECJ has boldly applied the covert discrimination principle to annul an article in the Regulation which had provided that workers in *France*, as distinct from other member states, were not under the Regulation to receive the family allowances provided by the state of employment when their dependent children were resident in another member state.[8] The Court held that although the Regulation was a coordination and not a harmonisation measure, it was contrary to the Treaty for it to add to the disparities between the social security systems of the member states by distinguishing France from other countries, thereby discriminating in effect against foreign workers in France, both in respect to French nationals and foreign workers in other countries.

B Aggregation of periods of insurance

The principle of aggregation of periods of insurance, employment or residence abroad for the purposes of satisfying the contribution conditions of the competent legislation is referred to in the Preamble of the Regulation, but not in its General Part. This is because it does not apply to all benefits or allowances, particularly those resulting from an industrial accident or disease[9] where entitlement is based on the employment alone. For each of the benefits for which the principle is relevant (sickness and maternity,[10]

---

5 [1976] ECR 553.
6 *Palermo* [1980] 2 CMLR 31. In *Re Residence Conditions* [1978] 2 CMLR 287 (*R(A) 2/78*), J G Monroe, Comr, ruled that the claimant, an Irish national born in Eire and widow of the Irish worker, should be treated for the purposes of the residence conditions for attendance allowance as if she had been born in Britain. But see *Re an Italian Widow* [1982] 2 CMLR 128.
7 [1978] 3 CMLR 651. For the further proceedings in this case, see p.370, above.
8 *Pinna* [1986] ECR 66, and see Raepenbush [1986] Cahiers de Droit Européen 475.
9 Though in this latter case there is partial recognition of the principle with regard to pneumoconiosis where periods of activity in a prescribed occupation in another member state may be aggregated: reg 1408/71, art 57(3). For some reason, the provision does not extend to other industrial diseases.
10 Ibid, art 18(1).

invalidity,[11] old age and death,[12] unemployment,[13] family[14] and orphans[15] benefits) the rule is stated explicitly in the Special Provisions in substantially the same form:

> the competent institution of a Member State whose legislation makes the acquisition, retention or recovery of the right to benefits conditional upon the completion of insurance periods or periods of employment or residence shall, to the extent necessary, take account of insurance periods or periods of employment or residence completed under the legislation of any other Member State as if they were periods completed under the legislation which it administers.[16]

It is this rule which enables a migrant to move from one state to another, confident that he is preserving rights which he is in the process of acquiring in the former state. The benefit which he may eventually claim from the competent institution of the second state is then assessed on the basis of the principles discussed in the next section. The aggregation rule is obviously easiest to apply when both systems employ contributory social security schemes, but it is clear that it also assists a migrant who moves from a state where there is such a system to another which determines entitlement purely on residence or some other territorial criterion.[17] It is for the competent state, and not others from which benefit might be claimed, to apply the aggregation principles.[18]

But what constitutes the appropriate 'insurance periods or periods of employment or residence' for the purposes of the rule quoted above is determined by the legislation under which they were completed or treated as completed.[19] So in *Murru*[20] an Italian worker claiming a disability pension in France was unable to rely on a period of unemployment in Italy, for while the period might have counted if it had been completed in France, in Italy it was not treated as equivalent to a 'period of employment'. Conversely, a period of employment under the law of a member state which does recognise it as an 'insurance period' must also be so recognised in the state where benefit (in the particular case, unemployment benefit under article 67) is claimed.[1] However, while the competent state is bound to respect the rules of the member state under which the periods of residence, etc. are completed, it is for the former then to determine whether the conditions of entitlement are met, e.g. whether the claimant is unemployed, or incapable of work for the purposes of sickness benefits.[2]

11 Ibid, art 38(1).
12 Ibid, art 45(1).
13 Ibid, art 67(1)–(2).
14 Ibid, art 72.
15 Ibid, art 79(1).
16 Ibid, art 18(1).
17 See the discussion in Holloway *Social Policy Harmonisation in the European Community* (1981) pp. 121–123, 177–178, and see Forde 1980/1 LIEI 23.
18 Case 150/82 *Coppola* [1983] ECR 43, and see *R(S) 13/83* for the Commissioner's decision applying this ruling. Further, see *R(G) 1/86*.
19 Reg 1408/71, art 1(r), 1(s) and 1(s)(a). Where for the purpose of invalidity or old age pension the competent legislation requires the completion of insurance periods in an occupation subject to a special scheme or in a special employment, periods completed in another member state may only be taken into account if they are involved in the same occupation or employment: arts 38(2) and 45(2).
20 [1972] CMLR 888.
 1 *Frangiamore* [1978] 3 CMLR 166.
 2 See *Baccini* [1983] ECR 583, and *R(S) 3/82*.

C Calculation and apportionment

Subject to the deterritoriality principle described below, it is for the member state under whose legislation benefit is claimed to assess the amount payable, but in so doing it is bound to apply certain rules of Community law. If the amount of benefit varies according to the number of dependants, those residing in the territory of another member state are to be treated as if residing in the territory of the determining member state.[3] As regards the short-term benefits for sickness, maternity, unemployment and industrial injury, where reference is made to the average earnings of the claimant, account is to be taken only of earnings received in the determining member state.[4] In the case of unemployment benefit, this will be based on the worker's last employment there, but if such employment did not exceed four weeks, reference is made instead to the normal earnings in the territory where the claimant is residing for an employment which is equivalent or similar to his last employment in another member state.[5] Any up-rating of benefits under national legislation must of course be applied to those workers claiming under the Regulation.[6]

The difficult question now arises as to the extent to which a benefit may be reduced on the ground of overlap with benefit payable for a similar risk for a similar period by another member state. The matter is governed by two principles formulated in the Regulation, but these may be ousted by a controversial third principle developed by the ECJ.

i Accumulation independently of Community law

This 'ousting' principle has been the subject of a number of the leading decisions on the scope of Community law and has given rise to considerable debate. In interpreting the overlapping provisions of the 1958 Regulation (the predecessor to that made in 1971) the ECJ took account of the wording of article 51 of the Treaty of Rome (set out on p 596) which the Regulation was designed to implement. That article was concerned to *extend* the rights of migrant workers, not to reduce them.[7] The Regulation, in furtherance of this aim, contained principles whereby rights acquired under different legislative systems might be aggregated and co-ordinated. The overlapping rules were complementary to these aggregation and co-ordination principles but had no force independently of them. If, without recourse to the Regulation, an individual had acquired rights under the legislation of different states, these could not be overridden by the Regulation:[8] an interpretation to the contrary would conflict with article 51 as reducing rather than extending the facilities of migrant workers.[9] Any limitation on the ability to accumulate had thus to be provided for in the national laws of the systems in question.[10]

---

3 Reg 1408/71, arts 23(3), 39(4), 58(3), 68(2).
4 Ibid, arts 23(1), 58(1), 68(1). Mutatis mutandis the same applies to awards based on 'standard' earnings.
5 Ibid, art 68(1). For frontier workers see *Fellinger* [1981] 1 CMLR 471.
6 Reg 1408/71, art 11.
7 Case 92/63 *Moebs* [1964] CMLR 338; *Guissart* [1967] ECR 425 at 433; *Niemann* [1974] ECR 571 at 579.
8 *Ciechelski* [1967] CMLR 192 at 205; *Guissart* n.7, above, at 433; *Duffy* [1971] CMLR 391 at 400.
9 *Duffy* n.8, above, at 339–400; *Kaufmann* [1974] ECR 517 at 525; *Niemann* n.7, above, at 578; *Massonet* [1975] ECR 1473 at 1481–1482.
10 *Guissart* n.7, above, at 434; *Massonet* n.9, above, at 1484.

The 1971 Regulation reformulated some of the rules and also introduced the provision in article 13(1) that workers governed by the Regulation were to be subject to the legislation of a single member state only. Although the ECJ has emphasised that under this article the Regulation precludes the ability of states, other than the competent one, to determine the beneficiaries of its social security system, this is not in its view incompatible with the principle that a migrant may accumulate benefits under two different member states' laws.[11] The survival of the principle subsequent to the 1971 Regulation was first confirmed in *Petroni*:[12]

> The Belgian Social Security institution, in calculating an old age pension payable on the basis of Belgian legislation alone to a worker, who also had acquired title under the Community aggregation and apportionment rules to benefit in Italy, sought to invoke an article of the 1971 Regulation[13] purporting to limit the maximum payable when a worker had been subject to the legislation of two or more member states in respect of the same risk. It was categorically held by the ECJ that, to the extent that the article in question imposed a limitation on the accumulation of two benefits acquired in different member states by a reduction in the amount of benefit acquired under national legislation alone, it was void as being inconsistent with the fundamental objective of article 51 of the Treaty of Rome: the aim of Community law was to extend the protection of social security systems to cover migrant workers, and unless there were compensating advantages for a worker under Community law, it was not to be interpreted as limiting his rights.

It follows that the two other principles shortly to be discussed apply only where a claimant invokes the Regulation for the purposes of benefitting from the aggregation principles.

The effect of the *Petroni* ruling is that migrant workers may obtain a social security advantage over persons who have stayed throughout their life in one member state: the former are able to accumulate a pension acquired under the Community Regulation with a pension to which they are entitled under national law alone, or, of course, two benefits both acquired under national law.[14] In this way, the Regulation does not effect perfect coordination of benefits. Despite this, the ECJ has repeatedly affirmed the principle.[15] In the *Giuliani* case[16] it held that it did not constitute unfair discrimination against non-migrants; their situation was not comparable with the position of those who experienced the difficulties of working abroad. The differences, the Court added, could not be resolved until there was a common social security system or harmonisation. Moreover, the *Petroni* principle was extended in this case, despite the submissions of Advocate-General Warner: it applied even where, as in the instant case, the claimant had to invoke the deterritoriality rule in article 10 to obtain payment, because he was resident outside the member state where he was entitled to benefit.[17] The Community

---

11 See *Vermoolen* Judgment of 7 July, 1986.
12 [1975] ECR 1149.
13 Art 46(3), p.608, below.
14 See Holloway *Social Policy Harmonisation in the European Community* (1981) pp. 178–181.
15 E.g. *Manzoni* [1977] ECR 1647; *Greco* [1977] ECR 1711; *Mura* [1979] ECR 1819.
16 [1977] ECR 1857, noted 3 European L Rev 49.
17 The deterritoriality principle is not relevant to the *acquisition* of benefit: see p.609, below.

overlap rules are only applicable when the claimant relies on the aggregation provisions of the EEC regulation to acquire title to benefit.

It is arguable, however, that the weaknesses of this approach are mitigated by another principle stated by the Court in a number of recent cases. Nothing in the Regulation precludes the member states applying their own overlap laws to benefits acquired under the laws of other member states, including benefits acquired there with the aid of Community law.[18] This does not apply, however, where the migrant is in receipt of benefits 'of the same kind in respect of invalidity, old age, death (pensions) or occupational disease' under the aggregation provisions of the Regulation, when the apportionment rules discussed below come into play.[19] There is now considerable case law on what constitutes a benefit 'of the same kind': for example, invalidity benefits converted into old-age pensions under the law of one state and not so converted under the law of another are so regarded.[20] Further, if the application of national overlap rules is less favourable to the claimant than the employment of the Community rules regarding aggregation and apportionment, the latter must be applied instead.[1] National law may in some situations, therefore, achieve the result which cannot be reached under the Community Regulation. The British overlapping regulations do not apply to benefits payable under the laws of other states, though there is power to introduce suitable provisions.[2]

ii No overlap of short-term or family benefits
Article 12(1) of the 1971 Regulation provides that:

> This Regulation can neither confer nor maintain the right to several benefits of the same kind for one and the same period of compulsory insurance. However, this provision shall not apply to benefits in respect of invalidity, old age, death (pensions) or occupational disease which are awarded by institutions of two or more Member States . . .

If, then, as a result of the aggregation provisions, a claimant acquires title for the same period under more than one system for a sickness, maternity, unemployment, industrial injury, family benefit, or death grant, he can receive no more than is payable under any one such system. The rule does not, however, apply to benefits payable under voluntary schemes,[3] nor, of course, if the aggregation arises independently of the Regulation.[4]

iii Apportionment of long-term benefits
The Regulation contains detailed and complicated rules for apportioning the amount payable where entitlement to the long-term benefits is based on an aggregation of periods completed in different member states. These rules therefore apply to all old-age and survivors' pensions, but as regards

---

18 *Greco*, n.15, above; *Mura*, n.15, above. See reg 1408/71, art 12(2).
19 Ibid, second sentence.
20 See Case 4/80 *D'Amico* [1982] 2 CMLR 733, and for cases stating the principle that benefits are 'of the same kind' when their purpose and basis of calculation are the same, see Cases 116, 117, 119–121/80 *Celestre* [1983] 1 CMLR 252 and *Van der Bunt-Craig* [1983] ECR 1385.
1 Case 83/77 *Naselli* [1979] 1 CMLR 270; *Viola* [1979] 1 CMLR 635.
2 SSA 1979, s.15. See *Re an Irish Widow* [1978] 2 CMLR 178 *(R(U) 2/78)* and *Re Industrial Disablement* [1979] 1 CMLR 653, where the Commissioner applied the *Petroni* principle.
3 The meaning of 'voluntary', however, remains obscure, cf reg 1408/71, art 1(a).
4 See *Walsh* [1980] 3 CMLR 573, where the ECJ construed reg 574/72, art 8 (prohibiting overlap of maternity benefits) only to apply where the claimant was actually entitled to two maternity benefits for the same period under the aggregation rules.

invalidity benefit an important distinction is made. If a claimant to such a benefit has completed periods of insurance *exclusively* under legislation of member states all of which calculate the amount of benefit independently of the duration of such insurance periods[5] (as e.g. the basic component in the UK invalidity pension), there is no need of apportionment and the ordinary rule in article 12(1) against overlap applies.[6] If, however, one or more of the legislations under which periods of insurance have been completed determine the amount according to the duration of such periods (as with the earnings-related component in the British invalidity pension)[7] then the apportionment rules òn old age pensions are applied by way of analogy.[8] These may be summarised as follows:

(1) Each state in which the claimant has completed periods of insurance of at least 12 months must make two calculations of the pension payable.[9]

(2) The first assessment is that payable under the legislation of that state without regard being had to periods completed in other member states.[10]

(3) The second assessment is based on the theoretical amount that would have been payable if all periods (including those of less than 12 months)[11] completed in other member states had been completed in the member state making the calculation – often referred to as the 'highest theoretical amount'. This amount is then reduced according to the proportion of the periods completed in the individual state to the total of periods completed in all member states.[12] (E.g. C has completed 300 months in state X and 100 months in state Y. If state X pays a pension of £60 a week on 300 months' contributions and £80 on 400 months', the second assessment will be £80 (highest theoretical amount) multiplied by ¾ = £60 a week.)

(4) The claimant is entitled from any of the relevant states to either (2) or (3) whichever is the higher.[13] But if and insofar as the total thereby acquired exceeds the highest theoretical amount, each state is to reduce the benefit payable on a proportionate basis.[14] (It was this rule which was the subject of the *Petroni* decision:[15] the highest theoretical amount can therefore be exceeded if the beneficiary is entitled under the competent legislation independently of the Regulation.)

(5) The amount payable under (4) may, however, be exceeded where a claimant is permanently resident in a member state under whose legislation he is entitled to a minimum pension. If that state would have granted a pension greater than (4) had all the periods of insurance

5 The legislation referred to is listed in Annex IV of reg 1408/71.
6 Ibid, art 37.
7 P.143, above.
8 Reg 1408/71, art 40(1). Classification of invalidity benefit into these two categories is rather oddly a question for the national law concerned, not for Community Law: *Dingemans* [1965] CMLR 144.
9 Reg 1408/71, arts 46(1) and 48(1).
10 Ibid.
11 Ibid, art 48(2).
12 Ibid, art 46(2). For examples of the calculation see: *Ciechelski* [1967] CMLR 192; Case 191/73 *Niemann* [1974] ECR 571. If the total number of periods exceeds the maximum required by the legislation of one of the member states in question, that state calculates the proportion according to such maximum rather than the total number of periods actually completed: reg 1408/71, art 46(2)(c): see *Mura* [1980] 3 CMLR 27.
13 Reg 1408/71, art 46(1).
14 Ibid, art 46(3).
15 [1975] ECR 1149.

aggregated under the Regulation been completed there, it must pay the claimant a supplement to raise the pension to that greater amount.[16]

D Deterritoriality

The deterritoriality principle necessary for a proper co-ordination of the systems is that the right to benefit acquired under the legislation of one member state should continue notwithstanding any change either in the legal system applicable or in the transfer of residence or presence to another member state. The principle is therefore concerned with the protection of acquired rights, rather than rights which are in the course of being acquired (the subject of the previous two sections).[17] It is particularly important for long-term benefits, where there is little need to maintain links between the claimant, wherever he is residing or staying, and the state under whose legislation the benefit has accrued. The 1971 Regulation thus provides that:

> invalidity, old age or survivors' cash benefits, pensions for accidents at work or occupational diseases and death grants acquired under the legislation of one or more Member States shall not be subject to any reduction, modification, suspension, withdrawal or confiscation by reason of the fact that the recipient resides in a territory of a Member State other than that in which the institution responsible for payment is situated.[18]

Within its scope, this overrides national legislation disqualifying claimants for absence abroad with, it seems, a retroactive effect on provisions already in force.[19] As regards short-term and family benefits, there is, however, a need for the national authorities to exert greater control on the activities of the claimant, in particular regarding his availability for work. The general principle quoted above therefore does not apply; instead there are special rules for the various categories of benefit.

i Sickness and maternity benefit

The availability of benefit in kind (medical services) is the reason for special provision here. Three situations are envisaged by the Regulation. In the first, the relevant person resides in a member state other than the competent state. If he satisfies the conditions of entitlement under the legislation of the latter, he is entitled to cash benefits and benefits in kind as provided by the state of residence.[20] The rule applies by analogy to benefits claimed by members of his family in the member state where they are permanently resident.[1] The second situation is that in which migrants and/or members of their family, while resident in another member state, return to the competent state for a visit. The obvious solution applies that they receive the benefit (cash or kind) from the competent state as if they were resident there, but it is rather surprisingly provided that this holds true even if they had already received benefit for the

16 Reg 1408/71, art 50(1). See *Torri* [1977] ECR 2299, and *R v Social Security Comr, ex parte Browning* [1982] 1 CMLR 427, where the ECJ ruled that in *parte* British law there is no 'minimum benefit'.
17 See the remarks of J G Monroe, Comr, in *R(S) 7/81*, para 9.
18 Reg 1408/71, art 10(1). There is no loss of entitlement if the migrant fails to notify his change of residence: Case 261/84 *Scaletta* [1985] ECR 2711.
19 *Re an Absence in Ireland* [1977] CMLR 5, where the Commissioner held SSA 1975, s.82(5)(a) inapplicable, an interesting application of the principle of supremacy of Community law.
20 Reg 1408/71, art 19(1).
1 Ibid, art 19(2).

same sickness or maternity before their stay.[2] The third and final situation is that in which the claimant (or a member of his family) is resident in the competent state but visits another member state. To claim the benefits from the latter state he must show that he satisfied the conditions of entitlement under the legislation of the competent state and: *either*

(1) his condition necessitated immediate benefits during the stay in the other state, *or*
(2) he was authorised by the competent state to transfer his residence to the other state[3], *or*
(3) he was authorised by the competent state to go to the territory of the other state to receive there treatment appropriate for his condition.[4]

Where, under these rules, cash benefits are payable under the legislation of the state of residence or presence, the rate and conditions for receipt (e.g. medical certification and examination) are governed by that legislation.[5] As regards benefits in kind, their cost is reimbursed by the institution of the competent state.[6]

ii Industrial injury benefits

As applied to the industrial injury benefits, the deterritoriality principle has two dimensions:[7] on the one hand, it enables benefit to be paid for accidents happening, or industrial diseases incurred, during work in a member state other than the competent member state;[8] on the other hand, in whichever member state the accident took place or disease was incurred, it provides for the receipt of benefit in kind or money in states other than the competent member state.[9] For this latter purpose, the rules described above for sickness and maternity apply.

iii Unemployment

The special considerations of unemployment requiring separate treatment are the problem of controlling the claimant's genuine availability for work, and the sometimes conflicting objective of encouraging him to transfer his search for employment to another member state where more vacancies exist.[10] The first objective is responsible for modifications to both the

2 Ibid, art 21.
3 The authorisation can be refused only if such a movement would be prejudicial to the claimant's state of health or his receipt of medical treatment: ibid, art 22(2).
4 Ibid, art 22(1). The authorisation cannot be refused if the treatment in question cannot be provided in the time normally necessary for obtaining the treatment in the territory of the competent state. See *Pierik* [1979] ECR 1977. The condition appears to be, for practical purposes, the same as that applied generally under the British legislation (p.359, above): see *Re a Visit to Holland* [1977] 1 CMLR 502; *R(S) 6/81* paras 13–14.
5 Reg 1408/71, art 19(1)(b).
6 Ibid, art 36.
7 See *Re a Visit to Italy* [1976] 1 CMLR 506 (*R(I) 1/76*).
8 Reg 1408/71, arts 52, 57. See e.g. *Bertholet* [1966] CMLR 191, and *Manpower* [1971] CMLR 222. Some industrial injury schemes cover journeys to work, others do not. In order that the position taken in the competent legislation should prevail, it is provided that 'an accident while travelling which occurs in the territory of a member state other than the competent state shall be deemed to have occurred in the territory of the competent state': reg 1408/71, art 56. See *Re a Car Accident in West Berlin* [1979] 2 CMLR 42.
9 Reg 1408/71, arts 52, 54 and 55.
10 Collins *The European Communities – The Social Policy of the First Phase* (1975) vol 2, pp. 63–77.

aggregation and the deterritoriality principles. The application of the normal aggregation rule is generally subject to the condition that the unemployed person must have been last employed (or insured) in the state under whose legislation he claims benefit.[11] He cannot simply move to a member state and claim unemployment benefit there on the basis of the contributions paid in another state. There are, however, exceptions in the case of frontier workers,[12] and for persons who make themselves available to the employment services of the country in which they reside; this latter group may receive benefit under the legislation of that state as if they had just been employed there.[13] The purpose of these provisions is to ensure that migrant workers receive benefit in the place most favourable to the search for new employment.[14]

More important is the restriction on the exportability of unemployment benefit. A person who is entitled to benefit in one member state and who travels to another to look for work may be paid benefit in the second state if:

(a) he has been registered with the employment services of the first state for at least four weeks prior to his departure, and
(b) he registers with the equivalent services of the second state and subjects himself to the control procedures there.[15]

Under this arrangement benefit is payable by the second state only for a maximum of three months (or less if the maximum period of entitlement under the legislation of the first state is exceeded).[16] If the person returns to the competent state within three months, he continues to be entitled to benefit from that state, but if he returns later he loses his right, though the competent institution may extend the time limit 'in exceptional cases'.[17]

It has recently been argued that the provision for loss of entitlement from the competent state after three months' absence is void, as restricting the free movement of workers guaranteed under article 48–51 of the Treaty of Rome.[18] But the Court rejected this, pointing out that in this area the Regulation was more than a coordination measure: the provisions created a new Community right, free from the requirement to observe the control procedures of the competent state for three months, and it was therefore reasonable to attach conditions to it. The *Petroni* principle was therefore inapplicable. If, however, the claimant is entitled to benefit from the state to which he has moved to look for work under the law of that state alone, the principle does apply and the Regulation is irrelevant.[19]

---

11 Reg 1408/71, art 67(3).
12 Ibid, art 71(a)(ii).
13 Ibid, art 71(b)(ii): see *Di Paolo* [1977] ECR 315; *Aubin* [1982] ECR 1991. For two British cases considering this provision, see *R(U) 7/85* and *R(U) 4/86*.
14 See Case 1/85 *Miethe* [1988] 1 CMLR 507 .
15 Reg 1408/71, art 69(1). For Commissioner's decisions applying these requirements, see *Re an Absence in Germany* [1978] 2 CMLR 603 (*R(U) 5/78); Re Search for Work in Ireland* [1978] 2 CMLR 174.
16 Reg 1408/71, art 69(1)(c). The cost of benefit is reimbursed by the state where the person was last insured: ibid, art 70(1).
17 Ibid, art 69(2). The principles to be applied by the state where the person returns late are discussed in *Coccioli* [1979] 3 CMLR 144.
18 *Testa* [1981] 2 CMLR 552, noted 6 European L Rev 296.
19 *Bonaffini* [1975] ECR 971.

iv Family benefits

The Regulation distinguishes between 'family allowances', i.e. periodical cash payments determined exclusively by reference to the number and, where appropriate, the age of the members of the family (e.g. the British child benefit); and 'family benefit', i.e. benefits in cash or kind, including 'family allowances', intended to meet 'family expenses' (other than childbirth) and coming within the scope of the Regulation.[19] The basic rule is that a migrant worker is entitled to claim family benefits from the competent state for members of his family resident in another member state, as if they were resident in the former country.[20] (The different rule that used to apply for France, justified on the ground of the high level of family benefits available in that country, has been held unlawful by the ECJ.[1]) Benefits are payable by the appropriate institution of the competent member state normally to the worker himself, but if it is established that the benefit is not being applied for the members of the family there is power to pay it instead to another person actually maintaining the members of the family, and if that person (and the family) is resident abroad this will be expedited by the social security institution in that country.[2]

In addition to these rules concerning the deterritoriality of family benefits, there are also some important overlapping provisions. Broadly they provide for the suspension of any entitlement to family benefits which may arise under the law of another state on the basis of, say, the claimant's residence, when there is also entitlement to benefit from the competent state.[3] This does not apply, however, when the worker's spouse or another person, carrying on a profession or trade, is entitled to family benefits from the state where the children are resident. In that situation, the worker's entitlement under the law of the competent state is suspended, and benefit is paid by the state of residence.[4] The ECJ has emphasised that benefit must actually be received in the other state for entitlement under the competent legislation to be suspended,[5] and that in any case where the amount of family benefit suspended is greater than the sum paid by the state of residence, the competent state must continue to pay the difference: otherwise the goal of free movement would not be reached.[6] Recently, the Court has applied the *Petroni* principle, so that a person does not lose family benefits under the relevant 'choice of legislation' provisions in the Regulation when he moves from one state to another, and under the law of the first state he was entitled to a higher benefit than that paid by the second state.[7]

20 Reg 1408/71, art 73.
 1 See p.603, above.
 2 Reg 1408/71, art 75(1).
 3 See Reg 574/72, art 10(1)(a), as interpreted in *Kromhout* [1985] ECR 2205.
 4 See Reg 1408/71, art 76 and Reg 574/72, art 10(1)(b) (reformulated in Reg 1660/85). (Prior to the reformulation in 1985, this latter overlapping provision only applied where the beneficiary in the state of the children's residence was the worker's spouse, whether divorced or not: see *Robards* [1983] ECR 171.)
 5 *Ragazzoni* [1978] ECR 963; Case 191/83 *Salzano* [1984] ECR 3741.
 6 *Rossi* [1979] ECR 831.
 7 See *Laterza* [1981] 1 CMLR 158 and *Patteri* [1984] ECR 3171 (construing art 77(2)(b)(i)), and *Gravina* [1981] 1 CMLR 529 (construing art 78(2)).

Appendix

Social security benefit rates

This list of the rates of benefit and contributions payable from April 1988 to April 1989 is not exhaustive. Fuller information can be found in Department leaflets, in particular NI 196 (general benefit and contributions rates) and MPL 154 (war pensions). Weekly rates are given unless otherwise stated.

BENEFIT	£
Attendance allowance	
Higher rate	32.95
Lower rate	22.00
Child benefit	7.25
Family credit	
Eligibility with net income of less than	96.50
plus allowances for each child under 11	8.50
11–15	16.00
16–17	21.00
18	30.50
Maximum rate of adult credit	32.10
plus for each child under 11	6.05
11–15	11.40
16–17	14.70
18	21.35
Guardian's allowance	8.40
Housing benefit – deductions for non-dependants (ND)	
from rent allowances where ND 18 + and in work	8.20
for boarders	8.20
for other NDs	3.45
low earnings threshold	49.20
from rate rebates where ND 18 +	3.00
Premium for lone parent	8.60
Income support – personal allowances	
Single person aged 16–17	19.40
aged 18–24	26.05
aged 25 +	33.40

Couple both aged under 18	38.80
one or both 18 +	51.45
One parent aged 16–17	19.40
aged 18 +	33.40
Dependent children under 11	10.75
11–15	16.10
16–17	19.40
18	26.05

Income support – premiums

Family	6.15
Lone parent	3.70
Pensioner – single	10.65
– couple	16.25
Higher pensioner – single	13.05
– couple	18.60
Disability – single	13.05
– couple	18.60
Severe disability – single	24.75
– couple where one qualifies	24.75
– couple where both qualify	49.50
Disabled child	6.15

Income support – reduction for strikers	17.70

Industrial injuries disablement benefit

100% disablement for person 18 +	67.20
– for person under 18 with no dependants	41.15
Constant attendance allowance	
Normal maximum rate	26.90
Exceptional rate	53.80
Exceptionally severe disablement allowance	26.90
Unemployability supplement basic rate	41.15
Reduced earnings allowance – maximum rate	26.88

Invalid care allowance	24.75

Invalidity benefit

Invalidity allowance	
Higher rate	8.65
Middle rate	5.50
Lower rate	2.75
Basic Invalidity Pension	41.15
for a couple	65.90

Maternity allowance	31.30

Mobility allowance	23.05

One-parent benefit	4.90

Retirement pension

Category A pension	41.15
for a couple	65.90
Category B pension	24.75
Category C pension	
Higher rate	24.75
Lower rate	14.80

Category D pension	24.75
Severe disablement allowance (SDA)	24.75
Sickness benefit	31.30
for a couple	50.70

Statutory maternity pay
Higher rate	– 90% of average earnings
Lower rate	34.25

Statutory sick pay
For average earnings of £79.50+	49.20
For average earnings of £41.00 to £79.50	34.25

Unemployment benefit	32.75
for a couple	52.95

War pensions
Basic award for 100% disablement	
for private	67.20
for Major-General	3809.00 per year
Unemployability supplement	
for officers	2279.00 per year
for other ranks	43.70
Constant attendance allowance	
full day rate for officers	1403.00 per year
full day rate for other ranks	26.90
Allowance for lowered standard of occupation	
maximum for officers	1402.00 per year
maximum for other ranks	26.88
Comforts allowance – normal rate for officers	605.00 per year
– normal rate for others	11.60
Exceptionally severe disablement allowance	
for officers	1403.00 per year
for other ranks	26.90 per year
Widow's pension: standard rate for privates	53.50
lower rate	12.35
widow of Major-General	3049.00 per year
Additions to widow's pensions:	
children's allowance in case of officers	625.00 per year
in case of other ranks	12.00 per year
rent allowance: maximum for all ranks	20.35
education allowance: maximum for all ranks	120.00 per year

Widow's benefits
Widowed mother's allowance (WMA)	41.15
Widow's pension (standard rate)	41.15
Age-related pension (examples only)	
Widow 50 when husband dies or WMA stops	26.75
Widow 45 when husband dies or WMA stops	12.35

Dependants' benefits
Child additions for long-term benefits	8.40
Dependant adults	
Retirement and invalidity pensions, and Unemployability supplement	24.75
Unemployment benefit	20.20

Invalid care allowance and SDA	14.80
Sickness benefit	19.40
Maternity allowance	19.40

Earnings limits

Retirement pension	75.00
Invalid care allowance	12.00
War pensions unemployability supplement	1404.00 per year
for dependent adults' additions (examples); where adult lives with claimant, for	
Retirement and invalidity pensions	32.75
where adult does not so live	24.75
for dependent child additions where spouse or partner lives with claimant	
for 1st child	90.00
for each extra child	11.00

CONTRIBUTIONS

Earnings limits

Upper earnings limit	305.00
Lower earnings limit	41.00

Non-contracted-out rates

Employee's weekly earnings (£)	Employee's contribution (full-rate)	Employer's contribution
under 41.00	none	none
41.00 – 69.99	5%	5%
70.00 – 104.99	7%	7%
105.00 – 154.99	9%	9%
155.00 – 305.00	9%	10.45%
over 305.00	9% of 305.00	10.45%

Contracted-out rates

For employees paying full-rate:

Employee's weekly earnings (£)	on the first £41.00	PLUS on earnings over £41.00
under 41.00	none	——
41.00 – 69.99	5%	3%
70.00 – 104.99	7%	5%
105.00 – 154.99	9%	7%
155.00 – 305.00	9%	7%
over 305.00	9%	7% up to £305.00

For employers:

Employee's weekly earnings (£)	on the first £41.00	PLUS on earnings over £41.00
under 41.00	none	——
41.00 – 69.99	5%	1.2%
70.00 – 104.99	7%	3.2%
105.00 – 154.99	9%	5.2%
155.00 – 305.00	10.45%	6.65%
over 305.00	10.45%	6.65% up to 305.00 PLUS 10.45% on earnings above

Class 2 (self-employed rate)
Flat-rate   £4.05
Small earnings exemption   £2250 per year

Class 3 (voluntary contributions rate)
Flat-rate   £3.95

Class 4 (self-employed rate)
Lower profits limit   £4750 per year
Upper profits limit   £15,860 per year
Contributions on profits between limits   6.3%

Index